Summer 1977

MINNESOTA COUNTIES

Cook
Lake
St. Louis
arlton
ine
Washington
Ramsey
odhue
Wabasha
Olmsted
Winona
ower
Fillmore
Houston

Publications of the

MINNESOTA HISTORICAL SOCIETY

Russell W. Fridley, *Director*
June Drenning Holmquist, *Managing Editor*

WARREN UPHAM as he looked in 1916

MINNESOTA GEOGRAPHIC NAMES
Their Origin and Historic Significance

By WARREN UPHAM

With an Introduction by
JAMES TAYLOR DUNN

Reprint Edition
MINNESOTA HISTORICAL SOCIETY 1969

Copyright © 1969, by the
MINNESOTA HISTORICAL SOCIETY, ST. PAUL

This work was first published by the Minnesota Historical
Society in 1920 as Volume 17 of the
Collections of the Minnesota Historical Society.

Library of Congress Catalog Card Number: 71–95570
Standard Book Number: 87351–051–8

INTRODUCTION TO THE REPRINT EDITION

WARREN UPHAM, geologist, archaeologist, and onetime librarian, was a compulsive collector of minutiae. A pedantic precisionist and a formalist of infinite old-world courtesy, he was exactly the right man to compile a major contribution to American place name literature — *Minnesota Geographic Names*. The half century which has passed since the initial publication of this book in 1920 has proven the basic thoroughness of Upham's research. In spite of an occasional error or a generality used to cover unknown facts, the volume has stood the test of time and its usefulness remains unimpaired. That these errors are not numerous is indicative of the author's careful work. It can safely be said that Upham's volume was a pioneering, pace-setting effort in place name literature. Even today *Minnesota Geographic Names* remains the best such guide for any state in the Union, approached only by Erwin G. Gudde's *California Place Names* (1960) and Lewis A. McArthur's *Oregon Geographic Names* (1944).

Because the first edition was a small one, this book has long been out of print and difficult to locate on the antiquarian market. No scholar of similar attainments has since appeared on the Minnesota scene to attempt a revision. Thus Upham's pioneering work is here republished essentially as it was issued in 1920. No attempt has been made to revise or update the text. To increase the usefulness of this reprint, however, Upham's own corrections are discussed below, and two supplements have been added, listing communities incorporated since 1920 and all the place names in the state covered by official decisions of the United States and Minnesota geographic boards.

Warren Upham, one of ten children born on a farm near Amherst, New Hampshire, was a graduate of Dartmouth College, class of 1871. From 1874 to 1878 he served as an assistant on the geological survey of New Hampshire, and he held the same position on the geological survey of Minnesota from 1879 to 1885 under state geologist Newton H. Winchell. During his first three years in Minnesota, Upham was engaged in field work, traveling, as the *St. Paul Daily Globe* reported on October 20, 1895, "11,000 miles, driving with horse about twenty-five miles daily, and thus thoroughly examining fifty of the . . . counties of Minnesota." He spent another two years — 1893 and 1894 — painstakingly surveying Aitkin and Cass counties, the area around Duluth, and northern St. Louis County.

Upham put the knowledge gained in his travels to good use, becoming a prolific writer in the field of geology. The Minnesota Historical Society's library contains at least ninety-four of his addresses and papers written (and mostly published) between 1877 and 1922. He contributed articles to periodicals such as the *American Geologist* and the Minnesota Academy of Science *Bulletin*; his books include *The Geology of Lake Agassiz* (1887) and *Geologic and Archaeologic Time* (1915). His total published works number 321, according to a bibliography compiled by Esther Jerabek.

An interruption in his Minnesota residency occurred in 1895 when he spent part of a year as archaeologist and librarian at the Western Reserve Historical Society in Cleveland. On January 1, 1896, Upham returned to Minnesota to succeed J. Fletcher Williams as superintendent and librarian of the Minnesota Historical Society, a dual post which he held until 1914 when he became the society's archaeologist, a position he kept until his death in 1934.

Although Upham's early notebooks and diaries are filled with place name references carefully recorded in his minuscule handwriting, the first official indication of his interest in this subject appeared in the society's minute books on May 8, 1899. Before a meeting of the institution's executive council on that date Upham "read a part of a paper prepared by him, entitled 'Origin of Minnesota Geographic Names.'" The minutes recorded that "the Council voted its thanks, and referred this paper to the Publication Committee." The society, however, made no further attempt to publish it at that time.

In 1901 Upham, anxious to get on with his place name study under the society's sponsorship, correctly argued that "the value and utility [of such research] can hardly be overestimated." By 1903 the society's *Biennial Report* recorded that plans were definitely afoot for a volume "giving the origin, meaning, and date, so far as can be ascertained, of all our proper names, as of the state, its counties and townships, cities, villages, railway stations, post-offices, creeks, rivers and lakes, hills and mountains, and the streets and parks in cities." In that year — 1903 — Upham began serious work on the subject — a task which was not to be completed until seventeen years later.

Research on the projected volume was taking up most of his time by 1916. That summer was spent on what he called "considerable journeys" to the eighty-six county seats. During the winter of 1916 Upham returned to desk research and was "chiefly occupied in gathering such information from published county histories of this state, early books and pamphlets and maps of the first and later explorers, descriptions by travelers, U.S. exploring expeditions, books relating to our Indian tribes, the series of this Society's publications, early newspaper files, and all other published sources of such information in this Society's Library or elsewhere in St. Paul and Minneapolis."

INTRODUCTION

The actual writing consumed about three years, and on January 23, 1919, Upham reported to his successor, the society's new superintendent Solon J. Buck, that the manuscript was "fully ready for printing." Dr. Buck gave his "cordial approval," and by mid-1920 the finished work made its appearance in an edition of 1,500 copies as volume 17 of the *Collections of the Minnesota Historical Society*.

Fifty years ago the study of place names in this country had not reached anything like the high point of acceptability it enjoyed in Europe, especially in England. The Upham volume, therefore, made hardly a ripple on the ocean of historical publications. No national scholarly magazine in the field gave the book a nod. Ignored by such prestigious publications as the *American Historical Review* and listed only in *Writings on American History* for 1920, the Upham volume garnered two short notices from the historical journals of nearby Midwestern states. A five-line item in the *Iowa Journal of History and Politics* called it a "distinct contribution." The *Michigan History Magazine* in its sixteen-line review correctly evaluated the book as a "model piece of workmanship," calling it (with tongue in cheek?) "prime material for the coming epic poet of the Gopher State."

Only in Upham's adopted state did the book receive the attention it deserved. Melvin R. Gilmore, ethnobotanist and then curator of the State Historical Society of North Dakota, reviewed the book for the August, 1920, issue of the *Minnesota History Bulletin*. "Whoever undertakes and faithfully carries out the task of compiling the place names of a state," Gilmore wrote, "with their derivation and significance, performs a praiseworthy accomplishment and does a distinct public service. . . . This is . . . a most noteworthy work, the result of a vast amount of diligent, persistent, and painstaking labor. . . . It is to be wished that every state might have wrought out for it as good and full an account of its place names as this which has been written for Minnesota."

Upham's interest in place names did not flag with the publication of his book. The library of the Minnesota Historical Society possesses the author's own copy, copiously and carefully annotated in his spidery handwriting. His notes include amplifications, additions, corrections, and peripheral information that he considered germane or that simply interested him. His copy indicates, for example, that he proposed to add the following useful information as an opening paragraph on page 1 of the book: "Minnesota was declared an organized territory June 1, 1849, in accordance with petition of August 26, 1848 (see page 4); and was admitted to the Union as a state on May 11, 1858, being the 32nd state, the 19th after the original thirteen of July 4, 1776."

Of the many changes jotted down in Upham's desk copy, the most notable is the establishment of the state's eighty-seventh county — Lake of the Woods — in 1922. He wrote that a petition was filed on August 8, 1922, "for division of Beltrami county, its former part north from twp. 157 to be named Lake of the Woods county" for the large body of water partially within its borders. Later he added: "Lake of the Woods County, 87th of this state . . . was proclaimed by Governor [Jacob A. O.] Preus on November 28, 1922, with Baudette as the county seat. The proposal carried by 507 votes in the Beltrami county election, Nov. 7, [1922]." The new county had "35 townships and included the Northwest Angle." Upham also noted that Penasse, a new post office in Angle Township had been established in 1921. He was not impressed by the name chosen for the new county. In a speech given in Duluth on July 28, 1922, Upham had strongly advocated that the area be named for French explorer Pierre de la Vérendrye. Users of this book will find the place names for both Lake of the Woods and Beltrami counties treated together in Upham's chapter on the latter.

Among the names which did not come into general use until after Upham's book was completed, is the state's sobriquet, "Land of Ten Thousand Lakes." Upham did use the phrase in part on page 235 when he called Lake Minnetonka in Hennepin County "an exceedingly attractive lake, of which I wrote in 1917 that it 'may well be called the Kohinoor of Minnesota's ten thousand lakes.'" In his annotated copy, however, the author expanded in several places on the origin of that inspired publicity catch phrase — from its first mention by Henry R. Schoolcraft in 1851 to its use in the Minnesota *Legislative Manual* of 1881. He called attention to volume I of *The Geology of Minnesota* (1884) in which N. H. Winchell stated: "The number of lakes in Minnesota is about ten thousand," and he recorded the appearance of the slogan "the country of ten thousand lakes" in the *St. Paul Dispatch and Pioneer Press Almanac and Year-Book for 1916*. Still another annotation recalled the organization "late in 1917" of the Ten Thousand Lakes of Minnesota Association, which from 1919 through 1922 expended a total of $102,000 appropriated by the state legislature for the promotion of tourism. It is interesting to note that 15,292 bodies of water over ten acres in size are listed in *An Inventory of Minnesota Lakes* published by the Minnesota Conservation Department in 1968.

The following list includes corrections and directly pertinent expansions on name origins noted by the author, as well as a few recorded by various members of the society's staff over the years. Upham's annotated copy, which contains many additional bits of information that he apparently wished to remember but that do not bear directly on place names, may be consulted in the society's library.

INTRODUCTION ix

ADOLPH (p. 477), a village in St. Louis County, was named for Adolph Bjorlin.

AITKIN COUNTY (p. 14) was named for William A. Aitken, whose name is properly spelled with an "e."

ANTRIM (p. 574), Watonwan County, was named by George W. Dodge, a settler from Antrim, New Hampshire.

AUSTIN (p. 359) — Austin Nichols died on April 15 (not April 5), 1914.

BABBITT (p. 478), a taconite town in St. Louis County first called Argo, was named for Judge Kurnal R. Babbitt of New York City in the 1920s.

BAYPORT (p. 568), Washington County, became the accepted name of Baytown.

BRANDON (p. 176, line 6 to the end), Douglas County, should be revised to read: Henry Gager, on a low hill about two miles north of the present railway village, which received its name of Brandon for the birthplace of Stephen A. Douglas in Vermont, as laid out in August, 1879. The township was also renamed. The village was incorporated November 22, 1881.

CARVER COUNTY (p. 10, lines 2, 3) — Jonathan Carver was born in Weymouth, Massachusetts, on April 13, 1710, rather than in Canterbury, Connecticut, in 1732.

CHAMPLIN (p. 220), a village in Hennepin County, was named by John B. Cook of St. Paul, one of its original proprietors, this being the family name of his wife Ellen, daughter of Stephen Champlin, commander of the "Scorpion," the gunboat which fired the first shots in the battle of Lake Erie on September 10, 1813. He was a cousin of Commodore Oliver H. Perry.

CHATFIELD (p. 192), Fillmore County, should be revised to show that Judge Chatfield presided over the first court held at Winona, not Chatfield.

COPAS (p. 569) in Washington County was named for an Italian settler, John Copas, who died in 1911, having lived there since 1859. The first store, post office, and mill have disappeared.

DARNEN TOWNSHIP (p. 535), Stevens County, was first named Darien, then Derrynane, a term used earlier in Le Sueur County. Darnen was coined from the latter.

DETROIT LAKES (p. 28), Becker County, was the name chosen for Detroit Township by a vote of its citizens on September 7, 1926.

DILWORTH (p. 115), Clay County, was perhaps named for eastern coffee importers, who owned land and had a large elevator in the neighborhood.

DULUTH (p. 481) — The birthplace of Daniel Greysolon, Sieur Du Luth, was St. Germain Laval near Roanne, France, not the Paris suburb of St. Germain-en-Laye.

―――― Chester Creek and Chester Park (p. 653, par. 6) were named for Charles Chester, a Duluth pioneer.

ERICKSONVILLE (p. 344), a village in Mille Lacs County, was named for Lars Erickson.

EVANSVILLE (p. 176), Douglas County, was named for Albert Evans.

EVELETH (p. 482), St. Louis County, was named for Erwin Eveleth, former postmaster and mayor of Corunna, Michigan, who died in 1922.

FARIBAULT COUNTY (p. 183, line 4) — Jean Baptiste Faribault was born at L'Ile Dupas, Quebec, on October 29, 1775. Lines 17 and 18 should be revised to read: Fort Snelling. Faribault and his family lived from 1826 to 1852 in Mendota, where he built a substantial stone house in 1838.

FORT CHARLOTTE (p. 136), Cook County, was named for Queen Charlotte (1744–1818), the wife of George III of England.

GLYNDON (p. 116), Clay County, was named by Major L. H. Tenney for Mrs. Edward W. Searing, an author and poet whose pen name was Howard Glyndon.

GRYGLA (p. 328), a small village on the east edge of Marshall County, was founded about 1902. It was named for Frank Grygla, better known as the "Father of the Polish National Alliance," of which he was president for ten years. His father was a count in one of the ancient and noble families of Poland.

HAGEN TOWNSHIP (p. 116), Clay County, was named for Norwegian settler Ole Hagen.

HALLOCK (p. 278, line 1), Kittson County, should indicate that Charles Hallock died on December 2, 1917.

HENDERSON TOWNSHIP (p. 519) and its village in Sibley County, founded in 1852 and platted in 1855 by Joseph R. Brown, who is commemorated by Brown County, were named by him in honor of his father's only sister, Mrs. Margaret Brown Henderson, and for her son Andrew Henderson.

HITTERDAL (p. 117), Clay County, was named for Bendt O. Hitterdal, the original town proprietor.

HOLLANDALE (p. 201), a new village of Hollanders in Freeborn County, was reclaimed from Rice Lake about twelve miles northeast of Albert Lea and opened for settlement in 1921.

HOYT LAKES (p. 484), a taconite town in St. Louis County developed by Pickands Mather and Company, was named in 1952 for Elton Hoyt II, head of that firm.

HUBERT (p. 158) in Crow Wing County, a railway village on the northeast end of the lake of this name, commemorates St. Hubert, the patron of huntsmen.

INTRODUCTION xi

KENYON (p. 207) in Goodhue County was more reliably named for Kenyon College in Gambier, Ohio, by James M. Le Duc, one of the original owners of the townsite, who wished to honor his alma mater.

KIMBALL PRAIRIE (p. 524), Stearns County, is now [1923] the village of Kimball.

KITTSON COUNTY (p. 276, line 17) should show that Norman Kittson died on May 10 (not May 11), 1888.

LAKES CHRISTINA AND ELLENORA (p. 182), Douglas County, were named in 1859 by James W. Taylor and Russell Blakeley in honor of Ellenora and Christina Sterling of Scotland.

LAKE SAGATAGAN (p. 530), Stearns County, was the name adopted for Lake St. Louis in 1920.

LEAF HILLS (p. 405) — The highest of the Leaf Hills has recently [1923] been named Inspiration Peak.

LINCOLN TOWNSHIP (p. 569), Washington County, received its name from Camp Lincoln, a group of summer homes about a mile north of Wildwood Park, named for President Lincoln by Samuel Bloomer, Civil War veteran and founder of Camp Lincoln about 1900.

LOCKHART TOWNSHIP (p. 383), Norman County, was named for a very large farm owned by Charles Lockhart.

LUXEMBURG (p. 525), a village in Stearns County, was named by its Luxembourg settlers for the grand duchy and its capital city in western Europe.

MILACA (p. 345) succeeded Princeton as the seat of Mille Lacs County in 1921.

MINNEAPOLIS (p. 223, par. 2, line 7) should read: "territorial" not "state."

MOUND TOWNSHIP (p. 468), Rock County, contains a mound now called Blue Mound.

NEVIS TOWNSHIP AND VILLAGE (p. 244), Hubbard County, may quite as probably have been named for Nevis, an island of the West Indies.

NISSWA (p. 158), Crow Wing County, bears an Ojibway name, probably related to *nessawae,* meaning "in the middle."

PARK REGION (p. 2), in Becker, Otter Tail, Douglas, and Pope counties, was named in 1869 by Charles Carleton Coffin, of the *Boston Journal,* who was with a Northern Pacific exploration party, writing from a camp on Floyd Lake in Becker County about two miles north of the site of Detroit Lakes. Coffin said: "On our second day's march eastward from the Red river we came to a section of country that might with propriety be called the Park Region of Minnesota. It lies amid the uplands of the divide. It is more beautiful even than the country around White Bear lake or in the vicinity of Glenwood. Throughout the day we rode amid such rural scenery as can only be found in the most lovely spots in England." This letter to the *Boston Journal* was dated at Floyd Lake, August 21–23, 1869.

PATTEN (OR PATTON) LAKE (p. 337), Martin County, named for Lieutenant Patton whose platoon of troops built a sod fort there in May, 1863, had previously been called Chanyaska Lake for its trees.

PIKE ISLAND (p. 441, par. 3 and elsewhere) is incorrectly located. It is in Ramsey County.

REDWOOD COUNTY (p. 449). Melvin R. Gilmore, who has been on the staff of the State Historical Society of North Dakota called in the MHS Library on May 24, 1923, on his way to enter service of the Museum of the American Indian, New York City. . . . He told me that Chanshayapi means in Dakota "they paint the tree red," referring to a former oak tree so painted for offerings and prayers on undertaking some serious business. He learned this from a well-informed Dakota, who formerly lived in southwestern Minnesota, now in the Standing Rock Reservation. H. M. Hitchcock . . . tells me on authority of Joe Coursolle, now living at the Lower Sioux Agency site, that a large oak tree on edge of the rock bluff near the west end of the bridge at Redwood Falls was repainted red by the Sioux yearly, being held in great veneration. Passing this tree was a trail leading down to the old ford used by the Indians and the early pioneers. Mr. Hitchcock avers that Joe Coursolle saw that red tree about 1858–62. This tree is regarded by Mr. H. and others as a memorial of a battle between Dakotas and the Cheyennes, perhaps about 1775. . . .

ST. PAUL (p. 439, line 1) Lucian should be spelled Lucien Galtier.

——— Carter Street (p. 632, par. 2) was named for W. C. Carter, who came to St. Paul in 1845.

——— Edgcumbe Road (p. 636, par. 1) was named by Charles B. Dunn of Philadelphia, owner of the property, for his home in Chestnut Hill, Pennsylvania, which in turn was named for Mount Edgcumbe in his native Cornwall.

——— Eustis Street (p. 631, par. 2) was named for Joseph M. Eustis (1827–98), proprietor of the Nicollet Hotel in Minneapolis.

——— Grace Street (p. 616, line 2) was named for Thomas L. Grace, bishop of St. Paul for twenty-five (not sixteen) years.

——— Jordan Avenue (p. 626, line 8) was named for James W. Jordan, chief clerk of the city department of public works.

——— Otto Avenue (p. 636, par. 1) was named for its earliest homesteader, Leberich Otto, a German immigrant (1812–84) who came to St. Paul in

INTRODUCTION

1840. He was a skilled musician who organized a band which for many years played for nearly all the dances in St. Paul and St. Anthony.

—— Pedersen Avenue (p. 626, line 9) was named for Jens Pedersen, a surveyor who arrived in St. Paul in 1857.

—— Riverview (p. 439, par. 2, line 6) should be read for Riverside.

—— Van Reed Street (p. 632, par. 5) was named for Henry Van Reed of Menomonie, Wisconsin.

SHELLY TOWNSHIP (p. 383), Norman County, was organized in 1879 and named for John Shely [sic], who came in 1870. . . .

SHOREHAM (p. 30), a village in Lake View Township, Becker County, between Lakes Sallie and Melissa, bears the name of a seaport in Sussex, England. The village was platted as early as 1904.

SIBLEY COUNTY (p. 518, par. 2, line 1) should be changed to read: In 1835–36 Sibley built at Mendota the oldest surviving stone dwelling house in Minnesota. . . .

SILVER BAY (p. 294), a taconite town in Lake County on the north shore of Lake Superior, was developed by Reserve Mining Company and named in 1954 for the bay on which it is located.

STARBUCK (p. 433), Pope County, was named for William Starbuck of New York, a railroad man.

TAYLORS FALLS (p. 110 and elsewhere), Chisago County, is customarily written without an apostrophe.

TIGER LAKE (p. 85), Carver County, was so named in May, 1855, by Martin McLeod on a journey with John H. Stevens and others. "On the evening of the 20th," wrote Stevens, "we camped on a lake, and wild animals prowled around us all night long, in consequence of which Mr. McLeod called the place of our discomfort Tiger Lake. . . ."

TODD COUNTY (p. 543, line 3), 1856 should read 1854. General Todd was a cousin of the wife of Abraham Lincoln.

TRAVERSE COUNTY (p. 550, par. 4, line 3), Wahnata should be spelled Wahnahta.

VIRGINIA (p. 491), St. Louis County, was named by David T. Adams.

WILLMAR (p. 272, par. 4, line 3), Kandiyohi County, was named by George L. Becker (not George F. Becker).

WUORI TOWNSHIP (p. 492), St. Louis County, has a Finnish name, meaning "a mountain." The southern part contains an exceptionally high area of the Mesabi Range, culminating in sections 25, 28, and 29, with crests of 1,825 to 1,925 feet above sea level.

In connection with these revised elevation figures, Upham noted (p.

504, par. 4, line 5) that the Wuori Township figure should be 500 feet rather than 700.

In addition to Upham's changes, the reader is referred to two new supplements compiled especially for this reprint. The years since 1920 have produced many new cities and incorporated villages as suburbia engulfs the fields and woods of yesteryear. Supplement 1 lists communities incorporated in Minnesota from 1920 to January 1, 1969. It was compiled from records in the office of the secretary of state, from files kept by the League of Minnesota Municipalities, and from *Village Laws and Government in Minnesota* by Harvey Walker (*Publication No. 6*, Bureau for Research in Government, University of Minnesota — 1927). Of the 171 place names listed in this supplement, it should be noted that at least a hundred appear in Upham's work as townships or physical features. The genesis of the nomenclature has, therefore, already been established by the indefatigable historian.

The second supplement offers for the first time a complete listing of the 1,167 official decisions made by the United States (753) and Minnesota (414) geographic boards concerning place names in the state. In 1890, by executive order of President Benjamin Harrison, the United States Board on Geographic Names was established to achieve "uniform usage in regard to geographic nomenclature and orthography." Since 1934 it has operated in the Department of the Interior. The Minnesota board was created by legislative action in 1937, the members being the commissioners of the conservation and highway departments, and the director of the Minnesota Historical Society. Its duties were to determine the correct and most appropriate names of various geographic features, as well as to assign names to undesignated features, eliminate duplication when feasible, and decide the official nomenclature when more than one name has been in use. The Minnesota Geographic Board was abolished by the 1969 legislature, and its functions were transferred to the commissioner of conservation, effective in 1971. Supplement 2 contains a full record of the state board's work from its establishment in 1937 to July 1, 1969.

In addition to giving the approved name and location of each feature, the supplement provides a list of previously used or erroneous designations. In some instances, the reader will find these older names in Upham's book. Marine Mills, Washington County, is a good case in point. Upham in his description on page 570 neglected to mention that in 1917 the post office elected to call the village Marine on St. Croix. Such an oversight, however, is understandable, since it was not until 1950 that the residents voted their approval and not until 1968 that the United States Board on Geographic Names made the name official, as noted in Supplement 2. The reader is warned that official names will not always appear in the index to this volume which has not been revised or corrected, and he is advised to check this introduction as well as the index and the alphabetical listings in Supplements 1 and 2.

MINNESOTA HISTORICAL SOCIETY
September 11, 1969

JAMES TAYLOR DUNN
Chief Librarian

PREFACE TO THE ORIGINAL EDITION

DURING sixteen years, from 1879 to 1894, of service for the geological surveys of Minnesota, the United States, and Canada, in travel over large areas of this state, the Dakotas, and Manitoba, my attention was often attracted to the origins of their names of places, partly received directly from the Indian languages, and in many other instances translated from the aboriginal names. Frequently our geographic names note remarkable topographic features, or are derived from the fauna and flora. Perhaps a greater number commemorate pioneer white explorers, early fur traders, and agricultural settlers.

Later work for the Minnesota Historical Society, since 1895, has permitted and even required more detailed consideration and record in this field. Many memorials of our territorial and state history are preserved in geographic names, and each nationality contributing to the settlement has its share in this nomenclature. As the first immigrants of the state along the Atlantic and Gulf coast brought many place names from England, France, Holland, and Spain, so in Minnesota many geographic names have come from beyond the sea. Here the influence of a large proportion of immigration from Germany is shown by such names as New Ulm, New Trier, Hamburg, Cologne, and New Munich. Old Bohemia is brought to mind by the city of New Prague. Sweden, Norway, and Denmark are well represented by Stockholm, Malmo, Bergen, Trondhjem, Denmark, and many other township and village names. In the early eastern and southern states, Plymouth, Boston, Portsmouth, Bangor, New York, Charleston, St. Augustine, and New Orleans recalled tender memories of the Old World. Likewise, these German and Bohemian and Scandinavian names have a great meaning to the immigrants from those countries who have made their new homes here.

To illustrate how this subject is like a garden of flowers, or like an epic poem, reference may be made to the names of the eighty-six Minnesota counties. Fifteen came directly, or through translation, from the Dakota or Sioux language, eight being retained as Sioux words, Anoka, Dakota, Isanti, Kandiyohi, Wabasha, Waseca, Watonwan, and Winona. Six are translated into English, namely, Big Stone, Blue Earth, Cottonwood, Redwood, Traverse, and Yellow Medicine; and one is received in its French translation, Lac qui Parle. Twelve counties bear names of Ojibway origin; but only five, Chisago,

Kanabec, Koochiching, Mahnomen, and Wadena, are Indian words, and the first was made by a white man's coinage. The seven others are Chippewa (the anglicized form of Ojibway), Clearwater, Crow Wing, Mille Lacs (a translation in French), Otter Tail, Red Lake, and Roseau (another French translation).

Fifty-two counties have received personal names, which may be arranged in four lists. The early explorers of this area are commemorated by seven counties; the fur traders of the early half of the last century, by four; citizens of Minnesota as a territory and state have been honored by the names of twenty-six counties; and citizens of other parts of the United States are similarly honored in fifteen counties. First enumerating the seven county names from explorers, we have Beltrami, Carver, Cass, Hennepin, Le Sueur, Nicollet, and Pope. The four named for early fur traders are Aitkin, Faribault, Morrison, and Renville. The twenty-six counties named for Minnesota citizens are Becker, Brown, Carlton, Cook, Freeborn, Goodhue, Hubbard, Jackson, Kittson, McLeod, Marshall, Meeker, Mower, Murray, Nobles, Olmsted, Pennington, Ramsey, Rice, Sherburne, Sibley, Stearns, Steele, Swift, Todd, and Wilkin counties. Among the fifteen counties named for citizens of this country outside of Minnesota, five are in honor of presidents of the United States, these being Washington, Polk, Fillmore, Lincoln, and Grant. The ten others in this list are Benton, Clay, Dodge, Douglas, Houston, Lyon, Martin, Scott, Stevens, and Wright.

Six of our counties have names given by white men for natural features, in addition to the larger number so derived from the Indian languages. These are Itasca, taking the name of the lake, formed of two Latin words; Lake county, named for Lake Superior; Pine county, so named for its extensive pine forests; Pipestone county, for the Indian pipestone quarry there; Rock county, for the very prominent rock outcrop near Luverne; and St. Louis county, for its river of that name. One county received its name, Norman, in honor of its large number of immigrants from Norway.

The earliest systematic endeavor to trace the origins of Minnesota county names was published by John Fletcher Williams, secretary of the Minnesota Historical Society, as an article in the St. Paul Pioneer, March 13, 1870. Another contribution to this subject, by Return I. Holcombe, of St. Paul, was in the Pioneer Press Almanac, 1896. Both these lists have been consulted, with much advantage, for the present volume.

In ascertaining derivations and meanings of Dakota and Ojibway names, very valuable aid has been obtained from a paper, "Minnesota Geographical Names derived from the Dakota Language, with some that are Obsolete," by Prof. Andrew W. Williamson, of Augustana College, Rock Island, Ill.,

PREFACE TO THE ORIGINAL EDITION xix

published in the Thirteenth Annual Report of the Geological and Natural History Survey of Minnesota, for 1884, pages 104-112; and from another paper, in the Fifteenth Report of the same survey, for 1886, pages 451-477, "Minnesota Geographical Names derived from the Chippewa Language," by Rev. Joseph A. Gilfillan, of White Earth, who also supplied in later letters many further notes of Ojibway names. These two papers are the most important sources of information on Minnesota geographic terms of Indian origin, supplementing the frequent references to origins of names by Hennepin, Carver, Mackenzie, Thompson, Pike, Long and Keating, Beltrami, Schoolcraft, Allen, Featherstonhaugh, Catlin, Lea, Nicollet, and other explorers of the area which is now Minnesota.

The narrations of these discoverers and explorers, and many later books, pamphlets, newspapers, atlases, and maps, have been examined in the library of the Minnesota Historical Society. Special acknowledgments are due to the following books and authors:

Grammar and Dictionary of the Dakota Language, edited by Rev. Stephen R. Riggs, published by the Smithsonian Institution, Washington, 1852; and a revised edition of the greater part, a Dakota-English Dictionary, issued in 1890 as volume VII, "Contributions to North American Ethnology."

An English-Dakota Dictionary, compiled by John P. Williamson, printed by the American Tract Society, 1902.

A Grammar of the Otchipwe [Ojibway] Language, 1878; a Dictionary of the Otchipwe Language, Part I, English-Otchipwe, 1878; and Part II, Otchipwe-English, 1880. These are editions published in Montreal, of volumes by Bishop Frederic Baraga, the Grammar having been first published in Detroit, 1850, and the Dictionary in Cincinnati, 1853.

A Glossary of Chippewa Indian Names of Rivers, Lakes, and Villages, by Rev. Chrysostom Verwyst, of Bayfield, Wis., in Acta et Dicta . . . of the Catholic Church in the Northwest, published in St. Paul, volume IV, pages 253-274, July, 1916.

Handbook of American Indians north of Mexico, edited by Frederick W. Hodge, published by the Smithsonian Institution as Bulletin 30, Bureau of American Ethnology, two volumes, 1907, 1910.

The Geological and Natural History Survey of Minnesota, 1872-1901, by Prof. N. H. Winchell, state geologist, and assistants: Annual Reports, 24 volumes; Bulletins, 10 volumes, treating partly of the mammals, birds, fishes, and the flora; Final Reports, 6 volumes, having chapters for all the counties and for the iron ore ranges.

Memoirs of Explorations in the Basin of the Mississippi, by Hon. J. V. Brower, of St. Paul, eight volumes, 1898-1905. Four of these volumes relate to parts of this state, being III, Mille Lac, 1900; IV, Kathio, 1901; V. Kakabikansing, 1902; and VI, Minnesota, 1903.

Minnesota Historical Society Collections, fifteen volumes, 1850–1915. Biographic references for places bearing names of personal derivation have been supplied in the greater part by the fourteenth volume, Minnesota Biographies, 1655–1912.

The Aborigines of Minnesota, a Report based on the collections of Jacob V. Brower, and on the field surveys and notes of Alfred J. Hill and Theodore H. Lewis, collated, augmented and described by N. H. Winchell; published by the Minnesota Historical Society, St. Paul, 1911.

The Origin of Certain Place Names in the United States, second edition, by Henry Gannett, published in 1905 as Bulletin 258 of the U. S. Geological Survey.

Complete Pronouncing Gazetteer or Geographical Dictionary of the World, published by the J. B. Lippincott Company, 1911, two volumes.

A History of the Origin of the Place Names connected with the Chicago & Northwestern and Chicago, St. Paul, Minneapolis & Omaha Railways, . . . compiled by one [W. H. Stennett] who for more than 34 years has been an officer in the employ of the system; Chicago, 1908.

In the early progress of this research, a paper by the author, "Origin of Minnesota Geographic Names," including quite full notes for each county name, was read at a monthly meeting of the executive council of the Minnesota Historical Society, May 8, 1899; and a second address, entitled "The Origin and Meaning of Minnesota Names of Rivers, Lakes, Counties, Townships, and Cities," was presented at an annual meeting of this Society, January 11, 1904. These papers were mainly published in a series of articles in the Office Blotter, a Minneapolis journal issued chiefly for the interest of Minnesota county officers, April to August, 1904; and they were again published with slight changes and additions in the Magazine of History, New York, volume VIII, September to November, 1908. More condensed and somewhat revised, they were embodied in a newspaper article, "Whence came the Names of Minnesota's Counties," in the St. Paul Pioneer Press, November 19, 1911. After further revision, notes of origins of the county names were published in numerous Minnesota daily newspapers, usually one county each day in alphabetic order, in the spring and summer of 1916.

For interviews with county officers, pioneer settlers, and others, twenty counties of northern Minnesota were visited by the author in the autumn of 1909; and in the year 1916, from April to October, all the eighty-six counties were visited. Such personal interviews, to some extent followed by correspondence, have been the chief sources of information for most parts of this

PREFACE TO THE ORIGINAL EDITION xxi

work, except for the considerable list of counties having published histories. Dates of organization of townships and villages are noted mainly from the county histories, so that comparatively few dates are given under other counties.

Published and personal sources consulted for each county are stated at the beginning of its catalogue of townships. To the many citizens who have contributed notes of the origins of place names, and of the names of streets and parks in our three great cities, the author and the people of Minnesota are enduringly indebted. Within the lifetime of pioneers who shared in the first settlement and in all the development of this commonwealth, a careful record has been made of a very significant portion of its history.

The first chapter of the book treats of general features, as districts bearing topographic names, the state name and sobriquets, and the larger lakes and rivers. Eighty-six chapters treat of the place names of the counties in alphabetic order. The name of each county is first somewhat fully noticed; next the townships and villages are listed in their alphabetic series, preceded by the due mention of books and persons supplying information for the county; and last are records of lakes and streams, hills, prairies, and, in some of the counties, Indian reservations, iron ore ranges, state and national forests, state parks, glacial lakes, beaches, and moraines. Localities of exceptional historic interest are found in nearly every county. Origins of the names of streets, avenues, and parks, in Minneapolis, St. Paul, and Duluth, are noted in the final three chapters, so that the whole volume comprises ninety chapters.

To find notations of any city, township, village, lake, river or creek, hills and prairies, iron ranges, etc., the reader will consult the Index, appearing on pages 657–735, which is the key to all its contents. An explanation of abbreviations used in the Index is given on its first page.

WARREN UPHAM

MINNESOTA HISTORICAL SOCIETY
    ST. PAUL

CONTENTS

GENERAL FEATURES 1
COUNTIES
Aitkin County	14	Jackson County	260
Anoka County	22	Kanabec County	265
Becker County	27	Kandiyohi County	268
Beltrami, Lake of the Woods Counties	34	Kittson County	276
		Koochiching County	281
Benton County	49	Lac qui Parle County	288
Big Stone County	53	Lake County	293
Blue Earth County	57	Le Sueur County	300
Brown County	67	Lincoln County	306
Carlton County	73	Lyon County	311
Carver County	80	McLeod County	316
Cass County	86	Mahnomen County	321
Chippewa County	102	Marshall County	326
Chisago County	107	Martin County	332
Clay County	114	Meeker County	338
Clearwater County	121	Mille Lacs County	343
Cook County	135	Morrison County	350
Cottonwood County	149	Mower County	359
Crow Wing County	154	Murray County	364
Dakota County	164	Nicollet County	371
Dodge County	171	Nobles County	376
Douglas County	175	Norman County	381
Faribault County	183	Olmsted County	385
Fillmore County	190	Otter Tail County	390
Freeborn County	198	Pennington County	406
Goodhue County	205	Pine County	410
Grant County	213	Pipestone County	416
Hennepin County	219	Polk County	421
Houston County	237	Pope County	430
Hubbard County	242	Ramsey County	436
Isanti County	249	Red Lake County	445
Itasca County	252	Redwood County	448

Renville County	455	Todd County	543
Rice County	461	Traverse County	550
Rock County	466	Wabasha County	555
Roseau County	470	Wadena County	560
St. Louis County	476	Waseca County	564
Scott County	507	Washington County	568
Sherburne County	513	Watonwan County	574
Sibley County	518	Wilkin County	577
Stearns County	522	Winona County	581
Steele County	531	Wright County	586
Stevens County	535	Yellow Medicine County	593
Swift County	539		

CITIES

Minneapolis	599	Duluth	643
St. Paul	611		

INDEX 657

SUPPLEMENTS
  No. 1. Minnesota Communities Incorporated Since 1920 739
  No. 2. Official Decisions of the Minnesota and
         United States Geographic Boards, 1890–1969 743

MINNESOTA
GEOGRAPHIC NAMES

GENERAL FEATURES

The most conspicuous geographic features of this state are its larger rivers and lakes, including the Minnesota river, whence the state is named, the Mississippi, largest of this continent, which here has its source and a great part of its course, the Red river, the Rainy, St. Louis, and St. Croix rivers, Lake Superior, adjoining Minnesota by 150 miles of its northwest shore, Rainy lake and the Lake of the Woods, Red lake, Winnebagoshish and Leech lakes, and Mille Lacs, each requiring mention as belonging partly to two or more counties. Likewise the origins and meaning of the names of many smaller rivers and lakes need to be given in this chapter, to which reference may be made under their several counties, unless their names, borne by counties, townships, or villages, are thus fully noticed.

DISTRICTS BEARING TOPOGRAPHIC NAMES.

Only limited areas of Minnesota have low mountains or even any noteworthy hills that have received names. Such are hilly or somewhat mountainous tracts on the Vermilion and Mesabi ranges, names which designate belts having immense deposits of iron ores, noted under Itasca, St. Louis, Lake and Cook counties. The first of these ranges was named from the Vermilion lake and river in St. Louis county. The second has an Ojibway name, spelled "Missabay Heights" by Nicollet, translated as Giant mountain by Gilfillan. It is spelled Missabe, pronounced in three syllables, by Baraga's Dictionary, which defines it as "Giant; also, a very big stout man."

The third and more southern belt of iron ores, latest discovered but now having many and large mines, was named the Cuyuna range by its discoverer, Cuyler Adams, from his own name and from his dog, Una, who accompanied him in many prospecting trips. This iron range has no prominently hilly tract.

From Duluth to the northeast corner of this state, the land rises generally 500 to 800 feet or more above Lake Superior within a few miles back from its shore, forming the southern margin of a high wooded area that reaches to the international boundary and is diversified by mostly low ridges and hills. Seen from passing boats, the eroded front of this highland for about thirty miles in Cook county, from Carlton peak to Grand Marais, presents a peculiarly serrate profile and is therefore commonly called the Sawteeth mountains, more definitely noted for that county.

Morainic hills of the glacial drift, amassed along the borders of the continental ice-sheet, are traced in twelve successive belts across this state. The most noteworthy development of these hills is found in Otter Tail county, where the eighth and ninth moraines are merged to form the Leaf hills, called "mountains" by the settlers in contrast with the lower hills in other parts of the state, rising in steep slopes to heights of 200 to 350 feet along an extent of about twenty miles. Their name, more fully considered in the county chapter, is translated from the Ojibway name, which was thence applied by the Ojibways to the Leaf lakes and river, and by the white people to Leaf Mountain township.

An important contrast is exhibited by the vegetation in different parts of Minnesota. Forest covers its northeastern two-thirds, approximately, while about one-third, lying at the south and southwest, and reaching in the Red river valley to the Canadian line, as also the part of this valley north to Lake Winnipeg, is prairie. Half of the state, on the northeast, had originally extensive tracts of very valuable white pine and red pine, which have been mostly cut off by lumbermen. Interspersed with these and other evergreen species, as the spruces, balsam fir, and arbor vitae, were tracts of maple, elm, bass, oaks, ash, and other deciduous trees. The Big Woods, a translation from the early French name, Grand Bois, occupied a large area west of the Mississippi, including Wright, Carver, Scott, and Le Sueur counties, with parts of adjacent counties. Until its timber was cleared off for cultivation of the land in farms, this area was heavily wooded with the deciduous forest, shedding its leaves before winter, lying south of the geographic range of the pines and their allies.

In the great prairie region of southwestern Minnesota, and extending northward into the northeast part of South Dakota, a large elevated district is inclosed by the contour line of 1,500 feet above the sea. This area comprises Pipestone county and the greater parts of Lincoln, Murray, Nobles, and Rock counties in this state, having an entire length in the two states of about 160 miles. It was named by the early French voyageurs and explorers the Coteau des Prairies, as on Nicollet's map, meaning, in English, the Highland of the Prairies.

The many beautiful lakes of Alexandria and its vicinity, of the adjoining country southward to Glenwood and northwest to Fergus Falls, and their landscapes of alternating woods and small openings of prairies, have given the name Park Region to that district, lying between the unbroken northeastern forest and the limitless prairie on the west.

Another area of many lakes and streams, having somewhat similar features as the foregoing, but with a mainly less rolling and diversified contour, excepting the valleys and inclosing bluffs of its rivers, was named by Nicollet the Undine Region, comprising the country of the Blue Earth river and its tributaries, as noticed in the chapter of Blue Earth county.

THE NAME OF THE STATE.

Minnesota received its name from the largest river which lies wholly within its area, excepting only that its sources above Big Stone lake are in South Dakota. During a hundred and fifty years, up to the time of the organization of Minnesota Territory, in 1849, the name St. Pierre, or St. Peter, had been generally applied to this river by French and English explorers and writers. March 6, 1852, the territorial legislature adopted a memorial to the President of the United States, requesting that this name should be discontinued, and that only the aboriginal name should be used for the river, the same as for the territory, by the different government departments; and this was so decreed on June 19 of the same year, by an act of Congress.

The old name, St. Peter's river, of French derivation, seems probably to have been given in commemoration of its first exploration by Pierre Charles Le Sueur. If so, however, his first journey up the Minnesota river was more than ten years before his expedition upon it in the year 1700, when he mined what he supposed to be an ore of copper in the bluffs of the Blue Earth river, near the site of Mankato; for the St. Peter and St. Croix rivers are mentioned by these names in Perrot's proclamation at his Fort St. Antoine, on Lake Pepin, taking possession of this region for France, dated May 8, 1689.

The Dakota or Sioux name Minnesota means sky-tinted water (Minne, water, and sota, somewhat clouded), as Neill translated it on the authority of Rev. Gideon H. Pond. The river at its stages of flood becomes whitishly turbid. An illustration of the meaning of the words was told to the present writer by Mrs. Moses N. Adams, the widow of the well known missionary of the Dakotas. She stated that at various times the Dakota women explained it to her by dropping a little milk into water and calling the whitishly clouded water "Minne sota."

Major Long in 1817 wrote that the Mississippi above the St. Croix had a name meaning Clear river, and Dr. Folwell in 1919 concludes that the Minnesota means this, contrasted with the very muddy Missouri.

In the years 1846 to 1848, Hon. Henry H. Sibley and Hon. Morgan L. Martin, the delegate in Congress from Wisconsin, proposed this name for the new territory, which thus followed the example of Wisconsin in adopting the title of a large stream within its borders. During the next few years, it displaced the name St. Peter as applied in common usage by the white people to the river, whose euphonious Dakota title will continue to be borne by the river and the state probably long after the Dakota or Sioux language shall cease to be spoken.

Gen. James H. Baker, in an address on the history of Lake Superior, before the Minnesota Historical Society at its annual meeting in 1879, published in the third volume of its Collections (1880, pages 333-355), directed attention, as follows, to a somewhat comparable Ojibway name for the wooded northern part of this state.

"In one of my expeditions upon the north shore, being accompanied by an intelligent Chippewa chief, I found the shrub, Balm of Gilead, a small tree of medicinal virtue, in great abundance. He gave me its Chippewa name as *Mah-nu-sa-tia,* and said it was the name given by their people to all that country west of the great lake, because it was the country yielding the Mah-nu-sa-tia. In conversing with other intelligent Chippewas, I found this statement was invariably confirmed. They claim it as the traditional name of the land to the west of the lake."

This Ojibway word, however, had no influence upon the selection of our territorial and state name. Indeed, it was generally unknown to the white people here until more than twenty years after the Sioux name was chosen.

The name Itasca, devised in 1832 by Schoolcraft with the aid of Rev. William T. Boutwell for the lake at the head of the Mississippi, was urged by Boutwell for the territory. Other names were suggested in the discussions of Congress, as Chippeway, Jackson, and Washington. Final choice of the name Minnesota was virtually decided in the convention held at Stillwater on August 26, 1848, which petitioned to Congress for territorial organization.

Carver, who wintered with the Sioux on the Minnesota river in 1766-67, was the earliest author to record its Sioux name. He spelled it Menesotor in his Travels and Menesoter on the accompanying map. It was spelled Menesota by Long and Keating; Menisothé by Beltrami; Minisotah by Nicollet; Minnay sotor by Featherstonhaugh; Minesota by Hon. M. L. Martin and Hon. Stephen A. Douglas, in bills introduced by them respectively in the House and Senate for organization of the territory; and Minnesota by Hon. H. H. Sibley at the Stillwater convention.

Sobriquets of Minnesota.

Like Michigan, which is frequently called the Wolverine state, and Wisconsin, the Badger state, Minnesota has a favorite sobriquet or nickname, the Gopher state. Its origin has been given by the late Judge Flandrau, who, in his "History of Minnesota," says that the beaver, as well as the gopher, was advocated to give such a popular title. The latter gained the ascendancy, soon after the admission of Minnesota to statehood, on account of the famous "Gopher cartoon," published in derision of the Five Million Loan bill, which was passed by the first state legislature to encourage the building of railroads. The striped gopher, common throughout our prairie region, is the species depicted by the cartoon. (Minnesota in Three Centuries, 1908, vol. I, pages 75-76.)

Minnesota is also often called the North Star state, in allusion to the motto, "L' Etoile du Nord," chosen by Governor Sibley for the state seal in 1858.

Another epithet for our fertile commonwealth more recently came into use from the Pan-American Exposition at Buffalo, N. Y., in 1901, where the superior exhibits of wheat, flour, and dairy products of Minnesota caused her to be called "the Bread and Butter state."

The Mississippi.

The chief river of Minnesota, and indeed of North America, bears for all time the Algonquian name which it received from the Ojibways who paddled their birch canoes on its head stream, within the area of this state, and on the lakes at its sources. This name, Mississippi, means simply the Great River. Such it is, being the second among the great rivers of the world, surpassed only by the Amazon.

Jean Nicolet, the first white explorer of Wisconsin, in the winter of 1634-35, went from Lake Michigan and Green bay to Lake Winnebago and the upper Fox river, and learned there from the Indians that the sea, as he understood them to say, was within three days' travel farther to the southwest. What he heard of was the Mississippi river.

It was first made known by name to Europeans in the Jesuit Relation of 1666-67, published in Paris in 1668, which mentions "the great river named Messipi." The Relation of 1670-71 gave a more definite description as follows: "It is a Southward course that is taken by the great river called by the natives Missisipi, which must empty somewhere in the region of the Florida sea, more than four hundred leagues hence (from the upper Great Lakes) * * * Some Savages have assured us that this is so noble a river that, at more than three hundred leagues' distance from its mouth, it is larger than the one flowing before Quebec; for they declare that it is more than a league wide [referring probably to its expansion in Lake Pepin]. They also state that all this vast stretch of country consists of nothing but treeless prairies."

Earlier names had been given by the Spaniards to this river in its lower part, seen by their expeditions. Thus, on the map resulting from Pineda's exploration of the Gulf coast in 1519, the Mississippi is named Rio del Espiritu Santo (River of the Holy Spirit) ; and it continued to be commonly or frequently mapped under that name until its present Algonquian designation was generally adopted.

Father Marquette, writing of his canoe voyage on this river in 1673, with Joliet, called it the Missisipi, but his map named it "R. de la Conception."

Hennepin, in the first edition of his travels, published in Paris in 1683, called the Mississippi the River Colbert, for the great French statesman who died that year, and so mapped it; but later editions named and mapped it as "Le Grand Fleuve Meschasipi."

La Salle, writing August 22, 1682, designated is as "the river Colbert, named by the Iroquois Gastacha, and by the Ottawas the Mississipy." Elsewhere, however, in the same and other writings, La Salle and his companions more commonly used only the latter name, spelling it Mississipi.

Perrot, after spending many years on the upper part of this river, in his Memoir written in 1718 or within two or three years later, spoke of "the Micissypy, which is now named the Louisianne;" and a French map published in 1718 gives the name as "the Missisipi or St. Louis."

Carver, who traveled into the area of Minnesota in 1766, described and mapped this river with its present spelling, Mississippi, which was followed by Pike, Cass and Schoolcraft, Long and Keating, Beltrami, and all later writers. Before this form became fully established, the name, as printed in books and maps, had many variations, which, according to an estimate by Dr. Elliott Coues, number probably thirty or more.

The first part of the name, Missi, means Great, being akin to the modern Ojibway word, Kitchi, great, or Gitche, as it is spelled by Longfellow in "The Song of Hiawatha"; and the second part, sippi, otherwise spelled sipi or sebe, or zibi, is the common Algonquian or Ojibway word for a river. This name, received from the Ojibways and other Algonquins by the earliest French missionaries and traders in the upper Mississippi region, though used by these Indians only for the upper part of the river as known to them, was extended by Marquette and Joliet and by La Salle to its entire course, displacing the numerous former Indian names which had been applied to its lower part.

Rev. J. A. Gilfillan wrote: "Below the junction of Leech Lake river, it is called Kitchi-zibi, or Great river. I cannot find by inquiry that the Chippewas have ever called it Missizibi (Mississippi) or Missazibi. But I consider it very probable that in remote times they did, for Missa-zibi (Mississippi) would express the same idea in their language, and would be proper, as witness Missa-sagaiigun (Mille Lacs), meaning Great lake. It so exactly corresponds with their language that it must have been taken from it."

Endeavoring to translate more fully the aboriginal significance of Missi, Gannett says that Mississippi means "great water," or "gathering in of all the waters," and "an almost endless river spread out."

The phrase, "Father of Waters," popularly given to this river, has no warrant in the Algonquian name. In 1854 Schoolcraft wrote: "The prefixed word Missi is an adjective denoting all, and, when applied to various waters, means the collected or assembled mass of them. * * * It is only symbolically that it can be called the Father of American rivers, unless such sense occurs in the other Indian tongues."

Red Lake and River.

Red lake is translated from its Ojibway name, which, like Vermilion lake, refers to the red and vermilion hues of the smooth water surface reflecting the color of the sky at sunset on calm evenings in summer, as noted in the chapters of Red Lake county and St. Louis county. The Red river, named from the lake, is the boundary of Minnesota at the west side of six counties, flowing thence to Lake Winnipeg. Its more distinctive name, Red river of the North, was used by Nicollet to distinguish it from the Red river tributary to the lower Mississippi.

An exceedingly flat plain adjoins the Red river, having an imperceptible descent northward, as also from each side to its central line. Along the axial depression the river has cut a channel twenty to sixty feet deep. It is bordered by only few and narrow areas of bottomland, in-

GENERAL FEATURES

stead of which its banks usually rise steeply on one side, and by moderate slopes on the other, to the broad valley plain which thence reaches nearly level ten to twenty-five miles from the river. This vast plain, lying half in Minnesota and half in North Dakota, with continuation into Manitoba and so stretching from Lake Traverse and Breckenridge north to Lake Winnipeg, a distance of 300 miles, is the widely famed Red River Valley, one of the most productive wheat-raising districts of the world.

GLACIAL LAKE AGASSIZ AND RIVER WARREN.

The farmers and other residents of this fertile plain are well aware that they live on the area once occupied by a great lake; for its beaches, having the form of smoothly rounded ridges of gravel and sand, a few feet high, with a width of several rods, are observable extending horizontally long distances upon each of the slopes which rise east and west of the valley plain. Hundreds of farmers have located their buildings on the beach ridges as the most dry and sightly spots on their land, affording opportunity for perfectly drained cellars even in the most wet spring seasons, and also yielding to wells, dug through this sand and gravel, better water than is usually obtainable in wells on the adjacent clay areas.

Numerous explorers of this region, from Long and Keating in 1823, to Gen. G. K. Warren in 1868 and Prof. N. H. Winchell in 1872, observed the lacustrine features of the valley; and the last named geologist first gave what is now generally accepted as the true explanation of the lake's existence, namely, that it was produced in the closing stage of the Glacial period by the dam of the continental ice-sheet at the time of its final melting away. As the border of the ice-sheet retreated northward along the valley, drainage from it could not flow as now freely to the north through Lake Winnipeg and into the ocean at Hudson bay, but was turned southward by the ice barrier to the lowest place on the watershed dividing this basin from that of the Mississippi. The lowest point is found at Brown's Valley, on the western boundary of Minnesota, where an ancient watercourse, about 125 feet deep and one mile to one and a half miles wide, extends from Lake Traverse, at the head of the Bois des Sioux, a tributary of the Red river, to Big Stone lake, through which the head stream of the Minnesota river passes in its course to the Mississippi and the Gulf of Mexico.

Detailed exploration of the shore lines and area of this lake was begun by the present writer for the Minnesota Geological Survey in the years 1879 to 1881, under the direction of Professor Winchell, the state geologist. In subsequent years I was employed in tracing the lake shores through North Dakota for the United States Geological Survey, and through southern Manitoba to the distance of 100 miles north from the international boundary to Riding mountain, for the Geological Survey of Canada. For the last named survey, also, Mr. J. B. Tyrrell extended the exploration of the shore lines more or less completely for 200 miles farther north, along the Riding and Duck mountains and the Porcupine and Pasquia hills, west of Lakes Manitoba and Winnipegosis, to the Saskatchewan river.

This glacial lake was named in the eighth annual report of the Minnesota Geological Survey, for the year 1879, in honor of Louis Agassiz, the first prominent advocate of the theory of the formation of the drift by land ice. The outflowing river, whose channel is now occupied by Lakes Traverse and Big Stone and Brown's Valley, was named, in a paper read before the American Association for the Advancement of Science at its Minneapolis meeting in 1883, the River Warren, in commemoration of General Warren's admirable work in the United States Engineering Corps, in publishing maps and reports of the Minnesota and Mississippi river surveys. Descriptions of Lake Agassiz and the River Warren were partly given in the eighth and eleventh annual reports of the Minnesota Geological Survey, and in the first, second, and fourth volumes of its final report. Monograph XXV of the U. S. Geological Survey, "The Glacial Lake Agassiz," published in 1896, treats of its entire explored extent (658 pages, with many maps). Its area exceeded that of the state of Minnesota, being about 110,000 square miles, or more than the united areas of the five Great Lakes that outflow to the St. Lawrence river.

LAKE SUPERIOR AND OTHER LAKES AND RIVERS.

The name of Lake county refers to its adjoining the Grand Lac of Champlain's map in 1632, which was mapped under its present name, Lake Superior, by Marquette in 1673. Its being the greatest lake in the series flowing to the St. Lawrence, or even the greatest freshwater lake in the world, was noted in the name used by Champlain, in translation from Kitchigumi of the Ojibways. Superior means simply the Upper lake in that series.

Rainy lake and river are likewise translations from their aboriginal and early French names. From the narration of a French voyageur, Jacques de Noyon, who was there in 1688 or within a year or two earlier or later, we have the name Ouchichiq or Koochiching, given by the Crees to this river and adopted by the Ojibways. Joseph la France, traveling there in 1740, noted the derivation of the name Lac de la Pluie, meaning in English the Lake of the Rain, from the mist of the falls of Rainy river at the present city named International Falls. Further consideration of these names is given for Koochiching county.

On the sketch map drawn in 1730 by an Assiniboine named Ochagach for Verendrye, the Lake of the Woods is unnamed, but the country at its north side is shown as inhabited by the Crees. In 1737 and 1754 it was mapped as Lac des Bois, from which the English name is translated.

La France, in 1740, recorded its aboriginal names, in translation, as "Lake Du Bois, or Des Isles," that is, the Lake of the Woods or of the Islands. It is entirely surrounded by woods, though the border of the great prairie region is not far westward; and its second name was given for the multitude of islands in its northern part. The Ojibway name of its broad southern part, adjoining Beltrami and Roseau counties, as noted by Gilfillan and Verwyst, refers to the sand dunes of Oak point and Sable island, at the mouth of Rainy river, whence this part was frequently called Sand Hill lake by the early fur traders.

The St. Louis river is duly noticed for the county named from it, with mention of its earlier French name as the river of Fond du Lac, so called because there the series of falls and rapids along its last fifteen miles descends to the level of Lake Superior. The Ojibways name it Kitchigumi zibi, Lake Superior river.

Cass lake, early known as Red Cedar lake in translation from the Ojibways, was renamed in honor of General Lewis Cass, who, with Schoolcraft as historian of his expedition, visited it in 1820, regarding it as the chief source of the Mississippi. He is also commemorated by Cass county, for which the names of this lake and of Winnebagoshish and Leech lakes are fully noticed.

Thief river, lying mostly in Marshall county and having its source in Thief lake, is translated from the Ojibway name, which is explained for the city at its mouth, Thief River Falls, in Pennington county.

Clearwater river, lying in three counties, one of which bears this name, is again a translation from the Ojibways, like Eau Claire, of the same meaning, which designates a river, a county, and its city and county seat, in Wisconsin.

The Wild Rice river, and the lakes so named near its source, are translations from Manomin or Mahnomen, the native grain much used and highly prized by the Ojibway people as a staple part of their food, noted more in detail for Mahnomen county.

Crow Wing river and the county named from it present another translation from these Indians, for the outline of an island at the junction of this river with the Mississippi, which they fancifully compared with the wing of a raven. Farther south, on the boundary between Wright and Hennepin counties, they applied to the Crow river a different name, correctly designating our American crow, the marauder of newly planted cornfields. These names, with the Ojibway words from which they were translated, are again noticed in the chapter of Crow Wing county.

Sauk river in Todd and Stearns counties, Osakis lake at its source, lying partly in Douglas county, and the villages and cities of Osakis, Sauk Center, and Sauk Rapids, the last being on the east side of the Mississippi opposite to the mouth of the Sauk river, derived their names from a small party of Sac or Sauk Indians, who came as refugees from their own country in Wisconsin and lived near Osakis lake, as related for the township and village of Sauk Rapids in Benton county.

Mille Lacs, as named by the French, meaning "a thousand lakes," bore a Sioux name, Mde Wakan, nearly like Mini Wakan, their equivalent name which is translated Spirit lake in Iowa. Its Ojibway name is Minsi or Missi sagaigon, as spelled respectively by Nicollet in 1843 and De L' Isle in 1703, meaning Great lake, just as the Mississippi is the Great river. These names are more elaborately reviewed in the chapter for Mille Lacs county, which also notes the origin of the name Rum river, the outlet of this lake.

Kettle river, in Carlton and Pine counties, is noticed for the latter in explanation of the name of Kettle River township.

The Pine lakes and river and the Ojibway village of Chengwatana, meaning Pine village, gave the names of Pine county and Pine City, its county seat.

Snake river is translated from the Ojibway name, Kanabec sibi, which has several other spellings. Kanabec, retained as the designation of a county, with its accent on the second syllable, is widely different in both pronunciation and meaning from the Kennebec river in Maine.

St. Croix river, which, with the expansion of its lowest twenty miles in Lake St. Croix, forms the boundary of this state on the east side of Pine, Chisago, and Washington counties, was called the River du Tombeau (Tomb or Grave river) by Hennepin in 1680, "R. de la Magdeleine" on Franquelin's map in 1688, and the River St. Croix (Holy Cross) by Perrot's proclamation in 1689 and by the Relation of Penicaut in 1700. A cross had been set at its mouth, as noted by Penicaut, probably to mark the grave of some French trader or voyageur. La Harpe, writing of Le Sueur's expedition in 1700, which was the theme of Penicaut's Relation, described this stream as "a great river called St. Croix, because a Frenchman of that name was wrecked at its mouth."

Lake Pepin bears this name on De L' Isle's map of Canada or New France, published in 1703. It may have been chosen, as stated by Gannett, in honor of Pepin le Bref, king of the Franks, who was born in 714 and died in 768. He was a son of Charles Martel, and was the father of Charlemagne. Very probably the name was placed on the map by De L' Isle under request of his patron, the king of France. Pepin was an infrequent personal surname among the French settlers of Canada, whence many explorers and traders came to this region, but history has failed to record for whom and why this large lake of the Mississippi was so named. Hennepin, in his narration and map, had called it Lac des Pleurs (Lake of Tears), because there, as he wrote, some of the Sioux by whom he had been taken captive, with his companions, "wept the whole night, to induce the others to consent to our death." Penicaut named it Lac Bon Secours, meaning Lake Good Help, apparently in allusion to the abundance of buffaloes and other game found in its vicinity. This name, Bon Secours, and another, River des Boeufs, that is, River of Buffaloes, were early applied to the Chippewa river in Wisconsin, which was the geologic cause of Lake Pepin by bringing much alluvium into the valley of the Mississippi below the lake. Its origin was thus like that of Lake St. Croix, and like Lac qui Parle on the Minnesota river.

Cannon river, joining the Mississippi at the head of Lake Pepin, is changed from its earlier French name, River aux Canots, meaning Canoe river, which alluded to canoes frequently left in concealment near its mouth by Indians and by French traders, especially when going on the hunt for buffaloes in the adjoining prairie country. The present erroneous name, losing its original significance, comes from the narratives of Pike's expedition in 1805-06 and of Long's expeditions in 1817 and 1823. Pike used both names, Canoe river when telling of his voyage up the Mississippi, and Cannon river in the journal of his return. Nicollet, in his report and map published in 1843, called it Lahontan river and also Cannon river, supposing it to be identifiable as the Long river of Baron Lahontan's "New Voyages to North America," which purported to relate his travel here in the winter of 1688-89. That stream, however, with later knowledge seems instead to be entirely fictitious (Minnesota in Three Centuries, 1908, vol. I, pages 239-241).

According to Nicollet, the name given by the Sioux to Cannon river was Inyan bosndata, in translation Standing Rock. It referred to the unequally eroded rock column or spire called by the white settlers Castle Rock, whence a township and railway station near this river in Dakota county are named.

Zumbro river bears a name more remarkably changed from its original form than the Cannon river, being derived from the early French name, River des Embarras, meaning River of Difficulties. Its surface in its lower course and on the Mississippi bottomland was obstructed by driftwood, as noted by Albert Lea in the expedition with Kearny in 1835. This burden and embarrassment prevented or hindered its navigation by the canoes of the French voyageurs for the fur trade. Two villages on the river are named Zumbrota and Zumbro Falls, respectively in Goodhue and Wabasha counties, for which these names are more fully considered. In St. Louis county, the large river whence it is named receives two tributaries that were likewise each named River des Embarras by the French, because of their burden of driftwood, the upper one being now the Embarrass river, and the lower now called Floodwood river. Forsyth in 1819 noted this stream as Driftwood river.

Beside the Zumbro in Goodhue county, the township and village of Pine Island recall its Sioux name, Wazi Oju, as the river is called on Nicollet's map, signifying Pines Planted, in allusion to the grove of large white pines adjoining this village.

Root river, the most southeastern large tributary to the Mississippi in this state, rising in Mower county and flowing through Olmsted, Fillmore, and Houston counties, was called Racine river by Pike, Root river by Long in 1817, and both its Sioux name, Hokah, and the English translation, Root, are used in Keating's Narrative of Long's expedition in 1823. With more strictly accurate spelling and pronunciation, the Sioux or Dakota word is Hutkan, meaning Racine in the French language and Root in English, while the Sioux word Hokah means a heron. Racine township and railway village in Mower county, and Hokah, similarly the name of a township and village in Houston county, were derived from the river.

Tributaries of the Minnesota river to be mentioned here are the Pomme de Terre and Chippewa rivers, from the north; the Lac qui Parle river, having the French name of a lake through which the Minnesota flows, and the Yellow Medicine, Redwood, Cottonwood, and Blue Earth rivers, from the southwest and south; and Watonwan and Le Sueur rivers, which flow into the Blue Earth. Each of these streams, excepting the first, is most fully noticed for a county bearing its name; and the Pomme de Terre lake and river, translated by the French from the Sioux, are noticed for a township so named in Grant county. It is noteworthy that our names of all these rivers, excepting Le Sueur, which commemorates the early French explorer, were originally received from the Sioux or Dakota people, who had long inhabited this part of Minnesota when the first explorers and settlers came. Only Watonwan, however, retains its form as a Sioux word.

Four streams that have their sources in this state and flow into Iowa, namely, the Rock, Des Moines, Cedar, and Upper Iowa rivers, will complete this list.

Rock river, translated from its Sioux name, refers to the prominent rock hill, commonly now called "the Mound," which rises precipitously west of this river in Mound township of Rock county, the most southwestern in Minnesota. Both the township and county, like the river, were named for this high outcrop of red quartzite. The same rock formation, continuing north in Pipestone county, includes the renowned Pipestone Quarry, whence came the names of that county, its county seat, and the creek that flows past the quarry.

The Des Moines river flows through Murray, Cottonwood, and Jackson counties, thence crosses Iowa, gives its name to the capital of that state, and joins the Mississippi at its southeast corner. Franquelin in 1688 and De L' Isle in 1703 mapped it as "R. des Moingona," the name being taken from an Indian village, Moingona, shown by Franquelin not far from the site of the present village of this name in Boone county, near the center of Iowa. The name was spelled by Pike as De Moyen and Des Moyan; Long called it De Moyen; and Beltrami, Le Moine and Monk river. It has three names on Nicollet's map: "Inyan Shasha of the Sioux," meaning Red Stone, in allusion to its flowing through a gorge of red sandstone in Marion county, Iowa; "Moingonan of the Algonkins," from the early maps; and "Des Moines of the French," meaning the River of the Monks. The third name, which has been too long in use to be changed, is an erroneous translation by the early traders, based merely on the pronunciation of the old Algonquian name. An interesting paper on its origin, by Dr. Charles R. Keyes, is in the Annals of Iowa (third series, vol. III, pages 554-9, with three maps, Oct., 1898).

Cedar river, flowing from Dodge and Mower counties in this state, is the longest stream of northeastern Iowa. Like the Missouri river, which exceeds the upper Mississippi in length, it is tributary to a shorter stream, the Iowa river, about twenty-five miles above the junction of the latter with the Mississippi. Red cedar trees, whose fragrant red wood is much esteemed for chests and other furniture, growing in many places along the bluffs of this river, supplied its aboriginal name, translated by Nicollet and on present maps as Red Cedar river. Its upper part, in this state, is more commonly called simply Cedar river; and its two chief cities, in Iowa, are named Cedar Rapids and Cedar Falls. The same name, Red Cedar, was derived in translation from the Ojibways for the lake of the upper Mississippi renamed as Cass lake, and for the present Cedar lake in Aitkin county, besides numerous other relatively small lakes, streams, and islands, in various parts of Minnesota. Far northward the full name Red Cedar was used in distinction from the arbor vitae, which often is called white cedar, having similarly durable wood of a light color.

Upper Iowa river begins in Mower county, runs meanderingly along parts of the south line of Fillmore county, and passes southeast and east in Iowa to the Mississippi near the northeast corner of that state, which is named from the larger Iowa river flowing past Iowa Falls and Iowa City. The application of the name to a district west of the Mississippi, and later to the territory and state, as first used for the district by Lieutenant Albert M. Lea in 1836, has been well told by Prof. Benjamin F. Shambaugh in the volume of Annals of Iowa before cited for the Des Moines river (third series, III, 641-4, Jan., 1899), with fourteen references to preceding papers and books that treat of the origin of the state name. It was originally the name of a Siouan tribe living there, whose hunting grounds extended north to the Blue Earth and Minnesota rivers at the time of Le Sueur's expedition in 1700-01. Their tribal name, spelled in many ways, was translated "sleepy ones" by Riggs, being analogous with the name of the Sioux chief Sleepy Eye, who is commemorated by a city in Brown county. The Handbook of American Indians gives more than seventy-five variations in the former spelling of the name that now is established in common use as Iowa (Part I, 1907, page 614).

AITKIN COUNTY

This county, established May 23, 1857, and organized June 30, 1871, was named for William Alexander Aitkin, a fur trader with the Ojibway Indians. He was born in Scotland in 1785; came from Edinburgh to America in his boyhood; and about the year 1802 came to the Northwest, being in the service of a trader named John Drew. Aitkin married into an influential Indian family; was soon a trader on his own account; and rapidly advanced until in 1831 he took charge of the Fond du Lac department of the American Fur Company, under John Jacob Astor, with headquarters at Sandy Lake, in this county, adjoining the east side of the Mississippi river. He died September 16, 1851, and is buried on the east bank of the Mississippi, opposite to the mouth of Swan river, in Morrison county, where he had a trading post during his last nine years, after 1842.

The name of Aitkin county was at first erroneously spelled Aiken, with which it is identical in pronunciation, and it was changed to its present spelling in 1872 by an act of the legislature.

Townships and Villages.

Information of the origins of township names was received from Thomas R. Foley, Jr., real estate and insurance agent, and Carl E. Taylor, court commissioner, both of Aitkin, during a visit there in May, 1916.

AITKIN township bears the same name as the county. Its village, also bearing this name, was founded in 1870, as a station of the Northern Pacific railroad, which in that year was built through the county; and the next year, in the county organization, it was made the county seat.

BAIN township, and its railway station of the same name, are in honor of William Bain, the hotel owner, who is one of the proprietors of the station site.

BALL BLUFF township should be Bald Bluff, being for the conspicuous morainic drift hill so named, having a bald grassy top without trees, in section 32 of this township, at the east side of the Mississippi.

BALSAM township is from two species of trees that are common or frequent in this county, the balsam fir and the balsam poplar.

BEAVER was named for beavers and their dams, found by the earliest settlers on the head streams of Split Rock river, in the south part of this township.

CLARK township had early settlers of this name, one being Frank Clark, who removed to McGregor.

CORNISH was named for Charles E. and Milo F. Cornish, settlers in section 34 of this township, coming from southern Minnesota.

DAVIDSON is for A. D. Davidson, senior partner in the Davidson and McRae Stock Farm Company, of Duluth, and later of Winnipeg, owners of numerous tracts of land in this township. He died in Rochester, Minn., April, 1916.

DICK township was named in honor of Miss Mildred Dick, assistant in the office of the county auditor.

ESQUAGAMAH township derived its name from Esquagamah lake, crossed by its east side. This is an Ojibway name, meaning the last lake, given to it as the last and most western in a series of three lakes lying mainly in Waukenabo township, which is named for the most eastern of these lakes.

FARM ISLAND township is from its lake of this name, having an island of 29 acres, on which the Ojibways formerly had large cultivated fields.

FLEMING township has Fleming lake, in section 22, named for an early settler there.

GLEN bears a euphonious name selected by its settlers at the time of the township organization.

HAUGEN township is named in honor of Christopher G. Haugen, former sheriff of this county.

HAZELTON is for Cutler J. Hazelton, a former county commissioner whose homestead was on Pine lake in this township. Cutler post office, on the south side of this lake, was also named for him.

Nichols post office, beside Mille Lacs in the southwest corner of Hazelton, was named for Austin R. Nichols, its postmaster, who settled there in 1879. A biographic sketch is given under the city of Austin, Mower county, also named in his honor.

HEBRON township was doubtless named by settlers coming from a town of this name in some eastern state. The original Hebron is a very ancient town in Palestine.

HILL LAKE township, and its village, named Hill City, as also its Hill lake, are all so designated from the prominent hill of morainic drift in section 25. This is the culminating point of a very knolly and broken tract of the same moraine extending into the adjoining sections, to which locality, and especially to its highest part, the Ojibways applied the name Pikwadina (or Piquadinaw), "it is hilly." Hence came the common name "Poquodenaw mountain," used by the lumbermen and given to this hill on the map of Aitkin county in the Minnesota Geological Survey.

IDUN township is named for a place in Sweden.

JEVNE township bears the surname of a Scandinavian family early settling there.

JEWETT township honors D. M. Jewett, a pioneer in section 20.

KIMBERLY township was named from its station established when the Northern Pacific railroad was built in 1870, in honor of Moses C. Kimberly, of St. Paul. He was born in Sandisfield, Mass., December 1, 1845; came to Minnesota in 1870, as a surveyor and engineer for this railroad; was during many years its general superintendent.

LAKESIDE township is at the east side of Mille Lacs.

LEE township was named in honor of Olaf Lee, a pioneer Norwegian farmer in section 18.

LE MAY township was named for Frank Le May, one of the first settlers.

LIBBY township is for Mark Libby, who long ago was a fur trader there with the Indians, on the outlet of Sandy lake.

LOGAN township was named for the long and narrow lakes, often shaped like a horseshoe or ox-bow, which lie in abandoned parts of the old channels of the Mississippi, occurring frequently in this and other townships. For these lakes of the alluvial land adjoining the river the name "logans" has been in common use in Aitkin county during the fifty years or more since the region was first invaded by lumbermen. (Geology of Minn., vol. IV, pages 26-27.)

MCGREGOR township was named after the station and village of the Northern Pacific railroad in section 31, which also became a station and junction of the Soo line.

MACVILLE township is for pioneer Scotch settlers there named McAninch and McPheters.

MALMO township is named for the large city of Malmo in southern Sweden, on the Sound opposite to Copenhagen.

MILLWARD township was named for one of its early settlers.

MORRISON township was named for Edward Morrison, one of its pioneer farmers.

NORDLAND township bears the name of a large district in northern Norway.

PLINY township has the name of a celebrated naturalist of ancient Rome.

QUADNA (each syllable having the sound of a in fall) is shortened from the earlier name of Piquadinaw, first given to this township on account of its tracts of knolly and hilly drift extending eastward from the high hill so named by the Ojibways, as before mentioned, in Hill Lake township.

RICE RIVER township received its name from its being crossed by the head streams of the Rice river, named, like the large Rice lake, from wild rice (Zizania aquatica), which was harvested by the Indians as a very valuable natural food supply.

SALO township was named by its Finn settlers for a town in southwestern Finland.

SEAVEY township was named for a family residing in Aitkin, one of whom, Frank E. Seavey, has been during many years the clerk of the county court.

SHAMROCK was named by Irish settlers for the trifoliate plant long ago chosen as the national emblem of Ireland.

SHOVEL LAKE township and its railway station were named for Shovel lake, crossed by the south line of the township.

SPALDING township was named in honor of John L. Spalding, former treasurer of this county.

SPENCER township is for William Spencer, who was a druggist in Aitkin, but removed to Texas.

TAMARACK is a village of the Northern Pacific railroad in Clark township.

TURNER township is for L. E. Turner, formerly a county commissioner.

VERDON township and post office were named for Verdon Wells, son of E. B. Wells, the postmaster.

WAGNER township was named for a former assistant in the office of the county register of deeds, Bessie Wagner, who now is Mrs. Hammond, living in Montana.

WAUKENABO township (accented on the syllable next to the last, with the sound of ah) has the Ojibway name of the eastern one of its series of three lakes. Gilfillan wrote it with a somewhat different spelling: "Wakonabo sagaiigun, the lake of the broth of wakwug or fish milt, or eggs-broth lake; or Broth-of-moss-growing-on-rocks-or-trees lake. The Indians use the latter in case of starvation. Both the above explanations are given by different Indians."

WEALTHWOOD is a name proposed by Mrs. Daniel J. Knox, of Aitkin, for the lakeside summer resort platted in section 20 of this fractional township, which previously was a part of Nordland.

WHITE ELK township bears the name of the lake crossed by its east line, translated from its Ojibway name.

WILLIAMS township was named in honor of George T. Williams, of Aitkin, who during many years was the county judge of probate.

WORKMAN township is thought to be named for a pioneer settler there, who later removed from the county.

LAKES AND STREAMS.

Nicollet's map, published in 1843, gives the following names of lakes and streams partly or wholly within the area of Aitkin county, as they have since continued in use: the Mississippi river, Willow and Little Willow rivers, West and East Savanna rivers, Lake Aitkin, Sandy lake, and Mille Lacs.

Other names which survive with slight changes from that map are Prairie river, tributary to the West Savanna, called Little Prairie river by Nicollet; Mud lake and river, tributary to the Mississippi at Aitkin, which were called Muddy lakes and river; and Cedar lake, Nicollet's Red Cedar lake, which Pike in 1805-06 called the Lower Red Cedar lake (to distinguish it from the Upper Red Cedar lake, far up the Mississippi, renamed in 1820 Lake Cassina, now Cass lake).

The very elaborate "Historico-Geographical Chart of the Upper Mississippi River," published by Dr. Elliott Coues in 1895 with his annotated edition of Pike's Expeditions, includes interesting notes of successive geographic names and their dates in Aitkin county.

Willow river was called Alder river by Schoolcraft in 1820 and likewise in 1855. It flows through a nearly level and largely swampy area, which bears abundant willows and alders. Its Ojibway name is translated Willow river by Gilfillan.

West Savanna river was so called in 1820 by Schoolcraft. The Savanna rivers, West and East, retain these names as given by the early French voyageurs; but this word, nearly equivalent to prairie, was originally of American origin. It was a Carib word, and was introduced into European languages by Spanish writers near the middle of the sixteenth century. By the Ojibways the East Savanna river was named Mushkigonigumi sibi, "the marsh-portage river," having reference to the very marshy portage made on this much used canoe route in passing to the West Savanna river and Sandy lake.

The early French name of Sandy lake was Lac au Sable or du Sable. The French and English alike translated it from the Ojibway name, recorded by both Gilfillan and Verwyst as Ga-mitawangagumag Sagaiigun, "the-place-of-bare-sand lake." The Northwest Company established a trading post on the west shore of this lake in 1794, which was visited by David Thompson in 1798 and by Pike in January, 1806; but before the time of Aitkin's taking charge there in 1831 the old post had been abandoned for a new site at the mouth of the outlet of Sandy lake, on the narrow point between the outlet and the Mississippi river.

Rice river and its tributary Rice lake (named Lake Dodge by Nicollet, probably for Governor Henry Dodge of Wisconsin), also another Rice lake, of very irregular outline, lying close south of Sandy lake, received their names, as before noted in connection with Rice River township, from their large and valuable supplies of the excellent native grain called wild rice. The Ojibway name of the wild rice, Manomin, is applied to this stream on Nicollet's map, in the common form of its spelling as given in Baraga's Dictionary. Another form is Mahnomen, given to a county of this state. Its French translation is Folle Avoine, meaning in our language "false or fool oat," nearly like the name, "Wild Oats river," used for this Rice river by Beltrami in 1823.

White Elk brook or creek, like the township of this name, is so called, in the Ojibway usage, for the lake of its source.

Moose river, tributary to Willow river, is translated from its Ojibway name, given by Gilfillan as Moz-oshtigwani sibi, Moosehead river. It receives the outflow of several small lakes, of which the most eastern, called Moose lake, in Macville, has been mainly drained.

Little Willow river is named, like the larger stream that often is called Big Willow river, for its plentiful willows.

Sisabagama lake (accented on the middle syllable, with the long vowel sound) and the outflowing creek or river of the same name, close east of Aitkin, have had various spellings. Gilfillan spelled and defined this Ojibway name as Sesabeguma lake, "Every-which-way lake, or the lake which has arms running in all directions"; but such description is not applicable to this lake, unless it be considered to include the group of several neighboring lakes which together are tributary to this stream.

Snake and Little Snake rivers, having their sources in the southeast part of Aitkin county and flowing south into Kanabec county, are translations from their Ojibway names, as is noted in the chapter on that county, which bears the aboriginal name of the Snake river.

Cowan's brook, in Williams township, tributary to the Snake river, was named for an early lumberman there.

Pine lake and Big Pine lake, in Wagner, the latter extending east into Pine county, gave their name to the outflowing Pine river. These lakes and great areas around them, in both Aitkin and Pine counties, originally had majestic white pine forests.

Dam lake and brook, in Kimberly, received this name from the low, ice-formed ridges of gravel and sand on the shores of this lake, especially at its mouth.

Sandy river, flowing west and then north into the lake of this name and outflowing by a very crooked course of more than two miles, though its junction with the Mississippi is only about a half mile from the lake, follows the Indian rule of nomenclature, that a lake gives its name to the stream flowing through it or from it.

Prairie river, like the West Savanna river, which unites with it, received its name from its small open spaces of grassy and bushy land without trees, in this generally wooded region.

Savanna lake, adjoining the old portage of the fur traders, and the Lower Savanna lake, through which their canoes passed to Sandy lake, also have reference to such small savannas, which are more commonly called prairies excepting in the southern states.

Tamarack river, flowing into Prairie river, was named for its plentiful growth of the tamarack, a very graceful species of our coniferous trees (the only one that is not evergreen).

Aitkin lake in sections 19 and 20, Turner, was named like this county for William A. Aitkin, the fur trader, who very probably often fished and hunted there.

Bald Bluff lake lies at the southern base of the hill of this name.

Birch lake, in section 19, Hazelton, is named for its yellow and paper birches, the latter being the species used for the Indian's bark canoe.

Blind lake, in T. 48, R. 27, is mainly inclosed by a large swamp and has no outlet, as its name implies.

Cedar lake, before mentioned, was named from the red cedars which in scanty numbers are found on its hilly shores and islands.

Clear lake, in sections 28 and 33, Glen, is exceptionally beautiful, with very clear water and inclosed by high shores.

Elm Island lake, at the center of Nordland, has a small island bearing elm trees.

Farm Island lake gave its name to that township, in allusion to the farming by Ojibways. The outflowing Mud river passes in the next two miles through Pine, Hickory, and Spirit lakes, which in the latest atlas are shown to be connected by straits, so that they might be termed a series of three bays continuous with the first named large lake.

Fleming, French, Jenkins, and Wilkins lakes, in Fleming township, are probably named for early settlers, trappers and hunters, or lumbermen. A larger lake of this group, now named Gun lake, was formerly called Lake Manomin (i. e., Wild Rice).

Hanging Kettle lake, translated from its Ojibway name, in sections 13 and 14, Farm Island township, is connected eastward by straits with Diamond and Mud lakes.

Horseshoe lake, in sections 23 and 24, Shamrock, is named for its curved shape.

Island lake, in sections 11 to 14, Turner, has a large central island.

Lone lake, in sections 29 and 30, Nordland, has no visible outlet; but it probably supplies the water of large chalybeate springs which issue close south of the road near the middle of the south side of Mud lake.

Mallard lake, in section 2, Hazelton, formerly called Rice lake, is named for its mallard ducks.

Nelson and Douglas lakes, section 23, Clark, now drained away, were named for M. Nelson and E. Douglas, owners of adjoining lands.

The name of Nord lake, in Nordland, is of similar origin with the township name, meaning north and given by Norwegian settlers.

Pine lake, named for its pine woods, in Hazelton township, was earlier known as Hazelton lake or Echo lake.

Portage lake, section 6, Davidson, was at the end of a portage on a former canoe route.

Rabbit lake, in Glen township, has high shores of irregular outlines, an excellent hunting ground.

Rat lake, in Workman, and Rat House lake, in sections 26 and 35, Cornish, are named for their muskrats.

Sugar lake, in Malmo, is named for its sugar maple trees, this species having been much used by the Ojibways for sugar-making.

Twenty lake, in Malmo, is named from the number of its section.

Vladimirof lake, mainly in section 10, Nordland, was formerly known as Section Ten lake, but has been renamed for a settler who owns lands close north and east of the lake.

This county also has the following names of lakes, which are of frequent occurrence elsewhere.

Bass lake, in section 28, Aitkin; another of this name in section 10, Farm Island (lately renamed as Hammal lake); and a third Bass lake in section 19, Turner.

Long lake, in Glen township.

AITKIN COUNTY 21

Mud lake, in Nordland; another in the north part of Logan; and a third and fourth in section 10, McGregor, and sections 14 and 23, White Elk.

Otter lake, in section 34, LeMay; and another in section 9, Logan.

Pickerel lake, in section 27, Aitkin.

Round lake, in section 31, Hazelton; another in Jevne; a third, crossed by the line between Haugen and Shamrock; and a fourth between Waukenabo and Esquagamah lakes.

GLACIAL LAKE AITKIN.

In the village of Aitkin and westward a beach ridge of gravel and sand, having a height of three to five feet, marks the south shore of a glacial lake which existed during a geologically very short time in the broad and shallow depression of this part of the Mississippi valley. It was first described and mapped by the present writer in Volume IV of the Final Report of the Geological Survey of Minnesota, published in 1899, being then known to extend from the edge of Crow Wing county eastward and northward in Aitkin, Spencer, and Morrison townships.

Later and more detailed examinations, by Leverett and Sardeson, show that this glacial lake reached northward along the Mississippi to the mouth of Swan river, in the north edge of Aitkin county (Bulletin No. 13, Minnesota Geological Survey, published in 1917). The length of Glacial Lake Aitkin was about fifty miles, but it had only a slight depth of water, nowhere exceeding twenty feet, above the Mississippi, Willow, and Rice rivers, and above the Sandy river and lake.

ANOKA COUNTY

The name of this county, established May 23, 1857, was taken from the town of Anoka, which was first settled in 1851-52 and was named in 1853. It is a Dakota or Sioux word, meaning, as Prof. A. W. Williamson wrote, "on both sides; applied by founders to the city laid out on both sides of Rum river, and since applied to the county," of which this city is the county seat. Rev. Moses N. Adams, who came as a missionary to the Sioux in 1848 and learned their language, stated that, as a Sioux word, Anoka means "the other side, or both sides."

According to the late R. I. Holcombe and others, including Albert M. Goodrich, the historian of this county, the Ojibways also sometimes used a name of nearly the same sound for the Rum river and for the site of Anoka near its mouth, meaning "where they work," on account of the extensive early lumbering and log-driving on this stream. The Ojibway verb, "I work," is Anoki, as given in Baraga's Dictionary, with many inflected forms and compound words from this root, all referring to work in some way as their central thought.

But the selection of the name Anoka had reference only to its use by the Dakota or Sioux people, whose language is wholly unlike that of the Ojibways. A newspaper article on this subject, written in 1873 by L. M. Ford, is quoted by Goodrich, as follows: "The name for the new town was a topic of no little interest, and the writer had something to do in its selection. It was decided to give it an Indian name. The Dakota Lexicon, just published, and of which I was the owner of a copy, was not infrequently consulted and at length the euphonious name Anoka was decided upon. . . . It was said to mean 'on both sides,' when rendered into less musical English, and to this day the name is by no means inappropriate, as the town is growing up and extending on either side of the beautiful but badly named river."

Townships and Villages.

Information for this county has been gathered from the "History of the Upper Mississippi Valley," 1881, in which Anoka county and its civil divisions are treated in pages 222-293; from the "History of Anoka county and the Towns of Champlin and Dayton in Hennepin County," 320 pages, 1905, by Albert M. Goodrich; and from Charles W. Lenfest, county treasurer, Frank Hart, clerk of the court, and Clarence D. Green, real estate agent, during a visit to Anoka in October, 1916.

Anoka was founded by Orrin W. Rice, Neal D. Shaw, and others, by whom its name was adopted in May, 1853. The "City of Anoka" was incorporated by the state legislature July 29, 1858, and later the "Borough of Anoka," March 5, 1869, but both these acts failed of acceptance by the vote of the township. Finally, under a legislative act of March 2, 1878, this city was set off from the township of the same name, the first city election being held on March 12.

BETHEL was first settled in 1856 by Quakers, and was organized the next year. Its name is from ancient Palestine, meaning "House of God," and was selected for this township by Moses Twitchell, who settled here as an immigrant from Bethel, Maine.

BLAINE township, settled in 1862, was the east part of Anoka until 1877, when it was separately organized and was named in honor of James Gillespie Blaine, a prominent Republican statesman of Maine. He was born in Pennsylvania, Jan. 31, 1830, and died in Washington, D. C., Jan. 27, 1893; was a member of Congress from Maine, 1863-76, being the speaker in 1869-75; U. S. senator, 1876-81; and secretary of state, March to December, 1881, and 1889-92. In the presidential campaign of 1884 he was an unsuccessful candidate. He wrote "Twenty Years of Congress," published in 1884-86.

BURNS township, settled in 1854 or earlier, was a part of St. Francis until 1869, being then organized and named, probably for the celebrated poet. This name was adopted on the suggestion of James Kelsey, who was elected the first township treasurer.

CENTERVILLE, settled in 1850-52, was organized in 1857. Its village of this name, thence given to the township, was platted in the spring of 1854, having a central situation between the Mississippi and St. Croix rivers. The settlers in the village and vicinity were mostly French, and this came to be known as the French settlement, while numerous German settlers in the western part of the township caused that to be called the German settlement.

The village of COLUMBIA HEIGHTS, a suburb of Minneapolis, in the south edge of Fridley tonwship, was platted and named by the late Thomas Lowry of that city.

COLUMBUS township, settled in 1855 and organized in 1857, was named for Christopher Columbus.

FRIDLEY, a fractional township comprising only about sixteen square miles, was established by legislative act as Manomin county (meaning Wild Rice), on the same date, May 23, 1857, with the establishment of Anoka county. "John Banfil settled in what is now Fridley in 1847, and kept a stopping place for the accommodation of travelers. Two years later Henry M. Rice acquired considerable land and built a country residence at Cold Springs, giving his name to the creek which flows through the town. . . . A ferry across the Mississippi river was established about 1854." (Goodrich, pages 162-3). This very small county continued nearly thirteen years, until in 1869-70 it was united with Anoka county as Manomin township. The name was changed to Fridley in 1879.

Abram McCormick Fridley, in whose honor this township received its name, was born in Steuben county, N. Y., May 1, 1817; came to Long

Prairie, Minn., in 1851 as agent for the Winnebago Indians; was afterward a farmer in this township, and in 1869 opened a large farm in Becker, Sherburne county; was a representative in the legislature in 1855, 1869-71, and 1879. He died in Fridley township, March, 1888.

GROW township, settled about 1853, was organized in 1857 with the name Round Lake, which in 1859 was changed to Grow, in honor of Galusha Aaron Grow, of Pennsylvania. He was born in 1823, and died in 1907; was a member of Congress, 1851-63, and again in 1894-1902; was the speaker of the House, 1861-3. "For ten years, at the beginning of each Congress, he introduced in the House a free homestead bill, until it became a law in 1862." This grand public service has caused him to be remembered gratefully by millions of homesteaders.

HAM LAKE township, settled in 1857, was attached to Grow township till 1871, when it was separately organized. It had been previously called Glengarry, a name from Scotland, which its Swedish settlers found difficult to pronounce. The county commissioners therefore named the new township Ham Lake, from its lake in sections 16 and 17, which had acquired this name on account of its form.

LINWOOD township, first settled in 1855 and organized in 1871, received its name from Linwood lake, the largest and most attractive one in a series or chain of ten or more lakes extending from northeast to southwest through this township and onward to Ham lake. The name doubtless refers to the lin tree or linden. Our American species (Tilia Americana), usually called basswood, is abundant here, and is common or frequent through nearly all this state.

OAK GROVE township, settled in 1855, was organized in 1857. "The name is derived from the profuse growth of oak trees, which are about equally distributed over the township." (Upper Mississippi Valley, page 285).

RAMSEY, first permanently settled in 1850, was organized in 1857, being then named Watertown; but in November, 1858, this township was renamed in honor of Alexander Ramsey, the first governor of Minnesota Territory, 1849-53, and later the second governor of this state, 1860-63.

Itasca was the name given by Governor Ramsey and others to a townsite platted in 1852 on sections 19 and 30 in this township, near an Indian trading post; and the first postoffice of Anoka county was established there and named Itasca in May of that year. The name was copied from Lake Itasca, at the head of the Mississippi, which had been so named by Schoolcraft in 1832. It was later applied during many years, after the building of the Northern Pacific railroad through this county, to its station near the former Itasca village site. Both the village and the railway station have been abandoned, but a new station, named Dayton, for the village of Dayton at the opposite side of the Mississippi, has been established on the Northern Pacific and Great Northern railways about a mile southeast from the former Itasca station. This old village name,

ANOKA COUNTY

which became widely known sixty years ago, is now retained here only by the neighboring Lake Itasca, of small size, scarcely exceeding a half mile in diameter.

St. Francis township, settled in 1855 and organized in 1857, bears the name given by Hennepin in 1680 to the Rum river. It was transferred by Carver in 1766 to the Elk river, and now is borne by the chief northern tributary of that river. The name is in commemoration of St. Francis of Assisi, in Italy, who was born in 1181 or 1182 and died in 1226, founder of the Franciscan order, to which Hennepin belonged.

Lakes and Streams.

The Mississippi has been considered in the first chapter; and the origin of the name Rum river, outflowing from Mille Lacs, is noted for Mille Lacs county.

A noteworthy series of lakes extends through Columbus and Centerville, including, in their order from northeast to southwest, Mud lake, Howard, Columbia, Tamarack, Randeau, Peltier, Centerville, George Watch, Marshan, Rice (or Traverse), Reshanau, Baldwin, and Golden lakes. The second to the fifth of these lakes are now much lowered or wholly drained away.

Peltier lake was named for early settlers, Charles, Paul, and Oliver Peltier, the first of whom built a sawmill.

Rice lake probably received its name from its wild rice, but Rice creek, flowing through this series of lakes, was named for Hon. Henry M. Rice, of St. Paul, United States senator, who was an early resident in Fridley township, as before noted. This Rice lake has been also known as Traverse lake, for F. W. Traverse, living at its northwest side.

Golden lake, the most southwestern in the series, lying in sections 25 and 36, Blaine, was named for John Golden, owner of land adjoining it, who was one of three brothers, early immigrants to this county from Ireland.

Another series of lakes, tributary in its northern part to the Sunrise river, and at the south to Coon creek, lies in Linwood, Bethel, and Ham Lake townships. This series includes, from northeast to southwest, Typo lake and Lake Martin; Island lake, named for its island; Linwood lake, giving its name to the township; Boot lake, named from its outline; Rice lake, having wild rice; Coon lake and Little Coon lake, named, like the creek, for raccoons, formerly much hunted here; and Lake Netta and Ham lake, the latter, as before noted, being named from its form, and giving name also to its township.

Cedar creek, and the adjoining Cedar station and village of the Great Northern railway, are named for the white cedar or arbor vitae, growing there in swamps.

Seeley, Trott, and Ford brooks, on the west side of Rum river, are named for their early settlers.

In Burns township, Norris lake, in section 1, was likewise named for Grafton Norris; and Hare lake, in section 21, now drained, for James U. Hare, who was formerly postmaster of Nowthen postoffice, lately discontinued, near this lake. (It is said that the name of this postoffice was recommended by Mr. Hare's neighbors, from his common use of it, "Now then," in conversation).

Other lakes named for pioneer settlers are Minard lake and Jones lake, in Bethel, the latter (now drained) having been also known as Lone Pine lake; Lake George, in Oak Grove township; Bunker lake in section 36, Grow township, named for Kendall Bunker, a homesteader there; and Lake Amelia, in section 35, Centerville.

The following lakes bear names that occur somewhat frequently in many other counties:

Cedar lake, in sections 33 and 34, Centerville.

Crooked lake, in section 33, Grow, and section 4, Anoka.

Deer lake, sections 15 and 22, Bethel.

Fish lake, in the north part of Bethel.

Goose lake, now drained, sections 15 and 16, Burns.

Grass lake, section 11, Oak Grove.

Mud lake, in section 16, Bethel; and another in section 13, Columbus.

Otter lake, sections 35 and 36, Centerville.

Pickerel lake, mostly drained, section 22, Burns.

The two Rice lakes, occurring in the series before noted.

Round lake, sections 20 and 29, Grow.

Swan lake, now drained. in section 25, Oak Grove.

Twin lake, section 19, Burns.

BECKER COUNTY

This county, established March 18, 1858, but not organized until thirteen years later by a legislative act approved March 1, 1871, was named in honor of George Loomis Becker, of St. Paul. He was born in Locke, Cayuga county, N. Y., February 4, 1829; was graduated at the University of Michigan in 1846; studied law, came to Minnesota in 1849, and began law practice in St. Paul; was mayor of this city in 1856; was Democratic candidate for Governor of Minnesota in 1859; was a state senator, 1868-71. He was commonly called General Becker, having been appointed by Governor Sibley on his military staff in 1858, with the rank of brigadier general. In 1862 he became land commissioner of the St. Paul and Pacific railroad, and was ever afterward occupied in advancing the railroad interests of Minnesota, being a member of the state railroad and warehouse commission from 1885 to 1901. He died in St. Paul, January 6, 1904.

October 13, 1857, Mr. Becker was elected as one of three members of Congress, to which number it was thought that the new state would be entitled. It was afterward decided, however, that the state could have only two representatives; and, in casting lots for these two, Becker was unsuccessful. His generous acquiescence was in part rewarded by this county name.

Townships and Villages.

Information has been gathered from "A Pioneer History of Becker County," by Alvin H. Wilcox, published in 1907, 757 pages; from H. S. Dahlen, county auditor, George D. Hamilton, editor of the Detroit Record, and Charles G. Sturtevant, formerly county surveyor, interviewed during a visit at Detroit in August, 1909; and from maps in the office of J. A. Narum, county auditor, examined during a second visit in September, 1916.

ATLANTA township, settled in 1871, was organized January 25, 1879, being then named Martin, perhaps for Martin Hanson, one of the first settlers. Two months afterward it was renamed Atlanta, "from the resemblance its undulating surface bears to the Atlantic ocean."

AUDUBON township was organized August 19, 1871, but was named successively Windom, Colfax, and Oak Lake, holding the last of these names from 1872 until 1881. The Northern Pacific station and village to be established here, also the small lake adjoining the village site, had received the name Audubon in August, 1871, in honor of John James Audubon (b. 1780, d. 1851), the great American ornithologist, celebrated for his pictures of birds. This name was proposed by his niece, a member of a party of tourists who "camped where the Audubon depot now stands." In January, 1881, the township name was changed to Audubon, and on February 23 of that year the village was incorporated.

BURLINGTON, organized August 26, 1872, "was so named from the city of Burlington in the state of Vermont, by Mrs. E. L. Wright, a Vermonter, whose husband took a leading part in the organization of the township."

Frazee village, on the Northern Pacific railroad in this township, was platted in 1873, but was not incorporated until 1891. It was named in honor of Randolph L. Frazee, owner of its lumber mill. He was born at Hamden Junction, Ohio, July 3, 1841; came to Minnesota in 1866, and to this place in 1872; was a representative in the legislature in 1875; removed in 1890 to Pelican Rapids, and died there June 4, 1906.

CALLAWAY township, organized March 30, 1906, is named for William R. Callaway, of Minneapolis, general passenger agent of the Soo railway, which had previously established a station and village of this name in section 32.

CARSONVILLE township, organized September 20, 1881, was named by Alvin H. Wilcox, then county treasurer, in honor of George M. Carson, a prominent pioneer, who in June, 1879, took a homestead in section 18, Osage (the east part of Carsonville till its separate organization in 1891).

CORMORANT township, organized February 26, 1872, received this name from its Big Cormorant and Upper Cormorant lakes, which are translated from the Ojibway names. Our species is the double-crested cormorant, which nests plentifully about these lakes.

CUBA, organized in the winter of 1871-72, was named for Cuba, Allegany county, N. Y., the native place of Charles W. Smith, who came as one of the first settlers of this township in 1871.

DETROIT township, settled in 1868 and organized July 29, 1871, derived its name from Detroit lake, which, according to the History of Becker county, had been so named by a French traveler here, who was a Catholic missionary. Having camped for a night on the north shore of the lake in full view of the long bar which stretches nearly across it and leaves a strait (detroit, in French) between its two parts, he thence applied this name to the lake. It appeared on our state maps in 1860. The Ojibway name of this lake refers also to its strait, being translated by Gilfillan as "the lake in which there is crossing on the sandy place." Detroit has been the county seat of Becker county from its organization in 1871; but during the first year some of the meetings of the county commissioners were held at or near Oak lake, a few miles distant to the northwest. The first village election was held March 3, 1881; and the city charter was adopted February 23, 1903.

ERIE township, first settled in 1872-3 and organized August 18, 1878, was named for Erie county in New York by settlers who came from the city of Buffalo, which is in that county.

EVERGREEN, organized January 4, 1888, was named for its abundant evergreen trees, including the pines, spruce, balsam fir, and the red and white cedars. It is estimated that in 1880 this township had "about five million feet of standing white pine."

GRAND PARK township, organized July 31, 1892, was so named for its beautiful scenery of rolling and hilly woodland, interspersed with lakes and traversed by the head stream of the Red river.

GREEN VALLEY, organized May 3, 1886, received this name from the valley of Shell river, which crosses the northeast part of this township.

HAMDEN township, organized September 19, 1871, was named for Hamden in one of the eastern states, this being a town or village name in Connecticut, New York, New Jersey, and Ohio.

HEIGHT OF LAND township, organized January 26, 1886, bears the name of the large lake crossed by its north boundary. The Red or Otter Tail river flows through this lake, from which a former canoe route led eastward to the Shell lake and river, tributary by the Crow Wing river to the Mississippi. Gilfillan translated the Ojibway name, "Ajawewesitagun sagaiigun, the lake where the portage is across a divide separating water which runs different ways, or Height of Land lake."

HOLMESVILLE township, which received its first settlers in 1871 and 1873, was organized March 19, 1889, as East Richwood; but this was soon changed to the present name, in honor of Elon G. Holmes. He was born in Madison county, N. Y., in 1841; served in the 26th New York regiment in the civil war; came to Minnesota in 1865; settled in Detroit in 1872, and was president of the First National Bank there; was a state senator, 1887-9.

LAKE EUNICE township, settled in 1870 and organized September 3, 1872, "was named by the United States surveyors in honor of Eunice McClelland, who was the first white woman to settle near the lake. She was the wife of John McClelland." (He was elected the first clerk of this township, and was also the first register of deeds of the county, holding the latter office six years).

LAKE PARK township, settled in 1870, was organized September 19, 1871, being then named Liberty, which was changed to the present name in 1876. Its many lakes were collectively named by the Ojibways, as translated by Gilfillan, "the lakes where there are streams, groves, prairies, and a beautiful diversified park country."

The name of LAKE VIEW, settled in 1870-71 and organized March 12, 1872, was suggested by Mrs. Charles H. Sturtevant, "as there were so many lakes in the township and so many pretty views from them."

OSAGE, settled in 1879, was united in township government with Carsonville until May 4, 1891, when it was separately organized, deriving this name from Osage, the county seat of Mitchell county, Iowa. It is also a geographic name in Arkansas, Missouri, Kansas, and Oklahoma; but originally it was adopted for the Osage tribe of Indians, "the most important southern Siouan tribe of the western division" (F. W. Hodge, Handbook of American Indians).

RICEVILLE, organized in 1912, derived its name from the South branch of the Wild Rice river, which flows through the northwest part of this township.

RICHWOOD township, organized June 23, 1871, was named from Richwood in the Province of Ontario, Canada, the native town of W. W. McLeod, who settled on the site of Richwood village in May, 1871, being one of the owners of a sawmill there.

RUNEBERG township, settled in 1882 and organized May 24, 1887, was named in honor of Johan Ludwig Runeberg, the great Swedish poet. He was born at Jakobstad, in Finland, February 5, 1804; and died at Borgå, near Helsingfors, May 6, 1877.

SAVANNAH township, organized October 12, 1901, was named for its several tracts of grassy meadow land along stream courses, "made in an early day by the backwater from the dams of the beavers." (The American origin of this word has been noted for the West Savanna river in Aitkin county).

SHELL LAKE township, first settled in 1881 and organized December 7, 1897, bears the name of its large lake, the source of the Shell river. These English names were derived probably from the shells found along the shore of the lake. The Ojibway name means, as translated by Gilfillan, "the lake lying near the mountain," having reference to the portage thence across the water divide to Height of Land lake.

SILVER LEAF, settled in 1882-83, was organized March 3, 1888, receiving its name "from the silvery appearance of the leaves of the poplar, with which the township abounds."

SPRING CREEK township, organized in 1912, is named for its small creeks and many springs, headwaters of the South branch of the Wild Rice river.

SPRUCE GROVE township, settled in 1880, was organized January 19, 1889. "As the predominant timber in the town was evergreens, it was called Spruce Grove. The township was heavily timbered with pine (five million feet), spruce, balsam, oak, poplar, birch, elm, basswood, ironwood, and tamarack."

TOAD LAKE township, settled in 1887 and organized January 5, 1892, received this name from its large lake, a translation from the Ojibway name, Mukuki (or Omakaki) sagaiigun. Thence also came the name of the outflowing Toad river, and of the prominent morainic drift hill in section 8, on the west side of this lake, called "Toad mountain," which commands an extensive view of the surrounding country.

TWO INLETS, settled in 1881 and organized September 20, 1898, was named from Two Inlets lake, in the east part of this township. It receives two inflowing streams close together at its north end, the larger one being the Fish Hook river, which flows through this lake.

BECKER COUNTY

WALWORTH township, settled in 1879 and organized April 3, 1883, was named by Albert E. Higbie, one of its first pioneers, for Walworth county, Wisconsin. He came from the adjoining Jefferson county in that state.

WHITE EARTH township, organized March 30, 1906, was named for its village of White Earth, the location of the United States government agency of the White Earth Indian Reservation, which lies in three counties, Becker, Mahnomen, and Clearwater. The removal of the Ojibways to this reservation began in 1868, the first party coming to the site of the agency on June 14, which is celebrated there each year as a great anniversary day.

The reservation and its agency were named from White Earth lake, the most beautiful one of the many fine lakes in the reservation, lying about five miles northeast of the agency. Its Ojibway name is given by Gilfillan, "Ga-wababigunikag sagaiigun, the-place-of-white-clay lake, so called from the white clay which crops out in places at the shore of the lake."

Ogema (with accent on the initial long o, g as in get, and a like ah), meaning in the Ojibway language a chief, is the railway village of this township.

WOLF LAKE township, first settled in 1888 by immigrants from Finland, was organized April 4, 1896, receiving this name from its large lake, which was so named by the settlers on account of its form. Many wolves, bears, and deer were killed here during the first years of settlement.

LAKES AND STREAMS.

The Otter Tail or Red river, traversing this county, received its name from the large Otter Tail lake in the next county on the south, which is named from that lake and the river, as noted in its chapter. Pelican river, flowing through the Detroit series of lakes to Otter Tail river, is noted in the same chapter, for Pelican township and the village of Pelican Rapids, named like this river, in translation of the Ojibway name for Lake Lida, which adjoins it and is tributary to it in Otter Tail county.

The origins of the names of several lakes of Becker county are noticed in the foregoing list of its townships. These are the Cormorant lakes in the township of this name, to which may be added the Little Cormorant lake in Audubon and Lake Eunice townships; Detroit lake, Height of Land lake and Lake Eunice; the many little lakes in Lake Park township; Shell lake, Toad lake, Two Inlets lake, White Earth lake, and Wolf lake.

Elbow lake, the most northern in the series through which the Red or Otter Tail river flows, is noted by Gilfillan as a translation of its Ojibway name, having reference to its sharply bent form. The next lake in this series is Little Bemidji lake, a mile long, this Ojibway word signifying a lake that is crossed by a stream.

Many Point lake is translated from the aboriginal name, referring to the many bays and intervening points of the shore. Round lake, likewise from the Ojibway name, requires no explanation, being one of our most common lake names throughout the state. The Upper and Lower Egg lakes, west of Round lake, and the outflowing Egg river, are again translations, referring to nests and eggs of water-loving birds.

Flat lake is another name of Indian origin, which perhaps should be better translated as Shallow lake. Below the junction of the Round Lake and Shallow Lake rivers, as they are named by the Ojibways, the Red river passes through a small lake in section 16, Grand Park, which Gilfillan translated as "the-blackbird-place-of-wild-rice lake." It has been more simply anglicized as Blackbird lake.

West of Height of Land lake are Pine, Tamarack, and Cotton lakes, the last probably named for a pioneer.

Other lakes whose Ojibway names are translated include Fish Hook lake (close west of White Earth lake), Big Rat lake, Big Rush lake, Ice Cracking, Green Water and Pine Point lakes, Basswood lake, Juggler lake, Lake of the Valley, Strawberry lake, the Big and Little Sugar Bush lakes (so named for maple trees and the making of maple sugar by the Indians), and Tulaby lake (named for a species of whitefish, the tullibee), these being in the White Earth Reservation. Straight lake and river are likewise translations from the aboriginal names.

The Buffalo river received its name from the white people, for a tributary having its sources in Audubon, which was called by the Ojibways, as translated, "Buffalo river, from the fact that buffaloes were always found wintering there." The present Buffalo lake, in the nomenclature of these Indians, is "the lake where it keeps crumbling away from the gnawing of beavers;" and they apply the same name, as stated by Gilfillan, to what we call Buffalo river, flowing into the Red river. In a word, therefore, the Ojibway name in translation would be Beaver lake and river.

Boot lake, in Savannah, and Moon lake, in sections 2 and 11, Richwood, are so named for their outlines. Mission lake, in White Earth, is named for the adjoining Catholic mission and church.

The following lakes, in the alphabetic order of their townships, were named for settlers on or near them: Balke lake and Lake Tilde, in Atlanta; Homstad, McKinstry, Marshall, and Reep lakes in Audubon; Chilton and Pearce lakes, in Burlington; Anderson and Fairbanks lakes, in Callaway; Floyd and Little Floyd lakes, in Detroit; Howe lake, in Erie; Collett lake, in Evergreen township; Momb's lake in Holmesville; Boyer lake, Lake Labelle, and Stakke lake, in Lake Park township; Lake Abbey, Curfman, Monson, Reeves, and Sauer's lakes, in Lake View; Campbell, Houg, and Sands lakes, in Richwood; Bisson and Trotochaud lakes, in Riceville; Lake Clarence, in Spring Creek township; and Du Forte and Morrison lakes, in White Earth.

Several lakes in the southwest part of this county were named for the wives or daughters of pioneer settlers, as Lakes Sallie and Melissa, through which the Pelican river flows below Detroit lake, Lake Eunice (giving name to its township), Lake Maud and Lake Ida. Excepting Lake Eunice, before noticed as named for Mrs. John McClelland, only one other of these has been identified with its surname, this being for Melissa Swetland, one of three daughters in the family of a pioneer from Canada, well remembered by Miss Nellie C. Childs, assistant county superintendent of schools.

This county has other lakes bearing the following names, for which their origin and significance have not been ascertained: Acorn and Eagle lakes, in Burlington; Brandy lake and St. Clair lake, in Detroit, and another St. Clair lake in sections 13 and 14, Callaway; Pearl lake, in Lake Eunice township; Lake Forget-me-not, in Lake Park; Dead lake and Hungry lake, in Silver Leaf township; Chippewa lake, in Grand Park; and Rock lake, in Holmesville.

Common lake names which need no explanation, occurring here, are two Bass lakes, in the White Earth Reservation; Long lake, in Detroit; Oak lake, the locality of an early settlement, between Detroit and Audubon; Loon lake, in section 24, Lake Eunice township; Fox lake, in section 7, Lake View; Pickerel lake and Perch lake, in Erie, Island lake, in Shell Lake township; Mud lake, close south of Toad lake, another a mile west of Little Toad lake, and a third in section 2, Silver Leaf; four Rice lakes, in Detroit, Erie, Grand Park, and Holmesville; Round lake, before noted, in the White Earth Reservation, and another in Holmesville; Turtle lake, in section 7, Cormorant; and Twin lakes, in sections 11 to 13, Height of Land.

HILLS.

In this large county wholly overspread by the glacial and modified drift deposits, with no outcrop of the underlying rock formations, most of the surface is only moderately undulating or rolling and in certain belts knolly and hilly, while other tracts in the northwest and southeast parts of the county have gentle and uniform slopes or are nearly level.

Two marginal moraine hills of exceptional height, though rising only about 150 or 200 feet above the lowest depressions near them, are popularly named Detroit mountain, about three miles east from the city of Detroit, and Toad mountain, close west of Toad lake. The former was called by the Ojibways, as noted by Gilfillan, "Ashiwabiwin, Looking out, from the Sioux having been always there on top of the mountain looking out for the Chippeways."

Smoky hill, in the north edge of section 15, Carsonville, is a steep hill of gravel and sand, about 200 feet above the mainly level surrounding country. It would be called by glacial geologists a kame, having been amassed where a drift-laden stream descended from the border of the melting and departing ice-sheet.

BELTRAMI and
LAKE OF THE WOODS COUNTIES

Thirty years intervened between the establishment of Beltrami county, February 28, 1866, and its organization, when its county seat and earliest settlement, Bemidji, received incorporation as a village, May 20, 1896.

The county name was adopted in honor of Giacomo Costantino Beltrami, the Italian explorer in 1823 of the most northern sources of the Mississippi river, near the center of the part of this county lying south of Red lake. Anglicized, his name was James Constantine, and on the title-page of his published works, relating his travels, it is given by initials as J. C. Beltrami. Except David Thompson in 1798, he was the first explorer to supply descriptions of Red and Turtle lakes, though undoubtedly they had been previously visited by roving traders and their canoe voyagers.

Beltrami was born at Bergamo, Italy, in 1779. His father advised him to the profession of the law, and he held numerous official positions as a chancellor and a judge; but in 1821, being accused of implication in plots to establish an Italian republic, he was exiled.

After traveling in France, Germany, and England, Beltrami sailed from Liverpool to Philadelphia, and arrived there February 21, 1823. About a month later he reached Pittsburgh, there made the acquaintance of Lawrence Taliaferro, the Indian agent at the new Fort St. Anthony (two years afterward renamed Fort Snelling), and traveled with him by steamboat down the Ohio and up the Mississippi, coming on May 10 to the fort.

From July 9 to August 7, Beltrami traveled to Pembina with the exploring expedition of Major Long, to whom he had been commended by Snelling and Taliaferro. He left that expedition at Pembina, and went southeastward along an Indian trail, with two Ojibways and a half-breed interpreter, to the junction of the Thief and Red Lake rivers, whence his journey was by canoe up the latter river to Red lake. From an Ojibway village near the mouth of the lake, Beltrami traveled with a canoe along its southwestern shore to the Little Rock or Gravel river, where he stopped at the hut of a half-breed, who became his guide. August 26 and 27 were spent in making long portages with the half-breed and an Ojibway, leaving the south shore of Red lake a short distance east from the site of the Agency and going south, passing small lakes and coming at last, by a few miles of canoeing, to Lake Puposky, now also called Mud lake. Proceeding still southward the next morning, Beltrami soon came to a lake named by him, for a deceased friend, Lake Julia, which he thought to have no visible outlet, but to send its waters by filtration through the swampy ground both northward and southward, being thus a source both of the Red Lake river, called by him Bloody river, and of the Turtle river, the most northern affluent of the Mississippi. The narrative of Beltrami shows that he arrived at Lake Julia by a short portage; but on the map of the United States land surveys it is shown as having an outlet into Mud lake, thus belonging to the Red river basin.

On September 4 Beltrami reached Red Cedar lake, since known as Cass lake; and during the next three days he voyaged down the Mississippi to the mouth of Leech Lake river. Thence he went up that stream to Leech lake, where he made the acquaintance of Cloudy Weather, a leader in the band of the Pillager Ojibways, by whom he was accompanied in the long canoe voyage of return to the Mississippi and down this river to Fort St. Anthony.

The next winter was spent by Beltrami in New Orleans, where he published his narration in 1824, written in French, bearing a title which in English would be "The Discovery of the Sources of the Mississippi and of the Bloody River." In 1828 he published in London his most celebrated work, entitled "A Pilgrimage in Europe and America, leading to the Discovery of the Sources of the Mississippi and Bloody River; with a Description of the Whole Course of the former and of the Ohio." This work of two volumes is cast in the form of a series of letters, addressed to an Italian countess. Eight letters, in pages 126 to 491 of Volume II, contain the account of his travels in Minnesota.

During his later years, until 1850, Beltrami resided in various cities of France, Germany, Austria, and Italy; and his last five years were spent on his land estate at Filotrano, near Macerata, Italy, where he died in February, 1855.

The city of Bergamo, his birthplace, in 1865 published a volume of 134 pages commemorating his life and work, dedicated to the Minnesota Historical Society. In translation from this book, Alfred J. Hill presented in the second volume of this society's Historical Collections a biographic sketch of Beltrami, together with a communication from Major Taliaferro, giving reminiscences of him.

Townships and Villages.

Information was received from John Wilmann, county auditor, during a visit at Bemidji in September, 1909; and from H. W. Alsop, deputy auditor, in a second visit there, August, 1916.

Alaska township was named by settlers who had traveled to Alaska.

Angle township received this name from its being bounded on the north by the inlet (about ten miles long) of the Lake of the Woods leading to its Northwest Angle, or "most northwestern point," as it was described by the treaty of 1783 and by later treaties defining the boundary between this country and Canada. The area thus named Angle comprises about 120 square miles, bounded by the lake on the south, east, and north. Excepting Alaska, it is the most northern tract of the United States, as it lies between 10 and 26 miles north of the 49th parallel.

ARNESEN is a fishing village on the shore of the Lake of the Woods in Lakewood township. Its site was formerly known as Rocky Point. The village was founded by Bernard A. Arnesen, who settled there in 1897.

BATTLE township is named for Battle river, flowing through this township into the east end of the south half of Red lake. The stream was so named by the Ojibways on account of their having fought here with the Sioux.

BAUDETTE township and village are named from the Baudette river, there tributary to the Rainy river. It is an early French name, probably in commemoration of a fur trader.

BEMIDJI township and city were named for an Ojibway chief whose band of about fifty people had their homes on and near the south end of Lake Bemidji and around Lake Irving, including the site where white settlers founded this town. The chief died in April, 1904, at the age of eighty-five years. His name was taken from the older Ojibway name of this lake, crossed by the Mississippi. Gilfillan translated it as "the lake where the current flows directly across the water, referring to the river flowing squarely out of the lake on the east side, cutting it in two as it were, very briefly Cross lake."

BENVILLE township was probably named for a pioneer settler.

BIG GRASS is named from the South branch of Roseau river, which has its sources in the north edge of this township. This French name, Roseau, translated from the Ojibway name of the Roseau lake and river, means the very coarse grass or reed (Phragmites communis), which is common or frequent in the edges of lakes and slow streams throughout this northwestern part of Minnesota.

BIRCH township has valuable timber of the paper or canoe birch, and also of the yellow or gray birch, the former species being greatly used by the Indians for making their birch bark canoes.

BIRCH ISLAND township, on the north side of the north half of Red lake, is named for its having a well wooded tract of canoe birch, elm, oak, ash, basswood, and other trees, along and near the lake shore between the Two rivers and for a mile eastward. This was a heavily timbered island, as it was called, rising 10 to 25 feet above the lake, in remarkable contrast with nearly all other parts of the north shore, which are a very extensive tamarack swamp only a few feet above the lake and reaching thence north 10 to 15 miles or more.

BLACK DUCK township received its name from its large Black Duck lake, the source of the river of the same name tributary to Red lake. The species popularly known by this name is, according to Dr. Thomas S. Roberts, the ring-necked duck (Marila collaris, Donovan), frequent or common throughout the state.

BROOK LAKE township, the most southeastern of this county, is named from a small lake in section 27, Moose Lake township, adjoining this on the north, and a brook flows from it into section 3 of this township.

BUZZLE township and Buzzle lake, in its section 21, were named in honor of an early settler beside the lake.

CHILGREN township was named for Albert Chilgren, of Swedish descent, who is a farmer and lawyer there.

CLEMENTSON, a small village on Rainy river at the mouth of Rapid river, in Gudrid township, was named for Helec Clementson, owner of a saw mill there, formerly a county commissioner, who came in May, 1896.

CORMANT is shortened from the Comorant river which flows through this township, named by Beltrami (in translation of the Ojibway name) for the double-crested cormorant, frequent in many parts of Minnesota. The full form of the name had been earlier applied to a township of Becker county, preventing its use elsewhere in this state; with the abridged spelling, however, it was admitted again into the list of our township names.

DURAND township is in honor of Charles Durand, a homesteader on the northeast side of Lake Puposky.

ECKLES township bears the name of an early landholder interested in the building of its branch of the Great Northern railway.

ELAND township was named by the early settlers, perhaps for the eland of South Africa, a large species of antelope or elk formerly found there in immense herds.

EUGENE township was named probably for Eugene V. Debs, of Indiana, candidate of the Socialist Party for president of the United States in 1904, 1908 and 1912.

FARLEY, a railway station in Port Hope township, was named for a lumberman and merchant there, who removed west several years ago and has since died.

FROHN was named for a district of Gudbrandsdalen, Norway, the former home of immigrants in this township.

FUNKLEY, a railway station and junction in Hornet township, was named for Henry Funkley, a lawyer in Bemidji.

GRANT VALLEY township and its Grant lake, in section 4, with Grant creek, its outlet, were named for an early settler or lumberman.

GUDRID township has a Norwegian feminine name, probably for the wife of an immigrant homesteader.

HAGALI was named for an early Norwegian settler of this township.

HAMRE township derived its name from a small district in Norway, whence some of its settlers came.

HINES, a railway station in Black Duck township, was named for William Hines, formerly a lumberman there.

HORNET township was originally named Murray, a duplication of an older Minnesota township name, and the change and selection of the present name caused much contention.

ISLAND LAKE, a village in the east part of Alaska township, at the end of a lumber railway branch, was named for the adjoining Island lake, which has a small island close to this village.

JONES township was named for a pioneer there, who moved away many years ago.

KEIL township was probably named for a German settler.

KELLIHER township and its village, at the end of a branch railway built for lumbering, were named for A. O. Kelliher, a former agent here for lumber companies.

KONIG township was named for a settler there from Germany.

LAKEWOOD township was named for its timber, and for its situation on the south shore of the Lake of the Woods.

LAMMERS was named for the Lammers Brothers (George A. and Albert J.), of Stillwater, who engaged in real estate and lumber business in this township.

LANGOR township received its name in honor of Henry A. Langord (the final letter being omitted), a settler of Norwegian descent, coming here from Wisconsin.

LEE township was named for settlers from Norway, their original name having been changed to this spelling.

LIBERTY township received this name in accordance with the petition of its settlers.

MAPLE RIDGE township was named for its sugar maple trees, and for its situation at the sources of streams descending north to Red lake. Sugar Bush township is also named for the maple trees and sugar-making, to be more fully noted in a later page.

McDOUGALD township was named for John McDougald, a member of the first board of county commissioners, now engaged in real estate business at Black Duck.

MEADOW LAND township is named for its grass lands along streams, open areas used for hay-making in this generally wooded region.

MINNIE township has the feminine name derived from the name of this state, perhaps chosen in honor of the wife or daughter of one of its pioneers.

MOOSE LAKE township is named for its Moose lake and Little Moose lake, which are probably translated from their Ojibway names.

MYHRE township was named for L. O. Myhre, of Norwegian descent, a former member of the board of county commissioners, residing near Bemidji.

NEBISH township and its lake of this name are from the Ojibway word anibish, tea, the much relished drink alike of the white settlers and the Indians.

NORTHERN township received this name because it includes the north part of Lake Bemidji.

NORTHWOOD township was named for its timber and its situation in the north part of this county.

NYMORE, the lumber manufacturing village near the city of Bemidji, was named for Martin Nye, a Bemidji pioneer, who was a veteran of the civil war.

BELTRAMI AND LAKE OF THE WOODS 39

O'BRIEN township was named for a lumberman there, William O'Brien, from Stillwater, Minn.

PIONEER township received this name in compliment to its pioneer settlers.

PONEMAH, a village on the north shore of the southern half of Red lake, having a United States government school for the Ojibway children, bears a name used by Longfellow in "The Song of Hiawatha." Minnehaha in dying, and afterward Hiawatha, depart

"To the Islands of the Blessed,
To the Kingdom of Ponemah,
To the Land of the Hereafter."

PORT HOPE township was named by one of its first settlers, Captain William Wetzel, a veteran of the Mexican war and the civil war, probably for Port Hope, Canada, on the north shore of Lake Ontario.

POTAMO township has the name of a town on the east coast of the island of Corfu, Greece.

PROSPER township received this name of good promise in accordance with the petition of its settlers.

PUPOSKY is a railway village in Durand township, on Lake Puposky, an Ojibway name recorded and translated by Beltrami, signifying "the end of the shaking lands," that is, swamps whose surface is shaken and sinks when walked on. It has been also translated as Mud lake, with Mud river outflowing from it.

QUIRING township needs further inquiry to learn why it is so named.

RAPID RIVER township was named for the stream crossing it, a tributary of the Rainy river. It was mapped and described by Keating of Major Long's expedition in 1823 as the River of Rapids, "so called from the fine rapids which it presents immediately above its mouth."

REDBY, a village on the south shore of Red lake and at the end of a railway branch, received its name from the lake.

ROOSEVELT township, including the greater part of Clearwater lake, crossed by the west line of this county, and also the railway village of Roosevelt, 78 miles farther north near the Lake of the Woods, in the east edge of the adjoining Roseau county, were named in honor of Theodore Roosevelt, president of the United States, 1901-09.

RULIEN township was named for William Rulien, who is engaged in real estate business in Baudette.

SHOOKS township was named for Edward Shooks, who was a merchant there at a former station of the Kelliher railway branch.

SHOTLEY township was probably named for a lumberman on its Shotley brook, here flowing into the north half of Red lake.

SOLWAY, a railway village in Lammers township, and the Solway Lumber Company, which formerly worked in its vicinity, were named after Solway Firth, the wide inlet from the Irish Sea between England and Scotland.

Spooner township is in honor of Marshall A. Spooner, of Bemidji, who was judge in this Fifteenth judicial district, 1903-08.

Spruce Grove township was named for its spruce timber, abundant on many tracts throughout northern Minnesota.

Steenerson township was named for Hon. Halvor Steenerson, of Crookston, representative in Congress since 1903.

Sugar Bush township was named, like Maple Ridge township also in this county, for its maple trees used by both the Indians and white people for sugar-making. Beltrami wrote of the Ojibway process of making maple sugar, as follows (in his "Pilgrimage," vol. II, page 402): "The whole of this territory abounds with innumerable maple or sugar trees, which the Indians divide into various *sugaries*. The sap of the trees flows through incisions made in them by the Indians in spring at the foot of the trunk. It is received in buckets of birch bark and conveyed to the laboratory of each respective sugary, where it is boiled in large cauldrons till the watery parts are evaporated. The dregs descend, and the saccharine matter remains adhering to the sides of the vessel. When this process is completed the sugar is made."

Summit township has the highest land crossed by the Minnesota and International railway, called therefore a "summit" by its surveyors.

Swift Water received its name, like Rapid River township before noted, from the Rapid river flowing through these townships.

Taylor township was named in honor of James Taylor, an early homesteader there, now a merchant at Tenstrike, the village on the west border of this township.

Tenstrike, a railroad village on the line between Port Hope and Taylor townships, was platted and named by Almon A. White of St. Paul, alluding to the completely successful bowling which with the first ball knocks down all the ten pins.

Turtle Lake township bears the name of its large lake, translated, as also the outflowing Turtle river, from the Ojibway name. Thompson, who traveled here in 1798, wrote of this lake that "its many small bays give it the rude form of a turtle."

Turtle River township likewise is named for its Turtle River lake, and for the river so named flowing through this lake, the most northern tributary of the Mississippi.

Wabanica township received its name from waban, the Ojibway word for the east and also for the twilight or dawn of the morning.

Walhalla township is named from Norse mythology, for the hall of Odin, also spelled Valhalla, into which were received the souls of warriors slain in battle.

Washkish township, at the east end of the north part of Red lake, is from the Ojibway word, wawashkeshi, the deer, which is yet common or frequent there, though much hunted.

WHEELER township, at the west side of the mouth of Rainy river, was named for Alonzo Wheeler, a pioneer farmer there.

WILTON, a railway village and junction in Eckles township, was named for some one of the fifteen or more villages and towns of this name in the eastern states, Canada, and England.

WOODROW township is in honor of the president of the United States, Woodrow Wilson.

ZIPPEL township was named for William M. Zippel, of German descent, who through many years has been a fisherman on the Lake of the Woods, living in this township, at the mouth of the creek which was earlier named for him. The aboriginal name of this stream, which continued until recently in use, was Sand creek. Mr. Zippel first settled at Rat Portage in 1884, and removed three years afterward to the mouth of this creek, where the fishing village bearing his name has since grown up.

LAKES AND STREAMS.

The names of the Lake of the Woods and Rainy and Mississippi rivers and Cass lake have been considered in the first chapter of this work; and Red lake will be later noticed in connection with Red Lake county.

In the preceding list of townships, sufficient mention is made of several lakes, rivers, and creeks, these being Battle river, Lake Bemidji, Black Duck lake and river, Brook lake, Buzzle lake, Cormorant river, Grant lake and creek, Moose lake and Little Moose lake, Nebish lake, Lake Puposky or Mud lake and the outflowing Mud river, Rapid river, Shotley brook, Turtle lake and river and the Turtle River lake, and Zippel's creek.

The longest southern tributary of Red lake on the canoe route of Beltrami is Mud river, the outlet of Lake Puposky or Mud lake, which he called "the river of Great Portage." This name, as he wrote, was given by the Indians, "because a dreadful storm that occurred on it blew down a vast number of forest trees on its banks, which encumber its channel, and so impede its navigation as to make an extensive or great portage in order to reach it." In accordance with the recommendation of Beltrami, it is sometimes called Red Lake river, indicating it to be the upper part of the river that outflows from Red lake.

Lake Julia, before noted as the highest source of this stream, was thought by Beltrami to send its waters partly southward, so that it supplied to him the title of "the Julian sources of Bloody river and the Mississippi."

Schoolcraft, in the Narrative of his expedition to Lake Itasca in 1832 (published in 1834), wrote the name of Lake Bemidji as "Pamitchi Gumaug or Lac Travers." On Nicollet's map, 1843, it is "Pemidji L."

Lake Irving, closely connected with Lake Bemidji by a strait and forming the south boundary of the city of Bemidji, was named by Schoolcraft for Washington Irving, the eminent American author (1783-1859).

It was frequently called Little Bemidji lake by the early settlers, which name has passed out of use.

Lake Marquette, in sections 29 to 31, Bemidji, was also named by Schoolcraft, for the zealous French missionary and explorer of the Mississippi (1637-75). It is on the Plantagenian or South Fork of the Mississippi, which Schoolcraft ascended on his way to Lake Itasca, now named Schoolcraft river (or Yellow Head river, for his Ojibway guide), more fully noticed in the chapter of Hubbard county.

The Mississippi for about six miles next below Lake Bemidji has a series of rapids, which were ascended in 1832 by Schoolcraft and were described by him as follows in his "Summary Narrative" (published in 1855). "Boulders of the geological drift period are frequently encountered in ascending them, and the river spreads itself over so considerable a surface that it became necessary for the bowsmen and steersmen to get out into the shallows and lead up the canoes. These canoes were but of two fathoms length, drew but a few inches of water, and would not bear more than three persons. . . . There were ten of these rapids encountered before we reached the summit or plateau of Lake Pemidjegumaug, which is the Lac Traverse of the French. These were called the Metoswa rapids, from the Indian numeral for ten" (Midasswi in Baraga's Dictionary).

A few miles below these rapids, the Mississippi in the southeast corner of Frohn township flows through Wolf lake, which was called Pamitascodiac by the Ojibways. It was thought by Schoolcraft to be so named for a tract of prairie adjoining it, "from pemidj, across, muscoda, a prairie, and ackee, land."

One to two miles farther east the Mississippi passes through the south end of Lake Andrusia, named by Schoolcraft in 1832 for Andrew Jackson, who was president of the United States, 1829 to 1837.

For the next two miles the course of this river is occupied by Allen's bay, which is connected with Cass lake by a short and narrow strait. This body of water was named also by Schoolcraft, for Lieutenant James Allen, a member of the expedition of 1832, "who, on his return down the Mississippi, was the first to explore it." Allen was born in Ohio, 1806; was graduated at the U. S. Military Academy, 1829; was promoted to be captain, First Dragoons, 1837; conducted an expedition to the sources of the Des Moines and Blue Earth rivers in 1844; and died at Fort Leavenworth, Kansas, August 23, 1846. He was author of a report to the government on each of these two Minnesota expeditions.

David Thompson's map of the international boundary survey from Lake Superior to the Lake of the Woods, in 1826, shows the mouths of Rapid river, Riviere Baudette, and Winter Road river, flowing into the Rainy river from this county. The first was named, as before noted, for its picturesque rapids or falls, descending about 20 feet, close above its mouth; and the second is thought to be a French personal surname.

The third of these streams received its name, as noted by Nathan Butler, of Minneapolis, who during many years was engaged in surveying and land examinations in northern Minnesota, for "a winter road, or dog sled trail, leaving the Rainy river at the mouth of the Winter Road river and running about S. 20° W. fifty miles, to the middle of the north shore of the north Red lake. The whole distance is one continuous swamp, tamarack and open, except where the streams have cut down into the ground from six to twelve feet below the surface, thus draining the land on either side for forty or fifty rods." (Geology of Minnesota, vol. IV, 1899, page 160.)

Winter Road lake, in Eugene township, is translated, like this outflowing river, from their Ojibway name.

Peppermint creek, tributary to the Winter Road river, is named for its native species of mint, including most notably the wild bergamot (Monarda fistulosa).

The following lakes bear names of early settlers: Campbell lake, Lake Erick, and Peterson lake (also called Mud lake), in Liberty township; Myrtle lake, in sections 4 and 9, Roosevelt; Buzzle and Funkley lakes, in Buzzle township; Movil lake, in Turtle Lake and Northern townships; Robideau and Gilsted lakes, in Birch township; and Swenson and Grace lakes, in Frohn township.

Pimushe lake, in Moose Lake township, which we receive from Nicollet's map, bears an Ojibway name, but it has not been identified in Baraga's Dictionary.

Kichi lake, on the south line of the same township, also mapped with this name by Nicollet, now spelled Kitihi lake, means in the Ojibway language Big lake. Its approved form is Kitchi, in Baraga's Dictionary, or Gitche, in Longfellow's "Song of Hiawatha." It is thus of exactly the same meaning as a second Big lake, three miles distant on the west, in Sugar Bush township.

Nearly all the other lakes of this county, not already noted, chiefly occurring only in its southern third part, have names of common or frequent use and evident origin, many indeed being translations of the aboriginal names. These include Moose and Turtle lakes, in Alaska township; Bass lake, in Nebish, also Bass and Little Bass lakes, in Turtle River township; Clearwater lake and river, to be more fully noticed for Clearwater county; two White Fish lakes, in Hagali and Buzzle townships; Loon lake and Medicine lake, in Hagali, the latter of Ojibway origin; Gull lake, in Hagali and Port Hope; Deer, Pony, and Long lakes, in Liberty township, and another Long lake in Turtle River township; Black lake, Fox, Gnat, and Three Island lakes, in Turtle Lake township; Twin lakes, in Taylor; Grass lake, on the line between Eckles and Grant Valley; Rice lake, on the east line of Sugar Bush, and another in Jones township, the latter more commonly known by its Ojibway name, Manomin lake, each referring to the luxuriant growths of wild rice; Boot and Fern lakes, in Grant Valley, the former named for its outline; and School lake, in Frohn, lying partly in the school section 16.

Points and Islands, Lake of the Woods.

The Rainy river enters the Lake of the Woods by flowing through Four Mile bay, so named for its length from east to west. This bay is separated from the main lake by Oak point, also four miles long, which is a narrow sand bar, bearing many bur oaks, a species that is common or abundant throughout Minnesota, excepting far northeastward.

On the Canadian side, opposite Oak point, a similar wave-built sand bar or barrier beach, named Sable island, skirts the original lake shore for about six miles northeastward. Its French name, if anglicized, would be Sand island. The geologic origin or formation of Oak point and Sable island is the same with Minnesota point and Wisconsin point, which inclose the harbors of Duluth and Superior.

The sand dunes of this island and of Oak point caused this large southwest part of the Lake of the Woods to be formerly often called Sand Hill lake.

From the mouth of Rainy river, at the east end of Oak point, the international boundary runs nearly due north across the main southern area of the lake, passing close west of Big island, which belongs to Canada. As it approaches the Northwest Angle inlet (called "Angle river" in the latest Minnesota atlas), which has been noted on a preceding page in its relation to Angle township, the boundary sets off to this state, on its west and south side, Oak, Flag, and Brush islands, in this order from southeast to northwest, besides several unnamed islands of smaller size.

Eight miles south of Oak island is Garden or Cornfield island, also belonging to Minnesota, named from its former cultivation by the Ojibways. John Tanner, the white captive who lived the greater part of his life among the Ottawas and Ojibways, had his home for some time on this island, as told in his Narrative, published in 1830.

In coasting along the south shore westward from the mouth of Rainy river, Long point and Rocky point are passed at the north side of Lakewood township.

Cormorant Rock, about a mile north from Rocky point, is a small island of bare rock, named from its being the nesting place of multitudes of the double-crested cormorant, the same species for which lakes and a township in Becker county are named, as also a river and a township in this county.

Next to the west, Muskeg bay, mostly adjoining Roseau county, is the most southwestern part of the lake, lying between Rocky point on the east and Buffalo point, in the edge of Manitoba, on the north. The bay received this Ojibway name from tracts of swamp on its shore, and the Buffalo point was named for its being on or near the northeastern limit of the former geographic range of the buffalo.

The site of Fort St. Charles, which was established by Verendrye in 1732 and named by him in honor of the governor of Canada, Charles de Beauharnois, was discovered in 1908, on the Minnesota shore of the Northwest Angle inlet, nearly three miles distant from the bend of the boundary at American point, the north end of a small island, where it turns from its north course to run westward up the inlet. From this fort the eldest son of Verendrye and a Jesuit missionary named Father Aulneau, with nineteen French voyageurs, started in canoes June 5, 1736, to go to Mackinac for supplies. Early the next morning, at their first camping place, they were surprised and murdered by a war party of the Prairie Sioux. This massacre, from which not one of the Frenchmen escaped, was on a small island of rock, since called Massacre island, in the Canadian part of the Lake of the Woods, about twenty miles distant from the fort by the canoe route. (Rev. Francis J. Schaefer, in Acta et Dicta, published by the St. Paul Catholic Historical Society, vol. II, pp. 114-133, July, 1909, with two maps between pages 240 and 241 in the same volume.)

TRIBUTARIES AND POINTS OF RED LAKE.

In September, 1885, the present writer made a canoe trip for geologic observations along the entire shore line of Red lake, starting east from the Agency. The journey, more than a hundred miles in extent and occupying six days, was wholly within the Red Lake Indian Reservation, which has since been greatly reduced in its area. My canoemen were two Ojibways, Roderick McKenzie and William Sayers, each of whom had received a fair education and could converse well in English. Mr. McKenzie, by his acquaintance with the Indians about the lake, was specially serviceable in obtaining information of the names applied by them to streams and points of land along the shore, and the translations of these are given in my report, published by the Geological and Natural History Survey of Minnesota (vol. IV, 1899, pp. 155-165). A sketch map of Red lake and its vicinity drawn during this travel and published by the U. S. Geological Survey, is Plate XII in Monograph XXV, 1896, "The Glacial Lake Agassiz." Much abridged from the report cited, the following are my notes of translations of the Ojibway names then in use.

The stream at the Agency is Pike creek, rendered Gold Fish creek by Beltrami; but by the English residents it is more commonly called Mill creek. A saw and grist mill, having ten feet head, is built on this stream about a quarter of a mile from its mouth. Its sources, according to Rev. F. W. Smith, are a series of three or four lakelets, the lowest of which, lying on the southwest side of the road to Cass lake, is called by the Indians Little lake, but by the white men Ten Mile lake, being about ten miles distant from the Agency. The highest, named Cranberry lake, has quite irregular outlines, lying mostly in sections 34 and 35, T. 150, R. 34, in the east part of Alaska township.

Near the chief's village, about five miles east of the Agency, is a slightly projecting point, called the Chief's point. It rises steeply 25 to 30 feet above the lake. Indian cornfields were seen on its top, in small clearings of the forest.

Mud river, called the Red Lake river on former maps, and Great Portage river by Beltrami, enters the lake about a half mile east of the Chief's point. This is larger than Pike creek, but smaller than Sandy river and Black Duck river. Its head stream passes through Lake Puposky, named on the township plats Mud lake, and through two lower small lakes called Wild Rice lakes.

Big point, a broad swell of the shore, standing out perhaps an eighth of a mile beyond the general outline westward, but little from that eastward, is nearly a mile east of Mud river.

In the distance of six miles from Big point to Black Duck river, four small creeks enter the lake, bordered by tracts of marsh grass along the lower part of their course. On these meadows we saw many stacks of hay which had been put up by the Indians, and the name Hay creek is applied to one of these streams. Hay is also cut by the Indians on the meadows of nearly all the streams about Red lake.

Black Duck river flows into the most southeast part of the southern half of the lake. It is called Cakakisciou river on Beltrami's map, and Cormorant river on Nicollet's and later maps; but it is known to the English-speaking residents only by the name of Black Duck river. Its principal tributary, coming in from the northeast, is now named the Cormorant river.

Battle river, from which a township is named, enters the lake about four miles farther north. It is of nearly the same size as Big Rock creek and Mud river.

In canoeing thence to the Narrows, only one small tributary was seen, called Sucker creek. About three miles west of this creek is Elm point, and nearly two miles beyond this we passed the more conspicuous Uninhabited point, so named by the Indians because of ancient clearings along the shore for a mile to the east, where in some former time, probably a century or longer ago, the Ojibway people had a village and cultivated fields. Their bark lodges and more permanent log-houses, with patches of corn and potatoes, were seen here and there all along this shore from its most eastern portion to the Narrows.

Beyond the Uninhabited point the shore trends west-northwest past Pelican, Halfway, and Rabbit points, successively about three fourths of a mile apart. About a mile northwestward from Rabbit point is Sand Cliff point. The base of this is the usual wall of boulders, derived from erosion of glacial drift; but its upper part, rising steeply from near the lake level to a height of 75 or 80 feet, is levelly bedded sand and fine gravel.

Next to the northwest a plain of sand and gravel, bearing no forest, and perhaps in part natural prairie, about 25 feet above the lake, extends two thirds of a mile or more, diminishing from a third to an eighth of a mile in width. On this tract, about a mile south of the Narrows, is the principal Ojibway village of Red lake, consisting in 1885 of forty or fifty lodges. This village was represented on Nicollet's map (1843), which was of so early date that it does not show St. Paul, Minneapolis, nor any other city or town in Minnesota.

A later note should be added, that, according to Miss Frances Densmore, of Red Wing, Minn., who has visited these Indians to write of their music, this village is called by them "Wabacing (where the wind blows from both sides)." The name refers to the exposed situation, between the south and north parts of the lake.

Big Sand Bar creek of 1885 is now named Shotley brook. At its mouth it has deposited a delta of sand and fine gravel, which projects fifteen rods into the lake. About three miles farther northeast is Little Sand Bar creek, in section 31, Washkish.

Tamarack river, called Sturgeon or Amenikaning river on Beltrami's map, comes in at the extreme east end of the lake. It is 50 to 100 feet wide near its mouth, and is bordered by shores of alluvial sand only three or four feet high.

Poplar creek, 15 to 20 feet wide and two or three feet deep, comes in about ten miles from the east end of the lake; and three miles farther west the Two rivers, each 30 feet wide and three or four feet deep, have their mouths about a half of a mile apart.

Some fifty rods west from the west one of the Two rivers is the beginning of the "winter road" to the Lake of the Woods, a trail used, as before noted, by the Indians in winter, when the vast swamps of the intervening country are frozen.

Wild Rice river (Manomin creek of the Ojibways) joins the lake at the extreme northwestern portion of this north half, where the shore turns in a graceful curve to the south. This is a large stream, 40 to 50 feet wide and five to seven feet deep for a distance of at least fifty rods from its mouth. Wild rice grows along its banks for a width of six to ten feet. About a mile southwest from its mouth this river flows through the north end of a shallow lake, called Wild Rice lake from its rank growth of this useful grain, which supplies a large part of the winter food of the Indians.

From the West Narrows point the north shore of the south half of Red lake trends west and southwest about four miles to Starting point, so named by the Indians because they gather there for starting in company in canoe trips to the outlet and down the Red Lake river.

Oak creek, about ten feet wide, comes in some six miles north of the outlet, deriving its name from the occurrence of several large oaks on the beach near its mouth. A marsh, destitute of trees, but with tamarack and spruce swamp beyond it westward, borders the lake thence about two miles to Last creek, which is of similar small size, being the last tributary passed in approaching the outlet.

Red Lake river receives no tributary, excepting recent drainage ditches, till it reaches the mouth of Thief river, 45 miles distant by a straight line from this lake.

Sandy river, which comes in at the most southwestern portion of the lake, is about 35 feet wide and four feet deep.

Big Rock creek, flowing into Red lake next eastward, is also called Shell creek for Shell lake from which it issues, where it is crossed by the road from the Red Lake agency to White Earth. It takes the former name from two large boulders, each about eight feet in diameter, which lie some five rods apart on the lake shore, one on each side of the mouth of this stream.

About four and a half miles farther east we passed Little Rock point and creek, a third of a mile apart, so called because of the beach of many little boulders, one to two feet in diameter, which extends an eighth of a mile each way from the mouth of the creek. It was called Gravel river by Beltrami, who visited and named a series of eight small lakes tributary to it. These lakes, which cannot now be exactly identified, he named for the children of a family endeared to him in friendship, Alexander, Lavinius, Everard, Frederica, Adela, Magdalena, Virginia, and Eleonora.

Red Water creek, very small, probably named thus in allusion to the bog iron ore of its springs, enters the lake between the Little Rock creek and the Agency. A pretty lake tributary to this creek, beside the road to White Earth, is called Green lake, probably from its reflection of the foliage of the surrounding woods.

It has been suggested that the Ojibway name, translated Red lake may have been taken from this Red Water creek, or from other inflowing streams and springs whose beds are made reddish and yellow by the rust-colored bog ore of iron. Beltrami imaginatively translated it as Bloody lake, attributing it to blood shed in Indian wars. More reliably, Rev. Joseph A. Gilfillan, through inquiries among the Indians, as noted for Red Lake county, learned that the aboriginal name was from the redness of the lake and sky reflected at evening from the bright red, vermilion, and golden hues of the sunset.

Beltrami Island of Lake Agassiz.

The only large island of the Glacial Lake Agassiz was between Red lake and the Lake of the Woods, in Beltrami and Roseau counties. The highest parts of that island, which was named in 1893 for Beltrami, are about 130 feet above Red lake and 1310 feet above the sea. When the glacial lake had fallen to the contour line of 1200 feet, the higher Beltrami island had an area of about 1160 square miles. (Journal of Geology, Vol. XXIII, pages 780-4, Nov.-Dec., 1915.)

BENTON COUNTY

This county, one of the first established in Minnesota Territory, October 27, 1849, and organized January 7, 1850, was named for Thomas Hart Benton, who was United States senator from Missouri during thirty years, 1821 to 1851. He was born near Hillsborough, N. C., March 14, 1782; and died in Washington, April 10, 1858. He studied law, and was admitted to the bar in Nashville in 1811; was an aide-de-camp of General Jackson in the War of 1812, and also raised a regiment of volunteers; removed to St. Louis in 1815, and established a newspaper which vigorously advocated the admission of Missouri to the Union; and in 1820 he was elected as one of the senators of the new state. In Congress his work for the original enactment of homestead land laws, in 1824-28, won the gratitude of pioneer settlers throughout the West. He is also honored by Benton township in Carver county, and by the name of Lake Benton in Lincoln county, applied by Nicollet in his expedition of 1838. Seven other states have counties named for him, and twenty states have cities, villages, and post offices of this name. In 1899 his statue was placed in the National Statuary Hall, at the Capitol, Washington, as one of the two representing Missouri.

Benton was the author of "Thirty Years' View: History of the American Government, 1820-1850," published in two volumes, 1854 and 1856. During the last two years of his life, with singular literary industry, he prepared the manuscript of his "Abridgment of the Debates of Congress, from 1789 to 1856," which was published in sixteen volumes, 1857 to 1863. Several biographies of him have been issued, one by Theodore Roosevelt in 1887 being in the "American Statesmen" series.

TOWNSHIPS AND VILLAGES.

Information for this county was gathered from the "History of the Upper Mississippi Valley," 1881, pages 340-369; from records in the office of J. E. Kasner, county auditor, at Foley, in a visit there in May, 1916; from William H. Fletcher, of Sauk Rapids, chairman of the board of county commissioners; and from Hon. Charles A. Gilman, of St. Cloud, who was a prominent pioneer of Benton county.

ALBERTA township, organized in 1868, was named for one of its early settlers, a farmer whose first name was Albert.

DUELM, a hamlet in section 34, St. George, was named by its German settlers.

EAST ST. CLOUD, in this county, is a part of the city of St. Cloud, which is mainly in Stearns county, west of the Mississippi, but also reaches east of the river into Benton and Sherburne counties.

FOLEY, a railway village and the county seat, was named for John Foley, its founder, one of five brothers who came to this state from Lanark county, Ontario. When this line of the Great Northern railway was built, in 1882-4, John and others of the brothers were contractors, camping on the site of this village, and he acquired lands here. Later he led in the effort, 1901-02, of transferring the county seat from Sauk Rapids to this place. He died in St. Paul, August 11, 1908.

GILMANTON township, organized in 1866, was named in honor of Charles Andrew Gilman, who was born in Gilmanton, N. H., February 9, 1833; came to Sauk Rapids, Minn., in 1855, and removed to St. Cloud in 1861. He was receiver, and afterward register, of the U. S. land office in St. Cloud for several years; was a member of the state senate, 1868-9, and of the House, 1875-9, being speaker the last two years, and again was a member of the House in 1915; was lieutenant governor, 1880-7; and state librarian, 1894-9. During about thirty years he was much engaged in lumbering in Benton and Morrison counties, and he located many permanent settlers in this township.

GLENDORADO township, organized September 20, 1868, received this name (partly Spanish, meaning the golden glen) by petition of its settlers.

GRANITE LEDGE township was named for its granite rock outcrops in sections 17, 18, 20, and 24, the last being on the West branch of Rum river.

GRAHAM township was named for one of its pioneer farmers.

LANGOLA township, organized July 12, 1858, has a unique name, unknown elsewhere, proposed by its petitioners for organization.

MAYHEW LAKE township, and also its lake and creek of this name, are in honor of George V. Mayhew, who was born in St. Lawrence county, N. Y., February 18, 1824; served in the Mexican War; came to Minnesota in 1854, and settled in the present Minden township of this county, beside the creek named for him; was a representative in the legislature in 1861; and served in the Seventh Minnesota regiment in the civil war, becoming a first lieutenant.

MAYWOOD township, organized in 1867, received this euphonious name on the request of its settlers. New Jersey, Kentucky, Indiana, Illinois, Missouri, and Nebraska, also have villages so named.

MINDEN township, organized in 1858, received its name from an eastern state, or more probably it was given by immigrants from Germany, for the ancient city of Minden in Prussia.

OAK PARK, a railway village in Maywood, is named for the oak groves of its vicinity.

PARENT, a small railway village in St. George township, was named for Auguste Parent and others of his family there, farmers, of French descent.

RICE, a railway village in Langola, is in honor of George T. Rice, who kept a hotel about three fourths of a mile farther west for the stage travel previous to the building of this railway. His name was also given to an extensive prairie that includes the western two thirds of Langola and the northwest part of Watab.

RONNEBY, another railway village, in Maywood, was named from a town near Karlskrona in southern Sweden, on the River Ronneby near its mouth in the Baltic Sea.

ST. GEORGE township, organized September 27, 1858, was named in compliment to three prominent early settlers of the south part of this county, George V. Mayhew, George McIntyre, and another who had the same first name.

SARTELL, a railway village, organized in November, 1907, adjoining the Mississippi in Sauk Rapids township, with extension west of the river in Le Sauk, Stearns county, was named for Joseph B. Sartell, who was the first settler of the west side, coming in 1854 as a farmer. Later he built and operated sawmills. He resided there, with seven sons, until his death, January 27, 1913, at the age of eighty-six years.

SAUK RAPIDS township was organized in 1854, and the village was platted in that year but was not separately organized until 1881. This village was the county seat from the organization of the county in 1850 until 1902, when the county offices were removed to Foley, as before noted. Sauk Rapids derived its name from the adjoining rapids of the Mississippi, called Grand Rapids by Pike in 1805 and mapped by him as Big Falls, falling about 20 feet in the first mile below the mouth of the Sauk river, mapped by Pike as Sack river, which comes in from Stearns county.

The origin of the names of Sauk river and of Osakis lake and village at its source, in Todd and Douglas counties, as also of the Sauk lakes and Little Sauk township in Todd county, of Sauk Center and Le Sauk townships in Stearns county, of Sauk Rapids, and of Osauka, an addition recently platted at the northwest edge of this village, was from refugee Sauk or Sac Indians, who came to Osakis lake from the home of this tribe, allied with the Fox Indians, in Wisconsin. This was told in a historical paper by the late Judge Loren W. Collins, as follows. "Five Sacs, refugees from their own tribe on account of murder which they had committed, made their way up to the lake [Osakis] and settled near the outlet upon the east side. . . On one of the excursions made by some of the Pillager bands of Chippewas to the asylum of the O-zau-kees, it was found that all had been killed, supposedly by the Sioux." (History of Stearns county, 1915, vol. I, page 24.)

WATAB township, organized in 1858, like its Indian trading post, which had been established ten years earlier, was named for the Watab river, called Little Sack river by Pike, tributary to the Mississippi from the west about five miles north of St. Cloud. This is the Ojibway word for the long and very slender roots of both the tamarack and jack pine, which were dug by the Indians, split and used as threads in sewing their birch bark canoes. Both these coniferous trees grow on or near the lower part of the Watab river.

Rev. F. W. Smith, an Ojibway pastor, of Red Lake Agency, informed the present writer in 1885, during my visit there, that in northern Minnesota the Ojibways principally use the roots of the jack pine as watab, although the roots of both tamarack and arbor vitae are also somewhat used (Minn. Geol. and Nat. Hist. Survey, Bulletin No. 3, 1887, page 53). The name of this river and township doubtless refers to the jack pines there, this being at the southwest limit of that species, whereas the geographic range of the tamarack extends considerably farther south and west.

The trading post named Watab was about two miles and a half north from the mouth of this river and on the opposite or eastern side of the Mississippi. During about ten years next following its establishment in 1848, Watab was the most important commercial place in Minnesota Territory northwestward from St. Paul, but later it was superseded by Sauk Rapids and St. Cloud, and before 1880 the village of Watab entirely disappeared.

Lakes and Streams.

The name of the Mississippi was fully noticed in the first chapter; the Elk and St. Francis rivers are considered in the chapter for Sherburne and Anoka counties, which respectively have the village and township of Elk River and St. Francis township; and a preceding page gives the origin of the name of Mayhew lake and creek.

Donovan lake, in section 34, Minden, named for John Donovan, a farmer near it, was formerly called Minden lake.

Halfway brook, tributary to the Mississippi close north of Sartell, received this name for its being nearly midway between Sauk Rapids and Watab.

The southern two thirds of Watab township has many outcrops of granite and syenite, continuing from their much quarried area in Sauk Rapids and East St. Cloud. At each side of the river road, in the vicinity of the Watab railway station, small hills and knobs of these rocks rise about 40 feet above the road and 75 to 90 feet above the river. One of these hills of rough, bald rock, called by Schoolcraft the Peace Rock, rises directly from the river's edge about a half mile south from the mouth of Little Rock creek, which, with its Little Rock lake, was thence so named. It is a translation of the Ojibway name, signifying, as more elaborately stated by Gilfillan, "where the little rocky hills project out every once in a while, here and there." Pike noted the large prairie here and northward as favorite grazing for elk, and he therefore mapped these as Elk lake and Lake river.

Peace Rock was named for its marking, with the Watab river, a part of the old line of boundary between the Ojibways and the Sioux, to which agreement was made by their chiefs in the Treaty of 1825 at Prairie du Chien.

BIG STONE COUNTY

This county, established February 20, 1862, and organized April 13, 1874, derived its name from Big Stone lake, through which the Minnesota river flows on the west boundary of the county and state. It is a translation of the Dakota or Sioux name, alluding to the conspicuous outcrops of granite and gneiss, extensively quarried, which occur in the Minnesota valley from a half mile to three miles below the foot of the lake. The city and county building in Minneapolis is constructed of the stone from these quarries, which also supplied four massive columns of the state capitol rotunda, on its north and south sides. The Sioux name, poorly pronounced and indistinctly heard, was written Eatakeka by Keating in his Narrative of Long's Expedition in 1823; but Prof. A. W. Williamson more correctly spelled it in two words, Inyan tankinyanyan, the first meaning stone, the second very great, as shown by the repetition of the first word and duplication of its final syllable.

Big Stone lake extends in a somewhat crooked course from northwest to southeast twenty-six miles; its width is one mile to one and a half miles; and its greatest depth is reported to be from 15 to 30 feet.

De L'Isle's map of Canada or New France in 1703 calls this the Lake of the Tintons, that is, the Prairie Sioux. The same name is given by the maps of Buache, 1754, and Bellin, 1755. Carver, who was on the Minnesota river in 1766-7, mapped this lake but left it unnamed. Long's expedition gave its earliest correct delineation, with its present name and the older equivalent Sioux and French names.

Townships and Villages.

Information has been gathered from "History of the Minnesota Valley," 1882, pages 973-986; and from Hayden French, of Ortonville, clerk of the court for this county, and Martin Irwin Matthews, who for many years was one of the county commissioners and later has been the municipal judge in Ortonville, each being interviewed during a visit there in September, 1916.

AKRON township, first settled in 1872, and organized July 25, 1881, was named for Akron, Ohio, whence some of its pioneers came.

ALMOND township, organized March 29, 1880, was named for the township and village of this name in Allegany county, New York, or for Almond township and village in Portage county, Wisconsin.

ARTICHOKE township, whose first settler came in May, 1869, received its name from the former Artichoke lake, now drained, which was five miles long, stretching from section 11 south to section 36. This name was probably translated from the Sioux name of the lake, referring to the edible tuber roots of a species of sunflower (Helianthus tuberosus), which was much used by the Indians as food, called pangi by the Sioux, abundant here and common or frequent throughout this state.

BARRY, a railway village in Toqua township, was named in honor of the Barry brothers, homesteading farmers there, who came from Lowell, Mass.

BEARDSLEY, the railway village of Brown's Valley township, was named for W. W. Beardsley, who platted it in November, 1880. He was born in Schuyler county, New York, in 1852; removed to Pennsylvania at the age of twenty-one years, and to Wisconsin in 1875; came to Minnesota in 1878, homesteading the farm which included the site of this village.

BIG STONE township, organized October 4, 1879, received its name, like the county, from the adjoining lake.

BROWN'S VALLEY township, first settled in 1875 and organized April 5, 1880, was named by Thomas Bailey, a homesteader there who came from Tennessee. The name was taken from the very remarkable valley between lakes Big Stone and Traverse, in which a trading post and the village of this name had been established by Hon. Joseph R. Brown, situated in the southwest corner of Traverse county. Brown county was named for him, and biographic notes are given in its chapter.

CLINTON, a railway village at the center of Almond township, was named probably for one of the many villages, towns, and counties bearing this name, which are found in our eastern and southern states.

CORRELL, a village on the main line of the Chicago, Milwaukee and St. Paul railway, bears a personal name given by the officers of the railway. Its more definite derivation has not been learned.

FOSTER, a village of summer residences on the shore of Big Stone lake. in Prior township, was platted in 1880 on the pre-emption claim of M. I. Matthews, who settled there in 1872. It was named for Foster L. Balch, of Minneapolis, president of the Big Stone Lake Navigation and Improvement Company.

GRACEVILLE township and its village, which was founded by Catholic colonists in 1877-8, were named in honor of Thomas Langdon Grace, who during twenty-five years was the bishop of St. Paul, 1859 to 1884. He was born in Charleston, S. C., Nov. 15, 1814, and died in St. Paul, Feb. 22, 1897.

MALTA township, organized February 14, 1880, was at first named Clarksville, for David K. J. Clark, its first settler, who came in June, 1876. It was renamed, after a town of New York and villages in Ohio and Illinois, for the island of Malta in the Mediterranean Sea.

MOONSHINE township took its name from its Moonshine lake which was named by D. K. J. Clark, mentioned as a settler in Malta. On his first coming here in 1876 from Wabasha county, his first camp was beside this lake, which he then named, intending to call it Moon lake for the surname of his wife, Mrs. Mary A. (Moon) Clark; but in the evening the bright moonlight caused the name to be thus changed.

BIG STONE COUNTY 55

ODESSA township, first settled in June, 1870, was named for the city of Odessa in southern Russia, whence seed wheat used in this vicinity was brought. The railway village of Odessa was platted in 1879, when this railway was being built.

ORTONVILLE township received its first settlers in 1871, and in September of the next year its village was platted by Cornelius Knute Orton, for whom the village and township were named. He was of Norwegian descent and was born in Dane county, Wisconsin, in 1846; came to Minnesota in 1857; settled on a land claim here in 1871; engaged in real estate business, and was a banker, merchant, and a member of the board of county commissioners. He died in Ortonville, December 24, 1890. This village was organized as a city on January 28, 1881.

OTREY township, first settled by Thomas and William Otrey from Illinois in June, 1869, was organized February 14, 1880. It was then named Trenton, but later was renamed in honor of these brothers, who had served in the civil war.

PRIOR township, settled in 1870 and organized in 1879, was named in honor of Charles H. Prior, of Minneapolis, superintendent of this Hastings and Dakota division of the Chicago, Milwaukee and St. Paul railway. He had large land interests in this township and in Ortonville.

TOQUA township (formerly spelled Tokua), first settled in 1877 and organized March 16, 1880, received its name from the two Tokua lakes in Graceville and the similar pair of lakes in this township, which latter were called by the Sioux, as translated, the Tokua Brothers lakes. This aboriginal name is spelled Ta Kara on Nicollet's map, 1843, Ta being the Sioux word for the moose, while Kara doubtless refers to the Kahra band of the Dakotas or Sioux.

Keating, the historian of Long's expedition in 1823, wrote as follows (in his Volume I, page 403), describing this band. "KAHRA (Wild Rice). These Indians dwell in very large and fine skin lodges. The skins are well prepared and handsomely painted. They have no permanent residence, but frequently visit Lake Travers. Their hunting grounds are on Red river. They follow Tatankanaje (the Standing Buffalo), who is a chief by hereditary right, and who has acquired distinction as a warrior."

Nicollet also used the word Kara as the final part of other names, Plan Kara and Manstitsa Kara, given on his map to two points or hillocks of the valley bluff east of the northern end of Lake Traverse. Riggs, however, in his Dakota Dictionary, published in 1852, rejected all use of the letter r in that language, so that the name Kahra or Kara may not be identifiable in that work. Tokua (or Toqua) was the white men's endeavor to spell the Sioux name for these pairs of lakes, which Nicollet spelled as Ta Kara.

Samuel J. Brown, of the village of Brown's Valley, has stated that this name "was taken from a picture carved on a tree, meaning probably some animal so pictured." This accords well with the meaning of the name given by Nicollet, as the moose of the Kara or Kahra band of Sioux, perhaps a family totem or their mystic patron of the clan (as we might say, a mascot).

LAKES AND STREAMS.

Since the first coming of the homestead farmers, nearly fifty years ago, the area of this county has witnessed the drying up of many of its former shallow lakes, partly because plowing and cultivation of the soil permit the rains and the water from the melting of the winter snows to sink in larger proportion into the ground, not running off to the hollows. In recent years others of the lakes have been drained by ditches, the lake beds being allotted fractionally to the adjoining landowners. The map of Big Stone county published by the Minnesota Geological Survey (vol. I, 1884, Chapter XXI) has more than fifty lakes; but the most recent Minnesota atlas, in 1916, shows only four or five yet remaining, these being unnamed.

Artichoke and Moonshine lakes, and the Tokua lakes and Tokua Brothers lakes, noted in the foregoing list of townships, have disappeared by drainage.

Only a few streams of noteworthy size and bearing names flow here into the Minnesota river and Big Stone lake. These include Five Mile creek, so named for its distance west of the Pomme de Terre river and the village of Appleton, in the adjoining Swift county; Stony run, in Big Stone and Odessa townships, named for the plentiful boulders along parts of this stream; and Fish creek, tributary to Big Stone lake at the northwest corner of Prior.

THE GLACIAL RIVER WARREN.

Big Stone lake, flowing south in the Minnesota river, and Lake Traverse, flowing north in the Bois des Sioux and Red rivers, are on the opposite sides of a continental water divide, one of these lakes sending its outflow to the Gulf of Mexico, the other to Hudson Bay. But they lie in a continuous valley, one to two miles wide, which was evidently channeled by a great river formerly flowing southward. The part of the ancient watercourse between these lakes, a distance of nearly five miles, is widely known as Brown's Valley. As noticed in the first chapter the former river here outflowing from the Glacial Lake Agassiz in the Red river basin has been named the River Warren, in honor of General G. K. Warren.

Fifteen miles below Big Stone lake, the Minnesota river flows through Marsh lake, on the south side of Akron, now mainly drained, which formerly was four miles long and about a mile wide. It was so named from its being shallow and full of reeds and grass.

BLUE EARTH COUNTY

This county was established March 5, 1853, and took its name from the Blue Earth river, for a bluish green earth that was used by the Sisseton Sioux as a pigment, found in a shaly layer of the rock bluff of this stream about three miles from its mouth.

The blue earth was the incentive and cause of a very interesting chapter of our earliest history. LeSueur, the French explorer, before his first return to France in 1695, had discovered the locality whence the savages procured this blue and green paint, which he thought to be an ore of copper, and he then took some of it to Paris, submitted it to L'Huillier, one of the king's assayers, and secured the royal commission to work the mines. But disasters and obstacles deterred him from this project until four years later, when, having come from a third visit in France, with thirty miners, to Biloxi, near the mouth of the Mississippi, he ascended this river in the year 1700, using a sailing and rowing vessel and two canoes. Coming forward along the Minnesota river, he reached the mouth of the Blue Earth river on the last day in September or the first in October.

LeSueur spent the ensuing year on this river, having built a camp or post named Fort L'Huillier, and in the spring mined a large quantity of the supposed copper ore. Taking a selected portion of the ore, amounting to two tons, and leaving a garrison at the fort, LeSueur again navigated nearly the whole length of the Mississippi, and arrived at the Gulf of Mexico in February, 1702. Thence with Iberville, the founder and first governor of Louisiana, who was a cousin of LeSueur's wife, he sailed for France in the latter part of April, carrying the ore or blue earth, of which, however, nothing more is known.

Thomas Hughes, of Mankato, historian of the city and county, identified in 1904 the sites of Fort L'Huillier and the mine of the blue or green earth, which are described in a paper contributed to the Minnesota Historical Society Collections (vol. XII, pages 283-5).

Penicaut's Relation of LeSueur's expedition was translated by Alfred J. Hill in the Minnesota Historical Society Collections (vol. III, 1880, pages 1-12); and a map showing the locations of the fort and mine, ascertained by Hughes, was published in 1911 by Winchell, on page 493, "The Aborigines of Minnesota." From that expedition and the mine, we have the name of the Blue Earth river and of this county, and also of the township and city of Blue Earth in Faribault county.

This name was probably received by LeSueur and his party from that earlier given to the river by the Sioux. The Relation of Penicaut, however, might be thought to indicate otherwise, as follows: "We called this Green river, because it is of that color by reason of a green earth which, loosening itself from the copper mines, becomes dissolved in it and makes it green." In the language of the Sioux the same word, *to,* is used both for blue and green, and their name of the Blue Earth river is Makato (*maka,* earth, *to,* blue, or green). Keating wrote, in the Narrative of Long's expedition, 1823: "By the Dacotas it is called Makato Osa Watapa, which signifies 'the river where blue earth is gathered.'"

The Sioux name is retained, with slight change, by the township and city of Mankato. On the earliest map of Minnesota Territory, in 1850, it appeared as Mahkahta for one of its original nine counties, reaching from the Mississippi above the Crow Wing west to the Missouri.

Townships and Villages.

Information of the origins of the local names has been gathered from "History of the Minnesota Valley," 1882, pages 532-637; from "The Standard Historical and Pictorial Atlas and Gazetteer of Blue Earth County," 1895, 147 pages; from the "History of Blue Earth County," by Thomas Hughes, 1909, 622 pages; and from Evan Hughes, judge of probate, Andrew G. Johnson, county treasurer, Thomas Hughes, and Judge Lorin Cray, during my visits in Mankato in July and October, 1916.

AMBOY, the railway village of Shelby township, was platted October 31, 1879, and was named by Robert Richardson, its first postmaster and merchant, for the town of his former home in Illinois.

BEAUFORD township was originally established under the name of Winneshiek (the Winnebago chief for whom a county of Iowa is named), April 16, 1858, when it was in the Winnebago Indian Reservation. It was organized March 13, 1865, with the present name, suggested by Albert Gates, "after a town in the east, from which some of the settlers had come." (The U. S. Postal Guide formerly had one post office of this name, this being in Floyd county, Virginia; but it was discontinued several years ago. Beaufort, nearly the same, is a frequent geographic name.)

BRADLEY railway station, five miles north of Mankato, was named for the Bradley crossing of the Minnesota river, established by the Bradley family, on whose farm this station was located. (Stennett, p. 169.)

BUTTERNUT VALLEY township, established January 6, 1857, organized in May, 1858, was named in accordance with the suggestion of Colonel Samuel D. Shaw, who had come from the town of Butternuts, in Otsego county, New York. The butternut tree is common or frequent, especially in river valleys, through the southeastern part of Minnesota.

CAMBRIA township, first settled in 1855, organized June 3, 1867, was named by Robert H. Hughes, a pioneer homesteader, who had come from Cambria, Wisconsin. This was the ancient Latin name of Wales, the native land of nearly all the settlers here, or of their parents.

CERESCO township, established July 8, 1857, organized May 11, 1858, was named by Isaac Slocum, for his former home town in Wisconsin.

CRAY, a railway station eight miles west of Mankato, was named for Judge Lorin Cray, who during many years was the Mankato attorney of this Chicago, St. Paul, Minneapolis and Omaha railway company.

DANVILLE township, established April 6, 1858, was then named Jackson; but because an earlier township of Minnesota had that name, it was changed October 14, 1858, in compliment to Lucius Dyer, a settler who had come from Danville, Vermont.

DECORIA township, named April 6, 1858, was in the Winnebago reservation, and it remained without organization till October 8, 1867, being the latest organized township of this county. The name is in commemoration of a Winnebago chief, called "One-Eyed Dekora," having lost an eye. This chief and the tribe aided the whites during the Black Hawk war of 1832, in which he displayed great ability and courage. He lived through the removals of the Winnebagoes from Wisconsin to northeastern Iowa in 1837-38, from Iowa to Long Prairie, Minnesota, in 1848, thence to Blue Earth county in 1855, next to a reservation in Dakota, 1863, and last to Nebraska in 1866. He was a renowned orator, and from his prowess in war and influence in council was known among his own people as Waukon Decorah, meaning in translation "Wonderful Decorah." Two important towns of Iowa, Waukon and Decorah, which are the county seats of its most northeast counties on the border of Minnesota, were named for him. This name, variously spelled also as De Kaury, Day Kauray, Day Korah, De Corrah, etc., belonged to a Winnebago family of hereditary chiefs through four generations or more, who had descended from a French army officer, Sabrevoir De Carrie. (Hodge, Handbook of American Indians, vol. I, 1907, page 384; Sparks, History of Winneshiek County, Iowa, 1877; Alexander, History of Winneshiek and Allamakee Counties, Iowa, 1882.)

EAGLE LAKE, a railway village in Le Ray township, was platted in November, 1872, and received its name from the neighboring lake, which had been so named by the United States land surveyors because many bald eagles had nests in high trees on the lake shore.

GARDEN CITY township was established April 6, 1858, but was then named Watonwan for the river. The village had been platted in June, 1856, being named Fremont for John C. Fremont, the Republican candidate for president in the campaign of that year. In October, 1858, it was replatted by Simeon P. Folsom, who renamed it Garden City, having reference to the native floral charms of the place. Stennett wrote of it, "Even to this day, in the spring the surrounding country is like a garden of wild flowers." In February, 1864, the township was changed to Garden City by an act of the state legislature. The name here antedates it on Long Island, N. Y., where the only town so named in the eastern states was founded in 1869 by A. T. Stewart, the multimillionaire merchant.

GOOD THUNDER, the railway village of Lyra township, platted in April, 1871, and incorporated March 2, 1893, was named for a chief of the Winnebagoes, whose village was close east of this site. The ford of the Maple river here had been previously called Good Thunder's ford. He was a friend of the white people, and in 1862 refused the overtures of the Sioux for the Winnebagoes to join in their outbreak and massacre of the white settlers. He died several years later on the Missouri river, after the removal of his tribe to Dakota.

This was also the name of a Sioux, Wa-kin-yan-was-te, in translation Good Thunder, who likewise was friendly to the whites, becoming General Sibley's chief of scouts during his expeditions against the Sioux after the massacre. He was converted to be a Christian in 1861, and was the first Sioux baptized by Bishop Whipple, receiving then the name Andrew. He lived as a farmer at the mission of Birch Cooley, and during many years was the warden of its Sioux church. In 1889 he was a guest of the village of Good Thunder at its celebration of the Fourth of July, when he and many of its people thought the name of the village to have been given in his honor. To make it more sure, by the speeches of that day it was so rechristened. (Good Thunder Herald, Feb. 21, 1901.) He died at the Sioux Agency near Redwood Falls, February 15, 1901. Portraits of this Good Thunder and his wife are given in "The Aborigines of Minnesota" at page 509, but he is there erroneously called a Winnebago; and another portrait of him is in Whipple's "Lights and Shadows of a long Episcopate," at page 128.

It seems most probable that when this name was first chosen for the village, although the greater number of those naming it had in mind the Winnebago chief, others of them and many in the county supposed it to be for the Sioux scout, the exemplary Christian convert. Both these Indians certainly were very well known by the people of this township and county.

JAMESTOWN, half of a government township, first settled in 1856, and organized May 11, 1858, then including also Le Ray township, was named by Enoch G. Barkhurst, "in honor of the first English colony of Virginia." The name there was given to honor James I, King of England in 1603-25.

JUDSON township, organized May 11, 1858, was "named by Robert Patterson, in honor of the great Baptist missionary." Patterson had earlier platted and named Judson village, December 10, 1856. Adoniram Judson was born in Malden, Mass., August 9, 1788; and died at sea, April 12, 1850. He went to Burma as a missionary in 1812, completed the translation of the Bible into Burmese in 1833, and completed a Burmese-English dictionary in 1849.

LAKE CRYSTAL, a railway village and junction, platted in May, 1869, incorporated by the legislature February 24, 1870, was named by Gen. Judson W. Bishop, of St. Paul, engineer of the survey and construction of this railway, for the adjoining lake, which, according to Stennett, "was named by John C. Fremont and J. N. Nicollet, who explored the country around it in 1838, because of the unusual brilliancy and crystal purity of its waters." (This lake and the others near are unnamed on Nicollet's map, 1843.)

LE RAY township, first settled in 1856, organized in 1860, was at first named Lake and was renamed Tivoli, but on September 5, 1860, received its present name. The only use of this name elsewhere is for a township of Jefferson county, N. Y., whence probably some of the settlers here had come.

LIME township, organized May 11, 1858, was named by George Stannard for its extensive outcrops of limestone, which have since been much quarried.

LINCOLN township, settled in 1856, was at first named Richfield, April 6, 1858; but it remained without separate organization until September 26, 1865, when it was renamed for the martyred War President.

LYRA township, at first named Tecumseh, April 16, 1858, was renamed Winneshiek in May, 1866; but at the time of its organization, September 22, 1866, it was finally named Lyra, as proposed by Rev. J. M. Thurston, "after a town he had come from in the east." (It appears in our eastern states only as a post office in Scioto county, Ohio.) "It comes to us from ancient mythology and was originally used to designate a northern constellation, . . . as it was supposed to represent the lyre carried by Apollo."

MCPHERSON was at first named Rice Lake township, August 21, 1855; was renamed McClellan, for Gen. George B. McClellan, September 2, 1863; and received its present name by an act of the state legislature in February, 1865, in honor of Gen. James B. McPherson. He was born in Sandusky, Ohio, November 14, 1828; was graduated at West Point, 1853; was appointed a major general in 1862; served with distinction in the siege and capture of Vicksburg; became commander of the Army of the Tennessee in the spring of 1864; and was killed near Atlanta, Ga., July 22, 1864.

MADISON LAKE, a railway village in Jamestown, was named for the adjoining lake, which had been so named by the government surveyors in honor of James Madison, fourth president of the United States, 1809-17.

MANKATO township was established April 6, 1858, and was organized in connection with the present city of Mankato, May 11, 1858. The city charter was adopted March 24, 1868; and the first election of the township, separate from the city, was held April 7, 1868. The first settlement of Mankato and of this county was in February, 1852, by Parsons King Johnson; and on the 14th of that month the Blue Earth Settlement Claim Association was organized in St. Paul by Henry Jackson, P. K. Johnson, Col. D. A. Robertson, Justus C. Ramsey, brother of the governor of the Territory, and others. Hughes writes of their choice of the name for the settlement to be founded, as follows: "The honor of christening the new city was accorded to Mrs. P. K. Johnson and Mrs. Henry Jackson, who selected the name 'Mankato,' upon the suggestion of Col. Robertson. He had taken the name from Nicollet's book, in which the French explorer compared the 'Mahkato' or Blue Earth river, with all its tributaries, to the water nymphs and their uncle in the German legend of

'Undine.' .... No more appropriate name could be given the new city, than that of the noble river at whose mouth it is located."

MAPLETON, first settled in April, 1856, was named Sherman in 1858 for Isaac Sherman, an old settler of Danville, or perhaps for Asa P. Sherman of this township. It was organized, with its first town meeting, April 2, 1861, taking its present name from the Maple river, which received this name from the government surveyors in 1854, for its plentiful maple trees. The site of the railway village of Mapleton was platted January 21, 1871, and it soon superseded the older village which had been platted in June, 1856.

MEDO, a township of the Winnebago reservation, was named by the county commissioners April 16, 1858, but it was not organized until September 2, 1863. This is a Sioux word, meaning a species of plant (Apios tuberosa), which has roots that bear small tubers much used by the Indians as food. It is common or frequent through the south half of this state, extending north to the upper Mississippi river. Dr. Parry, with Owen's geological survey in 1848, wrote of it as "Pomme de Terre of the French voyageurs; Mdo, or wild potato, of the Sioux Indians." It is also called ground-nut, and its nutlike tubers grow in a series along the root.

PERTH, a railway station in Lincoln township, was named in 1905 from the city in Scotland. It had formerly been called Iceland, for the native island of some of its immigrants.

PLEASANT MOUND township was first named Otsego, April 6, 1858; but on October 14 of that year it was renamed Willow Creek, "probably an eastern name familiar to some old settler." There is a creek of this name in the east part of the township, flowing northeast into the Blue Earth river. A post office named Pleasant Mound was established in 1863 at the home of F. O. Marks, near a series of hills of drift gravel, called kames, in section 25. The Sioux name of these hills, according to Hughes, was Ichokse or Repah Kichakse, meaning "to cut in the middle, perhaps from the fact that the ridge is divided into a number of mounds, or it may mean 'thrown down or dumped in heaps,' as the spelling is uncertain." September 6, 1865, this township was organized and was given its present name, on the suggestions of Mr. Marks and John S. Parks, taken like that of the post office from the knolly gravel ridge.

RAPIDAN township, which was in the Winnebago reservation, was at first named De Soto, April 16, 1858; but at its organization, April 15, 1865, it received the present name, suggested by C. P. Cook, from the civil war, for the Rapidan river of Virginia. This name is also given to rapids and a dam of the Blue Earth river in the northwest part of this township, about two miles west of Rapidan village on the railway.

ST. CLAIR, a railway terminal village in McPherson township, is on the site of the old Winnebago Agency, where after the removal of the Indians a village named Hilton was platted on land of Aaron Hilton in

1865. Its name was changed to St. Clair by officers of the Chicago, Milwaukee and St. Paul railway company.

SHELBY township, established by the county commissioners April 6, 1858, was then named Liberty, but was renamed as now on October 14, of that year. Its village of Shelbyville had been platted in April, 1856, which was superseded by the more centrally located railway village of Amboy, platted in 1879, so that the Shelbyville post office was discontinued in 1881. This village name was given by Rev. John W. Powell, who came here in October, 1855, from Shelbyville, Indiana.

Isaac Shelby, whose name is borne by nine counties in our central and southern states and also by numerous towns and villages, with several other cities and villages named Shelbyville, was born in Maryland, December 11, 1750; and died near Stanford, Kentucky, July 18, 1826. He served very honorably in the Revolutionary War, and again in the War of 1812; was the first governor of Kentucky, 1792-96, and also in 1812-16; returned from each period of his governorship to the cultivation of his farm; was six times a presidential elector, but declined other public service.

SOUTH BEND township "derived its name from the fact that the Minnesota river makes its great southern bend on its northern boundary." This name was proposed by David C. Evans, by whom, with Captain Samuel Humbertson and others, the village of South Bend was founded in the summer of 1853, as a rival of Mankato. Its plat was recorded September 22, 1854. The township was organized May 11, 1858.

STERLING township, first settled in 1855, was organized in April and May, 1858, then being named Mapleton; but on January 3, 1860, the county commissioners granted the petition of the settlers in this township to rename it Sterling. It was so organized, separate from the present Mapleton, April 3, 1860. Robert Taylor proposed the name for the city and county in Scotland, spelled Stirling; but, as Hughes writes, "William Russell contended for the name 'Sterling,' as more appropriate and expressive of the quality of the soil and people, and the majority sided with him."

STONE, a railway station three miles north of Mankato, "was originally called Quarry, owing to stone quarries in the vicinity. In 1902 the name was changed to Stone, and came from the same 'stone quarries' that had given it the earlier name." (Stennett, Origin of the Place Names of the Chicago and Northwestern Railways.)

VERNON CENTER township, settled in 1855, was at first named Montevideo by the county commissioners, April 6, 1858; but ten days later they renamed it Vernon, and on October 14 of the same year they changed this to the present name. A village had been platted here in June, 1857, by proprietors who came from Mount Vernon, Ohio, two of whom, Col. Benjamin F. Smith and Benjamin McCracken, gave to it the name Vernon. The many villages and cities of the United States that bear this name, including the home of Washington in Virginia, received it primarily in honor of the distinguished English admiral, Edward Vernon, (1684-1757), the hero of the expeditions capturing Porto Bello in 1739 and attacking Cartagena in 1741. When the railway was built through this township in 1879, the first name given to the station here was Edgewood, for its being at the edge of a grove; but it was renamed in 1885 for the township, although neither the township nor the station is quite centrally situated.

Lakes and Streams.

Minneopa creek, its falls, and the State Park, are noted in a later part of the present chapter.

In the foregoing notes of townships and villages, other streams and lakes have been noticed, namely, Maple river, Willow creek in Pleasant Mound township, Lake Crystal, and Eagle and Madison lakes.

The United States surveyors named Washington, Jefferson, and Madison lakes, in commemoration of the early presidents. These are notably large in a group of many lakes, the first and second being in the south edge of LeSueur county, adjoining Jamestown, and the third in Jamestown and Le Ray. Hughes records the Sioux name of Lake Washington as Okapah, meaning the Choke Cherry lake, and of Lake Madison as Wakonseche, that is, the Evil Spirit, or Abundant Mystery, or the Sacred Shade.

Government surveyors also named the Maple river, which the Sioux called the Tewapa-Tankiyan river (meaning Big Water-Lily root), and the Big Cobb river, which bore a Sioux name, Tewapadan (Little Lily root.) The names used by the Indians, copied thus from Nicollet's map (1843), referred to the roots which they dug for food in the shallow water of these streams and their tributary lakes. On the township plats the Big Cobb and Little Cobb rivers were spelled without their final letter, though probably named for some member or acquaintance of the surveying party.

Lake Lura is said to have been so designated by one of the early settlers, from the name "Lura" found carved on a tree upon its shore, and thence it was given to a neighboring township in Faribault county. It had two Sioux names, Tewapa (Water Lily) and Ata'kinyan or Ksanksan (crooked or irregular).

Jackson lake, on the east line of Shelby, named for Norman L. Jackson, the first settler of that township, who located on its shore, had the Sioux name Sinkpe (Muskrat). Hughes writes: "The southern half of its bed, being shallow, was thickly populated by these animals, whose rush-built homes literally covered that portion of the lake. The spot was noted among both the Indians and pioneers for trapping these fur-bearing rats."

Wita lake, in Lime township, retains its Sioux name, meaning Island lake, for its two islands.

The aborigines are also commemorated by two Indian lakes, in Le Ray and South Bend townships.

Names of pioneer settlers are borne by Ballantyne lake, in Jamestown, for James Ballantyne, a school teacher and homesteader; Gilfillin lake, in Jamestown and Le Ray, for Joseph Gilfillin, who left his home near this lake to join the Ninth Minnesota Regiment, Company E, and was killed only two weeks later in service against the Sioux near New Ulm, September 3, 1862; Kilby lake, on the line of Judson and Butternut Valley, for Benjamin E. Kilby; Armstrong, Dackins, Lieberg, Solberg, and Strom lakes, in Butternut Valley, for John Armstrong, Edward Dackins, Ole P. Lieberg, Olens Solberg, and Andrew Strom, the largest of these, Solberg lake, and also Dackins lake, having been recently drained by ditches; Mills lake, in Garden City township, for Titus Mills, whose farm bordered on this lake; Morgan creek, in Cambria, for Richard Morgan, also sometimes otherwise named for others of the settlers along its course; Rogers lake, in sections 7 and 18, Danville, for John E., Robert H., and Josiah Rogers, early settlers on its shore; Albert and George lakes, in Jamestown; and Lake Alice, in Le Ray, and Ida lake in Shelby, each probably named for the wife or daughter of a pioneer.

Other names are of obvious significance, as Cottonwood lake, in Medo; Duck lake, and also Long and Mud lakes, in Jamestown; another Mud lake, in Le Ray; Fox lake, in South Bend; Perch lake, and Perch creek; Lily and Loon lakes, adjoining Lake Crystal, the first very shallow and filled with lilies, water grasses, and rushes; Rice lake in McPherson, named for its wild rice, like many other lakes throughout this state; and Rush lake, in Judson.

THE UNDINE REGION.

Nicollet in 1841 gave to the area of Blue Earth county, with parts of other counties adjoining it, "the name of *Undine Region* . . . derived from that of an interesting and romantic German tale, the heroine of which belonged to the extensive race of water-spirits living in the brooks and rivers and lakes, whose father was a mighty prince. She was moreover the niece of a great brook (the Mankato), who lived in the midst of forests, and was beloved by all the many great streams of the surrounding country."

The author of "Undine," entitled for its heroine, published in 1811, was Friedrich Fouqué, who was born at Brandenburg, Prussia, in 1777, and died at Berlin in 1843. Her name is from the Latin unda, a wave, whence we derive several common words, as undulation and inundate, and speak of undulating prairies, where they have a broadly wavy surface.

On Nicollet's map the Undine Region extends from the Redwood river east to the upper part of Cannon river, and from the Minnesota river south to the north edge of Iowa.

MINNEOPA STATE PARK.

The state legislature in 1905 provided for the purchase of land containing the Minneopa Falls on the creek of this name in South Bend township, about four miles west of Mankato, for public use as a state park. Its area is about sixty acres, comprising the falls, two near together, of 60 feet descent, with the gorge below. The railway station, and townsite, named Minneopa, close to the falls, had been platted in September, 1870. This name is contracted from Sioux words, minne-hinhe-nonpa, which mean "water falling twice" or "two waterfalls." An early name of this stream was Lyons creek, for a pioneer. It flows from Strom, Lily, and Crystal lakes.

The Winnebago Reservation.

Green bay, of Lake Michigan, was known to the French in Radisson's time as the Bay of the Puants, or Winnebagoes, an outlying tribe of the Siouan stock, mainly surrounded by Algonquian tribes. Their name, meaning the People of the Stinking Water, that is, of the Sea, or of muddy and ill-smelling lakes, roiled by winds, was adopted by the French from its use among the Algonquins. In 1832 the Winnebagoes ceded their country south and east of the Fox and Wisconsin rivers to the United States, and afterward many of the tribe were removed to northeastern Iowa. Thence, in 1848, they were removed to Long Prairie, in the central part of what is now Minnesota; and in 1855 they were again removed, to a reservation in Blue Earth and Waseca counties of this state. In 1863, after the Sioux outbreak, they were removed to a reservation in Dakota; and in 1866 to a more suitable reservation in Nebraska.

The reservation that was provided here for this tribe by a treaty made at Washington, on February 27, 1855, included in Blue Earth county the townships of Rapidan, Decoria, McPherson, Lyra, Beauford, and Medo; and it continued six miles east in Waseca county, there including Alton and Freedom townships. By a later treaty at Washington, April 15, 1859, the Winnebagoes relinquished the west half of this Reservation, "to be sold by the United States in trust for their benefit;" and by an act of Congress, February 21, 1863, the east half, comprising McPherson, Medo, Alton, and Freedom, was directed to be similarly sold, another reservation having been provided in Dakota.

Glacial Lake Minnesota.

In the basins of the Blue Earth and Minnesota rivers, flowing northward from the edge of Iowa to the Mississippi at Fort Snelling, a glacial lake was held by the barrier of the departing continental glacier during its final melting. This temporary lake was mapped and named in my work for the United States Geological Survey (Monograph XXV, "The Glacial Lake Agassiz," 1896, plates III and XIII; pages 254 and 264). To the later and reduced condition of this glacial lake, when it outflowed to the Cannon river, Professor N. H. Winchell in 1901 gave the name of Lake Undine ("Glacial Lakes of Minnesota," Bulletin of the Geol. Society of America, vol. 12, pages 109-128, with a map).

BROWN COUNTY

Established by legislative act February 20, 1855, and organized February 11, 1856, this county was named in honor of Joseph Renshaw Brown, one of the most prominent pioneers of this state. He was born in Harford county, Maryland, January 5, 1805; and died in New York City, November 9, 1870.

In his boyhood he ran away from an apprenticeship for the printing business at Lancaster, Pa.; enlisted in the army as a drummer boy; and at the age of fourteen years came to the area of Minnesota, with the troops who built Fort St. Anthony (in 1825 renamed Fort Snelling). In May, 1822, with William Joseph Snelling, son of the commandant, he explored the creek and lake since named Minnehaha and Minnetonka.

John Fletcher Williams, secretary of the Minnesota Historical Society, wrote in 1871, as follows, of Brown's varied life work and of his personal qualities.

"On leaving the army, somewhere about 1825, he resided at Mendota, Saint Croix, and other points in the State, and engaged in the Indian trade, lumbering, and other occupations. His energy, industry and ability soon made him a prominent character on the frontier, and no man in the Northwest was better known. He acquired a very perfect acquaintance with the Dakota tongue, and attained an influence among that nation (being allied to them by marriage), which continued unabated to his death. He held, at different times during his life, a number of civil offices, which he filled with credit and ability. . . . He was also a leading member of the famous 'Stillwater Convention' of citizens held in August, 1848, to take steps to secure a Territorial organization for what is now Minnesota. He was the Secretary of the Territorial Councils of 1849 and 1851, and Chief Clerk of the House of Representatives in 1853, a member of the Council in 1854 and '55 and House in 1857, and Territorial Printer in 1853 and '54. He was also a member from Sibley county in the Constitutional Convention ('Democratic Wing') of 1857, and took a very prominent part in the formation of our present State Constitution. . . . He shaped much of the legislation of our early territorial days, and chiefly dictated the policy of his party, of whose conventions he was always a prominent member. . . .

"But it is as a journalist and publisher I desire principally to speak of him here. His first regular entrance into the printing business in Minnesota was in the year 1852, though he had before written considerable for the press. Shortly after the death of James M. Goodhue, which occurred in August of that year, Major Brown purchased the 'Minnesota Pioneer,' and edited and published it under his own name for nearly two years. In the spring of 1854, he transferred the establishment to Col. E. S.

Goodrich. During the period of his connection with the paper, he established a reputation as one of the most sagacious, successful and able political editors in the Territory, and as a sharp, interesting and sensible writer.

"In 1857 he established at Henderson, which town had been founded and laid out by him a short time before, a journal called the 'Henderson Democrat,' which soon became a prominent political organ, and was continued with much ability and success until 1860 or '61."

Joseph A. Wheelock wrote in the St. Paul Press, November 12, 1870: "A drummer boy, soldier, Indian trader, lumberman, pioneer, speculator, founder of cities, legislator, politician, editor, inventor, his career—though it hardly commenced till half his life had been wasted in the obscure solitudes of this far Northwestern wilderness—has been a very remarkable and characteristic one, not so much for what he has achieved, as for the extraordinary versatility and capacity which he has displayed in every new situation."

The village of Brown's Valley in Traverse county, founded by Joseph R. Brown and others, was the place of his trading post and home during his last four years; and an adjoining township of Big Stone county also bears this name.

Townships and Villages.

Information has been gathered from "History of the Minnesota Valley," 1882, pages 698-762, and "History of Brown County," L. A. Fritsche, M. D., Editor, two volumes, 1916, pages 519, 568; from Benedict Juni, Richard Pfefferle, and August Schwerdtfeger, each of New Ulm, and from the county offices of the register of deeds, judge of probate, and clerk of the court, during a visit at New Ulm in July, 1916.

ALBIN, settled in 1866, was organized June 23, 1870. "The preliminary meeting for the organization of the town was held at the house of S. Rima; a name for the town could not be agreed upon, and Albin was suggested by Mrs. Rima." (History, Minnesota Valley, p. 758.)

BASHAW township, organized in April, 1874, was named for Joseph Baschor (or Pascher), a Bohemian, who was the first settler, coming in the spring of 1869. He was yet living in 1916, in the village of **Springfield**. The name was changed in spelling, to give a more easy English pronunciation.

BURNSTOWN, first settled in 1857, was named for J. F. Burns, one of the early settlers, who came in 1858. This township was organized October 14, 1871. "In 1877 the village of Burns was surveyed . . . on the line of the Winona and St. Peter railroad. . . February 21, 1881, it was incorporated under the name of Springfield."

COBDEN, a railway village, was originally named North Branch, from its location near Sleepy Eye creek, the principal north branch of Cottonwood river; but in 1886 it was changed to Cobden, for the English statesman. The village was platted February 16, 1901, and was incorporated in 1905. Richard Cobden was born in Sussex, England, June 3, 1804; died in London, April 2, 1865. He entered Parliament in 1841; visited the United States in 1854; was especially noted as an advocate of free trade and of peace. During our civil war he was a supporter of the cause of the North.

COMFREY, the railway village on the south line of Bashaw township, was platted in 1902, taking its name from a near postoffice, which had been established in 1877. That had been so named "by A. W. Pederson, the first postmaster, from the plant, comfrey . . . that he had met with in his reading." (Stennett, Origin of Place Names of the Chicago and Northwestern Railways.)

COTTONWOOD township, first settled in 1855, organized October 24, 1858, was named for the Cottonwood river, on its north edge, and the Little Cottonwood river, flowing through its center, their names being translations from the Sioux, as noted more fully in the chapter for Cottonwood county.

DOTSON railway station, in Stately township, established in 1899, was named for Enoch Dotson, an early settler of the neighboring village of Sanborn in Redwood county.

EDEN township, which was a part of the Sioux reservation till 1863, was first settled by white immigrants in December, 1864, and was organized April 2, 1867. Its name was chosen by the settlers because of the beauty of its scenery and fertility of the soil. Lone Tree postoffice was established in Eden township in 1869, being named for the neighboring lake, which had received this name from a large lone cottonwood tree, once a famous landmark.

ESSIG, the railway village in Milford, "was named by C. C. Wheeler, then an officer of the Chicago and Northwestern Railway, to honor one of the Brothers Essig, who erected the first business building in the place." (Stennett.) The name is for John Essig, a farmer here since 1882, who was born in Will county, Illinois, May 29, 1851. He came to Minnesota in 1866, with his parents, who settled on a farm in Milford. His father, John F. Essig, who was born in Germany, lived in Milford till 1886, and later in Springfield, where he died in 1896.

EVAN, a railway village in section 8, Prairieville, was first platted as Hanson station in May, 1887, by Nels Hanson, and became an incorporated village March 22, 1904. A postoffice had been established in 1886, named Evan by the first postmaster, Martin Norseth, for his wife, Eva, and its name was transferred to this village.

HANSKA, the railway village in the east edge of Lake Hanska township, bears as its name, like the township, the common Sioux word meaning long or tall, which these Indians gave to the remarkably long and narrow lake in this township and Albin. The village was platted October 9, 1899, and was incorporated in May, 1901.

HOME, the largest township of this county, settled in 1857, organized June 30, 1866, was so named in accordance with the petition of its settlers.

IBERIA, a small hamlet near the center of Stark township, bears the ancient name of the Spanish and Portugese peninsula. The postoffice of this name was established February 1, 1870, and was finally discontinued February 24, 1893.

LAKE HANSKA township, first settled in 1857, organized June 21, 1870, was named for its long lake, as before noted for its village of Hanska.

LEAVENWORTH township, in which a village of this name was platted in October, 1857, was organized April 16, 1859. It was probably named in honor of Henry Leavenworth, commander of the troops who came in 1819 to found the fort at first called Fort St. Anthony, renamed as Fort Snelling in 1825.

LINDEN township, settled in 1856, organized in 1859, was named for its groves of the American linden, usually called basswood. The largest groves here bordered Lake Linden, which had been earlier so named.

MILFORD township, first settled in 1853, set apart by the county board for organization on June 28, 1858, was named from a sawmill built in 1854-55 on a small creek, tributary to the Minnesota river, where it was crossed by a ford. This was the first sawmill in the upper Minnesota valley.

MULLIGAN township, settled in 1865, organized April 26, 1871, was named for an early pioneer, probably from Ireland.

NEW ULM, the county seat, founded in 1854-55 by German colonists, coming from Chicago and Cincinnati, was named for Ulm in Germany, near the village of Erbach, which was, according to the late Hon. William Pfaender, the place of emigration of twenty in thirty-two of the first company of pioneer settlers, who came in the autumn of 1854. It was incorporated as a town by an act of the legislature, March 6, 1857; as a borough, February 19, 1870; and as a city, February 24, 1876. It received its present charter on March 1, 1887. Ulm is an important city of Würtemberg, in southwestern Germany, situated on the northwest side of the Danube at the head of navigation. Its population in 1900 was nearly 43,000. On the opposite Bavarian side of the Danube is Neu Ulm, which in 1900 had a population of 9,215.

NORTH STAR township, first settled in 1858, set apart for organization on January 9, 1873, received its name in allusion to the French motto, "L'Etoile du Nord," on our state seal, whence Minnesota is often called the North Star State.

PRAIRIEVILLE township, whose first settlers came in 1866, was organized in March, 1870, taking this name because it consists almost wholly of prairie land.

SEARLES, a railway village in Cottonwood township, was platted October 10, 1899, being named by officials of the Minneapolis and St. Louis Railway Company.

BROWN COUNTY

SIGEL township, settled in 1856, organized April 28, 1862, was named in honor of Franz Sigel, a general in the Civil War. He was born at Sinsheim, Baden, Germany, November 18, 1824; died in New York City, August 21, 1902. He came to the United States in 1852; settled in St. Louis, 1858, as a teacher in a German institute; organized a regiment of U. S. volunteers, 1861, of which he became colonel; won the battle of Carthage, Mo., July 5, 1861; was promoted to the rank of major general, March, 1862, and took command of a wing of the army of Virginia; was appointed to the command of the army of West Virginia in February, 1864; was U. S. pension agent in New York City, 1885-89. About the year 1873 General Sigel visited New Ulm and this township.

SLEEPY EYE, the city and railway junction in Home township, platted September 18, 1872, incorporated as a village February 14, 1878, and as a city in 1903, was named, like the adjoining lake, for a chief of the Lower Sisseton Sioux. His favorite home and village during some parts of many years were beside this lake. He was born near the site of Mankato; became a chief between 1822 and 1825; signed the treaties of Prairie du Chien, 1825 and 1830, of St. Peter's in 1836, and Traverse des Sioux, 1851. Doane Robinson wrote: "Sleepy Eyes died in Roberts county, South Dakota, but many years after his death his remains were disinterred and removed to Sleepy Eye, Minn., where they were buried under a monument erected by the citizens." (Hodge, Handbook of American Indians, Part II, 1910.) The monument, close to the railway station, bears this inscription, beneath the portrait of the chief in bas relief sculpture: "Ish-tak-ha-ba, Sleepy Eye, Always a Friend of the Whites. Died 1860."

An interesting biographic sketch of "Sleepy Eyes, or Ish-ta-hba, which is very literally translated," by Rev. Stephen R. Riggs, in the Minnesota Free Press, St. Peter, Jan. 27, 1858, is reprinted in the Minnesota History Bulletin, vol. 2, no. 8, pp. 484-495, Nov., 1918.

SPRINGFIELD, the railway village in Burnstown, platted in 1877, was then named Burns, but at its incorporation, February 21, 1881, received its present name. This is said by Stennett to be derived from the city of Springfield, Mass.; but Juni refers its origin to a very large spring there, on the north side of the Cottonwood river and high above it.

STARK township, settled in 1858, organized April 7, 1868, was named for August Starck, a German pioneer farmer there.

STATELY, settled in 1873, was the last township organized in this county, April 7, 1879. The origin of its name has not been ascertained, but as an English word, of frequent use, it means "having a grand and impressive appearance, lofty, dignified." The west part of the south line of Stately crosses the highest land of this county, commanding a far prospect northward and eastward.

LAKES AND STREAMS.

Cottonwood and Little Cottonwood rivers are noticed in connection with Cottonwood township, and most fully in the chapter on the county of that name. Lone Tree lake is mentioned under Eden township, and Lakes Hanska and Linden with the townships so named. Sleepy Eye lake and creek received their names, like the city, from the Sioux chief.

Only a few other names of streams remain to be noticed. Big Spring creek, also called Spring Branch creek, in Eden and Home townships, takes its name from its large springs; Mine creek, in North Star township, refers doubtless to prospecting or mining there; and Mound creek in Stately may have been named, as also this township, in allusion to the highland on its upper course.

The following lakes bear names of early pioneers, whose homes were usually beside them or in their vicinity: George lake, named for Captain Sylvester A. George, and Rose lake, for Fred Rose, in Home township, the former having been earlier called Cross lake in allusion to its four bays having somewhat the outline of a cross; Kruger lake, in Prairieville, for Louis Kruger, a German farmer; Lake Hummel, also named Clear lake, in Sigel; Lake Emerson, now drained, on the south line of Linden; Broome and Omsrud lakes, in Lake Hanska township; and Lake Altermatt, in Leavenworth, for John B. Altermatt, a Swiss farmer.

Lake Juni, in section 26, Sigel, is named in honor of Benedict Juni, of New Ulm. He was born in Switzerland, January 12, 1852; and came to the United States when five years old with his parents, who settled on a farm in Milford. In 1862 he was a captive of the Sioux, from August 18 to the surrender of the prisoners at Camp Release, as narrated by him in the "History of Brown County" (vol. I, pages 111-122). During more than thirty years he was a teacher in the public schools of this county.

School lake, also in Sigel, received this name from its lying mainly in the school section 16.

Dane lake, in Linden, was named for its several Dane settlers in a a mainly Norwegian township.

Bachelor lake, in Stark, was named for a lone homesteader there, unmarried; and Rice lake, mostly in section 29 of the same township, for its wild rice, a name that formerly was also applied to the present Lake Altermatt.

The origin of the name of Boy's lake, in Leavenworth, was not learned.

Reed lake, in section 6, Bashaw, was named for its abundant growth of reeds; and Wood lake, crossed by the south line of Mulligan and lying mainly in Watonwan county, for its adjoining groves, the source of firewood used by the early settlers.

CARLTON COUNTY

This county, established May 23, 1857, with a further legislative act of February 18, 1870, and organized September 26, 1870, was named in honor of Reuben B. Carlton, one of the first settlers of Fond du Lac, at the head of lake navigation on the St. Louis river, near the line between St. Louis and Carlton counties. He was born in Onondaga county, New York, March 4, 1812; came to Fond du Lac in 1847, as a farmer and blacksmith for the Ojibway Indians; was one of the proprietors of the townsite of Fond du Lac, being a trustee under the act of its incorporation in 1857; and was a member of the first state senate, 1858. He owned about eighty acres adjoining that village and the river, on which he resided until his death, December 6, 1863.

The village of Carlton, the county seat of this county since 1886, was also named for him; and he is further commemorated by Carlton's Peak, near Tofte in Cook county, the most prominent point on the north shore of Lake Superior in Minnesota, forming the western end of the Sawteeth Range.

Fifty years after Carlton's death, James Bardon of Superior, Wis., wrote the following personal remembrance and estimate of him to Henry Oldenburg of Carlton, dated September 10, 1913.

"'Colonel' Carlton, as he was called, was a man of large frame, fully six feet in height, a strong personality, of good looks and pleasing manners, a man of much intelligence. He became associated with the bright and enterprising men who laid out and established Superior, Duluth, and other places about the head of Lake Superior. An avenue here in Superior was named after him.... Colonel Carlton was more prominently identified with the westerly part of St. Louis county, now Carlton county, in the early days, than any other man; and when the new county was projected it is likely that all men agreed that Carlton was the appropriate name for it, ... a really noble character."

TOWNSHIPS AND VILLAGES.

For the origins and significance of local names in this county, information was gathered from F. A. Watkins, judge of probate, visited at Carlton in September, 1909, and again in August, 1916; and also from Hon. Spencer J. Searls, in the second of these visits.

ATKINSON township was named for John Atkinson, an early settler there, who during many years was employed as a land examiner for the St. Paul and Duluth railroad company.

AUTOMBA was named after the railway station of the Soo line in this township, but the origin of this name remains to be ascertained.

BARNUM township received its name in honor of George G. Barnum, now a resident of Duluth, who was paymaster of the Lake Superior and Mississippi railroad (later named the St. Paul and Duluth), when it was being built.

BESEMANN township was named for a former German landowner there, Ernst Besemann, who removed to Chaska.

BLACK HOOF was named for the creek which flows circuitously through this township to the Nemadji river. It is translated from the Ojibway name of the creek.

CARLTON village, the county seat, took its name, like the county, in honor of Reuben B. Carlton. During about fifteen years from the building of the Northern Pacific railway, in 1870, this place was called Northern Pacific Junction, being at the junction of that transcontinental line with the older Lake Superior and Mississippi line.

CLOQUET (retaining the French pronunciation of its last syllable, as in bouquet and sobriquet), incorporated as a city, was named for the Cloquet river, from which, and from other tributaries of the St. Louis river, came the logs of its lumber manufacturing. The map of Long's expedition, in 1823, shows that stream as Rapid river, and it is unnamed on the map by Thompson in 1826 for the proposed routes of the international boundary; but on Nicollet's map, published in 1843, it has the present title, Cloquet river. It is not used outside of Minnesota as a geographic name, and here was probably derived from some fur trader. It is applied also to an island of the Mississippi in section 10, Dayton township, Hennepin county.

CORONA, the Latin word meaning a crown, was first given to a station of the Northern Pacific railway, perhaps because it is near the highest land crossed between Lake Superior and the Mississippi; and thence it was given to the township, in accordance with the petition of the settlers.

CROMWELL, a railway village in the south edge of Red Clover township, was organized January 17, 1891, receiving its name from the Northern Pacific railway company.

EAGLE township was named for its Eagle lake. Our common species is the bald eagle, so called for his white head, found throughout Minnesota, nesting in large trees, preferably on lake shores or islands.

HOLYOKE township, organized in 1903, received its name from the earlier railway station, where it was given by the Great Northern railway company.

IVERSON station was named by the Northern Pacific railway company for Ole Iverson, a pioneer settler there.

KALEVALA township has many Finnish settlers, by whom it was given this name of the national epic poem of Finland, meaning "the abode or land of heroes." English translations of it have been published in 1888 and in 1907. "The elements of the poem are ancient popular songs. . . . The poem owes its present coherent form to Elias Lönnrot (1802-1884), who during years of assiduous labor collected the material in Finland proper, but principally in Russian Karelia eastward to the White Sea. . . . The Kalevala is written in eight-syllabled trochaic verse, with alliteration, but without rime. The whole is divided into fifty cantos or runes. Its subject matter is mythical, with a few Christian elements. Its central hero is Wainamoinen, the god of poetry and music. It is the prototype, in form and contents, of Longfellow's 'Hiawatha.'" (Century Cyclopedia of Names.)

KETTLE RIVER, the railway village of Silver township, is named for the river, a translation of its Ojibway name, Akiko sibi.

KNIFE FALLS township is named for the falls of the St. Louis river, falling 16 feet, in the west part of section 13, close east of Cloquet. On the canoe route used by fur traders during a hundred years, these falls were passed by a portage about a mile long on the south side of the river, of which Prof. N. H. Winchell wrote: "It is well named Knife portage, because where it starts, and for some distance, the slates are thin, perpendicular, and sharp like knives."

LAKE VIEW township, having Tamarack lake, nearly two miles long, adjoining tamarack woods, and several other lakes of small size, received this name by vote of the settlers.

MAHTOWA township has a name formed from the Sioux mahto and the last syllable of the Ojibway makwa, each meaning a bear.

MOOSE LAKE township has reference to its Moose lake and Moose Head lake, each probably translated from their original Ojibway names.

NEMADJI, the Soo railway station in Barnum township, received this Ojibway name from the Nemadji river, meaning Left Hand river. The name refers to its being next on the left hand when one passes from Lake Superior into the St. Louis river.

PERCH LAKE township is named for its Perch lake, which is somewhat larger than its adjacent Big lake, each being very probably translations of the aboriginal names.

PROGRESS has a euphonious and auspicious name, selected by the petitioners for the township organization.

RED CLOVER township was named similarly with the last noted. This beautiful and highly valued species of clover is of Old World origin, but it is nearly everywhere cultivated with grasses in the sowing of lands for hay.

SAWYER, a railway station in Atkinson township, was named by the officers of the Northern Pacific railroad company.

SCANLON, the lumber manufacturing village between Cloquet and Carlton, was named for M. Joseph Scanlon, president of the Brooks-Scanlon Company, Minneapolis. He was born in Lyndon, Wis., August 24, 1861; settled in Minneapolis in 1889, and has engaged in many large enterprises of logging, the manufacture of lumber, and building and operating railroads to supply logs. In addition to his company's very large lumber interests at this village, he has conducted similar lumbering and sawmills at Cass Lake, and also in Oregon and in Louisiana and Florida.

SILVER township has a euphonious name chosen by its settlers, for the Silver creek there tributary to Kettle river.

SKELTON township was named for two brothers, John and Harry E. Skelton, who lived in the village of Barnum. The former was the county surveyor in 1897-1901, and the latter was judge of probate for the county, 1901-04, dying in office.

SPLIT ROCK township was named for the small river flowing through it, on which ledges of slates and schists have been deeply channeled near its mouth, the rocks of the opposite banks appearing therefore as if split apart.

THOMSON township received its name from the station and village of the St. Paul and Duluth and Northern Pacific railroads, built in 1870. This village was the county seat from that date until 1886. The name was given by officers of the former line, in honor of David Thompson, the Canadian explorer and geographer; but it has been generally spelled as if for James Thomson (1700-1748), the Scottish poet, author of "The Seasons."

David Thompson was born in Westminster (now a part of London), England, April 30, 1770; and died in Longueuil, near Montreal, February 10, 1857. He was in the service of the Hudson Bay Company, 1784-97, and of the Northwest Fur Company the next eighteen years. In the spring of 1798 he traveled from the mouth of the Assiniboine river, the site of the city of Winnipeg, to Pembina; thence to the trading house of the Northwest Company on the site of Red Lake Falls; thence by the Clearwater and Red Lake rivers to Red lake; thence by Turtle lake and river to Red Cedar lake (now Cass lake); thence down the Mississippi to the Northwest trading post on Sandy lake; thence by the Savanna rivers and portage to the St. Louis river, and down this river, past the site of Thomson, to the trading post at Fond du Lac; and thence along the south shore of Lake Superior to the Sault Ste. Marie. Thompson's account of this journey through northern Minnesota, with descriptions of the rivers and lakes and the country traversed, forms Chapters XVI to XIX in his "Narrative of Explorations in Western America, 1784-1812," edited by J. B. Tyrrell, published in 1916 as Volume XII (pages xcviii, 582, with maps and sketches), Publications of the Champlain Society. This work is reviewed, with a biographic sketch of Thompson, in the "Minnesota History Bulletin" (vol. I, pages 522-7, November, 1916).

TWIN LAKES township was named for its two small lakes in section 36, on the first road laid out from St. Paul, through Chisago and Pine counties, to the head of Lake Superior. A map of Minnesota in 1856, by Silas Chapman, shows this road with a small settlement named Twin Lakes, which was the only locality indicated as having inhabitants in Carlton county. It was nominally the county seat until Thomson was so designated by the legislative act of February 18, 1870.

CARLTON COUNTY 77

WRENSHALL township was named from the railway station and village, which received this name from the Northern Pacific company. It is for C. C. Wrenshall, who during several years was in charge of maintenance and repairs of bridges for this railway.

WRIGHT, a railway village in Lake View township, recalls the work of George Burdick Wright, who during many years was engaged in land examinations and locating new settlers in northern and western Minnesota. He was born in Williston, Vt., June 21, 1835; and died at Fergus Falls, Minn., April 29, 1882. He came to Minnesota in 1856; and first settled in Minneapolis; was the principal founder of Fergus Falls, in 1871; and secured the building of a branch of the Northern Pacific railroad in 1881-2 from Wadena to Fergus Falls and Breckenridge.

The name also had a second and equal reason for being chosen, to commemorate Charles Barstow Wright of Philadelphia, Pa., who was a director of the Northern Pacific railroad company in 1870-74, and was its president from 1875 for four years, during a period of restoration of business credit and prosperity after the great financial panic and depression of 1873. For Minnesota, in 1877-78 he directed the construction of the Western railroad, a line between St. Paul and Brainerd, which became a part of the Northern Pacific system.

LAKES AND STREAMS.

The preceding list has sufficiently referred to Black Hoof creek, Cloquet river (north of Carlton county), Eagle lake, Knife falls and portage of the St. Louis river, Tamarack lake, Moose and Moose Head lakes, Nemadji river, Perch lake and Big lake, Split Rock river, and the Twin lakes.

West and East Net rivers (or creeks) in Holyoke are probably translated from their Ojibway names, referring to nets for catching fish.

Skunk, Deer, Mud, and Clear creeks, flowing into Nemadji river, need no explanations; and the same may be said of Otter creek, at Carlton, probably an Ojibway name translated, and of Midway and Hay creeks in Thomson, the former being midway between Thomson and Fond du Lac.

Stony brook, the outlet of Perch lake, Tamarack river, flowing west from Tamarack lake, Moose Horn and Dead Moose rivers and Otter brook (now called Silver creek), each flowing from the west into the Kettle river, and Moose river, its tributary from the east, are likewise of obvious or simple derivations, some or all of them being translations of the Ojibway names.

Portage river, an eastern branch of Moose river, refers to the portage from it to the head stream of Nemadji river, being an ancient aboriginal and French name.

Gillespie brook, in Silver township, bears probably the name of an early lumberman or trapper.

This county has two Silver creeks, one flowing to Kettle river in Silver township, the other a smaller stream heading about a mile south of Carlton and flowing three miles east to the St. Louis river.

In Ahkeek lake, Corona, lately called Kettle lake, we have the Ojibway name and its English translation, this lake being near the most northern sources of Kettle river.

Other names of lakes in this county, some being translations, and nearly all being of evident origin or meaning, include Dead Fish lake, in section 12, Progress; White Fish lake (lately called Big lake), one to two miles south of Barnum village; Bear lake, close east of Barnum, and another Bear lake in section 4, Black Hoof; Coffee, Echo, and Sand lakes, in the south part of Moose Lake township; Chub and Hay lakes, in Twin Lakes township; Rocky lake (now called Park lake), in Atkinson; and Island lake, on the Northern Pacific railway, whence the early name of its station there was Island Lake, later changed to Cromwell.

Cole lake, in sections 7 and 8, Lake View, was named for James Cole, a civil war veteran, who was a homesteader there; and Woodbury lake, section 31, Red Clover, similarly commemorates an early settler.

Hanging Horn lake, crossed by the west line of section 7, Barnum, translates its Ojibway name, as also probably Horn lake in section 3, Atkinson.

Moran lake, in section 8, Atkinson, was named for Henry P. Moran, an early Irish homesteader and trapper.

Venoah lake (formerly called Mink lake), three miles south of Carlton, received its present name in compliment to the daughters, Winona and Marie, of Judge F. A. Watkins, who kindly supplied much information for this chapter. The lake name was coined from their pet names as children about twenty years ago.

Jay Cooke State Park.

In the years 1915 and 1916, Minnesota received by donation from the estate of Jay Cooke more than 2,000 acres of land, bordering each side of the St. Louis river through its winding course of about ten miles, from the Northern Pacific railway at Carlton and Thomson, along it rapids and falls descending 395 feet in crossing Range 16, to the east line of the county and state. With additional adjoining lands of equal or greater area, expected to be obtained by further donations and by purchases, a large state park is planned, to preserve these Dalles of the St. Louis for the enjoyment and recreation of the people.

Jay Cooke was born in Sandusky, Ohio, August 10, 1821; and died at Ogontz, near Philadelphia, Pennsylvania, February 16, 1905. In 1861 he founded in Philadelphia the banking house of Jay Cooke and Company, and during the next four years of the civil war he was the principal financial agent of the Federal government, negotiating loans for the war expenses to a value of about $2,000,000,000. In 1873 his house failed, on account of too heavy investments in the Northern Pacific railroad bonds.

"Before the financial crash of 1873, Mr. Cooke regarded himself as one of the richest men of the country. He built in the beautiful suburbs of Philadelphia a palace which, for size and costliness, had scarcely an equal on this side of the Atlantic. In this palace, called 'Ogontz,' he dispensed a lavish hospitality. He had also a summer residence named 'Gibraltar,' on a rocky cape at the entrance of Sandusky Bay on Lake Erie. . . . After the crash came he lived for a long time in retirement in a little cottage, in the country, near Philadelphia,—to all appearances a broken man. But after getting through the bankruptcy courts, he reappeared in business circles in Philadelphia, occupied his old office on South Third street, and began to build up a second fortune. . . . His career offers the rare instance of a man losing one fortune and making another when past the meridian of life." (Smalley, "History of the Northern Pacific Railroad," 1883.)

Sixteen years later than the writing here cited, his wealth "was estimated to be as large as at any period of his life." He was a generous patron of education, of churches, and of charities; and in his later years spent much of his time in the recreations of hunting and fishing. An excellent biography, "Jay Cooke, Financier of the Civil War," by Ellis Paxson Oberholtzer, was published in 1907 (two vols., pages 658, 590, with portraits and many other illustrations).

Fond du Lac Reservation.

The reservation for the Fond du Lac bands of the Ojibway people, established by a treaty at La Pointe, Wisconsin, September 30, 1854, comprises the present Knife Falls and Perch Lake townships, with the edges of the adjoining townships in this county, and thence reaches north to the St. Louis river, thus including a tract in St. Louis county equivalent to about two townships. The name Fond du Lac, meaning the farther end or head of the lake, was applied by the early French traders and voyageurs to their trading post on the north side of the St. Louis river, where its strong current is slackened by coming nearly to the level of Lake Superior, which, in its extension of St. Louis bay, is about two miles away. The same name was given also to this river, called "R. du Fond du Lac" on Franquelin's map, 1688, renamed St. Louis by Vaugondy's map in 1755.

Glacial Lakes St. Louis, Nemadji, and Duluth.

Prof. N. H. Winchell, in the fourth volume (published in 1899) of the Final Report of the Geological Survey of Minnesota, gave the names St. Louis and Nemadji to two early and relatively small glacial lakes in Carlton county, which successively outflowed to the Moose and Kettle rivers by channels in Mahtowa and Barnum townships, respectively about 1125 and 1070 feet above the sea. They were followed by the slightly lower Glacial Lake Duluth, named by Frank B. Taylor of the United States Geological Survey, which in its maximum stage occupied a large area of the Lake Superior basin, with outlet at the head of the Brulé river in Douglas county, Wisconsin, to the Upper St. Croix lake and river.

CARVER COUNTY

This county, established February 20, 1855, was named for Captain Jonathan Carver, explorer and author, who was born in Stillwater, now Canterbury, Conn., in 1732, and died in London, England, January 31, 1780. He commanded a company in the French war, and in 1763, when the treaty of peace was declared, he resolved to explore the newly acquired possessions of Great Britain in the Northwest. In 1766 he traveled from Boston to the upper Mississippi river, and spent the ensuing winter with the Sioux on the Minnesota river in the vicinity of the site of New Ulm. On his return, according to statements published after his death, he negotiated a treaty, May 1, 1767, at Carver's cave, in the east edge of the present city of St. Paul, by which the Sioux granted to him a large tract of land on the east side of the Mississippi. Carver continued his explorations by a canoe journey along the north and east coast of Lake Superior. He returned to Boston in October, 1768, soon sailed to England, and spent the remainder of his life in London.

Carver's "Travels Through the Interior Parts of North America," a volume of 543 pages, with two maps, was published in London in 1778, and new editions were issued the next year in London and in Dublin. After the author's death, his friend, Dr. John C. Lettsom, contributed to the third London edition, in 1781, a biographic account of Captain Carver, in 22 pages, including the first publication of the deed or grant of land obtained by Carver from the Sioux chiefs.

Several American editions of this work, with abridgment and changes, were published during the years 1784 to 1838; and translations of it into German, French, and Dutch, were published respectively in 1780, 1784, and 1796.

The Minnesota river is noted on Carver's map of his Travels as "River St. Pierre, call'd by the Natives Wadapawmenesoter," this being one of the earliest records of the Sioux name of this river and state. At its north side, nearly opposite to the site of New Ulm, three Sioux teepees are pictured, with the statement that "About here the Author Winter'd in 1766."

Numerous endeavors made by heirs of Captain Carver and by others to whom their rights were assigned, for establishing their claims and ownership of the large tract deeded to him by the Sioux, have been narrated by Rev. John Mattocks in his address at the Carver Centenary celebration in 1867, published in Volume II of the Minnesota Historical Society Collections; by John Fletcher Williams in his "History of the City of St. Paul and of the County of Ramsey," forming Volume IV in the same series, published in 1876; and most fully, with many documents submitted to the United States Congress, relating to the Carver claims, in an article by

Daniel S. Durrie, to which Lyman C. Draper added important foot-notes, in Volume VI, pages 220-270, of the Wisconsin Historical Society Collections, published in 1872.

Between forty and forty-five years after Carver's death, the supposed rights of his heirs under the deed were denied and annulled in Congress by the Committees on Public Lands and on Private Land Claims. One of the grounds for this decision was that no citizens, but only the state, whether Great Britain, as in 1767, or the United States after the treaty of 1783, could so receive ownership of lands from the aborigines.

Townships and Villages.

Information of origins and meanings of geographic names in this county has been gathered from "History of the Minnesota Valley," 1882, pages 352-410; from "Compendium of History and Biography of Carver and Hennepin Counties," R. I. Holcombe, historical editor, 1915, pages 187-342; and from John Glaeser, judge of probate; Albert Meyer, register of deeds, and Hon. Frederick E. Du Toit, Sr., each of Chaska, interviewed during a visit there in July, 1916.

Assumption, a hamlet in section 18, Hancock, received its name from that of the Catholic church there, referring to the ascent of the Virgin Mary into heaven and its anniversary, celebrated on August 15.

Augusta, a railway station in section 3, Dahlgren, was named in honor of the wives of two settlers near, each having this name and having come from Augusta in Eau Claire county, Wisconsin.

Benton township, first settled in May, 1855, organized May 11, 1858, was named, like Benton county, in honor of the distinguished United States senator, Thomas Hart Benton, whose life and public services are more fully noted in the chapter for that county. He died April 10, 1858, a month before this township was organized and named. The village of Benton, on the northeast shore of the little Lake Benton, and a half mile north of Cologne, platted in June, 1880, was incorporated in March, 1881.

Camden township, settled in July, 1856, had a village platted and a postoffice established in the same year; but this township was not organized until the spring of 1859. It was named doubtless for some one of the eighteen villages and cities of this name in the older eastern and southern states, of which the largest is the city of Camden, N. J., on the Delaware river, opposite to Philadelphia.

Carver, a very small fractional township bordering on the Minnesota river, was named, like this county, in honor of Jonathan Carver. The first settlers came in 1851-52, and the township was organized May 11, 1858. The village of Carver was platted in February, 1857, and was incorporated February 17, 1877, comprising all the township. Carver creek, named by Captain Carver for himself, the outlet of Clearwater or Waconia lake and numerous other lakes of smaller size, here joins the Minnesota river. On Nicollet's map it is "Odowan R.," which is the Sioux word for a song or hymn.

CHANHASSEN township received its earliest settlers in June, 1852, and was organized May 11, 1858. The name, adopted on the suggestion of Rev. H. M. Nichols, means the sugar maple, being formed of two Sioux words, chan, tree, and hassen (for hasan, from haza or hah-zah, the huckleberry or blueberry), thus signifying "the tree of sweet juice."

CHASKA township and city, the county seat, has, unlike the preceding name, the French sound of Ch like sh. This was the name generally given in a Sioux family to the first-born child, if a son, as Winona was the general name of a first-born daughter. The earliest permanent settlers came in 1853, and the date of the township organization was May 11, 1858. The village was founded in June, 1854, by the Shaska Company "(the name was thus misspelled in the act of incorporation of the company)." March 6, 1871, it was incorporated as a village, and on March 3, 1891, as a city. A small lake at the southwest side of the city is named Chaska lake, and a creek here tributary to the Minnesota river is likewise called Chaska creek.

This word is pronounced by the Sioux, and by Riggs' Dictionary, with the English sound of ch (as in charm), and with the long vowel sound in the last syllable, as if spelled kay; but common usage of the white people has given erroneously the French pronunciation (ch as in charade), with the last syllable short, like Alaska.

COLOGNE, the railway village of Benton township, platted in August, 1880, and incorporated in 1881, was named by German settlers for the large and ancient city of Cologne (the German Köln) on the Rhine.

CONEY ISLAND, a railway hamlet and summer resort at the north side of Clearwater lake, was named from the island of thirty-seven acres in the southern part of the lake near Waconia village. The island had been named for the popular Coney Island beach of Long Island near New York City. The adoption of this name, however, was suggested by its similarity in sound with Waconia.

DAHLGREN township, settled in 1854, organized April 5, 1864, was named Liberty in 1863. "May 9, 1864, the name of the town was changed . . . to Dahlgren, at the suggestion of the state auditor, in honor of our distinguished admiral, because the name Liberty had already been appropriated by another town in the state." (History of the Minnesota Valley.) John Adolphus Bernard Dahlgren, of Swedish parentage, was born in Philadelphia, November 13, 1809; and died in the city of Washington, July 12, 1870. He became a lieutenant in the U. S. Navy in 1837; was assigned to ordnance duty in Washington, 1847, and introduced important improvements in the naval armament, including the Dahlgren gun, which he invented. He was appointed chief of the bureau of ordnance, July 18, 1862, became rear-admiral February 7, 1863, and gained renown for his service through the civil war. His biography, by his widow, was published in 1882 (660 pages, with two portraits).

GOTHA, a hamlet in section 1, Hancock, was named for the ancient city of Gotha, in central Germany.

CARVER COUNTY 83

HAMBURG, a railway village in sections 28 and 33, Young America, was named for the great German city and port of Hamburg, on the River Elbe, which was founded and fortified by Charlemagne about the beginning of the ninth century.

HANCOCK township, settled in the spring of 1856, organized March 23, 1868, was named in honor of Winfield Scott Hancock. He was born at Montgomery Square, Pa., February 14, 1824; died at Governor's Island, N. Y., February 9, 1886. After graduation at West Point, 1844, he served as lieutenant in the Mexican War; was a general during the Civil War; and was commander of the military department of the Atlantic, 1872-86. In the presidential campaign of 1880, he was the unsuccessful Democratic candidate.

HOLLYWOOD township, settled in 1856, organized April 3, 1860, had a small village near it southeast corner, platted in the autumn of 1856 and named Helvetia by John Buhler, an immigrant from Switzerland, of which this was the ancient Latin name. Matthew Kelly, an Irish settler, proposed the township name, saying that he had seen the shrub named holly, which is common in Ireland, growing here in the woods. After the name had been adopted, it was ascertained that the European holly does not occur in this country; but Minnesota has two species of this family, found rarely on bluffs of Lake Pepin, the St. Croix river, and northward.

LAKETOWN, so named on the suggestion of John Salter, for its ten small lakes and the large Clearwater lake on its west boundary, was first settled in April, 1853, and was organized May 11, 1858. It was at first called Liberty, but was renamed as now on June 12, 1858, a month after the organization. The Swedish community on the east side of Clearwater lake has been often called Scandia, the ancient Roman name for the southern part of Sweden.

MAYER, a railway village on the line between Camden and Waconia, was named by officers of the Great Northern railway company.

MINNEWASHTA, a village mainly of summer homes, on the northeast end of the largest lake in Chanhassen, received its name from the lake. It consists of two Sioux words, minne, water, and washta, good.

NEW GERMANY, the railway village in sections 4 and 5, Camden, was named in compliment to the many German settlers in its vicinity. In the World War, 1914-18, this name was changed to Motordale, on account of popular indignation against Germany.

NORWOOD, a village and railway junction in Young America, platted in 1872 and incorporated in 1881, is said to have been "named by Mr. Slocum, an early banker there, for an eastern relative or friend of his wife." Fifteen villages and postoffices in eastern and southern states have this name.

PLEASANT VIEW, a village and summer resort in section 1, Chanhassen, at the north end of Long lake, was thus euphoniously named by its proprietors.

SAN FRANCISCO, a fractional township beside the Minnesota river, settled in 1854 and organized May 11, 1858, was named by William Foster, who in 1854 platted and so named a village site on his claim, taking this name from the metropolis of California. The village flourished only about ten years, and its site then reverted to be farming land.

VICTORIA, a railway village in sections 13 and 14, Laketown, was named in honor of the queen of England.

VINLAND, a hamlet of summer homes in section 2, Chanhassen, at the south end of Christmas lake, was named for the region of temporary Norse settlement, about the beginning of the eleventh century, on the northeast coast of North America. The name is Icelandic, meaning wineland, bcause grapes were found there.

WACONIA township, settled in 1855, organized May 11, 1858, bears the Sioux name of its large lake, meaning a fountain or spring. The village of Waconia was platted and named by Roswell P. Russell in March, 1857. This lake is also called Clearwater lake. "It has about eighteen miles of shore, most of which is high with a gravelly beach. The water is very clear, hence its name, and well stocked with fish."

WATERTOWN, first settled in 1856, organized April 13, 1858, received this name "because of the township's large water supply," by five or six lakes and the South fork of Crow river. The village of Watertown, platted in 1858, was incorporated February 26, 1877.

In YOUNG AMERICA a village of this name was platted in the fall of 1856, which was incorporated March 4, 1879. The same name is also given to a small lake there. At the organization of the township in 1858, it was first named Farmington, but later in that year was renamed Florence; and in 1863 it was again changed to the present name, like its village. This name is a familiar expression for the vigor and progressiveness of the young people of the United States. Its only use elsewhere as a geographic name is for a village in Cass county, Indiana.

LAKES AND STREAMS.

At the Little Rapids of the Minnesota river, adjoining the southeast quarter of section 31, Carver, a ledge of the Jordan sandstone running across the river bed causes a fall of two feet; and again about a quarter of a mile up the river its bed is similarly crossed by this sandstone, having there a fall of slightly more than one foot. In the stage of low water, these very slight falls prevent the passage of boats; but at a fuller stage the river wholly covers the ledges, with no perceptible rapid descent, being then freely navigable. Fur trading posts were located there during many years. A lake there, close west of the river, is named Rapids lake.

In the list of townships and villages, the origins and meanings of the names of several lakes and streams have been noted, including Lake Benton, Carver creek, Chaska lake and creek, Clearwater or Waconia lake and its Coney Island, Lake Minnewashta, Long lake in Chanhassen, and Young America lake.

Names given in honor of early settlers, mostly having taken homesteads on or near the lake or stream so designated, include Bevins creek, flowing through San Francisco to the Minnesota river; Lakes Lucy, Ann, and Susan, in Chanhassen, the first and second being named respectively for the wives of Burritt S. and William S. Judd, and the third for Susan Hazeltine, who taught the first school in Carver county and is also commemorated here, with her father, by Hazeltine lake; Virginia lake, in section 6, and Bradford lake, in sections 24 and 25, Chanhassen, and Bavaria lake, crossed by the west line of that township, named for the native land of settlers near it; Pierson, Reitz, Schutz (or Goldschmidt), Stieger (or Herman), and Watermann's lakes, in Laketown, commemorating John Pierson, Frederick Reitz, Matthias Schuetz, Carl Stieger, and Michael Wassermann, settlers near these several lakes; Buran's lake, for a German farmer adjoining it, Adolph Burandt, Lake Donders, and Hyde, Patterson, and Rutz lakes, in Waconia, the last three being for Ernst Heyd, the first county surveyor, who owned land there, William Patterson, one of the earliest settlers, and Peter Rutz; Berliner lake, in section 12, Camden, for a German settler from Berlin; Campbell lake, section 18, Hollywood, for Patrick Campbell and his two brothers, Irish settlers; Miller's lake, in section 8, Dahlgren, for Herman Mueller; Gruenhagen's, Heyer's, Hoeffken's, Maria, and Winkler's lakes, in Benton, the first for H. F. Gruenhagen, the second for Louis Heyer, the third for Henry Hoeffken, and the last for Ignatz Winkler; and Barnes, Brandt and Frederick's lakes, in Young America, respectively for William Barnes, the earliest homesteader there, Leroy Brandt, and Frederick Ohland.

Eagle lake, in section 34, Camden, was named for an eagle's nest there, in a very great cottonwood tree.

For Lake Auburn and Parley and Zumbra lakes, in Laketown, no information of the origin of their names has been learned.

Swede lake, in Watertown, was named for its several Swedish settlers by the earliest of them, Daniel Justus, in August, 1856. This neighborhood was known as Götaholm (Göta, a river of southern Sweden, holm, a grove). The same name, Swede lake, was also formerly borne by the present Maria lake, section 36, Benton.

Tiger lake, in Young America, has reference to a "mountain lion," also named the cougar or puma, seen there by the first settlers. This species, very rare in Minnesota, more frequent in the region of the Rocky Mountains, was mentioned by Carver in the narration of his Travels as "the Tyger of America," one having been seen by him on an island of the Chippewa river, Wisconsin.

Several other lakes of this county have names of frequent occurrence and evident significance, as Rice lake on the north line of Benton, and a second Rice lake, section 36, Chanhassen, both named from their wild rice; Marsh lake, in section 26, Laketown; Mud and Oak lakes, Watertown; and Goose and Swan lakes, in Waconia.

CASS COUNTY

Established September 1, 1851, but having remained without organization till 1897, this county commemorates the distinguished statesman, Lewis Cass, who in 1820 commanded an exploring expedition which started from Detroit, passed through lakes Huron and Superior, and thence advanced by way of Sandy lake and the upper Mississippi as far as to the upper Red Cedar lake. This name, a translation from the Ojibway name, was changed by Schoolcraft, the narrator of the expedition, to be Cassina or Cass lake, in honor of its commander. He was born in Exeter, N. H., October 9, 1782, and died in Detroit, Mich., June 17, 1866. At the age of eighteen years he came to Marietta, the first town founded in southern Ohio, and studied law there; was admitted to the bar in 1803, and began practice at Zanesville, Ohio; and was colonel and later brigadier general in the War of 1812. He was governor of Michigan Territory, 1813 to 1831; negotiated twenty-two treaties with Indian tribes; was secretary of war, in the cabinet of President Jackson, 1831-36, including the time of the Black Hawk war; minister to France, 1836-42; United States senator, 1845-48; Democratic candidate for the presidency in the campaign of 1848; again U. S. senator, 1849-57; and secretary of state, in the cabinet of President Buchanan, 1857-60.

To voyage along the upper Mississippi river and to describe and map its principal source were the motives for the expedition undertaken in 1820 by Cass. At this time Michigan Territory, of which he was governor, included the northeastern third of Minnesota, east of the Mississippi; and Missouri Territory extended across the present State of Iowa and western two-thirds of Minnesota.

The report of this expedition, published the next year, is entitled "Narrative Journal of Travels from Detroit northwest through the Great Chain of American Lakes to the Sources of the Mississippi river in the year 1820, by Henry R. Schoolcraft... Albany, .. 1821" (424 pages, with a map and eight copper-plate engravings.) This title-page is engraved and is followed by another in print, which states that the author was "a member of the Expedition under Governor Cass." The explorations of the upper Mississippi by Cass and Schoolcraft, of whom the latter visited and named Lake Itasca in 1832, are related in a chapter of "Minnesota in Three Centuries" (1908, vol. I, pp. 347-356, with their portraits.)

Several extended biographies of General Cass were published during his lifetime, in 1848, 1852, and 1856, the years of successive presidential campaigns. In 1889 a marble statue of him was contributed by the State of Michigan as one of its two statues for the National Statuary Hall at the Capitol in Washington; and the proceedings and addresses in Congress upon the acceptance of the statue were published in a volume of 106 pages. Two years afterward, in 1891, a mature study of his biography, entitled "Lewis Cass, by Andrew C. McLaughlin, Assistant Professor of History in the University of Michigan" (363 pages), was published in the "American Statesmen" series.

TOWNSHIPS AND VILLAGES.

For the origins and meanings of these names, information has been gathered in October, 1909, from Iver P. Byhre, county auditor, and in September 1916, from Nathan J. Palmer, clerk of the court, Mack Kennedy, sheriff, James S. Scribner, former county attorney, and M. S. Morical, all of Walker, the county seat, during my visits there.

ANSEL township received the name of an earlier postoffice, which was given by its postmaster, Myron Smith, this being the first or christening name of one of the pioneers there.

BACKUS, the railway village in Powers township, was named in honor of Edward W. Backus, of Minneapolis, lumberman, president of the Backus-Brooks Company, and of the International Falls Lumber Company.

BARCLAY township bears the surname of one of its pioneers.

BECKER township was named for J. A. Becker, an early settler there.

BENA, a railway village adjoining the most southern bay of Lake Winnebagoshish, is the Ojibway word meaning a partridge, spelled biné in Baraga's Dictionary. This game bird species, formerly common throughout the wooded region of this state, is the ruffed grouse, called the "partridge" in New England and in Minnesota, but less correctly known as the "pheasant" in the middle and southern states. Longfellow used this word in his "Song of Hiawatha,"

"Heard the pheasant, Bena, drumming."

BEULAH township received its name in honor of Mrs. Olds, the wife of an early homesteader there, this being her first name, a Hebrew word meaning married.

BIRCH LAKE township was named for its lake adjoining Hackensack village. It is translated, as noted by Gilfillan, from the Ojibway "Ga-wig-wasensikag sagaiigun, the-place-of-little-birches lake." On the map of the Minnesota Geological Survey it is called Fourteen Mile lake, indicating its distance by the road south from the Leech Lake Agency.

BOY LAKE and BOY RIVER townships were named from their large lake and river, which are translations of the Ojibway names. Gilfillan wrote that Woman lake and Boy lake "are so called from women and boys, respectively, they having been killed in those lakes by the Sioux during an irruption made by them." The date and origin of the name of Boy lake, whence by Ojibway usage the outflowing river was likewise named, are stated by Warren in his "History of the Ojibway Nation" (Minnesota

Historical Society Collections, vol. V, pages 222-232), to have been about the year 1768, within a few years after the Ojibways had driven the Sioux southward from Mille Lacs. A war party of Sioux invaded the upper Mississippi region, by way of the Crow Wing and Gull rivers, and by a canoe route, with portages, through White Fish, Wabedo, and the Little Boy and Boy lakes, to Leech lake. At Boy lake they "killed three little boys, while engaged in gathering wild rice. . . . From this circumstance, this large and beautiful sheet of water has derived its Ojibway name of Que-wis-ans (Little Boy)." Warren's narration shows that this attack was on the lower one of the two Boy lakes, lying partly in the township named for it. Gilfillan's list of Ojibway names and translations has exactly the same Ojibway name for this lake, on the lower part of Boy river, and for the lake about ten miles south on the upper part of the river, which our maps name Little Boy lake.

Nicollet mapped the lower Boy lake under the name of Lake Hassler, in honor of Ferdinand Rudolph Hassler (b. in Switzerland, 1770, d. in Philadelphia, 1843), who was superintendent of the U. S. Coast Survey.

BULL MOOSE township was named in compliment to the Progressive or "Bull Moose" division of the Republican party, which supported former President Roosevelt as its candidate in the presidential campaign of 1912.

BUNGO township was named for descendants of a negro, Jean Bonga, who, according to Dr. Neill, was brought from the West Indies and was a slave of Captain Daniel Robertson, British commandant at Mackinaw from 1782 to 1787. His family intermarried with the Ojibways, and the name became changed to Bungo. George Bonga was an interpreter for Governor Cass in 1820 at Fond du Lac, and he or another of this family was an interpreter for the Ojibway treaty in 1837 at Fort Snelling. Rev. Joseph A. Gilfillan wrote in 1897 (M. H. S. Collections, vol. IX, page 56): "About Leech lake there are perhaps a hundred descendants of the negro Bungo; nearly all these are very muscular, and some have been of unusually fine physique." This township has a Bungo brook, which was earlier so named, flowing out at its northeast corner.

BYRON was named for Byron Powell, the first white boy born in this township, son of Philo Powell, who later removed to northwestern Canada.

CASS LAKE, a large railway village, received its name from the adjoining lake, which, as before noted, was named, like this county, in honor of General Cass.

CROOKED LAKE township took this name from its Crooked lake, half of which extends into Crow Wing county. It is a translation of the aboriginal name, Wewagigumag sagaiigun. By a resolution of the state legislature, March 6, 1919, this lake was renamed Lake Roosevelt, in honor of President Theodore Roosevelt, who two months previously, on January 6, died at his home, Oyster Bay, N. Y.

CUBA and SCHLEY, stations of the Great Northern railway, commemorate the Spanish-American war of 1898.

CYPHERS, a railway station five miles south of Walker, was named for a former resident, who removed into Hubbard county.

DEERFIELD township was named, on request of its people, for the plentiful deer there; but it also is a common geographic name, borne by townships, villages and postoffices in fourteen other states.

EAST GULL LAKE township was named for its comprising the greater part of the northeast end of Gull lake, with its continuation north to Upper Gull lake.

FAIRVIEW township received this euphonious name in accordance with the petition of its people for organization.

FEDERAL DAM is the railway village at the reservoir dam built by the United States government on Leech Lake river.

GOULD township was named for M. I. Gould, logger and farmer, who owned hay meadows there.

GULL RIVER station of the Northern Pacific railway, formerly a place of great importance for its lumber manufacturing, was named for the Gull lake and river, each a translation of the name given by the Ojibways, the latter, in accordance with their general rule, being supplied from the name of the lake. This aboriginal name is noted by Gilfillan as "Gagaiashkonzikag sagaiigun, the-place-of-young-gulls lake."

HACKENSACK, a railway village, was named for an earlier postoffice there, which derived its name from the town of Hackensack in New Jersey, on the Hackensack river, given by James Curo, who was the first postmaster, ranchman, and merchant there.

HIRAM township was named by the petition for organization, in honor of Hiram Wilson, an early settler, who was yet living there in 1916.

HOME BROOK township received the name of a postoffice earlier established, which had taken the name of the brook, given by lumbermen. (Brook and creek have the same meaning in this state, the latter being the more common, or the only term in use, through the greater part of the state; but lumbermen and settlers coming from Maine and others of the eastern states have in many cases named the small streams as brooks, especially in the wooded northeastern third of Minnesota.)

INGUADONA township has a name of probably aboriginal derivation, but its significance has not been learned. It was given to the township from its lake so named. If it is of the Ojibway language, its original form and pronunciation may have been so changed as to be now unidentifiable. Gilfillan gave the name of this lake as "Manominiganjiki, or The-ricefield." It was called Lake Gauss on Nicollet's map, for the celebrated German mathematician (b. 1777, d. 1855).

KEGO, the name of a township here, is a common Ojibway word, meaning a fish, used as a general term for any fish species. This is spelled Gigo in Baraga's Dictionary.

LEECH LAKE township was named for the lake, translated from the Ojibway name, noted by Gilfillan as "Ga-sagasquadjimekag sagaiigun, the-place-of-the-leech-lake; from the tradition that on first coming to it, the Chippeways saw an enormous leech swimming in it." Nicollet wrote that this aboriginal name "implies . . . that its waters contain a remarkable number of leeches."

LIMA township (pronounced here with the long English sound of i, unlike Lima in Peru) was named probably for the city of Lima in Ohio, where the pronunciation has been thus anglicized. Ten other states have towns and villages of this name.

LOON LAKE township was named for its lake in section 20. This large water bird was formerly frequent or common throughout this state, and is yet common in its wooded northeast part.

MCKINLEY township was named in honor of our third martyr president, William McKinley, who was born in Niles, Ohio, January 29, 1843, and died in Buffalo, N. Y., September 14, 1901, assassinated by an anarchist. He was president of the United States, 1897-1901.

MAPLE township received this name on the petition of its people for organization, referring to its plentiful sugar maple trees, a species that is common or abundant throughout Minnesota, excepting near its west side. The sap is much used for sugar-making, in the early spring, both by the Indians and the white people. Warren wrote of this Ojibway work about Leech lake: "The shores of the lake are covered with maple which yields to the industry of the hunters' women, each spring, quantities of sap which they manufacture into sugar."

MAY township was named in honor of May Griffith, daughter of a former county auditor, Charles Griffith, in whose office she was an assistant. Lake May, formerly called Lake Frances, in the southwest edge of Walker village, is also named for her.

MEADOW BROOK township took its name from a brook where a schoolhouse was built and so named before the township was organized.

MILDRED, a small railway village in Pine River township, was named in honor of Mrs. Mildred Scofield, first postmistress and wife of the merchant there, who, with her husband, removed to the west.

MOOSE LAKE township was named for its small lake in sections 10 and 15.

MUD LAKE township was named for its Mud lake, mostly shallow with a muddy bed and having much wild rice, through which the Leech Lake river flows. The Ojibway name is translated by Gilfillan, "meaning shallow-mud-bottomed lake." Nicollet mapped it as Lake Bessel, in honor of Friedrich Wilhelm Bessel (b. 1784, d. 1846), a distinguished Prussian astronomer.

NUSHKA, a Great Northern railway station in the Chippewa Indian Reservation, is an Ojibway word of exclamation, meaning "Look!" It is used by Longfellow in "The Song of Hiawatha."

PIKE BAY township includes the large Pike bay, more properly a separate lake, which is connected on the north with Cass lake by a very narrow strait or thoroughfare. The name commemorates Zebulon Montgomery Pike, the commander of the expedition sent to the upper Mississippi in 1805-06 by the United States War Department. Pike came to Cass lake (then known as the upper Red Cedar lake) on February 12, 1806, by a land march from Leech lake and across Pike bay; spent a day at the Northwest Company's trading post there; and returned on the 14th by the same route. His biography is presented in the chapter of Morrison county, where he is honored by the names of a creek, a township, and rapids of the Mississippi, beside the site of his winter stockade camp.

PILLAGER, a village of the Northern Pacific railway, the adjoining Pillager creek, and the lake of this name at its source, are derived from the term, Pillagers, applied to the Ojibways of this vicinity and of the Leech Lake Reservation. According to the accounts given by Schoolcraft and his associate, Dr. Douglass Houghton, in the Narrative of the expedition in 1832 to Itasca Lake (pages 111, 112, 254), this name, Mukkundwais or Pillagers, originated in the fall of 1767 or 1768, when a trader named Berti, who had a trading post at the mouth of Crow Wing river, was robbed of his goods.

Warren gave, in the "History of the Ojibway Nation," written in 1852, a more detailed narration of the robbery or pillage, referring it erroneously to the year 1781. The name Pillagers, given to the Leech Lake band of the Ojibways, had come into use as early as 1775, when the elder Henry found some of them at the Lake of the Woods.

PINE LAKE township, bordering the most southern part of the shore of Leech lake, contains eight lakes, with others crossed by its boundaries. It had abundant white pine timber, and thence came this name of its lakes, in sections 17 and 18, later given to the township. Its largest lake, in sections 28, 32, and 33, is called Boot lake, from its outline.

PINE RIVER township is on the upper part of Pine river, which flows eastward through White Fish lake and joins the Mississippi near the center of Crow Wing county. This township has, near Mildred station, a second but smaller Boot lake, named for its having a bootlike shape.

PONTO LAKE township has a lake of this name, in sections 3, 9, and 10; and an adjoining postoffice is named Pontoria. These are unique names, not in use elsewhere, and their derivation and significance remain to be learned.

POPLAR township had an earlier postoffice of this name, referring to the plentiful poplar groves.

PORTAGE LAKE, a station of the Soo line, in the Chippewa Indian Reservation, and the lake of this name, a half mile distant to the north, as also the neighboring Portage bay of the large north arm of Leech lake, refer to the canoe portage there between the waters of Leech and

Winnebagoshish lakes. On Nicollet's map this Portage lake is named in honor of Duponceau (b. in France, 1760, d. in Philadelphia, 1844), author of a "Memoir on the Indian Languages of North America," published in 1835; and the Portage bay bears the name of Pickering bay on this map, for an American writer of another work on the same subject, published in 1836.

POWERS township was named in honor of Gorham Powers, of Granite Falls, who was a landowner there, having a summer home on Sanborn lake, in section 27. He was born in Pittsfield, Maine, September 14, 1840; served in the civil war, 1862-5; was graduated at the Albany law school, 1866, and in the same year came to Minnesota, settling in Minneapolis; removed in 1868 to Granite Falls; was county attorney of Yellow Medicine county, 1872-7, and 1884-6; was a representative in the state legislature, 1879; and was judge in the Twelfth judicial district from 1890 until his death, at Granite Falls, April 15, 1915.

REMER township, and the earlier Remer postoffice and railway village, were named in honor of E. N. and William P. Remer, brothers, of whom the former is treasurer and manager of the Reishus-Remer Land Company, of Grand Rapids, and the latter was the first postmaster here.

ROGERS was named in honor of William A. Rogers, who had a homestead in this township, coming, as also his brothers Nathan and Frank, from St. John, N. B. He engaged in logging as a contractor, resided in Walker, and was killed by an elevator accident in Duluth. His son, Edward L. Rogers, has been the county attorney of Cass county since 1913.

SALEM was named by its settlers in their petition for township organization. It is the name of townships, cities, villages, and postoffices, in thirty-two states of our Union.

SCHLEY, a Great Northern railway station, was named in honor of Winfield Scott Schley, rear admiral of the United States Navy. He was born in Frederick county, Maryland, October 9, 1839; was graduated at the U. S. Naval Academy in 1860, and was an instructor there after the civil war; commanded the "Flying Squadron" in the Spanish-American war, 1898, and directed the naval battle off Santiago, Cuba; author of an autobiography, "Forty-five Years under the Flag" (1904, 439 pages); died in New York City, October 2, 1911.

Three successive stations and sidings of this railway in the north edge of Cass county, established in 1898-99, are commemorative of our short and decisive war with Spain, named Schley, Santiago, and Cuba..

SHINGOBEE township received this name from its creek, being the general Ojibway word for the spruce, balsam fir, and arbor vitae, species of evergreen trees that are common or abundant through northern Minnesota, excepting the Red River valley. It is spelled jingob in Baraga's Dictionary.

SLATER township was named for David H. Slater, a homestead farmer in section 6.

SMOKY HOLLOW was named by Levi Morrow, a settler who came from Missouri, in remembrance of his former home in the state of New York, near a locality so named (or perhaps for Sleepy Hollow, a quiet valley near Tarrytown, on the Hudson, of which Irving wrote in "The Sketch Book"). This township has in part a surface of marginal morainic drift, remarkably diversified with knolls, ridges, and hollows.

SYLVAN township is named for its Sylvan lake, which refers to the woods or groves on its shores. The Ojibway name, noted by Gilfillan, means Fish Trap lake.

THUNDER LAKE township is derived likewise from its lake of this name, which is probably a translation of the aboriginal name.

TRELIPE township (pronounced in three syllables, with accent on the first, and with the short sound of each) is named, with variation of spelling, for the tullibee, a very common fish in the lakes of northern Minnesota, having a wide geographic range from New York to northwestern Canada. This species, Argyrosomus tullibee (Richardson), closely resembles the common whitefish. The word was adopted, as noted by Richardson, from the Cree language. Tulaby lake, crossed by the line between Becker and Mahnomen counties, was also named for this fish, supplying another way of its spelling.

TURTLE LAKE township is named for its two lakes in sections 22, 23, 26, and 27, called by the Ojibways, as recorded by Gilfillan, "Mikinakosagaiigunun, or Turtle lakes."

WABEDO township (accenting the first syllable) received its name from its Wabedo lake. Warren, writing in 1852 in his "History of the Ojibway Nation" (M. H. S. Collections, vol. V, page 224), related that an invading war party of the Sioux, about the year 1768, came "into Wab-ud-ow lake, where they spilt the first Ojibway blood, killing a hunter named Wab-ud-ow (White Gore), from which circumstance the lake is named to this day by the Ojibways." The same party, advancing northward, killed three boys gathering rice, whence Boy lake and river received their name, as noted on a preceding page. Gilfillan spelled Wabedo lake as "Wabuto sagaiigun, or Mushroom lake."

WAHNENA (with accent on the second syllable) was named for an Ojibway chief who died about the year 1895.

WALDEN township bears the name of a pond near Concord, Mass., beside which Henry D. Thoreau, the author, built a hut and lived about two years, 1845-47, as told in his book, "Walden, or Life in the Woods," published in 1854. This is also the name of a town in northern Vermont, and of a large manufacturing village in Orange county, N. Y.

WALKER village, the county seat, was named in honor of Thomas Barlow Walker, who has large lumbering and land interests in Cass county and in several other counties of northern Minnesota. He was born in Xenia, Ohio, February 1, 1840; came to Minnesota in 1862, and was the surveyor of parts of the St. Paul and Duluth railway line; commenced in 1868 the purchase of great tracts of pine lands, and later built and operated, in Crookston and elsewhere, many large lumber mills. He resides in Minneapolis, and maintains a very valuable and choice art gallery to which the public are freely welcomed. An autobiographic paper by Mr. Walker is published in the Minnesota Historical Society Collections (vol. XV, 1915, pages 455-478, with his portrait).

WILKINSON township commemorates Major Melville Cary Wilkinson, who was killed in a skirmish with the Bear Island band of the Pillager Indians, at Sugar point on Leech lake, October 5, 1898. He was born in New York, November 14, 1835; served as a volunteer in the civil war, and in 1866 entered the regular army. The "battle of Sugar point," and dealings with these Ojibways preceding and following it, are narrated in Flandrau's "History of Minnesota" (1900, pages 229-234), and more fully by Holcombe in "Minnesota in Three Centuries" (1908, vol IV, pages 245-254).

WOODROW township received its name, by petition of its citizens for the township organization, in honor of President Woodrow Wilson. He was born in Staunton, Va., December 28, 1856; was graduated at Princeton University, 1879; was professor there, of finance and political economy, 1890-1902, and president, 1902-10; author of several books on United States history and politics; was governor of New Jersey, 1911-13; president of the United States since March 4, 1913.

BAYS, POINTS, AND ISLANDS OF LEECH LAKE.

The origin of the name of Leech lake has been noted for the township so named. It was translated from the Ojibway name, the French translation being Lac Sangsue (which in English is a bloodsucker, that is, a leech).

This lake has a very irregular outline, with numerous bays and projecting points, and it contains several islands. On the east is Boy River bay, named for its inflowing river, with Sugar point at its west entrance, named for its sugar maples, the site of the battle in 1898, when Major Wilkinson lost his life, as noted for the township of his name. Bear island stretches three miles from north to south, lying in front of this bay and of Rice bay at the southeast, and Pelican island lies far out in the southern central part of the broad lake, these names being translations from those given by the Ojibways.

Big point and Otter Tail point, respectively on the southwest and northwest borders of the main lake, guard the entrance to the more irregular western part. The Peninsula juts into that part from the south, having itself a small Peninsula lake, and bounded on the southeast by Agency bay and on the west by the South arm and West bay. At the south end of the Peninsula, a passage called the Narrows leads from the South arm to Agency bay; and on the north the Peninsula is separated from the main shore by the North Narrows, and it terminates northeastward in Pine point. Nearly all these names are self-explanatory, having an obvious significance. The Otter Tail point, at the end of a tapering tract of land about five miles long, is a translation of the Ojibway name, referring to its outline, which resembles an otter's tail, similarly as the large lake and county of this name have reference to a tapering point of land adjoining the eastern end of that lake.

On the north end of the Peninsula, at the North Narrows, was the village of Eshkebugecoshe (Flat Mouth, b. 1774, d. about 1860), the very intelligent, friendly, and respected chief of the Pillager Ojibways; and close east of this village, at the time of Schoolcraft's visit there in 1832, was the trading house of the American Fur Company. In the time of Pike's visit, 1806, the Northwest Company's trading post was about two miles distant to the northeast from the North Narrows, being opposite to Goose island.

West bay in its north part branches westward to the Northwest arm, entered by a very narrow and short strait, and opens northward, opposite to the North Narrows, into Duck bay, which is entered with Prairie point on the right, and with Aitkin point, succeeded westward by the small Aitkin bay, on the left. Proceeding five miles up the Duck bay, past Duck island (called in the latest atlas Minnesota island), one comes at the northwest corner of this bay to the mouth of the Steamboat river, "fringed with extensive fields of wild rice," whence a canoe route through several little lakes, with portages, leads to Pike bay of Cass lake.

Four years after the southward journey of Schoolcraft through Leech lake in 1832, Rev. William T. Boutwell, his companion of that travel, who a year later had established a mission here for the Ojibways, befriended Nicollet on his exploration of the upper Mississippi country, in his relations with these Indians. Nicollet spent a week on Leech lake in the middle of August, 1836, having his camping place generally on Otter Tail point. Boutwell's mission house was on or near the isthmus that connects the Peninsula with the mainland of the present Leech Lake Agency. On Nicollet's return from Lake Itasca, by way of the Mississippi and Cass lake, he again camped on Otter Tail point during the first week of September, visited with Boutwell, and had long interviews with Flat Mouth.

Sucker bay lies west and north of Otter Tail point, and receives Sucker brook at its north end. Flea point, called Sugar point on Schoolcraft's map of Leech lake, juts into the southern part of the western side of the bay; and the present Sucker brook is designated on that map by the nearly equivalent name of Carp river. The Sucker Family of fishes, Catostomidae, includes "some 15 genera and more than 70 species," wholly limited in geographic range to the fresh waters of North America, excepting that two species occur in eastern Asia. Ulysses O. Cox, in his "Preliminary Report on the Fishes of Minnesota," published in 1897, wrote of this family that "five genera and eleven species" were then known in this state. Our most plentiful species, known as the "common sucker," found in nearly all large lakes of Minnesota, "attains a length of 18 inches or more, . . . a food-fish of considerable importance."

On the northwest side of the northern part of the main lake are the Two points and Noon Day point; and this part ends in the little Portage bay, called Rush bay on Schoolcraft's map, whence this map notes the "Route to L. Winnipeg" (that is, Winnebagoshish). The present name of the bay, refers, as before mentioned, to that canoe route and its portage. Nicollet named this most northern bay of Leech lake as Pickering bay, in honor of John Pickering (b. 1777, d. 1846), of Massachusetts, a philologist, who in 1836 published "Remarks on the Indian Languages of North America." This is the only name connected with Leech lake as mapped in much crude detail by Schoolcraft and Nicollet, which they bestowed otherwise than by translation of the Ojibway names.

Islands of Cass Lake.

Of the Ojibway name of this lake, with its translation, Gilfillan wrote: "Cass lake is Ga-misquawakokag sagaiigun, or The-place-of-red-cedars lake, from some red cedars growing on the island; more briefly, Red Cedar lake." The same name was given also by these Indians to Cedar lake in Aitkin county, as noted in the chapter for that county. Until the adoption of the new name, Cassina or Cass lake, these were discriminated respectively as the upper and lower Red Cedar lakes.

Gilfillan further wrote: "The large island in the lake was anciently called Gamisquawako miniss, or the island of red cedars. It is now called Kitchi miniss, or Great island." Schoolcraft in 1832 described and mapped it as "Colcaspi or Grand island," having coined the former word from parts of the names of its three explorers, Schoolcraft, Cass, and Pike. "The town of Ozawindib" (Yellow Head, who was the guide of Schoolcraft and his party in their expedition to Lake Itasca) was on this island, being a village of 157 people, with "small fields of corn and potatoes, cultivated by the women." It is now commonly called Star island, and it has a small lake, about three-fourths of a mile long, which is called Lake Helen, this name having been given in honor of Miss Helen Gould, of New York City, on the occasion of her visit here about the year 1900.

Having set aside the Ojibway name of Red Cedar island for the new name, Colcaspi, Schoolcraft gave the name, "R. Cedar I." on his map, to a small island on the southeast. Garden and Elm islands of Allen's bay, in Beltrami county, each of very small area, are also mentioned by Schoolcraft, the former doubtless so named for its having been cultivated by the Indians.

Lake Winnebagoshish.

Thompson in 1798 gave this name as Lake Winepegoos in his Narrative, published under editorial care of J. B. Tyrrell in 1916; but on Thompson's map, reproduced in facsimile in that work, it is Winnipeg Lake.

Schoolcraft's Narrative Journal of the Expedition in 1820 under General Cass, published in 1821, called it Lake Winnipec in the text, while the map spelled it Lake Winnepec. An island of boulders in its western part, not shown on maps but probably lying off a narrow projecting point, had large numbers of various species of waterfowl, one of which, a pelican found dead, caused it to be named Pelican island.

The map in the Narrative of Long's expedition, 1823, notes it as "Lit. Winnepeek L.;" Beltrami in the same year called it Lake Winnepec; and Allen, in 1832, spelled this name Lake Winnipeg, the same as the lake in Manitoba. Warren, writing in 1852 in his "History of the Ojibway Nation," called it Lake Winnepeg.

In Nicollet's Report, from his exploration in 1836, published in 1843, it appears both in the text and on the map as Lake Winebigoshish; and this form has continued from that time in prevalent use, excepting that the letter n has been doubled. The accent is placed by the white people on the syllable next to the last, with the long o sound.

By the Ojibways of that region, however, this lake name is generally pronounced like the etymologically cognate name of the Winnebago Indians and Lake Winnebago in Wisconsin (which is accented on the next before the final syllable and has the English long sound of the a), with addition of another syllable, shish. Gilfillan followed the orthography introduced to cartographers by Nicollet, and defined the meaning as "miserable-wretched-dirty-water (Winni, filthy; bi, water; osh, bad, an expression of contempt; ish, an additional expression of contempt, meaning miserable, wretched)." The whole lake is shallow, with a mostly muddy bed at a depth probably nowhere exceeding 20 or 25 feet, so that the large waves of storms stir up the mud and sand of the lake bottom and shores, roiling the water upward to the surface upon nearly or quite all its area.

Similar shallowness and general muddiness of Lakes Winnipeg and Winnipegosis, in Manitoba, also caused them to receive these Ojibway names, the former meaning muddy water, as noted by Keating in 1823 (vol. II, page 77), and the latter meaning "Little Winnipeg," according to Hind's "Narrative of the Canadian Exploring Expeditions" (vol. II, page 42).

The spelling received from Nicollet, mispronounced by our white people, has been corrected, in accordance with the Ojibway usage, to Winnebagoshish, by treaties of the United States with the Ojibways under dates of May 7, 1864, and March 19, 1867, and in an executive order of President Grant, May 26, 1874. Rev. S. R. Riggs, in a paper written in 1880, spelled the name as "Lake Winnebagooshish or Winnipeg" (Minnesota Historical Society Collections, VI, 157, 158). The orthography in the treaties here cited was also used by the present writer in the U. S. Geological Survey Monograph XXV ("The Glacial Lake Agassiz"), published in 1896, and was recommended by me in 1899 for general adoption (Final Report of the Minn. Geol. Survey, vol. IV, page 57). It still seems to me desirable that the corrected spelling and pronunciation be adopted by Minnesota writers and speakers.

Other Lakes and Streams.

The list of townships and villages has included sufficient mention of numerous lakes and streams, including Birch lake, Woman lake, the Boy lakes and river, Cass lake, Crooked lake, Gull river and lake, Home brook, Inguadona lake, Leech lake, Loon lake, Lake May, Meadow brook, Moose lake (in the township of this name), Mud lake and the Leech Lake river, Pike bay of Cass lake, Pillager creek and lake, Pine and Boot lakes (in Pine Lake township), Pine river, with the second Boot lake in Pine River township, Ponto lake, Portage lake, Shingobee creek, Sylvan lake, Thunder lake, the Turtle lakes in the township named for them, and Wabedo lake.

On the canoe route from Cass lake and Pike bay to Leech lake, Schoolcraft named the first lake, in sections 2 and 3, Wilkinson, Moss lake, for the mosslike water-plants seen growing in large masses on the lake bottom, which the canoemen "brought up on their paddles." Thence they made a portage of about two miles southwest into a lake at the center of this township, which Schoolcraft named Lake Shiba, spelled by "the initials of the names of the five gentlemen of the party, Schoolcraft, Houghton, Johnston, Boutwell, Allen." About a mile farther southwest, they came into "a river of handsome magnitude, broad and deep but without strong current," since named Steamboat river because it is ascended by steamboats from Duck bay of Leech lake, some three miles distant. Steamboat lake, crossed by the west line of this county, lies a quarter of a mile west from the junction of the outlet of Lake Shiba with this river.

Going from Leech lake southwest to the Crow Wing river, Schoolcraft took a somewhat frequented canoe route, starting from West bay near the site of Walker and first portaging to the present Lake May (formerly called Lake Frances), then named the Warpool by the Ojibways, who there began their war expeditions to the country of the Sioux. Next and very near was the Little Long lake, in sections 33 and 34, May, and section 4, Shingobee. Thence they passed up a little inlet, through its four lakelets, and by portages through a series of three small lakes, each without outlet, coming next to the Long Water lake in Hubbard county, at the head of the Crow Wing, beginning its series of eleven lakes. Schoolcraft's Lake of the Mountain and Lake of the Island, passed on this route before coming to the Long Water, remain unnamed on later maps.

Distances of travel south from the Leech Lake Agency, on the road to Hackensack and Brainerd, are noted by Three Mile lake, Four Mile lake, Six Mile lake, Ten Mile lake, Fourteen Mile lake at Hackensack (called now Birch lake, translated from its Ojibway name), with the outflowing Fourteen Mile creek, the head of Boy river, and Twenty-four Mile creek, which outflows from Pine Mountain lake, being the head stream of Pine river. These names are recognized as given by white pioneers, being unlike the majority derived by translations.

Gilfillan wrote that the long lake of the northwest part of T. 144, R. 27, in the Chippewa Reservation, between Leech Lake river and Lake Winnebagoshish, is named "Kitchi-bugwudjiwi sagaiigun, meaning big-lake-in-the-wilderness or big-wilderness lake."

Bear river (also called Mud river), in Salem, flowing into the south end of Mud lake, and Grave lake at its head, in sections 10, 14, and 15, Slater, may be aboriginal names translated, but they are not identified in Gilfillan's list. Little Sand lake, section 28, Slater, and its larger companion, Sand lake, crossed by the south line of this township, probably originated as white men's names, for Gilfillan gave the Ojibway name of this Sand lake as "Mikinako sagaiigun, Turtle lake." Its outlet is noted on the map of the Minnesota Geological Survey as Swift river, flowing northwest through the long and very narrow Swift lake, which the Ojibways name "Ningitawonan sagaiigun, Separating-canoe-route lake."

Big and Little Vermilion lakes, the Upper Vermilion lakes, and the larger Sugar lake (on recent maps noted as Little Sugar lake), and Vermilion river outflowing from them to the Mississippi, are translations from their Ojibway names.

Willow river, Birch brook and lake in Lima township, Big Rice lake, Thunder, Little Thunder, and Turtle lakes, and the long and narrow Blind lake in Smoky Hollow township, are partly or all of Ojibway derivation.

Lakes George and Washburn, Lawrence, Leavitt, and Morrison, in Crooked Lake and Beulah townships, also the Washburn brook, were named for lumbermen who formerly cut pine logs in these originally well forested townships.

Little Norway lake, named for its red or Norway pines, lying five miles south of Wabedo lake, outflows westward to Ada brook and Pine river. This brook and Lakes Ada and Hattie, also Mitten lake and Lake Laura, outflowing by Laura brook to Lake Inguadona, need further inquiries for the origins of their names.

Mule lake, a mile west of Wabedo lake, is said to have been named by the lumbermen for its outline, resembling a mule's head. Goose lake, next on the west, was named for the wild geese.

Girl lake, in sections 33 and 34, Kego, and Baby lake, in sections 13, 14, 23, and 24, Powers, are names suggested probably by Woman and Boy lakes, which latter are of Ojibway origin, referring to persons of that tribe slain by the Sioux, as noted in the foregoing list of townships.

Whitefish and Little Whitefish lakes, on the Fourteen Mile creek near Hackensack, are named, like the larger Whitefish lake on the Pine river in Crow Wing county, for their highly valued fish of this species, common or abundant in many lakes of northern Minnesota. The Ojibway fisheries of Leech lake are mentioned by Warren as follows: "The waters of the lake abound in fish of the finest quality, its whitefish equalling in size and flavor those of Lake Superior, and they are easily caught at all seasons of the year when the lake is free of ice, in gill-nets made and managed also by the women."

The Jack Pine lakes, two of small size near together, in sections 28, 32, and 33, Hiram, the outflowing Pine Lake brook, the large Pine Mountain lake, which receives this brook, and its outlet, called Twenty-four Mile creek or Norway brook, flowing through Norway lake, are lumbermen's names of the headwaters of Pine river.

On the west side of section 31, Bull Moose, is Township Corner lake, so named from its location; and on the west line of sections 18 and 19, Bungo, is Spider lake, named from its irregular and branching shape.

Stony creek, flowing into the eastern end of Wabedo lake, Stony brook, tributary to the Upper Gull lake, and Mosquito brook and Swan creek, respectively emptying into Crow Wing river about seven and fourteen miles west of Pillager, are names that need no explanations for their significance.

A few other names of lakes remain to be noted, including Lake Kilpatrick, through which Home brook flows, probably named for a former lumberman there; War Club lake, in sections 9 and 16, Deerfield, named for its shape; Island lake, in section 7, Powers; Portage lake, in section 28, Shingobee, smaller than the other Portage lake near Lake Winnebagoshish; Bass lake, in sections 24 and 25, Shingobee; Duck or Swamp lake, a mile west from the north end of Duck bay of Leech lake; and Long lake, in the east half of Kego township.

Pillsbury State Forest.

In 1899 a tract of 1,000 acres of non-agricultural land, from which the pine timber had been cut, was donated to the State of Minnesota from the estate of the late Governor John S. Pillsbury, to be administered by the Forestry Board as a State Forest. In honor of the donors, this tract, lying near the west shore of Gull lake, has been named the Pillsbury Forest. In 1904 and later years, parts of this area, not naturally reseeding to pine, have been planted with white, red or Norway, jack, and Scotch pines, and with Norway and white spruce.

Minnesota National Forest.

By an act of Congress approved May 23, 1908, the Minnesota National Forest was established, comprising an area of about fourteen government survey townships. It lies mainly in the north part of Cass county, north of Leech lake and river, extending to Cass lake, and including Lake Winnebagoshish, with about four townships at its north and northwest sides in Itasca county. This large tract covers the Chippewa, Cass Lake, and Winnebagoshish Indian Reservations, which had been long previously established. The text of the law for this national forest, fully safeguarding the rights of the Indians to whom it had been reserved, is published in the Thirteenth Annual Report of the Forestry Commissioner of Minnesota, Gen. C. C. Andrews, for the year 1907.

Indian Reservations.

Cass county has the Chippewa Indian Reservation, as it is officially named, and the Leech Lake Indian Reservation. The former name is not clearly definitive, for all the reservations now remaining in this state have been set apart for bands of the Chippewas (Ojibways), excepting only the very small reservation, a mile square, at the red pipestone quarry in Pipestone county.

The Chippewa reservation adjoins the north side of Leech lake and its outlet, the Leech Lake river, extending thence north to the Mississippi, Cass lake and Lake Winnebagoshish, and it also extends east across the Mississippi to include a tract equal to about four townships in Itasca county. It was set apart for the Ojibways of the Mississippi, in a treaty at Washington, March 19, 1867.

The Leech Lake reservation, which has an earlier date, borders the south and east shores of this lake, between Shingobee creek and Boy river. It includes the village of the Leech Lake Agency, at the east side of Agency bay. This reservation, and another at the north side of Lake Winnebagoshish, whence it is named, also a third reservation, on the north side of Cass lake and including all its islands, named therefore the Cass Lake reservation, were set apart for the Pillager and Winnebagoshish bands of the Ojibways by a treaty at Washington, February 22, 1855; but their areas were enlarged, by executive orders of the President, in 1873 and 1874.

Boutwell wrote of the Pillager band at Leech lake in 1832, during the expedition with Schoolcraft to Lake Itasca: "This band is the largest and perhaps the most warlike in the whole Ojibway nation. It numbers 706, exclusive of a small band, probably 100, on Bear Island, one of the numerous islands in the lake" (Minn. Hist. Soc. Collections, vol. V, page 481). The national census in 1910 enumerated 1,172 Ojibways in this county, showing decrease of 257 from the census of 1900.

CHIPPEWA COUNTY

This county, established February 20, 1862, and organized March 5, 1868, is named for the Chippewa river, which here joins the Minnesota. The river was called Manya Wakan (of remarkable or wonderful bluffs) by the Sioux. Its present name was also given by the Sioux, because the country of their enemies, the Chippewa or Ojibway Indians, extended southwestward to the headwaters of this stream, at Chippewa lake in Douglas county. As the Chippewa river of Wisconsin received its name from war parties of this tribe descending it to the Mississippi, likewise the river in Minnesota was named for this tribe, whose warriors sometimes made it a part of their "war road" to the Minnesota valley, coming with their canoes from Leech lake and Mille Lacs by the Crow Wing, Long Prairie, and Chippewa rivers. The earliest publication of the name, Chippewa river, was by Keating and Nicollet, though only the other Sioux name, Manya Wakan, is given on Nicollet's map. Ojibway is more accurately the aboriginal tribal title, which is anglicized as Chippewa, with the final vowel long. The form Ojibway has been used in nearly all the publications of the Minnesota Historical Society. It is asserted by Warren, the Ojibway historian, that this name means "to roast till puckered up," referring to the torture of prisoners taken in war.

By the early French voyageurs and writers the Ojibways were commonly called Saulteurs, from their once living in large numbers about the Sault Ste. Marie. Their area, however, also comprised a great part of the shores of lakes Huron and Superior, with the adjoining country to variable distances inland. During the eighteenth century they much extended their range southwestward, driving the Sioux from the wooded part of Minnesota, and also spreading across the Red river valley to the Turtle mountain on the boundary between North Dakota and Manitoba.

William W. Warren, whose mother was an Ojibway, prepared, in 1851-53, an extended and very valuable "History of the Ojibway Nation," chiefly relating to its part in Minnesota and Wisconsin, which was published in 1885 as Volume V of the Minnesota Historical Society Collections. In Volume IX of the same series, published in 1901, Rev. Joseph A. Gilfillan, who during twenty-five years was a very devoted missionary among the Ojibways in the White Earth Reservation and other large parts of northern Minnesota, contributed a paper of 74 pages, vividly portraying the habits and mode of life of this people, their customs and usages in intercourse with each other and with the white people, their diverse types of physical and mental development and characteristics, and much of their recent history. The next paper in the same volume, 14 pages, is

CHIPPEWA COUNTY 103

by Bishop Whipple, entitled "Civilization and Christianization of the Ojibways in Minnesota."

TOWNSHIPS AND VILLAGES.

Information of the derivations and meanings of names in this county has been gathered from "History of the Minnesota Valley," 1882, in pages 913-937; from "History of Chippewa and Lac qui Parle counties," by L. R. Moyer and O. G. Dale, joint editors, two volumes, 1916; and from Frank E. Bentley, judge of probate, J. J. Stennes, county auditor, and Elias Jacobson, clerk of the court, also much from the late Lycurgus R. Moyer, court commissioner and editor of the recently published county history, each of these being interviewed during my visit to Montevideo in July, 1916.

ASBURY, a Great Northern railway station, was named, like the villages and postoffices of this name in nine other states, in honor of Francis Asbury, the first Methodist Episcopal bishop in the United States, who was born in England, 1745, and died in Virginia, 1816. He was sent by John Wesley as a missionary to the American Colonies in 1771.

BIG BEND township, first settled in July, 1867, organized April 7, 1874, received its name for the bend of the Chippewa river in the north part of this township.

CLARA CITY, a railway village on the line of Rheiderland and Stoneham, founded in 1887, was named in honor of the wife of Theodor F. Koch, one of the managers for a Holland syndicate buying farm lands and establishing colonies here.

CRATE township was at first named Willow Lake, for the lake, now drained, which was crossed by its south boundary. That name, however, could not be accepted by the state auditor, because it had been previously given to another township of this state. The present name was selected by the citizens July 23, 1888, in compliment to Fanning L. Beasley, an early homesteader in section 4, this being a nickname by which he was generally known. It had reference to his middle name, Lucretius.

GRACE township, first settled in October, 1869, and organized August 9, 1880, was named in honor of Grace Whittemore, daughter of Augustus A. Whittemore, a homesteader in section 8, who was the contractor and builder of the court house in Montevideo.

GRANITE FALLS township, settled in 1866, set apart for organization March 9, 1880, received its name from the rock outcrops and falls of the Minnesota river here. This name is also borne by the adjoining city of Granite Falls, which is the county seat of Yellow Medicine county, and which extends across the river to include a part of section 34 in this township.

HAVELOCK township, settled in June, 1872, organized October 6, 1873, was named by John C. and Aaron J. Mullin, brothers, and other settlers from the eastern provinces of Canada, in honor of the English general, Sir Henry Havelock (b. 1795, d. 1857), the hero who in 1857 relieved the siege of Lucknow, India.

KRAGERO, first permanently settled in 1867-68, organized April 7, 1873, was named for Hans H. Kragero, a pioneer farmer here, whose surname was taken from his native town, the seaport of Kragero in southern Norway, on an inlet of the Skagerrak. He was born June 17, 1841; was a sailor, and afterward lived in Chicago, 1866-69; and came to Minnesota in 1870, settling in section 12 of the south part of this township.

The trading post of Joseph Renville, and the early Presbyterian mission for the Sioux conducted by Williamson and Riggs, 1835-1854, were in what is now section 13 in the southern corner of Kragero, nearly opposite the mouth of the Lac qui Parle river and close southeast from the foot of the lake. The site of the old mission station is marked by a granite block, inscribed "Lac qui Parle Mission, 1835."

LEENTHROP township, settled in 1870, organized January 20, 1872, has probably a Swedish name, anglicized in spelling.

LONE TREE township, organized August 5, 1878, received it name for a lone and tall cottonwood tree near the west end of Bad Water or Lone Tree lake, which tree was a landmark for the first immigrants.

LOURISTON, settled in 1867, organized September 18, 1877, was named in compliment for Laura Armstrong, daughter of Henry Armstrong, who was a homesteader on section 8, and who was elected in the first township meeting as one of its justices and a member of its board of supervisors.

MANDT, first settled in 1869 and organized June 13, 1876, was named in honor of Engelbreth T. Mandt, an early settler in section 30, at whose house the first town meeting was held, in which also he taught the first school in the spring of 1875.

MAYNARD, a railway village in Stoneham, was platted in 1887 by John M. Spicer, of Willmar, superintendent of this division of the Great Northern railway, and was named "in honor of his sister's husband."

MILAN, the railway village of Kragero, was platted December 1, 1880, and was incorporated March 15, 1893. This name of the great city in northern Italy is borne also by villages in twelve other states of our Union.

MINNESOTA FALLS, a railway station in the southern corner of this county, established in 1879, bears the name of a township and former village in Yellow Medicine county, on the opposite side of the Minnesota river, where on a fall or rapids of the river a dam and a sawmill and a flouring mill were built in 1871-72.

MONTEVIDEO, the county seat, was platted May 25, 1870, was incorporated as a village March 4, 1879, and as a city June 30, 1908. This Latin name, signifying "from the mountain I see," or "Mount of Vision," was selected, according to the late L. R. Moyer, by Cornelius J. Nelson, a settler who came here in 1870 from the state of New York, platted additions to the village in 1876 and 1878, and was its president in 1881 and 1885-7. The village and future city "was given its high-sounding appella-

CHIPPEWA COUNTY 105

tion by its romantic founders, who were so delighted by the wonderful view gained from the heights overlooking the interlocking valleys of the Minnesota and Chippewa rivers at that point, that they translated their feeling into good, mouth-filling Latin." But this name, while very appropriate on account of the view here, was derived by Nelson from the large South American city, the capital of Uruguay, whence the mayor of that Montevideo about the year 1905 presented the Uruguayan flag to this municipality.

Another good reason for the choice of this name, in allusion to the grand prospect seen from the river bluffs, may have been found in the aboriginal Sioux name of the Chippewa river, before noted as Manya Wakan (meaning wonderful bluffs), quite probably so named by these observing people in their admiration, like our own, for the beautiful and noble panorama here spread around them.

An earlier settlement on the opposite side of the Chippewa river had been platted and named Chippewa City in the autumn of 1868, and the county seat was there until 1870, when it was changed to the new town of Montevideo by an act of the state legislature.

RHEIDERLAND township, organized August 15, 1887, was named by early settlers from Holland, probably taking this name from Rheydt or Rheidt, a city of Rhenish Prussia, about twelve miles east of the Holland boundary, which had a population of 34,000 in 1900.

ROSEWOOD, first settled in 1869, organized September 2, 1871, was named for a village in Ohio, whence several German settlers of this township came.

SPARTA, settled in 1868-9, organized March 22, 1870, was earliest called Chippewa, for the river; was renamed by petition of its people, several of whom had come from Sparta in Wisconsin. The name belonged to a renowned city of ancient Greece, extremely heroic in wars, and it is retained by a modern city partly on the same site, which has about 4,000 people. This township "received the first permanent white settlement in the county, it being within its limits that Chippewa City was situated, and a little later Montevideo."

STONEHAM, organized August 9, 1880, was so named on the suggestion of a settler who came from the town of Stoneham, Mass., near Boston. A further motive for adoption of this name was to honor another of its citizens, Hammet Stone.

TUNSBERG, first settled in the spring of 1865, organized March 21, 1870, is thought to have been named for a locality or a farm in Norway.

WATSON, the railway village of Tunsberg, platted in August, 1879, was named by officers of the Chicago, Milwaukee and St. Paul railway company.

WEGDAHL, a railway village in the southeast corner of Sparta township, was named in honor of the pioneer farmer on whose land it was platted, Hemming Arntzen Wegdahl, who was the first postmaster there.

His surname was probably derived from the farm of his native place in Norway.

WOODS township, settled in 1876, was organized in 1879. "Most of the odd sections were sold to a land syndicate headed by Judge William W. Woods, of Ohio. It was for him that the township was named." (History of Chippewa County, vol. I, page 214.)

STREAMS AND LAKES.

The origin and significance of the name of the Minnesota river, adopted by the state, are presented in the first chapter; the lake of this river, named Lac qui Parle, will be considered in the chapter for the county of that name; and the Chippewa river, giving its name to this county, is fully noticed at the beginning of the present chapter.

Hawk creek is translated from the Sioux name, "Chetambe R.," given on Nicollet's map.

Palmer creek was named for Frank Palmer, one of the first settlers there in 1866, and Brofee's creek was likewise named for an early settler, these being tributary to the Minnesota river between Granite Falls and Montevideo.

Spring creek, Dry Weather and Cottonwood creeks, flowing into the Chippewa river, need no explanation.

Shakopee creek and lake, in the north part of Louriston, flowing to the Chippewa river in Swift county, received their name, the Sioux word meaning six, from the Six Mile grove, which borders the river along that distance and reaches from the mouth of Shakopee creek northward into Six Mile Grove township at the center of that county. Another name of the Shakopee lake, in somewhat common use, is Buffalo lake.

Black Oak lake, which was mostly in section 12, Sparta, four miles east of Montevideo, has been drained. It was mapped by Nicollet with its equivalent Sioux and English names, "Hutuhu Sapah, or Black Oak L." A grove of about forty acres bordered it, as stated by the late L. R. Moyer, comprising many large bur oaks, but no black oaks, although the latter is generally a common or abundant species of southeastern Minnesota.

Willow lake, previously mentioned in connection with Crate township, as now drained, was named for its willows, of which eight species or more are found frequent or common throughout the state, ranging in size from low shrubs to small trees. Three shrubby willow species and one of tree size are listed in Chapter III of the History of Chippewa County, by the late L. R. Moyer, entitled "The Prairie Flora of Southwestern Minnesota."

Lone Tree lake, which gave its name to a township, as before noted, has also been known as Bad Water lake, being somewhat alkaline.

Epple lake, in sections 20 and 29, Woods, and Norberg lake, in section 26, Stoneham, bear the names of adjacent pioneer settlers.

CHISAGO COUNTY

Established September 1, 1851, and organized October 14 of that year, this county bears a name proposed by William H. C. Folsom, of Taylor's Falls, who wrote of its organization and the derivation of the name, as follows ("Fifty Years in the Northwest," 1888, on pages 298-9 and 306).

"The county takes the name of its largest and most beautiful lake. In its original, or rather aboriginal form, it was Ki-chi-sago, from two Chippewa words meaning 'kichi,' large and 'saga,' fair or lovely. For euphonic considerations the first syllable was dropped.

"This lake is conspicuous for its size, the clearness of its waters, its winding shore and islands, its bays, peninsulas, capes, and promontories. It has fully fifty miles of meandering shore line. Its shores and islands are well timbered with maple and other hard woods. It has no waste swamps, or marsh borders. When the writer first came to Taylor's Falls, this beautiful lake was unknown to fame. No one had seen it or could point out its location. Indians brought fish and maple sugar from a lake which they called Kichi-saga sagiagan, or 'large and lovely lake.' This lake, they said, abounded with 'kego,' fish. . . .

"The movement for the organization of a new county from the northern part of Washington commenced in the winter of 1851-52. A formidable petition to the legislature to make such organization, drawn up and circulated by Hon. Ansel Smith, of Franconia, and the writer, was duly forwarded, presented and acquiesced in by that body. The writer had been selected to visit the capital in the interest of the petitioners. Some difficulty arose as to the name. The writer had proposed 'Chi-sa-ga.' This Indian name was ridiculed, and Hamilton, Jackson, Franklin, and Jefferson, were in turn proposed. The committee of the whole finally reported in favor of the name, Chisaga, but the legislature, in passing the bill for our county organization, by clerical or typographical error changed the last 'a' in 'saga' to 'o,' which, having become the law, has not been changed."

In Baraga's Dictionary the second of the two Ojibway words, saga, used by Folsom to form this name, is spelled sasega, or sasegamagad, being defined, "It is fair, it is ornamented, splendid." In pronunciation, this name Chisago has the English sound of Ch, and it accents the second syllable, preferably with a as in father (but in prevailing use taking the broad sound as in fall).

TOWNSHIPS AND VILLAGES.

The sources of information for this county have been "Fifty Years in the Northwest," by William H. C. Folsom, 1888, pages 298-354; and Edward W. Stark, judge of probate, Alfred P. Stolberg, county attorney, and John A. Johnson, sheriff, interviewed during my visit at Center City, the county seat, in May, 1916.

ALMELUND, a hamlet in the south part of Amador, founded about 1887, means, in the Swedish language, Elm Valley. The name was adopted in compliment to the first postmaster there, Mr. Almquist, whose name means an elm twig or branch.

AMADOR, settled in 1846, organized in 1858, bears a name which means, in the Spanish language, a lover, a sweetheart. It is the name of a county and a village in central California, whence it was adopted here by settlers of this township who had previously visited California. In the same way, probably, came also this name as applied to small villages in Iowa, Kansas, and Michigan.

BRANCH, named from the North Branch of Sunrise river flowing through this township, "was set off from Sunrise and organized in 1872."

CENTER CITY, a village in Chisago Lake township, was platted in May, 1857, and has been the county seat since 1875. Its name refers to its central position, between Chisago City and Taylor's Falls.

CHISAGO CITY, also a village in Chisago Lake township, was platted in 1855, taking its name from the lake.

CHISAGO LAKE township, likewise named for the beautiful lake, was settled in 1851 and was organized in 1858. This name, given to the county, has been fully noticed on a preceding page.

FISH LAKE township, organized in 1868, having formerly been a part of Sunrise, is named for its lake in section 25 and the outflowing creek, both of which are translated from their Ojibway names.

FRANCONIA township, organized in 1858, received its name from the earlier village, which was first settled and named by Ansel Smith, who came from Franconia, N. H., in the region of the White Mountains. The village was platted in 1858, and was incorporated in 1884. This is an ancient name of a large district in Germany.

HARRIS township, first settled in 1856, and organized in 1884, received its name from its earlier railway village, which was platted in May, 1873, and was incorporated in 1882, being named in honor of Philip S. Harris, a prominent officer of the St. Paul and Duluth railroad company.

KOST, a small village in the south part of Sunrise, was named in honor of Ferdinand A. Kost, who built a flouring mill there in 1883.

LENT township, organized in 1872, was named in honor of Harvey Lent, one of its first settlers, who came in 1855.

LINDSTROM, a village platted in 1880 on the central part of Chisago lake, including many summer homes of city residents, was named for Daniel Lindstrom, a pioneer farmer. He was born in Helsingland, Sweden, in 1825; came to the United States, settling here; sold the greater part of his farm in 1878, which became the village site, and continued to reside here until his death in 1895.

NESSEL, set off from Rushseba and organized in 1870, bears the name of its earliest pioneer farmer, Robert Nessel, who was born in Germany,

CHISAGO COUNTY   109

1834, came to the United States in 1847 and to Minnesota in 1854, and settled here in 1856.

NORTH BRANCH, the railway village of Branch township, named for the North branch of Sunrise river, was platted in January, 1870.

RUSH CITY received this record by Folsom: "In 1868, at the completion of the St. Paul and Duluth railroad, a depot was built and a station established at the crossing of Rush river, around which rapidly grew up the village of Rush City. It was surveyed and platted by Benjamin W. Brunson, surveyor, in January, 1870, . . . was incorporated in 1874."

RUSHSEBA township, organized in 1858, is in its second part an Ojibway name, seba or sippi, meaning a river. Both the Rush lake, in Nessel township, and its outflowing Rush river, are translated from the aboriginal name. Several species of bulrushes and other rushes are common throughout this state, one of which (Scirpus lacustris), abundant in the shallow borders of lakes, was "in common use among the Indians for making mats."

ST. CROIX RIVER, a railway station in the east edge of Rusheba, is named for the river crossed there, of which an extended notice in respect to the origin of the name has been given in the first chapter.

SHAFER township is noticed as follows by Folsom: "A Swedish colony settled here in 1853. . . The town organized first as Taylor's Falls, but the name was changed to Shafer in 1873. . . . A railroad station . . . bears the name of Shafer, derived, together with the name of the township, from Jacob Shafer, who, as early as 1847, cut hay in sections 4 and 5. He seems to have been in no sense worthy of the honor conferred upon him, as he was but a transient inhabitant and disappeared in 1849. No one knows of his subsequent career. The honor ought to have been given to some of the hardy Swedes, who were the first real pioneers, and the first to make substantial improvements."

STACY, a railway village established in 1875, was named in honor of Dr. Stacy B. Collins, an early resident.

STARK, a small village in section 26, Fish Lake township, was named in honor of Lars Johan Stark, who was the first postmaster there. He was born in Westergotland, Sweden, July 29, 1826, and died in Harris, Minn., May 5, 1910. He came to the United States in 1850, and settled at Chisago Lake, Minn.; engaged in mercantile business and farming; was a representative in the state legislature in 1865 and 1875. His son, Edward W. Stark, born in Fish Lake township, December 5, 1869, was a merchant at Harris, 1890-1905; was a representative in the legislature in 1901-03; and has been judge of probate for this county since 1905, residing at Center City.

SUNRISE township, organized October 26, 1858, had earlier a village of this name, on the Sunrise prairie, where in 1853 a hotel and store were built by William Holmes. The name is received from the lake and river, whose Ojibway name, Memokage (pronounced in four syllables), is translated by Gilfillan as "Sun-keep-rising."

TAYLOR'S FALLS, a village at the head of the Dalles of the St. Croix river, platted in 1850-51, incorporated in 1858, during many years the county seat, was named for Jesse Taylor, who came in 1838, and Joshua L. Taylor, to whom the former sold his claim in 1846. Jesse Taylor, pioneer, was born in Kentucky; was employed as a stone mason at Fort Snelling; was the first settler here, in 1838, and owned a sawmill; removed to Stillwater in 1846, and resided there until 1853; was a representative in the territorial legislature, 1851-2. Joshua Lovejoy Taylor was born in Sanbornton, N. H., in 1816; and died in Ashland, Wis., April 27, 1901. He came to Minnesota in 1840, settling at Taylor's Falls; engaged in lumbering; pre-empted a part of the site of this village; lived in California, 1849-56; returned here in 1856; removed to Ashland in 1896.

Folsom wrote of this village and the adjacent part of the river, at the Interstate bridge: "Many of the later residents query as to why it was ever called Taylor's Falls. It takes a keen eye to discover any fall in the river at the point named. The falls indeed were once far more conspicuous than they are now, owing to the fact that a large rock rose above the water at the ordinary stage, around which the crowded waters roared and swirled. That rock, never visible in later days, was called Death Rock, because three hapless mariners in a skiff were hurled against it by the swift current and drowned."

WYOMING township, organized in 1858, derived its name from the Wyoming Valley in Luzerne county, Pennsylvania, which is traversed by the North branch of the Susquehanna river. A colony from that region had settled in the western part of this township in 1855, and the eastern part had been earlier settled by Swedes. The village of Wyoming was platted in 1869, the next year after the completion of the St. Paul and Duluth railroad, and ten years later the branch from Wyoming to Taylor's Falls was built.

This name, given also to the Territory of Wyoming, organized in 1868 and admitted to the Union as a state in 1890, is from the language of the Delaware or Lenape Indians, formerly a large branch of the Algonquian stock, signifying "large plains," "extensive meadows."

LAKES AND STREAMS.

In the preceding pages attention has been given to the names of several lakes and streams, including Chisago lake, the Sunrise river and its North branch, Fish lake, and the Rush lake and river. The St. Croix river, belonging to several counties, is considered in the first chapter with the large rivers of this state.

Names commemorating pioneer settlers include four in Fish Lake township. These are Alexis lake, in sections 5 and 8, for John P. Alexis; Mandall lake, in the northwest quarter of section 15, for Lars

Mandall; Molberg lake, in the northwest quarter of section 22, for Erick Molberg; and Neander lake, section 11, named for Nels P. Neander. All of these settlers came as farmers, themselves or their parents being immigrants from Sweden.

Browning creek, in Harris, was named for John W. Browning, a pioneer farmer from the eastern states and of English descent.

Colby lake, about a mile northwest of Taylor's Falls, was named for an early farmer who likewise came from the eastern states.

Bloom's lake, in section 7, Franconia, was named in honor of Gustaf Bloom, from Sweden, whose son, David Bloom, has been since 1909 the county register of deeds; and Ogren's lake, in section 12 of this township, for Andrew Ogren, who was a soldier in our civil war.

Linn lake, adjoining the south end of the eastern body of Chisago lake, was named for a family living at its west side.

Lake Comfort, in sections 22 and 27, Wyoming, bears the name of Dr. John W. Comfort, a physician who lived there and had a wide country practice. It is also very frequently called "the Doctor's lake."

Heim's lake, in sections 29 and 30, Wyoming, mostly drained, received its name for families living there, especially for Conrad Heim, the pioneer.

Martha and Ellen lakes, beside the railway in sections 1 and 12, Wyoming, and nearly adjoining the north end of Green lake, are also commemorative of early pioneers, but inquiries have failed to supply their surnames.

Other lakes and creeks in this county, mostly bearing names that scarcely need explanations of their derivation, are Asp lake, in the northwest quarter of section 21, Fish Lake township, having aspen or poplar groves; Pine lake, in sections 23 and 26, Nessel, for its white pines; another Pine lake, about a mile south from the most southwestern arm of Chisago lake, situated, like the foregoing, near the southwestern limit of the geographic range of our pines; Grass lake, about two miles northeast of Harris, shallow and having much marsh grass on its borders; the Little Duck lake in section 19, Franconia; the much larger Goose lake, and Goose creek, flowing thence eastward to the St. Croix river; Spring creek, tributary to the St. Croix three miles farther north; Rock creek, flowing through the northeast part of Rushseba, named for the conspicuous rock outcrops on the St. Croix river about a half mile northeast from its mouth; Dry creek, in section 2, Shafer; Hay creek, flowing into the Sunrise river three miles from its mouth; the Middle, West, and South branches of Sunrise river; Leech lake, sections 35 and 36, Nessel, named, like the great Leech lake in Cass county, for its plentiful leeches; Horseshoe and Little Horseshoe lakes, respectively in sections 23 and 22, Fish Lake township, named for their form; Horseshoe creek, their outlet; Chain lake, in section 6, Branch, named for its form or outline, and for the small lakes connected with it southward in

112 MINNESOTA GEOGRAPHIC NAMES

a chainlike series; Mud lake, in section 28, Lent, shallow, with muddy shores and bottom; School lake, in the school section 36, Lent; Spring lake, one to two miles west of Lindstrom; Little lake, a misnomer as it is nearly a mile long, lying a mile and a half northeast from Center City; Ice lake, in section 30, Franconia; Swamp lake, sections 14 and 23, Franconia; Spider lake, named for its branched outline, in section 27, near the south end of Chisago Lake township; First, Second, and Third lakes, consecutive in an east to west series, in sections 34 to 32, about a mile south and southwest of Spider lake; Green lake, after Chisago lake the second in size in this county, named for the clearness and beauty of its water, reflecting the verdure of the grass and trees on its banks; and White Stone lake, in sections 11 and 14, Wyoming, named for its white pebbles or boulders.

INTERSTATE PARK AT THE DALLES OF THE ST. CROIX.

The Legislative Manual of Minnesota, for 1907 and ensuing sessions, gives the following statement of the origin of this public park.

"In 1895 the State of Minnesota, by a legislative act, set aside a tract of about 110 acres in the town of Taylor's Falls, Chisago county, as a public park, to be called the State Park of the Dalles of the St Croix. An act was also passed by the Wisconsin legislature of the same year, which provided a commission to ascertain the probable cost of acquiring a larger tract for a state park on the opposite side of the St. Croix river; and in 1899 and 1901 the State of Wisconsin passed acts for the purchase of lands there, amounting to about 600 acres. The original park on the Minnesota side of the river has been extended to an area of about 150 acres, and plans are under consideration for further extension to a total of about 500 acres in Minnesota. The two states have thus established an Interstate Park, including the grand and picturesque rock gorge called the Upper Dalles of the St. Croix, where the river for a distance of two-thirds of a mile, at and just south of the village of Taylor's Falls, flows through a chasm walled by cliffs of rock 75 to 150 feet high.

"The first suggestion for devoting this tract of remarkable natural beauty to such public use was made by George H. Hazzard, a pioneer of Minnesota Territory, to members of the Minnesota legislature in 1893. His idea was welcomed with enthusiasm by newspapers, commercial bodies, and the people of the State."

The name Dalles, applied by the early French voyageurs to rock-walled gorges of the Wisconsin river, the St. Croix and St. Louis rivers in Minnesota, and the Columbia river on the boundary between Oregon and Washington, came from a French word, dalle, meaning a flagstone or slab of rock, referring in this name to the vertical and jointed rock cliffs enclosing the rivers at the localities so named, where in most instances (though not in the case of the St. Croix) the river flows through its gorge in rapids and falls.

CHISAGO COUNTY 113

In the Upper Dalles, at Taylor's Falls, and again in the Lower Dalles, situated two miles farther down the river and reaching a third of a mile, close above the village of Franconia, the rock walls of trap, Keweenawan diabase, rise almost or quite perpendicularly on each side of the river, inclosing it at each place by a very picturesque gorge.

A paper entitled "Giants' Kettles eroded by Moulin Torrents," contributed by the present writer to the Bulletin of the Geological Society of America (vol. 12, 1900, pages 25-44, with a map), was partly quoted as follows by the Legislative Manual in 1907 and 1909.

"To nearly every visitor the most interesting and wonderful feature of the Interstate Park consists in many large and small waterworn potholes, which are also, in their large examples, often called 'wells.' The languages of Germany, Sweden, and Norway, give the name 'giants' kettles' to such cylindric or caldron-shaped holes of stream erosion, which are everywhere characteristic of waterfalls and rapids, especially in crystalline rocks. These potholes, occurring most numerously near the steamboat landing of Taylor's Falls, at the central part of the Upper Dalles, and within a distance of fifty rods northward, are unsurpassed by any other known locality in the world, in respect to their variety of forms and grouping, their great number, the extraordinary irregularity of contour of the much jointed diabase in which they are eroded, and the difficulty of explanation of the conditions of their origin."

Like the giants' kettles of the Glacier Garden at Lucerne, Switzerland, these larger and deeper potholes are ascribed "to erosion by torrents of water falling through crevasses and vertical tunnels, called moulins, of an ice-sheet during some stage of the Glacial period. In this park they seem referable to the stage of final melting and departure of the ice-sheet from this area."

CLAY COUNTY

This county, established March 8, 1862, and organized April 14, 1872, was named for the greatly admired statesman, Henry Clay, of Lexington, Kentucky. He was born in Hanover county, Virginia, April 12, 1777; died in Washington, D. C., June 29, 1852. He began to study law in 1796, and in the next year, being admitted to practice, he removed to Kentucky; was U. S. senator, 1806-7 and 1810-11; was a member of Congress, 1811-21 and 1823-25, serving as speaker in 1811-14, 1815-20, and 1823-25; was peace commissioner at Ghent in 1814; was candidate for the presidency in 1824; secretary of state, 1825-29; again U. S. senator, 1831-42 and 1849-52; was Whig candidate for the presidency in 1832 and 1844; was the chief designer of the "Missouri Compromise," 1820, and of the compromise of 1850; was the author of the compromise tariff of 1833; said in a speech in 1850, "I would rather be right than be President."

Among the numerous biographies of Henry Clay, the most extended is by Rev. Calvin Colton, six volumes, containing speeches and correspondence, published in 1846-57; its revised edition, 1864; and its republication in 1904, ten volumes, with an introduction by Thomas B. Reed, and a History of Tariff Legislation, 1812-1896, by William McKinley.

Carl Schurz, on the final page of his "Life of Henry Clay," published in 1887 (two volumes, in the "American Statesmen" series), pointed to his greatest political motive: "It was a just judgment which he pronounced upon himself when he wrote, 'If any one desires to know the leading and paramount object of my public life, the preservation of this Union will furnish the key.'" Near the end of the dark first year of our civil war, and nearly ten years after Clay had died, this county was named. Minnesota had then raised four regiments for the defence of the Union.

Townships and Villages.

Information of the origins and meanings of names in this county has been received from "History of the Red River Valley," two volumes, 1909, pages 798-830; from Hon. Solomon G. Comstock, of Moorhead, and Andrew O. Houglum, county auditor, interviewed during my visit in Moorhead in September, 1916; and from Nathan Butler, of Minneapolis, who was formerly a resident in Barnesville during twenty years, 1883-1903.

ALLIANCE township was named for the Farmers' Alliance, a political party of considerable prominence in Minnesota during the campaign of 1890. Hon. George N. Lamphere, in a paper entitled "History of Wheat Raising in the Red River Valley" (Minn. Hist. Soc. Collections,

CLAY COUNTY

vol. X, 1905, pages 1-33), stated that the agitation for lower railroad freight rates, which was the cause of the formation of the Farmers' Alliance, began in 1883-4 in Clay county, spread thence throughout the wheat-raising districts of this state, and developed into the People's or Populist party.

AVERILL, a railway village on the boundary line of Moland and Spring Prairie, was named in honor of Gen. John Thomas Averill, who was born in Alma, Maine, March 1, 1825, and died in St. Paul, Minn., October 3, 1889. He was graduated at Wesleyan College; settled in Lake City, Minn., 1857; served during the civil war in the Sixth Minnesota regiment, becoming its colonel in 1864, and was brevetted a brigadier general in 1865. After the war he founded and conducted a wholesale paper house in St. Paul, under the name of Averill, Carpenter and Co. In 1858-60 he was a state senator; and in 1872-5 represented his district in Congress.

BAKER, a railway village in section 1, Alliance, was named for Lester H. Baker, a farmer there, who removed to the State of Washington.

BARNESVILLE township was named after its railway village, which was established in 1874 by George S. Barnes, a farmer and wheat merchant, who owned and managed a very large farm near Glyndon and died there about the year 1910. The village was incorporated November 4, 1881, and received its charter as a city April 4, 1889.

COMSTOCK, the railway village of Holy Cross township, was named in honor of Solomon Gilman Comstock, of Moorhead, for whom also a township in Marshall county was named. He was born in Argyle, Maine, May 9, 1842; came to Minnesota in 1869, settling in Moorhead; was admitted to the bar in 1871; was a representative in the state legislature, 1876-7 and 1879-81; a state senator, 1883-7; and a representative in Congress, 1889-91.

CROMWELL township, settled partly by immigrants from England, was named, in accordance with the petition of its citizens, for Oliver Cromwell (born 1599, died 1658).

DILWORTH, a village and division point of the Northern Pacific railway, three miles east of Moorhead, was named by officers of that railway company.

DOUGLAS, a Great Northern railway station two miles south of Georgetown, was named in honor of James Douglas, one of the first settlers of Moorhead. He was born in Scotland, March 13, 1821; came with his parents to the United States in 1832; came to Minnesota in 1871, settling in Moorhead, where he was a merchant, built the steamboats Manitoba and Minnesota in 1875 for the Red river trade, and secured the building of a flouring mill.

DOWNER, the railway village of Elkton township, was named by officers of the Great Northern railway company.

EGLON township bears the name of a city of ancient Palestine, also of postoffices in West Virginia, Kentucky, and Washington.

ELKTON township refers to the elk formerly common or frequent here and in many parts of Minnesota.

ELMWOOD township received this euphonious name in accordance with its petition for organization, alluding to its abundant elm trees along the South fork of Buffalo river.

FELTON township was named, after its railway station, in honor of S. M. Felton, by the officers of the Great Northern railway company.

FINKLE, a railway station four miles south of Moorhead, was named in honor of Henry G. Finkle, an early pioneer, of the firm of Bruns and Finkle, merchants in Moorhead.

FLOWING township has chiefly Scandinavian settlers, by whom this name was adopted, but its significance remains to be ascertained, unless it refers to artesian or flowing wells. The many flowing wells in the Red river valley, of which Clay county and this township have a good number, are the subject of a chapter in "The Glacial Lake Agassiz," (Monograph XXV, U. S. Geological Survey, 1896, pages 523-581, with a map).

GEORGETOWN was established as a trading post of the Hudson Bay Company in 1859; was abandoned in September, 1862, during the Sioux outbreak; and was reëstablished in 1864. The township received its name from the trading post.

GLYNDON was platted as a railway village in the spring of 1872, being named by officers of the Northern Pacific railroad company, and thence the township was named. It is also the name of small villages in Pennsylvania and Maryland.

GOOSE PRAIRIE township was named for the wild geese formerly plentiful in its lakes and sloughs.

HAGEN township commemorates an early Norwegian settler of this surname. A large manufacturing city in western Germany bears this name.

HAWLEY, a railway village settled by an English colony in 1871, incorporated February 5, 1884, and its township, at first called Bethel, were renamed in honor of Gen. Joseph Roswell Hawley, of Connecticut, one of the original stockholders of the Northern Pacific railroad company. He was born in Stewartsville, N. C., October 31, 1826; died in Washington, D. C., March 17, 1905. He was graduated at Hamilton College, 1847; was admitted to practice law, 1850; became editor of the Evening Press, Hartford, Conn., 1857; served as a brigade and division commander in the Union army during the civil war, and was brevetted major general in 1865; was president of the U. S. Centennial Commission, 1873-77; was member of Congress, 1872-75 and 1879-81; was U. S. senator, 1881-1905.

HIGHLAND GROVE township received its name for its location on the high ascent eastward from the Red river valley, and for the groves beside its lakes and on the Buffalo river, the surface all about being mainly prairie.

HITTERDAL, a railway village on the line between Goose Prairie and Highland Grove, is named for a valley and lake in southern Norway.

HOLY CROSS township was named for a conspicuous wooden cross set on the prairie at a cemetery about a half mile west of the Red river, in North Dakota, amid a Catholic community of French Canadian farmers. This township on the Minnesota side was settled by Norwegian farmers, Lutherans, and both sides of the river were comprised in the "Holy Cross neighborhood."

HUMBOLDT township, settled by a German colony, is named in honor of the celebrated German scientist, traveler, and author, Alexander von Humboldt, who was born in 1769 and died in 1859. In the years 1799 to 1804 he traveled in South America and Mexico, and later he published many books on his observations of natural sciences, history, and political affairs of this continent.

KEENE township was named for a homesteader there, who was a veteran of the civil war.

KRAGNES was named in honor of A. O. Kragnes, a prominent Norwegian farmer, one of the first settlers of that township, who came from Houston county in 1872. He was born in Norway and came to the United states in 1852, with his parents, who two years later settled in Houston county.

KURTZ township was named for Thomas C. Kurtz, formerly cashier of the Merchants' Bank, Moorhead, who removed to Portland, Oregon. He is a son of Colonel John D. Kurtz, of the United States Engineer Corps, who served with distinction during the civil war, and later was superintendent of the engineering works of Delaware bay and river.

LAMBS, the railway station in Oakport, was named for John and Patrick H. Lamb, brothers from Ireland, who were early settlers and engaged extensively in farming, brick-making, railroad construction, and banking.

MOLAND township was named by its Norwegian settlers.

MOORHEAD, first settled in 1871, when the building of the Northern Pacific railroad reached its site, was named in honor of William G. Moorhead, of Pennsylvania, who was a director of that railroad company. He was a partner of Jay Cooke, the Northern Pacific financial agent, and his first wife was a sister of Cooke. He was president of the Philadelphia and Erie railroad, and his brother, Gen. James Kennedy Moorhead, was likewise much interested in railway development, especially in the Northern Pacific finances. Moorhead was incorporated as a city February 24, 1881, and the township also bears this name.

The adjoining city of Fargo, in North Dakota, was named for William George Fargo, (b. 1818, d. 1881), of Buffalo, N. Y., founder of the Wells, Fargo Express Company and prominent as a Northern Pacific director.

Cass county, North Dakota, adjoining Clay county, and also its city of Casselton, are named for Gen. George W. Cass, of Pennsylvania, who was president of the Northern Pacific railroad company in 1872-75. He was born in Ohio, and was a nephew of Governor Lewis Cass, of Michigan; was graduated at the U. S. Military Academy, West Point, in 1832; was president during twenty-five years of the Pittsburg, Fort Wayne and Chicago railroad company; purchased a large tract adjoining the Northern Pacific line between fifteen and twenty miles west of Fargo, and, employing Oliver Dalrymple as farm superintendent, was the first to demonstrate in 1876 the high agricultural value of the Red river valley lands for wheat raising on a large scale.

MORKEN township was named in honor of T. O. Morken, its first homesteader, who came here from Houston county in 1875.

MUSKODA, a former station of the Northern Pacific railway in the east edge of section 7, Hawley, had an Ojibway name, meaning a meadow or tract of grass land, a large prairie. It is spelled Muskoday in Longfellow's "Song of Hiawatha," with accent on the first syllable. In Baraga's Dictionary it is spelled mashkode, to be pronounced in three syllables nearly as by Longfellow. A few miles east of Clay county, the traveler on the Northern Pacific line passes out from the northeast forest region, and thence crosses an expanse of prairie and plain, mainly treeless, for eight hundred miles to the Rocky mountains. (By a relocation of the railroad to secure an easier grade in the next seven miles west of Hawley, the site of Muskoda is left now about two-thirds of a mile distant at the north.)

OAKPORT township has many oaks in the narrow fringe of timber along the navigable Red river.

PARKE township was named probably in honor of a pioneer settler. A county in western Indiana bears this name.

RIVERTON township has reference to Buffalo river, which flows across its northern part.

RUSTAD, a railway village in Kurtz, was named in honor of Samuel Rustad, a Norwegian merchant there.

RUTHRUFF, a railway station in section 36, Moorhead, was named for an adjoining settler.

SABIN, a railway village in Elmwood, is in honor of Dwight May Sabin, who was born in Manlius, Ill., April 25, 1844, and died in Chicago, December 23, 1902. He came to Minnesota in 1867, and the next year settled in Stillwater, where he engaged in the lumber business, and in the manufacture of machinery, engines, and cars. He was a state senator, 1871-3, and a United States senator, 1883-9.

SKREE was named for Mikkel Skree, a Norwegian farmer, who was the first settler of this township.

SPRING PRAIRIE township, a euphonious name selected in the petition for organization, refers to its springs and rivulets.

TANSEM township was named for John O. Tansem, one of its pioneer farmers, a highly respected citizen. He was born in Eidsvold, Norway, in 1842; came to the United States in 1861; settled here, in the most southeastern township of this county, in 1862.

ULEN township was named in honor of Ole Ulen, its first settler. He was born in Norway, April 18, 1818, and died in Ulen village January 19, 1891. He came to the United States in 1851, and to Minnesota in 1853, settling in Houston county; was a farmer there until 1867; removed to this county in 1872.

VIDING township was named for a Swedish settler there.

LAKES AND STREAMS.

Buffalo river is translated from the Ojibway name of its southern tributary flowing from lakes in and near Audubon, in Becker county, of which Rev. Joseph A. Gilfillan wrote that it "is called Pijikiwi-zibi, or Buffalo river, from the fact that buffaloes were always found wintering there." Hence the white people have erroneously called the whole river Buffalo river. On Nicollet's map it is named "Pijihi or Buffalo R." The name used by the Ojibways for our Buffalo lake in Becker county, and for the Buffalo river, flowing thence to the Red river, would be correctly translated as Beaver lake and Beaver river.

Near the middle of the west side of Kragnes township, on the Red river opposite to the mouth of the Sheyenne, a townsite named LaFayette was surveyed in March, 1859; and there in April of that year, "the first steamboat on the Red river was built . . . the materials for which were transported across the country from Crow Wing on the Mississippi, where the steamer North Star was broken up for that purpose. The new boat was named the Anson Northup." (Lamphere, M. H. S. Collections, vol. X, 1905, pages 16, 17; History of the Red River Valley, 1909, pages 569-572.)

The Sheyenne river (here spelled unlike the Cheyenne river of South Dakota and the city Cheyenne, capital of Wyoming), flowing into the Red river from North Dakota, received this name, given by Nicollet as "Shayenn-oju R.," from the Sioux, designating it as the river of the Cheyenne tribe, meaning "people who speak a strange language." Rev. T. S. Williamson wrote (M. H. S. Collections, vol. I, pages 295-301) that when the Sioux first came to the Falls of St. Anthony, the Iowas occupied the country about the mouth of the Minnesota river, and the Cheyennes had their villages and cultivated fields "on the Minnesota between Blue Earth and Lac qui Parle, whence they moved to a western branch of Red river of the North, which still bears their name." Thompson recorded the narration in 1798 by an Ojibway chief, of an Ojibway war party who attacked and destroyed the Cheyenne village west of the Red river, probably about 1775 or 1780, but perhaps five or ten years later. (Thompson's Narrative, edited by Tyrrell, 1916, pages 236, 261-3). Next this tribe removed to a second Cheyenne river, west of the Missouri in South Dakota, and yet later they migrated farther across the plains to the west and south.

Wild Rice river, whose South branch runs through Ulen and Hagen, and the river of the same name in North Dakota, tributary to the Red river nine miles south of Fargo and Moorhead, are translated from the Ojibway names, referring to their valued native grain, the wild rice, much harvested by the Indian women for food. It also gave the name of Mahnomen county, and is more fully noticed in the chapter for that county.

No explanations seem needed for the names of Hay creek, tributary to the Buffalo river in section 33, Highland Grove, and a second Hay creek in Skree and Elkton; Spring creek, tributary to the last and joining it two miles southeast of Downer; and Stony and Willow creeks, flowing through Barnesville township to the South branch of Buffalo river. Each of the two creeks last named has been sometimes called Whiskey creek, in allusion to a great spree of the railway graders when the former railway line from Breckenridge to Barnesville was completed. Another name for Stony creek, crossed by the railway two miles north of the city of Barnesville, is Sieber's creek, for Rudolph Sieber, who had a milk farm at its north side.

Deerhorn creek, in Alliance township, flowing northwestward from Wilkin county to the South branch of Buffalo river, received its name from antlers shed by deer and found by the pioneer settlers.

The east margin of Clay county, above the Glacial Lake Agassiz, has numerous small lakes, but only a few have received names on maps. These bearing names are Silver lake, in section 26, Hawley, in allusion to its placid and shining surface; Moe lake, in sections 2, 11, and 12, Eglon, for Nels R. Moe, the farmer on its west side; Sand lake, in the east half of section 12, Eglon, for its sandy shore; Solum lake, in the southwest quarter of the same section, for H. H. Solum, whose farm adjoins it; Lee lake, in sections 9 and 16, and Perch lake in section 17, Eglon; Turtle lake, crossed by the east line of section 12, Parke; and Grove lake, partly in section 36, Tansem, lying mostly in Otter Tail county.

Buffalo Delta of Lake Agassiz.

Where the Buffalo river enters the area of the Glacial Lake Agassiz, a delta of stratified gravel and sand was deposited during the earliest and highest stage of the ancient lake. The Herman or first beach and the east edge of the delta were crossed by the Northern Pacific railroad at Muskoda, and the extent of the delta from north to south, on both sides of the river, is seven miles, with a width from two to three and a half miles. (U. S. Geological Survey, Monograph XXV, 1896, pages 290-292, with map and section.)

CLEARWATER COUNTY

This county, established December 20, 1902, received its name from the Clearwater river and lake, which lie partly within its area. For the formerly great industry of pine lumbering, this was a very important river, the logs being floated down from the head stream and its tributaries into Clearwater lake and thence to the Red Lake river and the sawmills at Crookston. Another Clearwater river, likewise flowing through a lake of the same name, empties into the Mississippi at the town of Clearwater in Wright county. Both of these rivers, with their lakes, and also the Eau Claire or Clearwater river in Wisconsin, derive their names by translation from those given by the Ojibways and other Indian tribes long before the coming of white men. According to Rev. Joseph A. Gilfillan, the Ojibway name of this river and the county, meaning Clearwater, is Ga-wakomitigweia. The name Clear Water river was used by Thompson in 1798, and on Nicollet's map, 1843. It was called Clear river on the map of Long's Expedition, 1823.

The quality denoted by this term, Clearwater, is in contrast with the more or less muddy and silty waters of the Missouri, Minnesota, and most other rivers, especially when they are in high flood stages, caused by the melting of winter snows at the return of spring or by exceptionally heavy rains, the inflowing drainage having washed down much mud, clay, and sand.

Another very remarkable contrast to clearness in river and lake waters is surprisingly shown by other streams of the northern woods and swamps, colored dark and yellowish by the drainage to them from decaying leaves, fallen branches and trunks of dead trees, and peaty soil, but most of all where extensive peat swamps and bogs supply water in any time of considerable drought, long saturated with the peat and decaying vegetation. In some cases, as the Rat Root river and Black or Rat Root bay of Rainy lake, in Koochiching county, seen during my travel in August, 1916, the very dark water, nearly or quite stagnant, although containing almost no mud or silty matter, is yet the antithesis of clearness or transparency, being too dark for one to see into it even to a depth of only two or three feet. From frequent acquaintance with similar peat-stained streams, the observant Ojibways were wont to distinguish other streams of opposite character by naming them for their crystal clearness.

Townships and Villages.

Information of the origins and meanings of names was gathered from F. A. Norquist, county treasurer, Frederick S. Kalberg, editor of the Clearwater Crystal, and Albert Kaiser, banker, of Bagley, during my visit in September, 1909; from T. L. Tweite, county treasurer, in my second visit, September, 1916; and for the Itasca State Park, lying mostly in this county, from Volumes VII and XI, Minnesota Historical Society Collections, 1893 and 1905, by the late Hon. J. V. Brower.

ALIDA (accented on the second syllable, with the long English sound of its vowel), a village in section 10, Bear Creek, was named by Governor John Lind. Indiana and Kansas also have postoffices of this name.

BAGLEY village, the county seat, was named in honor of Sumner C. Bagley, an early lumberman of this part of the Clearwater river, who removed to Fosston in 1885 and died there in 1915.

BEAR CREEK township is named for its Bear creek, flowing into the Mississippi river in section 26.

CHURNES, a former postoffice in section 35, Greenwood, was named for its postmaster, Alexander Churnes, a Norwegian pioneer farmer.

CLEARBROOK, the railway village in Leon, took its name from the brook there.

CLOVER township, organized in 1914, received this name on the suggestion of James N. Vail, an early settler.

COPLEY township was named in honor of Lafayette Copley, one of its first pioneers, who removed in 1916 to western Oregon. He came from Massachusetts; was the builder of five dams on the upper Clearwater river, used by T. B. Walker for log-driving.

DUDLEY was named in honor of Frank E. Dudley, who was a county commissioner of Beltrami county when this township was organized, before the establishment of Clearwater county. He was born in Geauga county, Ohio; came to Minnesota in 1881; was mayor of Bemidji, 1900-02.

EBRO, a railway station seven miles west of Bagley, has the name of a river in northeastern Spain.

EDDY township was named in honor of Frank M. Eddy, of Sauk Center, Minn. He was born in Pleasant Grove, Minn, April 1, 1856; was a school teacher, and later a land examiner for the Northern Pacific railroad company; was clerk of the district court of Pope county, 1884-94; was a representative in Congress, 1895-1903.

GONVICK, the railway village of Pine Lake township, was named for Martin O. Gonvick, an early Norwegian settler there.

GREENWOOD township was so named in its petition for organization, probably in allusion to the verdure of its woods.

HANGAARD township was named for Gunder G. Hangaard, its first homesteader, who came from Norway. Gunder postoffice, at his home in section 19, was also named for him.

HOLST township received its name in honor of H. J. Holst, a Norwegian pioneer farmer there, who was sheriff of this county in 1904-08.

ITASCA township lies next north of Itasca lake and the State Park.

LEON township is for Leon Dickinson, the first white child born there, son of Daniel S. Dickinson, who later removed to Montana.

LEONARD, the railway village of Dudley township, was named for Leonard French, first child of an early settler, George H. French, who became a merchant of this village.

MALLARD, a village in sections 5 and 8, Itasca, received it name for the adjoining lake, having many mallard ducks.

MEADOWS, a former postoffice in Greenwood, now discontinued, was named for the wide natural meadows of the Clearwater river.

MINERVA township was named for the Roman goddess of wisdom, by Frederick S. Kalberg, owner of the Pinehurst farm on the southeast side of Lake Minerva, section 13.

MOOSE CREEK township has the small creek so named, flowing from section 21 to the northeast and east.

NEVING, a postoffice near the mouth of Clearwater lake, in Sinclair township, was named for a lumberman and farmer there, Robert Neving, who removed to Saskatchewan about the year 1910.

NORA township was named in honor of Knut Nora, a Norwegian pioneer farmer there, who was a member of the first board of county commissioners. He removed to North Dakota several years ago.

OLBERG, a former small village in the north edge of section 22, Leon, named for Anton Olberg, a pioneer from Norway, was superseded by Clearbrook when the railway was built there.

PINE LAKE township has the large lake of this name, outflowing by Pine river, a tributary of Lost river. The original wealth of this region consisted in its timber of the white and Norway pines, but the timber lands are now largely changed into farms.

POPPLE township was named for its plentiful poplar woods, misspelled and mispronounced, by quite common usage, in this name.

RICE township refers to the headwaters of the Wild Rice river, with the Rice lakes. This river flows through the northwest corner of this township.

SHEVLIN township and railway village were named in honor of the late Thomas Henry Shevlin, of Minneapolis. He was born in Albany, N. Y., January 3, 1852; died in Pasadena, Cal., January 15, 1912. He came to Minnesota in 1886, settling in Minneapolis; was president of several logging and lumber manufacturing companies, cutting much pine timber in this county. He was donor of the Alice A. Shevlin Hall, University of Minnesota, built in 1906.

SINCLAIR township received its name in honor of an early land surveyor.

WEME (pronounced in two syllables), a small hamlet in section 18, Eddy, was named for Hans Weme, a Norwegian merchant, who was its first postmaster.

WILLBORG, a former postoffice in the south part of Eddy, was named for a Swedish farmer, Mart E. Willborg, who was the first postmaster and was the county judge of probate in the years 1904-09.

WINSOR township is in honor of Hans C. Widness, a Norwegian farmer, who was the first postmaster there. The name of the postoffice (now discontinued) and township was thus changed and anglicized in accordance with his suggestion.

Among names of discontinued postoffices, two of fanciful or romantic significance were Moonlight, in section 3, Eddy, and Starlight, in section 21, Sinclair.

LAKES AND STREAMS.

In the foregoing list of townships and villages, attention has been given to Bear creek, Clear brook, Mallard lake, Moose creek, and the Pine lake and river.

Rice lake and the Upper Rice lake, and the Wild Rice river, have probably borne these names in four successive languages, the Dakota or Sioux, the Ojibway, French, and English. The oldest printed reference is in the narrative of Joseph La France, a French and Ojibway halfbreed, who in 1740-42 traveled and hunted with the Indians of a large region in northwestern Minnesota and in Canada northward to Lakes Winnipeg and Manitoba and Hudson bay. In the story of his wandering, given by Dobbs in "An Account of the Countries adjoining to Hudson's Bay," published in London in 1744, La France described the Upper Rice lake, in Bear Creek and Minerva townships of this county, as follows: "The Lake Du Siens is but small, being not above 3 Leagues in Circuit; but all around its Banks, in the shallow Water and Marshes, grows a kind of wild Oat, of the Nature of Rice; the outward Husk is black, but the Grain within is white and clear like Rice; this the Indians beat off into their Canoes, and use it for Food." (Minnesota in Three Centuries, 1908, vol. I, pages 299-302.) This French name, Du Siens, seems probably to be from the Dakota word, psin, meaning wild rice.

Gilfillan gave the present Ojibway name of this Upper Rice lake as "Ajawewesitagun sagaiigun, meaning the lake where there is a portage from water running one way to waters running the opposite way, or briefly, Height-of-land lake." The portage was from the Mississippi river through this lake into the Wild Rice river.

Seven miles distant westward, lying on the course of the Wild Rice river, is the larger Rice lake, in T. 145, R. 38, of this county, where our names of both the river and lake are received from the Ojibway name, noted by Gilfillan as "Ga-manominiganjikawi zibi, The river where wild rice stalk or plant is growing; so called from the last lake through which it flowed." According to the prevalent usage of the Ojibways, they gave to the river their name of the lake whence it flows.

Nearly all the area of this lower Rice lake has only shallow water, one to five feet deep, so that the lake is filled with a luxuriant growth of wild rice. It presents in the late summer, when viewed from a distance, the appearance of a grassy marsh. The greater part of this

CLEARWATER COUNTY 125

valuable grain gathered for food by the Indians of the White Earth reservation is obtained from this lake and the Upper Rice lake.

Thompson's map, from his field notes in 1798, has Wild Rice river; Long's map, 1823, has this name, and also Rice lake; and Nicollet's map, 1843, has "Manomin R. or Wild Rice R." and "Rice L."

Four-legged lake, in Dudley, is a translation of its Ojibway name, given by Gilfillan as "Nio-gade (pronounced in four syllables) . . . from an old Indian of that name who lived there." Its outlet flows west into Ruffee creek, called by the Ojibways Four-legged creek, which flows north to the Clearwater river. Our name of this creek is in honor of Charles A. Ruffee, of Brainerd, who was appointed in 1874 by Governor Davis to make inquiries and report on "the condition of the several bands of Chippewa Indians of Minnesota," with recommendations for state legislation toward their "ultimately becoming citizens of the State." ("Aborigines of Minnesota," 1911, pages 671-3.)

Lost river, flowing from Holst and Eddy northwest and west to join the Clearwater river in Red Lake county, received its name for its formerly passing in section 17, Winsor, and for several miles onward, beneath a floating bog in a spruce swamp; but its course has been opened by a state ditch, with reclamation of adjoining lands for agriculture.

Peterson lake, in sections 4 and 5, Holst, was named for Nels M. Peterson, owner of the land on its south side.

Popple township has Minnow lake, named for its little fishes, in section 22, near the sources of Clearwater river; and Sabe lake, a name whose origin was not ascertained, on the south side of section 24.

Lake Lomond, adjoining the north end of Bagley village, was named by Randolph A. Wilkinson, of St. Paul, general solicitor of the Great Northern railway company, for the "bonny Loch Lomond" of Scotland, the largest and most beautiful lake in Great Britain.

Walker brook, flowing into the Clearwater river at the southeast corner of Bagley village, was named for Thomas B. Walker, of Minneapolis, who engaged extensively during many years in lumbering on the Clearwater river and its branches. He is also honored by the name of the county seat of Cass county, as noted, with a biographic sketch, in its chapter.

Nora township has Walker Brook lake, in section 1; Mud lake, crossed by the east side of sections 25 and 36; and Mosquito creek, flowing west and southwest, tributary to Rice lake.

Little Mississippi river, beginning in the north part of Shevlin, on a nearly level tract within a mile south of the Clearwater river, runs south and southeast to Manomin or Rice lake and the Mississippi in the southeast part of Jones township, Beltrami county. It was called Piniddiwin river by Schoolcraft in 1832, an abbreviation of the Ojibway name, meaning "the place of violent deaths, in allusion to an inroad and murder committed at this place, in former times, by the Sioux" (that is, at or near the mouth of this stream).

Tamarack lake, in sections 26 and 35, T. 146, R. 38, is named for the inclosing woods, consisting largely of the tamarack, our American larch.

Long lake, in section 24, Rice, extending southeast into Itasca township, and Heart lake, in section 25, Rice, are named from their shape.

Gill and Sucker lakes, in sections 20 and 29, Itasca, are named for their species of fish, caught in gill nets.

Big La Salle lake is crossed by the east line of sections 12 and 13, Itasca, lying partly in Hubbard county. It is tributary, with the smaller La Salle lake, a mile and a half farther north in that county, to the Mississippi by a short stream flowing north, which was named La Salle river by Glazier in 1881. These recent names, in the latest atlas of Minnesota, are adopted to preserve in this region one of the historic names used by Schoolcraft and Nicollet, who described and mapped a Lake Marquette and a Lake La Salle on the Schoolcraft or Yellow Head river, two to three miles south of the site of Bemidji. Only one lake is there, although nearly divided into two by a strait, and both parts are now named together as Lake Marquette.

ITASCA STATE PARK.

Lake Itasca, the head of the Mississippi, and the greater part of the State Park inclosing this lake lie in Clearwater county. Oldest of our state parks, its place at the source of the greatest river of North America gives to it national significance and value, geographic, historic, and educational.

The first expedition seeking to reach the head of the Mississippi was that of General Lewis Cass in 1820, penetrating the northern forest to Cass lake, which seems to have been regarded for some years afterward as the principal source of the river. A few years later, in 1823, Beltrami traversed the country between the Red River valley and the upper Mississippi, crossing Red lake and entering the Mississippi basin above Cass lake by way of the Turtle lake and river, which, from his giving the name Lake Julia to a little lake at the water divide, are called the Julian sources of the Mississippi. But another stream, somewhat larger than the Turtle river, was known to come from the west and southwest, and in 1832 Schoolcraft, under instructions from the government, conducted an expedition up that stream, which has ever since been rightly considered the main Mississippi, to the lake at its head, which the Indians called Omushkos, that is, Elk lake. Schoolcraft then named it Itasca, from the Latin words *veritas,* truth, and *caput,* head, supplied to him by Boutwell, the name being made by writing the words together and cutting off, like Procrustes, the first and last syllables. Four years later, in 1836, Nicollet more fully explored this lake, and claimed that its largest tributary, the creek or brook flowing into the extremity of its southwest arm, is "truly the infant Mississippi."

Here the question rested until Captain Willard Glazier in 1881, six years after the Government sectional survey of that area, made his expedition to Itasca and to the lake in section 22, T. 143, R. 36, called by the Government survey plats Elk lake, lying close southeast of the southwestern arm of Itasca, and thence voyaged in a canoe to the mouths of the Mississippi. His ridiculous re-naming of Elk lake for himself, with assertion that it should be regarded as the main source of this river, in his subsequently published books and maps, directed the attention of geographers anew to the determination of the source of the Great River.

Willard Glazier was born in Fowler, N. Y., August 22, 1841; and died in Albany, N. Y., in 1905. He served in New York regiments in the civil war, attaining the rank of captain, and published several books on the history of the war. His biography, entitled "Sword and Pen," by John Algernon Owens (written in large part by Glazier), was published in 1884, 516 pages, including 80 pages on his expedition in the summer and autumn of 1881 by the canoe route from Leech lake to Lake Itasca and Elk lake and thence down the Mississippi, with a map of the sources of this river. His later books on the Mississippi, are "Down the Great River," 1887, 443 pages, with the map redrawn, several names on it being changed; and "Headwaters of the Mississippi," 1893, 527 pages, with six maps, including the narrative of Glazier's second expedition, going again in 1891, with a large party, to the head of the river for reinforcement of the claims that Lake Glazier, as named in 1881, is the geographic head and chief source. In this expedition the route, both in going and returning, was by the wagon road from Park Rapids to Lake Itasca.

On account of the claims of Glazier and his friends, for Elk lake, renamed Lake Glazier, to be regarded as the head of the Mississippi, Hopewell Clarke, of Minneapolis and later of St. Paul, made in October, 1886, for Ivison, Blakeman, Taylor and Co., publishers, New York, a reconnoissance of Lake Itasca and its basin. His report, which appeared in Science for December 24, 1886, fully sustained the work and conclusion of Nicollet, before noted.

The Minnesota Historical Society next took up an investigation of the sources of this river, and the report of its committee, presented by Gen. James H. Baker at a meeting on February 8, 1887, repudiated Glazier's claims, and refused the substitution of his name for Elk lake. But a good result from this controversy was the great increase of public interest in the geography and history of the Itasca region, which brought within a few years the establishment of this State Park. In October, 1888, Hon. J. V. Brower began his explorations and surveys of Lake Itasca and its environs, which continued through four years, being commissioned in February, 1889, to this work by the Historical Society; and he was the chief factor in securing the establishment of the Park by an act of the state legislature, April 20, 1891, followed by an act of Congress, August 3, 1892, which granted to the state for this Park all undisposed lands of the United States within its area.

The earliest printed proposal for the Itasca Park was a letter of Alfred J. Hill, in the St. Paul Dispatch, March 28, 1889. Throughout the work of Brower in examination and surveys of the park area, Hill was a colaborer with him concerning the history of the early Spanish and French explorers of the whole extent of the Mississippi, contributing much of his excellent Volume VII of the Minnesota Historical Society Collections, entitled "The Mississippi River and its Source" (1893, pages xv, 360).

The claims of Glazier are effectually cancelled by Brower in this work. Emile Levasseur in France, and N. H. Winchell, state geologist of Minnesota, followed with papers indorsing Brower's conclusion, that Nicollet's "infant Mississippi . . . a cradled Hercules," in the southern part of the State Park, above Lake Itasca, is the veritable, highest, and farthest source of this river (Minnesota Historical Society Collections, vol. VIII, Part II, pages 213-231, published December 1, 1896).

Jacob Vradenberg Brower, archaeologist and author, was born in York, Mich., January 21, 1844; and died in St. Cloud, Minn., June 1, 1905. He came to Long Prairie, Minn., in 1860; served in the First Minnesota cavalry, 1862-3; served in the U. S. navy, 1864-5; studied law and was admitted to the bar in 1873; was a representative in the legislature, 1873; was register of the U. S. land office in St. Cloud, 1874-9; was the first commissioner of Itasca Park, 1891-95; explored and mapped many aboriginal mounds. He was author of Volume VII, M. H. S. Collections, before cited; Volume XI in the same series, entitled "Itasca State Park, an Illustrated History" (1905, 285 pages); "Prehistoric Man at the Headwater Basin of the Mississippi" (1895, 77 pages); "The Missouri River and its Utmost Source" (1896, 150 pages, and a second edition, 1897, 206 pages); Memoirs of Explorations in the Basin of the Mississippi, a series of eight quarto volumes: I. Quivira, 1898, 96 pages; II. Harahey, 1899, 133 pages; III. Mille Lac, 1900, 140 pages; IV. Kathio, 1901, 136 pages; V. Kakabikansing, 1902, 126 pages; VI. Minnesota, Discovery of its Area, 1903, 127 pages; VII. Kansas, Monumental Perpetuation of its Earliest History, 1541-1896, 1903, 119 pages; VIII. Mandan, 1904, 158 pages. Biographic sketches and portraits of Brower and his associates in archaeology, Alfred J. Hill and Theodore H. Lewis, are given by Prof. N. H. Winchell in "The Aborigines of Minnesota," 1911, pages vi-xiv.

The people of this state will forever remember Brower with gratitude, as the founder of Itasca Park, and its defender and guardian, amidst many difficulties and discouragements, through his last years. His heavy cares and efforts for truthfulness of the river history, and to protect the Park and Lake against ruthless damage by lumbermen, are shown throughout his latest book, the M. H. S. Volume XI; but in the darkest hour, when the biennial session of the state legislature in 1893 adjourned without providing for the maintenance of the Park, with unfailing courage he exclaimed, "Itasca State Park shall live forever!"

The Itasca Moraine.

Another subject of much interest is presented by the admirable development of a belt of marginal moraine hills, knolls, and short ridges, traversing the south and west edges of the Park. This is part of a very extensive course of such irregularly hilly deposits of glacial and modified drift crossing Minnesota, named the Itasca or Tenth moraine. It is one of twelve similar marginal moraines traced in this state by the present writer, formed at stages of temporary halt or readvance during the general recession and departure of the continental ice-sheet.

Nomenclature of the Park.

Most of the information for this list is from Brower's M. H. S. Volumes VII and XI, supplemented with various details from other sources.

The Ojibways call Itasca lake Omushkos, as before noted, meaning Elk lake, which also is their name of the river thence to Lake Bemidji, as similarly they call it Bemidji river thence to Cass lake. In translation of the Ojibway name, the early French fur traders called Itasca Lac La Biche, and Beltrami in like manner named it "Doe lake, west source of the Mississippi." Boutwell wrote in his Journal, 1832: "This is a small but beautiful body of water. . . . Its form is exceedingly irregular, from which the Indians gave it the name of Elk, in reference to its branching horns." (M. H. S. Collections, vol. I.) Brower wrote in Volume VII, page 119: "The topographical formation of the locality in its physical features,—the shape of an elk's head with the horns representing the east and west arms,—no doubt gave it the name 'Elk.'"

Gen. James H. Baker, surveyor general for Minnesota, transferred the name Elk lake on the plats of the government survey, in 1875-76, to the lake at the east side of the Southwest arm of Itasca, designated by the Ojibways, as noted by Gilfillan, "Pekegumag sagaiigun, the water which juts off from another water." The same name was also used by the Ojibways, and is retained without translation by the white people, for a lake and falls of the Mississippi in Itasca county, and for a lake and Indian battle-ground in Pine county, being for those places commonly spelled Pokegama.

This lake had been visited by Julius Chambers in 1872, who then called it "Dolly Varden" from the name of his canoe; and in 1881 Captain Glazier's party applied to it his name, which he endeavored strenuously but unavailingly to maintain, as related in preceding pages. A short time previous to Glazier's visit, Rev. Joseph A. Gilfillan, going there in May, 1881, had named it "Breck lake, in honor of the distinguished first missionary of the American [Episcopal] church to St. Paul and vicinity, who was afterwards first missionary of the church to the Chippewa Indians around the sources of the Mississippi." Although worthily renamed for James Lloyd Breck (b. 1818, d. 1876), the name Elk lake is yet more desirably retained, because it preserves in translation the aboriginal title which was superseded by Schoolcraft's Itasca.

The only island of Itasca was named for Schoolcraft by his party, 1832. The three branches or arms of Itasca are called by Brower the North, East, and West arms; but the latter two are also known as the Southeast and Southwest arms.

The largest affluent, Nicollet's "infant Mississippi," is mapped by Brower as "Mississippi River" in "Nicollet Valley." This stream is also often called Nicollet creek, as by Winchell, in 1896, and the map of the Mississippi River Commission, 1900. Three lakelets noted there by Nicollet, 1836, are "Nicollet's Lower, Middle, and Upper lakes." The head stream flowing into the Upper lake rises from the "Mississippi Springs," above which, with underground drainage to them, is Floating Moss lake; and close above, and flowing into it from the south, is Whipple lake, at the head of the visible surface drainage. This last name was given by Gilfillan in 1881, to honor Bishop Henry B. Whipple (b. 1822, d. 1901), renowned for his interest in missions for both the Ojibways and Sioux of this state.

Southward from Whipple lake, and ensconced in hollows among the low hills and ridges of the Itasca moraine, are the three little Triplet lakes; the much larger Morrison lake, named by Brower in honor of William Morrison, the early trader who was at Elk lake (since named Itasca) in 1804; Little Elk lake; Groseilliers and Radisson lakes, named by Brower for the first white men in Minnesota, whose travels here, in 1655-56 and again in 1660, are the theme of a paper by the present writer (M. H. S. Collections, vol. X, Part II, 1905, pages 449-594, with a map); the Picard lakes, named for Anthony Auguelle, "called the Pickard du Gay," a companion of Hennepin, 1680; Mikenna lake, named by Alfred J. Hill, of undetermined meaning; and the large Lake Hernando de Soto, commemorating the Spanish discoverer of the Mississippi, 1541, with its Brower island, named in honor of J. V. Brower by a committee of the Minnesota Historical Society. These many lakes of the morainic belt in the southwest part of the Park, with several smaller lakelets there remaining unnamed, are believed to send seeping waters northward to springs, rivulets, and creeks, which are tributary to the Mississippi above the West arm of Itasca and to Elk lake. For this reason their area is named on Brower's maps as "the Greater Ultimate Reservoir Bowl at the source of the Mississippi river."

Elk lake receives four small streams. At the west is Siegfried creek, named by Brower for A. H. Siegfried, a representative of the Louisville Courier-Journal, who with others made a recreational expedition to Itasca and Elk lakes in July, 1879. Hall lake, on the upper part of this creek, was also named by Brower, in honor of Edwin S. Hall, the U. S. surveyor in 1875 for several townships here, including the Park area. These names displace the Eagle creek and Lake Alice, names given in 1881 by Glazier, the latter being for his daughter, who ten years afterward, in 1891, was a member of the second Glazier expedition.

The three other tributaries of Elk lake are from the south, namely, Elk creek, on the southwest; Clarke creek, commemorating Hopewell Clarke, before mentioned as a surveyor here in 1886, with its mouth at the head of Chambers bay; and Gay-gued-o-say creek, named for Nicollet's Ojibway guide to Itasca in 1836. Clarke lake and Deer Park lake flow into the last of these creeks at stages of high water.

Chambers bay on the south side of Elk lake, and Chambers creek, its short outlet to Lake Itasca, honor Julius Chambers, the journalist and author, whose expedition here in 1872, before noted, probably became a chief incentive for his publication of a historical and descriptive book in 1910, entitled "The Mississippi River and its Wonderful Valley" (308 pages, with 80 illustrations and maps).

At the south end of the East arm of Itasca, Mary creek brings the inflow from a series of lakes. The lowest, Mary lake, is named like the creek, in honor of the wife of Peter Turnbull, a land surveyor and civil engineer from Canada, who opened the northern part of the road from Park Rapids to Itasca in 1883, and resided during the next two years on the east side of its East arm. In 1885 they removed to Park Rapids, where Mrs. Turnbull died in May, 1889.

The higher lakes of Mary Valley, in their order from north to south, are the small Twin lakes; Danger lake, so named by Mr. Turnbull on account of water "flooding the ice surface in winter at its south shore," renamed Deming lake for Hon. Portius C. Deming, of Minneapolis, a friend and promoter of the interests of Itasca Park, who later was the president of the Minneapolis Board of Park Commissioners; Ako lake, named for one of Hennepin's companions, 1680, whose name is also spelled Accault; and Josephine lake, in honor of a daughter of Commissioner Brower, who has been a teacher in the State Normal School at St. Cloud, and in the public schools of Minneapolis. The upper part of Mary Valley, holding these lakes, was called by Brower "the Lesser Ultimate Reservoir Bowl." This valley, excepting its mouth and west border, lies, with all its lakes, in the edge of Hubbard county, into which the Itasca Park extends a mile along its east side.

South and southwest of Josephine lake, and beyond the water divide, several small lakes lie in the southeast corner of the Park, mostly having no surface outlets but tributary by underground seepage to the basin of Crow Wing river. These include Sibilant lake, named for its form resembling the letter S; Ni-e-ma-da lake, of which Brower stated that "the name is composite in form, not of Indian origin;" a narrow northern arm of Little Man Trap lake, so named, like the larger Man Trap lake a dozen miles eastward, because many peninsulas and the tamarack swamps at the head of its bays baffled the hunter, or in former times the "cruiser" in search for pine lands, when attempting to pass around it; Gilfillan lake, in honor of Rev. Joseph A. Gilfillan (b. 1838, d. 1913), Episcopal missionary to the Ojibways in northern Minnesota during twenty-five years; and Frazier lake, named for a homesteader whose cabin was beside it.

Other streams flowing into Lake Itasca include Island creek, tributary to the west side of the North arm, opposite to Schoolcraft island; French creek, between Island creek and Hill point, named for George H. French, of the survey for the Mississippi River Commission, 1900; Boutwell creek, named for Rev. William Thurston Boutwell (b. 1803, d. 1890), who accompanied the Schoolcraft expedition in 1832; Sha-wun-uk-u-mig creek, commemorating the Ojibway guide of Rev. J. A. Gilfillan in his visit to the Itasca basin in 1881; and Floating Bog creek, emptying into the bay of this name about a half mile east of the island.

Tributaries from the west to the Mississippi river above Lake Itasca are Demaray creek, named in honor of Mrs. Georgiana Demaray, daughter of William Morrison, Spring Ridge creek, and Howard creek, named for Mrs. Jane Schoolcraft Howard, daughter of the explorer and author, Henry Rowe Schoolcraft.

Named points and bays of the Itasca shore, especially observed in canoeing, are Bear point, at the west side of Floating Bog bay; Turnbull point, on the west side of the East arm, commemorating Peter Turnbull, before mentioned; Comber bay and point, next on the north, for W. G. Comber, assistant in the survey of the Park area for the Mississippi River Commission, 1900; O'Neil point, a little farther northwest, for Hon. John H. O'Neil, of Park Rapids; Chaney bay and point, next south of Turnbull point, in honor of Josiah B. Chaney (b. 1828, d. 1908), newspaper librarian of the Minnesota Historical Society, who visited the Itasca Park in 1901 and 1903; Ray's bay and point, nearly a half mile farther south, for Fred G. Ray, of the Mississippi River Commission survey, 1900; Ozawindib or Yellow Head point, at the entrance to the West arm, for the Ojibway guide of Schoolcraft's party in 1832; Tamarack point, a quarter of a mile southwest from the last; Garrison point, on the west side of the West arm, commemorating Oscar E. Garrison (b. 1825, d. 1886), who examined the Lake Itasca region and the river below in 1880, for the Forestry Department of the United States Census; and Hill point, on the west side of the North arm, named in honor of Alfred J. Hill (b. 1823, d. 1895), the archaeologist, who, as before noted, was the first to propose the establishment of this State Park.

Several additional names of lakes are to be noted: Bohall lake, for Henry Bohall, an assistant with Brower in 1889; Hays lake, for an assistant in 1891; Kirk lake, for Thomas H. Kirk, author of an "Illustrated History

CLEARWATER COUNTY   133

of Minnesota" (1887, 244 pages), who visited Itasca and Elk lakes in 1887; Lyendecker lake, for a comrade of Brower in his first visit to Itasca, 1888; Allen lake, for Lieut. James Allen (b. 1806, d. 1846), who accompanied Schoolcraft's expedition in 1832, and whose very interesting report of it was published twenty-eight years afterward in the American State Papers (vol. V, Military Affairs, 1860, pages 312-344, with a map); Budd lake, "after an Ohio family name;" McKay lake, for Rev. Stanley A. McKay, of Owatonna, Minn., "who in the month of June, 1891, celebrated the ceremonies of baptism at Itasca lake;" Green lake, close west of Chaney bay; Iron Corner lake, near the iron post that marks the northeast corner of Becker county; and Augusta, Powder Horn, and Musquash lakes, named by the Mississippi River Commission, 1900, adjoining the southwest side of Morrison lake. The last of these lakes, Musquash, has the Algonquian name of the muskrat, a fur-bearer whose houses dot many of our shallow lakes.

Crescent springs, Elk springs, Nicollet springs, the Mississippi springs, and Ocano springs, the last bearing a name "found in Schoolcraft's Narrative," are shown on Brower's maps of the Park.

Rhodes hill was named for for D. C. Rhodes, of Verndale, Minn., photographer of the Brower survey; Morrison hill, like Morrison lake, for the first recorded white visitor at Itasca; Morrow Heights, in honor of A. T. Morrow, director of the survey of the Itasca basin for the Mississippi River Commission, 1900; Ockerson Heights, for J. A. Ockerson, also a surveyor for that Commission; Aiton Heights, after Prof. George B. Aiton, of Minneapolis and later of Grand Rapids, who made botanic examinations of the Park in 1891; and Comber island in Morrison lake, for W. G. Comber, who has thus threefold honors, of this island and of a point and a bay on the Itasca shore.

The Lind Saddle Trail was named in honor of Governor John Lind, who visited Itasca in 1899, then ordering this trail to be cut through the woods, as his personal donation for the improvement of the Park.

Close north of the Park limits, Division creek (also called Sucker creek) flows into the Mississippi from the heights on the west, "which divide the waters flowing to Hudson's Bay and the Gulf of Mexico."

McMullen lake (formerly known as Squaw lake), close outside the Park at the northwest, was named by Brower in honor of William McMullen, the first permanent settler at Itasca lake, in 1889, on the east side of the North arm. The former name is from the Algonquian word meaning a woman, anglicized as "squaw," used commonly among the Ojibways as the ending, qua, of feminine names, like the final syllable, win, of the same use among the Sioux.

Kakabikans rapids, noted by Schoolcraft in 1855 as a name from the the Ojibway language, meaning Little falls or rapids, are formed by very abundant glacial boulders in the channel of the Mississippi a few miles below Itasca lake.

Several names which had their origin from the expedition of Glazier in 1881 are retained by popular use in Hubbard county, but only one has been so retained within the limits of the Itasca Park, this being La Salle river, in the northeast corner, named, with the lakes on its course to the north, in honor of the renowned early French explorer. It was called Andrus creek by Brower in 1892, "after the treasurer of the Minnesota Game and Fish Commission." Schoolcraft in 1832 had mapped it as "Cano R." and on the map of his "Summary Narrative," published in 1855, it was called "De Witt Clinton's R.," but in the text it is named "Chemaun or Ocano." The former word, Chemaun, is Ojibway for a birch canoe, as used in Longfellow's "Song of Hiawatha;" and the latter word, Ocano, is from the French "aux canots," that is, at or of canoes, which was the ancient and original form that became anglicized into the name of Cannon river, in southeastern Minnesota.

A glacial lake was held temporarily in the Itasca basin by the barrier of the departing ice-sheet at the end of the Ice Age, with an area "several times the present size of Itasca lake," named by Brower in Volume XI, Winchell lake, in honor of Prof. N. H. Winchell. This may be preferably called Glacial Lake Winchell, to distinguish it from Winchell lake in Cook county.

Newton Horace Winchell was born in Northeast, Dutchess county, N. Y., December 17, 1839; and died in Minneapolis, May 2, 1914. Coming to Minnesota in 1872, and residing in Minneapolis, he was state geologist twenty-eight years, 1872-1900; was editor of the American Geologist, 1888-1905; and was the archaeologist of the Minnesota Historical Society, 1906-14. His contribution to the Itasca Park literature, entitled "The Source of the Mississippi," is in the M. H. S. Volume VIII (pages 226-231); a biographic memorial of him, in Volume XV (pages 824-830, with a portrait); and a more full memorial, in the Bulletin of the Minnesota Academy of Science (Volume V, pages 73-116).

Like the majestic progress of an epic poem or a grand drama, the history of the gradual discovery of the Mississippi river runs through four centuries. Begun when Amerigo Vespucci in 1498 mapped the delta and mouths of this mighty stream on the north shore of the Gulf of Mexico, it continued till Brower in 1889-92 mapped the shores and islands of Lake Hernando de Soto, in the south edge of Itasca Park. The moving picture of this history is portrayed in words and in maps by the volumes of the M. H. S. Collections. In the nomenclature of the Park a good number of the great explorers of the river are recalled, De Soto, Groseilliers and Radisson, La Salle, Schoolcraft, Nicollet. The vain endeavors of Glazier to link his name with those heroes aroused the just indignation of geographers and the officers of the Minnesota Historical Society. During a decade or longer a great strife raged concerning the true head of the Mississippi and the rightful name of Elk lake. In 1905 Glazier and Brower, chief opponents in the strife, died; but the Itasca State Park, which grew from it, "shall live forever."

COOK COUNTY

This county, established March 9, 1874, was named in honor of Major Michael Cook, of Faribault, a prominent citizen and a brave soldier in the civil war. He was born in Morris county, N. J., March 17, 1828; came to Minnesota, settling in Faribault, in 1855, and, being a carpenter, aided in building some of the first frame houses there; and was a territorial and state senator, 1857 to 1862. In September, 1862, he was mustered into the Tenth Minnesota regiment, in which he was appointed major, and served until he fell mortally wounded in the battle of Nashville, December 16, 1864, his death occurring eleven days later.

Colonel Charles H. Graves, the state senator from Duluth, introduced the bill to establish this county and to name it in honor of Verendrye, the pioneer of exploration on the northern boundary of Minnesota; but the name was changed before the bill was enacted as a law. It has been thought by some that the name adopted was in commemoration of John Cook, who was killed by Ojibway Indians, as also his entire family, in 1872, his house at Audubon, Minn., being burned to conceal the deed. Colonel Graves has stated, in a letter, that this name was selected to honor Major Cook.

It may well be hoped that some county, yet to be formed adjoining the north line of Minnesota, will receive the name Verendrye, in historic commemoration of the explorations, hardships, and sacrifices of this patriotic and truly noble French explorer. He was the founder of the fur trade in northern Minnesota, in Manitoba, and the Saskatchewan region, where it greatly flourished during the next hundred years; and two of his sons were the first white men to see the Rocky mountains, or at least some eastern range or outpost group of the great Cordilleran mountain belt.

Townships and Villages.

Information of the origins of geographic names in Cook county was gathered during my visit in August, 1916, at Grand Marais, the county seat, from Thomas I. Carter, the county auditor; Axel E. Berglund, county surveyor; George Leng, clerk of the court; William J. Clinch, superintendent of schools; and John Drourillard and George Mayhew, of Grand Marais.

Each of the organized townships in this county comprises several government survey townships; and Grand Marais and Rosebush are very irregular in their outlines, stretching from areas adjoining Lake Superior to areas on the international boundary, with narrow strips connecting their southern and northern parts.

COLVILLE township, organized in 1906, was named in honor of Colonel William Colvill, to whose name a silent *e* is added for the township. He was born in Forestville, N. Y., April 5, 1830; and died in Minneapolis, June 12, 1905. He came to Red Wing, Minn., in 1854, and the next year established the Red Wing Sentinel, a Democratic newspaper. He served as captain and colonel of the First Minnesota regiment, 1861-4; was colonel of the First Minnesota Heavy Artillery, 1865, and was brevetted brigadier general. He was a representative in the legislature in 1865, and again in 1878; and was attorney general of the state, 1866-8. In the battle of Gettysburg, 1863, he led his regiment in a famous charge, one of the noblest sacrifices to duty in all the annals of warfare. In his later years, Colonel Colvill homesteaded a claim on the Lake Superior shore in this township (section 9, T. 61, R. 2 E.), but his home previously, and also afterward, was near Red Wing. In 1909 his statue in bronze was placed in the rotunda of the state capitol.

GRAND MARAIS township received this French name, meaning a great marsh, in the early fur-trading times, referring to a marsh, twenty acres or less in area, nearly at the level of Lake Superior, situated at the head of the little bay and harbor which led to the settlement of the village there. Another small bay on the east, less protected from storms is separated from the harbor by a slight projecting point and a short beach. In allusion to the two bays, the Ojibways name the bay of Grand Marais as "Kitchi-bitobig, the great duplicate water; a parallel or double body of water like a bayou" (Gilfillan).

GRAND PORTAGE, a village and formerly a very important trading place, at the head of the bay of this name, and at the southeast end of the Grand portage, nine miles long, to the Pigeon river above its principal falls, has the distinction of being the most eastern and oldest settlement of white men in the area of Minnesota. Probably during the period of Verendrye's explorations, this place became the chief point for landing goods from the large canoes used in the navigation of the Great Lakes, and for their being dispatched onward, from the end of this long portage, in smaller canoes to the many trading posts of all the rich fur country northwest of Lake Superior. In 1767, when Carver went there in the hope of purchasing goods, Grand Portage was an important rendezvous and trading post. At the time of the Revolutionary War, as Gen. James H. Baker has well said, it was the "commercial emporium" of the northwestern fur trade.

Fort Charlotte was the name of the trading post and station of the Northwest Fur Company at the western end of the portage, on the Pigeon river.

HOVLAND, the oldest organized township of this county, is in compliment to a pioneer settler named Brunas, for his native place in Norway.

LUTSEN township was named by its most prominent citizen, Carl A. A. Nelson, for a town in Prussian Saxony, made memorable by the battle there, 1632, in which the renowned Gustavus Adolphus, king of Sweden, lost his life.

COOK COUNTY 137

MAPLE HILL township has extensive sugar maple woods, on the highland five to ten miles back from Lake Superior.

ROSEBUSH township, organized in 1907, took its name from Rose Bush river, as it is popularly known, in translation of its Ojibway name, Oginekan, though called "Fall river" on maps, in the east edge of T. 61, R. 1 W. The creek a mile farther west, mapped as "Rose Bush river," has no recognized name among the settlers.

SCHROEDER township and village are in honor of John Schroeder, president of a lumber company having offices in Ashland and Milwaukee, Wis., for whom pine logs have been cut and rafted away from the neighboring Temperance, Cross, and Two Island rivers.

TOFTE, likewise the name of a township and village, founded in 1898, is in honor of settlers having this surname, derived from their former home in the district of Bergen, Norway.

LAKES AND STREAMS.

Gilfillan, in his list of "Minnesota Geographical Names derived from the Chippewa language," wrote: "Pigeon river is Omimi-zibi, Omimi meaning pigeon, and zibi . . . . river." The accent of Omimi is on the second syllable, and *i* has the sound of the English long *e*. "The Song of Hiawatha" correctly anglicizes it,

"Cooed the pigeon, the Omemee."

Until 1870 or later, the passenger pigeon was common or abundant throughout Minnesota, coming early in April, breeding here, and returning southward in October and November. During the next thirty years they became scarce, and about the year 1900 they perished utterly from all that great region, eastern North America, where from time immemorial they had been very abundant. The species, once represented by countless millions, undoubtedly is extinct.

This river, which is the boundary between the United States and Canada, was delineated on "the oldest map of the region west of Lake Superior, ... traced by a chief of the Assiniboines, named Ochagach, for Verendrye, in 1730," which is published in the Final Report of the Geology of Minnesota (vol. I, 1884, pages 18, 19). A series of twelve lakes is shown by this map on the canoe route from the mouth of Pigeon river to "Lac Sesakinaga" (Saganaga), the fourth and eighth being named respectively "Lac Long" and "Lac Plat." Hence came the name "Long lake," given to the lower part of Pigeon river on the map of John Mitchell, 1755, which was used by the British and American commissioners in the Treaty of Paris, 1783, providing that the international boundary should run "through the middle of the said Long lake and the water communication between it and the Lake of the Woods, to the said Lake of the Woods; thence through the said lake to the most northwestern point thereof." (M. H. S. Collections, vol. XV, 1915, pages 379-392, with map.)

In 1775 this stream was called "the river Aux Groseilles," that is, Gooseberry river, by the older Alexander Henry.

Pigeon Falls, 70 feet high, on the Pigeon river about two miles from its mouth, are pictured in the "Geology of Minnesota" (vol. IV, 1899, plate PP, also page 509). About a mile up from these falls, the river has a sharp angle in its course, pointing northward, called "The Horn."

In Split Rock Canyon, noted on the map of Cook county by Jewett and Son, 1911, about a half mile to one mile below (northeast from) the western end of the Grand Portage road, Pigeon river has "Falls, 144 feet." These falls were called "the Great Cascades" by Norwood in 1852, who stated, in his report for the Owen Geological Survey, that the river there descends 144 feet in a distance of 400 yards, through a narrow gorge formed by perpendicular walls of rock, varying from 40 to 120 feet in height.

Partridge falls, an upper fall 30 feet high, and a lower fall, very close below, falling 10 feet, are on this river about two miles westward, by the zigzag course of the stream, from the end of the Grand portage. The height of these falls was exaggerated by Mackenzie, in his "Voyages from Montreal," published in 1801, to be 120 feet, probably confounding the Partridge falls with the much higher falls last mentioned. Dr. Alexander Winchell in 1887 called these falls "the Minnehaha of the boundary."

Fowl portage, and the South and North Fowl lakes, lowest in the series of lakes on the Pigeon river, are translated from their early French name, Outarde (a bustard, here in the usage of the voyageurs applied to the Canadian goose, Branta canadensis, our most common wild species), which was probably a translation from the aboriginal Ojibway name. More definitely, therefore, these would be Goose portage and lakes.

Next are Moose portage and Moose lake, which Mackenzie called Elk portage and lake, but which Thompson mapped, on the survey for the international boundary, 1826, as "Moose lake, d'Original." Both the English and French names came from the Ojibway, "Mozo sagaiigun" (Gilfillan),

Big Cherry portage, named for the wild cherries growing there, the Lower and Upper Lily lakes, "where there is plenty of water lilies," and the Little Cherry portage, translated from the French names used by Mackenzie, lead to Mountain lake, called Hill lake by Norwood, translated from its Ojibway name, given by Gilfillan as "Gatchigudjiwegumag sagaiigun, the lake lying close by the mountain." This refers to Moose mountain, shown on the Jewett map, at the south side of the east end of this lake.

"The small new portage" of Mackenzie, next west of Mountain lake, was called Watap portage by Thompson, on account of the growth of jack pines, which also are referred to in the names of Watab river and township (previously noted in the chapter for Benton county).

Rove lake, called Watab lake by Norwood and by Dr. Coues, through which the canoes next passed, was called by Mackenzie "a narrow line of water," and it was so mapped later by Thompson, very narrow and somewhat crooked, whence probably came the name, to rove or wander; but it is erroneously mapped as a rather broad lake in "Geology of Minnesota" (vol. IV, plates 69 and 83), which error is retained on the maps of Cook county in our latest atlas. The Ojibway name of this lake means "the lake lying in the burnt wood country."

A very rugged and difficult portage, about a mile and a half in length, called by Mackenzie "the new Grande Portage" (on the Geol. Survey map, "Great New Portage"), leads to Rose or Mud lake, which outflows eastward into Arrow lake and river in Canada, being thus tributary to the Pigeon river. In the language of the Ojibways, "Rose lake is Ga-bagwadjiskiwagag sagaiigun, or the shallow lake with mud bottom."

From Rose lake westward two short portages, named Marten and Perch portages, with an intervening "mud pond covered with white lilies," as noted by Mackenzie, lead to South lake, as it was named by Thompson, where, wrote Mackenzie, "the waters of the Dove or Pigeon river terminate, and which is one of the sources of the great St. Lawrence in this direction."

North lake, the first in the series flowing west to the Lake of the Woods, was so named by Thompson, his South and North lakes having that relationship to the portage across the continental water divide. Mackenzie called North lake "the lake of Hauteur de Terre" (Height of Land), and by Norwood is was named "Mountain lake."

Thence the canoes went down the outflowing stream into Gunflint lake, named from flint or chert obtained in its rocks, also occurring abundantly as pebbles of its beaches, sometimes used for the flintlock guns which long preceded the invention of percussion caps. The English name is translated from the earlier Ojibway and French names.

Northward in a distance of ten miles from the mouth of Gunflint lake to Saganaga falls and lake, the international boundary has Magnetic lake, Pine or Clove lake, Granite bay, Gneiss lake, and Maraboeuf lake, with intervening stretches of the stream, broken by frequent rapids and low falls, past which portages were made. The varying characters of the outcropping rocks supply a majority of these lake names. The most northern is a Canadian French name, used by Mackenzie, 1801, and on the latest maps of Cook county, 1911 and 1916, apparently for "marsh deer or buffalo" if it were anglicized; but this name, Maraboeuf, is not found in dictionaries. Thompson in 1826 mapped it, with no name, as a narrow and quite irregularly branched lake, nearly four miles long from south to north, its jagged eastern shoreline in Canada being wholly unlike its representation in our Cook county maps.

Maraboeuf lake was called Banks' Pine lake by Prof. N. H. Winchell in 1880 (Ninth Annual Report, page 84), for its forest of jack pine (Pinus Banksiana); but in the later reports of the Minnesota Geological Survey it is mapped as Granite lake, for its lying within the area of Saganaga granite.

Mackenzie wrote that Lake Saganaga "takes its name from its numerous islands." Thompson mapped it as "Kaseiganagah lake." Gilfillan wrote, "Saganaga lake is Ga-sasuganagag sagaiigun, the lake surrounded by thick forests." (The pronunciation places the principal accent on the first syllable, and a secondary accent on the last.)

Winchell, from information given by the Ojibways, wrote in the report before cited: "The word Saganaga signifies islands, or many islands, and seems to be the plural of Saginaw." Verwyst, however, defines Saginaw in Michigan (the river, bay, city, and county), as from an Ojibway word, "Saging or Saginang, at the mouth of a river." According to Gannett, Saginaw means "Sauk place," referring to the Sauk or Sac Indians. The Michigan name and our Saganaga, therefore, are probably not alike in their origin and meaning.

Three miles from Grand Portage village and bay, the Grand Portage road crosses Poplar river, tributary to Pigeon river.

Dutchman lake lies two miles west of Grand Portage, and Teal lake is two miles northeast of that village.

"Mesqua-tawangewi zibi, or Red Sand river," as it was called by Gilfillan, and a lake of the same name, form the greater part of the west boundary of the Pigeon River Indian Reservation. This stream is also called Reservation river, and the lake is named Swamp lake on the latest maps, 1911 and 1916. In the treaty of September 30, 1854, which established the reservation, this stream is mentioned as "called by the Indians Maw-ske-gwaw-caw-maw-se-be, or Cranberry Marsh river."

Tom lake, near the center of T. 63, R. 3 E., is at the head of Kameshkeg river, meaning Swamp river, which flows north to Pigeon river.

Devil Fish and Otter lakes outflow by the next tributary of Pigeon river, called Portage brook, and a mile farther northwest it receives Stump river. Greenwood lake, west of the Devil Fish, flows south to Brulé river.

West of the Fowl lakes, the northern tiers of townships in this county have a multitude of lakes, mostly narrow and much elongated from east to west, lying in eroded hollows of the bedrocks. These include Royal lake, John lake, McFarland lake, the East and West Pike lakes, Pine lake, Long lake, and Lakes Fanny and Marinda; Crocodile, East Bear Skin, Caribou, and Clearwater lakes, in Ts. 64 and 65, R. 1 E., lying south of Rove lake; Morgan lake, Misquah (Red) lake, Cross, Horseshoe, and Swamp lakes, Aspen and Flour lakes, Hungry Jack lake, Leo lake, Poplar lake, tributary by Poplar river to the North branch of Brulé river, Daniels lake, Birch or West Bear Skin lake, Duncan's, Moss, and Partridge lakes, in Ts. 64 and 65, R. 1 W., lying south of Rose lake; Winchell lake, Gaskan and Johnson lakes, Henson lake,

COOK COUNTY

Pittsburg lake, Stray lake, another Caribou lake, Meeds lake, Moon lake, Rush, Lum, and Portage lakes, No Name or Birch lake, Dunn lake, Iron and Mayhew lakes, Pope lake, Crab lake, and Lakes Emma and Louise, in Ts. 64 and 65, R. 2 W., lying south of the South and North lakes; Kiskadinna or Colby lake, Nebogigig or Onega lake, Davis lake, Trap and Cliff lakes, Ida, Jay, and Ash lakes, Long Island lake, Finn lake, Banadad or Banner lake, Ross, George, and Karl lakes, Tucker lake and river, and Loon lake, in Ts. 64 and 65, R. 3 W., being south of Gunflint lake; Frost, Irish, Don, Tuscarora, Snipe, and Copper lakes, in T. 64, R. 4 W., and Ham, Round or Bear, Brant or Charley, Cloud, Dingoshick, Akeley, Chub, Arc, and Larch lakes, in T. 65, R. 4 W., south of Maraboeuf lake; Hub or Mesabi, East and West, Crooked or Greenwood Island, Bullis or Gill's, Little Saganaga, Rattle, and Fern lakes, in T. 64, R. 5 W., and Gabimichigama, Howard, Peter or Clothespin, French or Kakigo, Bat or Muscovado lakes, Fay or Paulson lake and Chub river outflowing from it, Jap lake, Ray, Jasper or Frog Rock, Alpine or West Sea Gull, and Red Rock lakes, and the large and very irregularly outlined Sea Gull lake, with many islands, the largest being named Cucumber island, in T. 65, R. 5 W., south of Lake Saganaga.

Many of the names of lakes in this list are of obvious derivations, as from the fish in them, the animals and birds and trees adjoining them, or from their outlines, as long, round, crooked, or having the form of a horseshoe, the crescent moon, or an arc.

The origins of only a few of the personal names borne by others of these lakes, as next noted, have been ascertained by the present writer.

Hungry Jack lake refers to an assistant on the government surveys, Andrew Jackson Scott, a veteran of the civil war, who for some time at this lake was reduced to very scanty food supplies.

Winchell lake was named for Prof. N. H. Winchell, state geologist, who is also honored by the Glacial Lake Winchell in the Itasca State Park.

Meeds lake was named in honor of Alonzo D. Meeds, of Minneapolis, who was an assistant in the Minnesota Geological Survey.

Mayhew lake is for the late Henry Mayhew, of Grand Marais, who aided for this survey in Cook county.

Charley lake and Bashitanequeb lake, the latter renamed on recent maps as Bullis or Gill's lake, are for an Ojibway, "Bashitanequeb (Charley Sucker), Indian guide, cook, and canoeman," in this survey ("Geology of Minnesota," Final Report, vol. IV, 1899, page 522, with his portrait).

Howard lake was named for one of the Howard brothers, mining prospectors, of Duluth, and Paulson lake for the owner of iron mines near it, on the Port Arthur, Duluth and Western railroad, a branch of the Canadian Northern railway.

Gilfillan recorded the following Ojibway names for several of these lakes, which have been translated to their present names used by the white people.

"Pine lake, Shingwako sagaiigun . . . Shingwak is a pine; o, a connective vowel; sagaiigun, lake."

"Near Rove lake is Ga-wakomitigweiag sagaiigun, or Clearwater lake."

"Iron lake is Biwabiko sagaiigun," the same with the town of Biwabik on the Mesabi iron range in St. Louis county.

"Ushkakweagumag sagaiigun, or Greenwood lake," has been sometimes called East Greenwood lake, to distinguish it from another of this name in Lake county.

"Muko-waiani sagaiigun, or Bear-skin lake."

Baraga's Dictionary has "Kishkadina . . . there is a very steep hill, very steep ascent." This name, with slight change of spelling, is applied on recent maps to a lake that was not named by the maps of the Minnesota Geological Survey; and the lake called Kiskadinna by that survey is now Long Island lake.

The two Caribou lakes have the Canadian French name of the American reindeer, changed from kalibu of the Micmac Indians, meaning "'pawer or scratcher,' the animal being so called from its habit of shoveling the snow with its forelegs to find the food covered by snow." The reindeer was formerly common in the north half of Minnesota.

Flour lake, which received its name on account of a cache of flour placed there during the government surveys, is erroneously spelled Flower on recent published maps. The Ojibways call this lake Pakwejigan (Bread or Flour), in allusion to this cache.

Sea Gull lake, like the Gull lake in Cass county, is a translation from the Ojibway name, referring to the American herring gull and three other species, which frequent the large lakes throughout this state.

Turning to the streams and lakes tributary to Lake Superior from Cook county, in their order from southwest to northeast, we have first the Two Island river, named for Gull and Bear islands, near its mouth.

Cross river, at Schroeder, was so called by Thomas Clark, assistant state geologist, in 1864, but later was named Baraga's river by Whittlesey in 1866. It had previously been named by the Ojibways, as Gilfillan relates, "Tchibaiatigo zibi, i. e., wood-of-the-soul-or-spirit river; they calling the Cross wood of the soul, or disembodied spirit." The origin of this name was from a cross of wood erected by Father Baraga, who, as Verwyst relates, "landed here after a perilous voyage in a small fishing boat, across Lake Superior, 1845-6." Whittlesey, in his report of explorations, published in 1866, wrote: "At the mouth of this creek there was in 1848 a rough, weather-beaten cross nailed to the tall stump of a tree, on which was written in pencil the following words: 'In commemoration of the goodness of Almighty God in granting to the Reverend F. R. Baraga, Missionary, a safe traverse from La Pointe to this place, August, 1843.' . . . I have endeavored to perpetuate this incident, and the memory of Father Baraga, by naming the stream after him." Bishop Frederic Baraga was born in Austria, June 29, 1797; and died in Marquette, Mich., January 19, 1868. He was a Catholic missionary to the Indians in northern Michigan and Wisconsin and northeastern Minnesota, 1835-68; author of an Ojibway grammar and dictionary, often quoted in this book, and of various religious works.

Temperance river was called Kawimbash river by Norwood, of Owen's geological survey, 1848-52, and it retained that name, meaning "deep hollow," in Whittlesey's report, 1866; but it had received its present name in Clark's geological report, 1864, and was so mapped in 1871. Clark explained the origin of the name Temperance as follows: "Most of the streams entering the lake on this shore, excepting when their volumes are swollen by spring or heavy rain floods, are nearly or quite closed at their mouths by gravel, called the *bar,* thrown up by the lake's waves; this stream, never having a 'bar' at its entrance, to incommode and baffle the weary voyageur in securing a safe landing, is called no *bar* or Temperance river." Its sources include Temperance lake, close west of Brulé lake, which has two outlets, the larger flowing east to Brulé river, and the other flowing west to Temperance lake and river; Cherokee lake, as it is named on recent maps, called Ida Belle lake by the Minnesota Geological Survey, in honor of a daughter of Prof. Alexander Winchell, who became the wife of Horace V. Winchell; Saw Bill lake, named for a species of duck; and Alton, Kelso, and Little Saw Bill lakes.

Below Temperance lake, the river of this name flows through Jack, Kelly, Peterson, and Baker lakes. Other lakes near its course and tributary to it include Vern lake, Pipe lake, named for its outline, Moore, Marsh, and Anderson lakes, on the east; and Clam lake, Odd, Java, Smoke, and Burnt lakes, on the west.

Near the west side of the county, and ranging from the northern watershed down the general slope toward Lake Superior, are Mesabi lake, Dent, Bug, Poe, Wind, Duck, and Pie lakes; Grace, Ella, Beth, and Phoebe lakes; and Frear, Elbow, Whitefish, Twohey, Four Mile, and Cedar lakes.

Gilfillan wrote that, in the Ojibway language, "Poplar river is Gamanazadika zibi, i. e., place-of-poplars river." Clark in 1864 definitely translated it as "Balm of Gilead," a variety of the balsam poplar, common or frequent along rivers in northeastern Minnesota. Lakes tributary to this river include Gust lake, named for Gust Hagberg, a Swede homesteader near it; Long, Beaver, Pine, Rice, Haberstead, and Barker lakes; Elbow or Tait lake; and Lake Clara, Big, and Sucker lakes, the last recently renamed Lake Christine, in honor of the daughter of William J. Clinch, county superintendent of schools, who has a homestead there. East of Poplar river, mostly tributary to it, are the Twin lakes, Mark, Pike, Trout, Bigsby, and Caribou lakes, and Lake Agnes.

Small streams next eastward, flowing into Lake Superior, are named False Poplar, Spruce, and Indian Camp rivers.

Cascade river, named from its series of beautiful waterfalls near its mouth, has Cascade and Little Cascade lakes, Swamp lake, Eagle and Zoo lakes, and the large Island lake. About six miles above its mouth, it receives an eastern tributary named Bally creek in honor of Samuel Bally, a member of the board of county commissioners, who has a homestead there.

Cut Face, Rose Bush, and Fall rivers, small streams between Cascade river and Grand Marais, have no considerable lakes.

"Devil Track river," wrote Gilfillan, "is Manido bimadagakowini zibi, meaning the spirits (or God) walking-place-on-the-ice river." The Ojibways applied this name primarily to Devil Track lake, and thence, according to their custom, to the outflowing river. The name implies mystery or something supernatural about the lake and its winter covering of ice, but without the supremely evil idea that is given in the white men's translation. The wild rock gorge of the river below this lake may have suggested the aboriginal name, which was used by Norwood in 1851 and Clark in 1864. Its translation, as now used, dates from the settlement of Grand Marais by Henry Mayhew and others in 1871.

Tributary to Devil Track lake and river are Swamp lake and creek, Clearwater lake, Elbow lake, named like numerous others, from its outline, and Monker lake, named for Claus C. Monker, a Norwegian homesteader on its south side, who has been later a fisherman, living in Grand Marais.

Next eastward are Durfee and Kimball creeks, the latter having Kimball and Pickerel lakes. Durfee creek was named in honor of George H. Durfee, judge of probate of this county. Kimball creek was named by Thomas Clark, in the geological exploration of 1864, for Charles G. Kimball, a member of the party, who lost his life near this stream by drowning in Lake Superior.

Diarrhoea river, which receives the outflow of Trout lake, has this name on Norwood's map in the Owen survey, 1851, referring to illness thought due to drinking its water; and it is so named by Jewett's map, 1911. The maps of the Minnesota Geological Survey call it Greenwood river.

Brulé river, called Wisacodé by Norwood, is given by Gilfillan as "Wissakode zibi or Half-burnt-wood river." Its largest lake, at the source of its South branch, is Brulé lake, which, as before mentioned, has another outlet to Temperance river. One of the islands of Brulé lake is called Tamarack island, for an old Ojibway, John Tamarack, who lived on it. (Brulé, the French word meaning burnt, has two syllables, the second having the English sound of lay; but it is often printed without the mark of accent on the *e,* so that it is liable to be mispronounced in only one syllable, the *e* becoming silent.)

Juno, Homer, Axe, and Star lakes, the last probably named for its radiating arms, lie close south of Brulé lake.

The South branch flows through Brulé bay, which is a separate small lake, Vernon, Swan, and Lower Trout lakes. It receives from the north the outflow of Echo, Vance, and Little Trout lakes; and on the south are Abita, Keno, or Clubfoot, Pine, and Twin lakes. Abita lake, on the southern slope from Brulé mountain, has the distinction of being the highest lake in Minnesota, 2,048 feet above the sea.

The North branch of Brulé river receives the outflow from Poplar, Winchell, and Meeds lakes, and a large number more, in the list of lakes before noted for the most northern townships of the county.

Below the junction of its South and North branches, Brulé river flows through Elephant lake, as it is named on our maps, more commonly known by the people of the region as Northern Light lake; and it receives Greenwood river, the outlet of Greenwood lake.

Little Brulé river is tributary to Lake Superior about a mile west of the large Brulé river.

Between Brulé and Pigeon rivers, only small streams enter Lake Superior, including, in order from west to east, Flute Reed river, Swamp river, Red Sand or Reservation river, and Hollow Rock creek.

Points, Bays, and Islands of Lake Superior.

Sugar Loaf point is two miles northeast from the southwest corner of this county.

Gull and Bear islands gave the name of Two Island river, as before noted. At the mouth of this river the village of Saxton was platted by Commodore Saxton, Lyle Hutchins, and others, in August, 1856, but was abandoned two years later, as related by Robert B. McLean, of Duluth.

Between Poplar and Devil Track rivers are Caribou point, Black point, Lover's point and bay, Terrace point and Good Harbor bay, and the two bays at Grand Marais.

Cow Tongue point, as named in the Minnesota Geological Survey, a half mile southwest of Kimball creek, is more commonly known as Scott's point, for Andrew Jackson Scott, who is commemorated also by Hungry Jack lake in this county, before noted.

Fishhook point is about two miles and a half southwest of the mouth of Brulé river.

Chicago bay, into which the Flute Reed river flows at Hovland village, was called Sickle bay in the Geological Survey.

Thence northeastward are Horseshoe and Double bays, Cannon Ball bay, Red Rock bay, Red point, and Deronda bay. The last was named by Prof N. H. Winchell in 1880, from George Eliot's novel, "Daniel Deronda," published in 1876, read partly in camp there.

Two small unnamed islands lie about a half mile and one mile east of Cannon Ball bay, and Arch island is off the southwest point inclosing Deronda bay.

Between Red Rock bay and Red point, a craggy part of the shore is called the East Palisades.

Grand Portage island, which lies in front of the bay of this name, is now often called Ganon island, for Peter Ganon, who has a supply store on its northern point.

Hat point, in front of Mt. Josephine, projects into the lake between Grand Portage bay and Waus-wau-goning bay. The name of the latter bay, considerably changed from its proper Ojibway form, was translated by Gilfillan as "making-a-light-by torches," having reference to the spearing of fish at night, whence Clark in 1864 called it "Spear-fish bay," a more free translation.

East of this bay, within about three miles, Clark enumerated twelve islands, which he compared, in beauty of scenery and attractiveness for sportsmen, with the Apostle Islands near La Pointe, Wisconsin. The largest was named Governor's island by Dr. Augustus H. Hanchett, of New York City, state geologist of Minnesota in 1864, in honor of Gov. Stephen Miller, and this name is retained by maps; but it is more commonly known as Susie island, a name used by the later state geologist, Prof. N. H. Winchell, in 1880. The next in size, which rises highest, named by Clark as High island, was called Lucille island by Winchell. Others of this group were named Magnet and Syenite islands by Clark, and Birch, Belle Rose, Little Brick, and Porcupine islands, by Winchell.

Northeast of these islands are Morrison and Clark bays, the latter named by Hanchett in honor of his assistant, Thomas Clark, author of valuable reports on the geology of parts of Minnesota, published in 1861 and 1865. Clark was born in Le Ray, Jefferson County, N. Y., January 6, 1814; removed to Ohio about 1835, settling in Maumee; removed to Toledo in 1851; was a civil engineer, and came to Superior, Wis., in 1854; surveyed the original site of that city; later surveyed and settled at Beaver Bay, Minn., his home when a state senator, 1859-60; died in Superior, Wis., December 20, 1878.

Pigeon point and bay, named from the river, are the most eastern part of this state.

Mountains and Hills.

In voyaging along the north side of Lake Superior, the highland in Cook county within one to two or three miles back from the shore is seen as a succession of serrate hills and low mountains, the peaks being generally about two miles apart for distances of many miles. The visible crest line thus presents a remarkable profile, resembling the teeth of an immense saw. Between Temperance river and Grand Marais, through nearly thirty miles, a somewhat regular series of these sharp outlines on the verge of the interior plateau has received the name of Sawteeth mountains.

The most conspicuous and highest summit of this range, at its west end close back from the village of Tofte, was named Carlton peak in 1848

COOK COUNTY   147

by Colonel Charles Whittlesey, in honor of Reuben B. Carlton, of Fond du Lac, Minnesota, who in that year ascended this mountain with Whittlesey, for the geological survey of this region by David Dale Owen. He is likewise honored by the name of Carlton county. Another peak is called Good Harbor hill, rising about a mile west of the bay so named.

Farquhar peak, similarly situated near the lake shore two miles west of Reservation river, was named in honor of an officer of the U. S. Survey of the Great Lakes.

Mt. Josephine, at the east side of Grand Portage bay, was named for a daughter of John Godfrey, of Detroit, Mich., who had a trading post at Grand Marais during several years, up to 1858. With a party of young people, she walked from Grand Portage to the top of this mountain, about the year 1853.

Mountain lake, on the international boundary, has Moose mountain close south of its east end, and Mt. Reunion a mile west of its west end, the latter being a name given for its being a place of meeting for parties on the Minnesota Geological Survey.

Brulé mountain is the summit of the highland close south of Lower Trout lake on the Brulé river.

Eagle mountain is about five miles southwest of Brulé mountain and a mile east of Eagle lake.

Prospect mountain is between the west ends of Gunflint and Loon lakes.

The highest lands of Minnesota are the Misquah hills, an east to west range south of Cross and Winchell lakes, whose hilltops within four miles east and seven miles west of Misquah lake are about 2,200 feet above the sea, the highest being 2,230 feet. The name of the Misquah lake and hills is the Ojibway word meaning red, in allusion to their red granite rocks which are exposed in extensive outcrops. Prof. N. H. Winchell wrote in 1881: "Misquah lake is flanked on the northeast and east by high brick-red hills, some of them being 500 or 600 feet high. The trees, being nearly all fire-killed and even consumed, allow a perfect view of the rock."

In the west edge of this county, the Mesabi lake marks the eastern extension of the Mesabi Iron Range, which passes by Little Saganaga lake and northeast to Gunflint lake. This Ojibway name was given on Nicollet's map in 1843 as "Missabay Heights." It has been spelled in several ways, Mesabi being its form in the reports and maps of the Minnesota Geological Survey. Gilfillan translated it as "Giant mountain," with an additional note: "'Missabe is a giant of immense size and a cannibal. This is his mountain, consequently the highest, biggest mountain." Winchell wrote of it, "The Chippewas at Grand Portage represent Missabe as entombed in the hills near there, the various hills representing different members of his body." Gunflint and North lakes lie in the course of continuation of the Mesabi Range, about ten miles north from the range of the Misquah hills, with which it is parallel.

Superior National Forest.

Large tracts in Cook, Lake, and St. Louis counties, exceeding a million acres, deemed chiefly valuable for forestry, were set apart by the United States government as a public reservation and named the Superior National Forest, in a proclamation of President Roosevelt, February 13, 1909, to which subsequent additions through similar proclamations have been since made. The initial recommendation for forestry reservation of these Minnesota lands was addressed to the commissioner of the U. S. General Land Office by Gen. C. C. Andrews, chief forest fire warden of this state, in 1902; and the authority for such national reservations had been vested in the President of the United States by an act of Congress in 1891.

Pigeon River Indian Reservation.

An area of about 65 square miles, including the trading post and village of Grand Portage, the portage road to Pigeon river, and the tract southward to the lake shore and west to Cranberry Marsh or Red Sand river, now commonly known as Reservation river, was set apart in a treaty with the Ojibways at La Pointe, Wis., September 30, 1854, for the Grand Portage band of these Indians. In the national census of 1910 the number of Indians in Cook county, nearly all of whom have their homes in this Reservation, was 220.

Glacial Lakes Duluth and Omimi.

The great glacial lake which was held by the barrier of the departing ice-sheet in the western part of the basin of Lake Superior, forming beach lines at Duluth 535 and 475 feet above Lake Superior, was named by the present writer in 1893 as the "Western Superior glacial lake." In 1897 and 1898, respectively, this cumbersome name was changed by Frank B. Taylor and Arthur H. Elftman to be Glacial Lake Duluth. The heights of its strand lines on Mt. Josephine had been determined by leveling in 1891 by Prof. Andrew C. Lawson, as 607 and 587 feet above Lake Superior, which is 602 feet above the sea.

A somewhat higher and much smaller glacial lake, existing for a relatively short time in the Pigeon river basin in eastern Cook county and extending slightly into Canada, was described and named Lake Omimi by Elftman, as follows (Am. Geologist, vol. XXI, p. 104, Feb. 1898): "Before the ice had receded beyond mount Josephine it retained a lake of about 40 square miles in area lying in the upper valley of the present Pigeon river. The lake bed has an altitude of 1,255 to 1,360 feet above the sea. Its lowest point is thus about 50 feet higher than the upper stage of Lake Duluth. .... When the ice receded from the vicinity of Grand Portage, Lake Omimi disappeared. The name Omimi is taken from the Chippewa name for Pigeon river."

COTTONWOOD COUNTY

This county, established May 23, 1857, organized July 29, 1870, derived its name from the Cottonwood river, which touches the northeast corner of Germantown in this county, and to which its northwest townships send their drainage by several small streams flowing northward. It is a translation of Waraju, the Dakota or Sioux name, noted by Keating and by Nicollet's report and map. Keating wrote that the river was so named "from the abundance of this tree on its banks," and Nicollet stated that the most important village of the Sisseton Sioux was on its north bank near its junction with the Minnesota river. The cottonwood, also called the necklace poplar, is a fast-growing, tall tree, common or frequent through the south half of this state and along the Red river valley, but reaches its northeastern limit on the headwaters of the St. Croix and the Mississippi. It is extensively planted for shade, as a shelter from winds, and for fuel; but at its time of shedding the seed from its tassels, which is in the spring, "the cotton from the seeds proves a source of much annoyance to the tidy housewife."

The Canadian French traders and voyageurs gave to the cottonwood the name Liard, meaning a farthing, perhaps in allusion to the nearly worthless quality of its lumber for constructive uses. Their translation of this Dakota name was "Rivière aux Liards," as recorded by Keating in 1823. In the Journal of the younger Alexander Henry, published in 1897 as edited by Dr. Elliott Coues, Henry wrote in 1803-04 of another Rivière aux Liards, a tributary of Red Lake river, probably the Clearwater river, which also has given its name to a county of Minnesota.

Townships and Villages.

The information of origins and meanings of geographic names in this county was received from "History of Cottonwood and Watonwan Counties," John A. Brown, editor, two volumes, 1916; from "A History of the Origin of the Place Names connected with the Chicago and Northwestern and Chicago, St. Paul, Minneapolis and Omaha Railways," by W. H. Stennett, 202 pages, 1908; from S. A. Brown, county auditor, S. J. Fering, register of deeds, and A. W. Annes, judge of probate, during a visit in Windom, July, 1916; and from E. C. Huntington, of St. Paul, who for thirty-six years, 1871-1907, was editor of the Windom Reporter.

AMBOY township, organized October 10, 1872, was named by settlers from the eastern states. Townships or villages of this name are in Ohio, Indiana, Illinois, Michigan, New Jersey, and New York.

AMO township, organized March 4, 1873, was named by W. H. Benbow, then clerk of court for the county, to inculcate the principle of friendship, the meaning of the name, in Latin, being "I love."

ANN township, organized in 1876, was named in honor of the wife of Hogan Anderson, then a member of the board of county commissioners, who was a homestead farmer in this township, wagonmaker and merchant.

BINGHAM LAKE, a railway village, platted July 28, 1875, and incorporated in 1900, "was named from a nearby lake. The lake was named by the United States surveyor, for Senator K. S. Bingham, of Michigan." Kinsley Scott Bingham was born at Camillus, N. Y., December 16, 1808; removed to Michigan in 1833, and engaged in farming; was a representative in the state legislature, 1836-40; was a member of Congress, 1847-51; governor of Michigan, 1855-59; and a U. S. senator, 1859-61, until his death at Oak Grove, Mich., October 5, 1861.

CARSON township, organized in July, 1871, bears the name of the widely known frontiersman, trapper, guide, soldier, and Indian agent, Christopher (commonly called Kit) Carson (b. 1809, d. 1868), for whom Carson City, the capital of Nevada, was named.

DALE township was organized March 30, 1872, having a name suggested by its valley and lakes. "When first discovered, there was a beautiful chain of lakes in the central eastern portion of this township. These were filled in their season with wild fowls, and many fish abounded in their waters. With the settlement of the country, several of these lakes have been drained out and are now utilized for pasture and field purposes by the farmers who own the property. Some of the lakes are still intact and are highly prized by the citizens of the county."

DELFT, established as a railway station in 1892 and platted as a village June 18, 1902, "was named for the city in Holland by John Bartsch and Henry Wieb. Previous to adopting this name the village was called Wilhelmine, a female name common in Holland."

DELTON township, organized September 17, 1872, bears the same name with villages in Virginia, Michigan, and Wisconsin.

GERMANTOWN, organized January 24, 1874, received its name from its many German settlers, who were a large majority of the early homesteaders in this township.

GREAT BEND township, organized August 27, 1870, "derives its name from the big bend in the Des Moines river within its borders." More exactly the apex of this bend or angle of the river is in the extreme southeast corner of Amo township.

HIGHWATER, organized January 24, 1874, is named for Highwater creek, which crosses the east half of this township, so called by the pioneer settlers "on account of its quick rising after a rain storm."

JEFFERS, platted and incorporated in September, 1899, was named in honor of George Jeffers, now a wealthy landowner, from whose homestead a part of the site of this railway village was purchased.

LAKESIDE township, organized August, 1870, received its name for its several fine lakes, including Bingham, Clear, Cottonwood, Fish, and

COTTONWOOD COUNTY

Wolf lakes, of which the third and fifth nearly adjoin the village of Windom. Fish lake has been renamed Willow lake.

MIDWAY township was organized March 16, 1895, having previously been a part of Mountain Lake township. Its name refers to its situation on the railway, equidistant between St. Paul and Sioux City.

MOUNTAIN LAKE township, organized May 6, 1871, derived its name from its former large lake, in which a mountain-like island rose with steep shores and nearly flat top about 40 feet above the lake, having similar outlines to those of the surrounding bluffs and general upland. "The upper part of the island was covered with trees, which could be seen for many miles. This spot served as a landmark and a guide for many of the early settlers. . . . . The lake, as known to pioneers, is no more; it has long since been drained, and grains and grasses grow in its old bed." Mountain Lake village, on the railway in the south edge of Midway township, was platted May 25, 1872.

ROSE HILL township, organized April 5, 1879, received its name for its plentiful wild prairie roses and its low ridges and hills of morainic drift.

SELMA township, organized April 4, 1874, bears a Scandinavian feminine Christian name, given to the first child born there.

SOUTHBROOK, the most southwestern township of this county, was organized in July, 1871. It is crossed by the Des Moines river, to which this township sends small brooks and rivulets from springs in the river bluffs.

SPRINGFIELD, organized August 27, 1870, was named by settlers from eastern states, many of which have townships, villages, and cities of this name.

STORDEN township, organized March 30, 1875, was first named Norsk, for its many Norwegian pioneers, but later was renamed in honor of its first settler, Nels Storden, an immigrant from Norway. Its railway village of the same name was platted July 8, 1903.

WESTBROOK, organized September 17, 1870, was named for the west branch of Highwater creek, which flows across the southeast part of this township. The railway village of Westbrook was platted June 8, 1900.

WINDOM, the county seat, was platted June 20, 1871; was incorporated as a village in the spring of 1875, the first ordinance of the village council being passed April 15; and was re-incorporated September 9, 1884. It was named by Gen. Judson W. Bishop, of St. Paul, chief engineer for construction of the railway, in honor of the distinguished statesman, William Windom, of Winona. He was born in Belmont county, Ohio, May 10, 1827; and died in New York City, January 29, 1891. He received an academic education, and studied law; came to Winona, Minn., in 1855; was a representative in Congress, 1859-69, and U. S. senator, 1871-81; was a member of the cabinet of President Garfield, in 1881, as secretary of the treasury, but retired on the accession of President Arthur; was again U. S. senator, 1881-83. On the inauguration of President Harrison, in

1889, Windom was re-appointed secretary of the treasury, and held the office till his death, which was very sudden, from heart failure, just after making an address at a banquet of the New York Board of Trade. A volume entitled "Memorial Tributes to the Character and Public Services of William Windom, together with his Last Address," 161 pages, was printed in 1891.

LAKES AND STREAMS.

Little Cottonwood river, and several streams flowing to the Cottonwood, namely, Mound, Dry, and Highwater creeks, and Dutch Charley's creek, receive the drainage of the northern part of this county. Mound creek was named in allusion to the massive ridge of quartzite, mainly overspread with the glacial drift, whence it derives its highest springs; Dry creek, because it becomes very small, or is wholly dried up, in severe droughts; Highwater creek, as before noted, for its sudden rise after heavy rains; and Dutch Charley's creek, for the earliest settler of Cottonwood county, Charles Zierke, whom the government surveyors found living beside that creek when they first came.

Several lakes have been sufficiently noticed in the foregoing list of townships, including Mountain lake, Bingham lake, and others in Lakeside.

The former Glen and Summit lakes, about two miles east of Windom, are now dry.

Bartsch, Eagle, Long, Maiden, and Rat lakes are in Carson, the first named for Jacob Bartsch, a farmer there, and the last named for its muskrats.

Swan, Lenhart's, and Wilson's lakes, in Dale, have been drained. The latter two, named respectively for John F. Lenhart and Samuel Wilson, settlers adjoining them, and a third, named Harder's lake, were formerly called "the Three lakes." Arnold's lake, close north of these, was named for a settler who came from Owatonna.

Lake Augusta was named in honor of the wife of a pioneer homesteader adjoining it. The outlet, Harvey creek, flowing south to the Des Moines, commemorates Harvey Carey, like the lake to be later mentioned.

Hurricane lake, now drained, had reference to a tornado which prostrated trees on its shore.

Bean lake was named for an early settler, Joseph F. Bean, who had remarkable talent of memorizing what he read.

Double lakes, a mile south of the last, are separated only by space for a road.

Berry and Carey lakes were named for settlers near them, the latter for the brothers Harvey, John, and Ralph Carey.

Long lake, a half mile west of Carey lake, was formerly called the Twin lakes.

COTTONWOOD COUNTY

Oaks lake may have been so called by the early surveyors, to preserve the name, "Lake of the Oaks," which Allen in 1844 applied to Lake Shetek, sixteen miles distant up the Des Moines river.

The two String lakes, in the southwest part of the Great Bend township, are named for their lying in a single winding string-like course, scarcely separated.

Clear lake, crossed by the south line of Southbrook, like another Clear lake before mentioned in Lakeside, refers to the clearness of its deep water, not covered by grass and water plants as many shallow lakes.

Talcott lake, through which the Des Moines river flows in Southbrook, is one of the names placed by Nicollet on his map, published in 1843, to commemorate friends and prominent men of science. His generous use of such names in the upper Mississippi region has been noticed in the chapter of Cass county. On and near the upper Des Moines river, he has Lakes Talcott and Graham, of which the latter is preserved as the name of two lakes and a township in Nobles county. These names are in honor of Andrew Talcott and James D. Graham, who, with James Renwick, were commissioners, in 1840-43, to survey the disputed northeastern boundary of the United States. Andrew Talcott was born in Glastonbury, Conn., April 20, 1797; and died in Richmond, Va., April 22, 1883. He was graduated at the U. S. Military Academy, West Point, 1818; was engineer on many government works; was astronomer in surveys of the boundary between Ohio and Michigan, 1828-35; was chief engineer of railway work in Mexico during the civil war.

The upper Des Moines river and adjoining region were explored in 1844 by Captain James Allen and a company of dragoons, of which he presented a report and journal, published by Congress in 1846. Morainic drift hills along the southwest side of the Des Moines, two to five miles northwest of Windom, were noted by Allen as "high bluffs, ... 150 or 200 feet above the general level of the country." These are named Blue Mounds in the description and map of this county by the Minnesota Geological Survey (vol. I, 1884, chapter XVI).

CROW WING COUNTY

This county, established May 23, 1857, organized March 3, 1870, was named for the Crow Wing river, translated from the Ojibway name, spelled Kagiwigwan on Nicollet's map, and Gagagiwigwuni by Gilfillan, who would preferably translate it, following Schoolcraft, as "Raven Feather river."

Pike in 1805 and Schoolcraft in 1820 and 1832 used the French name of this river, de Corbeau, meaning of the Raven; but its more complete name in French was rivière à l'Aile de Corbeau, river of the Wing of the Raven, as translated by the voyageurs and traders from the Ojibway name. In the "Summary Narrative," published in 1855, Schoolcraft referred to the somewhat erroneous English translation, Crow Wing river, as follows: "The Indian name of this river is Kagiwegwon, or Raven's-wing or Quill, which is accurately translated by the term Aile de Corbeau, but it is improperly called Crow-wing. The Chippewa term for crow is andaig, and the French, corneille,—terms which are appropriately applied to another stream, nearer St. Anthony's Falls."

Mrs. E. Steele Peake, widow of an early missionary in 1856-61 to the Ojibways at the mission stations of Gull Lake and Crow Wing, wrote in a letter of her reminiscences in the Brainerd Dispatch, September 22, 1911, concerning the aboriginal name of Crow Wing river: "Where the river joins the Mississippi was an island in the shape of a crow's wing, which gave the name to the river and the town."

The North American crow, common or frequent throughout the United States, has been confounded in this name with "his regal cousin, the raven," a larger bird, not addicted like the crow to uprooting and eating newly planted corn. Our American variety of the raven inhabits the country "from Arctic regions to Guatemala, but local and not common east of the Mississippi river." Dr. P. L. Hatch, in "Notes on the Birds of Minnesota," 1892, wrote of ravens, "they are rarely seen in the vicinity of Minneapolis and St. Paul, but from Big Stone lake to the British Possessions they seem to become increasingly common." Probably because the early English-speaking travelers and employees in the fur trade came from the eastern states, where the raven is practically unknown, they anglicized this name as Crow Wing, used only once by Schoolcraft in his "Narrative" of 1832, and criticized by him in 1855, as before cited.

After the adoption of the English name of the river, and twenty years or more before the county was outlined and named, the important Crow Wing trading post was established on the east side of the Mississippi opposite to the mouth of the Crow Wing river north of its island, and was surrounded by a village of the Ojibways and white men.

CROW WING COUNTY   155

The earliest record of a trader near this site is in the list of licenses granted in 1826 by Lawrence Taliaferro, as Indian agent, one of these being for "Benjamin F. Baker, Crow Island, Upper Mississippi," in the service of the American Fur Company (Minnesota in Three Centuries, 1908, vol. II, p. 54). Among the traders licensed in 1833-34, none is mentioned for that post, which seems to have been abandoned.

There was again a station of the fur traders at Crow Wing, facing the northern mouth of the Crow Wing river, "about the year 1837," and it became a few years later "the center of Indian trading for all the upper country, the general supply store being located at this place. . . . In 1866, the settlement and village contained seven families of whites, and about twenty-three of half-breeds and Chippewas, with a large transient population. . . . The entire population was, from reliable estimates, about six hundred. . . . Crow Wing, as a business point, has passed away, most of the buildings having been removed to Brainerd, and the remaining ones destroyed." (History of the Upper Mississippi Valley, 1881, pages 637-8.)

By an act of the Legislature, February 18, 1887, which was ratified by the vote of the people of the county at the next general election, the part of Crow Wing county west of the Mississippi river, previously belonging to Cass county, was annexed to this county, somewhat more than doubling its former area.

Townships and Villages.

Information for this county was gathered from "History of the Upper Mississippi Valley," 1881, pages 637-659; from Anton Mahlum, city clerk of Brainerd, Samuel R. Adair, county treasurer, and William H. Andrews, during my visit in Brainerd, May, 1916; and by correspondence from John F. Smart, former county auditor, now of Fairhope, Alabama.

ALLEN township was named for its first settler, a pioneer from the eastern states.

BARROWS railway station and the Barrows mine, five miles southwest from Brainerd, are named for W. A. Barrows, Jr., of Brainerd.

BAXTER township commemorates the late Luther Loren Baxter, of Fergus Falls, who during many years was an attorney for the Northern Pacific company. He was born in Cornwall, Vt., in 1832; was admitted to practice law, 1854, and soon afterward settled in Minnesota; enlisted in the Fourth Minnesota regiment, served at first as captain, and was promoted to the rank of colonel; was a state senator in 1865-8 and 1870-6, and a representative in the legislature in 1869 and 1877-82; was judge in the Seventh judicial district, 1885-1911. He died at his home in Fergus Falls, May 22, 1915.

BAY LAKE township received its name from its large lake, which was so named for its irregular outline, with many bays, projecting points, and islands. Its Ojibway name, like that of another lake of similar form in Aitkin county, was Sisabagama (accented on the third syllable), meaning, according to Gilfillan, "Every-which-way lake, or the lake which has arms running in all directions."

BRAINERD, founded in 1870, when the Northern Pacific survey determined that the crossing of the Mississippi should be here, was organized as a city March 6, 1873; but an act of the legislature, January 11, 1876, substituted a township government. It again became a city November 19, 1881. "The name first suggested for this place was 'Ogemaqua,' in honor of Emma Beaulieu, a woman of rare personal beauty, to whom the Indians gave the name mentioned, meaning Queen, or Chief Woman. The present name was chosen in honor of the wife of J. Gregory Smith, first president of the Northern Pacific Railroad Company, Mrs. Smith's family name being Brainerd." (History, Upper Mississippi Valley, p. 640.)

Mrs. Ann Eliza (Brainerd) Smith was a daughter of Hon. Lawrence Brainerd, of St. Albans, Vt. Her husband, John Gregory Smith (b. 1818, d. 1891), also a resident of St. Albans, honored by the name of Gregory Park or Square in Brainerd and by Gregory station and village in Morrison county, was governor of Vermont, 1863-65; was president of the Northern Pacific company, 1866-72; and later was president of the Vermont Central railroad until his death. Mrs. Smith was author of novels, books of travel, and other works. Her father, Lawrence Brainerd (b. 1794, d. 1870), was a director of the St. Albans Steamboat Company, a builder and officer of railroads in northern Vermont, a noted abolitionist, and was a United States senator, 1854-5.

Portraits of Mrs. Smith, for whom Brainerd was named, and her father, with extended biographic notices, are in "The Genealogy of the Brainerd-Brainard Family in America" (three volumes, published in 1908), The biographic sketch of her is in Volume II, pages 162-3, from which the following is quoted: "She was president of the board of managers for the Vermont woman's exhibit at the Centennial Exposition of 1876, at Philadelphia, and was frequently chosen in similar capacities as a representative Vermont woman. Her patriotic feeling was shown in the Civil War, at the rebel raid on St. Albans and the plunder of the banks, Oct. 19, 1864, and a commission as Lieutenant-Colonel was issued to her for gallantry and efficient service on that occasion by Adjutant-General P. T. Washburn." She was born in St. Albans, Vt., October 7, 1819; and died at her home there, January 6, 1905.

The Northern Pacific railroad ran its first train to Brainerd, a special train, on March 11, 1871; and its regular passenger service began the next September. The first passenger train from the Twin Cities, by way of Sauk Rapids, came November 1, 1877. Crow Wing, the former trading post, was soon superseded by Brainerd, which the Ojibways named "Oski-odena, New Town."

CROSBY, a mining village on the Cuyuna Iron Range branch of the "Soo" railway, was named in honor of George H. Crosby, of Duluth, manager of iron mines.

CROW WING township was named for its including the site of the early Indian village and trading post of this name.

CUYUNA, a mining village, and the iron ore range on which it is situated, were named by and for Cuyler Adams, of Deerwood, prospector, discoverer, and mine owner of this range, and for his dog, Una, who accompanied him in many lone prospecting trips, so that he affirmed that the discovery of workable ore deposits here should be credited jointly to himself and the valuable aid of Una. This iron range is more fully noticed at the end of this chapter.

DAGGETT BROOK township was named for the brook flowing through it meanderingly to the Nokasippi river, which brook commemorates Benjamin F. Daggett, an early lumberman who cut much pine timber there. He was born in Wiscasset, Maine, September 31, 1821; and died in Sauk Rapids, Minn., August 31, 1901. He came to Minnesota in 1855, settling at Elk River, and engaged in lumbering; afterward resided at Little Falls and Sauk Rapids. (Another Daggett brook, likewise named for this lumberman, is in the north part of this county, outflowing from Crooked lake, through Mitchell, Eagle, Daggett, and Pine lakes, to Cross lake.)

DAVENPORT township has the name given by Nicollet to Cross lake on the Pine river, in honor of Colonel William Davenport of the U. S. Army. He was a captain in the war of 1812; was promoted to the rank of lieutenant colonel, 1832, and colonel, 1842; was brevetted colonel in 1838, for meritorious service in Florida; resigned from the army, 1850; died April 12, 1858. He was commandant of Fort Snelling in the summer of 1836, and there became acquainted with Nicollet.

DEAN LAKE township, with its Dean lake and brook and the Upper Dean lake, bears the name of a pioneer lumberman, Joseph Dean of Minneapolis, who cut its pine timber.

DEERWOOD railway station and village, at first called Withington, "after the maiden name of the wife of one of the railway officials," was renamed for the plentiful deer in its woods, the name being thence given to the township. This change was made to avoid confusion with Worthington, Nobles county.

EMILY township was named from Emily lake, one of its group of four lakes having feminine names, Anna, Emily, Mary, and Ruth; but whether they were of one family, or what was the surname of any of them, has not been ascertained. Probably they were the daughters or wives of early lumbermen.

FAIRFIELD township has a euphonious name, perhaps derived from the township and large manufacturing village of this name in Maine. It is the name of counties, villages, and cities, in many states.

FORT RIPLEY, a railway village near the east bank of the Mississippi, bears the name of the fort formerly on the opposite bank of this river, from 1849 to 1878, named in honor of Gen. Eleazar W. Ripley, more fully noticed in the chapter for Morrison county.

GARRISON township was named in honor of Oscar E. Garrison, a land surveyor and civil engineer, who was born at Fort Ann, N. Y., July 21, 1825, and died on his farm in this township, April 2, 1886. He came to Minnesota in 1850; explored Lake Minnetonka, and platted the village of Wayzata in 1854; removed to St. Cloud in 1860; served in the Northern Rangers against the Sioux, 1862; was agent of the United States Census, Department of Forestry, 1880, examining the region of the Upper Mississippi, on which his observations were published (49 pages) in the Ninth Annual Report of the Minnesota Geological Survey. He took his homestead claim here in 1882.

IDEAL township, a fancy name, was originally called White Fish, for the large lake of that name comprised almost wholly in this township.

IRONTON is a mining and railway village of the Cuyuna Iron Range.

JENKINS railway village and township were named for George W. Jenkins, a lumberman, who platted this village.

KLONDIKE township was named from the Klondike placer-gold region in the Yukon district, Canada, discovered in 1896, which took its name from the Klondike river (Indian, "Throndiuk, river full of fish"). This name was adopted in allusion to the large and valuable deposits of iron ore in the Cuyuna Iron Range, discovered by Cuyler Adams in 1895 as the result of magnetic surveys, several of the best mining locations being in this township.

LAKE EDWARD township bears the name of the largest one of its numerous lakes, given at the time of the government survey, probably in honor of a member of the surveying party.

LEAKS, a station of the Minnesota International railway about three miles north of Brainerd, was named for John Leaks, a locomotive engineer of that railway.

LITTLE PINE township received its name for its lake and river of this name, tributary to the Pine river.

LONG LAKE township received its name from its Long lake, through which the Nokay river flows. Our name of this lake is a direct translation of its Ojibway name, "Gaginogumag sagaiigun."

MANGANESE, a mining village in Wolford, has reference to its manganiferous iron ores, which have from 1 to 25 per cent of manganese. These mines are on the northern border of this Cuyuna district.

MAPLE GROVE township has groves of sugar maple, interspersed with the other timber of its general forest.

MERRIFIELD, a railway village seven miles north of Brainerd, bears the name of the former owner of its site.

MISSION township and its two Mission lakes were named for an early missionary station there for the Ojibways.

NOKAY LAKE township has the lake of this name on the upper course and near the head of the Nokasippi or Nokay river, as it is spelled on Nicollet's map. This was the name of an Ojibway chief and noted hunter, whom the "Handbook of American Indians" (Part II, 1910) mentions as follows: "A chief of the western Chippewa in the latter half of the 18th century, who attained some celebrity as a leader and hunter. The chief incident of his life relates to the war between the Mdewakanton [Sioux] and the Chippewa for possession of the banks of the upper Mississippi. In 1769, the year following the battle of Crow Wing, Minn.,—where the Chippewa, though maintaining their ground, were hampered by inferior numbers,—they determined to renew the attack on the Mdewakanton with a larger force. This war party, under the leadership of Noka, referred to as 'Old Noka' evidently on account of his advanced age, attacked Shakopee's village on Minnesota river, the result being a drawn battle, the Chippewa retiring to their own territory without inflicting material damage on their enemy." Warren, the historian of the Ojibways, wrote of Nokay's skill in hunting (M. H. S. Collections, vol. V, page 266).

OAK LAWN township was named for its "oak openings," tracts occupied by scattered oak trees with small grassed spaces, somewhat like a prairie, interrupting the general woodland.

OUTING, a small village on the southeastern shore of Crooked lake, in Emily township, was platted in 1907 by William H. Andrews, as a place for "outings" or short visits of city people and sportsmen in summer.

PELICAN township was named for its large Pelican lake, which was first mapped by the United States government surveys, about the year 1860. The remarkably fine group of large lakes in this county between Gull and White Fish lakes was represented on earlier maps only by several quite small lakes, one of which is named Lake Taliaferro on Nicollet's map, in honor of the Indian agent at Mendota. As Pelican lake is the largest in this group, it may be thought to be the one so designated. It is translated from the Ojibway name, given by Gilfillan as "Shede sagaiigun, Pelican lake." Longfellow's "Song of Hiawatha" spells this Ojibway word Shada, which has the long *a* sound in both syllables. The pelican, our largest bird species of Minnesota, was formerly common or frequent here, as attested by its name given to rivers, lakes, and islands.

PEQUOT, a railway village in Sibley township, bears the name of a former tribe of Algonquian Indians in eastern Connecticut. This village is the sole instance of its use as a geographic name.

PERRY LAKE township and its lake of this name probably commemorate an early lumberman.

PLATTE LAKE township received its name from the lake at its southeast corner, the central and largest one of a group of several lakes forming the headwaters of Platte river. This is a French word, meaning flat. The translation of the Ojibway name of this lake, according to Gilfillan, is "Hump-as-made-by-a-man-lying-on-his-hands-and-knees."

RABBIT LAKE township similarly took the name of its Rabbit lake, the head of Rabbit river, a short tributary of the Mississippi. The Ojibway name of the lake, given by Gilfillan, is "Wabozo-wakaiiguni sagaiigun, Rabbit's-House lake."

RIVERTON is a mining village of the Cuyuna Iron Range, beside Little Rabbit lake, through which Rabbit river flows just before joining the Mississippi.

ROOSEVELT township was named in honor of Theodore Roosevelt, then President of the United States.

ROSS LAKE township and its lake of this name are in honor of a pioneer lumberman there.

ST. MATHIAS township was named from its Catholic church, dedicated to Christ's disciple who was chosen by lot to be one of the twelve apostles, in the place of Judas.

SIBLEY township was named from its Lake Sibley, a name given by Nicollet on his map, published in 1843, in honor of Henry Hastings Sibley, for whom also Sibley county was named.

SMILEY township, having a common English or American surname, remains of undetermined derivation.

TIMOTHY township, at first called Clover, received the popular name of a European species of grass, much cultivated in Europe and America for hay, more commonly called "herd's grass" in New England. The seed of this grass was carried from New England to Maryland about the year 1720 by Timothy Hanson, whence came its prevalent American name. It grows very luxuriantly under cultivation in Minnesota, and frequently is adventive by roadsides and about logging camps.

WATERTOWN has many lakes and the Pine river. In the central part of the west half of this township, the river flows into the west side of Cross lake and out from its east side, whence the lake received this name. It is translated from the Ojibway name, meaning the same as Lake Bemidji, "the lake which the river flows directly across." This lake was named Lake Davenport on Nicollet's map in honor of Col. William Davenport, of the United States Army, for whom also a township in this county is named.

WOLFORD township, recently organized, comprising the mining villages of Manganese and Iron Mountain, at the north edge of the Cuyuna Range, was named in honor of Robert Wolford, a pioneer farmer there.

LAKES AND STREAMS.

The preceding pages have noticed a number of the lakes and streams, including several given by Nicollet's map. Other names thus applied by Nicollet are Lake Plympton, now called Rush lake, crossed by the Pine river between White Fish and Cross lakes, in honor of Captain Joseph Plympton (b. 1787, d. 1860), who was commandant of Fort Snelling in the years 1837-41; Lake Gratiot now Upper Hay lake a mile east of Jenkins village, named in honor of Gen. Charles Gratiot (b. 1788, d. 1855), in charge of the U. S. engineer bureau and inspector of West Point; Manido river, the Ojibway name for Spirit river, outflowing from

CROW WING COUNTY 161

Lake Gratiot to White Fish lake; Lake Stewart, in Timothy township, for the gallant U. S. naval officer, Charles Stewart (b. 1778, d. 1869), famous for his services in the War of 1812; and Lakes Enke and Chanche, now respectively Lakes Washburn and Roosevelt, the former wholly and the latter partly in Cass county, tributary by the northern Daggett brook to Cross lake.

White Fish lake is called Kadikomeg lake on Nicollet's map, an attempt to record the aboriginal name, which Gilfillan noted more fully, "Ga-atikumegokag, the place of white fish." Another lake of this name, much smaller, is crossed by the east line of Roosevelt, lying partly in Mille Lacs county. The next lake across which Pine river passes below White Fish, named Lake Plympton by Nicollet, now known as Rush lake, is called by the Ojibways "Shingwakosagibid sagaiigun, the lake of the pine sticking up out of the water." Their name of the Pine river, which we retain in translation, is "Shingwako zibi;" and Serpent lake is translated from "Newe sagaiigun, Blow-Snake lake." Pike or Borden lake, named for David S. Borden, an adjacent settler, in sections 10, 11, and 14, Garrison, is called "Wijiwi sagaiigun, the lake full of muskrat houses or beavers," as noted by Gilfillan; and the aboriginal name for Round lake, through which the Nokay river flows in sections 11 and 14, St. Mathias, is Nokay lake.

The larger Round lake, in Smiley township, is translated from "Gawawiiegumag;" and the Ojibway name of Lake Hubert, recorded by Gilfillan, is "Ga-manominiganjikag sagaiigun, Wild Rice lake." Gull lake, a translation from the Ojibways, has been more fully noticed in the chapter on Cass county.

In this region of plentiful game, finny, furred, and feathered, Lake Hubert, and the adjoining village of this name, may well have been so designated in honor of St. Hubert, the patron saint of huntsmen.

An enumeration of other lakes and streams in this county, not previously noticed, is as follows, taking first the part southeast of the Mississippi, in the order of townships from south to north, and of ranges from east to west, and next, in the same order, taking the northwest part of the county. Personal names, applied to many of these lakes, are nearly all commemorative of early settlers.

Camp or Crooked lake, Erskine, Mud, Bass, Rock, and Bull Dog lakes, in Roosevelt township.

Sebie, Mud, and Crow Wing (or Thunder) lakes, in Fort Ripley township.

Clearwater, Miller, Barber, and Holt lakes, in Garrison.

Chrysler lake, in Maple Grove township.

Russell lake, in Long Lake township, named for T. P. Russell, a setiler there at its north side.

Buffalo creek, in Crow Wing township, named for buffaloes frequenting its oak openings and small tracts of prairie.

A second and larger Clearwater lake, Crooked, Hanks, Portage, Rice, and Birch lakes, and a small Long lake in section 1, Bay Lake township.

Eagle, Pointon, Perch, and Grave lakes, in Nokay Lake township.

Sand and Whitely creeks, and Rice or Whitely lake, in Oak Lawn township.

Agate and Black lakes, Cedar creek and lake, Shine or Shirt lake, and Hamlet, Portage, Rice, and Reno lakes, in Deerwood. The last was named in honor of Gen. Jesse Lee Reno, who served in the Mexican and Civil wars, and was killed in the battle of South Mountain, Md., September 14, 1862.

Manomin, Portage, Blackhoof, Little Rabbit, Rice, Crocker, and Wolf lakes, in Klondike.

Black Bear lake, in Wolford.

Little Sand or Perch lake, White Sand, Red Sand, and Whipple lakes, in Baxter, the first township northwest of the Mississippi. The last is in honor of the eminent Bishop Whipple, under whose direction and care were many missions for the Ojibways and Sioux in Minnesota, including the Ojibway mission of St. Columba, at Gull lake in the adjoining edge of Cass county.

Long lake, Love lake, Bass, Carp (or Mud), Gilbert, and Hartley lakes, in Township 134, Range 28 and the east half of Range 29.

The two Mission lakes, named for an early Ojibway mission near them, and Perch, Silver, Bass, Fawn, Spider, and Camel lakes, in T. 135 N., R. 27 W.

Markee and Twin lakes, Garden, Rice, Clark, Hubert and Little Hubert, Gladstone, Mollie, and Crystal lakes, in Lake Edward township.

Cullen, Fawn, Fish Trap (or Marsh), Roy, and Mud lakes, in Smiley.

Nelson lake, in Dean Lake township, named for H. M. Nelson, the first settler having a family in that township.

Bass lake, Fool's lake, and Indian Jack lake, in Perry Lake township.

Lizard, Sandbar or Horseshoe, and Bass lakes, and the northern Mission lake, in Mission township.

Long, Schaffer, and Upper Cullen lakes, in Pelican.

Twin lakes, in Sibley.

Island, Mud, and Rogers lakes, Upper Dean lake, Twin lakes, and Stark lake, in Ross Lake township.

Grass, Pickerel, and Trout lakes, Dolney's lake, Mud, Bass, and Adney lakes, in Fairfield.

Ox, Island, Hen, Rush, Daggett, Bass, Goodrich, O'Brien, Phelps, Big Bird, and Greer lakes, in Watertown, with two Pine lakes, one in the northeast part of this township, and the other in sections 32 to 34.

Big Trout, Mud, Bertha, Pig, Star, Bass, Kimball, Long, and Clear lakes, in White Fish township.

The Upper and Lower Hay lakes, and Nelson lake, in Jenkins.

Little Pine lake, Low's, Duck, Moulton, Bass, and Birchdale lakes, in Little Pine township.

CROW WING COUNTY 163

Papoose, Butterfield, and Dahler lakes, in Emily township.

Mitchell, Eagle, East Fox, West Fox, and Kego lakes, in Allen, the last an Ojibway name meaning Fish lake.

Jale, Big Rice, and Swede lakes, in the east half of T. 138, R. 29, the most northwestern in this county.

The Mississippi has "an island in the mouth of Pine river, well timbered with pine, elm, and maple," as described by Schoolcraft in 1820; French rapids, shown on Nicollet's map, about three miles north of Brainerd; Whitely island, close below these rapids; three or four other small islands between this and the Crow Wing river; and, at the mouth of that river, Crow Wing island. Another name sometimes given to the last is McArthur's island, as on the map accompanying the chapter for this county by the Minnesota Geological Survey, having reference to a Scotch trader, named McArthur.

In the vicinity of the Buffalo creek and the mouth of Crow Wing river, as Schoolcraft wrote in 1820, "the Buffalo Plains commence and continue downward, on both banks of the river, to the falls of St. Anthony. These plains are elevated about sixty feet above the summer level of the water, and consist of a sandy alluvion covered with rank grass and occasional clumps of the dwarf black oak."

AHRENS HILL.

A remarkable series of gravel knolls and ridges, called kames and eskers, borders the Mississippi on its northwest side at Brainerd and for a distance of about three miles up the river. Its culmination and northern end is a hill that rises about 175 feet above both the river on its east side and Gilbert lake on the west, being 100 feet higher than the mainly level sand and gravel plain of the river valley. This high and short esker was named Ahrens hill in the Geological Survey (vol. IV, 1899, p. 73), for Charles Ahrens, the farmer of its southern and western slopes.

CUYUNA IRON RANGE.

The origin of the name of this belt of iron ore deposits has been noted for the village of Cuyuna, in the preceding list; and the date of discovery of these beds of ore by Cuyler Adams, in 1895, was mentioned in the notice of Klondike township. Mining and shipments of ore from the Cuyuna range were begun in the years 1910 to 1912, and its production in 1915 was 1,137,043 tons. The explored extent of this iron ore district, lying in Crow Wing and Aitkin counties, has no prominent hills or highlands, and only very scanty outcrops of the bed-rocks, which, with the ore deposits, are deeply covered by the glacial and modified drift.

DAKOTA COUNTY

This county, established October 27, 1849, was named for the Dakota people, meaning an alliance or league. Under this name are comprised a large number of allied and affiliated Indian tribes, who originally occupied large parts of Minnesota and adjoining states. The Dakotas called themselves collectively by this name, but they have been more frequently termed Sioux, this being a contraction from the appellation, Nadouesioux, given with various spellings by Radisson, Hennepin, and LaSalle, a term evidently of Algonquian origin, adopted by the early French explorers and traders.

Radisson says (Voyages, p. 154) that the first part of the Algonquian name for the Dakotas, spelled, in the translation of his manuscript, Nadoneceronons, means an enemy.

Rev. Moses N. Adams informed me that the Dakotas dislike to be called Sioux, and much prefer their own collective name, borne by this county, which implies friendship or even brotherly love.

Townships and Villages.

For the origins and meanings of the names of townships, villages, post offices, lakes, creeks, etc., in this county, we are mainly indebted to its three published histories: "Dakota County, Its Past and Present, Geographical, Statistical, and Historical," by W. H. Mitchell, 1868, in 162 pages; "History of Dakota County," by George E. Warner and Charles M. Foote, 1881, 551 pages; and "History of Dakota and Goodhue Counties," edited by Franklyn Curtiss-Wedge, 1910, two volumes, the first, in 662 pages, being for this county. Especial acknowledgment is due to the excellent contribution by the late Judge Francis M. Crosby, of Hastings, entitled "Origin of Names," in the third of these histories, pages 131-133.

BURNSVILLE township, organized May 11, 1858, was named for its first settlers, "William Burns and family, consisting of his wife and five sons, who emigrated from Canada the same year [1853]. He settled in the northwest corner of the town, near the mouth of Credit river."

CASTLE ROCK township, organized April 6, 1858, was named, on the suggestion of Peter Ayotte, an early settler, for a former well known landmark, a pillar or towerlike remnant, spared by erosion and weathering, of "a sandstone rock which stands alone on a prairie in that town. This geologic formation, before its partial disintegration which left it in ruins, closely resembled a castle." Nicollet's Report, in 1843, gives its Sioux name, Inyan bosndata, Standing Rock, which, he adds, on the authority of LeSueur in the year 1700, was the Sioux name also of the

Cannon river. Prof. N. H. Winchell's Final Report of the Geology of Minnesota, in Volume II, 1888, has a good description and historical notice of Castle Rock, pages 76-79 in Chapter III, "The Geology of Dakota County," with three pictures of it from photographs. Its height was 44 feet above the ground at its base, and 70 feet above an adjoining hollow; but the slender pillar, 19 feet high, forming its upper part, has since fallen, about twenty years ago.

DOUGLASS township, established April 6, 1858, "was named for Stephen A. Douglas, the statesman." Its earliest spelling by the petitioners and county commissioners has been continued, though differing from that of the great politician and orator. He is also commemorated by the name of Douglas county.

EAGAN township, established by legislative act in 1861, was named for Patrick Eagan, one of the first settlers, coming in 1853.

EMPIRE was named "for Empire, N. Y., the native place of Mrs. A. J. Irving, wife of one of the early settlers." This township, organized and named May 11, 1858, had previously an early neighborhood settlement, which in 1854-55 was called "Empire City."

EUREKA township, organized May 11, 1858, has for its name a Greek word, meaning "I have found it!" This was the exclamation of members of its "Indiana settlement," when they first arrived, in 1854.

GREENVALE, also organized May 11, 1858, "probably received its name from the name given to a Sunday School in the southern part of the township. The name was doubtless inspired by the picturesque surroundings."

HAMPTON township, established April 6, 1858, was named for "a place of that name in Connecticut. This appellation was suggested by Nathaniel Martin in honor of his birthplace."

HASTINGS, the county seat, platted as a village in 1853 and incorporated as a city in 1857, was named in drawing lots by its several proprietors, this second name of Henry Hastings Sibley, later governor and general, having been his preference. "Judge Solomon Sibley, of Detroit, Mich., studied law in Massachusetts with Judge Hastings, whom he greatly admired, and gave this name to his son."

Before the platting and naming of Hastings, this locality had been known during thirty-three years as Oliver's Grove, often ignorantly changed to "Olive Grove." The origin of this early name is told by John H. Case in Volume XV of the Minnesota Historical Society Collections (page 377), as follows: "The site of the city of Hastings was earlier called Oliver's Grove, after Lieut. William G. Oliver, who was ascending the Mississippi with one or more keel boats in the autumn of 1819, but was prevented from going farther by a gorge of ice in the bend of the river opposite to this city. The boat or boats were probably run up to the outlet of Lake Rebecca, to be out of the way of the ice when the river broke up in the spring of 1820. Lieutenant Oliver was on his way from Fort Crawford at Prairie du Chien with supplies for the soldiers at St. Peter's camp, now Fort Snelling, among whom was the first settler of Hastings, Joe Brown, the drummer boy, then about fourteen years of age."

INVER GROVE township was organized May 11, 1858. "The town was named by John McGroarty, the name Inver Grove being given in recollection of a place in Ireland from which many of the settlers came."

LAKEVILLE township, established April 6, 1858, was named for Prairie lake, which about fifteen years ago was renamed Lake Marion, as is further noted in the list of lakes of this county.

LEBANON received its name "from Lebanon, N. H., from whence came Charles and H. J. Verrill, early settlers." It was organized May 11, 1858.

MARSHAN township "was named for Michael Marsh and his wife, Ann." Previous to its organization, May 11, 1858, it was known as Bellwood, for Joseph Bell, who took a claim there in 1854. It then had a small village, called Bellwood, with the first hotel of the township and a Catholic church; but the site "soon was abandoned."

MENDOTA township, established in April, 1858, bears a Sioux name, meaning the mouth of a river, because here the Minnesota river joins the Mississippi. This name was adopted about the year 1837, instead of the former name St. Peter's, taken from the St. Peter's or Minnesota river, as applied to the early settlement of traders opposite to Fort Snelling.

NININGER township, established April 6, 1858, was named from its earlier "city of Nininger," which was platted in the summer of 1856 by John Nininger, for whom it was named. He resided in Pennsylvania, and was a brother-in-law of Governor Ramsey. In the winter of 1857-8 an act of incorporation of this city was passed by the legislature. In the spring of 1858, when it reached the height of its progress, Nininger "numbered nearly, if not quite, 1,000 inhabitants, and cast a vote of over 200."

RANDOLPH township, established April 20, 1858, was then named Richmond, "in honor of John Richmond, the first settler within its limits." This name was rejected September 18, 1858, because there was another Richmond in the state; and on October 30, 1858, it was renamed Randolph. "D. B. Hulburt, an admirer of the Virginia statesman, John Randolph, suggested that his distinguished surname be given to the town." This was "Randolph of Roanoke," as he was generally known, who was born in 1773 and died in 1833.

RAVENNA township, separated from the city of Hastings on June 5, 1860, was named by Albert T. Norton for Ravenna, Ohio, where his wife had taught school.

ROSEMOUNT township, established April 6, 1858, "was named by Andrew Keegan and Hugh Derham, from the picturesque village of that name in Ireland."

DAKOTA COUNTY 167

SCIOTA township, organized May 11, 1858, "was named from Sciota, Ohio," as related by Judge Loren W. Collins.

SOUTH ST. PAUL and WEST ST. PAUL, recently incorporated cities, received their names from their situation "in reference to the city of St. Paul." West St. Paul township was organized May 11, 1858, and by an act of the legislature, approved March 9, 1874, its village (as it then was) of this name was detached from Dakota county and annexed to Ramsey county, being made a part of St. Paul.

VERMILLION township, organized April 5, 1858, was named for the Vermillion river, which bears a translation of its Sioux name, as more fully noted on an ensuing page.

WATERFORD township, established April 20, 1858, "received its name from the fact that there was a ford across Cannon river within its limits. This ford was on the old trail from St. Paul to Faribault."

The villages of this county, in alphabetic order, are as follows:

CASTLE ROCK, a railway station, named like its township.

ETTER, a railway station, named for Alexander Etter, its first merchant.

FARMINGTON, incorporated in March, 1872, an important railway town, "received its name from its situation in a district exclusively devoted to farming."

HAMPTON and INVER GROVE railway villages are named for their townships.

LAKEVILLE, named like the township, received its first settlers in 1855. When the Hastings and Dakota railroad was built there, in 1869, a new village site was chosen, at first called Fairfield. This village superseded the older Lakeville and adopted that name in its act of incorporation, March 28, 1878.

MENDOTA, the oldest village of this county, gave its name to a township.

MIESVILLE was named for John Mies, by whom this little village was founded in 1874.

NEW TRIER was "named for Trier, Germany, the native place of some of the early settlers in this vicinity."

NICOLS, a railway station, was named for John Nicols, of St. Paul, the former owner of its site.

NININGER, once a large village and incorporated as a city, but now nearly deserted, has been noticed for the township named from it.

PINE BEND, on the Mississippi river, includes the site of the village of a Sioux chief, Medicine Bottle, who seceded from the Kaposia village. "It is named from the fact that pine trees stand on the banks where the river makes a decided turn or bend." This is also the name of a station, on the upland, of the new St. Paul Southern electric railway.

RANDOLPH, a railway junction, is named for its township.

RICH VALLEY was named "from its location in a valley of very fertile soil."

Rosemount, Vermillion, and Waterford, railway villages, bear the names of their townships.

Wescott, a railway station, usually spelled Westcott, was named for a prominent pioneer, James Wescott, who settled there in 1854. He served in the First Minnesota heavy artillery in the civil war; was treasurer of this county in 1860-62; and died on his farm near this station, May 4, 1910.

Lakes and Streams.

Three small lakes lying within about a mile south of the village of Mendota were named lakes Charlotte, Lucy, and Abigail, on the earliest map of the vicinity of Fort St. Anthony, which in 1825 was renamed Fort Snelling. These names were given respectively in honor of the wives of Lieutenant Nathan Clark, Captain George Gooding, and Colonel Josiah Snelling. None of these names is retained at the present time. The most northeastern and largest of these lakes now bears the name Lake Augusta, which was given to it probably more than fifty years ago, in honor of the eldest daughter of General Sibley, who later was married to Captain Douglas Pope. It is the lake that was named at first for Mrs. Abigail Snelling.

Chub lake and Chub creek (or river) are named for the well known species of fish, being quite probably a translation of their Sioux name.

Of Crystal lake it is said that "when the government survey was made, its clear shining surface led to the adoption of its present name."

Black Dog lake, four miles long, lying in the bottomland of the Minnesota river and occupying a deserted rivercourse, was named for a Sioux, Black Dog, whose village was near the northeast end of the lake.

For the Big Foot creek and Black Hawk lake, apparently translations of ancient Sioux names, no definite information has been obtained.

Lake Farquhar was named for John Farquhar, a pioneer who took a land claim near it.

Lake Isabel, adjoining the east edge of the city of Hastings, was stated by the late Gen. William G. Le Duc to be named in honor of a daughter of Alexis Bailly, one of the original proprietors of this city. The Sioux name of this lake was Mahto-waukan, Spirit Bear.

Keegan lake was named for Andrew Keegan, owner of a farm there.

Le May lake commemorates settlers who lived near it.

Lake Earley was named for "William Earley, who settled on its western shore in 1854."

Orchard lake, formerly called Round lake, is named for the native crab-apple trees and wild plum trees in the woods of its vicinity.

Lake Marion, formerly Prairie lake, was renamed in honor of the late Marion W. Savage, owner of the famous trotting stallion "Dan Patch," and president of the Minneapolis, St. Paul, Rochester and Dubuque Electric Traction Company, whose railway line, (commonly called "the Dan Patch line") passed by the east side of this lake. At its southeast end are summer homes and pavilions for picnics and for boating, fishing, and hunting parties, this station being named Antlers Park, in allusion to the former abundance of deer in this region. For the village named Savage, beside the Minnesota river in Scott county, a biographic sketch of Mr. Savage is presented, with a note of the recently changed ownership of this electric railway.

Rice lake, on the west line of Eureka and crossed by the line dividing Dakota and Scott counties, was named for its wild rice.

Lake Rebecca, nearly two miles long, lying close northwest of Hastings, occupying a deserted channel of the Mississippi, was named, as told by General Le Duc, for Miss Rebecca Allison, daughter of a pioneer settler, who, after a few years residence here, returned to the east.

Spring lake, on the southwest edge of the Mississippi bottomland, is named for its contiguous springs issuing from the base of the river bluffs.

Sunfish lake is named for this species of fish; and Pickerel lake, similarly, for its large and abundant pickerel.

Rogers lake commemorates E. G. Rogers, who owned a farm on its southeast side.

Vermillion lake, quite small, in section 18, Eureka, and the Vermillion river, which lies wholly in this county, are a translation, first published by Nicollet's map in 1843, of the Sioux name. Its origin was probably from the very bright red and orange-colored ocher obtained by the Sioux in seams of Chimney Rock in Marshan, more fully noted on an ensuing page, and of other outcrops of the St. Peter sandstone beside or near the course of this river.

The lower parts of the Vermillion river, after it reaches the Mississippi bottomland, there flowing in two streams northwestward and southeastward to the great river, are named the Vermillion slough. Four miles southeast of Hastings, this slough or river is joined by the Truedell slough, named for a pioneer settler, by which it is connected with the Mississippi. Thence southeastward these two rivers, the Vermillion and the Mississippi, inclose Prairie island, ten miles long, lying mostly in Goodhue county, under which its name and history are again noticed. The name is a translation of its earliest French name, Isle Pelée, called by Radisson "the first landing isle." (Minnesota Historical Society Collections, vol. X, part II, pages 462-473, with a map of this island.)

Dudley island, in the Mississippi between one and two miles east of Hastings, belonging to Ravenna township, was named, as stated by Irving Todd, Sr., for John Dudley, of Prescott, Wis., owner of sawmills adjoining the mouth of the St. Croix river.

Belanger island, in Nininger, south of the main channel of the Mississippi, bears the name of the first settler in this township, a French Canadian, whose cabin was on the bank of Spring lake.

Pike island, at the mouth of the Minnesota river and adjoining Mendota, is named for Lieutenant (later General) Zebulon M. Pike, who in 1805 on the west end of this island made a treaty with the Sioux for the tract on which Fort St. Anthony, later named Fort Snelling, was built in the years 1820-24.

Kaposia, the village of the successive hereditary Sioux chiefs, named Little Crow, was situated from 1837 to 1862 on a part of the site of South Park, a suburb of South St. Paul. Previously, in the time of the expeditions of Pike, Cass, and Long, this movable Indian village had been located on the eastern side of the Mississippi, as noted for Ramsey county. In 1820 and till 1833 or later, it was on the upper side of Dayton's bluff, within the area of St. Paul; but earlier, during a dozen years or more, in 1805 and in 1817, it was at the Grand Marais, one to two miles south of that bluff. Concerning the name Keating wrote: "The Indians designate this band by the name of Kapoja, which implies that they are deemed lighter and more active than the rest of the nation." (Minnesota in Three Centuries, vol. I, pages 366-368.)

Hills and Rocks.

The hilly tracts or belts of Dakota county consist of morainic glacial drift, amassed in abundant knolls, short ridges, and small hills, of which only a few rise to such prominence that they are named.

The most conspicuous hill, rising to about 1175 feet above the sea, being about a hundred feet above any point in the view around it, is Buck hill, near Crystal lake, described as follows in the History of this county published in 1881: "At the west end of the lake is a high hill, . . . called by the early settlers 'Buck Hill.' From the top of this high eminence the Indians would watch the deer as they came to drink from the cool waters of the lake."

Another conspicuous height, near Mendota, is commonly called Pilot Knob; but on the oldest map of the vicinity of Fort Snelling, before mentioned, it is more properly named Pilot hill.

In section 1, Marshan, are two prominent drift hills, which have been long known as "the Mounds."

Besides the Castle Rock, in the township so named, this county has several other somewhat similar castlelike or columnar rock masses. One of these, about ten miles north of the Castle Rock, is called Castle Hill on Nicollet's map, but since the settlement of the county it is named Lone Rock. About a mile and a half east of this is a Chimney Rock. Again, about eight miles distant east-southeast from the last, there is another and more remarkable Chimney Rock. This is in the east edge of section 31, Marshan, about seven miles south of Hastings. As described in 1905 by the present writer (Bulletin of the Minnesota Academy of Sciences, vol. IV, page 302, with a view from a photograph which well shows the reason for its name), this Chimney Rock "is the most picturesque and perfect example of columnar rock weathering in Minnesota. . . . It is a vertical pillar, measuring 34 feet in height and about 6 and 12 feet in its less and greater diameters, being no thicker near the base than in its upper part."

DODGE COUNTY

Established February 20, 1855, this county received its name in honor of Henry Dodge, governor of Wisconsin, and his son, Augustus C. Dodge, of Iowa.

Henry Dodge was born in Vincennes, Indiana, October 12, 1782; and died in Burlington, Iowa, June 19, 1867. He served in the war of 1812; was a colonel of volunteers in the Black Hawk war, 1832; commanded an expedition to the Rocky mountains in 1835; was governor of Wisconsin territory and superintendent of Indian affairs, 1836-41; delegate in Congress for Wisconsin, 1842-6; again governor of that territory, 1845-8; and was one of the first U. S. senators from the state of Wisconsin, 1848-57.

Governor Dodge on July 29, 1837, at Fort Snelling, then in Wisconsin, made a treaty with the Ojibways, by which they ceded to the United States all their pine lands and agricultural lands on the upper part of the St. Croix river and its tributaries, in the present states of Wisconsin and Minnesota. The tract ceded also reached west to include the upper part of the basin of Rum river, and onward to the Mississippi between Sauk Rapids and the mouth of Crow Wing river. In September of the same year, under direction of Governor Dodge, about twenty chiefs and braves of the Sioux went with the agent, Major Taliaferro, to the city of Washington and there made a treaty ceding all their lands east of the Mississippi, together with the islands in this river. By these treaties a large tract of eastern Minnesota (then a part of Wisconsin), including the sites of St. Paul and St. Anthony, was opened to white settlement.

Augustus Caesar Dodge was born in St. Genevieve, Missouri, January 12, 1812; and died in Burlington, Iowa, November 20, 1883. He was the delegate in Congress for Iowa territory, 1840-7; was one of the first U. S. senators of Iowa, 1848-55, his father being also a senator at the same time; and was minister representing this country in Spain during four years, 1855-9.

Biographies of both the father and son, with their portraits, by Louis Pelzer, have been published, respectively in 1911 and 1908, by the State Historical Society of Iowa, in its Iowa Biographical Series.

Townships and Villages.

For the origins and meanings of the geographic names of this county, information has been gathered from "An Historical Sketch of Dodge County," by W. H. Mitchell and U. Curtis, 1870, 125 pages; "History of Winona, Olmsted, and Dodge Counties," 1884 (this county having pages

769-1266); "Atlas of Dodge County," by R. L. Polk and Co., 1905, having pages 61-129 of text, historical and biographic, with illustrations; and from the offices of George L. Taylor, county auditor, and George H. Slocum, editor of the Mantorville Express, visited in April, 1916.

ASHLAND township, first settled in May, 1854, organized June 15, 1858, was named from its original village plat in 1855 by William Windom, Thomas Wilson, and Daniel S. Norton, of Winona, with others. Each of the three proprietors here noted, then new immigrants to this territory, afterward attained great prominence in Minnesota history. This name, applied to townships, villages, cities, and counties, occurs in twenty-six other states of our Union.

BERN, a former post office in Milton, established in 1858, was named for the capital of Switzerland.

BUCHANAN, formerly a small village having a sawmill, on the North Middle branch of the Zumbro river, was named in honor of James Buchanan, elected in 1856 to the presidency of the United States.

CANISTEO township, settled in 1854 and organized in 1858, was named by its numerous immigrants from Canisteo, a village and a township in Steuben county, N. Y., on the Canisteo river, which is about sixty miles long, flowing to the Tioga and Chemung rivers, the latter a tributary of the Susquehanna. An early village there, of the Delaware tribe of Indians, was called Canisteo, being the origin of this name, said to mean "board on the water." This Indian village was described as "the largest of the Delaware towns, consisting of sixty good houses with three or four fire-places in each." (Roberts, Historical Gazetteer of Steuben County, 1891, pages 15-17.)

CHENEY, the post office at Eden railway station, in Wasioja, was named in honor of B. P. Cheney, a farmer there.

CLAREMONT township, first settled in September, 1854, organized May 11, 1858, was named for the town of Claremont, N. H., whence several of its settlers came, including George Hitchcock, its first postmaster. Claremont village was incorporated in 1878.

CONCORD township, settled in April, 1854, organized May 11, 1858, was named in like manner for the city of Concord, N. H., the capital of that state. The village plat was recorded June 7, 1856.

DODGE CENTER, the railway village in the south edge of Wasioja, founded in 1866, was platted in July, 1869, and was incorporated February 29, 1872. This name was proposed by D. C. Fairbank, on account of the location at the center of the county. The first passenger train arrived here, on the Winona and St. Peter railroad, July 13, 1866.

EDEN, the railway station and village having Cheney post office, was named by officers of the Chicago Great Western Railway Company.

ELLINGTON township, settled in July, 1855, organized May 11, 1858, had been at first named Pleasant Grove, but was renamed for the town of Ellington in Connecticut. Mrs. John Van Buren, who proposed this change of name, "wrote the votes by which the matter was decided."

DODGE COUNTY 173

HAYFIELD township was organized March 30, 1872, having previously been a part of Vernon. Its name was adopted from a township of Crawford county in northwestern Pennsylvania. The railway village of Hayfield was incorporated January 7, 1896.

KASSON, a railway village in the south edge of Mantorville, was named in honor of Jabez Hyde Kasson, owner of the original town site. He was born in Springville, Pa., January 17, 1820, and came to Minnesota in 1856, settling on a farm in this township. When the Winona and St. Peter railroad reached this place, in the fall of 1865, this village was laid out by Mr. Kasson and others, the plat being recorded October 13, 1865, and in November the first passenger train came.

MANTORVILLE township was first settled in April, 1854; was incorporated under legislative acts of 1854 and 1857; and was organized under the state government, May 11, 1858. The village was platted March 26, 1856, by Peter Mantor, H. A. Pratt, and others, and in 1857 it was designated by a vote of the county to be the county seat. This name was adopted in honor of three brothers, Peter, Riley, and Frank Mantor, who came here in 1853 and 1854 from Linesville, Crawford county, Pa. Peter Mantor, the oldest of these brothers and the leader in founding this town, was born in Albany county, N. Y., December 15, 1815; settled on the site of the village of Mantorville, April 19, 1854, and built a sawmill and gristmill there; was a representative in the legislature, 1859-60; was captain of Company C, Second Minnesota Regiment, 1861; removed to Bismarck, Dakota, in 1874, where he was register of the U. S. land office until 1880; died in Mantorville, September 23, 1888.

MILTON township, settled in May, 1854, organized May 20, 1858, had been successively called Watkins, Buchanan, and Berne. Georgia has a Milton county, and thirty other states have townships, villages, and cities of this name, honoring the grand poet and patriot of England (b. 1608, d. 1674).

OSLO, a hamlet at the center of Vernon township, was made a post office in 1879, lately discontinued. This name is now borne by a village of the Soo railway in the southwest corner of Marshall county. It was the name of the original city founded in 1048 by Harald Sigurdsson near the site of Christiania, the capital of Norway. Oslo (or Opslo) became the chief city of Norway, but it was built mainly of wood, and after a great conflagration the city was refounded on the present site by the king, Christian IV, who gave his name to it in 1624.

RICE LAKE, a village in the northwest corner of Claremont, received its name from the neighboring lake, crossed by the west line of this county. It refers to the growth of wild rice in this shallow lake, which was used as an important food supply by the Indians.

RIPLEY township, first settled in September, 1854, organized May 14, 1858, may probably have been named for some eastern township or village, as in Maine, New York, Ohio, Indiana, Illinois, or West Virginia, in each of which states this name is found.

SACRAMENTO was a village platted in the fall of 1855, on the Zumbro river in the west edge of Mantorville, against which it was a rival for election as the county seat, but it was defeated by the popular vote in 1857. Within the next decade its buildings were removed, and its site reverted to farm use. The name, from California, had reference to scanty occurrence of placer gold in the drift of some localities on branches of the Zumbro and Root rivers, as noted in reports of the Minnesota Geological Survey. One of the places of ill repaid gold washing by the early settlers was near the site occupied a few years by this "deserted village."

VERNON township, settled in October, 1855, organized March 4, 1858, was named from Mount Vernon, Virginia, the home of Washington, for Admiral Edward Vernon (b. 1684, d. 1757), of the British navy.

VLASATY, a railway station in Ashland, was named by officers of the Chicago Great Western railway.

WASIOJA township, settled in October, 1854, organized in 1858, bears the Sioux name of the Zumbro river, spelled Wazi Oju on Nicollet's map in 1843. It is translated as "Pine river" by Nicollet, and is defined as meaning "pine clad." Large white pines, far west of their general geographic range, grow on the Zumbro bluffs in the east part of this township, as also in Mantorville, and at Pine Island in Goodhue county. The village of Wasioja was platted May 24, 1856.

WEST CONCORD, a village of the Chicago Great Western railway, was platted June 1, 1885.

WESTFIELD township, settled in 1855, organized March 22, 1866, probably commemorates an eastern village or township whence some of its settlers had come. The name is so used in a dozen eastern states, and it is also borne by a river in Massachusetts.

LAKES AND STREAMS.

The North Middle branch of Zumbro river, its South Middle branch, and its South branch, gather their head streams in this county; and from Hayfield and Westfield the Cedar river, a long and large stream of Iowa, receives its highest sources, its East, Middle, and West forks.

Milliken and Harkcom creeks, in Concord and Milton, flowing into the North Middle Zumbro, were named for pioneer settlers, as also Maston's branch, flowing northeastward past Kasson to the South Middle fork.

La Due's bluff, the site of the quarries in Mantorville, was named for Hon. A. D. La Due, a prominent early citizen, who died at Mantorville on January 12, 1899.

On the South branch of the Zumbro, in the southwest quarter of section 12, Vernon, was the Indian Grove, named for a large number of Sioux who had their camp there in the winter of 1856-7.

Hammond or Manchester lake and Prince lake, in Ripley, were named for adjoining farmers.

The origins of the names of Zumbro and Cedar rivers are noticed in the first chapter, treating of the large rivers of this state.

DOUGLAS COUNTY

This county, established March 8, 1858, and organized June 15, 1866, was named in honor of Stephen Arnold Douglas, statesman and leader in the Democratic party, eminent in his patriotic loyalty to the Union at the beginning of the Civil War. He was born in Brandon, Vermont, April 23, 1813; and died in Chicago, June 3, 1861. He lived in Vermont to the age of seventeen years; studied law, and was admitted to practice in Illinois in 1834; was elected to the state legislature in 1835, and won there the sobriquet of "the Little Giant," by which he was ever afterward well known; was elected a judge of the state supreme court in 1841; was a member of Congress, 1843-47; and U. S. Senator, 1847-61. On the application of Minnesota to be admitted as a state, in 1857-58, Douglas earnestly advocated it, being then chairman of the Senate Committee on Territories.

In a series of debates in Illinois in 1858, with Abraham Lincoln, his Republican opponent, nominated for the United States senate, Douglas defended his view that Congress had no authority for exclusion of slavery from territories not yet received into the Union as states. Each of these great political leaders then aroused extraordinary interest throughout the nation, and two years later they were opposing candidates for the presidency, Lincoln was elected, the southern states seceded, and in 1861 the great Civil War began.

Several biographies of Douglas have been published, in the presidential campaign of 1860, again new editions of one of these in the midst of the Civil War and at its close, and more complete and dispassionate studies in recent years. The influence of his loyalty for preservation of the Union was an inestimable contribution to the making of history and the welfare of the world.

Townships and Villages.

Information for this county was gathered from the "History of Douglas and Grant Counties," Constant Larson, editor, 1916, two volumes, 509, 693 pages; "Plat Book of Douglas County," 1886, 82 pages, including a "Historical Sketch" in four pages; and from George P. Craig, judge of probate, Gustav A. Kortsch, president of the Douglas County Bank, R. C. Bondurant, local editor of the Alexandria Post News, Mrs. Charles F. Canfield, and Mrs. James H. Van Dyke, interviewed during a visit at Alexandria, the county seat, in May, 1916.

ALEXANDRIA, settled in 1858, established as a township, June 15, 1866, was named in honor of Alexander Kinkaid, because he and his brother William were its first settlers, coming from Maryland. The form of the name follows that of the large city in Egypt, which was founded in the year 332 B. C. by Alexander the Great. Fifteen other states have villages or cities of this name. The village of Alexandria was incorporated February 20, 1877; and its charter as a city was adopted in 1908. The first passenger train on the railroad reached this place November 5, 1878.

Alexander Kinkaid removed to California, and additional record of him has not been learned. William Kinkaid was born in Elkton, Md., December 3, 1835; came to Minnesota in 1856; served in the Second Minnesota Battery, 1862-3; was afterward chief clerk in the hospital at Washington for returned prisoners of war; died in St. Cloud, Minn., May 22, 1868.

BELLE RIVER township, settled in 1865, was established March 8, 1870, being then named Riverdale. January 4, 1871, the present name was chosen by vote of the people. Each of these names was suggested by the Long Prairie river, which flows meanderingly through the north half of this township, on its way toward the Long Prairie that borders it in Todd county, being what the French first word of the township name signifies, beautiful.

BRANDON, settled in 1860, was established as a township September 3, 1867, and was then called Chippewa, for its lakes and river of that name, used as a "road of war" by the Ojibways in their forays to the Sioux country. Previously it had a station, named Chippewa, of the Burbank stage route from St. Cloud to the Red river, at the home and hotel of Ole Brandon, on a low hill about two miles north of the present railway village, which received his name, whence also the township was renamed. The village was incorporated November 22, 1881.

CARLOS, first settled in 1863, was made a township May 1, 1868. Its railway village was incorporated July 7, 1904. The name was adopted from the beautiful, large and deep Lake Carlos, which had received it before 1860, given by Glendy King, a homesteader adjoining Alexandria, who had been a student at West Point. Lakes Carlos and Le Homme Dieu were named by him for two of his friends in the eastern states.

EVANSVILLE, permanently settled in 1865, established as a township January 7, 1868, commemorates the first mail carrier, named Evans, of the route opened in 1859 from St. Cloud to Fort Abercrombie, who had a log cabin here for staying over night. He was killed in the Sioux outbreak of 1862. The village of Evansville was platted in the fall of 1879, with the coming of the first railway train, and was incorporated in 1881.

FORADA, the railway village in Hudson, platted in July, 1903, by Cyrus A. Campbell, of Parker's Prairie, Otter Tail county, incorporated April 6, 1905, has the first name of Mrs. Campbell, Ada; but that name was already widely known as the county seat of Norman county, and therefore it received the prefixed syllable.

GARFIELD, the railway village of Ida township, platted February 17, 1882, incorporated September 9, 1905, was named in honor of President

DOUGLAS COUNTY 177

Garfield, who was shot July 2, 1881, by the assassin Guiteau, and died at Elberon, N. J., our second martyr president, September 19, a few months before this village was founded.

GENEVA BEACH, a village of summer homes at the south end of Lake Geneva, received its name from this lake, which, as also the adjoining Lake Victoria, was named by Walter Scott Shotwell. The former name was derived from the lake and historic city in Switzerland; the latter is in honor of Queen Victoria. The sponsor of these names was a son of Daniel Shotwell from New Jersey, whose homestead claim, taken in 1859, was between these lakes. The son studied medicine, traveled to California, and died many years ago.

HOLMES CITY, settled in 1858, established as a township October, 4, 1866, was named in honor of Thomas Andrew Holmes, leader of its first group of settlers. He was born in Bergerstown, Pa., March 4, 1804; and died in Cullman, Ala., July 2, 1888. He established an Indian trading post in 1839 at Fountain City, Wis., and in 1849 removed to Sauk Rapids, Minn.; was a member of the first territorial legislature; founded the towns of Shakopee and Chaska in 1851. Before engaging in the Indian trade, he had been one of the founders of Janesville, Wis., in 1836. Following the receding frontier, he went to Montana in 1862, and there participated in founding Bannack City, at an early locality of placer gold mining, which became the first capital of Montana Territory.

HUDSON township, first settled in 1864, organized April 16, 1869, was named from Hudson, Wis., whence some families of its pioneers came, including Mrs. S. B. Childs, who proposed this name.

IDA township, settled in 1863, organized April 7, 1868, received the name of its large Lake Ida, which had been so named by Myron Coloney, one of its first settlers, for a friend, probably residing in an eastern state.

INTERLACHEN PARK, a summer village in Carlos township, bordering the north shore of Lake Le Homme Dieu and having its western end beside Lake Carlos, derived this name, with a slight change of spelling, from Interlaken, Switzerland, much visited by tourists, between Lakes Thun and Brienz. It means "between the lakes."

KENSINGTON, the railway village of Solem township, was platted by Hon. William D. Washburn in March, 1887, and was incorporated June 6, 1891. This is the name of a western section of the city of London, and it is also borne by villages and townships in seven other states. On the farm of Olof Ohman, about three miles northeast from this village, the famous Kensington rune stone was found in November, 1898. It is described in the Minnesota Historical Society Collections, volume XV, pages 221-286, with illustrations and maps.

LA GRAND township, first settled in 1860, was organized September 23, 1873, being then called West Alexandria; but in December of that year it was changed to La Grand, taking the name of an early resident of Alexandria.

LAKE MARY township, settled in 1863, established September 3, 1867, was named for its large lake, which commemorates Mary A. Kinkaid, a homesteader of 1861 in section 24, La Grand, sister of Alexander and William Kinkaid, before mentioned as the first settlers in Alexandria. Her homestead adjoined Lake Winona, which she probably named.

LEAF VALLEY, to which the first settler came in 1866, was established as a township November 23, 1867. Its name refers to its situation at the southern border of the Leaf hills, commonly called "mountains," which rise conspicuously in the adjoining edge of Otter Tail county.

LUND, first settled in 1866, made a township March 1, 1872, is named for the very ancient city of Lund in southern Sweden, which has a famous university founded in 1666. In pagan times Lund attained great importance, and during a long period of the Middle Ages it was the seat of an archbishopric and was the largest city of Scandinavia.

MELBY, the railway village of Lund, was platted in April, 1902, being named probably for a farming locality in Sweden, whence some of the adjoining settlers came, receiving from it their own personal surnames.

MILLERVILLE, established as a township November 23, 1867, was named for John Miller, an early and prominent German settler. Its village was incorporated June 29, 1903.

MILTONA township was established December 19, 1871, receiving its name from the large Lake Miltona, which occupies more than a sixth part of its area. The lake was named for Mrs. Florence Miltona Roadruck, wife of Benjamin Franklin Roadruck, who had a homestead in section 22, Leaf Valley, at the west end of this lake. In 1877 they returned to their former home in Indiana. (Letter from George L. Treat, of Alexandria.) Tradition tells that her family washing was often done on the lake shore.

MOE, settled in 1863, was established as a township September 3, 1867, being at first called Adkinsville in honor of Thomas Adkins, one of the first settlers. "Later the name was changed to Moe, in memory of a district in Norway, from which a number of the pioneers came."

NELSON, a railway village on the east line of Alexandria township, founded about the year 1875, was incorporated August 31, 1905. The post office and village were at first named Dent, in honor of Richard Dent, who settled at Alexandria in 1868, and died in Spokane, Wash., May 19, 1915. The name was changed to Nelson, after 1881, in honor of Senator Knute Nelson, the most eminent citizen of this county. He was born in Vossvangen, Norway, February 2, 1843; came to the United States when six years old, with his mother; served in the Fourth Wisconsin Regiment, 1861-4; was admitted to the bar in 1867; came to Minnesota in 1871, and settled on a farm near Alexandria; practiced law in Alexandria after 1872; was a state senator, 1875-8; representative in Congress, 1883-9; governor of Minnesota, 1893-5; and resigned to accept the office of U. S. senator, which position he has since filled with very distinguished ability and grand loyalty to this state and the nation. His

DOUGLAS COUNTY 179

biography is in "Lives of the Governors of Minnesota," by Gen. James H. Baker (M. H. S. Collections, vol. XIII, 1908, pp. 327-355, with portrait).

ORANGE was settled in 1863-4, and was established as a township January 7, 1868. Eight states have counties of this name, and it is borne in twenty states by cities, villages, and townships.

OSAKIS, first settled in 1859, was established June 15, 1866, this and Alexandria being the oldest townships of the county. The name was received from Osakis lake, which, as also the Sauk river outflowing from it, has reference to Sauk Indians formerly living here, as narrated in connection with Sauk Rapids in the chapter of Benton county. In 1859 the stages running to Fort Abercrombie had a station on the site of Osakis village, and the earliest settlers took claims; but the Sioux outbreak in 1862 caused these claims to be abandoned. The village was founded in 1866, and was incorporated February 21, 1881. The date of the first passenger train was November 1, 1878.

SOLEM, settled in 1866, was established as a township March 10, 1870. "The township takes its name from a district in Norway, from which place many of the pioneers came."

SPRUCE HILL township, the latest established in this county, was organized March 9, 1875. Its low timbered hills of morainic drift bear the black spruce, balsam fir, white pine, paper or canoe birch, balsam poplar, and blueberries, with other trees and shrubs, the several species thus named reaching here the southwestern limits of their geographic range. This township has two hamlets, named Spruce Hill and Spruce Center.

URNESS, first settled in 1862-3, was established as a township, March 22, 1869, to be called Red Rock, from its lake of that name, referring to reddish boulders on its shore, one being especially noteworthy on the northeast shore of the main lake. On February 7, 1871, the commissioners received a petition requesting that the name of the township be changed to Urness, "in memory of a certain district in Norway." Two of its pioneer farmers, Andrew J. and Ole J. Urness, respectively in sections 24 and 12, coming in 1865, were immigrants from that district.

LAKES AND STREAMS.

The foregoing list of the names of townships has included sufficient references to several rivers and lakes.

Only a few other names of streams are to be noticed, as Spruce and Stormy creeks in Spruce Hill township, and Calamus creek named for its growth of the calamus or sweet flag (Acorus Calamus, L.), in Osakis and Belle River townships. More recently the last has been named Fairfield creek, in honor of Edwin, George, and Lloyd D. Fairfield, early settlers in Osakis and Orange, having homesteads near the farthest sources of this stream.

But there remains a multitude of lakes, unsurpassed in beauty and diversity. Some of these are named for pioneers whose homes adjoined the lakes; others for their outlines, as Horseshoe lake, Moon lake, two

Crooked lakes, Lobster lake, and several Long lakes; and others for their trees and animals, as Maple lake, Elk, and Turtle lakes.

The complex and recurving series or chain of lakes, large and small, through which the head stream of Long Prairie river takes it course, consists in descending order of Lake Irene, earlier called Reservation lake; Lakes Miltona and Ida, respectively the largest and the next in size in this series; Lakes Charlie and Louise, named for a son and a daughter of Charles Cook, who settled in Alexandria in 1858, had been a fur merchant in London and a member of the Hudson Bay Company, was the first postmaster of Alexandria, and after a few years returned to the eastern states and later to London, where he spent the remainder of his life; Union lake, where this series receives an important inflowing stream from another large series of lakes at the west and south; Stone and Lottie lakes; Lake Cowdry, named for Samuel B. Cowdry, a pioneer farmer in Alexandria, who removed in 1862, later attended the Seabury Divinity School, Faribault, and became an Episcopal rector in southern Minnesota; Lake Darling, commemorative of Andrew Darling, a pioneer who settled on the shore of this lake in 1860, an exceptionally successful farmer; and Lake Carlos, lowest of this series, sounded by Rev. C. M. Terry and found to have in some places a depth of 150 feet, being the deepest lake of this state.

Lake Irene, in sections 14, 22, and 23, Miltona, is in honor of Irene Roadruck, for whose mother Lake Miltona is named, as noted for this township.

A second series, mentioned as tributary to Union lake of the preceding series, has, in like descending order, Lake Andrews, named probably in honor of the first physician of Alexandria; Lake Mary, largest in this series; Mill and Lobster lakes, the latter having numerous arms or claws; and Lake Mina, Berglin's lake, and Fish lake (the last formerly called Mill lake). Lake Mina is again noticed on page 182.

A third series of lakes, tributary to Lake Carlos, includes another and smaller Union lake, covering parts of four sections in Hudson; Burgan's lake, named for William P. Burgan, a farmer who settled near its southwest shore in 1869; and Lakes Victoria, Geneva, and Le Homme Dieu, each having many summer homes along the shores.

To the eastern arm of Lake Victoria a fourth series sends its outflow, comprising Lover's lake, Childs lake, and Lake Jessie, the second being for Edwin R. Childs, who came there as a homesteader in 1867.

Many lakes yet remain, not hereinbefore noticed. In the order of townships from south to north, and of ranges from east to west, these are listed as follows, so far as they have names on our maps and atlases. A goodly number having relatively small areas lack published names.

Swims or Clifford lake, Myer's, Owings, and English Grove lakes, in Orange, the last named for its grove on the homestead of William T. English, who settled there in 1863. These lakes are shallow, and in the latest atlas, of 1916, they are mapped as drained.

Maple lake, in Hudson.

Turtle, Long, and Mud lakes, in Lake Mary township, the last recently drained.

Van Loon's lake, Grubb lake, Lake Rachel, Echo lake, Grant's and Blackwell lakes, Holmes City lake, Oscar lake, South Oscar lake, and Freeborn, Mattson, and Olaf lakes, in Holmes City township. Early settlers commemorated in these names include Noah Grant, who settled on section 2 in 1858; George Blackwell, on section 3, 1868; Miner Van Loon, section 24, 1865; John Freeborn, section 30, 1868; and John Mattson, section 32, 1868. (For the origin of the name of Lake Oscar, see the end of this chapter.)

Long lake, Eng, Hegg, and Roland lakes, in Solem. Among the pioneer settlers in this township were Erick Pehrson Eng, Erick Hegg, and John Roland, for whom these lakes were named.

Lake Smith, Bird lake, Crooked and Hanford lakes, in Osakis township, the last two now drained.

Lakes Agnes and Henry, close north of the city of Alexandria, the former named for the eastern "lady love" of William Kinkaid by Mrs. Caroline Cook, wife of Charles Cook, the merchant pioneer from London, and the latter for one of their children, brother of Charlie and Louise Cook (for whom other small lakes, previously noted, are named), and of Fanny Cook, who became the wife of James Henry Van Dyke, first merchant of Alexandria; Lake Winona, at the west side of Alexandria, and extending into La Grand, for which lake and for this county the first white child born here was named Winona Douglas James, daughter of Joseph A. James, a settler who came from Philadelphia in 1858; Lake Conie, at the southeast edge of the city, and Shadow lake in section 23, these all being in Alexandria township.

Lake Alvin, Lake Latoka, (of origin and meaning yet to be ascertained), Nelson lake (for O. W. Nelson, an adjoining farmer), and Lake Cook, in Le Grand, the last being in honor of Charles Cook.

Elk lake, Lakes Elizabeth, Gilbert, and William, Crooked lake, Lake Brandon (named for John Brandon, a farmer whose home is at its east side), Thorstad and Minister lakes, in Moe, the last being near a Norwegian Lutheran church.

Amos lake, for Amos Johnson, Thorson lake, Barsness lake, for Albert and Oscar Barsness, Holleque lake, Quam lake, for P. J. Quam, and Lake Venus, with the much larger Red Rock lake, before noticed, in Urness.

Mud lake, at the corner of sections 27, 28, 33, and 34, Carlos.

Baumbach, Hunt, Stowe's, and Grassy lakes, Long and Moon lakes, Lakes Aldrich and Nelson, Burrows, Whiskey, and Devil's lakes, in Brandon. The first was named in honor of Frederick von Baumbach, who was born in Prussia, August 30, 1838; and died at his home in Alexandria, Minn., Nov. 30, 1917. He came to the United States with his father in

1848; served in the Fifth and Thirty-fifth Wisconsin regiments during the civil war, attaining the rank of major; came to Minnesota, settling at Alexandria, in 1867; was auditor of this county, 1872-78, and again in 1889-98; secretary of State of Minnesota, 1880-87; and internal revenue collector for this state, 1898-1914. Lake Mina, before noted in the second series tributary to Long Prairie river, was named for his mother.

Others of these Brandon lakes were named for Joseph Hunt, homesteader on section 6 in 1867; Martin Stowe, on section 18 in 1862; John D. Aldrich, section 23, 1868; and John Nelson, section 26, 1865.

Another Long lake, Jennie, Erwin, Alberts, Solberg, Hubred, Davidson, Mahla, and Fanny lakes, in Evansville. Adjacent farmers commemorated by these names include George Erwin, Ole Alberts, A. H. Solberg, Oliver Hubred, D. J. Davidson, and M. H. Mahla.

Vermont and Wood lakes, in Miltona, the former named by settlers from that state.

Spring and Kelly's lakes, in Leaf Valley, the latter in honor of Patrick Kelly, an Irish homesteader at its east side in 1873.

Lakes Moses and Aaron, Lorsung, Wilken, Stockhaven, and Stockhousen lakes, in Millerville. The first two were named for the great Hebrew lawgiver and his brother, deliverers of their nation from Egyptian bondage and leaders toward the promised land of Palestine. The third and fourth of these lakes, named for Joseph Lorsung and John and William Wilken, have been drained, the bed of each being subdivided to the adjoining farms. The last was named, with change of spelling, in honor of Hans G. von Stackhausen, who took a homestead claim there in 1870.

Lund, the most northwestern township, has the large but shallow Lake Christina, the small Lakes Anka and Ina, bordering the south shore of that large lake, and Horseshoe lake and Lake Sina. The last, in section 25, bears on maps of thirty to forty years ago this name of Mount Sinai (called Sina in the seventh chapter of the Acts), where the Decalogue and other laws were received, the name being suggested by Lakes Moses and Aaron, a few miles distant.

Lake Christina and its companion, the large Pelican lake in the adjoining corner of Grant county, appear, though with inaccurate outlines, on an early map of this state, dated January 1, 1860, their names being given as Lakes Christina and Ellenora. These were probably names of pioneer women, the first and perhaps both being from Sweden. It may be true, however, that the first was bestowed in honor of Queen Christina, who was regent of Sweden in 1632-44 and queen during the next ten years.

Similarly the name of Lake Oscar, in Holmes City township, though a common christening name, was quite surely not adopted to honor any settler there, but for Oscar I, the king of Sweden and Norway in 1844-59, father of Oscar II, who was the king in 1872-1907.

FARIBAULT COUNTY

This county was established February 20, 1855, being named in honor of Jean Baptiste Faribault, who was engaged during the greater part of his long life as a trader among the Sioux, at first for the Northwest Fur Company. He was born at Berthier, Province of Quebec, in 1774, and came to the Northwest in 1798, taking charge of a trading post on the Kankakee river near the south end of Lake Michigan. During the years 1799 to 1802, he was stationed at the Redwood post, situated on the Des Moines river, "about two hundred miles above its mouth," being in what is now the central part of Iowa. Coming to Minnesota in 1803, he took charge of a post at Little Rapids, on the Minnesota river a few miles above the present sites of Chaska and Carver, where he remained several years. Afterward he was a trader on his own account at Prairie du Chien, Wis., whence he removed to Pike island, at the mouth of the Minnesota river, in the spring of 1820, having been promised military protection by Colonel Leavenworth, who had come there with troops in the preceding August for building the fort which in 1825 was named Fort Snelling. After 1826 Faribault and his family lived in Mendota, having built there a substantial stone house, the first in Minnesota, and in the winters during many years he traded with the Sioux at Little Rapids. His influence with the Indian tribes west of the Mississippi, from the Missouri to the Red river, was very great. He endeavored to teach them agriculture, and was the first white settler to cultivate the soil in this state. He spent his last years in the town of Faribault, in Rice county, founded, at first as an Indian trading post, by his eldest son, Alexander Faribault, for whom it was named. He died at the home of his daughter there, August 20, 1860.

An appreciative memoir of him, by Gen. Henry H. Sibley, in the Minnesota Historical Society Collections (vol. III, pages 168-179), closes with these words: "Among the pioneers of Minnesota, there are none whose memory and whose name better deserve to be respected and perpetuated."

Townships and Villages.

Information of the origins and meanings of the geographic names in this county was received from "The History of Faribault County . . . to the close of the year 1879," by Judge J. A. Kiester, 1896, 687 pages; and from John Siverson, register of deeds, and Henry P. Constans, proprietor of the Constans Hotel, interviewed at Blue Earth during my visit there in July, 1916.

BARBER township, settled in June, 1857, established September 27, 1858, and organized June 10, 1864, was named in honor of Chauncey

Barber, whom the commissioners supposed to be a resident of this township. He came from Pennsylvania to Wisconsin, and in 1856 to this county, settling in Minnesota Lake township, was its first hotelkeeper, and platted its railway village on his lands in 1866. About twelve or fifteen years later he removed to Oregon.

BLUE EARTH township, first settled in May, 1855, organized October 20, 1858, derived its name from its village, called Blue Earth City, which had been platted in July, 1856, and has ever since been the county seat. The village was named from the river, which the Sioux called Mahkahto, meaning green or blue earth, as more fully noticed in the chapter of Blue Earth county. By an act of the legislature, March 1, 1872, the village was incorporated; it received a new and improved charter by a second act, January 27, 1879; and it adopted the city form of government in 1900.

BRICELYN, the railway village in Seely township, was named for John Brice, who owned and platted it.

BRUSH CREEK township, settled in May, 1856, and established September 27, 1858, received the name of its small creek which joins the East fork of Blue Earth river in section 26. The reason for the application of this name to the creek was "the thick growth of small trees, thickets and brush along its banks."

CLARK township, settled in June, 1862, and organized September 7, 1869, had been named Cobb by the county commissioners in 1858, from their erroneous supposition that the Cobb river (of Blue Earth county) received a portion of its headwaters in this township. At its organization, in 1869, the name was changed to Thompson, in honor of Clark W. Thompson, "the largest land owner of the town and county." Because that name, however, was already in use for another township in Minnesota, it was renamed Clark, March 24, 1870, taking his first name. He was born near Jordan, Canada, July 23, 1825; and died at Wells, the railway village of this township, October 11, 1885. He came to Minnesota in 1853; engaged in milling in Houston county until 1861; was Indian agent, by appointment of President Lincoln, 1861-5; built the Southern Minnesota railroad from the Mississippi river to Winnebago City, and afterward owned an extensive farm at Wells; was a representative in the territorial legislature, 1855; member of the state constitutional convention, 1857; a state senator, 1871; and president of the State Agricultural Society, 1880-85.

DELAVAN, settled in May, 1856, organized October 20, 1858, was at first named Guthrie, in honor of Sterrit Guthrie, one of the pioneer settlers. May 1, 1872, the name was changed to Delavan, to agree with that of the railway village which had been platted October 11, 1870, in the southeast corner of this township. The proprietors of the village were Henry W. Holley, chief engineer of this Southern Minnesota railroad, and Oren Delavan Brown, in whose honor the village name was

FARIBAULT COUNTY   185

suggested by Mrs. Holley. He was born in Jefferson county, N. Y., in 1837; came to Minnesota in 1856 with his father, Orville Brown, a prominent newspaper editor; was an engineer on the surveys for the Southern Minnesota railroad, 1865-75, and later for the St. Paul and Sioux City railroad; afterward resided in Luverne, Minn. The first passenger train arrived here December 19, 1870. The village was incorporated February 7, 1877.

DUNBAR, settled in 1856, organized April 3, 1866, was named Douglas by the county commissioners September 27, 1858, in honor of Stephen A. Douglas, for whom also Douglas county had been earlier named in the same year. But this name had been previously given to another Minnesota township, hence it was changed January 4, 1859, to be in honor of William Franklin Dunbar, then the state auditor. He was born in Westerly, R. I., November 10, 1820; and died in Caledonia, Minn. He came to Minnesota in 1854, settling in Caledonia, and opened a farm near that town; was a member of the territorial legislature, 1856; and was the first state auditor of Minnesota, 1858-60.

EASTON, the railway village in Lura township, platted in September, 1873, and incorporated March 9, 1874, was named for Jason Clark Easton, one of the original proprietors. He was born in West Martinsburg, N. Y., May 12, 1823; and died in La Crosse, Wis., April 25, 1901. He came to Minnesota in 1856, and settled at Chatfield. There and in several other towns of southern Minnesota he had extensive interests in banking, farm lands, and railways. He removed to La Crosse in 1883.

ELMORE, first settled in November, 1855, and organized in 1858, was then named Dobson, in honor of James Dobson, who came from Indiana, settling here as a homesteader in April, 1856. This name was changed to Elmore in 1862, commemorating Andrew E. Elmore, a prominent citizen of Wisconsin, who numbered among his friends several early settlers of this township. He was born in Ulster county, N. Y., May 8, 1814; and died at Fort Howard, Wis., January 13, 1906. He came to Wisconsin in 1839, settling in Mukwonago, Waukesha county, where he was a merchant during twenty-five years. In 1864 he removed to Green Bay, and after 1868 he resided at Fort Howard, near Green Bay. He was a member of the Wisconsin territorial legislature, 1842-44; of the first constitutional convention, 1846; the state legislature, 1859-60; and was during many years president of the State Board of charities and reform. He was commonly called "the Sage of Mukwonago."

EMERALD, settled in 1856, organized April 3, 1866, was named by the county commissioners for Ireland, the "Emerald Isle," supposing erroneously that it had Irish settlers.

FOSTER, settled in June, 1856, organized September 24, 1864, was named in honor of Dr. Reuben R. Foster, one of the earliest settlers of the county. He was born in Jefferson county, N. Y., in 1808; came to Minnesota in 1856, settling in Walnut Grove township; removed in 1858 to

Blue Earth City, and was its first resident physician; removed to Jackson, Minn., in 1869, and to St. Paul, about 1880, where he died.

FROST, a railway village in the north edge of Rome, "was named for Charles S. Frost, an architect of Chicago." (Stennett, Place Names of the Chicago and Northwestern Railways, 1908.)

HUNTLEY, a railway village in Verona, founded in August, 1879, is named for Hon. Henry M. Huntington, a pioneer farmer. He was born in Yates county, N. Y., in 1835; came to Minnesota in 1857, settling in this township; served in the Sixth Minnesota Regiment during the civil war; was a representative in the legislature in 1872; removed to his old home in New York in 1879, but returned in 1892, and afterward resided in Winnebago City. Because the name Huntington was previously in use in Minnesota, this shorter form was adopted.

JO DAVIESS township, (pronounced as Davis, and on recent maps so spelled erroneously), settled in 1855, organized January 26, 1864, was named Johnson in 1858 by the county commissioners, in honor of James and Alexander Johnson, who were early settlers of the county. It was found, however, that this name had been before given to another Minnesota township, and it was accordingly changed, the present name being adopted January 4, 1859, on the suggestion of James L. McCrery, one of the commissioners and the first settler in this township, a native of Kentucky. It is the name of the most northwestern county of Illinois; and Kentucky, Indiana and Missouri have each a county named Daviess. It commemorates Joseph Hamilton Daviess, a brave soldier and an able lawyer and orator, who "in the early days of Kentucky ranked with her most gifted and honored names." He was born in Bedford county, Virginia, March 4, 1774; and was killed in the battle of Tippecanoe, November 7, 1811.

KIESTER township, settled in May, 1866, organized in January, 1872, was named Lake by the county commissioners in 1858, from their supposition that it had a number of lakes. Because another Minnesota township had previously received this name, it was changed January 4, 1859, in honor of Jacob Armel Kiester, who later became the historian of this county. He was born at Mount Pleasant, Pa., April 29, 1832; and died in Blue Earth City, December 13, 1904. He was a student in Mt. Pleasant and Dickinson colleges, Pa.; studied law, and was admitted to practice, 1855; came to Minnesota in 1857, settling in Blue Earth City, which ever afterward was his home; was a representative in the legislature in 1865, and during many years was an officer of this county, being successively county surveyor, register of deeds, county attorney, and from 1869 to 1890 was judge of probate; was a state senator, 1891-3. He collected materials during more than twenty years for "The History of Faribault County," before mentioned as the source of much information for this chapter; and he also wrote a continuation of that work, from 1880 to 1904 inclusive, of which typewritten copies (717 pages) are in the

Etta Ross Memorial Library, Blue Earth, and the Library of the Minnesota Historical Society, St. Paul.

LURA, settled in May, 1856, organized September 7, 1864, derived its name from Lake Lura, crossed by the north line of the county about a mile west from the northwest corner of this township. Its name is said to have been given "by one of the early settlers, from the name 'Lura' being carved on a tree upon its shore." In the chapter of Blue Earth county, its Sioux names are also noted.

MINNESOTA LAKE township, settled in 1856, was organized in 1858, and was then named Marples by the commissioners, in honor of Charles Marples, an early settler. He was an Englishman, and had served seven years in the British army. After long residence here, he removed to Missouri. This township name was changed February 23, 1866, to Minnesota Lake, for the former large lake, which has been lately drained and apportioned to the adjoining farms. It is a name received from the Sioux or Dakotas, meaning slightly whitish water, which they also applied to the Minnesota river, thence adopted by this state. The railway village of Minnesota Lake was platted in October, 1866, and was incorporated February 14, 1876.

PILOT GROVE township, first settled in June, 1856, organized in January, 1864, "was so named because of the fine grove of native timber on the northern boundary of the town; and this grove was named Pilot Grove because in the early days, before roads were established, this grove was a sort of landmark, on the wide prairies, by which the immigrant was piloted on his way westward. It may be added, too, that this grove, with its fine lake of sparkling waters and rich grasses surrounding it, was, in the days of immigrants, a sort of capacious inn, or caravansary, or camping ground." (Kiester's History.) We regret to note that Pilot Grove lake has in recent years been wholly drained away.

PRESCOTT, settled in September, 1855, organized September 16, 1861, received its name in 1858 for a settler who soon afterward moved away. "All that has been ascertained of him is, that he was a carpenter by trade, and that he was known by the name of 'Old Honesty.'"

ROME township, settled in March, 1863, organized in 1868, was named Campbell by the commissioners in 1858, for James Campbell, one of the first settlers in Elmore township. At its organization, it was renamed Grant, in honor of General Grant, who later in that year was elected president of the United States. This name, however, had been earlier given to another Minnesota township, wherefore it was again changed in March, 1868, the present name being adopted, for the city of Rome, N. Y., on the suggestion of Fred Everton, the second settler in this township, who during many years was chairman of its board of supervisors.

SEELY, settled in June, 1856, organized in 1858, commemorates Philander C. Seely, one of its earliest settlers. He was born in Cayuga county, N. Y., in 1823; came to Minnesota and to this county in 1857; was elected sheriff in 1861, receiving every vote polled; served in the civil war; resided several years in this township, and later in Blue Earth City.

VERONA, settled in June, 1855, organized in October, 1858, was named after its post office, established in 1856 at the home of Henry T. Stoddard, in the southeast quarter of section 11, the name having been proposed by A. B. Cornell, of Owatonna, for this terminus of the mail route. It is the name of an important province in northern Italy, and of its chief city, whence came the title of the Shakespeare drama, "Two Gentlemen of Verona." Seventeen other states of our Union have villages or townships of this name.

WALNUT LAKE township, settled in June, 1856, organized in 1861, bears the name of its large lake, referring to its butternut trees, also called oil-nut and white walnut. It is translated from the Sioux name Tazuka.

WALTERS, the railway village of Foster, was named by officers of the Chicago, Rock Island and Pacific railway company.

WELLS, the railway village of Clark township, was founded and named July 1, 1869, receiving the maiden surname of Mrs. Clark W. Thompson. The Southern Minnesota railroad was completed to this place in January, 1870, and the railroad from Mankato to Wells in 1874. This village was incorporated March 6, 1871. Within the next few years numerous flowing wells, twenty or more, were obtained in and near this village, by boring through the glacial drift to depths of 110 to 120 feet, securing excellent water which rises from the bottom to a height of five to fifteen feet above the surface. These are the most remarkable wells of a large region in southern Minnesota, but the presence of artesian water here was unknown when the village was named.

WINNEBAGO township, settled in June, 1855, organized in October, 1858, was then named Winnebago City, after the village of this name which was founded here by Andrew C. Dunn and others in September, 1856. The townsite was platted in January, 1857, being named for the Winnebago tribe of Indians, whose reservation during the years 1855 to 1863 was in the adjoining Blue Earth county. It was named "City" for discrimination from the Winnebago Agency near Mankato, but this part of the name was discontinued in 1905.

LAKES AND STREAMS.

In the preceding list, sufficient mention has been made for the Blue Earth river, Brush creek, Cobb river (flowing through the northeast corner of this county), Lura lake, Minnesota lake, and Pilot Grove and Walnut lakes.

Maple river, named for the maple trees along its course, flowing northward into Blue Earth county, gave the name there of Mapleton township and village. Rice lake, in Delavan, near the head of the west branch of this river, was named Maple lake on the state map of 1860. Its present name refers to its wild rice, like another Rice lake in Foster.

FARIBAULT COUNTY 189

Bass lake, in section 9, Delavan, was named for the well known fish, and it gave the name of the first post office in this township, Bass Lake, which was established about the year 1859, but was discontinued after the Delavan railway village was founded. An oak grove overlooking Bass lake is named "Camp Comfort," much used in summers for picnics, reunions of the old settlers, and other meetings.

Hart lake, in section 28, Delavan, commemorates John and George Hart, who were pioneer farmers there.

Gorman's lake, now drained, in section 17, Jo Daviess, was named in honor of Patrick Gorman, an early Irish settler beside it.

Goose and Swan lakes were in sections 11 and 14, Brush Creek township, but have been drained. Another Swan lake, in section 15, Barber, was called Lake Kanta in 1860, a Sioux name, meaning Plum lake, for its wild plum trees.

The two largest lakes of this county, Minnesota lake, before noticed, and Ozahtanka lake in Barber and Emerald townships, have been drained, their beds being now cultivated farm lands. Both these names are on the map of 1860, each being the Sioux language. Tanka, like tonka, means great, but Ozah is not defined in Riggs' Dakota Dictionary.

The former Mud lake in section 23, Lura, is now traversed by a ditch and drained.

Jones creek, in Foster, commemorates a settler or a trapper.

Coon creek, tributary to the Blue Earth river from the east, and Badger creek from the west, are named for fur-bearers, the first formerly common here, but the latter rare in Minnesota, though common in parts of Wisconsin, giving its name as the sobriquet of that state.

Elm, Center, and South creeks, in Verona, flowing to the Blue Earth river from Martin county, are to be noticed in the chapter for that county.

THE KIESTER MORAINE AND GLACIAL LAKE MINNESOTA.

The fourth in the series of twelve terminal and marginal moraines formed in Minnesota by the continental ice-sheet during its wavering departure, at the close of the Glacial period, is called the Kiester moraine, from its prominent Kiester hills in the township of this name. These marginal drift hills and the continuation of their morainic belt northwesterly in this county and onward through the state, probably passing into South Dakota in the vicinity of Big Stone lake, were noted in Volume I of the Final Reports of the Minnesota Geological Survey, published in 1884.

At the time of formation of the Kiester moraine, the Glacial Lake Minnesota, described in the chapter of Blue Earth county, overspread the greater part of Faribault county, reaching thence northwestward along its ice border, and outflowing south by the Union slough in Iowa, at the head of the Blue Earth river, being thence tributary to the Des Moines river.

FILLMORE COUNTY

This county, established March 5, 1853, was named for Millard Fillmore, who was president of the United States, 1850 to 1853, retiring from office on the day previous to the approval of the act creating this county. He was born at Summer Hill, Cayuga county, N. Y., February 7, 1800; and died at Buffalo, N. Y., March 8, 1874. He studied law, and was admitted to practice in 1823; was a member of Congress, 1833-35 and 1837-43; was comptroller of the state of New York, 1847-49; was elected vice president on the Whig ticket headed by Zachary Taylor, 1848; and succeeded to the presidency by the death of Taylor, July 9, 1850. Fillmore visited St. Paul in a large excursion of eastern people, June 8, 1854, as noted in the Minnesota Historical Society Collections (vol. VIII, pages 395-400).

Biographies of Fillmore were published in 1856, when he was nominated as presidential candidate of the American party; and in 1915 Rev. William Elliot Griffis published a memorial review of his life and character, 159 pages, entitled "Millard Fillmore, Constructive Statesman, Defender of the Constitution, President of the United States." He is also commemorated by Fillmore county in Nebraska, by Millard county in Utah, and by villages named Fillmore in a dozen states.

TOWNSHIPS AND VILLAGES.

Information of these names has been gathered from "History of Fillmore County," by Ellis C. Turner and others, 1882, 626 pages; the later History of this county, compiled by Franklyn Curtiss-Wedge, 1912, two volumes (continuously paged), 1170 pages; and from Archibald D. Gray and Andrew W. Thompson, of Preston, and Calvin E. Huntley, of Spring Valley, interviewed in April, 1916.

AMHERST, settled in 1853, organized May 11, 1858, was named by one of its pioneer colonists, E. P. Eddy, "in honor of the place in which his wife was born." This was Amherst in Lorain county, Ohio, where her father, Henry Onstine, leader of these colonists, formerly lived. The settlers of the Ohio township came from New England, where towns of New Hampshire and Massachusetts had been named Amherst in honor of General Jeffery Amherst, the English commander and hero of the siege and capture of Louisburg from the French in 1758.

ARENDAHL, first settled in 1854, organized April 1, 1860, was named by Isaac Jackson, a Norwegian immigrant, who had lived twelve years in Dane county, Wisconsin, and came to this township in 1856, the name being for the seaport city of Arendal on the southeast coast of Norway. "He named the town in remembrance of old associations, secured a post office, and was the first postmaster."

FILLMORE COUNTY 191

BEAVER, settled in 1854, organized May 11, 1858, received its name from the Beaver creek (doubtless a home of beavers), which flows through this township, joining the Upper Iowa river in section 34. A former post office near its center, established in 1859, was called Alba, meaning white, because the name was "short, eastern, and ancient."

BELLVILLE, a former village in Newburg township, was founded in 1853 by two brothers, Edmund and Henry Bell.

BLOOMFIELD, first settled in 1854, was organized May 11, 1858. Eighteen other states have villages or cities of this "spring reminding name."

BRATSBERG, a hamlet in the southeast corner of section 10, Norway, bears the name of a district in southern Norway, comprising an area of about 5,500 square miles.

BRISTOL, settled in July, 1853, organized May 11, 1858, has the name of a large city in England, near the head of the Bristol channel. It is also the name of counties in Massachusetts and Rhode Island, and of villages and townships in twenty other states of our Union.

CANFIELD, a hamlet on the east line of section 21, York, was named for S. G. Canfield, who established a store there in 1876.

CANTON, first settled in March, 1851, was organized May 11, 1858. "There was a spirited contest over the name, and quite a number were suggested, but the struggle was finally narrowed down to two names, 'Elyria,' suggested by E. P. Eddy, and that of 'Canton,' proposed by Fred Flor. The vote declared in favor of Canton, but the Elyria party gave up reluctantly. . . . . On the records up to 1860, the name Elyria is carried along in the town books, when it dropped out of sight." These are names of cities in northeastern Ohio, near the former homes of many settlers in this township. Canton is a large and very ancient city of southeastern China, and thence twenty-three states of our Union have given this name to villages, cities and townships. The railway village of Canton was incorporated April 29, 1887.

CARIMONA, first settled in 1852, organized May 11, 1858, has the village of this name, founded in 1853-4, which was the county seat in 1855-56, being succeeded by Preston. During several years this village was a busy station of the stage route from Galena and Dubuque to St. Paul, as shown by the hotel register of the Carimona House, 1855-59, presented to the Library of the Minnesota Historical Society. This was the name of a prominent chief of the Winnebagoes, who signed by his mark seven successive treaties of the United States with this tribe, in 1816, 1825, '27, '28, '29, 1832, and 1837. His name, borne also by his son, had much variety of spellings, and is translated as "Walking Turtle." Dr. L. C. Draper wrote of him: "Naw-Kaw, or Car-a-mau-nee, or The Walking Turtle, went on a mission with Tecumseh in 1809 to the New York Indians, and served with that chief during the campaign of 1813, and was present at his death at the Thames." (See Wisconsin Historical Society Collections, vols. II, III, V, VII, and VIII; Minnesota H. S.

Collections, vol. IV, Williams' History of St. Paul, page 256; and "Waubun, the 'Early Day' in the North-West," by Mrs. John H. Kinzie, 1856, page 89.)

At a grand council held by Governor Ramsey in St. Paul, March 14, 1850, with Winnebago chiefs who had come from their reservation at Long Prairie, Carimona was one of the seven chiefs whose names are given by Williams. This chief, doubtless a son of the older Carimona, removed from Wisconsin to Iowa, later to Minnesota, and died, after 1850, on the Yellow river in Allamakee county, Iowa. For him this village and township were named.

CARROLLTON, settled in the spring of 1854, organized May 11, 1858, received its name in honor of Charles Carroll, of Carrollton, in Maryland, the last survivor of the signers of the Declaration of Independence. He was born in Annapolis, Md., September 20, 1737; and died in Baltimore, November 14, 1832.

CHATFIELD, settled in 1853, organized in 1858, was named in honor of Judge Andrew Gould Chatfield, who presided here at the first court held in the county, June 27, 1853. He was born in Butternuts, Otsego county, N. Y., January 27, 1810; and died in Belle Plaine, Minn., October 3, 1875. He was an associate justice of the supreme court of Minnesota Territory, 1853-7; was one of the founders of the town of Belle Plaine, and practiced law there, 1857-71; was judge of the Eighth judicial district, 1871-5. The village of Chatfield, platted in the spring of 1854 and incorporated in 1857, was the first county seat for two years, but was succeeded in 1855 by Carimona, and by Preston since 1856. This village was incorporated as a city, by the legislature, Februry 19, 1887.

CLEAR GRIT, a former hamlet on the South branch of Root river, in section 21, Carrollton, took the name given by John Kaercher to a flouring mill operated there by him with much success, 1872-81, retrieving ill fortune and losses that he had experienced through panics, fire, and flood, from 1857 onward in Preston, Chatfield, Fillmore, etc. (M. H. S. Collections, vol. X, page 42.)

ELLIOTA, a former village in section 32, Canton, was laid out in 1853 by Captain Julius W. Elliott, its earliest settler and first postmaster and blacksmith. He was born in Vermont in 1822; came to this county from Moline, Illinois, in 1853, bringing thence a company of the first settlers. In 1871 he removed to Missouri, where he died in 1876.

ETNA, a hamlet in section 25, Bloomfield, received its name, from several that were suggested, by drawing lots when its post office was established in 1856, now discontinued. This name of the lofty volcano in Sicily is borne by villages and post offices in sixteen other states.

FILLMORE township, settled in August, 1854, organized May 11, 1858, was named, like the county, in honor of President Fillmore, taking this name from its village, which had been founded in 1855.

FILLMORE COUNTY

FORESTVILLE township, first settled in 1852 and organized in 1855, received its name in honor of Forest Henry, the first probate judge of the county, who settled here in 1854 and in the next year was the first postmaster here. He was also one of the proprietors of the village of Forestville, platted in 1854.

FOUNTAIN, settled in 1853, organized May 11, 1858, was named for its large "Fountain Spring" in section 4, whence the railway village of Fountain, platted when the railway was built, in 1870, derives its water supply. The village was incorporated, by an act of the legislature, in 1876.

GRANGER, a village in the south edge of Bristol, was platted in 1857 by C. H. Lewis and B. Granger, of Boston, Mass., who also opened its first store.

GREENLEAFTON, a little hamlet in section 1, York, "was named in honor of Miss Mary Greenleaf, of Philadelphia, who generously gave three thousand five hundred dollars to build the Dutch Reformed Church edifice."

HAMILTON, a small village in the southwest corner of Sumner, was platted in 1855. Ten states have Hamilton counties, and twenty-six states have townships, villages, or cities of this name, mostly in honor of Alexander Hamilton, patriot in our American Revolution, and first secretary of the treasury of the United States, 1789-95.

HARMONY township, settled in the fall of 1852, was organized, May 11, 1858. Its village was founded in 1880. This name is borne by villages and townships in fifteen states of our Union.

HENRYTOWN, a hamlet in Amherst, platted in 1854, was named in honor of Henry Onstine, who was the leader in the settlement of that township, as before noted.

HIGHLAND, a hamlet in sections 35 and 36, Holt, received the name of its former post office, established in 1857, referring to its elevation which gives broad views over the valleys on the north and south.

HOLT, settled in the spring of 1854, organized May 11, 1858, was at first called Douglas, in honor of the statesman, Stephen A. Douglas, for whom a county of this state is named. Because that name had been applied to another Minnesota township, it was changed to Holt in 1862, honoring Gilbert Holt, a pioneer farmer in section 30, who "early in the seventies" removed to Dakota.

ISINOURS, a railway station in Carrollton, established about 1870, was named, with change of spelling, for George Isenhour, on whose land it was located.

JORDAN township, settled in 1853, organized May 11, 1858, was named for its North and South Jordan creeks, which unite and flow into the Middle branch of Root river. The name was given to these small streams by John Maine, one of the first settlers, who came from New England, fancifully deriving it from the River Jordan in Palestine.

LANESBORO, the railway village in Carrollton, was platted in the spring of 1868. Some of its early settlers came from Lanesboro township in

Berkshire county, Mass., and F. A. Lane was one of the stockholders in the townsite company.

LENORA, a village in sections 2 and 11, Canton, was founded in 1855 by Rev. John L. Dyer. It was named by him for one of his family or for a friend.

MABEL, a railway village in Newburg, was platted by Frank Adams, chief engineer of this railway, giving it the name of his little daughter who had died.

NEWBURG, first settled in 1851, was organized May 11, 1858, taking the name of its village in section 8, which had been founded and named in 1853 by Hans Valder, a native of Norway, who with others came to this place from LaSalle county, Illinois. Eighteen states of our Union have villages and post offices of this name.

NORWAY, settled in 1854, was organized April 3, 1860. "The name of the town is said to have been suggested by John Semmen, in honor of the native country of almost every inhabitant of the township."

OSTRANDER, the railway village of Bloomfield, platted in 1890, was named for William and Charles Ostrander, who gave to the railway company parts of the village site. William Ostrander was born in the state of New York, in 1819; and came to Minnesota in 1857, settling here as a farmer.

PETERSON, a railway village in section 30, Rushford, was founded in 1867, when the railway was built, on land donated for this use by Peter Peterson Haslerud, who settled here in July, 1853. It was incorporated in February, 1909. He was born in Norway, July 21, 1828; came to the United States in 1843; was a representative in the legislature, 1862; died September 23, 1880.

PILOT MOUND township, settled in 1854, organized May 11, 1858, is named for a flat-topped limestone hill in the southwest part of section 11. "It forms a prominent and striking object in the landscape, and formerly guided many a weary traveler as he wended his way toward the West."

PREBLE, settled in 1853-4, organized May 11, 1858, was named in honor of Edward Preble (b. 1761, d. 1807), of the United States Navy, commander of the expedition against Morocco and Tripoli in 1803-4.

PRESTON, first settled in 1853, organized May 11, 1858, received the name which had been given to its village, platted in the spring of 1855, by John Kaercher, its founder and mill owner, "in honor of his millwright, Luther Preston." In the same year a post office bearing this name was established, and Preston was appointed the first postmaster. This village, situated at the center of the county, has been the county seat since 1856. It was incorporated March 4, 1871.

PROSPER is a railway village in sections 35 and 36, Canton, auspiciously named.

RUSHFORD, settled in July, 1853, organized May 11, 1858, was named on Christmas day, 1854, by unanimous vote of the pioneer settlers, taking the name from Rush creek here tributary to the Root river. The men and women so voting numbered nine, these being all the settlers at that date. "Rush creek was so called on account of the tall rushes that grew along its banks, where cattle and ponies could obtain a subsistence all winter." The village of Rushford, founded in 1854, was named at the same time with the township. It was incorporated as a city in 1868, and often was called "the Trail City, on account of the intersection of several Indian foot paths."

SPRING VALLEY township, settled in 1852, organized May 11, 1858, was named for its several very large springs, one being about a mile east of the village, and two nearly as large within the townsite limits, one of these being walled up and used as a pumping supply for the water works. This village, founded in 1855, incorporated in 1872, has become a junction of railways.

STRINGTOWN village, begun in 1860, in section 27, Amherst, has its name "from the fact that all the settlers built their houses along the road in the ravine in which the would be village is located, thus stringing it out for some distance."

SUMNER, settled in May, 1853, organized May 11, 1858, was named by the earliest settlers in honor of the statesman, Charles Sumner (b. 1811, d. 1874), United States senator for Massachusetts from 1851 till his death, an uncompromising opponent of slavery, and during and after the civil war chairman of the senate committee on foreign affairs, 1861-71.

WAUKOPEE, a former hamlet in section 25, Carimona, founded in 1853, derived its name "from an Indian chief, who used to have a fishing and hunting camp at this place."

WHALAN, the railway village in Holt, founded in 1868, is on land previously owned by John Whaalahan, "but usage dropped the redundant a's and an h, and it became Whalan." It was incorporated in March, 1876.

WYKOFF, another railway village, in Fillmore, platted in 1871, and incorporated March 8, 1876, commemorates Cyrus G. Wykoff, of LaCrosse, Wis., who was the surveyor for construction of this railway and was one of the proprietors of this townsite.

YORK, settled in 1854, organized May 11, 1858, bears the name of a very ancient walled city in England, which was one of the principal seats of Roman dominion there. Thence came the name of the city and state of New York, and numerous villages, cities, and counties, in seventeen states of the Union are named York, this being the Saxon form derived from Eboracum, the Latin name.

RIVERS AND CREEKS.

A large area of southeastern Minnesota, comprising Fillmore county, also Houston county on the east, Winona and Olmsted counties on the north, Wabasha and Goodhue counties, farther north, and Mower county on the west, has no lakes, being strongly contrasted with the abundance of lakes in nearly all other parts of this state. The southeastern lakeless area includes the edge of the great Driftless Area of Wisconsin, which reaches into Houston and Winona counties. On its other and larger part, in Fillmore county and the other counties named, the formations of glacial and modified drift, spread by the continental ice-sheet and by waters from its melting, are relatively ancient and thin, not dominating the surface outlines. The region therefore lacks the more or less uneven contour of alternate swells and depressions, or sometimes more noteworthy ridges, hills, and hollows, which elsewhere are characteristic of the drift, causing it generally to have plentiful lakes.

Root river, more fully noticed in the first chapter, is translated from the Dakota or Sioux name, Hokah, both being used on Nicollet's map in 1843. This river may be said to be formed by the union of its North and Middle branches in Chatfield township. A mile and a half below Lanesboro it receives the South branch. Another large southern affluent, called the South fork of Root river, drains southeastern Fillmore county and joins the main stream in Houston county.

On the state map published in 1860, the Middle and South branches and the South fork were respectively called Fillmore, Carimona, and Houston rivers, taking these names from the three villages.

Tributaries of the Root river from the north in this county include Rush creek, before noted, in Rushford; Pine creek, in the north edge of Arendahl, which is a branch of Rush creek; and Money and Trout creeks, in Pilot Mound township.

Houston county has another Money creek, for which a township is named. There it originated from an incident of the early history; but the reason for its duplication in Fillmore county has not been ascertained, though the two are believed to have some relationship.

Lost creek, tributary to the Middle branch, is so named because it flows underground in the creviced limestone beds for two miles, through sections 14 and 13, Jordan.

The North and South Jordan creeks, before mentioned as giving the township name, and the Brook Kedron, flowing into the Middle branch in Sumner, are names from the Bible, the latter being a very small stream with a deep valley at the east side of Jerusalem.

Bear, Deer, and Spring Valley creeks flow into the Middle branch from the southwest.

Sugar creek, named for its sugar maples, is tributary to Root river in section 13, Chatfield.

The South branch receives Watson creek near the center of Carrollton, commemorating Thomas and James Watson, pioneers of Fountain township; and from the south it receives Canfield, Willow, and Camp creeks, the first (which in two parts of its course flows underground) being named for S. G. Canfield, of York, and the last having been a favorite camping place for immigrants. A small eastern tributary of

FILLMORE COUNTY 197

Camp creek was formerly called Duxbury creek, for pioneer families there; but on recent maps it is named Partridge creek, for the well known game birds.

Weisel creek, flowing into the South fork of Root river in Preble, was named for David Weisel, who in 1855 built a sawmill and gristmill near its mouth. The mill was carried away, and himself and family were drowned, by a flood of this stream, August 6, 1866.

Beaver creek, before noticed as the source of the name of Beaver township, was called Slough creek on the map of 1860.

The head stream of Upper Iowa river, to which Beaver creek is tributary, flows meanderingly past the south side of Beaver, York, and Bristol, several times crossing the state boundary. Its name, previously considered in the first chapter, like that of the state of Iowa and of the larger Iowa river, farther south, commemorates a Siouan tribe who lived on these rivers, nearly related with the Winnebagoes.

EAGLE ROCKS AND CHIMNEY ROCK

are craggily eroded and weathered forms of the limestone strata, left in the process of very slow channeling of the valley of the South branch of Root river in section 27, Forestville. The Eagle Rocks are pictured in the Final Report of the Minnesota Geological Survey (vol. I, 1884, page 296); and on the same page the Chimney Rock is described, "on the side of the bluff of a ravine, . . . having a fancied resemblance to an oven with a low chimney."

FREEBORN COUNTY

Established February 20, 1855, this county was named in honor of William Freeborn, member of the Council in the Territorial Legislature for the years 1854 to 1857. He was born in Ohio in 1816; came to St. Paul in 1848, and removed to Red Wing in 1853, where he had large interests, as also at Cannon Falls; emigrated in 1864 to the Rocky mountains, and spent the next winter as a gold miner in Montana; was engaged three years in fruit culture in Oregon; and finally, in 1868, settled in California, on a ranch at Santa Margarita, in San Luis Obispo county. He was the second mayor of Red Wing, in 1858, but resigned before the end of the year. Although he had traveled much, he wrote in 1899 from his California home that he had never ridden on a railroad train. Newson, in his "Pen Pictures of St. Paul" (1884), wrote of Freeborn as follows: "He was a man of progressive and speculative ideas, energetic, always scheming, and had a happy faculty of getting other parties interested in his enterprises. He was a quietly spoken man, of rugged appearance; self-possessed, and never was afraid to venture." This county was organized March 4, 1857, with Albert Lea as the county seat.

Townships and Villages.

Notes of the origins of geographic names have been gathered from "History of Freeborn County," 1882, 548 pages, including the "Centennial History," by Daniel G. Parker (forming pages 281-292); the later History of this county, compiled by Franklyn Curtiss-Wedge, 1911, 883 pages; and from Martin Van Buren Kellar, of Albert Lea, interviewed in April, 1916.

ALBERT LEA township, first settled in the summer of 1855, organized in 1857, took the name of its village, which was platted in October, 1856, and was incorporated as a city March 11, 1878. The name was adopted from the large adjoining lake on the southeast, to which Nicollet gave it in honor of Albert Miller Lea who in 1835 explored and mapped streams and lakes in this county.

Lea was born in Richland, Grainger county, Tennessee, July 23, 1808; was graduated at West Point in 1831; aided Major Long in 1832, in surveys of the Tennessee river; was an assistant on surveys of Lake Michigan in 1833; was in military service on the Missouri and Mississippi rivers during 1834; and in the summer of 1835 was second lieutenant of a company on the exploring expedition here noticed, in which he was designated as ordnance officer and volunteered his services as topographer and chronicler.

The expedition, under the command of Lieut. Col. Stephen Watts Kearny, traveled along the northeast side of the Des Moines river from

FREEBORN COUNTY				199

the Mississippi to the mouth of Boone river, thence northeast to the Mississippi at the mouth of Zumbro river, (named Embarras river by Lea, because it was encumbered by a raft of driftwood near its mouth), thence southeast to Wabasha's village and the site of Winona, and thence westward to headwaters of the Cedar and Blue Earth rivers, and southwestward through the present Winnebago and Kossuth counties in Iowa, to the Des Moines river. Descending the Des Moines in a canoe from the site of the city of this name to its mouth, Lea mapped it and described it in his journal of the expedition, which was the basis of an unpublished report to the War Department, and of a pamphlet in 53 pages, with a map, published the next year in Philadelphia. In this publication, Lea first gave the name Iowa to the district obtained by treaty at the close of the Black Hawk war, in 1832. It was an eastern part of the large area later called Iowa as a territory and state, having reference to the Iowa Indians and the river bearing their name.

An extended autobiographic sketch, written by Albert M. Lea for the Minnesota Historical Society, was published in the Freeborn County Standard, March 13, 1879. He resigned from the army in 1836; resided in Tennessee, was a civil engineer, and in 1838 was U. S. commissioner for the survey of the southern boundary of the Territory of Iowa; was professor of mathematics in the East Tennessee University, at Knoxville, 1844-51; removed to Texas in 1857; was an engineer of the Confederate service during the civil war; lived in Galveston, 1865-74, and later in Corsicana, Texas, where he died, January 17, 1891. Two of his brothers were Pryor Lea, a member of Congress, and Luke Lea, who, as Commissioner of Indian Affairs, was associated with Governor Ramsey in 1851 in making the treaties of Traverse des Sioux and Mendota.

Further details of this expedition, and notes of the names applied by Lea to lakes and streams in Freeborn county, are given in the later part of this chapter.

ALDEN, settled in 1858, was organized April 3, 1866. The railway village was platted in 1869, and the track was completed to this place January 1, 1870. It was incorporated in 1879. This name is borne by villages and townships in seven other states.

ARMSTRONG, a railway station in section 4, Pickerel Lake, was established in 1878, and was named for Hon. Thomas Henry Armstrong, who in that year erected a grain elevator there. He was born in Milan, Ohio, February 6, 1829; was graduated at Western Reserve College, 1854; came to Minnesota in 1855, settling in High Forest, Olmsted county; and in 1874 removed to Albert Lea, where he died, December 29, 1891. He was a representative in the legislature, 1864-5, being speaker in 1865; was lieutenant governor, 1866-70; and a state senator, 1877-8.

BANCROFT, first settled in July, 1855, organized May 11, 1858, had a temporary village of this name, platted in the fall of 1856, in sections 28 and 29, which on March 4, 1857, was an unsuccessful candidate for the county seat. The name was chosen in honor of George Bancroft (b. 1800, d. 1891), who was author of "History of the United States," ten volumes, published 1834-74; U. S. secretary of the navy, 1845-6, and founder of the Naval Academy, Annapolis; minister to Great Britain, 1846-49, and to Berlin, 1868-74.

BATH, settled in the spring of 1856, was organized in January, 1858, under the name of Porter, but was renamed Bath, April 15, 1859, after the name of the county seat of Steuben county, New York, the native town of Frederick W. Calkins, who had settled here in 1857.

CARLSTON, first settled in August, 1855, was organized in January, 1858, being then named Stanton, in honor of Elias Stanton, a settler on the shore of Freeborn lake, who had suffered amputation of his feet because of their being frozen, and who died in the spring of 1858. This name was earlier used for another Minnesota township, so that in September, 1859, it was changed, the present name being adopted "in respect to the memory of a distinguished Swede of that name, who settled in that town in an early day, and who was drowned in Freeborn lake." He was Theodore L. Carlston (or Carlson), the second settler, drowned in 1858.

CLARK'S GROVE, the railway village in Bath, was founded in 1890, ten years before the railway was built. Its name had been long borne by a grove a mile east of the present village, in which grove J. Mead Clark settled "in the early days."

CONGER, a railway village in the east edge of Alden, was named by officers of the Chicago, Rock Island and Pacific railway.

EMMONS, a railway village in the south edge of Nunda, on the state line, was incorporated March 14, 1899. Here Henry G. Emmons settled in 1856, and "in 1880 his sons started a store on the present site of the village." He was born in Norway, October 16, 1828; came to the United States in 1850, settling at first in Wisconsin; was postmaster of the State Line post office here fifteen years; was a representative in the legislature, 1877-8; died in this village, October 2, 1909.

FREEBORN township was first settled in July, 1856, and was organized May 11, 1858. Its village, platted in June, 1857, and the lake beside which it lies, were named like the county, in honor of William Freeborn, whence also the township received this name.

FREEMAN, first settled in 1854, organized April 2, 1861, was named in honor of John Freeman, a native of Northampton, England, who in 1855 "secured, under the pre-emption law, the whole of section fifteen for himself and three sons."

GENEVA, settled in 1855-6, was organized May 11, 1858. Its village, platted in the winter of 1856-7, had been named by Edwin C. Stacy, the first postmaster here and the first probate judge for the county, "in remembrance of Geneva, N. Y.," whence the large adjoining lake and the township received the same name.

FREEBORN COUNTY   201

GLENVILLE, the railway village and junction in Shell Rock township, was named by officers of the railway company. It was incorporated in 1898. Previous to the building of the railway here in 1877, this had been the site of a smaller village, platted in 1856, bearing the name Shell Rock, for the river on which it is situated, thence given also to the township.

GORDONSVILLE, a railway village in section 32, Shell Rock, platted in 1880, received its name from a post office that was established about 1860 or earlier, of which T. J. Gordon and his son, W. H. H. Gordon, were successively postmasters after 1865, residing as farmers in section 28, near the site of this village.

HARTLAND, settled in the spring of 1857, organized May 11, 1858, was named for Hartland in Windsor county, Vermont, whence some of its early settlers came. This name was proposed by the wife of O. Sheldon, the first postmaster. The railway village of Hartland was platted in 1877, and was incorporated in 1893.

HAYWARD, settled in 1856, organized April 5, 1859, was named in honor of David Hayward, one of its earliest settlers, who came from Postville, Iowa, and returned to that state after living here only two years. The railway village, founded in 1869, was replatted in 1886.

ITASCA was a small village or hamlet in section 31, Bancroft, platted in the winter of 1855-6, adjoining a lakelet which also was named Itasca. In 1857 it was an aspirant to be designated as the county seat, but, failing in that ambition, it lasted only a few years. The name was derived from that given by Schoolcraft to the source of the Mississippi river.

LONDON, settled in 1855, organized in 1858, received its name for the city and county of New London, Connecticut. It was proposed by William N. and James H. Goslee, natives of Hartford county in that state, who settled here respectively in 1856 and 1857. The railway village of London was platted in October, 1900.

MANCHESTER, first settled in June, 1856, organized in January, 1858, was then named Buckeye, but in May it was renamed Liberty. In October of that year it received the present name, suggested by Mathias Anderson, who came here in 1857 from a township of this name in Illinois. Its railway village, founded in 1877-8, was platted in 1882.

MANSFIELD, settled in June, 1856, was organized in January, 1866, being the latest township of this county. Its name, suggested by Captain George S. Ruble, founder of the city of Albert Lea, is borne by a city in Ohio, near his former home, and by villages and townships in fourteen states of our Union. Originally the name is from a town of Nottinghamshire in England, whence the first Earl of Mansfield (b. 1705, d. 1793), a distinguished British jurist and statesman, received his title. The History of this county (1882) refers to him as commemorated by this township name.

Moscow, first settled in May, 1855, was organized in January, 1858. "Some years previous to settlement, the heavy body of timber which covered section seventeen, in Moscow, was set on fire in a dry season, creating such a conflagration as to suggest scenes in Russia under the great Napoleon. From that time it was known as the Moscow timber, and thus the name of the town had its origin." (History, 1882, page 292.) The little village of this name was platted in June, 1857.

MYRTLE, the railroad village in section 7, London, was founded "in 1900, when the railroad came through."

NEWRY, settled in 1854, organized May 11, 1858, was named on the suggestion of Thomas Fitzsimmons, who was the first township clerk, for a seaport and river in northern Ireland, whence several pioneers of this township came.

NUNDA, settled in 1856, organized May 11, 1858, was named by Patrick Fitzsimmons, a native of Ireland, who was one of the first settlers and a prominent citizen, "in honor of towns of the same name in which he had lived in New York and Illinois." This name is "derived from the Indian word *nundao,* meaning 'hilly,' or according to another authority, 'potato ground.'" (Gannett, The Origin of Certain Place Names in the U. S., 1905.)

OAKLAND, settled in 1855, organized April 5, 1857, received its name from the small and scattered oak trees, with occasional groves, which originally occupied fully half of its area, commonly called "oak openings," while the remainder consisted of prairie land and grassy sloughs.

PICKEREL LAKE township, first settled in 1855, organized September 8, 1865, bears the name of the lake crossed by its east boundary, widely known for its abundance of this fish. The lake had been called Bear lake by the Indians because previous to the coming of white settlers they killed a large bear near it. The present name was given by Austin R. Nichols, through whose mistake in 1854 the former names of Pickerel and Bear lakes became transposed. (History, 1882, page 291.)

RICELAND, settled in August, 1856, organized in January, 1858, was at first named Beardsley, in honor of Samuel A. Beardsley, one of the first pioneers, who "came by ox team from Illinois, brought considerable stock, and settled on the south side of Rice lake." This large but shallow lake, well filled with wild rice, for which the township was soon renamed, covered some 2,000 acres, but it has been wholly drained away, the lake bed being now farm lands.

ST. NICHOLAS was the first village in this county, platted in the summer of 1856, on the south side of Lake Albert Lea, in sections 25 and 26 of Albert Lea township. In March, 1857, it aspired to be elected as the county seat, but, after the failure of that hope, its buildings were removed and the village site became farming land.

SHELL ROCK township, settled in June, 1853, organized in 1857, received the name of its river, the outlet of Lake Albert Lea, which along its course in Iowa is bordered by rock strata containing fossil shells. The early village of Shell Rock has been noticed in this list as Glenville, its present name.

FREEBORN COUNTY

TWIN LAKES, a railway village in section 12, Nunda, was partly platted in 1858, being the site of a sawmill and a flouring mill many years previous to the building of the railway in 1877-8. The fall of Goose creek, outflowing from the neighboring Twin lakes, supplies valuable water power.

LAKES AND STREAMS, WITH NOTES OF THE EXPEDITION IN 1835.

The pamphlet before mentioned as published by Lieut. Albert M. Lea, entitled "Notes on the Wisconsin Territory, particularly with reference to the Iowa District or Black Hawk Purchase" (53 pages, 1836), has a folded map of the country extending from northern Missouri to the foot of Lake Pepin and from the Mississippi to the Missouri river, comprising the present southeast part of Minnesota and nearly all of Iowa. In the area of Freeborn county Lea mapped and named five lakes, each of which is clearly identified on the present more accurate maps.

Fox lake, doubtless named for a fox seen there, is the largest of these lakes, to which Nicollet's map in 1843 gave its present title, Lake Albert Lea. The outflowing Shell Rock river received this name on Lea's map, which Nicollet copied but called it a creek. Where Lea crossed it on the outward journey of the expedition, "limestone filled with petrifications was abundant," whence he derived the name. (Iowa Historical Record, vol. VI, page 548.)

Chapeau lake, meaning in French a hat, so named by Lea for its outline, which reminded him of the old-fashioned three-cornered hat, left unnamed by Nicollet, is now White Lake, commemorating Captain A. W. White, an early settler who lived beside it till 1861, then removing into the village of Albert Lea.

Fountain lake, adjoining the north side of the city of Albert Lea, is produced by a dam, so that it does not appear on early maps.

Council lake of Lea's map, referring to some parley there with "a few straggling Indians," as mentioned in his autobiographic letter to the Minnesota Historical Society, is now Freeborn lake, outflowing by the Big Cobb river northwesterly to the Blue Earth and Minnesota rivers. This lake and two others continuing northward are mapped by Nicollet as Ichiyaza lakes, a Sioux name meaning a row or series.

Trail lake, named probably for an Indian trail passing by it, mapped too large by Lea, copied by Nicollet, but without a name, is the Upper Twin lake, outflowing by Lime creek, which was also named by Lea, now Goose creek. A very little lakelet of Lea's map, northwest of Trail lake, represents the Little Oyster lakes in sections 23 and 26, Pickerel Lake township, "so called because of their shape."

Lake Boone, named by Lea in honor of Nathan Boone, captain of one of the companies of dragoons in this expedition, is now Bear lake in Nunda, which was at first called Pickerel lake in 1853 by the white settlers, as noted in the History of this county (1882, page 291). Lea mapped it erroneously as the source of Boone river in Iowa, named on his map likewise for Captain Boone. In this error he was followed by Nicollet, whose map, however, leaves both the lake and river unnamed. Nathan Boone (b. 1780, d. 1857), was the youngest of the nine children of the renowned frontiersman, Daniel Boone.

"Paradise Prairie," noted by Lea, northward of his Chapeau lake, was described in the History of the county in 1882, that it enters Bancroft township "in the southwestern corner and extends northeasterly almost across the entire town, gradually disappearing towards Clark's Grove, in the northeast corner."

In the list of townships, sufficient reference has been made to several lakes, besides those noted by Lea, namely, Geneva lake, Itasca lake, Pickerel and Rice lakes, and the Twin lakes.

Nicollet's Ichiyaza lakes, before noticed, doubtless included Lake George, and Spicer and Trenton lakes, in Freeborn, named for and by early settlers. Another, the little Prairie lake, also named Penny lake, is in section 31 of this township.

Le Sueur or Mule lake, in the east part of Hartland, lies at the head of Le Sueur river. Its second name alludes to the loss of "a fine span of mules belonging to B. J. Boardman," drowned there in 1857.

Lake George, in section 22, Bath, was named in honor of George W. Skinner, Jr., son of a prominent pioneer there.

Newry lake derived its name from its location, in section 2, Newry township.

Deer and Turtle creeks, in Newry and Moscow, Goose lake in section 3, Albert Lea, and Elk lake, section 21, London, need no explanations.

Spring lake, in the city of Albert Lea, and Fountain lake at its north side, the latter a mill pond, are named for springs on their shores.

Bancroft creek is in the township of this name.

Manchester had a notable group of small lakes, namely, Lake Peterson, Silver, Sugar, and Spring lakes; but the first two have been drained.

Peter Lund creek, in Hayward, commemorates a pioneer farmer, an immigrant from Norway, who came to America in 1850, settled here in 1856, and was the first township treasurer.

Steward's creek, in Alden and Mansfield, was named in honor of Hiram J. Steward, who was born near Bangor, Maine, September 21, 1831; served in the civil war, 1862, being severely wounded; came west, and in 1869 settled as a farmer in section 12, Mansfield.

Lime creek is the outlet of Bear lake and State Line lake, flowing into Iowa and there tributary to Shell Rock river. It was thought by Lea to be the head stream of Boone river, as before noted.

Grass lake, in sections 26 and 35, Freeman, now drained, was named for the grasses and sedges growing in its shallow water.

Woodbury creek, in Oakland and London, flowing into Mower county, received the name of a settler there.

GOODHUE COUNTY

This county, established March 5, 1853, was named in honor of James Madison Goodhue, who was the first printer and editor in Minnesota, beginning the issue of the Minnesota Pioneer on April 28, 1849. He was born in Hebron, N. H., March 31, 1810, and died in St. Paul, August 27, 1852; was graduated at Amherst College in 1833; studied law in New York City, and was admitted to the bar about 1840; afterward was a farmer three years in Plainfield, Ill.; practiced law in Galesburg, Ill., and in Platteville and Lancaster, Wis.; became editor of the Wisconsin Herald, published in Lancaster; removed to St. Paul in the spring of 1849, and was a most earnest and influential journalist here during the three remaining years of his life.

Goodhue was a man of very forcible character and of high moral principles. As a vigorous writer, he did much to upbuild St. Paul and Minnesota, and made strong personal friends and enemies. Because of his scathing editorial against the U. S. marshal, Alexander Mitchell, and Judge David Cooper, a brother of the latter attacked Mr. Goodhue, January 15, 1851, on the street in front of the building in which the legislature was in session, and stabbed him twice, severely wounding him, and being shot in return. From that injury he never fully recovered.

Biographic sketches of Goodhue as founder and editor of the first newspaper of the new Minnesota Territory are in the Minnesota Historical Society Collections, by Col. John H. Stevens (vol VI, pages 492-501) and D. S. B. Johnston (X, 247-253). His successor as editor of the Pioneer, Joseph R. Brown, wrote of him in an editorial tribute a year after he died: "James M. Goodhue was a warm and fast friend of Minnesota to the day of his death. He will be remembered with the small band of sturdy men who labored constantly and with iron resolution to establish the pillars of society in our Territory upon a sound moral basis. His press was always found on the side of law, order, temperance, and virtue."

Townships and Villages.

Information of origins and meanings of these names has been gathered from the "Geographical and Statistical Sketch . . . of Goodhue County," by W. H. Mitchell, 1869, 191 pages; "History of Goodhue County," 1878, 664 pages; "Goodhue County, Past and Present, by an Old Settler" (Rev. Joseph W. Hancock), 1893, 349 pages; the later History, edited by Franklyn Curtiss-Wedge, 1909, 1074 pages; and from Dr. William M. Sweney, Albert E. Rhame, city engineer, and Charles S. Dana, clerk of the court, interviewed at Red Wing in April, 1916.

BELLE CREEK township, settled in 1853, organized in 1858, received this French name of its creek, meaning beautiful.

BELVIDERE, settled in the spring of 1855, organized May 11, 1858, was at first called York, and later Elmira, the present name being adopted December 28, 1858. Illinois has a city of this name, which also is borne by villages and townships in seven other states.

BURNSIDE, settled in 1854, organized in 1858, was known at first as Union, and in 1859-61 as Milton, but was renamed as now in March, 1862, in honor of Ambrose Everett Burnside (b. 1824, d. 1881), a distinguished general in the civil war, 1861-65, governor of Rhode Island, 1866-9, and United States senator, 1875-81.

CANNON FALLS township, settled in 1854, organized in 1858, derived its name from the falls of Cannon river, as it was named by Pike in 1806, by Keating's Narrative of Long's expedition in 1823, and on Nicollet's map, 1843, erroneously changed from the early French name, Riviere aux Canots, which alluded to canoes left near its mouth by parties of Indians on war or hunting expeditions. Cannon Falls village, platted August 27, 1855, was incorporated March 10, 1857, and adopted its city charter in February, 1905.

CENTRAL POINT, a township of very small area, settled about 1850, was organized in 1858. Its name refers to a point of land here extending into Lake Pepin, about midway between the head and foot of the lake.

CHERRY GROVE, settled in 1854, organized in 1858, received its name from a cherry grove in the central part of this township, where a log schoolhouse was built in 1857. The wild red cherry (also called bird cherry) and the wild black cherry are common throughout the greater part of this state.

CLAY BANK, CLAY PITS, and BELLE CHESTER, in Goodhue township, are railway stations for supply of pottery clay, used extensively in Red Wing for manufacture of stoneware and sewer pipe.

DENNISON, a railway village in the west edge of Warsaw, on the county line, was named in honor of Morris P. Dennison, a settler near its site in 1856, on whose land the village was located.

EGGLESTON, a railway station in Welch, was likewise named for an early settler and land owner. John E. and Joseph Eggleston settled in the adjoining township of Burnside in the spring of 1855, and Harlan P. and Ira E. Eggleston were volunteers in the civil war from that township, which included Welch until 1864.

FAIRPOINT, a small village euphoniously named, in section 33, Cherry Grove, was platted in 1857.

FEATHERSTONE, first settled in 1855, organized in 1858, "derived its name from William Featherstone, who with a large family settled there in 1855."

FLORENCE, settled in 1854, organized 1858, was named in honor of Florence Graham, oldest child of Judge Christopher C. Graham, of Red Wing. She was married January 8, 1872, to David M. Taber, who died

April 1, 1880. Mrs. Taber, yet living in Red Wing in 1916, "is known for her interest in all matters which tend toward the betterment of the city and county." Her father (b. 1806, d. 1891) served in the Mexican war; came to Red Wing in 1854, as receiver of the U. S. land office, and filled that position until 1861; was the municipal judge after 1869.

FRONTENAC, a railway village and neighboring lakeside village of summer homes, in Florence township, had the early Indian trading post of James Wells, before 1850, and was permanently settled in 1854-57. The name commemorates Louis de Buade de Frontenac, who was born in Paris, 1622, and died in Quebec, November 28, 1698. He was the French colonial governor of Canada in 1672-82 and 1689-98. There is no record of his traveling to the Mississippi river.

GOODHUE township, settled in 1854, organized September 13, 1859, was then named Lime, but was renamed as now in January, 1860, honoring James M. Goodhue, like the county name. The village was incorporated April 26, 1897.

HAY CREEK township, settled in the spring of 1854, organized in 1858, received its name from the stream, which had natural hay meadows.

HOLDEN, settled in 1854-5, organized in 1858, has a name that is borne by townships in Maine and Massachusetts, and by a city in Missouri.

KENYON, settled in 1855, organized in 1858, was named for a pioneer merchant, who in 1856 built the first store there. The village, now a railway junction, was also originally platted in 1856.

LEON, settled in the fall of 1854, organized in 1858, bears a foreign name, that of a medieval kingdom, which was later a province of Spain. It is also the name of townships in New York and Wisconsin.

MINNEOLA, settled in May 1855, organized December 15, 1859, has a name from the Dakota or Sioux language, meaning much water.

PINE ISLAND, settled in 1854, organized in 1858, took the name of its village, which was platted in the winter of 1856-7. "The island proper is formed by the middle branch of the Zumbro, which circles around the present village, enclosing a tract once thickly studded with tall pine trees. . . . This spot was one of the favorite resorts of the Dakota Indians. They called it Wa-zee-wee-ta, Pine Island, and here in their skin tents they used to pass the cold winter months, sheltered from the winds and storms by the thick branches of lofty pines. The chief of Red Wing's village told the commissioners of the United States, when asked to sign the treaty that would require his people to relinquish their home on the Mississippi river, that he was willing to sign it if he could have his future home at Pine Island." (Hancock, page 288.) "Between the two branches of the Zumbro river, which unite a short distance below, there was quite a forest of pine, which could be seen for a long distance over the prairie, giving it quite the appearance of an Island in the sea." (Mitchell, page 118.)

RED WING, the location of a mission to the Sioux in 1837 by two Swiss missionaries, Samuel Denton and Daniel Gavin, was first settled for farming and Indian trading in 1850-52; was chosen to be the county seat in 1853; was incorporated as a city March 4, 1857; and received new municipal charters on March 3, 1864, and February 21, 1887.

Doane Robinson, historian of the Sioux, writes in the "Handbook of American Indians" (Hodge, Part II, 1910, page 365): "RED WING. The name of a succession of chiefs of the former Khemnichan band of Mdewakanton Sioux, residing on the west shore of Lake Pepin, Minn., where the city of Red Wing now stands. At least four chiefs in succession bore the appellation, each being distinguished by another name. The elder Red Wing is heard of as early as the time of the Pontiac war, when he visited Mackinaw, and was in alliance with the English in the Revolution. He was succeeded by his son, Walking Buffalo (Tatankamani), who enlisted in the British cause in 1812. The name was maintained during two succeeding generations, but disappeared during the Sioux outbreak of 1862-65. The family was less influential than the Little Crows or the Wabashas of the same tribe."

Colonel William Colvill, in a letter to Prof. N. H. Winchell, wrote (Geology of Minnesota, Final Report, vol. II, 1888, page 60): "Red Wing's titular name was Wacouta—'the shooter.' This was always the head chief's title,—the same as that of the chief who captured Hennepin. He had the name of Red Wing, Koo-poo-hoo-sha [Khupahu, wing, sha, red], from the swan's wing, dyed scarlet, which he carried."

Pike in 1805-06 called the second of these hereditary chiefs Talangamane, which should be more correctly written Tatanka mani, meaning Buffalo walking; and he also gave his titled name in French, Aile Rouge, with its direct English translation, Red Wing.

The Sioux name of this place was Rhemnicha or Khemnicha, applied by Nicollet's map to the present Hay creek as Remnicha river. It means the Hill-Water-Wood place, formed by three Sioux words, Rhe, a high hill or ridge, mini, water, and chan, wood, referring to the Barn bluff and other high river bluffs, and to the abundance of water and wood, which made it an ideal camp ground.

ROSCOE, settled in 1854, organized in 1858, was named by Charles Dana, one of the pioneers, "from the township of Roscoe, Illinois, where he had previously lived."

STANTON, settled in the fall of 1854, organized in 1858, was named in honor of William Stanton, who, with his son of the same name and others, immigrants from New England, came in 1855, settling on Prairie creek. Rev. J. W. Hancock, who conducted the first religious services of this township at his home in the winter of 1855-6, wrote: "The log house built by William Stanton, Sr., near the road leading to Faribault from the nearest Mississippi towns, was for several years the only place for the entertainment of travelers between Cannon Falls and further west. Mr. Stanton's latch string was always hanging out, and every civil appearing stranger was welcome to such accommodations as he had. He frequently entertained fifty persons the same night."

GOODHUE COUNTY 209

VASA, settled in 1853, organized in 1858, "was named in honor of Gustavus Vasa, king of Sweden, more generally known as Gustavus I, the Christian king, and the founder of the Lutheran Church." (History, 1878, page 428.) He was born in Lindholmen, Upland, Sweden, May 12, 1496, and died in Stockholm, September 29, 1560; was king 1523-60.

WACOUTA, settled in 1850, organized 1858, was named by George W. Bullard, the first settler, who was an Indian trader and in 1853 platted a village around his trading post, which was a rival of Red Wing for designation as the county seat. Hancock wrote as follows of the last chief bearing this name, commemorated by this little township.

"The nephew of Scarlet Wing [Red Wing] was the last reigning chief of this band of Dakotas. His name was Wacouta, the shooter. It was this chief who informed the writer that his uncle, the Scarlet Wing, was buried on a bluff near Wabasha. Wacouta was a man of peace. He was not accustomed to lead in the warpath, although his braves had the privilege of forming war parties and making raids against their enemies whenever they desired.

"Wacouta was very tall, straight, and dignified in his demeanor. He was also a man of good judgment. His authority was not absolute. He rather advised his people than commanded them. He encouraged industry and sobriety; was a friend to the missionaries, and sent his own children to their schools when he was at home himself."

As before mentioned by Colvill in the notice of Red Wing, this name was borne as a title of chieftaincy. With slight difference, it was the name of the head chief of the Issati Sioux about Mille Lacs at the time of the captivity of Hennepin and his companions in 1680. Hennepin wrote of him as "Ouasicoudé, that is, the Pierced-pine, the greatest of all the slati chiefs."

Keating in 1823, as historian of Major Long's expedition, gave this name, under another spelling, "Wazekota (Shooter from the pine-top)," for the old Red Wing chief, Walking Buffalo, whom Pike had met eighteen years before. It is from two Dakota words, wazi, pine, and kute, to shoot.

WANAMINGO, settled in 1854, organized in 1858, is almost wholly occupied by prosperous Norwegian farmers. The origin and meaning of the name remain to be learned. It appears to be of Indian derivation, "the name of a heroine of a novel popular in those days." (History, 1910, p. 222.)

WARSAW was first settled in June, 1855, and was organized in 1858. Indiana has a city of Warsaw, and twelve states of our Union have villages and townships that bear this name of the large capital of the former kingdom of Poland.

WELCH, settled in 1857, organized March 23, 1864, was then named Grant, in honor of General U. S. Grant; but it was renamed as now in January, 1872, to commemorate Abraham Edwards Welch, of Red Wing. He was born at Kalamazoo, Mich., August 16, 1839; and died in the army at Nashville, Tenn., February 1, 1864. He volunteered at Lincoln's first call for troops, and was first lieutenant in the First Minnesota regiment; was taken prisoner, paroled, and served as major against the Sioux in 1862. Later he was major in the Fourth Minnesota regiment, and died from the effect of wounds received at Vicksburg. He was the son of William H. Welch, jurist, who was born in Connecticut about 1812, was a graduate of Yale College and later of its law school, came to Minnesota in 1850, and resided at first in St. Anthony and afterward in St. Paul. He was chief justice of the supreme court of Minnesota Territory, 1853-58, removed in 1858 to Red Wing, and died there January 22, 1863.

ZUMBROTA, settled in 1854, organized in 1858, received the name of its village, platted in September, 1856, on the Zumbro river, which flows across the southern part of this township. The Sioux named this river Wazi Oju, meaning Pines Planted, having reference to the grove of great white pines at Pine Island, before noticed; and it bears this name on Nicollet's map, 1843, and the map of Minnesota Territory in 1850. It was called Riviere d'Embarras and River of Embarrassments by Pike, 1805-6, adopting the name given it by the early French traders and voyageurs; Embarrass river by Major Long, 1817; and Embarras, the more correct French spelling, by Lea's map, 1836. From the reminiscences written by Lea in 1890, of his explorations, we learn that the French name referred to obstruction of the river near its mouth by a natural raft of driftwood. Pronounced quickly and incompletely, with the French form and accent, as heard and written down by the English-speaking immigrants, this name, Rivière des Embarras, was unrecognizably transformed into Zumbro, which is used on the map of Minnesota in 1860. The village and township name adds a syllable, the Sioux suffix, ta, meaning at, to, or on, that is, the town on the Zumbro, being thus a compound from the French and Dakota languages.

LAKES, STREAMS, ISLANDS, AND BLUFFS.

The Mississippi river, which has the large Prairie Island at its west side above Red Wing and extending into Dakota county, and the enlargement of the Mississippi named Lake Pepin, adjoining Goodhue and Wabasha counties, have been considered in the first chapter.

Cannon and Zumbro rivers are also noticed in that chapter, the former especially in its presumed identification with the fictitious Long river of Lahontan; but the origins and significance of the names of these streams are again mentioned in the foregoing pages for Cannon Falls and Zumbrota townships.

Other names of streams, etc., whose origins are presented in the list of townships, include Belle creek, Central Point of Lake Pepin, Hay creek, and the so-called Pine Island of Zumbro river.

Excepting Lake Pepin, Silver lake (very small) in Red Wing, and the few small lakes on Prairie Island, this county is destitute of lakes.

Several streams need no explanations for their names, as Pine creek, tributary to Cannon river from the north in Cannon Falls township,

GOODHUE COUNTY

Prairie creek in Stanton, Little Cannon river, Spring creek in Featherstone and Burnside, and the North and South branches of the Zumbro.

Bullard creek, in Hay Creek township and Wacouta, was named in honor of George W. Bullard, early trader, founder of the former village of Wacouta.

Wells creek commemorates James Wells, often called "Bully" Wells, an early fur trader on Lake Pepin near the site of Frontenac, who was a member of the Territorial Legislature in 1849 and 1851.

"Rest Island," at the west side of Lake Pepin near the Central Point, was the location of a home for reform of drunkards, founded in 1891 under the earnest work of John G. Woolley, of Minneapolis, who in 1888 entered the lecture field as an advocate of national prohibition.

Prairie Island, translated from its early French name, Isle Pelée, visited by Groseilliers and Radisson in 1655-56, as narrated in the M. H. S. Collections (vol. X, part II, pages 449-594, with maps), has Sturgeon lake, Buffalo slough, North lake, Clear and Goose lakes, and the Vermilion river or slough, continuing from this river in Dakota county and being the western boundary of this large island, which forms mainly the northern parts of Burnside and Welch townships. Buffalo slough recalls the old times, long before agricultural settlements here, when buffaloes sometimes grazed on the extensive prairie of this island.

Sturgeon lake was named for the shovel-nosed sturgeon, frequent in the Mississippi here and in this lake, a very remarkable and large species of fish, esteemed for food, having a projecting snout, broad and flat, resembling a shovel or a canoe paddle, which was particularly described by Radisson and Hennepin, the first writers on the upper Mississippi.

Assiniboine bluff in Burnside, nearly isolated from the general upland by the erosion of the Mississippi and Cannon valleys, commemorates the former presence of Assiniboine Indians here, of whom Col. William Colvill wrote in the Final Report of the Geological Survey of this state (vol. II, 1888, pages 57-60).

Barn bluff, at Red Wing, is translated from its early French name, La Grange, meaning the Barn, which refers to its prominence as a lone, high, and nearly level-crested bluff, quite separated from the side bluffs of the valley, and therefore conspicuously seen at a distance of many miles up the valley and yet more observable from boats passing along Lake Pepin. Major Stephen H. Long in 1817 ascended this hill or bluff, called in his journal "the Grange or Barn," of which he wrote: "From the summit of the Grange the view of the surrounding scenery is surpassed, perhaps, by very few, if any, of a similar character that the country and probably the world can afford. The sublime and beautiful are here blended in the most enchanting manner." (M. H. S. Collections, vol. II, page 45.)

Other bluffs in Red Wing, adjoining the western border of the river valley or forming a part of it, include Sorin's bluff, named in honor of

Rev. Matthew Sorin, who settled here in 1853, was the first treasurer of this county and the second president of the trustees of Hamline University, later was a pastor in Missouri and Colorado, and died in 1879; the Twin bluffs, on opposite sides of a street leading southwestward; and College hill, the site of the Red Wing Seminary.

Jordan bluff in Wacouta, and a short stream and ravine called Jordan creek in Red Wing, were probably named for a pioneer.

Post bluff, next eastward in Wacouta, commemorates Abner W. and George Post, early settlers there.

Waconia bluff, in Florence, rising on the valley side west of Frontenac, bears a Sioux name meaning a fountain or spring, from a spring at its base.

Near this southeastward is Point No-point, "from whose summit one may see the whole length of the lake. . . . Persons going in boats down the river see this point for six or eight miles, while the boat seems all the time approaching it, yet none of the time getting any nearer till just as they arrive at Frontenac." (Mitchell, 1869, pages 96-97.)

Sand point, translated from the French name, Pointe au Sable, is a wave-built spit of sand and gravel, a narrow projection of the shoreline jutting half a mile into Lake Pepin, adjoining Frontenac. Wells creek, here flowing into the lake, was called "Sand Point R." on Nicollet's map in 1843.

Westward from Point No-point, the large and high area of Garrard bluff in the northern part of Florence, between the railway and the lake, was named in honor of the Garrard brothers, who founded and named Frontenac village. After they had first visited this place in 1854 on a hunting trip, they purchased large tracts of land here, several thousand acres.

Louis H. Garrard settled at Frontenac in 1858, and engaged in farming and development of this estate; was a representative in the legislature in 1859; removed to Lake City in 1870, and was for three years president of the First National Bank there; resided in Cincinnati, Ohio, his native city, after 1880; and died at Lakewood, N. Y., July, 1887, aged fifty-eight years.

The older brother, Israel Garrard, was born in Lexington, Ky., October 22, 1825; and died at his home in Frontenac, Minn., September 21, 1901. He was graduated at the Harvard law school; settled here in 1854, and after the completion of the land purchase, in 1857-8, built the family home, St. Hubert's Lodge, named for the patron saint of huntsmen. At the beginning of the civil war, he raised a troop of cavalry in Cincinnati; served as colonel of the Seventh Ohio Cavalry regiment, and was promoted to be brigadier general; returned here in 1865, and was widely known for his liberality.

GRANT COUNTY

This county, established March 6, 1868, and organized in 1874, was named in honor of Ulysses Simpson Grant, whose generalship terminated the Civil War, in 1865, with preservation of the Union, after which he was president of the United States, 1869 to 1877. He was born at Point Pleasant, Clermont county, Ohio, April 27, 1822; and died at Mount McGregor, near Saratoga, N. Y., July 23, 1885. Having been graduated at West Point in 1843, he served through the Mexican war of 1846-48; left the army in 1854, and settled in St. Louis; and removed to Galena, Illinois, in 1860. He entered the Civil War in June, 1861, as a colonel, and on April 9, 1865, received the surrender of Lee, which ended the war.

On the occasion of the completion of the building of the Northern Pacific railroad across the continent, General Grant visited Minnesota, and was present at the grand celebration held in St. Paul and Minneapolis, September 3, 1883.

Many excellent biographies of Grant have been published. One of his latest biographers, Louis A. Coolidge in 1917, writes: "His success as President in setting our feet firmly in the paths of peace, and in establishing our credit with the nations of the world, is hardly less significant than his success in war."

The grand courage displayed in his last severe and incurable illness, when during the final months of his life he diligently toiled with the pen in the completion of his Memoirs, to win a competence for his family, and to aid toward payment of creditors after great financial disaster, revealed heroic traits of his character which could never otherwise have found expression.

In twelve states of our Union counties have been named for him. In New York City his Tomb, completed in 1897, has been rightly called "the most imposing memorial structure on the Western Continent."

Townships and Villages.

Information of geographic names in this county has been gathered from the "Illustrated Souvenir of Grant County," by W. H. Goetzinger, 1896, 42 pages; "History of Douglas and Grant Counties," Constant Larson, editor, 1916, two volumes (pages 361-509 in Volume I being description and history of this county); and from C. M. Nelson, county auditor, and Hon. Ole O. Canestorp, interviewed during a visit at Elbow Lake, the county seat, in May, 1916.

Ashby, the railway village of Pelican Lake township, platted in 1879, was named in honor of Gunder Ash, a pioneer farmer from Norway, who lived close east of the village site.

BARRETT, a railway village in section 12, Lien, platted in May, 1887, and incorporated in 1889, and the adjoining Barrett lake, commemorate Gen. Theodore Harvey Barrett, who after the civil war owned and conducted an extensive farm in Grant and Stevens counties, residing near Moose Island station in Stevens county. He was born in Orangeville, Wyoming county, N. Y., August 27, 1834; and died in this county at Herman, July 20, 1900. He settled in St. Cloud, Minn., 1856; was a captain in the Ninth Minnesota regiment, 1862-3; was colonel of the 62d U. S. Colored Infantry, 1864-5, and was breveted brigadier general, March 13, 1865.

CANESTORP, a railway station one mile west of Elbow Lake, platted in March, 1887, was named for Hon. Ole O. Canestorp, who was born in Sweden, May 21, 1847; came to the United States in 1862, and to Minnesota in 1871, settling at Elbow Lake; was judge of probate of this county, 1878-82, county treasurer, 1882-89, and a state senator, 1891-3 and 1907-09. He died at his home March 24, 1917. The place is also frequently called West Elbow Lake.

DELAWARE township, organized October 6, 1879, was named by pioneer settlers from that state.

ELBOW LAKE township, organized April 3, 1877, received its name from the adjacent lake in Sanford, shaped like an arm bent at the elbow, to which this name had been given many years previously by early traders and immigrants. Major Samuel Woods and Captain John Pope, in their expedition in the summer of 1849, were the earliest to apply this name, which they each, in their official reports, derived from the shape of the lake.

ELBOW LAKE village, on a site chosen in 1874 to be the county seat, in Sanford township, was also named from this lake, was platted October 28, 1886, and was organized September 13, 1887.

ELK LAKE township, organized January 4, 1876, was named for its Elk lake and Lower Elk lake, tributary to the Chippewa river, where elk were plentiful before agricultural settlers came. The route of Woods and Pope in 1849 passed this Elk lake, named by the former in his report, writing "Here we saw an elk, . . . the first one that crossed our path."

ERDAHL, organized July 30, 1877, was "named in remembrance of a district in Norway, from which some of the early settlers had come." The same name was borne also by a pioneer Lutheran pastor of this county, Gullik M. Erdahl, who was born in Hardanger, Norway, October 5, 1840, and came to America at the age of seven years with his parents who settled in Madison, Wisconsin. He was graduated at Luther College, Decorah, Iowa, 1866, and at the Concordia Seminary, St. Louis, 1869; was a missionary and founder of churches in Kansas, Nebraska, and Iowa; was pastor of five congregations in this county, 1875 to 1900, and later of two until his death at his home near Barrett on March 25, 1914. The railway village of Erdahl was platted in October, 1887.

GORTON, organized July 21, 1879, received the name given by officials of the railway to a former siding in this township, northwest of Norcross.

HEREFORD, a railway village in section 1, North Ottawa, was platted in September, 1887. The History of the county notes the origin of this name as follows: "In 1886, when the railroad was about to establish a station at this point, it was the intention to call the place Culbertson, in honor of the man who owned a tract of land there, but the modest man said that if they wished to compliment him in any way to call the place 'Hereford,' after his beautiful herd of white-faced cattle kept on his farm, 'Hereford Park,' near Newman, Illinois. Accordingly the place was so christened." The breed of cattle came from a county so named in western England.

HERMAN, the railway village in Logan, platted in September, 1875, was incorporated March 15, 1881, and would doubtless have been chosen as the county seat if its location were near the center of the county. In 1914 it was selected by the State Municipality League, on account of its civic merit, as the "model town" of Minnesota. Its name was given by the railway officials, in honor of Herman Trott, land agent of the St. Paul and Pacific railroad company. He was born in Hanover, Germany, February 25, 1830; and died in St. Paul, December 29, 1903. He came to this state in 1856, and settled in St. Paul two years later; removed to the state of Washington in 1890, but returned to reside in St. Paul after 1899.

HOFFMAN, a railway village in Land township, platted in April, 1887, incorporated June 23, 1891, was named in honor of Robert C. Hoffman, of Minneapolis, who during many years has been chief engineer of the Minneapolis, St. Paul and Sault Ste. Marie railway.

LAND township, organized March 6, 1878, was named, on the suggestion of Erik Olson, a Norwegian farmer there, "for the town of Land, Wisconsin, whence some of the early settlers had come." In the Norwegian language, it is a general word meaning land or country.

LAWRENCE was organized March 29, 1880. "The first settlers . . . came here in 1870 from St. Lawrence county, New York. It was they who gave the township its name in remembrance of their former home."

LIEN, organized July 28, 1874, was named in honor of Ole E. Lien, who was one of its first settlers, coming in 1867 or 1868. He was born in Norway; came to the United States in 1861, settling in Minnesota, and served during the civil war in the Tenth Minnesota regiment.

LOGAN, first settled in 1871, organized July 29, 1874, commemorates John Alexander Logan, who was born in Jackson county, Illinois, February 9, 1826, and died in Washington, D. C., December 26, 1886. He served in the Mexican war; was a member of Congress from Illinois, 1859-61; was a general in the civil war, 1861-5; was again a representative in Congress, 1867-71, and a senator, 1871-77 and 1879-86. In 1884 he was the Republican candidate for vice president.

MACSVILLE, organized September 23, 1878, was named in compliment for Francis McNabb, an early settler and chairman of the first board of supervisors, and for John McQuillan, another early settler, who was the first township clerk, also for Coll McClellan, who in 1875 was chairman of the board of county commissioners.

NORCROSS, the railway village in Gorton, platted in December, 1881, and incorporated in 1903, received its name from Henry Allyn Norton and Judson Newell Cross, of Minneapolis, proprietors of the village site. Norton was born in Byron, Ill., October 17, 1838; died in Minneapolis, February 3, 1906. He served in the army, 1861-5, attaining the rank of major; resided in Chicago until 1882, when he removed to Minneapolis. Cross was born in the state of New York, January 16, 1838; died in Minneapolis, August 31, 1901. He was a student at Oberlin College when the civil war began; enlisted in the Seventh Ohio regiment, and during the first year in service was promoted to the rank of captain; in 1864 was made adjutant general of the military district of Indiana. After the war he studied law, and in 1875 settled in Minneapolis.

NORTH OTTAWA was organized July 24, 1882. "Thomas H. Toombs, from Ottawa, Illinois, gave the township its name." The first township meeting was held at his house, and he was then elected chairman of the supervisors.

PELICAN LAKE township, organized January 4, 1876, has an extensive lake of this name, which "was noted for the large flocks of pelicans found there in the early days." It was named Lake Ellenora on the earliest state map, in 1860.

POMME DE TERRE township, organized July 17, 1877, took the name of the large lake at its southeast border, whence also the Pomme de Terre river, flowing from it to the Minnesota river, was named. It is received from the early French voyageurs and traders, meaning literally apple of the earth, that is, a potato; but it was here applied to the edible ovoid-shaped root of the Dakota turnip (Psoralea esculenta), called Tipsinah by the Dakota or Sioux people. This much esteemed aboriginal food plant, very valuable to these Indians, formerly was common on dry and somewhat gravelly parts of upland prairies throughout southwestern Minnesota. The old village of Pomme de Terre, in section 24, platted in 1874, was the first village in the county, now superseded by railway towns.

ROSEVILLE was organized July 24, 1878. "Many names were suggested . . . but the settlers finally decided upon a name which would remind them of the appearance of the virgin prairie when they located there, beautiful with thousands of wild roses." (History, 1916, page 383.)

SANFORD, organized July 24, 1882, was named by the county commissioners in honor of Henry F. Sanford, who was the first settler in the township, coming here in 1869. He was born in Pleasantville, Pa., June 2, 1845; came to Minnesota, and served in Hatch's Battalion of cavalry against the Sioux, 1863-6; was chairman of the first board of county commissioners, 1873; and was county auditor in 1875-8 and 1887-91. He was killed by an accident in New Mexico in 1914.

GRANT COUNTY

STONY BROOK township, first settled in 1870, organized July 30, 1877, derived its name from the small Stony brook and lake in its north part, which are headwaters of Mustinka river.

WENDELL, the railway village in Stony Brook, platted in July, 1889, and incorporated in April, 1904, received its name from the railway officials when the road was being built, with location of a depot here, in 1887. It is also the name of a town in Massachusetts and a village in North Carolina.

LAKES AND STREAMS.

The foregoing pages have noticed Barrett lake, Elbow and Elk lakes, Pelican lake, the Pomme de Terre river and lake, and Stony brook.

Mustinka river has a Dakota or Sioux name, meaning a rabbit, the reference being to the common white rabbit, which also is called the "varying hare," because its fur is gray in summer and white in winter. The Dakota dictionaries by S. R. Riggs (1852) and John P. Williamson (1902) give it as Mashtincha. The larger jack rabbit or hare, also formerly common on the prairies of western Minnesota and on the great plains farther west, was called mashtintanka, which means great rabbit.

Another stream of this county is named Rabbit river, having its sources in Lawrence and flowing west in Wilkin county to Bois des Sioux river.

Two early routes or trails of traders, traveling with trains of Red river carts from the Selkirk and Pembina settlements, in the lower Red river valley, to St. Cloud and St. Paul, passed across the area of Grant county. Both are delineated on the state map of 1860, the more northern passing by Pelican lake, then called Lake Ellenora, and the central route by Elbow lake. A more southwestern route led from the Red and Bois des Sioux rivers to the Minnesota valley and past Swan lake and Traverse des Sioux to St. Paul.

Woods and Pope, in the expedition of 1849, before mentioned, took the middle route, passing Elk lake, the Little Pomme de Terre lake (now named Barrett lake), and onward northwest, having on the left hand, successively, Long, Worm, Elbow, and Lightning lakes. Three of these last have been named for their shape or outline, the most remarkable being Worm lake, of very irregular and wormlike form.

Lightning lake, in Stony Brook township, and Upper Lightning lake, a few miles farther northwest, in the edge of Otter Tail county, perhaps derived their names from an incident during the expedition of Woods and Pope, when they so named two lakes where they had camped, in reference to "a stroke of lightning, which tore in pieces one of the tents, and prostrated nearly all the persons who were in the camp." (Pope's Report, 1850, pages 18-19.) But the detailed narration of Pope shows that their Lightning lakes were those now named Grove lake and McCloud's lake, in Pope county, on a more southeastern part of the route, distant about two or three days' journey from these lakes. In a paper by D. S. B. Johnston, who went over this route in 1857, it is stated that the Lightning lake of Grant county, according to Pierre Bottineau, the famous guide, "took its name from a man in a former expedition being struck by lightning and killed." (M. H. S. Collections, vol. XV, 1915, page 417.) In the tradition of guides, possibly the experience of the expedition in 1849 had given origin to a misplaced Lightning lake in 1857, which has been permanently retained.

A large number of other lakes are named mostly in honor of early settlers near them, or for trees, as Cottonwood lake, birds, as Cormorant lake, or other animals, as Turtle lake; or for their size or outlines, as Big, Horseshoe, and Round lakes. These are noted in the following list, arranged in the numerical order of the townships and ranges, but omitting many lakes of relatively small size, for which the maps have no names.

Patchen, Shauer, and Silver lakes, in Roseville.

Big and Cottonwood lakes, Burr, Johnson, Olstrud, Neimackl, Barrows, Graham, and Nelson lakes, in Macsville.

Pullman lake, adjoining Herman, named for Charles Pullman, proprietor of the first hotel there.

Lake Katrina or Sylvan lake, (bordered by a grove), Peterson, Thompson, Torstenson, Ellingson, Olson, and Retzhoff lakes, Round lake, Spring and Turtle lakes, Church lake (beside a church), and Island lake, in Elk Lake township.

Cormorant lake, Eide, Huset, and Jones lakes, in Lien.

Moses lake or slough, in Delaware.

Island and Round lakes, in Sanford.

Four Mile lake (so far from the old Pomme de Terre stage station), Field, Horseshoe, and Scott's lakes, in Pomme de Terre township, of which the second and fourth were named for adjacent farmers.

Stony Brook lake, in sections 3 and 10 of Stony Brook township.

Stony lake, in section 12, Lawrence, and Ash lake in sections 24 and 25 of this township, the last being named for an early immigrant farmer from England.

HERMAN AND NORCROSS BEACHES OF LAKE AGASSIZ.

From their excellent development near Herman and at Norcross, the first and uppermost beach and the second beach, which is next lower, of the Glacial Lake Agassiz, received their names as respectively the Herman and Norcross beaches or shore lines. Along northern parts of this great ancient lake, which filled the Red river valley, as more fully noticed in the first chapter of this volume (pages 7, 8), each of these beaches is divided, on account of the northward uplift of the land during the existence of the lake, into two or several beaches, distinct and separate strand lines at small vertical intervals, which there are distinguished as the upper and lower Herman beaches, or the first, second, third, etc., and likewise the upper and lower Norcross beaches. The earliest published use of these names is in the Eleventh Annual Report of the Geological Survey of Minnesota, for 1882.

HENNEPIN COUNTY

This county, established March 6, 1852, commemorates Louis Hennepin, the Franciscan missionary, explorer, and author, who was born in Ath, Belgium, about 1640, and died in Holland about 1701. He entered the order of the Recollects of St. Francis, probably in his early youth; spent many years in services of that order in France, Belgium, Holland, Italy, and Germany; and was present, as a regimental chaplain, at the battle of Senef, in 1674. The next year he sailed to Canada, in the same ship with Laval, the bishop of the newly established see of Quebec, and La Salle, destined to be the greatest French explorer of the New World, arriving at Quebec in September. In 1678 Hennepin joined La Salle's expedition for exploration of lakes Ontario, Erie, Huron, and Michigan, and the Illinois and Mississippi rivers.

By direction of La Salle, whom he left near the site of Peoria, Hennepin descended the Illinois river with two companions in a canoe, and thence ascended the Mississippi. On their way up the Mississippi they were captured by a band of Sioux, living near Mille Lacs, spent eight months with them, and were rescued by Du Luth, who enabled Hennepin to reach Green Bay. In the midsummer of 1680, after the early part of their captivity by the Sioux in the region of Mille Lacs, Hennepin and one of his French companions, Anthony Auguelle (also called the Pickard du Gay), were the first white men to see the Falls of St. Anthony, which Hennepin named in honor of his patron saint, Anthony of Padua.

He returned to Quebec in 1682, and to Europe soon afterward. In 1683 he published in Paris an account of his explorations, entitled "Description de la Louisiane." A translation of it, by John Gilmary Shea, was published in New York in 1880, with dedication to Archbishop Ireland and John Fletcher Williams, who were respectively the president and secretary of the Minnesota Historical Society. This volume has an introductory notice of Father Hennepin and an account of his published works, in 45 pages; and the main translation is followed by others from La Salle and Du Luth, and by a bibliography of Hennepin's works and their many editions and translations.

Extensive quotations from Shea are given in chapter VII (pages 205-241) in volume I of "Minnesota in Three Centuries," published in 1908, which narrates the explorations of Du Luth and Hennepin in the area of this state, with biographic sketches of these great pioneers of New France.

Two hundred years after Hennepin visited and named the falls of the Mississippi at the center of the present city of Minneapolis, a great celebration was held there by the Minnesota Historical Society and the people of the Twin Cities, on the grounds of the State University, within view of the falls, on Saturday, July 3, 1880. The description of this Hennepin Bi-Centenary celebration, and the addresses of Governor C. K. Davis, Governor Ramsey, General W. T. Sherman, and Archbishop Ireland, with a poem by A. P. Miller, are published in the M. H. S. Collections (vol. VI, pages 29-74).

The name of Hennepin, instead of Snelling, which latter had been proposed by Colonel John H. Stevens in the original bill, was adopted for this county on request of Martin McLeod, member of the Territorial Council.

TOWNSHIPS, VILLAGES, AND MINNEAPOLIS.

The origins and meanings of these names have been gathered mostly from the "Geographical and Statistical History of the County of Hennepin," by W. H. Mitchell and Col. John H. Stevens, 1868, 149 pages; "History of Hennepin County and the City of Minneapolis," by George E. Warner and Charles M. Foote, 1881, 713 pages; "History of Minneapolis, edited by Judge Isaac Atwater, and Hennepin County, edited by Colonel John H. Stevens," 1895, two volumes, continuously paged, 1497 pages; "Compendium of History and Biography of Minneapolis and Hennepin County," by Return I. Holcombe and William H. Bingham, 1914, 584 pages; and from Hon. John B. Gilfillan, Dr. Lysander P. Foster, and Major Edwin Clark, each of Minneapolis, the second and third being respectively president and secretary of the Hennepin County Territorial Pioneers' Association.

BLOOMINGTON township, first settled in 1843, organized May 11, 1858, was the home of bands of the Dakotas, "those of Good Road and Man of the Clouds. They occupied the bluff on the river near the residence of Rev. G. H. Pond." The name was given by settlers from Illinois, who came in 1852. Twelve other states have villages and cities of this name, the two largest being in Illinois and Indiana.

BROOKLYN township, settled in 1852, organized May 11, 1858, was named by pioneers from southern Michigan, who came in 1853, for the former township and present railway village of Brooklyn in that state, about twenty miles northwest of Adrian.

BROOKLYN CENTER is an incorporated village, mainly a farming area, adjoining the northwest corner of Minneapolis.

CHAMPLIN, first settled in 1852, organized May 11, 1858, was named from its village, platted in 1853, opposite to Anoka and the mouth of Rum river. It bears a personal surname, but why it came to be applied to this village and the township remains to be learned. No other place in the United States is so named. A farmer of Vernon Center, in Blue Earth county, Ezra T. Champlin, born in Ferrisburg, Vt., April 2, 1839, came to this state in 1860; served in the Third Minnesota regiment in the civil war, attaining the rank of captain; and was a representative in the legislature in 1875, 1887, and 1891, being speaker of the House in 1891.

CORCORAN, settled in 1855, organized May 11, 1858, was named in honor of Patrick B. Corcoran, who was the first school teacher here, the first merchant, and first postmaster. He was highly commended as a good citizen by Colonel Stevens. He was born in Ireland, 1825; came to the United States in 1847, and to this county in 1855, being one of the earliest settlers of this township.

CRYSTAL village, as it is now named, incorporated January 11, 1887, would be more suitably termed a small township, under which form of government it was organized April 3, 1860, being then called Crystal Lake. It has the Twin lakes and the smaller Crystal lake, which boasts "a good depth of water and better shores." Besides the title of the township and village, its Crystal prairie, four miles long and a mile wide, but dotted originally with many small groves, like islands, was also named from the lake.

DAYTON township, settled in 1851, organized May 11, 1858, was named, like its village, platted in 1855, in honor of Lyman Dayton, of St. Paul, one of the original proprietors. He was born in Southington, Conn., August 25, 1810; and died in St. Paul, October 20, 1865. He came to Minnesota in 1849, and invested largely in real estate; was the projector and president of the Lake Superior and Mississippi railroad (later named St. Paul and Duluth).

DEEPHAVEN, a village in Excelsior and Minnetonka, founded about 1880, was named for its excellent harbor.

EDEN PRAIRIE township, settled in 1852, organized in 1858, had a fine natural prairie in its southern portion. "The town was named, in 1853, by a Mrs. Elliot, who gave it the name Eden, in expressing her admiration of this beautiful prairie." (History, 1881, page 231.) The reference should be for Mrs. Elizabeth F. Ellet, an author of national reputation, who visited Lake Minnetonka in August, 1852, less than three months after it was visited and named by Governor Ramsey. Other names proposed by her, for bays and a point of Minnetonka are noted on a later page in this chapter.

EDINA, a southwestern village suburb of Minneapolis, was incorporated December 18, 1888, having been previously a part of Richfield. Its name was derived from the Edina flouring mill, owned by Andrew and John Craik, who so named the mill in memory of their boyhood home, in or near Edinburgh, Scotland.

EXCELSIOR, organized May 11, 1858, "owes its name and settlement to a colony, under the title of the Excelsior Pioneer Association," which was formed in New York City, November 12, 1852. "They were headed by George M. Bertram and arrived in the summer of 1853." The colony adopted this name in allusion to Longfellow's world-famous short poem, "Excelsior," which was written September 28, 1841, and was published a few days later.

GOLDEN VALLEY, a western suburb of Minneapolis, euphoniously named for its beautiful valley inclosing a small and narrow lake, was incorporated December 17, 1886, under a village charter, though it is chiefly a farming community. It had been formerly the northwest part of Minneapolis township.

GREENWOOD, settled in 1855, organized May 11, 1858, took the name of a former village, which aspired to be a city, platted by Thomas A. Holmes (founder of many towns) and others in the winter of 1856-7. It was soon superseded by Rockford, on the Wright county side of the Crow river about a mile below the Greenwood city site. "The origin of the name was the charming appearance of the woodlands, as seen by the first settlers, in the early days of summer." (History, 1881, page 311.)

HAMEL, a railway village in section 12, Medina, founded in 1886, was named for J. O. and William Hamel, merchants there.

HASSAN, first settled in 1854, organized April 3, 1860, received its name from a Dakota or Sioux word, chanhasan, meaning the sugar maple tree (chan, tree; hasan, from haza, the whortleberry or huckleberry, also blueberries; that is, the tree having similarly sweet sap). Carver county has a township named Chanhassen, close south of Lake Minnetonka, settled two years earlier and organized in 1858. Not to conflict with that name, the syllable meaning tree was here omitted.

HENNEPIN, a short-lived village platted in 1852, in sections 34 and 35, Eden Prairie, on the Minnesota river, was during several years a shipping point for grain.

HOPKINS, a railway village in St. Louis Park, Edina, and Minnetonka, was named in honor of Harley H. Hopkins, its postmaster. He was born in 1824; came to this county in 1855; engaged in farming on a part of the village site; died in Minneapolis, February 19, 1882.

INDEPENDENCE, settled in 1854-5, organized May 11, 1858, bears the name of the largest one of its several lakes. "The lake derived its name from a party of Fourth of July excursionists. Kelsey Hinman, one of the party, named it Lake Independence, in honor of the national holiday." (History, 1881, page 263.)

LONG LAKE, a Great Northern railway village in Orono, was named for the adjoining Long lake, one of our most abundant lake names.

LORETTO, a Soo railway village in section 6, Medina, founded in 1886, was named from a Roman Catholic mission for refugees of the Huron Indians near Quebec, Canada, called Lorette, founded and named in 1673, and from the village of Loretto, Kentucky, where a society of Catholic "Sisters of Loretto at the Foot of the Cross" was founded in 1812. Many schools are conducted by members of this society in the central and southern United States. The original source of the name is Loreto, a small town in Italy, which has a noted shrine of pilgrimage. (Catholic Encyclopedia, vol. IX, 1910, pages 360-361; vol. XIII, 1912, pages 454-6.)

MAPLE GROVE township, first settled in 1851, organized May 11, 1858, and MAPLE PLAIN, a railway village in Independence, platted in 1868, when the railway construction was completed to that station, were both named for the abundance of the hard or sugar maple in their forests.

HENNEPIN COUNTY 223

MEDINA, settled in 1854, organized May 11, 1858, had been previously called Hamburg by the county commissioners, which name was then changed to Medina by a unanimous vote of the thirty-seven settlers present. This name of a city in Arabia, where Mohammed spent his last ten years and died, is borne by villages and townships in eight states of our Union, and by counties in Ohio and Texas.

MINNEAPOLIS, founded by Col. John H. Stevens, builder of the first house on the west side of the Mississippi here in 1849-50, organized as a township May 11, 1858, was transformed in 1886 to the village organizations of Golden Valley and St. Louis Park, excepting the eastern part of the township, which had been comprised in the city area. On the original site of this city, platting of village lots was begun in the spring of 1854 by Stevens, to which other plats were added in 1854-5. The state legislature, in an act approved March 1, 1856, authorized a town government with a council, which was inaugurated July 20, 1858. The city of Minneapolis was incorporated under an act of March 2, 1866, and its first election of officers was held February 19, 1867. It was enlarged, through union of the former cities of Minneapolis and St. Anthony, by a legislative act approved February 28, 1872, and the new city council was organized April 9, 1872.

The earliest announcement and recommendation of this name was brought by Charles Hoag to the editor of the St. Anthony Express, George D. Bowman, on the day of its publication, November 5, 1852. It was then published, without time for editorial comment, which was very favorably given in the next issue, on November 12. Soon this new name, compounded from Minnehaha and the Greek "polis," city, displaced the various earlier names which had attained more or less temporary acceptance, including All Saints, proposed by James M. Goodhue of the Minnesota Pioneer, Hennepin, Lowell, Brooklyn, Albion, and others.

The distinguished parts borne by both Hoag and Bowman in this opportune coinage of the name Minneapolis have been many times related, with gratitude to Hoag for the bright idea and to Bowman for his effective advocacy of it by his newspaper.

But a new claim, for the origination of the name by Bowman during a horseback ride from St. Anthony to Marine Mills, on the St. Croix river, was published in the summer of 1915 by a posthumous letter of Benjamin Drake, Sr., a cousin of Bowman, printed on page 1583 in Volume III of the late Captain Henry A. Castle's History of Minnesota. The circumstantial evidences of truthfulness there shown for Bowman, as the first to receive the inspiration of uniting "Minnehaha" and "polis" to form this city name, seem quite conclusive.

It is probable, however, that Bowman had mentioned this idea to his friend, Mr. Hoag, and that some days or weeks later, when Hoag had entirely forgotten this, it may have come again to his mind and been thought new and original with himself, immediately before his writing the short article by which this name was proposed in November, 1852.

So each of these excellent early citizens of Minneapolis may have honestly believed himself the favored first originator of the city's name. They worked together unselfishly and successfully for its adoption, and they seem equally deserving of enduring fame for this service to the young city.

The claims for each are quite fully stated and discussed in the Minneapolis Journal, by Hon. John B. Gilfillan, January 7, 1917, and by the present writer a week later, on January 14.

MINNETONKA township, first settled in the spring of 1852, organized May 11, 1858, received the name of the adjoining large lake. The earliest recorded exploration of this lake by white men was in 1822, by two youths, Joseph R. Brown, who became a leading figure in Minnesota history, and William Joseph Snelling, son of the commandant of the fort, accompanied by two soldiers. From their meager and magnified description, Keating, the historian of the United States exploring expedition under Major Stephen H. Long, in 1823, mentioned this lake, though it was not named nor shown on their map.

Twenty years later, in 1843, Nicollet's map and report of this region, based on preceding maps and filled out by much information from his own explorations and from Indians and white voyageurs whom he questioned, had no intimation of the existence of Minnetonka. It seems to have been entirely forgotten by the officers of the fort, with whom Nicollet was intimately acquainted. Because it was in the Sioux country, not ceded for white immigration until the treaties of Traverse des Sioux and Mendota in 1851, ratified by Congress the next year, this fairest one of our myriad lakes remained to be named and published when its first white settlers came.

In the chapter on this township, contributed by Judge Henry G. Hicks to the History of the county in 1895, the exploration of the lower part of this lake by Simon Stevens and Calvin A. Tuttle in April, 1852, is well narrated. Two days after their return, the St. Anthony Express, for April 16, published an article entitled "Peninsula Lake," in which it is truly remarked that "almost the entire shore appears to be a succession of bays and peninsulas."

The present more felicitous name was coined about six weeks later by Governor Alexander Ramsey, when, near the end of May, he made a journey to this lake in a company of several prominent citizens from St. Anthony and St. Paul. An article by Goodhue in his newspaper, the Minnesota Pioneer, for July 1, says: "The lake was named by Governor Ramsey, Minnetonka, or 'Big Water,' who expressed great admiration of the beauties of the country surrounding."

Minne (also spelled mini) is the common Sioux word for water, and tonka (also spelled tanka) is likewise their common word meaning big or great; but the name thus compounded seems not to have been used by the Sioux till Ramsey coined it for the lake. So far as we have records, in-

HENNEPIN COUNTY 225

deed, the Sioux or Dakota people appear to have had no term for this large and many-featured body of water.

MINNETONKA BEACH is a railway village of summer hotels and homes, on the north side of the lake, between Crystal and Lafayette bays, in Orono.

MINNETRISTA, settled in 1854, organized in the spring of 1859, was at first named German Home by the county commissioners, but was changed to the present name by vote of the settlers at the date of organization. "Several names were proposed and rejected. The name of Minnetrista was finally proposed and accepted, Minne (meaning waters) and trista (meaning crooked); and from the fact that the town contained so many crooked lakes, this name was considered as the most appropriate." (History, 1881, page 260.)

To be more definite, this name seems to have been chosen primarily in allusion to the very irregular and curiously zigzag outline of Whale Tail lake, which thus not only suggested its own name, but also this name for the township. Another lake of curious crookedness, in sections 5 and 6, is called Ox Yoke lake, from its shape. Minnetrista is partly of Dakota derivation, in its first half; but trista is not found in either the Dakota or Ojibway languages. It is another example of words coined by white men, as if used by Indians. The letter r, occurring in trista, is not employed by Riggs or Baraga in their dictionaries of these aboriginal languages; nor are their words meaning crooked similar in sound with trista, which we may therefore think to be of Yankee invention, to signify twisted or twister.

MOUND, a railway village of summer homes, with other homes of permanent residents, in Minnetrista, on and near the northwestern shore of Lake Minnetonka, is named for its aboriginal mounds. Three groups of these mounds within the area of the village, mapped by Winchell, have respectively four, eighteen, and nine mounds; and at the distance of about a mile westward is a remarkable series of sixty-nine mounds, on the north side of Halsted's bay. (Aborigines of Minnesota, 1911, pages 224-6, with maps of these mound groups.)

Around all the shores of Lake Minnetonka, and on some of its islands, are many mounds, mostly in groups. The aggregate number of these mounds mapped and described by Winchell, in the work cited (pages 224-242, with 36 maps or plats), is 495, in more than thirty groups, which range in their separate numbers from two or three up to 98 mounds.

ORONO township was organized in 1889, having previously been the south half of Medina. The name, adopted from the township and village of the same name in Maine, was suggested by citizens who had come to Minnesota from that state. Several years before this township was organized and named, George A. Brackett, of Minneapolis, purchased for his summer home a point on this part of the lake shore, before called Starvation point, which he then renamed as Orono point. In an address by Hon. Israel Washburn, Jr., at the centennial celebration of Orono, Maine, on March 3, 1874, this name is stated to have been borne by a prominent chief of the Penobscot Indians, who was born in 1688 and died February 5, 1801, aged 113 years. Washburn wrote: "Orono was always inclined to peace and good neighborhood. . . . What the grand and sonorous name he bore signified, or whence it was derived, I have never heard."

OSSEO, a village in Brooklyn and Maple Grove townships, platted in 1856, occupies a part of Bottineau prairie, where Pierre Bottineau, the noted half-breed guide, took his land claim in 1852. The village "remained under the township governments . . . until the spring of 1875, when it was incorporated by act of Legislature." The source of the name is "The Song of Hiawatha," by Longfellow, published in 1855, which presents the story of Osseo, "son of the Evening Star," told by Iagoo at the wedding of Hiawatha and Minnehaha. This name, received likewise from Longfellow, is borne also by villages in Michigan and Wisconsin.

PLYMOUTH, first settled in October, 1853, organized May 11, 1858, took the name of its village previously platted on Parker's lake, in 1856; but the village was only of short duration, in contrast with the township name, which, however, some of the settlers at first wished to change to Medicine Lake. Like all the many Plymouths of the United States, it commemorates the city of Plymouth at the mouth of the River Plym in Devonshire, England, whence the Pilgrims in the Mayflower sailed in 1620 to the site of Plymouth, Mass., landing there on a boulder of world renown, called Plymouth Rock.

RICHFIELD, settled in 1849-52, organized May 11, 1858, was then so named by vote of the people, in preference to Richland, its previous name. Twelve other states have Richfield townships, villages, or cities.

ROBBINSDALE, a suburban village adjoining Minneapolis on the northwest, was named for Andrew B. Robbins, who purchased lands there in 1887 and platted the village, which a few years later was incorporated.

ROGERS, the railway village of Hassan, was named by officers of the Great Northern railway company.

ST. ANTHONY, incorporated as a city March 3, 1855, and its outlying area which was organized as a township May 11, 1858, received the name of the adjacent falls of the Mississippi, which Hennepin in 1680, as he wrote, "called the Falls of St. Anthony of Padua, in gratitude for the favors done me by the Almighty through the intercession of that great saint, whom we had chosen patron and protector of all our enterprises." St. Anthony was born in Lisbon in 1195, became a Franciscan friar at the age of twenty-three years, and spent his last five years in a convent at Padua, Italy, where he died in 1231.

ST. ANTHONY FALLS was platted as a village in 1849, and was included in Ramsey county until March 4, 1856. Another plat, in 1848-9, named St. Anthony City, comprised the site of the State University and adjoining area southeastward, which later was popularly called "Cheevertown," in honor of William A. Cheever, a pioneer who settled there in 1847, builder of an observatory tower.

HENNEPIN COUNTY 227

An act of the Legislature, "consolidating the cities of St. Anthony and Minneapolis, and incorporating the same into one city by the name of Minneapolis," was approved February 28, 1872.

ST. BONIFACIUS, a railway village in Minnetrista, was named from its Catholic church, consecrated to St. Boniface, the Apostle of the Germans. He was born in Devonshire, England, about 680, the son of a West Saxon chieftain; was ordained to the priesthood in 710; went as a missionary to Bavaria in 720, and became archbishop of Mentz; resigned that position as primate of Germany at the age of seventy-four years, resumed his missionary work, and in the next year suffered "martyrdom at the hands of the pagans of Utrecht." The name Bonifacius is Latin, meaning "of good fate or fortune."

ST. LOUIS PARK, a suburban village adjoining the west side of Minneapolis, was formerly included in Minneapolis township. It was incorporated October 4, 1886, being named in allusion to the Minneapolis and St. Louis railway.

TONKA BAY, a summer village having a large hotel, north and west of Gideon bay, in Excelsior, bears a name abbreviated from Minnetonka.

WAYZATA, a village in sections 5 and 6, Minnetonka, lying on the north side of Wayzata bay, was platted in 1854, and was incorporated in 1884. This name was formed by slight change from Waziyata, a Dakota (Sioux) word, meaning "at the pines, the north." Wazi is defined as "a pine, pines"; and Waziya, "the northern god, or god of the north; a fabled giant who lives at the north and blows cold out of his mouth. He draws near in winter and recedes in summer." The suffix ta, denotes "at, to, on." (Riggs, Dictionary of the Dakota Language, 1852, pages 192, 239.) The name Wayzata, originated by white men, refers to the location, at the north side of the east end of Lake Minnetonka; not to pine trees, which are found nearest, in very scanty numbers, on the Mississippi bluffs at Dayton, and on Bassett's and Minnehaha creeks in Minneapolis.

FORT SNELLING, AT FIRST NAMED FORT ST. ANTHONY.

The naming of Fort Snelling was preceded by three or four other names. First, when the troops came in August and September, 1819, with Colonel Leavenworth, for construction of the fort, they spent the fall and winter, as also two succeeding winters, in a cantonment or barracks of log-houses, on the southeastern or Dakota county side of the Minnesota river, about a third of a mile southeast from the site of the fort. St. Peter's Cantonment took the French and English name of the river. It was also called New Hope, noting cheer and trust for the future of this outpost in the wilderness, far from civilized settlements.

At the time of high water of the river in the spring, they were compelled to remove to another camping place, which was selected on the upland prairie, about a mile northwest from the fort site. Copious springs of clear and cool water issue on the face of the river bluff below that second camp ground, which was mostly of tents, named Camp Cold Water.

After three years of alternation in cabin and tent life at New Hope and Camp Cold Water, the troops moved into their barracks within the inclosure of the fort, in the late autumn of 1822. Its corner stone had been laid September 10, 1820, soon after Colonel Snelling succeeded Leavenworth in the command; and its construction was well completed in 1824, when General Winfield Scott visited it in May or early June, on a tour of inspection of western army posts. Up to that time and till the beginning of 1825, it was called Fort St. Anthony, in allusion to the neighboring St. Anthony falls.

In the report of the tour of review and inspection, dated at West Point, November, 1824, General Scott wrote in part as follows, concerning Fort St. Anthony: "I wish to suggest to the general-in-chief, and through him to the War Department, the propriety of calling this work *Fort Snelling,* as a just compliment to the meritorious officer under whom it has been erected. The present name is foreign to all our associations, and is, besides, geographically incorrect, as the work stands at the junction of the Mississippi and Saint Peter's rivers, eight miles below the great falls of the Mississippi, called after Saint Anthony. Some few years since the Secretary of War directed that the work at the Council Bluffs should be called Fort Atkinson in compliment to the valuable services of General Atkinson on the upper Missouri. The above proposition is made on the same principle."

In accordance with this recommendation, "it was directed in War Department General Orders No. 1, dated January 7, 1825, that the military post on the Mississippi at the mouth of the Saint Peter's, theretofore called Fort Saint Anthony, be thereafter designated and known as Fort Snelling." (Letter of Gen. Henry P. McCain, U. S. Adjutant General, Sept. 24, 1915.)

Josiah Snelling was born in Boston, Mass., 1782; and died in Washington, D. C., August 20, 1828. He was commissioned first lieutenant in the Fourth Infantry, U. S. Army, 1808; served in the War of 1812; was promoted to be colonel of the Fifth Infantry, 1819; took command of Fort St. Anthony in 1820, and in the next three years erected its permanent buildings. In 1827 his regiment was removed to St. Louis. (Much history of the officers and their families at Fort St. Anthony, especially for Col. and Mrs. Snelling, is given in a paper contributed by the present writer to the Magazine of History, vol. XXI, pages 25-39, July, 1915.)

Lakes and Streams.

The first chapter has given attention to the origins of the names of the Mississippi, Minnesota, and Crow rivers, which together form two-thirds of the boundary inclosing this county.

Islands of the Mississippi in the area of Minneapolis, in their descending order, include Boom island, where log booms formerly retained the lumbermen's logs until they were gradually supplied to the sawmills; Nicollet island, a residential portion of the city, named, like an avenue, in honor of the French explorer and geographer, Joseph Nicolas Nicollet; Hennepin island, named also like an avenue and like this county; Cataract island and Carver's island, just below the falls, the latter being named for Captain Jonathan Carver, who visited the falls in 1766; Spirit island, close below the preceding, formerly a high remnant of the rock strata, held in awe by the Indians; and Meeker island, an alluvial tract between the Franklin Avenue bridge and the Milwaukee Railway bridge, which was owned by Judge Bradley B. Meeker, for whom also a county is named.

In the preceding list of townships, sufficient mention has been made for Crystal lake and Lake Independence, Long lake in Orono, Lake Minnetonka, Whale Tail and Ox Yoke lakes, the Falls of St. Anthony, and Wayzata bay.

The earliest detailed map of any part of this state was drafted during the building of the fort, in 1823, entitled "A Topographical View of the Site of Fort St. Anthony," as described in the historical paper before cited. Lakes Harriet and Calhoun and the Lake of the Isles, in the series at the west side of Minneapolis, are there mapped and named, with numerous others of the lakes, rivers and creeks, in the contiguous parts of Hennepin, Ramsey, and Dakota counties. The region east of the Mississippi river was designated as Michigan, and that on the west as Missouri.

Lake Harriet was named for the wife of Colonel Leavenworth. Her maiden name was Harriet Lovejoy, her home being in Blenheim, Schoharie county, N. Y. She was born in 1791; was married to Leavenworth in the winter of 1813-14; and died at Barrytown, N. Y., September 7, 1854. She came here with her husband and the first troops, August 24, 1819, and was here about one year. Leavenworth received the brevet rank of brigadier general in 1824, and died at the age of fifty-one, July 21, 1834, in an expedition against the Pawnees and Comanches. Fort Leavenworth, in Kansas, and a city and county there, were named in his honor.

Lake Calhoun commemorates John Caldwell Calhoun (b. 1782, d. 1850), the eminent statesman of South Carolina, who was Secretary of War from 1817 to 1825. He was vice president of the United States, 1825-32; was U. S. senator, 1833-43; and was Secretary of State under President Tyler, 1844-5, when he was again elected to the Senate, of which he remained a member until his death. The Dakota or Sioux name of this lake is given as "Mde Medoza, Lake of the Loons," by Major T. M. Newson in his "Indian Legends of Minnesota Lakes" (No. 1, 1881, page 18).

The Lake of the Isles was named for its islands (now two, but formerly four, as mapped in Andreas' Atlas, 1874); and Cedar lake, for the red cedar trees of its shores.

Minnehaha Falls received the name of Brown's Falls on the Fort map of 1823, in honor of Jacob Brown, major general and commander in chief of the army from 1814 until his death, February 24, 1828; but Minnehaha creek on that map, quite erroneous in its course, bears no name. A journey up this creek to Lake Minnetonka, which was made, as before mentioned, by Joseph R. Brown and William J. Snelling in May, 1822, when they were each only seventeen years old, could scarcely have caused the name of that subsequently prominent citizen of Minnesota to be so applied on a map drafted by an army officer.

The name Minnehaha is cited by Longfellow's "Song of Hiawatha," published in 1855, as used by Mrs. Mary H. Eastman in the introduction of her book, "Dakotah, or Life and Legends of the Sioux around Fort Snelling," published in 1849. She there wrote: "The scenery about Fort Snelling is rich in beauty. The Falls of St. Anthony are familiar to travelers, and to readers of Indian sketches. Between the fort and these falls are the 'Little Falls,' 40 feet in height, on a stream that empties into the Mississippi. The Indians call them Mine-hah-hah, or 'laughing waters.'"

The common Sioux word for waterfall is "haha," which they applied to the falls of St. Anthony, to Minnehaha, and in general to any waterfall or cascade. To join the words "minne," water, and "haha," a fall, seems to be a suggestion of white men, which thereafter came into use among the Indians.

The late Samuel W. Pond, Jr., in his admirable book, "Two Volunteer Missionaries," narrating the lives and work of his father and uncle, Samuel W. and Gideon H. Pond, wrote: "The Indian name, 'Little Waterfall,' is given . . . in speaking of the falls now called by white people 'Minnehaha.' The Indians never knew it by the latter name, bestowed upon it by the whites."

Somewhat nearly this name, however, was used in 1835 by Charles J. Latrobe, in his book, "The Rambler in North America," telling of his travels in 1832-3, in which he wrote as follows, applying it, with parts of the name transposed, to the larger falls of the Mississippi: "But the Falls of St. Anthony! . . . the Hahamina! 'the Laughing Water,' as the Indian language, rich in the poetry of nature, styles this remote cataract."

Another early book of travel using the same form of the name, under a different spelling, is "A Summer in the Wilderness; embracing a Canoe Voyage up the Mississippi and around Lake Superior," by Charles Lanman, 1847 (208 pages). He described the present Minnehaha creek as "a small river, without a name, the parent of a most beautiful waterfall." Of the Falls of St. Anthony he wrote: "Their original name, in the Sioux language, was Owah-Menah, meaning falling water." The same spelling and translation had been given in Schoolcraft's Narrative, 1820.

Soon this Sioux or Dakota name took its present form, an improvement devised by white people, probably first published in Mrs. Eastman's book, in 1849, previously quoted. It was more elaborately presented by Rev. John A. Merrrick, in a paper describing the Falls of St. Anthony, contributed to the Minnesota Year Book for 1852, published by William G. LeDuc. Merrick wrote: "By the Dahcota or Sioux Indians they are called Minne-ha-hah or Minne-ra-ra (Laughing water), and also Minne-owah (Falling water), general expressions, applied to all waterfalls; but *par eminence* Minne-ha-hah Tonk-ah (the great laughing water). By the Ojibways they are termed Kakah-Bikah (the broken rocks)."

The noble American epic of Longfellow, in which he pictured Hiawatha, "skilled in all the crafts of hunters," and

. . . "the Arrow-maker's daughter,
Minnehaha, Laughing Water,
Handsomest of all the women,"

so well appealed to the imagination of both the United States and Great Britain, indeed of all where English is spoken, that soon after its publication, in 1855, this name became known around the world, the most widely honored and loved name in Minnesota history and legends.

The names of other streams and lakes in this county are noted in their order from south to north and from east to west, this being the numerical order of the townships and ranges in the government surveys.

Rice lake, through which Minnehaha creek flows, was named for its wild rice, formerly gathered for food by the Indians.

Lake Nokomis was called Lake Amelia by the Fort map in 1823, probably for the wife or daughter of Captain George Gooding, who came with the first troops in 1819. The name was changed to Nokomis by the Park Commissioners of Minneapolis in 1910, for the grandmother of Hiawatha.

Next to the south and southwest are Mother lake (lately drained), Diamond, Pearl, Mud, and Wood lakes.

Nine Mile creek received its name from its distance southwest from Fort Snelling.

Long lake (now mostly drained), Grass lake (on a recent map named Terrell lake), and Rice lake (having wild rice), are on the bottomland of the Minnesota river in Bloomington and Eden Prairie.

On the upland in these townships are another Long lake (also named Bryant's lake), Anderson, Bush, Hyland, Neill, Staring, Red Rock, and Moran lakes, Lake Riley, Mitchell, Round, and Duck lakes, mostly named for farmers adjoining them.

Minnetonka township has Shady Oak lake, in section 26, and Glen lake in section 34.

In Excelsior are Galpin's lake, Christmas lake, and Silver lake, the first named for Rev. Charles Galpin, the first pastor there, and the second for Charles W. Christmas, of Minneapolis, the first county surveyor.

Minnetrista, named for its two remarkably crooked lakes, has also Dutch lake, adjoining a German settlement; Lake Langdon, which commemorates R. V. Langdon, the first township clerk; and Long lake, in sections 9, 15, and 16.

Minneapolis, in addition to its western series of lakes before noted, has Sandy lake, northeast of the Mississippi; Powderhorn lake, named for its original shape, now changed as the center of a park; and Loring Park lake, named in honor of Charles M. Loring, who was prominent during more than thirty years in the development of the Minneapolis system of parks and public grounds. Glenwood park, on the west border of this city, includes Glenwood and Brownie lakes.

Bassett creek, flowing through the village area of Golden Valley and the city of Minneapolis, was named for Joel Bean Bassett, an early settler and lumberman, who was born in Wolfborough, N. H., March 17, 1817, and died in Los Angeles, Cal., Feb. 1, 1912. He came to Minnesota in 1849, settling in St. Paul, but soon pre-empted a tract adjoining the Mississippi in Minneapolis, near the mouth of this creek; removed there in 1852, and afterward engaged in lumbering and flour milling; was a member of the Territorial Council, 1857; was Indian agent for Minnesota 1865-69.

The village area of Golden Valley has Virginia lake, Sweeney lake, and Twin lake.

Again Twin lakes are found three to four miles farther north, in the area of Crystal village, which was named, as before noted, for its Crystal lake.

Shingle creek, which crosses Brooklyn township and the Brooklyn Center village, joining the Mississippi in the north edge of Minneapolis, had near its mouth the first shingle mill in this county, built in 1852. It flows through Palmer lake, named for a pioneer.

Plymouth has Bass lake, Pomerleau, Smith, and Turtle lakes, in its northern half. The much larger Medicine lake, in its southeastern part, was named by the Indians after one of their number was drowned there by the capsizing of his canoe in a sudden storm. This name, in their use, means mysterious, and was given to the lake because they could not find his body. Parker's lake, and Gleason and Kraetz lakes, in the southwest part of Plymouth, were named for adjoining settlers, the first being for six Parker brothers who came from Maine, in 1855 and later, opening farms around this lake.

Medina township has Medina lake in section 2; Lake Peter in sections 4 and 5; School lake in the school section 16; Seig and Half Moon lakes, in sections 17 and 18; Hausmann lake, in section 24; Wolfseld lake, in sections 22 and 27; and Lake Katrina, in sections 19, 20, 29, and 30.

Orono has Lydiard lake, close east of Long lake; Classen lake, a mile and a half west of Long Lake village; and French and Forest lakes, adjoining the bays and arms of Lake Minnetonka.

Independence has Mud lake, Haughey, and Fox lakes; and Pioneer creek, the outlet of Lake Independence, flows southwestward across this township.

Elm creek flows through Rice lake, at the center of Maple Grove township, and Hayden's lake, in the southeast corner of Dayton. Midway between these lakes, Rush creek is tributary to it from the west.

Maple Grove also has Mud lake, in section 2; Weaver lake, in sections 17 to 20; and Fish lake, Cedar Island, and Eagle lakes, the last being the largest in the township.

Corcoran has only very small lakes, the largest (which alone is named on maps) being Jubert's lake, in sections 29 and 32.

Lake Sarah, the largest in Greenwood, outflowing to the Crow river by Edgar creek, was named in 1855 for the wife or sweetheart of a pioneer; and in the same year Lake Rebecca received its name in honor of Mrs. Samuel Allen. Sections 23 and 24 of this township had a series of small lakes, recently drained, which were named Hafften, Schendel, Schauer, and Schnappauf lakes, for German farmers.

Besides Hayden's lake, before mentioned, Dayton has French lake, named for a settlement of French families there, who came in 1853; Grass, Diamond, and Lura lakes, next northward; Goose lake, at the southeast corner of this township; and Powers lake, in section 34.

Hassan has Lake Harry, Sylvan lake, and Cowley lake. The last is also known as Parslow's lake, in honor of Septimus Parslow, who in 1856 was appointed the first postmaster of Hassan, and held the office twenty-five years or more.

BAYS, POINTS, AND ISLANDS OF LAKE MINNETONKA.

The origin of the name of this lake, and also the story of its early white explorers, have been told for Minnetonka township. Shortly after its exploration and naming in 1852, it was visited on August 11 of that summer by a prominent author, Mrs. Elizabeth Fries Ellet, of New York City, who gave to Minnesota and Minnetonka nearly twenty pages in her "Summer Rambles in the West." Besides her notes of the journey to this lake, she named Eden Prairie, which gave its title to a township.

Her name for the first water sheet at the east end of Minnetonka, now named Gray's lake or bay, was Lake Browning, for the poet, Elizabeth Barrett Browning. The next part, wider and larger, which was soon afterward named Wayzata bay, as before noted, Mrs. Ellet called Lake Bryant, for our American poet, from whom she "read aloud a few lines . . . appropriate to the scene."

Between her Lake Bryant and the third large sheet of water, "an extremely narrow . . . headland half a mile in length, running out from the southern shore," since named Breezy point, was by her named Point Wakon, "the Dakota term for anything spiritual or supernatural." There an oval stone, a waterworn boulder about a foot in diameter, had been found, which the Dakotas had "painted red, and covered with small yellow spots, some of them faded to a brown color," around which stone the Dakota or Sioux braves were accustomed, after raids against the Ojibways, to celebrate their scalp dance.

Cedar point projects into Wayzata bay from the south, named for its red cedar trees.

Proceeding westward along the south side of the lake, we pass Robinson's bay, with Sunset point southwest of it; Carson's bay at Deephaven; and St. Alban's bay and Gideon's bay, respectively east and west of Excelsior.

Hotel Keewaydin, a name from Longfellow's "Song of Hiawatha," meaning "the Northwest wind, the Home wind," was at Cottagewood, close west of Carson's bay. Keewaydin is the same name as the differently spelled Keewatin, a former large province of northwestern Canada, lying west of Hudson bay.

Gluek's point and Solberg's point are passed southwestward, before coming to Excelsior.

A summer village that failed to grow, called St. Albans, was platted in 1856 on the north shore of the bay which thence took its name.

Gideon's bay (also called Tonka bay) commemorates Peter M. Gideon, the horticulturist, who there originated the renowned Wealthy apple, named by him in honor of his wife. He was born in Champaign county, Ohio, February 9, 1820; came to Minnesota in 1853, settling beside this bay, where later he was superintendent of the State Fruit Farm. A small memorial park and a tablet in his honor, at Manitou Junction, about a mile west of Excelsior, were dedicated June 16, 1912.

Hull's Narrows, joining the lower and upper parts of Minnetonka, received this name for Rev. Stephen Hull, who settled on a farm there in February, 1853. Originally a short creek, it was widened and deepened as a canal, and was opened to steamboat navigation in 1873.

On the south side of the upper lake are Lock's point, Howard's point, and a less noteworthy projection of the shore at Zumbra Heights, west of Smithtown bay.

Hard Scrabble point on the west, and Cedar point on the east, divide this upper lake from Cook's and Priest's bays, at the west end of Minnetonka.

Yet farther west, connected by a strait with Priest's bay, is Halsted's bay, named for Frank William Halsted, who was born in Newark, N. J., in 1833, and died here in June, 1876. He came to Minnesota in 1855; served in the U. S. navy during the civil war; resided in a picturesque house near the shore of this bay, called the Hermitage. His older brother, George Blight Halsted, was born in Elizabethtown, N. J., March 17, 1820; and died here September 6, 1901. He was graduated at Princeton college; studied law; served in the navy, and later in the army, through the civil war; came to this state in 1876, and afterward resided in the home where his brother had lived.

Phelps island (originally a peninsula) lies east of Cook's bay, and is indented on its southeast side by Phelps bay. These names were given in honor of Edmund Joseph Phelps, of Minneapolis, who was born near Brecksville, Ohio, January 17, 1845. He came to Minnesota in 1878, set-

HENNEPIN COUNTY   235

tling in Minneapolis; organized, with others, the Minneapolis Loan and Trust Company in 1883, of which he was secretary and treasurer.

Pelican point and Casco point are respectively west and east of Spring Park bay, on the north side of the upper lake.

Carman's bay, named for a farmer, John Carman, who settled here in September, 1853, and Lafayette bay, named from the Hotel Lafayette, are respectively west and east of the Narrows, on the north side.

Huntington point and Starvation or Orono point jut into the lower lake from the north, respectively west and east of Smith's bay.

Branching off from Smith's bay westward is Crystal bay, and connected with the latter are Maxwell and Stubbs bays, the North Arm, and the West Arm and Harrison's bay.

East of Orono point is Brown's bay, and next east are Lookout point and an upland with fine residences, named Ferndale, which, with the opposite Breezy point, before noted, are at the entrance of Wayzata bay.

So we have traversed the entire shore line, with its multitude of indenting bays and projecting points, of this exceedingly attractive lake, of which I wrote in 1917 that it "may well be called the Kohinoor of Minnesota's ten thousand lakes." For the archaeologist and historian, this lake has great interest in its many groups of aboriginal mounds, before noticed in connection with the village named Mound. For the naturalist, in addition to its beautiful scenery, it has treasures of the native flora and fauna, notably its abundant species of trees and shrubs and its many kinds of fishes and birds. Two points, one near the east end of the lake and another near the west end, are named for their red cedars; and islands in the upper part of the lake received names from their formerly plentiful cranes and more rare nests of the bald eagle.

The islands of Minnetonka include Big island in the lower lake, which at first was known as Meeker's island, for Judge Bradley B. Meeker, of Minneapolis, who visited this lake with Governor Ramsey and others in 1852; Gale island, near the southwest shore of Big island, named for Harlow A. Gale (b. 1832, d. 1901), of Minneapolis, whose summer home was there; and, in the upper lake, Wild Goose island, Spray island, Shady, Enchanted, Wawatasso, Eagle, and Crane islands. The longest of these names may be akin with one in Longfellow's "Song of Hiawatha,"

"Wah-wah-taysee, little firefly."

"Picturesque Lake Minnetonka," published in yearly editions by S. E. Ellis (1906, 102 pages), referred the name of Enchanted island to its being long ago a favorite place of Dakota or Sioux medicine dances, with wierd incantations; and related that Wawatasso was a young Dakota brave who rescued the daughter of a white pioneer trapper from drowning. Other Dakota legends about Minnetonka have been written in prose by Thomas M. Newson, in 1881, and in poetry by Hanford L. Gordon ("Indian Legends and Other Poems," 1910, 406 pages). Like Hiawatha and Minnehaha, and like the geographic names in this county that are partly of Dakota derivation, these writings present more white than red ways of thought and imagery.

THE FORT SNELLING MILITARY RESERVATION IN 1839.

A map of "Fort Snelling and Vicinity," surveyed and drafted by Lieut. E. K. Smith in October, 1837, comprises the near vicinity of the fort, Camp Cold Water, and the post of the American Fur Company, on the site of Mendota, having probably been made mainly to show the cabins and fields of settlers permitted to locate on the Military Reservation.

Two years later a more extended survey and map, for the U. S. War Department, by Lieut. James L. Thompson, showed the boundaries established or adopted for the Military Reservation, "done at Fort Snelling, October and November, 1839, by order of Major Plympton."

This map, on the scale of two inches to a mile, is limited to the Reservation area, reaching west to the Lake of the Woods (now called Wood lake), the series of Harriet, Calhoun, and the Lake of the Isles, and northwest to the lower part of Nine Mile creek (now Bassett's creek). On the east the Reservation was bounded by the middle of the channel of the Mississippi to the island next below the present Meeker island. From the upper end of that island, the boundary on the north side of the part of the Reservation east and north of the Mississippi extended due east five miles, to a point near the present intersection of St. Peter and Tenth streets in the city of St. Paul. Next it extended due south two miles and ten chains, crossing the Mississippi very close west of the upper end of Harriet island, to a point near the present corner of Annapolis street and Manomin avenue in West St. Paul. Thence the southeastern boundary of the Reservation ran eight miles and 42 chains southwestward, nearly in parallelism with the Mississippi and Minnesota rivers and about a mile distant from them. Finally the most southern line of this area ran due west one mile and 75 chains, to the Minnesota river at the place of beginning, about six miles distant from the fort.

Reserve township of Ramsey county, now included in the city of St. Paul, had its north boundary very near the north line of the Reservation, whence the township was named.

The history of the opening for settlement of the greater parts of the Reservation, in 1852-55, including the southwestern areas of St. Paul and Ramsey county, and the area of Minneapolis west of the river, has been related by Dr. Folwell in a paper, "The Sale of Fort Snelling, 1857," in the M. H. S. Collections (vol. XV, 1915, pp. 393-410).

On the Reservation map of 1839, "Land's End" is a part of the bluff on the northwest side of the Minnesota river, nearly two miles southwest from the fort, where the bluff is intersected by a tributary ravine; Minnehaha falls and creek were called Brown's falls and Brown's creek; an "Indian Village" adjoined the southeast shore of Lake Calhoun; and the "Mission," with three cultivated fields, comprising probably 30 acres, was on the northwest side of Lake Harriet.

HOUSTON COUNTY

Established February 23, 1854, this county was named in honor of Samuel Houston, who was president of Texas before its annexation to the United States and afterward was a senator from that state. He was born near Lexington, Virginia, March 2, 1793; and died in Huntsville, Texas, July 26, 1863. In his youth he lived several years with the Cherokee Indians, near his home in eastern Tennessee; later he served in the Creek war, 1813-14, winning the admiration of Gen. Andrew Jackson by his bravery in a battle, after being severely wounded; studied law, and was admitted to practice, 1818-19; was a member of Congress from Tennessee, 1823-7; and was governor of that state, 1827-9.

On account of an uncongenial marriage, he resigned the governorship, retired to savage life in the Arkansas Territory, whither the Cherokees had been removed, and again lived with them, becoming an Indian trader. In December, 1832, he went to Texas under a commission from President Jackson, looking toward its purchase for the United States. In 1835 he was elected commander-in-chief of the Texans, and in the battle of San Jacinto, April 21, 1836, he defeated the Mexicans and captured their general, Santa Anna, ending the war.

Houston was president of the Texas republic, 1836-8 and 1841-4. Texas was annexed to the United States in 1845, being admitted as a state, and Houston was elected one of its senators, which position he held by re-elections for thirteen years, until 1859. Later he was governor of Texas, 1859-61, being an opponent of secession.

In the years 1854-6, when antagonism between the North and South on slavery questions gave presages of the civil war, Houston aspired to nomination as the Democratic candidate for the national presidency; and in October, 1854, the general Democratic committee of New Hampshire earnestly recommended him to be "the people's candidate" for the campaign in 1856. His popularity in Minnesota at that time is attested by the name of this county; and he is likewise commemorated by counties in Tennessee and Texas, and by names of cities and villages in Texas, Mississippi, Missouri, and other states.

Several biographies of Sam Houston, as he always styled himself, have been published from 1846 to 1900.

Marble statues of him and Stephen F. Austin, sculptured by Elisabet Ney, of Texas, and erected as the gift of that state in Statuary Hall of the national capitol, were accepted February 25, 1905, with memorial addresses by members of Congress representing Texas, Tennessee, Missouri, and Arkansas.

Townships and Villages.

Information for the origins of geographic names in this county has been gathered from the "History of Houston County," 1882, 526 pages; and from Charles A. Dorival, judge of probate, interviewed during a visit at Caledonia, the county seat, in April, 1916.

BLACK HAMMER township, first settled in 1852, organized in April, 1859, received this name, meaning Black Bluff, from an exclamation of Knud Olson Bergo, an early Norwegian settler in the adjoining township of Spring Grove, on seeing a prairie bluff here blackened by a fire. It was the name of a bluff at his birthplace in Norway. Hammer, as a Norwegian word, has the same spelling and meaning as in English. Doubtless the name was suggested, both in Norway and here, by the shape of the bluff or hill.

BROWNSVILLE, first settled in November, 1848, organized May 11, 1858, was named for its steamboat landing and village, platted in 1854, by Job and Charles Brown, brothers, who came to Minnesota in 1848 from the state of New York. Biographic notes of both are in the M. H. S. Collections, volume XIV.

CALEDONIA, settled in 1851, organized May 11, 1858, took the name of its village, which was platted and named in 1854-5 by Samuel McPhail, who had served in the Mexican war and later was colonel of the First Minnesota mounted rangers in the Sioux war, 1862-3. This was the ancient Roman name of Scotland north of the firths of Clyde and Forth, and in modern use it is the poetic name of Scotland. Caledonia village was incorporated by a legislative act, Feb. 25, 1870.

CROOKED CREEK township, settled in 1852-3, organized May 11, 1858, was named for the creek which flows through it in an exceptionally crooked course, entering a western channel of the Mississippi at Reno. Its valley is the route of the railway from Reno nearly to Caledonia.

EITZEN, a village in section 32, Winnebago, was named for a place in Germany whence some of the early settlers came.

FREEBURG, a railway village in section 30, Crooked Creek township, was named by German settlers, for the city of Freiburg in the Black Forest region of Germany.

HOKAH township, settled in 1851, organized May 11, 1858, bears the Dakota or Sioux name of the Root river, which is its English translation. Hutkan is the spelling of the word by Riggs and Williamson in their Dakota dictionaries, 1852 and 1902; but it is spelled Hokah on the map by Nicollet, published in 1843, and on the map of Minnesota Territory in 1850. A part of the site of the village, which was platted in March, 1855, had been earlier occupied by the village of a Dakota chief named Hokah. This railway village was incorporated March 2, 1871.

HOUSTON township, settled in 1852 and organized in 1858, was named, like the county, for General Sam Houston, of Texas. The village was incorporated April 7, 1874.

HOUSTON COUNTY   239

JEFFERSON township, organized in 1858, received its name, on the suggestion of Eber D. Eaton, of Winnebago township, for Jefferson county, New York, whence he came to Minnesota. Jefferson village, on the west channel of the Mississippi, was at first called Ross's Landing for John and Samuel Ross, brothers, who came here as the first settlers in 1847.

LA CRESCENT township, settled in 1851, organized May 11, 1858, was named, like its village, platted in June, 1856, in allusion to the town of La Crosse, Wisconsin, which had been previously founded on the opposite side of the Mississippi. That French name, meaning the bat used in playing ball and thence applied to the ball game often played by the Indians, had been given to La Crosse prairie before the settlement of the town, because the ground was a favorite place for their meeting to play this game. The origin and meaning of the Wisconsin name, however, were disregarded, if known, by the founders of La Crescent, who confused it with La Croix, the Cross. "Recalling the ancient contests of the Crusaders against the Saracens and Turks in their efforts to recapture the Holy Sepulchre, where the Cross and the Crescent were raised aloft in deadly strife, and being mindful of the fate that overtook those who struggled under the banner of La Crosse, they resolved to challenge their rival by raising the standard of La Crescent, and thus fight it out on that line." (History of Houston County, 1882, page 426.)

MAYVILLE, settled in 1855 and organized in 1858, was named for Mayville, N. Y., the county seat of Chautauqua county, whence Dr. John E. Pope and others of the early settlers of this township came.

MONEY CREEK township, settled in 1853-4, organized May 11, 1858, and its village, which was platted in the autumn of 1856, received their names from the creek here tributary to the Root river. "Some man having got his pocket-book and contents wet in the creek, and spreading out the bank notes on a bush to dry, a sudden gust of wind blew them into the water again, and some of it never was recovered, so this circumstance suggested the name of the stream, after which the town was named." (History, 1882, page 436.)

MOUND PRAIRIE township, settled in 1853-4, was organized in April, 1860. "The name of the town was suggested by Dr. Chase, an old resident, in remembrance of a remarkable rounded bluff in section four, surrounded by a wide valley on all sides."

RENO, a railway village and junction in Crooked Creek township, at first called Caledonia Junction, was renamed by Capt. William H. Harries, of Caledonia, in honor of Jesse Lee Reno. He was born at Wheeling, West Virginia, June 30, 1823; was graduated at West Point in 1846; served in the Mexican war; was a brigadier general, and later a major general, of United States volunteers in the civil war; was killed in the battle of South Mountain, Md., September 14, 1862.

RICEFORD, a village in section 6, Spring Grove township, platted in 1856, was named in honor of Henry M. Rice, of St. Paul, who also is commemorated by the name of Rice county. He visited this place in 1856, following an Indian trail and fording the creek here, which thence is called Riceford creek.

SHELDON, settled in June, 1853, organized May 11, 1858, took the name of its village, founded in 1854-7, of which Julius C. Sheldon, who came from Suffield, Conn., was one of the proprietors.

SPRING GROVE township, settled in 1852 and organized in 1858, received the name of its first post office, which was established in 1854 at the home of James Smith, the earliest settler, beside a spring and a grove.

UNION township, settled in 1853, was organized April 5, 1859. Thirty other states have townships and villages of this name.

WILMINGTON, first settled in June, 1851, organized May 11, 1858, has a name that is likewise borne in fourteen other states by townships, villages, and cities.

WINNEBAGO, settled in March, 1851, organized May 11, 1858, is drained by Winnebago creek, which, with the township, received its name from the Winnebago Indians, many of whom, after the cession of their Wisconsin lands, in 1832, were removed to northeastern Iowa. Their hunting grounds then extended into this adjoining edge of Minnesota, until they were again removed in 1848 to Long Prairie, in central Minnesota.

The head chief of the Winnebagoes, Winneshiek, for whom an adjacent county in Iowa is named, lived and hunted much in this county. "His principal home was about seven miles west of the village of Houston, on the Root river, Houston county, Minnesota; here he lived, during the winter, in a dirt wigwam." (History of Winneshiek County, Iowa, by Edwin C. Bailey, 1913, vol. I, p. 34.)

YUCATAN, settled probably in 1852 and organized in 1858, was at first called Utica; but to avoid confusion with other places of that name, which are found in sixteen states, one being Utica township in Winona county, it was changed to the present name of somewhat similar sound, which is used nowhere else in the United States. It was taken from the large peninsula of Yucatan, forming the most southeastern part of Mexico, and from the Yucatan channel, between that country and Cuba.

LAKES, RIVERS, CREEKS, AND BLUFFS.

Houston county lies in a large Driftless Area, exempted from glaciation and therefore having none of the glacial and modified drift formations by which it is wholly surrounded. This area also includes parts of several other counties of southeastern Minnesota, but its greatest extent is in Wisconsin, with small tracts of northeast Iowa and northwest Illinois. Its length is about 150 miles from north to south, with a maximum width of about 100 miles. It is characterized by absence of lakes, excepting on the bottomlands of rivers, where they fill portions of deserted watercourses. Such lakes occur in this county along the Mississippi and Root rivers, one of which, two to three miles southeast of La Crescent, is named Target lake, from former rifle practice there.

HOUSTON COUNTY 241

The preceding pages have noted the origins of the names of Crooked creek, Root river, Money creek, and Riceford and Winnebago creeks.

Pine creek, flowing through La Crescent to the Mississippi, has here and there a few white pines on its bluffs, this region being at the southwestern limit of this tree.

Tributaries of the Root river from the north are Storer, Silver, and Money creeks; and from the south, in similar westward order, Thompson creek (formerly also known as Indian Spring creek), Crystal creek, and Badger, Beaver, and Riceford creeks. Thompson creek was named in honor of Edward Thompson and his brother, Clark W. Thompson, the principal founders of Hokah, for whom biographic notices are given in the M. H. S. Collections, volume XIV.

A prominent bluff of the Root river valley at Hokah is named Mt. Tom.

Wild Cat creek flows into the Mississippi at Brownsville, and Wild Cat bluff is a part of the adjacent high bluffs forming the west side of the Mississippi valley. These names, and those of Badger and Beaver creeks, tell of early times, when the fauna of this region included many furbearing animals that have since disappeared or become very scarce.

HUBBARD COUNTY

This county, established February 26, 1883, was named in honor of Lucius Frederick Hubbard, governor of Minnesota from 1882 to 1887. He was born in Troy, N. Y., January 26, 1836; came to Minnesota in 1857, established the Red Wing Republican, and was its editor till 1861; enlisted in December, 1861, as a private in the Fifth Minnesota regiment; within a year was promoted to be its colonel; and in December, 1864, was breveted brigadier general. In the Spanish-American war, 1898, he again served as brigadier general. In 1866 he engaged in the grain business at Red Wing, and after 1870 also in flour milling. From 1877 to 1890 he took a leading part in the construction and management of new railway lines, built to promote the business development of Red Wing and Goodhue county. He was a state senator, 1872-5; and was governor, 1882-7, his second term consisting of three years on account of the change to biennial sessions of the legislature. He removed to St. Paul in 1901, and afterward lived there, except that his home during the last two years was with his son in Minneapolis, where he died February 5, 1913.

In the Minnesota Historical Society Collections, volume XIII ("Lives of the Governors of Minnesota," by Gen. James H. Baker, published in 1908), pages 251-281 give the biography and portrait of Governor Hubbard, with extracts from his messages.

By an act of the Legislature, April 16, 1889, Hubbard was appointed a member of a board of commissioners for preparing and publishing a history entitled "Minnesota in the Civil and Indian Wars, 1861-1865." In this work of two volumes he contributed the "Narrative of the Fifth Regiment," forming pages 243-281, and followed by the roster of this regiment in pages 282-299, of volume I, published in 1890.

Five other papers by Hubbard, relating to campaigns, expeditions, and battles of the Civil War, are in the M. H. S. Collections, volume XII, 1908, pages 531-638; and the same volume has also an article by him, in pages 149-166, entitled "Early Days in Goodhue County."

Townships and Villages.

Information for these names, and for lakes and streams in this county, was gathered from Joseph F. Delaney, who was the county auditor from 1907 to 1915, M. M. Nygaard, register of deeds, and Dr. Pearl D. Winship, a resident since 1887 at Park Rapids, the county seat, interviewed during visits there in October, 1909, and September, 1916.

AKELEY township and its railway village were named in honor of Healy Cady Akeley, who built large sawmills here and during many years engaged very extensively in logging and manufacture of lumber. He was born in Stowe, Vt., March 16, 1836; and died in Minneapolis, July

30, 1912. He was admitted to practice law in 1858; served in the Second Michigan cavalry in the civil war; settled in Minneapolis in 1887, as a lumber merchant; was president of the Flour City National Bank, and of the Akeley Lumber Company. In 1916 these sawmills were closed, having exhausted the available supplies of pine timber.

ARAGO township received its name from Lake Arago on Nicollet's map, of 1843, at the place of the present Potato lake, in the southeast part of this township. The name commemorates Dominique Francois Arago, an eminent French physicist and astronomer, who was born at Estagel, France, February 26, 1786, and died in Paris, October 2, 1853.

BADOURA township was named for Mrs. Mary Badoura Mow, wife of David Mow. They were pioneer settlers on the Hubbard prairie, where she died a few years ago, after which he removed to southern Minnesota. This was the name of a princess in "Arabian Nights."

BENEDICT, a railway station in section 35, Lakeport, and Benedict lake, about two miles distant to the south, were named for a homestead farmer.

CLAY township was named for its generally clayey soil of glacial drift, in contrast with other tracts having more sandy and gravelly soil.

CLOVER township derived its name from its abundance of white clover, growing along the old logging roads of the lumbermen.

CROW WING LAKE township was named for its group of nine lakes on and near the Crow Wing river, in its course through this township.

DORSET, a railway village in sections 10 and 11, Henrietta, was named by officers of the Great Northern railway company. This is the name of a county in southern England, a town in Vermont, and a village in Ohio.

FARDEN township was named for Ole J. Farden, a Norwegian homesteader there, who removed to West Hope in Saskatchewan.

FARRIS is a railway village of the Great Northern and Soo lines in sections 14 and 15, Farden.

FERN township was named in honor of Richard Fern, who owned a homestead in Lake Emma township, but in 1916 removed to Park Rapids.

GUTHRIE township, named after its railway village, commemorates Archibald Guthrie, a contractor for the building of this Minnesota and International railway.

HART LAKE township was named for its heart-shaped lake in section 17, but the names of the lake and township are misspelled.

HELGA bears the name of a daughter of John Snustad, probably the first white child born in that township.

HENDRICKSON township commemorates John C. Hendrickson, the former owner of a sawmill there, who removed to Sauk Center.

HENRIETTA township was named for the wife of William H. Martin, whose homestead adjoined the southwest end of Elbow Lake. He served during the civil war in an Ohio regiment, attaining the rank of lieutenant colonel; was a member of the board of county commissioners when this township was organized; and later returned to his former home in Dayton, Ohio, where he died several years ago.

HORTON, a station of the Great Northern railway in section 34, Straight River township, was named for Edward H. Horton, a cruiser selecting lands for lumbering, who lived many years in Park Rapids, but removed to Montana in 1908.

HUBBARD township, notable for its large prairie, was named, like the county, for General Hubbard.

LAKE ALICE township received its name from a lake which was called Lake Elvira by Captain Willard Glazier, in memory of his eldest sister, on the maps of his expeditions to Lake Itasca in 1881 and 1891. The lake was renamed by the pioneer settlers to commemorate Alice Glazier, who accompanied her father in the large party of his second expedition, and to whom his book, "Headwaters of the Mississippi" (1893, 527 pages), was dedicated.

LAKE EMMA township was named for a beautiful though small lake in the north half of section 23, which is much surpassed in size by several others in this township.

LAKE GEORGE township has a large lake at its center, which was thus named by Glazier in 1881 for his brother, a member of his first expedition to Lake Itasca, in July of that year.

LAKE HATTIE township bears the name of its largest lake, derived from Glazier's map in 1881.

LAKEPORT township was named, with a change of spelling, for its railway village, LAPORTE (meaning, in French, the door or gate), which is the name of a city and county in Indiana, and of villages in seven other states.

LATONA was the name of the post office, now discontinued, at Horton railway station.

MANTRAP township was named for the large Mantrap lake at its northwest corner, which, by its many bays and peninsulas, entrapped and baffled travelers through this wooded country in their endeavors to pass by it or around it. Crooked and Spider lakes, in this township, were also named for their similarly winding and branched outlines.

NARY, a railway station in Helga township, was named for Thomas J. Nary, of Park Rapids, who during many years was a cruiser selecting timber lands for purchase by lumber manufacturers in Minneapolis.

NEVIS township and its railway village were probably named for Ben Nevis in western Scotland, the highest mountain of Great Britain.

PARK RAPIDS, the county seat, was named by Frank C. Rice, proprietor of the townsite, who came from Riceville, Iowa, a railway village which he had previously platted. The name was suggested by the parklike groves and prairies here, beside the former rapids of the Fish Hook river, now dammed and supplying valuable water power.

ROCKWOOD township was at first named Rockwell, in honor of Charles H. Rockwell, a homesteader there. A lake also bears his name in sections 16 and 17, Henrietta, where likewise he had a farm.

ROSBY, a station of the Great Northern and Soo railways in the northeast corner of Helga township, was named for Ole Rosby, an adjoining Norwegian farmer.

SCHOOLCRAFT township was named for its river, along which Henry Rowe Schoolcraft and his party canoed in 1832, ascending and portaging to Elk lake, which he then renamed Lake Itasca. He was born in Albany county, N. Y., March 28, 1793; and died in Washington, D. C., December 10, 1864. He was educated at Middlebury college, Vt., and Union college, Schenectady, N. Y., giving principal attention to chemistry and mineralogy. In 1817-18 he traveled in Missouri and Arkansas; in 1820 was in the expedition of General Lewis Cass to the upper Mississippi river, which turned back at Cass lake, regarded then as the principal source of the river; in 1822 was appointed the Indian agent for the tribes in the region of the Great Lakes, with headquarters at the Sault Ste. Marie, and afterward at Mackinaw; and in 1832 he led a government expedition to the head of the Mississippi in Lake Itasca. He published, in 1821, 1834, and 1855, narrative reports and maps of the two expeditions up the Mississippi, which supplied many geographic names. During the greater part of his life, Schoolcraft held various official positions connected with Indian affairs; and in 1851-57, under the auspices of the United States government, he was the author and compiler of a most elaborate work in six quarto volumes, finely illustrated, entitled "Historical and Statistical Information respecting the History, Condition, and Prospects of the Indian Tribes of the United States."

STRAIGHT RIVER township was named for the river flowing from Straight lake in Becker county eastward through the north part of this township. In the usage of the Ojibways, from whom these are translations, the river took the name of the lake whence it flows.

THORPE was named for Joseph Thorpe, an early schoolteacher of Hubbard county, who took a homestead claim in this township.

TODD was named, as proposed by Frank C. Rice, of Park Rapids, which is situated in this township, for Smith Todd, a homesteader here. He served during the civil war in the Eighth Maine regiment; removed about 1910 to Spokane, Wash., and died there in 1915.

WHITE OAK township was named for this species of oak, having "strong, durable, and beautiful timber," which is frequent or common in southeastern and central Minnesota. Its geographic range continues northwest through this county to the upper Mississippi river and the White Earth reservation.

LAKES AND STREAMS.

The foregoing pages have noted the names of Benedict lake and railway station, and of Hart lake, Lakes Alice, Emma, George, and Hattie, Mantrap lake, and Straight river, for each of which a township is named.

The remarkable series or chain of lakes along the head stream of Crow Wing river, in the southeast part of this county, was mapped by

Schoolcraft in 1832. On his return from the expedition to Lake Itasca, his party traveled by canoes from Leech lake southwest to the head of the Crow Wing and through its lakes, this being a route well known to the Ojibways and frequently used in their war raids against the Sioux. In the descending order, these eleven lakes on Schoolcraft's map, published in 1834 with his Narrative of this expedition, are Kaginogumag, Little Vermilion, Birch lake, Lac Plè, Ossowa lake, Lac Vieux Desert, Summit lake, Long Rice lake, Allen's and Johnston's lakes, and Lake Kaichibo Sagitowa. Two of these names were given in honor of Lieutenant James Allen and George Johnston, members of the expedition.

On the map of Hubbard county by the Minnesota Geological Survey (in Volume IV, 1899), this series of names is copied, excepting that the first is Longwater lake, as it was translated by Schoolcraft's Narrative.

Lac Plè (or Pelé) was named in allusion to its being partly bordered by a prairie. Lake Ossowa of the map is named Lake Boutwell in the Narrative, in honor of Rev. William T. Boutwell, of this expedition. Lac Vieux Desert is there translated from its French name, as "the Lake of the Old Wintering Ground." Summit lake was named "from its position," where the river turns southeastward from its previous southwest course. The lowest lake of the series is translated as "the lake which the river passes through at one end."

In the latest atlas of Minnesota, published in 1916, these original names are replaced by a numerical list, which came into use by lumbermen and the pioneer settlers. The lowest is called First or Sibley lake, and the Third and Fourth lakes are also named respectively Swift and Miller lakes, these names being for early governors of Minnesota. The other lakes are designated only by their numbers, up to the Eleventh lake, which, as noted by Schoolcraft, is called Kaginogumag by the Ojibways, meaning Longwater lake.

The stream now named Schoolcraft river was called by him the "Plantagenian or South fork of the Mississippi." Lake Plantagenet, through which it flows in the north edge of this county, retains the name that he gave in 1832. These names, for a line of kings of England, who reigned from 1154 to 1399, were derived from the flowering broom (in Latin, planta genista), chosen as a family emblem by Geoffrey, count of Anjou, whose son was Henry II, the first of the Plantagenet kings. Another name sometimes given to this river is Yellow Head, for Schoolcraft's guide, whose Ojibway name, Oza Windib, has this meaning. It was called River Laplace by Nicollet's map in 1843, for the great French astronomer, who was born in 1749 and died in 1827.

Hennepin lake and river, La Salle river, and its Lake La Salle, tributary to the Mississippi from the northwest part of this county, bear names given in honor of these early French explorers by Glazier in his first expedition to Lake Itasca, in 1881.

Other names received from Glazier's map of his route in that year, passing from Leech lake west to Itasca, are Garfield lake, for the president, James Abram Garfield (b. 1831, d. 1881); Lake Sheridan, in sections 24 and 25, Lake George township, for Philip Henry Sheridan, (b. 1831, d. 1888), the renowned cavalry commander in the civil war; and Lake Paine, for Barrett Channing Paine, who accompanied Glazier in that expedition.

Steamboat river and lake were named for their being ascended by steamboats from Leech lake.

Fish Hook river and lake are translations from their Ojibway name, given by Rev. J. A. Gilfillan as Pugidabani.

Elbow lake, named by the white settlers for its sharply bent outlines, has an Ojibway name which means, as translated by Gilfillan, "the lake into which the river pitches and ceases to flow,—dies there." It has no visible outlet, the inflow being discharged south to the Crow Wing river by springs, or perhaps westward to the north part of Long lake, in Henrietta and Hubbard townships.

Kabekona, the Ojibway name of a lake and river tributary to Leech lake, is defined by Gilfillan as "the end of all roads," which may be nearly equivalent with Schoolcraft's earlier translation, "the rest in the path."

Many other lakes remain to be noted as follows, in the order of the townships from south to north and of ranges from east to west.

Badoura has Wolf lake in sections 17 and 18, and Tripp lake on the south line of section 20, the last being named for Charles Tripp, an early settler beside it.

Crow Wing lake township, in addition to the four lower lakes of the Crow Wing river series, has another Wolf lake; Bladder and Ham lakes, named for their shape; Palmer lake, in section 29; and Duck lake, in section 31.

Hubbard has Stony lake in sections 1 and 2, and Little Stony lake on the east side of section 1, named for ice-formed ridges of boulders and gravel on their shores; Long lake, extending north from the village six miles; and Upper Twin lake, partly in section 31, lying on the Wadena county line.

Straight River township has Lake Moran, nearly three miles long and very narrow, reaching from section 13 to section 27, named for an early settler; and Bass lake and Hinds lake in section 24, the last being named for Edward R. Hinds, of Hubbard, representative of this county in the legislature in 1903-5, 1909, and 1915-19, who about thirty years ago had a logging camp at this lake.

White Oak township has Williams lake in section 13, Hay lake in section 10, and Loon lake in section 30.

Nevis has the Fifth to the Eighth lakes of the Crow Wing series; Elbow lake, before noted; and Deer lake, Shallow lake, and Clausen's lake, in sections 4, 5, and 6.

Henrietta has Bull lake, named by the Ojibways for a bull moose killed there; and Swietzer, Rockwell, and Peysenski lakes, named for pioneer farmers.

Portage lake, in Todd township, was named for a portage from it westward on an Ojibway canoe route.

Shingob lake, in sections 25 and 26, Akeley, and the creek flowing thence to Leech lake, are named, like the adjoining Shingobee township in Cass county, from the Ojibway word, jingob, applied as a general term to several species of evergreen trees, including the balsam fir, spruce, and arbor vitae.

Mantrap township, with its Mantrap, Crooked, and Spider lakes, before noticed, has Waboose lake in section 2, meaning a rabbit in the Ojibway language; and Dead lake in section 18, which, though receiving an inlet from Crooked lake, has no outlet.

Lake Emma township, besides the small lake of this name, has Bottle lake, named for the narrow strait, like the neck of a bottle or hourglass, connecting its two broad areas; Stocking lake, named for its shape; Pickerel lake, having many fish of this species; Rice lake, having much wild rice; Blue lake, named for its depth and color; Big Sand lake, and Little Sand lake; and Gilmore and Thomas lakes, the last being named for the owner of a hotel there, frequented for hunting and fishing.

Arago has Potato lake, named for the wild artichoke, a species of sunflower with tuberous roots, much used as food by the Indians; Eagle lake, named by timber cruisers for a nest in a large tree near the middle of its east shore; Island lake; and Sloan lake, in section 32, named for John Sloan, an adjacent farmer.

Mud lake is in sections 19 and 30, Thorpe.

Clay township has Schoolcraft lake, crossed by its north line, near the highest sources of Schoolcraft river; Fawn lake, on the west side of section 6; Skunk lake, in sections 29, 30, and 32; and Bad Axe lake, in sections 26 and 35.

Clover township has Little Mantrap lake on its west boundary, named for its irregularly branching bays, lying about ten miles west of the larger Mantrap lake.

Lakeport, with Garfield and Kabekona lakes, before noted, has also Mirage lake.

Lake Alice township, including the eastern edge of the Itasca State Park, which reaches one mile into this county, has Lake Alice in sections 2 and 11, Beauty lake in section 28, and numerous other little lakes not yet named.

Dow's lake, in section 32, Schoolcraft, was named for William Dow, who built a sawmill on the Schoolcraft river near this lake, taking a homestead there, but later removed to Laporte.

Farden has Midge, Grace, Wolf, Mud, and Long lakes, all lying in the northeast part of this township.

Rockwood, with the large Plantagenet and Hennepin lakes, before noticed, has Spearhead and Little Spearhead lakes, probably named for their shape.

Fern township has Diamond lake and Lake La Salle.

ISANTI COUNTY

Established February 13, 1857, this county bears the former name, now obsolete, of a large division of the Dakotas or Sioux, anciently Izatys, now Santees, who lived two hundred years ago in the region of the Rum river and Mille Lacs, called by Hennepin respectively the river and lake of the Isantis. Under different forms of spelling, this name was used by DuLuth, Hennepin and La Salle, the first two seeing these Indians in 1679 and 1680; and the name, spelled Issati, appears on Franquelin's map of 1688.

Prof. A. W. Williamson wrote of this word, and of its probable derivation from the Sioux name of Knife lake in Kanabec county: "Isanti (isanati or isanyati), —isan, knife; ati, dwell on or at; the Dakota name of the part of the nation occupying Minnesota, and comprising the Sissetons as well as those now known as Santees; it is supposed the name was given as this lake was their chief location for a time on their westward journey."

Neill's History of Minnesota (page 51) mentions the Isanti division of the Dakota people as follows: "From an early period, there have been three great divisions of this people, which have been subdivided into smaller bands. The first are called the Isanyati, the Issati of Hennepin, after one of the many lakes at the head waters of the river marked, on modern maps, by the unpoetic name of Rum. It is asserted by Dahkotah missionaries now living, that this name was given to the lake because the stone from which they manufactured the knife (isan) was here obtained. The principal band of the Isanti was the M'dewakantonwan. In the journal of Le Sueur, they are spoken of as residing on a lake east of the Mississippi. Tradition says that it was a day's walk from Isantamde or Knife lake." The two lakes so referred to are doubtless Mille Lacs (the lake of the Isantis) and Knife lake, on the Knife river, fifteen miles distant southeastward.

Hon. J. V. Brower has shown that the Knife lake and the Isanti or Knife Sioux probably derived their name from the first acquirement of iron or steel knives there by these Indians, in the winter of 1659-60, through their dealings with Groseilliers and Radisson, and with the Hurons and Ottawas of their company. (Memoirs of Explorations in the Basin of the Mississippi, Volume VI, entitled "Minnesota," 1903, pages 119-123.),

TOWNSHIPS AND VILLAGES.

Information for this county was received from Hans Engberg, president of the First National Bank of Cambridge, who was the county auditor during the years 1878-88, from Sidney S. Bunker, an early pioneer, and G. G. Goodwin, county attorney, each a resident of Cambridge, the county seat, interviewed during a visit there in August, 1916.

ATHENS township bears the name of the most renowned city of ancient Greece, which is now the largest city and capital of that country. An Ohio county and its county seat, townships in Maine, Vermont, and New York, and cities and villages in fourteen other states of our Union, are also named Athens. Probably settlers coming from one or more of these states proposed this name.

BRADFORD was named by Rev. Charles Booth, an Episcopal pastor who took a homestead claim in this township, for his native city of Bradford in Yorkshire, England.

BRAHAM, a railway village in Stanchfield, was named by officers of the Great Northern railway company.

CAMBRIDGE township was named by settlers from Maine, for the township of Cambridge in the central part of that state. The village was incorporated in 1876. The old university city of Cambridge in England, whence we have the names of several cities and villages in the United States, is built on both sides of the little River Cam.

DALBO township has a Swedish name, meaning the home of people from the former province of Dalarne, also called Dalecarlia, in central Sweden.

GRANDY is a Great Northern railway village in Cambridge.

ISANTI township and its railway village were named, like the county, for the eastern Sioux who inhabited this region when the first white explorers and traders came.

MAPLE RIDGE township was named for its broad low ridge and the plentiful maples of its original forest.

NORTH BRANCH township is crossed by the North branch of the Sunrise river.

OXFORD township was named by its settlers, for Oxford county, township, and village in Maine. Twenty-five states of our Union have Oxford townships or villages, the earliest having derived the name from the ancient city and university of Oxford in England. It is of Anglo-Saxon origin, meaning the oxen's ford.

SPENCER BROOK township received the name of its brook, on which a pioneer from Maine, commonly called Judge Spencer, opened a farm.

SPRINGVALE township has a euphonious name that is also borne by a village in Maine, and by townships and villages in seven other states.

STANCHFIELD township, the Lower Stanchfield brook and lake, and Stanchfield creek or upper brook, with its two Upper Stanchfield lakes, are named in honor of Daniel Stanchfield, who was the first, in September, 1847, to explore the extensive pineries of Rum river. He was born in Leeds, Maine, June 8, 1820; and died at Fort Logan, Colorado, May 23, 1908. He settled at St. Anthony in 1847; engaged in logging on this river, and in mercantile business at St. Anthony; was a representative in the territorial legislature in 1853; removed to Iowa in 1861; and returned to Minneapolis in 1889, which was afterward his home. He contributed to the Minnesota Historical Society Collections, volume IX, 1901, a paper entitled "History of Pioneer Lumbering on the Upper Mississippi and its Tributaries, with Biographic Sketches" (pages 325-362, with his portrait.)

STANFORD township has the name of a township in New York, villages in Indiana and Illinois, and a small city in Kentucky.

WYANETT township was named after a village in northern Illinois, which was platted in 1856. It is noted by Gannett as an Indian word, meaning beautiful.

LAKES AND STREAMS.

The foregoing list has referred to the North branch of the Sunrise river, Spencer brook, and the Stanchfield brooks and lakes.

Sunrise river is translated from its Ojibway name, given by Gilfillan as "Memokage zibi, Keep sunrising river."

Rum river is noticed in the chapter on Mille Lacs county, the name of this river having been suggested by the Sioux name of Mille Lacs.

Oxford has Horse Shoe lake and Horse Leg lake, the latter extending into North Branch, each named for their shape; Twin lakes, and Upper and Lower Birch lakes; and Hoffman, Tamarack, Long, and Typo lakes.

Athens has Stratton lake in section 18, named for an early settler.

Marget lake, of section 3 in the east part of Stanford, named for farmers adjoining it, has been drained. Seelye creek, flowing south from section 12, Stanford, was named for Moses Seelye, a pioneer settler who came from New Brunswick.

North Branch has Big Pine lake in sections 4 and 9, named for a large white pine there, near the southern limit of its geographic range.

Isanti township has Lakes Fanny and Florence, named for wives or children of pioneers.

Bradford has Lakes Elizabeth and Francis, Long lake, and German lake, the last being named for German settlers there. The second and third have been also called respectively Lake St. Francis, from the old French name of Rum river, and Lake Henrietta.

In Spencer Brook township are Tennyson, Baxter, Blue, and Mud lakes.

Cambridge has Skogman's lake, named for an early Swedish settler beside it. This township has two Long lakes, one in sections 4 and 9, and another in sections 12 and 13.

Green lake in Wyanett is mainly shallow, named for its green scum in summer; and the smaller but deeper Spectacle lake is named for its shape, like a pair of eyeglasses.

Troolin and Linderman lakes, in Stanchfield, were named respectively for a blacksmith and a farmer near them; Mud lake, for its muddy shores; and the Upper and Lower Rice lakes, for their wild rice.

Lory lake, in section 5, Maple Ridge, was named for H. A. Lory, the former owner of the east half of that section.

ITASCA COUNTY

This county, established October 27, 1849, having originally a much greater area than now, derived its name from Itasca lake, which was named by Schoolcraft in his expedition to this source of the Mississippi in 1832. The translation of its previous Ojibway and French names is Elk Lake. Schoolcraft gave no explanation of the origin and meaning of the name Itasca in his narrative of this expedition published in 1834; but in his later book, on the Cass expedition of 1820 and this of 1832, published in 1855, the following statement is made, relating to the meaning of Itasca lake. "I inquired of Ozawindib the Indian name of this lake; he replied *Omushkos,* which is the Chippewa name of the Elk. Having previously got an inkling of some of their mythological and necromantic notions of the origin and mutations of the country, which permitted the use of a female name for it, I denominated it Itasca."

The existence of this lake, and its French name, Lac la Biche, were known to Schoolcraft by information from Indians and voyageurs, before this expedition; and the actual history of his coining this new word, as narrated fifty years afterward by his companion in the expedition, Rev. William T. Boutwell, is told by Hon. J. V. Brower in the Minnesota Historical Society Collections (vol. VII, pp. 144, 145).

"Schoolcraft and Boutwell were personal associates, voyaging in the same canoe through Superior, and while conversing on their travels along the south shore of the great lake, the name 'Itasca' was selected in the following manner, in advance of its discovery by Schoolcraft's party.

"Mr. Schoolcraft, having uppermost in his mind the source of the river, expecting and determined to reach it, suddenly turned and asked Mr. Boutwell for the Greek and Latin definition of the headwaters or true source of a river. Mr. Boutwell, after much thought, could not rally his memory of Greek sufficiently to designate the phrase, but in Latin selected the strongest and most pointed expressions, 'Veritas,' and 'Caput,'—Truth, Head. This was written on a slip of paper, and Mr. Schoolcraft struck out the first and last three letters, and announced to Mr. Boutwell that 'Itasca shall be the name.'"

The origin of this name had perplexed experts acquainted with the Ojibway and Sioux languages, as related by Charles H. Baker in the St. Paul Pioneer, May 26, 1872. Three weeks later the same newspaper for June 16 published letters received by Alfred J. Hill, from Gideon H. Pond, the missionary to the Sioux; Mrs. Mary H. Eastman, citing a supposed Ojibway myth or tradition in her "Aboriginal Portfolio;" and Rev. William T. Boutwell, telling how Schoolcraft coined the name by using

ITASCA COUNTY 253

parts of the two Latin words, Veritas, Caput. Twenty years later, Brower's publication of his interview with Boutwell, as here cited, settled this very interesting question beyond any further doubt.

The chapter of Clearwater county contains a review of the explorations of the sources of the Mississippi, which were completed by detailed surveys of the Itasca State Park, lying mainly in that county.

Townships and Villages.

Information of the names in this county was received from Edward J. Luther, deputy county auditor, and John A. Brown, county surveyor, during a visit at Grand Rapids, the county seat, in September, 1909; and from Hugh McEwen, deputy auditor, during a second visit there in August, 1916.

ALVWOOD township is mainly occupied by Swedish settlers, and the first part of its name is probably derived from Sweden.

ARBO township was named for an early lumberman, John Arbo, who settled there.

ARDENHURST, at first called Island Lake township, was renamed by its settlers from England. The first part of this name refers to the ancient Ardennes forest, which covered a large area in northern France, Belgium, and western Germany; and hurst is an Anglo-Saxon word, meaning a grove or a wooded hill.

BALL CLUB is the name of a railway village at the south end of Ball Club lake, which is translated from its Ojibway name, suggested by the form of the lake. The Indians were fond of playing ball, and their club or bat used in this game was called La Crosse by the French, being the source of the name given to a city and county in Wisconsin.

BALSAM township was named for the Balsam lake and creek, and for its abundance of the balsam fir, which also is common throughout northeastern Minnesota. The bark of this tree supplies a transparent liquid resin or turpentine, called Canada balsam, used in mounting objects for the microscope and in making varnish.

BASS BROOK township and BASS LAKE township were named for their brook and lake, having many fish of our well known bass species. The Ojibway name of the lake is noted by Gilfillan as Ushigunikan, "the place of bass," and the outflowing brook, according to the Ojibway usage, bears the same name.

BEARVILLE township is named for its principal stream, Bear river, flowing from Bear lake.

BIG FORK township and its railway village are named from their location on the Big fork of Rainy river.

BLACKBERRY township and its railway station are similarly named for the Blackberry lake and brook.

BOWSTRING township adjoins the east side of Bowstring lake, which is a translation of its Ojibway name, noted as Atchabani or Busatchabani by Gilfillan. This name is also applied by the Ojibways to the **Big fork**, because the Bowstring lake is its source.

BUSTICOGAN, a township name, is probably of Ojibway derivation.

CALUMET, a mining railway village of the Mesabi iron range, bears the French name (from the Latin calamus, a reed) of the ceremonial pipe used by the Indians in making treaties or other solemn engagements. Assent was expressed by smoking the calumet, which, from treaties preventing or terminating wars, was often called the peace pipe.

CARPENTER township was named in honor of Seth Carpenter, an aged homesteader, who in 1906 headed the petition for its organization.

COHASSET, the railway village of Bass Brook township, received its name from the town of Cohasset on the east coast of Massachusetts. It is an Indian word, meaning, as noted by Gannett, "fishing promontory," "place of pines," or "young pine trees."

COLERAINE, a mining railway village at the west end of the Mesabi range, bears the name of a township in western Massachusetts. It was chosen in honor of Thomas F. Cole, who was prominent in the early development of these iron mines, but later removed to Arizona, becoming president of a copper mining company there.

DEER LAKE township and DEER RIVER township and railway village are named for this lake and river, which are translated from the Ojibway name, Wawashkeshiwi, as noted by Gilfillan.

DEWEY township was named in honor of George Dewey, victor in the battle of Manila Bay, May 1, 1898. He was born in Montpelier, Vt., December 26, 1837; was graduated at the United States Naval Academy, 1858; served in the civil war; was promoted as lieutenant commander in 1865, captain in 1884, commodore in 1896, and admiral in 1899.

EFFIE, a station of the Minneapolis and Rainy River railway, was named for Effie Wenaus, daughter of the postmaster there.

FAIRVIEW township has the euphonious name chosen by its settlers in their petition for organization.

FEELEY township was named for Thomas J. Feeley, of Aitkin, who had logging camps there during several years. He has lived in this township since 1899.

FRANKLIN township, like the counties of this name in twenty-four states of the Union, and townships, villages, or cities, in thirty states, commemorates Benjamin Franklin, philosopher, statesman, and diplomatist, who was born in Boston, January 17, 1706, and died in Philadelphia, April 17, 1790.

GOOD HOPE, named by the settlers of this township, is also the name of villages in eight other states.

GOODLAND township has another auspicious name, found likewise in Indiana, Michigan, and Kansas.

GRAN township was named for an early settler.

GRAND RAPIDS township received its name from the location of its village, the county seat, beside rapids of the Mississippi, having a fall of five feet in a third of a mile. The river is ascended to this place by steamers from Aitkin.

GRATTAN township was named for the Irish orator and statesman, Henry Grattan (b. 1746, d. 1820).

GREENWAY township was named for John C. Greenway, who formerly had charge of iron mining at Coleraine for the Oliver Mining Company, but removed to be a superintendent of copper mining in Bisbee, Arizona.

HARRIS township was named for Duncan Harris, who took a homestead claim there, on which he has a fruit farm.

INGER township was named for one of its pioneer settlers.

IRON RANGE township contains the iron mining railway villages of Colerane, Bovey, and Holman, which have the most western mines of the Mesabi range.

KEEWATIN, an iron mining town in the east edge of this county, has an Ojibway name, spelled giwédin by Baraga's Dictionary, meaning north, also the north wind. It was the name of a former large district of Canada, at the west side of Hudson bay. This word is spelled Keewaydin, as it should be pronounced, in Longfellow's "Song of Hiawatha," with translation as "the Northwest wind, the Home wind."

KINGHURST township, formerly called Popple (a mispronunciation of the poplar tree, very abundant here), was renamed in honor of Cyrus M. King, of Deer River, who during many years was a member of the board of county commissioners. (See also Ardenhurst, before noted in this list.)

LAKE JESSIE township has a lake of this name, and another called Little Jessie lake, probably in commemoration of the wife or daughter of one of the early lumbermen.

LA PRAIRIE, a railway village and junction, is near the mouth of Prairie river, which flows through Prairie lake.

LONG LAKE township is similarly named for one of its lakes, this name and also Round lake being of very frequent occurrence among the almost countless lakes of Minnesota.

MCCORMICK and MCLEOD townships, and MCVEIGH railway station, were named for pioneers.

MARCELL township was named in honor of Andrew Marcell, the first conductor of trains on the Minneapolis and Rainy River railway, which was originally built for transportation of logs to sawmills.

MOOSE PARK township received this name by the suggestion of C. H. Harper, a pioneer farmer there, who was one of the petitioners for its organization.

NASHWAUK township has an Algonquin name, from Nashwaak river and village, near Fredericton, New Brunswick. It is probably allied in meaning with Nashua, "land between," the name of a river and a city in New Hampshire.

NORE township was named for Kittil S. and Syver K. Nohre, immigrant settlers from Norway.

ORTH is a railway village of Nore, in the north edge of this county.

OTENEAGEN was named by William Hulbert, a farmer and lumberman of this township, who came from Michigan. In a different spelling, Ontonagon, it is the name of a river in northern Michigan, tributary to Lake Superior, and of its village and county. Gannett has defined the Michigan name as an Ojibway word, meaning "fishing place," or, in another account of its origin, adopted because an Indian maiden lost a dish in the stream and exclaimed "nindonogan," which in her dialect meant "away goes my dish."

POKEGAMA township derived this Ojibway name from the Pokegama lake, translated by Gilfillan as "the water which juts off from another water," and "the lake with bays branching out." This large lake, having a very irregularly branched shape, nearly adjoins the Mississippi river.

The Pokegama falls of the Mississippi, named from this lake, about three miles above Grand Rapids, had a descent of fifteen feet in a sixth of a mile; but the dam built there in the Upper Mississippi reservoir system increases the fall to twenty-one feet, raising also the level of the lake. Schoolcraft, in his Narrative of the expedition with Governor Cass in 1820, wrote: "The Mississippi at this fall is compressed to eighty feet in width and precipitated over a rugged bed of sand stone, highly inclined towards the northeast. There is no perpendicular pitch, but the river rushes down a rocky channel."

ROUND LAKE township and railway station are named for the central and smallest one of the three Round lakes in the north half of this county. The next in size closely adjoins Long lake, and the largest is at the east side of Good Hope.

SAGO township received this name after several others had been successively chosen but found inadmissible, being previously used elsewhere in Minnesota. It was suggested by one of the county commissioners because sago pudding was served at their dinner.

SAND LAKE township bears the name of its large lake, through which the Big fork flows, next below Bowstring lake.

SPANG township was named in honor of Matthew A. Spang, a lumber manufacturer at Grand Rapids, who was the county auditor when this township was organized.

SPLIT HAND township received the name of its principal lake and creek, translated from the Ojibway name as "Cut Hand" on Nicollet's map.

SWAN RIVER, a railway village and junction, is named for the river near it, which flows from Swan lake. This is a translation of the Ojibway name, Wabiziwi, noted by Gilfillan.

THIRD RIVER township is crossed by the river of this name, the third in the order from east to west, tributary to the north side of Lake Winnebagoshish.

ITASCA COUNTY 257

TROUT LAKE township is named for its largest lake, translated from Namegoss or Namegosi, as the Ojibway word is spelled respectively by Baraga and Gilfillan.

WARBA, a railway village in Feeley township, was formerly called Verna, but was renamed by officers of the Great Northern railway company, probably for Waiba, the Ojibway word meaning soon.

WAWINA, the most southeastern township of this county, received the name of its earlier railway village, an Ojibway word, meaning "I name him often, . . . mention him frequently," as defined in Baraga's Dictionary.

WELLER'S SPUR is a railway village five miles southeast of Deer River.

WINNEBAGOSHISH is a township of the Indian Reservation at the north side of the large lake of this name, which has been fully noticed in the chapter for Cass county.

WIRT township was named by O. E. Walley, its first settler, probably for a township in New York or a county in West Virginia, where the name was given in honor of William Wirt (b. 1772, d. 1834), who was the attorney general of the United States in 1817-29.

ZEMPLE village needs further inquiry for the origin of its name.

LAKES AND STREAMS.

The preceding pages have given sufficient mention of Ball Club lake, Balsam lake and creek, Bass brook and lake, Bear river and lake, the Big fork of Rainy river, Blackberry lake and brook, Bowstring lake, a name that is also given to the Big fork by the Ojibways, Deer lake and river, Lake Jessie and Little Jessie lake, Prairie river and lake, Long lake, Pokegama lake and falls, the three Round lakes, Sand lake, Split Hand lake and creek, Swan river and lake, Third river, and Trout lake.

Lake Winnebagoshish, as it should be spelled in accordance with its Ojibway pronunciation, lies in the course of the Mississippi on the boundary between Cass and Itasca counties, so that it has previously received attention.

In addition to the southern Deer lake and river, which gave their names to townships and a large village, this county has a second lake and river of this name, tributary to the Big fork.

The following lakes remain to be mentioned, in their order from south to north, and from east to west.

Cowhorn lake is named for its shape.

Lake Siseebakwet, as spelled on recent maps, but given by Gilfillan as Sinzi-ba-quat, is a name received from the Ojibways, meaning Sugar lake, having reference to their making maple sugar.

Rice lake, in Bass Brook township, is named for wild rice.

Southeast of Swan lake are Hart, Helen, and Beauty lakes.

Trout Lake township has Mud lake, one of our most frequent lake names.

Grand Rapids township has Horseshoe lake, Lily, Hale, and Crystal lakes. The third was named in honor of James T. Hale, a member of the State Tax Commission, who formerly lived here.

White Oak point on the Mississippi, a lake of the same name, and the little White Oak Indian Reservation, are translated from the Ojibway name of this point, Nemijimijikan, as noted by Gilfillan.

Northwest and west of Swan lake are Ox Hide, Snowball, and Panasa lakes. The last is an Ojibway name, meaning a young bird.

Shoal lake lies between Prairie and Bass lakes.

Chase lake, near the west end of Deer lake, was named for Jonathan Chase, who was born in Sebec, Maine, Dec. 31, 1818, and died at his home in Minneapolis, February 1, 1904. He came to Minnesota in 1854, engaged in lumbering in Mille Lacs county, and later owned an interest in the large sawmills at Gull River, Cass county.

Crooked lake has very irregularly branched outlines.

Lawrence lake was named for Hugh Lawrence, a Minneapolis lumberman who had a logging camp there.

Wabano lake and the Little Wabano lake are nearly like an Ojibway word, waban, the east, the morning twilight. Wabun is its spelling in "The Song of Hiawatha," and Waupun as the name of a city in Wisconsin. Longfellow also used another word, wabeno, a magician or juggler, spelled Wabanow by Baraga, which is more directly the source of the name of these lakes. Wabeno is a village name in northeastern Wisconsin, defined by Gannett as "men of the dawn" or "eastern men."

Next westward are Blue lake, Johnson, Moose, and Island lakes.

Buck lake was named for a male deer.

Pioneer lumbermen, or their forest cruisers who selected tracts of timber for purchase, are commemorated by Lake Buckman, King, Gunn, Dick, and Smith lakes.

A further list of lakes, with those last named and westward, comprises another Island lake, Ruby, Spider, and Little Long lakes; Wolf lake, Carriboo lake (more correctly spelled Caribou), Dead Horse and Grave lakes, Little Bowstring lake, and Potato lake; and Portage lake, lying between Bowstring and Sand lakes.

Northward are Eagle, Coon, and Fox lakes; Turtle and Little Turtle lakes; Cameron and Sandwick lakes, the second named for John A. Sandwick, a pioneer farmer; Bustie's lake and Shine lake, close north of the most eastern bend of the Big fork; Lakes Bella and Dora; Spring, East, and White Fish lakes; and Four Towns lake, of small area, named for its lying in the corner of four townships.

Cut Foot Sioux lake is translated from its Ojibway name, referring to a maimed Sioux who was killed there in a battle in 1748. (Warren, "History of the Ojibway Nation," M. H. S. Collections, vol. V, p. 184; Winchell, "The Aborigines of Minnesota," 1911, p. 534.) The outlet of this lake is the first stream found flowing into the north side of Lake

ITASCA COUNTY 259

Winnebagoshish, in the order from east to west. Next are Pigeon river and Third river, the last giving its name to a township.

Downes creek, flowing into the west part of Round lake, is the most western stream of the Big Fork basin.

Island lake in Ardenhurst, the third so named in this county, has Elmwood island, which is more than a mile long, but very narrow, indicating by its mapped outline that it is an esker gravel ridge of the glacial drift.

Maple Ridge.

The highest point of Itasca county is a hill four miles west of Grand Rapids, in sections 22 and 23, Bass Brook, adjoining the north part of Pokegama lake, above which it rises about 350 feet. It is commonly called Maple Ridge or Sugar Tree Ridge. Other hills or ridges in this county rarely have even a third of this height, being so low that they have not been named.

Indian Reservations.

In a treaty made at Washington, February 22, 1855, a delegation of the Ojibways of the upper Mississippi ceded to the United States large areas of their lands, but reserved other tracts. The Winnebagoshish reservation, lying at the north side of the lake of this name, was set apart by this treaty for Pillager and Lake Winnebagoshish bands of these Indians. Its boundaries reached from the mouth of the lake north to the head of the first river tributary to it, thence west to the Third river, down this river to the lake, and thence in a direct line across the lake to the place of beginning.

Another reservation for these bands, on the north side of Cass lake, also made in the same treaty, was later extended eastward to the west side of Lake Winnebagoshish and to Third river, including about fifty square miles in the present Itasca county.

Again in a treaty at Washington, March 19, 1867, a large tract at the south side of these lakes and reaching to the Leech lake and river, was reserved to the Ojibways. This reservation, lying mainly in Cass county, continues east across the Mississippi to include an area in Itasca county nearly equal to four townships.

The Winnebagoshish reservation, enlarged under executive orders by the President in 1873 and 1874, is wholly in Itasca county. The other two areas, known as the Cass Lake and Chippewa reservations, extend partly into this county, so that the three together reach from its western border past Winnebagoshish and Ball Club lakes to Deer River village.

Adjoining the southeast corner of the Chippewa reservation, an executive order of October 29, 1873, reserved a small area of about sixteen square miles, through which the Mississippi flows, including White Oak point and the lake of this name, whence it is known as the White Oak reservation. This lies in Itasca county, excepting about a quarter part in Cass county, on the southwest side of the river.

JACKSON COUNTY

This county, established May 23, 1857, is stated by its best informed old citizens, as also by J. Fletcher Williams, who from 1867 to 1893 was secretary of the Minnesota Historical Society, and by Return I. Holcombe, writing in the Pioneer Press Almanac of 1896, to be named "for Hon. Henry Jackson, the first merchant in St. Paul." He was born in Abingdon, Virginia, February 1, 1811; came to St. Paul in June, 1842; was appointed the first justice of the peace, 1843; was the first postmaster, 1846-49; was a member of the first Territorial Legislature, and a charter member of the Historical Society; removed to Mankato in 1853, where he was one of the first settlers; and died there, July 31, 1857. In the summer of 1842 he opened the first store at St. Paul, in a cabin built of tamarack logs on the river bank near Jackson street, which was named for him.

The late William P. Murray, who was a member of the legislature in 1857, at the time of formation of Jackson county, dissented from this derivation of the name, asserting that according to his recollection it was their intention to commemorate Andrew Jackson, the seventh president of the United States.

The county seat also has this name, with which its site was christened a few weeks before the legislative act forming the county was passed. So it appears that the name was first adopted by pioneers on the ground, but whether they meant to honor Andrew Jackson, the military hero and statesman, or Henry Jackson, a founder of St. Paul and Mankato, on their route from the east to this area, is not certainly determined.

Counties in twenty other states of the Union are named Jackson, which with only one exception, are noted by Gannett as in honor of the president. Twenty-four states have townships, villages, or cities of this name. Pennsylvania, the previous home of some of the pioneers of this county and of Jackson, its county seat, has seventeen townships thus named, in so many different counties, surpassing any other state in such expression of admiration of Andrew Jackson.

TOWNSHIPS AND VILLAGES.

Information for this county was gathered from "An Illustrated History of Jackson County, Minnesota," by Arthur P. Rose, 586 pages, 1910; and from I. W. Mahoney, county abstractor, at the office of the register of deeds, and Alexander Fiddes, an early settler, who was the postmaster many years at Jackson, interviewed during a visit there in July, 1916.

ALBA township, organized September 21, 1872, has a Latin name, meaning white, which is also the name of villages in Pennsylvania, Michigan, Missouri, Texas, and Oregon.

ALPHA, a railway village in Wisconsin township, platted in 1895, and incorporated July 25, 1899, bears the name of our letter A in the Greek alphabet, which word is formed from the first and second Greek letters. It is also the name of villages in Maryland, Indiana, Illinois, and other states.

BELMONT township was organized January 5, 1867, receiving its name from a settlement of Norwegian immigrants who came here in 1860. One of their leaders, Anders Olson Slaabaken, was also often called Anders Belmont, probably for a locality in Norway. This is also a frequent English name of villages and townships in many other states.

CHRISTIANIA township, organized March 4, 1871, was named by its settlers for the capital city and chief seaport of Norway. This name was given to the city in honor of Christian IV, king of Denmark and Norway, by whom it was founded in 1624.

DELAFIELD township, finally so named March 4, 1871, was organized October 11, 1870, being then called Pleasant Prairie and afterward Orwell and Bergen, which names were not accepted because they had been earlier given to townships elsewhere in Minnesota. This name is borne by villages in Illinois and Wisconsin.

DES MOINES township, organized April 2, 1866, was at first called Jackson, for the county seat thus named in the eastern part of this township. About six weeks later, on May 16, it was renamed as now by the county commissioners, for the river which flows through the township and county. The very interesting origin of this name has been noted in the first chapter.

ENTERPRISE, organized March 4, 1871, was named in accordance with the suggestion of Samuel D. Lockwood and Anders Roe, early settlers of this township.

EWINGTON, organized March 28, 1873, was named in honor of Thomas C. Ewing and family, who were its first settlers.

HERON LAKE township, organized September 7, 1870, was named for the large lake on its west side, which, as noted by Prof. A. W. Williamson, is translated from its Sioux or Dakota name, Okabena, (*hokah,* heron; *be,* nests; *na,* diminutive suffix), meaning the nesting place of herons. Minnesota has three common species, the great blue heron or crane, from which Crane island of Lake Minnetonka was named, the green heron, and the black-crowned night heron. The last, found by Dr. Thomas S. Roberts in considerable numbers at Heron lake, was formerly plentiful or frequent through the greater part of this state.

HUNTER, organized February 13, 1872, was named in honor of James Wilson Hunter, a pioneer merchant of Jackson, who at that time was the county auditor. He was born in Scotland, August 16, 1837; came to the

United States in 1855, and to Minnesota in 1858; settled at Jackson in 1868, where he died August 13, 1900. He was a representative in the state legislature in 1869.

JACKSON village, the county seat, is on the site of the earliest white settlement within the area of this county, founded and named Springfield in the summer of 1856. It consisted of a log store building on the west side of the Des Moines river and a few cabins, quite scattered, on the east side. Several of its settlers were killed, March 26, 1857, by a marauding band of Sioux under the leadership of Inkpaduta, coming from their massacre of many settlers at Spirit Lake, Iowa. Soon afterward the site of Springfield was renamed Jackson, and on May 23 of that year it was designated to be the county seat by the act establishing this county. But the financial panic of 1857 checked immigration, the civil war followed, and the village was not platted until the fall of 1866. It was incorporated April 19, 1881. The origin of this name, which was adopted for the county, is discussed at the beginning of this chapter.

KIMBALL township, organized March 23, 1872, was named in honor of Wilbur S. Kimball, the pioneer hardware merchant of Jackson. He was born in Chelsea, Vt., in 1835; came to Minnesota at the age of twenty-one years, engaging in hardware business at Austin; served in the Fourth Minnesota regiment during the civil war; removed to Jackson in 1867, and was a merchant there many years; was later a traveling salesman; and died in Jackson, December 13, 1892.

LA CROSSE township, organized in September, 1872, was named for the city of La Crosse, Wisconsin, whence many of its settlers came. This name refers to the favorite game of ball often played there by the Indians, the stick or club used to catch and throw the ball being called *la crosse* by the French.

LAKEFIELD, a railway village founded in 1879 with the completion of the railway to this point, was named for the adjoining Heron lake. It was incorporated September 1, 1887.

MIDDLETOWN, lying between Petersburg and Minneota, was organized May 10, 1869. "The fact that the township was situated between the two older organized townships suggested the name."

MILOMA, the station at the intersection of the Milwaukee and Omaha railways, has a compound name, recently formed by putting together the first three letters of each. This crossing was laid August 1, 1879, and for about twenty-five years it was called Prairie Junction.

MINNEOTA township, organized October 15, 1866, has a Sioux or Dakota name, meaning "much water," given partly for its group of several small lakes, but mainly for the adjoining large Spirit lake and Lake Okoboji in the edge of Iowa.

OKABENA, a railway station in West Heron Lake township, was founded in September, 1879, taking the Sioux name of the lake, which means, as before noted, "the nesting place of herons."

JACKSON COUNTY 263

PETERSBURG, organized April 2, 1866, received its name in honor of Rev. Peter Baker, a pioneer Methodist minister, who settled in this township in 1860 and was its first postmaster.

ROST township, organized February 3, 1874, was named in honor of Frederick Rost, an early settler who came there in 1869. It was at first erroneously spelled Rust in the record of the county commissioners and on maps.

ROUND LAKE township, organized in October, 1869, was named for the beautiful lake in its western part.

SIOUX VALLEY township, organized February 27, 1874, the latest in this county, was named for the Little Sioux river, which flows through it and continues south across northwestern Iowa to the Missouri river. The Little and Big Sioux rivers, the latter forming the northwest boundary of Iowa, were named for the Dakota or Sioux Indians, who inhabited this region. The name Sioux is the terminal part of Nadouesioux, a term of hatred, meaning snakes, enemies, which was applied by the Ojibways and other Algonquins to this people.

WEIMER, organized May 27, 1871, was then named Eden, which was changed to the present name October 20, 1871. "Charles Winzer, the township's first settler, selected the name in honor of his home town in Germany, Saxe-Weimar." It was correctly spelled in the petition for its adoption, but was copied erroneously in the county records.

WEST HERON LAKE township was organized January 7, 1874, "its geographical location suggesting the name."

WILDER, a railway station in Delafield, was located and named in November, 1871, in honor of Amherst Holcomb Wilder, of St. Paul. He was born in Lewis, N. Y., July 7, 1828; and died in St. Paul, November 11, 1894. He came to Minnesota in 1859, and engaged in mercantile business and also in stage and steamboat transportation. Later he was interested in building numerous railways in Minnesota and adjoining states. By his will, and by the later wills of his widow and daughter, the Amherst H. Wilder Charity was founded, providing a fund of about $3,000,000, of which the income is used to aid the worthy poor of St. Paul. The building of this village was begun in 1885. It was platted December 7, 1886, and was incorporated March 28, 1899.

WISCONSIN township, organized April 10, 1869, was named in honor of the state from which a majority of its settlers came. This name, given to the state from its large river, is noted by Gannett as "a Sauk Indian word having reference to holes in the banks of a stream, in which birds nest."

LAKES AND STREAMS.

The preceding pages have noticed the Des Moines river, Heron lake, Round lake, and the Little Sioux river.

Elm creek, draining the northeastern part of this county, flows east across Martin county to the Blue Earth river.

Independence lake, on the south line of Christiania, was named by the United States surveyors, who came to it on the fourth of July. Long lake and Fish lake are crossed respectively by the east and north boundaries of this township. Lower's lake, in sections 15 and 22, has been drained.

The east part of Wisconsin township has small creeks flowing into Martin county, which are sources of the East fork of Des Moines river.

Minneota has Loon lake, Pearl, Rush, and Little Spirit lakes. The last is named in contrast with the much larger Spirit lake in Iowa, which is translated from its Sioux name, Mini wakan, noted by Nicollet. In its most northern part, Spirit lake touches the boundary of the state and of this township at the south side of section 36.

Tributary to the West fork of the Little Sioux river are Skunk and Rush lakes in Spring Valley, Round lake in the township bearing its name, and also Illinois lake, Plum Island lake, named for the grove of native plum trees on its island, and Iowa or State Line lake, crossed by the Iowa boundary at the southwest corner of this county.

Des Moines township has Clear lake at the middle of its west side, remarkable for the depth and purity of its water.

Heron Lake township has Lake Flaherty, an early name, but for whom it was given remains to be ascertained.

Timber lake, named for its lone grove in this broad prairie region, adjoins the south side of Wilder village. It has been also called Lake Minneseka, a Sioux name meaning "bad water."

Lake Carroll, formerly mapped in section 4, Delafield, has been drained.

Jack and Okabena creeks flow into the west side of Heron lake, the former being probably named from jack rabbits, and the latter bearing the Sioux name for Heron lake.

KANABEC COUNTY

Established March 13, 1858, and organized in 1882, this county bears a name proposed by William H. C. Folsom, of Taylor's Falls, who, as a member of the state senate in 1858, introduced the legislative bill for the formation of the county. Kanabec is the usual word for a snake in the language of the Ojibways, given by them to the Snake river flowing through Kanabec and Pine counties to the St. Croix. It has a heavy accent on the second syllable, with the English long sound of the vowel, being thus pronounced quite unlike the name of the Kennebec river in Maine. The latter name, accented on the first syllable, is of different etymology, meaning "long lake,—a name of Moosehead lake transferred to the river."

This Ojibway word is variously spelled, but has only slight difference of pronunciation. On Nicollet's map it is Kinebik; in Wilson's Manual of this language, kenabig; and in Baraga's Dictionary, which is followed by Gilfillan and Verwyst in their lists of Ojibway names, it is ginebig, but this is pronounced, in French style, nearly like our English form of the word in the county name.

Townships and Villages.

Information of geographic names in this county has been received from "Fifty Years in the Northwest," by W. H. C. Folsom, 763 pages, 1888; and from A. V. Sander, county auditor, A. M. Anderson, register of deeds, Olof P. Victorien, judge of probate, and Hon. J. C. Pope, each of Mora, the county seat, interviewed during a visit there in May, 1916.

ANN LAKE township, its lake of this name, and the outflowing Ann river, tributary to the Snake river, commemorate an Ojibway woman who lived beside the lake. ("Kathio," by J. V. Brower, 1901, page 114.)

ARTHUR township, organized in 1883, was named by Charles E. Williams, of Mora, in honor of Chester Alan Arthur, the twenty-first President of the United States, who was born in Fairfield, Vt., October 5, 1830, and died in New York city, November 18, 1886. He was graduated at Union College in 1848; practiced law in New York city; was inspector general of state troops during the civil war; was collector of the port of New York, 1871-78; was elected Vice-President in 1880, and succeeded Garfield, who died September 19, 1881. His term as President extended to March 4, 1885.

BRUNSWICK township, organized in 1883, received its name from Brunswick village and township in Maine, at the head of navigation on the Androscoggin river, whence many pioneer lumbermen came to the pineries of the St. Croix and Snake rivers. A village of this name, platted in 1856 in section 1 of this township, was the first county seat.

COMFORT township bears a surname of early settlers.

FORD township, organized in 1916, the latest in this county, was formerly included in Peace township. It was named for Henry Ford, of Detroit, Mich., a wealthy manufacturer of automobiles, who conducted a large delegation from this country to Europe in December, 1915, to confer with the nations at war and to intercede for restoration of peace.

GRASS LAKE township, organized in 1883, formerly had a small lake of this name, now drained, in sections 13 and 24, which was mostly filled with tall marsh grass, the water being very shallow. From this lake was also derived the name of GRASSTON, the railway village in section 12.

HAY BROOK township was named for the brook flowing through it, having meadows which supplied hay for winter logging camps.

HILLMAN township was named in honor of William F. Hillman, a pioneer farmer there.

KANABEC township, like the county, bears the Ojibway name of the Snake river.

KNIFE LAKE township received its name from the Knife lake and river, which are translated from their Sioux and Ojibway names. The first knives of iron or steel obtained by the Sioux, in the winter of 1659-60, were brought here by Groseilliers and Radisson and the Huron and Ottawa Indians who accompanied them, as noted for Isanti county.

KROSCHEL township was named in honor of Herman Kroschel, one of its first settlers.

MORA, a village on the railway in Arthur township, was platted in 1882, when by popular vote it succeeded Brunswick as the county seat. It was named by Myron R. Kent, owner of its site, for the city of Mora at the northwest end of Siljan lake in central Sweden.

OGILVIE, the railway village of Kanabec township, commemorates Oric Ogilvie Whited, for whom also Whited township was named.

PEACE township was named by vote of its people, this name being suggested in contrast with its village of Warman.

POMROY township was named, as also Pomroy lake, crossed by its west line, in honor of John Pomroy, a pioneer lumberman who had a logging camp beside the lake.

QUAMBA, a railway village in Whited, was named by officers of the Great Northern railway company.

SOUTH FORK township is crossed by the South branch or fork of the Ground House river.

WARMAN, a village in sections 5 and 6, Peace, having granite quarries, was named in honor of S. M. Warman, a quarry owner there, who was killed by the fall of a derrick.

WHITED township, like Ogilvie village, was named in honor of Oric Ogilvie Whited, of Minneapolis. He was born in Fitchville, Ohio, January 20, 1854; was graduated at the State Normal School, Winona, Minn.,

KANABEC COUNTY

1872; taught school several years in Olmsted county, and later was the county superintendent of schools; was admitted to practice law, 1884; settled in Minneapolis in 1890, engaged in real estate business and law practice, and owned numerous tracts of land in this county. He died in Minneapolis, August 6, 1912.

Lakes and Streams.

The foregoing pages have noted the Snake river, Ann lake and river, Grass lake, Hay brook, Knife lake and river, Pomroy lake, and the South fork of Ground House river.

A tradition among the Sioux and Ojibways, cited by Winchell in "The Aborigines of Minnesota" (page 67), told of Hidatsa Indians, a branch of the great Dakotan stock, anciently living in Minnesota, who were driven westward to the Missouri river by the coming of the Sioux. These Indians lived in wooden huts covered with earth, whence probably came the aboriginal name that we retain in translation as the Ground House river, draining the southwest part of this county. It is called Earth Fort river on the map of Owen's Geological Report, published in 1852.

Tributaries of the Snake river, in their order from south to north in this county, include, on its east side, Mud creek, flowing through Mud lake, Chesley brook, also called Little Snake river, and Cowan's brook, the second and third being named for pioneer lumbermen; and, on the west side, Rice creek, named for its wild rice, Ground House, Ann, and Knife rivers, previously noticed, Moccasin brook, into which Snow Shoe brook flows, Hay brook, and Bergman's brook, near the north line of the county. The last bears the name of a lumberman whose logging camp was on this brook.

The picturesque Upper falls and Lower falls of the Snake river are respectively about two miles and three miles south of the north boundary of this county.

Among the few lakes that remain to be mentioned, Brunswick has Devil's lake, in section 4; Pennington lake, in section 13, now drained, named for James Pennington, who near it opened the first farm in the county; and Lewis lake, in the southwest corner of this township, named for a pioneer settler beside it.

Arthur township has Spring lake, in sections 1 and 12; Lake Mora, in the village of this name; Kent lake, in sections 16 and 21, commemorating Myron R. Kent, who platted and named this village; and Fish lake, through which Ann river flows, in sections 33 and 34.

A lake beside Snake river in sections 10 and 15, Peace, is mapped as "Full of Fish lake," a translation from its Ojibway name.

Kroschel has Bass lake, in section 1; Loon lake, in sections 3 and 4; Long lake and Bland lake, in sections 4 and 5; Beauty lake, in section 10; Lake Eleven, in the section having this number; Pike lake, in section 13; Feathery lake and Muskrat lake, in section 24; and White Lily lake, in section 27, named for its abundance of the fragrant white water-lily.

KANDIYOHI COUNTY

This county, established March 20, 1858, bears the Dakota or Sioux name of one or several of its lakes, meaning "where the buffalo fish come." Williamson states that it is from *"kandi,* buffalo fish; *y,* euphonic; *ohi,* arrive in." Our three species of buffalo fish, Ictiobus cyprinella, I. urus, and I. bubalus, at their spawning season in May and June leave the large rivers, in which they live the greater part of the year, and come, sometimes in immense numbers, to the lakes at the head of the small streams. The first named species, when mature, often attains the weight of 30 to 40 pounds; and the second and third are about two thirds as large.

Lawson, the historian of the county, writes:

"It is believed that in early times the Indians applied this name to the entire group of lakes which form the sources of the Crow river. Until very recent years buffalo fish and other kindred species came up the rivers and small streams every spring to find spawning places in these waters. . . .

"The name Kandiyohi was first made known to white men by Joseph Nicholas Nicollet, who in 1836-41 explored the region now comprising Minnesota. . . . He did not personally visit this section, but secured his information about the sources of the Crow from Indians. . . . It was not until 1856 that white men acquired any definite knowledge as to the extent and character of these lakes. In that year four different parties of townsite promoters visited the region now embraced within the boundaries of our county and gave separate names to the different lakes which attracted their attention. The name Kandiyohi was appropriated by one of these companies, and two of the lakes in the southern group were by them named Big and Little Kandiyohi. When a new county was organized the historic Indian name was adopted."

In the accepted pronunciation, which differs somewhat from the Dakota usage, this name accents its first and last syllables, the last having the English long sound of the vowel.

At first the area of this county was divided under legislative acts of March 8 and 20, 1858, in two counties, each comprising twelve congressional townships. The north half was named Monongalia county, and during twelve years Kandiyohi county had only the south half of its present area, until in 1870 they were united. The name Monongalia was derived from the county so named in Virginia (now in West Virginia), being Latinized from the Delaware Indian word, Monongahela, "river with the sliding banks," given to the stream which unites with the Allegheny at Pittsburg, forming the Ohio river.

KANDIYOHI COUNTY 269

TOWNSHIPS AND VILLAGES.

The origins and meanings of the geographic names in this county have been learned from the "Illustrated History and Descriptive and Biographical Review of Kandiyohi County," by Victor E. Lawson and Martin E. Tew, 446 pages, 1905; and from interviews with Samuel Nelson, county auditor, and Mr. Lawson, editor of the Willmar Tribune and principal author of the admirable folio History here cited, during a visit at Willmar, the county seat, in May, 1916.

ARCTANDER township, organized April 4, 1879, was named in honor of John W. Arctander, who during ten years, 1876-86, was a resident of this county, being an attorney in Willmar, and thence removed to Minneapolis. He was born in Stockholm, Sweden, October 2, 1849; was graduated at the Royal University of Norway, 1870, and the same year came to the United States; came to Minnesota in 1874, and soon afterward was admitted to practice law. In 1875 he published a handbook of the laws of Minnesota in the Norwegian language.

ATWATER, the railway village in Gennessee, founded in 1869, was named in honor of E. D. Atwater, secretary of the land department of the St. Paul and Pacific railway. It was incorporated February 17, 1876.

BURBANK township, organized in August, 1866, was named in honor of Henry Clay Burbank, a well known merchant in St. Paul and St. Cloud "held in high esteem by the early settlers for favors extended." He was born in Lewis, N. Y., May 4, 1835; and died in Rochester, Minn., February 23, 1905. At the age of eighteen years he came to St. Paul, and with his brother, James C. Burbank, engaged in forwarding and commission business and wholesale grocery trade. The firm transported supplies and furs for the Hudson Bay Company, and owned wagon trains and steamboats on the Red river. He was a state senator in 1873.

COLFAX township, organized June 24, 1871, was at first called Lake Prairie, but in September of the same year it was renamed in honor of Schuyler Colfax (b. 1823, d. 1885), who in 1869-73 was Vice-President of the United States.

DOVRE township, organized April 6, 1869, received its name from its prominent morainic hills in sections 20 and 21, which the early Norwegian settlers called the Dovre hills, in remembrance of the Dovrefjeld mountains and high plateau on the boundary between Norway and Sweden.

EAST LAKE LILLIAN township, organized March 6, 1893, had been since 1872 the east half of Lake Lillian, named for the lake crossed by the boundary between these townships.

EDWARDS township, established September 7, 1871, was named in honor of S. S. Edwards, a pioneer settler who was the leader for its organization.

FAHLUN, established March 20, 1877, bears "the popular name of the home county in Sweden of a number of the early settlers." The chief city of that district, also named Fahlun or Falun, is sometimes called "the Treasury of Sweden," having mines of copper, silver, and gold.

GENNESSEE, organized in 1858, was named (with changed spelling) for the Genesee river in New York, whence several of its first pioneers had come in 1857. This name means, according to Gannett, "shining valley" or "beautiful valley," in its native Indian language of New York; but the too liberal spelling here used, yet without change in pronunciation, came from Tennessee.

GREEN LAKE township, established in January, 1868, received its name from the large lake on its north boundary, which was named August 10, 1856, by the first party of settlers. On that day they selected a townsite on the southwestern shore of this lake, now occupied by the village of Spicer, in sections 3 and 4 of this township. "They were enraptured by the beautiful sheet of water, and from its peculiar shade of bottle green christened it Green lake. To their future city they gave the name of Columbia."

HARRISON township, established April 25, 1858, was named in honor of Joseph D. Harris, who settled here in August, 1857, and was the first postmaster and the first town clerk. He was born in Nova Scotia in May, 1834, and died May 7, 1878.

HOLLAND township was established July 23, 1888. Its settlers "were principally Hollanders, or of Holland descent, but with a sprinkling of Swedes and Germans."

IRVING township, organized March 27, 1868, took its name from a townsite platted on the east side of Green lake in 1856 by Eugene M. Wilson, of Minneapolis, who later was a congressman, and others. This name was probably selected in honor of the distinguished American author, Washington Irving (b. 1783, d. 1859).

KANDIYOHI township was established March 1, 1868, then including also the present townships of Fahlun, Whitefield, and Willmar. It was named, like the county, for the Kandiyohi lakes. The railway village, named for the township, was founded when the railway was built, in 1869, and was incorporated May 7, 1904.

An earlier townsite of this name, platted in October, 1856, in section 25 of this township and the adjoining section 30 of Gennessee, at the north side of Lakes Kasota and Minnetaga, aspired to become the capital of Minnesota, for which purpose a bill was passed by the legislature in March, 1869, but was vetoed by Governor Marshall. This project was again brought to the attention of the legislature in 1871, and also in 1891 and 1893, but received no favorable action. In 1901 the "capitol lands," which had been acquired here by the state in 1858, were sold for use in farming.

LAKE ANDREW township, organized March 19, 1872, received the name given to this lake in the summer of 1857 by Andrew Holes, one of the first two settlers, being carved by him "in large, plain letters upon one of the cottonwood trees" of its south shore.

KANDIYOHI COUNTY 271

LAKE ELIZABETH township, organized April 16, 1869, bears the name of the lake crossed by its north boundary, given "in honor of the wife of A. C. Smith, the early lawyer and receiver at the United States land office at Forest City." Lakes Ella and Carrie, closely adjoining the north side of this lake, in Gennessee, were named for her daughters.

LAKE LILLIAN township was organized January 23, 1872. The lake was named in honor of the wife of an artist and author, Edwin Whitefield, who accompanied the first exploring party to the Kandiyohi lakes in the summer of 1856.

MAMRE township, organized April 6, 1870, took the name given in 1866 to the lake in sections 11, 12, and 14, by one of the first three settlers, John Rodman, whose homestead claim was on the southwest arm of this lake. "He gave the name Mamre to his new home locality, from the Biblical reference to the home of Abram in the Promised Land."

NEW LONDON township, organized August 25, 1866, derived its name from the village, which was founded in 1865, by building a sawmill, and was incorporated April 8, 1889. The name was chosen by Louis Larson, "from a similarity he saw with the location of New London, Wis., a prospering village of his old home county."

NORWAY LAKE township, organized in August, 1866, at first included also the present townships of Arctander, Lake Andrew, Mamre, and Dovre. It was named for the largest lake of its original area, lying mainly in Lake Andrew township, around which many Norwegian immigrants settled.

PENNOCK, the railway village of St. John's township, founded in 1870-71, with the building of this railway, at first bore the township name. In the fall of 1891 it was renamed in honor of George Pennock, of Willmar, superintendent of this division of the Great Northern railway.

PRINSBURG, a hamlet at the center of Holland township, platted in 1886, commemorates Martin Prins, member of a land firm in Holland, who came here and in 1884 acquired about 35,000 acres of railroad lands, mostly in this county. He died in 1887.

RAYMOND, a railway village in Edwards, platted in 1887, was named for Raymond Spicer, a son of John M. Spicer, of Willmar, who was the founder of Spicer village.

ROSELAND township was organized March 16, 1889, its name being chosen by Peter Lindquist, the first settler, who same in the spring of 1869. "In Swedish the name is the usual designation for a flower garden."

ROSEVILLE township, organized August 25, 1866, was named as suggested by Joseph Cox, "on account of the profusion of wild roses growing and in bloom upon the prairie."

ST. JOHN'S township, first settled in 1868, was established by a special act of the legislature, February 27, 1872, and was organized a month later. It bears a name given to a locality on its north line by an early map of the state, published in 1860, probably noting a proposed site for a Catholic colony, whence the lake in sections 1 and 2 became known as St. John's lake.

SPICER, a railway village in the north edge of Green Lake township, was platted in 1886, on the deserted early townsite of Columbia, and was named in honor of John M. Spicer, its founder and owner of the site, who was the president of the company building this railway line. Raymond village was named for his son, as before noted.

WHITEFIELD township was established June 6, 1870. Its name is from a proposed townsite selected by an exploring party in the early autumn of 1856, on the northwest shore of Lake Wagonga, in sections 1 and 11, named in honor of Edwin Whitefield, a landscape artist, who was a member of the party. Lake Lillian, named for his wife, is the source of another township name, as before noted.

WILLMAR township, established January 4, 1870, took the name of its village, platted in 1869 when the railroad here was built. The townsite was selected and named by George F. Becker, president of the railroad. "Leon Willmar, a native of Belgium, at that time residing in London, was the agent for the European bondholders of the St. Paul and Pacific railroad company, and it was in his honor that the town was named. He afterwards secured several hundred acres of land around the northeastern shores of Foot lake, and presented the same to his son, Paul Willmar, who a few years before had served as a soldier of fortune under Maximilian, the adventurous invader of Mexico." Expensive buildings were erected in 1871 for the Willmar farm, on section 1 of this township, where during ten years Paul Willmar conducted operations on an extensive scale. In 1881 he sold this large farm and returned to Belgium, his native land. Willmar village was incorporated January 16, 1874; and its city charter was adopted November 19, 1901.

LAKES AND STREAMS.

The foregoing pages have noted the names of the Kandiyohi lakes, Green lake, Lakes Andrew, Elizabeth, and Lillian, Lakes Ella and Carrie, Lake Mamre, Norway lake, and St. John's lake.

Shakopee creek, flowing west to the lake of this name in Chippewa county, is noticed in the chapter for that county; and Hawk and Chetamba creeks, having their sources here, are noticed under Renville county.

Many lakes remain to be mentioned, but a considerable number have names that require no explanation, and others of small size are unnamed. The list follows the numerical order of the townships from south to north, and of the ranges from east to west.

Dog lake, in East Lake Lillian township, and others smaller and without names, have been drained and are now farm lands.

Fox lake, crossed by the south line of Lake Lillian township, and Grove lake on its west side, named for the grove on its island, have been drained.

KANDIYOHI COUNTY 273

Lake Elizabeth township has Johnson lake in sections 10 and 11, and Otter lake in sections 10 and 15. Lakes Charlotte and Mary, now drained, were in its southwest part.

Fahlun has Lake Fanny and Wagonga lake, which was formerly called Grass lake, in translation of this Dakota or Sioux name. The latter, reaching west into Whitefield, is erroneously spelled Waconda by some maps.

Lake Milton was in sections 7 and 18, Whitefield, and Stevens lake in section 20, but both are drained.

Edwards has Bad Water lake, through which Hawk creek flows at Raymond; Olson lake, in section 26; and Vick lake, drained, in sections 29 and 30.

Gennessee has Summit lake, in sections 9 and 10, referring to the building of the railroad, which very near the west line of this township crosses its highest land between St. Paul and Breckenridge; Pay lake, of smaller size, in section 10, where the paymaster in that work had his camp; Lakes Ella and Carrie, before noticed in their relationship with Lake Elizabeth; and Lake Minnetaga, compounded of Dakota words, *minne,* water, and *taga,* froth, foam.

In Kandiyohi township are Lake Kasota, a Dakota name, meaning a cleared place, and Swan lake, each lying close to the north side of Little Kandiyohi lake, with which Lake Kasota is connected by a strait.

Willmar has Foot lake, adjoining the city, named in honor of the first settler here; Willmar lake, which adjoins the former Willmar farm, being a northeastern bay of Foot lake, connected therewith by a narrow passage; and Grass lake, which was shallow and mostly filled with marsh grass, but is now drained.

Solomon R. Foot, commemorated by the lake bearing his name, was born in Dover, Ohio, May 30, 1823; came to Minnesota in 1857, and in June took a homestead claim on the shore of this lake, being the first settler of Willmar township; removed about six years later to Melrose, in Stearns county, where he built a hotel and was the first postmaster; removed to Minot, N. D., in 1888; spent his last few years in California, with his children, and died March 15, 1903. Another lake, in Dovre, is also named for him.

The largest lake in Harrison was visited in September, 1856, by a party of explorers who came from St. Peter. "The crystal brightness of the lake impressed them, and they named it Diamond lake." Other lakes in this township are Jessie lake, crossed by the north line of section 6; Rieff and Swenson lakes, drained, in section 15; Sperry lake, section 16; Tait's lake, section 19; Thomas lake, drained, in sections 21 and 22; Schultz lake, in sections 23 and 26; and Wheeler lake, in sections 26, 27, and 34.

Green Lake township has Henderson lake in section 6; Twin lakes, sections 7 and 8; Elk Horn lake, sections 9 and 16, where a pair of very large elk antlers were found in 1857; Eagle lake, crossed by the west line of this township; and Bur Oak lake, in section 33.

Dovre has Ringo lake, Florida Slough lake, and Long or Nevada lake, each of large size, in its northeast part; Point lake, King, Skataas, and Swan lakes, at the southeast, the second and third being named for pioneer farmers; and Solomon lake at the southwest, named, like Foot lake in Willmar, for Solomon R. Foot, who often visited this lake as a hunter and trapper.

In Mamre township, besides the lake of this name, are Swan lake, of clear water, in sections 9 and 10, and Church and Lindgren lakes, respectively in sections 23 and 26, which are shallow and grassy.

Irving has Calhoun lake, named for an early settler who raised cattle there; Otter lake, very small, in section 4, and Shoemaker lake, crossed by the south line of section 6, both drained; and Long lake, in the north part of section 6, extending into Roseville.

New London has Bear lake, in section 7; Cedar Island lake, in section 17, named for its red cedar trees; Nest lake, in sections 28 and 29, remarkable for the former abundance of nests of double-crested cormorants, commonly called "black jacks," on the trees of its larger island; and George and Woodcock lakes, respectively in sections 32 and 33, extending south into Green Lake township. The last was named for Elijah T. Woodcock, the first settler near it. Lake Eight, in sections 5 and 8, translated from the name given by Swedish settlers, is a marsh, only covered by water in wet seasons.

Lake Andrew township, with its lake so named, has also Middle lake and Norway lake; Lake Mary, on the west line of section 19; Norstedt lake, small and shallow, in section 24; and, near the south side of the township, Lake Florida and Crook lake, the last being named from its crooked outline. "Lake Florida is said to have been first so designated by the early settlers of Norway Lake on account of its location to the south."

Arctander has Swenson lake, in sections 24 and 25. West and Sand lakes, in sections 16 and 17, have been drained.

Burbank has Lake Twenty, in the section so numbered, and Mud lake, on the south line of this township.

Colfax has Prairie and Stauffer lakes, shallow, or sometimes dry, in its southeast part; Timber lake, Skull and Swan lakes, and Games lake, at the southwest; and Sand, Thompson, and Hystad lakes, in its north half, the last being named for Andrew O. Hystad, an early farmer there.

In Norway Lake township are Lake Bertha and Even's or Glesne lake, near its center; and Deer lake, Lake Ole, Lake of Hefta, and Brenner lake in its north part, with Crook lake on its north line. Glesne lake was named for Even O. Glesne, a pioneer farmer beside it, and Lake Bertha for his daughter. "Lake of Hefta was so called in honor of Mrs. Marie Hefta, . . . who was born on a place of that name in Norway;" and

KANDIYOHI COUNTY 275

Brenner lake was named for Andreas Hanson "Brenner," the added surname having reference to "his vocation in Norway as manufacturer of tar."

When the first pioneers came, their settlements or small neighborhoods preceding the organization of townships were designated by the adjoining lakes, as the Diamond Lake, Eagle Lake, and Nest Lake settlements. Finally nine townships, among them being Kandiyohi, Mamre, and St. John's, were thus named for their lakes.

HILLS OF THE WACONIA AND DOVRE MORAINES.

The north half of this county is crossed by two belts of morainic drift hills, very irregular in contour and attaining heights of 100 to 200 feet above the lowlands and lakes. Names applied to parts of these hilly tracts, and to some of the more conspicuous separate elevations, are Cape Bad Luck and Sugarloaf, in the south edge of Roseville; the Blue hills, culminating in Mount Tom, about a mile north of Lake Andrew; the hills before noted as giving their name to Dovre township; and Ostlund's hill, in section 22, Mamre, named for Lars Ostlund, a farmer at its west side.

Derived from the hills in Dovre, this name is extended to the seventh or Dovre moraine in the series of twelve marginal moraine belts formed successively along the receding border of the continental ice-sheet during its final melting in Minnesota.

Eastward in New London, Irving, and the edge of Roseville, the drift hills are referred to a somewhat earlier stage of the glacial retreat, being a part of the sixth or Waconia moraine, named from Waconia in Carver county. At Mount Tom, and thence northwest for about twenty-five miles, the Waconia and Dovre moraines are merged in a single belt of drift hills, knolls, and short ridges.

SIBLEY STATE PARK.

Adjoining Lake Andrew with a shore line of one and a half miles, this park, named in honor of Governor Henry Hastings Sibley, was provided through purchase by the state in July, 1919. It is a tract of 356 acres, consisting of high morainic hills, short ridges, and hollows, sprinkled with drift boulders and covered with hardwood timber. Its acquirement as a state park was advocated by Victor E. Lawson, of Willmar, and Peter Broberg, of New London; and its supervision and development are to be directed by Carlos Avery, state game and fish commissioner.

KITTSON COUNTY

Forming the northwest corner of this state, Kittson county was established by being thus renamed, March 9, 1878, and by reduction from its area, making Marshall county, February 25, 1879. Previously it had been a part of Pembina county, one of the nine large counties into which the new Minnesota Territory was originally divided, October 27, 1849. It was named in honor of Norman Wolfred Kittson, one of the leading pioneers of the territory and state. He was born in Sorel, Canada, March 5, 1814; came to the area that afterward was Minnesota in 1834, and during four years was engaged in the sutler's department at Fort Snelling; was later a fur trader on his own account, and became manager for the American Fur Company in northern Minnesota; engaged in transportation business, at Fort Snelling, Pembina, and St. Paul; was a member of the territorial legislature, 1851-55, and mayor of St. Paul, 1858; became director of steamboat traffic on the Red river for the Hudson Bay Company, in 1864; and established a line of steamers and barges known as the Red River Transportation Company, whence he was often called "Commodore." He died suddenly, May 11, 1888, on a railway train in his journey of return to Minnesota from the east. The Catholic Cathedral in St. Paul is built on the site of his home.

With the adoption of the present name of Kittson county, the former Pembina county ceased to exist in Minnesota, but it is still represented by a North Dakota county bearing that name, on the opposite side of the Red river. It was first the name of a river there, was thence applied to an early fur trading post at the junction of this stream with the Red river, was given in 1849 to the great Pembina county, and later to the town that became the county seat of its part in Dakota Territory, near the site of the old trading post. Keating wrote, in his Narrative of Long's expedition in 1823, that it was derived from the Ojibway word for the fruit of the bush cranberry, "anepeminan, which name has been shortened and corrupted into Pembina." This tall bush (Viburnum Opulus, L.) is common along the Pembina and Red rivers, as also through the north half of Minnesota, and its fruit is much used for sauce by the Ojibways and the white people. Neill translated the name as follows (History of Minnesota, p. 868): "The Pembina river, called by Thompson 'Summer Berry,' was named after a red berry which the Chippeways call Nepin (summer) Minan (berry), and this by the voyageurs has been abbreviated to Pembina, which is more euphonious."

KITTSON COUNTY 277

TOWNSHIPS AND VILLAGES.

Information has been gathered from "History of the Red River Valley," two volumes, 1909, the chapter for this county, by Edward Nelson, former register of deeds, being pages 923-966; and from interviews with Mr. Nelson and Axel Lindegard, a merchant in Hallock, the county seat, during a visit there in August, 1909, and Edward A. Johnson, clerk of court, and again with Mr. Lindegard, in a second visit there, September, 1916.

ARVESON township, organized July 14, 1902, was named in honor of Arve Arveson, a settler in Davis, who was then chairman of the county commissioners.

BRONSON, a railway village in Percy, was named for Giles Bronson, an early farmer in section 32 of that township, well known for entertaining sportsmen at his home.

CANNON township, organized July 11, 1904, was named for Thomas Cannon, a merchant in Northcote, who was one of the county commissioners.

CARIBOU township, organized January 8, 1908, had a few reindeer, of geographic limitation in the wooded and partly swampy region of northern Minnesota and Canada, named Rangifer caribou. The second word of the name is of Algonquin Indian origin, meaning a pawer or scratcher, in allusion to the habit of this animal in winter, pawing in the snow to eat the reindeer moss beneath.

CLOW township commemorates several brothers of that name, early settlers there, who came from Prince Edward Island.

DAVIS township, organized July 24, 1882, was named in honor of Edward N. Davis a settler in section 30, who was a county commissioner, but removed to Georgia.

DEERWOOD was organized July 23, 1888, receiving this name from its deer and its tracts of woodland.

DONALDSON, the railway village of Davis township, was named for Captain Hugh W. Donaldson, a veteran of the civil war, manager of an adjoining farm of several thousand acres, owned by the Kennedy Land Company.

GRANVILLE township, organized July 27, 1885, took a name that is borne by villages and townships in twelve other states.

HALLOCK township, which includes the county seat, was organized August 2, 1880, and was named in honor of one of the founders of its village, Charles Hallock, the widely known sportsman, journalist, and author. He was born in New York city, March 13, 1834; was graduated at Amherst college, 1854; was during many years editor of "Forest and Stream," which he founded in 1873; erected a large hotel here in 1890, which was a noted resort of sportsmen until it was burned in 1892; is author of many magazine articles and books on hunting, fishing, travel in Alaska, Florida, etc.; now resides in Washington, D. C. Hallock village, platted in 1879-80, was incorporated June 11, 1887.

HALMA is the railway village of Norway township.

HAMPDEN township was the earliest organized in this county, July 28, 1879. It was named on the suggestion of officers of its railway, for John Hampden (b. 1594, d. 1643), the celebrated statesman and patriot of England.

HAZELTON township, organized July 23, 1888, was probably named for its plentiful growth of wild hazelnut bushes. Minnesota has two species, each being common through its northern part.

HILL township, organized January 11, 1901, is named in honor of the distinguishd railway builder and president, James Jerome Hill, who owned and farmed large tracts in and adjoining this township. He was born near Guelph, Ontario, September 16, 1838; and died at his home in St. Paul, May 29, 1916. He came to Minnesota in 1856, and engaged in steamboat and railway transportation. In 1871 he consolidated the transportation business, of Norman W. Kittson in the Red river region with his own; and Donald A. Smith (since Lord Strathcona) managed the company jointly with himself. He was the prime mover in the effort to secure the bonds of the St. Paul and Pacific railroad, successfully accomplishing this in 1878, with reorganization under the name of the St. Paul, Minneapolis and Manitoba Railway Co., of which he was general manager, 1879-82; and president, 1883-90. This railway and its new branches were again changed in name in 1890 to be the Great Northern railway system, of which Mr. Hill continued as president till 1907, becoming then chairman of its board of directors. His biography, by Joseph G. Pyle, in two volumes, with portraits, was published in 1917. The extensive Hill farm, comprising about 15,000 acres in Hill and St. Vincent townships, was sold during the summer of 1917, in 127 parts, to make small farms for settlers.

HUMBOLDT is a Great Northern railway village in the southeast part of St. Vincent township. This name, borne by counties in Iowa, Nevada, and California, and by villages or small cities in seven states, commemorates Baron Alexander von Humboldt (b. 1769, d. 1859), an eminent German scientist and author, who in 1799 to 1804 traveled in South America and Mexico.

JUPITER township, organized November 10, 1883, was named for the planet Jupiter by Nels Hultgren, an early Norwegian settler there, who had been a sea captain.

KARLSTAD, a Soo railway village in the east edge of Deerwood, was named for the city of Karlstad in Sweden.

KENNEDY, a Great Northern railway village, was named in honor of John Stewart Kennedy (b. 1830, d. 1909). From his former home in Scotland he came to America in 1856, settled in New York city, and was an iron merchant, banker, and railway director. He was a generous donor to many public charities, and for educational and religious work.

KITTSON COUNTY

LANCASTER is a Soo railway village in the east edge of Granville. Eighteen states have villages, cities, or townships of this name, derived from a city and county of England.

McKINLEY township, organized July 14, 1902, was named in honor of William McKinley (b. 1843, d. 1901), who was a member of Congress from Ohio, 1877-91; governor of Ohio, 1892-6; and president of the United States, 1897-1901.

NORTHCOTE, the railway village in Hampden, was named in honor of Sir Stafford Henry Northcote (b. 1818, d. 1887), an eminent English statesman and financier. He was a commissioner at the treaty of Washington in 1871, which referred the Alabama claims of the United States against England to an international tribunal of arbitration.

NORWAY township, organized January 9, 1901, was named for the country from which nearly all its settlers came.

NOYES, a station of the Great Northern and Soo railways adjoining the international boundary, was named in honor of J. A. Noyes, the U. S. customs collector there.

ORLEANS, a Soo railway village in the east edge of Clow, was named by officers of that railway. Derived from the city of Orleans in France, this name is borne by counties in Vermont and New York, and by townships and villages in Massachusetts and seven other states.

PELAN township, organized April 20, 1900, was named for Charles H. Pelan, a pioneer settler there.

PERCY township, organized July 9, 1900, was named for Howard Percy, an early trapper and hunter.

POPPLETON, organized April 8, 1893, received its name, by a common mispronunciation, for the plentiful poplar trees and groves in this township.

RED RIVER township, organized January 5, 1881, having a length of twelve miles from south to north, is named for the river that is its western boundary.

RICHARDVILLE township, organized January 8, 1895, was named for George Richards, one of its first settlers, whose homestead claim is the southwest quarter of section 30.

ST. JOSEPH township, organized January 9, 1901, was named by its settlers, including Catholic immigrants from Poland, for St. Joseph, husband of the Virgin Mary. The north part sends its drainage west to the Joe river, a small stream so named by the early fur traders and voyageurs.

ST. VINCENT township, organized March 19, 1880, is opposite to Pembina, N. D. Its name had been earlier given, before 1860, to a post of fur traders here, in honor of the renowned St. Vincent de Paul, founder of missions and hospitals in Paris, who died September 27, 1660, at the age of eighty years.

SKANE township, organized May 10, 1887, was named for the old province of Scania, the most southern part of Sweden.

SPRING BROOK township, organized January 2, 1884, received the name of a brook flowing through its southern part.

SVEA township, organized February 15, 1884, bears a name given in poetry to Sweden, the native country of many of its settlers.

TEGNER, organized July 24, 1882, was named in honor of Esaias Tegner (b. 1782, d. 1846), a famous Swedish poet. In 1811 he was awarded the prize of the Academy of Sweden for a long poem entitled "Svea;" and in 1825 he published his most celebrated work, "Frithjofs Saga," based on the old Norse saga of this name.

TEIEN, organized April 5, 1882, was named for Andrew C. Teien, an early Norwegian homesteader in section 4.

THOMPSON, organized July 24, 1882, was named for William, Robert, and George Thompson, brothers, who took homestead claims in this township as pioneer farmers.

Townships 161 and 162, in Range 45, are yet unorganized.

LAKES AND STREAMS.

This county, lying wholly within the great area of the Glacial Lake Agassiz, has now only very few and very small lakes. These are the Twin lakes in Arveson, Scull lake in section 22, St. Joseph, and Lake Stella (a star), adjoining the village of St. Vincent. The last was called "Lac du Nord Ouest" on the map of Minnesota in 1860, meaning, in its use by the French voyageurs, "Lake of the Northwest" corner of this North Star State.

Spring brook, giving its name to a township, is one of the sources of Tamarack river, (a translation of the Ojibway name), which, after flowing through large swamps, joins the Red river in the southern half of Red River township.

The South branch of Two rivers receives the Middle branch at Hallock, and it unites with the North branch about two miles above the mouth of the united stream. The Ojibway name, given by Gilfillan, "is Ga-nijoshino zibi, or the river that lies two together as in a bed; no doubt, from its two branches running parallel."

Joe river, before noted, deriving its headwaters from St. Joseph township, and flowing through Richardville, Clow, and the northeast part of St. Vincent, reaches the Red river about three miles north of the international boundary. In Clow the channel is lost for several miles in a wide swamp.

KOOCHICHING COUNTY

This county, established December 19, 1906, bears the Cree name applied by the Ojibways to Rainy lake, and also to the Rainy river and to its great falls and rapids at International Falls. It is translated by Rev. J. A. Gilfillan as Neighbor lake and river, or, under another interpretation, a lake and river somewhere. He remarked that this word is of difficult or uncertain meaning, and that, although in common Ojibway use, it does not strictly belong to that language.

Jacques de Noyon, a French Canadian voyageur, who was probably the first white man to traverse any part of the northern boundary of Minnesota, about the year 1688, found this name used in the Cree language for the Rainy river. As narrated by an official report of the Intendant Begon, written at Quebec, November 12, 1716, published in the Margry Papers (vol. VI, pages 495-8), DeNoyon, about twenty-eight years previous to that date, had set out from Lake Superior by the canoe route of the Kaministiquia river, under the guidance of a party of Assiniboine Indians, in the hope of coming to the Sea of the West. He passed through Rainy lake, called the Lake of the Crees, and wintered on its outflowing river, the Takamaniouen, "otherwise called Ouchichiq by the Crees," evidently the Koochiching or Rainy river and falls, from which this county is named.

Another early narrative of travel, 1740-42, by a French and Ojibway half-breed named Joseph la France, containing a description of the Rainy lake and river, is given in a book published by Arthur Dobbs in London in 1744, entitled "An Account of the Countries adjoining to Hudson's Bay." La France passed through Rainy lake in the later part of April and early May, 1740, and staid ten days at the Koochiching falls on the Rainy river near the outlet of this lake. For the purpose of fishing, the Moose band of Ojibways had "two great Villages, one on the North Side, and the other on the South Side of the Fall," being respectively on or near the sites of Fort Frances and International Falls. The narrative tells the origin of the French name, Lac de la Pluie (Lake of the Rain), which in English is Rainy lake, that it "is so called from a perpendicular Water-fall, by which the Water falls into a River South-west of it, which raises a Mist-like Rain." This refers to the outflowing Rainy river, in its formerly mist-covered falls, since 1908 dammed and supplying water-power in the city of International Falls for the largest paper-making mills in the world.

The original meanings of Ouchichiq (for Koochiching,) the Cree name of Rainy river two hundred years ago, and Takamaniouen, variously spelled, an equally ancient Indian name of the Rainy river and lake, are uncertain; but it may be true that one or both gave in translation the French and English names, which refer to the mists of the falls, resembling rain.

Takamaniouen, as written by Begon in 1716, placed in another spelling on the map drawn by Ochagach for Verendrye in 1728, was received from the Assiniboines. It is thought by Horace V. Winchell and U. S. Grant (Geology of Minnesota, vol. IV, p. 192), that this name was translated to Lac de la Pluie.

Townships and Villages.

Information for this county was gathered from Louis A. Ogaard, county surveyor, during a visit at International Falls, the county seat, in September, 1909; and from L. H. Slocum, county auditor, during a second visit there in August, 1916.

BALDUS is a recently organized township, probably named for a pioneer settler.

BANNOCK township received this Gaelic name from Scotland by vote of its bachelor settlers, for their bannock bread, "in shape flat and roundish, . . . baked on an iron plate or griddle."

BEAR RIVER township is crossed by a little river of this name, flowing north to the Big fork.

BEAVER township had formerly many beaver dams on its Beaver brook, a tributary of the Little fork.

BIG FALLS township includes the railway village of this name near its northeast corner, at the Grand falls of the Big fork. Its north side adjoins Grand Falls township.

BRIDGIE township was named for a girl, Bridgie Moore, the first white child born there.

CALDWELL township and the Caldwell brook, flowing to the Big fork, were named for an early pioneer.

CINGMARS township was named for E. F. Cingmars, a French settler there, who removed to the west.

CROSS RIVER township was named for this small stream, flowing northeastward through it to the Little fork.

DENTAYBOW township uniquely honors three of its homestead farmers, named Densmore, Taylor, and Bowman, each represented by a syllable in the name.

DINNER CREEK township is crossed by a creek so named, where timber cruisers and estimators had a meeting place for dinner, tributary northwestward to the Sturgeon river.

ENGELWOOD township received its name in compliment to its numerous settlers named Engelking, who came from the vicinity of Fort Ridgely, Nicollet county.

ERICSBURG, a railway village on the Rat Root river, was named in honor of the late Eric Franson, of International Falls, a real estate dealer, by whom it was platted.

KOOCHICHING COUNTY 283

EVERGREEN township has a general forest of the evergreen trees, including black and white spruce, balsam fir, arbor vitae or white cedar, and our three species of pines.

FELDMAN, a township organized in 1916, is named for one of its first settlers.

FOREST GROVE township received this descriptive name by the vote of its people.

GEMMELL, the railway village of Evergreen township, was named in honor of W. H. Gemmell, of Brainerd, general manager of the Minnesota and International railway.

GOWDY township commemorates its several pioneers of this name, who took homestead claims on and near the Big fork.

GRAND FALLS township is crossed meanderingly by the Big fork. Its Grand falls, in the southeast edge of this township, with descent of 29 feet over ledges of gneiss and mica schist, gave also the name Big Falls to the adjoining railway village and township on the south.

HARRIGAN and HENRY were named for prominent pioneers in these townships.

INDUS township received this name of a great river in western India by the suggestion of Rev. M. F. Smootz, a homesteader beside the Rainy river here, who had been a missionary in that country.

INTERNATIONAL FALLS, the county seat, founded as Koochiching village in the township of this name, was incorporated as a city in 1909. Its name notes its location on the international boundary at the Koochiching falls of Rainy river. The descent of the river here, in broken rapids on irregularly jutting ledges of granitoid gneiss, was 23 feet, mainly within a distance of about 300 feet; but a dam close above the falls, completed in 1908, increased their head to 26 feet, raising the river to the level of Rainy lake and permitting the lake steamboats to come to this city. Before the stream was thus used for its water-power, operating the great paper mills of International Falls, the plentiful mists and spray of the falls, which nearly always formed a rainbow in the sunshine, well accounted for the aboriginal origin of the names of Rainy lake and river.

Fort Frances, the village on the Canadian side of Rainy river opposite to this city, was built around a former fur trading post, which was so named in honor of Frances Ramsey Simpson (d. 1853), wife of Sir George Simpson (b. 1792, d. 1860). He was governor for the Hudson Bay Company in Canada nearly forty years, from 1821 until his death, September 7, 1860, at his home in Lachine, near Montreal.

JAMESON township was named in honor of Charles S. Jameson, a homesteader on the site of the village of Little Fork in this township. He came from Northfield, Minn.; founded the first newspaper of Koochiching (now International Falls); is editor of the Little Fork Times.

KLINE township, recently organized, was named for a pioneer settler.

KOOCHICHING township, like the county, took this name from the falls of Rainy river.

LINDFORD township was named in honor of L. A. Lindwall, a Swedish farmer beside the Big fork in section 13, who also owned a store and was the Lindford postmaster.

LITTLE FORK, the railway village of Jameson, is named for its location on the Little fork of the Rainy river.

MANITOU received its Ojibway name, meaning a spirit, from the Manitou rapids of Rainy river, which forms the north boundary of this township. The river falls about three feet in these rapids, "a short pitch over solid rock on the bottom and in both banks."

MEADOW BROOK township has a small stream of this name, tributary to the Bear river.

MEDING township was named for Paul Meding, an early German farmer here.

MIZPAH, the name of a railway village in Engelwood, is the Hebrew word for a watchtower. It is used as a parting salutation, meaning "The Lord watch between me and thee, when we are absent one from another" (Genesis, xxxi, 49).

MURPHY township was named in honor of an Irish pioneer, whose homestead farm here nearly adjoined the Rainy river.

NET LAKE township and NET RIVER township border on the Bois Fort or Net Lake Indian Reservation, which is more fully noticed, with the origin of these names, at the end of this chapter.

NORDEN township and its earlier Norden post office were named for Norwegian settlers.

NORTHOME, a railway village near the southwest corner of the county, was named North Home by Harris Richardson, of St. Paul, who with others platted this village. The name was changed to its present form by request of the U. S. Post Office Department.

PELLAND, a hamlet at the mouth of the Little fork, was named for Joseph Pelland, a French farmer, who was its postmaster.

PINE TOP township was named for an exceptionally tall white pine, which had at its top a peculiar cluster of small branches.

PLUM CREEK township has a little stream so named for its wild plum trees.

"RAINY LAKE CITY" was a gold mining station, during a few years, at the east side of the strait between Rainy lake and Black bay (also called Rat Root lake). A stamp mill was built there in 1894 for crushing the ore mined on the southwest end of Dryweed island, less than a mile distant; but the work failed to repay its expenses, and about fifteen years later the proposed city site was abandoned.

RANIER is a village of the Duluth, Winnipeg and Pacific railway at the mouth of Rainy lake, named by officers of this railway.

RAPID RIVER township contains the sources of the East fork of the river so named, flowing thence north to the Rapid and Rainy rivers.

RAT ROOT township is crossed by the circuitous course of the river so named, tributary to Rat Root lake, which also is very commonly called

KOOCHICHING COUNTY 285

Black bay, connected with Rainy lake by a strait. The name of the river and lake, adopted for the township, is a translation of the Ojibway name, referring to roots eaten by muskrats. All the streams in this district become somewhat darkly stained by the peaty swamps through which they sluggishly flow, so that they give the same dark color to the water of the Rat Root lake, whence came its other name, Black bay.

The muskrat is the most abundant fur-bearing animal of the northern United States and Canada, a small brother or cousin of the beaver, which it almost equals in its industry and skill for house-building. Its favorite food, stored for winter use in the houses of mud and rushes built in shallow lakes, consists of the roots of the common yellow water-lilies, which gave the name of Rat Root. Another place named for the muskrat is Rat Portage, now Kenora, at the mouth of the Lake of the Woods.

RAY township was named for Edwin Ray Lewis, of Grand Rapids, who was a land surveyor and timber cruiser, often traversing this region.

REEDY township commemorates David Reedy, its first settler, an immigrant from Ireland, who took a land claim at the west side of the mouth of the Big fork.

SAULT township received its name, the French word for a leap or jump, from the Long Sault rapids of Rainy river, which is its north boundary. The rapids are about a mile long, falling about seven feet.

SCARLETT and STEFFES townships were named in honor of pioneers.

STURGEON RIVER township is traversed in its south part by this river, flowing east to the Big fork. The name, probably translated from the Ojibways, refers to the ascent of the lake or rock sturgeon to this stream.

SUMMERVILLE township was named by vote of its people. There are villages or townships of this name in Pennsylvania, North and South Carolina, Georgia, and other states of the Union, and also in Nova Scotia and Ontario.

WARREN township, organized in 1916, has a name that is borne by counties in fourteen states, and by townships, villages and cities in twenty-four states, a large majority being in commemoration of Joseph Warren, who fell in the battle of Bunker Hill.

WATROUS township was named for Charles B. Watrous, from Pennsylvania, who was a farmer here and owned a large sawmill on the Rainy river near the east line of this township.

WHITE BIRCH township has an abundance of the paper or canoe birch, used by the Indians to make their birch bark canoes.

WICKER township was named for Harry Wicker, a homesteader in its sections 10 and 11, on the Big fork.

WILDWOOD township received this name in the petition of its people for organization.

WILLIAMS township was named in honor of James Williams, well known for his operating a portable sawmill, whose homestead farm on the Rainy river is in sections 6 and 7, at the northwest corner of this township and of the county.

LAKES AND STREAMS.

Foregoing pages have sufficiently noted the names of the Rainy lake and river, the Koochiching or International falls, the Big and Little forks of Rainy river, Bear river, Beaver brook, Caldwell brook, Cross river, Dinner creek, the Grand falls of the Big fork, the Manitou and Long Sault rapids of Rainy river, Meadow brook, Plum creek, the East fork of Rapid river, the Rat Root river and lake (this lake, united to Rainy lake by a strait, being also named Black bay), and the Sturgeon river.

Names of islands, bays, and points of the part of Rainy lake belonging to this county, in their order from east to west, are Dryweed island before mentioned for its gold mining, Sha Sha point and Black bay, Grindstone island, Grassy island and Grassy narrows separating it from the south shore, Red Sucker island, Jackfish island and bay, Stop island, Kingston island, and Sand bay and Pither's point at the mouth of the lake.

The Big fork is known by the Ojibways as Bowstring river, from its source in the large Bowstring lake, which is translated from the name Atchabani or Busatchabani, given by them to the lake and its outflowing stream, before noticed in the chapter for Itasca county.

The Little fork bears a peculiarly descriptive Ojibway name, recorded by Gilfillan as Ningtawonani zibi, "the river separating canoe routes," which name is also applied, with a slight change, to the Net river. In the thought of these Indians, expressed by the name, canoe voyageurs ascending the Little fork may go forward to its source or may turn aside and go up Net river, having thus the choice of separate routes.

The Ojibway name of Net lake was written Asubikone by Gilfillan, meaning "taken or entangled in the net." Its origin, as told by the Bois Fort Ojibways, is presented in the notice of their reservation.

Only a few other names of streams and lakes in this county remain to be listed.

South of Net lake, Prairie creek and Willow creek flow into the Little fork from the east; Reilly creek is a small eastern tributary of the Big fork, about ten miles south of Big Falls; Black river, named for its peat-stained water, joins Rainy river about three miles west of the Big fork; Tamarack river flows from Gemmell northwestward to the north part of Red lake; and the headstream of Battle river, (formerly mapped here as Armstrong creek), tributary to the south part of that lake, crosses Bridgie township, in the southwest corner of this county.

Among the few and little lakes, limited to the south edge of the county above the highest shoreline of Lake Agassiz, only Bartlett lake, at Northome, and Battle lake, through which the Battle river flows, are named on maps.

BOIS FORT OR NET LAKE INDIAN RESERVATION.

This small Ojibway reservation, comprising the whole or parts of nine surveyed townships and inclosing Net lake, lies in Koochiching and St.

KOOCHICHING COUNTY

Louis counties. By a census in 1909 the number of the Bois Fort band was 641. They call themselves Sugwaundugah wininewug, meaning "Men of the thick fir woods;" but the early French traders named them Bois Forts, "Hard Wood Indians."

In the treaty at Washington, April 7, 1866, providing this reservation, the name given to Net lake by the Ojibways was spelled As-sab-a-co-na. Albert B. Reagan, who was the United States agent here in 1909-14, writes the traditional origin of this name, received as a myth of the Bois Fort medicine men. The Ojibways, coming first by the route of Vermilion and Pelican lakes, are said to have found on the little island of Net lake many strange beasts, "half sea-lion and half fish," who fled westward by swimming and wading though the shallow and mostly rice-filled lake. "On coming to the island the canoemen paddled around it, and by the track of the muddied water pursued the beasts across the lake and up a creek till they found where the earth had swallowed them, as if they had been caught in a net." The myth is thought to refer to the flight and escape of a party of their enemies, the Sioux, whom the Ojibways by many raids and battles drove away from the wooded north part of Minnesota.

The northeast side of this island, which is named Picture island by the white people, but Drum island by the Ojibways, has a smoothly glaciated rock surface, as described by Reagan, "covered with crudely made pictographs of human beings, dance scenes, and outlines of the animal gods worshipped by the men making the pictures. . . . The drawings seem to be similar to those at Pipestone, Minnesota, which are known to be Siouan. Furthermore, the Ojibways say that their people did not make the rock pictures."

COUTCHICHING ROCK FORMATION.

Reports on the geology of the parts of Canada and Minnesota surrounding Rainy lake, published in 1889-1901, give the name Coutchiching to a large series of Archaean mica schists, outcropping in this county on Rainy lake, around Black bay, and southward on the Little and Big forks and at and near Net lake. (Geology of Minnesota, Final Report, vol. IV, 1899, chapter VIII, pages 166-211, with maps and sections; vol. VI, 1901, plate LXV.) This name is a variant form of the Cree and Ojibway name of Rainy lake and river, which is applied to this county and a township, the pronunciation in the two forms being alike.

LAC QUI PARLE COUNTY

This county was established March 6, 1871. Nine years earlier a county bearing this name, but of entirely different area, situated north of the Minnesota river, had been authorized by a legislative act, February 20, 1862, but it was not ratified by the people. This French name, meaning "the Lake that Talks," is translated from the Dakota or Sioux name, Mde Iyedan (*mde,* lake; *iye,* speaks; *dan,* a diminutive suffix), applied to the adjacent lake, which is an expansion of the Minnesota river. The lake, nearly ten miles long with a maximum width of one mile and a maximum depth of twelve feet, owes its existence to the deposition of alluvium from the Lac qui Parle river, which enters the Minnesota valley near the foot of the lake. Its name most probably was suggested to the Indians by echoes thrown back from its bordering bluffs. Prof. Andrew W. Williamson wrote: "It is very uncertain how it received the name; one tradition says from an echo on its shores, but it is doubtful if any such existed; another tradition is that when the Dakotas first came to the lake voices were heard, but they found no speakers; some think the word has changed its form." The Qu' Appelle river in Saskatchewan, also a French translation of its Indian name, having nearly the same significance, "the River that Calls," is similarly inclosed by somewhat high bluffs, likely to reply to a loud speaker by echoes.

Rev. Moses N. Adams, who during our territorial period resided as a missionary at Lac qui Parle, told of a very remarkable creaking, groaning, and whistling of the ice on the lake in winter and spring, due to fluctuations of the water level allowing the ice to rise and fall, grating upon the abundant boulders of the shores. At the same time these strange sounds are echoed and reverberate from the inclosing bluffs. To these "voices" he ascribed the Dakota and French name.

In the History of the county (1916, page 99), a different explanation is offered, "that at times when the wind was from the right quarter the breaking of waves against the stones on the shore gave off a distinct musical note, or sound, which accounted for the giving of the name to the lake by the early voyageurs."

Townships and Villages.

Information of the origins and meanings of these names has been gathered from "History of the Minnesota Valley" (1882, 1016 pages), in which pages 937-955 relate to this county; "History of Chippewa and Lac qui Parle Counties" (1916, two volumes, 605 and 821 pages), edited by Lycurgus R. Moyer and Hon. Ole G. Dale; and from interviews with these

LAC QUI PARLE COUNTY 289

editors and Hon. J. F. Rosenwald, of Madison, the county seat, during a visit there in July, 1916.

AGASSIZ township, settled in 1870, organized April 12, 1887, was named for the Glacial Lake Agassiz, in the basin of the Red river and of Lake Winnipeg, which outflowed by the River Warren along the Minnesota valley at the north side of this township. Jean Louis Rudolphe Agassiz, in whose honor that ancient lake received its name, was born in Motier, Switzerland, May 28, 1807, and died in Cambridge, Mass., December 14, 1873. His observations of the Swiss glaciers and his principal writings concerning them and the glacial origin of the drift were during the years 1836 to 1846. In the autumn of 1846 Agassiz came to the United States, and the remainder of his life was mostly spent here in zoological researches and in teaching in Harvard College, where he founded the Museum of Comparative Zoology.

ARENA, a Latin word meaning sand, is the name of a township settled in 1878, organized January 3, 1880. Its earliest pioneers came from southern Wisconsin, where this name was earlier given to a township and village on the Wisconsin river in Iowa county.

AUGUSTA township, organized February 5, 1880, was named for Augusta in Eau Claire county, Wisconsin, the former home of its first settlers, a party of eleven families, who came in April, 1879.

BAXTER township, settled in the summer of 1870 and organized September 30, 1871, was named in honor of Hiram A. Baxter, at whose home the township meeting for organization was held.

BELLINGHAM, a Great Northern railway village, platted September 12, 1887, was named for Robert Bellingham, one of the original owners of its site, who came from Dane county, Wisconsin.

BOYD, a railway village in Ten Mile Lake township, platted in 1884 and incorporated in 1893, was named by officers of the Minneapolis and St. Louis railway company.

CAMP RELEASE township, first settled in 1868, organized April 5, 1871, has the site of Camp Release, marked by a monument, where the captives taken by the Sioux in the outbreak of 1862 were surrendered on September 26 to General Sibley.

CERRO GORDO township, settled in the spring of 1868, organized April 7, 1871, received this Spanish name, meaning "Big Mountain," in accordance with the suggestion of Colonel Samuel McPhail, who participated in the battle of Cerro Gordo in the Mexican war, April 18, 1847.

DAWSON, a railway city near the center of Riverside township, platted in 1884, incorporated as a village in 1885 and as a city in 1911, was named in honor of William Dawson, a banker of St. Paul, who was one of the proprietors of its site. He was born in County Cavan, Ireland, October 1, 1825; came to America in 1846; settled in St. Paul in 1861, was its mayor, 1878-81, and died there February 19, 1901.

FREELAND was settled in 1877 and organized in March, 1880. The petitioners at first requested that the name Freedom be given to the new township, in compliment to J. P. Free, one of its pioneers; but this was changed, because another township of the state was earlier so named.

GARFIELD township, settled in 1873, organized January 24, 1881, was named in honor of James Abram Garfield, President of the United States. He was born at Orange, Ohio, November 19, 1831; was an instructor and later president of Hiram College, Ohio, 1856-61; served in the civil war, and was promoted major general in 1863; was a member of Congress from Ohio, 1863-1880; was elected President in 1880, and was inaugurated March 4, 1881; was shot at Washington by Guiteau, July 2, and died at Elberon, N. J., September 19, 1881.

HAMLIN township, settled in April, 1874, and organized September 10, 1879, commemorates its first settler, John R. Hamlin, who died in 1876.

HANTHO township, organized November 4, 1878, was also named for its first settler, Halvor H. Hantho, an immigrant from Norway, who took a homestead on section 15 in 1872. Later in the same year his brothers, Nels and Ole, located on section 13.

HAYDENVILLE, a railway station in section 20, Arena, platted October 10, 1910, was named in honor of Herbert L. Hayden, owner of the site. He was born in Onondaga county, N. Y., March 23, 1850; and died in Madison, Minn., November 20, 1911. He came to Minnesota in 1875; settled at Lac qui Parle in 1878; was admitted to practice law, 1881; removed to Madison in 1884, was secretary and treasurer of the townsite company, and engaged in banking and farming; was county attorney, 1891-2 and 1895-6.

LAC QUI PARLE township, first settled by homesteaders in 1868, organized January 12, 1873, took its name, like the county, from the lake on its northern boundary. Its village was the county seat until May, 1889, when the county offices were permanently located in Madison.

LAKE SHORE township, settled in 1874, organized March 11, 1879, received this name because it borders on Marsh lake, four miles long, through which the Minnesota river flows, a body of shallow water, or more generally in the summer a grassy marsh.

LOUISBURG, a Great Northern railway village, platted September 12, 1887, was named by officers of that railway company.

MADISON township, first settled in 1877, organized in October, 1879, was named on the suggestion of C. P. Moe, "in memory of his former home at Madison, Wisconsin." Its railway village, which became the county seat in 1889, was platted in October, 1884, was incorporated in 1886, and adopted its city charter March 12, 1902.

MANFRED township, settled in 1876, was organized March 11, 1879, being then named Custer, in honor of General George A. Custer (b. 1839, d. 1876). The name was changed to Manfred in 1884, for the principal character in a wild and weird dramatic poem by Byron, having its scenes in the Alps of Switzerland.

MARIETTA, a railway village in Augusta, platted in 1884 and incorporated in 1899, was named by officers of the Minneapolis and St. Louis rail-

LAC QUI PARLE COUNTY 291

way company. This name is borne by cities in Ohio and Georgia, and by villages in eleven other states. Pioneers from Marietta, Ohio, had settled here.

MAXWELL township, settled in 1871 and organized in 1878, was named in honor of Joseph Henry Maxwell, one of its earliest pioneers. He was born in West Virginia, March 5, 1840; served in a West Virginia regiment during the civil war; came to Minnesota in 1871, taking a homestead claim in this township; died in Minneapolis, January 27, 1916.

MEHURIN township, organized October 14, 1879, was named in honor of its first homesteader, Lucretia S. Mehurin, and her father, Amasa Mehurin, who each came to this township in 1877. He was born in Rutland county, Vermont, June 28, 1808; lived in Iowa twenty-one years, 1833-54, and later in Freeborn county, Minn.; came to Lac qui Parle county in 1873, being the first settler in Garfield.

NASSAU, a Great Northern railway village in the west edge of this county, was platted in December, 1893. This name, received from Germany, is borne by counties of New York and Florida.

PERRY township was settled in 1878 and organized in 1880. Its name is borne by counties of ten states of our Union, and by townships and villages or cities in nineteen states, mostly in honor of Oliver Hazard Perry (b. 1785, d. 1819), victor in the celebrated battle of Lake Erie, September 10, 1813. Some of the first settlers here had come from a township of this name in Dane county, Wisconsin.

PROVIDENCE township, settled in 1877, organized October 31, 1878, received its name from the large city and capital of Rhode Island, founded by Roger Williams in 1636. Villages and townships in twelve other states also bear this name.

RIVERSIDE, settled in 1868 and organized September 21, 1872, took its name from Lac qui Parle river, which traverses this township, being formed here by the union of its West and East branches.

TEN MILE LAKE township, first settled in 1876, organized November 4, 1878, was named for its former lake, now drained, which was ten miles distant from the Lac qui Parle mission and trading post. The lake outflowed by Three Mile creek, so named because it joins Lac qui Parle river about three miles south of the mission site.

WALTER township, settled in 1878 and organized October 18, 1884, was named in honor of Henry Walter, who was its first settler, served as a county commissioner, and after living here about thirty years removed to the state of Washington and died there.

YELLOW BANK township, organized January 28, 1878, received the name of Yellow Bank river, referring to the yellowish glacial drift seen in its newly eroded bluffs. This stream, having its sources on the high Coteau des Prairies, was called by Keating the Spirit Mountain creek, translated from its Sioux name, in the narrative and map of Long's expedition in 1823. It is Yellow Earth river on the map of Minnesota published in 1860.

LAKES AND STREAMS.

Keating mapped Lac qui Parle river as Beaver creek, adopting this name from the fur traders. His narrative adds that the Sioux called it Watapan intapa, 'the river at the head," because they considered Lac qui Parle as the head of the Minnesota river, probably referring rather to the limit of favorable canoe travel during the usually low stage of water in the summer. Its name on Nicollet's map, published in 1843, is Intpah river; and this is repeated on maps of Minnesota in 1850 and 1860.

Canby or Lazarus creek, which flows past Canby in Yellow Medicine county, crosses several sections in Freeland and Providence, thence being tributary southeastward to the East branch of the Lac qui Parle river; and Cobb or Florida creek, from sources in Florida township, Yellow Medicine county, flows north to the West branch.

Salt lake, also called Rosabel lake, is crossed by the state boundary at the west side of sections 5 and 8, Mehurin.

Emily creek, in Hantho township, flows to Lac qui Parle.

Yellow Bank river has South and North forks.

Whetstone river flows from South Dakota through the northmost corner of this county, being tributary to the Minnesota at Ortonville. It is a translation of the Sioux name, given as Izuzah river by Nicollet.

ANTELOPE HILLS AND MORAINES.

Through the west border of this county runs a narrow belt of low morainic hills, knolls, and irregular short ridges. In Freeland the most prominent of these glacial drift accumulations are named the Antelope hills. Northward in Mehurin and Augusta the belt is called Stony Ridge, one of its knolls or hillocks at the north side of the West branch of Lac qui Parle river being styled Mt. Wickham. Farther north it is known as Yellow Bank hills, cut through by the river of that name.

It is a part of the Antelope or Third moraine of the continental ice-sheet, in the series of twelve mapped in Minnesota. At its west side in this county a wider tract of lowlands is known as the Antelope Valley, named, like this moraine, for their once frequent antelope herds.

The only American species of these graceful deerlike animals is Antilocapra americana, the prong-horn antelope, proverbially timid and fleet in escape from pursuers. Prof. Clarence L. Herrick wrote of their geographic range as follows, in his "Mammals of Minnesota," published in 1892. "The habitat is limited to the temperate parts of North America west of the Mississippi river. Formerly their range included all of the territory between the tropics and about fifty-four north latitude and from the Mississippi to the coast, except in the wooded and mountainous portions. At the present time they are restricted to the less accessible and arid regions between the Missouri river and the Mountains and southward. Southwestern Minnesota once furnished them congenial pasturage, but they have long since retired beyond the Missouri."

LAKE COUNTY

This county, established March 1, 1856, received its name from its being bounded on the southeast by Lake Superior, which the Ojibways call "Kitchigumi, meaning great water," as spelled by Gilfillan, or "Gitche Gumee, the Big-Sea-Water," of Longfellow in "The Song of Hiawatha." Its very early French name, Lac Superieur, used by Marquette, Hennepin, and Franquelin, denotes its situation as the highest in the series of five great lakes tributary to the St. Lawrence river, which are named collectively the Laurentian lakes. This largest body of fresh water in the world has a mean level 602 feet above the sea, and a maximum depth of 1,026 feet.

TOWNSHIPS AND VILLAGES.

Information of origins and meanings of the geographic names was gathered from John P. Paulson, county auditor, and A. E. Holliday, assistant superintendent of the Duluth and Iron Range railroad, each being interviewed during a visit at Two Harbors, the county seat, in August, 1916.

ALGER, a railroad station and junction, nine miles north of Two Harbors, was named for Hon. Russell A. Alger, senior member of a lumbering firm in Saginaw, Mich., formerly owning much pine timber in this county and large sawmills in Duluth. He was born in Medina county, Ohio, February 27, 1836; served in the Union army during the civil war, and was breveted major general in 1865; was governor of Michigan, 1885-87; was secretary of war, 1897-9, and United States senator from Michigan, 1902-07; and died in Washington, D. C., January 24, 1907.

BEAVER BAY township, the first organized in this county, before 1885, received its name from Beaver Bay village, platted in 1856 by Thomas Clark, on the west side of the small bay bearing this name, where the Beaver river flows into Lake Superior. The Ojibway name of this bay is noted by Gilfillan and Verwyst alike, "Ga-gijikensikag, the place of little cedars." The village was the first county seat until 1888, when it was succeeded by Two Harbors.

BRITTON, a railroad junction eight miles northwest of Two Harbors, was named for a superintendent of logging in its vicinity.

CRAMER township, organized July 14, 1913, and its railway village, were named in honor of J. N. Cramer, a homesteader and later a merchant in the village, who removed to Pennsylvania.

CRYSTAL BAY township, organized April 26, 1904, received this name from a very little bay of Lake Superior, having such crystalline rocks as were formerly worked at two localities farther southwest on the lake shore in this county to supply emery, a variety of corundum, used for grinding and polishing.

DRUMMOND, a railroad station twelve miles northwest of Two Harbors, was named for the owner of adjacent logging camps.

FALL LAKE township, organized April 4, 1899, comprising the northern quarter of this county, received its name from Fall lake, in the southwest part of the township area. The Ojibways apply the name Kawasachong to this lake, meaning mist or foam lake, referring to the mist and spray rising from rapids and falls of the Kawishiwi river, which descends about 70 feet in a short distance between Garden lake and Fall lake. This aboriginal name of the falls and lake, noted by Prof. N. H. Winchell (Geology of Minnesota, vol. IV, p. 408), is in origin and meaning like the French and English names of Rainy lake and river, and in form it is somewhat like Koochiching, their Cree and Ojibway name.

FINLAND, a railroad village in Crystal Bay township, was named for the native country of many of its settlers, including some whose parents came there from Sweden.

HIGGINS, a railroad station in Two Harbors township, was named for a former owner of an adjacent tract of pine timber.

HIGHLAND, a Duluth and Iron Range railroad station, is near the highest land crossed between Lake Superior and the Cloquet river.

KNIFE RIVER, a railroad village in the southwest corner of this county, incorporated October 2, 1909, is at the mouth of the river of this name, which is translated from Mokomani zibi of the Ojibways.

LARSMONT, a railroad station between Knife River and Two Harbors, was named for an adjoining settler, who is a farmer and fisherman.

LAX LAKE, a railroad station in Beaver Bay township, and its lake of this name, commemorate John Waxlax, a Swedish immigrant from Finland, whose homestead farm adjoined the lake.

LITTLE MARAIS, a small village port of Lake Superior, in Cramer township, was named by the early French voyageurs for its little marsh, in contrast with the larger marsh of Grand Marais, in Cook county.

SILVER CREEK township, organized May 3, 1905, received the name of a creek flowing into Lake Superior four miles northeast of Two Harbors, translated from the Ojibway name.

TWO HARBORS township, organized February 20, 1894, was named after the lake port of the Duluth and Iron Range railroad, bearing the same name, which was incorporated as a village March 9, 1888, and as a city February 26, 1907. The city lies on two little bays, natural harbors, named Agate and Burlington bays, the ore docks being on the western Agate bay. Beach sand and gravel here contains frequent pebbles of banded chalcedony, called agate.

WALDO township, organized August 3, 1909, took its name from an earlier Duluth and Iron Range railroad station. This is also the name of a county in Maine, and of villages and townships in nine other states.

LAKE COUNTY

LAKES AND STREAMS.

Much aid for the following pages has been received from the descriptions and maps of the Minnesota Geological Survey, which in the fourth volume of its Final Report has a long chapter on Lake county and three other chapters on its parts of the Vermilion and Mesabi iron ranges.

The coast of Lake Superior in this county has the following islands, points, bays, and tributary streams bearing names, in their order from southwest to northeast: Knife island and Granite point, near the mouth of Knife river; Agate and Burlington bays, before mentioned, at Two Harbors; Burlington point, at the east side of the latter bay, which received its name from a townsite platted on its shore in 1856; Flood bay, named for a man who took a land claim there in the same year; Stewart river, where likewise in 1856 John Stewart and others took claims; Silver creek, which gave its name to a township; Encampment river, and an island of this name, about a mile and a half farther east, named in Norwood's geological report, as assistant with Owen, published in 1852; Gooseberry river, a name given on the map of Long's expedition in 1823, noted by Gilfillan as a translation of the Ojibway name; Split Rock river and point, named from the rock gorge of the stream near its mouth; Two Harbor bay (not to be confounded with the bays at the city of Two Harbors); Beaver river and bay, whence the village and township of Beaver Bay are named; the Great Palisades, turretlike rock cliffs, rising vertically 200 to 300 feet at the lake shore; Baptism river, named Baptist river on Long's map; Cathedral bay, bordered by rock towers and pinnacles; Crystal bay, source of the name of a township; an unnamed bay and point at Little Marais; Manitou river, retaining its Ojibway name, which means a spirit; and Pork bay, in notable contrast with the grandeur and awe of some of the preceding names.

Lakes tributary to Lake Superior include Stewart lake and Twin lakes, sources of Stewart river; Highland lake, close west of Highland station; Thomas, Christensen, Amberger, Clark, Kane, and Spruce lakes, mostly named for cruisers selecting tracts of timber, or for lumbermen in charge of logging camps; Bear lake, three miles northwest of Beaver Bay; Lax lake (formerly called Schaff's lake), for which a railroad station is named, as before noted; Nicado, Micmac, and Nipissiquit lakes, having aboriginal names; Moose, Nine Mile, and Echo lakes, outflowing south to Manitou river; Long lake, Shoepack, Crooked, Artlip, and East lakes; and, farther north, Harriet lake, Wilson lake and Little Wilson lake, Windy lake, Elbow, Lost, and Frear lakes, the last three being crossed by the east line of the county.

On the north, the basin of Rainy lake comprises about three fifths of Lake county. Its chief streams, sending their waters to the series of lakes on the international boundary, are Isabella river, Stony and Birch rivers, and Kawishiwi river. The last is an Ojibway name, meaning, as defined by Gilfillan, "the river full of beavers' houses, or, according to some, muskrats' houses also."

The abundant lakes of this northern district include Bellissima or Island lake, Parent and Syenite lakes, Lake Isabella, Gull, Bald Eagle, and Gabbro lakes, the last being named from the rock formation of its shores; Copeland's lake, Clearwater, Pickerel and Friday lakes; Greenwood lake, named for George C. Greenwood, who was a hardware merchant in Duluth, often called West Greenwood lake, in distinction from a lake of this name in Cook county; Sand, Slate, Birch, White Iron, Farm, and Garden lakes, the last two noting that the Ojibways had cultivated ground adjoining them; Fall lake, called Kawasachong lake by the Ojibways, noticed on a preceding page for the township named from it; Boulder lake, Lake Polly, Lake Alice, and Wilder lake; Fraser and Thomas lakes, named for John Fraser and Maurice Thomas, who selected timber lands and engaged in lumbering near these lakes; Gabimichigama and Agamok lakes, each extending into Cook county; Ogishke Muncie lake, somewhat changed from its Ojibway name, meaning a kingfisher, spelled ogishkimanissi by Baraga's Dictionary; Cacaquabic or Kekequabic lake, translated by Gilfillan as "Hawk-iron lake;" Marble lake, Cherry, Currant, Doughnut, Spoon, Pickle, and Plum lakes; Lake Vira and Ima lake, the latter named in honor of the eldest daughter of Prof. N. H. Winchell, the state geologist; Illusion lake, Jordan, Alworth, Disappointment, and Round lakes; Ensign lake, named in honor of Josiah D. Ensign, of Duluth, judge in this district since 1889; Snowbank lake, a translation of its Ojibway name, which means, as Gilfillan defined it, "snow blown up in heaps lying about here and there;" Newfound lake, Moose, Jasper, Northwestern, and Crab lakes; Manomin lake, meaning wild rice; Wood or Wind lake, Pine, Sucker, Oak Point, and Saturday lakes; Triangle and Urn lakes, whose names were suggested by their outlines; Newton lake, named by Dr. Alexander Winchell in honor of his brother, Newton H. Winchell; and, near the northwest corner of the county, Horse lake and Jackfish lake.

Snowbank lake has Boot and Birch islands, the first being named for its shape; and a small lake between Ensign and Snowbank lakes is for a like reason named Boot lake.

During the examination of this region for the Minnesota Geological Survey, much care was taken to secure correctly the Ojibway names of the streams and lakes. Their translations were commonly used in that survey, as also by the earlier explorers and fur traders, government surveyors, and lumbermen. But nearly all the lakes of relatively small size lacked aboriginal names, and in many instances they yet are unnamed. The need for definite description and location of geologic observations led frequently to arbitrary adoption of names, where

LAKE COUNTY 297

none before existing could be ascertained. For example, Dr. Alexander Winchell in 1886 gave to six little lakes on the canoe route between Kekequabic and Ogishke Muncie lakes, occurring within that distance of less than two miles, the names of the first six letters of the Greek alphabet, the series being Alpha, Beta, Gamma, Delta, Epsilon, and Zeta lakes. When farmers and other permanent settlers come, new names will doubtless replace some that have been thus used or proposed without local or historical significance.

The lakes on the north side of this county were surveyed and mapped, with full details of their shores and islands, by David Thompson in 1822-3, for determination of the course of the international boundary, following a canoe route that had been long used by the fur traders. An excellent description of this route, from Grand Portage to the Lake of the Woods, was published in 1801 by Sir Alexander Mackenzie in his "General History of the Fur Trade from Canada to the Northwest."

Cypress or Otter Track lake is the most eastern in this series bordering Lake county. Its first name, used by Thompson, refers to its plentiful cypress trees, now commonly called arbor vitae or white cedar. Otter Track is for the Ojibway name, noted by Gilfillan, "Nigig-bimi-kawed sagaiigun, the lake where the otter make tracks, from four tracks of an otter on the rocks by the side of the lake, as if he had jumped four times there." More probably, however, the name alludes to peculiar slides where otters took amusement by sliding into the water from a bank of snow or rock or mud, as described in Herrick's "Mammals of Minnesota" (pages 129-135).

Next westward is Knife lake, having several branches or arms, translated from Mokomani sagaiigun of the Ojibways. Prof. N. H. Winchell in 1880 wrote of their reason for this name, derived from an adjoining rock formation, "a blue-black, fine-grained siliceous rock, approaching flint in hardness and compactness, with conchoidal fracture and sharp edges; sometimes it is nearly black. It is this sharp-edged rock that gave name to Knife lake. It is only local, or in beds, or sometimes in ridges."

The outlet of Knife lake flows through three little lakes, which Dr. Alexander Winchell named in 1886, from east to west, Potato, Seed, and Melon lakes. Next are Carp lake (also called Pseudo-Messer lake) and Birch or Sucker lake, named for their fish and trees, succeeded westward by the large and much branched Basswood lake, on the northern limit of the geographic range of this tree, which is generally common throughout Minnesota and is very abundant in the Big Woods.

For the last of these lakes Mackenzie used the French name of the basswood, Lac Bois Blanc (white wood), adding, "but I think improperly so called, as the natives name it the Lake Pascau Minac, or Dry Berries." This Ojibway name was spelled Bassimenan by Prof. N. H.

Winchell, and Bassemenani by Gilfillan, whose translation of it is "Dried blueberry lake." Although the first syllable may have suggested the English name, Basswood, which is a translation from that given by the early French voyageurs, the Indians had no reference to the tree, but only to their gathering and drying berries here for winter use.

Adjoining the northwest part of Lake county, the river flowing from Basswood lake along the boundary enters Crooked lake, translated from its old French name, with reference to its very irregularly crooking and branching outlines.

Hunter's Island.

Nicollet's map, published in 1843, shows a more northern route of canoe travel from Saganaga lake west to Lac la Croix, which follows the stream and series of lakes outflowing from Saganaga, whereas the international boundary crosses a water divide between Saganaga and Cypress or Otter Track lake, thence passing westward along a continuous stream and its lakes. The tract between that northern route of waterflow and the southern or boundary route, bordering the north side of Lake county, is named Hunter's Island by Nicollet's and later maps. It is estimated by Dr. U. S. Grant to have an area of about 800 square miles. (M. H. S. Collections, vol. VIII, 1898, pages 1-10.)

Greenwood Mountain and other Hills.

This county is traversed from southwest to northeast by the continuations of the Vermilion and Mesabi iron ranges, belts of rock formations more fully noticed in the chapter for St. Louis county, where they contain vast deposits of iron ores. These belts are not marked by ridges or hills along large parts of their course, and they nowhere attain heights worthy to be called mountains.

The general highland rises about 1,000 feet above Lake Superior, or 1,600 feet above the sea, within eight or ten miles north from the lake shore. Onward this average height, much diversified by valleys, low ridges, and hills, reaches nearly to the international boundary, on which Otter Track and Crooked lakes are respectively 1,387 feet and 1,245 feet above the sea. Names have been given to only a few of the highest hills. Though these vary in their altitude to about 500 feet above the adjoining lowlands and lakes, they are unduly dignified by being called mountains and peaks.

Greenwood mountain is only 145 feet above the lake of this name at its north side.

Disappointment hill, a mile east of the lake so named, has a height of 350 feet above it.

Mallmann's peak, named for John Mallmann, employed by the Minnesota Geological Survey, situated close north of the east end of Kekequabic lake, rises steeply to the height of 230 feet.

LAKE COUNTY 299

About two miles southeast from the last are the Twin peaks, and nearly two miles farther east is Mount Northrop, named in honor of Cyrus Northrop, president of the University of Minnesota from 1884 to 1911, attaining altitudes about 2,000 feet above the sea, or 500 feet above Kekequabic lake.

SUPERIOR NATIONAL FOREST.

A great part of the north half of Lake county is included in this National Forest, which also comprises considerable areas in Cook and St. Louis counties. The date of its establishment, in 1909, and the steps taken by an act of Congress and by a special recommendation from Minnesota, leading to the designation of these lands as a public reservation for forestry uses, have been noted in the chapter for Cook county.

GLACIAL LAKE ELFTMAN.

When the continental ice-sheet of the Glacial period was finally melting away from this area, its northwardly receding border held temporarily an ice-dammed lake in the basin of Kawishiwi river, with outflow southward and westward. This ancient lake, first described by Arthur H. Elftman, an assistant of the Minnesota Geological Survey, was named in his honor by Prof. N. H. Winchell in the Bulletin of the Geological Society of America (vol. XII, 1901, page 125). "It had an area of about 100 square miles at the time of its greatest extent and an elevation of about 1,700 feet above the sea."

LE SUEUR COUNTY

Established March 5, 1853, this county commemorates a Canadian French trader and explorer, Pierre Charles Le Sueur, before mentioned in the chapter for Blue Earth county as mining a supposed copper ore there in 1701, whence the name of the Blue Earth river and of that county was derived. He was born in 1657, of parents who had emigrated to Canada from the ancient province of Artois in northern France. At the age of twenty-six years, in 1683, he came to the Mississippi by way of the Wisconsin river. The remaining years of the century, excepting expeditions for the sale of furs in Montreal and absence in voyages to France, he spent principally in the country of the Sioux or Dakotas. He was at Fort St. Antoine, on the eastern shore of Lake Pepin, with Perrot at the time of his proclamation in 1689, which he signed as a witness. At some time within a few years preceding or following that date he made a canoe trip far up the Mississippi, this being the first recorded exploration of its course through the central part of Minnesota.

Within the first few years after Le Sueur came to the area of this state, he had acquired acquaintance with the language of the Sioux, and had almost certainly traveled with them along the Minnesota river. From his first Christian name, Pierre, as Neill and Winsor think, came the French name St. Pierre, in English the St. Peter, by which this river was known to the white people through more than a century and a half, until its aboriginal Sioux name was adopted for the new Minnesota Territory.

A letter of Cadillac, written in 1712, cited in the Margry Papers, states that after the appointment of Iberville, a cousin of Le Sueur's wife, to be the first governor of Louisiana, LeSueur had his family remove there, and that his wife and children were then living in Louisiana, where he had died. Another account indicates that he died during the return voyage from France, after his visit there in 1702, carrying the green or blue earth, supposed to be an ore of copper, which he mined on the Blue Earth river.

Townships and Villages.

Information for these names was gathered from "History of the Minnesota Valley" (1882, 1016 pages), having pages 477-532 for this county, and "History of Nicollet and Le Sueur Counties" (1916, two volumes, 544 and 538 pages, edited by Hon. William G. Gresham; and from Edward Solberg, register of deeds, who has made many land surveys throughout the county, Frank Moudry, former register of deeds, and

LE SUEUR COUNTY 301

Patrick G. Galagan, former judge of probate, each being interviewed during a visit at LeSueur Center, the county seat, in July, 1916.

CLEVELAND township, organized in 1858, was named for the city of Cleveland, Ohio, several of the first settlers here, in 1855-6, having come from that state. The village, founded and thus named in 1857, was the county seat during one year, 1875-6, being succeeded by Le Sueur Center. In Ohio this name refers to General Moses Cleaveland (b. 1754, d. 1806), agent of the Connecticut company that colonized the Western Reserve, under whose direction the site of the city named in his honor was surveyed in 1796.

CORDOVA township, settled in 1856 and organized in 1858, bears the name of an ancient city of Spain, renowned for its Moorish antiquities, which in the middle ages was "the most splendid seat of the arts, sciences, and literature in the world." The village of this township was platted September 28, 1867.

DERRYNANE township, organized in 1858, was settled partly by immigrants from Ireland. Its name was derived from Derrynane Abbey beside the little bay of this name on the southwest coast of Ireland. It is also borne by a village in the province of Ontario, Canada.

EAST HENDERSON, platted December 22, 1877, and EAST ST. PETER, platted October 1, 1856, are small villages with railway stations at the east side of the Minnesota river, opposite to Henderson in Sibley county and St. Peter in Nicollet county.

ELYSIAN township, organized in 1858, received this name from its village which had been platted September 20, 1856, and was incorporated in January, 1884. It was adopted from Greek names, Elysium and the Elysian Fields, "the dwelling place of the happy souls after death, placed by Homer on the western margin of the earth, by Hesiod and Pindar in the Isles of the Blessed in the Western Ocean." The village adjoins the northeast end of Lake Elysian, called Okaman lake on Nicollet's map in 1843, which is crossed by the county line and lies almost wholly in Waseca county.

HEIDELBERG, platted December 4, 1878, is a hamlet four miles southwest of New Prague, named by its German people for the city of Heidelberg in Germany, widely known for its great university which was founded in 1386.

KASOTA township, settled in 1851, organized May 11, 1858, took the Sioux name of its village, which was platted March 23, 1855, and was incorporated in April, 1890. It means, as noted by Prof. A. W. Williamson, "clear, or cleared off; the name sometimes applied by the Dakotas to the naked ridge or prairie plateau south of the village." This Kasota terrace of the valley drift, three miles long from north to south and averaging a half mile wide, is about 150 feet above the river and 75 feet lower than the general upland.

KILKENNY township, settled in 1856, was named by its Irish people for a city and county of southeastern Ireland. Its village on the Minneapolis and St. Louis railway was platted in 1877, and was incorporated June 3, 1883.

LANESBURG township was named in honor of its first settler, Charles L. Lane, who came in 1854 and opened a farm in section 33.

LE SUEUR township and city were founded in 1852, with the village plats bearing this name, which in the next year was given to the new county. Two rival villages, one called Le Sueur and the other Le Sueur City, were incorporated respectively on June 10 and 17, 1858. Nine years later, by an act of the state legislature, March 9, 1867, they were united in a borough town, Le Sueur, which was incorporated as a city March 16, 1891. It was the first county seat until 1875, being then succeeded by Cleveland for one year, and by Le Sueur Center since 1876.

A stream here tributary to the Minnesota river is called LeSueur creek or river, and its northern branch is known as Little LeSueur creek or "Forest and Prairie creek." The last name refers to its course through an originally wholly wooded area, but near its mouth coming to the north end of the extensive LeSueur prairie, five miles long and two to four miles wide, which is a terrace of valley drift similar to the much smaller Kasota prairie terrace, previously noted.

LE SUEUR CENTER, a village platted December 2, 1876, at the geographic center of the county, in sections 28 and 29, Lexington, has been the county seat from that date, its site being "cut out of a dense forest growth in 1876-77." It was incorporated in the spring of 1890.

LEXINGTON township, settled in 1855 and organized in 1858, was named after its village, which was platted by pioneers from New England in 1857. This name is borne by a village of Massachusetts, where the battle of Lexington was fought, beginning the Revolutionary War, April 19, 1775, by cities in Kentucky and Missouri, and villages and townships in nineteen other states.

MARYSBURG, a hamlet in the south edge of Washington township, platted January 24, 1859, was named by its first settler, John L. Meagher, an immigrant from Ireland, who was its postmaster during many years and was also the probate judge for this county.

MONTGOMERY township was settled in 1856 and organized in 1859. Its city, incorporated in 1902, was platted as a village September 5, 1877, when the Minneapolis and St. Louis railway was built there, its site being "in the midst of a dense forest of very heavy timber." Fifteen states of the Union have counties of this name, and it is borne also by a similar number of villages and townships, commemorating General Richard Montgomery, who in the American Revolution commanded an expedition invading Canada, in which he was killed December 31, 1775, while leading an attack on Quebec.

NEW PRAGUE, incorporated as a village in March, 1877, and as a city in April, 1891, is crossed along its main street by the line of Le Sueur

LE SUEUR COUNTY 303

and Scott counties. It was named for the ancient city of Prague, the capital of Bohemia, from which part of Austria many immigrants came here.

OKAMAN, at the east side of the northern end of Lake Elysian, was an early village, platted March 30, 1857, lying partly in Waseca county. Its site was vacated in 1867 and reverted to farm uses. The name Okaman, supplied by the Sioux, was given to this lake by Nicollet, derived, according to Williamson, from *hokah,* heron, *man,* nests. It thus had the same meaning as the Okabena creek and lakes in Jackson and Nobles counties.

OTTAWA township was settled in 1853 and organized in 1858. Its village, platted April 4, 1855, was then named Minnewashta, from Sioux words meaning water and good, in allusion to its excellent springs. June 20, 1856, it was surveyed anew and renamed Ottawa, for a tribe of the great Algonquian family, nearly related to the Ojibways. Their name, originally meaning traders, is given to the Ottawa river and the capital of Canada, to cities in Illinois and Kansas, a village in Ohio, and a township in Wisconsin.

SHARON township was settled in 1854 and organized in 1858. Its name, derived from the fertile plain of Sharon in Palestine, is borne also by villages and townships in nineteen other states of the Union.

TYRONE township, settled in 1855-6 and organized in 1858, was named, on the suggestion of Irish immigrants, for a county in northern Ireland. New York and Pennsylvania have townships of this name.

WASHINGTON, first settled in 1858 and in the same year designated as a township, has two large lakes which the government surveyors had named in honor of Washington and Jefferson, presidents of the United States.

WATERVILLE township, settled in 1855 and organized in 1858, received this name from its village platted December 5, 1856, which was incorporated as a village in 1878 and as a city in 1898. It is also the name of a city in Maine, and of villages and townships in ten other states. The choice of the name had reference chiefly to the adjoining Lakes Tetonka and Sakata (Sioux names, used by Nicollet), through which the Cannon river flows, and to White Water creek, here tributary to Lake Sakata.

LAKES AND STREAMS.

Lakes Elysian, Washington, Jefferson, Tetonka, and Sakata, Le Sueur creek or river, the Little Le Sueur creek, and White Water creek, are noted in the preceding list of townships.

Other lakes and creeks of this county are as follows, in the order of the townships and ranges, from south to north and from east to west.

Horseshoe lake is crossed by the east line of Waterville, and Goose lake is in its section 2.

Elysian has Lake Francis, Ray's lake (named for George E. Ray, a pioneer farmer there), and Lake Tustin (partly drained), at the north side of the village; Rice lake, in section 3, named for its wild rice; German lake, mostly in sections 4 and 5, bordered by farms of German settlers; Sasse lake, in section 10, named for early German homesteaders, William and Frederick Sasse; Silver lake, in section 20; Steele lake, on the north line of section 22; Fish lake, in sections 23 and 24; and Round lake in sections 29 and 30.

Kasota is crossed by Chankaska creek (a Sioux name, used by Nicollet, meaning forest-inclosed), the outlet of Lake Washington; Spring creek, about three miles farther north; and Cherry creek at the north end of this township, flowing into the Minnesota river near Ottawa village. Lake Williams or Plaza, and Long lake, each very small, are in the southern part of Kasota, and the larger Lake Emily near its center. Another Lake Emily is mapped in section 31, Cleveland, only two miles southeast from the last.

Kilkenny has Sunfish, Saber, and Diamond lakes, in its south half, which is crossed by Little Cannon creek or river; and its north half has Lakes Dora, Mabel (recently drained), and Volney, the last being named for Volney J. Brockway, a pioneer farmer in section 31, Montgomery, at its north side.

Cordova township has Lake Gorman, named in honor of Willis Arnold Gorman (b. 1816, d. 1876), who was governor of Minnesota Territory, 1853-7, and served in the civil war as colonel of the First Minnesota regiment in 1861, and later as a brigadier general; Sleepy Eye lake, in section 15, named for the Dakota or Sioux chief who is also commemorated by a lake and village of Brown county; Goose lake, in section 28; and Bossuot lake, in sections 29 and 32.

Scotch lake in Cleveland received its name for pioneers from Scotland; Lake Henry, Decker lake (also called Silver lake), and Savidge and Goldsmith lakes, were likewise named for adjacent settlers; and this township also has a little Rice lake in sections 7 and 8, Dog lake in sections 32 and 33, and no less than three Mud lakes, in sections 24, 25, and 33.

Montgomery has another Rice lake, named for the wild rice (but also called Hunt lake), in section 1; another Mud lake, in section 27; Kuzel lake, in section 16; Borer lake, in section 19, commemorating Felix A. Borer, formerly county auditor; and Green Leaf lake, named from the foliage of the surrounding woods, in sections 19, 20, 29, and 30.

Beside Hockridge lake, in the northeast corner of Lexington, a farm claim was taken by Granville Hockridge in October, 1860, and a second claim was taken by his brother in 1863; Clear lake and Lake Mary adjoin Lexington village; and farther south in this township are Tyler lake, named for William L. Tyler, who settled there in 1858, and Mud lake in sections 24 and 25.

Sharon has a large Rice lake, shallow in wet seasons and filled with wild rice, but only a marsh in the summer, this being the fourth Rice lake noted in Le Sueur county.

In the northwest part of Lanesburg are Graham lake and yet another Mud lake, the sixth so named on a recent map of this county; and in its southern part, outflowing east and north into Scott county by Sand creek, are Eggert lake, Lake Pepin, named for some reason after the large Lake Pepin of the Mississippi river, and Lake Sanborn, the last being in honor of Edwin Sanborn, who took a homestead here in April, 1857.

In Derrynane are Shea's lake, named for Timothy Shea, an early settler whose farm adjoined it, and School lake, in the school section 36.

Elysian Moraine.

Le Sueur county is crossed at and near its southern border by a belt of low morainic drift hills, ridges, and small knolls, much strewn with boulders, occupying a width of three to four miles, reaching from Waterville and Elysian northwesterly by Lake Jefferson and the two Lakes Emily to the wide Minnesota valley at St. Peter and Traverse des Sioux. In Nicollet county this belt continues, but is less clearly developed, passing westward by the north side of Swan lake. It is named the Elysian moraine by the chapters on these counties in the Final Report of the Minnesota Geological Survey, being the fifth in a series of twelve marginal moraines partly mapped in their courses through this state.

LINCOLN COUNTY

This county, established March 6, 1873, was named in honor of Abraham Lincoln, president of the United States during the civil war, who was born February 12, 1809, near Hodgenville, Kentucky, and died in Washington, April 15, 1865. In his youth and early manhood he was a farm laborer, a salesman, a merchant, and a surveyor. He served in the Black Hawk war, 1832; was a member of the Illinois legislature, 1834-42; began practice of law at Springfield, Illinois, in 1837; was a member of Congress, 1847-49; was Republican candidate for United States senator in 1858, and held a series of debates throughout Illinois with the Democratic candidate, Stephen A. Douglas, on questions of national legislation against slavery; was president from 1861 until his death, and was assassinated five days after the surrender of Lee, which had ended the war.

Born of humble but worthy parents in their small log cabin on the lonely frontier, Lincoln became the foremost statesman of our American republic, its preserver in the direful war of secession, emancipator of the millions of slaves, and his life was crowned by martyrdom for the sacred cause of justice, liberty, and law.

The patriotic legislature of Minnesota in the year 1861 desired to honor Lincoln by giving his name to a county established from the northeastern part of the present Renville county, with addition of the two most southern townships now in Meeker county; but this act failed of the requisite ratification by the people of the counties thus changed. Next, by an act approved March 9, 1866, the name of Rock county was changed to Lincoln. This law, however, was ineffectual, being ignored by the people of Rock county. Therefore a third unsuccessful attempt was made, by an act of February 12, 1870, on the anniversary of Lincoln's birthday, to establish a county named Lincoln, taking it, as in 1861, from eastern Renville county, but not with the same boundaries as before. It again failed of adoption by the people. Finally, in 1873, Lincoln county was made from the former western part of Lyon county, the legislative act was ratified by the popular vote in November, and the new county was proclaimed by Governor Austin, December 5, 1873. Counties have been named for President Lincoln in fifteen other states.

Among the many biographies of Lincoln the most complete is by John G. Nicolay and John Hay, in ten volumes, published in 1890. "Lincoln Bibliography, a List of Books and Pamphlets relating to Abraham Lincoln," by Judge Daniel Fish, of Minneapolis, 380 pages, was published in 1906.

LINCOLN COUNTY

TOWNSHIPS AND VILLAGES.

Information was received from Leroy P. Sisson, register of deeds, and George Graff, clerk of the court, during a visit at Ivanhoe, the county seat, in July, 1916.

ALTA VISTA township, meaning "high view," was named by Colonel Samuel McPhail, whose home as a farmer during several years was in the southeast quarter of its section 12. This area is 300 to 600 feet above the Minnesota river, about 30 miles distant to the northeast, in which direction it has a very extensive view.

ARCO, a railway village in Lake Stay township, platted in 1900, was named by the Chicago and Northwestern railway officials for the ancient city of Arcola in Italy, the last syllable being omitted to avoid confusion with a railway station named Arcola in Washington county.

ASH LAKE township received the name of its lake in section 17, which was bordered by a grove of white ash trees, a species that is frequent or common throughout Minnesota, excepting far northward.

DIAMOND LAKE township was named from its lake of diamond shape in sections 23 and 24, adjoining the north side of Lake Benton.

DRAMMEN township was named by its Norwegian settlers for the seaport, river, and fjord in Norway, bearing this name, about twenty-five miles southwest of Christiania.

HANSONVILLE, the most northwestern township and the last organized in this county, was named in honor of one of its earliest settlers, John Hanson, who was a representative in the state legislature in 1887. During recent years he has been the historian of the Lincoln county Old Settlers Association.

HENDRICKS township and railway village received their name from Lake Hendricks, crossed by the state boundary at the west side of this township. The lake has this name on the map of Minnesota published by Sewall and Iddings in 1860, which shows the boundary line and its relation to Lakes Hendricks, Shaokatan, and Benton. Such delineation was derived from a survey after the passage in 1857-58 of the acts of Congress defining the western limits of Minnesota for its admission as a state. The name Hendricks was given to the lake during that survey, in honor of Thomas Andrews Hendricks, commissioner of the General Land Office from 1855 to 1859, who was born near Zanesville, Ohio, September 7, 1819, and died in Indianapolis, Ind., November 25, 1885. He was a member of Congress from Indiana, 1851-55; United States senator, 1863-69; governor of Indiana, 1873-77; and was vice-president of the United States in 1885.

HOPE township was named by vote of its settlers. Fourteen other states have villages and townships of this auspicious name.

IVANHOE village, platted in 1900, was named by officers of the Chicago and Northwestern railway, for the hero of the novel thus entitled, written by Sir Walter Scott. It succeeded Lake Benton as the county seat in 1902.

LAKE BENTON township, the first organized in the area of Lincoln county, and its village, which was the county seat for twenty years, 1882-1902, succeeding Marshfield, bear the name given to the lake on Nicollet's map, published in 1843. In his journey to the Pipestone Quarry and to this lake in the summer of 1838, Nicollet was accompanied by John C. Fremont, then a young man, who afterward was known as "the Path Finder," for his explorations of the Rocky mountains, and who in 1856 was the presidential candidate of the newly organized Republican party. Lake Benton was named by Fremont and Nicollet for Senator Benton, whose daughter Jessie was married to Fremont in 1841; and a lake in North Dakota was named Lake Jessie in honor of her on this map. Thomas Hart Benton was born near Hillsborough, N. C., March 14, 1782; and died in Washington, D. C., April 10, 1858. He was United States senator from Missouri during thirty years, 1821-1851.

The depth and area of Lake Benton vary much with fluctuations of average moisture or dryness during successive years. At its high stage the water surrounds an island in the east part, called Bird island.

LAKE STAY township has a lake, adjoining Arco village, named in honor of Frank Stay, who was wounded there in 1865, near the end of his service of three years in campaigns against the Sioux after their outbreak in 1862. He was born in Canada, June 10, 1837; came to Minnesota in 1854; was farming on the site of Hanley Falls, Yellow Medicine county, at the time of the Sioux massacre, in August, 1862, and only escaped after great exposure and suffering. Since 1868 he has lived on his homestead farm in the township of Camp Release, Lac qui Parle county, where he was the first settler.

LIMESTONE township, occupied in its greater part by the knolly and hilly glacial drift of the Gary moraine, which is more fully noticed near the end of this chapter, received its name in allusion to the plentiful limestone boulders, with many others of granite and gneiss.

MARBLE township, likewise mainly belonging to the Gary moraine, was similarly named for its light yellowish magnesian limestone boulders, some of which resemble marble in hardness, durability, and adaptation to be polished for building or ornamental uses.

MARSHFIELD township received the name of its village, previously platted in 1873 in the northeast quarter of section 30, which was the first county seat until 1882, being then succeeded by Lake Benton. It was named in honor of Charles Marsh and Ira Field, pioneer settlers. The former, who came here in 1871, was the owner of its site, and was appointed the first auditor of the county in January, 1874. The village site is now farming land.

ROYAL township was so named, signifying kingly, to express the satisfaction and pride and loyalty of its people for their new homes here.

SHAOKATAN township has the Sioux name of its lake, found on an early map of this state, before mentioned for Lake Hendricks, published January 1, 1860. Its origin and meaning remain to be learned.

LINCOLN COUNTY 309

TYLER, a railway village platted in 1879, was named in honor of C. B. Tyler, who was born in Montrose, Pa., September 2, 1835; came to Minnesota in 1857; was register of the United States land office in New Ulm after 1873; owned and edited the New Ulm Herald, 1875-8; removed to Tracy in 1880 and later to Marshall, where he engaged in banking.

VERDI township was named for the renowned Italian operatic composer, Giuseppe Verdi (b. 1813, d. 1901). This name means verdant or verdure, descriptive of the greenness of the township, which in all its extent is during the spring and summer a far-reaching green prairie.

LAKES AND STREAMS.

The preceding pages have noticed Ash and Diamond lakes; three lakes of special geological interest, named Benton, Shaokatan, and Hendricks, which will be again noticed at the end of this chapter; and Lake Stay, which in dry seasons is represented by two lakelets.

Other lakes bearing names to be listed are Swan lake, a mile south of Tyler; Cottonwood lake, which has been drained, close north of Tyler; Lake Nova or Dead Coon lake, in the northeast corner of Marshfield; Blackman and Rush lakes, in sections 9 and 16 of Diamond Lake township; Perch lake in section 17, Royal, and Eagle lake in sections 25 and 36, which are the only lakes named among the several of that township, most of them, however, being marshes or mainly dry in years of deficient rainfall; and the Twin lakes, in sections 28 and 29, Hansonville.

The streams of this county are named only as branches of the Redwood, Yellow Medicine, and Lac qui Parle rivers.

ALTAMONT AND GARY MORAINES.

The description and map of Lincoln county in the Final Report of the Minnesota Geological Survey (vol. I, 1884, chapter XX, pages 589-612) direct attention to its two well developed belts of marginal drift hills and short low ridges and knolls, abundantly sprinkled with boulders. The western or outer moraine, lying on the crest of the great highland called the Coteau des Prairies, extends north-northwestward through the southwestern part of the county, past the western ends of Lakes Benton, Shaokatan, and Hendricks; and thence it continues in South Dakota, to cross the Chicago and Northwestern railway at Altamont, a dozen miles west of the interstate boundary. Parallel with this and about fifteen miles distant to the northeast, the similar but broader second moraine passes across the northeast part of this county, where its profusion of limestone boulders gave the names of Limestone and Marble townships. It crosses the same railway at and west of Gary, in the east edge of South Dakota.

From these localities, described by the Minnesota reports, these first and second marginal moraines of the continental ice-sheet, in a successive series of twelve traced partly in this state, were named in 1883 by Prof. T. C. Chamberlin as the Altamont and Gary moraines. Next northeastward, being also parallel with these, is the Antelope or Third moraine, also named by him in 1883, noted in the chapter for Lac qui Parle county.

The Hole in the Mountain.

The outer or Altamont moraine belt, and the thick sheet of till that descends thence westward, are cut in the west part of Lake Benton township by a deep channel or valley, which is called, translating the Sioux name, the "Hole in the Mountain." The railroad between Lake Benton and Verdi village goes south-southwest four miles through this gap, bounded on each side by picturesque bluffs. Its depth, wholly in the glacial drift, is from 150 to 200 feet below the knolly surface of the moraine, and its highest point is about ten feet above Lake Benton, which has its outlet eastward into the Redwood river. This valley, from an eighth to a fourth of a mile wide, was evidently excavated by a river that flowed from northeast to southwest across this great ridge, which is the highest land in southwestern Minnesota, being 1,000 feet above the Minnesota river on the northeast, 350 feet above the Big Sioux river on the west, and about 1,960 feet above the sea.

At three other places, 11, 14, and 18 miles northwest from Lake Benton, similar channels have been eroded through the massive ridge of this moraine and through the smooth sheet of drift that slopes downward from its west side. The first of these channels begins at the southwest end of Lake Shaokatan, and extends about two miles southwest in the same course with this lake, through the knolly belt of the moraine, beyond which its course for the next three miles is northwest along its west side, crossing the state line. Lake Shaokatan outflows northeastward to the Yellow Medicine river, but the highest part of the valley that extends from it westerly is only slightly elevated above the lake.

The most northwestern of these remarkable channels or valleys, lying in Brookings county, South Dakota, and extending southward from the southwest end of Lake Hendricks, was called by the Sioux "the Brother of the Hole in the Mountain," because of its close likeness to the pass southwest from Lake Benton.

While the ice-sheet covered the basin of the Minnesota river and deeply overspread all the country northward, rising high above the Coteau des Prairies, streams outflowed from its melting border in the courses of these channels, at the same time with the accumulation of the Altamont moraine. Much glacial drift was borne away by the streams from the lower part of the ice in which it had been held, producing hollows when that drift was deposited, in which lie the Lakes Benton, Shaokatan, and Hendricks, respectively about 10, 15, and 20 feet in depth. The general surface of the drift is about 10 feet above these lakes, showing that the drift inclosed in the basal part of the ice-sheet adjoining the outermost moraine, measured by the action of the glacial rivers and the resulting hollows of the three lakes, was equal to a thickness of 20 to 30 feet.

LYON COUNTY

This county, established by two legislative acts, March 6, 1868, and March 2, 1869, was named in honor of General Nathaniel Lyon, who was born in Ashford, Conn., July 14, 1818, and was killed in the battle of Wilson's Creek, Mo., August 10, 1861. He was graduated at the United States Military Academy in 1841; served in Florida during the later part of the Seminole war, 1841-2, and also served in the Mexican war, 1846-7; was promoted captain in 1851, and was on frontier duty during the years 1853-61 in Kansas, Dakota, Minnesota, and Nebraska. At the beginning of the civil war he took a prominent part in the contest against secession in Missouri, rendered efficient aid to the national government as commander of the United States arsenal in St. Louis, and was appointed general of the Department of Missouri in June, 1861.

A series of his letters in 1860, in which he advocated the election of Lincoln as president, entitled "The Last Political Writings of Gen. Nathaniel Lyon," was published in 1861, soon after his death (275 pages, including a memoir of his life and military services). His biography was more fully written by Dr. Ashbel Woodward (360 pages, 1862); and his devotion to the Union, for which he gave his life, is the theme of a volume by James Peckham, "Gen. Nathaniel Lyon and Missouri in 1861, a Monograph of the Great Rebellion" (447 pages, 1866). He is also commemorated by the names of counties in Iowa, Kansas, and Nevada.

TOWNSHIPS AND VILLAGES.

Information of the origins of names was gathered from "History of the Minnesota Valley" (1882, 1016 pages), having pages 848-882 for this county, "History and Description of Lyon County," by C. F. Case, (1884, 98 pages), and "An Illustrated History of Lyon County," by Arthur P. Rose (1912, 616 pages); and from interviews with Mr. Rose, author of the later work, and Richard R. Bumford, former register of deeds, visited at Marshall, the county seat, in September, 1916.

AMIRET township, settled in 1868 and organized March 17, 1874, was at first called Madison, which was changed in 1879 to the present name, taken from its railway village. The name was chosen in honor of Amiretta Sykes, wife of M. L. Sykes, vice president of the Chicago and Northwestern railway company. The first townsite in the area of Lyon county had been platted in 1857 about three miles southwest from the site of this village and was named Saratoga, which name was given in 1874 to the railway village then platted. When the railway was being built, in 1872, a post office had been established here and named Coburg, in honor of William Coburn, the pioneer merchant and first postmaster. In 1879 the name Amiret was chosen, superseding both these names and the former township name of Madison.

BALATON, the railway village of Rock Lake township, platted in July, 1879, and incorporated in 1892, was named for the large and picturesque Lake Balaton in western Hungary.

BURCHARD, a railway station in Shelburne, received this name in 1886, in honor of H. M. Burchard, a Chicago and Northwestern land agent at Marshall.

CLIFTON township, settled in 1872 and organized October 7, 1876, bears a name proposed by Christopher Dillman, which is also borne by villages and townships in twenty-one other states.

COON CREEK township, organized August 4, 1883, has a creek so named from Dead Coon lake near its source, in Lincoln county, to which that name was given by the early government surveyors because they found a dead raccoon there.

COTTONWOOD, a Great Northern railway village in Lucas township, platted in July, 1888, received its name from the adjacent lake, which has cottonwood trees on its shore.

CUSTER township, settled in 1868 and organized October 14, 1876, was named in honor of George Armstrong Custer, who was born in Ohio, December 5, 1839; was graduated at the United States Military Academy in 1861; served through the civil war; was brevetted a major general in 1866; commanded an exploring expedition to the Black Hills in 1874; and was killed with all his attacking troops, by the Sioux in Montana, June 25, 1876.

DUDLEY, a railway station in Clifton, platted December 20, 1901, was named for Dudley village and township in Massachusetts.

EIDSVOLD township, first settled in June, 1871, and organized September 20, 1873, was named by vote of its Norwegian settlers for a parish in Norway, noted as the meeting place of the National Assembly in 1814.

FAIRVIEW, settled in June, 1870, organized April 1, 1873, was described by Case in 1884, "as its name implies, a beautiful prairie township, which, especially in early summer, spreads out a landscape of loveliness nowhere else equalled but on the green, rolling prairies, and under the clear atmosphere of Minnesota."

FLORENCE, a Great Northern railway village in Shelburne, platted October 9, 1888, was named for Florence Sherman, daughter of its founder.

GARVIN, a Chicago and Northwestern railway village in Custer, platted April 30, 1886, was at first called Terry and afterward Kent, which was changed to the present name in July, 1891, in honor of H. C. Garvin, traveling freight agent of this railway.

GHENT, the railway village of Grandview, platted in June, 1878, and incorporated May 15, 1899, at first bore the name of the township, but was renamed in September, 1881, for the ancient city of Ghent in Belgium, in compliment to Belgian colonists coming in 1880-81, who were led by Bishop Ireland to settle in this part of the county.

GRANDVIEW township, first settled in August, 1871, and organized two years later, was named, like Alta Vista in Lincoln county, for the extensive outlook northeastward from the Coteau des Prairies.

GREEN VALLEY, a railway village in Fairview township, platted in May, 1888, refers to the vast green prairie there traversed by the Redwood river.

HECKMAN, a station of the Chicago and Northwestern railway, five miles southeast of Marshall, was named for a dining-car superintendent.

ISLAND LAKE township, first settled about the year 1868, organized in March, 1879, was named for its lake in section 34, having a small wooded island.

LAKE MARSHALL township, settled in 1869 and organized March 8, 1872, received the name of its lake, given in honor of Governor William Rainey Marshall, for whom also a county is named.

LUCAS was settled in 1871. "The town was set off for organization.in July, 1873, as Canton, which was changed to Lisbon, and again to Moe, and lastly to Lucas. The first town meeting was held August 5, 1873." (History, Minnesota Valley, p. 865.) This name is borne by counties in Ohio and Iowa, a township in Wisconsin, and villages in these and other states.

LYND township, settled in 1867, organized January 9, 1873, was named in honor of James W. Lynd, who had a fur trading station in section 5, Lyons, during 1855-57, and afterward removed one or two miles down the Redwood river to the northeast quarter of section 33 in this township. He was born in Baltimore, Md., November 25, 1830; and was killed in the Indian massacre at the Lower Sioux Agency, August 18, 1862. He came to Minnesota about 1853, and lived among the Sioux to learn their language, habits, and characteristics, on which he intended to publish a book. The manuscript for it was completed, but was mostly destroyed in the Sioux outbreak, of which Mr. Lynd was the first victim. He was a state senator in 1861. Lynd railway village, near the site of his second trading post, was platted November 6, 1888.

LYONS township, first settled in January, 1868, organized April 1, 1873, received its name from that of the county, with an added letter which gives to it the English form of the name of the ancient and large city of Lyon in France.

MARSHALL, the county seat, platted in August, 1872, with the building of the Chicago and Northwestern railway, incorporated as a village March 18, 1876, and as a city February 20, 1901, was named for Governor Marshall, like Lake Marshall township, in which it is situated.

MINNEOTA, a railway village in Eidsvold, platted in 1881, has a Sioux name, meaning "much water." Prof. A. W. Williamson wrote of its origin, that it is "said to be so named by an early settler on account of an abundance of water flowing into his well."

MONROE township, first settled in 1871, organized January 5, 1874, was named by Louis and Ole Rialson, pioneers who came from Monroe, the county seat of Green county in southern Wisconsin. Seventeen states of the Union have counties of this name, and a larger number have townships and villages or cities, including eight townships in Pennsylvania, all being named in honor of James Monroe (b. 1758, d. 1831), who was the fifth president of the United States, 1817-25.

NORDLAND township, settled in 1870, organized May 9, 1873, has the name of a northern district of Norway, crossed by the Arctic circle. Nearly all its settlers came from that country.

ROCK LAKE township, organized October 26, 1876, took its name from the lake in its northwest corner, which refers to the abundance of boulders around the shore, pushed up in some places by the lake ice to form a rock wall.

RUSSELL, a Great Northern village in Lyons, founded in May, 1888, and incorporated August 30, 1898, was named for Russell Spicer, son of a promoter of the building of this branch railway.

SHELBURNE township, settled in 1871, organized September 6, 1879, has a name that is borne also by townships and villages in New Hampshire, Vermont, and Massachusetts, and by a county and its county seat in Nova Scotia.

SODUS township, first settled in the spring of 1871, organized October 27, 1876, was named for Sodus township and village in Wayne county, N. Y., adjoining Sodus bay of Lake Ontario. This name is of Indian origin, but its meaning is uncertain.

STANLEY township, settled in 1867, was organized in March, 1877. A city in Wisconsin, villages and post offices in a dozen other states, and a county in South Dakota, bear this name.

TAUNTON, a Chicago and Northwestern railway village in Eidsvold, platted in April, 1886, and incorporated June 5, 1900, was named by C. C. Wheeler, an officer of this railway company, for the city of Taunton in Massachusetts.

TRACY, a village and junction of the Chicago and Northwestern railway, platted in 1875, incorporated as a village February 5, 1881, and as a city August 3, 1893, was named in honor of John F. Tracy, a former president of this railway company.

VALLERS township, organized October 7, 1876, was named by ·Ole O. Brenna, a pioneer settler from Norway. "His desire was to name it Valla, a Norwegian word, meaning valley, but because of incorrect spelling in the petition or illegibility the county commissioners made the name read Vallers." (History of Lyon County, by Rose, p. 57.)

WESTERHEIM township, first settled in June, 1871, and organized May 9, 1876, received this Norwegian name, meaning western home, by vote of its people, mostly immigrants from Norway.

LYON COUNTY

LAKES AND STREAMS.

Coon creek, Cottonwood lake, Island lake, Lake Marshall, and Rock lake, giving their names to townships, a city, and a village, have been duly noticed in the foregoing list.

Meadow creek is a name given on a recent map to the stream flowing from Lake Marshall to the Cottonwood river.

Three Mile creek is a northern tributary of the Redwood river, with which it is nearly parallel and three to five miles distant along all its course.

Monroe has Lake Sigel and the shallow or sometimes dry Twin lakes, the former being named in honor of General Franz Sigel (b. 1824, d. 1902), distinguished for his service in the civil war.

The Lake of the Hills, often dry, is in sections 20 and 21, Custer. Long lake, on the south line of this township, and Lake Yankton, named for a division of the Sioux or Dakota people, adjoining Balaton, outflow southeastward to Lake Shetek and the Des Moines river.

Black Rush lake, recently drained, was in Lyons; Marguerite or Wood lake is in Coon Creek township; and Goose lake lies about a mile west of Island lake.

Swan lake is on the east side of section 12, Stanley.

School Grove lake was in the school section 36 of Lucas; Lady Slipper and Lady Shoe lakes were in the south half of this township, having species of the Minnesota state flower, commonly known by these names, also called moccasin flower; and Sham lake was in section 3. These former lakes, however, have lately been drained. Only Cottonwood lake, beside the village named from it, and Lone Tree lake, in sections 5 and 6, remain in Lucas township.

Between the lakes of Stanley and Lucas, in the northeast corner of this county, and the numerous lakes before mentioned, in its higher southwest part, a wide tract extending from southeast to northwest through its center is destitute of lakes, excepting Lake Marshall, named for a governor of this state and giving his name to the county seat.

McLEOD COUNTY

Established March 1, 1856, this county was named in honor of Martin McLeod, a pioneer fur trader of Minnesota, who was born in Montreal, August 30, 1813, of Scotch parentage, and there received a good education. In 1836 he came to the Northwest, voyaging in an open boat on Lake Superior from its mouth to La Pointe, Wisconsin, and thence walking more than six hundred miles to the Pembina settlement on the Red river, where he arrived in December. The next March, having set out with two companions, young British officers, and Pierre Bottineau as guide, he came to the trading post of Joseph R. Brown at Lake Traverse, arriving March 21, after a journey of nineteen days and a most perilous experience of hunger and cold due to successive blizzards, by one of which the two officers perished. Coming forward to Fort Snelling in April, 1837, he was afterward during many years engaged as a fur trader for Chouteau and Company, under the direction of General Sibley, being in charge of trading posts successively on the St. Croix river, at Traverse des Sioux, Big Stone lake, Lac qui Parle, and Yellow Medicine.

McLeod was a member of the Council in the Territorial legislature, 1849-53, being president of the Council in 1853. With Colonel John H. Stevens and others, he was one of the founders of Glencoe in 1855. He died November 20, 1860, on his farm to which he had removed his family in 1849, at Oak Grove, in Bloomington, Hennepin county. He was a charter member of the Minnesota Historical Society, and was one of its two vice presidents elected at the time of its organization, November 15, 1849. (The name is pronounced as if spelled McLoud, with English sound of the diphthong.)

Townships and Villages.

Information of the origins of geographic names has been received from an address by R. H. McClelland at the fiftieth anniversary of the founding of Hutchinson, October 4, 1905; "History of McLeod County," 862 pages, 1917, edited by Franklyn Curtiss-Wedge and Return I. Holcombe; and interviews with Captain Axel H. Reed, Henry L. Simons, and Henry Wadsworth, each of Glencoe, the county seat, during a visit there in July, 1916.

Acoma township was named by Dr. Vincent P. Kennedy, for the Indian pueblo village of Acoma in western New Mexico, about fifty miles west of Albuquerque.

Bergen township was named by its Norwegian settlers, for the large city and seaport of Bergen in southwestern Norway.

BISCAY, a railway village in Hassan Valley township, received its name from the large Bay of Biscay adjoining Spain and France.

BROWNTON, a railway village in Sumter, platted October 15, 1877, incorporated February 12, 1886, was named in honor of Alonzo L. Brown, whose farm included this townsite. He was born in Auburn, N. Y., November 8, 1838; and died at his home in Brownton, October 11, 1904. He came to Minnesota in 1857, settling here; served in the Fourth Minnesota regiment in the civil war, and became captain in a colored regiment; was author of the History of the Fourth Regiment, Minnesota, 594 pages, published in 1892.

COLLINS township was named in honor of one of its early settlers. This name is borne by a township in New York, and by villages in ten other states.

GLENCOE township received the name of its village, founded in June 11, 1855. It was chosen by Martin McLeod, for whom this county was named, and who was a member of the townsite company, in commemoration of the historic valley called Glencoe in Scotland, where the MacDonalds were massacred in February, 1692. This village was incorporated in 1873 and adopted its charter as a city March 4, 1909. From the beginning of the county, it has been continuously the county seat.

HALE township "was named either for an early settler or for John P. Hale, of New Hampshire, a distinguished American statesman and the Free Soil candidate for president in 1852. It is said that the Hutchinsons and other anti-slavery men of the county induced the county board to name the township for the eminent New England Free Soiler." (History of this county, page 264.) John Parker Hale was born in Rochester, N. H., March 31, 1806; and died in Dover, N. H., November 19, 1873. He was a member of Congress from New Hampshire, 1843-45; United States senator, 1847-53 and 1855-65; and was minister to Spain in 1865-69.

HASSAN VALLEY township, the last organized in this county, is crossed by the Hassan river, as it was named on maps of Minnesota in 1860 and 1869, but on later maps called the South fork of Crow river. This Sioux word, hassan, is derived from haza or hah-zah, the huckleberry or blueberry. With another Sioux word, chan, tree, it supplied the name of the sugar maple, chanhassan, "the tree of sweet juice," whence came the name of Chanhassen township in Carver county, and Hassan township in Hennepin county.

HELEN township was named in honor of Mrs. Helen Armstrong, its first white woman resident, whose husband, J. R. Armstrong, was sheriff of the county.

HUTCHINSON township took the name of its village, founded November 19, 1855, by the brothers, Asa, Judson, and John Hutchinson, with others. These brothers were members of the famous family of many singers, born in Milford, N. H., who gave concerts of popular and patriotic songs throughout the United States after 1841 until the close of the civil war.

Hutchinson was incorporated as a village February 9, 1881, and as a city in 1904.

Asa Burnham Hutchinson, youngest of the brothers founding Hutchinson, where he afterward lived, was born March 14, 1823, and died at his home here November 25, 1884. Adoniram Judson Joseph Hutchinson, commemorated by the name of Judson lake, recently drained, about a mile north of this city, was born March 14, 1817, and died in Lynn, Mass., January 10, 1859. John Wallace Hutchinson, born January 4, 1821, resided many years in Lynn, Mass., and was author of the "Story of the Hutchinsons," two volumes, 495 and 416 pages, published in 1896.

KONISKA, a village platted in 1856 on the South fork of Crow river, for utilization of its water-power, has been mainly superseded by the villages and cities on railways.

LESTER PRAIRIE, a railway village in Bergen, platted in 1886 and incorporated in 1888, was named in honor of John N. Lester and his wife, Maria Lester, whose homestead farm included a part of its site.

LYNN township was named probably by recommendation of the Hutchinson brothers, for the city of Lynn in Massachusetts.

PENN township, settled largely by Germans from Pennsylvania, was named for William Penn, the founder of that state.

PLATO, a railway village of Helen township, bears the name of a renowned Greek philosopher (d. 347 B. C.), who was a disciple of Socrates and the teacher of Aristotle. This is also the name of small villages in New York, Illinois, Kentucky, and Missouri.

RICH VALLEY was named on the suggestion of A. B. White, an early settler at its village of Koniska, for the fertility of its soil and for the South fork of Crow river flowing through this township.

ROUND GROVE township was named for the large grove in the northwest quarter of its section 6, adjoining the east side of Round Grove lake, less than a mile southwest from Stewart village.

ST. GEORGE is a hamlet on the South fork of Crow river in the east edge of Rich Valley.

SILVER LAKE, a village platted in 1881 and incorporated in 1889, is situated at the north side of Silver lake, in sections 33 and 34, Hale, about a mile north of its Great Northern railway station.

STEWART, a village on the Chicago, Milwaukee and St. Paul railway in section 31, Collins, platted in 1878 and incorporated in 1888, was named in honor of its founder, Dr. D. A. Stewart, of Winona.

SUMTER township was named for Fort Sumter, built on a small artificial island three miles southeast of Charleston, S. C., as a defence of its harbor. The bombardment of this fort by the Confederates, April 12 and 13, 1861, with its evacuation by Major Anderson on April 14, began the civil war.

WINSTED township. its village, and the adjoining Winsted lake, received their name from Winsted in Connecticut, one of the county seats of

MC LEOD COUNTY 319

Litchfield county, the native place of Eli F. Lewis, founder of this village. The lake was originally named by him Lake Eleanor, in honor of his wife.

LAKES AND STREAMS.

Crow river, belonging to several counties, has been considered in the first chapter. McLeod county lies mostly in the basin of its South fork, which in early years of the county was called Hassan river, as before noted. That name, received from the Sioux and meaning sugar maple, is applied to a township, Hassan Valley; and the next township on this stream, also named from it, is Rich Valley. Its chief tributary, flowing across the south half of the county, is Buffalo creek, named for abundant buffalo bones found throughout the area when it was first settled and brought under cultivation.

Silver creek, in Bergen township, is a smaller southern tributary of the South fork; and from the north it receives Crane, Otter, and Bear creeks, the last being the outlet of Bear lake, Lake Harrington, and Silver lake.

High Island creek, crossing the two most southern townships, flows eastward through Sibley county to the Minnesota river, passing High Island lake, whence came its name, as noted for that county.

The list of townships and villages contains due notice of Judson lake, near Hutchinson, Round Grove lake, Silver lake, and Winsted lake.

It is noteworthy that the long and narrow Otter lake, intersected by the course of the South fork or Hassan river, Lake Marion in the northeast edge of Collins, Lake Addie at Brownton, and Baker's lake, crossed by High Island creek in Penn township, form together an almost straight series, extending seventeen miles from north to south, more than half of which is water. This series of lakes may be of similar origin with the three very remarkable series or chains of lakes in Martin county, described and named in its chapter.

Lakes Addie and Marion were named before 1860 by Charles Hoag, for his two daughters. He lived here during a few years, though previously and also afterward his home was in Minneapolis, where in 1852 he bore a principal part in naming that city.

Baker's lake was named in honor of Augustus C. Baker, who settled here as a farmer in 1865. He was born in Freedom, Ohio, December 19, 1838; came to Minnesota, and served during the last year of the civil war in the Fourth Minnesota regiment; engaged in mercantile business in Brownton after 1878, and in recent years was its postmaster.

King's lake, in sections 10 and 15, Penn, and Ward's lake, crossed by the south line of Round Grove township, were named for early settlers.

Helen township formerly had Kennison lake in sections 1 and 12, and Bear and Brian lakes in section 32, but they have been recently drained.

Glencoe has Rice and Swan lakes in sections 7 and 8, and Brewster and Thoeny lakes in its southwest part. Mathias Thoeny, for whom the last is named, was born in Switzerland, September 28, 1837; served through the civil war in the Second Minnesota regiment, rising to the rank of captain; was a merchant in Glencoe, 1865-70, auditor of this county in 1873-83, and afterward was cashier of the First National Bank of Glencoe during thirty years.

Sumter, with Lake Addie before noted, has Lake Mary in section 17, Clear lake in section 13, and Nobles lake adjoining Sumter village. The last was named for three brothers, Alexander, Daniel, and Jeremiah Nobles, whose homesteads were on or near this lake.

In Collins, with Lake Marion, are Eagle lake and Lake Whitney, the last being named for a pioneer farmer.

Lake Barber, similarly named, is in sections 26 and 27, Lynn; but Lake Allen, formerly in its sections 22 and 23, and another shallow lake, unnamed, in section 34, have been drained.

Winsted has South lake, lying a half mile south of Winsted lake; Roach and Higgins lakes, each recently drained, in the east edge of this township; Grass lake in sections 3 and 10; Coon lake, crossed by the north line of section 5; and Cloustier lake, in section 31. Crane and Otter creeks, in the south half of Winsted, flow southeastward to the South fork of Crow river.

With Silver lake, beside the village of this name in Hale township, are Mud lake, on the east, and Swan lake, about a mile distant northwestward. Another Mud lake, in sections 23, 24, and 26, Hale, has been drained, as also the former Bullhead lake, in section 21, named for its small species of catfish, called the bullhead or horned pout.

Hutchinson township has Lake Byron, in section 2, and a group of a dozen other lakes in its northern half, including Bear and Little Bear lakes, Emily and Echo lakes, Lakes Harrington, Hook, and Todd, and Loughnan's lake, with others unnamed.

Lewis Harrington, honored by one of these lakes, was born in Greene, Ohio, November 22, 1830; was surveyor of the townsite of Hutchinson, 1855-56, and its first postmaster; was captain of a company defending this place against the Sioux in 1862; was a representative in the state legislature, 1866-68; and died by an accidental fall, August 14, 1884, while engaged on government surveys in the state of Washington.

Lake Hook was named for Isaac Hook, who came in the spring of 1856 and lived beside this lake many years as a recluse.

Lake Todd commemorates Daniel S. Todd, a pioneer farmer.

Walker's lake, two miles northeast from the city of Hutchinson, and Judson lake, before noticed, have been drained for use of their beds as farming land.

In the north half of Acoma are Cedar and Belle lakes, crossed by the north line of the township and county, and Stahl's lake, in sections 10 and 11, named for Charles Stahl, a German farmer, who settled there in June, 1857. Ferrel lake, formerly in sections 16 and 17, is drained.

MAHNOMEN COUNTY

This county, established December 27, 1906, was previously the east part of Norman county. It comprises half the area of the White Earth Indian Reservation, which also extends south into Becker county and east into Clearwater county, the name of the reservation as noted in the chapter for Becker county, being derived from White Earth lake. The south line of Mahnomen county crosses the north end of this lake, and its outlet, the White Earth river, flows through the south half of this county to the Wild Rice river.

Mahnomen is one of the various spellings of the Ojibway word for the wild rice. From this excellent native grain we receive the English name, through translation, of the Wild Rice lakes, in Clearwater county, and of the Wild Rice river, which has its source in these lakes and flows across Mahnomen and Norman counties to the Red river. The same word has been more commonly written Manomin, as in Baraga's Dictionary of the Ojibway language, and in this spelling it was the name of a former very small county in this state, between Anoka and St. Anthony (the east part of Minneapolis), existing from 1857 to 1869. With other orthographic variations, it gave the names of the Menominee tribe of Indians, Menominee river, county, and city, in Michigan, and Menomonee river, as well as the towns of Menomonee Falls and Menomonie, in Wisconsin.

The county seat of Mahnomen county has the same name, which was given to this railway village before the county was established. Its spelling here adopted is similar to Mahnomonee, written by Longfellow in "the Song of Hiawatha."

In the Dakota or Sioux language, according to its Dictionary by Riggs, wild rice is called psin. From that word probably came the earliest published name, Du Siens, for the Wild Rice lake and river, given by the narration of Joseph la France in 1744, as noted in the chapter for Clearwater county. He described the plant as "a kind of wild Oat, of the Nature of Rice." It was commonly known by the early French traders and voyageurs as folle avoine, meaning fool oat or false oat; and thence their name for the Menominee tribe, living in the north part of Wisconsin and Michigan, was Folles Avoines, and that region of many lakes and streams, having abundance of wild rice, was named the Folle Avoine country. Dr. Douglas Houghton, writing in 1832 as a member of Schoolcraft's expedition to Lake Itasca, defined this term to comprise "that section of country lying between the highlands southwest from Lake Superior and the Mississippi river."

A very interesting monograph, entitled "The Wild Rice Gatherers of the Upper Lakes," was contributed by Prof. Albert E. Jenks in the Nineteenth Annual Report of the Bureau of American Ethnology, for 1897-98, published in 1900, forming its pages 1013-1137, illustrated with thirteen plates. Derived mainly from that elaborate work, a summary notice of the wild rice and its use by the Ojibways was given by Prof. N. H. Winchell, in part as follows. "The plant is an annual, springing from seed every year, growing in lakes and slow-flowing streams which have a mud-alluvial bottom. The grain is from about a half an inch to nearly an inch in length, cylindrical, dark slate color when ripe, and is embraced in glumes, or husks, arranged in an appressed panicle at the top of the long stem. . . . Its leaves are broad (for a grass) and numerous. Its botanical name in *Zizania aquatica*. The fruit is ripe in September. While it is perpetual when once established in favorable situations, it becomes necessary to sow it artificially when it is destructively gathered either by wild fowl or by Indians. . . . In August the green, standing, rice stalks are tied into bunches by the women. This is for protecting the grain from injury and loss by water-fowl as well as by winds, and also to facilitate the subsequent harvesting. The twine used is the pliable inner bark of the basswood. . . . Much rice is gathered, however, without previous tying. When it is ripe it is gathered in canoes which are pushed through the rice-field, one woman acting as canoeman and the other as harvester. The stalks, whether tied in bundles or not, are bent over the gunwale and beaten with a stick so as to dislodge the grain. As the fruit is easily loosened, whether by the wind or by birds, as well as by handling, it is necessary to gather it just before maturity, and subsequently subject it to a process of drying and ripening." (The Aborigines of Minnesota, 1911, pages 592-4.)

About 10,000 bushels of wild rice were formerly harvested yearly by the Ojibways in northern Minnesota, being an average of a bushel or more for each of the population. Since many have adopted in later years the ways of civilization, making farms and permanent homes on the White Earth reservation, the amount of wild rice used is much diminished. Its salable value, as partly purchased by white people, is five to ten cents per pound, or from three to six dollars per bushel.

Rev. Joseph A. Gilfillan, in his paper on "The Ojibways in Minnesota" (M. H. S. Collections, vol. IX, 1901, pp. 55-128), presented a vivid description of the gathering of wild rice, as seen at a large rice lake in the north part of this reservation.

Townships and Villages.

Information of the origins and meanings of names in this county was received from Alfred Aamoth, auditor, and Arthur J. Andersen, treasurer, during a visit at Mahnomen, the county seat, in September, 1909; and from John W. Carl, auditor, and Martin M. Bowman, clerk of the court, in a second visit there in September, 1916.

BEAULIEU township and village were named for Henry and John Beaulieu, who served in the civil war and afterward owned farms here.

MAHNOMEN COUNTY 323

John Beaulieu was during many years the village postmaster. Records of the Beaulieu family and allied families, prominent in the history of the Ojibways in this state, descendants of a French fur trader, Bazille Beaulieu, and his Ojibway wife, "Queen of the Skies," are given by Winchell in "The Aborigines of Minnesota," page 722.

BEJOU township and its railway village received this name, changed in pronunciation and spelling, from the French words, Bon jour ("Good day"), of the former fur traders and voyageurs. It is the common Ojibway salutation on meeting friends or even strangers, used like the familiar English and American greeting, "How do you do?"

CHIEF township was named in honor of May-sha-ke-ge-shig (also spelled Me-sha-ki-gi-zhig), the principal chief of the Ojibways on the White Earth Reservation, described by Winchell as "a man revered for many noble qualities and for his distinguished presence." He died "nearly 100 years old," August 29, 1919, at the Old Folks Home in Beaulieu; had lived as a farmer on this reservation since 1868.

GREGORY was named for Joseph Gregory, an early farmer here, who was one of the first taking an allotment of land in this township.

HEIER township commemorates Frank Heier, who was teacher of an Ojibway school in this township, and later was superintendent of the government school at Pine Point, Becker county, near the southeast corner of the White Earth Reservation.

ISLAND LAKE township has a large lake of this name, containing an island of many acres.

LAGARDE township was named for Moses Lagarde, who served in the civil war, received a farm allotment here, and was owner of a hotel in Beaulieu village.

LAKE GROVE township is mostly a broadly undulating and rolling prairie, but has several small lakes bordered with groves.

MAHNOMEN, the county seat, is a railway village close north of the Wild Rice river, whence came this Ojibway name, later given to the county.

MARSH CREEK township bears the name of the creek flowing across it.

PEMBINA township, like Pembina river and county in North Dakota, is named from the bush cranberry, excellent for making sauce and pies, called by the Ojibways nepin ninan, summer berry. The Ojibway words were transformed into this name by the French voyageurs and traders.

POPPLE GROVE township has mainly a prairie surface, interspersed with occasional groves of the common small poplar, often mispronounced as in this name.

ROSEDALE township, consisting partly of prairie and partly of woodland, was named for its plentiful wild roses.

SCHNEIDER LAKE township has a lake of this name, beside which Frank Schneider, a German married to an Ojibway, formerly lived as a farmer, but later removed to Waubun village.

TWIN LAKES township is named for its two lakes, separated by a narrow strip of land with a road.

WAUBUN, a railway village, has an Ojibway name, meaning the east, the morning, and the twilight of dawn. It is spelled waban in Baraga's Dictionary, and wabun by Longfellow in "The Song of Hiawatha," with definition as the east wind. Another spelling of this name is borne by Waupun, a city in eastern Wisconsin.

LAKES AND STREAMS.

The foregoing pages have sufficiently noticed the White Earth and Wild Rice rivers, Island lake, Marsh creek, Schneider lake, and the Twin lakes.

The origins of the names of White Earth and Tulaby lakes, crossed by the south line of this county, are given in the chapter for Becker county.

Numerous other lakes are to be here listed, in the order of townships from south to north and of ranges from east to west; but many lakes of relatively small size are yet unnamed.

Big Bass lake was named for its fish, and Little Elbow lake for its bent form.

Simon lake, crossed by the middle part of the east boundary of the county, commemorates Simon Roy, who had a cattle farm there and died many years ago, leaving several sons yet living in the White Earth Reservation.

Lake Erie is in section 7, Lagarde. Why it received this name remains to be learned.

Rosedale has Gardner, Sandy, and Fish lakes. The first was named for Charles Gardner, who was a log driver on the Snake and Pine rivers and later was a successful farmer at this lake.

Lone lake is two miles north of Simon lake, and Washington lake lies four miles northwest of Lone lake, being close north of Wild Rice river.

Aspinwall, Vanoss, and Warren lakes, in Chief township, were named respectively for Henry Aspinwall, a farmer beside the lake of his name, Francis Vanoss, of Canadian French and Ojibway descent, who in his old age took a land allotment, and Budd Warren, a nephew of William W. Warren, the historian of the Ojibways. This township also has Chief lake, named, like the township, for the Ojibway chief.

Sugar Bush lake, in section 7, Island Lake township, received its name from its maple trees used for sugar-making.

Gregory township has Lake Beaulieu and Church lake. The first was named for Alexander H. Beaulieu, who long ago was allotted land there, which he farmed until 1916, then removing to Fosston. Church lake was named for Charles Church, an American farmer there, having an Ojibway wife.

Tamarack lake, in section 29, Bejou, is partly bordered by tamarack woods. Sand Hill river, flowing through the northwest part of this township, is named from the dunes or wind-blown sand hills of its delta, in Polk county, which was deposited at the highest stage of the Glacial Lake Agassiz.

WHITE EARTH RESERVATION.

Because Mahnomen county is wholly included within this Reservation, special attention should be here directed to the concise notice of its name and date before given for Becker county, in which are the Reservation Agency, at White Earth, and the lake whence the name is taken. It is the largest of the several Ojibway reservations that remain in this state, having an area of thirty-two townships. Aside from its many lakes, mostly of small size, it has space for about 4,000 farms like the usual homestead of white settlers, measuring 160 acres or a quarter of a section in the government survey.

The Ojibway name of the White Earth lake, which is retained in its translation, being given also to the Reservation, is noted on page 31 of the Becker county chapter.

The White Earth reservation was established by a treaty at Washington, March 19, 1867. In the summer of the next year many Ojibways of the Mississippi and Gull Lake bands, led respectively by their chiefs, Wa-bon-a-quot (White Cloud) and Na-bun-ash-kong, removed there. June 14, 1868, was the day of arrival of the pioneers in the removal, and its anniversary is celebrated at White Earth each year. Twelve townships in Becker county, the entire sixteen townships of Mahnomen county, and the next four of Range 38 in Clearwater county, are included in the reservation area, being as fertile farming land as is found in any part of Minnesota.

MARSHALL COUNTY

This county, established February 25, 1879, was named in honor of William Rainey Marshall, governor of Minnesota. He was born near Columbia, Missouri, October 17, 1825; but his boyhood was spent in Quincy, Illinois, to which place his parents removed in 1830. At the age of fifteen years, in company with his older brother Joseph, he went to the lead mines of Galena, where he worked several years and learned land surveying.

In 1847 he came to St. Croix Falls, Wisconsin, and in 1849 to Minnesota, settling at St. Anthony Falls and opening a general hardware business, with his brother Joseph. For Franklin Steele and others he surveyed the St. Anthony Falls townsite, his plat being dated October 9, 1849. Two years later he removed to St. Paul, which thenceforward was his home, and became its pioneer hardware merchant. In 1855 he founded a banking business, which failed in the financial panic of 1857; and subsequently he engaged in farming and stock-raising, and brought to Minnesota its earliest high-bred cattle.

Marshall was commissioned in August, 1862, as lieutenant colonel of the Seventh Minnesota regiment; aided in the suppression of the Sioux outbreak, and in the expedition of 1863 against the Sioux in North Dakota; and afterward served through the civil war in the South, being promoted colonel of his regiment in November, 1863, and brevetted brigadier general March 13, 1865. He was governor of Minnesota during two terms, 1866-70, being "one of the best chief magistrates the state has ever had." In 1876-82 he served as the state railroad commissioner.

In 1893 he was elected secretary of the Minnesota Historical Society, of which he had been president in 1868; but he resigned in 1894, on account of ill health, and went in hope of recovery to Pasadena, California, where he died January 8, 1896. An obituary sketch, by Rev. Edward C. Mitchell, was published in the eighth volume of this society's Historical Collections (1898, pages 506-510, with a portrait); and the thirteenth volume of this series, "Lives of the Governors of Minnesota," by General James H. Baker, published in 1908, has a more extended biography (pages 145-165, with a portrait), including extracts from his addresses and messages as governor.

Townships and Villages.

Information of the origins of names was received from "History of the Red River Valley," two volumes, 1909, having pages 831-859 for this county; from August G. Lundgren, county auditor, and Peter Holan, deputy auditor, John P. Mattson, editor of the Warren Sheaf, and Hon.

MARSHALL COUNTY 327

Andrew Grindeland, district judge, each being interviewed during a visit at Warren, the county seat, in August, 1909; and again from Mr. Lundgren, also from Alfred C. Swandby, clerk of the court, R. C. Mathwig, Albert P. McIntyre, and Charles L. Stevens, editor of the Warren Register, during a second visit there in September, 1916.

AGDER township, organized in 1902, has the name of a district in southern Norway, southwest of Christiania.

ALMA, organized in 1882, was named for Alma Dahlgren, the first child born in this township, daughter of Peter O. Dahlgren, who during several years was the county treasurer.

ALVARADO, a railway village in Vega township, has the name of a seaport and river in Mexico, about forty miles southeast of Vera Cruz. It is also the name of a small city in Texas, and of villages in Indiana and California.

ARGYLE, a large railway village in Middle River township, bears the name of a county in western Scotland, which is borne also by a township in Maine and by villages in nine other states. This name was proposed by Hon. S. G. Comstock, for whom a township of this county is named.

AUGSBURG township, organized in 1884, was named by its Lutheran people for the ancient city of Augsburg in Bavaria, Germany. The chief Lutheran creed, called the Augsburg confession, was submitted to the Diet of Augsburg in 1530; and a treaty was made there between the Lutheran and Catholic states of Germany, September 25, 1555, which secured the triumph of the Reformation by granting authority for the separate states to prescribe the form of worship within their limits.

BIG WOODS township, organized in 1882, has a wide border of timber along the Red river.

BLOOMER township, also organized in 1882, received its name from the village of Bloomer in Chippewa county, Wisconsin, whence some of its settlers came.

BOXVILLE township, organized in 1884, was named for William N. Box, an early homesteader there, who removed to Northfield, Minn., and later to the Pacific coast.

CEDAR township, organized in 1892, has groves of the arbor vitae, more often called white cedar.

COMO township, organized in 1900, received its name from Lake Como in St. Paul, as probably proposed by George F. Whitcomb, a land owner here who lived in that city. Seven states of the Union have villages of this name, derived from the Italian city and province and their mountain-bordered lake so named at the south side of the Alps.

COMSTOCK township, organized in 1881, was named in honor of Solomon G. Comstock, an attorney for the Great Northern railway company, who named the village of Argyle. He was born in Argyle, Maine, May 9, 1842; came to Minnesota in 1869, settling in Moorhead; was admitted to practice law in 1871; was a representative in the state legislature, 1876-7 and 1879-81; a state senator, 1883-7; and a representative in Congress, 1889-91.

DONNELLY township, organized in 1895, commemorates Ignatius Donnelly, who was born in Philadelphia, November 3, 1831, and died in Minneapolis, January 1, 1901. He was admitted to practice law in his native city; came to Minnesota in 1857; was lieutenant governor, 1860-3, and a representative in Congress, 1863-9; later served several terms in the state legislature, and was a national leader in the Farmers' Alliance movement, and in the Populist party; author of many published speeches and addresses, and of numerous books. He lived many years at Nininger, a few miles west of Hastings, and was often called "the Sage of Nininger."

EAGLE POINT, organized in 1890, was named from an eagle's nest near the center of this township, at a point of the woods which reached eastward from the Red river.

EAST PARK, organized in 1899, is the second township east of Nelson Park, previously organized, whence this name was suggested.

EAST VALLEY township, organized in 1896, crossed by the Thief river, had settlers from the earlier West Valley township on the Middle river.

ECKVOLL township, organized in 1901, received this Norwegian name, meaning "Oak Vale," in allusion to its abundant oak groves. It was proposed by Nels K. Nelson, previously a resident of Warren, being taken from a former Eckvoll post office in Oak Park township.

ESPELEE township, organized in 1903, is likewise named from Norwegian words, meaning "Poplar Slope," for its many groves of poplars.

EXCEL township, organized in 1884, was named from the village and township of Excelsior in Hennepin county, being shortened to avoid exact repetition of that name, which was taken from the well known poem entitled "Excelsior," written by Longfellow in 1841.

FOLDAHL, organized in 1883, is named for a locality in Norway, the country from which most of the settlers in this township came.

FORK township, organized in 1896, was so named because the Red river receives the Snake river at its west side. Boatmen ascending the Red river may here take either one of two routes, like prongs or tines of a fork.

GRAND PLAIN township, organized in 1898, is in the nearly level and plainlike east part of the county.

HOLT township, organized in 1890, and its railway village, were named in honor of a pioneer Norwegian settler. This is an ancient Anglo-Saxon and Scandinavian word, meaning a grove or a wooded hill.

HUNTLEY township, organized in 1902, having been a noted hunting ground for moose, was at first called Huntsville, which was changed because an earlier township in Polk county had received that name.

LINCOLN township, organized in 1892, was named in honor of the martyr president of the United States in the civil war.

LINSELL, the most northeastern township of this county and one of the latest organized, in 1908, was named by its Swedish people for the town of Linsell in central Sweden.

MCCREA township, organized in 1882, was named for Hon. Andrew McCrea, farmer and lumberman, who had land interests in this county, and whose sons were residents of Warren during many years, thence removing to the west. He was born in New Brunswick in 1831; came to St. Paul in 1854; afterward lived in Colorado and other states, but in 1870 settled in Perham, Minn.; was a representative in the legislature in 1877, and a state senator in 1879.

MARSH GROVE township, organized in 1884, formerly had numerous marshes and poplar groves, now mostly changed to well cultivated farms.

MIDDLE RIVER township, the earliest organized in this county, October 14, 1879, and the railway village of this name, in Spruce Valley township, are on the stream so named, which flows through the central and western part of this county, being tributary to the Snake river near its mouth.

MOOSE RIVER township, organized in 1904, took the name of its river, flowing into Thief lake.

MOYLAN township, organized in 1902, was named for Patrick Moylan, an Irish settler, who removed to Oregon or Washington.

MUD LAKE township, organized in 1914, includes the east half of the area of Mud lake, tributary to Thief river, now mainly drained.

NELSON PARK township, organized in 1884, was named for James Nelson, a Yankee hunter and trapper, who was its earliest homesteader, and for several other settlers named Nelson, immigrants from Sweden and Norway.

NEW FOLDEN township, organized in 1884, and its railway village, received their name from a seaport in northern Norway, on the south branch of the Folden fjord.

NEW MAINE township, organized in 1900, was named in compliment to settlers from the state of Maine.

NEW SOLUM township organized in 1884, is named for a district in Norway.

OAK PARK township, organized in 1883, has many oaks in its woods bordering the Red river. The name of a discontinued post office of this township, Eckvoll, meaning "Oak Vale," was transferred, as before noted, to a township in the east part of this county.

OSLO, the railway village of Oak Park, bears the name of a large medieval city which occupied the site of Christiania, Norway. The old city was mostly burned in 1547 and again in 1624, and the new city was founded and named at the later date by Christian IV, king of Denmark and Norway.

PARKER township, organized in 1884, was named for George L. Parker, a pioneer settler there, who after several years moved away.

RADIUM is a small village of the Soo railway in Comstock township, named for the very wonderful metallic element, radium, discovered in 1902; and ROSEWOOD is another station of the Soo railway, in New Solum.

ROLLIS, organized in 1899, was named for Otto Rollis, formerly of Warren, who became a storekeeper in this township, but later removed to Colorado.

SINNOTT township, organized in 1883, had two settlers of this name, J. P. Sinnott in section 8 and P. J. Sinnott in section 20.

SPRUCE VALLEY township, organized in 1888, is named for its spruce trees along the Middle river, which are common or abundant throughout northeastern Minnesota, but here reach their southwestern limit.

STEPHEN, a village of the Great Northern railway in Tamarac township and close north of Tamarac river, was named in honor of George Stephen, a prominent financial associate of James J. Hill in the building of this railway system. He was born at Dufftown, in Banffshire, Scotland, June 5, 1829; came to Canada in 1850, settling in Montreal, and engaged in dry goods business and manufacturing cloth; was president of the Bank of Montreal, 1876-81, and president of the Canadian Pacific railway company, 1881-87; was knighted by Queen Victoria in 1886; was a founder in 1887, with Sir Donald Smith, of the Royal Victoria Hospital, Montreal; removed to England in 1888, and has since resided in London. In 1891 he received the title of Baron Mount Stephen, referring to a peak of the Rocky mountains named for him during the construction of the Canadian Pacific railway.

STRANDQUIST, a Soo railway village in Lincoln township, was named in honor of J. E. Strandquist, a merchant there, who was born in Sweden in 1870 and settled in this county in 1892.

TAMARAC township, organized in 1879, received its name from the Tamarac river, here crossed by the Great Northern railway.

THIEF LAKE township, organized in 1896, is named for its large lake, the source of the Thief river. The origin of these names, related by Warren in the "History of the Ojibways," is given in the chapter for Pennington county, which has its county seat at Thief River Falls.

VALLEY township, organized in 1900, is crossed by Mud river or creek, tributary to Mud lake by a valley scarcely below the general level.

VEGA township, organized in 1883, bears the name of the ship in which Baron Nordenskjöld, the Swedish explorer, in 1878-9 traversed the Arctic ocean along the north coast of Russia and Siberia, passed through Bering strait to the Pacific, and returned around Asia and through the Suez canal.

VELDT township, organized in 1902, was at first called Roosevelt, for the president of the United States. Because that name had been earlier given to another township of Minnesota, it was changed to this Dutch word, used in South Africa, meaning "a prairie or a thinly wooded tract."

VIKING township, organized in 1884, was named by Rev. Hans P. Hansen, a Norwegian Lutheran pastor in Warren. This Scandinavian word, often translated as a sea king, more correctly denoted any member of the early medieval pirate crews of Northmen who during several centuries ravaged the coasts of western and southern Europe.

WANGER township, organized in 1882, was named for a German hunter and trapper who lived there before the coming of agricultural settlers.

WARREN, the county seat, platted in 1879-80, incorporated as a village in 1883, and as a city April 3, 1891, was named in honor of Charles H. Warren, general passenger agent of the St. Paul, Minneapolis and Manitoba railway company, which in 1890 was renamed the Great Northern company. The railway was built to the site of Warren in the summer of 1878, and in November of that year trains ran through to Winnipeg.

WARRENTON township, organized in 1879, has a name of the same origin as the city of Warren, which is at its southeast corner.

WEST VALLEY township, organized in 1884, is named from the Middle river, which here is inclosed by low bluffs.

WHITEFORD township, organized in 1910, has a name that is borne also by small villages in Maryland and Michigan.

WRIGHT township, organized in 1884, probably received this name in honor of one of its first settlers.

STREAMS AND LAKES.

Middle river was named by the fur traders, whose trains of Red river carts crossed it on the old Pembina trail about halfway between Pembina and their crossing of the Red Lake river.

Snake river is translated from its Ojibway name, written by Gilfillan as Ginebigo zibi.

Tamarac river is also noted by him as a similar translation, from Gamushkigwatigoka zibi. Tamarack is elsewhere the common spelling for the tree and geographic names derived from it.

In the place of these three streams, only one is found on the map of Long's expedition in 1823, named Swamp creek, where the present Tamarac ditch in Donnelly and Eagle Point townships carries to the Red river the drainage of a large swamp area, in which Tamarac river was formerly lost, thence emerging northward and joining the Red river in the southwest part of Kittson county. Swamp creek, translated from the Ojibway name of Tamarac river, was copied on Nicollet's map in 1843 and on the map of Minnesota Territory in 1850; but the state map of 1860 has the present Tamarac, Middle, and Snake rivers, although their courses are erroneously drawn.

Preceding pages have noticed Moose river, Thief lake and river, and Mud river and lake, whence three townships are named.

Green Stump lake and Elm lake, each shallow and drained for use as farm lands, were respectively about one mile and three miles southwest of Mud lake, which, as before noted, is also mainly drained.

Whiteford has two little lakes, about midway between Thief and Mud lakes, of which the eastern one is named Olson lake.

Marshall county is wholly in the area of the Glacial Lake Agassiz.

MARTIN COUNTY

This county was established May 23, 1857, being named, according to the concurrent testimony of its best informed early citizens yet living, in honor of Henry Martin, of Wallingford, Conn., who then was a resident of Mankato, having land interests here and probably expecting to live permanently in Minnesota. He was born in Meriden, Conn., February 14, 1829; went to California in 1849, and engaged in auction business in San Francisco until 1851; returned to Connecticut, and was state bank commissioner, 1854-56; came to Minnesota in 1856, and selected and purchased, for eastern associates and himself, about 2,000 acres of lands in Mower, Fillmore, and other counties, including the area, then in Brown county, which in 1857 was set apart as Martin county; resided temporarily in Mankato, and visited the chains of lakes in this county for hunting and fishing, one of which, Martin lake in the northwest corner of Rutland township, was named for him. Beside this lake he built a house, and partly planned to settle here. Within about one year he returned to Wallingford, Conn., where his family had continuously resided, and that town was ever afterward his home. He engaged in manufacturing there, was deputy sheriff of New Haven county, 1884-87, and after 1895 was assistant town clerk. (These biographic notes are in a letter and personal sketch received from him in 1905.) He died in Wallingford, July 18, 1908, in the home to which he brought his bride in 1853.

Members of the Territorial legislature, who passed the act establishing Martin county, may have been partly influenced in favor of this name by remembering that Morgan Lewis Martin, of Green Bay, Wis., as delegate in Congress from Wisconsin Territory, on December 23, 1846, introduced the bill for the organization of the Territory of Minnesota. He was born in Martinsburg, Lewis county, N. Y., March 21, 1805; was graduated at Hamilton College, 1824; came to Green Bay in 1827, and during his long life resided there, being, as a lawyer and judge, prominently identified with the history of his state. He died December 10, 1887. An autobiographic narrative by him, with notes by R. G. Thwaites, was published in the Wisconsin Historical Society Collections, vol. XI, 1888, pages 380-415; and his portrait is given in vol. IX of that series, facing page 397.

The honor of the county name, ascribed to Henry Martin by William H. Budd (History, page 114), was again so stated, with historical details given by George S. Fowler, in an article published by the Martin County Sentinel, July 15, 1904. Two weeks later, a second article on this subject, by A. N. Fancher, presented the rival claim that the honor belongs in an equal or larger degree to Morgan L. Martin.

MARTIN COUNTY

TOWNSHIPS AND VILLAGES.

Information of geographic names has been gathered from "History of Martin County," by William H. Budd, published in 1897, 124 pages; from George S. Fowler and Christian N. Peterson, interviewed during a visit at Fairmont, the county seat, in October, 1910; and from R. M. Tyler, clerk of the probate court, Hon. Albert L. Ward, state senator, Hon. Frank A. Day, and Miss Minnie Bird, librarian, during a second visit at Fairmont, in July, 1916.

CEDAR township, established January 2, 1872, was named for Cedar lake, at its east side, which has red cedar trees on its shores.

CENTER CREEK township bears the name of the creek flowing through it from the Central Chain of lakes.

CEYLON, a railway village in Lake Belt township, has the name of a large island adjoining India. It is also the name of villages in Pennsylvania and Ohio.

DUNNELL, the railway village of Lake Fremont township, was named in honor of Mark H. Dunnell, congressman, who was born in Buxton, Maine, July 2, 1823, and died in Owatonna, Minn., August 9, 1904. He was graduated at Waterville college in 1849, and was admitted to practice law in 1856; was appointed United States consul to Vera Cruz in 1861; came to Minnesota in 1865, settling at Winona, and later removed to Owatonna; was a representative in the legislature in 1867; state superintendent of public instruction, 1868-71; and a member of Congress, 1871-83, and again in 1889-91.

EAST CHAIN township was named for the East Chain of lakes, described in the later part of this chapter.

ELM CREEK township, established in March, 1867, is crossed by the creek of this name, which flows through the north half of the county, having many elms in the woods along its course.

FAIRMONT, the county seat, platted as a village in October, 1857, from which the township also took this name, was incorporated February 28, 1878, and adopted its city charter in 1902. It was at first called Fair Mount, referring to its situation beside and above the Central Chain of lakes, having a fine outlook across the lakes and the adjoining county.

Fox LAKE township, established January 2, 1872, is named for the long and narrow lake at its south side, which also gave this name to the railway village at its east end, platted in 1899.

FRASER township was named in honor of Abraham N. Fraser, who took one of its first homestead claims, on Elm creek.

GALENA township was named by settlers from the city of Galena in Illinois, which received this name from mines of galena, a lead ore.

GRANADA, the railway village of Center Creek township, bears the name of a renowned medieval Moorish city and kingdom in Spain.

IMOGEN, a railway village in Pleasant Prairie township, platted in 1900, has the name of the daughter of Cymbeline, in one of the Shakespearean plays.

JAY township, established January 2, 1872, has the name of a county in Indiana, and of villages and townships in Maine, Vermont, and New York, commemorating John Jay (b. 1745, d. 1829), who was an eminent statesman of the American Revolution, first chief justice of the United States supreme court, 1789-95, and governor of New York, 1795-1801.

LAKE BELT township, established in March, 1867, was named for its series of three lakes, to be again noticed in the later part of this chapter.

LAKE FREMONT township, established January 2, 1872, formerly had a small lake, now drained, in the west part of section 34, which was named in honor of John C. Fremont (b. 1813, d. 1890), assistant with Nicollet in his expedition through this region in 1838. He was later called "the Pathfinder," from explorations of the Rocky mountains and the Pacific slope in 1842-45, and was the Republican candidate for the presidency of the United States in 1856.

MANYASKA township bears a Sioux name, given to lakes of this vicinity on Nicollet's map, probably meaning white bank or bluff, but to be then more correctly spelled mayaska. It has been otherwise translated as "white iron" or silver, from maza, iron, ska, white. This name is also borne by a lake in section 19, and by a railway station.

MONTEREY, a railway village on the south line of Galena, has a Spanish name, meaning "king mountain," from the city of Monterey in Mexico, captured September 24, 1846, after severe fighting, by the United States army under General Zachary Taylor. Thence a city and county in California are also named, and villages in fifteen other states.

NASHVILLE was named in honor of A. M. Nash, a pioneer farmer, at whose home this township was organized, May 3, 1864.

NORTHROP, a railway village in Rutland, platted in 1899, was named in honor of Cyrus Northrop, who was born in Ridgefield, Conn., Sept. 30, 1834; was professor of rhetoric and English literature in Yale University, 1863-84; and was president of the University of Minnesota, 1884-1911.

ORMSBY is a railway village on the north line of Galena.

PLEASANT PRAIRIE township, organized March 7, 1865, has a euphoniously descriptive name, chosen by its settlers.

ROLLING GREEN township bears a name similarly chosen, for its undulating and rolling contour of the green and far-viewing prairie.

RUTLAND township was named, on the suggestion of one of its early settlers, Amasa Bowen, register of deeds, for the city and county of Rutland in Vermont.

SHERBURN, a railway village and junction, was named in honor of the wife of an officer of the Chicago, Milwaukee and St. Paul railway company, living in McGregor, Iowa.

SILVER LAKE township has the South and North Silver lakes in the Central Chain.

TENHASSEN township, established March 7, 1865, received this Sioux name, changed in form, from the "Tchan Hassan lakes," mapped in this vicinity by Nicollet. More correctly spelled, it is the name of Chanhassen township in Carver county, meaning the sugar maple, from chan, tree, and hassen, related to haza, huckleberry or blueberry, thus denoting "the tree of sweet juice."

TRIUMPH, a railway village platted in 1899, on the line between Galena and Fox Lake townships, was named by John Stein, in compliment for the Triumph Creamery company.

TRUMAN, a railway village in Westford, platted in 1899, was named for Truman Clark, a son of J. T. Clark, who was then the second vice president of the Chicago, St. Paul, Minneapolis and Omaha railway company. Several families named True live near this village.

WAVERLY township was named by a pioneer settler, from the large village of Waverly in Tioga county, New York.

WELCOME, a railway village eight miles west of Fairmont, was named in honor of Alfred M. Welcome, whose farm lies at its southwest side.

WESTFORD township has a name that is borne also by villages and townships in Vermont, Massachusetts, Connecticut, New York, Pennsylvania, and Wisconsin.

CHAINS OF LAKES.

Three remarkable series of lakes in this county, named the East, Central, and West chains, are of great interest in glacial geology, because they give evidence of a prolonged warm or temperate interglacial stage or epoch, preceded and followed by long stages of severe cold, when the continental ice-sheet covered this area and extended far to the south.

The East chain extends in a somewhat irregular northerly course for 12 miles from the Iowa line, with outflow northeastward by South creek. This chain comprises eight lakes, varying from a half mile to two miles in length, with a half to two-thirds as great widths. The lakes are bordered by rolling areas of till, to which their shores ascend 30-40 feet, mostly by quite steep slopes. Between the lakes are, in some cases, marshes as wide as the narrower parts of the lakes; but some of the adjoining lakes are connected by contracted channels, such as may have been cut by the outflowing stream. Thus the series does not occupy depressions in any well-marked continuous valley.

About 20 lakes form the Central chain, which extends 22 miles in an almost perfectly straight course from south to north, lying three to six miles west of the East chain. Its outlets are South, Center, Elm and Perch creeks, all flowing eastward. The shores and the country on both sides consist of till, which rises to a moderately undulating expanse 30 to 40 or 50 feet above the lakes. Though forming a very distinct, straight series, these lakes do not occupy a well-defined valley, for its width varies from one mile or more to less than an eighth of a mile, and it is interrupted in three places by water-divides, their lowest points being 10 to 15 feet above the adjoining lakes.

The West chain is less distinctly connected than the East and Central chains, from which it also differs in having the longer axes of some of its lakes transverse to the course of the chain, and in having shorter series of lakes joined with it as branches. Tuttle lake at the south end of the chain lies on the state line, about four miles west of Iowa lake, the south end of the Central chain. Thence the West chain reaches 20 miles northwesterly, then nine miles northerly, and then northwest and west for eight miles to Mountain lake in Cottonwood county, its whole extent being 37 miles. Its successive portions from south to north are tributary to the East fork of Des Moines river, to Center and Elm creeks, and to the South fork of Watonwan river. This West chain comprises about 25 lakes, extending through a region of undulating till, the direct deposit of the ice-sheet, with no noteworthy areas nor unusually thick included layers of water-deposited gravel and sand, as is true of all this county.

A series of three lakes in Lake Belt township lies somewhat west of the direct course of the West chain, and may be regarded as a branch of it; and three miles east of this lake belt, another series of seven lakes, very plainly a branch of the West chain, diverges from it, and reaches almost due north 12 miles from Tuttle and Alton lakes. To these, as a continuation of the same branch, ought perhaps to be added four other lakes, which are situated four to nine miles farther north.

The explanation of these series of lakes which appears most probable is that they mark interglacial avenues of southward drainage and occupy portions of valleys that were excavated in the till after ice had long covered this region and had deposited most of the drift sheet, but before the later Glacial stage or epoch again enveloped this area beneath a lobe of the continental glacier, partially refilling these valleys, and leaving along their courses the present chains of lakes.

In the order from north to south, the East chain includes Lone Tree lake, named for a tall cottonwood tree beside it, which was a landmark for travelers; Lake Imogene, whence the neighboring railway village was named; Rose lake, having many roses along its shores; Sager lake, named for a pioneer settler; and Clear lake and East Chain lake. This chain also has two lakes of small size that are mapped without names.

In the same order, the Central chain has Perch lake, outflowing northward by Perch creek; Murphy lake, named for John Murphy, an early Irish homesteader; Martin lake, named for Henry Martin, as before noted; High lake, Lake Charlotte, Twin lakes, Canright lake, and Buffalo lake, in Rutland, the last being named for its buffalo fish; Lake George, named for George Tanner, a settler there in the north edge of the present city of Fairmont; Lake Sisseton, bearing the name of a tribal division of the Sioux, this region being noted on Nicollet's map as the "Sissiton Country;" Budd lake, named in honor of William H. Budd, historian of the county, who took a land claim here in July, 1856; Hall lake, commemorating E. Banks Hall, who also came in the summer of 1856; Amber lake, Mud lake, and Bardwell and Wilmert lakes; North and South Silver lakes, the former also called Summit lake; and Iowa lake, crossed by the Iowa line.

MARTIN COUNTY 337

The West chain comprises in this county, besides several nameless small lakes, Fish, Buffalo, and North lakes, the second named for the buffalo fish; Cedar lake, which gave the name of a township; Big Twin lakes, the smaller one of which has been drained; Seymour and McGowan lakes, the latter now dry, named respectively for W. S. Seymour and Daniel McGowan, pioneers; Fox lake, naming a township; Temperance lake, Munger lake, now drained, named for Perry Munger, an early farmer, and Manyaska and Prairie lakes, the latter lately drained, in Manyaska township; Smith lake, formerly called Goose lake, and Holmes lake, each recently drained, on the north line of Lake Belt; and Alton or Inlet lake and Tuttle lake, in Tenhassen. The last, crossed by the state line, is named in honor of Calvin Tuttle, one of the earliest settlers in Martin county, who came in March, 1856. This lake was called Okamanpidan lake on Nicollet's map, a Sioux name referring to its nests of herons.

A western branch of the West chain, before noted, giving the name of Lake Belt township, consists of Susan, Fish, and Clear lakes.

Between the Central and West chains, a longer but less continuous branch of the latter includes, with several small lakes unnamed and several lately drained, Long and Round lakes in Waverly; Patten lake in section 25, Galena, and Creek lake on Elm creek, crossed by the south line of section 36; Eagle and Swan lakes, in Fraser; Pierce and Mud lakes, in Rolling Green; and a second Mud lake or Rice lake, Babcock or Bright lake, and Clayton lake, in Tenhassen.

OTHER LAKES AND STREAMS.

Only a few lakes and fewer streams remain to be noted, in addition to the chains of lakes and the streams outflowing from them.

Burnt Out lake, adjoining a burned peat bed, in sections 21 and 28, East Chain, was formerly called Calkins lake, for pioneer farmers of this name at its east side. Ash lake, shown by early maps in sections 26 and 27 of this township, has been drained.

Timber lake or marsh, mostly in section 2, Rolling Green, is named for its grove.

The head stream of the East fork of the Des Moines, flowing across Jay and Lake Belt townships, and through Alton lake to Tuttle lake, has given to the former of these lakes a second name, Inlet lake.

Lily creek, having water lilies, is the outlet of Fox lake, flowing east into Swan and Eagle lakes.

Clam lake is in sections 15 and 16, Fox Lake township.

Badger lake, shallow and to be drained, in sections 17 to 20, Galena, now crossed by a road, was named for its badgers, formerly frequent here, but more common in Wisconsin, "the Badger State."

Duck lake, once noted for its wild ducks, in sections 2 and 11, Elm Creek township, and Watkins lake, in sections 8, 9, and 16, have been drained.

MEEKER COUNTY

Established February 23, 1856, this county was named in honor of Bradley B. Meeker, of Minneapolis, who was an associate justice of the Minnesota supreme court from 1849 to 1853. He was born in Fairfield, Conn., March 13, 1813; studied at Yale College; practiced law in Richmond, Ky., 1838 to 1845, and later in Flemingsburg, Ky.; was appointed judge in the new territory of Minnesota in 1849, and presided at the first term of court on the site of Minneapolis, which was held in the old government grist mill on the west side of the river below the falls, August 20, 1849. Judge Meeker was a charter member of the Minnesota Historical Society, 1849; and was one of the first Board of Regents of the University of Minnesota, elected by the Territorial Legislature in 1851. After leaving the bench, he engaged in real estate business and was a member of the constitutional convention, 1857. He purchased a large tract of land on the Mississippi below St. Anthony, including Meeker island and extending eastward; and he foresaw and often spoke of the coming great prosperity of Minneapolis. He died very suddenly in Milwaukee, where he had halted on a journey to the east, February 20, 1873.

TOWNSHIPS AND VILLAGES.

Information of the origin and meaning of names has been gathered from "A Random Historical Sketch of Meeker County," by A. C. Smith, 1877, 161 pages; "Album of History and Biography of Meeker County," 1888, 610 pages; and from Norris Y. Taylor, who during many years was county surveyor, J. W. Wright, who was county superintendent of schools, 1879-87, and a state senator, 1907-09, and William H. Greenleaf, for whom a village and township are named, each being interviewed during a visit at Litchfield, the county seat, in May, 1916.

ACTON, organized in April, 1858, was named for the village of Acton in Ontario, Canada, whence the Ritchie family came to settle in this township in 1857.

CEDAR MILLS township, organized January 25, 1870, received the name of its village founded in 1860, which was named from the large Cedar lake, about two miles distant to the east. This lake has many red cedars on its shores and islands, as noted by its name on Nicollet's map, Rantesha Wita or Red Cedar Island lake.

COLLINWOOD, organized May 8, 1866, bears the name (changed in spelling) of Collingwood, a port on the southern part of Georgian bay in Ontario. This township was at first called New Virginia, but was renamed as now in 1868, taking the name of the village platted in its north-

MEEKER COUNTY 339

east corner by Canadian settlers in 1866, beside Lake Collinwood, which is crossed by its east line.

COSMOS township, organized January 25, 1870, has a name proposed by Daniel Hoyt, one of its first settlers, who came in 1867, was a surveyor, and was elected the first township clerk. It is an ancient Greek word, meaning order, harmony, and thence the universe as an orderly and harmonious system.

DANIELSON, settled in 1857, organized March 12, 1872, was named for Daniel Danielson, its first township clerk and assessor, and for Nels Danielson, an immigrant from Norway, who took a land claim here in 1861 and died in 1870.

DARWIN township, organized April 5, 1858, was then called Rice City, which was changed in 1869 to the name of its railway village, platted in October of that year. It was chosen in honor of E. Darwin Litchfield, of London, England, a principal stockholder and promoter of the St. Paul and Pacific (now the Great Northern) railroad, for whom also, as well as for his wife and his brothers, the village and township of Litchfield were named.

DASSEL township, first settled in 1856, was organized in the fall of 1866 under the name of Swan Lake, from the Big Swan lake in its northeast part; but it was renamed in 1871 for its railway village, platted in 1869, which was incorporated March 4, 1878. The village and township thus commemorate Bernard Dassel, who in 1869 was secretary of the St. Paul and Pacific railroad company.

EDEN VALLEY, a railway village in the north edge of Manannah, platted in 1886, was euphoniously named by officers of the St. Paul, Minneapolis and Sault Ste. Marie railway company.

ELLSWORTH township, first settled in June, 1856, organized September 1, 1868, was named at the suggestion of Jesse V. Branham, Jr., in honor of Ephraim Elmer Ellsworth, colonel of a Zouave regiment from New York city, who soon after the beginning of the civil war was killed in Alexandria, Va., May 24, 1861.

FOREST CITY township, on the west border of the Big Woods, organized April 5, 1858, received the name of its village, platted in the summer of 1857, which was the county seat until the autumn of 1869, being then succeeded by Litchfield.

FOREST PRAIRIE township, consisting mainly of woodland but having a small prairie nearly a mile long in its northwest corner, was organized in the summer of 1867.

GREENLEAF township, settled in 1856 and organized August 27, 1859, was named, like the village on its east border, in section 30, Ellsworth, platted in 1859, in honor of William Henry Greenleaf, one of the founders of the village. He was born in Nunda, N. Y., December 7, 1834; came to Minnesota in 1858, settling here; was county treasurer, 1860-2; county surveyor, 1864-70; and a representative in the legislature, 1871-3. He removed to Litchfield in 1872, where he has since lived, excepting several years, next after 1878, of absence as receiver of the United States land office in Benson.

GROVE CITY, a railway village in the north edge of Acton and adjoining Swede Grove township, was platted in the summer of 1870 and was incorporated February 14, 1878.

HARVEY township, settled in the spring of 1856, organized in 1867, was named for James Harvey, who took a homestead claim here in 1860.

KINGSTON, settled in 1856 and organized April 5, 1858, took the name of its village, platted in the fall of 1857, proposed by George A. Nourse, a lawyer of St. Anthony. Twenty-five other states, and also the Canadian provinces of Ontario and New Brunswick, have villages or cities and townships of this name.

LITCHFIELD township, organized April 5, 1858, was at first named Ness, in honor of Ole Halvorson Ness, one of its original party of Norwegian settlers, who came in July, 1856. It continued to bear that name until its village was platted in 1869 on the St. Paul and Pacific railroad, then being built. By petition of its citizens, the township received the village name, Litchfield, in honor of a family who prominently aided in the construction and financing of the railway, including three brothers, Egbert S., Edwin C., and E. Darwin Litchfield. They were the contractors by whom the line from St. Paul to St. Cloud and Watab was built in 1862 to 1864, and later they aided to provide the means for building this more southern line through Meeker county to Breckenridge. (Life of James J. Hill, by J. G. Pyle, 1917, two volumes.) Partly in appreciation of the honor of the name given to the village and township, generous donations to the Episcopal church here were received from Mrs. E. Darwin Litchfield in London. Another of this family, William B. Litchfield, was in 1869 the general manager of this railroad; and his son, Electus D. Litchfield, was the architect, in 1915-17, of the new building of the St. Paul Public Library and the Hill Reference Library. Litchfield village succeeded Forest City as the county seat in the fall of 1869, and was incorporated February 29, 1872.

MANANNAH township, organized October 13, 1857, took the name of its early village, which was platted and named by Ziba Caswell and J. W. Walker in December, 1856. "Search in an old Scottish history gave them the name of Manannah." (Album of History, 1888, p. 554.) The present village of this name was platted in 1871.

SWEDE GROVE township, organized March 15, 1868, bears the name of a post office established there in 1864, referring to its many Swedish settlers and the frequent tracts of woodland.

UNION GROVE township, settled in 1856 and organized April 18, 1866, received its name from the grove where a union church had been built, this name for the settlement being proposed by Lyman Allen, one of its pioneer farmers, who came from Massachusetts in 1856 and returned there in 1860.

WATKINS, a railway village in Forest Prairie township, was named by officers of the Soo railway company.

LAKES AND STREAMS.

The foregoing pages have noticed Cedar lake, crossed by the south line of Ellsworth, which gave a part of the name of Cedar Mills township; Collinwood lake, adjoining the township of this name; and Big Swan lake, whence Dassel township was originally named.

Crow river, having its North, Middle, and South forks in Meeker county, is considered in the first chapter, treating of rivers and lakes that belong partly to several counties.

In the order of the townships from south to north, and of the ranges from east to west, this county has the following many lakes and creeks.

The north line of Cedar Mills crosses Harding, Coombs, and Atkinson lakes, named for pioneers, extending also into Greenleaf, the first being in honor of Rev. W. C. Harding, who later was a Presbyterian pastor in Litchfield. Vincent Coombs and John Atkinson were farmers beside the lakes bearing their names. Hoff lake is in section 1, and Pipe lake, named for its shape, was in sections 16 and 21, but has been drained. Mud lake, also drained, was crossed by the west line of this township.

Cosmos has Thompson lake, named for an early homesteader, and the greater part of the dry bed of Mud lake.

Collinwood has Butternut lake, named for its trees, in section 3; Washington lake, on the northwest, named for the first president of the United States, extending into Dassel, Darwin, and Ellsworth; Pigeon or Todd lake and Spencer lake, each lately drained; Maple, Long, and Wolf lakes, and Lakes Byron and Jennie. Silver creek flows into Collinwood lake from this township.

Belle lake and Cedar lake, named for its red cedars, as before noted, are crossed by the south line of Ellsworth, continuing into McLeod county. Fallon lake, mostly drained, a small Long lake, in section 23, Lake Erie, Sioux lake, and Greenleaf and Willie lakes are in the south half of the township, the last two being named for William H. Greenleaf, like the next township, and for U. S. Willie (or Wiley), a young lawyer, a member of the legislature in 1859, who lived a year or two at Forest City and died there. In the north half are Birch, Hurley, Benton, and Manuella lakes; and Stella lake is on the north line, reaching into Darwin.

In Greenleaf, besides the three lakes on its south side, lying partly in Cedar Mills township, are Goose and Mud lakes, the second now drained, Lake Minnie Belle, Evenson lake, Hoosier lake, and Star lake, the last, extending into Litchfield, being named for its arms like rays of a star.

Danielson has King lake, beside which Hon. William S. King, of Minneapolis, had a large stock farm, raising Durham cattle, later called March lake for a subsequent owner of this farm, with King creek outflowing to the South fork of Crow river; and Bell lake and creek, similarly named for another farmer.

In Dassel township are Spring and Little Spring lakes, Long lake, Sellards lake, named for Thomas Sellards, a settler from Kentucky, Big

Swan lake, before noted, Lake Arvilla, and Maynard lake, with Washington creek, outflowing from Washington lake to the North fork.

Darwin township has Lake Darwin, Stevens and Casey lakes, Rush lake, Mud lake (drained), and Round lake, the last being crossed by the west line of sections 30 and 31.

Adjoining Litchfield village is Lake Ripley, which commemorates Dr. Frederick N. Ripley, frozen to death there in the winter of 1855-6. The township has also Stone lake, in section 3, and Lake Harold, in sections 19 and 30, with five or six other small lakes mapped and named, which are merely marshes or dry lake beds, excepting in the spring or in very rainy summers.

Acton has a large Long lake, most frequent of our geographic names; Hoop lake (mapped wrongly as Lake Hope), named because its water, like a hoop, surrounds a central island; and fully a dozen marshes that sometimes become shallow lakes, including Kelly, Butter, and Lund lakes.

Lake Francis, outflowing by Eagle creek to the North fork, and Lake Betty, on the Clearwater river, are in Kingston.

Powers, Dunn, Richardson, Plum, Rice, and Mud lakes, are in Forest City township, besides the Mill pond, formed by a dam on the North fork of Crow river. Michael Powers, Timothy Dunn, and William Richardson, were pioneer farmers adjoining the lakes named for them.

Harvey has Schultz lake, Lake Mary, Half Moon lake, named for its shape, and Tower lake. The first was named for three brothers, German farmers, and the last for an early homesteader who was killed by the Sioux in 1862. Jewett and Battle creeks here flow to the North fork of Crow river, the second being translated from its Indian name.

In Swede Grove township are Helga lake or marsh, Peterson lake, and Wilcox, Miller, and Mud lakes, the last two being shallow and mainly drained. Peterson lake was named for Hans Peterson, an adjoining settler, father of the late Hon. Peter E. Hanson, of Litchfield, who was a state senator, 1895-7, and secretary of this state, 1901-07.

Clear lake, named for its deep and clear water, situated in the center of Forest Prairie township, is the chief source of Clearwater river, which flows thence eastward to the Mississippi. This is a translation from the Ojibways, who named the river for the lake at its source, their name of each being Kawakomik, as spelled on Nicollet's map, Ga-wakomitigweia in the lists of Gilfillan and Verwyst. It was a frequent Ojibway name, being retained in Wisconsin by the equivalent French name of the Eau Claire lakes, river, city, and county.

Manannah has Swift's lake, in section 33, and Pigeon lake, crossed by its west line. Stag creek runs south in this township to the North fork. Horseshoe lake, formerly in section 23, nearly adjoining the north side of Tyrone prairie, has been drained.

Union Grove township comprises a part of Pigeon lake, on its east side; Lake Emma and Mud lake, mostly in section 10; and a part of the large Lake Koronis on the north, which lies mainly in Paynesville, Stearns county.

MILLE LACS COUNTY

This county, established May 23, 1857, was named for the large lake, called Mille Lacs, meaning a thousand lakes, which is crossed by the north boundary of the county. It was named Lac Buade by Hennepin in 1680, for the family name of Count Frontenac. By the Sioux it was called Mde Wakan, that is, Wonderful lake or Spirit lake. Le Sueur's journal, written in 1700 and 1701 and transcribed by La Harpe, states that the large part of the Sioux who lived there received from this lake their distinctive tribal name, spelled, by La Harpe, Mendeouacantons. The same name, with better spelling, was given by Keating in 1823, and the lake, on the map accompanying his Narrative, is named Spirit lake; but this group of the Sioux, the Mdewakantons, had before that time been driven from the Mille Lacs region by the Ojibways, and then lived along the Mississippi.

Wakan island, noted on a following page for the present village of Wahkon, was the source of the name Mde Wakan, given to the lake and to this great subtribe of the Siouan people, and was also accountable, by a punning translation, for the Rum river, the outlet of this lake.

The Ojibway name of the lake, as given by Nicollet, is Minsi-sagaigon, which is also applied to the adjoining country, "from *minsi,* all sorts, or everywhere, etc., *sagaigon,* lake." He adds that the first is an obsolete word, "pronounced *misi* or *mizi.*" Gilfillan gave the meaning of the Ojibway name as "Everywhere lake or Great lake." This name, spelled Mississacaigan, appeared on Delisle's map in 1703. It is evidently of the same etymology as Mississippi (great river).

The French voyageurs and traders, as Nicollet states, following their usual practice of translating the Indian name, called the country, having "all sorts of lakes," the Mille Lacs [Thousand Lakes] region; whence this name came to be applied more particularly to this largest lake of the region. It was used by Pike, in application to the lake, being well known at the time of his expedition in 1805; and Carver learned much earlier, in 1766, of the name, but supposed it to refer to "a great number of small lakes, none of which are more than ten miles in circumference, that are called the Thousand Lakes."

Dr. Elliott Coues discussed this name somewhat lengthily in his edition of Pike (vol. I, pp. 311-314).

Mille Lacs has an area of about 200 square miles, slightly exceeding Leech and Winnebagoshish lakes, but much surpassed by Red lake. It is shallow near the shore, and there it is often made muddy by the waves of storms; but its large central part is always clear water, varying mainly from 20 to 50 feet in depth, with a maximum depth of 84 feet.

Townships and Villages.

Information of geographic names has been received from "History of the Upper Mississippi Valley," 1881, having pages 663-680 for Mille Lacs county; "Memoirs of Explorations in the Basin of the Mississippi," by Hon. J. V. Brower, vol. III, Mille Lac, 1900, pages 140, and vol. IV, Kathio, 1901, pages 136, each having maps and many other illustrations; and from Hon. Robert C. Dunn, Judge Charles Keith, and Joseph C. Borden, deputy county treasurer, each being interviewed during a visit at Princeton, the county seat, in October, 1916.

BOCK, the railway village of Borgholm, was named by officers of the Great Northern railway company.

BOGUS BROOK township bears the name of its large eastern tributary of Rum river, derived from the early Maine lumbermen; but the reason for the adoption of this name, meaning spurious and originally referring to counterfeit money, remains to be learned.

BORGHOLM township has the name of a seaport of Sweden, on the island of Oeland, whence some if its settlers came.

BRICKTON, a railway village about two miles north of Princeton, has several brickyards, making excellent cream-colored bricks.

DAILEY township was named in honor of Asa R. Dailey, an early settler there, who removed to Montana.

EAST SIDE township adjoins the east shore of Mille Lacs.

FORESTON, a railway village about three miles west of Milaca, is partly surrounded by a hardwood forest.

GREENBUSH township, settled in 1856, organized in 1869, was named for the township of Greenbush adjoining the east side of Penobscot river in Maine. Many of the settlers in this county, both for its pine lumbering and for farming, came from that "Pine Tree State," being therefore commonly called "Mainites."

HAYLAND township was named for the natural meadows on its several brooks, supplying hay for oxen and horses of winter logging camps.

ISLE, a railway village and port of Mille Lacs, and its ISLE HARBOR township, are named from their excellent harbor, partly inclosed and sheltered in storms by Great or Big island.

IZATYS, a lakeside village of summer homes in South Harbor township, has the name given by Du Luth in the report of his service to France, writing of his first visit to the Sioux at Mille Lacs: "On the 2d of July, 1679, I had the honor to plant his Majesty's arms in the great village of the Nadouecioux, called Izatys, where never had a Frenchman been." It is a variation of Issati or Isanti, noting this division of the Sioux.

KATHIO township, adjoining the southwest shore of Mille Lacs and including its outlet, Rum river, here flowing through three small lakes, bears an erroneously transcribed form of the foregoing name, Izatys, published by Brodhead in 1855 (Documents relating to the Colonial History of New York, vol. IX, page 795). In the original manuscript of

MILLE LACS COUNTY   345

Du Luth's report, before cited, Brodhead copied *Iz* of *Izatys* as "K," and *ys* as "hio," giving to that name a quite new form, Kathio, which error was followed by Neill, Winchell, Hill, Brower, Coues, and others. It has been so much used, indeed, that it will be always retained as a synonym of Izatys or Isanti. (Minnesota Historical Society Collections, vol. X, Part II, 1905, page 531.)

LONG SIDING, a railway village about four miles north of Princeton, was named for Edgar C. Long, a lumberman and landowner.

MILACA village and railway junction, at first called Oak City, and MILACA township, organized after the village was platted, have a shortened and changed name derived from Mille Lacs.

MILO township, settled in 1856 and organized in 1869, received its name from a township and its manufacturing village in the central part of Maine, on the Sebec river.

MUDGETT township, organized in 1916, was named in honor of Isaiah S. Mudgett, who was born in Penobscot county, Maine, June 7, 1839, came to Minnesota in 1858, settled at Princeton in 1865, and was during several years the county auditor. His son, Harold Mudgett, is a farmer in section 30 of this township.

ONAMIA township bears the name given on the government survey plats by Oscar E. Garrison, surveyor, to the third and largest of the three lakes through which Rum river flows next below the mouth of Mille Lacs. A railway village on the south side of Onamia lake also has this name. It was received from the Ojibways, but its meaning is uncertain, unless it be like Onamani, noted in Baraga's Dictionary, whence Vermilion lake in St. Louis county is a translation.

OPSTEAD is the name of a post office and a hamlet of Swedish settlers in East Side township.

PAGE township was named in honor of Charles H. and Edwin S. Page, lumbermen there, who came from Maine.

PEASE, a railway village in section 13, Milo, was named by officers of the Great Northern railway company.

PRINCETON village, the county seat, which received its first permanent settlers in 1854, was named in honor of John S. Prince, of St. Paul, who with others platted this village in the fall or winter of 1855, the plat being recorded April 19, 1856. He was born in Cincinnati, Ohio, May 7, 1821; came to St. Paul in 1854 as agent of the Chouteau Fur Company; afterward engaged in insurance, real estate, and banking; was a member of the constitutional convention of Minnesota, 1857; mayor of St. Paul, 1860-2 and 1865-6; was president of the Savings Bank of St. Paul for many years; and died in that city, September 4, 1895. Princeton township was organized in 1857, and the village was incorporated March 3, 1877.

SOUTH HARBOR township was named for its good harbor on the south side of Mille Lacs.

VINELAND, a village and port of Mille Lacs near its outlet, in Kathio, was named for the early Norse settlement on the northeast coast of North

America in the year 1000, visited by numerous later voyages, which was called in the Icelandic language Vinland, meaning Wineland, from grapes found there.

WAHKON, a railway village and port in Isle Harbor township, bears the Sioux or Dakota name of Mille Lacs, spelled wakan in the Dakota Dictionary by Riggs, defined as "spiritual, sacred, consecrated, wonderful, incomprehensible." The Sioux applied this name especially to a very remarkable but small island far out in the lake, about seven miles northwest from Wahkon, consisting of rock, granitic boulders piled by the ice of the lake to a height of nearly 20 feet, a noted resort of gulls and pelicans, called on maps Spirit island or Pelican island. Only one or two feet below the lake level, and visible under the water for 100 feet or more to the north and east, is a ledge of the bedrock, described by David I. Bushnell in Brower's memoir of Mille Lac (page 121, with a picture, on page 118, of the heaped rock masses forming the island.) Wonderful as the island is, it was the origin of the Sioux name of the lake, of this village, and, by a punning perversion noted on a later page, the name of Rum river.

BAYS, POINTS, AND ISLANDS OF MILLE LACS.

From the map and descriptive notes of this lake by Hon. J. V. Brower, in his memoirs entitled "Mille Lac" and "Kathio," the following names are copied for its south half in Mille Lacs county, with their derivations or significance, and with notes of more recent names.

Halfway point, now called Hunter's point, is in the north edge of Mille Lacs county, near the middle of the east shore.

Accault bay is next south, named for one of the two Frenchmen who were at Mille Lacs with Hennepin in 1680.

Big point and Cedar point are the northwest and southeast limits of Radisson bay, named for the earliest writer of travels in the area of Minnesota, who came with Groseilliers to Prairie island in 1655 and to the region of Kanabec county, not far southeast of Mille Lacs, in the midwinter of 1659-60.

Next in order southward are Cedar bay and island, Ojibway point, North and South Courage bays, now renamed Twin bays, with Courage point between them, Boulder point, now named Hawk Bill point, Big island, and Gim-i-nis-sing bay. The Courage bays and point were named for an Ojibway, "A-ya-shintang, He-is-encouraged;" and the bay last named, now called Isle Harbor, bears on Brower's map the Ojibway name which is translated for Big island. On a recent map this island is named Malone island, for Charles Malone, a resident of Isle village.

West of Isle Harbor are Be-dud, Na-gwa-na-be, and Wadena points, named for Ojibways of Mille Lacs, the second a medicine chief, and the third a chief who was severely wounded in their last battle against the Sioux, near Shakopee, May 27, 1858.

Wahkon bay, adjoining the village of this name, was mapped by Brower as Sa-ga-wa-mick bay, meaning a long shoal or sand bar, which in this

MILLE LACS COUNTY

bay extends from its shore to Mulvey island, named for a lumberman of the Snake river and Stillwater. Other islands farther north in this bay, named by Brower as Sumac and Pelican islands, are on a later map called Half Moon island, for its shape, and Wilson island, for its owner, Guy G. Wilson, of Mora. Northeast from the last is Pine or Spider island.

Between Wahkon bay and Cove bay or South Harbor, called South End bay by Brower, are Coming-in-sight point, translated from its Ojibway name, Carnelian beach, named from its carnelian pebbles, Maple point, and Mo-zo-ma-na point, named for a former Mille Lacs chief, signer of treaties in 1863 and 1889.

Portage bay, next westward, was the usual starting place for canoe journeys down the Rum river, making first a portage about a mile long from the south side of Mille Lacs to the east end of Lake Onamia.

Anderson point, next west of Portage bay, is named for a recent Swedish settler, owner of its summer hotel. Thence to Sah-ging point and Outlet bay, a nearly straight shore reaches four miles, named Rogers shore by Brower for Oren S. Rogers, drowned near there June 27, 1896.

Sah-ging, the Ojibway word meaning an outlet, was applied by Brower to the point southeast of Outlet bay; but later maps rename these as Libby's point and Vineland bay. Hay island and the small Robbins bay adjoin Vineland village, and at the north limit of Vineland bay is Cormorant point, with Robbins island, named by Brower for David H. Robbins, which is recently called Rainbow island.

Shore View bay and Sa-gutch-u point, next northward, as they were mapped by Brower, the latter being named for an Ojibway living there, are called on a recent map Sha-bosh-kung bay and point, commemorating a former head chief of Mille Lacs, who signed treaties in 1863, 1867, and 1889. This name, spelled in several ways, is translated "Who passes under." (Aborigines of Minnesota, pages 726-7.)

Wigwam bay, west of the last named point, is succeeded northward by Reel point, Fenley shore, named for William E. Fenley, and Aitkin and Crow Wing points, which adjoin the corner of the counties so named.

Hennepin island, also named Prisoner's island, alluding to the captivity of Hennepin, who probably, however, never came to this island, lying nearly five miles north of Wahkon village, is a small and low reef of boulders, called Deception Crest by Brower. The only other island far from the shore is the Wakan or Spirit island, before noted as the source of the old Sioux name for Mille Lacs, Mde Wakan, and the differently spelled village name, Wahkon. By proclamation of the President of the United States in 1915, Spirit island is a bird refuge or reservation, for protection of water-loving birds that have resting places and nests there.

A very interesting and reliably historic locality, identified and named by Brower, is Aquipaguetin island, a tract of hard ground about a half mile long and a quarter of a mile wide, in the northeast part of section 25, Kathio, inclosed by Rum river on the east, the western part of Third or Onamia lake on the south, and a swamp on the west and north.

In a Sioux village there the chief Aquipaguetin lived, who adopted Hennepin as his son and befriended him during his enforced stay in the vicinity of Mille Lacs from May to September in 1680, excepting their midsummer absence on a great hunting expedition far down the Mississippi.

Brower mapped twenty-two ancient village sites, scattered around the entire circuit of Mille Lacs, which were probably all occupied for some time by the Sioux or Dakota people. They are most frequent about the southwestern third of the lake, from Wahkon to Aquipaguetin island, Vineland, and the west side of Wigwam bay, thirteen sites of the former villages being found in that distance of about twenty miles. "The great village," called Izatys by Du Luth, misread "Kathio" by Brodhead, is thought to have been near the present Vineland.

OTHER LAKES AND STREAMS.

The name of Rum river, which Carver in 1766 and Pike in 1805 found in use by English-speaking fur traders, was indirectly derived from the Sioux. Their name of Mille Lacs, Mde Wakan, translated Spirit lake, was given to its river, but was changed by the white men to the most common spirituous liquor brought into the Northwest, rum, which brought misery and ruin, as Du Luth observed of brandy, to many of the Indians. The map of Long's expedition in 1823 has these names, Spirit lake and Rum river. Nicollet's map, published in 1843, has "Iskode Wabo or Rum R.," this name given by the Ojibways, but derived by them from the white men's perversion of the ancient Sioux name Wakan, being in more exact translation "Fire Water." More frequently, as noted by Gilfillan, the Ojibway name for Rum river was taken from their name for the lake and meant simply the Great Lake river.

Three lakes on the course of the Rum river in its first eight miles from the mouth of the Mille Lacs were called Rice lakes by Daniel Stanchfield in the autumn of 1847, for their abundance of wild rice then being harvested by the Ojibway women. On a map of Minnesota published in 1850 they are Roberts' lakes. In the government survey, by Oscar E. Garrison, they were named Ogechie, Nessawae, and Onamia lakes. The first was from the Ojibway word for an intestinal worm, referring to its long, narrow, and curved shape; but its more common name used by the Ojibways, as noted by Gilfillan, is "Netumigumag, meaning First lake." In the Ojibway Dictionary the second name is spelled Nassawaii, meaning "in the middle;" but on recent maps this is called Shakopee lake. The third name, Onamia, meaning Vermilion lake, given to a township and village, probably referred, like the larger Vermilion lake and Red lake in northern Minnesota, to the vermilion and red hues of the western sky and of the lake at sunset, as seen from the eastern shore. According to Gilfillan, however, the Ojibways commonly call this "Eshquegumag, the Last lake."

Whitefish lake is a half mile west of Wigwam bay, to which it outflows.

MILLE LACS COUNTY 349

Chase brook, named for Jonathan Chase, of Minneapolis, who had a logging camp there, flows into Mille Lacs from East Side township. He was born in Sebec, Maine, December 31, 1818; came to Minnesota in the spring of 1854, and engaged in lumbering on Rum river; later owned an interest in the large sawmills at Gull River in Cass county; died in Minneapolis, February 1, 1904.

Tributaries to Rum river from the east include, in their order from north to south, Black brook, darkly colored by peat swamps; Whitney, Mike Drew, O'Neill, and Vondel brooks, named for early lumbermen; and Bogus brook, before noticed for its naming a township.

From the west, Rum river receives Bradbury brook, having North and South forks; Hanson brook, named for Gilbert S. Hanson, a lumberman from Maine; Burnt Land, Whiskey, and Tibbetts brooks, the last being named for two brothers, lumbermen, who lived in Princeton; Chase brook, named for Nehemiah Chase (a brother of Jonathan, before mentioned), killed by an accident when breaking a log jam on the Rum river at the mouth of this brook.

The West branch of Rum river receives Stony brook, Estes brook, named for Jonathan Estes, of St. Anthony, and Prairie brook.

Battle brook, in Greenbush, named from a fight there between employees of Sumner W. Farnham, a Minneapolis lumberman, flows through Rice lake, named for its wild rice, and thence is tributary southward to the St. Francis and Elk rivers in Sherburne county.

Mud lake is crossed by the north line of section 1, Princeton; Fogg lake is at the southeast corner of section 17, named for Frederick A. Fogg, an early homesteader, who removed to Sauk Rapids; and Silver lake is a mile east of Princeton village.

Branches of the Ground House river, and of Ann and Knife rivers, drain eastern parts of this county, being tributary to Snake river.

MILLE LACS INDIAN RESERVATION.

By a treaty in Washington, February 22, 1855, the three surveyed townships adjoining the south side of Mille Lacs, with their islands, and the small fractional township at its west side, all lying in the later area of this county, were reserved to the Ojibways living on this excellent hunting ground, with its abundant wild rice and fine fishing in the great lake.

Nine years afterward, in another treaty at Washington, May 7, 1864, this tract was conditionally ceded to the United States, except one section granted to Sha-bosh-kung, for whom a bay and point on the west side of Mille Lacs are named, as before noted. But according to article 12 of this treaty the Ojibway people were accorded the right to occupy the reservation so long as they would not molest the persons and property of adjoining white settlers. Under this condition they continued here during thirty-six years, and were reluctantly persuaded in the year 1901 and later to remove to the White Earth reservation.

MORRISON COUNTY

This county, established February 25, 1856, was named in honor of William and Allan Morrison. The older of these brothers, William, was born in Montreal, March 7, 1785, and died on Morrison's Island, near Sorel, Canada, August 7, 1866. He entered the service of the XY fur company in 1802, coming to Grand Portage, Leech lake, and the headwaters of Crow Wing river. From 1805 to 1816 he was engaged here for a new company formed by the coalition of the XY and Northwest companies. Later, through ten years, he was in service of the American Fur Company, under John Jacob Astor, and established a series of trading posts on or near the northern boundary of Minnesota from Grand Portage west to the Lake of the Woods. In 1826 he retired, and afterward lived in Canada. During his journeys as a fur trader he explored a large region of northern Minnesota. In 1804 he visited Lake Itasca, then called Lac La Biche or Elk lake, thus long preceding Schoolcraft in the discovery of the source of the Mississippi, as is related by Hon. J. V. Brower in Volume VII of the Minnesota Historical Society Collections, with publication of the full text of a letter on this subject, which William Morrison wrote to his brother Allan, January 9, 1856. This letter was forwarded to Governor Ramsey, then president of the Historical Society, a few days before the act was passed establishing this county.

Allan Morrison, who is also commemorated by this name, was born at Terrebonne, near Montreal, June 3, 1803, and died at White Earth, Minn., November 21, 1877. He came to Fond du Lac and northern Minnesota, in the fur trade, associated with his brother William, in 1820; had charge of trading posts at Sandy lake, Leech lake, Red lake, and Mille Lacs; was the first trader at Crow Wing, continuing there many years; and finally removed in 1874 to the White Earth reservation. He was a representative in the first territorial legislature.

Townships and Villages.

Information has been gathered from "History of the Upper Mississippi Valley," 1881, having pages 586-636 for this county; "The History of Morrison County," by Nathan Richardson, a series of weekly articles in the Little Falls Transcript during 1876, collected in a scrap-book in the Public Library of Little Falls; "History of Morrison and Todd Counties," by Clara K. Fuller, 1915, two volumes, 708 pages; and from Edward F. Shaw, judge of probate, interviewed during a visit at Little Falls, the county seat, in May, 1916.

AGRAM township received this name by request of its settlers, in July, 1886, for the city of Agram in Austria-Hungary, the capital of Croatia and Slavonia.

MORRISON COUNTY 351

BELLE PRAIRIE township, first settled in 1849, organized April 6, 1858, adopted this name, meaning "beautiful prairie," from the French fur traders and voyageurs, for its tract of grassland five miles long and averaging about a mile in width, nearly adjoining the Mississippi river.

BELLEVUE township, settled in 1852, organized in the spring of 1858, has another French name, meaning "beautiful view," in reference to the outlook from its prairie beside the Mississippi, which reaches south into Benton county.

BOWLUS, a railway village in Two Rivers township, platted in July, 1907, was named by officers of the Minneapolis, St. Paul and Sault Ste. Marie railway company.

BUCKMAN township, organized in 1874, was named in honor of Clarence B. Buckman, one of its first settlers. He was born in Bucks county, Pa., April 1, 1850; came to Minnesota in 1872, settling here as a farmer and lumberman; removed to Little Falls in 1880; was a representative in the legislature, 1881, and a state senator in 1889 and 1899-1901; was a member of Congress in 1903-07; and died in a sanitarium at Battle Creek, Mich., March 1, 1917.

BUH township, organized in July, 1895, was named in honor of Joseph Francis Buh, a Catholic priest, who was born in Austria, March 17, 1833; came to the United States in 1864; was a missionary in Minnesota during eighteen years, until 1882; and later through more than twenty years was a pastor at various places in this state.

CLOUGH township, organized in October, 1890, was named in honor of David Marston Clough, who engaged extensively in lumbering here, with sawmills and manufacturing in Minneapolis. He was born in Lyme, N. H., December 27, 1846; came to Minnesota in 1857 with his father's family, who settled at Spencer Brook, Isanti county; removed to Minneapolis in 1866; was a state senator, 1886-90; lieutenant governor, 1893-5, and governor of Minnesota, 1895-99; removed in 1899 to Everett, Washington, and there also engaged in a large lumber business.

CULDRUM township, organized June 2, 1870, was named by John Workman, who had previously lived at Little Falls and settled here soon after the civil war, this being the name of his birthplace in Ireland.

CUSHING township, organized October 30, 1891, and its railway village, platted in December, 1907, probably were named for an eminent jurist, congressman, and diplomatist, Caleb Cushing (b. 1800, d. 1879), of Massachusetts, who in 1847 was financially associated with Franklin Steele and others in founding St. Anthony and beginning the great lumber industries of the upper Mississippi.

DARLING township, established January 7, 1891, at first called Randall, which continues as the name of its railway village, in section 7, was renamed in October, 1907, for William L. Darling, of St. Paul. He was born in Oxford, Mass., March 24, 1856; was graduated at Worcester Polytechnic Institute, 1877; settled in St. Paul, engaged in railway engineering, and since 1905 has been chief engineer of the Northern Pacific railway. This is also the name of a railway station in section 35.

ELM DALE township, settled in 1865, organized April 11, 1881, has abundant elms in its woods, and its western part has many low morainic hills and dales.

FLENSBURG, a railway village in Culdrum, platted in March, 1890, was named for a seaport and fjord of Schleswig, a province of Prussia, adjoining Denmark.

GENOLA is a railway village in Pierz township, platted in August, 1908, at first called New Pierz, but in 1915 taking this name of a village in Piedmont, Italy.

GRANITE township, organized in July, 1902, has in its section 21 many outcrops of a granitic rock, coarse gray gneiss, adjoining the Skunk river for a half mile or more, where a village named "Granite City" was founded by Tallmadge Elwell in 1858. It had a sawmill, hotel, and other buildings, which were deserted in 1861-62, on account of the civil war and the Sioux war, the site being permanently abandoned.

GRAVELVILLE, a former village on the Platte river in the southeast corner of Belle Prairie township, was founded in 1876 by Charles Gravel, who, with his older brother Narcisse, built a sawmill and gristmill here and also engaged in mercantile business.

GREEN PRAIRIE township, organized in the spring of 1868, was named in honor of its first settler, Charles H. Green, a native of Glens Falls, N. Y., who came here in 1855, enlisted in the Third Minnesota regiment, 1861, and was killed in the battle of Murfreesboro, July 13, 1862. The prairie in this township, bordering the Mississippi, was about three miles long and nearly a mile wide.

GREGORY is a station and small village of the Northern Pacific railway in the north edge of Bellevue, named for John Gregory Smith, of Vermont, president of the Northern Pacific company in 1866-72, more fully noticed in the chapter for Crow Wing county, where the city of Brainerd was named in honor of his wife.

HILLMAN township, organized July 7, 1902, the railway village of this name in Leigh township, platted in July, 1908, and the brook much earlier so named, with its southern tributary, Little Hillman brook, commemorate a pioneer of the county.

LAKIN township, organized July 6, 1903, was named for Fred H. Lakin, a settler from Maine, who during many years was one of the county commissioners, living in Royalton.

LEIGH township, organized February 15, 1908, was named in honor of Joseph P. Leigh, a pioneer farmer there, who came from Maine.

LINCOLN, a railway village in Scandia Valley township, platted in September, 1893, having numerous summer homes beside Fish Trap lake, was named for the martyr president of the United States in the civil war.

LITTLE FALLS, the county seat, first settled in 1848 and platted in 1855, was incorporated as a village February 25, 1879, and as a city in July,

1890. The city area mainly belonged to Little Falls township, which was organized May 11, 1858; but it extends also into the adjoining Belle Prairie township, and its part west of the Mississippi is in Pike Creek township. Pike in 1805-06 called the rapids or falls of the river here "Painted Rock or Little Falls," the first of these names being translated from the French traders. Mill island, a slate outcrop a quarter of a mile long, divides the river into east and west channels; and the original descent of the rapids at this island and southward was 11 feet in three-fourths of a mile. About the year 1890 a dam was built, which raises the river nine feet above the former head of the rapids, giving thus a total fall of 20 feet and holding the river as a mill pond for about three miles to the middle of the Little Elk rapids, which previously had a descent of seven feet in one mile.

During an exceptionally high flood stage of the Mississippi in June, 1858, the steamboat North Star from Minneapolis passed over the Sauk rapids and the Little falls, and made a pleasure trip to the Grand rapids in Itasca county. (M. H. S. Collections, vol IX, page 48.)

The discovery in 1878 by Miss Frances E. Babbitt, a school teacher at Little Falls, of artificially flaked quartz fragments in the Mississippi valley drift, gave evidence of the presence of primitive men here during the closing part of the Ice Age. "Kakabikansing," the Ojibway name of Little Falls, meaning "the place of the little squarely cut-off rock," is the title of a memoir on this subject, by Hon. J. V. Brower, published in 1902 (126 pages, with maps and many illustrations from photographs).

MORRILL township, settled in 1874, organized April 11, 1881, was at first called Oakwood, but after a few years was renamed in honor of Ashby C. Morrill, a member of the board of county commissioners. He was born in Canterbury, N. H., January 9, 1830; was graduated in the law school of Harvard College; came to Minnesota in 1857, settling in Minneapolis; engaged after 1868 in milling and lumbering, and had a farm in Buckman township; resided after 1884 at Little Falls, where he erected the Little Elk mills; and died in Minneapolis, May 5, 1904.

MOTLEY township, organized in the spring of 1879, took the name of its railway village, founded in 1874, which was named by officers of the Northern Pacific railway company.

MOUNT MORRIS township, organized March 17, 1897, was named by Dunkard settlers who came from Pennsylvania and Ohio. This name is borne also by townships and villages in New York, Pennsylvania, Illinois, Michigan, and Wisconsin.

NORTH PRAIRIE, a small village in Two Rivers township, platted in the summer of 1885, is in the oldest Polish settlement of this county, founded by its pioneer immigrants in 1868-70.

PARKER township, organized in the spring of 1880, was named in honor of George F. Parker, its first settler. He was born in Bridgewater, Mass., December 26, 1846; served during the civil war in Massachusetts regiments; and came here as a homesteader, April 17, 1879.

PIERZ township, organized March 9, 1869, was named in honor of Francis Xavier Pierz (or Pirec), a Catholic missionary. He was born in Godic, Carniola, Austria, November 20, 1785; was ordained a priest in 1813; came to the United States in 1835; was a missionary to the Ottawa Indians in Michigan, and from 1852 to 1873 labored mainly among the Ojibways in northern Minnesota; was a leader in forming the Benedictine community of St. John's, Collegeville, and in bringing German colonists to Stearns and Morrison counties; returned to Austria in 1873, and died in Laibach, Carniola, January 22, 1880. The village of Pierz was platted in 1891, and was incorporated in January, 1892. The railway village, formerly New Pierz, has been renamed Genola, as before noted.

PIKE CREEK township, organized in 1880, with its creek of this name, commemorates Zebulon Montgomery Pike, explorer of the upper Mississippi, whose stockade camp in the winter of 1805-06 was on its west bank in Swan River township, about a quarter of a mile south from the mouth of Swan river. He was born in Lamington, N. J., January 5, 1779; entered the United States army in 1799, and became a captain in 1806; conducted an expedition to the headwaters of the Mississippi in 1805-06, being overtaken by an early snow and cold on October 16, so that his party then made their winter encampment, as noted, at the west side of Pike rapids; advanced thence afoot in the midwinter, with a few of his men, to Sandy, Leech, and Cass lakes; discovered Pike's peak of the Rocky mountains in the next year, on an expedition to the headwaters of the Arkansas and Red rivers; was promoted in the War of 1812 to the rank of brigadier general, and was killed April 27, 1813, while commanding an attack at York (now Toronto), Canada. In 1807 and 1810 he published accounts of his explorations in Minnesota and in the Southwest. His journals and reports of these expeditions were more fully published in 1895, edited and annotated by Dr. Elliott Coues, in three volumes. A paper in the Somerset County (N. J.) Historical Quarterly, October, 1919 (vol. VIII, pp. 241-251), shows that Pike's birthplace was at Lamington in that county.

PLATTE township, organized January 24, 1899, was named for the Platte river, which crosses it. This stream has its main source in a large Platte lake on the north line of the county, and it flows through a smaller Platte or Rice lake in the east part of Little Falls township. Its name, given by the early French fur traders, meaning "dull, flat, shallow," is borne also by a remarkably shallow river, though long, in Nebraska and Colorado.

PULASKI township, organized in January, 1899, was named in honor of the Polish general, Casimir Pulaski, who greatly aided Washington in the Revolutionary War. He was born in Poland, March 4, 1748; entered the American service in 1777; formed a corps called "Pulaski's Legion" in 1778; defended Charleston in 1779; was mortally wounded near Savannah, Ga., October 9, 1779, and died two days later.

RAIL PRAIRIE township, organized January 27, 1890, was named in honor of Case Rail, a pioneer farmer in section 18, beside the Mississippi, whose homestead was mostly a prairie.

MORRISON COUNTY 355

RANDALL, a railway village in Darling township, platted in March, 1890, and incorporated in July, 1900, was named in honor of John H. Randall, of St. Paul. He was born in Roxbury, Mass., in 1831; came to Minnesota in 1856; engaged in official service for the St. Paul and Pacific railway company, and from 1887 to 1907 for the Northern Pacific company; and died in St. Paul, March 11, 1916. This township was originally named Randall in 1891, after the village, and received its present name in 1907, as before noted.

RICHARDSON township, organized January 7, 1903, was named in honor of Nathan Richardson, who was the author of a newspaper history of this county in 1876. He was born in Clyde, N. Y., February 24, 1829; came to Minnesota in 1854, and in the next year settled at Little Falls; was during many years register of deeds for the county, and later was judge of probate; was postmaster of Little Falls for about ten years; was a representative in the legislature in 1867, 1872, and 1878; and died at his home in Little Falls, January 9, 1908.

RIPLEY township received its name from Fort Ripley, built in 1849-50 on the west bank of the Mississippi in the eastern section 7 of Clough township, opposite to the mouth of Nokasippi river, which continued in use as a military post of the United States until July, 1878. It was at first named Fort Gaines, in honor of Edmund Pendleton Gaines (b. 1777, d. 1849), who served in the War of 1812 as a colonel and later as a brigadier general. Eleazar Wheelock Ripley, for whom this fort was renamed November 4, 1850, was born in Hanover, N. H., April 15, 1782; served in the War of 1812, being promoted to the rank of brigadier general, and was brevetted major general; was a member of Congress from Louisiana, 1835-9; and died in Louisiana, March 2, 1839.

ROSING township, organized July 7, 1902, was named in honor of Leonard August Rosing, who in that year was the Democratic candidate for governor of Minnesota. He was born in Malmo, Sweden, August 29, 1861; came to the United States in 1869 with his parents, who settled in Goodhue county, Minn.; resided in Cannon Falls after 1881, being a merchant there; was private secretary of Governor Lind, 1899-1901; was a member of the State Board of Control, 1905-09; and died in St. Paul, April 14, 1909.

ROYALTON, a railway village in Bellevue, platted in 1878 and incorporated in October, 1887, was named by settlers from the township and village of Royalton in Vermont.

SCANDIA VALLEY township, organized in October, 1893, was named by its Scandinavian settlers. In ancient times the name Scandia designated what was supposed to be a large island north of the Baltic sea, before exploration made it known as the south part of the peninsula of Sweden and Norway.

SWAN RIVER township, organized in December, 1874, bears the name of the stream flowing through its northern part to the Mississippi. Its source is Swan lake in Todd county, the name of both the lake and river being received by translation from their Ojibway name, spelled Wabisi by Baraga and Wabizi by Gilfillan. When the first settlers came, Minnesota had two species of swans, the whistling swan, which is yet rarely seen here, and the trumpeter swan, believed now to be extinct, like the passenger pigeon.

SWANVILLE township, organized October 12, 1892, likewise crossed by the Swan river, took the name of its railway village, platted in November, 1882, and incorporated May 24, 1893.

Two RIVERS township, first settled in 1855 and organized in September, 1865, received the name of its streams tributary to the Mississippi, a translation from the Ojibways, as noted by Gilfillan. The larger one of the Two rivers is formed by the South and North Two rivers, which unite about three miles above its mouth, the former being the outlet of Two River lake in Stearns county. Little Two river flows into the Mississippi a third of a mile north from the mouth of the larger stream.

UPSALA is a hamlet in Elm Dale township, named from the ancient city of Upsala in Sweden, renowned for its university founded in 1477.

VAWTER, a small village of the Soo railway in the north edge of Bellevue, was platted in the summer of 1908.

LAKES AND STREAMS.

The preceding pages have noticed the Hillman and Little Hillman brooks, Pike creek, Platte lake and river, Swan lake and river, and the Two rivers.

Near the northwest corner of the county, Scandia Valley township has a fine group of lakes, beautiful for their hilly and wooded shores, numerous points, bays, and islands, and abounding in fish and water-fowl. Lake Alexander, the largest of this group, named before 1860 for Captain (and later Major) Thomas L. Alexander, stationed at Fort Ripley, has Crow, Potato, and High islands. It outflows to Fish Trap lake, and thence by Fish Trap brook to the Long Prairie and Crow Wing rivers. Shamano lake, about two miles farther north, has this spelling on the map of Minnesota in 1860, derived, according to Gilfillan, "from an old Indian named Shamanons, who lived there long ago;" but on the most recent maps it is spelled Shamineau, a French form of this Ojibway name.

Smaller lakes in Scandia Valley are Stanchfield lake, named for a lumberman, on the south line of sections 1 and 2; Duck lake, in sections 9 and 10; Round lake, in section 13; McDonald lake, section 17; Lena lake, section 18; and Ham lake, named for its shape, adjoining the northeast shore of Fish Trap lake.

Mud lake is in section 36, Rosing.

Tamarack and Aiott lakes are respectively in section 11 and 34, Rail Prairie. The latter, erroneously printed Mott lake on a recent map, was named for F. Aiott, a pioneer farmer there.

Clough township has Round lake in section 27, and Goose and Clough lakes in sections 26 and 35.

Lake Madaline is in sections 5 and 8, Cushing.

Fish lake is on the east line of Darling township.

In the northwest part of Elm Dale are Long, Pine, and Cedar lakes.

Little Elk river, translated from its Ojibway name, is tributary to the Mississippi from the west, giving name to Little Elk rapids of the great river, between two and three miles north of Little Falls. Hay creek, named from its meadows which supplied hay for winter logging teams, flows into the North fork of Little Elk river; and the South fork receives Tidd, Shingle, and Sturgis brooks.

Another Hay creek flows to the Mississippi from the south part of Swan River township.

Below the Little Elk river and rapids, the Mississippi has Big island, a mile north of Mill island at Little Falls; Newton and Hobart islands, about a mile north of Pike rapids; and between three and five miles south of Swan river are Cash's, Muncy's, and Blanchard's rapids.

On its east side the Mississippi receives Fletcher Boundary creek from Ripley and Belle Prairie.

At the head of Platte river are Platte lake, before noted, and Sullivan lake, the latter crossed by the east line of Pulaski. Skunk river, the large eastern tributary of the Platte, was called Little Platte river on the map of Minnesota in 1860. Nicollet mapped the Platte as "Pekushino river;" it was named "Flat river" on the map of Minnesota territory in 1850; and Norwood's map in Owen's geological report, published in 1852, first presented its French name, Platte river.

Four small lakes are tributary to the lower part of this river, namely, Fish lake, in sections 13 and 14, Agram; Pelkey lake, bearing the name of pioneer farmers beside it, in sections 34 and 35, Belle Prairie; Rice lake, formerly mapped as Platte lake, having much wild rice, through which the river flows in Little Falls township; and Skunk lake, closely adjoining this Rice lake and also very near the mouth of Skunk river.

Little Rock creek flows into Benton county.

Mount Morris and Lakin townships are drained to the Rum river by its West Branch and Tibbetts brook.

PRAIRIES AND HILLS.

Four townships of this county, Belle Prairie, Bellevue, Green Prairie, and Rail Prairie, are named for small natural prairies on the valley drift bordering the Mississippi. A larger area, called Rich prairie, consisting mainly of similar valley drift, adjoins the Platte and Skunk rivers in Buh, Pierz, Agram, and the southeast part of Little Falls township. With the exception of these and some other such limited grasslands, Morrison county originally was well wooded, and amidst its principally hardwood forests it had numerous extensive tracts of valuable white pine timber.

Considerable parts of this county are occupied by belts of low morainic drift hills, but only two hills are named on maps. One is widely known as "Hole-in-the-Day's bluff," because the second hereditary Ojibway chief of this name was buried on its top. He was born in 1828, and died at Crow Wing, June 27, 1868, being assassinated by three of his own people, members of the Pillager band. This hill is on the south edge of Belle Prairie, about a mile and a half northeast of Little Falls. It rises 40 feet above the average height of neighboring hillocks in the same belt, being about 150 feet above the Mississippi, but even this slight elevation commands a wide prospect of the adjoining valley plain.

The second morainic hill distinguished by a name is in the eastern section 26 of Belle Prairie, known as Tanner's hill, which has a height of only about 100 feet above the country around it.

PIKE'S WINTERING PLACE.

The site of log houses and a stockade built by Pike and his soldiers as their winter quarters, in 1805-06, on the west bank of the Mississippi at Pike rapids, before noticed for Pike Creek township, is marked by a bronze memorial tablet, upon a cairn of stones, given by the Daughters of the American Revolution and unveiled September 27, 1919, with an address by Mrs. James T. Morris, of Minneapolis, state regent.

The Mississippi at its stage of low water falls three feet by its rapids in the distance between about a quarter and an eighth of a mile north of this site. Its bed, strewn with boulders, has many low outcrops of staurolite-bearing mica schist.

MOWER COUNTY

Established February 20, 1855, this county was named in honor of John E. Mower, who was born in Bangor, Maine, September 15, 1815, and died in Arcola, Minn., June 11, 1879. He came to St. Croix Falls, Wis., in 1842; removed to Stillwater, Minn., in 1844; and settled at Arcola, near Stillwater, in 1847, where he afterward resided, being chiefly engaged in lumbering. He was a member of the council of the territorial legislature, 1854-5, and a representative in the state legislature, 1874-5. His brother, Martin Mower, born in Stark, Maine, in 1819, came to Stillwater in 1843; had large business interests of building, manufactures, and lumbering, in Stillwater and Arcola; selected the latter place as his home in 1846; and died there in July, 1890.

The family name here has been pronounced with the long sound of *o*, as for one mowing grass, not like a mow of hay in a barn; but the county title, by common usage, is divergently spoken in both ways.

Townships and Villages.

Information of the origin and meaning of names has been gathered from "History of Mower County," 1884, 610 pages; the later History of this county, edited by Franklyn Curtiss-Wedge, 1911, 1006 pages; and from Henry Weber, Jr., judge of probate, Eugene Wood, register of deeds, and Mrs. Flora Crane Conner, librarian, each interviewed during a visit at Austin, the county seat, in April, 1916.

ADAMS township was organized in May, 1858. Its railway village of the same name was platted January 30, 1868, and was incorporated March 2, 1887. This name is borne by counties in nine states of the Union, and by villages and townships in fourteen states, mostly in honor of John Adams, the second president of the United States in 1797-1801, and his son, John Quincy Adams, the sixth president, 1825-29.

AUSTIN, the county seat, platted in the spring of 1856, incorporated as a village in 1868 and as a city in 1873, and also Austin township, organized in 1858, were named for Austin R. Nichols, their first settler. He was born in Lawrence county, N. Y., June 13, 1814; came to Minnesota in 1851, and took a land claim in 1853 on the site of this city; built a sawmill here in 1854, but sold this claim later in the same year; was a pioneer farmer subsequently at several other places in this state; removed to Minneapolis in 1865, and to the northwest shore of Mille Lacs in 1879, where Nichols post office, named in his honor, was established at his home, in the west edge of Aitkin county. He died there, almost a century old, April 5, 1914.

BENNINGTON township, at first named Andover by the county commissioners in 1858, was organized in the autumn of 1860, then receiving its present name from Bennington, Vermont, renowned for a battle of the

Revolutionary War, August 16, 1777, in which the British were defeated by the Americans.

BROWNSDALE, the village of Red Rock township, was platted in the summer of 1856 by Andrew D. and Hosmer A. Brown, and was incorporated in February, 1876. Andrew D. Brown was born in North Stonington, Conn., in 1818; came to Minnesota in 1856, settling here, and engaged in lumber business and milling; died in Minneapolis in May, 1911. Hosmer A. Brown was born in North Stonington, Conn., September 30, 1830; came to this state in 1855, settling on the site of Brownsdale as a farmer and carpenter; was a representative in the legislature in 1870 and 1877.

CLAYTON township, originally named Providence in 1858, was organized June 20, 1873 being then renamed in honor of William Z. Clayton, owner of a large tract of land in this township. He was born in Freeman, Maine, in 1837; came to Minnesota about 1857; served in the First Minnesota Battery of Light Artillery, 1861-5, becoming its captain; later resided in Winona county, and during several summers in this township, being a farmer and dealer in real estate; removed to Bangor, Maine.

DEXTER township, organized June 6, 1870, was named for Dexter Parritt, who came from Ohio with his father, Mahlon Parritt, in 1857, these being the first settlers. Dexter railway village was platted in 1874, and was incorporated February 28, 1878.

ELKTON, a village of the Chicago Great Western railway in Marshall, platted January 25, 1887, has a name of villages in eleven other states.

FRANKFORD township was organized May 11, 1858, taking the name of its village which had been platted in 1856. It is the name of a township in New Jersey, and of villages in Delaware, West Virginia, and other states, and in Ontario, Canada.

GRAND MEADOW township, named by the county commissioners in 1858, in allusion to its being an extensive prairie, was organized April 20, 1862. Its village of this name, on the Chicago, Milwaukee and St. Paul railway, was platted in 1870, when this railway line was built through the county.

HAMILTON, a former village on the east line of Racine, lying mainly in Fillmore county, was platted in 1855, as noted for that county.

LANSING township, organized May 11, 1858, received this name from the capital of Michigan, in compliment to Alanson B. Vaughan, a pioneer settler, on account of its similarity in sound with his first name. Lansing village, of which he was the first proprietor, was also platted in 1858. He was born in Clinton county, N. Y., June 6, 1806; removed to Rock county, Wisconsin, in 1843; came to Minnesota in 1854, and settled in this township, with his five sons, in 1855; was the first merchant and first post master in the adjoining village of Austin; was a member of the state constitutional convention in 1857, and the first judge of probate in this county; died October 3, 1876.

LE ROY township was organized May 11, 1858. Its railway village, bearing the same name, was platted in 1867, when this Iowa and Minne-

MOWER COUNTY 361

sota division of the Chicago, Milwaukee and St. Paul railway was being built. Fourteen other states have villages and townships of this name.

LODI township, organized in February, 1874, had received this name from the county commissioners in 1858. It is borne by villages and townships in New York, New Jersey, Wisconsin, and several other states, being derived from a medieval city of Lombardy in Italy, made famous by a victory won at the bridge of Lodi, by Napoleon against the Austrians, May 10, 1796.

LYLE township, organized in 1858, was named in honor of Robert Lyle, a native of Ohio, who settled here in November, 1856, was judge of probate for the county, and in 1868 removed to Missouri. Lyle railway village, platted in 1870, was incorporated March 9, 1875.

MARSHALL township, which had been called York by the county commissioners in 1858, was organized June 6, 1870, being named in honor of William Rainey Marshall, who was governor of this state from 1866 to 1870.

NEVADA township, first settled in 1854, was organized in May, 1858, receiving this name from the Sierra Nevada, meaning "Snowy Range," which forms the eastern border of the great valley of California. Nevada Territory was organized three years later, in 1861, and was admitted to the Union as a state in 1864.

PLEASANT VALLEY township, organized May 11, 1858, was named by Sylvester Hills, its pioneer settler, who came here in 1854 from the village and township of Pleasant Valley in Dutchess county, New York.

RACINE township, organized May 11, 1858, bears the French name, meaning root, of the Hokah or Root river, which receives tributaries from this township. Racine railway village was platted October 3, 1890.

RAMSEY, a railway junction and small village three miles north of Austin, was named in honor of Governor Ramsey, for whom a biographic sketch is presented in the chapter of Ramsey county.

RED ROCK township, organized in 1858, was named by its first settler, John L. Johnson, who came from Rock county, Wisconsin, in October, 1855. His first home here was in Red Rock grove in section 4, this name being suggested "by a large red rock in the grove, the only one of the kind to be found for miles around."

RENOVA, a little village of the Chicago Great Western railway in Dexter, was platted March 30, 1900.

ROSE CREEK, a railway village in Windom, founded as a flag station in 1868, was incorporated February 14, 1899. It is situated beside the creek of this name, which is the largest eastern tributary of Cedar river in this county.

SARGEANT township, organized September 16, 1873, was named in honor of Harry N. Sargeant, one of its pioneer farmers. He was born in the Province of Quebec, June 19, 1817; came to Wisconsin in 1858, and to this county in 1865, settling in section 11 of this township; was elected the first township clerk; died January 25, 1884. Sargeant railway village was platted September 7, 1894, this railway having been built in 1887.

TAOPI, a railway village and junction in Lodi township, platted in 1875, incorporated in 1909, was named in honor of Taopi (Wounded Man), chief of the Farmer band of the Santee Sioux, who died in March, 1869. He was one of the first converts to Christianity at the Redwood mission on the Minnesota river, and at the time of the Sioux outbreak, 1862, was friendly to the whites and aided in the rescue of many. He is commemorated in a book, "Taopi and His Friends, or the Indians' Wrongs and Rights," by Rev. S. D. Hinman, Bishop Whipple, and others, 125 pages, with his portrait, published in 1869.

UDOLPHO township, organized in 1858, was named by one of its pioneers, Col. Henry C. Rogers, from his having read "The Mysteries of Udolpho," by Mrs. Ann Ward Radcliffe of England, published in 1794. This is a highly fanciful and weird romance of Italy in the seventeenth century, representing Udolpho as a medieval castle in the Apennines.

VARCO, a railway station four miles south of Austin, was platted November 17, 1875, on the farm of Thomas Varco, in whose honor it was named. He was born in England, came to Minnesota in 1856, settling here, and died February 12, 1893.

WALTHAM township, organized June 4, 1866, had been named April 16, 1858, at a meeting of the county commissioners, one of whom, Charles F. Hardy, of Red Rock, was a native of Waltham in Massachusetts. Waltham railway village was platted September 8, 1885.

WINDOM township, organized May 11, 1858, at first called Brooklyn and later Canton, was renamed in May, 1862, in honor of William Windom, of Winona, who then was a member of Congress. His name is borne also by the county seat of Cottonwood county, for which a biographic notice of him is presented.

RIVERS AND CREEKS.

Mower county, with a large adjoining tract of southeastern Minnesota, differs from nearly all other parts of this state by the absence of lakes.

The North and South branches of Root river, and Bear and Deer creeks, head streams of its Middle branch, drain the northeast part of the county, the French name of this river, Racine, being given to its most northeastern township.

Upper Iowa river flows eastward from Lodi, receives the Little Iowa river in Le Roy, and crosses the state line at the southeast corner of this county.

Cedar river, called Red Cedar river on Nicollet's map in 1843, flows through the west part of this county. Its tributaries here received from the east, in the order from north to south, are Wolf creek, Dobbin's creek, Rose creek, before noted as giving its name to a railway village, and Otter creek. Little Cedar river, another of its eastern tributaries, which joins the Cedar river much farther south in Iowa, has its sources in Marshall, Clayton, and Adams townships. From the west, Cedar river in this county receives Turtle, Orchard, and Woodbury creeks.

HORACE AUSTIN STATE PARK.

In the northern part of the city of Austin a tract of fifty acres, including "water of the Red Cedar river and a number of deeply wooded islands," was acquired by the state in 1914 as a public park, named in honor of the sixth governor of this state. An expedition of three companies of the First United States Dragoons, under Lt. Col. Stephen W. Kearny, whose route was sketched by Albert M. Lea, camped here in 1835. Later the site of this park was a camping ground of parties of hunters and trappers in 1836, 1841, and 1846, including Major Taliaferro, Henry H. Sibley, Alexander Faribault, William H. Forbes, and others prominent in the history of Fort Snelling and of the fur trade within the area that afterward was Minnesota.

Horace Austin was born in Canterbury, Conn., October 15, 1831, and died in Minneapolis, November 7, 1905. He settled in St. Peter, Minn., in 1854; served in the Indian war, 1863, as captain of cavalry; was judge of the Sixth judicial district, 1865-9; governor of Minnesota, 1870-4; later was third auditor of the U. S. Treasury, and afterward was connected with the Department of the Interior seven years. In 1887-9 he was chairman of the railroad commissioners of Minnesota. He resided at Lake Minnetonka, and during his last years engaged in mining in California.

MURRAY COUNTY

This county, established May 23, 1857, and organized June 17, 1872, was named in honor of William Pitt Murray, who was born in Hamilton, Ohio, June 21, 1825, and died in St. Paul, June 20, 1910. He studied at Miami University, Oxford, Ohio; was graduated in law at the State University of Indiana, 1849, and came to Minnesota the same year, settling in St. Paul; was a member of the territorial legislature in 1852-3 and in 1857, and of the council, 1854-5, being its president in 1855; was a member of the state constitutional convention, 1857; a representative in the state legislature in 1863 and 1868; and a state senator, 1866-7 and 1875-6. He was a member of the St. Paul city council, 1861-8 and 1870-79, being six years its president; and for thirteen years was the city attorney, 1876-89. He contributed a paper, "Recollections of Early Territorial Days and Legislation," in the Minnesota Historical Society Collections (vol. XII, 1908, pages 103-130, with his portrait); and was a member of the board of editors of "Minnesota in Three Centuries," four volumes, published in 1908. During more than sixty years he was an eminently useful and greatly beloved citizen of the capital of this state.

Townships and Villages.

Information of geographic names in Murray county was received from Alfred Terry, of Slayton, during many years a dealer in real estate here, E. V. O'Brien, county auditor, W. J. McAllister, judge of probate, and Robert Hyslop, clerk of the court, each being interviewed during a visit at Slayton, the county seat, in July, 1916; and from Neil Currie, interviewed several times in St. Paul, in 1918.

Avoca, a railway village in Lime Lake township, was named in 1879 by Archbishop Ireland, who founded near it a Catholic colony of immigrant farmers. The name is taken from a river in County Wicklow, Ireland, about forty miles south of Dublin, noted for the picturesque beauty of its valley, called "Sweet Vale of Avoca" in a poem by Thomas Moore. From the fame given by the poet's praise, this name also has been chosen for villages in thirteen other states of the Union.

Belfast township, organized July 19 and September 3, 1878, bears the name of a large seaport city in northern Ireland, whence the city of Belfast in Maine, on Penobscot bay, was named, as also villages of eight other states and townships in New York and Pennsylvania.

Bondin township, organized November 2, 1874, received the name of a post office previously established at the home of William M. Davis, a pioneer farmer in the northwest quarter of its section 24.

MURRAY COUNTY

CAMERON township, organized September 10, 1878, has a name that is borne also by villages or cities or townships in fourteen other states. It was selected here in compliment for Charles Cameron Cole, an early settler.

CHANARAMBIE township, organized July 25, 1879, is drained by the head streams of "Hidden Wood creek or Tchan Narambe creek," as it is named on Nicollet's map, published in 1843. This Sioux name referred to trees or a grove in its valley concealed from any distant view, called "Lost Timber" by the early settlers.

CHANDLER, a railway village in the northeast corner of Moulton, was named in honor of John Alonzo Chandler, who was in official service of the Chicago, Milwaukee and St. Paul railway company more than forty years, beginning this service in 1856. He was born in West Randolph, Vt., January 18, 1831; was captain in the Nineteenth Wisconsin regiment, 1861-2, and a state senator in Wisconsin, 1864-5; came to Minnesota in 1870, settling in St. Paul, where he died March 31, 1902.

CURRIE, the village of Murray township, was founded in 1872, when Neil Currie and his father, Archibald Currie, built a flour mill here, using water power of the Des Moines river about a mile below the mouth of Lake Shetek. Archibald Currie was born in Argyllshire, Scotland, November 13, 1816; came with his parents to America when five years old, and to Minnesota in 1862; was a merchant in Winona county until 1874; then removed to Currie, where he engaged in merchandising and milling; was treasurer of this county, 1879-83; died July 15, 1904. This village, which was the first county seat, from 1872 to 1889, being succeeded by Slayton, was named in honor of him and of Neil Currie, who was born in Canada, December 15, 1842. He built the first store here in 1872, and aided in organizing the Murray County Bank in 1874; was postmaster of Currie, 1872-90, and clerk of the court, 1874-87; resided here as a merchant until 1905, when he removed to St. Paul.

DES MOINES RIVER township, organized May 31, 1878, is crossed by the river of this name, which has its sources in the west edge of this county.

DOVRAY township, organized March 18 and April 22, 1879, was named for Dovre, a village in Norway, and for the Dovrefjeld, a high mountainous plateau of that country, this name being given by Nels S. Taarud, the county treasurer. Ten years earlier, in 1869, a township of Kandiyohi county received the name Dovre, having the same derivation, for which reason the spelling was changed here, while retaining nearly the original pronunciation. Dovray railway village was platted in 1904.

ELLSBOROUGH township, organized March 21, 1874, has an unusual name, unknown elsewhere either as a place name or a surname, which was adopted in honor of Knut Ellingson, one of its first settlers.

FENTON township, the latest organized in this county, March 19, 1886, was named in honor of P. H. Fenton, a pioneer farmer, who removed to the state of Washington.

FULDA, the railway village in Bondin, was named for an ancient city in central Germany, on the river Fulda, noted for its early medieval abbey, founded in 744, and its beautiful cathedral, built in 1704-12.

HADLEY, a railway village in Leeds, has a name that is borne by villages and townships in Massachusetts, New York, Pennsylvania, and other states.

HOLLY, the name of one of the oldest townships of this county, organized June 17, 1872, was chosen in honor of John Z. Holly, one of its early pioneers, who after a few years returned to Illinois.

IONA township, organized March 17, 1880, was named after its railway village, platted in 1878 by Rev. Martin McDonnell, who here founded a Catholic industrial school for orphans. This is the name of a small island on the west coast of Scotland, celebrated for its ancient abbey, founded by St. Columba in the sixth century, and for a ruined cathedral, which was founded in the thirteenth century.

LAKE SARAH township, organized March 11, 1873, was named for its largest lake, doubtless commemorating, like the companion Lake Maria, the wife or daughter of one of the government land surveyors or of a pioneer settler, but surnames for these lakes remain to be learned.

LAKE WILSON, the railway village in Chanarambie, platted in 1883, was named by Jonathan E. Wilson, "formerly of Chicago, Illinois, who also named the nearby lake for himself. He owned at one time seventeen thousand acres of land in this vicinity." (W. H. Stennett, Place Names of the Chicago and Northwestern and the Chicago, St. Paul, Minneapolis and Omaha Railways, 1908, p. 180.)

LEEDS township, organized March 11, 1873, received its name from Leeds township and village in Columbia county, Wisconsin. It is near Lowville in that county, whence the Low brothers came to Murray county.

LIME CREEK, a little railway village in Belfast, and LIME LAKE township, organized September 24, 1873, are named from this creek and lake, which have plentiful boulders of limestone, especially abundant around the lake and pushed up by its ice into ridges along parts of its shore.

LOWVILLE township, organized September 2, 1873, was named for John H. and Bartlett M. Low, brothers, who came here from New York and Wisconsin. Each of these states has a township named Lowville in honor of their family. John H. Low came first in the winter of 1865-6, for trapping in the vicinity of the Bear lakes. In 1866 the brothers took land claims in and adjoining "the Great Oasis" of timber, as the extensive grove beside these lakes was named on Nicollet's map, in allusion to the surrounding region of treeless prairie. John H. Low was the county auditor in 1881-84; continued as a farmer on his homestead forty-eight years; and removed to Slayton in 1914. Bartlett Marshall Low was born in Poughkeepsie, N. Y., in 1839; served in the 42d Wisconsin regiment during the civil war; came to Minnesota in 1865, and settled here a year later; was a representative in the legislature, 1887-89. (The family and township names here have an exceptional pronunciation, like how, now.)

MURRAY COUNTY 367

MASON township, organized July 20, 1872, was at first called Okcheeda, but in 1879 was renamed in honor of Milo D. Mason, one of its pioneer settlers, who was a mail carrier between Currie and Pipestone.

MOULTON township, organized October 28 and November 18, 1879, was named in honor of Justin P. Moulton, of Worthington. He was born in Gilbertsville, N. Y., July 4, 1828; came to Minnesota in 1855; kept a hotel in Saratoga, Winona county, and later engaged in mercantile business in Rochester; was a representative in the legislature, 1862-3; was receiver of the United States land office in Worthington, 1875-81.

MURRAY township, organized July 20, 1872, was named, like this county, for William Pitt Murray, of St. Paul.

OWANKA, a Sioux or Dakota word, meaning a camping place, is the name of grounds platted for summer homes in Shetek township, on and near the northeastern shore of Lake Shetek. A part in the southwest quarter of section 29 had been earlier named Tepeeota, meaning a place of Sioux tents or tepees. About a mile southward, in the center and southwest part of section 32, the high shore is called "Ball's bluff," for Ezra Ball, a pioneer settler there, on whose land a party of state cavalrymen camped as rangers through this region after the Sioux massacre in 1862.

SHETEK township, at first called Lake Shetek, organized July 20, 1872, was named for its large lake, of which the broadest expanse is in the southwest part of this township, and which also reaches south into Mason and Murray. Nicollet wrote of his visit here in the summer of 1838: "I pitched my tents, during three days, about the group of Shetek or Pelican lakes, that occupy a portion of the space forming the Coteau des Prairies. This name belongs to the language of the Chippewas and has been given to them by the voyageurs. The Sioux call this group of lakes the *Rabechy,* meaning the place where the pelicans nestle" [have nests]. (Report, 1843, page 13.) Shetek is thus noted as an Ojibway word, meaning a pelican, but it differs somewhat from its original form. It is spelled Shada in Longfellow's "Song of Hiawatha," Shede (each vowel being pronounced like long *a*) by Gilfillan, and jede (nearly the same as each of the preceding in pronunciation) by Verwyst.

Six years after Nicollet was here, Captain James Allen, with a company of dragoons, explored the Des Moines valley in August and September, 1844, from its junction with the Mississippi to Lake Shetek, which, not having Nicollet's report and map, he called "the Lake of the Oaks, . . . the highest source of the Des Moines that is worth noticing as such."

SKANDIA township, first settled in 1870 and organized January 7, 1873, bears the ancient name of southern Sweden, whence a longer form of the same name, Scandinavia, is used to designate the great peninsula of Sweden and Norway, or, in a wider sense, to include also Denmark and Iceland.

SLAYTON township, organized July 20, 1872, was then called Center, for its central position in the county; but in 1882, a year after Slayton railway village was platted, the township was thus renamed, in honor of Charles W. Slayton, its founder and chief proprietor. He was a real estate dealer, lived in this village about two years, 1881-2, removed afterward to New Mexico, but returned to Minnesota and lived in St. Paul several years. The county seat was removed from Currie to Slayton, by a vote of the county, June 11, 1889.

Charles Wesley Slayton was born at West Potsdam, N. Y., August 24, 1835; came to Wisconsin, with his parents, in 1855; was a farmer, and after 1868 a manufacturer of furniture in Berlin, Wis., and a traveling salesman; removed to Minnesota in 1878, settling in St. Paul as a land agent of the St. Paul and Sioux City railroad company; platted Slayton village in 1881; went to England early in 1882, and returned in April with 67 colonists, most of whom settled in or near this village; was a partner after 1882 in gold and silver mining in New Mexico, but thereby in failure of his associates he lost his entire property; removed in 1892 to Phoenix, Arizona, there engaging again in real estate business and in mining. (History of the Slayton Family, 1898, pages 123-124, with his portrait.) On account of failing health, he went in hope of recovery to Little Rock, Arkansas, and died there, June 5, 1906.

Lakes and Streams.

The foregoing pages have noticed the Des Moines river, Chanarambie creek, Lakes Sarah and Maria, Lake Wilson, Lime lake and creek, and Lake Shetek.

Okshida creek, as named on Nicollet's map, called also Oksida or Beaver creek on later maps, being the head stream of Des Moines river, gave its name in the early years to Okcheeda township, from 1872 to 1879, since called Mason. This is evidently the same Sioux word that in Nobles county is applied to Lake Ocheeda and Ocheyedan creek or river, south of Worthington. Its meaning is indicated by Nicollet on his map, which, in the belt of morainic drift hills that is intersected by this lake and its outflowing stream, has "Ocheyedan Hillock or Mourning Ground." In the Dakota Dictionary by Riggs, 1852, acheya and akicheya are verbs meaning to mourn, as for a dead relative, these words being allied closely with the names cited in Nobles county, and with Okshida, variously spelled, in Murray county. Here the name commemorates the mourning for two boys killed by a war party of enemies.

The southeast part of Moulton is drained by Champepadan creek, flowing southward into Nobles and Rock counties. Its Sioux or Dakota name, given by Nicollet, with translation, as "Tchan Pepedan river, or Thorny Wood river," was derived from its thorn bushes and small trees.

Currant lake, on the west line of Skandia, and Plum creek, in Holly township, each flowing northeast to the Cottonwood river, received these names from their wild currants and wild plum trees.

Skandia also has Iron lake and Lake Oscar.

Hawk or Rush lake, crossed by the south line of Skandia, was the most northeastern of the group of Bear lakes, four in number, lying mainly in Lowville, the others being Crooked and Bear lakes and Tibbetts or Great Oasis lake. The first and third are now represented by dry lake beds, having become valuable farming lands. The fourth is called Great Oasis lake on recent maps, from this name applied by Nicollet to the adjoining grove, which had an area of more than 300 acres, before noted for Lowville township.

Lake Wilson, close east of the railway village so named, was earlier called Sand lake. It is shallow and becomes dry in seasons of scanty rainfall.

Summit lake adjoins Hadley village, whence the railway descends both to the east and west.

Lake Elsie, now drained and in cultivation, in the east part of Slayton village, was named for a daughter of Arthur Simpson, a settler beside it, who came from England, was the first owner of the Park hotel, and removed to southern California.

Lake Cora Belle, in Iona, and Lake Iva Delle, (spelled Ivedalle on recent maps), in Ellsborough, were named by the United States surveyors, in honor of daughters of the proprietor of the principal hotel in Worthington.

The Badger lakes, in the northeast corner of Iona, named for badgers formerly found here, are expected soon to be drained.

In the southeast part of Mason are Lake Beauty, so called by Henry Edwards, a settler near it, and Mud and Clear lakes, which are described by their names.

Another Clear lake, now dry, was crossed by the west line of section 6, Shetek; and James lake, named for James P. Corbin and James W. Matthews, early settlers beside it, is in the east half of section 4, outflowing eastward to Plum creek.

"The Inlet" is a long and narrow northwestern arm or branch of Lake Shetek, receiving a tributary creek from Long lake, which is crossed by the north line of this county.

Several small lakes adjoin the northeast end of Lake Shetek, named Bloody lake, for victims of the Sioux massacre in 1862, Fox lake, Isabella or Round lake, and Lake Fremont. The last commemorates John C. Fremont (b. 1813, d. 1890), who was here with Nicollet in 1838, renowned later as an explorer, and as the Republican candidate in 1856 for the presidency of the United States.

Smith lake, named for Henry Watson Smith, a pioneer farmer, at its west side, is near the southeast shore of Lake Shetek, in sections 6 and 7, Murray. He settled here before the Sioux massacre, left his claim at that time, and never returned.

In Dovray are Skow lake, in section 1; Long lake, on the west side of sections 3 and 10; Rush lake, in section 15; Lake Buffalo, in section 18;

Duck lake, a half mile southeast of Dovray village; and Star lake, at the middle of the south line of this township.

Lake Louisa (earlier mapped as Lake Eliza) is in sections 11 and 12, Des Moines River.

Seven Mile lake, close south of Fulda, was named for its distance on an old trail from the Graham lakes in Nobles county.

Center lake, also called Central lake, is at the center of Belfast. Talcott lake, on the east line of its sections 24 and 25, was named by Nicollet in honor of Andrew Talcott (b. 1797, d. 1883), as noted in the chapter of Cottonwood county.

Buffalo Ridge.

The highest land in this county, extending about two miles along the crest of the Coteau des Prairies in the central part of Chanarambie, is called Buffalo Ridge, in translation of its Sioux name. It rises 100 to 200 feet above the lowest adjoining valleys. On its highest knoll the Sioux had delineated various animals by "a series of boulder outlines, mostly formed of small stones. The best preserved of these figures apparently represents a buffalo. . . . It heads to the northeast, and its greatest length is nearly 12 feet." (T. H. Lewis, in the *American Anthropologist,* July, 1890, quoted in "The Aborigines of Minnesota," 1911, pages 106-108, with a diagram of the buffalo outline.)

NICOLLET COUNTY

Established March 5, 1853, this county was named in honor of Joseph Nicolas Nicollet, geographer and explorer, whose admirable map and report of the region that now comprises Minnesota and the eastern parts of North and South Dakota were published in 1843, soon after his death. His name is also commemorated by an island of the Mississippi at Minneapolis, and by a principal avenue of that city. (In pronunciation the name is anglicized, with accent on the first syllable, and sounding the final letter.)

Nicollet was born July 24, 1786, at Cluses, in Savoy; completed his studies in Paris, where in 1817 he was appointed an officer of the astronomical observatory; in 1819 he became a citizen of France, and in 1825, or earlier, he received the Cross of the Legion of Honor. He was financially ruined by results of the Revolution of 1830, and came to the United States in 1832, to travel in unsettled parts of the South and West. Under the direction of the U. S. War Department and Bureau of Topographical Engineers, he made a canoe journey in 1836, from Fort Snelling up the Mississippi to Itasca lake, and in 1838 a trip up the Minnesota river and past Lake Shetek to the red pipestone quarry. He died in Washington, D. C., September 11, 1843.

In the United States government reports and maps of his work, his name appears varyingly as I. N. or J. N. Nicollet; and it is given as Jean N. by General Sibley, Dr. Neill, Prof. N. H. Winchell, and other writers of Minnesota history. Researches by Horace V. Winchell, however, in 1893, published in the American Geologist (vol. XIII, pages 126-128, for February, 1894), show that his name was Joseph Nicolas Nicollet. A biographic sketch of him, with a portrait, was given by N. H. Winchell in the American Geologist (vol. VIII, pages 343-352, December, 1891); and additional details were given by H. V. Winchell in the article before cited.

The error of this name, during half a century so generally mistaken, may have come from its being confounded with that of the much earlier French explorer, Jean Nicolet (also spelled Nicollet), who came to Canada in 1618, and who was a most energetic and honored agent of the proprietors of Canada for the promotion of the fur trade. In 1634 this Nicolet visited the Sault Ste. Marie, and thence came to Green bay in eastern Wisconsin, being the first white man known to explore any part of that state. He died on the last day of October, 1642, being drowned by shipwreck on the St. Lawrence river near Quebec.

Townships and Villages.

Information of geographic names has been gathered from "History of the Minnesota Valley," 1882, having pages 637-697 on this county; "History of Nicollet and Le Sueur Counties," edited by Hon. William G. Gresham, two volumes, pages 544 and 538, 1916; and from Judge Gresham, the editor here cited; Z. S. Gault, cashier of the Nicollet County Bank, Henry Moll, judge of probate, and Mrs. Mary Briggs Aiton, widow of Rev. John F. Aiton, each being interviewed during a visit at St. Peter, the county seat, in July, 1916.

BELGRADE township, first settled in 1854 and organized in 1858, was named from a township and village in Kennebec county, Maine, and from the ancient city of Belgrade, the capital of Serbia, on the River Danube.

BERNADOTTE township, settled in 1859, organized January 23, 1869, received this name at the suggestion of John Miller, one of its pioneer settlers, in honor of Charles XV (b. 1826, d. 1872), king of Sweden and Norway. He was the son of Oscar I, and was the grandson of a French general, Jean Baptiste Jules Bernadotte (b. 1764, d. 1844), who was elected crown prince of Sweden in 1810 and became the king in 1818, with the title Charles XIV. A township and village in Illinois also bear this name.

BRIGHTON, settled in 1855, but the latest township organized in this county, October 16, 1877, had several families who came from Brighton township in Kenosha county, Wisconsin.

COURTLAND township, organized in 1858, was then called Hilo, from its post office established in 1856, which received that name from a bay and town in Hawaii. It was renamed in 1865, for Cortland county and its county seat in New York, whence some of its settlers came. The village of this township, having the same name, designated as a railway station in 1872, was platted February 14, 1882.

GRANBY township, settled in May, 1855, organized May 11, 1858, has the name of townships and villages in Vermont, Massachusetts, Connecticut, New York, and the Province of Quebec.

KLOSSNER, a railway village in Lafayette, platted in October, 1897, was named for Jacob Klossner, proprietor of its site. He was born in Switzerland, December 23, 1846; came with his parents to the United States when three years old, and to Minnesota in 1856; served against the Sioux, with the First Minnesota Mounted Rangers, 1862-3; owned a farm in New Ulm; was a representative in the legislature in 1878.

LAFAYETTE township, settled in 1853 and organized May 11, 1858, was named, like townships and villages or cities of twenty other states of the Union, with counties of six states, in honor of the Marquis de Lafayette (b. 1757, d. 1834), of France, who came to America and greatly aided Washington in the Revolutionary War, and later was an eminent French statesman and general. The railway village of this name, in the northeast corner of the township, was platted in 1897.

NICOLLET COUNTY 373

LAKE PRAIRIE township, settled in the summer of 1853, organized in 1858, was mainly an extensive prairie, with numerous small lakes, some of which have been drained.

NEW SWEDEN township, organized January 25, 1864, has many Swedish settlers; but its earliest settlement, in 1855-57, was by immigrants from Norway, taking homesteads near a grove in its north part, which therefore was named Norwegian Grove.

NICOLLET township, named after the county, was first settled in the spring of 1854 and was organized May 11, 1858. An early village of this name, in section 17, was platted in 1857, but lasted only three years. The present Nicollet railway village was incorporated November 17, 1881.

NORTH MANKATO, in Belgrade township, is a village on the Minnesota river, opposite to the city of Mankato, Blue Earth county.

OSHAWA township, first settled in 1852, organized in 1858, received its name from the Canadian town of Oshawa on the northwest shore of Lake Ontario, noted by Gannett as an Indian word, meaning "ferry him over," or "across the river."

REDSTONE, a village site platted in 1856, on sections 34 and 35 in the west part of the present Courtland township, was named for adjacent outcrops of red quartzite beside the Minnesota river. A few years later this site was mostly vacated by removal of its settlers to New Ulm, Brown county.

RIDGELY township, organized September 26, 1871, was named for Fort Ridgely, in its section 6, built in 1853-54, which was used as a United States military post until the spring of 1867. The fort was named in 1854 by Jefferson Davis, then secretary of war, in honor of three army officers from Maryland who died in the Mexican war, Lieut. Henderson Ridgely, Captain Randolph Ridgely, and Captain Thomas P. Ridgely. During thirteen years before its organization, from 1858 to 1871, this township was a part of West Newton, which was named from the steamboat that brought the first troops and supplies to build Fort Ridgely, as noted for that township.

ST. PETER, the county seat, first settled in the fall of 1853 by Captain William B. Dodd, platted in June, 1854, was incorporated as a borough March 2, 1865, and as a city January 7, 1873. It was named for the St. Pierre or St. Peter river, as the Minnesota river was called by the early French and English explorers and fur traders, probably in honor of Pierre Charles Le Sueur, whose surname is borne by the adjoining county on the east side of this river.

TRAVERSE township, organized May 11, 1858, took the name of its village, platted in 1852, commonly called Traverse des Sioux, "Crossing of the Sioux," because the Minnesota river was crossed here on a much used trail from St. Paul and Fort Snelling to the upper Minnesota valley and the Red river valley. In 1823 this place was named "the Crescent" by Long's expedition, referring to a bend of the river; but before 1838, when Nicollet was here, it had received this French name, Traverse des Sioux.

The Dakota Dictionary, published in 1852, notes its Sioux name as Oiyuwege, meaning "the place of crossing, a ford."

WEST NEWTON township, settled in the spring of 1856 and organized May 11, 1858, originally included Fort Ridgely and the present Ridgely township. It was named partly in compliment to James Newton, one of its first settlers, who was born in Kentucky in 1829, took a homestead claim here in 1856, and served in the Second Minnesota regiment in the civil war. A further and principal reason for the choice of this township name was the steamboat named West Newton, under command of Captain D. S. Harris, which made the trip from Fort Snelling to the site of Fort Ridgely in the last four days of April, 1853, bringing two companies of the Sixth regiment, with lumber and supplies for building the fort. "This was the first steamer that had ascended the Minnesota river any distance above the mouth of the Blue Earth," as Major Benjamin H. Randall wrote in a paper on the history of Fort Ridgely, especially narrating its defence against the Sioux, August 18-22, 1862, published in the Winona Republican, 1892.

The steamboat, West Newton, 150 feet long and of 300 tons burden, was built for Captain Harris in 1852, for the Mississippi river traffic between Galena and St. Paul. It was the earliest boat arriving at St. Paul in the spring of 1853, on April 11, and during that season it made twenty-seven trips to and from St. Paul, until in September it was sunk near Alma, Wisconsin. (George B. Merrick, "Old Times on the Upper Mississippi," 1909, page 293.)

LAKES AND STREAMS.

The Sioux name, Mini Sotah, borne with changed spelling by the river which borders this county and by the state, is also applied on Nicollet's map to the lake crossed by the county line on the north side of West Newton, translated as Clear lake. The outlet of Clear lake is Eight Mile creek, crossed eight miles from Fort Ridgely on the road to Traverse des Sioux.

Little Rock creek or river, also called Mud creek, joins the Minnesota river near the east line of Ridgely. About three miles northwest from its mouth is an outcrop of gneiss and granite in the Minnesota valley, adjoining the site of a former Indian trading post, called Little Rock in translation of the French name, Petite Roche, given to it by the early traders and voyageurs.

Fort creek, flowing past the east side of the site of Fort Ridgely, is the most western tributary of the Minnesota river in this county.

Nicollet creek, flowing south through Nicollet township to the Minnesota, is the outlet of the large Swan lake, which Nicollet mapped as Marrah Tanka (for *maga,* goose, *tanka,* great), the Sioux name of the swan. Keating, in the Narrative of Long's expedition in 1823, wrote of this lake, "The Indian name is Manha tanka otamenda, which signifies the

NICOLLET COUNTY 375

lake of the many large birds." Two species, the trumpeter swan and the whistling swan, were formerly found in Minnesota. The first, which now is extinct, nested here; but the second, which yet is rarely seen in this state, has its breeding grounds far north of our region.

Eastward from Swan lake are Middle lake, Little lake, Horseshoe lake, named for its shape, Timber lake, having trees and groves on its shores and on its large island, Fox lake, and Rogers lake, the last, in section 3, Traverse, being named for a pioneer farmer.

Oak Leaf lake, formerly called Cowan's lake, in section 25, Oshawa, received its present name in honor of H. J. Eckloff, an adjoining Swedish farmer, whose name has this meaning.

Goose lake, named for its wild geese, on the line between Traverse and Oshawa, has been drained.

Several small creeks flowing to the Minnesota river, mostly in the east part of the county, remain unnamed on maps.

SITE OF THE SIOUX TREATY, 1851.

Near the ford of the Minnesota river, called the Traverse des Sioux, whence Traverse village and township were named, a treaty with the Dakotas or Sioux had been made in 1841 by Governor James D. Doty of Wisconsin, which, however, failed of ratification in the United States Senate. Ten years later, on July 23, 1851, a treaty with the Wahpeton and Sisseton Sioux of the Minnesota valley was concluded here by Governor Ramsey and Colonel Luke Lea, whereby these Indians ceded to the United States, for white settlement, the greater part of their lands in southern Minnesota. A year later this treaty, with changes afterward accepted by the Sioux, received ratification by the Senate, and it was proclaimed by President Fillmore on February 24, 1853. (See the account of these Treaties, by Thomas Hughes, M. H. S. Collections, vol. X, 1905, pages 101-129.)

The site of the Treaty of Traverse des Sioux in 1851 was appropriately marked June 17, 1914, by a brass tablet on a granite boulder, unveiled by Mrs. Mary B. Aiton. This historic memorial was presented to the state, from the Captain Richard Somers Chapter of the Daughters of the American Revolution, St. Peter, by Mrs. H. L. Stark, regent. (St. Peter Herald, June 19, 1914.)

NOBLES COUNTY

Established May 23, 1857, and organized October 27, 1870, this county was named for William H. Nobles, who was a member of the Minnesota territorial legislature in 1854 and 1856. In the autumn of the latter year he began the construction of a wagon road for the United States government, crossing southwestern Minnesota and this county, to extend from Fort Ridgely to the South pass in the Rocky mountains. This work was continued in 1857, but was not completed.

Nobles was born in New York state in 1816; was a machinist by trade, and came to St. Croix Falls, Wisconsin, in 1841, to assist in building the first mill there, but soon removed to Hudson, Wis., then called Willow River; in 1843 he began his residence in Minnesota, at Stillwater; and in 1848 came to St. Paul, where he commenced wagon-making and blacksmithing, building for Henry H. Sibley the first wagon made here. In 1849 he went to California, and lived there, in Shasta county, until May, 1852, when he led a party of citizens to inspect a pass which he had discovered, crossing the Sierra Nevada, since bearing his name. Returning to Minnesota, he earnestly advocated the building of an immigrant road (and ultimately a railroad) from St. Paul, by way of the South pass and Nobles pass, to San Francisco. He served as lieutenant colonel in the 79th New York regiment during a part of the civil war, and afterward held several government positions. A few years of ill health ensued, and he died in St. Paul, December 28, 1876, having returned a few days previous from seeking in vain for recovery.

The United States steamship Nobles, named in honor of this county's Liberty Loan record in the World War, was launched August 23, 1919.

TOWNSHIPS AND VILLAGES.

Information of geographic names has been received from "An Illustrated History of Nobles County," by Arthur P. Rose, 637 pages, 1908; and from Dr. George O. Moore, president of the State Bank of Worthington, and Julius A. Town, attorney, who came here as pioneer settlers in 1872, interviewed at Worthington, the county seat, in July, 1916.

ADRIAN, a village in Olney and West Side townships, platted in May, 1876, and incorporated November 17, 1881, was named in honor of Adrian Iselin, who was the mother of Adrian C. Iselin, one of the directors of the St. Paul and Sioux City railroad company. In the vicinity of Adrian a Catholic colony of immigrant farmers was founded by Archbishop Ireland in 1879.

BIGELOW township, organized May 20, 1872, and its railway village, platted in the same year, were named in honor of Charles Henry Bigelow, who was born in Easton, N. Y., June 4, 1835, and died in St. Paul,

Minn., July 31, 1911. He settled at St. Paul in 1864, engaged in lumber business and insurance, and was president of the St. Paul Fire and Marine Insurance Company, 1876-1911. This village was incorporated March 14, 1900.

BLOOM township, organized in April, 1879, was named in honor of Peter Bloom and his family, including three sons, who were its first settlers, locating on section 22 in 1874.

BREWSTER, the railway village of Hersey township, platted April 22, 1872, was called Hersey until August, 1880, being then renamed for the village and township of Brewster in Barnstable county, Mass. William Brewster, honored in the name of that township, was born in Scrooby, England, about 1560, was one of the founders of the Plymouth colony in Massachusetts, coming on the Mayflower in 1620, and died in Plymouth, Mass., April 10, 1644.

DEWALD township, organized September 20, 1872, was named in honor of Amos and Hiram Dewald, pioneer settlers, who came in April, 1872.

DUNDEE, a railway village in the northeast corner of Graham Lakes township, platted in 1879 and incorporated February 15, 1898, has the name of a city in Scotland, which is also borne by villages in twelve other states.

ELK township, established September 16, 1872, took the name given by early trappers to the creek which has its sources here, flowing eastward. A lone elk was seen in this township ten days before the petition for its organization was granted by the county commissioners.

ELLSWORTH, the railway village and junction in Grand Prairie township, platted in September, 1884, and incorporated January 13, 1887, was named in honor of Eugene Ellsworth, of Cedar Falls, Iowa.

GRAHAM LAKES township, organized April 21, 1871, received this name from its East and West Graham lakes, mapped as Lake Graham by Nicollet. James Duncan Graham and Andrew Talcott, for whom Nicollet named Lake Talcott in the southwest corner of Cottonwood county, were commissioners in 1840-43, with James Renwick, for the survey of the northeastern part of the international boundary between the United States and Canada. Graham was born in Virginia, April 4, 1799; and died in Boston, Mass., December 28, 1865. He was graduated at the United States Military Academy in 1817, served in the corps of topographical engineers after 1829, and was brevetted lieutenant colonel for his valuable work on the northeastern boundary survey.

GRAND PRAIRIE township, organized October 30, 1873, is in a very extensive prairie region, which has mostly an undulating or rolling surface, but the greater part of this township is nearly level.

HERSEY township, organized June 11, 1872, took the early name of its railway village, which was changed to Brewster in 1880, as before noted. The township name commemorates Samuel Freeman Hersey, of Bangor, Maine, who was a director of the St. Paul and Sioux City railroad company. He was born in Sumner, Maine, April 12, 1812; engaged in lumber business and banking in Maine, Minnesota, and Wisconsin, and established large sawmills in Stillwater, Minn.; was a member of Congress from Maine, 1873-75; and died in Bangor, February 3, 1875.

INDIAN LAKE township, established April 22, 1871, bears the name of its lake in sections 27 and 34, where the first white settlers, coming in 1869, found the camp of a considerable band of Sioux who remained in this vicinity during several years.

KINBRAE village, in Graham Lakes township, founded in 1879 by the Dundee Land Company of Scotland, was at first called Airlie and later De Forest, but received the present Scottish name in August, 1883. It was incorporated February 17, 1896.

LARKIN township, the latest organized in this county, March 27, 1883, was named in honor of John Larkin, of New York city, a prominent worker in the Catholic colonization association which brought many settlers to southwestern Minnesota.

LEOTA township was organized April 5, 1879. "The name was suggested by W. G. Barnard, one of the township's earliest settlers. It is the only township, village or physical feature in Nobles county named in honor of an Indian. Leota was an Indian maiden who figured in a story of Indian adventure." (History of this county by Rose, p. 102.)

LISMORE township, organized August 9, 1880, to which many Irish Catholic settlers came during that year, was named after a village of County Waterford in Ireland, noted for a fine baronial castle. Lismore railway village was platted in the summer of 1900, and was incorporated May 27, 1902.

LITTLE ROCK township, organized September 20, 1872, is crossed by the Little Rock river, which here receives its West branch. Thence it flows southwestward through Lyon county in Iowa to the Rock river, which is named, like Rock county of Minnesota, from the Mound, a precipitous hill of red quartzite near Luverne in that county.

LORAIN township was organized September 20, 1872, being then named Fairview, from its beautiful panoramic outlook over this great prairie region, but was renamed June 15, 1874, "after the town of Loraine, Adams county, Ill., the superfluous 'e' being dropped." This name in Ohio and Illinois came from the ancient large district of Lorraine in France and Germany.

OLNEY township, established July 10, 1873, was at first called Hebbard in honor of William F. Hebbard, an early settler. June 15, 1874, it received the present name, after the county seat of Richland county, Illinois, which was namd for Nathan Olney of Lawrenceville in that state.

ORG, a railway station and junction about four miles southwest of Worthington, was formerly Sioux Falls Junction, but received this name, of unknown derivation, in 1890, the change being ordered by W. A. Scott, then general manager of the Chicago and Northwestern railway.

RANSOM township, organized September 20, 1872, was at first named Grant, for General and President Grant, but was changed because he had

NOBLES COUNTY 379

been thus honored earlier by another Minnesota township. July 10, 1873, the present name was given by the county commissioners, in honor of Ransom F. Humiston, the founder of Worthington. He was born in Great Barrington, Mass., July 3, 1822; was educated in the Western Reserve College, Ohio, and was principal of a classical school which he established in Cleveland, Ohio; organized the National Colony Company in 1871, and brought many settlers to Worthington and other parts of this county; returned to live in the east, and died in April, 1889.

READING, the railway village of Summit Lake township, platted in June, 1900, was named in honor of a pioneer farmer, Henry H. Read, the original owner of a part of the village site.

ROUND LAKE village, on the railway in Indian Lake township, founded in 1882, was named for the adjoining Round lake, in Jackson county, on request of O. H. Roche, who owned a ranch of nearly 2,000 acres surrounding that lake. It was incorporated August 10, 1898.

RUSHMORE village, platted in July, 1878, on the Sioux Falls branch of the Omaha railway, bears the name of its pioneer merchant, S. M. Rushmore. It was incorporated March 27, 1900.

SEWARD township, organized October 30, 1872, commemorates William Henry Seward, the noted statesman, who was born in Florida, N. Y., May 16, 1801, and died in Auburn, N. Y., October 10, 1872. He was governor of New York, 1839-42, and a United States senator, 1849-61; was secretary of state, 1861-69, and concluded the purchase of Alaska from Russia in 1867.

SUMMIT LAKE township, organized June 5, 1873, was first called Wilson, later Akin, and received its present name July 27, 1874, from its former lake in section 11, whence the general surface descends in very gentle slopes both eastward and westward.

WEST SIDE township, organized February 24, 1877, is at the west side of the county.

WILLMONT township was organized December 12, 1878. "One faction wanted the township named Willumet, the other Lamont. When the commissioners, on November 22, provided for the organization, they named the township Willmont, a combination of parts of the names suggested by the two factions." (History by Rose, p. 100.)

WILMONT railway village, platted in December, 1899, omitting one letter of the township name, was incorporated May 29, 1900.

WORTHINGTON, the county seat, platted in the summer of 1871, was incorporated as a village March 8, 1873, and as a city in 1912. Its site had been called Okabena during the grading of the railway in 1871, for the two adjoining lakes, meaning the nesting place of herons, a Sioux name from *hokah,* heron, *be,* nests, and *na,* a diminutive suffix, as noted by Prof. A. W. Williamson. In the autumn of 1871 that name was changed to Worthington, in honor of the mother of Mrs. Mary Dorman Miller, wife of Dr. A. P. Miller, who was intimately associated with Ransom F. Humiston in forming the National Colony Company and founding Worthington, before noticed because Ransom township was named for him. Mrs. Miller in 1888 wrote of the origin of this name: "My mother's maiden name was Worthington. Her father was Robert Worthington, of Chillicothe, Ohio, who was the brother of Thomas Worthington, governor of Ohio; and the now beautiful, prosperous town of Worthington, Minn., was named for the Chillicothe family." Worthington township was organized May 20, 1872.

Dr. A. P. Miller, whose wife and her family were thus honored, came from Ohio to Minnesota in 1871; was editor and owner of the Worthington Advance, 1872-87; removed to California, and in 1908 was in newspaper business at Los Angeles. He is author of an excellent poem read at the Hennepin Bi-Centenary celebration in Minneapolis, 1880 (M. H. S. Collections, vol. VI, pages 55-61).

Lakes and Streams.

The foregoing pages have noticed Elk creek, from which Elk township is named, the Graham lakes, Indian lake, Little Rock river, and Summit lake, all of which likewise give their names to townships. The railway village of Round Lake is for a lake and township of Jackson county.

Another Elk creek, formed by small streams from Lismore and West Side townships, flows southwest into Rock county, to the Rock river.

Okabena creek, flowing east from Worthington to Heron lake in Jackson county, is the outlet of the West Okabena lake, whence the site of Worthington was at first named Okabena, as before noted. From this name, given to Heron lake on Nicollet's map in 1843, the present name of that lake was translated, while the Sioux name, referring to these lakes and the creek as "the nesting place of herons," was retained for the creek and for two lakes at Worthington, of which the east one has been drained.

Jack creek, in the northeast part of this county, probably named for its jack rabbits, also flows into Heron lake.

Lake Ocheeda (or Ocheda lake), its outflowing Ocheyedan creek, and Okshida creek in Murray county, are names received by Nicollet from the Sioux, having reference to their mourning for the dead, as before noted in the chapter of Murray county.

Kanaranzi creek, which gathers its head streams from the central part of Nobles county, running southwest to the Rock river and giving its name to a township in Rock county, was mapped by Nicollet as "Karanzi R., or R. where the Kansas were killed," referring to Kansas or Kaw Indians who had ventured thus far into the Dakota or Sioux country.

Champepadan creek, crossing the northwest corner of this county, is likewise a Sioux name given by Nicollet, somewhat transformed in spelling, which his map translates as "Thorny Wood river," from its having thorn bushes and trees.

Eagle lake, formerly in sections 4 and 9, Graham Lakes township, has been recently drained. Clear lake adjoins Kinbrae village in this township, and State Line lake is at the southeast corner of this county.

NORMAN COUNTY

This county, established February 17, 1881, has been thought by R. I. Holcombe and others to be named, like Kittson county three years before, in honor of Norman W. Kittson, who accomplished much for the extension of commerce and immigration to the Red River valley. The actual choice of this name, however, as better known by residents of the county and by surviving members of the convention held at Ada for securing its establishment by the state legislature, was for commemoration of the great number of Norwegian (Norseman or Norman) immigrants who had settled there. Norse delegates were a majority in the convention, and the name was selected on account of patriotic love and memories of their former homes across the sea. Similarly a township organized in March, 1874, in Yellow Medicine county, had been named Norman; and another township there in the same year received the name Normania. "In Norway a native is referred to as a Norsk or Norman."

By the census of 1910, in a total population of 13,446 in Norman county, 2,957 were born in Norway; and both parents of 4,651 others, among those born in America, were Norwegian. No other county of Minnesota has so large a proportion of Norwegian people.

Townships and Villages.

Information of the origins and meanings of names has been gathered from "History of the Red River Valley," two volumes, 1909, having pages 967-972 for Norman county; and from David E. Fulton, county auditor, historian for the Norman County Old Settlers' Association, and Conrad K. Semling, clerk of the court, interviewed during visits at Ada, the county seat, in September, 1909, and again in September, 1916. Additional notes were also received in 1916 from Alexander Holden, of Ada, and Anund K. Strand, of Lake Ida township, pioneers who came respectively in 1872 and 1880.

ADA, the county seat, founded in 1874, and incorporated as a village February 9, 1881, was named in honor of a daughter of William H. Fisher, of St. Paul, then attorney and superintendent of the St. Paul and Pacific railroad, under whose superintendency this line of the Red river valley was constructed. A biographic notice of him is given in the chapter of Polk county, where his name is borne by Fisher township and village. Ada Nelson Fisher died at the age of six years, in 1880, but this prosperous and beautiful village and the county perpetuate her name and memory.

ANTHONY township, organized in 1879, was named for Anthony Scheie, one of its first settlers, who came here in 1872. His father, Andreas A.

Scheie, the first pastor in this county, was born in Vigedal, Norway, February 17, 1818; came to the United States in 1840; was ordained to the ministry in 1855; was pastor in Fillmore county, Minn., 1857-76, and afterward in Ada; died in 1885.

BEAR PARK township, organized in 1881, received this name in accordance with the request of its settlers in the petition for organization.

BORUP, a railway village in Winchester township, was named in honor of Charles William Wulff Borup, who was born in Copenhagen, Denmark, December 20, 1806, and died in St. Paul, July 6, 1859. He came to the United States in 1828, and to St. Paul in 1848, where in 1854 he established the banking house of Borup and Oakes, the first in Minnesota. His sons, Gustav J. and Theodore Borup, were also prominent business men in St. Paul.

FLAMING is a Northern Pacific railway village in Sundahl.

FLOM township, at first called Springfield, organized in 1881, was named for Erik Flom, a native of Norway, who came here as a pioneer farmer in 1871.

FOSSUM township, settled in 1872 and organized in 1881, was named for a village in southern Norway.

GARY, the railway village of Strand township, founded in 1883, received this name in compliment to Garrett L. Thorpe, its first merchant, who came here from Manchester, Iowa, became an extensive land owner in this county, and settled at Ada.

GOOD HOPE township was the latest organized, in 1892, its auspicious name being chosen by vote of its people.

GREEN MEADOW township, organized in 1880, bears a name that was likewise chosen by its people, having reference to the summer verdure of its prairie surface.

HADLER, a railway village in Pleasant View township, was named for Jacob Hadler, an early settler there, who in 1909-15 was a member of the board of county commissioners.

HALSTAD township, organized in 1879, and its railway village, were named for Ole Halstad, a pioneer farmer, who came from Norway. During many years he was the postmaster of Marsh River post office in this township, now discontinued.

HEGNE township, organized in 1881, was named for Andrew E. Hegne, one of its first settlers, coming from the district of Stavanger, Norway, who removed to Evansville, Minn., and was a hardware merchant there.

HEIBERG, a railway village in Wild Rice township, was named in honor of Jorgen F. Heiberg, owner of its flour mill.

HENDRUM township, organized in 1880, and its railway village, founded in 1881, are named from a district or group of farms in Norway, whence some of the early settlers of this township came.

HOME LAKE township, organized in 1881, has two lakelets in section 13, to which this name was given as a compliment for John Homelvig, the former clerk of this township.

NORMAN COUNTY 383

LAKE IDA township, organized in 1879, bears the name of a small lake in its sections 7 and 8, given in honor of Ida Paulson, daughter of an early homesteader in Anthony township.

LEE township, at first called Norman, organized in 1882, was named for Ole Lee, a pioneer settler, who came from Kongsberg, Norway. His son, B. O. Lee, of this township, was in 1909-17 a member of the board of county commissioners.

LOCKHART township, organized in 1882, was named for its very large Lockhart farm, which bore the name of the owner, a resident in Pennsylvania. Lockhart railway village, in the north edge of section 29, has superseded the former Rolette station and village in section 17.

McDONALDSVILLE township. the first organized in the area of this county, in 1874, was named in honor of one of its pioneer farmers, Finnen McDonald, a native of Scotland, who came to Minnesota from Glengarry, Ontario, settling here beside the Wild Rice river.

MARY township, organized about the year 1880, was named in honor of the wife of Jacob Thomas, an early settler here.

PERLEY, the railway village of Lee township, was named in honor of George Edmund Perley, of Moorhead. He was born in Lempster, N. H., August 19, 1853; was graduated at Dartmouth College, 1878; was admitted to practice law in 1883, and came to Minnesota the next year, settling in Moorhead; was a representative in the legislature in 1903-05.

PLEASANT VIEW township, organized in 1880, received this euphonious name by suggestion of James Preston, one of its pioneers, who later removed to Duluth.

ROCKWELL township, at first called Wheatland, organized in 1882, was named by settlers who came from Rockwell in Cerro Gordo county, Iowa.

ROLETTE, a former railway village in Lockhart township, was superseded by Lockhart village. Its name commemorates Joe Rolette, who was born at Prairie du Chien, Wis., October 23, 1820, and died at Pembina, Dakota, May 16, 1871. He was employed by the American Fur Company at their trading post at Pembina in 1840; established a cart route from the Red river to St. Paul, extending the fur trade of that city into a large region in competition with the Hudson Bay Company; was a representative in the territorial legislature of Minnesota, 1853-5, and a member of the territorial council, 1856-7. During the latter year occurred his notorious exploit of carrying away the bill to remove the seat of government to St. Peter, and thus he saved the capital to St. Paul.

SHELLY township, organized in 1879, was named for John Shelly, a trapper, who was the first homestead farmer of this township, was later a wheat buyer at Ada, and thence removed to Duluth as an assistant grain inspector for the state. Shelly railway village was platted in 1896.

SPRING CREEK township, organized in 1880, was named for the creek flowing through it, a tributary of the Marsh river.

STRAND township, organized in 1880, was so named by the Norwegian settlers because its poplar groves bordering the beaches of the glacial

Lake Agassiz, seen at a long distance from the vast prairie of the Red river valley, resembled an ocean strand or shore.

SUNDAHL, organized in 1880, received its name from a village and a river in Norway.

SYRE is the railway village of Home Lake township.

TWIN VALLEY, a railway village in Wild Rice township, was named from its situation between the Wild Rice river and a tributary creek.

WAUKON township, organized in 1880, has a Dakota or Sioux name, meaning "spiritual, sacred, wonderful." It probably refers to the grandeur of the view westward over the broad Red river valley, this township being crossed by the highest shoreline of Lake Agassiz.

WHEATVILLE is a railway village in Winchester.

WILD RICE township, organized in 1881, is crossed by the Wild Rice river, translated from its Ojibway name, Manomin or Mahnomen.

WINCHESTER township, organized in 1854, was named by settlers from Winchester in Van Buren county, Iowa. This name is borne by townships and villages or cities of twenty-one states of the Union.

LAKES AND STREAMS.

The Red river has been considered in the first chapter, and the Wild Rice river is most fully noticed for Mahnomen county, which bears the aboriginal name of that river and of the lakes at its source.

Marsh river, which diverges from the Wild Rice river about two miles southeast of Ada, flowing thence northwest to the Red river, is a sluggish and marshlike stream in dry seasons, but carries a great part of the Wild Rice waters during flood stages.

Spring creek, for which a township is named, receives a tributary, South Spring creek, from Green Meadow township.

Two tributaries of the Wild Rice river in this county are named on maps, these being its South branch, a considerable stream, and the little Marsh creek in Fossum.

With Lake Ida and Home lake, in the townships so named, only two other lakes are mapped with names, these being Long lake, close east of Ada, and Love lake, a former rivercourse in the northwest corner of Lee.

Several other lakelets are found in the most eastern townships, above the highest beach of Lake Agassiz; but for these no names were learned, excepting Stene lake on the farm of Mons L. Stene, in section 35, Fossum.

FRENCHMAN'S BLUFF.

The first settlers of Flom, coming in 1871, found three old log cabins, long deserted, in a grove adjoining a prominent and irregularly outlined hill of morainic drift near the center of the area of that township. Thinking the cabins to have been built by early fur traders, they named the hill "Frenchman's bluff." It rises 150 feet or more above the upper shoreline of the former Lake Agassiz, about three miles distant at the northwest, and affords a wide view on all sides.

OLMSTED COUNTY

This county, established February 20, 1855, was named in honor of David Olmsted, first mayor of St. Paul, in 1854, who in 1855 removed to Winona, in the county of that name, adjoining Olmsted county. He was born in Fairfax, Vt., May 5, 1822; came to the Northwest, first to the Wisconsin lead mining region, in 1838; was a pioneer settler of Monona, Iowa, in 1840; engaged in trading with the Indians at Fort Atkinson, Iowa, in 1844; was a member of the convention which framed the state constitution of Iowa, in 1846; came in 1848 to Long Prairie, Minn., when the Winnebago Indians were transferred there, and established a trading post which he continued several years. He was a charter member of the Minnesota Historical Society, and a member of the council of the first territorial legislature, 1849 and 1850, being its first president. In 1853, having removed to St. Paul, he became proprietor and editor of the Minnesota Democrat, which under his management began its issue as a daily newspaper in May, 1854. After his removal to Winona, ill health compelled him, in 1857, to give up business, and he then returned to his old home in Vermont, where he died February 2, 1861.

Another prominent citizen of this name, but of another family, with slightly different spelling, for whom, however, some have supposed this county to be named, was S. Baldwin Olmstead, a farmer and contractor, of Belle Prairie and Fort Ripley, who was a member of the territorial council in 1854 and 1855, when this county was created, having been president of the council in the former year. He was born in Otsego county, N. Y., in 1810; came to the Northwest in early manhood, and resided in Iowa and Minnesota; was engaged with government contracts about Fort Ripley for a time; removed to Texas at the close of the civil war, and settled on a farm in Burnett county, where he died, January 27, 1878.

Townships and Villages.

Information of geographic names has been gathered from the "Geographical and Statistical History of the County of Olmsted," by W. H. Mitchell, 121 pages, published in 1867; "History of Olmsted County," pages 617-1148, in the "History of Winona and Olmsted Counties," 1883; "History of Olmsted County," by Hon. Joseph A. Leonard and others, 674 pages, 1910; and from Hon. Charles C. Willson and Timothy H. Bliss, each of Rochester, the county seat, interviewed during a visit there in April, 1916.

BYRON, a railway village in Kalmar township, platted in 1864 and incorporated in 1873, was named at the suggestion of G. W. Van Dusen, an early grain buyer, for his former home, Port Byron, N. Y. (W. H. Stennett, Origin of the Place Names of the Chicago and Northwestern Railway, 1908, page 50.)

CASCADE township, organized in 1859, was named for the beautiful Cascade creek, which flows through the south edge of this township, joining the Zumbro river in the city of Rochester.

CHATFIELD village, of Fillmore county, reaches north into the southwest corner of Elmira townsip.

CHESTER, a railway village six miles east of Rochester, has a name that is also borne by townships and villages or cities in twenty-five other states.

CUMMINGSVILLE, a former village on the North branch of Root river, in Orion township, was platted by Francis H. Cummings, who settled here in 1855, building a sawmill.

DOUGLASS, a railway village eight miles northwest of Rochester, was named for Harrison Douglass, owner of its site. He was born in Macedon, N. Y., March 21, 1825; came to Minnesota in 1855, settling here as the first blacksmith in the county; built a grain elevator at this village in 1878; died in Fargo, N. D., March 7, 1902.

DOVER township, originally named Whitewater in 1858, for its river flowing east into Winona county, was organized in May, 1859, being then renamed for Dover in New Hampshire, whence some of its settlers came. The railway village of this name, platted in the spring of 1869, was at first called Dover Center, from its location at the center of this township.

ELMIRA township, organized May 11, 1858, was named by settlers from the vicinity of Elmira, New York,

EYOTA township, organized in 1858, was at first named Springfield, which was changed in 1859 to this Dakota or Sioux word, spelled iyotan by Riggs in the Dakota Dictionary, meaning "greatest, most." Eyota railway village, platted in November, 1864, was incorporated March 9, 1875.

FARMINGTON, organized in 1858, is an excellent farming township, whence it received this name, borne also by a railway village in Dakota county, and by townships and villages or cities in twenty-five other states of the Union. Five counties in Wisconsin have each a Farmington township.

GENOA, a little village in section 34, New Haven, first settled in 1856 and platted in 1865, bears the name of an ancient seaport in northern Italy, the birthplace of Columbus. Nine other states of the Union have villages of this name.

HAVERHILL township, organized in 1858, originally called Zumbro for the principal river of this county, was renamed Sherman in 1865 and Haverhill in 1866, this name being suggested by settlers who had come from Haverhill in Massachusetts.

HIGH FOREST township, organized in 1858, took the name of its village, platted in 1855, on high land partly surrounded by forest trees growing along the North branch of the Root river.

OLMSTED COUNTY 387

HORTON railway station, in the south part of Eyota, was named for Charles Horton, a lumber merchant of Winona. He was born in Niles, N. Y., March 31, 1836; came to Minnesota in 1858, settling in Winona; founded the Empire Lumber Company in 1858, and was its president; died in Winona, May 15, 1913.

JUDGE, a railway station in High Forest township, was located on the farm of Edward Judge, a native of Ireland, who came here as a pioneer settler in 1854, and died in September, 1904.

KALMAR township, organized in May, 1858, bears the name of a seaport in southern Sweden, noted for a treaty made there July 20, 1397, uniting the kingdoms of Sweden, Norway, and Denmark.

LAIRD, a railway station in section 26, Eyota, was named in honor of William Harris Laird, of Winona, who was born in Union county, Pa., February 24, 1833, and died at a hospital in Baltimore, Md., February 5, 1910. He came to Minnesota in 1855, settling in Winona, and in the firm of Laird, Norton and Co., formed in 1856, engaged extensively in lumbering and lumber manufacturing. He was donor of the Public Library building in Winona, and president of the trustees of Carleton College.

MARION township, organized in 1858, received the name of its village, founded in 1855-6. Seventeen states of the Union have counties of this name, and it is borne also by townships and villages or cities of twenty-five states, in honor of Francis Marion (b. 1732, d. 1795), of South Carolina, a distinguished general in the Revolutionary War.

NEW HAVEN township, organized in May, 1858, was named for the city of New Haven in Connecticut.

ORION township, organized in 1858, received this name of a constellation from a township and village in Richland county, Wisconsin.

ORONOCO township, organized in 1858, was named for its village, founded in 1854, which Dr. Hector Galloway, one of its first settlers, named for the large Orinoco river (differently spelled) in South America, in allusion to the valuable water power of the Middle branch of Zumbro river at this village.

PLEASANT GROVE township, organized May 11, 1858, and its village, platted in 1854, derived their name "from a beautiful grove of oaks, where the little village is located."

POTSDAM, a village in Farmington, founded about the year 1860, was named by its German settlers for the Prussian city of Potsdam, noted for its royal palace and beautiful parks, sixteen miles southwest of Berlin.

PREDMORE, a railway station in the southeast corner of Marion, established in 1891, was named for J. W. Predmore, who came in 1854 as one of the pioneer settlers of this township.

QUINCY township, organized May 11, 1858, bears the name of cities in Massachusetts and Illinois, and of villages and townships in fourteen other states.

ROCHESTER, the county seat, often called "the Queen City," was platted in October, 1855, and was incorporated as a city August 5, 1858. It was named for Rochester, N. Y., by George Head, a pioneer settler, who had lived there and afterward in Wisconsin before coming to this place in July, 1855. The rapids of the Zumbro river here reminded him of the Genesee river in New York and its great water power at Rochester, having a vertical fall of 95 feet. (Leonard, History of this county, p. 185.)

ROCK DELL township, organized May 11, 1858, has narrow gorges or dells, with ragged cliffs of limestone, eroded by little streams flowing northward to the South branch of the Zumbro river.

SALEM township, organized in 1858, was named by Cyrus Holt, a pioneer who came here in 1855 and was appointed postmaster of an office established in the winter of that year. The post office, and later the township, received this name from Salem, the county seat of Marion county, Illinois.

SIMPSON, a railway village and junction in Pleasant Grove township, platted in 1890, was named in honor of Thomas Simpson, of Winona, Minn., secretary of the Winona and Southwestern railroad company. He was born in Yorkshire, England, May 31, 1836; came to the United States with his parents while quite young; studied surveying, and in 1853 took the government contract for running the meridian and parallel lines in the southeast part of Minnesota Territory; settled in Winona in 1856; was admitted to the bar in 1858; practiced law, engaged in many important business enterprises, and during many years was president of the State Normal School board; died in Winona, April 26, 1905.

STEWARTVILLE, in High Forest township, was founded by Charles Stewart, who came from the state of New York in the spring of 1857 and built a mill here in 1858. When the railroad passing this place was constructed, in 1891, additions to the village were platted by Charles N. Stewart and others.

VIOLA township, at first named Washington, organized in May, 1858, was renamed at the suggestion of Irwin N. Wetmore, for the village of Viola in Wisconsin, about forty miles southeast of La Crosse. The railway village in this township, bearing the same name, was platted in September, 1878.

LAKES AND STREAMS.

Olmsted county is drained by the Zumbro, Whitewater, and Root rivers, flowing to the Mississippi.

The origin and meaning of the first of these names are fully noticed in the chapter of Goodhue county, where a village and township on this river are named Zumbrota. Its earlier Sioux name, Wazi Oju, applied to the river by Nicollet, referring to its large grove of white pines at the village of Pine Island, is also duly explained for that village and township in Goodhue county.

Large affluents of the Zumbro in Olmsted county are its Middle branch, formed at Oronoco village by union of the North and South Middle

OLMSTED COUNTY 389

branches, Cascade creek, whence a township is named, the South branch, Silver creek, Bear creek, to which Badger run is a tributary, and Willow creek.

Bear creek has its farthest source in a spring on the farm in Eyota which was taken as a homestead claim in 1853 by Benjamin Bear, a pioneer from Pennsylvania, the first settler in that township, for whom the creek received this name.

Whitewater river, having in this county its North, Middle, and South branches, is translated from its Sioux name, Minneiska, borne by a township and village in Wabasha county at the mouth of this stream.

Root river, to which its North branch flows through the south edge of Olmsted county, is also a translation of the Sioux name, Hutkan, spelled Hokah on Nicollet's map, which gave the name Hokah of the village and township adjoining the mouth of Root river in Houston county.

Partridge creek is a small tributary to this branch of Root river from the south in Pleasant Grove township.

The only lakes in this county are two picturesque mill ponds formed by dams, Shady lake at the village of Oronoco, and Lake Alice or Florence at Stewartville. The second "was named Lake Alice by Charles N. Stewart, in compliment to his wife" (as noted in the History of this county by Leonard, 1910, page 270); but in the latest atlas of the state, 1916, it is called Lake Florence.

HILLS.

The bed rocks, sculptured by rains and streams before the Ice Age and only thinly overspread by the glacial drift, present beautiful valleys and ravines, most noteworthy in Rock Dell township, and in some places form hills or small and low plateaus. College hill is such a plateau, about 75 feet high, in the west part of the city of Rochester; Sugarloaf Mound, more conspicuously seen, rises close south of the railroad two miles east of this city; and Lone Mound is in section 11, Farmington.

OTTER TAIL COUNTY

This county, established March 18, 1858, and organized September 12, 1868, received its name from the Otter Tail lake and river. The lake, from which the river was named, derived its peculiar Ojibway designation, thus translated, from a long and narrow sand bar, having an outline suggestive of the tail of an otter, formed very long ago and now covered with large woods, which extends curvingly southeast and south between the last mile of the inflowing Otter Tail or Red river and the lake, at its eastern end, in section 10 of Otter Tail township. At its northwestern base the bar is connected with the main shore by a gradually widening higher tract between the river and lake, to which, with the prolonged bar, the Indians very fittingly, in view of their geographic outlines, gave this name. Its Ojibway form is given by the late Rev. J. A. Gilfillan as Nigigwanowe, that is, Otter Tail, both for the lake and for the outflowing river to its junction with the Bois des Sioux river. The otter was formerly frequent or common in and near the rivers and lakes of all parts of this state, but is now rare. It subsists on fish, capturing them by rapid and expert swimming.

The late Hon. J. V. Brower, who visited the locality three times, in 1863, 1882, and 1899, on the latter occasion giving it a careful examination as a part of his archaeologic survey of the region, stated that the height of the bar varies from 10 to 25 feet above the lake; that its length slightly exceeds a mile, while its width, somewhat uniform, is only about 50 to 75 feet; and that it appears to have been amassed by wave and ice action of the lake. It was probably built by the waves during storms, nearly to its present extent and form, within the first few centuries after the lake began its existence, which was at the time of uncovering this region from the receding ice-sheet at the close of the Glacial period.

Otter Tail City, which about the years 1850 to 1860 was an important trading post on the route from the then flourishing town of Crow Wing to Pembina and the Selkirk settlements, stood on the main shore at the northeastern end of Otter Tail lake, adjoining the mouth of the river and the end of the Otter Tail bar. The United States Land Office for this district was located there during several years, and was thence removed to Alexandria in 1862. But all the buildings of the "city" were long since removed or destroyed, and only the cellar holes now remain.

The Red river was known to the Ojibways at the time of Owen's geological exploration, in 1848, as the Otter Tail river from this lake to its junction with the Red Lake river at Grand Forks. Present usage by many of the older white people retains the name Otter Tail for the river

OTTER TAIL COUNTY   391

above the lake of this name (though other names, derived from successive lakes, are used there by the Ojibways); and indeed occasionally it is still called Otter Tail river along its portion continuing below this lake to the axis of the Red River Valley at Breckenridge and Wahpeton, where it receives the Bois des Sioux river and turns from a westward to a northward course.

TOWNSHIPS AND VILLAGES.

Information of the origins and meanings of geographic names has been supplied by the "History of Otter Tail County," edited by John W. Mason, 1916, two volumes, pages 694, 1009; from William Lincoln, county auditor, and P. A. Anderson, register of deeds, interviewed during visits at Fergus Falls, the county seat, in September, 1909, and again in September, 1916; and from Hon. E. E. Corliss, formerly of Fergus Falls, custodian of the state capitol, 1910-17.

AASTAD township, organized March 14, 1871, was named for Gilbert Aastad, one of its early settlers, a native of Norway.

ALMORA is a Soo railway village in Elmo township.

AMOR, organized April 5, 1879, has a Latin name, meaning love, adopted in the Norwegian language of the settlers of this township as the name of Cupid, the god of love in the ancient Roman mythology.

AURDAL township, organized January 24, 1870, was named for a village in Norway, 80 miles northwest of Christiania.

BALMORAL, a lakeside village of summer homes in section 31, Otter Tail township, received its name from Balmoral Castle in Scotland, which was a favorite summer residence of Queen Victoria.

BATTLE LAKE, a railway village, platted October 31, 1881, and incorporated April 28, 1891, adjoins the western end of the large West Battle lake, which lies mainly in Everts and Girard townships. Near this lake and the East Battle lake, in the southeast part of Girard, a desperate battle was fought, about the year 1795, by a war party of fifty Ojibways, coming from Leech lake, against a much greater number of Sioux. A graphic narration of the battle, in which more than thirty of the Ojibways were killed, is given in Warren's "History of the Ojibways" (M. H. S. Collections, vol. V, 1885, pp. 336-343).

BLOWERS township, organized April 9, 1884, was named "in honor of A. S. Blowers, one of the prominent citizens of the early history of the county, and a member of the board of commissioners for many years."

BLUFFTON township, organized July 17, 1878, and its railway village, platted in March, 1880, incorporated February 24, 1903, received this name in allusion to the high banks or bluffs of the Leaf river along its course in the south edge of this township. North Bluff creek is tributary here to the Leaf river from the north, and South Bluff creek from the south.

BUSE was organized October 3, 1870. "Ernest Buse, in whose honor the township was named, was one of the earliest settlers and became one of the most influential men of the county." He was born in 1836; came to Minnesota in 1857, when his parents settled at Red Wing; served in the Third Minnesota regiment, 1864-5; was the first homesteader on the site of Fergus Falls, 1869; removed to Vancouver, B. C.; returned to Minnesota, and resided at Red Lake Falls; died during a visit in Lodi, California, February 1, 1914.

BUTLER township, organized August 15, 1883, was named in honor of Stephen Butler, of Fergus Falls, who during many years was the county treasurer.

CANDOR township, organized January 8, 1880, has a name that is also borne by a township and village in New York, and by villages in Pennsylvania and North Carolina.

CARLISLE township, organized February 24, 1881, received the name of its village on the Great Northern railway, which was platted in December, 1879. A city in England, a county in Kentucky, and villages and townships in eleven other states, bear this name.

CLITHERALL township, the first organized in this county, October 24, 1868, and Clitherall village, in Nidaros township, settled in 1865, platted in October, 1881, and incorporated October 4, 1898, received their name from Clitherall lake, lying in these townships and adjoining the village. "The lake took its name from Major George B. Clitherall, who was register of the United States land office at Otter Tail City from 1858 to 1861." (History of this county, 1916, page 169.) He was born at Fort Johnson, N. C., June 13, 1814; and died in Mobile, Ala., October 21, 1890. He is well remembered by the Minnesota Historical Society for his donation to its museum, a carved mahogany armchair that was owned by Washington in his home at Mount Vernon.

COMPTON township, organized July 31, 1875, commemorates James Compton, an early pioneer of this county. He was born near Meadville, Pa., January 14, 1840; served during the civil war in Pennsylvania and Illinois regiments, attaining the rank of captain; came to Minnesota in 1872, settling at Fergus Falls; assisted in organizing the First National Bank there, and was its cashier until 1891; was a state senator, 1883-9; was commandant of the Minnesota Soldiers' Home, at Minnehaha, after 1900; and died in Minneapolis, January 14, 1908.

CORLISS township, organized January 3, 1884, was named in honor of Eben Eaton Corliss, of Fergus Falls, who was born in Fayston, Vt., September 1, 1841, and died in St. Paul, July 21, 1917. He came to Minnesota in 1856, when his parents settled in Winona county; served during the civil war in the Second Minnesota regiment; was admitted to practice law in 1870, and in the same year settled near Battle Lake, building the first frame house in Otter Tail county; removed to Fergus Falls in 1874; was the first county attorney, 1871-75, and again held this office in 1879-85; was a representative in the legislature in 1872; was a member of the State Capitol Commission, 1893-1908; and after 1910 **was custodian** of the capitol.

OTTER TAIL COUNTY 393

DALTON, a Great Northern railway village in Tumuli township, platted in 1882 and incorporated May 2, 1905, was named in compliment for Ole C. Dahl, proprietor of its site.

DANE PRAIRIE township, organized May 10, 1870, received this name by choice of its people, nearly all being natives of Denmark. It has much timber beside its many lakes, with small intervening prairies.

DAYTON, probably named for Lyman Dayton, of St. Paul, was a village founded before 1860 with the building of a sawmill on the Red river, about four miles southwest from the site of Fergus Falls, and its post office was named Waseata; but this settlement was permanently abandoned in August, 1862, on account of the Sioux outbreak.

DEAD LAKE township, the last organized in this county, April 10, 1897, took the name of its large lake, which extends west into the townships of Star Lake and Maine. It is translated from the Ojibway name, referring to a grave, given by Gilfillan as Tchibegumigo, "House of the Dead, . . . from the custom of the Indians to build the resemblance of a little house over a grave." Dead river, named from the lake, is its outlet.

About the year 1843, beside the eastern part of this lake, some thirty or forty Ojibways, comprising only old men, women, and children, were killed by a war party of Sioux, whence the lake and river were named. (History of Becker county, by Wilcox, 1907, pages 212-214.)

DEER CREEK township, organized July 1, 1873, and its railway village, platted in May, 1882, and incorporated December 26, 1899, are named for the creek flowing north through the east part of this township to the Leaf river.

DENT, a village on the Soo railway in Edna township, platted August 19, 1903, was incorporated September 6, 1904.

DOPELIUS, a village of the Northern Pacific railway in Newton, was platted in the summer of 1901. With change of the initial letter, this was the name of a distinguished Swedish editor, educator, historian, poet, and novelist, Zachris Topelius (b. 1818, d. 1898), of Helsingfors, Finland.

DORA township, organized August 9, 1879, was probably named in honor of the wife or daughter of a pioneer homesteader, but her surname remains to be learned.

DUNN township, organized March 16, 1880, was named in honor of George W. Dunn, at whose home the first election was held.

EAGLE LAKE township, organized September 5, 1870, has the name of its largest and deepest lake.

EASTERN, organized July 29, 1875, is the most southeastern township of this county. Its name was chosen with reference to Western, the township forming the southwest corner of the county, which had been organized in January, 1873.

EDNA township, organized March 21, 1882, was named probably for one of its pioneer women.

EFFINGTON, organized March 21, 1872, received its name on the suggestion of Matthew Evans, an early settler, who had found it in a novel. (History of this county, 1916, pages 216-218.)

ELIZABETH township, organized September 5, 1870, was named in honor of the wife of Rudolph Niggler, a pioneer merchant, at whose store the first township meeting was held. Its railway village, bearing this name, platted in 1872, was incorporated November 21, 1884.

ELMO township, organized March 16, 1880, has a name that is borne also by villages in Wisconsin, Missouri, and other states, and by a lake near Stillwater in this state, with the railway village of Lake Elmo beside it.

ERHARD'S GROVE, a township organized September 24, 1870, was named for Alexander E. Erhard, a signer of the petition for organization, at whose house the first election was held. Erhard village, on a branch of the Great Northern railway, was platted in July, 1882.

EVERTS township, organized July 22, 1879, was named in honor of Rezin Everts and his son, Edmund A. Everts, pioneers of this township. A biographic sketch of the latter, contributed by E. E. Corliss in the History of Otter Tail county, notes that he was born in Carroll county, Illinois, November 12, 1840; came to Minnesota in 1855 with his parents, who settled in Winona county; served in the Second Minnesota regiment during the civil war; settled as a homestead farmer in section 27 of this township in the spring of 1871; removed to Battle Lake village in 1881, and was a merchant there until his death, March 9, 1915.

FERGUS FALLS, platted in August, 1870, on a site that had been selected and named in 1857, was incorporated as a village February 29, 1872, and as a city March 3, 1881. Within the city limits, along a course of about three miles, the Red river descends nearly 70 feet, having originally comprised here a nearly continuous series of rapids, flowing over boulders of the glacial drift. The county seat was first located in 1868 at Otter Tail City, and was removed to Fergus Falls in the later part of 1872. The township of this name, which included the north half of the present city area, was organized June 29, 1870.

James Fergus, for whom the township and city were named, was born in Lanarkshire, Scotland, October 8, 1813. "At the age of nineteen he came to America with the idea of improving his fortune. He located in Canada at first, where he spent three years and learned the trade of millwright. . . . In 1854 he removed to Little Falls, Minnesota, and, in company with C. A. Tuttle, built a dam across the Mississippi and platted a village. Here he remained for two or three years. During the townsite speculation fever, in the winter of 1856 and 1857, Joseph Whitford, a blacksmith and steamboat engineer, a natural frontiersman, possessed of uncommon courage, energy and prudence, proposed to go out and take up a townsite at what was known as Graham's Point, on the Red river. Mr. Fergus furnished the necessary outfit for this expedition. Procuring a dog train and a half-breed guide, Whitford went to Graham's Point

OTTER TAIL COUNTY 395

and staked out a town. On their way back, at Red river, an Indian family told them of a better place for a town twenty miles distant. Leaving his half-breed to recruit, Whitford took an Indian as a guide and went to the place designated and staked off what is now Fergus Falls, the name being given by the exploring party in honor of the man who had furnished the outfit for the expedition. Mr. Fergus himself never visited the place."

"In 1862 Mr. Fergus drove his own team from Little Falls, Minnesota, to Bannock, Montana territory. He became quite prominent in territorial affairs and was influential in the organization of the new county of Madison in that territory, and held many positions of trust and responsibility. He served two terms in the Montana legislature, and was a member of the constitutional convention of 1887." (History of Otter Tail County, 1916, pages 479, 480.)

Fergus county in Montana was named in his honor. He died near Lewistown in that county, June 25, 1902.

FOLDEN township, organized February 24, 1881, bears the name of a seaport on the Folden fjord in Norway, about 70 miles north of the Arctic circle.

FRENCH is a station of the Northern Pacific railway in Carlisle, six miles west of Fergus Falls.

FRIBERG township, organized January 6, 1874, was at first called Florence and later Woodland, but was renamed June 1, 1874, for the city of Germany, spelled Freiberg, in Saxony.

GIRARD township, organized March 21, 1882, has a name that is borne by townships and villages or cities in Pennsylvania, Ohio, Illinois, Kansas, and other states, in honor of Stephen Girard (b. 1750, d. 1831), of Philadelphia, a wealthy merchant and philanthropist, founder of Girard College.

GORMAN township, organized September 4, 1873, was named in honor of John O. Gorman, at whose home the first township election was held.

HENNING township, organized July 17, 1878, was at first called East Battle Lake, which was changed August 1, 1884, to the present name, borne also by villages in Illinois and Tennessee. The railway village of this township, incorporated September 17, 1887, had several years earlier received this name, in honor of John O. Henning, of Hudson, Wis., who during many years was a druggist there and died April 15, 1897.

HOBART township, organized July 10, 1871, and its village on the Northern Pacific railway, platted in the spring of 1873, have a name that is borne also by villages and post offices in New York, Indiana, and several other states.

HOMESTEAD township, organized July 26, 1880, received this name in allusion to the many homestead farms received by its settlers from the United States government.

INMAN township, organized March 18, 1878, was named in honor of Thomas Inman, a pioneer homesteader from Indiana, noted as a deer hunter, at whose house the first township election was held.

LEAF LAKE township, organized July 22, 1879, was named for its West and East Leaf lakes, further noticed also for the next township.

LEAF MOUNTAIN township, organized January 7, 1874, was at first called Dovre Fjeld, for the mountainous plateau of that name in Norway. It was renamed March 18, 1874, for its Leaf hills or "mountains," a belt of conspicuous morainic drift hills, more fully noticed at the end of this chapter. Their aboriginal name, given by Gilfillan as Gaskibugwudjiwe, translated as "Rustling Leaf mountain," was applied alike by the Ojibways to these drift hills, the two Leaf lakes, and their outflowing Leaf river, the lakes and river being named from the hills.

LIDA township, organized March 19, 1879, bears the name of its largest lake, which probably commemorates the wife or daughtetr of a pioneer settler, or of the government surveyor of the sections in this township. On the early state maps published in 1860-70, Lake Lida is incorrectly outlined and named Lake Anna; but it is rightly mapped, with the present name, in the first Atlas of Minnesota, 1874.

LUCE, a village on the Northern Pacific railway in Gorman township, was platted in May, 1884, and was incorporated June 13, 1905.

MAINE township, organized September 5, 1871, was named at the request of R. F. Adley, one of its first settlers, a native of the state of Maine, at whose home the first election of this township was held.

MAPLEWOOD township, organized July 26, 1880, was then called St. Agnes, but was renamed May 2, 1882. The sugar maple is a common or abundant tree throughout nearly all of the forested region of this state.

NEWTON township, organized March 22, 1877, was at first called NEW YORK MILLS, which remains as the name of its principal village on the Northern Pacific railway, platted in 1883 and incorporated May 27, 1884. The township name was changed July 26, 1883, the present name being adopted for its having the same first syllable as before.

NIDAROS township, organized September 5, 1871, bears an ancient name for the city of Trondhjem in Norway, derived from Nidrosia, its medieval Latin name, which has reference to its situation at the mouth of the River Nid.

NORWEGIAN GROVE township, organized January 7, 1873, was settled entirely by people from Norway.

OAK VALLEY township, organized January 2, 1877, is drained northward to the Leaf river by two small streams, named Oak and South Bluff creeks.

ORWELL township, organized July 27, 1886, had been previously known as West Buse, but was then called Liberty, which was changed November 3, 1886, to the present name. This is borne also by townships and villages in Vermont, New York, Pennsylvania, and Ohio. It was adopted here in compliment to Charles D. Wright, who was born in Orwell, Vt., November 8, 1850; came to Minnesota in 1869, and was employed seven years in the office of the U. S. surveyor general in St. Paul; settled in

OTTER TAIL COUNTY 397

Fergus Falls in 1877; was mayor in 1885 and 1888, and president of the First National Bank, 1882-1912.

OSCAR township, organized July 1, 1873, was named in honor of Oscar II, who was born in Stockholm, January 21, 1829, and was the king of Sweden and Norway from 1872 until his death, December 8, 1907.

OTTER TAIL township, organized September 5, 1870, and its railway village, platted in the summer of 1903 and incorporated May 3, 1904, were named like this county, for its largest lake. OTTER TAIL CITY, the early station on a route of fur traders in going from St. Paul and Crow Wing to the Red river valley, noted at the beginning of this chapter, was in the area of this township, being for several years the place of the U. S. land office, and later it was the first county seat.

OTTO township, organized March 22, 1883, was named thus by the county commissioners, who disregarded the request of the petitioners that it be called Lake View. Whether the commissioners intended to honor a pioneer, or derived it from the county name, was not recorded. Eight other states have Otto townships and post offices.

PADDOCK township, organized March 21, 1882, was named for L. A. Paddock, at whose sawmill the first election was held.

PARKDALE, a small village of the Great Northern railway in section 3, Tumuli, was platted in 1876 as Hazel Dell, which was changed to the present name by an act of the state legislature, February 7, 1878.

PARKER'S PRAIRIE township, organized January 4, 1870, being then called Jasper, was renamed March 1, 1873, for an early settler on its principal tract of prairie. Its railway village of the same name, platted in the summer of 1880, was incorporated November 17, 1903.

PARKTON is a railway station in section 5, Inman.

PELICAN township, organized September 5, 1870, took its name from the Pelican river flowing through it. In sections 22 and 27, where the river descends with rapids over drift boulders, PELICAN RAPIDS village was platted in 1872 and incorporated May 16, 1882. The Ojibways gave to Lake Lida their name of the pelican, spelled Shada by Longfellow's "Song of Hiawatha," and they applied the same name to the Pelican river from this lake and Lake Lizzie to its junction with Red river.

PERHAM township, organized March 19, 1872, was then called Marion Lake township, for the lake adjoining its southwest corner; but March 1, 1877, it was renamed, to be like its village, by an act of the legislature. Josiah Perham, commemorated in this name, was the first president of the Northern Pacific railroad company, in 1864-65. He was born in Wilton, Maine, in 1803, and died in Boston, Mass., in 1868. Very interesting biographic notes, with narration of his enthusiastic efforts for construction of this transcontinental railway line, are given in Eugene V. Smalley's "History of the Northern Pacific Railroad" (1883, chapters XI-XV, pp. 97-132). Perham village, on this railroad, platted March 6, 1873, was incorporated February 14, 1881.

PINE LAKE township, organized January 5, 1883, was named for its large Pine lake, through which the Red river flows, originally bordered by valuable white pine timber. The three pine species of this state, each common or frequent through northeastern Minnesota, reach the southwestern limit of their geographic range in the east part of this county.

RICHDALE, the railway village of Pine Lake township, was platted in September, 1899. This village and the next were named in honor of Watson Wellman Rich, civil engineer, who was born in Dayton, N. Y., March 9, 1841, and died in Shanghai, China, January 12, 1903. He served in the Fourth Minnesota regiment in the civil war, attaining the rank of captain; engaged in engineering work for several railroad lines in Minnesota, and after 1897 was chief consulting engineer of the Imperial Chinese Railway Administration.

RICHVILLE, on the Soo railway in Rush Lake township, platted in the fall of 1903, was incorporated October 25, 1904. Under Richdale, preceding, the origin of this name has been noted.

RUSH LAKE township, organized January 3, 1871, bears the name of its large lake, which is translated from the name given to it by the Ojibways, used also by them for the Roseau lake and river. Rush lake gives its name, in the usage of the Ojibways, to the part of the Red river flowing from it to Otter Tail lake.

SAINT OLAF township, organized March 20, 1869, was at first called Oxford, but was renamed May 10, 1870, in honor of St. Olaf, born in 995, an early king of Norway, in 1015-30, who consolidated the kingdom and aided the establishment of Christianity, but was killed in a battle with his rebellious subjects, July 29, 1030. He is the patron saint of Norway, and is regarded by its people as the great champion of national independence.

SCAMBLER township, organized August 8, 1871, was named for Robert Scambler, a homesteader, at whose house the first township election was held.

STAR LAKE township, organized January 18, 1880, has a large and remarkably branched Star lake in its northern part, "which in shape bears a striking resemblance to a star fish."

SVERDRUP township, organized March 18, 1878, was at first called Norman. Because that name had been previously given to another Minnesota township, it was renamed July 17, 1878, in honor of George Sverdrup, president of Augsburg Seminary, Minneapolis. He was born in Balestrand, Norway, December 16, 1848; was graduated in theology at the University of Norway, 1871; became a professor of Augsburg Seminary in 1874, and its president in 1876; died in Minneapolis, May 3, 1907.

TORDENSKJOLD township, organized September 8, 1869, as Blooming Grove, was renamed May 10, 1870, in honor of Peder Tordenskjold, a renowned Norwegian admiral in the Danish service. He was born in Trondhjem, Norway, October 28, 1691; and was killed in a duel at Hanover, Germany, November 20, 1720. His original surname was Wessel,

OTTER TAIL COUNTY

and the name of this township, meaning "Thunder Shield," was conferred on him by the king of Denmark as a title of nobility.

TRONDHJEM township, organized July 7, 1873, bears the name, meaning "Throne Home," of an ancient city in Norway, on the south side of the great Trondhjem fjord, noted for its cathedral, an early burial place for the kings of Norway and in later times the place of their coronation.

TUMULI township, organized September 8, 1869, was then called Union, but on May 10, 1870, received this Latin name, meaning mounds, as of burial, having reference probably to the morainic drift hills in the east part of this township.

UNDERWOOD, a railway village in Sverdrup, platted in the fall of 1881 and incorporated November 2, 1912, was named in honor of Adoniram Judson Underwood, who was born in Clymer, N. Y., May 26, 1832, and died in Fergus Falls, December 21, 1885. He came to Minnesota in 1854; served in the First Minnesota and other regiments in the civil war; was a representative in the legislature, 1871-72; settled at Fergus Falls in 1873, and was the founder and editor of the Journal, 1873-85.

VERGAS, a Soo railway village in Candor township, was platted under the name of Altona in the fall of 1903, and was so incorporated February 21, 1905. Its present name, adopted November 6, 1906, is not found recorded elsewhere, either as a geographic name or a personal surname.

VINING, a railway village in Nidaros, platted in the fall of 1882 and incorporated April 20, 1909, has a name, given by officers of the Northern Pacific company, which is borne also by villages in Georgia, Iowa, and Kansas.

WALL LAKE, a Northern Pacific station in Aurdal, is near the north end of the lake so named for a low and flat-topped gravel ridge, like a wall, on its west side, through which the lake has cut its outlet, leaving a distinct old shoreline at its formerly higher level.

WESTERN, organized January 7, 1873, received its name as the most southwestern township in the county. Eastern township was named similarly, in July, 1875, at its southeast corner.

WOODSIDE, organized January 2, 1877, was then called WRIGHTSTOWN, for several pioneer settlers named Wright, which remains as the name of a hamlet in section 2. The present name of the township was adopted March 22, 1877, referring to its original woodlands and its situation at the east side of the county.

LAKES AND STREAMS.

The preceding pages have considered the names of Otter Tail lake and river, the Red river, the West and East Battle lakes, the North and South Bluff creeks, Clitherall lake, Dead lake and river, Deer creek, Eagle lake, the West and East Leaf lakes and Leaf river, Lake Lida, Oak creek, Pelican river, and Pine, Rush, Star, and Wall lakes.

Pomme de Terre river, receiving its headwaters in the south part of this county, has been previously noted, with derivation of its name, in the chapter for Grant county, which has a township named from it.

Wing river, flowing from southeastern Otter Tail county northward to join the Leaf river in Wadena county, gives its name to a township there, so that it is to be better noticed for that county.

Similarly the Red Eye river, crossing the northeast corner of Otter Tail county, passes a township that bears this name in Wadena county, and is to be again mentioned there, with the origin of the name from species of fish in this stream.

Toad river, the outlet of Toad lake in a township of that name in Becker county, each translated from their Ojibway name, flows into the north end of Pine lake.

Only a few other streams remain for notation, as Willow creek, tributary from Henning to the East Leaf lake; Belle river, flowing from Eastern township into Douglas county, and there giving the name of Belle River township; Pelican creek, which flows from St. Olaf southwest through Pelican Lake township of Grant county to the Pomme de Terre river; and the head stream of Mustinka river, running south across Aastad into Grant county. The last name is from a Dakota or Sioux word, mashtincha, meaning a rabbit.

"According to Rev. J. B. Hingeley, there are 1,029 lakes, by actual count, in Otter Tail county, not including sloughs and ponds." (Geology of Minnesota, vol. II, 1888, page 535.) A large majority of these lakes, however, are yet unnamed. To give a systematic enumeration of such as are named on maps, excepting those on the courses of the Red and Pelican rivers, they may well be arranged in the order of the townships from south to north, and of ranges from east to west.

The Red river, also called Otter Tail river, as stated at the beginning of this chapter, runs through Rice lake in Hobart, Mud lake and Little Pine lake in the southeast corner of Gorman, Big Pine lake in the township named for it, Rush and Otter Tail lakes, Deer lake in the northwest corner of Everts, East Lost lake in the northeast corner of Sverdrup, West Lost lake in Maine township, and three smaller unnamed expansions of the river, which might well be termed lakes, in sections 25 and 27 to 29, Friberg.

On the Pelican river in this county are Pelican lake, as it is named by the white people, called by the Ojibways, in Gilfillan's translation, "the lake with the smooth-shorn prairie coming down to it on one side;" Lake Lizzie, probably commemorating a pioneer woman, possibly the Elizabeth who is honored by the name of a township on this river, but here lacking knowledge of her surname; and Prairie lake, in Pelican township, lying in the eastern edge of the great prairie region.

Eastern township has Lake Annalaide, Long lake, Lake Mary, Rice lake, named for its wild rice, and North and South Maple lakes.

OTTER TAIL COUNTY

Parker's Prairie township has Horsehead lake, Cora lake and Lake Augusta, Rainy lake, Lake Adley, and Clarino, Resser, Nelson, and Fish lakes.

In Effington are Mud lake, Meyer, Arken, Block, and Stemmer lakes.

In Leaf Mountain township are Jessie's lake, Lake George, Tom's lake, Johnson, Samson, and Spitser's lakes.

In Eagle Lake township, besides the lake of that name and several others unnamed, Lake Jolly Ann is crossed by its west line.

St. Olaf township has Long lake, Lakes Johannes, Johnson, Lacy, and Sewell, Vinge lake, and Sonmer lake.

In Tumuli the Pomme de Terre river runs through Rose and Ten Mile lakes, the second being the largest of this township, which also has Clear lake, Hansel lake, and Mineral and Alkali lakes. The last two are sometimes reduced to mostly dry lake beds, with alkaline crystals resulting from evaporation. Ten Mile lake tells, by its name, the distance on an old Indian trail from the lake to the crossing of the Red river.

Aastad has Mud lake in sections 23 and 24.

Western township has Upper Lightning lake, more than three miles long, lying about four to seven miles northwest from Lightning lake of the Mustinka river in Grant county. The chapter of that county has comments on the origin of these names.

Woodside, which is township 132 in the most eastern range, has no lakes named on maps.

Elmo township, next westward, has Wing River lake, the largest and the only one named among several little lakes near the sources of this stream.

Folden has about twenty small lakes or lakelets, but none of sufficient size to be named.

In Nidaros are Stuart, Bredeson, Siverson, Johnson, and Belmont lakes; Bullhead lake, having the small species of catfish known by this name, also called the horned pout; and the northeast end of Clitherall lake.

In Clitherall township, besides the large lake of this name and the southwest edge of West Battle lake, are Crane lake and Lake Lundeberg, the last shallow and being drained.

Tordenskjold has German and Dane lakes, named from the nationality of their first settlers, and Fiske, Tamarack, Long, Volen, Black, Stalker, and Sugar lakes.

In Dane Prairie township, with Wall lake, before noted for the railway station so named, are Stang lake, recently drained, Rosvold and Larson lakes, Indian lake, Bronseth, Fossen, Lye, and Swan lakes, with many others unnamed.

Buse township has One Mile lake, at the southeast edge of Fergus Falls, Pebble, Horseshoe, and Iverson lakes. In the southeast part of the city area of Fergus Falls, originally belonging to this township, are Lake Charles and Grotto lake.

Orwell has Rush lake in section 12, and an unnamed lake is crossed by the west line of sections 6 and 7.

Oak Valley, Inman, and Henning, the townships numbered 133 in the three eastern ranges, have no lakes bearing names, except that East Battle lake, before noted, lies partly in Henning.

Girard, with the East and West Battle lakes, has Beauty Shore lake, shallow and in prospect of being drained, Mason, Tamarack, and Hanson lakes, and Lakes Emma and Ethel.

In the eastern edge of Everts, the outlet of West Battle lake flows through the Mollie Stark lake, Annie Battle lake, and Lake Blanche, the first being named for the wife of John Stark, a noted general of the Revolutionary War, who won the victory of Bennington, August 16, 1777. In the west part of this township are Elbow lake, the two Silver lakes, and Round and Deer lakes.

Sverdrup has the South and North Turtle lakes, Bass lake, Lake Onstad, Norway lake, Crooked and Horseshoe lakes, East Lost lake, Lake John, Anna and Little Anna lakes, and Pleasant lake.

Aurdal has Loon, Mud, and Nelson lakes, Little lake, and Spring lake. Its formerly large but shallow Fish lake has been mostly drained.

Fergus Falls township has Lake Alice in the city area, Opperman and Hoot lakes, nearly adjoining the city, and Wedell lake in section 6.

Carlisle, with several unnamed lakes in its northeast part, has also Oscar lake, crossed by its north line and extending into Oscar township.

Compton and Deer Creek townships, numbered 134 in the two eastern ranges, have no lakes.

Leaf Lake township, in addition to the East and West Leaf lakes, whence it is named, has Grass lake in section 19, and Portage lake, to which the traders and canoemen made a portage from the West Leaf lake on their route to the Red river valley.

Otter Tail township, with the west part of Portage lake and the northeastern half of Otter Tail lake, has Lake Buchanan, named by Major Clitherall in honor of President James Buchanan (b. 1791, d. 1868), two Long lakes, respectively northwest and southeast of the old Otter Tail City, Donald's lake, Gourd lake, named for its curved outline, with a strait connecting its larger and smaller parts, and Pickerel and Round lakes.

Amor has Walker lake, through which Dead river flows, close above its mouth, Mud lake, and the eastern one of the Twin lakes.

Maine township has the western Twin lake, Pickerel and Peterson lakes, Leon lake, and the West Lost lake, the last being on the course of the Red river.

Friberg, although containing nearly forty lakes from a quarter of a mile up to more than a mile in length, yet lacks any so distinctly noteworthy as to be named on maps.

Elizabeth township has Long lake, Reed and Zimmerman lakes, Lakes Jewett and Mason, the last having been recently drained, and Devil's lake.

OTTER TAIL COUNTY 403

Oscar township contains about a dozen lakes on its map, but only one is named, this being Oscar lake, which commemorates King Oscar II, like this township. Its southern part, lying in Carlisle, has an island of twenty-nine acres.

Bluffton and Newton, the two most eastern townships numbered 135, have no lakes; and Otto, next westward, has none named, excepting the east half of the large Rush lake, which gave its name to the fourth township of this tier.

In Rush Lake township, besides the west half of the lake so named, are Round and Head lakes, the greater eastern part of Marion lake, and Rice and Boedigheimer lakes, the last two being on the outlet of Marion lake.

In Dead Lake township, with the eastern part of that large lake and the west part of Marion lake, are seven small lakes, unnamed by maps.

Star Lake township, with the great and triply branched Star lake, includes a major part of the western body of Dead lake and much of Mud lake, both being crossed by the south line of the township. Fifteen smaller lakes, or more, remain without names.

Maplewood township has Beers lake, Twin and Crystal lakes, and Lake 21, named from its section, besides a great number of unnamed lakes.

Erhard's Grove township has Sandberg and Grandrud lake, and Lake Knobel, with about thirty others that are smaller and wait to be named on maps.

In Trondhjem nine lakes, from a third of a mile to more than a mile long, thus wait for names.

Returning again to the east side of the county, we find no lakes in Blowers and Homestead, the townships numbered 136 in the two eastern ranges.

Pine Lake township has the Big Pine lake, but only three additional lakelets, each unnamed.

Perham has the southern parts of Little Pine lake and Mud lake, also the southeast part of Devil's lake, each of which reaches north into Gorman.

In Edna township are the Big and Little McDonald lakes, Pickerel, Rice, Wolf, Paul, Ceynowa, Moenkedick, Grunard, Wendt, and Mink lakes, with a part of Lake Sibyl (incorrectly spelled Sybil) in the north edge of sections 5 and 6.

Dora township has the western continuation of Lake Sibyl, the south half of Loon lake, which reaches north into Candor, and Spirit lake, these being in its northern half, and the two long Silent lakes in its southern border, with about fifteen smaller lakes waiting for names.

Lida township has the large Lakes Lida and Lizzie, before noted, with several nameless lakelets.

In Pelican township are Prairie lake, the lowest through which the Pelican river flows, and numerous unnamed lakelets, the largest of these being in section 19.

Norwegian Grove township has Grove lake at its northeast corner, reaching northeastward into Scambler and Pelican, and having a grove on its large island, which is mostly in section 1, of this township; also Lakes Alfred, Olaf, Jacob, and Annie, with many others that are smaller and without names.

Paddock, the most northeastern township, has Mud lake, one of our most abundant names, likely to be given to any lake with mainly muddy shores.

Butler has Bear and Edna lakes, each crossed by its west line.

Corliss, with parts of the two lakes last noted and also parts of Big and Little Pine lakes, has also Indian lake in its sections 8 and 9.

Gorman, in addition to the three lakes on its south side, reaching into Perham, as already mentioned, has a small Dead lake in section 1, and Silver lake in sections 6 and 7.

In Hobart are Gray and Keyes lakes, Rice lake on the Red river, Graham, Wimer, and Fairy lakes, Five and Six lakes, named from their being in sections 5 and 6, Scalp lake, and Rose, Jim, and Long lakes.

Candor township has Sauer lake, crossed by its north line, Cook's and Schram lakes, Hand lake and T lake, named from their outlines, and Leek, Lawrence, Hook, and Otter lakes.

Dunn township, with the northwest part of Lake Lizzie, Pelican lake, and Little Pelican lake, which are on the Pelican river, has also Lake Emma, Elbow lake, and Franklin lake.

Scambler, at the west end of this northern tier of townships, with the west part of Pelican lake, has Tamarack and Sand lakes, Lake Harrison, Ranklev, Pete, and Grove lakes. The last has been earlier mentioned for its reaching southwest into Norwegian Grove township.

While only a relatively small portion of the lakes in this county are named and here listed, it is evident that if we could narrate the stories of pioneers by whom or for whom they were named, with origins also of the many impersonal names, the interesting information so to be recorded would require a long search to gather it somewhat fully, and would fill many printed pages. In general, only the rivers and a few large lakes retain names used by the Indians, or translations from them. Nearly all the other names, of townships, villages, and lakes, numbering hundreds in this very large county, were selected or invented by the incoming white agricultural settlers.

Hills of the Marginal Moraines.

In the series of twelve marginal moraines of the continental ice-sheet mapped for parts of their courses across Minnesota, the eighth and ninth are very prominently developed in this county, being thence named respectively the Fergus Falls and Leaf Hills moraines. These belts of drift hills, extend in a semicircle from Fergus Falls southeast to the south line of the county and thence east and northeast to East

OTTER TAIL COUNTY

Leaf lake, a distance of fifty miles. Through five townships, Tordenskjold, St Olaf, Eagle Lake, Leaf Mountain, and Effington, the two moraines are merged together and form a range five to three miles wide, composed of very irregular, roughly outlined hills, 100 to 300 feet high, commonly called the "Leaf mountains." This is a translation from the Ojibways, as was noted for Leaf Mountain township, and they also applied their name of the hills to the Leaf lakes and river. The common designation as "mountains" has currency because they are the only hills in this part of Minnesota which are conspicuously seen at any great distance. In the highest portions they rise 200 to 350 feet above the adjoining country, which is itself deeply covered with drift. (Geology of Minnesota, Final Report, vol. II, 1888, pages 544-551.)

From the crests of the Leaf hills, extensive views are obtained northward over the greater part of this county, and southward across Douglas and Grant counties; but the separate hills, of which there are many supplying such wide and grand views, have not received names on maps.

Indian hill, in section 9, Oscar, near the middle of the west side of this county, has a fine outlook eastward upon that part of the Fergus Falls moraine; and at the west it overlooks the plain of Wilkin county, which was the bed of the Glacial Lake Agassiz, stretching with a slight descent twenty miles to the Red river.

PENNINGTON COUNTY

This county, the latest established in the state, November 23, 1910, was named in honor of Edmund Pennington, of Minneapolis. He was born in La Salle, Illinois, September 16, 1848; began his life work in railroad service in 1869; was since 1888 successively superintendent, general manager, and vice president of the Minneapolis, St. Paul and Sault Ste. Marie railway company, and since 1909 has been its president.

From 1858 to 1896 this area was included in Polk county, and from 1896 to 1910 it was a part of Red Lake county.

Townships and Villages.

Information of geographic names in Pennington county was received from Edward L. Healy, real estate dealer, of Red Lake Falls, interviewed during a visit there in August, 1909; and from Harry E. Ives, clerk of the court, Lars Backe, former mayor, and Joseph Johnson, each of Thief River Falls, the county seat, interviewed there in September, 1916.

BLACK RIVER township slopes mostly southwestward, sending its drainage to the stream of this name, given on Nicollet's map in 1843, which alludes to its dark water, stained by the peaty soil of some parts of its course.

BRAY township was named in honor of Damase Simon Bray, one of its pioneer farmers. He was born at Cedars, near Montreal, Canada, March 17, 1828; came to Minnesota in 1880, settling on a homestead in this township, as it was later organized; removed to Red Lake Falls, 1886; and died there, September 24, 1908.

CLOVER LEAF township was named for its white clover, growing abundantly in many places beside roads and on pastured lands.

DEER PARK township was formerly a favorite hunting ground for deer, which under legal protection continue to be found sparingly in this eastern part of the county.

ERIE post office, in Star township, was named by the late Alex F. Latimore, who came from near Erie, Pa. He was editor of "The Eleven Towns," a newspaper especially representing a group of eleven townships in the eastern part of this county, formerly in the Red Lake Indian Reservation, but opened to white settlers June 20, 1906.

GOOD RIDGE township and its village on an electric railway, in section 21, are named for a broad but very low ridge, only a few feet above the adjoining areas at each side, which reaches from the village about four miles southeastward.

HAZEL is a village of the Soo railway in section 1, River Falls. Two species of hazel, much sought by children and squirrels for their ex-

PENNINGTON COUNTY 407

cellent nuts, are generally common in this county and throughout northern Minnesota.

HICKORY township, the most southeastern in the county, is at or near the northwestern limit of the swamp hickory or bitternut. This species furnished nearly all the hoop-poles for flour barrels cut in the southern and central parts of the state.

HIGH LANDING township and its village, on the north bank of the Red Lake river, are named from the relatively high ground there adjoining the stream, which makes this a favorable place for the landing of steamboats on their passage between Thief River Falls and Red lake.

HILDA, a post office in section 1, Deer Park, was named in honor of the wife of Olaf Hanson, a pioneer farmer, who was its first postmaster.

KRATKA township and village, beside Red Lake river, were named in honor of Frank H. Kratka, an early merchant of this county. He was born at Sugar Island, Wis., May 21, 1850; settled in 1884 at the site of Thief River Falls, then called Rockstad as a trading post for the Ojibways of the adjacent Red Lake and Pembina Indian Reservation; learned their language, and was an interpreter; was the first postmaster of Thief River Falls, in 1887-88, when the village was platted and named; was its president in 1891 and 1893, the first mayor after its incorporation as a city, 1896-97, and again in 1902-03; likewise for a second time was the postmaster, 1907-14; removed to Pasadena, Cal., where he died January 27, 1915. The Ojibways called him Ogema, meaning a chief; but in 1896 he opposed an endeavor to rename this city as Ogema Falls.

MAVIE is a village on the electric railway in Clover Leaf township.

MAYFIELD township was named in honor of A. C. Mayfield, who was one of its early homesteaders, coming from Wisconsin.

NORDEN township, at the north side successively of Polk, Red Lake, and Pennington counties, received this name, meaning northern, from the languages of its Norwegian and Swedish settlers.

NORTH township, next east of Norden, is named similarly for its location, and for its including the most northern part of the Red Lake river, at the city of Thief River Falls.

NUMEDAL township bears the name of a river in Norway, and of the series of farms and pasture lands along its valley.

POLK CENTER township, the most southwestern in this county, was named for its situation near the center of the orginal area of Polk county.

REINER township was named in compliment for Reinhart Johnsrud, who later was the township treasurer.

RIVER FALLS township has rapids of the Red Lake river, flowing over glacial drift boulders, at St. Hilaire village, and in other parts of its course through this township.

ROCKSBURY township was named in honor of Martin Rockstad, one of its first settlers, whose homestead farm in section 4 nearly adjoined Thief River Falls. ROCKSTAD, more exactly bearing his name, was the earliest post office there, established about the year 1882, at a trading station in or near the south edge of the present city area, as before mentioned in the notice for Kratka township.

ST. HILAIRE, a Great Northern railway village, on the west side of the Red Lake river in the northwest corner of River Falls, platted in 1882, was named by Hon. Frank Ives for the French statesman and author, Jules Barthelemy-Saint-Hilaire, who was born in Paris, August 19, 1805, and died November 24, 1895. The former railway branch from Crookston to St. Hilaire began its regular train service on July 4, 1883.

SANDERS township was named in compliment for Sander Engebretson, a native of Hallingdal, Norway, who was one of its pioneer farmers.

SILVERTON township received this euphonious name by vote of its people. It is near the eastern limit of the silverberry, a shrub having whitish leaves and bearing edible berries of the same silvery color, common along the Red river valley and thence far westward.

SMILEY township was named in honor of William C. Smiley, who in 1904 was the county surveyor of Red Lake county and in recent years has practiced law in St. Paul.

STAR township, for which the name Zenith had been proposed by Joseph Johnson, received its name by vote of its people, who thought Zenith difficult to pronounce. It has reference to the polar or north star, in the French language "L'Etoile du Nord" of the state seal, whence Minnesota is popularly called "the North Star State."

SUNBEAM, a post office in High Landing township, was named by W. G. Hunt, publisher of its local newspaper, which has the same name.

THIEF RIVER FALLS, the county seat, in North township, was platted as a village in 1887, and was incorporated as a city September 15, 1896. The Red Lake river within the city area originally flowed in rapids over boulders. Above the present dam, which has a head of 15 feet, supplying valuable water power, this river is navigable by steamboats to Red lake. On the northeast side of the city it receives Thief river, which is translated from the Ojibway name, noted by Gilfillan as "Kimodakiwi zibi, the Stolen Land river or Thieving Land river." The map of Long's expedition, in 1823, and Nicollet's map, published in 1843, give the present name.

Warren's "History of the Ojibways" (Minnesota Historical Society Collections, vol. V) explains the origin of this name and notes its true translation, as it was at first used. "For a number of years, on the headwaters of Thief river . . . a camp of ten Dakota lodges succeeded in holding the country by evading or escaping the search of the Ojibway war parties. Here, loath to leave their rich hunting grounds, they lived from year to year in continual dread of an attack from their conquering foes. They built a high embankment of earth, for defence, around their lodges, and took every means in their power to escape the notice of the Ojibways—even discarding the use of the gun on account of its loud report, and using the primitive bow and arrows, in killing such game as

PENNINGTON COUNTY

they needed. They were, however, at last discovered by their enemies. The Crees and Assiniboines, during a short peace which they made with the Dakotas, learned of their existence and locality, and, informing the Ojibways, a war party was raised, who went in search of them. They were discovered encamped within their earthen inclosure, and after a brave but unavailing defence with their bows and arrows, the ten lodges, with their inmates, were entirely destroyed." From the Sioux earthwork, constructed for concealment and defence, the Ojibways gave to the stream its early name, meaning "Secret Earth river," as translated by Warren, in allusion to the hiding and protecting earth embankment. Through erroneous pronunciation of the name, however, with a misunderstanding of its intended significance, the French and English fur traders, and afterward also the Ojibways, changed it to "Stealing Earth river," and thence to Thief river. The same name is applied by the Ojibways to Thief lake, the head of this stream, the lake and nearly all the course of the river being in Marshall county.

TORGERSON, a post office in Reiner, was named for Mikkel Torgerson, a homestead farmer, who was the first clerk of this township.

WYANDOTTE township bears the aboriginal name of a confederation of four Iroquoian tribes, called Hurons by the French, who lived in the part of Canada southeast of Lake Huron and the Georgian bay. It is also the name of counties in Ohio, Michigan, and Kansas. In the year 1655, Huron and Ottawa exiles, driven from their homes by raids of the Iroquois, accompanied Groseilliers and Radisson to Prairie island of the Mississippi on the southeast boundary of the present state of Minnesota.

RIVERS.

Black river and Thief river have been noted in the preceding pages, for the township and city named for them.

Red lake and the streams to which its name is given, Red Lake river, crossing this county, and the Red river on the west boundary of the state, are considered in the first chapter, which treats of lakes and rivers that belong partly to several counties, and they are again somewhat fully noticed in the chapter of Red Lake county.

The glacial and modified drift in Pennington county, and the relatively thin lacustrine and alluvial beds which in some parts of this area cover the drift, were spread very evenly on the bed of the Glacial Lake Agassiz, so that the surface has no hollows holding lakes.

PINE COUNTY

Established March 1, 1856, and organized in 1872, this county was named with reference to the extensive pineries, of white and red (Norway) pine, in various parts of this district, since much worked and practically all cut off by lumbermen. Perhaps also this name was adopted partly for the Pine lakes and river, here tributary from the west to the Kettle river. Pine City, the county seat, received its name from that of the county, and also from the adjacent Ojibway village, Chengwatana.

Minnesota has three pine species, each limited to its northeastern part. The white pine is the most abundant, and is commercially the most valuable for its excellent lumber; the red pine, more commonly but wrongly called the Norway pine, is also plentiful in many large tracts, preferring a more sandy soil, and is nearly as much esteemed for its lumber as the foregoing; and the jack pine, of smaller size, grows on areas of yet more sandy and gravelly soil, being least valued for lumber and commonly utilized only as fuel.

Townships and Villages.

Information of names in Pine county has been gathered from "Fifty Years in the Northwest," by William H. C. Folsom, 1888, having pages 260-285 for this county; and from W. H. Hamlin, county auditor, and Robert Wilcox, judge of probate, interviewed during a visit at Pine City, the county seat, in May, 1916.

ARLONE township, organized May 22, 1911, was named in honor of Lois Arlone Hamlin, daughter of the county auditor.

ARNA township, organized March 11, 1910, has a name proposed by W. H. Hamlin, county auditor, not known in use elsewhere, either as a personal or place name.

ASKOV is a Great Northern railway village in Partridge.

BANNING is a hamlet on a branch of the Northern Pacific railway, in section 34, Finlayson, having sandstone quarries beside the Kettle river. It was named in honor of William L. Banning, who was born in Wilmington, Del., Jan., 1814; settled in St. Paul, Minn., 1855, and engaged in banking; served in the Third Minnesota regiment in the civil war; afterward was a contractor in railroad construction; died in St. Paul, November 26, 1893.

BARRY township was named in honor of Edward Barry, a heroic engineer of the Great Northern railway train which rescued nearly five hundred people of Hinckley and its vicinity from death in a great forest fire, September 1, 1894, carrying them to West Superior, when the vil-

PINE COUNTY 411

lages of Hinckley and Sandstone were burned. ("Memorials of the Minnesota Forest Fires," by Rev. William Wilkinson, 1895, pages 127-187.)

BELDEN is a station of the Soo railway, sixteen miles north of Markville.

BEROUN is a Northern Pacific railway village, six miles north of Pine City.

BIRCH CREEK township, the most northwestern in this county, was named for the creek that flows through it, tributary to the Kettle river.

BREMEN township was named by its German settlers, for the city of Bremen in Germany.

BROOK PARK township and its village on the Great Northern railway have a euphonious name suggested by its brook tributary to Pokegama creek.

BRUNO township and its railway village were named in honor of an early hotel owner there.

CHENGWATANA township, organized in 1874, bears an Ojibway name, stated by Folsom to be formed by the words meaning pine and city, which are spelled *jingwak* and *odena* in Baraga's Dictionary. It was the name of "an Indian village which from time immemorial had been located near the mouth of Cross lake. This locality had long been a rallying point for Indians and traders."

CLOVER township was named for its profuse growth of the cultivated red clover in fields and of the native white clover in pastures and beside roads, both giving evidence of a rich clayey soil.

CLOVERTON is a station of the Soo railway, five miles north of Markville.

CROSBY was named in honor of Ira Crosby, a pioneer farmer in this township.

DANFORTH was named for N. H. Danforth, of Sandstone, a landowner in this township, who removed to the state of Washington.

DELL GROVE township was named for the valley of Grindstone lake and the North branch of Grindstone river, and for its groves of pines which were burned by the forest fires in September, 1894.

DENHAM is a Soo railway village in Birch Creek township.

DOSEY township was named in honor of Julius Dosey, a former lumberman there, who in 1916 was the mayor of Pine City.

DUQUETTE is a village of the Great Northern railway in the east edge of Kerrick township.

FINLAYSON township, and its village, on the Northern Pacific railway, were named in honor of David Finlayson, the former proprietor of a sawmill in this village.

FLEMING township was named for a lumberman from Stillwater, who had logging camps there.

FRIESLAND, named for a province of Holland, is a Northern Pacific railway station, five miles north of Hinckley.

GRONINGEN, the next Northern Pacific station, in the northeast corner of Dell Grove township, bears the name of the most northeastern province of Holland, adjoining the east side of Friesland.

HARLIS is a Soo railway station in the northeast corner of this county.

HENRIETTE village, formerly called Cornell, is on the Great Northern railway in Pokegama.

HINCKLEY township, organized in 1872, and its railway village, incorporated in 1885, were named in honor of Isaac Hinckley, who was born in Hingham, Mass., in 1815, and died in Philadelphia, Pa., March 28, 1885. During sixteen years, from 1865 to 1881, he was president of the Philadelphia, Wilmington and Baltimore railroad company. He was a stockholder for building the St. Paul and Duluth railroad, now owned by the Northern Pacific company.

KERRICK township and its Great Northern railway village have a name that is borne also by a village in central Illinois. It was chosen in honor of Cassius M. Kerrick, who was born at Greensburg, Ind., in 1847; came to Minnesota, settling in Minneapolis, as master mechanic for the Great Northern railway; later was a contractor, erecting many railway bridges; removed to Pasadena, Cal., in 1913, and died there March 12, 1918.

KETTLE RIVER township, organized in 1874, received the name of the river flowing through it, a translation from the Ojibway name, noted by Gilfillan, "Akiko zibi; Akik, kettle, zibi, river, and o, connective." This name was given to the river in allusion to the waterworn rocks, copper-bearing trap rock and conglomerate, of its rapids along a distance of five miles next above its junction with the St. Croix river. Through the central part of the county, from the south line of this township to the mouth of Grindstone river, the Kettle river flows fifteen miles in a valley or gorge about a quarter to two-thirds of a mile wide, eroded in horizontally bedded sandstone which forms bluffs on each side 75 to 100 feet high, their upper half being usually vertical cliffs.

KINGSDALE is a Soo railway village five miles north of Cloverton.

MARKVILLE is on the Soo railway in Arna township.

MISSION CREEK township, organized in 1880, and its railway station in section 10, bear the name of the creek flowing through the east part of this township. It joins the Snake river close east of Lake Pokegama, and received its name from a mission to the Ojibways founded beside that lake in 1836, which was broken up by the attack of a large war party of the Sioux, May 24, 1841.

MUNCH township was named in honor of three brothers, natives of Prussia, who were lumbermen in this county. Adolph Munch, born in 1829, came to the United States in 1850, and to Minnesota in 1854; resided at Taylor's Falls, Chisago county, and at Pine City; removed to St. Paul in 1871, and died there November 26, 1901. Emil Munch, born in 1831, came to this country in 1849, and settled at Taylor's Falls in 1852; was a representative in the legislature, 1860-1; was captain of the First Minnesota Battery, 1861-5; was state treasurer, 1868-72; owned a flouring mill at Afton, Washington county, after 1875; died August 30, 1887. Paul Munch, born in 1833, came to the United States in 1854, settling at Taylor's Falls; served in the First Minnesota light artillery in the civil war, attaining the rank of first lieutenant; removed to Chengwatana, where he died July 26, 1901.

NICKERSON township and its railway village were named in honor of John Quincy Adams Nickerson, of Elk River, Sherburne county, who promoted the building of this line of the Great Northern railway. He was born in New Salem, Maine, March 30, 1825; came to St. Anthony, Minn., in 1849, and four years later settled at Elk River, buying land on which a part of that village was afterward built; conducted a hotel, and also engaged in lumbering; was postmaster of Elk River, and treasurer of Sherburne county.

NORMAN township was named by its Swedish and Norwegian settlers to commemorate their Scandinavian origin as Northmen, being thus like the names of Norman county and Norman township in Yellow Medicine county.

OGEMA township, organized in 1915, has an Ojibway name, meaning a chief.

PARTRIDGE township was named in honor of one of its first settlers.

PINE CITY township, organized in 1874, and its railway village, the county seat, platted in 1869 and incorporated February 14, 1881, were named from the county. It is also especially significant that the name of the nearly adjacent Ojibway village, Chengwatana, was derived, as before noted, from the two words for pine and city. Probably this aboriginal village, as well as the pine forests, shared in the naming of the village and township of Pine City, and also in the earlier selection of the county name.

PINE LAKE township has the Big Pine lake and the Upper and Lower Pine lakes, which outflow northeastward by the Pine river, all these names, as likewise of the county and of its ancient Ojibway village, being derived from the majestic pine woods.

POKEGAMA township bears the Ojibway name of its creek and lake, meaning "the water which juts off from another water," applied to this lake because its south end is very near the Snake river. It is also the name of a large lake beside the Mississippi in Itasca county, and likewise was given by the Ojibways to the little lake now called Elk lake, closely adjoining Lake Itasca.

ROCK CREEK township, settled in 1872, organized in March, 1874, and its railway village, bear the name of the creek that here flows south into the northeast corner of Chisago county, tributary to the St. Croix river.

ROYALTON, the most southwestern township of Pine county, was named in honor of Royal C. Gray, who in 1854 settled on section 15, at the south side of the Snake river, on a farm that had been opened in 1849 by Elam Greeley, a pioneer lumberman.

RUTLEDGE is a railway village in section 28, Kettle River.

SANDSTONE township and its railway village, platted in June, 1887, were named for their extensive quarries of sandstone in the bluffs of the Kettle river, which were first worked in August, 1885.

STURGEON LAKE township and its railway village were named for the large lake in Windemere township, two miles east of this village.

WILLOW RIVER, a village of the Northern Pacific railway, is at its crossing of this stream, the largest eastern tributary of the Kettle river.

WILMA township, organized October 22, 1907, was named in honor of a daughter of William H. Abbott, a former resident of this township, who removed to Caledonia, Minn.

WINDEMERE township, organized January 3, 1882, received its name, with change in spelling, from Lake Windermere, the largest lake in England.

LAKES AND STREAMS.

The foregoing list has noticed Birch creek, Kettle river, Mission creek, the Pine lakes and river, Pokegama creek and lake, Rock creek, Sturgeon lake, and Willow river, from which seven townships and four villages in this county received their names.

The St. Croix and Snake rivers are considered in the first chapter, treating of large rivers and lakes that are partly included in several counties; and the Snake river, translated from Kanabec, its Ojibway name, is also noticed in the chapter of Kanabec county.

Cross lake, so named from its being crossed by the Snake river, is a translation of its Ojibway name, Bemidji. The same aboriginal name is borne by a lake and city on the upper Mississippi, in Beltrami county. In each case, the name alludes to the river flowing across the lake.

Grindstone river, formed by union of its South and North branches, and Grindstone lake, outflowing by the North branch, are named from the finely gritty sandstone outcrop at the north side of this river adjoining Hinckley village, which was used for sharpening iron and steel tools by the Ojibways and early fur traders. Quarrying to supply stone for bridge masonry and other building uses was begun there in 1878, and seven years later more extensive quarries were opened in the similar rock beds at the village of Sandstone.

Other lakes and streams in this county, mostly needing no explanations of the derivations and meanings of their names, include Rock lake, one of the sources of Rock creek, and Devil's lake, of small area, respectively about two miles and one mile south of Pine City, each bordered by low morainic drift hills, abundantly strewn with boulders; Hay creek, in the west part of Royalton, flowing north to the Snake river; Cedar lake, in Munch township; Deer and Skunk creeks, tributary to the Kettle river from the west in Barry and Sandstone townships; Elbow and Bass lakes, crossed by the north line of Dell Grove township;

PINE COUNTY 415

Indian and Fish lakes, in the east edge of Pine Lake township; Little Pine river, flowing through the Upper and Lower Pine lakes; Moose river, a large eastern branch of Kettle river, coming from several lakes in Carlton county which are named from moose formerly abundant in this region; Island and Grass lakes, in the north edge of Windemere; Oak lake in Kerrick, near the head of Willow river; Net lake and river, flowing northeastward into Carlton county; Bear creek, Sand river, its East fork, and Hay creek, also flowing to Sand river from the east, Crooked creek, with its West and East forks, Tamarack river, with its West fork, and Spruce river, these numerous streams, in their order from west to east, being tributary to the St. Croix between the Kettle river and the east line of the county and state; and Rock lake, Lake Lena, and fourteen other little lakes that are mapped without names, in Ogema.

The Kettle river at its Upper falls or Dalles, close east of Banning, flows in rapids about a half mile, through a narrow gorge formed by ragged cliffs of sandstone, 50 to 100 feet high. Its Lower falls, on each side of an island a half mile southeast of Sandstone village, descend about eight feet within a distance of an eighth of a mile. In the three miles between these falls the river flows with a gentle current.

Opposite the mouth of this river, and for three miles above and one mile below, the St. Croix river is turned in two channels by three long islands, which together are called the "Big island." The eastern large channel is the state boundary, and the western is commonly called "the Slough." In both the river has a strong current, with numerous rapids, so that this extent of four miles on the St. Croix is named Kettle River rapids.

Between four and five miles farther south, the St. Croix has its Horse-race rapids, a half mile long, over a smooth rock bed, not broken by boulders.

PIPESTONE COUNTY

This county, established May 23, 1857, was organized twenty-two years later, by a legislative act approved January 27, 1879. Its name was at first applied, however, by an error of the original act in 1857, to the area that is now Rock county, while that name was given to the present county of Pipestone. These counties therefore exchanged names by an act of the legislature, February 20, 1862. The transposition was needful, as Pipestone county now includes the celebrated Indian quarry of red pipestone, to which its name refers; and Rock county now has the prominent rock mound near Luverne, which similarly was the source of its name.

Carver, wintering in 1766-7 with the Sioux on the Minnesota river, near the site of New Ulm, learned of the highland farther west, since named Coteau des Prairies, as "a mountain, from which the Indians get a sort of red stone, out of which they hew the bowls of their pipes." George Catlin, the painter of Indian portraits, wrote the earliest printed description of this quarry, which he visited in the summer of 1836. Two years later it was visited by Nicollet, as noted in the report with his map of the upper Mississippi region. These descriptions are reprinted in the Final Report of the Geological Survey of Minnesota (vol. I, 1884, pages 62-70). The great veneration of many tribes of Indians for the stone here quarried, and the legend of its first use to make the peace pipe or calumet, are known to all readers of Longfellow's "Song of Hiawatha," published in 1855, which derived its account of the pipestone from Catlin and Nicollet.

The red pipestone, also called catlinite, occurs as a layer about eighteen inches thick, inclosed in strata of red quartzite. It has been quarried by the Indians along an extent of nearly a mile from north to south, their earliest quarrying having been done hundreds of years ago. This tract is now comprised in an Indian reservation, one mile square, which was set apart for the Yankton Sioux in accordance with a treaty made in Washington, April 19, 1858. The reservation was provided solely for this quarrying by the Indian tribes, and no trespassing there by white men is permitted. Pipestone, the county seat, is a flourishing city about a mile south of the quarry.

Townships and Villages.

Information of the origin and meaning of names has been gathered from "An Illustrated History of the Counties of Rock and Pipestone," by Arthur P. Rose, 1911, having pages 241-421 and 657-802 for this county; and from Charles H. Bennett, Warrington B. Brown, and L. G. Jones,

PIPESTONE COUNTY   417

the county treasurer, each of Pipestone, interviewed during a visit there in July, 1916.

AETNA township, the latest organized, July 19, 1880, was named in honor of Aetna Johnson, a step-daughter of Christ Gilbertson, an immigrant from Norway, who settled in this township in 1878.

AIRLIE, a railway village six miles west of Pipestone, was founded in 1879 by a land corporation of Scotland, being named in honor of the earl of Airlie, who was its president.

ALTONA township, organized February 28, 1880, received its name by vote of its settlers, for the city of Altoona in Pennsylvania; but an error in spelling changed it to the name of a city in Germany, adjoining Hamburg. Altona is also the name of a village and township in New York, and of villages in Michigan, Indiana, Illinois, and Missouri.

BURKE township, organized April 26, 1879, was at first called Erin, but was renamed a few weeks later in honor of Rev. Thomas N. Burke, of Ireland, who in 1871 had visited America on a lecturing tour in defence of the political rights of that country.

CAZENOVIA, a railway village in Troy, founded in 1884, was named for a town and lake in Madison county, N. Y., whence many farmers of this vicinity had come.

EDEN township, organized September 27, 1879, was named by a popular vote, on the recommendation of Richard O'Connell, after much discussion of other proposed names. "The beautiful stretch of country comprising the township suggested the Garden of Eden to the pioneers."

EDGERTON, the railway village of Osborne township, platted in September, 1879, and incorporated October 14, 1887, was named in honor of Gen. Alonzo J. Edgerton, who was born in Rome, N. Y., June 7, 1827, and died in Sioux Falls, S. D., August 9, 1896. He was graduated at Wesleyan University in 1850; came to Mantorville, Minn., in 1855, and was there admitted to practice law; served as captain of the Tenth Minnesota regiment, 1862-4, and in 1865 was brevetted brigadier general; removed to Kasson in 1878; was a state senator in 1859, and again in 1877-8; and was a United States senator by appointment from March to December, 1881.

ELMER township, organized August 28, 1879, has a name that is also borne by villages in New Jersey, Pennsylvania, Michigan, and Missouri.

ETON, a railway station in Gray township, established in 1895 as Gray siding, was renamed in November, 1906, for the town of Eton in England, having a celebrated school where founders of an English colony of this county were educated.

FOUNTAIN PRAIRIE, organized June 2, 1879, was named by Charles Heath, one of its early settlers, for his former home township in Columbia county,. Wisconsin.

GRANGE township, organized April 26, 1879, received this name in compliment to the Patrons of Husbandry, a secret agricultural order whose lodges are called granges, from French words, grange, a barn, and grangier, a farmer. This order was founded in 1867 by Oliver H. Kelley (b. 1826, d. 1913), who since 1849 had been a Minnesota farmer in Sherburne county.

GRAY township, organized June 28, 1879, was named in honor of Andrew O. Gray, its first permanent settler.

HATFIELD, a railway village in the southeast part of Gray, founded in 1880, has a name that is borne by a township and village in Massachusetts, and by villages of Pennsylvania, Wisconsin, and other states.

HOLLAND, a Great Northern railway village nine miles northeast of Pipestone, founded in 1888, was incorporated May 10, 1898, being named for "a large colony of Hollanders in that vicinity."

IHLEN, a railway village in section 9, Eden, was named in honor of Carl Ihlen, on whose land it was platted in July, 1888.

JASPER, a railway village in the south edge of Eden, extending also into Rock county, platted in April, 1888, and incorporated May 9, 1889, was named for its quarries of red quartzite, commonly called jasper, an excellent building and paving stone.

OSBORNE township, organized March 31, 1879, was named on the suggestion of William J. Dodd, an early settler, in honor of his cousin, J. C. Osborne, of Newark, New Jersey.

PIPESTONE, the county seat, at first named Pipestone City, platted in October, 1876, was incorporated as a village February 10, 1881, and as a city July 23, 1901. Its area was mostly in section 12 of Sweet township, adjoining the south border of the Pipestone Reservation and Indian quarry, before noted at the beginning of this chapter, which are mostly comprised in section 1.

ROCK township, organized June 2, 1879, has several small streams, sources of the Rock river flowing southward past "the Mound" of red quartzite in Rock county, whence the river and that county received their name, given also to this township for its location at the head of the river.

RUTHTON, the railway village of Aetna township, platted in June, 1888, and incorporated November 2, 1897, was named in honor of the wife of W. H. Sherman, one of the townsite proprietors.

SWEET township, organized February 20, 1879, was named in honor of Daniel E. Sweet, the first settler of this county. He was born in Pennsylvania, April 10, 1838; came to Wisconsin with his parents, and in 1860 removed to Iowa; served in the Eleventh Iowa regiment during the civil war; took a land claim on the site of Pipestone in 1874; platted Pipestone city, in company with Charles H. Bennett, in 1876, was its first postmaster, and later was the county surveyor and probate judge; removed to Louisiana in 1886, where he had charge of a steamboat line and engaged in other business enterprises; died at Siloam Springs, Ark., October 2, 1902.

TROSKY, the railway village of Elmer township, platted in September, 1884, was incorporated June 10, 1893. The significance of this name, not found elsewhere in the United States, remains to be ascertained.

PIPESTONE COUNTY 419

TROY township, organized December 3, 1879, received its name from Troy, N. Y., by vote of the settlers after many other names had been proposed and rejected. Daniel B. Whigam, at whose home in section 10 the township meeting was held, finally suggested this name from its being stamped on his kitchen stove as its place of manufacture. "The stove instrumental in supplying the name of the township had a history of its own. It was the first stove sold by the first dealer in Pipestone county, and came from the store of William Wheeler, of Pipestone." (Rose, History of this county, page 277.)

WOODSTOCK, the railway village of Burke, platted in September, 1879, and incorporated June 23, 1892, "was named after Woodstock, the county seat of McHenry county, Illinois, which was named after Woodstock, Vermont, and that after a town in England."

STREAMS AND LAKES.

The Rock river has been noticed in the first chapter, and again for the township in this county named from it.

Redwood river, having sources in Aetna, the most northeastern township of this county, is fully noticed in the chapter for Redwood county.

Flandreau creek, in Fountain Prairie and Altona townships, flowing southwest to the Big Sioux river in South Dakota, and the village of this name near its mouth, commemorate Charles Eugene Flandrau (but with a change in spelling), who was born in New York city, July 15, 1828, and died in St. Paul, Minn., September 9, 1903. He was admitted to practice law in 1851; came to Minnesota in 1853, settling in St. Paul; was a member of the state constitutional convention, 1857; was associate justice of the supreme court of Minnesota, 1857-64; author of "The History of Minnesota and Tales of the Frontier" (408 pages, 1900), and many papers in the Minnesota Historical Society Collections. During the Sioux outbreak, in August, 1862, Judge Flandrau commanded the volunteer forces in their defence of New Ulm against the attacks of the Sioux, and on account of his important services received from Governor Ramsey the commission of colonel.

Pipestone creek, named from its flowing past the red pipestone quarry, has a series of four little lakes on its course, Pipestone, Crooked, Duck, and Whitehead lakes, the first being in the east part of the reservation and the others within about a mile west from the quarry. These are the only lakes in the county.

At the quartzite bluff between Pipestone lake and the quarry, this stream "passes over the ledge from the upper prairie to the lower with a perpendicular fall of about 18 feet," as noted by Prof. N. H. Winchell (Geology of Minn., Final Report, vol. I, 1884, p. 539). His later map of the pipestone quarry names this cascade as Winnewissa falls (Aborigines of Minn., 1911, plate at page 564), from a Sioux verb, winawizi, to be jealous or envious. The name had been used much earlier in an excellent poem by Mrs. Adelaide George Bennett, of Pipestone, entitled "The Peace-Pipe Quarry," first read at a celebration there July 4, 1878, which was reprinted as pages 77-85 in "Indian Legends of Minnesota," compiled by Mrs. Cordenio A. Severance and published in 1893. In the reprint Mrs. Bennett inserted new lines with this name, "Falls of Winnewissa."

Close west of the falls are Leaping rock, a little columnar cliff left by erosion in front of the verge of the bluff and within leaping distance from it, and Inscription rock, bearing the name of J. N. Nicollet and initials of five members of his exploring party, inscribed when they visited the pipestone quarry in July, 1838.

Nearly on the south line of the reservation, about a half mile south from the falls and the present quarry pits, an exceptionally huge granite boulder, the largest known in Minnesota, lying on the quartzite, has fallen in six pieces under the action of frost, separating it along the natural seams or joints. "The largest three pieces, each about twenty feet long and twelve feet high, are the Three Maidens, so called . . . from the tradition that after the destruction of all the tribes in war, the present Indians sprang from three maidens who fled to these rocks for refuge." (Geology of Minn., vol. I, page 546.)

Split Rock creek, named from its flowing through gorges eroded in the quartzite at Jasper and on lower parts of its course, in Rose Dell township of Rock county and in South Dakota, receives its head streams from Sweet and Eden townships in the southwest corner of Pipestone county.

In Osborne, the most southeastern township, the West fork of Rock river flows to it from Elmer; and nearly opposite to that stream it receives Chanarambie creek, bearing a Sioux name that means "hidden wood," as noted for Murray county, which has a township of this name.

The Altamont moraine, the outermost marginal belt of knolly and ridged glacial drift, forms the crest of the Coteau des Prairies in the northeast part of this county, extending across Rock and Aetna townships, with the sources of the Des Moines and Redwood rivers on its slope declining eastward and the highest springs of Rock river on its western slope.

POLK COUNTY

Established July 20, 1858, and organized in 1872-73, this county was named in honor of James Knox Polk, the eleventh president of the United States. He was born in Mecklenburg county, N. C., November 2, 1795, and died in Nashville, Tenn., June 15, 1849. His home was in Tennessee after he was eleven years old. He was admitted to practice law in 1820; was a member of Congress, 1825-39, and served as speaker the last four years; was governor of Tennessee, 1839-41; and as Democratic candidate for president was elected in 1844. On March 3, 1849, the next to the last day of his presidential term, he approved the act of Congress which organized Minnesota Territory.

Holcombe, in the History of this county, wrote of Polk as follows: "He advocated the war against Mexico and was an efficient President during that contest. But he was opposed to wars in general, and it was largely his great influence during his administration which prevented war with Great Britain in 1846 over the Oregon question—a war of which many unwise Americans were decidedly in favor—and when he was in Congress he and some other Congressmen prevented a war with Spain. He was a man of pure and high character and personally popular. This county need be well satisfied with its name."

TOWNSHIPS AND VILLAGES.

Information of names has been gathered from "History of the Red River Valley," 1909, two volumes, continuously paged, having a chapter for this county, pages 860-886, by Judge William Watts and Arthur A. Miller; "Compendium of the History and Biography of Polk County," by Return I. Holcombe and William H. Bingham, 1916, 487 pages; interviews with Judge Watts and Arthur A. Miller, of Crookston, the county seat, during a visit there in August, 1909; from Henry J. Welte, county auditor, Amund L. Hovland, judge of probate, Hans L. Waage, clerk of court, Elias Steenerson, David H. Turner, and Judge Watts, during a second visit at Crookston in September, 1916; and from A. F. Cronquist and Thomas Vollen, of Erskine, interviewed there in September, 1916, for the southeast part of this county.

ANDOVER township, organized in 1877, has a name that is also borne by townships and villages in Maine, New Hampshire, Massachusetts, and ten other states.

ANGUS township, organized in 1879, and its earlier railway village, were named in honor of Richard Bladworth Angus, a banker of Montreal, who financially aided the construction of this line of the Great

Northern railway. He was born in Bathgate, Scotland, May 28, 1831, came to Canada in 1857; was successively a director, general manager, and president in 1910-14, of the Bank of Montreal; was a principal promoter for building the Canadian Pacific railway, which was completed in 1885.

BADGER township has a lake of this name, adjoining Erskine village, and its outlet, Badger creek, flows northwest through this township. The lake and creek were named for the burrowing animal, formerly frequent in Minnesota, which gave to Wisconsin its sobriquet as the "Badger State."

BELGIUM township, organized in 1880, had immigrants from Belgium as its first settlers.

BELTRAMI, the railway village in Reis township, was named in honor of Giacomo Costantino Beltrami (b. 1779, d. 1855), an Italian exile, who traveled to the Red river and the upper Mississippi in 1823, as narrated in the chapter of Beltrami county.

BRANDSVOLD township was named in honor of one of its pioneer settlers, an immigrant from Norway.

BRANDT township has a name that is borne by villages in Pennsylvania, Ohio, and South Dakota.

BRISLET township, organized in 1880, was probably named for one of its early settlers.

BUFFINGTON is a station of the Northern Pacific railway on the south line of Euclid.

BYGLAND township, organized in 1877, was named for a village in southern Norway, whence several of its pioneer settlers came.

CHESTER township has a name that is borne also by townships and villages or cities in twenty-five other states, by counties in Pennsylvania, South Carolina, and Tennessee, and by a city and county in England.

CLIMAX, a railway village in Vineland, is named with an ancient Greek word, meaning a ladder or a stairway, hence the highest point attained in an oration or in any series of endeavors, chosen here from its use in an advertisement of "Climax Tobacco."

COLUMBIA township has a name borne by counties in eight states, townships and villages or cities in twenty-seven states, and the largest river of our Pacific coast, in honor of Christopher Columbus, the discoverer of America.

In 1896 several propositions for the establishment of new counties from the eastern part of Polk county were submitted to the vote of the people, resulting in the formation of Red Lake county. One of the petitions had sought to form a county named Columbia, and this was again attempted in 1902, for the southeast part of the present Polk county, which then received a large vote in its favor. Columbia county was proclaimed by the governor in December, 1902, as established; but the proceedings in the popular vote, when three different names, Nelson, Columbia, and Star, had been submitted and adopted to be applied to the new county, were declared invalid and of no effect by a decision of the state supreme court, April 16, 1903.

CROOKSTON, the county seat, first settled in 1872, incorporated as a city February 14, 1879, was named in honor of Colonel William Crooks, of St. Paul, who was the chief engineer in locating the first railroad here, then known as the St. Paul and Pacific railroad, which was constructed in 1872 from Glyndon through Crookston to the Snake river at the site of Warren in Marshall county. He was born in New York city, June 20, 1832; was graduated from the department of civil engineering at West Point military academy; settled in St. Paul in 1857, as engineer for this railroad; served as colonel of the Sixth Minnesota regiment in the civil war; was a representative in the state legislature, 1875-7, and a state senator, 1881; died in Portland, Oregon, December 17, 1907. The first locomotive used in Minnesota, in 1862, was named William Crooks in his honor.

His father, Ramsay Crooks, who was born in Greenock, Scotland, January 2, 1787, and died in New York city, June 6, 1859, was probably also intentionally honored by the adoption of this name for the largest Minnesota city in the Red river valley. As a member, and subsequently president, of the American Fur Company, he was well known throughout the Northwest. During many years he was identified with the fur trade in Minnesota, and had great influence with the Indians.

Crookston township was organized March 28, 1876. The city area was taken partly from this township, and also from Lowell, Andover, and Fairfax.

DUGDALE is a railway village in Tilden.

EAST GRAND FORKS, incorporated as a city March 7, 1887, is at the east side of the Red river, opposite the city of Grand Forks, N. D., where the confluence of the large Red Lake river with the upper part of the Red river presents two navigable courses or forks for ascending boats.

EDEN township, was named, like a township of Pipestone county and Eden Prairie township in Hennepin county, for the Garden of Eden, to express the happiness of the settlers in their new homes.

ELDRED, a Great Northern railway village in Roome township, bears the name of a village in New York and six townships of different counties in Pennsylvania, commemorating Judge Nathaniel B. Eldred, of Bethany, Pa. He was born in Orange county, N. Y., in 1795; was admitted to practice law in 1816, and in the same year settled at Bethany, Pa.; was a district judge, 1835-57; and died in January, 1867.

ERSKINE, a Great Northern village in Knute township, founded in 1889, was named in honor of John Quincy Erskine, who was born in Vermont in December, 1827, and died at Crookston in January, 1908. He came from Racine, Wis., to this county about 1885, and was president of the First National Bank of Crookston.

ESTHER township was named in honor of the daughter of Grover Cleveland, president of the United States.

EUCLID township, organized in 1879, and its railway village, were named by Springer Harbaugh, manager of the large Lockhart farm in Norman county, for the beautiful Euclid avenue in Cleveland, Ohio, where he had formerly lived.

FAIRFAX township, organized in 1879, bears the name of a county in Virginia, and of townships and villages in Vermont, Ohio, Indiana, Iowa, and several other states.

FANNY township, organized in 1880, commemorates the wife or daughter of a pioneer, but her surname remains to be learned.

FARLEY township, organized in 1878, was named in honor of Jesse P. Farley, who was born in Tennessee in 1813, and died in Dubuque, Iowa, May 9, 1894. He was a merchant in Dubuque, and established a steamboat line to St. Paul; came to Minnesota in 1873, as receiver of the St. Paul and Pacific railroad; resided in St. Paul several years, engaging in railroad enterprises.

FERTILE, a Northern Pacific railway village in Garfield, was named for Fertile village of Worth county in northern Iowa, whence some of its first settlers came.

FISHER township, organized in 1876, and its railway village of the same name, received it from the earlier railway terminal village of FISHER'S LANDING, founded here in the fall of 1875 on the Red Lake river at its head of practicable steamboat navigation. During a few years, until the railway lines to Winnipeg and Grand Forks were completed, respectively in 1878 and 1879, Fisher's Landing surpassed Crookston in population and business. It closely adjoined the site of the present village, by which it was superseded, so that the old Landing village area "has changed to an unpretentious cow pasture." These names were adopted in honor of William H. Fisher, who was born in Hunterdon county, N. J., December 24, 1844; engaged in railroad business after 1864; settled in St. Paul in 1873, as attorney for the receiver of the St. Paul and Pacific railroad, and as its assistant manager and superintendent; later was president and manager of the St. Paul and Duluth railroad company, 1883-99; was vice president and general manager of the Duluth and Winnipeg railroad company, 1888-93.

FOSSTON, the railway village in Rosebud township, was named in honor of Louis Foss, its earliest merchant, who removed to Tacoma, Wash.

GARDEN township, organized in 1881, was named by its people for its beauty and fertility, like Eden before noted.

GARFIELD township, organized in 1880, commemorates James Abram Garfield, who was born at Orange, Ohio, November 19, 1831, and died at Elberon, N. J., September 19, 1881. He was an instructor and later president of Hiram College, Ohio, 1856-61; served in the civil war, and was promoted major general in 1863; was a member of Congress, 1863-80; was president of the United States in 1881.

GENTILLY township, organized in 1879, received its name from a village on the St. Lawrence river in the Province of Quebec, which was named for the town of Gentilly in France, a southern suburb of Paris.

GIRARD is a Great Northern railway station in Andover.

GODFREY township, organized in 1881, was named in honor of Warren N. Godfrey, an early settler at the southwest end of Maple lake in this township, who removed to the state of Washington.

GRAND FORKS township, organized in 1882, has a translated name, like the adjoining city of East Grand Forks and the city in North Dakota on the opposite side of the Red river, from the Ojibway name of the junction of the Red river and the Red Lake river, noted by Gilfillan as "Kitchi-madawang, the big forks, that is, where the rivers are so large in either fork that you don't know which to go into."

GROVE PARK township, organized in 1880, has groves bordering the northeast part of Maple lake, with Lakeside Park on the shore of this lake in the adjoining edge of Woodside township.

GULLY township and its railway village are named for a gully or ravine there crossed by the railway, adjoining the highest beach ridge of the Glacial Lake Agassiz.

HAMMOND township, organized in 1880, was named in honor of one of its early settlers.

HELGELAND township was so named by its Norwegian people for the district of Helgeland in the north part of Norway.

HIGDEM township, organized in 1879, was named in honor of Arne O. Higdem, a pioneer farmer there, who was a member of the board of county commissioners.

HILL RIVER township has a stream that was so named for morainic hills adjoining its course near the north line of this township. It has also been called the South fork of Clearwater river.

HUBBARD township, settled in 1871 and organized in 1882, was named in honor of Lucius Frederick Hubbard, governor of Minnesota in 1882-87, for whom a biographic notice is presented in the chapter of Hubbard county.

HUNTSVILLE, the first township organized in the county, March 17, 1874, was named in honor of Bena Hunt, one of its first settlers, who came here from Winona in 1871.

JOHNSON township, organized in 1898, was named in honor of John O. Johnson, a Norwegian homesteader in Columbia, who then was one of the county commissioners.

KERTSONVILLE township, organized in 1881, was named for one of its pioneer settlers.

KEYSTONE township, also organized in 1881, had the very large Keystone farm, owned by capitalists in Pittsburg, Pa. This farm was named for Pennsylvania, the "Keystone State," which was at the center in the series of the thirteen original states, like the keystone of an arch.

KING township was named in honor of Ephraim King, an early settler, who was the first postmaster there.

KITTSON, a station of the Great Northern railway seven miles south of Crookston, was named for Norman W. Kittson, of whom a biographic sketch has been given in the chapter for Kittson county.

KNUTE township was named for Knute Nelson, a Norwegian farmer near Fertile, who was a member of the board of county commissioners. He had the same name as Governor Nelson, who since 1895 has been a United States senator.

LAKESIDE PARK is a village of summer homes in Woodside, on the northwest shore of Maple lake.

LENGBY is a railway village in Columbia.

LESSOR township received its name, changed in spelling from Lessard, in honor of a French Canadian pioneer farmer.

LIBERTY township, organized in 1880, was named by its people in the petition for township organization.

LOWELL township, organized in 1877, was named for the city of Lowell in Massachusetts, whence some of its settlers came.

MCINTOSH, the railway village of King township, was named for the owner of a part of the village site, who kept a hotel there. He was of Scotch and Ojibway descent, and removed to the White Earth reservation.

MALLORY, a railway village in Huntsville, was named in honor of Charles P. Mallory, a lumber merchant in Fisher. He was born in the Province of Quebec, March 7, 1844; came to Minnesota in 1871, settling in Minneapolis; and removed to Fisher in 1878.

MAPLE BAY is a village of summer homes at the southwest end of Maple lake, in Godfrey township.

MENTOR, a railway village in Grove Park township, was named for the village of Mentor in northeastern Ohio, where President Garfield purchased a farm which was his country home during his last three years.

NESBIT township, organized in 1880, was named in honor of James and Robert Nesbit, brothers, born in Lanark county, Canada, who settled here in 1875.

NIELSVILLE is a Great Northern railway village in Hubbard.

NORTHLAND township was named for Norway, the native land of many of its settlers.

ONSTAD township, organized in 1882, was named in honor of Ole P. Onstad, one of its pioneer farmers, an immigrant from Norway.

PARNELL township was named by settlers from Ireland, in honor of Charles Stewart Parnell, the Irish statesman. He was born in Avondale, Ireland, in 1846; was a member of Parliament, 1875-91; visited the United States in the interest of the Irish agitation for home rule, in 1879-80; and died in Brighton, England, October 6, 1891.

POLK COUNTY 427

QUEEN township is the second east of King township, which suggested this name.

REIS township, organized in 1880, was named in honor of George Reis, an early settler, who came here from Pennsylvania, and after a residence of several years removed to Michigan.

RHINEHART township was named in honor of Captain A. C. Rhinehart, of East Grand Forks, who was a member of the board of county commissioners.

ROOME township, organized in 1879, was named for one of its pioneer farmers.

ROSEBUD township has a name that is borne also by villages in Pennsylvania, Illinois, Missouri, South Dakota, and other states. Wild roses are common, or in many places abundant, throughout this state.

RUSSIA township, organized in 1882, and its railway village, bear the name of the largest country of Europe, and of a township and village in New York.

SANDSVILLE township, organized in 1882, was named in honor of Casper and Martin Sand, brothers, natives of Norway, who came here as homesteaders in 1880, opening a large stock farm. After 1888 they also conducted a meat market in Crookston.

SCANDIA township bears the ancient name of the southern part of the peninsula of Sweden and Norway, whence those countries, and also Denmark and Iceland, are together named Scandinavia.

SHIRLEY, a station of the Great Northern railway seven miles north of Crookston, has a name that is borne by townships and villages in Maine, Massachusetts, and several other states.

SLETTEN township was named in honor of Paul C. Sletten, who was receiver of the United States land office in Crookston.

SULLIVAN township, organized in 1880, was named in honor of Timothy Sullivan, municipal judge in East Grand Forks.

TABOR township, settled by Bohemians, was named for a city of Bohemia, about fifty miles south of Prague.

TILDEN township, organized in 1882, was named in honor of Samuel J. Tilden, who was born in New Lebanon, N. Y., February 9, 1814, and died at Greystone, near Yonkers, N. Y., August 4, 1886. He was governor of New York in 1875-76, and was the Democratic candidate for president of the United States in 1876.

TRAIL, a Soo railway village in Gully township, was named for its location where a former trail between the Red river valley and the Red Lake Indian Agency was crossed by the railway.

TYNSID township, settled in 1871, and organized in 1879, was named for Tönset, a railway village in Norway, about 100 miles south of Trondhjem. It was thus incorrectly written in the petition for the township organization.

VINELAND township, organized in 1876, was named in compliment to Leif Steenerson, its first settler, who took a homestead claim here in

May, 1871. The name refers to the voyage of Leif Ericson from Greenland, about the year 1000, when he discovered a country to which he gave the name Vinland or Wineland, for its grape vines, having sailed probably to the coast of Maine and Massachusetts.

WINGER township was named by Norwegian settlers, for a group of farms in the valley district called Gudbrandsdal in central Norway.

WOODSIDE township, organized in 1882, lies mainly on the wooded southeastern side of Maple lake, which is bordered westward by the vast prairie area of the Red river valley.

LAKES AND STREAMS.

The Red river and the Red Lake river are noticed in the first chapter, and they are more fully considered in the chapter of Red Lake county.

An older channel of the Red Lake river, branching from it in Fisher, extending about twenty-five miles northwestward, and joining the Red river near the north line of Esther, was named the Grand Marais, meaning Great marsh, by the early French fur traders and voyageurs. Like Marsh river, which similarly extends from the Wild Rice river at Ada northwest to the Red river, in Norman county, it has during most of the year only a small and nearly stagnant stream, which is changed into a great river with the snow melting of spring and at times of heavy rains.

The Snake river, translated from Kanabec, its Ojibway name, crosses the north line of this county for a few miles in Sandsville, and by several unnamed creeks receives the drainage of its northeastern townships, from Belgium and Euclid northward.

Lost river, in Gully and Chester, flowing west to the Clearwater river in Red Lake county, was formerly lost in a large swamp along a part of its lower course.

Hill river, from which a township received its name, was translated from Peqwudina zibi of the Ojibways, as written by Gilfillan.

Poplar river, having its sources in Columbia and joining the Clearwater river near the northwest corner of Poplar River township in Red Lake county, is a translation of the Ojibway name, Asadi zibi.

Badger lake and creek, giving their name to a township of Polk county, have been before noticed.

Burnham and Anderson creeks are southern tributaries of the Red Lake river in Fisher.

Sand Hill river, flowing westward through the south edge of this county from unnamed lakes near its sources in Rosebud township, is another translation from the Ojibways, given more fully by Gilfillan as "Ga-papiqwutawangawi zibi, or the river of sand hills, scattered here and there in places." The short English name is used on the map of Long's expedition in 1823. Plentiful dunes of wind-blown sand, forming hillocks 25 to 75 or 100 feet high, to which this name refers, occur within two miles west of Fertile and thence for a distance of five miles south-

POLK COUNTY 429

ward, lying on the sand delta deposited here at the highest level of the ancient Lake Agassiz.

The southeastern part of this county, above the highest shoreline of Lake Agassiz, has abundant lakes, but they are mostly unnamed on maps.

Maple lake, before noticed for its villages of Lakeside Park and Maple Bay, has many sugar maple trees in the forest at its southeast side.

Cable lake is about a mile west of Lakeside Park.

Union lake, in Woodside and Knute townships, was named for its comprising three wide parts united by straits.

Crystal lake, in Woodside, has exceptionally transparent water.

Lake Sarah, in the southwest part of Knute township, adjoins the east end of Union lake. In the north part of this township are Lake Cameron beside Erskine village, named for Daniel Cameron, an early homesteader on the site of this village, and Oak lake, named for its oak groves.

Lake Arthur, in Garfield township, was named in honor of Chester Alan Arthur (b. 1830, d. 1886), who succeeded Garfield as president of the United States, 1881-85.

Cross lake, named from its outline, on the head stream of Hill river in the central part of Queen township, had a very long Ojibway name, translated by Gilfillan as "the lake with pines on one side of the water."

Turtle lake, a mile west of Cross lake, is translated from the Ojibways, their name, noted by Gilfillan, being "Mekinako sagaiigun, or Turtle lake, from its form, which, seen from a canoe in the middle, closely resembles a turtle."

Perch lake adjoins the west side of Cross lake, and Connection lake forms the greater part of a canoe route between Cross and Turtle lakes.

White Fish lake, on the south line of Queen township, a mile south of Turtle lake, is one of the sources of the Poplar river, which also receives the outflow of six smaller lakes mapped without names in the west part of Columbia.

POPE COUNTY

This county, established February 20, 1862, and organized September 4, 1866, was named in honor of General John Pope, who was born in Louisville, Ky., March 16, 1822, and died in Sandusky, Ohio, September 23, 1892. He was graduated at West Point in 1842, and served as a lieutenant in the Mexican war. In the summer of 1849 he was a member of an exploring expedition, under the command of Major Samuel Woods, which went from Fort Snelling up the Mississippi and Sauk rivers and past White Bear lake (since named Lake Minnewaska), in the present Pope county, to the Red river, and thence northward by a route at a considerable distance west of the river to Pembina. On the return, in order to make a thorough examination of the Red river, Pope and a small number of the party embarked in canoes and ascended this river to Otter Tail lake, made the portage to Leaf lakes, and thence descended the Leaf, Crow Wing, and Mississippi rivers. He wrote in his report: "On the 27th of September we arrived at Fort Snelling, and completed a voyage of nearly one thousand miles, never before made by any one with a like object."

At the time of this expedition, Pope was a captain. He was afterward, in 1853 to 1859, commander of the expedition making surveys for a Pacific railroad near the 32d parallel. In the civil war he was a most energetic defender of the Union, and early in 1862 was commissioned major general of volunteers. September 6, 1862, shortly after the outbreak of the Sioux war in Minnesota, General Pope was appointed commander of the Department of the Northwest, with headquarters at St. Paul, and he continued in charge of this department until January, 1865. To his efficient direction and coöperation was due, in a large degree, the success of Generals Sibley and Sully in their campaigns of 1863 and 1864 against the Sioux.

TOWNSHIPS AND VILLAGES.

Information of the origins and meanings of names was received from the "Illustrated Album of Biography of Pope and Stevens Counties," 1888, having pages 145-364 for Pope county; and from Ole Irgens, county auditor, Casper T. Wollan, a pioneer merchant, and his brother, M. A. Wollan, president of the Pope County State Bank, each of Glenwood, the county seat, interviewed during a visit there in May, 1916.

BANGOR township bears the name of a city in Maine, and of villages and townships in New York, Pennsylvania, Michigan, Wisconsin, and several other states.

POPE COUNTY 431

BARSNESS township was named in honor of three brothers, Nels N., Erik N., and Ole N. Barsness, born in Norway respectively in 1835, 1842, and 1844, who settled in this township in 1865-66.

BEN WADE township was named in honor of Benjamin Franklin Wade, who was born near Springfield, Mass., October 27, 1800, and died in Jefferson, Ohio, March 2, 1878. He removed to Ohio, with his parents, about 1820; began law practice in 1827; was a district judge, 1847-51; and was a United States senator, 1851-69. He was an anti-slavery leader, and favored the Homestead bill.

BLUE MOUNDS township is crossed by a belt of low morainic drift hills, to which this name was given by settlers from Blue Mounds village in Dane county, Wisconsin. The hills thus named in each of these states appear bluish when seen from a distance.

CHIPPEWA FALLS township was named for its falls in Terrace village, descending 16 feet, on the East branch of the Chippewa river, supplying water power for a flour mill. This village and its post office at first were called Chippewa Falls, but were renamed by request of the settlers to prevent their mail from going to the City of Chippewa Falls in Wisconsin.

CYRUS is the railway village of New Prairie township, platted in the spring of 1882.

FARWELL, a railway village in the northwest corner of Ben Wade township, platted in April, 1887, has a name that is borne also by villages in Michigan and Nebraska.

GILCHRIST township was probably named in honor of a pioneer settler beside its Lake Gilchrist, which lies mainly in section 7.

GLENWOOD township, on the southeast side of Lake Minnewaska, was named for the great glen or valley occupied by this lake and for the woods around its shores, contrasted with the prairies that form the far greater part of this county. The city of Glenwood, the county seat at the northeast end of the lake, in Glenwood and Minnewaska townships, first platted in part on September 26, 1866, was incorporated as a village February 23, 1881, and as a city in 1912. This name is borne also by cities in Wisconsin and Iowa, and by villages and townships in twenty other states.

GROVE LAKE township has Grove lake and McCloud lake near its south side, which are more fully noticed in the later part of this chapter.

HOFF township was named for the village of Hof in Norway, about 50 miles north of Christiania.

LAKE JOHANNA township bears the name given to its large lake on the map of Minnesota in 1860, probably in honor of the wife or daughter of an early settler, but her surname remains to be learned.

LANGHEI township has a Norwegian name, meaning "a long highland." Its northeastern part gradually rises to an elevation about 300 feet above Lake Minnewaska, being the highest land in the south half of the county, with a very extensive prospect on all sides.

LEVEN township was named for a loch or lake in eastern Scotland, the Leven river outflowing from it, and the seaport at its mouth, on the north side of the Firth of Forth.

LOWRY, a Soo railway village in the east edge of Ben Wade township, platted in March, 1887, was named in honor of Thomas Lowry, who was born in Logan county, Illinois, February 27, 1843, and died in Minneapolis, February 4, 1909. He was admitted to the bar in 1867, and in the same year came to Minnesota, settling in Minneapolis, where he practiced law and dealt in real estate; was president and principal stockowner of the company operating the street railways of Minneapolis and St. Paul, called the Twin City Rapid Transit Company.

MINNEWASKA township, adjoining the northern shore of the largest lake in this county, bears the name given to the lake by the white settlers made from two Dakota or Sioux words, mini or minne, water, and washta or waska, good. Prof. N. H. Winchell wrote of the lake and its successive names, as follows: "This lake, according to statements of citizens of Glenwood, was originally designated by an Indian name, meaning *Dish lake,* because of its being in a low basin. After that, when the chief, White Bear, was buried in a high hill on the north shore, it was called *White Bear* lake. After a time it was changed to *Lake Whipple,* from Bishop Whipple, of Faribault, and by act of the state legislature in 1883 it was again changed to *Minnewaska,* or Good-water. It is said to be 85 feet deep in its deepest part and averages about 40 feet, and there is no known evidence of its having ever stood at a higher level." (Geological Survey of Minnesota, Thirteenth Annual Report, for 1884, p. 14.)

Nicollet's map, published in 1843, has no delineation nor name for this lake, which, with its grandly picturesque basin and inclosing bluffs, is the most noteworthy topographic feature of the county. Major Woods and Captain Pope, in their exploration in 1849, first mapped it as White Bear lake. The name Lake Whipple, in honor of Henry Benjamin Whipple (b. 1822, d. 1901), the revered and beloved Episcopal bishop of Minnesota, was applied to it during several years, when it was confidently expected that an Episcopal school would be founded at Glenwood.

NEW PRAIRIE township was named by its settlers, as their new home in the great prairie area of western Minnesota.

NORA township is reputed to have been named for Norway, the native country of many of its people.

RENO township received the name of its large lake, commemorating Jesse Lee Reno, major general of United States volunteers, who was born in Wheeling, West Virginia, June 20, 1823, and was killed in the battle of South Mountain, Md., September 14, 1862. He was graduated at West Point in 1846; served in both the Mexican and civil wars; and made a survey in 1853 for a military road from Mendota, Minn., to the mouth of the Big Sioux river.

ROLLING FORKS township was named for its contour as an undulating and rolling prairie, crossed by the East branch or fork of the Chippewa river, which here receives a considerable tributary from the north.

SEDAN, a Soo railway village in the northwest corner of Bangor township, is named for a city of France, famous for the battle fought on September 1, 1870, between the Germans and the French, which resulted in the surrender of the French army, leading directly to the establishment of France as a republic.

STARBUCK, platted in the spring of 1882, is a village of the Northern Pacific railway, adjoining the western end of Lake Minnewaska.

TERRACE is a village formerly called Chippewa Falls, in the township of that name, platted in June, 1871. The village is built on a terrace plain of the valley drift bordering both sides of the Chippewa river.

VILLARD, a village of the Northern Pacific railway in the east edge of Leven, platted in August, 1882, was named in honor of Henry Villard, who was born in Bavaria, April 11, 1835, and died at Dobbs Ferry, N. Y., November 12, 1900. He came to the United States in 1853; engaged in journalism, and in the management of railroads; and was president of the Northern Pacific railroad company in 1881-83, when the construction of its transcontinental line was completed. E. V. Smalley, in his History of this railroad, devoted two chapters (pages 245-276) to the very remarkable career of Villard, up to the time of its publication in 1883.

WALDEN township has the name of a township and village in Vermont, and of villages in New York, Georgia, and Colorado. Henry D. Thoreau lived alone in 1845-47 beside Walden pond, near Concord, Mass., as narrated in his book, "Walden, or Life in the Woods," published in 1854.

WESTPORT township and its railway village, which was platted in October, 1882, have a name that is borne by townships and villages in Maine, Massachusetts, Connecticut, New York, Wisconsin, and ten other states.

WHITE BEAR LAKE township includes the western end of this lake, which has been known by several names, before mentioned for Minnewaska township. The grave of the Ojibway chief, White Bear, is an elongated mound on a knoll in the south edge of section 3, Minnewaska, about 90 feet above the lake, as described by Prof. N. H. Winchell (Aborigines of Minnesota, 1911, p. 298).

"Waube-Mokwa (the White Bear), who was a chief among the Ojibways and dwelt by these waters," is represented to have lived here more than two centuries ago by "The Tribe of Pezhekee, a Legend of Minnesota" (1901, 232 pages), written by Alice Otillia Thorson, of Glenwood. It is known in history, however, that the warfare of the Ojibways against the Dakotas, acquiring the region of northern Minnesota by conquest, took place much later.

Lakes and Streams.

Excepting its eastern border, this county is drained by the Chippewa river, which is fully noticed, for the origin of its name, in the chapter of Chippewa county. Its tributaries in Pope county are the Little Chippewa river, Outlet creek, which flows from Lake Minnewaska and through Lake Emily, and the East branch, from which Chippewa Falls and Rolling Forks townships are named, flowing into Swift county.

Signalness creek, tributary to Outlet creek from the north side of the Blue mounds, and a small lake crossed by the south line of section 14 in Blue Mounds township, were named in honor of Olaus Signalness, a pioneer farmer in the northwest quarter of that section. He was born in Norway, November 12, 1851; came to the United States in 1864, with his parents, who settled in Wisconsin; and in 1869 they removed to this county, being the first settlers in this township.

Mud creek flows from Lake Johanna township southwestward to the East branch.

Grove lake, having a grove beside it, which gives its name to a township, and McCloud lake, closely adjoining its west end, are at the head of the North fork of Crow river, flowing east into Stearns county. These lakes were on the route of Woods and Pope, for the latter of whom this county is named, in the expedition to the Red river in 1849, and their party camped here during a week, from June 27 to July 3; but they were then named Lightning lakes, referring to a severe thunderstorm, with "a stroke of lightning, which tore in pieces one of the tents, and prostrated nearly all the persons who were in the camp." The name of the Lightning lakes, however, although clearly shown by Pope's journal to belong to the Grove and McCloud lakes, has been transferred to two other lakes much farther west on their course, in Grant county and southwestern Otter Tail county.

Westport lake, in the township of this name, is the source of Ashley creek, which flows into Stearns county and is a tributary of Sauk river.

The other lakes of Pope county, including many named for pioneer settlers, are noted as follows, in the order of the townships from south to north, and of the ranges from east to west.

Lake Johanna township, with the large lake of this name, has several of small size not yet named on published maps.

Gilchrist township has Lakes Gilchrist, Linka, Nilson, and Johnson, Scandinavian lake, and Goose and Simon lakes. Lake Linka was named in honor of the wife of Rev. Peter S. Reque, a Lutheran pastor.

Rolling Forks township has Lakes Hanson, Helge, Anderson and Rasmusson. The first named, which is the largest, was formerly called Woodpecker lake.

Langhei has Lake Benson and Swan lake.

Hoff, the most southwestern township, and Bangor, the most eastern of the townships numbered 124, have no lakes.

Chippewa Falls township has Round lake and Lakes Swenoda and Anderson. The second is a composite name, for its adjoining Swedish, Norwegian, and Danish settlers; and Swenoda township, 25 miles distant to the southwest, in Swift county, was named in the same way.

Barsness has Lakes Stenerson, Gilbertson, Ben, Mary, Celia, Nelson, and Edwards.

Lake Emily, on Outlet creek in Blue Mounds and Walden townships, quite surely commemorates the wife or daughter of a pioneer; but her surname, as for other feminine names of lakes in this county, remains to be ascertained for a more definite historical record.

Grove Lake township, beginning the tier numbered 125, has Lake Lincoln and Mud lake, with Grove and McCloud lakes, which earlier had been named Lightning lakes, as before noted.

Lake Alice is mainly in section 12, Glenwood, and Camp lake is crossed by the west line of its sections 30 and 31.

Minnewaska township, with its large and beautiful lake of this name, has also Pelican lake.

White Bear Lake township has Lake Malmedard, crossed by its north line, named for Christian Malmedard, a pioneer Norwegian farmer there; and several smaller lakes are mapped without names.

On the west line of New Prairie township are Lakes Charlotte and Cyrus, the latter being close southwest of Cyrus village.

In Westport, the most northeastern township, Westport lake, as before mentioned, is connected southward by a strait with the wider Swan lake.

Leven has a series of four lakes, the most southern being Lake Amelia, the source of the East branch of the Chippewa river; Lake Villard, next northward, adjoining the village of this name; and Lakes Leven and Ellen. Rice lake, close west of Lake Villard, is named for its wild rice.

In Reno township, with its lake so named, are Lakes Ann and John, Mud lake, crossed by its north boundary, and a dozen unnamed lakelets.

Ben Wade township has Lake Jorgenson, but its six other small lakes are nameless on maps.

Nora, the most northwestern township, has Pike lake, named by Woods and Pope in 1849 for many pike fish caught there; and in this township are also ten lakelets that have no names.

HILLS.

The Blue mounds, before mentioned for the township named for them, are overtopped by the great highland of Langhei, also before noted in the list of townships. The very massive Langhei hill and the deep basin and high bluffs of Lake Minnewaska are undoubtedly due to the contour of the bedrocks, though no outcrop of them is seen because of their concealment under the glacial drift.

RAMSEY COUNTY

Established October 27, 1849, this county was named in honor of Alexander Ramsey, the first governor of Minnesota Territory. He was born near Harrisburg, Pa., September 8, 1815; studied at Lafayette College; was admitted to the practice of law in 1839; was a Whig member of Congress from Pennsylvania, 1843 to 1847; was appointed by President Taylor, April 2, 1849, as governor of this Territory; arrived in St. Paul, May 27; and commenced his official duties here June 1, 1849. He continued in this office to May 15, 1853. In 1851 Governor Ramsey negotiated important treaties with the Sioux at Traverse des Sioux and Mendota, and in 1863 with the Ojibways where the Pembina trail crossed the Red Lake river, by these treaties opening to settlement the greater part of southern and western Minnesota. He was the second mayor of St. Paul in 1855. After the admission of Minnesota as a state, he was elected its second governor, and held this office from January 2, 1860, to July 10, 1863, during the very trying times of the civil war and the Sioux war. Being in Washington on business for the state when the news of the fall of Fort Sumter was received, he at once tendered to President Lincoln a regiment of one thousand men from Minnesota, this being the first offer of armed support to the government. Ramsey was United States senator, 1863 to 1875; and secretary of war, in the cabinet of President Hayes, 1879 to 1881. He was president of the Minnesota Historical Society, 1849-63, and from 1891 until his death in St. Paul, April 22, 1903. The Minnesota legislature has provided that his statue will be placed in the Statuary Hall of the national capitol, being one of the two in this state thus honored.

When this county was first established in 1849, as one of the nine counties into which the new territory was originally divided, it reached north to Mille Lacs and to the upper Mississippi in the present Aitkin county. In 1857, with the formation of Anoka, Isanti, Mille Lacs, and Aitkin counties, Ramsey retained only a small part of its former area and became the smallest county of Minnesota. Its county seat, St. Paul, has been continuously the capital of the territory and state.

Townships, Villages, and St. Paul.

Information of the origins of names has been gathered in "A History of the City of St. Paul and of the County of Ramsey," by John Fletcher Williams, published in 1876 as Volume IV of the Minnesota Historical Society Collections, 475 pages; "History of Ramsey County and the City of St. Paul," 1881, 650 pages; "Fifty Years in the Northwest," by Wil-

RAMSEY COUNTY 437

liam H. C. Folsom, 1888, having pages 532-590 for this county; and "History of St. Paul," edited by Gen. C. C. Andrews, 1890, 603 pages, with biographical sketches, 217 pages, by R. I. Holcombe.

BALD EAGLE is a village on the southern shore of Bald Eagle lake, in White Bear township, consisting largely of summer homes and also having permanent residents. The lake was so named because "a small island near the center was the home of several bald eagles at the time of the government surveys."

GLADSTONE, a village and junction of the Northern Pacific and Soo railways, in New Canada, was named in honor of William Ewart Gladstone (b. 1809, d. 1898), the eminent British statesman, for whom villages are also named in New Jersey, Illinois, Michigan, and other states.

HAZEL PARK, a railway station nearly four miles northeast from the Union station in St. Paul, "was so named because it was located in the midst of a dense hazel shrubbery." (Stennett, Place Names of the Chicago and Northwestern Railways, 1908, p. 178.)

HIGHWOOD is a railway station in the southeast part of the area of St. Paul, having the same name with villages in Connecticut, New Jersey, and Illinois.

McLEAN township, organized in April, 1858, was named in honor of Nathaniel McLean, who in 1853 settled on its sections 3 and 4, close east of Dayton's bluff adjoining the Mississippi. He was born in Morris county, N. J., May 16, 1787; came to St. Paul in 1849; was the Sioux agent at Fort Snelling, 1849-53; and died in St. Paul, April 11, 1871. This former township was annexed to the city of St. Paul in 1887.

MERRIAM PARK, a large residential district in the western part of St. Paul, was named for Hon. John L. Merriam (b. 1825, d. 1895) and his son, Governor William R. Merriam, who with others were the original proprietors of this addition to the city.

MOUNDS VIEW township, organized May 11, 1858, has a tract of hills of morainic drift extending from south to north about three miles through its central part, affording a fine panoramic view from their northern and highest points, which are about 200 feet above the surrounding country.

NEW BRIGHTON, a railway village of Mounds View, having stockyards and meat-packing business, was named from Brighton, Mass., which formerly was an important cattle market with abattoirs, now a suburban district of Boston.

NEW CANADA township, also at first called Little Canada, organized May 11, 1858, was named in compliment for its French Canadian settlers.

NORTH ST. PAUL, a railway village in New Canada, adjoining Silver lake, was at first named Castle, in honor of Captain Henry Anson Castle (b. 1841, d. 1916), of St. Paul, by whom it was founded in 1887, the next year after the Wisconsin Central railroad was built there.

RESERVE township, organized May 11, 1858, had been until 1853 a part of the Fort Snelling military reserve. The north line of this reservation east of the river, surveyed in 1839, as noted in the chapter of

Hennepin county, coincided nearly with the north line of this township, and with the present Iglehart avenue of St. Paul. In 1887, with the enlargement of St. Paul to the present area, this township became a suburban part of the city, but much of it yet is a farming district.

RIVERVIEW, formerly called West St. Paul or simply the West Side, being the part of the city on the western (but here really the southern) side of the Mississippi, received this name February 15, 1918, by action of the city council. Its high river bluffs, in part known as Cherokee Heights, give very extensive and grand views of this valley. The petition for the change to the name Riverview bore 3,434 signatures, while 50 opposing it preferred that the new name should be South Side.

ROSE township, organized May 11, 1858, was named in honor of Isaac Rose, who settled here in the summer of 1843, purchasing 170 acres of land, which included the site of Macalester College. He was born in New Jersey, in 1802; was a land agent, selecting farms for immigrants; died at Traverse des Sioux, Minn., in February, 1871.

ST. ANTHONY PARK, the most northwestern part of St. Paul, includes a residential area of nearly two square miles, adjoining the Minnesota Agricultural College and Experimental Farm, departments of the State University, with the State Fair Ground, which are in Rose township. The name was applied to additions of the city area, in allusion to the former city of St. Anthony, now the east part of Minneapolis, bordering the west side of St. Anthony Park. Both refer to St. Anthony falls of the Mississippi, named by Father Hennepin in 1680 after his patron saint.

ST. PAUL, the county seat and the capital of Minnesota, first settled by Pierre Parrant in 1838, received its name from a little Catholic chapel built in 1841 under the direction of Father Lucian Galtier, who in the preceding year had come to Mendota, near Fort Snelling. The history of the building and naming of the chapel, with the adoption of the name for the village and city, was written in part as follows by Galtier in 1864, at the request of Bishop Grace.

"In 1841, in the month of October, logs were prepared and a church erected, so poor that it would well remind one of the stable at Bethlehem. It was destined, however, to be the nucleus of a great city. On the 1st day of November, in the same year, I blessed the new *basilica,* and dedicated it to 'Saint Paul, the apostle of nations.' I expressed a wish, at the same time, that the settlement would be known by the same name, and my desire was obtained. I had, previously to this time, fixed my residence at Saint Peter's [Mendota], and as the name of PAUL is generally connected with that of PETER, and the gentiles being well represented in the new place in the persons of the Indians, I called it Saint Paul. The name 'Saint Paul,' applied to a town or city, seemed appropriate. The monosyllable is short, sounds well, and is understood by all denominations of Christians. . . . Thenceforth the place was known as 'Saint Paul Landing,' and, later on, as 'Saint Paul.'" (History of the City of St. Paul, by Williams, 1876, pages 111-112.)

RAMSEY COUNTY 439

Lucian Galtier was born in France in 1811, and died at Prairie du Chien, Wis., February 21, 1866. He studied theology in his native land; came to the United States in 1838, with a band of missionaries; was ordained a priest at Dubuque, Iowa, in 1840, and the same year settled at Mendota. In 1844 he removed to Keokuk, Iowa, and four years later returned to France. Afterward he again came to America, and resided at Prairie du Chien until his death.

St. Paul was organized as a village or town November 1, 1849, and was incorporated as a city March 4, 1854, then having an area of 2,560 acres, or four square miles. It received a new city charter March 6, 1868, when its area was 5.45 square miles, to which about seven square miles were added February 29, 1872, and again three square miles March 6, 1873. West St. Paul, now Riverside, which had belonged to Dakota county, was annexed November 16, 1874, by proclamation of the popular vote ratifying the legislative act of March 5, 1874, whereby the total area of the city was increased to 20 square miles. Further large annexations, March 4, 1885, and February 8, 1887, adding the former McLean and Reserve townships, extended St. Paul to its present area, 55.44 square miles, which is very nearly the same as the area of Minneapolis.

Prof. A. W. Williamson, in his list of geographic names in this state received from the Sioux, wrote: "Imnizha ska,—*imnizha*, ledge; *ska*, white; the Dakota name of St. Paul, given on account of the white sandstone cropping out in the bluffs." In the simplest words, this Sioux name means "White Rock."

As a familiar sobriquet, St. Paul is often called "the Saintly City;" Minneapolis similarly is "the Mill City" or "the Flour City;" and the two are very widely known as "the Twin Cities."

A few districts of St. Paul have been noted in the preceding list, namely Merriam Park, Riverview, and St. Anthony Park; and the railway stations of Hazel Park and Highwood, likewise before noted, also are in St. Paul. This city has numerous other residential or partially mercantile and manufacturing districts, which may properly be briefly mentioned here, in advance of more definite notice in a later chapter, which will treat especially of the streets, avenues, and parks. Several districts designated as parks, however, are wholly or partly occupied by residences, this being the case with each of the districts called parks in the following list.

Dayton's bluff, at the east side of the Mississippi in the southeast part of St. Paul, has a large residence district on the plateau extending backward from its top. The name commemorates Lyman Dayton, a former landowner there for whom a village and township in Hennepin county were named. On the edge of the southern and highest part of the bluff, in Mounds Park, is a series of seven large aboriginal mounds, 4 to 18 feet high, from which a magnificent prospect is obtained, overlooking the river and the central part of the city. Dayton was born in

Southington, Conn., August 25, 1810, and died in St. Paul, October 20, 1865. He came to Minnesota in 1849, settling in this city, and invested largely in real estate; was the projector and president of the Lake Superior and Mississippi railroad.

Arlington Hills and Phalen Park are northeastern districts, the second being named from Phalen lake and creek, for Edward Phelan (whose name was variously spelled), one of his successive land claims, in the earliest years of St. Paul, having been on this creek.

Como Park, the largest public park of the city, with adjoining residences, incloses Lake Como, named by Henry McKenty in 1856 for the widely famed Lake Como adjoining the south side of the Alps in Italy. He was born in Pennsylvania in 1821, settled in St. Paul at the age of thirty years, dealt largely in city lots and farm lands, and died in this city August 10, 1869.

Lexington Park is a western central district, named from Lexington, Mass., where the first battle of the Revolutionary War was fought, April 19, 1775.

Farther northwest and southwest, respectively, are the districts of Hamline and Macalester Park, having the Methodist Hamline University and the Presbyterian Macalester College, named in honor of Bishop Leonidas Lent Hamline (b. 1797, d. 1865), of Ohio, and Charles Macalester (b. 1798, d. 1873), of Philadelphia, a generous donor to this college.

In and near Groveland Park, a district at the west side of the city, bordering on the Mississippi, are three large Catholic institutions, St. Paul Seminary, St. Thomas College and St. Catherine's College.

St. Anthony Hill, often called simply the Hill district, comprises a large residential area on a broad plateau that was crossed by the earliest road leading from the central part of St. Paul to the Falls of St. Anthony and the city of this name, which in 1872 was united with Minneapolis.

At Seven Corners, close southwest from the business center of St. Paul, streets radiate in seven directions, with buildings on the intervening corners of the city blocks.

WEST ST. PAUL, which had been incorporated as a city in Dakota county, March 22, 1858, returned to township government in 1862, but was annexed to Ramsey county in 1874, becoming a ward of the city of St. Paul, and was renamed Riverview in 1918, as before noted.

WHITE BEAR township, organized May 11, 1858, and its village, which was incorporated in 1881, received the name of the large White Bear lake, "from an old Indian legend, in which they suppose it to be possessed with the spirit of a white bear, which was about to spring on the wife of one of their young braves, but was shot by him, and its spirit had haunted the island and lake since and had mysteriously disposed of several of their braves. The island, which they named Spirit island, is located near its northwestern shore and has about fifty-four acres of land, covered with quite a heavy growth of timber." (History of this county, 1881, p. 281.) It is now commonly called Manitou island, its original Ojibway name.

William H. C. Folsom, in his "Fifty Years in the Northwest" (1888, on its page 545), wrote of the Dakota or Sioux name, as follows: "The Indians called this a grizzly, polar, or white bear, and named an adjacent locality [now a village on the northeastern shore, in Washington county] 'Mah-to-me-di,' or 'M'de, i. e., Mahto, gray polar bear, and M'de, lake. It is not probable, however, that a polar bear ever reached this spot, and a visit from a grizzly is nearly as improbable. Indian legends are very frequently made to order by those who succeed them as owners of the soil."

Lakes and Streams.

Pike island, on the Dakota county side of the Mississippi at the mouth of the Minnesota river, adjoining the former Reserve township (now the most southwestern part of St. Paul), was named in honor of Zebulon Montgomery Pike, who in 1805 there purchased from the Dakotas or Sioux, for the United States, a large tract as a military reserve, on which Fort Snelling (at first called Fort St. Anthony) was built in 1820-24.

Beside the center of St. Paul, at the foot of the bluff of Riverview, are Harriet and Raspberry islands of the Mississippi. Harriet island, containing 28 acres, donated to this city by Dr. Justus Ohage, May 26, 1900, is used as a public playground, bathing place, and zoological park. It was named very long ago in honor of Harriet E. Bishop, who was born in Vergennes, Vt., January 1, 1817, and died in St. Paul, August 8, 1883. She came to St. Paul in 1847, to open the first permanent school in this city. Through her influence a Sunday school also was soon organized, and in the next year a public building was erected to accommodate the school, preaching services, etc. She was the author of "Floral Home, or First Years of Minnesota" (1857), and other books.

The little Cozy lake, in Como park, adjoins Lake Como.

Rice creek, the outlet of White Bear and Bald Eagle lakes, flows through shallow lakes having much wild rice in Centerville township, Anoka county, thence passing into Mounds View, and reaching the Mississippi in Fridley, Anoka county, a few miles north of Minneapolis. Hon. Henry M. Rice, of St. Paul, was an early landowner and summer resident near the lower course of this creek, in Fridley township, the stream being named in his honor, as noted in the chapter for that county.

Shadow Falls creek, a very little stream, is named for its cascade in springtime or after any heavy rains, on its descent to the great river, close north of the St. Paul Seminary. Finn's glen, having a similar brooklet, is about a mile farther south, named for William Finn, the first permanent settler in Reserve township.

Trout brook, flowing through St. Paul, which was tributary to Phalen creek just before their united waters reached the Mississippi, is the outlet of McCarron lake, in Rose township. John E. McCarron, a farmer who lived beside this lake, was born in 1839; came there in 1849; served in the Fourth Minnesota regiment in the civil war; and died in St. Paul, March 27, 1897.

Phalen creek and lake have been previously noted for the northeastern district and public park of St. Paul adjoining this lake, which was the original source of the city water supply. Northward a series of lakes has been added to that first source, partly by artificial channels, including Spoon lake, named for its outline, Gervais, Fitzhugh (or Kohlman), Bass, Vadnais, Lambert, Pleasant, and Charles lakes, Long and Deep lakes, and Wilkinson and Otter lakes, reaching to the north line of the county.

Gervais lake commemorates Benjamin Gervais, a pioneer French Canadian farmer, who was born at Riviere du Loup, Canada, July 15, 1786, and died here in January 1876. He settled on the Red river in the Selkirk Colony in 1812; came to Fort Snelling in 1827; and when settlers were ordered to leave the military reservation, in 1838, he opened a farm in the central part of the present area of St. Paul. In 1844 he removed to this lake, being the first settler in the area of New Canada.

Vadnais lake was named "for John Vadnais, who made a claim on its banks as early as 1846;" Lambert lake, for Louis Lambert, who purchased a part of its island; and Wilkinson lake, for "Ross Wilkinson, who first took up a claim on its shores."

Pig's Eye lake and marsh, on the alluvial bottomland of the Mississippi about two miles southeast from Dayton's bluff and the Indian Mounds, were named in allusion to Pierre Parrant, a whiskey dealer, before mentioned as the first settler in St. Paul, who about the year 1842 removed to the vicinity of that lake. He had a defective eye, whence he received this nickname, applied also to the village of St. Paul at its beginning, until displaced by the present name in 1841. Pig's Eye lake had been previously called Grand Marais, meaning the Great marsh, by the early French fur traders and voyageurs. (History of Saint Paul, by Williams, 1876, pages 64-88.)

Battle creek, named for the battle of Kaposia in 1842, between the Ojibways and Sioux, flows into Pig's Eye lake from the high land east of the river valley. Another great ravine there, having numerous tall white pines, is named Pine Cooley, from a French word, coulée, meaning a ravine or run. (History by Williams, pages 122-125.)

Kaposia, the Sioux or Dakota village of the successive hereditary chiefs named Little Crow, early located on the east bank of the Mississippi near the Grand Marais, where Pike saw it in 1805 and Long in 1817, was several times changed in place, being even removed to the vicinity of the mouth of Phalen creek or near the site of the union depot in St. Paul, as known by the narratives of Cass and Schoolcraft at this village in 1820, Long and Keating in 1823, and Latrobe in 1833. Again in 1835 it was near the Grand Marais, as noted by Featherstonhaugh. After the treaty at Washington in 1837, by which the Sioux ceded their lands east of the Mississippi here, the Kaposia band had their village at its west side, occupying a part of South Park, a suburb of South St. Paul in Dakota county, which was its site at the time of the battle. The approach of the Ojibways for the attack, and the course of their retreat, were by way of these ravines of Battle creek and Pine Cooley.

The name Kaposia, changed from Kapozha in the Dakota language, means light or swift of foot in running, as defined by Williamson in his list of Sioux geographic names, before cited for the city of St. Paul. Little Crow's band had received this name, which thence was applied to their village, "in honor of their skill in the favorite game of lacrosse."

The following lakes remain to be noticed in this county.

Beaver lake is about two miles east from the south end of Lake Phalen.

New Canada has Silver lake, adjoining North St. Paul, and Savage lake in sections 6 and 7, the latter being so named because "the Indians frequented its shores in large numbers."

White Bear township, with its numerous lakes before noted, has also Birch, Black, Poplar, Sucker, and Gilfillan lakes, the last being named in honor of Charles D. Gilfillan, of St. Paul.

The north line of Rose township crosses Lake Owasso, formerly called Big Bass lake, and Lake Josephine. The first of these names is nearly like "the bluebird, the Owaissa," in Longfellow's "Song of Hiawatha." For the companion lakes Josephine and Johanna, the latter lying in Mounds View township, Judge Bazille states that the surname McKenty may be added, these names being in honor respectively of the daughter and wife of Henry McKenty, by whom Lake Como was named.

Other lakes in Mounds View are Turtle, Maryland (formerly Snail), Grass, Island, Valentine, Long, and Silver lakes. Marsden and Round lakes have been drained.

Hills and Caves.

The Mounds View hills, in the township named for them, are the highest points in the county.

The Arlington hills, in a district of St. Paul platted with that name, are merely an undulating and somewhat prominently rolling tract of morainic drift. St. Anthony hill, another district in this city, is an extensive plateau about 225 to 240 feet above the Mississippi. Dayton's bluff and Cherokee heights, respectively east and west or south of this river in St. Paul, are parts of the prolonged series of river bluffs which bound the valley on each side, rising from its bottomlands to the general level of the adjoining country.

Carvers' cave, in the lower part of Dayton's bluff, was named for Captain Jonathan Carver, who there on May 1, 1767, received a deed written by himself and signed by two Sioux chiefs, granting to him and his heirs a large tract of land in the present states of Minnesota and Wisconsin. This cave was well known to the Sioux or Dakota people, whose name for it, as noted by Carver, was "Wakon-teebe, that is, the Dwelling of the Great Spirit."

A biographic sketch of Carver is given in the chapter for the county bearing his name. All the vast inheritance that had been claimed for his heirs and others, under the Sioux deed, was denied and annulled in 1821-1825 by the United States Congress. Long afterward Carver's lake, which is in the edge of Washington county, five miles southeast from Carver's cave and the Mound Park, was named for one of his descendants who settled as a farmer beside it.

Fountain cave, about four miles farther up the Mississippi, at the base of its bluff in the southwest part of St. Paul, was discovered in 1811. Major Long explored and described it in 1817, giving to it this name because a brook runs through the cavern and issues, like a fountain, at its mouth. Cass and Schoolcraft examined it in 1820, but erroneously called it Carver's cave.

GLACIAL LAKE HAMLINE.

A map and description of a glacial lake, lying mostly within the area of St. Paul, are presented by the present writer in the Bulletin of the Geological Society of America (vol. VIII, 1897, pages 183-196). Its deposits form nearly level sand and gravel plains and plateaus, 260 to 225 feet above the river, extending from near the State Agricultural College eastward to the northwest end of Lake Como, thence southward past Hamline University, with a narrow connection southeast to another wide expanse in the Hill district or plateau crossed by Summit avenue. The length of the glacial Lake Hamline was thus about six miles, with maximum widths exceeding one mile.

RED LAKE COUNTY

Established December 24, 1896, this county received its name from the Red Lake river, which flows through it, giving also its name to Red Lake Falls, the county seat. The river derives its name, in turn, from Red lake, these both being translations of their Ojibway names.

Why these Indians originally so designated the lake was uncertain until it was ascertained by the late Rev. Joseph A. Gilfillan. It had been affirmed, with poetic license, by Beltrami, who traveled here in 1823, publishing in 1824 and 1828, that the aboriginal names of Red lake and its outflowing river, the latter translated by him Bloody river, refer to the "blood of the slain," in the wars between the Ojibways and Dakotas. Gilfillan, who was a missionary to the Ojibways of northwestern Minnesota from 1873 to 1898, wrote in 1885 that the Ojibway name of this lake, written by him "Misquagumiwi sagaiigun, Red-water lake," perhaps alludes to "reddish fine gravel or sand along the shore in places, which in storms gets wrought into the water near the edges," or to the reddish color of streams flowing into the lake from bogs on its north side, probably reddened by bog iron ore. He later wrote, however, in a letter of February, 1899, that these are erroneous conjectures of some of the Ojibways, and that he had obtained more reliable information, so that he could then confidently state the origin of this name, as follows: "Red lake is so called from the color of the lake [reflecting the redness of sunset] on a calm summer evening, when unruffled by wind and in a glassy state, at which times it is of a distinctly wine color. . . .It is not called Red lake from any battle fought on its shores."

Red lake and Red river appear with these names, in French, on the map by Verendrye (1737) and on Buache's map (1754); and the lake is so named on the somewhat later maps of Jefferys and Carver. From information obtained during his travels in Minnesota in 1766 and 1767, Carver mapped Red lake and the Red Lake river, giving them exactly their present names. Their earliest delineation, however, from personal examination, was by Thompson (in 1813-14), who in April, 1798, reached Red lake, coming by way of the Red Lake and Clearwater rivers, and thence going onward to Turtle and Cass lakes.

It tells us something of the appreciation of natural beauty and grandeur by the Indians, that they took from the hues of sunset the name of the largest lake in Minnesota, whence we now have, by derivation, the names of two large rivers, of a county, and its county seat.

Townships and Villages.

Information of names was received from Edward L. Healy, real estate dealer, Z. A. Chartier, deputy county auditor, Ovide Emard, county treasurer, and Frank Jeffers, register of deeds, each of Red Lake Falls, interviewed during visits there, the first in August, 1909, and the others in September, 1916.

BROOKS is a village of the Soo railway in Poplar River township. This name is borne also by a township and village in Maine, and by villages and post offices in twelve other states.

BROWN'S CREEK township has a stream so named, tributary to the Black river, probably commemorating a pioneer settler or an early hunter and trapper.

DELORME, a station of the Northern Pacific railway in the south edge of Lake Pleasant township, was named for Ambrose Delorme, an adjoining homestead farmer.

DOROTHY, a Northern Pacific station in Louisville, was named by J. F. Matthews of Red Lake Falls. This feminine name, derived from the ancient Greek language, means "the gift of God."

EMARDVILLE township received its name in honor of Pierre Emard, who was born in Longueuil on the St. Lawrence river in Canada, opposite to Montreal, in 1835, and came to Minnesota in 1878, settling as a homesteader in section 24, Red Lake Falls. One of his sons is the county treasurer.

EQUALITY township was named by its people in the petition for its organization.

GARNES township bears the name of one of the earliest settlers, E. K. Garnes, an immigrant from Norway.

GERVAIS township was named in honor of Isaiah Gervais, who was born at Fort Garry (now Winnipeg), Manitoba, December 10, 1831; came to Minnesota, and lived in St. Paul; settled as a homestead farmer in section 26, Red Lake Falls, in 1876; and died there, November 2, 1888.

HUOT is a little village on the Red Lake river in section 28, Louisville. The village and township were each named for Louis Huot, an early French Canadian homesteader there.

LAKE PLEASANT township was named for the former lake and marsh in its section 18, now drained.

LAMBERT township was named for Francois Lambert, who was born at St. Ursule, P. Q., March 10, 1847. He came to Minnesota in 1881, settling as a farmer on section 10 in this township, of which he was the treasurer during many years.

LOUISVILLE township, like its village of Huot, before noted, commemorates Louis Huot, a pioneer farmer.

OKLEE, a Soo railway village in Lambert, bears the name of Ole K. Lee, a Scandinavian settler, on whose farm the village was built.

RED LAKE COUNTY 447

PERRAULT, a Northern Pacific station near the center of Lake Pleasant township, was named for Charles Perrault, an adjacent homestead farmer, who died in 1915. His son, Joseph Perrault, is the county judge of probate.

PLUMMER, the Soo railway village and junction in Emardville, received its name in honor of Charles A. Plummer, who about the year 1881 built a sawmill and gristmill on the Clearwater river near the site of this village. He removed to Iowa.

POPLAR RIVER township is crossed by this stream, tributary to the Clearwater river. Its name, which is translated from the Ojibways, appears as Aspen brook on Thompson's map from his travel here in 1798. Two species of poplar or aspen are common throughout most of this state, one of them being especially plentiful northward.

RED LAKE FALLS, the county seat, near the center of a township bearing this name, was incorporated as a village February 28, 1881, and as a city in 1898. The name has reference to rapids and falls within the city area, supplying valuable water power, on both the Red Lake and Clearwater rivers. These are translations of their Ojibway names, received from the lakes whence they flow.

RIVER township is named for the Red Lake river flowing through it.

TERREBONNE township has a French name, meaning good land, received from the county and town of this name in the Province of Quebec.

WYLIE township and its railway village were named in honor of an early farmer there.

STREAMS AND LAKES.

Lost river, Hill river, Poplar river, and Badger creek, southern tributaries of Clearwater river in this county, have their headwaters in the southeast part of Polk county, so that the origins and meaning of their names have been given in the chapter for that county. The second of these streams was mapped by Thompson in 1798 as "Wild Rice rivulet," for several small lakes of its upper course, having much wild rice.

Black river, flowing from the north through Wylie and Louisville to the Red Lake river at Huot, is named from the dark color of its water received from peaty swamps. Its largest tributary is Brown's creek, for which a township is named.

This county, like others lying within the area of the Glacial Lake Agassiz, has a smoothed surface of its drift sheet, with no hollows holding lakes. Formerly it had a single lake, which gave the name of Lake Pleasant township; but that was rather a marsh, becoming occasionally a shallow lake, which has been drained, its bed being now good farming land.

REDWOOD COUNTY

Established February 6, 1862, this county was named for the Redwood river, whence also comes the name of the county seat, Redwood Falls, situated on a series of cascades and rapids of the river. Prof. A. W. Williamson wrote of this name: "Chanshayapi;—*chan,* wood; *sha,* red; *ayapi,* are on; Redwood river; so called by the Dakotas on account of the abundance of a straight slender bush with red bark, which they scraped off and smoked, usually mixed with tobacco. This name is spelled by Nicollet Tchanshayapi." Keating and Featherstonhaugh each gave both the Dakota and English names of this river; and the latter traveler expressly defined their meaning, as follows: "This red wood is a particular sort of willow, with an under bark of a reddish colour, which the Indians dry and smoke. When mixed with tobacco it makes what they call *Kinnee Kinnik,* and is much less offensive than common tobacco."

The inner bark of two Cornus species, C. sericea, the silky cornel, and C. stolonifera, the red-osier dogwood, were used by the Indians, both the Sioux and the Ojibways, to mix with their tobacco for smoking. The Algonquian word, kinnikinnick, for such addition to the tobacco, included also the leaves of the bearberry and leaves of sumach, gathered when they turn red in the autumn, which were similarly used.

Cornus sericea is frequent throughout Minnesota, excepting far northward; and C. stolonifera abounds through the north half of this state, and is common southward to Winona, Mower, and Blue Earth counties, but its southward geographic range scarcely reaches into Iowa. Dr. C. C. Parry stated that the bark of the former species, wherever it is found, is preferred for use as kinnikinnick; and that the bark of the latter is commonly substituted for it by the Indians about Lake Superior.

It has been supposed also that the Dakota name of the Redwood river alludes to the red cedar trees on its bluffs at Redwood Falls, or to trees there marked by spots of red paint for guidance of a war party at some time during the ancient warfare between the Ojibways and the Sioux for ownership of this region, as told in a Sioux legend to early white settlers (History of this county, 1916, pages 613-614). Either of these alternative suggestions has seemed to many of the settlers more probable than the testimony for the kinnikinnick, which was received from an earlier and more intimate knowledge of the Dakota people and their language. Chan, as a Dakota word, may mean a tree or any woody shrub, being a more general word than wood in our language, which in its most common use is applied only to trees.

REDWOOD COUNTY   449

But two or even all three of these reasons for the naming of the river may be included together as each contributing to its origin, namely, the kinnikinnick, the red cedars, and also painted trees. In support of the third as a part of the origin, we should quote from Beltrami who was here in 1823, accompanying Major Long's expedition, for he wrote that the Redwood river was "so called from a tree which the savages paint red every year and for which they have a peculiar veneration." (Beltrami's Pilgrimage, vol. II, p. 316.)

TOWNSHIPS AND VILLAGES.

Information of the origins and meanings of names has been gathered from "History of the Minnesota Valley," 1882, having pages 762-798 for this county; "The History of Redwood County," compiled by Franklyn Curtiss-Wedge, reviewed by Julius A. Schmahl, 1916, two volumes, 1016 pages; and William H. Gold, Hiram M. Hitchcock, Major M. E. Powell, and Hon. Orlando B. Turrell, each of Redwood Falls, the county seat, interviewed during a visit there in July, 1916.

BELVIEW, a village of the Minneapolis and St. Louis railway in Kintire, platted in 1889 and incorporated January 3, 1893, has a name derived from French words, meaning a beautiful view.

BROOKVILLE township, settled in 1869 and organized April 19, 1873, has a name that is borne also by villages in Pennsylvania, Ohio, Indiana, Illinois, Wisconsin, and six other states.

CHARLESTOWN, organized May 25, 1872, was named in honor of Charles Porter, who was the first settler in this township, coming in 1864.

CLEMENTS, a railway village in Three Lakes township, platted in 1902, was named in honor of Peter O. Clements, an adjoining farmer. He was born in Sweden, April 17, 1847; came to the United States, settling first in Washington county, Minn.; and removed in 1877 to section 32 in this township. One of his sons, Arthur E. Clements, born April 13, 1878, is a hardware merchant here.

DELHI township, first settled in 1865, organized February 19, 1876, was named by Alfred M. Cook, builder and owner of a flour mill at Redwood Falls, who came from Delhi, a village in Ohio, near Cincinnati. Six other states have villages of this name, derived from the large city of Delhi in India. The railway village of this township, bearing the same name, was platted in 1884, and was incorporated November 25, 1902.

GALES township, organized July 18, 1876, received its name in honor of its first settlers, A. L. and Solon S. Gale, who came in May, 1872.

GILFILLAN, a railway station in Paxton, eight miles southeast of Redwood Falls, was named in honor of Charles Duncan Gilfillan, owner of a very large farm there, comprising about 8,000 acres, who was born in New Hartford, N. Y., July 4, 1831, and died in St. Paul, December 18, 1902. He came to this state in 1851, and settled in St. Paul in 1854; was for three terms a representative in the legislature, and a state senator in 1878-85. During his later years he engaged largely in farming in this county, and was president of the Minnesota Valley Historical Society, interested in the erection of monuments and tablets commemorating events of the Sioux massacre and war in 1862.

GRANITE ROCK township, first settled in 1871-2 and organized in 1890, has small outcrops of the granitic bedrock in sections 6 and 12. Excepting these outcrops and the similar but far more extensive rock exposures along the Minnesota valley and in the adjacent gorge of the Redwood river at and below its falls, all the surface of the county is a moderately undulating sheet of glacial drift, which deeply covers the bedrocks.

HONNER township, first settled in 1864 and organized January 24, 1880, was named for J. S. G. Honner, who was one of the first settlers of Redwood Falls and later took a claim on the Minnesota river in this township. He was born in New York in 1831; came to Minnesota in 1856, and to this county in 1864; was the first register of deeds for the county, and was a representative in the legislature in 1865 and 1870, and a state senator in 1872.

JOHNSONVILLE township, settled in 1872, organized January 9, 1879, "was named for the Johnsons living in it." Four members of the first board of township officers had this surname.

KINTIRE township, first settled in the summer of 1872 and organized May 25, 1880, received its name from the large peninsula of Kintyre, 40 miles long, on the southwestern coast of Scotland.

LAMBERTON township, settled in July, 1864, organized April 1, 1874, and its railway village, founded in 1873 and incorporated March 3, 1879, commemorate Henry Wilson Lamberton, who was born in Carlisle, Pa., March 6, 1831, and died in Winona, Minn., December 31, 1905. He settled there in 1856; became president of the Winona Deposit Bank in 1868; was elected president of the Winona and Western railway company in 1894; and was one of the state capitol commissioners from the organization of that board until his death.

LOWER SIOUX AGENCY, established in 1853-4, on the southern bluff of the Minnesota river in the present northwest quarter of section 8, Sherman, had several government buildings and became a considerable village before its abandonment on account of the Sioux outbreak and massacre, August 18, 1862.

LUCAN, the railway village of Granite Rock, platted in January, 1902, and incorporated March 29, 1904, was named for a village in Ireland, seven miles west of Dublin.

MILROY, a railway village in Westline, next west of Lucan, platted in March, 1902, and incorporated on November 15 of the same year, "was named for Major General Robert H. Milroy, a gallant Union soldier during the early days of the war of the rebellion" (Stennett, Place Names of the Chicago and Northwestern Railways, 1908, p. 102). He was born near Salem, Ind., June 11, 1816; was graduated at Norwich University, Vermont, 1843; served in the Mexican war and in the civil war; was superintendent and agent for Indian affairs in Washington Territory, 1872-85; and died in Olympia, Wash., March 29, 1890.

MORGAN township, organized in May, 1880, and its railway village, platted in August, 1878, and incorporated February 23, 1889, were named in honor of Lewis Henry Morgan, the eminent soldier, explorer and author, who has been called "the Father of American anthropology." He was born near Aurora, N. Y., November 21, 1818, and died in Rochester, N. Y., December 17, 1881. Among the numerous books of his authorship is a history of the American beaver and its works, for which in 1861 he traveled through Minnesota to the Red river settlements in Manitoba, and in 1862 for this research he ascended the Missouri river to the Rocky mountains.

MORTON village, lying mainly in Renville county, includes also a suburb on the south side of the Minnesota river in the extreme eastern corner of Honner.

NEW AVON township, first settled in March, 1870, organized September 5, 1872, was named in compliment to Joshua S. and Jonathan P. Towle, early settlers there, who had come from Avon township in Maine.

NORTH HERO township, settled in 1871 and organized September 27, 1873, "was named by Byron Knight, after his old home, the island of North Hero in Lake Champlain, Vermont. This island was named in honor of Ethan Allen, of Revolutionary fame." (History of this county, 1916, p. 360.)

NORTH REDWOOD, a railway village in Honner, two miles distant from Redwood Falls, was platted in the autumn of 1884, and was incorporated August 14, 1903.

PAXTON township, organized September 13, 1879, was named in honor of James Wilson Paxton, a lawyer of Redwood Falls, who became owner of a large tract of land in this township, but removed to Tacoma, Wash. He was born in Pennsylvania, December 21, 1827, and died January 6, 1892. (The Paxton Family, 1903, p. 399).

REDWOOD FALLS, the county seat, first settled by Col. Samuel McPhail, J. S. G. Honner, and others, in the spring and summer of 1864, was platted October, 1865, and was incorporated as a village March 9, 1876, and as a city April 1, 1891. The name is taken from the falls of the Redwood river, which descends about 140 feet by vertical falls and by rapids in its last three miles. The greater part of this descent takes place in a picturesque gorge close below the city area, within a distance of less than a half mile. The township of this name, having the city in its northeast corner, was organized January 22, 1880.

REVERE, a railway village in the east edge of North Hero, platted in May, 1886, and incorporated February 17, 1900, was named in honor of Paul Revere, a patriot in the American Revolution, renowned for his ride from Boston to Lexington, April 18-19, 1775, to arouse the minutemen, as told by Longfellow in "The Midnight Ride of Paul Revere." He was born in Boston, January 1, 1735, and died there May 10, 1818.

ROWENA, the railway village of New Avon, platted in March, 1902, bears the name of a ward of Cedric in Scott's "Ivanhoe." She is the rival of Rebecca the Jewess, and marries Ivanhoe.

SANBORN, a village and junction of the Chicago and Northwestern railway in Charleston, platted in October, 1881, and incorporated November 17, 1891, was named in honor of Sherburn Sanborn, who during many years was an officer of this railway company.

SEAFORTH, the railway village in Sheridan, platted in October, 1899, and incorporated in December, 1900, received its name from Loch Seaforth, an arm of the sea in the Hebrides, which partially divides Lewis from Harris.

SHERIDAN township, organized January 22, 1870, was named for Philip Henry Sheridan (b. 1831, d. 1888), a famous Union general in the civil war.

SHERMAN township, organized October 4, 1869, was named for William Tecumseh Sherman (b. 1820, d. 1891), a heroic general of the civil war, renowned for his march through Georgia, "from Atlanta to the sea," November 15 to December 21, 1864.

SPRINGDALE township, at first called Summit, having the highest land of this county, at its southwest corner, was first settled in June, 1867, and was organized November 21, 1873, being named for its numerous springs and brooks or creeks, flowing in dales and ravines.

SUNDOWN township, settled in 1871 and organized in 1873, has an almost unique name meaning the sunset. It is also the name of a village in Ulster county, New York.

SWEDE'S FOREST township, first settled in September, 1865, and organized September 21, 1872, was named in compliment to its many immigrant settlers from Sweden. It is mostly prairie, but has a continuous forest along the bluff fronting the Minnesota river valley.

THREE LAKES township, settled in 1868, organized April 4, 1876, derived this name from the former group of three lakes in its northern part, now drained.

UNDERWOOD township, settled in August, 1869, organized May 2, 1876, has a name that is borne also by a village in Otter Tail county, and by villages in Iowa and North Dakota.

VAIL township, first settled in 1869 and organized September 16, 1879, was named in compliment for Fred Vail Hotchkiss, who was chairman of the board of county commissioners.

VESTA township, settled in 1868, organized May 29, 1880, was named on the suggestion of F. V. Hotchkiss for the goddess Vesta of ancient Roman mythology, who guarded the home hearth fire and thence was a guardian of the city and the nation. Vesta railway village was platted in 1899, and was incorporated February 6, 1900.

WABASSO, a railway village and junction in Vail township platted in September 1899, was incorporated April 28, 1900. Its name is from Long-

REDWOOD COUNTY 453

fellow's "Song of Hiawatha," for the Ojibway word, wabos (pronounced wahbose), meaning a rabbit.

WALNUT GROVE, a railway village in the west edge of North Hero, platted in April, 1874, and incorporated March 3, 1879, was named for a grove of about 100 acres, including many black walnut trees, on Plum creek in the southeast corner of Springdale, from one to two miles southwest of this village. It is at the northern limit of the geographic range of this tree.

WANDA, the railway village of Willow Lake township, platted in September, 1899, and incorporated April 10, 1901, is named from "the Ojibway Indian word *wanenda,* and means 'to forget' or 'forgetfulness'" (Stennett, Place Names of the Chicago and Northwestern Railways, p. 135).

WATERBURY township, settled in the spring of 1872 and organized April 9, 1878, was named for the township and large village of Waterbury in Vermont.

WAYBURNE, a railway station in the north edge of Brookville, was platted in 1902.

WESTLINE township, settled in 1872 and organized October 14, 1878, was named for its situation on the west side of the county.

WILLOW LAKE township, first settled in 1871, organized September 27, 1873, was named for its lake adjoining Wanda village.

STREAMS AND LAKES.

Tributaries of the Minnesota river in this county include Big Spring creek, in Swede's Forest; Rice creek, in Delhi; the Redwood river, noticed in the first pages of this chapter; Crow creek, five miles farther east; and Wabasha creek, in Sherman. Beside Crow creek were the villages of Little Crow and Big Eagle, after their removal from the Mississippi, till the time of the Sioux outbreak in 1862; and the villages of two other Sioux chiefs, Wabasha and Wacouta, adjoined Wabasha creek. The Lower Sioux Agency, before noticed, was nearly midway between these creeks.

The Redwood river receives Ramsey creek from the south edge of Delhi, flowing from Ramsey lake (now drained), each named in honor of Governor Alexander Ramsey; and an unnamed southern tributary, from Granite Rock township, joins this river at Seaforth.

The Cottonwood river, crossing the southern part of this county, has been well noted in the chapter of Cottonwood county. It may be here added that a very large and lone cottonwood tree beside this stream, about seven miles northwest of Lamberton village, was reputed to be a chief reason for its name; but the Sioux had used the name, Waraju in their language, as spelled by Nicollet, which the white traders and explorers translated, for probably more than a century before the growth of that tree began.

Sleepy Eye creek, flowing from this county east to join the Cottonwood river in Brown county a few miles south of the city of Sleepy Eye, has been noticed under that county.

On its north side the Cottonwood river receives no tributary in Redwood county. On the south it receives three creeks from Gales township, unnamed on maps; Plum creek, from Springvale and North Hero, named for its wild plums; and farther east, flowing from Cottonwood county, Pelt creek, Dutch Charley's creek, to which Highwater creek is a tributary, and Dry creek, so named from its being often dried up during summer droughts.

The preceding pages have noticed the former Ramsey lake, in Delhi; the Three lakes, now drained, which were formerly in the township named for them; and Willow lake, also giving its name to a township.

Only a few other lakes remain to be listed, as Hackberry lake in Brookville, now drained, which was named for its hackberry trees; Snyder lake in section 33, Morgan, now dry; Rush lake, also now dry, two miles southeast of Willow lake; Nettiewynnt lake (formerly Hall lake), now drained, in Gales township, bearing the fanciful name of a large farm that adjoins it and extends more than two miles south, containing about 3,000 acres; Horseshoe lake, of curved shape, now drained, in Westline; Goose and Swan lakes, in the northwest part of Underwood; and Tiger lake, on the Minnesota bottomland in Honner, named probably for a puma or "mountain lion." This animal, also often called a panther, was described by Captain Jonathan Carver as "the Tyger of America."

RAMSEY STATE PARK.

Adjoining the city of Redwood Falls, a mainly wooded tract of about a hundred acres was acquired by the state of Minnesota in 1911 as a public park. It includes a half mile of the picturesque gorge of the Redwood river below its falls, with the tributary gorge of Ramsey creek, which in this park has a waterfall descending nearly fifty feet. The Redwood river flows one and a half miles in its gorge before it opens into the broad bottomland of the Minnesota valley, being quite unique in its grand and beautiful scenery. The state park is named in honor of Governor Alexander Ramsey, who was prominent in making treaties in 1851 with the Sioux, by which they ceded the great prairie region of southwestern Minnesota for white settlers and agricultural development. Soon after the establishment of the Lower Sioux Agency, about eight miles east of Redwood Falls, it was visited by Governor Ramsey, for whom then Ramsey creek and lake were named.

RENVILLE COUNTY

This county, established February 20, 1855, and organized March 1 and November 8, 1866, was named for Joseph Renville, a "bois brulé" (son of a French father and Indian mother), of whom Dr. E. D. Neill gave an appreciative sketch in the first volume of the Minnesota Historical Society Collections. Renville was born at or near the Kaposia village of the Sioux, on the Mississippi a few miles below St. Paul, about the year 1779. After a few years at school in Canada, he became a voyageur for an English company in the fur trade of the Northwest. In the war of 1812 he received the appointment and rank of a captain in the British army, and led a company of Sioux warriors against the United States frontier. He was employed by Long as the interpreter of his expedition to the Red river and Lake Winnipeg, in 1823; and Keating, the historian of the expedition, derived from him a large amount of information relating to the Sioux people. Afterward, having become an agent of the American Fur Company, Renville erected a trading house at Lac qui Parle, and resided there until his death, which was in March, 1846.

He was a friend of Rev. T. S. Williamson, who came as a missionary to the Sioux of the Minnesota valley in 1835. "Renville warmly welcomed him," wrote Dr. Neill, "and rendered invaluable assistance in the establishment of the missions. Upon the arrival of the missionaries at Lac qui Parle, he provided them with a temporary home. He acted as interpreter, he assisted in translating the Scriptures, and removed many of the prejudices of the Indians against the white man's religion."

TOWNSHIPS AND VILLAGES.

Information of names has been gathered in "History of the Minnesota Valley," 1882, having pages 798-848 for this county; "The History of Renville County," compiled by Franklyn Curtiss-Wedge, 1916, two volumes, 1376 pages; and from Charles N. Matson, judge of probate, and Hon. Darwin S. Hall, each of Olivia, the county seat, interviewed during a visit there in July, 1916.

BANDON township, first settled in April, 1869, and organized January 4, 1871, was named by its Irish settlers for a town in southern Ireland, on the River Bandon, about twenty miles southwest of Cork.

BEAVER FALLS township, organized April 2, 1867, and its village, platted July 25, 1866, and incorporated January 21, 1890, received their name from Beaver creek, which is a translation of the Sioux name, Chapah river, noted on Nicollet's map in 1843. This village was the first county seat, until a very long contest, begun in 1885, was finally decided in October, 1900, by removal of the county offices to Olivia.

BIRCH COOLEY township, organized April 2, 1867, and its former village, platted in June, 1866, but burned in 1871, were named for their small stream. "Coulée is a French word meaning the bed of the stream, even if dry, when deep and having inclined sides. The original name of the stream in the coulèe was La Croix creek, but the vicinity was known from the early days as Birch coulée, and this was finally corrupted to Birch Cooley, now the official name of the township." (History of this county, 1916, p. 1290.) This name was translated from Tampa creek of the Sioux, as it was mapped by Nicollet, referring to its many trees of the paper or canoe birch, which in this vicinity reaches the southwest limit of its geographic range.

BIRD ISLAND township, settled in the spring of 1872, was organized October 21, 1876; and its railway village of the same name, platted in July, 1878, was incorporated March 4, 1881. The name was derived from a grove of large trees, including many of the hackberry, in section 15, about a mile west of the village and on the south side of the railway, surrounded by sloughs, like an island, whereby it was protected from prairie fires. This grove, named Bird Island for its plentiful wild birds, was a favorite camping place of Indians and trappers, and it supplied timber for the early settlers.

BOON LAKE township, organized September 6, 1870, bears the name of its largest lake, probably given in honor of a pioneer settler.

BROOKFIELD township, settled in 1871 and organized April 7, 1874, has a name that is borne also by a city in Missouri and by villages and townships in twelve other states.

BUFFALO LAKE, the railway village of Preston Lake township, platted in 1881, is a half mile south of the picturesque little lake whence it received this name.

CAIRO township, settled in 1859 and after the Sioux war again settled in 1864, was organized April 7, 1868. It was at first called Mud Lake township, for its lake on Mud creek, but received its present name July 8, 1869. This name, derived from the capital of Egypt, is borne also by a city of Illinois and by villages and townships in ten other states.

CAMP township, organized April 2, 1867, needs further inquiry for the origin of its name.

CROOKS township, the latest organized in this county, December 9, 1884, was named in honor of H. S. Crooks, who settled here as a homestead farmer in 1870.

DANUBE is a railway village in Troy township, founded in 1899 and incorporated in 1901. This name, received from the large river in Europe, is borne also by a township and village in New York.

EMMET township, first settled in June, 1869, and organized September 21, 1870, was named in honor of Robert Emmet (b. 1778, d. 1803), the Irish patriot.

ERICSON township, settled in 1871 and organized January 27, 1874, was named in honor of Eric Ericson, a prominent pioneer of this county, who served as county auditor and during many years was the county superintendent of schools.

FAIRFAX, the railway village of Cairo, platted August 22, 1882, and incorporated January 18, 1888, was named by Eben Ryder, president of the Minneapolis and St. Louis railway company, for his native county in Virginia.

FLORA township, first settled in the spring of 1859 and again (after the Sioux war) in 1865, was organized April 2, 1867, receiving the name of "the first horse brought here after the massacre by Francis Shoemaker."

FRANKLIN is a railway village in Birch Cooley township, platted in 1882. Eighteen townships in so many counties of Pennsylvania, and also townships and villages or cities in twenty-nine other states, bear this name, with counties in twenty-four states, mostly in honor of Benjamin Franklin (b. 1706, d. 1790).

HAWK CREEK township, organized April 2, 1867, received the name of its creek, translated from its Sioux name, Chetambe, noted on Nicollet's map.

HECTOR township, settled in 1873 and organized June 30, 1874, was at first called Milford, but was renamed a month later for the township and village of Hector in Schuyler county, New York, whence many of its settlers had come. The railway village of this township, bearing the same name, was platted in September, 1878, and was incorporated February 23, 1881.

HENRYVILLE township, settled in May, 1866, and organized March 16, 1871, was named in honor of Peter Henry, one of its pioneer farmers.

KINGMAN township, settled in May, 1877, organized September 3, 1878, was named by S. T. Salter, the first township clerk, in honor of W. H. Kingman, his former fellow townsman in Winn, Maine, who removed to Wisconsin and purchased much land in this township, but did not settle here.

MARTINSBURG township, settled in 1873, organized September 3, 1878, was named for Martin Grummons, whose father, W. F. Grummons, of this township, was then a member of the board of county commissioners.

MELVILLE township, settled in 1872 and organized January 1, 1878, needs further search to learn the reason for its name.

MORTON, a railway village adjoining the Minnesota river in Birch Cooley township, platted in 1882 and incorporated in September, 1887, was named by officers of the Minneapolis and St. Louis railway company.

NORFOLK township, settled in the fall of 1868 and organized July 26, 1869, was at first called Houlton, but on January 4, 1871, was renamed Marschner, which in 1874 was changed to Norfolk. This name, derived from a county in England, is borne also by counties in Massachusetts and Virginia, and by townships and villages or cities in these states and in Connecticut, New York, and Nebraska.

OLIVIA, the county seat, a railway village in the west edge of Bird Island township, platted in September, 1878, and incorporated March 4, 1881, was named by Albert Bowman Rogers, an eminent civil engineer, who located this railway. "The first station agent to be placed at Ortonville, Minn., was a woman. Her name was Olive. She was a particular friend of Chief Engineer Rogers, and it was for her he named Olivia." (History of this county, p. 1359.) After much contention extending through fifteen years for removal of the county seat from Beaver Falls to Olivia, this was finally provided by a vote of the county October 25, 1900.

OSCEOLA township, settled in 1875 and organized September 30, 1879, was named by L. L. Tennis, then a county commissioner, for the village of Osceola in Wisconsin. Counties in Florida, Michigan, and Iowa, and townships and villages or cities in fifteen states of our Union, are named in commemoration of a patriot Seminole chief, Osceola, who was born in Georgia in 1804, and died at Fort Moultrie, S. C., January 30, 1838.

PALMYRA township, organized January 2, 1872, was named by settlers who came from Palmyra in southeastern Wisconsin. Sixteen other states also have villages and townships named from the ancient Palmyra, "city of palms," which was in an oasis of the Syrian desert.

PRESTON LAKE township, settled in 1866 and organized September 7, 1869, was named for its largest lake, probably commemorating a pioneer settler or a hunter and trapper.

RENVILLE, a railway village in Emmet township, platted in September, 1878, and incorporated February 19, 1881, was named in honor of Joseph Renville, like this county.

SACRED HEART township, organized April 6, 1869, was settled mostly by Lutherans, so that the adoption of a name apparently Roman Catholic in origin seems surprising. It was derived, however, from the name given by the Sioux or Dakota people to an early trader, Charles Patterson, who about 1783 established a trading post at the rapids of the Minnesota river in the present section 29, Flora, since called Patterson's rapids. He wore a bearskin hat, whence, "the bear being a sacred animal to the Indians, they called him the 'Sacred Hat' man, which gradually became Sacred Heart" (History of the Minnesota Valley, p. 817). The name so applied to the trader was afterward used by the Sioux for the site of his trading post, and thence it was given, in this accepted translation, to the adjacent township.

Another explanation for the origin of this name has been told by Louis G. Brisbois, a French pioneer of Hawk Creek township. "He declared that in the early days the mouth of the Sacred Heart creek formed in the shape of a heart, and that a French missionary priest, inspired by this, had given the name of Sacred Heart to a mission of French half-breeds and Indians that he had established here, and that the locality gradually took the name of this early mission, still retaining it long after the mission had passed into oblivion." (History of this county, p. 1332).

Sacred Heart railway village was platted in October, 1878, and was incorporated in 1883.

TROY township, settled in 1871-72, organized March 21, 1876, has the name of a very ancient city in Asia Minor, renowned as the scene of the Trojan war, the theme of the Iliad of Homer. It is also the name of a large city in New York, and of townships and villages or small cities in twenty-five other states.

VICKSBURG, a former village in section 19, Flora, platted in 1867, was superseded in 1878 by the railway village of Sacred Heart, to which its buildings were removed. Its name was from Vicksburg, Miss., which was besieged in the civil war and surrendered July 4, 1863.

WANG township, settled in 1867 and organized July 28, 1875, was named for a district or group of farms in Norway.

WELLINGTON township, settled in 1868 and organized June 4, 1873, commemorates the Duke of Wellington (b. 1769, d. 1852), victor over Napoleon at Waterloo in 1815. A city of Kansas and villages and townships in ten other states bear this name.

WINFIELD township, settled in 1872, organized December 27, 1878, was named in honor of General Winfield Scott (b. 1786, d. 1866), chief commander in the Mexican war. Winfield is the name also of a city in Kansas and of villages and townships in sixteen other states.

STREAMS AND LAKES.

The Minnesota river flows in strong rapids over a bed of glacial drift boulders adjoining section 29, Flora, named Patterson's rapids for a fur trader, as was noted under Sacred Heart township. The descent here is about five feet within a third of a mile.

On the southwest border of this county the Minnesota river receives Hawk creek and Sacred Heart creek in the townships bearing these names, the first being a translation from its Sioux name, Chetamba, which is now given to a creek flowing into it from Ericson and Wang; Middle creek, in Flora; Beaver creek, with West and East forks, translated from the Sioux, as noted for Beaver Falls township; Birch cooley or creek, also from the Sioux and before noticed for the township named from it; and Three Mile creek, in Camp, so named for its distance northwest from the former Fort Ridgely. Farther east, in Cairo, are Fort creek and Mud or Little Rock creek, flowing into Nicollet county and there tributary to the Minnesota river respectively near Fort Ridgely and near the site of a former trading post called Little Rock, adjoining an extensive rock outcrop in the Minnesota valley.

Buffalo creek flows eastward into McLeod county, from Brookfield and Preston Lake townships.

Besides Boon, Buffalo, and Preston lakes, whence two townships and a village are named, these townships have Hodgson, Phare, and Allie (or Alley) lakes, named for early settlers.

In section 23, Brookfield, Boot lake, named from its outline, has been drained; and a lake formerly in the central part of Wellington has also been drained.

Mud lake is on Mud or Little Rock creek, in Cairo.

Fox lake, formerly about four miles long, crossed by the county line at the north side of Kingman, and another lake on the north line of Ericson, have been drained. Thus too the former Pelican lake, adjoining the southeast side of Bird Island village, and Long or Lizard lake in Winfield, have disappeared.

Monuments of the Sioux War, 1862.

Through the work of the Minnesota Valley Historical Society, under the direction of its president, Hon. Charles D. Gilfillan, many localities in Renville and Redwood counties, of great historical interest in events of the Sioux outbreak and massacre in August, 1862, and of the war against these Sioux in 1862-63, were carefully identified and marked in 1895-1902 by granite monuments and tablets. A report of this work, including many illustrations and much history and biography, written by Return I. Holcombe, was published in 1902 (79 pages).

Two of these monuments are erected beside the railway close southeast of Morton village, one being in memory of the soldiers killed in the battle of Birch Cooley, September 2, 1862, and the other in memory of several Sioux who were friendly to the white people, doing all they could to rescue them from the massacre.

In Redwood county, this society erected numerous tablets in the vicinity of the Lower Sioux Agency, and also similarly marked the site of Camp Pope, about a mile northwest from the present city of Redwood Falls, named, like Pope county, in honor of General John Pope. There General Sibley and his troops were encamped from April 19 to June 16, 1863, in preparation for his expedition against the Sioux in the present area of North Dakota.

RICE COUNTY

Established March 5, 1853, this county was named in honor of Henry Mower Rice, one of the two first United States senators of Minnesota, 1858 to 1863. He was born in Waitsfield, Vt., November 29, 1816; came west, to Detroit, in 1835, and four years later to Fort Snelling; was during many years an agent of the Chouteau Fur Company; aided in the negotiation of several Indian treaties, by which lands were ceded for white immigration in Minnesota; and was the delegate from this territory in Congress, 1853 to 1857. Excepting when absent in Washington, he resided in St. Paul from 1849 onward, and was a most generous benefactor of this city. To Rice county he presented a valuable political and historical library. Mr. Rice was a charter member of the Minnesota Historical Society, and was its president for the years 1864 to 1866. He died in San Antonio, Texas, while spending the winter months there, January 15, 1894. His portrait and a sketch of his life and public services, written by Governor Marshall, are published in the M. H. S. Collections (vol. IX, 1901, pages 654-8).

In accordance with the state enactment, a statue of Senator Rice is one of the two selected to represent Minnesota in the Statuary Hall of the U. S. capitol in Washington, as unveiled February 8, 1916.

Townships and Villages.

Information of the origin and significance of names has been gathered from "History of Rice County," 1882, 603 pages; "History of Rice and Steele Counties," compiled by Franklyn Curtiss-Wedge, 1910, two volumes, in which pages 1-628, in vol. I, are the history of this county; and from Frank M. Kaisersatt, county auditor, and Martin M. Shields, judge of probate, interviewed at Faribault, the county seat, during a visit there in April, 1916.

All the townships of this county were organized May 11, 1858, on the date of admission of Minnesota as a state.

BRIDGEWATER township, first settled in 1853, has a name that is borne by a seaport city in southern England, and by townships and villages in Maine, New Hampshire, Vermont, Massachusetts, and ten other states.

CANNON CITY township, settled in October, 1854, was named like its village, platted in the fall of 1855, for the Cannon river, flowing across the west part of the township. Ambitiously called a city, this village had the honor of being the first place of meeting of the county commissioners, in 1855, but within that year Faribault was selected as the county seat. The village and its vicinity were the scene of a widely read story by Edward Eggleston, "The Mystery of Metropolisville," published in 1873.

DEAN was the name of the post office at Cannon City after 1880, in honor of J. W. Dean, an early merchant there, and this name is borne by the present hamlet on the site of that formerly large village; but the post office was discontinued in 1901, by free delivery from Faribault.

DENNISON is a village of the Chicago Great Western railway on the east line of Northfield, lying mostly in Goodhue county. It was named for the previous owner of its site, Morris P. Dennison, a farmer, who removed to the city of Northfield.

DUNDAS, a railway village in Bridgewater, platted in 1857 and chartered in 1879, bears the name of a large town in Ontario, and of villages in Ohio, Illinois, and Wisconsin, commemorating Henry Dundas (b. 1742, d. 1811), an eminent British statesman. This village was named by its founders, Edward T. and John M. Archibald, who came from Dundas in Ontario, built a flour mill here and made the best flour in the state. (M. H. S. Collections, vol. X, 1905, Part I, p. 41; XIV, 1912, p. 19.)

ERIN township, settled in the spring of 1855, received this ancient and now poetic name of Ireland at the time of its organization, in 1858, by vote of its people, many of whom were Irish immigrants.

FARIBAULT, the county seat, platted in February, 1855, organized as a township of small area May 11, 1858, and incorporated as a city February 29, 1872, was named in honor of Alexander Faribault, the eldest son of Jean Baptiste Faribault, who is commemorated by the county of this name. Alexander was born at Prairie du Chien, Wis., June 22, 1806, and died in this city which he had founded, November 28, 1882. He came to the Cannon river as a trader among the Indians in 1826, and during the next eight years he established trading posts on the sites of Waterville in LeSueur county and Morristown in this county, and also at a large Sioux village on the northwest shore of Cannon lake. In 1834-35 he persuaded these Sioux to remove their village to the site of Faribault. The next white settlers, Peter Bush and Luke Hulett, came in 1853.

FOREST township, first settled in 1854, was named probably for the originally wooded condition of nearly all its area. Townships and villages in ten other states, and counties in Pennsylvania and Wisconsin, bear this name.

LONSDALE is a railway village in Wheatland, founded in 1903, having the same name as villages in Rhode Island and Arkansas.

MILLERSBURG, a village in Forest township, was platted in 1857 by George W. Miller. Its post office was discontinued in 1901, and the village site is now mostly farming land.

MORRISTOWN, a village platted in the autumn of 1855, and its township, organized May 11, 1858, received this name in honor of Jonathan Morris, who was born in Pennsylvania, January 9, 1804, and died here November 27, 1856. After being for twenty-five years a minister of the denomination called Christians or Disciples, in Indiana and Ohio, he came to Minnesota in 1853 and settled here in 1855. Hard work and exposure in building a sawmill caused the illness in which he died.

RICE COUNTY 463

NERSTRAND, the railway village of Wheeling township, platted in 1855 and incorporated January 30, 1897, bears the name of an earlier post office, established in 1878, which was named by Osmund Osmundson for his former home in Norway.

NORTHFIELD, platted in October, 1855, incorporated as a village in 1871 and as a city February 26, 1875, and the adjoining township of this name, organized in 1858, commemorate John W. North, principal founder of the village, who was born in Onondaga county, N. Y., in February, 1815, and died in Oleandar, Cal., February 22, 1890. He was educated at Wesleyan University, Middletown, Conn.; was admitted to practice law in 1845; came to Minnesota in 1849, and settled here in 1855; was a member of the territorial legislature in 1851, and presided over the Republican wing of the convention in 1857 that framed the state constitution; was influential in founding the University of Minnesota, and was treasurer of its board of regents, 1851-60. In 1861 he removed to Nevada, being appointed by President Lincoln surveyor general of that territory. He presided over the convention that formed the state constitution of Nevada, in 1864, and was one of the judges of its supreme court. Later he organized the company that established the fruit-growing settlement of Riverside, near Los Angeles, Cal., and was United States judge for that state.

Another citizen of Northfield, who has been thought to be included in the honor of this name, was Ira Stratton Field, born in Orange, Mass., January 25, 1813, who came to Minnesota early in 1856, settling in Northfield as a blacksmith and farmer, and died here June 2, 1892. For twenty years before his coming here, he had lived in Jamaica, Vt., and had been elected twice to the Vermont legislature. He was an earnest advocate for temperance and for abolition of slavery. His removal to Northfield with his family very soon after the village was platted and received its name, and the tradition that the name was intended to honor each of these prominent early settlers, may be explained by acquaintance between North and Field before the latter came west. An obituary sketch of Field in the Northfield Independent, June 9, 1892, states that "early in 1856 . . . he was gladly welcomed by Mr. North and the other few here at that time."

RICHLAND township, settled in 1854, has a name borne by counties in Wisconsin and five other states, and by villages and townships in twenty states.

SHIELDSVILLE township, settled in 1855, was named in honor of General James Shields, who induced many Irish colonists to take homestead farms in this township and in Erin. He was born in Atmore, Tyrone county, Ireland, December 12, 1810; came to the United States in 1826; studied law, and in 1832 began practice in Kaskaskia, Ill.; was a member of the legislature in that state, 1836-39, state aduitor in 1840-43, and a judge in its supreme court, 1843-5; served in the Mexican war, attaining the brevet rank of major general; was United States senator from

Illinois, 1849-55; settled in Faribault, Minn., 1855, being attorney for the townsite company; was one of the senators elected to Congress when this state was organized, and served in 1858-9; removed to California in 1860; served in the civil war, 1861-3; resided on a farm in Carrollton, Mo., after 1866, devoting much time to lecturing, and was again a United States senator in 1879, from Missouri; died in Ottumwa, Iowa, June 1, 1879. At the unveiling of his statue in the Minnesota capitol, October 20, 1914, an address was given by Archbishop Ireland, which, with the portrait of Shields and a biographic paper by Captain Henry A. Castle, was published in the M. H. S. Collections (vol. XV, 1915, pages 711-740). His statue is also placed in the National Statuary Hall at Washington, as one of the two representing Illinois. The village of Shieldsville, in the northeast corner of this township, was platted June 12, 1856.

VESELI, a village in Wheatland, incorporated in 1889, was named for the city of Weseli in southern Bohemia, whence its early settlers came.

WALCOTT township, first settled in February, 1854, "was named in honor of Samuel Walcott, from Massachusetts, who was a very able, energetic and talented man, but after a time his mind became distraught, and he found an abiding place in an insane retreat in his native state" (History of this county, 1910, p. 147).

WARSAW township, settled in 1854 and organized in 1858, was at first called Sargent, but was renamed in 1864, then taking the name of its first post office, which had been established in 1856. This name was given "in honor of a town in New York, from whence a number of the early settlers had come" (History of this county, 1882, pp. 507, 513).

WEBSTER township, first settled in the spring of 1855, commemorates Ferris Webster, one of its most prominent pioneers. He was born in Franklin, N. Y., February 2, 1802; came to Minnesota in 1856, settling here as a farmer; died August 24, 1880.

WELLS township, settled in 1853, was named for James Wells, more commonly called "Bully Wells," a fur trader and farmer. He was born in New Jersey in 1804; served fifteen years in the U. S. army, having come to Minnesota with Colonel Leavenworth in 1819; was a trader at Little Rapids, near the site of Chaska, and in 1836 established a trading post on the site of Okaman in Waseca county; removed in 1837 to the head of Lake Pepin, being a trader there sixteen years; came to this township in 1853, and founded a trading post on section 34, beside Wells lake on the Cannon river, but gradually gave his attention mainly to farming; was murdered mysteriously in 1863, probably by treacherous Indians.

WHEATLAND township, settled in 1855-6, has a name that is borne also by townships and villages in New York, Pennsylvania, Indiana, Wisconsin, Iowa, and six other states.

WHEELING township, first settled in June, 1854, bears the name of a city in West Virginia and villages in Indiana, Illinois, and Missouri.

RICE COUNTY 465

LAKES AND STREAMS.

The name of the Cannon river and lake has been noticed in the first chapter, and it is also considered for Cannon Falls, Goodhue county.

Straight river, lying mainly in Steele county, is noted in its chapter.

Cannon river has its source in Shields lake, crossed by the north line of Shieldsville, named like that township for General James Shields. It flows through Rice lake, named for its wild rice, and Hunt lake is tributary to it, before passing westward into Le Sueur county. Returning into Rice county, from Waterville, it flows through the Lower or Morristown lake, Cannon lake, and Wells lake, the last named, like its township, for the fur trader, James Wells.

From the north and west, the Cannon river receives Devil creek, which brings the outflow of Cedar and Mud lakes; three creeks, unnamed on maps, flowing from Peterson, Florer, Dudley, French, and Roberds lakes; Wolf creek, deriving outflow from Mazaska, Fox, Circle, and Logue lakes; and Heath creek, flowing from Knowles lake and through Union lake.

In the preceding list, we may additionally note that Cedar lake has red cedars on its shores; Roberds lake was named for William Roberds, a native of North Carolina, who settled beside it and built a sawmill; Mazaska, meaning "white iron," is the Sioux word for silver; Circle lake encircles a large island, containing 97 acres; and in Union lake the two head streams of Heath creek are united.

Small tributaries of Cannon river from the south and east, nameless on maps, are outlets of Poole's lake and Sprague lake in Morristown; Mackenzie's creek flows through Warsaw to Cannon lake; and Prairie creek, flowing northeastward from Cannon City through Northfield, passes across an eastern prairie area, contrasted with the mainly wooded country west of the Cannon river.

Straight river in this county receives Mud creek from the west, and Kush and Falls creeks from the east.

Crystal lake, named for the clearness of its water, adjoins Dean village in Cannon City.

The northeast part of Morristown has three little lakes, namely, Pat's lake and Boneset and Mormon lakes. The second is named for its abundance of boneset, also called thoroughwort; and the third was used by a Mormon missionary as a place for baptism of converts.

Hatch lake, in sections 16 and 17, Wheatland, was named in honor of Zenas Y. Hatch, a pioneer homesteader, who was prominent in township affairs. Other lakes in Wheatland are Rezac lake, in section 20, named for Frank Rezac, a farmer near it, who served in the Union army; Cody lake, named in honor of Patrick Cody, an adjacent farmer; and Phelps lake, formerly called Cedar lake, extending across the township line into Erin. Their outflow goes west and north by Sand creek, tributary to the Minnesota river near Carver.

ROCK COUNTY

This county was established May 23, 1857, and was oganized by a legislative act March 5, 1870. Its name and also that of the Rock river refer to the prominent rock outcrop (called "The Rock" on Nicollet's map in 1843) of reddish gray quartzite, forming a plateau of gradual ascent from the west and north, but terminated precipitously on the east and south, which occupies an area of three or four square miles, situated about three miles north of Luverne, on the west side of the Rock river, above which it has a height of about 175 feet. In this generally prairie region, "the Mound," as this plateau is now called, commands an extensive prospect. The name is translated from the Sioux "Inyan Reakah or River of the Rock," as it was mapped by Nicollet.

By the original legislative act of 1857, the names of Rock and Pipestone counties were respectively transposed from their intended and appropriate areas, which error was corrected by the legislature in 1862.

Townships and Villages.

Information of names has been gathered from "History of Rock County," pages 5-8 in a Plat Book of this county, published in 1886; "An Illustrated History of the Counties of Rock and Pipestone," by Arthur P. Rose, 1911, having pages 31-239 on this county, with pages 423-655 for its biographical history; and from Joseph H. Adams, county register of deeds, Charles O. Hawes, and Mrs. Caroline M. Watson, each of Luverne, the county seat, interviewed during a visit there in July, 1916.

Ash Creek, a railway village in Clinton, platted in August, 1883, is near the mouth of the creek so named for its ash trees. The owner of this townsite, Colonel Alfred Grey, an English capitalist and an extensive landowner in this section of Minnesota and Iowa, "was fully honored in the names bestowed upon the streets running east and west, which were Colonel, Grey, and Alfred" (History of this county, 1911, p. 209).

Battle Plain township, organized July 16, 1877, was at first called Riverside, but was renamed March 19, 1878, for "the Indian battlefield located within its boundaries."

Beaver Creek township, organized September 16, 1872, received this name from its creek, on the suggestion of James Comar, a homesteader on section 14. Rose, in the History of the county (page 234), gives an interesting account of the former great abundance of the beaver, as follows: "Beaver and other fur-bearing animals were taken along the streams for many years after the county was settled. During the early seventies quite a number of beaver were trapped by the settlers along

ROCK COUNTY 467

Beaver creek in the township of the same name. A pioneer settler of the precinct tells me that at the mouths of the many deep holes, which are a feature of the stream, these cunning animals would cut down the willows and build formidable dams within a few days if unmolested. The local press in the fall of 1876 reported Rock river lined with implements of destruction for the taking of the valuable pelts. Beaver were taken along this stream up into the eighties." The railway village of Beaver Creek was platted in October, 1877, and was incorporated October 2, 1884.

BRUCE, a railway station in Martin township, platted in May, 1888, was named in honor of one of the chief officials of the Illinois Central railway company.

CLINTON township, organized February 18, 1871, was named by vote of its people, for the village of Clinton in Oneida county, New York, the seat of Hamilton College.

DENVER township, the latest organized in this county, July 24, 1878, was at first called Dover until January 6, 1880. It was renamed with this slight change in spelling, after the capital of Colorado, "Queen City of the Plains," because another township of Minnesota had been earlier named Dover.

HARDWICK, the railway village of Denver, platted in September, 1892, and incorporated October 10, 1898, was named in honor of J. L. Hardwick, the master builder of the Burlington railway company.

HILLS, a railway village and junction in Martin, platted in November, 1889, and incorporated November 15, 1904, was at first called Anderson, in honor of Goodman Anderson, a resident there, but was renamed March 1, 1890, for Frederick C. Hills, who then was president of the Sioux City and Northern railroad company.

JASPER, a railway village on the north line of Rose Dell and reaching into Pipestone county, platted April 19, 1888, and incorporated May 9, 1889, was named for its excellent quarries of "jasper," more correctly to be termed red quartzite.

KANARANZI township, organized January 15, 1873, bears the name of its creek, which is spelled Karanzi on Nicollet's map, a Sioux word, translated as meaning "where the Kansas were killed." The railway village of this name was platted in August, 1885.

KENNETH, a railway village in the northeast corner of Vienna, platted in July, 1900, was named for a son of Jay A. Kennicott, owner of "a section farm half a mile south of the new town."

LUVERNE, the county seat, first settled in 1867-68, platted as a village in 1870, was incorporated by a legislative act February 14, 1877, and by vote of its people November 12, 1878. Nearly twenty-six years later, on September 7, 1904, it was organized as a city. This name was adopted for the post office in the winter of 1868, being in honor of Eva Luverne Hawes, the eldest daughter of the first settler here, Philo Hawes. She was born at Cannon Falls in Goodhue county, November 14, 1857; accompanied her parents to the Rock river home in 1868; was married to P. F. Kelley, September 5, 1876; and died in Luverne, June 9, 1881. In the early years the name was spelled as two words, Lu Verne, "but the style was gradually replaced by the present form." The personal name was found in a novel or romance, then probably a new book or published in a magazine, which was read by Philo Hawes' cousin, Lucy Cotter, of Red Wing, at whose request the baby Luverne was so named.

As her father and mother are also honored by the name of the village and city, this notice may desirably add that he was born in Danby, N. Y., December 18, 1830, and died at Luverne, August 10, 1908. He came to Minnesota in 1853; served as second lieutenant in the Eleventh Minnesota regiment in the civil war; was a mail-carrier in 1867 between Blue Earth, Minn., and Yankton, Dakota territory; settled on the site of Luverne in March, 1868; was chairman of the board of county commissioners, 1871-73; was postmaster of Luverne, 1871-74 and 1888-93; and engaged in real estate and insurance business.

Luverne township, named from its earlier village, was organized February 16, 1871. Villages in Alabama and Iowa also have this name.

MAGNOLIA township, organized November 27, 1872, was named for the township and village of Magnolia in Rock county, Wisconsin, on suggestion of Philo Hawes, who had lived there. The railway village of this name, platted in October, 1891, was incorporated September 4, 1894. When first established as a station, in 1877, it was called Drake, for Hon. Elias F. Drake, of St. Paul, president of the Omaha railway company, who owned a large farm here; but May 2, 1886, the name was officially changed to that of the township.

MANLEY, a railway station in the south edge of Beaver Creek township, platted in October, 1889, was named in honor of W. P. Manley, cashier of the Security National Bank in Sioux City, Iowa, one of the leading stockholders of the Sioux City and Northern railroad company. The former village has dwindled, until it remains only as a wheat-buying station.

MARTIN township, organized March 12, 1873, was named for John Martin, its first settler, who located on section 13 in 1869 and built the first house in this township.

MOUND township, established April 21, 1877, contains the large plateau of rock, called "the Mound" by the white settlers, whence the Rock river and this county are named, as before noted. An earlier township, named Gregory, at first including all the north half of the county, had been organized May 2, 1873, at the home of Horace G. Gregory in section 35 of the present Mound township; but the six surveyed townships originally forming Gregory were later separately organized under other names. The quarries of the Mound, worked since 1875, have supplied to Luverne the stone used in building the court house, high school, and numerous other buildings.

ROCK COUNTY 469

ROSE DELL township, organized August 17, 1877, bears a name proposed by W. T. Vickerman, for "a rocky gorge, filled in the summer months with beautiful wild roses." This gorge is about 200 feet wide and 40 feet deep, on section 25, "a few rods west of Mr. Vickerman's pioneer home." (History of the county, 1911, p. 67.)

SPRINGWATER township, organized May 5, 1874, was then called Albion, but was renamed as now on June 15 in that year. "Mike Mead had immigrated to the township from Springwater, New York, and when he discovered a large spring on section 32 it doubtless suggested to him the appropriateness of Springwater for the township, which through his eloquence he persuaded the majority of the citizens to accept." (History of the county, p. 65.)

STEEN, a railway village in Clinton, platted in the summer of 1888, was named in honor of John P. Steen and his brother, Ole P. Steen, immigrants from Norway, who were respectively homesteaders of its site and an adjoining quarter section.

VIENNA township, organized February 10, 1874, was named by D. A. Hart, at whose home the first township meeting was held. This name, received from the large capital city of Austria-Hungary, is borne by villages and townships in Maine, New York, Ohio, Wisconsin, and thirteen other states of our Union.

RIVERS AND CREEKS.

This is one of the very few counties in Minnesota having no lakes. It lies south and west of the remarkable marginal moraines referable to the later part of the Ice Age, and therefore it has a relatively smooth drift sheet destitute of low hills or swells, with hollows and lakes, which are characteristic of the drift generally in this state.

The Rock river, Ash creek, Beaver creek, and Kanaranzi creek, have been already noticed.

Elk creek, flowing through Magnolia, testifies of former pasturage of elk there.

Champepadan creek in Vienna, flowing from Nobles county, has a Sioux name, translated "Thorny Wood" on Nicollet's map.

Mud creek flows south from Martin into Iowa, and Brush and Four Mile creeks flow southwestward into South Dakota.

Beaver creek receives Little Beaver and Springwater creeks as tributaries.

In Rose Dell township are Split Rock and Pipestone creeks, which have been noted in the chapter of Pipestone county.

ROSEAU COUNTY

This county was established December 31, 1894, and received an addition from Beltrami county, February 10, 1896. It is named from the Roseau lake and river, of which the former appears, with this name, on Verendrye's map (1737). The river is shown on Thompson's map (1814), with the name Reed river, translated from this French name, which is in turn a translation of the Ojibway name. Gilfillan wrote it, "Ga-shash-agunushkokawi-sibi or the-place-of-rushes-river, or briefly, Rush river." It is more accurately called Reed-grass river on Long's map (1823) and on Pope's map (1849). The very coarse grass, or reed, referred to is Phragmites communis, which is common or frequent in the shallow edges of lakes throughout the prairie region of Minnesota and Manitoba. During a canoe trip around all the shore of Red lake in September, 1885, this species was observed in great abundance at many places, growing 8 to 12 feet in height.

Townships and Villages.

Information of the origins and meanings of geographic names has been received from Syver G. Bertilrud, county auditor, interviewed at Roseau, the county seat, during a visit there in September, 1909; and from him a second time, also from D. H. Benson, dealer in real estate, and J. W. Durham, janitor of the High School, each of Roseau, interviewed there in September, 1916.

ALGOMA township bears a name of Indian derivation, "formed by Schoolcraft from *Algonquin* and *goma* meaning 'Algonquin waters.'" It designates a large district in Canada, bordering Lakes Huron and Superior.

AMERICA township was named by its settlers, mostly born in the more eastern states and thence called Americans, in distinction from the foreign immigrants who settled many townships of this county.

BADGER, a railway village in the east edge of Skagen, took its name from the Badger creek, flowing northwestward, tributary to the Roseau river.

BARNETT township was named in honor of Myron E. Barnett, one of its American homesteaders.

BARTO township was named for a Bohemian settler there.

BEAVER township was named for its former colonies of beavers, living on the head streams of the North fork of Roseau river.

BLOOMING VALLEY is the most northwestern township of the county, named for its prairie and woodland flowers in the slight depression of the Roseau valley.

CASPERSON post office, in Golden Valley township, was named for brothers who took homestead claims near it.

CEDAR BEND township has a bend of the West branch of War Road river, bordered by many trees of white cedar, also known as the American arbor vitae.

CLEAR RIVER township received this name in allusion to the clearness of the West branch of War Road river in its southwestern part, contrasted with the frequently dark color of streams in this region, stained by seepage from peaty ground.

DEER township had formerly many deer, being a favorite hunting ground.

DEWEY township commemorates Admiral George Dewey, hero in the Spanish-American war, 1898, who was born in Montpelier, Vt., December 26, 1837, and died in Washington, D. C., January 16, 1917. He was graduated at the U. S. Naval Academy, 1858; served in the civil war; was promoted to be a captain, 1884, commodore in 1896, and admiral in 1899. Soon after the outbreak of the war with Spain, he destroyed the Spanish fleet off Cavite in the Bay of Manila, May 1, 1898; and on August 13 his fleet aided the troops under General Merritt in the capture of Manila.

DIETER township was named in honor of a German settler, Martin Van Buren Dieter, who later removed to Montana.

DUXBY post office, in Pohlitz, was named for its first postmaster.

EDDY post office, in Stafford, was named in honor of Frank Marion Eddy, of Sauk Center. He was born in Pleasant Grove, Minn., April 1, 1856; taught school a few years, and was land examiner for the Northern Pacific railroad company; was clerk of the district court of Pope county, 1884-94; representative in Congress, 1895-1903; and later was editor of the Sauk Center Herald.

ELKWOOD township had elk formerly on its small prairie tracts, but most of its area is woodland.

ENSTROM township received its name in honor of Louis Enstrom, a homestead farmer and lawyer in Malung, who was a member of the board of county commissioners. He was born in Sweden in 1873, and settled here in 1889.

FALUN township bears the name of an important mining town in central Sweden, famous for its mines of copper, silver, and gold, whence it is sometimes called "the Treasury of Sweden."

Fox is a railway village in Ross, named for foxes, as the next village and creek westward are named for badgers.

GOLDEN VALLEY township, crossed by the South fork of Roseau river, was thus auspiciously named by vote of its settlers.

GREENBUSH, a railway village in Hereim, was named for the first evergreen trees seen near the "ridge road," as one comes eastward from the Red river valley. These are spruce trees, about two miles northeast of the village. An early trail, later a wagon road, and latest the railway, here began a curving course along a gravel beach ridge of the glacial Lake Agassiz, following this beach for about twenty miles, or nearly to the site of Roseau.

GRIMSTAD township was named for John Grimstad, a Norwegian homesteader there, who removed several years ago to North Dakota.

HAUG post office, in Soler, was named for Theodore E. Haug, a homestead farmer from Norway.

HEREIM township was named for another Norwegian farmer, Ole Hereim.

HOMOLKA post office, in the south edge of Poplar Grove township, was named for Anton Homolka, a Polish settler.

HUSS township bears the name of the great Bohemian religious reformer and martyr, John Huss (b. 1369, d. 1415). He followed Wyclif of England, "the Morning Star of the Reformation."

JADIS, the township in which Roseau is situated, was named in honor of Edward W. Jadis, agent for the Sprague Lumber Company of Winnipeg. He was born in England, and received a liberal education there; came from eastern Canada to Minnesota before 1875, and was a lumberman on Mud and Pine creeks, floating the logs down the Roseau and Red rivers to Winnipeg; removed to Hallock, was auditor of Kittson county, 1887-92, and died November 1, 1892.

JUNEBERRY post office, in T. 162, R. 44, is named for a small tree, variously called Juneberry, service berry, or shad bush, which is common or frequent throughout Minnesota.

LAONA township was at first called Roosevelt, like its railway village, but was renamed because another Minnesota township, in Beltrami county, had earlier received that name.

LEO post office, in Barto, was named in honor of Leo XIII (b. 1810, d. 1903), who was the Pope twenty-five years, from 1878 until his death.

LIND, the most southwestern township, is in honor of John Lind, the fourteenth governor of this state. He was born in Kanna, Sweden, March 25, 1854; came to the United States in 1867 with his parents, who settled in Goodhue county, Minn. He attended the University of Minnesota in 1875-6; was admitted to the bar in New Ulm in 1877, and practiced there, excepting terms of absence in official duties, until 1901; represented his district in Congress, 1887-93; was governor of Minnesota, 1899-1901; removed to Minneapolis in 1901, and was again a member of Congress, 1903-05; president of the Board of Regents of the University of Minnesota, 1908-13; was envoy of President Wilson in Mexico, 1913-14.

LONGWORTH, a railway station in Algoma, six miles north of Warroad, is named in honor of Nicholas Longworth, of Cincinnati, Ohio, where he was born November 5, 1869. He was graduated at Harvard University, 1891, and in its Law School, 1893; was married to Alice Lee Roosevelt, daughter of President Roosevelt, in 1906; was a member of Congress, 1903-13; and since 1916.

MALUNG township and village have the name of a town in western central Sweden.

MANDUS railway station, formerly called Lucan, was named for Mandus Erickson, an adjoining Swedish farmer.

MICKINOCK township commemorates a petty chief of the Ojibways, whose home was near Ross post office, west of Roseau lake. He was described as "one of the best Indians that ever lived, intelligent, sociable, and honest."

MOOSE township was named for its formerly frequent moose. This is one of our few English words received, with slight change, from the Algonquian languages.

MORANVILLE township received its name in compliment for Patrick W. Moran, its first settler, who came here in 1894.

NERESEN township was named in honor of Knut Neresen, one of its Norwegian homesteaders.

NORLAND township, meaning Northland, adjoins the international boundary.

OAKS township was named for Charles Oaks, an American homesteader near the center of this township, who was a stage-driver between Stephen and Roseau but removed several years ago to the Peace river valley in Alberta.

PALMVILLE township was named in compliment for Louis Palm, a Swedish homesteader there.

PENCER, a post office in Mickinock, was intended to honor John C. Spencer, a traveling salesman from St. Paul, but the proposed name was thus changed by the U. S. postal department. He took a homestead claim near Wannaska, about six miles distant to the southwest.

POHLITZ township was named for one of its pioneer homesteaders, an immigrant from Iceland.

POLONIA township was settled mostly by immigrants from Poland.

POPLAR GROVE township was named by vote of its people, this being chosen from the ten or more names proposed.

ROOSEVELT, a railway village in the southeast corner of Laona, adjoining the east boundary of the county, was named in honor of Theodore Roosevelt, the eminent author and statesman. He was born in New York City, October 27, 1858; served as a colonel in the Spanish-American war, 1898; was governor of New York, 1899-1900; president of the United States, 1901-09; was later an editor of "The Outlook;" died at his home, Oyster Bay, N. Y., January 6, 1919.

ROSEAU, the county seat, a village in Jadis, was named like this county, for the Roseau lake and river.

Ross, one of the earliest townships organized, needs further inquiry for the selection of its name, which is borne by a county in Ohio, and by villages in Ohio, Indiana, Iowa, and other states.

SALOL, a railway village in Enstrom, was named by Louis P. Dahlquist, formerly a druggist clerk, who was county superintendent of schools and later the county treasurer. Salol is a white crystalline powder, used as a remedy for rheumatism and neuralgia.

SANWICK, a former post office in Dewey, was named for Aven Sanwick, a Norwegian settler.

SKAGEN township is in honor of Albert O. Skagen, of Ross, who was chairman of the county commissioners. This is the name of a seaport and cape at the north extremity of Denmark.

SOLER township is named for the district of Solör in Norway.

SPRUCE township had formerly much spruce timber. Our larger species, called black spruce, attaining a height of 70 feet and diameter of one to two feet, is much used for paper-making; but the white spruce, of somewhat more northern range, is a smaller tree, here growing to the height of about 20 feet, with a diameter of six to eight inches. Both are common in northern Minnesota, extending westward to the Roseau river.

STAFFORD township was named for William Stafford, a settler who came from Michigan.

STOKES township was named for George Stokes, who lived in Badger village, adjoining the west line of this township.

STRATHCONA, a railway village in Deer township, commemorates Donald Alexander Smith, later Lord Strathcona, who was born in Forres, Scotland, August 6, 1820, and died in London, January 21, 1914. He came to Canada in 1838 in the service of the Hudson Bay Company; was stationed during thirteen years at trading posts on the Labrador coast, and later in the Canadian Northwest; was promoted to be resident governor for that company; was one of the principal financial promoters for construction of the transcontinental Canadian Pacific railway, and was a friend of James J. Hill, under whose leadership the Great Northern railway was built; was during many years a member of the Dominion House of Commons; after 1896 was High Commissioner for Canada in London, and in 1897 was raised to the peerage as Baron Strathcona and Mount Royal; was a very generous donor from his great wealth to many institutions of education and charity.

The compound title of his peerage referred to Glencoe, his summer home in the county of Argyle, Scotland, and to Mount Royal in Montreal, his former home in Canada. "Glencoe, the glen or valley of Conan, has its equivalent in Strathcona." (The Life of Lord Strathcona, by Beckles Willson, 1915, vol. II, p. 265.)

TORFIN, a former post office in the east edge of Palmville, was named in honor of Iver Torfin, a Norwegian pioneer, who was the first clerk of the court for this county, 1895-1905, now a farmer in that township.

WANNASKA, a hamlet in Grimstad, on a camping ground of the chief Mickinock, is said to bear an early Ojibway name of the Roseau river. Probably it referred rather to a deep place of the river, being derived from *wanashkobia*, defined by Baraga as "a reservoir or basin of water."

WARROAD, a township of small area on the southwest side of the Lake of the Woods, and its village on the Warroad river near its mouth, in-

ROSEAU COUNTY

corporated November 9, 1901, are named from this river, which was in a neutral tract between the warring Ojibways and Sioux. Carver's map from his travel to the Minnesota river in 1766-67, explains this term, as follows: "All Countries not Possessed by any one Nation, where War Parties are often passing, is called by them the Road of War."

Lakes and Streams.

The name of the Lake of the Woods is fully considered in the first chapter, treating of our large rivers and lakes; and Roseau lake and river are noticed at the beginning of this chapter.

An unnamed lake near the international boundary, in Algoma, and Mud lake, quite small, in sections 10 and 11, T. 160, R. 37, complete the meager list of lakes in this county, which lies within the area of the glacial Lake Agassiz, having therefore a smoothed surface, with few hollows for lakes or sloughs.

Mud and Pine creeks, flowing from the edge of Manitoba, join the Roseau river and lake, and were formerly routes of driving pine logs to Winnipeg.

In Laona is Willow creek, tributary to the Lake of the Woods; and iu Moranville the Warroad river is formed by union of its East and West branches, having also between them a small affluent called Bull Dog run.

Roseau river, formed by its North and South forks, which unite in Malung, receives also Sucker creek, Hay creek, flowing into the North fork, and Cow creek, these being tributaries above Roseau lake; and farther west it receives Badger creek, which runs in a drainage ditch along most of its course.

On the southwest, the head stream of the South branch of Two rivers flows past Greenbush, and thence it crosses Kittson county to the Red river.

ST. LOUIS COUNTY

This county, established by legislative acts of March 3, 1855, and March 1, 1856, is named from the St. Louis river, the largest entering Lake Superior, which flows through this county. The river was probably so named by Verendrye (born 1685, died 1749), who was a very active explorer, in the years 1731 and onward, of the vast country from Pigeon river and Rainy lake to the Saskatchewan and Missouri rivers, establishing trading posts and missions. The king of France, in 1749, shortly before the death of Verendrye, conferred on him the cross of St. Louis as a recognition of the importance of his discoveries, and thence the name of the St. Louis river appears to have come. On Franquelin's map (1688) and Buache's map (1754), it is called the Riviére du Fond du Lac; and the map by Vaugondy (1755) and Carver's map (1778) are the earliest to give the present name. St. Louis county has the distinction of being the largest county in this state, having an area of 6,611.75 square miles.

Saint Louis was born at Poissy, France, near Paris, April 25, 1215, and died near Tunis, Africa, August 25, 1270. From 1226 he was King Louis IX of France, his mother Blanche being regent during his minority. He undertook a crusade to the Holy Land in 1248, from which, after a terrible war, he returned to France in 1254. His second crusade was undertaken in 1267, for which he finally sailed from France on July 1, 1270; but in this expedition he died by an illness, less than two months later. He is commemorated by the name of the city of St. Louis, but Louisiana was named for Louis XIV, who was king of France from 1643 to 1715.

Townships, Villages, and Cities.

Information of names has been gathered from "History of the Upper Mississippi Valley," 1881, having pages 681-699 for this county; "History of Duluth, and of St. Louis County, to the Year 1870," by Hon. John R. Carey, in the M. H. S. Collections, vol. IX, 1901, pages 241-278; "History of Duluth and St. Louis County," edited by Dwight E. Woodbridge and John S. Pardee, 1910, two volumes, pages 1-412, 413-899; and from J. O. Walker, deputy county auditor, George H. Vivian, county treasurer, Edward K. Coe, county engineer of roads, J. W. Marvin, of the Land Department, Duluth, Missabe and Northern railway, Hon. Josiah D. Ensign, district judge, Hon. William E. Culkin, Jerome E. Cooley, Leonidas Merritt, and John G. Williams, each of Duluth, the county seat, and James Bardon, of Superior, Wis., and J. D. Lamont, of the Cole-McDonald Exploration Company, Virginia, all being interviewed during visits in Duluth, Superior, and Virginia, in August, 1916.

ST. LOUIS COUNTY 477

ADOLPH, a railway village in Herman, twelve miles west of Duluth, has a personal name derived from the old German language, meaning "noble wolf, that is, noble hero."

ALANGO township received its name, probably from Finland, by choice of its settlers.

ALBORN township was similarly named by its settlers, the Norwegians being probably more numerous than those of any other nationality. Its railway station was at first named Albert, for Albert S. Chase, brother of Kelsey D. Chase, who was president of the Duluth, Missabe and Northern railway company in 1890-93.

ALDEN LAKE is the name of a hamlet on the Cloquet river, beside a lake through which the river flows.

ALICE, a Great Northern railway station one mile south of Hibbing, was named for a daughter of a proprietor of its site.

ALLEN township was named in honor of William Prescott Allen, lumberman, who was born in Thomaston, Me., September 1, 1843, and died in Portland, Me., in August, 1908. He served in the First Iowa Cavalry, and later in the 65th U. S. Infantry, attaining the rank of captain; settled in Minnesota at the close of the war; after 1881 resided at Cloquet, and was general manager and vice-president of the C. N. Nelson Lumber Company; was a member of the state senate, 1891-5.

ALLEN station and ALLEN JUNCTION are railway stations about seven miles east of Aurora, named, like the preceding township, which is 12 to 18 miles distant northward, for the late William P. Allen, of Cloquet.

ANGORA township and railway village bear the name of a town in Asiatic Turkey, celebrated for its long-haired goats, whose wool is largely exported.

ARBUTUS is the most northwestern station of the Duluth, Winnipeg and Pacific railway in this county, named for the fragrant spring flower, Epigaea repens, often called "trailing arbutus," commonly known in New England as the Mayflower. This locality is near the western limit of its geographic range.

ARTHUR is a station of the Duluth and Iron Range railroad about three miles east of French River.

ASH LAKE is a station of the Duluth, Winnipeg and Pacific railway, adjoining a small lake of this name, about eight miles north of Cusson and Pelican lake.

ATHENS, a railway station six miles south of Tower, was named for the capital city of Greece.

AULT township bears the name of a village on the coast of France near the mouth of Somme river, also of a village in Colorado.

AURORA, founded in 1898 and incorporated in 1903, is a large mining village of the Duluth and Iron Range railway, about six miles east of Biwabik. This Latin name, meaning the morning, is borne by cities in Illinois, Indiana, Missouri, and Nebraska, a township of this state in Steele county, and villages and townships in thirteen other states.

BALKAN township was named for the Balkan mountains of Bulgaria.

BARTLETT is a station of the Duluth, Winnipeg and Pacific railway, three miles south of Cloquet river.

BASSETT township was named for William Bassett, a cruiser, who selected tracts valuable for their pine timber.

BEATTY township honors five brothers, pioneers there in lumbering and farming.

BIRCH, a station of the Duluth, Missabe and Northern railway, four miles north of Alborn, was named in honor of Charles J. Birch, of Proctor, trainmaster of this railway.

BIWABIK township and its large mining village, founded in 1892, on the Mesabi Iron Range, have an Ojibway name, meaning iron.

BREDA, a station of the Duluth and Iron Range railroad, four miles southeast of Fairbanks, was named for one of its Norwegian settlers.

BREITUNG township was named in honor of Edward Breitung, of Negaunee, Mich., who opened the Minnesota mine, the first worked on the Vermilion Iron Range. He was born in Schalkau, Germany, November 10, 1831; was educated at the College of Meiningen, Germany; was mayor of Negaunee, 1879-82; was a member of Congress in 1883-85.

BREVATOR is a station of the Great Northern railway, eleven miles northwest of Cloquet.

BRIMSON, a village of the Duluth and Iron Range railroad, near its crossing of the Cloquet river, was named in honor of W. H. Brimson, who was superintendent of this railroad in 1888-89.

BRITT is a station of the Duluth, Winnipeg and Pacific railway, eight miles north of Virginia.

BROOKLYN is a southeastern suburb of Hibbing, having a station on the Duluth, Missabe and Northern railway.

BROOKSTON is a village of the Great Northern railway in Culver township.

BUCHANAN, a townsite platted in October, 1856, "named after James Buchanan, then candidate for the presidency of the United States, . . . was located on the shore of Lake Superior southwestward from the mouth of Knife river. Like many other paper towns on the north shore, it never amounted to anything." (Carey, p. 272.) It had the U. S. land office from 1857 until May, 1859, when the office was removed to Portland, later a part of Duluth.

BUHL, a mining village of the Mesabi range, incorporated in 1901, "was named in honor of Frank H. Buhl, of Sharon, Pa., president of the Sharon Ore Company, which corporation opened the first mines in this locality in the spring of 1900." (History of the county, 1910, p. 727.)

BURNETT, a station of the Duluth, Missabe and Northern railway in Industrial township, was named for a roadmaster of this railway.

BUYCK township was named for one of its pioneers, Charles Buyck, who became treasurer of this township, but later removed to Canada.

ST. LOUIS COUNTY 479

CANOSIA township was named for a lake crossed by its west line, now more commonly called Pike lake. This widely used Algonquian word for the pike fish, spelled kinoje in Baraga's Ojibway Dictionary, is the same with Kenoza, the name of a lake in Haverhill, Mass., theme of a short poem by Whittier, who translated it "Lake of the pickerel." It is spelled Kenosha as a city and county of Wisconsin.

CANYON is a hamlet in the north edge of New Independence township.

CEDAR VALLEY township is named for its abundant growth of the arbor vitae, more frequently called "white cedar," bordering the Floodwood river.

CENTRAL LAKES is a village of the Duluth, Winnipeg and Pacific railway, about six miles south of the St. Louis river.

CHISHOLM, a very large mining village, which was incorporated July 23, 1901, was burned September 5, 1908, but was soon rebuilt, and has a population of about 10,000 people. Its great mine, first worked in 1889, and the village, are named in honor of Archibald Mark Chisholm, a principal explorer of the Mesabi range. He was born in Alexandria, Ontario, April 25, 1864; came to Minnesota, and in 1888-94 was paymaster of the Chandler and Ely mines on the Vermilion range; removed in 1894 to Hibbing, where he was a bank cashier, dealing also in real estate and mining properties; was discoverer and partner of several very productive Mesabi mines, including this one bearing his name; has large interests of copper mining in Arizona and New Mexico; removed in 1900 to Duluth.

CLIFTON was the first village site platted in this county, in October, 1855, "on the north shore of Lake Superior about nine or ten miles from Duluth. The plat of the townsite showed two long parallel piers or breakwaters extending for hundreds of feet into the lake, indicating a commodious harbor; but it was all on paper; the name was the only existence that Clifton ever had." (Carey, p. 253.) A railway station of this name is on the old village site.

CLINTON township was named in honor of Clinton Markell, who was one of the proprietors of Portland, removed from Superior to Duluth in 1869, was mayor of Duluth in 1871-2, and aided much in making this city a market for shipment of grain.

COLBY is a railway station three miles east of Aurora.

COLVIN township was named for Frank S. Colvin, a lumber dealer in Biwabik.

COOK, a village of the Duluth, Winnipeg and Pacific railway in Owens township, platted in 1903, was named in honor of Wirth H. Cook, a lumber dealer of Duluth, chief promoter of the construction of this railway, who became its president.

COSTIN, a mining townsite near the large village of Mountain Iron, was platted about 1912 by John Costin, Jr., of Virginia, who was born in Hancock, Michigan, and came here in 1893.

COTTON township was named in honor of Joseph Bell Cotton, a lawyer of Duluth. He was born in Albion, Ind., January 6, 1865; was graduated at the Michigan Agricultural and Mechanical College, Lansing, 1886; was admitted to the bar, and two years later settled in Duluth; was a representative in the legislature in 1893.

CULVER township and its railway village commemorate Joshua B. Culver, one of the founders of Duluth. He was born in Delaware county, N. Y., September 12, 1829; came to Minnesota in 1848, and engaged in the Indian trade on the upper Mississippi until 1855, when he removed to Superior, Wis.; but two years later he settled at Duluth as a proprietor of its site. He was in that year appointed the first postmaster, and was also the first clerk of the district court; was register of the U. S. land office in 1860, and till May, 1861. Soon after the civil war began, he removed to Michigan, helped to organize the Thirteenth Michigan regiment, went with it as adjutant, and succeeded to its command as colonel. He served with this regiment through the war, being in its later part brigade commander. In 1868 he returned to Duluth, and in 1869 was appointed the first county superintendent of schools; was elected the first mayor of Duluth, in 1870; and "continued as one of its most honored and leading citizens until his death on July 17th, 1883." (Carey, p. 257.)

CUSSON is a village of the Duluth, Winnipeg and Pacific railway near Pelican lake, named by officers of this railway, which here has repair shops.

DEWEY LAKE, a station of the Great Northern railway about ten miles north of Hibbing, bears the name of its adjacent lake, perhaps given in honor of Admiral George Dewey, who was previously noticed for Dewey township in Roseau county.

DINHAM LAKE, a station of the Duluth, Winnipeg and Pacific railway three miles north of White Face river, is beside a lake of this name.

DULUTH, the county seat, first settled in 1850-51, platted and named in 1856, was incorporated as a town May 19, 1857, as a city March 5, 1870, and received a new city charter March 2, 1887. "In 1868, Duluth, Portland, and Rice's Point, until then three separate organizations, were consolidated, and all assumed the name of Duluth." Later the city area was extended on the west to include Oneota and Fond du Lac, and eastward to Endion, Lakeside, and Lakewood.

The choice of the name of this city is narrated by Hon. John R. Carey, as follows: "In February, 1856, . . . Rev. Joseph G. Wilson, of Logansport, Ind., then sojourning at Superior as a home missionary, under the home mission board of the New School Presbyterian Church, was appealed to, to suggest a name for the future city. Mr. Wilson, who that winter lived with the writer and his family, informed me that he was promised two lots by the proprietors in the new town, in case he would suggest an appropriate name which they would accept. He asked for any old books in my possession, which might mention the name of some early missionary or noted explorer in the Lake Superior country, but I had then but a few books and not of the kind required. Mr. Wilson set about his task to earn the reward of the deed of the two lots in the great city. He visited the homes of citizens that he expected might be possessed of a library, and in his search found among some old books belonging to George E. Nettleton, an old English translation of the writings of the French Jesuits, relating to themselves and the early explorers and fur traders of the Northwest. In this he ran across the name of Du Luth, along with others of those early traders and missionaries who visited the head of the lake in the remote past. With other names, that of Du Luth was presented by Mr. Wilson to the proprietors at their meeting one evening in the home of George E. Nettleton, and after discussion of the relative merits of the several names submitted, the name Du Luth was selected." (M. H. S. Collections, vol. IX, p. 254.) On the first plat of Duluth, surveyed by Richard Relf and recorded May 26, 1856, the name appeared in its present form.

Daniel Greysolon Du Luth was born at St. Germain-en-Laye, a few miles west of Paris, in 1649; and died at his home in Montreal, February 25, 1710. His surname was otherwise variously spelled, as Du Lhut, Du Lhud, and Du Lud. It seems most suitable to adopt the spelling here first given, which, written as a single word, is borne in his honor by this great city, built on or near the site of his convocation of many Indian tribes in the early autumn of 1679.

With seven Frenchmen, Du Luth made the canoe journey to Lake Superior, in 1678, for the purpose of exploring the country farther west, occupied by the Sioux and Assiniboines, among whom he spent the next two years, endeavoring to bring them into alliance with the French for fur trading. In the summer of the second year, 1680, Du Luth met Hennepin and his two French companions and secured their liberation from captivity with the Sioux of Mille Lacs.

The sobriquet of Duluth, "the Zenith City of the Unsalted Seas," was originated by Dr. Thomas Foster (b. 1818, d. 1903), who established the first newspaper in Duluth in 1869. It was an expression in an enthusiastic speech by Foster at a celebration of July 4, 1868, by Duluth and Superior people, in a park on Minnesota Point. It has been sometimes erroneously attributed to a very famous speech in Congress, January 27, 1871, by James Proctor Knott (b. 1830, d. 1911), who was a member from Kentucky, ridiculing Duluth in connection with the bill for a land grant to the St. Croix and Superior railroad company.

"Twin Ports" is a name frequently used for these adjoining great cities of Duluth and Superior, as the term "Twin Cities" is applied to Minneapolis and St. Paul.

DULUTH township adjoins the east boundary of the county, including the former sites of Buchanan and Clifton.

DUNKA is a railway station for logging on the Dunka river about a mile south of Birch lake.

ELLSBURG township was named by its Swedish settlers for a place in Sweden.

ELLSMERE is a railway station in Ellsburg.

ELSDON is the railway station next north of Cusson.

ELY, a city on the Vermilion range, platted as a village in 1887, incorporated as a city March 3, 1891, was named in honor of Arthur Ely, of Cleveland, Ohio, one of the financial promoters of the construction of the Duluth and Iron Range railroad, which was opened to traffic here in July, 1888. He also was prominent in the development of the iron mines at Tower.

Another citizen distinguished in the history of the county, for whom this city has been thought to be named, was Rev. Edmund Franklin Ely, who was born in Wilbraham, Mass., August 3, 1809, and died in Santa Rosa, Cal., August 29, 1882. He came to Minnesota in 1832, as a missionary to the Ojibways, under appointment by the American Board for Foreign Missions, and located at Sandy lake. In 1834 his mission school was removed to Fond du Lac, where he labored until May, 1839, then removing to Pokegama. In 1854 he came as a homesteader to the site of Superior, Wis., and in the next year he settled at Oneota, now a part of Duluth. He platted the Oneota townsite, built a steam sawmill and docks, and was the postmaster six years, but removed in 1862 to St. Paul.

EMBARRASS township and its railway station received this name from the Embarrass river, referring to the driftwood formerly on some parts of this stream, which was a difficulty and hindrance to canoes.

ENDION, the name of a village site platted in 1856, now a part of Duluth, is an Ojibway word, meaning "my, your, or his home."

EVELETH, a mining city on the Mesabi range, founded in 1894, but mostly removed about one mile in 1900, was given this name "after a woodsman named Eveleth sent up here from Michigan about twenty years ago, in the interests of Robinson, Flinn and Fowler, to pick up pine lands." (History of the county, 1910, p. 705.)

FAIRBANKS, a village of the Duluth and Iron Range railway, formerly called Bassett Lake, eight miles south of the St. Louis river, was named in honor of Charles Warren Fairbanks, of Indiana. He was born in Union county, Ohio, May 11, 1852; was graduated at the Ohio Wesleyan University, 1872; was admitted to practice law, 1874, and settled in Indianapolis; was U. S. senator, 1897-1905; and vice-president of the United States, 1905-09; died at his home in Indianapolis, June 4, 1918.

FAYAL township and the great Fayal iron mine were named for the most western island in the central group of the Azores, which has an excellent harbor.

ST. LOUIS COUNTY 483

FERMOY is a station and junction of the Great Northern railway, four miles north of Kelsey.

FERN township received its name by vote of its people, who represent several nationalities.

FIELD township was named for a newspaper editor, one of the organizers of the township, who later removed to Canada.

FINE LAKES township was named by its Scandinavian people, for its numerous little lakes.

FLOODWOOD township and its railway village, at the mouth of Floodwood river, received their name from the stream, which formerly was obstructed by natural rafts of driftwood. It was called Embarras river by Nicollet's map in 1843, which designated the present river of that name as Second Embarras river. Both these streams, like the Zumbro river in southeastern Minnesota, derived their old French name, Embarras, from their driftwood hindering canoe travel.

FOND DU LAC, bearing a French name that signifies "Farther end of the lake," or, as we should commonly say, "Head of the lake," was a trading post of the Northwest Fur Company in 1792, being then on the south or Wisconsin shore of the St. Louis river where it comes to the still water level of Lake Superior, twelve miles distant in a straight line from the Minnesota Point. Later the post of this name occupied by the American Fur Company was on the opposite or Minnesota side of the river on a part of the village site which was platted in 1856, now included in the Duluth city area.

FORBES is a railway village in the north edge of McDavitt township.

FREDENBERG township was named in honor of Jacob Fredenberg, one of its German pioneer settlers.

FRENCH township was named for William A. French, an early homesteader, who became an officer of this township.

FRENCH RIVER is a village of the Duluth and Iron Range railroad, at its crossing of this river in Duluth township.

GHEEN, a village of the Duluth, Winnipeg and Pacific railway, six miles southeast of Pelican lake, was named in honor of Rear Admiral Edward Hickman Gheen, of the United States Navy, who was born in Delaware county, Pa., December 11, 1845. His wife is a daughter of the late Delos A. Monfort, of St. Paul.

GILBERT, a mining village of the Mesabi range, platted in August, 1907, and incorporated in May, 1908, was named in honor of E. A. Gilbert, a prominent business man of Duluth.

GLENDALE is a railway station about two miles south of Orr.

GNESEN township was named by Polish settlers for a city in the province of Posen, Prussia, reputed to be the oldest of Polish cities, where until 1320 the kings of Poland were crowned.

GRAND LAKE township and railway station received their name from a lake, which is large or grand in comparison with smaller neighboring lakes.

GREANEY, a hamlet ten miles west of Gheen, is named for Patrick Greaney, a merchant there.

GREAT SCOTT township was named by the board of county commissioners, this being a common expletive of one of the board members.

HALDEN township is named in honor of Odin Halden, of Duluth. He was born in Norway, May 6, 1862; came to the United States in 1881, and settled at Duluth in 1882; was a grocer, 1883-90; was deputy auditor of this county, 1890-94, and has since been the county auditor.

HALEY is a railway station five miles northwest of Cook.

HARRIS LAKE is a railway station about eight miles southwest of Fairbanks, adjoining a small lake of this name.

HERMAN township was named by German settlers, in honor of the early German hero, who was born in the year 17 B. C. and died in 21 A. D., renowned for his defeating the Roman troops in Germany.

HIBBING, a large mining city of the Mesabi range, yet continuing under a village government as incorporated August 15, 1893, was named in honor of Frank Hibbing, its founder. He was born in Germany in 1857; came to the United States with his parents when a boy; engaged in lumbering in Duluth, and also acquired large interests in the Mesabi iron mines; discovered the Hibbing ore beds in the autumn of 1892; died in Duluth, July 30, 1897.

HINSDALE is a railway station two miles north of Mesaba village.

HORNBY, a railway station two miles south of Fairbanks, and HORNBY JUNCTION, a station eight miles southwest of the preceding, are named for Henry Cook Hornby, of Cloquet. He was born in Gilbert, Iowa, April 29, 1866; came to Minnesota in 1884, and since 1888 has been in employment of the Cloquet Lumber Company, being assistant manager, 1897-1904, and afterward manager and president.

HUTTER, a railway station in the west part of Biwabik township, was named for H. A. Hutter, of Duluth, an ore dock agent.

IDINGTON is a railway station in Angora township.

INDEPENDENCE is the name of a hamlet and post office in New Independence township.

INDUSTRIAL township received this name by choice of its settlers. It is also the name of a village in West Virginia.

IRON is the post office name of IRON JUNCTION, a village of the Duluth, Missabe and Northern railway in Clinton township.

IRONTON is a western district of the city of Duluth, containing the great manufacturing plant of the United States Steel Corporation.

ISLAND is a Great Northern railway station, six miles northwest of Floodwood village, named for its having a tract of dry farming land, surrounded by a very extensive swamp region.

JONES is a railway station in the west part of Biwabik township, named in honor of John T. Jones, one of the discoverers of the iron mines of Biwabik and Virginia.

ST. LOUIS COUNTY 485

KEENAN is a railway station in the south part of Clinton, named for C. J. Keenan, a station agent.

KELLY LAKE, a village of the Great Northern railway, four miles southwest of Hibbing, is beside a little lake so named.

KELSEY township and its railway village were named in honor of Kelsey D. Chase, of Faribault. He was born in Little Valley, N. Y., December 1, 1841; came to Minnesota in 1860; served in the Second Minnesota regiment during the civil war; engaged in mercantile business, real estate, and railway and mining development, residing successively in Rochester, Owatonna, Duluth, Crookston, and since 1887 in Faribault; was president of the Duluth, Missabe and Northern Railway Co., 1890-3; president of the Chase State Bank in Faribault.

KINMOUNT is a station of the Duluth, Winnipeg and Pacific railway, five miles northwest of Ash Lake.

KINNEY, a mining village three miles northeast of Buhl, was named in honor of O. D. Kinney, a discoverer of the iron mines of Virginia and a founder of that city.

KITZVILLE is a mining village two miles southeast of Hibbing.

KUGLER township was named in honor of Fred Kugler, a former member of the board of county commissioners.

LAKESIDE is an eastern residential district in the city of Duluth.

LAKEWOOD township, beside Lake Superior, is an area of woodland.

LAVELL township is named in honor of a French homesteader, who has developed a good farm.

LEANDER is a railway station in the south edge of Owens.

LEIDING township was named for one of its families of Scandinavian settlers.

LESTER PARK, a residential district in the east part of Duluth, has a small public park, and a station so named on the Duluth and Iron Range railroad, at its crossing of Lester river.

LINDEN GROVE township is named for its timber of basswood, our American linden tree.

LUCKNOW is a railway station for freighting iron ore, about a mile east of Buhl. It is named after a city of India, where the British garrison made a heroic defence against the Sepoy mutineers in 1857.

LYNWOOD, formerly called Stuart, is a railway station twelve miles southwest of Hibbing.

McDAVITT township was named for J. A. McDavitt, of Duluth, who was a pioneer lumberman here.

McKINLEY, a mining village of the Mesabi range, first settled in 1890, and incorporated in the autumn of 1892, is named from the mine developed by "the McKinley brothers, John, William, and Duncan."

MANEY, a station of the Duluth, Missabe and Northern railway in Alborn township, was named for E. J. Maney, of Duluth, general superintendent of the Shenango Furnace Company.

MARKHAM post office, near a lake of this name, in Colvin township, was named for a pioneer.

MEADOWLANDS township has a tract of natural mowing and farming land, called meadows, adjoining the White Face river and giving the name of the railway village and the township; but much of its area consists of extensive swamps, called muskegs.

MERRITT, a mining townsite one mile east of Biwabik, was named in honor of Alfred and Leonidas Merritt, of Duluth, widely known for the discovery and development of the iron ore of the Mesabi range, and for promoting the construction of the Duluth, Missabe and Northern railroad, and of the great ore docks in Duluth. Leonidas Merritt, the older of these brothers, commonly called "Lon," was born in New York state in 1845; served in Brackett's Battalion, Minnesota Cavalry, in the civil war; was a representative in the legislature in 1893; and is shown as one of the statues at the base of that of Governor Johnson in front of the state capitol, being the prospector carrying a pack on his back.

MESABA township and mining railway village were named from the Mesabi iron range. The diverse spellings of this Ojibway name, and its significance as "the Giant's range," are considered on a later page of this chapter.

MIDWAY township is named from Midway creek, halfway between Fond du Lac and the head of the falls and rapids on the St. Louis river.

MIRBAT is a Great Northern railway station, five miles southeast of Floodwood village.

MISSABE MOUNTAIN township has a high portion of the Mesabi range, with the large mining cities of Virginia and Eveleth and the village of Gilbert.

MITCHELL, a mining railway station about two miles east of Hibbing, was named in honor of Pentecost Mitchell, vice-president of the Oliver Mining Company.

MORCOM township was named in honor of Elisha Morcom, of Tower, a Cornishman, one of the promoters of mining development on the Vermilion range, being the first superintendent of the Soudan mine, who was chairman of the board of county commissioners when the new Court House was built.

MORSE township, in which the mining city of Ely is situated, was named in honor of the late J. C. Morse, of Chicago, who was one of the members of the Minnesota Iron Company.

MOUNTAIN IRON, a mining village of the Mesabi range, in Nichols township, first settled in the spring of 1892, was incorporated in the fall of that year. Its name is from the Mountain Iron mine, the earliest to ship ore from this range, in August, 1892.

MUNGER, a railway village in Solway township, was named in honor of Roger S. Munger, of Duluth. He was born in North Madison, Conn., February 25, 1830; came to Minnesota in 1857, and was partner with his brother, Russell C. Munger, in the pioneer music store of St. Paul; removed to Duluth in 1869, engaging in lumber business; in 1872 organized a firm, Munger, Markell and Co., who built grain elevators and made this city a great grain buying and shipping market; and was president of the Imperial Mill Company, organized in 1888, and of the Duluth Iron and Steel Company, organized in 1898.

MURRAY, a railway station five miles east of Tower, was named for a foreman or superintendent of the Tower Lumber Company.

NAGONAB, a station of the Great Northern railway in the south edge of this county, bears the name of an Ojibway, the head chief of Fond du Lac, who was born in 1795 and died at Fond du Lac in June, 1894. He was influential in persuading the Ojibways and Sioux to sign a treaty at Prairie du Chien in 1825, acknowledging the sovereignty of the United States; was a signer of a treaty at La Pointe, Wis., in 1854, in which the Ojibways ceded large tracts of land in northern Minnesota and Wisconsin, including the Vermilion and Mesabi iron ranges; and in 1889, at the age of ninety-four years, he with his son signed further agreements for cessions of lands and rights in the Fond du Lac and Red Lake reservations. His name, spelled in five or six ways, with accent on the second syllable, is translated as "Sitting ahead." (Aborigines of Minnesota, 1911, pages 719, 720, 722.)

NEW DULUTH is an extreme western part of Duluth, between Spirit Lake Park and Fond du Lac.

NEW INDEPENDENCE township was named by choice of its settlers, who came mostly from Norway when that country and Sweden had the same sovereign.

NICHOLS township was named in honor of James A. Nichols, a foreman or captain of ore prospectors, who discovered for the Merritt brothers the first large bed of iron ore found on the Mesabi range.

NORMAN is the post office name for the railway village of Skibo, five miles southeast of Allen Junction, chosen in honor of Peter Norman, foreman of a railway section.

NORMANNA township was named in compliment for immigrants from Norway.

NORTHLAND township, like the two foregoing, has many Norwegian settlers.

ONEOTA, a village on the northwest shore of St. Louis bay, platted in 1856 and annexed to Duluth in 1889, received its name from a book published by Schoolcraft in 1845, entitled "Oneota, or Characteristics of the Red Race of America." In the preface he wrote: "The term Oneota is the name of one of these aboriginal tribes (the Oneidas). It signifies, in the Mohawk dialect, the people who are sprung from a rock." His larger work, "History, Condition, and Prospects of the Indian Tribes" (six volumes, 1851-57), has an article of Part I (pages 176-180) on "An Aboriginal Palladium, as exhibited in the Oneida stone," with a large colored picture of it. This stone, named Oneota, visited by Schoolcraft in the summer of 1845, was found to be a boulder of syenite on the top of one of the highest hills in the country of the Oneida Indians in western New York.

ORR, a village at the east end of Pelican lake, is the nearest railway station for the Bois Fort Indian Reservation. William Orr is the postmaster and owner of a general store.

OWENS township was named in honor of three brothers, John L., Samuel H., and Thomas Owens. The first, who owns a farm near Cook village in this township, was formerly a lumberman and owner of a sawmill at Tower, was one of the first to ship ore from the Vermilion range, and now lives at Lakeside, an eastern suburb of Duluth. The second came to Tower in 1883, was engineer at its first sawmill, and since 1902 has been yardmaster in Eveleth for the Fayal mine. Thomas Owens, of Two Harbors, has been superintendent of the Duluth and Iron Range railroad since 1892.

PALMER'S is a post office and hamlet on the Duluth and Iron Range railroad about two miles east of French River.

PALO, a Spanish word meaning a tree, is the name of a lumber-manufacturing hamlet about ten miles south of Biwabik.

PAUPORI, a Great Northern railway village eight miles west of Brookston, is diversely spelled, Poupore (in three syllables) being the post office name. The postmaster, Phil Poupore, and the railway agent, W. S. Poupore, are sons of an Ojibway farmer who is yet living here.

PAYNE, a station of the Duluth, Missabe and Northern railway nine miles north of Alborn, was named in honor of a former secretary of this railway company.

PEARY is a station of the Duluth, Winnipeg and Pacific railway, at its crossing of the St. Louis river, named in honor of Robert Edwin Peary, the noted Arctic explorer. He was born at Cresson, Pa., May 6, 1856; traversed the inland ice of northwestern Greenland in 1891; traced the northern limit of the Greenland archipelago in 1900; and on April 6, 1909, he reached the north pole.

PEYLA is a hamlet in Vermilion Lake township, of which Peter Peyla is the postmaster.

PIKE township has Pike river flowing through it, tributary to Vermilion lake. This stream, called Vermilion river on the map of Owen's geological survey, published in 1852, is named from the fish.

PORTLAND, a townsite platted in 1855 on the north shore of Lake Superior, adjoined the original plat of Duluth, to which it was annexed in 1868.

PRAIRIE LAKE township is named from the Prairie lake and river, flowing through it, tributary to Sandy lake in Aitkin county. Mushkodensiwi, meaning little prairie, is the Ojibway name, noted by Gilfillan, for the lake and river.

PROCTOR KNOTT, a village adjoining the west side of Duluth, usually now called simply Proctor, commemorates the late James Proctor

ST. LOUIS COUNTY 489

Knott, of Kentucky, before mentioned for his humorous speech in Congress in 1871, ridiculing Duluth, but really aiding the young city much by its advertisement. He was born near Lebanon, Ky., August 29, 1830; was a representative in Congress, 1867-71 and 1877-83; governor of Kentucky, 1883-87; professor of civics and law in Center College, Danville, Ky., 1892-1901; and died at Lebanon, Ky., June 18, 1911.

RENO is a railway station three miles north of Fairbanks.

RICE LAKE township is named for the Wild Rice lake, crossed by its west line. The Ojibway name of this lake means, according to Gilfillan, "the place of wild rice amidst the hills."

RICE'S POINT, a district of Duluth, between the harbor and St. Louis bay, was named in honor of its pioneer landowner, Orrin Wheeler Rice, of Superior, Wis., who was a younger brother of Henry M. and Edmund Rice, very prominent citizens of St. Paul. He was born in Waitsfield, Vt., October 6, 1829, and died in Minneapolis, March 9, 1859. He filed a land claim for this point in 1854, and was a member of the first town council of Duluth in 1857. The first election in St. Louis county was held at his house on this point in September, 1855.

RIVERS is a railway station about two miles south of Tower, named from its location near the crossing of the West Two rivers. The eastern one of these rivers flows through Tower.

ROBINSON, a railway station nine miles west of Ely, was named for a lumberman whose logging camp was beside a small lake there.

ROLLINS, a railway station two miles southeast of Brimson, was likewise named for an adjacent lumberman.

RUSH LAKE, a railway station for logging on the Duluth and Northeastern railroad, is beside a lake of this name.

SAGINAW is a railway village eight miles east of Brookston, named probably by lumbermen from the city and county of Saginaw in Michigan.

ST. LOUIS township is named like this county, for the St. Louis river, crossed in its south part by the Duluth and Iron Range railroad.

SANDY township is named for Sandy lake and an adjacent Sand lake, each tributary by Pike river to Vermilion lake.

SAXE, a railway station about nine miles southeast of Buhl, was named for Solomon Saxe, of Eveleth, who was a landowner there.

SHAW is a station of the Duluth, Winnipeg and Pacific railway, four miles south of White Face river.

SHENANGO, a mining railway station two miles southeast of Chisholm, was named for the Shenango Furnace Company of Pennsylvania.

SKIBO, a station of the Duluth and Iron Range railway at its crossing of the St. Louis river, was named for Skibo Castle, the summer home of Andrew Carnegie, on the north shore of Dornoch Firth in the northern part of Scotland.

SOLWAY township was named for the Solway Firth, an arm or inlet of the Irish sea, between Scotland and England.

SOUDAN, a large mining village near Tower, and its mine, which was the first in this state to ship iron ore, in 1884, were so named by D. H. Bacon, general manager of this mine, because the severe winter cold here is very strongly contrasted with the tropical heat of the Soudan (or Sudan) region in Africa.

SPARTA is a mining village in Missabe Mountain township, incorporated in 1897, named from ancient Greece, like Athens station near Tower, but probably by pioneers coming from Sparta in Wisconsin.

SPAULDING is a townsite at the east end of Long lake, between Ely and Winton.

STEVENSON is a mining village of the Mesabi range in the west edge of this county.

STROUD is a logging station of the Duluth and Northeastern railway, six miles southwest of Rush Lake.

STUNTZ township, which includes Hibbing, was named in honor of George R. Stuntz, of Duluth. He was born in Albion, Erie county, Pa., December 11, 1820; came to the site of Duluth in 1852; was a land surveyor and civil engineer, and made extensive surveys in northern Wisconsin and northeastern Minnesota, including the iron ore lands along the Mesabi range; died in Duluth, October 23, 1902.

STURGEON township was named from the Sturgeon river, which flows through it northwestward, being tributary to the Little fork of Rainy river. The rock sturgeon of northern Minnesota attains a length of six feet and weight of a hundred pounds. "On portions of the Lake of the Woods sturgeon fishing is the chief occupation, thousands of large fish being taken annually." (Cox, Fishes of Minnesota, 1897, p. 13.)

TABER is a railway station six miles southeast of Angora.

TAFT is a station of the Duluth, Winnipeg and Pacific railway three miles north of the Cloquet river, named in honor of William H. Taft. He was born in Cincinnati, Ohio, September 15, 1857; was graduated at Yale University, 1878; was United States circuit judge, 1892-1900; was president of the U. S. Philippine Commission, 1900-01; first civil governor of the Philippine Islands, 1901-04; U. S. secretary of war, 1904-08; and president of the United States, 1909-13.

TOIVOLA township bears a Finnish name, equivalent to "Hopeville" or "Land of Promise," given by Thomas Arkkola, a pioneer immigrant from Finland. Toijala is a village in the southwest part of that country.

TOWER, first occupied by white men and platted as a townsite in 1882, reached by the Duluth and Iron Range railroad in 1884, and incorporated as a city March 13, 1889, was named in honor of Charlemagne Tower, Sr., of Philadelphia, Pa. He was born in Paris, N. Y., April 18, 1809; was graduated at Harvard College, 1830; studied law, and was admitted to the bar in 1836; practiced law in Pennsylvania twenty-five years; was captain in the Sixth Pennsylvania regiment in the civil war; was connected with the Minnesota Iron Company and the Duluth and

Iron Range railroad company, and was thus instrumental in opening in 1884 the great iron industry of Minnesota.

The name also honors Charlemagne Tower, Jr., who was born in Philadelphia, April 17, 1848; was graduated at Harvard University, 1872; was admitted to the bar in 1878; resided in Duluth, 1882-87, where he was president of the Duluth and Iron Range railroad company, and managing director of the Minnesota Iron Company; was U. S. ambassador to Austria-Hungary, 1897-9, to Russia, 1899-1902, and to Germany, 1902-08; resides in Philadelphia.

TWIG is a railway village in Grand Lake township.

VAN BUREN township was named in honor of Martin Van Buren, who was born at Kinderhook, N. Y., December 5, 1782, and died there, July 24, 1862. He was United States senator from New York, 1821-28; governor of New York, 1828-9; secretary of state under President Jackson, 1829-31; vice-president of the United States, 1833-7; and president, 1837-41.

VERMILION GROVE is a proposed village site for summer homes, on the south side of Frazer bay (formerly called Birch bay) of Vermilion lake.

VERMILION LAKE township, adjoining the most southern arm of this lake, thence derived its name, a translation of Onamuni, the Ojibway name of the lake. George H. Vivian, the county treasurer, who formerly lived in Tower, states that the aboriginal name refers to the red and golden reflection from the sky to the smooth lake surface near sunset, being thus of the same significance as the Ojibway name of Red lake.

VIRGINIA, a mining and lumber manufacturing city, the largest of the Mesabi range and after Duluth the largest in this county, having a court house as the seat of the judicial district for the north part of the county, was founded in September, 1892, and was incorporated as a city in 1894, after having been almost entirely destroyed by a fire in June, 1893. It was again almost wholly burned in the summer of 1900, from a forest fire. This name was proposed by a lumberman from the state of Virginia, living in Duluth, who was a cruiser for selecting valuable tracts of pine timber. The site of the city was originally heavily wooded.

WAASA township was named for the province of Vasa (or Waasa) in western Finland.

WAGONER is the post office in Alango township.

WAHLSTEN, a railway station in Kugler township, was named for August Wahlsten, a Swedish lumberman and homesteader in this township.

WALLACE, a railway station four miles north of Kelsey, was named for a lumberman there, who later lived in Duluth.

WHITE township was named in honor of a mining captain on the Mesabi range, in the employ of the Kimberly Mining Company.

WILLOW VALLEY township, recently organized, needs no explanation of its name.

WILPEN is a railway village five miles east of Hibbing.

WINTON, a large mining village in the east edge of this county four miles northeast of Ely, was named in honor of William C. Winton, a member of the Knox Lumber Company of Duluth, which did much logging around Ely and Winton. He was superintendent for building the first sawmill at Winton in 1898.

WOLF is a railway station and junction, two miles north of Iron Junction.

WUORI township has a Finnish name, meaning a mountain. The southwest part of this township has an exceptionally high and massive hill of the Mesabi range, culminating in section 28, with its top about 2,150 feet above the sea, being the highest land in this county, 700 feet above the mining city of Virginia, three miles distant to the southwest.

WYMAN, a railway junction three miles south of Mesaba village, was named in honor of an old sea captain, George Wyman, who lived at Two Harbors.

ZIM, a railway village in McDavitt township, is near the former site of the logging camp of a lumberman named Zimmerman.

Many other townships in this county yet await agricultural settlements and organization, requiring citation therefore by the township number and range number.

LAKES AND STREAMS.

The foregoing pages contain notes of the St. Louis river, Alden lake, Ash lake, Canosia or Pike lake, the Central lakes, Dewey and Dinham lakes, Dunka river, Embarrass river, the Fine lakes, Floodwood river, French river, Grand lake, Harris and Kelly lakes, Midway creek, Pike river, Prairie lake and river, Wild Rice lake, the West and East Two rivers of Tower, Robinson lake, Rush lake, Sandy and Sand lakes, Sturgeon river, and the large Vermilion lake.

VICINITY OF DULUTH

Knife river, having its sources in Duluth township, is the most eastern flowing into Lake Superior from this county. Its name is noted by Gilfillan as translated from Mokomani zibi of the Ojibways.

Sucker river, next westward, is likewise a translation from the Ojibway name, Namebini zibi.

French river, "R. des Français" of Owen's geological report in 1852, is called Angwassago zibi in the Ojibway language, meaning Floodwood river, the aboriginal name being thus of the same significance with two tributaries of the St. Louis river.

Talmadge river, the next considerable stream westward, was named for Josiah Talmadge, a north shore pioneer at Clifton in 1856.

Lester river, named by the white people in honor of a pioneer, is called Busabika zibi by the Ojibways, meaning "Rocky Canyon river, or the

ST. LOUIS COUNTY 493

river that comes through a worn hollow place in the rock," as translated by Gilfillan. Its aboriginal name comes from its picturesque gorge in Lester Park. Amity creek is tributary to it from the west.

Farther west, within the city limits of Duluth, are Tischer's creek, Chester creek, Miller, Keene, and Kingsbury creeks, Knowlton's creek, Stewart creek, Sargent's creek, and Mission creek. The last, flowing into St. Louis river at Fond du Lac, was named from the early mission there for the Ojibways.

Miller creek was named for Robert P. Miller, who enlisted from Duluth in the Fourth Minnesota regiment in December, 1861, and was promoted as first lieutenant in the 50th U. S. Colored Infantry in 1863.

Kingsbury creek was named in honor of William Wallace Kingsbury, who was born in Towanda, Pa., June 4, 1828, and died April 17, 1892. He settled in Endion (later a part of Duluth) ; was a member of the Territorial legislature, 1855-6, and of the constitutional convention, 1857; was delegate to Congress from Minnesota Territory, 1857-8; later returned east.

On the Lake Superior shore are Knife island, very small, and Granite point, each about a quarter of a mile south from the mouth of Knife river; Stony point and Sucker bay, adjoining the mouth of Sucker river; Crystal bay, a mile northeast from Lester river; and Minnesota point, a very prolonged and somewhat broad sand bar beach reaching from the north shore near the center of Duluth about seven miles southeastward, which, with the similar but shorter Wisconsin point, incloses the Duluth and Superior harbor, also known as the Bay of Superior. Through the base of this long point a ship canal was cut in 1871, which, with its lighthouse and the long piers built out into the lake, gives a protected and deep entrance to the harbor.

West of the main harbor are two shorter and wider sandbar points, namely, Rice's point, before noted on the Minnesota side, and Connor's point of Superior, Wisconsin, which divide the harbor or Bay of Superior, from St. Louis bay. Proceeding thence up the St. Louis river, one passes Grassy point, the large Clough island, Spirit lake and its Spirit island, Mud lake, and Bear island, before coming to Fond du Lac, Nekuk island, and the foot of the long series of rapids and falls of the St. Louis river, which were passed in the former canoeing travel by a portage of seven miles to the head of these falls near Cloquet.

Along a distance of about six miles, from Thompson and Carlton nearly to Fond du Lac, the river flows in a rock-inclosed gorge, called the Dalles of the St. Louis, with frequent reaches of towering cliffs. It makes a descent of 400 feet, utilized by a canal and penstocks to supply water power for Duluth, and to generate for the Twin Ports electric power, light, and heat. In the chapter of Chisago county, which has the Dalles of the St. Croix river, the derivation and significance of this French name have been previously noted.

494 MINNESOTA GEOGRAPHIC NAMES

BAYS, POINTS, AND ISLANDS OF VERMILION LAKE.

For Vermilion Lake township the aboriginal origin and meaning of this name have been stated, being the same as for Red lake. In the Fifteenth Annual Report of the geological survey of Minnesota, for 1886, Prof. N. H. Winchell presented a large map of Vermilion lake, with the names of its many bays, points, and islands, noting for most of these features both the Ojibway name and its translation. It will be sufficient here to note the translated names, and to designate other names that are applied only by the white people, either on that map or in later maps and atlases.

Beginning at the east end of the lake and taking the names in their order from east to west, we have Armstrong river flowing into Bear bay and Armstrong bay, the river and bay being named for a white pioneer, who prospected for the Minnesota Iron Company; the large Bear island, later named Ely island in honor of Arthur Ely, like the city of this name; the very little Ant island and Kid island, respectively at the northwest side and west end of Ely island; Stuntz island, named, like a township, in honor of George R. Stuntz, at the entrance of Pelican Rock bay, which has Stuntz bay as its indented southern part; Beef bay, and its western part called Jones bay, names from white men, with Basswood and Birch islands, the former called by the white men Whiskey island; Hoodoo point, projecting into the east part of Beef bay, and Sucker point, with the little Fish island, the last two names being from the Ojibways, at the north side of its entrance; Mission bay, also called Sucker bay, next west of Beef bay, and Beef lake, about two miles farther west, these being named from an Indian mission school, and from provisions used by mining and timber prospectors; Birch point, three miles long and narrow, and Black Duck point, the latter a wide peninsula of very irregular outline; Black Duck bay, and Tree island; and Birch bay, called in the latest atlas Frazer bay.

The foregoing names belong to the southern side of the eastern and relatively broad two-thirds of Vermilion lake. On the northern side of that part, in the same order from east to west, are the very little Newfoundland island, a white man's name; Cedar island, called Key island by white people in allusion to its outline; Brush bay and river; Spring and Rice lakes, the latter connected by a very narrow strait, a mile long, with the main lake; Pine island, six miles long, of very irregular form, having a Narrows north of its east end, a Little portage crossing an isthmus of this island, and Porcupine bay and island north of its western part; Bear Trap creek, a mile west of the Narrows; Trout river, Short portage, at its rapids, and the large Trout lake, with Pine island in its northern part; Silver island, at the northeast side of Birch or Frazer bay; and Menan island, the most eastern in a series of five islands on the north side of Birch bay.

Advancing northward and westward beyond Birch or Frazer bay, one passes Avis island, nearly two miles long, named for a daughter of Prof. N. H. Winchell; Birch river or narrows and Oak island, coming to Outlet bay and the rapids in the Vermilion river at the mouth of this lake; Bear narrows, leading into the West bay; Farm island, named from its cultivation by the Ojibways, at the center of this bay; Long bay, its northeast arm; Partridge bay on the north, connected by a long strait, called the Partridge river, with the West bay; and Big island, Little Farm island, Little Sucker river, and Sturgeon portage, at the west end of the lake.

The map of Long's expedition, in 1823, gives the name of Vermilion lake, as if it were on or very near the international boundary; Nicollet mapped it somewhat correctly; and the map of Owen's survey, published in 1852, shows both the lake and the inflowing Pike river, which it calls Vermilion river, a name now restricted to the outflowing stream.

On a later map of Vermilion lake by Prof. N. H. Winchell, in the Final Report of the geological survey (vol. IV, 1899), the same nomenclature is presented as in 1886, excepting omission of minor details and insertion of Wakemup's village on the southwest shore of West bay.

A very large drafted map of the county, used in the office of the county auditor, agrees with the latest atlas of the state, published in 1916, by designating the several broad parts of Vermilion lake, in order from east to west, as Armstrong bay, east of Ely island; Pike bay, close west of Tower, formerly called Beef bay, into which the Pike river flows; Big bay, the main broad body of the lake; Daisy bay, next northwest of the very long and narrow Birch point; Frazer bay, called Birch bay by the Ojibways; Niles bay, also known as Outlet bay; and Wakemup bay, formerly called West bay. Armstrong, as before noted, was a mining prospector; Frazer bay commemorates the late John Frazer, of Duluth, who was a timber explorer or cruiser; and Wakemup was the anglicized name of an Ojibway chief, Way-ko-mah-wub, a signer of the treaty or agreement in 1889, whose village was at the southwest side of that western bay.

Other changes from Winchell's map in 1886 are found in the atlas of 1916, including Lost lake, instead of Beef lake, two miles west of Mission bay; Hillsdale island, instead of Avis island; Norwegian bay, for the Long bay of the Ojibways, branching off northeast from Wakemup bay; and Black bay, for Partridge lake and river, the long northern arm of Wakemup bay. Here immigrants from Norway, and the dark, peat-stained water, have given the newer names last noted.

Railway advertising pamphlets claim 365 islands in Vermilion lake, counting many formed by rock ledges, very small in area; but nearly all these islands are unnamed.

THE INTERNATIONAL BOUNDARY.

Lakes and streams, flowing westward to Rainy lake, were traversed by the former canoe route on the boundary of St. Louis county in the following order from east to west as described by Sir Alexander Mackenzie in his "General History of the Fur Trade from Canada to the Northwest" (forming a part of his "Voyages from Montreal . . . in the Years 1789 and 1793").

Crooked lake, adjoining also the northwest corner of Lake county, is translated from its old French name, Croche, meaning crooked, bent, given by the early voyageurs and traders in allusion to its exceedingly irregular outlines. Next was the Portage de Rideau, meaning Curtain portage, 400 paces long, named "from the appearance of the water, falling over a rock of upwards of thirty feet." About three miles farther, after crossing the similarly very irregular Iron lake, the canoemen passed over the Flacon portage, meaning a flagon or decanter, hence translated as Bottle portage, "which is very difficult, is 400 paces long, and leads to the Lake of La Croix [the Cross], so named from its shape."

Thence the route on Lac la Croix, for nearly thirty miles, was first northward, next a long distance westward, and at last southward, to the Portage la Croix, 600 paces long. Beyond are the Loon lake and river, the latter also called Little Vermilion river, reaching about four miles to the Little Vermilion lake, narrow and riverlike, "which runs six or seven miles north-northwest, and by a narrow strait communicates with Lake Namaycan [also spelled Namekan or Nemeukan, an Ojibway word, meaning Sturgeon], which takes its name from a particular place at the foot of a fall, where the natives spear sturgeon."

Sand Point lake, as named on later maps, and the Lake Namekan, connected by a winding and riverlike strait, having a descent of only a few inches, were described by Mackenzie as a single lake, spelled by him Namaycan. Thence the descent to Rainy lake is nine feet, at the Chaudiere falls and portage, which is the French name given to the fall, meaning a great boiling kettle. The preferred canoe route, however, passed westward a few miles on Lake Namekan and thence crossed the Nouvelle or New portage as a more expeditious route to Rainy lake.

Early maps by Long, Nicollet, Owen, and Andreas, from 1823 to 1874, note Namekan or Sturgeon lake as reaching far west toward the Black bay, near the west end of Rainy lake; but on later maps the western half of this irregular and partly constricted body of water bears another Ojibway name, Kabetogama lake, meaning, as defined by Gilfillan, "the lake that lies parallel or double, namely with Rainy lake." Thompson, in 1826, mapped this western part as "Lac Travere," (probably meant for Travers), and the east part as "Lake Nemeukan." The French name, "Travere" or Travers, which may be translated as "abreast or alongside," referred doubtless to the aboriginal name, Kabetogama.

ST. LOUIS COUNTY   497

Within the half of Rainy lake that borders St. Louis county, it is nearly divided in two by the "Grande Detroit," as named on Thompson's boundary map in 1825-6, meaning the Great strait. The part of the lake east of this strait was mapped by Thompson with an aboriginal name "Wapesskartagar or Rainy lake," which is not found in Baraga's Ojibway Dictionary, needing therefore additional search to learn its origin and meaning. The larger part west of the strait is designated by his map as "Koocheche sakahagan or Rainy lake," for which a full consideration has been presented in the chapter of Koochiching county.

Returning to the northeast corner of this county, we need to note that it borders on the western part of Hunter's Island, a large tract of Canada, as before explained in the chapter for Lake county.

Adjoining the Flacon or Bottle portage, a very large island on the Canadian side of the southeast part of Lac la Croix is called Shortiss island by the latest atlas, but it was named Irving island on the map of St. Louis county in the Final Report of the Minnesota geological survey. Next northwestward this lake has Coleman island, about four miles long and irregularly branched, on the Minnesota side of the boundary.

For this large and very diversified lake, named La Croix by the French, "from it shape," the map by Thompson, in 1826, gives also an Ojibway name, Nequawkaun, spelled Nequowquon on recent maps, which seems to be the same word as Negwakwan, defined by Baraga as "a piece of wood put in the incision of a maple tree" (apparently the spout to collect sap for sugar-making). Throughout northern Minnesota the Ojibways, according to Clark, commonly made much maple sugar at the time of sap-running each spring, averaging north of Lake Superior from 100 to 500 pounds for each lodge. A different name used by the Ojibway people for this lake is given by Gilfillan, "Sheshibagumag sagaiigun, the lake where they go every which way to get through."

Loon lake is translated from its Ojibway name.

Gilfillan noted their name of the river north of Hunter's Island, "Gawasidjiwuni zibi, or River shining with foam of rapids." This stream, the outlet of Lake Saganaga, lies in Canada; and the international boundary, following the canoe route, crosses a water divide between Saganaga and the Otter Track or Cypress lake. Thereby Hunter's Island, an area of about 800 square miles, is set off to Canada, although it lies south of the continuous watercourse from North and Saganaga lakes to Rainy lake.

Again the boundary, if it followed the natural waterflow, instead of the established route of canoe travel, would lead from Lake la Croix by its outlet, Namekan river, more directly westward into Namekan lake, instead of taking the circuitous course, easier for canoes, through Loon, Little Vermilion, and Sand Point lakes, thus giving to Canada a tract of about 125 square miles south of the natural and uninterrupted watercourse. These and other features of our northern boundary are more fully noted in two papers by Dr. U. S. Grant and Prof. Alexander N. Winchell in the Minnesota Historical Society Collections (vol. VIII, 1898, pages 1-10 and 185-212, with a map at page 40).

Another very interesting historical paper, with references to early surveys by David Thompson and his admirable detailed maps, published in 1898, is also included in these Collections (vol. XV, 1915, pages 379-392), entitled "Northern Minnesota Boundary Surveys in 1822 to 1826, under the Treaty of Ghent," by Hon. William E. Culkin, of Duluth.

BAYS, POINTS, AND ISLANDS OF RAINY LAKE.

From a geological map of Rainy lake by Horace V. Winchell and Dr. U. S. Grant (Final Report, Geol. of Minnesota, vol. IV, 1899, p. 192), the following names are noted.

Near Kettle falls, between Namekan and Rainy lakes, the latter lake has Tierney point, Hale bay, and a large Oak Point island, these being on the Canadian side of the boundary.

Westward, along the Minnesota shore, are Lobstick point, Rabbit island, and Sand Narrows; a nameless coast for the next seven miles; then Big island, the Pine islands, Saginaw bay, and Point Observe; Brulé Narrows, which Thompson called "Grande Detroit," the newer French name Brulé being given in allusion to adjacent burned woodlands; Cranberry bay, and Dryweed island, which has its east extremity at the northwest corner of St. Louis county and reaches west three miles, beside the Itasca county shore.

In both Namekan and Kabetogama lakes this map shows many islands, from the smallest size to a mile or more in length; but only one, Big Pine island in Kabetogama, is named.

OTHER PARTS OF THIS COUNTY.

There remain many other lakes and streams, to be additionally catalogued, but considerable numbers of relatively small lakes and creeks are yet unnamed. The further names are arranged in the order of the townships from south to north, and of the ranges from east to west.

White Pine creek flows from Canosia or Pike lake, through Mud lake, to the St. Louis river about a mile above Nagonab.

Lake Antoinette is in section 28, Rice Lake township.

Caribou lake, named for reindeer formerly frequent here, adjoins the west side of Canosia township.

Close south of Grand lake is the smaller Second Grand lake, and the stream flowing thence west and north to the Cloquet river is named Grand Lake river.

Sunset lake is in section 15, Industrial.

Cloquet river received this French surname on Nicollet's map in 1843, but twenty years earlier it was called Rapid river on the map of Long's expedition.

ST. LOUIS COUNTY 499

Artichoke river, joining the St. Louis river in Culver, is named from its wild artichokes, a sunflower species having tuberous roots, much used as food by the Indians, which is common or frequent throughout this state.

East Savanna river, having its mouth near Floodwood village, was a part of the canoe route from Lake Superior and the St. Louis river to the West Savanna river, Sandy lake, and the upper Mississippi. The word Savanna, more frequently used in Georgia and Florida, is of American Indian origin, meaning a treeless area, and it is here applied to tracts of partly marshy grassland, over which the portage between the East and West Savanna rivers was made.

Gnesen township has Eagle lake, named for nesting eagles, and Dalka, Jacobs, and Schultz lakes, named for pioneer farmers.

Fredenberg has Cook's, Gibson, and Orchard's lakes, each named for a pioneer, and Beaver river, the outlet of Wild Rice lake.

In New Independence township are Artichoke or Benson lake and Schelin's lake; and in Alborn are Crooked lake and Olson and Schellin lakes.

T. 52, R. 19, has Spider lake, probably named for its small tributary creeks, reminding one of the legs of a spider.

White Face river, joining the St. Louis in the east edge of Van Buren, was first mapped and named by Owen in 1852, the name being translated from the Ojibways.

T. 53, R. 13, has Alden, Barr's and Lienau lakes, named for lumbermen and trappers.

The next township westward has Island lake, on the Cloquet river, and Boulder and Thompson lakes, the last being named for an early lumberman.

T. 53, R. 15, has Otter lake and Boulder creek, flowing southward to Cloquet river.

T. 53, R. 16, is crossed by Ushkabwahka river, and Leora lake is in its northwest corner. The Ojibway name of the river is translated by Gilfillan as "the place of the wild artichokes," being thus of the same meaning as another stream before noted, tributary to the St. Louis river.

Northland township has Nichols lake.

T. 54, R. 12, has Pequaywan lake, an Ojibway name of undetermined meaning, and seven other lakes of smaller size unnamed.

T. 54, R. 16, has Witchel lake, with three others larger but unnamed; and Bug creek is there tributary to the White Face river.

T. 54, R. 17, has Kaufit and Williams lakes.

Sand creek is a western tributary of the St. Louis river in Toivola.

Floodwood lake, source of the river of this name, which was earlier noted, is in the west edge of this county in T. 54, R. 21.

T. 55, R. 12, has Brown, White, and Stone lakes.

T. 55, R. 14, has Sullivan lake in sections 23 and 24.

T. 55, R. 15, has Comstock and Wasuk lakes, the second being of small area in sections 17 and 18.

Among seven lakes mapped in T. 55, R. 16, only Dinham lake has a name, which it gave also to the adjacent railway station.

The next township westward has Young lake, and these townships are crossed by Pale Face river, tributary to the White Face.

East Swan river, and its tributary, West Swan river, are translated from the Ojibway name.

T. 56, R. 13, has Wolf and Harris lakes on its southern border, the latter giving its name to a railway station.

Linnwood lake is in T. 56, R. 14, and Markham lake in T. 56, R. 15.

Next are Mud Hen lake and creek, and Long lake, which outflows westward by the Water Hen river.

T. 56, R. 17, has in its southern half Elliott, Fig, Anchor, Murphy, and Stone lakes. The singularly branched form of Anchor lake suggested its name.

McDavitt has eight unnamed lakes in its east edge; and in its section 18 the St. Louis river receives from the north two small tributaries, named the East and West Two rivers.

T. 57, R. 12, has Bassett and Cadotte lakes in its southwest corner, Pine lake at its northeast corner, and its north line crosses Long lake, which also has been called Jack Pine lake.

T. 57, R. 16, has Bass lake in its sections 1 and 2.

Fayal township, next west, has Ely lake, which was formerly called Cedar Island lake, St. Mary lake, and Forbes lake.

Clinton has Elbow lake, named from its shape; and the next township has McQuade lake.

Hibbing and its vicinity have Carson and Kelly lakes, Lake Alice, and Carey lake.

T. 58, R. 12, has Seven Beaver lake, the principal head of the St. Louis river, named by the Ojibways for beavers trapped or shot there; Big lake, named Dead Fish lake on Nicollet's map, but on some recent maps called Devil Fish lake; also Swamp and Stone lakes, and on its south line are Pine and Long lakes, before noted.

Partridge river, flowing through the lake of this name, is a northern affluent of the St. Louis river; and Sunfish lake lies close southwest of Partridge lake.

Embarrass river, previously noticed, flows through a series of three long lakes, where it intersects the Mesabi range, named Wine, Embarrass, and Eshquaguma lakes, the first and second being translated from their Ojibway names. The first, which is the most northern, is renamed Sabin lake on several maps; but the people of the Mesabi mining range universally know it by the translation of its aboriginal name, given by Gilfillan as "Showiminabo, or Wine lake, literally Grape-liquid lake." The name of the second of these lakes, as of the river, comes through the

French language of the former fur taders and voyageurs, referring to driftwood which obstructed parts of the river; and the third name, Eshquaguma, means "Last water or Last lake."

Wanan lake is in the west edge of Biwabik township; and in the southeast part of Missabe Mountain township are Crooked and Lost lakes.

In the city of Virginia are Silver and Virginia lakes.

Nichols township has Manganika and Mashkenode lakes, Ojibway names that need further inquiry for their meanings; and the first is also called on some maps Three Mile lake.

Longyear lake, at Chisholm, was named in honor of brothers superintending mines there.

T. 58, R. 21, has Rock, Day, and Moran lakes.

T. 59, R. 15, has Little Mesabi lake.

T. 59, R. 20, has Long lake; and in the next township are Dewey, Island, Hobson, and Gansey lakes, with ten other small lakes that are mapped but not named.

In T. 60, R. 13, Iron lake has been also called Thevot lake.

Big Rice lake is in T. 60, R. 17, outflowing by Rice river to the South branch of the Little Fork of Rainy river.

Sturgeon lake, on the west line of the county, is the head of Sturgeon river, tributary to the Little Fork; and adjoining it on the east is Side lake, named from its position.

In the townships numbered 61 are Birch lake, Bear Island lake, which is called Stuntz lake on the map of this county by the Minnesota geological survey, Bear's Head lake, and Putnam lake; the East and West Two rivers, tributary to Vermilion lake; and, in the west edge of the county, Bear river, flowing to Sturgeon river.

T. 62, R. 12, has White Iron lake and One Pine lake.

T. 62, R. 14, has the Eagle Nest lakes; Gem lake, in section 29; Sand or Armstrong lake, flowing west to Armstrong bay of Vermilion lake, before noted; and Mud lake and river.

T. 63, R. 12, has Long lake, adjoining Ely, besides several unnamed lakes in its northern part.

Burntside lake and river are translated from their Ojibway name, referring to burned tracts of forest. The scenery of this lake, having more than sixty islands on our maps, all nameless, was highly praised by Prof. Alexander Winchell.

T. 63, R. 15, has Pine, Long, and Crab lakes, the last being named from the four arms or claws stretching out from its north side.

Trout lake, of large area, has been noticed in connection with Vermilon lake.

Next westward are Sea Gull and Wolf lakes.

In T. 63, R. 18, Black lake and creek are tributary to Black bay of Vermilion lake, each being named from the peat-stained water.

Willow river and Beaver creek flow westward to the Little Fork.

Many unnamed lakes are in the townships numbered 64, with Clear lake, very irregularly branched, in T. 64, R. 14.

Hawkinson creek is a western tributary of Vermilion river in T. 64, R. 17.

Elbow and Susan lakes outflow by Elbow river, through Rice lake, to the Pelican river at Glendale.

Pelican lake and river are translated from their Ojibway name, given as Shetek on Owen's map in 1852, which also is the name of a large lake in Murray county.

T. 65, R. 15, has in its east part the Indian Sioux river, also called Loon river, which flows north to Loon lake on the international boundary; and in its west part are Lakes Crellin and Jeannette.

Fensted lake is in section 30, T. 65, R. 16; Olive lake, in sections 27 and 28, T. 65, R. 17; Kjorstad and Myrtle lakes are in T. 65, R. 18; Moose lake, in sections 28 and 33, T. 65, R. 19; and Net lake, into which Lost creek flows, is crossed by the west line of T. 65, R. 21, which is the county boundary.

The townships numbered 66 to 71, extending to the Canadian line, have many lakes, of which those along the boundary have been already noticed. Others bearing names on maps include Shell lake, close east of Loon river; Rachel, Herman, Echo, and Rice lakes, east of the Vermilion river; Crane lake, through which that river flows near its mouth; Lake Marion, in sections 16 and 17, T. 67, R. 18; Elephant and Black Duck lakes, in T. 66, R. 19; Ash lake, at the railway station of that name, with Ash river running thence north to Kabetogama lake; Long lake and Moose lake and river, tributary to Namekan lake; Spring and Johnson lakes, flowing by the small Namekan river to the lake so named, before considered; and a little Net lake, in sections 4 and 9, T. 68, R. 18.

HILLS, MOUNTAINS, AND THE IRON RANGES.

The highest elevations in this county, popularly designated as "mountains," would be classed merely as hills in any really mountainous region. Furthermore, it must be noted that the so called "iron ranges" are belts of land along which very great beds of iron ore have been found, comprising hills and ridges in parts of their course, but in other large parts having no considerable height above the adjoining country on each side.

With topographic exaggeration, Schoolcraft in 1820 and again with Allen in 1832 called the belt of highland north and west of the west end of Lake Superior, adjoining the sites of Duluth and Fond du Lac, the Cabotian mountains. This name was derived from Cabotia, applied by Bouchette, a French author, "to all that part of North America lying north of the Great Lakes," in honor of John and Sebastian Cabot, father and son, who were the earliest making voyages of discovery to the mainland of this continent, in 1497 and 1498. The Dalles of the St. Louis river, before noted, are in the westward extension of this range, as mapped by Allen, but his delineation of its continuation farther west has no warrant in the land contour. Eastward from this river, the Cabotian range may be regarded as continuous along all the northwest shore of Lake Superior in this state, since practically the same highland adjoins all the lake coast to the Sawteeth mountains and Mt. Josephine in Cook county. Within the western limits of Duluth, about a mile west of Morgan Park, one of the hills of the range is called Bardon's peak, in honor of James Bardon, of Superior, Wis.

Grandmother hill is in section 8, T. 57, R. 13.

Bald mountain, merely a hill, is in section 23, T. 64, R. 19.

The Vermilion iron range, named from Vermilion lake on its north side, has Sunset peak in section 15, T. 63, R. 12, about two miles west of Winton; Chester peak, three miles east of Tower, named in honor of Prof. A. H. Chester, but often by error called Jasper peak; and the North and South ridges, respectively near Soudan and Tower.

Albert Huntington Chester, commemorated by Chester peak, was born at Saratoga Springs, N. Y., Nov. 22, 1843; was graduated at the Columbia School of Mines, 1868; was professor of chemistry, mineralogy and metallurgy in Hamilton College, 1870-91, and later in Rutgers College; and died in 1903. For the Minnesota Iron Company in 1875, he made explorations of both the Mesabi and Vermilion ranges; but his observations remained unpublished until 1884, when they were presented in the Eleventh Annual Report of the Minnesota Geological Survey, for 1882 (pages 154-167).

To work the Vermilion iron mines, the construction of the Duluth and Iron Range railroad was completed to Tower in 1884, and to Ely in 1888. The first trainload of ore was taken from Tower to Two Harbors, the Lake Superior port of this railroad, in August, 1884.

On the very productive central part of the Mesabi iron range, the Mountain Iron mine was the first discovered, November 16, 1890, "by a crew of workmen under Capt. J. A. Nichols," for whom Nichols township, including this mine, was named, as before noted. "In August, 1891, the next large deposit was discovered by John McCaskill, Capt. Nichols, and Wilbur Merritt; this has since developed into the Biwabik group of mines. In 1892 two railroads were built to the range, and in 1893 the shipments amounted to 620,000 gross tons." (Horace V. Winchell, "Historical Sketch of the Discovery of Mineral Deposits in the Lake Superior Region," 23d Annual Report, Minn. Geol. Survey, for 1894, pages 116-155.) More full description and history of this range are presented in "The Mesabi Iron-bearing District of Minnesota," by Charles K. Leith, this work being Monograph XLIII, U. S. Geol. Survey, 1903 (pages 316, with maps and many other plates).

Nicollet mapped this highland range as "Missabay Heights," the earliest published form of the name; but Dr. Joseph G. Norwood, who explored the St. Louis, Embarrass, and Vermilion rivers in 1848, for

Owen's geological survey, wrote it "Missabé Wachu, or 'Big Man Hills,' which form a portion of the dividing highlands between the waters of Hudson's Bay and Lake Superior." Gilfillan noted the Ojibway name as "Missabe wudjiu or Giant mountain," in which spelling the final *e* is to be pronounced with the English sound of long *a,* as if having the accent given by Norwood, being thus equivalent to Nicollet's spelling. Verwyst, in his later list of Ojibway geographic names, uses the same orthography; and both these lists copy the spelling of Baraga's Dictionary, published in 1880, which defines this word as "Giant; also, a very big stout man." Gilfillan added the following note in his list: "Missabe is a giant of immense size and a cannibal. This is his mountain, consequently the highest, biggest mountain."

But the spelling used by Norwood, Baraga, Gilfillan, and Verwyst, having a final *e* sounded as in French and other European languages, is apt to be mispronounced by American and English readers, who would in analogy with the usage of our language pronounce Messabe in two syllables, with *a* as in fate or babe. Although the Duluth, Missabe and Northern railway company adopted that form, as also the township of Missabe Mountain, while another township makes it Mesaba, the Minnesota and United States geological surveys use the preferable form of Mesabi, which readers will surely pronounce in three syllables. Yet they must by analogy give to the last syllable the short sound of *i,* as in Mississippi, whereas Nicollet's spelling is strictly in accordance with the Ojibway pronunciation, requiring the final syllable to be sounded as *bay.* More satisfactory would be Missabi, if we should not fully follow the spelling by Nicollet, for then the name would show its meaning, great, like Mississippi, Great river.

Henry H. Eames, state geologist of Minnesota in 1865-66, wrote this name as Missabi Wasju; and Col. Charles Whittlesey, in his report on the "Mineral Regions of Minnesota" published in 1866, set the example of spelling it as "the Mesabi Range."

Several references along this range to mountainous heights attained in portions of its extent, including Mesaba (that is, Giant), Wuori, and Missabe Mountain townships, and the village of Mountain Iron, would seem to imply greater altitudes than from 200 to 300 feet above the average of the adjoining region, up to the exceptional 700 feet in Wuori above Virginia city. Such ridges and hills, however, are very noteworthy in comparison with the relatively slight elevations found generally throughout this state.

Marginal Moraines and Glacial Lakes.

In the series of twelve successive marginal moraines formed along the borders of the continental ice-sheet at pauses that slackened or interrupted its final melting, the latest two are well exhibited on or near the iron ore ranges. Thence they are named the Mesabi or Eleventh and the Vermilion or Twelfth moraines.

ST. LOUIS COUNTY 505

Contemporaneous with the wavering retreat of the ice-border, the basins of the Red and Rainy rivers and of Lake Superior were filled by great ice-dammed lakes, called glacial lakes. Prof. N. H. Winchell, the state geologist, reviewed the evidences of these glacial lakes, enumerating twenty-six for this state, in a paper read before the Geological Society of America and published in its Bulletin (vol. XII, 1901, pages 109-128, with a map).

Within the basin of Lake Superior and lying partly in the area of St. Louis county, the list includes Lake Upham, first described and named in 1901 (Final Report, Geology of Minnesota, vol. VI, plate 66), which had an estimated extent of about 1,000 square miles in the St. Louis basin, outflowing past Sandy lake to the Mississippi; and Lakes St. Louis, Nemadji, and Duluth, flowing to the St. Croix river, the first two by way of Carlton county and the Kettle river, and the last by the Brulé river in Wisconsin to the Upper St. Croix lake and river. Lakes St. Louis and Nemadji received their names from the present rivers, of which the latter, emptying into Lake Superior in the city of Superior, was called Nemadji by the Ojibways, meaning Left Hand, because in entering Superior bay, west of the Wisconsin and Minnesota points, which inclose the harbor, that stream was on the left hand, the St. Louis river being on the right.

The basin of Lake Winnipeg held a much larger glacial lake, named Lake Agassiz in 1879, described most fully in the U. S. Geol. Sur. Monograph XXV (1896, 658 pages, with many maps and other plates). In the 22d Annual Report of the Minnesota survey, for 1893, this ancient lake was mapped as reaching eastward, during its highest stage on the international boundary, to the west part of Hunter's Island. By the recent field work and map of Frank Leverett and Frederick W. Sardeson for the Minnesota and United States geological surveys, published in 1917, the highest shore of Lake Agassiz is traced eastward in the Little Fork valley nearly to the middle of the south side of Vermilion lake. Other observations by Prof. N. H. Winchell imply that this glacial lake stood about 10 or 15 feet above the level of Vermilion lake (Final Report, Geology of Minn., vol. IV, 1899, page 523). Hence we know that it must have extended east along the boundary to Knife and Otter Track lakes, on the southeast side of Hunter's Island, if the ice-sheet there was melted away before Lake Agassiz receded from its highest stage.

Between its mouth, at Lakes Traverse and Big Stone, and Vermilion lake, in a distance of 240 miles, the old lake level at its highest or Herman stage shows now an ascent from 1050 to 1370 feet above the sea, or an average gradient of one foot and a third per mile. In other words, since the time of the Herman level of the glacial lake, this area in northern Minnesota has been differentially uplifted or tilted, giving now to the highest and earliest lake beach an ascent of 320 feet in 240 miles from southwest to northeast.

506   MINNESOTA GEOGRAPHIC NAMES

NATIONAL AND STATE FORESTS.

In the chapters for Cook and Lake counties, the large area of the Superior National Forest has been previously considered, with the date, February 13, 1909, when its earliest part was reserved by the United States government for foresty uses. From western Cook county this public forest area crosses north central Lake county, and it continues halfway across northeastern St. Louis county, to Echo lake and nearly to the Vermilion river.

South of the National Forest, this state owns two tracts, comprising together about 20,000 acres, or more than 30 square miles, of rocky land, lying in T. 63, R. 14, and T. 64, R. 13, close west and north of Burntside lake. These tracts, named the Burntside State Forest, were "granted to the state by act of Congress, April 28, 1904, for tree propagation and playground purposes. . . . The forest contains forty-three lakes, all connected, and one of the noted canoe routes of the state passes through it. The entire district can be developed into a splendid playground. The abundance of fish and big game make it especially attractive." (Legislative Manual of Minnesota, 1917, p. 223.)

INDIAN RESERVATIONS.

By a treaty at La Pointe, Wis., September 30, 1854, the Ojibways ceded to the United States a great tract in northeastern Minnesota, including Cook and Lake counties and the greater part of St. Louis county, reaching west to the St. Louis, East Swan, and Vermilion rivers. Less than a year later, in a treaty at the city of Washington, February 22, 1855, they ceded lands farther west and southwest, from the St. Louis and East Swan rivers to the Red river, Otter Tail lake, and Crow Wing river; and in another treaty at Washington, April 7, 1866, the Ojibway lands of northwestern St. Louis county and eastern Koochiching county were ceded, excepting the Bois Fort reservation, including and surrounding Net lake. This reservation, more fully noticed under Koochiching county, reaches three miles into the west edge of St. Louis county, with an extent of twelve miles from north to south.

The Fond du Lac reservation, in St. Louis and Carlton counties, was provided under the treaty of La Pointe in 1854, comprising a tract on the southwest side of the St. Louis river, reaching from Cloquet, Nagonab, and Brevator, west nearly to the middle of Range 19.

Latest provided, by an executive order of the President, December 20, 1881, the Vermilion Lake reservation comprises only about two square miles, being an irregular tract between Pike bay and Mission or Sucker bay, between two and four miles west of Tower.

SCOTT COUNTY

Established March 5, 1853, this county was named in honor of General Winfield Scott, who was commander in chief of the United States army from 1841 to 1861. He was born near Petersburg, Va., June 13, 1786, and died at West Point, N. Y., May 29, 1866; entered the army as captain in 1808; served with distinction in the War of 1812, and was made a brigadier general and brevet major general in 1814; was chief commander in the Mexican war, 1847; and was an unsuccessful Whig candidate for President in 1852. General Scott visited Fort St. Anthony in the spring of 1824, for inspection of its construction, then completed, and on his recommendation its name was changed to Fort Snelling by a general order of the War Department, January 7, 1825.

Townships and Villages.

Information of names was gathered in "History of the Minnesota Valley," 1882, having pages 290-351 for Scott county; and from Nicholas Meyer, judge of probate since 1880, and William F. Duffy, clerk of the court, interviewed at Shakopee, the county seat, during a visit there in July, 1916.

BARDEN, a railway station six miles east of Shakopee, received its name in 1885, in honor of J. W. Barden, "who was largely interested in grain elevators and other business enterprises here and hereabouts" (Stennett, Place Names of the Chicago and Northwestern Railways, 1908, page 167).

BELLE PLAINE township, first settled in 1852-53, and its village, founded in 1854, were named by Hon. Andrew G. Chatfield, an associate justice of the supreme court of Minnesota Territory, who settled here in 1854. It is a French name, meaning "beautiful plain."

BLAKELEY, settled in 1853 and established as a township by a legislative act, March 9, 1874, received the name of its railway village, founded in 1867 by Elias F. Drake and I. N. Dean, by whom it was named in honor of Captain Russell Blakeley, who was born in North Adams, Mass., April 19, 1815, and died in St. Paul, February 4, 1901. His connection with steamboating from Galena to St. Paul began in 1847, and he continued in it, as clerk and afterward as captain and traffic manager, during many years. Later he engaged in staging and expressing in Minnesota and Dakota, and had large interests in banking, insurance, and railway companies. He settled in St. Paul in 1862. He was president of the Minnesota Historical Society in 1871, and vice-president from 1876 until his death, and contributed to its Collections the "History of the Discovery of the Mississippi River and the Advent of Commerce in Minnesota" (vol. VIII, 1898, pages 303-418, with his portrait and eleven plates of early steamboats). A biographic sketch of him is in these Collections (vol. IX, 1901, pages 665-670).

BRENTWOOD, a village site platted in September, 1860, was united with Jordan when that place was incorporated as a village in 1872.

CEDAR LAKE township, settled in 1855 and organized April 11, 1858, was named from the lake crossed by its west line, having red cedar trees on its shores.

CREDIT RIVER township, settled in 1854 and organized in 1858, bears the name of the stream flowing through it, called Credit or Erakah river on Nicollet's map in 1843. Twenty years earlier it was named Elk creek on the map of Long's expedition.

EAGLE CREEK township, first settled by Rev. Samuel W. Pond in the fall of 1847, was organized in 1858, receiving the name of a creek which has its source in Pike lake, in section 23, and flows northeastward to the Minnesota river.

ELKO, a railway village in New Market, has a name that is also borne by villages in Virginia, South Carolina, and Georgia, and by a county and its county seat in Nevada.

GLENDALE township, first settled in the spring of 1852, has a name borne by villages in Massachusetts, Ohio, Wisconsin, and fourteen other states.

GRAINWOOD is the name of a railway station, with a village mainly consisting of summer homes, between Prior and Long lakes, in the south edge of Eagle Creek township.

HELENA township, first settled in 1854, organized May 12, 1858, and the railway station on its north line, bear the name of an earlier village platted in 1856 on section 11 by John C. Smith. It is the name also of the capital of Montana, a city in Arkansas, and villages in eight other states.

JACKSON, a township of small area, adjoining the city of Shakopee, was first settled in the spring of 1851, and was organized May 11, 1858. It was called Shakopee township until the incorporation of the city, when the remaining part of the township was renamed Jackson by a legislative act, January 17, 1871. Like many counties, townships, villages, and cities, throughout the United States, it was probably named in honor of President Andrew Jackson (b. 1767, d. 1845).

JORDAN, platted by Thomas A. and William Holmes in 1854, incorporated as a village February 26, 1872, and as a city March 11, 1891, was named by William Holmes for "the River Jordan in Palestine. The name was given at the end of a somewhat angry and prolonged discussion amongst the citizens as to what the name should be." (Stennett, Place Names of the Chicago and Northwestern Railways, page 180.)

LOUISVILLE township, named like its former village for the large city of Louisville in Kentucky, the previous home of H. H. Spencer, who settled here in 1853, was originally a part of Shakopee, from which it was set off April 13, 1858. The village of Louisville, platted in 1854, grew well during four or five years, until it had thirty houses or more; but within a few years later its buildings were mostly removed to Carver, or were torn down, and the site is now farming land.

MERRIAM, a proposed village of the St. Paul and Sioux City railroad, platted in 1866 but abandoned in 1871, and the present station of Merriam Junction in Louisville, established in 1875, were named by Gen. Judson W. Bishop, chief engineer of this railroad, in honor of John L. Merriam, who was born in Essex, N. Y., February 6, 1825, and died in St. Paul, January 12, 1895. He came to Minnesota in 1860, settling in St. Paul, where he engaged with J. C. Burbank and Capt. Russell Blakeley in the staging and expressing business. He helped to organize the First National Bank and the Merchants' National Bank of St. Paul, and was president of the latter. In 1870-1 he was a representative in the legislature, being speaker of the House.

NEW MARKET township, settled in the spring of 1856, was at first named Jackson, when it was organized in May, 1858; but it was renamed as now at the election held October 12, 1858. The name is thought to have been adopted from the town of New Market near Cambridge in England, famous for its horse races. Thirteen other states have villages of this name.

NEW PRAGUE, founded in 1856, incorporated as a village March 1, 1877, and as a city April 4, 1891, was named for the ancient city of Prague, the capital of Bohemia, whence many of its first colony of settlers came. This city lies, in about equal parts, in Scott and Le Sueur counties; the main street, running east and west, is on the county line.

PRIOR LAKE, a railway village near the lake so named, in the north edge of Spring Lake township, was platted in 1875, taking the name of a post office that had been established in 1872. The lake, post office, and village, thus successively named, are in honor of Charles H. Prior, of Minneapolis, who in 1871-86 was superintendent of the Minnesota divisions of the Chicago, Milwaukee and St. Paul railway, and since 1886 has been a dealer in real estate. He was born in Norwich, Conn., August 1, 1832; studied at Oberlin College and the Ohio State University.

ST. LAWRENCE township, first settled in 1854, was organized May 11, 1858. Its village, platted in the fall of 1858, was all vacated for farming uses before 1882. New York has a county and a village of this name, which also is borne by villages and townships in five other states, derived from the river and gulf of St. Lawrence. The name was first applied by Cartier to a bay at the north side of the gulf, August 10, 1536, this being the festal day of St. Lawrence, who suffered martyrdom on August 10, A. D. 258.

SAND CREEK township was first named Douglass at its organization, May 11, 1858; but in September it was changed to St. Mary, and in

December to Jordan. The present name was adopted at the annual town meeting, April 5, 1859, being taken from the stream that flows through this township and supplies water power at Jordan. It was mapped by Nicollet as "Batture aux fieves," meaning, "shallow, with fevers." Next on the map of Minnesota dated January 1, 1860, it is called Fever river, and also has a Sioux name, Chankiyata river, of undetermined meaning, while a settlement near the site of Jordan is named Sand Creek. Numerous outcrops of soft white sandstone occur there, whence the stream and township were named.

SAVAGE, a railway village in the northeast corner of Glendale, after being called Hamilton during many years, was renamed in honor of Marion Willis Savage, who here owned a horse-training farm, with a covered track for practice in racing. He was born near Akron, Ohio, March 26, 1859; removed to Minneapolis in 1886, and engaged in manufacture of stock foods; purchased the world's champion racing horse, Dan Patch, for $60,000, in 1902; constructed the Dan Patch electric railway, from Minneapolis to Savage, Northfield, and Faribault; died in Minneapolis, July 12, 1916, on the next day after his famous horse died. The Dan Patch railway soon afterward became insolvent, but in July, 1918, it was purchased by a reorganized company, being renamed the Minneapolis, Northfield and Southern railway.

SHAKOPEE, the county seat, was founded by Thomas A. Holmes in 1851 as an Indian trading post, to which he gave this name of the chief of a Sioux band living here. The village, platted in 1854, was incorporated as a city May 23, 1857, but surrendered its charter in 1861, returning to township government. It again received a city charter March 3, 1870, and the former township of Shakopee, excepting the city area, was renamed Jackson, as before noted, January 17, 1871. The Sioux name of their village here was Tintonwan, signifying "the village on the prairie;" and Rev. Samuel W. Pond, who settled as their missionary in the adjacent edge of Eagle Creek township in 1847, translated the native name as Prairieville.

Shakopee (or Shakpay, as it was commonly pronounced), meaning Six, was the hereditary name, like Wabasha, of successive chiefs, in lineal descent from father to son. The first of whom we have definite knowledge is the Shakopee who was killed when running the gauntlet at Fort Snelling in June, 1827, as related by Mrs. Charlotte O. Van Cleve ("Three Score Years and Ten," 1888, pages 74-79). The second, who is commemorated by the name of this city, characterized by Samuel W. Pond, Jr., as "a man of marked ability in council and one of the ablest and most effective orators in the whole Dakota Nation," died in 1860. His son, who had been called Shakpedan (Little Six), born on the site of the city in 1811, became at his father's death the chief of the band, numbering at that time about 400. He was hung at Fort Snelling, November 11, 1865, for participating in the massacres of 1862.

SCOTT COUNTY

SPRING LAKE township, first settled in 1853, organized May 11, 1858, was named from "Spring lake, a large and beautiful body of water, situated in the northern part of the town, which in turn derives its name from a large spring tributary to it." (History of the Minnesota Valley, p. 341.)

LAKES AND STREAMS.

At the Little Rapids, in the north part of the southeast quarter of section 31, Louisville, the Minnesota river has a descent of two feet, very nearly, at its stage of low water, flowing across an outcrop of the Jordan sandstone. About a quarter of a mile up the river, which turns at a right angle between these points, there is another rapid, in the east part of the same quarter section, which at the lowest stage of water has a fall of one foot.

In the foregoing pages attention has been directed to the names of Cedar lake, Credit river, Eagle creek and Pike lake, Prior lake, Sand creek, and Spring lake.

Other lakes and streams to be noticed are arranged in the order of the townships from south to north, and of the ranges from east to west.

New Market has Rice lake, crossed by its east line, named from its wild rice; Goose lake, on its south line; and Vermilion lake, in section 28.

Cedar Lake township is crossed from southeast to northwest by Porter creek, named for George Porter, a pioneer farmer there, which flows through Bradshaw and Mud lakes. This township also has Ready's or Lennon lake, in sections 11 and 12; O'Connor's lake, in section 22; McMahon or Carl's lake, St. Catherine's lake, and Cynthia lake, on its north line; and Hickey's and Cedar lakes at its west side.

Helena has Pleasant lake and Raven stream, a tributary of Sand creek.

Belle Plaine had a Rice lake, now drained, in the western section 25; and Brewery creek joins the Minnesota river close east of the village.

From Blakeley the Minnesota river receives Robert creek, named in honor of Captain Louis Robert, of St. Paul, who established an Indian trading post on this creek in 1852; and Big and Little Possum creeks, flowing through the village, but it seems doubtful that the geographic range of the opossum, common in the southern states, reaches into Minnesota. Clark's lake, near the center of this township, has an outlet that flows southward into Le Sueur county and joins the Minnesota river at East Henderson. Though unnamed on later maps, this stream was called Abert river on Nicollet's map in 1843, in honor of Colonel John James Abert, of the U. S. topographical engineer corps, under whose commission Nicollet conducted his surveys in the Northwest.

Credit River township has Murphy lake in section 3 and 4, and Cleary lake in section 7, the last being named for John, Peter, and Patrick Cleary, who settled here in 1855.

Spring Lake township has Kane's and Markley lakes, crossed by its east line; Crystal and Rice lakes, in section 10 and 11; Fish lake, in sections 27 and 28; Spring, Prior, and Little Prior lakes; and Campbell lake in sections 5 and 6.

In Sand Creek township are Geis and Sutton lakes.

Glendale has Lake Hanrahan, named for a farmer, Edward Hanrahan, whose home was near its western end.

Eagle Creek township has Long lake, the most northeast and longest in a noteworthy series of three lakes, named Long, Prior, and Spring lakes. The first two, connected by a strait, have been sometimes called Credit lake, from the Credit river to which they have probably an underground flow. This township also has Howard, O'Dowd, Pike, Dean's, Rice, Fischer, and Blue lakes. O'Dowd lake was named for three brothers, farmers near it; Dean's lake commemorates Matthew Dean, a settler who came there in 1855; and the last three lakes are on the bottomland of the Minnesota river.

Thole's (or Haam) and Gifford lakes are in Louisville.

Strunk's lake, beside the Minnesota river in Jackson, was named in honor of H. H. Strunk, an adjacent farmer, who afterward was a druggist in Shakopee.

Spirit Hill and Shakopee Prairie.

The eastern part of a high terrace of the Minnesota valley drift, adjoining the Sand creek at Jordan, was named Spirit hill by the Sioux, who frequently held councils and medicine dances there.

Another remnant of this valley drift is the plateau called the "Sand prairie," which lies a mile north of Spirit hill.

Through Jackson and Eagle Creek townships a similar but longer and wider valley drift terrace, 140 to 125 feet above the Minnesota river and nearly 100 feet below the crest and general expanse of the adjoining upland, has a width from a half mile to one and a half miles, with a length of about ten miles. All of this county was originally wooded, excepting much of the bottomland of the Minnesota valley and large parts of its terraces, such as those of Belle Plaine and near Jordan and this close south of Shakopee, which last has therefore received the name of "Shakopee prairie."

SHERBURNE COUNTY

This county, established February 25, 1856, was named in honor of Moses Sherburne, who was an associate justice of the Supreme Court of Minnesota Territory from 1853 to 1857. He was born in Mount Vernon, Kennebec county, Maine, January 25, 1808; came to St. Paul in April, 1853, and resided there fourteen years, engaging in law practice after 1857; was one of the two compilers of the statutes of Minnesota, published in 1859; removed to Orono, in Sherburne county, 1867, and died there, March 29, 1868.

An interesting biographic sketch of Judge Sherburne, with his portrait, was contributed by Rev. Simeon Mills Hayes in the M. H. S. Collections (vol. X, part II, 1905, pages 863-6). This paper includes special notice of his life and public services in Maine before coming to Minnesota. His professional and personal character is portrayed as follows: "Sherburne was a successful lawyer from the beginning of his practice. His absolute integrity, imposing presence, accurate learning, and oratorical endowments drew clients from neighboring counties, and brought him almost immediately into prominence. Although never an office-seeker, his popularity and the general respect felt for his abililty made him a recipient of public offices during the greater portion of his professional life. . . . When the Territory of Minnesota applied for admission to the Union as a state, Judge Sherburne took a prominent part in the deliberations which resulted in the adoption of the State Constitution, and his remarks during the Constitutional Convention are among the valuable original sources to which the future historian of Minnesota will apply for an insight into the problems and motives of the Fathers of the North Star State."

Townships and Villages.

Information of the origin and meaning of geographic names has been gathered from "History of the Upper Mississippi Valley," 1881, having pages 294-339 for Sherburne county; "Fifty Years in the Northwest," by W. H. C. Folsom, noting this county in pages 453-459; and from Charles S. Wheaton, attorney at Elk River since 1872, and Hiram H. Mansur, photographer, each being interviewed during a visit at Elk River, the county seat, in October, 1916.

BAILEY, a railway station in Big Lake township, five miles west of Elk River, was named in honor of Orlando Bailey, a pioneer farmer there. He was born in Chautauqua county, N. Y., in 1820; came to Minnesota in 1852, settling in this township; kept a stage station and hotel nine years;

was the first sheriff of this county; and his son, Albert Bailey, is the present probate judge.

BALDWIN township, first settled in 1854 and organized September 13, 1858, received this name in honor of Francis Eugene Baldwin, of Clear Lake township. He was born in Wayne county, Pa., March 7, 1825; was graduated at Illinois College in 1846; was admitted to practice law in 1847; came to Minnesota in 1855, and resided in Minneapolis and at Clear Lake in this county; was the county attorney two years, and owned a farm; was a state senator in 1859-60.

BECKER township, settled in 1855, organized in 1871, and its railway village, founded in 1867, were named in honor of George Loomis Becker, of St. Paul, for whom a biographic sketch has been presented in the chapter of Becker county.

BIG LAKE township, settled in 1848, organized in 1858, and its village, at first called Humboldt, are named from the lake adjoining the village, a favorite place for picnics. Humboldt was the county seat until 1867, being succeeded by Elk River, and its name was changed to that of the township when the railroad was built, in 1867.

BLUE HILL township, settled in 1857 or earlier, organized March 20, 1877, had previously been a part of Baldwin. It has a lone hill of glacial drift in the northwest quarter of section 28, called the Blue Mound from its appearance when seen at a far distance, which rises about 75 feet above the surrounding flat plain of sand and gravel.

CLEAR LAKE township, settled in 1850, organized in 1858, and its railway village, founded in 1867 and platted in 1879, were named for a lake in sections 10 and 11, two miles west of the village.

ELK RIVER township, settled in 1848 by Pierre Bottineau, who established an Indian trading post near the site of the village, received its first farming settlement in 1850. Its village of Orono, to be again noticed, was platted in 1855; and the village of Elk River, platted in 1865, was incorporated in 1881, the two villages being united under the latter name. The county seat was first established at Humboldt, now Big Lake village, as before noted; but its offices were removed in 1867 to Elk River village, then known, in distinction from Orono, as "the Lower Town."

The river, whence this township and village are named, was called the St. Francis river by Carver, Pike, Long, and Schoolcraft, taking the name given to the present Rum river by Hennepin. Nicollet's map, in 1843, applied the name St. Francis as it is now used, for the chief northern tributary of Elk river. Beltrami and Nicollet used an Ojibway name for Elk river, translated as Double river, or by Allen as Parallel river, alluding to its course nearly parallel with the Mississippi. On account of the herds of elk found there by Pike and later explorers and fur traders, the present name was given to this river, and to Elk lake, through which it flows, on the first map of Minnesota Territory in 1850.

FITZPATRICK is a railway station six miles north of Elk River.

SHERBURNE COUNTY 515

HAVEN township, first settled in 1846, organized in 1872, had previously been a part of Briggs (now Palmer) township. Its name is in honor of John Ormsbee Haven, who was born in Addison county, Vermont, October 3, 1824, and died at his home in Big Lake township, September 1, 1906. He was graduated at Middlebury College, 1852; came to Minnesota in 1854; settled on a farm at Big Lake in 1866; was register of deeds, county auditor, county superintendent of schools, and clerk of the district court. In 1872-3 he was a representative in the legislature.

HOULTON, a railway station about three miles north of Elk River, was named for William Henry Houlton, who was born in Houlton, Maine, March 29, 1840, and died at his home in Elk River township, August, 1915. He came to Monticello, Minn., in 1856; served in the Eighth Minnesota regiment, 1862-5; entered partnership with his brother Horatio at Elk River in 1866, and engaged in mercantile business, manufacture of lumber and flour, banking, and farming; was a state senator in 1878 and 1883-85; was superintendent of the State Reformatory, 1896-1900.

LAKE FREMONT, a village on the Great Northern railway in Livonia, incorporated in 1912, is called Zimmerman by the railway company and as a post office, in honor of Moses Zimmerman, who was owner of the farm on which the village was located. The adjoining lake received its name in 1856, when John Charles Fremont (b. 1813, d. 1890) was the Republican candidate for president of the United States. He was the assistant of Nicollet, 1838-43, in the surveys and mapping of the upper Mississippi region including Minnesota.

LIVONIA township, settled in 1856 and organized in 1866, is said to bear the Christian name of the wife of Benjamin N. Spencer, who settled in this township in 1864 and was the probate judge of the county for two terms. This is the name of a province in Russia, adjoining the Gulf of Riga.

ORONO, a village that in 1881 became a part of the village of Elk River, as before noted, was platted in May, 1855, by Ard Godfrey of Minneapolis, who named it for his native town in Maine. Much interesting biographic information of Orono, the Penobscot chief, for whom the Maine town and village are named, was given in an address of Hon. Israel Washburn, Jr., at the Centennial Celebration of that town, March 3, 1874. Orono was born in 1688 and died at Oldtown, Maine, February 5, 1801, aged 113 years. His life is also sketched somewhat fully in the "Handbook of American Indians," edited by F. W. Hodge (Part II, 1910, p. 155).

ORROCK township, settled in 1856 and organized in 1875, after being previously a part of Big Lake, was named in honor of Robert Orrock, its earliest settler. He was born in Scotland, July 15, 1805; came to America in 1831; settled here in 1856 as a farmer; and died at his home January 4, 1885.

PALMER township, settled in 1855, "was organized in 1858, with the name of Briggs, in honor of Joshua Briggs, who resided on the west bank of the lake bearing his name. . . . A few years afterwards, the name was changed to Clinton Lake, and subsequently to Palmer, in honor of Robinson Palmer, the father of Mrs. Joshua Briggs." (History, Upper Mississippi Valley, p. 336.)

Benjamin Robinson Palmer, physician, was born in South Berwick, Maine, March 15, 1815; came to Minnesota in 1856, settling in St. Cloud; was assistant surgeon in the United States army, 1862-6, being stationed at Sauk Center and Fort Ripley, Minn.; lived afterward at Sauk Center, had an extensive medical practice, and died there May 6, 1882.

ST. CLOUD, the county seat of Stearns county, extends also as an incorporated city across the Mississippi to include wards 5 and 6 in Benton county and ward 7 in the northwest corner of Sherburne county. The State Reformatory, established in 1889, is in the part of St. Cloud lying in this county. Its ground, 1,057 acres, includes a large granite quarry.

SANTIAGO township, settled in 1856, organized in 1868, and its village, platted in April, 1857, have the Spanish name for St. James, borne by the capital of the republic of Chile, as also by a city and province in Cuba.

ZIMMERMAN, the railway village in Livonia, named for a farmer there, has been before noticed as Lake Fremont, its corporate village name.

LAKES AND STREAMS.

In the foregoing pages, attention has been given to Big lake, Clear lake, the Elk river and lake, St. Francis river, Lake Fremont, and Briggs lake, the last being named in honor of Joshua Briggs, a former English sea captain who settled there.

The other lakes and streams bearing names on maps of this county include Twin lake, on the east line of Elk River, outflowing by Trott brook, named for Joseph Trott, its earliest settler, who came in 1854; Tibbetts brook, the outlet of Lake Fremont, named for four brothers from Maine, Joshua, Nathaniel, Ben, and Jim, who were lumbermen and farmers; Battle brook, named from a fight of two white men, as noted in the chapter for Mille Lacs county, flowing through a second Elk lake; Rice lake, on the St. Francis river, filled with wild rice, called St. Francis lake on old maps; Catlin and Sandy lakes, in the south part of Baldwin; Stone lake, in sections 25 and 36, Livonia, and a Lake of the Woods in its section 30; Lakes Ann and Josephine, Big Mud lake, and Eagle lake, in Orrock; Birch, Mud, and Thompson lakes, in Big Lake township; Lake Julia and Rush lake, joined by straits with Briggs lake; Rice or Strong creek, in Palmer, flowing through a lake having much wild rice; Pickerel and Long lakes, crossed by the south line of Haven; and Biggerstaff creek in Haven, named for a pioneer farmer, Samuel Biggerstaff.

RAPIDS AND ISLANDS OF THE MISSISSIPPI.

From the "Historico-Geographical Chart of the Upper Mississippi River," accompanying Coues' edition of Pike's Expeditions, published in 1895, the following names are listed, in the descending course of the

SHERBURNE COUNTY

river on the border of Sherburne county, from St. Cloud to the mouth of Crow river at Dayton.

The Thousand Islands, within two miles south of St. Cloud, so named, with great exaggeration, in allusion to the Thousand Islands of the St. Lawrence river along many miles next below the mouth of Lake Ontario, were called Beaver islands by Pike in 1805, and an "archipelago" by Beltrami in 1823.

Next southward are Mosquito rapids and Grand island, which is more than a mile long.

Boynton's island and Smiler's rapids adjoin the south side of Clear Lake township.

Bear island, Cedar rapids, Cedar island, and Lane's island, are at the south side of Becker.

Boom island, Battle rapids, Brown's island, Spring rapids, and Bakers' and Dimick's islands, adjoin Big Lake township. The Boom island has reference to booms for storing logs. Battle rapids, adjoining section 32, received this name in commemoration of the battles of Elk river, between the Ojibways and the Sioux, narrated by Warren in his "History of the Ojibways" (M. H. S. Collections, vol. V, 1885, pages 235-241). These battles are referred by Winchell to the years 1772 and 1773 (Aborigines of Minnesota, 1911, page 539). "From the circumstances of two battles having been fought in such quick succession on the point of land betweeen the Elk and Mississippi rivers, this spot has been named by the Ojibways, Me-gaud-e-win-ing, or 'Battle Ground'" (Warren, page 240).

Next are Davis, Wilson, Jameson, and Nickerson islands, extending to the vicinity of the mouth of the Elk river; and near the southeast corner of Elk River township and of this county are Dayton island and Dayton rapids, named, like the adjoining village and township in Hennepin county, for Lyman Dayton of St. Paul.

CRAIG PRAIRIE.

A large opening in the woods in the west part of Orrock, having an area of about two square miles, is named Craig prairie, in honor of Hugh E. Craig, its pioneer farmer. Other and more extended open tracts, originally prairies but unnamed, or partly brushland, adjoined the Mississippi through this county and are now mainly occupied by farms.

SIBLEY COUNTY

Established March 5, 1853, this county was named in honor of General Henry Hastings Sibley, pioneer, governor, and military defender of Minnesota. He was born in Detroit, Mich., February 20, 1811; went to Mackinaw, entering the service of the American Fur Company, in 1829; came to what is now Minnesota in 1834, as general agent in the Northwest for that company, with headquarters at Mendota (then called St. Peter's), where he lived twenty-eight years; removed to St. Paul in 1862, and resided there through the remainder of his life. He was delegate in Congress, representing Minnesota Territory, 1849 to 1853; was first governor of the state, 1858 to 1860; and during the Sioux war, in 1862, led in the suppression of the outbreak, and in the next year commanded an expedition against these Indians in North Dakota. He was during more than twenty years a regent of the State University; was a charter member of the Minnesota Historical Society; and was its president in 1867, and from 1876 until his death, at his home in St. Paul, February 18, 1891.

In 1835 Sibley built at Mendota the first stone dwelling house of Minnesota, in which he and his family lived until their removal to St. Paul. This house is now owned by the Daughters of the American Revolution, and is used as a historical museum.

His biography, in 596 pages, by Nathaniel West, D. D., was published in 1889; an excellent memoir of him, by J. Fletcher Williams, is in the Minn. Historical Society Collections (vol. VI, pages 257-310); and a shorter biography, by Gen. James H. Baker, is in his "Lives of the Governors of Minnesota" (M. H. S. Collections, vol. XIII, pages 75-105).

Among the Sioux or Dakota people, with whom Sibley had a very intimate and wide acquaintance, he was called "Wah-ze-o-man-ee, Walker in the Pines, a name that had a potent influence among them far and near, as long as the Dakota race dwelt in the state." (Williams, p. 167.)

Townships and Villages.

Information of names has been gathered from "History of the Minnesota Valley," 1882, having pages 410-477 for Sibley county; and from Florenz Seeman, register of deeds, and Julius Henke, a pioneer who came here in 1860, during a visit at Gaylord, the county seat, in July, 1916.

ALFSBORG township, organized January 26, 1869, received this name of a district in Sweden by vote of its Scandinavian settlers.

ARLINGTON township, settled in 1855, organized May 11, 1858, and its village, platted in 1856 and somewhat changed in location when the railway was built in 1881, have a name that is borne also by a village in Virginia, and by villages and townships in twenty-five other states.

BISMARCK township, settled in 1867, organized July 24, 1874, was named by its German settlers in honor of the great Prussian statesman, "the

SIBLEY COUNTY 519

creator of German unity." He was born at Schönhausen, Prussia, April 1, 1815, and died at Friedrichsruh, July 30, 1898.

CORNISH township, settled in 1868, organized January 25, 1871, received this name on the recommendation of J. B. Wakefield, who settled here in 1869, "in memory of his native town in New Hampshire."

DRYDEN township, settled in 1854 and organized May 11, 1858, was at first called Williamstown, but was renamed by request of Hamilton Beatty and others, he being chairman of the first township board of supervisors. This name, in honor of the celebrated English poet and dramatist, John Dryden (b. 1631, d. 1700), is borne also by villages and townships in Maine, New York, Virginia, Michigan, and Arkansas.

FAXON township, first settled in May, 1852, organized May 11, 1858, and its former village, platted in April, 1857, were named for a member of its townsite company.

GAYLORD, a railway village in Dryden, platted in 1881, and GIBBON, a railway village in Severance, were named by officials of the Minneapolis and St. Louis railway company. Gaylord succeeded Henderson in 1915 as the county seat. Edward W. Gaylord, of Minneapolis, was master of transportation for this railway, 1874-77, and its superintendent, 1878-80. General John Gibbon (b. 1827; d. 1896) was temporarily stationed at Fort Snelling in 1878, and was its commandant during parts of 1880-82; was commander-in-chief of the Loyal Legion when he died.

GRAFTON township, settled in 1870 and organized in September, 1873, has a name that is borne by a county and a town in New Hampshire, and by villages and townships in seventeen other states.

GREEN ISLE township, settled in 1857, and organized May 11, 1858, received its name, referring to Ireland, "the Emerald Isle," by suggestion of Christopher Dolan, an Irish immigrant. The railway village of this name, in the adjacent section 18 of Washington, was platted in August, 1881. Lake Erin, next eastward from this village, testifies similarly to the loyal spirit of its settlers from Ireland.

HENDERSON township and its village, founded in 1852 and platted in 1855 by Joseph R. Brown, who is commemorated by Brown county, were named by him in honor of his mother and of her father, Andrew Henderson, of Frederick, Pa. During several years this village was Brown's home, and he founded and edited its first newspaper, the Henderson Democrat, 1857-61. It was the county seat until 1915, when the county offices were removed to Gaylord. It was incorporated as a town in 1855; as a borough, January 23, 1866; and as a city, March 23, 1891.

JESSENLAND township, settled in 1853, organized May 11, 1858, is "supposed to have received its name from the fact that Jesse Cameron was the first to arrive; it was for some time known as "Jesse's Land.'" (History, Minn. Valley, p. 428.)

KELSO township, settled in 1855-6 and organized in 1858, bears a name that was originally given by A. P. Walker, a surveyor, in 1854 or 1855, which "is of Scotch derivation," being the name of a town on the Tweed river in southern Scotland.

MOLTKE township, settled in 1875 and the latest organized in this county, August 21, 1878, was named by its German pioneers in honor of the famous Prussian general, Count von Moltke (b. 1800, d. 1891).

NEW AUBURN township, settled in 1855, organized May 11, 1858, and its village, platted in 1856, were named by settlers from Auburn, N. Y.

SEVERANCE township, settled in 1867-8 and organized in 1870, was at first called Clear Lake, for the lake crossed by its south line; but, because that name had been earlier given to another Minnesota township, it was renamed in honor of Martin Juan Severance, of Mankato. He was born at Shelburne Falls, Mass., December 24, 1826, and died in Mankato, Minn., July 11, 1907. He was admitted to practice law in 1853; came to this state in 1856, locating at Henderson; served in the Tenth Minnesota regiment, 1862-5, attaining the rank of captain; afterward lived in LeSueur till 1870, then removing to Mankato; was a representative in the legislature in 1862; judge of the Sixth judicial district, 1881-1900.

SIBLEY township, settled in 1856 and organized July 9, 1864, was named like the county, in honor of General Sibley.

TRANSIT township, settled in 1858, organized in 1866, has a unique name, as if from the transit instrument used for railway surveys.

WASHINGTON LAKE township, settled in 1854-5, organized May 11, 1858, bears the name of a large lake at its center, which "was so called from the fact that two of the first settlers on its borders were from Washington, D. C." (History, Minn. Valley, p. 435.)

WINTHROP, a railway village in Alfsborg and Transit townships, incorporated as a village before 1891 and as a city in 1910, was named by officers of the Minneapolis and St. Louis railway.

LAKES AND STREAMS.

The Minnesota river, forming the east border of Sibley county, and Clear lake in Severance, crossed by the south boundary, had the same Dakota or Sioux name, printed "Mini sotah" on Nicollet's map (Mini, water, sotah, whitishly clouded).

High Island lake, the largest in the county, has a small but high island of glacial drift in its northern part, rising 20 or 30 feet above the lake. The same name is given likewise to the outflowing High Island creek, being partly a translation of the Sioux name, recorded by Nicollet as Witakantu, meaning Plum island (Wita, island, kantu, plum trees).

Nicollet also noted the Sioux name, Wanyecha Oju river, and its translation, Rush river, which, with its North and South branches, drains the southern part of the county.

Bevens creek, the outlet of Washington lake in the township of that name, flows northeastward into Carver county.

Buffalo creek, lying mainly in McLeod county, traverses also the north edge of New Auburn.

SIBLEY COUNTY 521

Round Grove lake, giving its name to a township of McLeod county, lies partly in the northeast corner of Grafton.

Other lakes having names on maps include Rice's lake, in section 34, Sibley, named for Andrew Rice, a homesteader who settled at its east end and made proof of his claim in 1860; Sand lake and Cummings or Mud lake, on the west line of Alfsborg, lying respectively in the course of the South and North branches of Rush river, the latter being named for A. Cummings, a pioneer who built a hotel there for travelers on the old road from Henderson to Fort Ridgely; Cottonwood and Swan lakes, respectively in the west parts of Cornish and Severance; Alkali lake, having somewhat bitter water, in Moltke; Ward's lake, on the north line of Bismarck; Buck's lake, in the north part of Grafton, named in honor of Adam Buck, of Henderson; Indian lake, in section 21, Transit; Titlow, Mud, Beatty, Duff, and Kirby lakes, in Dryden; Silver lake, in Jessenland; Kerry lake, in sections 20 and 21, Faxon; Lake Erin, or Mud lake, in Washington; Lake Severance, in Green Isle, named, like a township, in honor of Judge Severance, who in June, 1858, made proof for a homestead in section 17, beside this lake; and Fadden, Hahn, and Schilling lakes, in New Auburn.

Adam Buck was born in Germany, October 12, 1830; came to the United States, and in 1852 settled as a farmer in this county; removed to Henderson in 1862, and opened a drug store; served in the Sioux war, 1862, and as a captain in the Eleventh Minnesota regiment, 1864-5; was county surveyor, 1868-79; was a representative in the legislature in 1862, 1868, and 1872, and a state senator in 1867; died at his home in Henderson, about 1895.

Robert Beatty was born in the north of Ireland in 1803; came with his parents to Pennsylvania; and removed, with his several sons, in 1857 to Dryden in this county. His son Samuel B. Beatty, born in Pennsylvania in 1841, settled in Dryden in 1857; served in the Tenth Minnesota regiment, 1863-5; was a representative in the legislature in 1877.

Duff lake was named for Bernard Duff, a farmer who made proof on his homestead there in October, 1860.

Joseph Patterson Kirby was born in Ireland, August 6, 1838; came to the United States when very young, with his parents; settled as a homestead farmer in New Auburn, 1856; served in the Third Minnesota regiment, 1861-65, attaining the rank of first lieutenant; lived in Le Sueur, 1865-74; removed to Henderson in 1874, and was judge of probate for Sibley county, 1875-94.

Fadden lake was named for James Fadden, who in May, 1869, made proof of his homestead at its north side in section 14, New Auburn.

Hahn lake was similarly named for William Hahn, who was born in Prussia in 1849; came to America at the age of five years, with his parents; and settled in New Auburn in 1879, beside this lake.

Schilling lake commemorates John Schilling, whose homestead was the southwest quarter of section 5 in this township.

STEARNS COUNTY

This county, established February 20, 1855, was named for Hon. Charles Thomas Stearns, member of the council of the Territorial Legislature, 1854 and 1855. The name, however, was decided by a mistake, told in the "History of the Upper Mississippi Valley," as follows: "The bill, as originally introduced, bore the name of Stevens county, in honor of Governor Stevens, then prominently connected with the survey of the Northern Pacific railroad and passed both branches of the Legislature in that shape; but in the enrollment of the bill the change occurred from Stevens to Stearns, and when discovered, it was concluded best to let the matter stand, as the name was still in the line of honorable mention, and Mr. Stearns well entitled to public recognition in this way."

Stearns was born in Pittsfield, Mass., January 9, 1807; came from Illinois to Minnesota in 1849, and first settled in St. Anthony; thence removed in 1855 to St. Cloud, the county seat of Stearns county, where he was proprietor of a hotel during fourteen years; and, about the year 1870, having sold his hotel to be one of the buildings of the State Normal School, he removed to Mobile, Ala. Later he resided in New Orleans, La., and died there May 22, 1898. He was the last survivor of the founders of the Masonic Grand Lodge of Minnesota.

Townships, Villages, and Cities.

Information of the origins and meanings of names has been gathered from "History of the Upper Mississippi Valley," 1881, which has pages 369-483 for this county; "History of Stearns County," by William Bell Mitchell, 1915, 1536 pages, in two volumes, continuously paged; from the author of this county history, also from Hon. Charles A. Gilman and John Coates, each of St. Cloud, the county seat, interviewed during a visit there in May, 1916; and from Edwin Clark, of Minneapolis, formerly of Melrose for twenty-five years, 1867-92.

ALBANY township, settled in 1863, organized in 1868, and its railway village, incorporated in January, 1890, have a name that is borne by the capital of New York, and by townships, villages, and cities in seventeen other states.

ASHLEY, the most northwestern township, settled in 1865 and organized in 1870, received its name from Ashley creek, flowing through this township, which was named in 1856 by Edwin Whitefield, an eastern artist traveling to Stearns, Todd, and Kandiyohi counties, in honor of his friend, O. D. Ashley, of Boston and New York city. Ossian Doolittle Ashley was born in Townshend, Vt., April 9, 1821; was a member of the Boston Stock Exchange, 1846-57, being its president in 1856-7; removed to

New York city in 1857, and was a member of its Stock Exchange; was elected president of the Wabash Western railway in 1887.

AVON township, settled in 1856 and organized in 1866, and its railway village, founded in 1873 and incorporated in February, 1900, bear the name of three rivers in England and two in Wales, and of villages and townships in Maine, Massachusetts, Wisconsin, and twelve other states of our Union.

BELGRADE, a village of the Soo railway in the west edge of Crow River township, has the name of the capital of Serbia, of a township and its village in Maine, and of villages in Missouri, Nebraska, and Montana.

BROCKWAY township, settled in 1855 and organized in 1858, was then called Winnebago, but was renamed as now in 1860, after a post office established in September, 1857, honoring a lumberman and farmer there.

BROOTEN, a railway village in North Fork township, founded with the building of the Soo line in 1886, was named for one of its Scandinavian farmers.

CLEARWATER, a village lying for its greater part in the township of this name in Wright county, reaching also into Lynden in Stearns county, received its name from the river there tributary to the Mississippi, called on Nicollet's map "Kawakomik or Clear Water R."

COLD SPRING, a village in Wakefield, was platted in the fall of 1856. "The vicinity abounds in natural mineral springs, and the two companies that have made the water famous over a wide territory do a business amounting to some $20,000 a year." (History of this county, p. 1333.)

COLLEGEVILLE township, settled in 1858, organized in January, 1880, is named for St. John's College, which was chartered by the legislature March 6, 1857. The college was opened in the fall of that year, being at first in St. Cloud, but in 1867 it was removed to its present site, in section 1, Collegeville. "In 1880 the name of the Monastery, St. Louis on the Lake, was changed to correspond with the name of the college, . . . as St. John's Abbey." (History, Upper Mississippi Valley, p. 373.) By an act of the legislature, February 27, 1883, the legal name of the college was changed to St. John's University. Its railway village, named also Collegeville, one mile and a half distant, is in section 32, St. Wendel.

CROW LAKE township, settled in 1861, organized in 1868, and CROW RIVER township, settled in 1860 and organized in 1877, are named respectively for Crow lake, in the former township, and the North branch of Crow river, which flows across the township bearing that name. The stream, belonging partly to several counties, is fully noticed in the first chapter and again in the chapter of Crow Wing county.

EDEN LAKE township, settled in 1856, organized February 16, 1867, and EDEN VALLEY railway village, on the south line of this township and reaching into Manannah in Meeker county, received these names by choice of their people, expressing their very high admiration. The lake of this name lies mostly in sections 25 and 26, and outflows northward to the Sauk river.

ELROSA is a village of the Soo railway in Lake George township.

FAIR HAVEN township, organized April 5, 1859, and its village, platted in May, 1856, received their name from an exclamation of Thomas C. Partridge, "This is a fair haven!" when in the spring of 1856 he came there in an exploring tramp from Clearwater. (County History, p. 1267.)

FARMING township, settled in 1858 and organized March 11, 1873, has a rare name, adopted in allusion to the occupation of all its people.

FREEPORT, a Great Northern railway village in Oak township, incorporated in September, 1892, was named by settlers who came from the city of Freeport in Illinois.

GEORGEVILLE is a Soo railway village in Crow River township.

GETTY township was organized in 1865. "John J. Getty, in honor of whom the town is named, was undoubtedly the first permanent settler. He came on the 6th of July, 1857, and settled on section nineteen, in what has since been known as Getty's Grove." (History, Upper Mississippi, p. 416.) He was born in Onondaga county, N. Y., September 15, 1821.

GREENWALD is a village of the Soo railway in Grove township. Wald is a German word, meaning a grove.

GROVE township, settled in the fall of 1858, was organized in 1867. It had previously been a part of Oak Grove township, organized in 1860, which included this surveyed township and another next east. When they took separate organizations, in 1867, they adopted respectively the names Grove and Oak.

HOLDING township, organized in 1870, was named in honor of its first permanent settler, who made a homestead claim in May, 1868. Six years later he platted the village of Holding's Ford, giving it this name from its fording place of the South stream of the Two rivers. For its post office the name is printed as Holdingford, and the village now includes a later village site platted on the east side of the river, which was at first named Wardeville. Randolph Holding was born in McHenry county, Ill., July 27, 1844; came to Minnesota in 1861, settling at Clearwater; served in the Eighth Minnesota regiment, 1862-65; engaged in freighting from St. Cloud to the Red river, 1866-8; settled in this township, 1868; was the township clerk, 1870-81; and a representative in the legislature, 1872.

KIMBALL PRAIRIE, a Soo railway village in Maine Prairie township, founded in 1886, incorporated in February, 1892, was named in honor of Frye Kimball, an early farmer there.

KRAIN township, settled in 1868, and organized in 1872, bears the name of a province of southern Austria, also called Carniola. This was the native province of Rev. Francis Xavier Pirec (or Pierz), who was a leader in founding St. John's College and in bringing German colonists to Stearns county and other adjoining counties, for whom Pierz township in Morrison county was named.

LAKE GEORGE township, settled in 1856 and organized in 1877, has a lake so named in honor of George Kraemer, one of its pioneer settlers. It was called Lake Henry by the expedition of Woods and Pope in 1849.

STEARNS COUNTY 525

LAKE HENRY township, settled in 1855 and organized in 1869, took the name of a lake in sections 10 and 15, which has been drained. This lake name, as noted for the last preceding township, was received from the expedition of Woods and Pope, whose route passed the north ends of Lakes David and Henry, named by their journals and maps, identifiable respectively as Lakes Henry and George of later maps.

LE SAUK township, settled in 1854, organized in 1860, received this French name, meaning "the Sauk," from the same derivation as Sauk Rapids, the Sauk river, Sauk Center, and Lake Osakis, before explained in the chapter for Benton county.

LUXEMBURG township, settled in 1861 and organized in 1866, was named by its German settlers for the province and city in western Germany.

Luxemburg village or hamlet is eight miles northeast from this township, being in the west part of St. Augusta.

LYNDEN township, settled in 1853, organized January 15, 1859, was then named Lyndon, like townships in Vermont and Wisconsin, and like townships and villages in five other states, honoring Josiah Lyndon (b. 1704, d. 1778), governor of Rhode Island in 1768-69, a patriot for the American revolution. From near its earliest record, however, the name has been spelled Lynden, in analogy with the linden tree.

MAINE PRAIRIE township, organized in 1858, was named by its many pioneers from Maine, who came as its first settlers in 1856. One of its villages or hamlets, named MAINE PRAIRIE CORNERS, founded in 1865-6, is on the site of a stockade and fort constructed in 1862 as a refuge from the Sioux outbreak. The name of this township was proposed by Aaron Scribner, who came from Aroostook county, Maine, and who later removed to Otter Tail county and there proposed the name of Maine township. He died in Washington state in March, 1916.

MEIRE GROVE is a village in Grove township, two miles north of Greenwald.

MELROSE township, settled in 1857 and organized in 1866, was named by Warren Adley, in honor of Melissa (or Melvina) and Rose, who were his daughters or were other near kindred or friends. The village of Melrose, platted in December, 1871, by Edwin and William H. Clark, cousins, was the terminus of the railroad from November 18, 1872, until 1878, was incorporated March 3, 1881, and received a city charter in 1898. This is elsewhere a frequent name, received from the town of Melrose in Scotland, having ruins of an ancient abbey, near the home of Sir Walter Scott. It is the name of a city in Massachusetts, and of villages and townships in seventeen other states.

MILLWOOD township, settled in 1866 and organized in 1871, has a name that is borne also by villages in Massachusetts, New York, Pennsylvania, and seven other states.

MUNSON township, settled in 1856, organized in 1859, has the name of villages in Ohio and Pennsylvania.

NEW MUNICH, a village in Oak township, first had a post office in 1859. "It received its name from a Bavarian hunter, who came from Munich, Bavaria, and stayed with the first settlers for several years." (History of the county, p. 1298.)

NEW PAYNESVILLE, platted as a village on the Soo railway, was organized in 1890, being situated about a mile east of the previous village of Paynesville. In the fall of 1904 it received the old townsite by annexation, and in 1905 its name was changed to Paynesville by popular vote.

NORTH FORK township, settled in 1864 and organized in 1867, is crossed by the North fork of Crow river.

OAK township, settled about 1856, organized in 1860, was then called Oak Grove. Its present name dates from 1867, when Grove township, formerly a part of Oak Grove, was separately organized, as before noted.

PAYNESVILLE township, organized September 20, 1867, had previously been included in Verdale. Edwin E. Payne was its first settler, coming in 1857 and making a homestead claim, on which in the same year he platted and named the first village site. This village, incorporated in 1887, was annexed to New Paynesville in 1904; and the resultant village in March, 1905, dropped "New" from its name.

PEARL LAKE, a hamlet adjoining the lake of this name in the north part of Maine Prairie, founded by the building of a church in 1889-90, received a post office in 1901, named Marty, which has been discontinued.

RAYMOND township, settled in 1860, but deserted from 1862 to 1866, was organized in 1867, being named in honor of Liberty B. Raymond, one of its early settlers.

RICHMOND, a village on the Sauk river in Munson, bears the surname of one of its earliest settlers; and it also partly commemorates Reuben Richardson, by whom this village was platted in 1856.

ROCKVILLE township, settled in 1855, organized June 25, 1860, and its village, platted in 1856, received their name from the outcrops of granite adjoining the Sauk river and Mill creek.

ROSCOE, a Great Northern railway village, formerly called Zion, is on the east side of Zion township.

ST. AUGUSTA township, settled in 1854 and organized in 1859, was originally called Berlin and later Neenah, but in 1863 adopted the present name, which had been given by Father Pierz in 1856 to the first church here. The village of St. Augusta, first platted in 1855, has a station of the Great Northern railway.

ST. CLOUD, the county seat, first settled in October, 1851, was platted in the fall of 1854 by John L. Wilson, "familiarly called the 'Father of St. Cloud.'" The History of the county says: "The choosing of St. Cloud as the name for his new town was due to the fact that while reading the life of Napoleon I, Mr. Wilson had observed that the Empress Josephine spent much of her time at the magnificent palace at St. Cloud, a few miles out of Paris, a circumstance which appealed so strongly to his fancy that he adopted it."

STEARNS COUNTY 527

Saint Cloud, or Clodvald or Chlodvald, was the youngest son of Clodomir, the king of Orleans, who was the son of Clovis. The History of France, by Guizot (eight volumes), tells in its first volume how the two brothers of Clodvald were murdered by their uncles, king Childebert of Paris and king Clotaire of Soissons, in A. D. 524. The murdered brothers were ten and seven years old, and they were greatly mourned by their grandmother, Queen Clotilde. Of the younger brother, Saint Cloud, Guizot wrote: "The third, named Clodvald (who died about the year 560, after having founded, near Paris, a monastary called after him St. Cloud), could not be caught, and was saved by some gallant men. He, disdaining a terrestrial kingdom, dedicated himself to the Lord, was shorn by his own hand, and became a churchman; he devoted himself wholly to good works, and died a priest. And the two kings divided equally between them the kingdom of Clodomir."

St. Cloud was incorporated as a town March 1, 1856, and as a city March 6, 1868. A more ample city charter was granted by the legislature April 13, 1889. This township was organized in 1858. The city extends across the Mississippi, including wards 5 and 6 in Benton county, and ward 7 in Sherburne county. Alluding to the granite quarries in the wards east of the river, St. Cloud is called "the Granite City;" and in 1916 the Street Department automobile, used for street sprinkling, bore the popular slogan, conspicuously painted in large letters, "Busy, gritty, Granite City."

St. Joseph township, settled in 1854, organized in 1858, and its village, founded in 1855 and incorporated January 29, 1890, bear the name of its church.

St. Martin township, settled in 1857 and organized in 1863, and its village, founded in 1866 and incorporated in 1891, are named in honor of St. Martin, bishop of Tours, who was born about the year 316, for whom November 11 is celebrated as Martinmas.

St. Stephen is a village in Brockway, incorporated May 2, 1914, including the former townsite named Brockway, which was platted in 1857.

St. Wendel township, settled in 1854 or earlier, was organized under the name of Hancock in the spring of 1868, but was renamed as now in the summer of the same year.

Sartell, a village on the Mississippi in Le Sauk, at the mouth of Watab river, opposite to the great paper mill of the Watab Pulp and Paper Company, is named in honor of Joseph B. Sartell, the first settler of Le Sauk, who came in 1854, built a sawmill in 1857, and continued to reside here, with seven sons, until his death, January 27, 1913. He was born at East Pepperell, Mass., January 15, 1826. The paper mill and dam of the Mississippi were built in 1905-07, and the bridge over the Mississippi in 1914. This village, including the mill and railway station in Benton county and the workmen's homes mainly in Stearns county, was incorporated in November, 1907.

SAUK CENTER township, settled in 1856 and organized in 1858, received this name in allusion to its central location on the Sauk river, between the Sauk rapids of the Mississippi and Lake Osakis, which likewise was named for its former occupation by a small band of Sauk Indians, as related in the chapter of Benton county. The village of this township, platted in 1863, was incorporated February 12, 1876, and received a city charter March 5, 1889.

SPRING HILL township, settled in 1857, organized July 10, 1871, was named from its springs and low morainic hills.

STILES, a Great Northern station in Ashley, five miles west of Sauk Center, commemorates A. M. Stiles, a pioneer farmer. He was born in Steuben county, N. Y., April 10, 1838; came to Minnesota in 1862, settling first in Rochester; was a miner in Idaho, 1864-6; removed in 1866 to the farm in section 11, Ashley, which was afterward his home; was chairman of the first board of township supervisors, 1870, and was town clerk, 1871-80; was a representative in the legislature, 1879.

VERDALE was a large township or district, organized in 1858, originally including St. Martin, Spring Hill, Lake Henry, Zion, and Paynesville. All its surveyed townships, when separately organized, took the other names here noted.

WAITE PARK, a western suburb of St. Cloud, containing the Great Northern railway shops, which were built in 1890-91, was incorporated as a village March 20, 1893, being named in honor of Henry Chester Waite, of St. Cloud. He was born in Rensselaerville, N. Y., June 30, 1830; was graduated at Union College, Schenectady, in 1851, and was admitted to practice law in 1853; came to Minnesota in 1855, settling in St. Cloud as its first lawyer; later engaged in banking, flour milling, and as a merchant; was register of the U. S. land office, 1865-69; was a member of the state constitutional convention, 1857, a representative in the legislature, 1863, and a state senator in 1870-71 and 1883-85; died on his farm near the city of St. Cloud, November 15, 1912. He owned flouring mills at Cold Spring and in Clearwater.

WAKEFIELD township, settled in 1855, and organized May 27, 1858, was at first called Springfield, but was renamed as now in 1870, in honor of Samuel Wakefield, chairman of its first board of supervisors in 1858.

ZION township, settled in 1860 by German Lutherans, organized in 1867, is named from the hill or plateau of Mount Zion, the highest part of the city of Jerusalem, praised in the 48th psalm for the beauty of its situation. The railway village of this township, formerly called Zion, is renamed Roscoe.

LAKES AND STREAMS.

The rapids and islands of the Mississippi at St. Cloud and southeastward are noted in the chapter for Sherburne county.

In the foregoing pages, attention has been given to the names of Ashley creek, Clearwater river, Crow lake and river, with the North fork of this river, Eden lake, the South stream of Two rivers, Lakes George and Henry, Pearl lake, and the Sauk river.

Watab river, joining the Mississippi at Sartell, received this name from jack pines growing near its mouth. The long and slender roots of this pine, as also of the tamarack, were called watab by the Ojibways and were used for sewing their birch bark canoes. In the treaty of 1825 at Prairie du Chien, this river was designated as a part of the boundary agreed upon to be a dividing line between the country of the Ojibways and that of the Sioux. The entire course of this boundary was noted by Prof. N. H. Winchell in "The Aborigines of Minnesota" (page 617).

Other tributaries of the Mississippi in this county, smaller than the Sauk, Watab, and Clearwater rivers, include the southern one of the Two rivers, which was crossed by "Holding's ford," with its affluent Hay creek; Spunk brook, translated from the Ojibway name, "Sagatagon or Spunk R." on Nicollet's map in 1843, meaning exceptionally dry and shredded wood or punk, used as tinder for making a fire; St. Augusta creek, in the township of this name, also called Johnson's creek, in honor of L. P. Johnson, a pioneer who came here in 1854 and was the first chairman of the township supervisors, in 1859; and Plum creek, in Lynden, named for its wild plum trees.

Sauk river receives from its north side Adley and Getchell creeks, named for prominent pioneers; and from its south side Silver and Ashley creeks, in Ashley township, Stony creek in Spring Hill, another stream which is the outlet of Eden lake and of the Rice lakes, and Mill creek at the village of Rockville.

Warren Adley was born in Maine in 1822; came to Minnesota in 1856; served in the Fourth Minnesota regiment in the civil war; kept a hotel first at Melrose, and later at Osakis; was a representative in the legislature in 1873.

Nathaniel Getchell was born in Wesley, Maine, November 9, 1828; came to Minnesota in 1852, and three years later was one of the founders of Brockway township in this county; served in the Minnesota Mounted Rangers, 1862-3.

From the township of Crow Lake flow Skunk river or creek, the outlet of Skunk or Tamarack lake, and the Middle fork or branch of Crow river, having its source in Crow lake.

Lakes that are named on the maps, in addition to such as have already been noticed, are Lakes Louisa, Maria, Caroline, and Augusta, and Clearwater, Grass, and Center lakes, a series through which the Clearwater river flows on the southern boundary of Fair Haven and Lynden; another Lake Maria, Crooked and Long lakes, Holman's lake, and Belle and Warner lakes, on Plum creek; Beaver and Block lakes, in the southwest corner of St. Augusta; Lake Lura and Otter lake, in Fair Haven; Goodner's and Day's lakes, Island lake, Carnelian and Willow lakes, and School lake, named from its situation in the school section 36, all being in Maine Prairie; Grand and Pleasant lakes, in Rockville; Cedar Island lake, Great Northern, Kray's, Park, and Knaus lakes, on the course of the Sauk river in Wakefield; Mud, Eden, Brown's, and Long lakes, in a series running from south to north through the east part of Eden Lake township; the large Rice lake and a small Pirz lake, in the west part of that township; Big lake, Schroeder, Becker, and Horseshoe lakes, in Munson, the last being on the Sauk river; Lake Koronis in Paynesville, extending south into Meeker county; Fish, Grass, and Halvorson lakes, in Crow Lake township; Sand lake, in the southeast corner of Raymond; Lake Isabelle, and Black Oak and Ellering lakes, in Grove township; a little Lake George, in the city of St. Cloud; Kraemer lake, in St. Joseph; Lake St. Louis and Stump lakes, adjoining St. John's University, and Island lake, Big Fish lake, Long and Sand lakes, Pitts, Thomas, and Kreighl lakes, and Big Watab and Little Watab lakes, all in Collegeville, the last two being on the South fork of Watab river; another Watab lake, on the middle course of this river in St. Wendel, and yet another and smaller Watab lake, on a northern tributary of this river, in sections 8 and 17, Le Sauk; Shepard lake, in Brockway; Achman and Kepper lakes, Lakes Anna and Lizzie, Linneman and Minnie lakes, and the Big, Middle, and Lower Spunk lakes, in the south half of Avon; Pelican and Pine lakes, in northwestern Avon; the large Two River lake, in Holding; Clear and Mud lakes, Big and Little Rice lakes, Lake Henn, another Mud lake, and Sand lake, in Farming; North lake, at the north side of Albany village; Vos lake, Lake St. Mary, and Lake St. Anna, in Krain; Gravel lake, in section 1, St. Martin; Sand and Getchell lakes, Lake Maria, Frevel's and Uhlenkott's lakes, in Oak township; King's lake, Long lake, Swamp, Cedar, and Wolf lakes, in the south half of Millwood, and Lake Mary and Birch Bark lakes, crossed by its north line; Lake Sylvia and Middle Birch lake, in the northeast part of Melrose, the former being named for the wife of Alfred Townsend; and McCormick, Cedar, and Sauk lakes, the last being on the Sauk river, in Sauk Center township.

Hills and Prairies.

Among many morainic hills from 50 feet, or less, to about 100 feet in height, or rarely 150 to 200 feet high, occurring in numerous long tracts or belts in this county, maps name only Cheney hill, in section 1, Melrose.

Winnebago prairie, also known as Brockway prairie, adjoins the Mississippi for about four or five miles in Le Sauk and Brockway; and the North prairie similarly borders the river in the northeast part of Brockway, continuing into Morrison county.

Besides these relatively small prairie areas of the valley drift in the generally wooded part of this county, it has a large area of prairie west of Richmond and southwest of the Sauk river, continuous with the great prairie region of southern and western Minnesota.

STEELE COUNTY

Established February 20, 1855, this county was named in honor of Franklin Steele, a prominent pioneer of Minneapolis. He was born in Chester county, Pennsylvania, May 12, 1813; came to Fort Snelling as sutler of that frontier post, in 1838; became owner of valuable lands at the falls of St. Anthony; and was active in improvements of the water power, and in the building up of St. Anthony and Minneapolis. He was a charter member of the Minnesota Historical Society, and at the time of his death was chairman of its Department of American History. In 1851 Mr. Steele was elected by the Legislature as one of the first board of regents of the University of Minnesota; and during all his later life he was identified with the promotion of many public interests, but never held political office. He died in Minneapolis, September 10, 1880.

Biographic notes, with portraits, of Franklin Steele and his associates in founding the lumber industries on the upper Mississippi, with the sawmills of Minneapolis, are given in the M. H. S. Collections (Volume IX, 1901, pages 325-362).

Townships and Villages.

Information of names has been gathered from "History of Steele and Waseca Counties," 1887, 756 pages; "History of Rice and Steele Counties," by Franklyn Curtiss-Wedge, 1910, having pages 629-1026 for this county; and Hon. Charles S. Crandall, Jesse Healey, Willard E. Martin, and W. E. Kenyon, judge of probate, these being interviewed at Owatonna, the county seat, during visits there in April and October, 1916.

ANDERSON is a railway station in Havana, seven miles east of Owatonna. Its village or hamlet is called Lysne (pronounced in two syllables). Each is the name of Scandinavian residents there.

AURORA township, first settled in 1856, organized February 17, 1857, was named by Hon. Amos Coggswell for the city of Aurora in Illinois. He was born in Boscawen, N. H., September 29, 1825; settled in 1856 on a homestead claim in this township; removed to Owatonna, and was a lawyer there; was speaker of the legislature in 1859, and a state senator in 1872-75; died in Owatonna, November 15, 1892. The name Aurora, from the Latin language, means the morning, or especially the redness of the dawning light.

BERLIN township, organized February 17, 1857, was named from the city of Berlin in Wisconsin. Twenty-three other states of our Union have townships and villages or cities likewise named after the capital of Germany.

BIXBY, a railway village in the south edge of Aurora, founded about 1890, was named in honor of John Bixby, who was born in Moretown, Vt., January 28, 1814, and died in Aurora January 15, 1890. He came to Minnesota in 1856, settling on a homestead claim a mile west of the site of this village. His eldest son, Jacob S. Bixby, on whose farm the new railway station was located, was the first postmaster there. The name Oak Glen, to be later noticed, was proposed for the post office, but was changed to Bixby by Hon. Mark H. Dunnell of Owatonna, member in Congress for this district.

BLOOMING PRAIRIE township, settled in 1856, was organized in 1867, being then called Oak Glen, as further noted in this list. The township was renamed as now in January, 1873, taking the name of its railway village, which was platted in 1868. It is euphonious, referring to the abundant flowers of this prairie region, and it has the merit of uniqueness, no other village or post office in the world having adopted this name.

CLINTON FALLS township, settled in 1854, organized May 11, 1858, and its village, platted in 1855, are named from the falls of the Straight river, having 10 feet head at its dam here. Nine other states have counties named Clinton, and thirty states have townships and villages or cities of this name, mostly commemorating George and DeWitt Clinton, who were governors of New York, the latter being also the projector of the Erie canal.

DEERFIELD township, first settled in May, 1855, and organized in the spring of 1858, has a name that is also borne by townships and villages in New Hampshire, Massachusetts, New York, Ohio, Wisconsin, and nine other states.

ELLENDALE, a village of the Chicago, Rock Island and Pacific railway in Berlin, was platted in the autumn of 1900 and was incorporated August 15, 1901, its site having been selected by the railway officials, C. J. Ives being president. "The name was given in memory of Mrs. C. J. Ives, who died a few years previous to this time. She was the laboring man's friend. She seemed to know every section man and every brakeman on the road; and her many acts of tender, thoughtful kindness endeared her to the hundreds of employees. Her maiden name was Ellen Dale, so this beautiful, prosperous village will perpetuate the memory of that good woman." (History, 1910, p. 944).

HAVANA township, settled in 1855, was organized February 27, 1857, being then called Lafayette. In September, 1858, the name was changed to Freeman, and in the next month to Dover. Thus it continued till 1869, when it was renamed Havana, on request of Elijah Easton, for Havana, the county seat of Mason county, Illinois. As a Spanish word, meaning a haven, a harbor, it became the name of the chief city and capital of Cuba. The village of Havana was founded and so named in 1867, with the completion of the Winona and St. Peter railroad.

STEELE COUNTY 533

HOPE is a station of the Rock Island railway in the west edge of Somerset.

LEMOND township, settled in 1856 and organized in April, 1858, bears probably a personal surname, but it is nowhere else used as a geographic name, excepting a railway station in Queensland, Australia.

LYSNE is a Scandinavian name, in two syllables, of a railway village in Havana, before noted as Anderson, which is its official railway name.

MEDFORD township, first settled in 1853, was organized August 29, 1855, and its village was platted in 1856. The first township meeting was held at the house of William K. Colling, an Englishman who had come here in 1854 and taken a homestead claim, but who after several years residence returned finally to England. "At a meeting of the settlers to consult upon a name wherewith to christen the town, Mr. Colling said that he had a son who was born on board the ship Medford, and was named Medford, in honor of the ship, and proposed that the town should be named Medford in honor of the boy, which proposition was unanimously adopted." (History, 1887, p. 303.) This is the name of a township and hamlet in Maine, a city in Massachusetts, and villages and townships in five other states.

MERIDEN township, settled in 1855 and organized in 1857-58, was named by F. J. Stephens, one of its founders, from the city of Meriden in Connecticut, which is famed for its manufacture of silver ware and thence is sometimes called the "Silver City." The railway village of Meriden was founded in 1867.

MERTON township, settled in 1855, was at first called Union Prairie, but was organized in 1857-8 as Orion, and was renamed Merton in 1862, probably for the township and village of Merton in Wisconsin. This is the name of a village in Surrey, England, which in the Middle Ages had a famous Augustinian abbey.

OAK GLEN was a stage coach station at the lakes of this name in the northeast part of the present township of Blooming Prairie, where a village site named Oak Glen was platted in 1856. Thence the township took this name when it was organized in 1867, but it was renamed Blooming Prairie, as before noted, in 1873.

OWATONNA, the county seat, earliest settled in 1854 and platted in September, 1855, was incorporated as a town August 9, 1858, and as a city February 23, 1865. The township was organized, with its present area, February 27, 1857. This was the Dakota or Sioux name of the Straight river, which is its translation. The river was mapped, but not named, on the map of Minnesota Territory in 1855; on the early state maps, in 1860 and 1869, it is called Owatonna river; but in 1870 it is named Straight river.

PRATT, a railway hamlet in the northwest corner of Aurora, was named in honor of William A. Pratt, an adjacent farmer.

SACO is a Rock Island railway station six miles south of Owatonna, named from the Saco river and city in Maine.

SOMERSET township, first settled in 1855 and organized in 1857-8, received the name of its first post office which was established in 1857, with Dr. Thomas Kenyon as postmaster, who came in the spring of 1856. The name of the settlement and post office is said to have come from the overturning of his tent by a high wind, when dinner was ready in it. The somersault of the tent, with change of spelling, became the township name. It is a common geographic name, thus spelled Somerset, for a county in England, counties in Maine, New Jersey, Pennsylvania, and Maryland, and villages and townships in fifteen states of our Union.

SUMMIT township, settled in the summer of 1856, organized May 10, 1858, has near its south line the summit or water divide between the sources of Straight river and Geneva lake in Freeborn county, which outflows southward to the Cedar river.

LAKES AND STREAMS.

Straight river, translated from its Sioux name, Owatonna, as before noted, has been said to be so named "in derision, as it is about the crookedest river in the state" (Stennett, Place Names of the Chicago and Northwestern Railways, 1908, p. 11) ; but, while the stream meanders, the general course of its valley is remarkably straight, from south to north.

Its tributaries from the east are the outlet of the three Oak Glen lakes and of Rickert lake, in Blooming Prairie; Turtle creek, four miles south of Owatonna; Maple creek, flowing from Rice lake, named for its wild rice, crossed by the east line of Havana; and Rush creek, flowing northwest into Rice county.

From the west this river receives the outlet of Lonergan, Beaver, and Mud lakes, in Berlin, and Crane creek, which flows through Bradley lake, on the line between Meriden and Deerfield.

Only three other lakes bearing names in this county remain to be noted, these being Wilker or Willert lake or slough, now drained, in section 6, Lemond, and Pelican and Swan lakes in Deerfield. The last two, with the adjacent Crane creek, tell of large wild birds that formerly were frequent here.

STEVENS COUNTY

Established February 20, 1862, this county was named in honor of Isaac Ingalls Stevens, who in 1853 commanded the expedition making the northern surveys for a Pacific railroad. The expedition started from St. Paul and traveled to the present sites of Sauk Rapids and St. Cloud, and by White Bear (now Minnewaska) and Elbow lakes, to the Bois des Sioux river, thus passing near the northeast corner of this county. Stevens was born in Andover, Mass., March 28, 1818; was graduated at West Point in 1839; served in the Mexican war; was governor of Washington Territory, 1853-57; was a delegate to Congress, 1857-61; and was a gallant leader for the Union in the civil war, entering it as colonel of the 79th Regiment of New York Volunteers, known as the Highlanders; attained the rank of major general, July 4, 1862; and lost his life in the battle of Chantilly, in Virginia, on the first day of September in the same year. An earlier attempt to give his name to a county of Minnesota, in 1855, was frustrated by a clerical error in the enrollment of the legislative act, which changed it to Stearns county.

Townships and Villages.

Information for the origins and meanings of names has been received from a pamphlet, "Stevens County, Minnesota, Its Villages, History," etc., 22 pages, published in 1879 by the Board of Trade of Morris; "Illustrated Album of Biography of Pope and Stevens Counties," 1888, having pages 367-530 for this county; and from Edwin J. Jones, a life member of the Minnesota Historical Society, who has resided in Morris since 1878, and A. L. Stenger, judge of probate, each being interviewed at Morris, the county seat, during a visit there in May, 1916.

ALBERTA, a railway village in Scott township, formerly called Wheeler, was renamed in honor of the wife of E. B. Lindsey, a farmer there.

BAKER township, originally called Potsdam, has a common personal surname, which is also borne by counties in Georgia and Florida, a county and city in Oregon, and villages in eight other states.

CHOKIO (accented on the second syllable, like Ohio) is a railway village in Baker. This name is a Dakota or Sioux word, meaning the middle.

DARNEN township, first settled at a stage station in section 12 by Henry Gager in 1866, has many immigrants from Ireland, who may have proposed this name, but its use elsewhere as either a geographic or personal name has not been ascertained. The site of Gager's station, at the crossing of the Pomme de Terre river on a state road from Glenwood to Brown's

Valley, was later occupied by the Riverside mill, owned by Hon. H. W. Stone and Company.

DONNELLY township, and its railway village, founded in 1872 and at first called Douglas, are named in honor of Ignatius Donnelly, the distinguished politician and author, who owned a farm in section 31, Rendsville, about a mile east of this village. He is also honored by the name of a township in Marshall county, for which a biographic sketch has been presented.

ELDORADO township has a Spanish name, meaning literally "the gilded," which is borne by a county in California, a city in Kansas, and villages in ten other states.

EVERGLADE township, originally called Potsdam, bears a unique name, received from the Everglades in southern Florida, a large marshy region which has much area of water from 1 to 10 feet deep, inclosing "thousands of little islands, covered with dense thickets of palmetto, cypress, oaks, vines, and shrubs, and in part inhabited by remnants of the Seminole tribe of Indians."

FRAMNAS township is settled mostly by Scandinavians, who selected this name. It is only used elsewhere, as a geographic name, for a cape near the Antartic circle in West Antartica.

HANCOCK, a village of the Great Northern railway in the north edge of Moore township, founded in 1871 when this railway line was completed to Morris, received its name in honor of Joseph Woods Hancock, who was born in Orford, N. H., April 4, 1816, and died in Minneapolis, October 24, 1907. He came to Red Wing in 1849, as a missionary teacher among the Indians; organized a Presbyterian church there in 1855, and was its pastor until 1861; was superintendent of schools for Goodhue county, 1864-1881; author of "Goodhue County . . . Past and Present, by an Old Settler," 349 pages, published in 1893. He continued to reside in Red Wing until about a week before his death.

HODGES township was named in honor of Leonard Bacon Hodges, tree planter for the St. Paul, Minneapolis and Manitoba (now the Great Northern) railway, who set out trees in many villages along this railway, including the hundred evergreen trees, or more, of the Court House square in Morris. He was born in West Bloomfield, N. Y., July 15, 1823, and died in St. Paul, April 14, 1883. He came to Minnesota in 1854, opened a farm in Olmsted county, and founded the town of Oronoco; was a state senator in 1871; removed to St. Paul in 1872; and afterward was much engaged in forestry.

HORTON township was named in honor of William T. Horton, its earliest settler, who was a farmer in section 14. He was born in Ulster county, N. Y., in 1825; came to Minnesota, and engaged in farming in Fillmore and Mower counties; served in the Eleventh Minnesota regiment, 1863-64; removed to this township in 1878, and here gave attention largely to stockraising.

STEVENS COUNTY

MOORE township was named for a family of its pioneer settlers.

MOOSE ISLAND, a railway station in the north edge of Donnelly, was named for the former Moose Island lake, noted in the list of lakes, 5 to 8 miles distant southward, which now is mostly drained.

MORRIS, the county seat, platted in 1869, incorporated as a village February 21, 1878, and as a city in 1902, was named in honor of Charles A. F. Morris, who was born in Ireland in 1827, and died in Excelsior, Minn., June 2, 1903. He came to the United States in 1849, and to St. Paul, in 1854; was connected with the engineering departments of several railroads, among them being the Manitoba and the Northern Pacific; removed to Oregon, but a few years later returned to Minnesota, and resided in Excelsior. Morris township was organized in 1871.

PEPPERTON township was named for Charles A. Pepper, its first settler, who in the fall of 1875 took a soldier's homestead claim in section 34. He was born in Burlington, Iowa, June 1, 1845; served in the Seventh Iowa Cavalry, 1863-6; came to Minnesota in 1871, first settling in Washington county; removed to his homestead in this township, 1875, and to Morris in 1883, where he was a dealer in farm machinery, and also in grain; is now a resident of St. Paul.

RENDSVILLE township has a name not elsewhere found, and its origin and meaning remain to be ascertained.

SCOTT township had settlers from southern Minnesota, and may thence have received this name from Scott county.

STEVENS township was named like this county.

SWAN LAKE township, formerly called Sahlmark, was renamed for its fine lake in sections 26 and 35.

SYNNES township has a Scandinavian name, derived from a group of farms whence some of its settlers came.

STREAMS AND LAKES.

Pomme de Terre river, flowing across this county, has been noticed in the first chapter, and also in the chapter for Grant county, where this river flows through the upper Pomme de Terre lake and gives its name to a township.

The Chippewa river, flowing through the east edge of Swan Lake township, was a route of travel for Chippewa or Ojibway war parties, in coming from their wooded northern country to the prairie region of the Sioux in the Minnesota valley.

Mud creek is a western tributary of the Pomme de Terre river, and Twelve Mile creek, flowing from Echo or Fish lake through Eldorado, joins the West branch of Mustinka river in Traverse county.

The following lakes are found in Stevens county, bearing names on maps, in the order of townships from south to north and of ranges from east to west.

Page lake, in Hodges, was named for the late William H. Page, who owned a farm beside it.

Scott township has Frog and Little Frog lakes, Lake Hattie, and Clear and Mud lakes.

Baker township has Clark and Gravel lakes, the first being named for a pioneer farmer who lived near Chokio.

Framnas has Long lake, formerly called Morse lake, crossed by its south line; Cyrus lake, in sections 25 and 36; Olson, Hanse, and Hanson lakes, Lake Moore, and Scandia lake, forming a very noteworthy group in the east part of this township; and Foss lake, in sections 8 and 17.

Crystal lake lies in the southwest part of the city of Morris; Gould's lake is a mile farther west, in sections 4 and 5, Darnen, named for John L. Gould, an adjoining farmer; and Maughan lake, named similarly for George W. Maughan, was two miles north of Morris, mostly in section 22, but it has been drained.

Wintermute lake, in sections 1 and 12, Morris, the largest lake of this township, was a favorite resort of the Sioux for fishing and hunting. It was named in honor of Charles Wintermute, one of the earliest settlers of the county, who came in 1871, purchased the Gager stage station, before mentioned, and also took a homestead and bought other land. He was born in Chemung county, N. Y., March 14, 1834; came to Minnesota in 1861; served against the Sioux, after their outbreak, 1862-3; was a trader at Fort Wadsworth, S. D., 1865-71; was a farmer beside this lake, 1871 to 1885, when he removed to Morris; and later continued in farming, with interests in mercantile business and in the lumber trade. In 1875-77 he was chairman of the board of county commissioners.

Moose Island lake, branched like the horns of a moose, lying in Pepperton and Donnelly, remains now only in part, as a large marsh; and Fish lake, formerly also called Echo lake, is mostly in sections 6 and 7 of this township.

Swan Lake township, with the lake so named, has two Pomme de Terre lakes, on the course of that river.

Harstad lake, in the southwest part of Rendsville, commemorates Lars E. Harstad, an early settler there.

Cottonwood lake, crossed by the north line of section 1, Donnelly, lies for its greater part in Grant county.

SWIFT COUNTY

Established February 18, 1870, this county was named in honor of Henry Adoniram Swift, governor of Minnesota in 1863. He was born in Ravenna, Ohio, March 23, 1823; was graduated at Western Reserve College; was admitted to the practice of law in 1845; came to Minnesota in 1853, first settling in St. Paul, but removing in 1856 to St. Peter; and was a member of the state senate, 1862 to 1865. For the latter half of the year 1863, having been elected lieutenant governor in place of Hon. Ignatius Donnelly, who resigned in consequence of his election as a representative in Congress, Swift succeeded to the governorship when Governor Ramsey had resigned to take his seat in the U. S. Senate. In 1865, Governor Swift was appointed register of the U. S. land office in St. Peter, and held this office until his death, February 25, 1869.

A memoir of Governor Swift, by John Fletcher Williams, secretary of the Minnesota Historical Society, is in its Volume III, pages 91-98, published in 1870. Gen. James H. Baker, in the "Lives of the Governors of Minnesota" (M. H. S. Collections, vol. XIII, 1908), presented his biography in pages 109-127, with his portrait. In the closing pages of this sketch General Baker wrote: "The memory of Governor Swift will ever be held in the highest regard by the people of this state. The integrity of his character, his fidelity to public duty, his exemplary and spotless life as a citizen, and his devotion to family ties, made him a model worthy of the regard and admiration of the youth of Minnesota."

Townships and Villages.

Information of geographic names has been gathered in "History of the Minnesota Valley," 1882, having pages 955-972 for Swift county; and from J. N. Edwards, judge of probate, H. C. Odney, register of deeds, and the late Ernest R. Aldrich, each of Benson, the county seat, the two former being interviewed during a visit there in May, 1916, and the last at later visits by him in St. Paul.

APPLETON township, organized in 1870, was at first called Phelps, in honor of its first settler, Addison Phelps, who came in the autumn of 1868. Appleton village, named for the city of Appleton in eastern Wisconsin, was founded in 1871-2; the railway was built there in 1879; and the village was incorporated in the spring of 1881. The township was renamed Appleton, on request of Mr. Phelps, who was one of the county commissioners, September 4, 1872. In Wisconsin this name commemorates Samuel Appleton, one of the founders of Lawrence University, located there.

BENSON, the county seat, platted for the railway company by Charles A. F. Morris, for whom Morris in Stevens county was named, in the spring of 1870, was incorporated as a village February 14, 1877, and as a city in 1908. Benson township, first settled in 1867, was organized in April, 1871. The name was adopted in honor of Ben. H. Benson, who was born in Norway in 1846, came to the United States in 1861, and settled in this township in 1869, engaging in mercantile business. After 1875 he owned a farm in Hantho, Lac qui Parle county. (History, Minnesota Valley, p. 950.) Later he removed to Duluth.

Others have regarded this name as chosen in honor of Jared Benson, of Anoka, who at that time and during many years was a prominent citizen and a political leader. He was born in Mendon, Mass., November 8, 1821; came to Minnesota in 1856, settling at Anoka, and engaged in farming and cattle raising; was a member and speaker of the House of Representatives in the state legislature in 1861-2 and 1864, and was again a representative in 1879 and 1889; and died in St. Paul, May 18, 1894.

CAMP LAKE township, first settled in 1866, was named from its lake, which was the site of the camp of government surveyors for this and adjoining townships.

CASHEL township, settled in 1873 and organized March 23, 1878, received its name from the ancient city of Cashel in Tipperary county, southern Ireland.

CLONTARF township, which received its first settler in June, 1876, was organized January 16, 1877. "The town was named by Bishop Ireland. The inhabitants are mostly Irish, a colony having settled here in 1878." (History, Minnesota Valley, p. 969.) The village of Contarf was platted in 1876. This name is from the town and watering place in Ireland, a suburb of Dublin.

DANVERS, a railway village in the east edge of Marysland, bears the name of a township and villages in Massachusetts and of a village in Illinois.

DE GRAFF, a railway village in Kildare, founded in 1875, was incorporated February 18, 1881, being named in honor of Andrew De Graff, of St. Paul. He was born near Amsterdam, N. Y., October 21, 1811; came to Minnesota in 1857, and built many railroads in this state, including the Great Northern line through this county; died in St. Paul, November 7, 1894.

DUBLIN township, organized February 14, 1878, having chiefly Irish settlers, is named for the capital and largest city of Ireland.

EDISON township, settled in 1872 and organized March 23, 1878, was originally called New Posen, for a Polish city and province of Prussia, but was renamed in honor of Thomas Alva Edison, the great inventor. He was born in Milan, Ohio, February 11, 1847; was a newsboy, and afterward a telegraph operator; removed to New York city, 1871, to Menlo Park, N. J., 1876, and later to West Orange, N. J. Among his inventions are the duplex telegraph, the phonograph, and the incandescent electric lamp.

FAIRFIELD township, settled in 1867, organized April 16, 1872, has a name borne by counties in Connecticut, Ohio, and South Carolina, and by townships and villages or cities in twenty-nine states of the Union.

HAYES township, settled in 1868 and organized in 1877, was named in honor of Rutherford Birchard Hayes, nineteenth president of the United States. He was born in Delaware, Ohio, October 4, 1822; served in the Union army during the civil war, and was brevetted major general of volunteers in 1865; was a member of Congress, 1865-7; governor of Ohio, 1868-72 and 1876-7; was president, 1877-81; died at Fremont, Ohio, January 17, 1893.

HEGBERT township was first settled by Ole Hegstad, in 1869, and was organized in a meeting at his house, April 8, 1876.

HOLLOWAY is a railway village in Moyer, named by officers of the Great Northern railway in honor of an adjacent pioneer farmer.

KERKHOVEN township, first settled in 1865, and the railway village of this name, in Pillsbury township, platted in 1870 and incorporated in January, 1881, received this Scottish name in honor of a stockholder of the Great Northern railway company.

KILDARE township, settled in 1868 and organized April 20, 1875, was named for a county and a town in Ireland.

MARYSLAND township, organized March 11, 1879, was settled and named by Catholic immigrants from Ireland.

MOYER township was first settled in June, 1869, by William Moyer, in whose honor it received this name at its organization, January 25, 1879.

MURDOCK, a railway village in Dublin, was platted by S. S. Murdock in 1878 and was incorporated in 1881. He removed to Phoenix, Arizona.

PILLSBURY township, settled in 1869, organized January 29, 1876, was named in honor of John Sargent Pillsbury, who was born in Sutton, N. H., July 29, 1827, and died in Minneapolis, October 18, 1901. He came to Minnesota in 1855, settling in St. Anthony, now the east part of Minneapolis, engaged in the hardware business until 1875, and afterward in lumbering and flour milling; was a state senator, 1864-8, and 1871-5; and governor, 1876-82. He was greatly interested in upbuilding the state university; one of its chief buildings was donated by him, and is named in his honor; and he was a member of the Board of Regents from 1863 until his death, being president of the board after 1891. His biography and portrait are in "Lives of the Governors of Minnesota," by General Baker (M. H. S. Collections, vol. XIII, 1908, pages 225-250).

SHIBLE township, organized July 8, 1876, was named for Albert Shible, its earliest settler, who came here in August, 1869, but removed in 1870.

SIX MILE GROVE township, settled in April, 1866, and organized November 1, 1877, is named for its grove, six miles distant from Benson.

SWENODA township, first settled in the spring of 1869, organized April 7, 1873, has a composite name, in compliment to its Swede, Norwegian, and Dane settlers. The same name is borne by a lake about 25 miles distant northeastward, in Pope county.

SWIFT FALLS is a hamlet on the East branch of the Chippewa river, in Camp Lake township.

TARA township, settled in the spring of 1877, organized December 21, 1878, is named for a hill in County Meath, Ireland, about 20 miles northwest of Dublin. "It was in antiquity a chief seat of the Irish monarchs, and is regarded with patriotic veneration by the Irish people."

TORNING township, organized April 5, 1879, bearing the name of a village in central Denmark, had previously been the south part of Benson township. It has the city of Benson in its northwest corner.

WEST BANK township, settled in 1868 and organized March 11, 1879, lies at the west side of the Chippewa river.

STREAMS AND LAKES.

The Minnesota river, forming a part of the south boundary of Appleton, and the Chippewa and Pomme de Terre rivers, which cross this county, are considered in the first chapter; and the second and third are also noticed in chapters for Chippewa, Grant, and Stevens counties.

Mud creek is tributary to the East branch of Chippewa river; Shakopee creek, flowing through Shakopee lake in Chippewa county, joins the Chippewa river in Swenoda; and it also receives Cottonwood creek, from West Bank township.

This county has relatively few lakes, of which only the following are named on maps.

Lake Manson and Frank lake are crossed by the line between Hayes and Kerkhoven. The former was named for Andrew Manson, a pioneer farmer from Norway.

Lake Mollerberg, in Kildare, was likewise named for a pioneer farmer beside it.

Shible township has Lake Hart, in section 20; but its former Lake Shible and Pelican lake are now dry. The first was named for Isaac Hart, an early settler; and the second for Albert Shible, like the township.

Camp lake has been before noticed, for the township so named.

In Benson township are Lakes Hassel, Moore, Frovold, and Johnson. The first is a Norwegian name, meaning the hazel; and the third is in honor of Knut P. Frovold, one of the earliest settlers, who was county auditor and removed to Benson.

Hegbert has Lakes Oliver and Henry in its southern part, and Lake Griffin at the northwest, which is more commonly called Dry Wood lake, with outflow in rainy seasons by Dry Wood creek to the Pomme de Terre river. The names Oliver and Griffin are derived from the plat of the government survey of this township. In its southwestern edge Artichoke creek, flowing only in wet years, runs northwesterly to the now drained bed of Artichoke lake, in the township of this name in Big Stone county. The name refers to a species of wild sunflower having tuberous roots, much used by both the Sioux and Ojibways for food.

TODD COUNTY

This county, established February 20, 1855, and organized January 1, 1867, was named for John Blair Smith Todd, commander of Fort Ripley (at first called Fort Gaines), 1849 to 1856, which was in the part taken from Todd county in 1856 to form a part of Morrison county. Todd was born in Lexington, Ky., April 4, 1814; was graduated at the U. S. Military Academy, West Point, 1837; served in the second Seminole war and the Mexican war; resigned from the army in 1856; was an Indian trader at Fort Randall, Dakota, till 1861; was a brigadier general in the civil war; was delegate in Congress for Dakota, 1861 and 1863-65, and governor of that territory, 1869-71. He died in Yankton, Dakota, January 5, 1872.

Townships and Villages.

Information ot names has been received from "History of Morrison and Todd Counties," by Clara K. Fuller, two volumes, 1915, having pages 211-307 on the history of this county; from E. M. Berg, county auditor, Otis B. De Laurier, Hon. William E. Lee, John H. Sheets, and Mrs. John D. Jones, each of Long Prairie, the county seat, interviewed during a visit there in May, 1916; and from Wilfred J. Whitefield, the oldest resident of Sauk Center, in Stearns county, also interviewed at his home in May, 1916.

BARTLETT township, organized March 22, 1883, was named for a family of pioneer homesteaders.

BERTHA township, organized January 4, 1878, and its railway village, platted in August, 1891, and incorporated in 1897, commemorate Mrs. Bertha Ristan, the first white woman settler there.

BIRCHDALE township, organized March 24, 1869, was named from its Birch lakes, to be more fully noticed on a later page, and its morainic hills and dales.

BROWERVILLE, a railway village in Hartford, platted in 1882, when the Sauk Center branch of the Great Northern railway was built, commemorates Abraham D. Brower, one of the first settlers of this county, who came in 1860, settled in Round Prairie township, and was chairman of the first board of county commissioners, in 1867; his fourth son, Jacob Vradenberg Brower (b. 1844, d. 1905), who was the first auditor of this county, 1867; and a younger son, Walter C. Brower (b. 1852), who was editor of the Stearns County Tribune, Sauk Center. These sons were proprietors of the townsite. The biography of Hon. Jacob V. Brower is presented by Josiah B. Chaney in the M. H. S. Collections (vol. XII, 1908, pages

769-774), and by Prof. N. H. Winchell in "The Aborigines of Minnesota," 1911, pages x-xiv, with his portrait and autograph.

BRUCE township was named by George Balmer, a Scotch pioneer farmer there, who was a county commissioner, in honor of Robert Bruce (b. 1274, d. 1329), a famous king and national hero of Scotland.

BURLEENE township, organized in 1888, has a unique name, for which further inquiry is needed to learn its origin and significance.

BURNHAMVILLE township, organized September 8, 1870, and its railway village, platted in February, 1883, are named in honor of David Burnham, who was a blacksmith for the Winnebago Indians at Long Prairie, and settled as a homestead farmer here soon after the civil war.

BURTRUM is a railway village in Burnhamville, platted in April, 1884, and incorporated in April, 1901.

CLARISSA, a railway village in Eagle Valley township, "was platted in 1877 by Lewis Bischoffsheim and wife, of London, England. The place was named in honor of the wife." (History, 1915, p. 298.) It was incorporated in 1897.

EAGLE BEND, a railway village in Wykeham township, received this name from its location at a notable bend of Eagle creek.

EAGLE VALLEY township, organized March 17, 1880, is crossed by Eagle creek, which was named for the bald or white-headed eagle, "the bird of freedom," emblem of the United States, formerly frequent throughout Minnesota.

FAWN LAKE township, organized July 28, 1881, bears the name early given to a lake in the east part of its section 30.

GERMANIA township, organized March 17, 1880, was named by its German settlers, this name being proposed by Paul Steinbach, from the ship Germania in which he came to America.

GORDON township, organized in January, 1869, was named in honor of J. M. Gordon, a pioneer farmer, who was a member of the first board of county commissioners.

GREY EAGLE township, organized September 15, 1873, and its railway village, platted in September, 1882, were named from an eagle shot here in 1868 by A. M. Crowell, who many years afterward removed to Bemidji and was its municipal judge.

HARTFORD township, organized March 12, 1867, has a name that is borne by a city and county in Connecticut, and by townships and villages or cities in Maine, Vermont, New York, Wisconsin, and twelve other states.

HEWITT, a railway village in Stowe Prairie township, platted in April, 1891, was named in honor of Henry Hewitt, an adjacent farmer.

IONA township, at first called Odessa, organized January 6, 1881, has the name of a historic island of the Hebrides, which also is borne by a railway village in Murray county.

KANDOTA township, organized in April, 1870, took the name of a proposed townsite platted here in 1856, on the shore of Fairy lake, by Edwin Whitefield, an artist from Massachusetts. This name, derived by him from the Dakota or the Ojibway language, is said to mean "Here we rest."

LEE'S SIDING, a railway station three miles north of Long Prairie, is named for Hon. William E. Lee, who was born in Alton, Ill., January 8, 1852; came to Minnesota with his parents in 1856; organized the Bank of Long Prairie in 1882, was its cashier, and in 1896 was elected its president; was a representative in the legislature, 1885-7 and 1893, being speaker of the House in 1893; was a member of the state board of control, 1901-03; was Republican candidate for governor in 1914.

LESLIE township, organized in September, 1876, and its railway village, platted in May, 1898, were named in honor of John B. Leslie, a pioneer settler from Kentucky.

LITTLE ELK township is crossed in its northeast part by the head stream of the South fork of the Little Elk river, flowing east into Morrison county.

LITTLE SAUK township, organized in the spring of 1870, and its railway village, on the Sauk river at the mouth of the Little Sauk lake, refer to a band of five Sauk Indians formerly living at Lake Osakis, as previously noted for the cities of Sauk Rapids and Sauk Center.

LONG PRAIRIE township, organized March 12, 1867, had been occupied 1848-55 by the agency of a reservation for the Winnebago Indians. Long Prairie village, the county seat, was platted in May, 1867, and was incorporated in 1883. The name is received from the Long Prairie river, flowing through this county to the Crow Wing river; and the stream was named for a long and relatively narrow prairie, from a half mile to one mile wide, bordering its east side for about twenty miles, from Lake Charlotte and Long Prairie village northward to the west line of Fawn Lake township.

MORAN township, organized March 27, 1877, is crossed by Moran brook, here joining the Long Prairie river, named for an early lumberman.

OAK HILL is a hamlet in Leslie township, named for its plentiful oak trees and morainic drift hills.

OSAKIS, a village lying mainly in Douglas county, but also extending into Gordon township, on the south shore of Osakis lake, received its name, like the lake and its outflowing Sauk river, from a small band of Sauk Indians, before noted for Little Sauk township.

PHILBROOK, a railway village in Villard and Fawn Lake townships, platted November 10, 1889, was named by officers of the Northern Pacific railway.

REYNOLDS township has a name that is borne by a county in Missouri and by villages in Pennsylvania, Indiana, Illinois, and seven other states.

ROUND PRAIRIE township, having one of the earliest settlements in this county, was named for the Round prairie, so called, about five miles long from north to south and two miles wide, in the western third of this township and the east edge of Little Sauk. The railway village of this name was platted in October, 1903.

STAPLES township, organized January 5, 1882, and the city of this name on the Northern Pacific railway, founded in 1885, platted as a village called Staples Mill in June, 1889, and incorporated as a city in 1906, commemorate Stillwater lumbermen named Staples, who had logging and manufacturing interests here. Two prominent pioneer lumbermen of this family, coming to Stillwater in 1853-54 from Topsham, Maine, were Samuel Staples (b. 1805, d. 1887), and Isaac Staples (b. 1816, d. 1898).

STOWE PRAIRIE, the most northwestern township, organized March 27, 1877, was named for three brothers, Amos, Isaac, and James Stowe, who were early settlers on and near a prairie area in the north part of this township, continuing also northward into Wadena county.

TURTLE CREEK township, organized in July, 1890, has Turtle creek, flowing through its west edge, and Turtle lake at its northwest corner.

VILLARD township, organized July 28, 1882, was named in honor of Henry Villard (b. 1835, d. 1900), president of the Northern Pacific railroad company in 1881-83, when its transcontinental line was completed. This name is also borne by a village in Pope county, for which a biographic notice has been presented.

WARD township, organized in July, 1877, was named for a township in Randolph county, Indiana, by settlers who had come from there.

WARD SPRINGS, a railway village in Birchdale township, platted by J. W. and Martha J. Ward, was previously called Birch Lake City, from its location beside Little Birch lake.

WEST UNION township was organized March 12, 1867; and its railway village, platted in June, 1881, was incorporated in 1900.

WHITEVILLE was the name commonly given to an early settlement in 1865-6, about five miles west of Long Prairie, for three sisters, wives of L. S. Hoadley, Albert Madison, and Horace Pierce, "whose maiden name was White." (History, 1915, p. 225.)

WYKEHAM township, originally called Eden, organized January 10, 1880, has a unique name, received from England.

STREAMS AND LAKES.

Crow Wing river has been fully noticed in the chapter of Crow Wing county. Long Prairie river is a translation of its Ojibway name, given by Gilfillan as "Ga-shagoshkodeia zibi, Long-narrow-Prairie river." These streams were described by Schoolcraft as "the war road between the Chippewas and Sioux," the country through which they flow being found by him in 1832 quite uninhabited. No dwelling place, "even a temporary wigwam," was observed in his canoe journey from the head of the Crow Wing along all its course to the Mississippi. (Summary Narrative, 1855, p. 267.)

Gilfillan wrote of Ojibway names in this county, with their translations, as follows:

"Osakis lake is Osagi sagaiigun, the Sauk's lake."

"Sauk lake" [in Kandota and extending south to Sauk Center] "is Kitchi-osagi sagaiigun, the great lake of the Sauks."

"Birch Bark Fort lake" [called Big Birch lake on recent maps], "Gawigwassensikag sagaiigun, the-place-of-little-birches lake."

"Sauk river, Osagi zibi, the river of the Sauks."

Wing river flows northeastward through Bertha and Stowe Prairie, being tributary to the Leaf river in Wadena county.

Bear creek, Little Partridge creek, and Egly creek, are tributary to Partridge river in Bartlett, which runs northeast to Crow Wing river.

From its north and west side, Long Prairie river receives Dismal creek, Freeman's creek, Dick's creek, Eagle creek, to which Harris creek is tributary, Moran brook, and Stony brook; and from the east this river receives Turtle creek and Fish Trap brook.

In the southeastern borders of the county are Prairie brook, flowing into Little Birch lake; Swan river, having Manley creek tributary to it from the south, and Little Swan creek from the north; and head streams of both the South and North forks of Little Elk river.

The south boundary of Todd county crosses Crooked lake, Big and Little Birch lakes (formerly called respectively Birch Bark Fort lake and Middle Birch Bark lake), and the large and long Sauk lake, through which the river of this name flows.

Grey Eagle township, besides the Crooked and Big Birch lakes, on its south line, has also Goose, Mound, Buck Head, Bass, Twin, and Trace lakes, the last being named for Ferdinand Trace, a homesteader beside it. Twin lake has two wide parts, united by a strait.

Birchdale has Long lake, mostly in section 19, and a second Twin lake in section 25.

Fairy lake, in Kandota, was thus fancifully named by Edwin Whitefield, mentioned in connection with this township.

Lake William is at the east side of section 12 and 13, West Union; and in section 1 the Sauk river flows through Lake Guernsey.

In Burnhamville are Buck and Moose lakes, Lady lake, named for its plentiful flowers of the lady's slipper, Big Swan lake, Looney or Long lake, Bass, Mons, and Little Swan lakes.

In Round Prairie township are Felix, Hansman, and Center lakes, and Lakes Latimer and Lashier. The largest is named for Alfred Eugene Latimer, of South Carolina, who, being a lieutenant in the U. S. army, was in service at Fort Ripley. In the winter of 1859-60 he was detailed, with his company, to be stationed at Long Prairie, as is noted by Mrs. Van Cleve ("Three Score Years and Ten," p. 158).

Little Sauk township has Cedar lake, in section 35, reaching south into Kandota. The northwest part of Little Sauk has Mud lake and Maple lake. The last, extending west into Gordon, is also often called Henry lake, for Lewis Henry, a pioneer farmer beside it.

Gordon has Slawson and Stallcopp lakes, named for William Slawson and Levi E. Stallcopp, early settlers there, and Faille lake, adjoining the east edge of Osakis village.

Bruce has Little Rice lake and Lake Beauty.

In Long Prairie township are Lake Charlotte and Meyer's lake, the former being named in honor of Mrs. Charlotte O. Van Cleve, who, with her husband, Gen. Horatio P. Van Cleve, and their family, lived at Long Prairie from 1856 to 1861. Charlotte Ouisconsin Clark Van Cleve was born at Prairie du Chien, Wis., July 1, 1819, and died in Minneapolis, April 1, 1907. Her parents, Lieut. and Mrs. Clark, accompanied the troops who came to the present state of Minnesota to establish the first military post, afterward named Fort Snelling. Their destination was reached when she was a few weeks old, and her childhood was passed there and at other army posts. She was married, March 22, 1836, to Lieut. (afterward General) Van Cleve. After resignation of his commission, they lived a few years in other states, but in 1856 returned to Minnesota, settling at Long Prairie, and five years later removed to Minneapolis, where Mrs. Van Cleve afterward resided, greatly honored and beloved. She wrote an autobiography, "Three Score Years and Ten," 176 pages, published in 1888. Two chapters in this book narrate remembrances of her life at Long Prairie.

Two miles west of Lake Charlotte is McCarrahan lake, in Reynolds, named for the late William McCarrahan, a Scotch-Irish farmer.

Leslie has Little Osakis lake, through which the Sauk river flows. On the long northeastern arm of Lake Osakis, which projects into this township, are Long point, Gutches, Coon, Buck, and Babbett points.

Little Elk township has Mill lake, Coal lake, named from the frequent fragments of lignite coal in its glacial drift, and Long and Round lakes.

Burleene has Lake Gray, Lowe's lake, and Lake Eli. The second was named for Lewis Lowe, a farmer there, who removed to Long Prairie; and the third for Isaac N. Eli, who lived in Reynolds, several miles southeast from that lake.

In Turtle Creek township are Big lake, Pine Island, and Thunder lakes; Mud lake, on the course of Turtle creek; Rice and Little Rice lakes, having wild rice; Star, Cranberry, and Long lakes, the last reaching north into Fawn Lake township; and Peat and Turtle lakes, in section 6.

Horseshoe lake, named from its curved outline, is in sections 27 and 34, Ward, near the Long Prairie river.

Pendergast lake is in sections 7 and 8, Wykeham.

Bertha has Deer lake, in the east edge of section 5.

In Fawn Lake township, with the lake so named, are also a second Pine Island lake, Little Fish Trap lake and creek (or brook), and Mud lake.

Villard has Nelson lake, in section 36, and Hayden lake and brook, flowing north to the Crow Wing river.

In Staples township are Rice lake, named from the wild rice, in sections 25 and 36, and Dower lake, about two miles west of the city, named in honor of a prominent pioneer settler, Sampson Dower, who came from England.

HILLS AND PRAIRIES.

Though Todd county is traversed by several belts or series of morainic drift hills, mostly from 50 to 100 feet high, only two localities of these hills have received names on maps. The Dromedary hills, rising with rounded outlines like a camel's hump, are in the northwest part of section 28, Little Elk; and Mount Nebo, in sections 4 and 9, Stowe Prairie, is named for the peak east of the north end of the Dead Sea, whence Moses viewed the Promised Land.

With the Long and Round prairies and Stowe prairie, which gave their names to townships, Pleasant prairie is also to be noticed, a mile in diameter, in the south edge of Round Prairie township, at the east side of Prairie brook.

The northeast boundary of the great prairie region of southwestern Minnesota crosses the southwest corner of this county, and includes sections 31 and 32 and parts of adjoining sections in Gordon, nearly all of West Union, and the south edge of Kandota. From the higher parts of West Union, an extensive view of limitless prairie is seen toward the south and southwest.

TRAVERSE COUNTY

This county, established February 20, 1862, organized March 8, 1881, received its name from Lake Traverse (Lac Travers in French), a translation of the Sioux name. Keating wrote of its significance: "The lake has received its present appellation from the circumstance that it is in a direction nearly transverse to that of the Big Stone and Lac qui Parle lakes, these being directly to the northwest, while Lake Travers points to the northeast." Williamson gave its Sioux name and meaning: "Mdehdakinyan, lake lying crosswise."

By the way of Lakes Traverse and Big Stone, whence two counties are named, and by the Minnesota river valley, whence this state is named, the River Warren outflowed from the Glacial Lake Agassiz, which in the closing part of the Ice Age filled the basin of the Red river and Lake Winnipeg. The Ojibways have given quite another name to Lake Traverse, referring to this deeply channeled ancient watercourse of the continental divide, noted by Gilfillan as follows: "Lake Travers is Ga-edawaii-mamiwung sagaiigun, the lake with a breast or pap (like a woman's) on either end; one on the northern, and one on the southern (flowing into Big Stone lake in high water); so flowing either way."

In exceptionally high flood stages of the upper Minnesota river, flowing into this channel of the Glacial River Warren at the village of Brown's Valley, a part of its water goes northward into Lake Traverse, so that canoes or boats can then have a continuous water passage from Big Stone lake to Lake Traverse; but probably no flood conditions in recent time have permitted any southward outflow from Lake Traverse.

At the east side of the southwest end of Lake Traverse, Major Long and his party in 1823 were entertained by Wanotan, chief of the Yankton Sioux, for whom, with changed spelling, Wahnata county of Minnesota Territory in 1849 was named, including the present Traverse county.

Townships and Villages.

Information of the origin and meaning of names has been gathered in "History of Traverse County, Brown's Valley and its Environs," by J. O. Barrett, 1881, 32 pages; "History of the Minnesota Valley," 1882, having pages 986-990 for this county; and from E. J. Fortune, judge of probate, Patrick H. Leonard, sheriff, George G. Allanson, postmaster, James H. Flood, and Ole Odenborg, all of Wheaton, the county seat, interviewed during a visit there in September, 1916.

ARTHUR township, organizd in 1881, originally called Hoff in honor of Abel Hoff, its first settler, was renamed on the suggestion of James H. Flood for Arthur village, Ontario, about 70 miles west of Toronto.

TRAVERSE COUNTY 551

BOISBERG, a village site platted in the northwest corner of Monson, is named from the Bois des Sioux river, to be noticed on a later page, and from the large granite boulder (berg) on the opposite or South Dakota side of this river in the village of White Rock, whence that village derived its name.

BROWN'S VALLEY, in Folsom township, a village founded in 1866-7 by Joseph R. Brown, platted in 1878, was the first county seat, being succeeded by Wheaton in 1886. The settlement and post office, established in 1867, were at first called Lake Traverse, but were renamed Brown's Valley after the death of the founder in 1870. Biographic notes of him are presented in the chapter of Brown county, which also was named in his honor. His son, Samuel J. Brown, who during fifty years has been a resident of this village, was its first postmaster, 1867-1878. A vivid sketch of Joseph Renshaw Brown was given in the pamphlet history of this county by J. O. Barrett in 1881.

CLIFTON township, the latest organized in this county, was named for a township in Monroe county, Wisconsin, about 40 miles east of La Crosse, as proposed by Bartlett Ashbough, a former settler here, who removed to Saskatchewan.

COLLIS, a railway village in Tara, comes from the Latin word, collis, a hill, this name being proposed by a priest, with reference to the hill Tara in Ireland, whence the township was named.

CROKE township, organized in 1881, was named, on the suggestion of P. D. O'Phelan, a homestead farmer in Tara, who was a member of the board of county commissioners, in honor of Thomas William Croke, who was born in County Cork, Ireland, May 24, 1824, and died at Thurles, Ireland, July 22, 1902. He was a Catholic bishop in Australia, 1870-74, and afterward was archbishop of Cashel in Ireland taking an active interest in political affairs and in support of the Home Rule movement. In 1876 the Catholic Colonization Bureau was organized, with Bishop Ireland as president and Dillon O'Brien, secretary, each of St. Paul, through whose efforts many Irish colonists were brought to this county, and to Swift, Murray, and other counties in southwestern Minnesota.

DOLLYMONT township, organized in 1881, bears the name of a seaside suburb of Dublin, Ireland, about four miles northeast from the center of that city. It was chosen also partly or mainly in honor of Anthony Doll, who was a pioneer settler here.

DUMONT, a railway village in Croke, was named by officers of the Chicago, Milwaukee and St. Paul railway company. The same name is borne by villages in New Jersey, Iowa, and Colorado.

FOLSOM township, organized September 2, 1880, was named in honor of Major George P. Folsom, who came from New Hampshire and was one of the first merchants of Brown's Valley. In the north part of this township, adjoining the shore of Lake Traverse in sections 2 and 10, a trading post for the Indians was established about the year 1815 by Robert Dickson, "a red-haired Scotchman," whom the British government had appointed "superintendent of the western tribes." In 1823, the expedition of Long and Keating found the Columbia Fur Company occupying this post (or another location near it), under the superintendence of "Mr. Moore," probably Hazen Mooers (b. 1789, d. 1858). He was also trading here in 1835 when Joseph R. Brown first came to this post; and a few years later, in 1838-39, Mooers and Brown were associated at Gray Cloud island, below St. Paul, in trading and farming.

LAKE VALLEY township, organized in 1881, is named for the northern part of Lake Traverse bordering its west side. This part of the lake, northward from its marshy tract at the mouth of Mustinka river, is called Buffalo lake on the map of Long's expedition, and Nicollet's map called it Intpah lake, a Sioux name meaning the end. It has an extent of eight or ten miles from south to north, being at the ordinary stage of low water an area of marsh one to two miles wide, in which are several spaces of open water a mile or two in length.

LEONARDSVILLE township, organized in 1881, commemorates Patrick Leonard, who came from Philadelphia, Pa., settled in Hastings, Minn., 1855, removed to this township as a homestead farmer in May, 1878, and died here in 1900.

MAUDADA, a townsite platted in 1881 on the shore of Lake Traverse close south of the mouth of Mustinka river, was designated in the first county election, November 8, 1881, to be the county seat; but business of the new county had been earlier transacted at Brown's Valley, from which its offices were not removed until in 1886 they were transferred to Wheaton. The name Maudada was in honor of Maud and Ada, daughters of A. C. Earsley and Charles F. Washburn, of Herman, the original proprietors of the townsite. This proposed village, though manifesting much vigor in its first year, had only a brief existence.

MONSON township, organized in 1881, was named for Peter Monson, a Swedish pioneer homesteader.

PARNELL township, also organized in 1881, was named, like Croke and Tara, by P. D. O'Phelan, one of the county commissioners, in honor of Charles Stewart Parnell (b. 1846, d. 1891), the prominent Irish statesman, who visited the United States in 1879-80.

REDPATH township, organized in 1881, was named by its Swedish settlers for a trail or path of the Sioux there.

TARA township, organized in 1881, received this name on recommendation of one of its pioneer settlers, P. D. O'Phelan, a county commissioner, for the renowned hill of Tara in Ireland. This extensive hill, adjoining the village of Tara, has a height of about 500 feet. Here was the "ancient seat of sovereignty in Ireland from a remote period to the middle of the sixth century."

TAYLOR township, organized in 1881, was named for one of its pioneer homesteaders.

TINTAH township, organized in 1881, received its name from the Dakota or Sioux people, this being their common word meaning a prairie.

TRAVERSE COUNTY 553

Hennepin wrote of the Sioux as "the Nation of the prairies, who are called Tintonha," a name derived from tintah. Later it has been written Tintonwans, Titonwans, or Tetons, comprising many Sioux bands ranging over southern and western Minnesota and onward to the vast country of plains west of the Missouri.

Shorelines of the Glacial Lake Agassiz extending past the railway village of Tintah are therefrom named the Tintah beaches, being traced, like other shorelines higher and lower, along great distances on each side of the Red River valley.

WALLS township, organized in 1881, was named for three brothers, William, Robert, and George Walls, Scotchmen, who came from New Brunswick, taking homestead claims in this township.

WHEATON, which succeeded Brown's Valley in 1886 as the county seat, is a railway village at the center of Lake Valley township, named in honor of Daniel Thompson Wheaton, of Morris, a surveyor for the Fargo Southern railway company. He advised that this new village be named Swedenburg in compliment to the Swedish owners of its site, Swan C. and Ole Odenborg, but they preferred to give it this name of the surveyor. He was born in Barre, Vt., January 21, 1845; was graduated at Dartmouth College, 1869; came to Minnesota in 1871, and settled at Morris in 1876; was county surveyor of Stevens county, 1877-1910.

WINDSOR township, first settled in September, 1871, organized in 1881, was named by one of its pioneer farmers, William J. Smith, who came here from Hastings, Minn. This name is borne by an ancient borough on the River Thames in England, a seaport town of Nova Scotia, a city in Ontario, and townships and villages or cities in nineteen other states of the Union.

LAKES AND STREAMS.

Lake Traverse, whence the county is named, has been noticed at the beginning of this chapter. Its northern part, often called Mud lake, is more definitely described, with comments on its nomenclature, under Lake Valley township.

The most southern island of Lake Traverse, about halfway across the lake opposite to the former trading post, which has been noticed for Folsom township, is called Snake island, "covering about 20 acres, once the village home of the Indians."

Battle point, in section 29, Windsor, commemorates a battle between the Ojibways and the Sioux, about the year 1830, narrated by Barrett (History of this county, 1881, p. 8).

Two other islands, nearer to the South Dakota shore, lie about one to two miles north of Battle point, the more southern being Plum island and the other North island. The former translates a Sioux name, Kanta Wita, which is placed farther north on Nicollet's map, in the extreme northern end of this lake.

Bois des Sioux river, outflowing from Lake Traverse to the Red river, has an early French name, meaning Woods of the Sioux, with reference to the woods or narrow groves by which it is bordered along its lowest five miles, next to Breckenridge and Wahpeton. On the map of Long's expedition, in 1823, it is called Sioux river; and in the Narrative by Keating, as also in the description of the country by Long, it is mentioned as the Sioux river or Swan river. The name Bois des Sioux was used by Keating to note only its fringe of timber. On Nicollet's map, 1843, it is named Sioux Wood river.

Keating's Narrative spells the name of the Mustinka river, tributary to Lake Traverse, with a more correct rendering of its Sioux pronunciation, Mushtincha, meaning Rabbit. The main stream receives in this county South and West branches or forks, and the latter has an affluent named Twelve Mile creek.

Hills.

Pelican hill, two miles northeast of Brown's Valley, is a knoll on the crest of the bluff of Lake Traverse, about 25 feet higher than the adjoining portions of the bluff.

Similar knolls or hillocks on or near the lake bluff close south of the Mustinka river were mapped by Nicollet with Sioux names, Plan Kara and Manstitsa Kara. One of these is now called Round Mound, from which, as noted by Barrett, very impressive views are obtained, especially when the effects of mirage bring Herman and the Tokua lakes into sight.

WABASHA COUNTY

This county, established October 27, 1849, commemorates a line of Dakota or Sioux chiefs, whose history is told by Hon. Charles C. Willson in the M. H. S. Collections (vol. XII, 1908, pages 503-512). Wapashaw (variously spelled) was the name, in three successive generations, of the hereditary chiefs having greatest influence among the Mississippi bands of the Sioux. McKenney and Hall, in the first volume of their "History of the Indian Tribes of North America" (1836), gave a portrait of the second chief bearing this name, who wore a covering over his left eye. The third Wapashaw's band occupied the country below Lake Pepin, his principal village being on the Rolling Stone creek, near the site of Minnesota City. A beautiful prairie in the Mississippi valley three to five miles southeast of this village, commonly called Wapashaw's prairie 60 to 80 years ago, became the site of the city of Winona.

The town (now a city) of Wabasha, which was named in 1843 for the last of these three chiefs, is situated at a distance of thirty miles up the Mississippi from his village. It was at first called Cratte's Landing, for the earliest white man to build his home there, in 1838.

From this town the county containing it, which was later established, received its name. The more remote origin of the name, which means "red leaf," and thence "red hat or cap," and "red battle-standard," as applied to the first chief named Wapashaw, was on the occasion of his return, as tradition relates, from a visit to Quebec, at some time after the cession of Canada to Great Britain in 1763. He had received from the English governor presents of a soldier's uniform, with its red cap, and an English flag, which, being displayed triumphantly on his arrival among his own people, led to their hailing him as Wapashaw (History of Winona County, 1883, page 31).

This name is widely different, as to its origin and meaning, from the Wabash river, which is said to signify in its original Algonquian, "a cloud blown forward by an equinoctial wind." In pronunciation, Wabasha should have the vowel of its accented first syllable (formerly spelled *Waa* and *Wah*) sounded like the familiar word, *ah;* and its final *a,* like *awe.* There is, however, a tendency or a prevalence of usage departing from the aboriginal pronunciation for each of the four names of Wabasha, Wadena, Waseca, and Watonwan, by giving to the first *a* its broad sound as in *awe* or *fall.*

Townships and Villages.

Information of names has been collected from the "Geographical and Statistical Sketch of the Past and Present of Wabasha County," by W.

H. Mitchell and U. Curtis, 1870, 164 pages; "History of Winona and Wabasha Counties," 1884, having pages 561-1314 for this county; and from Joseph Buisson, Jr., and David Cratte, sons of founders of Wabasha, the county seat, interviewed during a visit there in April, 1916.

BEAR VALLEY, a hamlet in Chester, is in a valley tributary to the Zumbro river. "Through this valley a bear was pursued by the early settlers."

BELLE CHESTER, a village in the north edge of Chester, founded in 1877, prefixes to the township name the French word meaning beautiful.

CHESTER township, organized May 11, 1858, has a name borne also by a city and county of England, counties in Pennsylvania, South Carolina, and Tennessee, and townships and villages or cities in twenty-six states of the Union.

DUMFRIES, a railway station in Glasgow township, received its name from a town and county of Scotland, the town being the former home and now the burial place of Robert Burns.

ELGIN township, first settled in April, 1855, organized May 11, 1858, likewise bears the name of an ancient town and its county in Scotland. It is also the name of a city in Illinois, having important manufactures of watches, and of villages in ten other states. Elgin village was founded in November, 1878, when the railway branch from Eyota to this place and Plainview was completed.

GILLFORD township, organized May 11, 1858, was named for Mr. and Mrs. Gill from Illinois. He came here and took a homestead claim in the summer of 1855, returned to Illinois, and soon died there. "His widow, in order to carry out her husband's wishes, removed to the claim he had selected, and entered upon the toils and privations of a frontier life. In honor of her energy and perseverance, and in memory of her husband, the town was called Gillford." This uniquely spelled name has the same pronunciation as Guilford, which is the name of townships and villages in Maine, Vermont, New York, and nine other states.

GLASGOW township, settled in 1855 and organized in 1858, "was named in honor of the city of Glasgow, Scotland, there being several Scotchmen in the township, and the first settler was a Scotchman."

GREENFIELD township, settled in 1854, organized May 11, 1858, has a name borne by townships and villages or cities in fourteen other states.

HAMMOND, a railway village in Zumbrota, was named for Joseph Hammond, the farmer on whose land it was platted. He was born in New Hampshire, March 28, 1816, and came to Minnesota, settling here, in 1856.

HIGHLAND township, organized May 13, 1858, was at first called Smithfield, but soon "the more euphonious title of Highland was substituted, which also truthfully implies the fact of its elevated surface."

HYDE PARK township, organized in 1858, was at first called Troy and later Zumbro, but received its present name in 1862, in accord with the suggestion of an Englishman, "so that the township is named after one

WABASHA COUNTY 557

of the most famous places in London." (History of the county, 1884, p. 788.) The choice of this name was decided mainly in compliment for John E. Hyde, of Mazeppa. He was born in Portland, Maine, in 1819; came to Platteville, Wis., in 1849, and to this state in 1855, settling in Mazeppa, where he was a merchant ten years; served in the 156th Illinois regiment, 1865, receiving a sunstroke, after which he never regained good health; but his mercantile business was continued by his wife until 1872. He was the first postmaster of Mazeppa, 1856, and was one of its most useful citizens.

JARRETT, a railway hamlet in Hyde Park, is near a former crossing of Zumbro river, called Jarrett's Ford, for the nearest original settler.

KEEGAN, another railway hamlet, in the north edge of Oakwood, was named for an Irish settler there.

KELLOGG, a railway village in Greenfield, founded in 1870, incorporated February 14, 1877, was named by officers of the Chicago, Milwaukee and St. Paul railroad company, "in honor of a Milwaukee gentleman who furnished the depot signs." (History, 1884, p. 885.)

KING'S COOLEY, a railway station in Pepin township, bears the name of a cooley or ravine there, on the farm of a settler named King.

In LAKE township, beside Lake Pepin, first settled in 1853-54, the village named LAKE CITY was platted in 1856; and on May 13, 1858, this township was "named Lake City by a vote of the people." The city was incorporated February 26, 1872, and the remaining part of the township "one year thereafter received by legislative enactment the curtailed name of 'Lake,' as it now is." (History, 1884, p. 796.)

MAZEPPA township, settled in 1855, organized May 11, 1858, and its village, platted in 1855 and incorporated in 1877, are named for Ivan Mazeppa (b. 1644, d. 1709), a Cossack chief, commemorated in a poem by Byron.

McCRACKEN, a railway station in Glasgow, is named in honor of William McCracken, from Scotland, the first settler in that township. He was born August 15, 1815; came to New Brunswick in 1841, and to Minnesota in 1855, settling here.

MIDLAND JUNCTION is a railway station in Greenfield, one mile north of Kellogg.

MILLVILLE, a railway village in the west edge of Oakwood, has a fine water power of Zumbro river, falling 14 feet.

MINNEISKA township, settled in 1851, organized April 5, 1859, and its village, platted in 1854, are named from the White Water river, which is a translation of its Dakota or Sioux name (Minne or Mini, water, ska, white).

MOUNT PLEASANT township, first settled in June, 1854, was organized May 11, 1858. "The appropriate name was suggested by the magnificent view presented to an observer from the tops of some of the elevations in the south central part, and from the summit of Lone Mound the sight is truly grand." (History, 1884, p. 752.)

OAK CENTER is a hamlet in Gillford, named "on account of the abundance of oak trees in that vicinity."

OAKWOOD township, similarly named as the preceding, was settled in 1855 and organized in 1859. It was at first called Pell, in honor of John H. Pell, an early settler, who was a state senator in 1861 and later was captain of Company I in the First Minnesota regiment, 1861-63; was renamed Sherman in 1868; but, because another Minnesota township had earlier received that name, it was finally changed to Oakwood in 1872.

PAUSELIM, for which the origin and meaning need further inquiry, was an early village in Greenfield, platted in 1863, which was superseded by Kellogg.

PEPIN township, organized May 11, 1858, is named from Lake Pepin, receiving thus an ancient and honored French name, as noticed in the first chapter.

PLAINVIEW township, settled in 1854 and organized May 11, 1858, took the name of its village, platted in the summer of 1857 and incorporated in 1875. The village was at first called Centerville, but was changed because another place in this state had been earlier so named. "In view of location, it being the watershed of the Zumbro and White Water rivers, and in plain view of a large tract of surrounding country, the name was changed to Plainview." (Mitchell and Curtis, 1870, p. 140.) Villages in Illinois, Nebraska, and four other states, also bear this name.

READ'S LANDING, a village in the east part of Pepin, adjoining the city of Wabasha, is on the site occupied as a Sioux trading post by Augustine Rocque from about 1810 to 1825 or 1830; by his son bearing the same name, from 1835 till his death, about 1860; by an Englishman named Hudson, from 1840 till he died, in 1845; and by Charles R. Read, who came here in 1847. Read was born about 1820 in England; came to the United States when ten years old; served in the American army in the Canadian rebellion 1837-8, was captured by the British and sentenced to be hung; was pardoned and returned to the United States; in 1847 took charge of this trading post; died at Millville in this county, October 9, 1900. The village of Read's Landing was platted in 1856 and incorporated March 5, 1868, and during ten to fifteen years later had flourishing commercial and transportation business, but afterward was superseded by Wabasha.

SMITHFIELD, a hamlet in Highland, retains the original name of that township.

TEPEEOTA, an early village in Greenfield, was founded in 1856 on an island of the Mississippi, a former camping ground of Wapashaw's band; but its hopes came to naught by the financial panic of 1857. On a March night in 1859, its deserted steam sawmill, three-story hotel, stores, etc., mostly then empty, were burned by incendiarism. This Sioux name means "many houses." (Mitchell and Curtis, 1870, pages 93-96.)

THEILMAN, a railway village in the southeast corner of West Albany, was named for Henry Theilman, on whose land this village was platted.

WABASHA COUNTY 559

WABASHA, the county seat, founded and named in 1843, as related at the beginning of this chapter, was platted in 1854 and was incorporated as a city March 20, 1858.

WATOPA township, settled in 1855 and organized May 11, 1858, has a Dakota or Sioux name, being a verb, "to paddle a canoe."

WEAVER, a railway village in Minneiska, platted in 1871, was named in honor of William Weaver, a pioneer settler, who came from the state of New York in 1857 and was one of the proprietors of this village site.

WEST ALBANY township, first settled in June, 1855, organized May 3, 1858, took this name from its village, which was platted in the spring of 1857 by settlers from Albany, N. Y.

ZUMBRO township, settled in 1855, was originally a part of Mazeppa and Troy townships, which were organized in 1858, and had for each the area of a township of the government survey. The inconvenience of crossing the Zumbro river, flowing through these townships, led to the organization of Zumbro, March 19, 1861, comprising the area east and south of the river; and the north part of Troy was renamed Hyde Park.

ZUMBRO FALLS is a railway village at falls of the Zumbro river in the southwest corner of Gillford.

RIVERS AND CREEKS.

Zumbro river is derived, by changes of pronunciation and greater change of spelling, from the early French name, Rivière des Embarras, meaning River of Difficulties or Encumbrances, that is, a stream on which canoeing was hindered by driftwood. On Nicollet's map, 1843, this stream is named Wazi Oju, "Place of Pines," referring to its grove of large white pines at Pine Island, in Goodhue county. The North and South branches of the Zumbro unite at the east side of Mazeppa.

From the north the Zumbro receives Skillman brook, West Albany creek, and Trout creek; and from the south its tributaries are Long, Middle, and West Indian creeks. Skillman brook, previously called Trout brook, was named from its mill in section 19, Chester, built by brothers of this name. Francis M. Skillman was born at Riverhead, Long Island, N. Y., November 23, 1812; came to Minnesota in 1856, settling on a farm in this county; was a representative in the legislature in 1859-60. Evander Skillman, born in German, N. Y., May 12, 1838, came to this county in 1856; served as first lieutenant in the Third Minnesota regiment in the civil war; engaged in mercantile business in Mazeppa, and in 1873 with his brother built this mill.

White Water river, before noticed for Minneiska township, flows through the southern edge of this county.

Lake Pepin, whence Lake City and Lake and Pepin townships are named, receives Gilbert Valley creek and Collins and King's creeks.

The Zumbro river in its southward course, after coming to the Mississippi bottomland, receives Dady's creek, flowing from Cook's Valley, Snake creek, and Indian creek.

WADENA COUNTY

Established June 11, 1858, and organized February 21, 1873, this county took its name from the Wadena trading post of the old trail from Crow Wing to Otter Tail City and Pembina, situated on the west bluff of the Crow Wing river at its crossing in the present township of Thomastown. The former ferry and trading post were between the mouths of the Leaf and Partridge rivers. Hon. J. V. Brower, who visited the place in 1863 and again examined it in May, 1899, stated that in its most populous period, about the years 1855 to 1860, more than a hundred people lived at this trading post; but that in 1899, like Crow Wing and the original Otter Tail City, its buildings had disappeared, and only their cellar holes remained to mark the spot, the trail or road having been long previously abandoned. Soon after the building of the Northern Pacific railroad, the county seat was located on this railroad, in 1872, fifteen miles west of the original Wadena trading post, from which its name was transferred.

This name, an archaic Ojibway word, signifies "a little round hill," according to Rev. J. A. Gilfillan. It probably had reference, as Mr. Brower thought, to the rounded outlines of the Crow Wing bluffs at the old Wadena ferry. It is also a somewhat frequent personal name among the Ojibways. One of this name, the eldest son of Bad Boy, the last Gull Lake chief, was living in 1899, an old man, on the White Earth reservation. Prof. N. H. Winchell defined his name as "Sloping Hill," with notation that he signed treaties in 1857 and 1889 (Aborigines of Minnesota, 1911, p. 729). Asher Murray, of Wadena, has a portrait of him. The name accents the middle syllable, and sounds each *a* as in *father*.

TOWNSHIPS AND VILLAGES.

Information of origins and meaning of geographic names was received from Eugene Boss, county auditor since 1903, and Asher Murray, each of Wadena, the county seat, interviewed during a visit there in May, 1916. Mr. Murray came to Minnesota in 1880, and has since resided in Wadena, being the county judge of probate in 1889-1902.

ALDRICH township received the name of the railway village, given by officers of the Northern Pacific railroad company, in honor of Cyrus Aldrich, who was born in Smithfield, R. I., June 18, 1808, and died in Minneapolis, October 5, 1871. He came to this state in 1855, settling in Minneapolis, and engaged in real estate business; was a representative in Congress, 1859-63; a member of the state legislature, 1865; and postmaster of Minneapolis, 1867-71.

WADENA COUNTY

BLUEBERRY township has Blueberry river and lake, which are translated from their Ojibway name. The low blueberry, supplying abundant berries much prized as food by both red and white people, is common in northern Minnesota, extending somewhat farther south and west than our species of pine, spruce, and fir.

BULLARD township was named in honor of Clarence Eugene Bullard, who was born at Fort Madison, Iowa, in 1843; served in the Sixth Wisconsin regiment in the civil war, attaining the rank of first lieutenant; came to Minnesota in 1864; settled in Verndale in 1878; was clerk of the district court of this county, 1881-6; removed to Wadena, and during many years was the county attorney; died at his home in Wadena in April, 1916.

HUNTERSVILLE township was named for its being a "hunters' paradise."

LEAF RIVER township, crossed by the river of this name, and its railway village are a translation from the Ojibway name of the Leaf hills or "mountains" and the Leaf lakes and river, before noted in the chapter of Otter Tail county. It is written by Gilfillan as "Gaskibugwudjiwe, Rustling Leaf mountain," the same name being also applied to the lakes and river.

LYONS township was named in honor of Harrison Lyons, of Verndale, who for many years was a member of the board of county commissioners.

MEADOW township was named for its relatively small tracts of prairie, natural grassland, inclosed in the general woodland.

MENAHGA, a railway village in Blueberry township, platted in 1891, very appropriately bears the Ojibway name of the blueberry, spelled Meenahga by Longfellow in "The Song of Hiawatha."

METZ was a post office in North Germany township, now discontinued, bearing the name of the chief city of Lorraine, which on October 27, 1870, after a siege of two months, was surrendered to the Germans.

NIMROD, a post office and hamlet in Orton, is named for the grandson of Ham, called, in Genesis, "a mighty hunter before the Lord," who is reputed to have directed the construction of the Tower of Babel.

NORTH GERMANY township was named by its many German settlers.

ORTON township was named in honor of one of its pioneer farmers.

OYE and OYLEN were post offices, lately discontinued, in Lyons.

RED EYE township is traversed by Red Eye river, named, in translation from the Ojibways, for its red-eye fish, a species that is also called "blue-spotted sunfish" or "green sunfish" (Cox, "Fishes of Minnesota," 1897, p. 67); but a later manual ("American Food and Game Fishes," by Jordan and Evermann, 1902) places this name, red-eye, as a synonym for the rock bass. The two species are nearly allied, and the latter is stated by Cox to be "a very common and valuable food fish in all the lakes and streams of the state." (p. 56).

ROCKWOOD township is thought to have been named from its glacial drift boulders and hardwood timber.

SEBEKA, a railway village in Red Eye and Rockwood townships, beside the Red Eye river, founded in 1891, was named, like Menahga, by Col. William Crooks, chief engineer of the Manitoba (now Great Northern) railway. Like Menahga, this is a name of Ojibway derivation, from sibi or zibi, a river, meaning "the village or town beside the river."

SHELL CITY is a hamlet in SHELL RIVER township, each of these names being from the mussel or clam shells of this river and of Shell lake, at its source in Becker county. The Ojibways, according to Gilfillan, call the lake by a different name, meaning "the lake lying near the mountain," that is, near a portage crossing the water divide between the Crow Wing and Otter Tail rivers. Thence they also give that name to the Shell river.

THOMASTOWN, the most southeastern township of this county, was named in honor of Thomas Scott, a pioneer homesteader, who was a lumberman and farmer; but he removed about the year 1875 to the state of Washington.

VERNDALE, a railway village in the west part of Aldrich, was named in honor of Vernie Smith, a granddaughter of Lucas W. Smith, one of its pioneers. He was born in Caledonia county, Vt., September 15, 1816; settled on a homestead claim near the site of this village, which he named; built the first house here, and engaged in mercantile business.

WADENA township, and its railway village, the county seat, first settled in the fall of 1871, incorporated February 14, 1881, are named, like this county, from the old trading post.

In WING RIVER township the stream of this name, flowing from Otter Tail and Todd counties, joins the Leaf river. Its name probably was translated from the Ojibways, like the Crow Wing river.

STREAMS AND LAKES.

On the map of Long's expedition, in 1823, the Crow Wing river is named "R. de Corbeau," meaning River of the Raven, the Leaf river is called its "West Fork," and the other streams of this county are unnamed, being indeed mostly without delineation. Nicollet's map, published in 1843, names the Crow Wing, Leaf, Red Eye, and Shell rivers; and the Partridge river bears its equivalent French name, "Riv. aux Perdrix." The early state map of 1860 adds Union creek and Wing and Partridge rivers.

Blueberry river and lake, and Leaf, Red Eye, Shell, and Wing rivers, from which townships are named, have been noticed in the preceding pages; and the French and English names of Partridge river are translations of its Ojibway name. The origin of the name of Union creek remains to be learned.

The Twin lakes, on the course of the Shell river, are crossed by the north line of this county.

Kettle creek is a tributary of Blueberry river.

Stocking lake, named from its shape, outflows by Stocking creek to the Shell river.

Spirit lake, without outlet, adjoins Menahga.

Jim Cook lake was named for an early farmer, who cut logs there.

Finn lake has several adjacent settlers from Finland.

In Meadow township, Yaeger lake was named for an early German or Swiss homesteader beside it; Mud lake lies close west, and Rice lake close south, the latter being named for its wild rice.

Cat river, flowing to the Crow Wing, was named for wildcats encountered by the pioneer settlers. This species, also called the lynx, was formerly frequent throughout Minnesota.

This county has two Hay creeks, one a tributary of Red Eye river, the other of Leaf river, each being named for their small tracts of natural hay meadows.

Lovejoy lake, in section 16, Thomastown, was named for Charles O. Lovejoy, a homesteader beside it; Hayden creek, also named for a pioneer, flows through the southeast corner of this township; and Simon lake is in its section 12.

From its east side, the Crow Wing river receives Big and Little Swamp creeks, Beaver creek, and Farnham brook, the last being named in honor of Sumner W. Farnham, a Minneapolis lumberman. He was born in Calais, Maine, April 2, 1820; came to Minnesota in 1848, and engaged in logging and lumber manufacturing; opened the first bank at St. Anthony Falls in 1854; was a member of the territorial legislature in 1852 and 1856; died in Minneapolis, April 2, 1900. A lake crossed by the east line of Bullard, about a mile east from the mouth of Farnham brook, is also named for him; and Sand lake is in section 1 of this township.

WASECA COUNTY

This county was established February 27, 1857. Its name is a Dakota or Sioux word, which has been explained by Prof. A. W. Williamson, as follows: "Waseca (wasecha), —rich, especially in provisions. I was informed in 1855 by a gentleman who was a stranger to me, who professed to be one of the first settlers, that this name was given in response to inquiries as to the Indian word for fertile, and adopted as a name. In Dakota writing and books the word *waseca* is spelled as we spell the name, and is a word likely to be given in answer to such a question. The soil is also very fertile." The name was first applied to the earliest farming settlement in 1855, near the present city of this name.

The county seat, originally located in Wilton, which became an important village, was removed to Waseca in 1870, soon after the building of the Winona and St. Peter railroad.

The Dictionary of the Dakota language, by Rev. S. R. Riggs, published in 1852, shows that this word was pronounced as if written *washecha*. It has the same accent and vowel sounds as Wadena.

TOWNSHIPS AND VILLAGES.

Information of names has been derived from "History of Steele and Waseca Counties," 1887, having pages 413-733 for this county; "History of Waseca County," by James E. Child, 1905, 848 pages; from Edward A. Everett and John F. Murphy, each of Waseca, the county seat, who came here respectively in 1867 and 1857, interviewed during a visit at Waseca in October, 1915; and from later letters of Mr. Everett, giving testimony from D. J. Dodge, the county clerk of the court, Edward Hayden, of Alton, and Mrs. A. C. Cleland.

ALMA CITY, a village in Alton and Freedom, platted in 1865, was named in honor of Alma Hills, daughter of Elijah Hills, one of the first settlers in Alton. Alma is also the name of a city in Wisconsin, and of townships and villages or cities in eighteen other states.

ALTON township, organized April 27, 1866, was named for the city of Alton, Illinois, by James Hayden and William Stewart, pioneers.

The origin of the name of BLOOMING GROVE township, organized April 5, 1858, is told by Mrs. A. C. Cleland, whose father, E. R. Connor, was one of the committee for selecting the township name. "A meeting was held at the residence of a Mr. Isaacs, . . . one mile north of Rice lake. This section of the township is a series of hills, like large and small islands surrounded by meadows and sloughs, which give the appearance of groves rather than a solid forest; and on all edges of these groves grew great plum thickets, and at the time the name was suggested by Mr. Isaacs the plums were in bloom, which gave them their idea of calling the township Blooming Grove." Townships and villages in New York, Pennsylvania, Indiana, and Texas, bear this name.

BYRON township, organized November 1, 1858, was named for Byron F. Clark, then a resident of Wilton. He was a money lender, accepting six per cent monthly interest, even from this county, during the financial depression after the panic of 1857. (County History, 1905, pages 95-96.)

FREEDOM township, organized in March, 1864, was named by Fletcher D. Seaman, one of its homestead farmers, who settled there in the spring of that year. Ten other states have townships and villages so named.

IOSCO township, organized April 5, 1858, has a rare name, borne elsewhere only by a county and village in Michigan. It is from Algonquian derivation, coined by Schoolcraft in his book, "The Myth of Hiawatha and other Oral Legends . . . of the North American Indians," published in 1856. Gannett defined the word as meaning "water of light," or "shining water."

JANESVILLE township, organized May 17, 1858, received the earlier name of its village. The original village was called Empire, but an addition was platted in 1856 by J. W. Hosmer, who "named it Jane for Mrs. Jane Sprague, and then, by general consent of the villagers, the 'Jane' was enlarged by adding to it 'ville,' and Janesville resulted and was accepted as the name of the whole village" (Stennett, Place Names of the Chicago and Northwestern Railways, 1908, p. 87). During the winter of 1869-70 nearly all the buildings of the previous townsite were removed to the new railway village site, called East Janesville, platted in August, 1869, for the Winona and St. Peter railroad company. May 10, 1870, the new village was incorporated as Janesville. (History of the county, 1887, pages 616, 617, 622.)

MATAWAN, a railway village in the southwest corner of Byron, bears the name of a village and township in New Jersey.

NEW RICHLAND township, first settled by a colony from Wisconsin in June, 1856, organized November 2, 1858, and its railway village, platted in August, 1877, received this name from the township and county of Richland in Wisconsin.

OKAMAN, a former village on the northeast shore of Lake Elysian, in section 1, Janesville, platted in May, 1857, extended also north into the edge of Le Sueur county. This Sioux name has nearly the same meaning as Okabena in Jackson and Nobles counties, each being from hokah, a heron, having reference to these localities as nesting places of herons.

OTISCO township, settled in 1856 and organized April 5, 1858, had a village so named which was platted in July, 1857; but its railway village dates only from the building of the Minneapolis and St. Louis railway in 1877. This is the name of a lake and a township in Onondaga county, New York, and of villages in Indiana and Michigan.

PALMER, an early railway station in Iosco, was platted as a village in September, 1915.

Ross is a station of the Chicago and Northwestern railway, two miles east of Janesville, "named for Ross Redfield, who lived nearby."

ST. MARY township, organized April 5, 1858, was named from its Catholic church, which was organized in 1856.

SMITH'S MILL, a railway village on the west line of Janesville, "was named for Peter Smith, the earliest settler here, who owned a mill here before the railroad reached the place." (Stennett, p. 125.)

VIVIAN township, settled in the summer of 1856, organized April 5, 1858, has a name borne by villages in West Virginia and Louisiana.

WALDORF, a railway village in the north edge of Vivian, has the name of a village in Maryland.

WASECA, the county seat, in Woodville township, platted in July, 1867, on the line of the Winona and St. Peter railroad, was incorporated as a village March 2, 1868, and as a city February 23, 1881. It succeeded Wilton as the county seat in 1870.

WILTON township, first settled in August, 1854, and organized May 11, 1858, took the name of its village, platted in the autumn of 1855, which was the county seat from the date of the county organization in 1857 until 1870, when the county offices were removed to Waseca. Wilton is the name of a town in Wiltshire, England, famous for its manufacture of carpets, and of townships and villages in Maine, New Hampshire, Connecticut, New York, Wisconsin, and seven other states.

WOODVILLE township, organized April 5, 1858, was named in honor of Eri G. and Loren Clark Wood, brothers, who were pioneer settlers here in 1856. Eri G. Wood was born in Franklin county, N. Y., March 17, 1832, and died at his home in this township, February 10, 1903. The first township meeting, May 11, 1858, was held at his house.

LAKES AND STREAMS.

The map of Minnesota Territory in 1855 has the Le Sueur and Cobb rivers, the latter being named by the government surveyors, and the former in honor of Pierre Charles Le Sueur (b. 1657, d. before 1712), of whom biographic notice is given in the chapter for Le Sueur county.

Boot creek is a western tributary of the Le Sueur river, and it receives the Little Le Sueur river and McDougal creek from the east. The last is named for Robert McDougal, who was born in Scotland, March 26, 1821; came to Canada in boyhood with his parents, and to Minnesota in 1855, taking a homestead claim in section 6, Otisco, beside this creek and the Le Sueur river; traveled in 1858-60 to the gold mines of the Saskatchewan river and to the Pacific coast; returned to Minnesota in 1861, but soon went back to Canada; came again to this state in 1866, and was a farmer in Otisco until his death, January 15, 1887.

Little Cobb river and Bull run, the outlet of Silver lake, flow west into Blue Earth county.

Iosco creek, to which Silver creek is tributary, flows into Lake Elysian; and Crane creek has its source in Rice lake, named for its wild rice.

WASECA COUNTY

Other lakes of this county include Trenton lake, crossed by the south line of Byron; Thompson lake, in section 13, New Richland, which on recent maps is named Norwegian lake, but also is often called St. Olaf's lake; Wheeler lake, in section 5, Vivian, named for John A. Wheeler, who took a claim on section 4 in 1858, served in the Tenth Minnesota regiment, 1862-4, afterward was first lieutenant in the 66th U. S. Colored Infantry, and died about 1876; Lake Canfield, in the northeast corner of Otisco, named in honor of Job A. Canfield, who was born in Ohio, settled here in 1856, was county judge of probate, 1857-60 and 1870-77, served in the Tenth Minnesota regiment, 1862-65, and died January 28, 1884; Mott lake, in sections 23 and 26, Freedom; Goose and Watkins lakes in the northeast part of Woodville, the latter named for Henry Watkins, who came here in 1856 and took a claim on the banks of the lake, but about fifteen years later removed to Iowa; Clear lake, remarkable for the clearness of its water, close northeast of Waseca; Gaiter lake, named for its shape, a quarter of a mile south of Clear lake, and Loon lake, adjoining the northwest side of this city; Buffalo lake, in Alton; Hayes, Remund, Everson, and Knutsen lakes, in Blooming Grove township; Toner's, Reed's, and Lily lakes, the last having many white water-lilies, in the northwest part of Iosco; Helena lake, in section 31, Iosco, and section 36, Janesville; and Rice lake, having wild rice, Willis, Lilly, and Fish lakes, in the northwest part of Janesville.

Lake Elysian, extending nearly across Janesville township, is the largest and most beautiful in this county, extending also north into Le Sueur county, where a township and village bear this name.

Samuel Remund, for whom a lake in Blooming Grove is named, was born in Canton Berne, Switzerland, January 26, 1833; came to the United States in 1855, and in 1856 settled on section 9 in this township; died February 8, 1903.

Gullick Knutsen, commemorated by another lake, was born in Roldat, Norway, May 25, 1840; came to the United States in 1851 with his parents, who settled in Dane county, Wisconsin, and removed to Blooming Grove in June, 1856; he served against the Sioux in 1862-3, in Company B, First Minnesota Mounted Rangers; was township treasurer and later township clerk; died at his home, August 11, 1901.

Richard Toner, a blacksmith, for whom Toner's lake was named, settled in Iosco in 1856, and was burned to death in a fire that destroyed his house, August 27, 1878.

Reed's lake was named for John Reed, a veteran of the War of 1812, who settled in Iosco in 1856.

Willis lake was named for Abner Willis, who was born in Connecticut, August 15, 1816, and was a farmer in section 8, Janesville.

Lilly lake, a mile west of Willis lake, commemorates Terrence Lilly, a cooper, who was born in 1808 at Enniskillen, Ireland, came to the United States in 1849, and to this state in 1857, settling in St. Mary township, and died May 15, 1891.

WASHINGTON COUNTY

Established October 27, 1849, this county was named for George Washington, "first in war, first in peace, and first in the hearts of his countrymen." He was born in Westmoreland county, Va., February 22, 1732; was commander-in-chief during the Revolutionary War, 1775-83; was the first president of the United States, 1789-97; and died at his home, Mount Vernon, Va., December 14, 1799. Thirty-two counties in as many states bear his name. This is one of the nine original counties into which Minnesota Territory was divided in 1849. Five others of these counties yet remain, namely, Benton, Dakota, Itasca, Ramsey, and Wabasha, each, like Washington county, being much reduced from its original area.

Townships and Villages.

Information of names has been gathered from "History of Washington County and the St. Croix Valley," 1881, 636 pages; "Fifty Years in the Northwest," by William H. C. Folsom, 1888, having pages 355-431 for this county; "History of the St. Croix Valley," edited by Augustus B. Easton, 1909, two volumes, paged continuously, 1290 pages; and from Nicholas A. Nelson, county auditor, and Alpheus E. Doe, judge of probate, each of Stillwater, the county seat, interviewed during a visit there in October, 1916.

AFTON township, first settled in 1837, organized in May, 1858, has an early village, platted in May, 1855, named by C. S. Getchell, "from Burns' poem, 'Afton Water,' which gives a fine description of the 'neighboring hills, and the clear winding rills.'" (History of the county, 1881, p. 402.)

ARCOLA, a former village of sawmills on the St. Croix about four miles south of Marine Mills, was founded in 1846-47. Its name is borne by an ancient town of Italy, and by villages in Pennsylvania, Indiana, Illinois, Georgia, and seven other states.

BAYTOWN, a small township on the south side of Stillwater, organized in May, 1858, was named by Socrates Nelson for the adjoining bay of Lake St. Croix, divided from the main lake by Mulvey's point.

COPAS, a village of the Soo railway, adjoins the former site of Vasa. It has a unique name, not known elsewhere.

COTTAGE GROVE township was settled in 1844 and organized in May, 1858; and its village, bearing the same name, in allusion to the mingled tracts of groves and prairies, was platted in April, 1871.

DELLWOOD, a railway village of euphonious name, having many summer homes beside White Bear lake, was platted in September, 1882.

DENMARK township, the most southern of this county, was first settled in 1839, and was organized October 20, 1858. Maine and New York

WASHINGTON COUNTY 569

have townships and villages of this name, which also is borne by villages or hamlets in thirteen other states.

FOREST LAKE township, organized March 11, 1874, took the name of its railway village, which was platted in 1868, at the west end of a large lake so named from the heavy timber skirting its shores.

GRANT township, organized in May, 1858, was then named Greenfield by Socrates Nelson, for his former home in Massachusetts; but, because that name had been previously given to another Minnesota township, it was renamed in 1864, in honor of General Ulysses S. Grant (b. 1822, d. 1885), whose biography is presented in the chapter of Grant county.

HUGO, a village of the St. Paul and Duluth railroad (now a branch of the Northern Pacific system) in Oneka township, was formerly called Centerville, for the adjacent township and village of Anoka county; but was renamed in honor of Trevanion William Hugo, of Duluth. He was born in Cornwall, England, July 29, 1848, came to America in 1852, with his parents who settled in Kingston, Ontario; was a marine engineer on the Great Lakes, 1869-1881; settled in Duluth, 1882, and has since been chief engineer of the Consolidated Elevator Company, the largest such company in the United States; was mayor of Duluth, 1900-1904.

LAKE ELMO, a railway village in Oakdale, was named for the adjoining lake, which was formerly called Bass lake but was renamed Lake Elmo in 1879 by Alpheus B. Stickney, of St. Paul, "from the novel, 'St. Elmo.'" (Stennett, Place Names, C. and N. W. Railways, 1908, p. 180.)

LAKELAND township, settled in 1839 and organized October 20, 1858, received the name of its village, platted in 1849 beside Lake St. Croix.

LAKEVIEW is a village site platted in sections 20 and 29, Lincoln.

LANGDON, a railway village in Cottage Grove township, platted in 1871, was named in honor of Robert Bruce Langdon, who was born in New Haven, Vt., November 24, 1826, and died in Minneapolis, July 24, 1895. He came to St. Paul in 1858, and removed to Minneapolis in 1866; was prominently engaged in the construction of railroads in Minnesota and other northwestern states, and in Manitoba and westward, besides the construction of canals, bridges, and many city blocks and flouring mills in Minneapolis and elsewhere. He was a state senator, 1873-8 and 1881-5; and was a member of the Republican national conventions of 1876, 1884, 1888 and 1892.

LINCOLN township, named in honor of President Lincoln, formerly the western third of Grant, was organized December 7, 1918, having been established by the board of county commissioners November 19. It includes the villages of Dellwood, Mahtomedi, and Wildwood, with the east half of White Bear lake.

MAHTOMEDI, a village consisting mostly of summer homes, on the northeast shore of White Bear lake, was platted in July, 1883, by the Mahtomedi Assembly of the Chautauqua Association. This is "the Dakota name of White Bear lake" (from *mato,* the white or polar bear, or *matohota,* the grizzly bear, with *mde,* a lake).

MARINE township, which was organized October 20, 1858, comprised from 1860 to 1893 the present townships of May and New Scandia. It received this name from the Marine Lumber Company, coming from Marine, a village in Madison county, Illinois, who in 1838-9 began lumber manufacturing here. The village of Marine Mills, platted in 1853 and incorporated in 1875, is included in the present Marine township, which since 1893 has an area of only about five square miles. The Illinois village was "so named because settled by several sea captains from the east." (Gannett, Place Names in the U. S., 1908, p. 199.)

MAY township, organized in 1893, having previously been the south part of Marine, was named in honor of Morgan May, a farmer here and owner of much land, who was a native of England.

MIDVALE, a railway village in the west edge of Oakdale, was formerly called Castle, in honor of Captain Henry A. Castle (b. 1841, d. 1916), of St. Paul, author of a History of St. Paul (1912) and History of Minnesota (1915), each in three volumes.

NEW SCANDIA township, organized in January, 1893, was formerly the north part of Marine. The first Swedish settlement in Minnesota was made in this township in October, 1850, whence this name was chosen, in allusion to the ancient name of the Scandinavian peninsula.

NEWPORT township, organized in May, 1858, received the name of its village, platted in 1857, which was so named by Mrs. James H. Hugunin. This is also the name of cities in Rhode Island and Kentucky, and of villages and townships in thirty other states.

OAK PARK was a village site, platted in May, 1857, in the present section 3 of Baytown.

OAKDALE township, settled in 1848 and organized in May and November 1, 1858, "originally was covered with white, black, and bur oak timber." (Folsom, Fifty Years, p. 386.)

ONEKA township, organized September 9, 1870, bears the name of its principal lake, in sections 9 and 16, of Dakota or Sioux origin, but of undetermined meaning.

POINT DOUGLAS, a former village near the point so named, at the west side of the mouth of Lake St. Croix, was platted August 18, 1849, commemorating Stephen A. Douglas (b. 1813, d. 1861).

RED ROCK, a railway village one mile north of Newport, is near the site of a mission for the Sioux in 1837-42. Since 1869 it has been the place of summer sessions of the Red Rock Camp Meeting Association, organized in that year by the Methodist Episcopal churches of this state. The name is from an ovally rounded boulder of granite, about five feet long, which originally lay on the neighboring bank of the Mississippi, but it has been removed recently to the west side of the railroad at the station. This rock was held in great veneration by the Sioux, who often visited it till 1862, and less frequently afterward, bringing offerings and renewing its vermilion paint. Folsom wrote of it in 1888: "It is painted in stripes, twelve in number, two inches wide and from two to six inches

WASHINGTON COUNTY 571

apart. The north end has a rudely drawn picture of the sun, and a rude face with fifteen rays."

ST. PAUL PARK is a railway village in Newport and Cottage Grove.

SCANDIA is a hamlet in New Scandia township.

SOUTH STILLWATER is a village in Baytown, platted in 1852 and originally named Baytown, like this township, for the adjoining bay of the Lake St. Croix. It is about a mile south of the New State Prison, which is built on a part of the former Oak Park village site.

STILLWATER, the county seat, was founded in 1843, and on October 26 of that year its name, "proposed by John McKusick, was adopted. This name was suggested by the stillness of the water in the lake, the anomaly of building a mill beside still water, and by fond recollections of Stillwater, Maine." (History of the county, 1881, p. 500.) The city was incorporated on the same date as St. Paul, March 4, 1854; and the township was organized in May, 1858. The earliest settlement here was by Joseph R. Brown, 1838-41, platting a townsite which he named Dahkotah, on the north part of the present city area.

VASA township, organized or at least named in 1858, was united with Marine on September 7, 1860. Its former village, named to honor Gustavus Vasa (b. 1496, d. 1560), king of Sweden, was platted in 1856.

WILDWOOD, a village site having many summer homes and noted as a place of picnics and amusements, at the southeast corner of White Bear lake and extending also north to Mahtomedi, was partly platted in 1883, with additions at later dates.

WOODBURY township, organized in 1858, was then called Red Rock, but was renamed in 1859, in honor of Judge Levi Woodbury of New Hampshire, a special friend of John Colby, who was chairman of the board of county commissioners. The fractional area which has the "Red Rock," before noticed, at first forming a part of this township, was annexed to Newport in 1861. Levi Woodbury was born in Francestown, N. H., December 2, 1789; was graduated at Dartmouth College, 1809, and was admitted to practice law in 1812; was a judge of the state supreme court, 1817; removed to Portsmouth, N. H., 1819; was governor of the state, 1823-4; U. S. senator, 1825-31; secretary of the navy, 1831-4, and of the treasury, 1834-41; again U. S. senator, 1841-45; and was a justice of the U. S. supreme court, 1846-51; died in Portsmouth, N. H., September 4, 1851.

LAKES AND STREAMS.

Lake St. Croix and the River St. Croix, bearing their early French name, are noticed in the first chapter. A minor feature of the St. Croix lake is the Catfish bar, near the middle of the length of the lake, reaching into it from the east shore, named in allusion to a legend of the Ojibways, whence their name for this lake is "Gigo-shugumot, Floating Fish lake," as noted by Gilfillan.

Painted Rock, a ledge of sandstone rising about 30 feet above the St. Croix river in the east part of section 15, Stillwater, has ancient Sioux pictographs, of which sixteen are reproduced on a scale of one eighth by Winchell in "The Aborigines of Minnesota," pages 567-8.

Cedar bend, a southeastward curve in the St. Croix river about a half mile southwest from the northeast corner of this county, marked the boundary between the country of the Sioux on the south and that of the Ojibways on the north, named for "an old cedar tree standing on a high bluff," and also for other "cedars that lined the banks of the stream at this turn in its course." (History of the county, 1881, p. 185.) This boundary was agreed to in a treaty at Prairie du Chien, August 19, 1825, defining its course across the area of Minnesota, and referring to this place as "the Standing Cedar, about a day's paddle in a canoe above the lake."

Battle Hollow, in the city of Stillwater, tributary to the St. Croix lake at the site of the old State Prison, is named from a battle there, July 3, 1839, between the Sioux and the Ojibways. (History, 1881, p. 103.)

From changes in the ownership of the point east of the bay in Baytown, it is now known as Mulvey's point, for James Mulvey, a lumber manufacturer, but was formerly called Kittson's point.

Belonging to the townships of Newport and Cottage Grove are the large Gray Cloud and Freeborn islands of the Mississippi, separated from the main land by small but permanent channels. Gray Cloud island was named for Mahkpia-hoto-win, in translation Gray Cloud, a noted Sioux woman, who lived on this island. She was first married to a white trader named Anderson, and after his death to the more widely known trader, Hazen P. Mooers. (M. H. S. Collections, vol. IX, 1901, p. 427.) Freeborn island, formerly called Kemp's island, commemorates William Freeborn, more fully noticed in the chapter for the county bearing his name. The minor rivercourse along the north side of Gray Cloud island is commonly called "Gray Cloud slough."

Medicine Wood, a translation from the Sioux, was a camping place on or near the western end of Gray Cloud island, occupied for a night by Leavenworth, Forsyth, and the first troops coming in 1819 for building the fort later named Fort Snelling. Forsyth wrote of it in his journal: "Medicine Wood takes its name from a large beech tree, which kind of wood the Sioux are not acquainted with, and supposing that the Great Spirit has placed it there as a genii to protect or punish them according to their merits or demerits." (M. H. S. Collections, vol. III, pages 153, 156.)

Bolles creek, in Lakeland and Afton, outflowing from Lake Elmo and Horseshoe lake, is renowned as the stream on which the first flouring mill in Minnesota was built in the winter of 1845-6 by Lemuel Bolles, a farmer in Afton, where he also owned a grindstone quarry. He was a native of New York state, and died in Stillwater in 1875.

Other lakes and streams are noted in the following list, in the numerical order of the townships from south to north.

WASHINGTON COUNTY

In Denmark are Allibone lake and creek and Trout brook, flowing to Lake St. Croix. The former were named for John Allibone, coming in 1851, whose farm included this lake.

Two lakes on the west part of Gray Cloud island were mapped by Hon. J. V. Brower as Baldwin and Moore lakes (Memoirs, vol. VI, Minnesota, 1903, p. 42); but the latter was named for the early fur trader of this island, Hazen P. Mooers, and it should therefore be spelled as Mooers lake.

Pine cooley, named for its tall and old white pines, twenty or more, is a ravine joining the Mississippi a half mile east of Freeborn island.

In Woodbury are Colby's lake, named for John Colby, an adjacent farmer, who was a member of the board of county commissioners, Powers, Wilmes, Carver, and Mud lakes. The next to the last was named for a farmer beside it, a descendant of Captain Jonathan Carver.

In Oakdale, with horseshoe lake, named for its shape, and Lake Elmo, before noticed, are Eagle Point lake, having a peninsula on its east side, where eagles nested, Clear lake, Lake Jane, Lake De Montreville (formerly mapped as Emma lake), and Long lake. De Montreville honors a dentist of St. Paul, whose country home was beside this lake.

The city area of Stillwater has McKusick's lake and Lily lake, the latter having white water-lilies. The former was named in honor of John McKusick, who was born in Cornish, Maine, December 18, 1815, and died in Stillwater, October 26, 1900. He came to Minnesota in 1840, settling in this county; built its first sawmill, was a state senator, 1863-66.

In Stillwater township are the southern Carnelian lake, having many carnelian pebbles on its shores, and a half dozen smaller lakes, unnamed on maps. Brown's creek, named in honor of Joseph R. Brown, before mentioned as sponsor of a townsite named Dahkotah, flows into Lake St Croix at the north edge of the city.

Grant township has Ben's lake, Man lake, Pine Tree lake, and Echo, Long, and Hamline lakes, the last three being near Mahtomedi.

White Bear lake has been noticed for Mahtomedi village, and more fully in the chapter of Ramsey county.

May township has the northern and larger Carnelian lake; Twin lake, shaped somewhat like a dumb-bell; Square lake, named from its shape; Terrapin lake, named for its turtles; Clear lake, Boot lake, having a bootlike outline, Bass lake, and Mud and Long lakes. Carnelian creek flows from Big lake southward across this township.

Oneka lake, before noticed, a second Horseshoe lake, Egg lake, Rice lake, having wild rice, Sunset and School Section lakes, the last lying partly in the school section 36, are in Oneka township.

New Scandia has Big lake (formerly called Big Marine lake), Long, Hay, and Sand lakes, and Fish, Goose, and Bonny lakes.

With the large Forest lake, the township named from it has also Clear and Mud lakes, whereby the list comprises three Clear lakes in this county, and also three named for their muddy shores and beds.

WATONWAN COUNTY

This county, established February 25, 1860, was named from the Watonwan river, whose head streams flow through it. Prof. A. W. Williamson, in his paper on our Dakota or Sioux geographic names, wrote: "This word might mean 'I see,' or 'he sees,' intransitive; it may have been applied to this branch of the Blue Earth as being a prairie country and presenting a good prospect, but it is uncertain whether this is the meaning on which the appellation was given." Rev. M. N. Adams later stated the significance of this name without doubt, that in being anglicized it was misspelled, and that it should be Watanwan, meaning fish bait, or where fish bait abounds, as he had been informed by the Dakotas. Our earliest knowledge of the Watonwan river is supplied by Nicollet's report and map, published in 1843. Its accent is on the first syllable; and the first *a* has its sound as in *father*, the last as in *fall*.

Townships and Villages.

Information of the origins and meanings of geographic names has been gathered from "History of Cottonwood and Watonwan Counties," John A. Brown, editor, 1916, two volumes, pages 595, 486; and from Fred Church, register of deeds, and Elwin Zillora Rasey, a resident of this county since 1871, each of St. James, the county seat, interviewed during a visit there in July, 1916. Mr. Rasey was chairman of the local committee of Watonwan county for compilation of its history in the work here cited, which was published in October of that year.

ADRIAN township, organized in June, 1871, has a name that is borne also by a city in Michigan, villages in New York, Pennsylvania, Georgia, and other states, and also a village in Nobles county of this state.

ANTRIM township, organized in January, 1867, has the name of the most northeastern county in Ireland, a county in Michigan, and townships and villages in New Hampshire, Pennsylvania, Ohio, and Louisiana.

BUTTERFIELD township, organized in January, 1872, and its railway village, which was platted September 13, 1880, and was incorporated April 5, 1895, were named "for William Butterfield, the owner of the townsite and its first settler." (Stennett, Place Names of the Chicago and Northwestern Railways, 1908, p. 50.)

DARFUR, a railway village in Adrian, platted in April, 1899, and incorporated in 1904, was named from a country of Egyptian Sudan.

ECHOLS, a railway village in the north part of Long Lake township, was named by officers of the Minneapolis and St. Louis railway company. It is a rare geographic name, borne elsewhere only by a county in Georgia and a village in Kentucky.

WATONWAN COUNTY 575

FIELDON township, organized in March, 1868, was then named Wakefield, but was renamed Fieldon in September of that year. Like the foregoing, it is a rare name, found elsewhere only for a village in Illinois.

GROGAN, a railway village five miles northeast of St. James, "was named in 1890 for Matthew J. Grogan, an early settler." (Stennett, p. 177.)

LA SALLE, a railway village in Riverdale, platted October 12, 1899, is named like a county and city of Illinois, a county in Texas, and a village on the Niagara river in New York, for the renowned French explorer, Robert Cavelier, Sieur de La Salle (b. 1643, d. 1687).

LEWISVILLE, a railway village in Antrim, platted May 3, 1899, and incorporated in 1902, was named in honor of Richard, James and Nelson Lewis, adjacent farmers, whose father, Thomas Lewis, a native of Ireland, came here from Ontario, Canada, in 1869, taking a homestead claim which included the site of this village. Richard Lewis was its first postmaster, and James Lewis is president of its Merchants' State Bank.

LONG LAKE township, settled in 1857, organized in March, 1868, bears the name of one of its three principal lakes.

MADELIA township, organized in 1858, before this county was established, took the name of its village, platted in July, 1857, and incorporated in 1872. The name was chosen in honor of the daughter of General Hartshorn, one of the townsite proprietors. It is "an elision and reconstruction of the name Madeline." This village was the first county seat, from 1860 until it was succeeded by St. James in 1878.

NELSON township, organized in September, 1870, had among its pioneer settlers several Swedish families of this name.

ODIN township, settled in 1868, organized in January, 1872, and its railway village, platted in March, 1899, and incorporated in 1902, bear the name of one of the chief gods in the ancient Norse mythology, called Woden by the Anglo-Saxons, for whom Wednesday (Woden's day) was named. "He is the source of wisdom, and the patron of culture and of heroes."

ORMSBY, a railway village on the south line of Long Lake township, platted October 14, 1899, and incorporated in 1902, was named in honor of Colonel Ormsby, of Emmetsburg, Iowa.

RIVERDALE township, organized in November, 1869, was named for the Watonwan river, which flows through it.

ROSENDALE township, organized in March, 1871, was named by Mrs. Samuel W. Sargeant, who had formerly lived in the township of this name in Fond du Lac county, Wisconsin.

ST. JAMES township, first settled in the spring of 1869, organized in March, 1870, received the name of its railway village, which was platted July 13, 1870. The St. Paul and Sioux City railway was so far constructed in that year that its first passenger train arrived here on November 22, bringing an excursion party from St. Paul, which included General

Henry H. Sibley, one of the directors of the railway, and Hon. Elias F. Drake, its president. The name had been selected for the village about three years previously, when it was designated to be the end of the first division of the railway. President Drake then requested Sibley to name the proposed division point, for which Sibley accordingly recommended a long Dakota or Sioux name. On the next day, however, neither of them could remember the proposed name, and Sibley said that he would consult papers at his home, "which will help me to think of it again."

"'Never mind, General, never mind,' said the President, 'we will have a name for that town that we *can* think of. I propose that we call it St. James.' Whereupon, by common consent, the point was called St. James by the railroad men some three years before it had any local existence." (Andreas' Atlas of Minnesota, 1874, p. 229.)

The village was incorporated in 1871, succeeded Madelia as the county seat in 1878, and received a city charter April 27, 1899. It is the largest place of this name, surpassing villages so named in eight other states.

SOUTH BRANCH township, organized in March, 1869, is crossed by the South branch or fork of the Watonwan river.

SVEADAHL, the name of a hamlet on the boundary between Adrian and Nelson, means "Sweden valley or dale." Sveahand is one of the three great divisions of Sweden, having its chief city and capital, Stockholm.

LAKES AND STREAMS.

Nearly all of this county is drained by the Watonwan river and its South branch, from each of which a township is named; and the minor streams tributary to these are unnamed on maps.

Perch creek flows from Perch lake in Martin county, crossing Antrim, and joining the Watonwan river in Blue Earth county.

With Long lake, the township named from it has also Mary lake and Kansas lake. "John Kensie was a scholarly gentleman and of a well-to-do family in England. He had a wife and three or four children and built a log hut on the south side of the grove by the lake, which still bears his name, though in a distorted form, 'Kansas lake.' The original and historic name is Kensie's lake." (History of the county, 1916, p. 436.)

In Odin are Irish lake and School lake (partly in the school section 16), and Sulem lake. Beside the last are farmers named Sulheim. Another family, named Sulem, immigrants from Norway in 1873, live in Long Lake township and in Butterfield village.

Rosendale has Bullhead lake, named for its small species of catfish.

Beside the city of St. James is a fine lake bearing this name.

Madelia has Hopkins, Fedje, and Lau lakes, a group one to two miles northeast from the village, and School lake, partly in section 16. Emerson lake, formerly on the north line of Madelia, extending into Brown county, has been drained.

Adrian has Cottonwood lake, in section 25, and Wood lake, named for its adjacent groves.

WILKIN COUNTY

This county, established with its present name March 6, 1868, commemorates Colonel Alexander Wilkin, who in the civil war gave his life for the Union, being shot and instantly killed in the battle of Tupelo, Mississippi, July 14, 1864. He was born in Orange county, N. Y., December, 1820; served as a captain in the Mexican war; came to St. Paul in 1849, and entered the practice of law; was United States marshal for Minnesota, and also secretary of the territory, 1851 to 1853; went to Europe in 1855, and studied the art of war before Sebastopol in the Crimea; afterward again was engaged in law practice in St. Paul; recruited the first company of the First Minnesota regiment for the civil war; served also in the second regiment, and was colonel of the ninth regiment. Physically he was of small size and stature; but he stood very high in courage and skill for military leadership.

An earlier county, somewhat corresponding to this in area and likewise having Breckenridge as its county seat, but named Toombs county, was established March 8, 1858. It was named for Robert Toombs (b, 1810, d. 1885), of Georgia, who had been a member of Congress in 1845-53, and was U. S. senator, 1853-61. He became a leading disunionist, was Confederate secretary of state, 1861, and later was a Confederate general. His disloyalty against the Union so displeased the people of the county that in 1862 they petitioned the legislature to change its name. "In 1863 the act changing the name from Toombs to Andy Johnson became a law. But the subsequent political attitude of Andrew Johnson [succeeding Lincoln as president of the United States] was no less displeasing to the people, and in 1868 the law was again amended and the name changed from Andy Johnson to Wilkin." (History of the Red River Valley, 1909, pages 908-9.)

TOWNSHIPS AND VILLAGES.

Information of names was learned from "History of the Red River Valley," 1909, two volumes, continuously paged, 1165 pages; and from John T. Wells, clerk of the court, and Halvor L. Shirley, president of the First National Bank, each of Breckenridge, the county seat, interviewed during a visit there in September, 1916.

AKRON township has a name that is borne by a city in Ohio and villages in nine other states. It is received from the ancient Greek language, meaning the extreme, hence a summit or hilltop.

ANDREA township is named in honor of Mrs. Andrea Heider, wife of Philip Heider, a pioneer homesteader here. He died in 1915, and she in 1916.

ATHERTON township was named for a former extensive landowner of this township, but not a resident.

BRADFORD township was similarly named for an owner of lands along the Red river north of Breckenridge.

BRANDRUP township was named in honor of Andrew Brandrup, one of its pioneer farmers, who became clerk of the court.

BRECKENRIDGE township, organized May 23, 1857, and its village, the county seat, platted in the spring of 1857, incorporated as a city in 1908, are in honor of John Cabell Breckenridge, who was born near Lexington, Ky., January 21, 1821, and died in that city May 17, 1875. He was a member of Congress, 1851-55; vice-president of the United States, 1857-61; general in the Confederate army, 1861-4; and Confederate secretary of state, January to April, 1865.

BRUSHVALE, a railway village in the southwest corner of Nordick, was named for Joseph Brush, on whose farm it was located.

CAMPBELL railway village, founded in 1871, and the township, organized in the fall of 1879, were named by the St. Paul and Pacific (now the Great Northern) railway company. This Scotch name is borne by counties in five states, and by villages of fourteen states.

CHAMPION township was named in honor of Henry Champion, a pioneer homesteader, who during several terms was the county auditor.

CHILDS, a railway village in the west part of Campbell, was named for Job W. Childs, an adjoining farmer, who was a member of the board of county commissioners, but later removed to California.

CONNELLY township was earliest settled by Edward Connelly, a homestead farmer, who came in 1868 and was a county commissioner.

DEERHORN township was named for the creek flowing through its northeast part.

DORAN, a railway village in Brandrup, was named in honor of Michael Doran, of St. Paul, who was born in County Meath, Ireland, November 1, 1829, and died in St. Paul, February 20, 1915. He came to the United States in 1850, and in 1856 to Le Sueur county in this state, where he engaged in farming and banking; removed to St. Paul in 1877; was a state senator, 1875-9.

EVERDELL, a railway village in Sunnyside township, was named in honor of Lyman B. Everdell, an early lawyer in Breckenridge.

FOXHOME township received the name of its railway village, from Robert A. Fox, a real estate dealer, who was proprietor of this townsite, but removed to Oklahoma.

KENT, a railway village in McCauleyville, was named by officers of the Great Northern railway company. This is the name of a county in England, counties in five states of the Union, and villages in twelve states.

LAWNDALE is a railway village, euphoniously named, in Prairie View.

MCCAULEYVILLE township, and its village on the Red river opposite to the site of Fort Abercrombie, were named in honor of David McCauley, sutler of the fort, who later founded this village and was county

WILKIN COUNTY 579

superintendent of schools many years. He was born in Merrimack, N. H., July 27, 1825; came to Minnesota in 1858; opened a store here in 1864, which was the beginning of the village.

MANSTON township received the name of its former railway village, given by officers of the St. Paul, Minneapolis and Manitoba (now the Great Northern) railway. It is the only place known bearing this name.

MEADOWS township was named for its being a part of a vast area of prairie, natural hayland.

MITCHELL township was named in compliment to Charles Mitchell Corliss, a homestead farmer here, a brother of the late Hon. Eben E. Corliss, of Fergus Falls and St. Paul.

NASHUA, a railway village in Champion, was named for its Nash families, but took the spelling of a city and river in New Hampshire, and of a village in Iowa.

NILSEN township, the latest organized in this county, has the name of one of its early settlers.

NORDICK township was named for Barney and Gerhard Nordick, German farmers, who came here from Iowa.

PRAIRIE VIEW, the most northeastern township, has from its high eastern part a very extensive view over the flat Red River valley.

ROBERTS township was named in honor of Michel Roberts, a French homesteader here, who was a cousin of the widely known Captain Louis Robert, of St. Paul. The old French surname is anglicized by the addition of *s*.

ROTHSAY, a railway village in the east edge of Tanberg, was named by officers of the railway company, for Rothesay, a seaport and watering place about thirty miles west of Glasgow, Scotland. This is the only use of the name in the United States.

SUNNYSIDE township, crossed by the Red river, was at first called Riverside; but, because that name had been elsewhere used in this state, it was changed, taking this euphonious name. It is borne also by villages and post offices in sixteen other states.

TANBERG township was named in honor of Christian Tanberg, a Norwegian pioneer settler, who was proprietor of its Rothsay townsite.

TENNEY, a railway village in the south part of Campbell, was named for the owner of its site.

WOLVERTON, the most northwestern township, was named in honor of Dr. W. D. Wolverton, physician of Fort Abercrombie, who owned much land in this township, but removed to the Pacific coast.

It seems desirable to add two names in North Dakota.

WAHPETON, the county seat of Richland county, on the west side of the Red river opposite to the city of Breckenridge, was settled in 1869, and was reached by the construction of the railway crossing the river in 1880. It bears the name of a large division of the Dakota or Sioux people, meaning "leaf dwellers," so named when they lived in the wooded country of Mille Lacs and farther north and east (from *Wakhpe,* leaf, *tonwan,* a village).

FORT ABERCROMBIE, on the west side of the Red river opposite to McCauleyville, was established in 1858, and was abandoned and dismantled in 1877-78, its buildings being sold and removed or torn down, to be used by settlers for making their homes on the surrounding prairie. It was named in honor of John Joseph Abercrombie, its first commander, who was born in Tennessee in 1802, and died in Roslyn, N. Y., January 3, 1877. He was graduated at West Point, 1822; served in the Florida and Mexican wars, and was breveted lieutenant colonel; was in this state when the civil war began, through which he served, being breveted brigadier general at its close.

LAKES AND STREAMS.

The only lake of this county, now drained, was crossed by its east boundary two miles east of Foxhome village. It is mapped as Lake Alice, but was more commonly known as Shaw lake, for Thomas Shaw, an adjoining farmer.

The Red river has been noticed in the first chapter, and again in part under Red Lake county; and the Bois des Sioux was noted in the chapter of Traverse county.

Deerhorn creek, for which a township is named, flows northward into Clay county, to the South branch of Buffalo river. Mushroom creek is tributary to the Deerhorn from the south.

Whiskey creek flows ten miles nearly parallel with the Red river, to which it is tributary a mile north of McCauleyville. It was named from unlawful sales of whiskey in dugout huts beside this stream to soldiers of Fort Abercrombie.

Rabbit river, crossing the southern end of the county, is named for its rabbits, like the larger Mustinka river in Traverse county, which is a Dakota word having the same meaning.

CAMPBELL AND MCCAULEYVILLE BEACHES.

While the Glacial Lake Agassiz flowed south along the valley of Lakes Traverse and Big Stone, its outlet stream, named the River Warren, eroded that remarkable valley, with gradual reduction of the lake level. Five stages of the ancient lake during its southward outflow are shown by so many distinct beaches, each lower than the preceding. In their descending order they are named, from places where they are well developed and were first recognized and mapped, being the Herman and Norcross beaches, for villages in Grant county, the Tintah beach for a village in Traverse county, and the Campbell and McCauleyville beaches in this county. Thence each of these old lake levels, recorded by the successive low beach ridges of sand and gravel, are traced far along each side of the Red river valley, in Minnesota and North Dakota and onward in Manitoba.

WINONA COUNTY

Established February 23, 1854, this county was named for a Dakota woman, Winona, cousin of the last chief named Wabasha, both of whom were prominent in the events attending the removal in 1848, of the Winnebago Indians from Iowa to Wabasha's prairie (the site of the city of Winona) and thence to Long Prairie in Todd county. This name belonged, says Prof. A. W. Williamson, in any Dakota or Sioux family, to the "first born, if a daughter, diminutive of wino, woman;" and similarly the name of the "first born child, if a son," was Chaska. In pronunciation, Winona is accented on the middle syllable, and the first and last syllables have the short vowel sounds. The first, however, is often incorrectly given the long sound, as in *wine;* it should be short, as in *win,* or may be quite rightly given the sound of long *e,* as *we.*

Keating gave an impressive narration of the death of a Dakota maiden named Winona, who threw herself to death from the precipice known as "the Maiden's Rock," on the east shore of Lake Pepin, in preference to being married, as her parents requested, to one whom she did not love. (Narrative of Long's Expedition, 1823, vol. I, pages 289-295.) With much amplification, including change of the home of the maiden from Wabasha's village of Keoxa to a Dakota village represented to have been near St. Anthony Falls, Hon. Hanford L. Gordon retold this tragedy in a poem bearing her name, "Winona," published in 1881, reprinted in his collected writings ("Indian Legends and Other Poems," 1910, pages 43-74).

This name was first applied, about a year before the establishment of the county, to the village of Winona, which became the county seat.

TOWNSHIPS AND VILLAGES.

Information of names has been gathered from "History of Winona County," by Dr. L. H. Bunnell and others, 1883, 966 pages; "Winona (We-no-nah) and its Environs on the Mississippi," by Lafayette Houghton Bunnell, M. D., 1897, 694 pages; "The History of Winona County," compiled by Franklyn Curtiss-Wedge, editor, assisted by William Jay Whipple, 1913, two volumes, continuously paged, 1125 pages; and from interviews with the late Mr. Whipple and Prof. John M. Holzinger, of the State Normal School, each of Winona, during a visit there in April, 1916.

ALTURA, a railway village in Norton, is named for a town in Valencia, Spain.

BEAVER, a hamlet in Whitewater township, platted in 1856, is on the Beaver creek near its mouth, where it was found obstructed by a beaver dam when the first white settlers came.

BETHANY, a railway village in the south edge of Norton, bears the name of a village in Palestine. It is the name of villages or townships in twelve states, and of a city in Missouri.

CENTERVILLE is the name of a hamlet in the southeast part of Wilson.

DAKOTA is a railway village beside the Mississippi on the line between Dresbach and New Hartford.

DRESBACH township and its railway village, platted in September, 1857, were named in honor of George B. Dresbach, who was born in Pickaway county, Ohio, August 27, 1827, came to Minnesota in 1857, founded this village, owned a farm and stone quarries, and was a representative in the legislature in 1868 and 1878.

ELBA township, organized May 11, 1858, and its village, founded in 1856, bear the name of an island of Italy, famed for its rich deposits of iron ore. Napoleon had his residence there in 1814-15.

ENTERPRISE is a hamlet in the southeast edge of Utica.

FREMONT township, organized May 11, 1858, was named in honor of John Charles Fremont (b. 1813, d. 1890), who assisted Nicollet in his expedition through southwestern Minnesota in 1838, and was the first Republican candidate for president of the United States, 1856.

HART township was also organized May 11, 1858. It bears a personal surname, but for whom should be learned by further inquiry.

HILLSDALE township, likewise organized May 11, 1858, was named for its hills or stream bluffs, inclosing dales or valleys.

HOMER township, organized May 11, 1858, and its village, previously platted in 1855, were named by Willard B. Bunnell, a brother of the historian of this county, for "his birthplace, the village of Homer, New York state." Fourteen states of the Union have villages and townships bearing this name of the early Greek epic poet.

LAMOILLE, a village on the Mississippi in the north corner of Richmond, platted in May, 1860, has the name of a river and county in northern Vermont.

LEWISTON, a railway village in Utica, incorporated February 23, 1875, "was named in 1873 for S. J. Lewis, an early settler." (Stennett, Place Names of the Chicago and Northwestern Railways, 1908, p. 94.)

MINNESOTA CITY, a village in Rollingstone township, was platted in March 1852, for the Western Farm and Village Association, a colony of settlers from New York, this place being named by Robert Pike for the Territory. The association was organized in New York city in October, 1851.

MOUNT VERNON township, organized May 11, 1858, is named from the home of Washington in Virginia, on the Potomac river, commemorating Admiral Edward Vernon (b. 1684, d. 1757). Twenty-one other states have townships and villages or cities of this name.

NEW HARTFORD township, organized in 1858, and its earlier village, platted in August, 1857, were named by settlers from Connecticut.

WINONA COUNTY   583

NORTON township, organized May 11, 1858, at first called Sumner, and later Jefferson, bears an honored name of this county. James L. Norton (b. 1825, d. 1904) and Matthew George Norton (b. 1831, d. 1917), brothers who came from Pennsylvania in 1856, were members of the widely known lumber firm of Laird, Norton and Co., in Winona. Daniel S. Norton was born in Mount Vernon, Ohio, April, 1829, and died in Washington, D. C., July 14, 1870. He received his education at Kenyon College, Gambier, Ohio; served in the Mexican war, and afterward studied law. In 1855, in company with Hon. William Windom, he came to Minnesota, and settled in Winona, where he practiced law ten years. He was a member of the state senate in 1857, 1861, and 1864; and of the United States senate from 1866 until his death.

OAK RIDGE is a hamlet in the south part of Mount Vernon.

PICKWICK, a village in Homer, platted in 1857, was named from the "Pickwick Papers," published serially by Charles Dickens in 1836-7.

PLEASANT HILL township has many bluffs and ridges, 200 to 300 feet high. Its name originated with the first permanent settler, Joseph Cooper, who, coming in December, 1854, "to the ridge at the head of the south branch of Pine creek," exclaimed "What a pleasant hill!" He immediately took "a claim of 160 acres of land, lying on the ridge and embracing the heads of South Branch and Money Creek valleys." (History of the county, 1883, p. 582.)

RICHMOND township, organized May 11, 1858, took the name of its village, platted in 1855. "In 1850, a Frenchman named Richmond established a wood-yard on the site of the landing where George Catlin, the noted artist, was forced by obstructing ice to winter his boat, when he was painting his celebrated Indian portraits and pursuing his voyage up the Mississippi in early days. For years, on a conspicuous sand rock in a cove where his boat lay out of danger from running ice, the name of George Catlin could be seen in glaring red, and the landing was well known to steamboat men and pioneers as 'Catlin's Rocks.' Finally, the name of Catlin disappeared by the action of frost and rain, and Richmond's name was given to the landing and perpetuated in village and township." (Bunnell, Winona and its Environs, 1897, p. 473.)

ROLLINGSTONE township and its village are named from their river or creek. Its Dakota name is "Eyan-omen-man-met-pah, the literal translation of which is 'the stream where the stone rolls.'" (History of the county, 1883, p. 144.) The journal of Forsyth, with Leavenworth and the troops who came in 1819 for building the fort that in 1825 was named Fort Snelling, called this stream "the Tumbling Rock."

ST. CHARLES township, organized May 11, 1858, and its village, founded in 1854, incorporated as a city February 28, 1870, were named "for St. Charles of Italy, who was born in 1538 and who became cardinal of Milan and secretary to Pope Pius IV." (History of the county, 1913, p. 597.)

SARATOGA township, organized May 11, 1858, and the village in its west edge, were named by settlers from New York, where this is the name of a lake, a county, and a town having famous medicinal springs. It is an Indian word, said to mean "place of miraculous water in a rock." (Gannett, Place Names in the U. S., 1905, p. 275.)

STOCKTON, a village in Hillsdale, platted in 1856, was named in honor of J. B. Stockton, who was the proprietor of this townsite.

TROY, a village in Saratoga, was named from the city in New York, which took this name from the ancient city in Asia Minor, the scene of the Trojan war, narrated by Homer in the Iliad.

UTICA township, organized May 11, 1858, and its railway village, platted in 1866, are named, like Troy, from a city in New York, which, with villages and townships in fourteen other states, derived this name from the ancient city of Utica, founded by the Phoenicians in North Africa.

WARREN and WILSON townships, side by side, each organized May 11, 1858, and the village of Wilson, are thought to have been named in compliment for Warren Wilson, a prominent early settler.

WHITEWATER township and its village of WHITEWATER FALLS bear the name of the river flowing through them northward to the Mississippi, derived in translation from two Dakota words, *mini,* water, *ska,* white. In Wabasha county this stream has a township and village named Minneiska.

WINONA, the county seat, platted June 19, 1852, was at first named Montezuma by Ervin H. Johnson, one of the proprietors of the site, for the Aztec war chief of Mexico at the time of the Spanish conquest, who was born in 1477 and died June 30, 1520. It was changed to Winona through request of Henry D. Huff, who in 1853 bought an interest in the townsite and platted an addition. This Dakota name has been fully noticed at the beginning of this chapter. A sobriquet recently coming into use is "the Gate City."

"The site of Winona was known to the French as La Prairie aux Ailes (pronounced O'Zell) or the Wing's prairie, presumably because of its having been occupied by members of Red Wing's band." It was latest occupied by Wabasha, the last of the Dakota chiefs for whom the county next northward was named, whose village here was called Keoxa, "difficult of translation, but it may be rendered as 'The Homestead,' because in the springtime there was here a family reunion to honor the dead and invoke their blessings upon the land." (History of the county, 1883, p. 25.) Prof. A. W. Williamson spelled and defined this name more correctly, that "the name of the band was *Kiyuksan,* breakers in two, or violators, so called because they violated the custom forbidding relatives, however distant, to marry."

Winona township, at first having a much larger extent than now, was established as an electoral precinct April 29, 1854. The city was incorporated March 6, 1857.

WISCOY township bears the name of a creek and a village in Allegany county, New York, "an Indian word meaning 'under the banks,'

WINONA COUNTY

or, according to another authority, 'many fall creek.'" (Gannett, Place Names in the U. S.)

WITOKA, a hamlet in the north edge of Wiscoy, platted in 1855, was named for "the daughter of the war chief of Wabasha's band. Witoka was captured by the Sacs (Sauks) near the present site of Witoka, and was rescued by her father's daring dash." (History of the county, 1913, p. 549.)

Lakes and Streams.

Beaver creek and the Rollingstone and Whitewater rivers are noticed in the foregoing list, for a village or hamlet and two townships named from them.

West, Middle, and South branches of Rollingstone creek unite in the township of this name; and similarly the North, Middle and South branches of Whitewater river unite in Elba.

The presence of brook trout is noted by Trout creek in Mount Vernon, a second creek so named in Saratoga, and Big Trout creek in Homer and Richmond.

White pine and red cedar trees, growing sparingly on stream bluffs, are the source of names of Pine creek in Pleasant Hill and New Hartford townships, a second Pine creek in the southwest part of Fremont, and Cedar creek in Homer.

Rush and Money creeks flow south into Fillmore and Houston counties, there giving names to Rushford and Money Creek townships.

Other small streams, directly tributary to the Mississippi here, are Gilmore creek, West and East Burns creeks, Pleasant Valley creek, and Dakota creek, the last having its mouth near Dakota village.

Relatively narrow channels of the Mississippi between its large alluvial islands and the west shore, within a few miles northwest from the city of Winona, are named Crooked slough and Straight slough.

Lake Winona, about two miles long, adjoining this city, occupies a part of a former rivercourse, which also was the character of a similarly long but shallow lake formerly mapped three to five miles northwest of the city.

Above the river bottomlands, this county has no lakes, like several other counties in southeastern Minnesota, which belong wholly or partly to an extensive area that was exempt from glaciation. The greater part of this tract lies in Wisconsin, so that it is commonly called by geologists the Wisconsin driftless area.

Sugarloaf bluff, south of Lake Winona, rises about 550 feet above the lake and river; Minneowah bluff, in Homer, and Gwinn's bluff, also called Queen bluff, in Richmond, have nearly the same height; and the bluffs adjoining the village of Dresbach, including Mineral bluff, rise 600 feet above the river, or about 1230 feet above the sea.

WRIGHT COUNTY

Established February 20, 1855, this county was named in honor of a statesman of New York, Silas Wright, who was born in Amherst, Mass., May 24, 1795, and died in Canton, St. Lawrence county, N. Y., August 27, 1847. It is said that the name "was adopted as a compromise after a somewhat animated discussion." Wright had been a personal friend of W. G. McCrory, who was a member of the committee chosen by the citizens of Monticello to go before the territorial legislature and urge the establishment and organization of the county. On their journey to St. Paul the committee discussed several proposed names for it, but were unable to agree. Finally, at the suggestion of this member, the name of Wright was adopted. He was graduated at Middlebury College, 1815; studied law, and settled for its practice at Canton, N. Y., 1819; was a member of Congress, 1827-29; was comptroller of the State of New York, 1829-33; was a United States senator, 1833-44; and was governor of New York, 1845-47. "He refused several offers of cabinet offices and foreign missions. After his term as governor he retired to his farm in Canton, which he cultivated with his own hands." Biographies of Governor Wright have been published in 1847, 1848, 1852, 1874, and 1913.

TOWNSHIPS AND VILLAGES.

Information of names has been gathered from "History of the Upper Mississippi Valley," 1881, having pages 483-585 for this county; a series of thirty-five newspaper articles on the county history, by Daniel R. Farnham, published in the Delano Eagle, Jan. 6 to Sept. 22, 1881; "History of Wright County," by Franklyn Curtiss-Wedge, 1915, two volumes, continuously paged, 1111 pages; and from Oscar J. Peterson, register of deeds, Hon. John T. Alley, formerly county surveyor and judge of probate, and William H. Cutting, attorney, each of Buffalo, the county seat, interviewed during a visit there in October, 1916.

ALBERTVILLE is a village of the Great Northern railway in the north edge of Frankfort. Its railway station name during many years was St. Michael, for the village of that name two miles distant to the south.

ALBION township, settled in 1855, organized May 11, 1858, bears an ancient name of England, meaning "white land," in allusion to the white chalk cliffs of its south coast.

ANNANDALE, a Soo railway village in Corinna, platted in October, 1886, was incorporated April 21, 1888. It was named for the Annan river and the seaport of Annan at its mouth on the Solway firth, in southern Scotland. Five other states of the Union have villages of this name.

WRIGHT COUNTY 587

BUFFALO village, the county seat, platted in 1856, incorporated May 24, 1887, took its name, given also to the township, which was first settled in April, 1855, and organized May 11, 1858, from their Buffalo lake, "named by the Indian traders on account of the large numbers of buffalo fish found in its waters." For Kandiyohi county, also named from these species of fish, they are more fully noticed.

CHATHAM township, settled in 1855, organized March 2, 1868, commemorates, with townships and villages so named in twelve other states, the distinguished English statesman, William Pitt (b. 1708, d. 1778), first earl of Chatham, who was a friend of the American colonies and an opponent of the British policy which brought on the Revolutionary War.

CLEARWATER township, settled in 1854, organized May 11, 1858, and its earlier village, platted in the spring of 1856, received this name from the Clearwater lake and river, there tributary to the Mississippi.

COKATO township, settled in the early spring of 1856, was organized August 4, 1868. Since 1861 this township had been called Mooers Prairie, being united in administration with Stockholm. Josiah P. Mooers, the first settler, was born in Deerfield, N. H., December 27, 1804; came to Minnesota in 1852, and settled here in 1856; was the first postmaster, the post office being named like the township in his honor. The Dakota or Sioux name, Cokato, adopted in 1868, which had been previously borne by the largest lake of the township, signifies "at the middle." The railroad was built to this place in 1869, the village of Cokato was then founded, and it was incorporated February 16, 1878.

CORINNA township, settled in August, 1856, by several families from Maine, was organized May 11, 1858. "The name is said by the late Levi M. Stewart, of Minneapolis, to have been given to the township by Elder Robinson, a Baptist preacher, who was a boyhood chum of Stewart's, and, like him, a native of Corinna, Maine." (History of the county, 1915, p. 708.)

DAYTON village, lying mainly in Hennepin county, for which its name has been explained, reaches also across the Crow river into the most eastern corner of Otsego.

DELANO, a railway village in Franklin, platted in 1868 and incorporated February 11, 1876, was at first called Crow River, but was renamed in honor of Francis Roach Delano, who was born in New Braintree, Mass., November 20, 1823, and died in St. Paul, February 6, 1887. He came to Minnesota in 1853, and engaged in lumbering in the St. Croix valley; was the first warden of the Minnesota state prison; settled in St. Paul in 1860, and became general superintendent of the St. Paul and Pacific railroad; was largely interested in railroad construction in the state, and during the later years of his life was right of way agent for the Manitoba, (now the Great Northern) railway. In 1875 he was a representative in the legislature.

DICKINSON, a Soo railway station in Rockford township, was named in honor of A. C. Dickinson, on whose farm it was located.

FRANKFORT township, settled in the summer of 1854, organized May 11, 1858, took the name of its earlier village, platted in January, 1857. Many of its pioneer settlers came from Germany, whence they chose this name of an ancient city in Prussia, one of the most important banking cities of the world.

FRANKLIN township, settled in 1855 and organized in 1858, was then called Newport; but, because that name had been early given to a township in Washington county, it was renamed September 14, 1858, in honor of Benjamin Franklin (b. 1706, d. 1790), the American philosopher, statesman, diplomatist, and author.

FRENCH LAKE township, settled in October, 1856, organized June 9, 1865, bears the name of its largest lake and of the outflowing creek, given in compliment for French Canadian settlers.

HANOVER, a village in Frankfort on the Crow river, founded in 1877 by Vollbrecht brothers, was named "in honor of their birthplace in Germany." It was incorporated October 9, 1891.

HASTY, a railway village on the boundary dividing Clearwater and Silver Creek townships, was platted about 1895 on the farm of Warren Hasty, who later removed to Minneapolis.

HOWARD LAKE, a railway village in the north edge of Victor, platted in the spring of 1869, incorporated in 1879, "takes its name from the beautiful sheet of water, on the south of which it is located, and which, tradition informs us, was named by the first surveyors who visited this region, in honor of John Howard, the English philanthropist." (History of the Upper Mi. Valley, 1881, p. 575.) He was born, probably at Hackney, London, Sept. 2, 1726; died at Kherson, Russia, Jan. 20, 1790; was celebrated for his exertions in behalf of prison reform.

MAPLE LAKE township, first settled in 1856 and organized in 1858, received the name of its largest lake, which is bordered by woodlands of the sugar maple. The railway village on the Soo line, bearing the township name, was founded in 1886 and was incorporated December 23, 1890.

MARYSVILLE township, settled in 1855, organized May 14, 1866, was named by its early Roman Catholic settlers.

MIDDLEVILLE township, settled in 1856, organized in 1858, was named by M. V. Cochran, "from his old home in Virginia."

MONTICELLO township, settled in 1852, organized May 11, 1858, and its village, platted in the autumn of 1854 and incorporated in 1856, were named by Thomas Creighton, one of the townsite proprietors, "from the 'Little Mountain,' a hill of modest proportions, about two miles from the village to the southeast. Previous to this in September [1854] Ashley C. Riggs and Moritzious Weissberger laid out the town of Moritzious." These were respectively the upper and lower parts of the present village of Monticello, being rivals during many years. "Monticello was first incorporated by an act of the Territorial Legislature approved March 1st, 1856. . . . Moritzious was also incorporated by an act of the State Legislature approved August 13th, 1858 . . . In after years, difficulties relating to titles led to some change in the corporation of Monticello, and on the 27th of April, 1861, the present organization was consummated." (History of the Upper Mississippi Valley, 1881, pages 537-9.) The home of Thomas Jefferson, in Virginia, three miles southeast of Charlottesville, bore this name, which thence has been given to townships, villages, and cities, in twenty-two other states of the Union.

MONTROSE, a railway village in the southeast edge of Marysville, was platted in 1878 and was incorporated in 1881, being named, like villages in fifteen other states, from a royal burgh and seaport of Scotland.

OTSEGO township, first settled in October, 1852, organized in 1858, and its village on the Mississippi, were named for a lake, a township, and a county in New York. Gannett notes this name as an Indian word, meaning "welcome water," or "place where meetings are held."

ROCKFORD township, settled in 1855, organized in 1858, received the name of its village, founded in 1856 at a rocky ford of the Crow river, having its bed strewn with boulders, where a sawmill was built. The village was platted in the spring of 1857, and was incorporated October 21, 1881. Near the millsite the Winnebago Indians had a village during the years 1850-54.

ST. MICHAEL, a village in Frankfort, incorporated February 10, 1890, was named from its Catholic church, which was built in 1856.

SILVER CREEK township, named for its creek, was settled in 1854 and organized in 1858.

SMITH LAKE, a railway village in Middleville, platted in July, 1869, bears the name of the adjoining lake, beside which Eugene Smith settled in 1858.

SOUTH HAVEN village, on the Soo railway in Southside township, had its first trains in 1887, was platted in 1888, and was incorporated in 1902. This name is derived from its township and from Fair Haven township and village on the north in Stearns county.

SOUTHSIDE township, named from its relation to the Clearwater river and the series of lakes through which that stream flows, was settled in 1857 and was organized March 9, 1868.

STOCKHOLM township, first settled in 1856, received its first Swede settlers in 1862 and many more in 1866. It was organized August 15, 1868, being named in compliment to these immigrants.

VICTOR township, settled in 1855, organized January 24, 1866, was named at the suggestion of Mark Fosket, an early settler, "in honor of Victor in Ontario county, New York."

WAVERLY, a railway village on the south line of Marysville, was founded in 1869, when the building of the St. Paul and Pacific railroad reached this site, and it was incorporated in 1881. Its name was received from the adjacent Big and Little Waverly lakes, and from an earlier Waverly village, having a sawmill and gristmill, platted in 1856 at the outlet of the Little Waverly lake. The name was originally given by the Colwell brothers, who with others were proprietors of that earlier townsite, for Waverly in Tioga county, N. Y., their former home, which derived it from Scott's Waverley novels, published in 1814-28.

WOODLAND township, settled in 1855, organized in 1858, was named for its originally heavily forested condition, being in the central part of "the Big Woods," a large area noticed in the first chapter.

LAKES AND STREAMS.

The origin and meaning of the names of the Crow and Clearwater rivers have been considered in the chapters for Crow Wing and Clearwater counties. The North and South branches of Crow river unite on the east side of Rockford.

Buffalo, Clearwater, and Cokato lakes, French lake and creek, Howard lake, Maple lake, Silver creek, Smith lake, and the Waverly lakes, are noticed for the townships and villages named from them in the preceding list.

Other lakes and creeks are arranged as follows, in the numerical order of the ranges from east to west, and of the townships from south to north.

Fountain, Cedar, and Rice lakes, in Franklin, are named respectively for their springs, red cedar trees, and wild rice.

Woodland has Carrigan, Ruckle's, and Lauzer's lakes, with two or three others unnamed.

Victor has the southern end of Howard lake, Mud and Dutch lakes, close southeastward, and Lakes Ann, Emma, and Mary. Tuey and Little Rice lakes and Spring lake, in the northwest part of this township, are scarcely more than marshes during the greater part of the year.

Big Rice lake or slough and Shakopee lake, in Stockholm, have been mostly drained. Butternut lake, at the south side of Stockholm, reaches into McLeod county; and Collinwood lake on the west extends into Meeker county, where a township bears this name.

Rockford has Moore, Wagner, Charlotte, and Mary lakes, crossed by its north line, named for pioneers. Frederick creek, outflowing from Mary lake, and Dean, Crawford, and Ilstrup lakes, are also similarly named. Mink and Tamarack lakes are crossed by the west line of sections 6 and 7.

Marysville has Deer lake, close southwest of Buffalo lake, and the Waverly lakes, adjoining its south line. Twelve Mile creek is the outlet of Little Waverly lake, and of Lake Ann in Victor and Rice lake in Stockholm.

In Middleville, besides Howard and Smith lakes, are also Doerfler and Junkins lakes.

With Cokato lake, the township of this name has Brooks and Skifstrom lakes, named in honor of early settlers. Beaver Dam and Swan lakes, on the west line of this township, are now mainly dry. Sucker creek, named for its fish, flows into Cokato lake.

Frankfort has Lake Foster in its eastern section 3; Goose, Mud, and School lakes, the last named for its situation in the school section 16; Eull's lake, Williams lake, Wagner, Beebe, and Schmidt lakes, each commemorating a pioneer farmer; and the southeastern part of Pelican lake, the largest of this county.

The west part of Schmidt lake, extending into Buffalo township, but now mostly drained, had Crane island, of 13 acres. This township includes also, with large parts of Pelican and Buffalo lakes, the beautiful Lake Pulaski, named for the Polish patriot and friend of Washington in our Revolutionary War; Green Mountain lake, named by settlers from Vermont; Washington lake, and Constance and Gilchrist lakes, the last reaching north into Monticello.

In Chatham, with about half of Buffalo lake, are Birch lake, Lakes Abbie and Albert, Cochrane lake, small Twin lakes in the northeast quarter of section 22, Lake Mary in section 19, and Rock lake, on the west line, named from it boulders.

Albion comprises Camp, Granite, Maxim, White, Henshaw, Albion, Edward, and Swartwatts lakes. The former William and Henry lakes, on the south sides of sections 5 and 6, have been lately drained.

In French Lake township, with its lake and creek so named, are Dan's lake and Lake Francis, the latter now renamed Hutchins lake, which extends west into Meeker county.

Otsego has School lake, in the western school section 36.

Monticello, having the northern part of Pelican lake, includes also the north part of Gilchrist lake; and farther west it has the series of Black, Cedar, North, Burch, Bertram, and Long lakes, outflowing by Otter creek to the Mississippi. With these are to be noted the little Twin lakes, in the west edge of this township.

In Maple Lake township are Maple and Ramsey lakes, the second being named for Governor Ramsey, Lightfoot and Angus lakes, and Lake Mary.

Silver Creek township comprises Eagle and Ida lakes, near its southeast corner; Silver, Marie, and Locke lakes, on Silver creek; and Ember, Limestone, and Mill Stone lakes. The former Melrose lake, in the north part of section 36, is now a marsh.

Corinna has Sugar lake, named for its sugar maples, Indian and Mink lakes, Cedar and Pleasant lakes, Bass lake, and the greater part of Clearwater lake, with its Eagle island.

Southside has Lake John, Goose lake, crossed by its south line, Lake Sylvia and Twin lake, connected by a strait, and, along the course of the Clearwater river, forming the northern boundary of this township and of the county, Lakes Louisa, Maria, Caroline, and Augusta.

On the west boundary of Clearwater township are Grass and Wiegand lakes, through which the Clearwater river flows; Nixon and Connelly lakes, named for early settlers, are on the east side of sections 22 and 27; Sheldon lake or marsh is in section 24; Fish lake has its outlet by Fish creek at the south end of an ox-bow of the Mississippi, which flows around Boyington island; and Rice lake, having wild rice, lies a mile farther east.

Prairies.

Relatively small areas of prairie, noteworthy for their occurrence in this mainly well wooded county, were Clearwater prairie, nearly adjoining the Mississippi eastward from the Clearwater river; Sanborn prairie, named for a pioneer farmer, in Silver Creek township; Monticello prairie, one to two miles southwest of the village of this name; Winneshiek prairie, near the Crow river in Frankfort, named "in honor of the Winnebago chief who spent several years in this vicinity," for whom a county in northeastern Iowa is named; and Mooers prairie, in Cokato, for which township it has been more fully noticed.

Winneshiek, previously chief of a band of the Winnebagoes, was appointed in 1845 by the United States War Department to be head chief of this tribe, which had been removed from Wisconsin to northeastern Iowa in 1840. He was thus the head chief while the Winnebagoes were in Minnesota, from 1848 to 1855 on the Long Prairie reservation, and later in Blue Earth county until 1863, being then removed to a reservation in Dakota. He died after 1880, while making a canoe journey down the Missouri river.

YELLOW MEDICINE COUNTY

This county, established March 6, 1871, is crossed by the Yellow Medicine river, whence the name is derived. It is a translation of the Dakota or Sioux name, which Prof. A. W. Williamson spelled and defined thus: "Pajutazee (Pezhihutazi, abbreviated from Pezhihutazizi kapi),— *peji*, generic name, including grasses and all other erect plants without wood stems; *huta*, root; *zi*, yellow; *kapi*, they dig; diggings of yellow plant root, or yellow medicine diggings; the Dakota name of the Yellow Medicine river, written by Nicollet Pejuta zizi. The name as first spelled was given by Dr. T. S. Williamson to his station, and is found in this form on a number of maps."

The late Dr. Thomas M. Young, who was during several years in charge of the government school for Indian children at the Sisseton Agency, South Dakota, stated that the "yellow medicine" is the long, slender, bitter, yellow root of the moonseed (Menispermum Canadense), which grows abundantly in thickets in this region. From the root of this plant came thus the name of the river and the county.

It was proposed in 1878-9 to establish a new county, named like the village and city of Canby, in honor of General E. R. S. Canby, whose biography is presented in the notice of that city. The legislative act passed for this purpose, subject to ratification by the people, received the governor's approval February 27, 1879. The proposed county was to comprise the western six townships of Yellow Medicine county, the three most northern of Lincoln county, and three from southwestern Lac qui Parle county. The vote in Yellow Medicine county was 463 yes, 370 no; but the vote in Lincoln county defeated it.

Townships and Villages.

Information of geographic names here, with their meanings, has been gathered from "History of the Minnesota Valley," 1882, having pages 882-912 for this county; "An Illustrated History of Yellow Medicine County," by Arthur P. Rose, 1914, 562 pages; and from George H. Wilson, county auditor, Charles F. Hall, judge of probate, Hon. Ole O. Lende, and Frederic W. Pearsall, each of Granite Falls, the county seat, interviewed during a visit there in July, 1916.

Burr, a village of the Northwestern railway in Florida township, founded in 1886, was called Stanley until its post office was established in 1895. Because the name Stanley had been given to an earlier postoffice in this state, the name Burr was adopted at the suggestion of Alfred Froberg, the merchant and grain-buyer here, "that being a Froberg family name." (History of the county, 1914, p. 247.)

BURTON township, settled in 1877 and organized May 20, 1879, was named "in honor of Burton French, the father of Palmer O. French, a pioneer settler."

CANBY, a city in Norman township, was platted in the summer of 1876, three years after the building of this line of the Northwestern railway, was incorporated as a village in 1879, and as a city March 1, 1905. It was named in honor of Edward Richard Sprigg Canby, as before noted in relation to a proposed county bearing his name. He was born in Kentucky in 1819; was graduated at the U. S. Military Academy, 1839; served during the Mexican war, 1846-8, and the civil war, 1861-5; was commander in Louisiana, and of the U. S. army departments west of the Mississippi, in 1864; captured Mobile, April 12, 1865; was promoted to major general of volunteers, and in 1866 became a brigadier general in the regular army; was treacherously killed by the Modoc Indians during a conference in Siskiyou county, northern California, April 11, 1873.

CLARKFIELD, a village of the Minneapolis and St. Louis railway in Friendship, platted October 7, 1884, incorporated October 10, 1887, was "named in honor of Mr. Clark, who was connected with the railroad company."

ECHO township, first settled in 1869, was organized March 31, 1874, being then named Empire, which was changed in the next month to Rose, "and on July 17, 1874, the name Echo was bestowed upon it. . . . The difficulties encountered in selecting a name not borne by some other township suggested the final name. This was one case where echo answered." (Arthur P. Rose, History of the county, p. 95.) The railway village, bearing the township name, was founded in August, 1884, and was incorporated May 31, 1892.

FLORIDA township, organized January 27, 1879, is crossed by Florida creek, which was named for a railway contractor, whose camp was there in 1873, when the railway was built.

FORTIER township, settled in the fall of 1873, was the latest organized in this county, May 30, 1881. "The name of Le Roy was first given to it, but, as there was already a town of that name, Fortier was substituted in honor of Joseph Fortier." He was born in Napierville, Canada, April 12, 1835; came to Minnesota in 1854, and from 1855 to 1862 was employed at the Upper Sioux Agency; was in the battle of New Ulm, the defence of Fort Ridgely, and the battle of Wood Lake, 1862; served also in Sibley's and Sully's expeditions, 1863 and '64; later was a merchant in Yellow Medicine City, and after 1874 at Granite Falls; was sheriff of this county, 1877-87; died at Granite Falls, March 27, 1898.

FRIENDSHIP, settled in the spring of 1872, organized March 11, 1879, was named in the petition of its people to the county commissioners for organization.

GRANITE FALLS, the county seat, platted May 7, 1872, incorporated as a village March 17, 1879, and as a city in April, 1889, received its name

YELLOW MEDICINE COUNTY   595

from the granite and gneiss outcrops of the Minnesota river here, over which and on boulders in the river bed it falls 38 feet.

HAMMER township, settled in June, 1872, organized July 2, 1877, has a name that is borne by villages in Bavaria and Prussia, and also by a village in Tennessee.

HANLEY FALLS, a railway junction village on the Yellow Medicine river, was founded in the summer of 1884, the Minneapolis and St. Louis track being laid to this place on August 19, and it was incorporated January 8, 1892. The name was given in honor of an officer of that railway company.

HAZEL RUN township, settled in 1871 and organized in 1877, bears the name of its creek, tributary to the Minnesota river. The railway village, named like the township, was platted in September, 1884, and was incorporated May 16, 1902.

HAZELWOOD, a mission station of Revs. T. S. Williamson and S. R. Riggs during the years 1854 to 1862, was in section 15, Minnesota Falls. Here were a mission school and numerous families of Christian Sioux, who were organized under a plan of self government, called the Hazelwood Republic.

LISBON township, settled in June, 1871, organized September 20, 1873, has the name of the capital of Portugal, borne also by townships and villages in nineteen other states.

LORNE, a station of the Great Northern railway five miles south of Granite Falls, established in 1898, was named in honor of the Marquis of Lorne, a British statesman, the eldest son of the eighth Duke of Argyll. He was born in London, August 6, 1845; represented Argyllshire in Parliament, 1868-78; was governor general of Canada, 1878-83; and succeeded to the dukedom in April, 1900. He married the Princess Louise, fourth daughter of Queen Victoria, in 1871.

MINNESOTA FALLS township, settled in October, 1865, organized April 5, 1873, and its former village, platted in 1871, which flourished during a few years, but whose buildings were partly burned and the others removed before the end of 1882, derived their name from the falls of the Minnesota river. At the sawmill and flour mill of Governor Austin and Park Worden, the utilized fall was 10 feet.

NORMAN, settled in 1870, was organized April 7, 1874. "The first settlers of this township were Norwegians exclusively, and the name was given in consequence. In Norway a native is referred to as a Norsk or Norman." (History of the county, 1914, p. 94.)

NORMANIA township, settled in 1867-8, was organized March 12, 1872, being then named Ree, for "a prominent group of farms in Norway," which was changed in 1874 to the present name, of the same significance as the last preceding.

OMRO township, settled in April, 1878, organized January 29, 1880, was named on suggestion of Robert North, the first chairman of the board of supervisors, "after a town in Mr. North's old home county [Winnebago] in Wisconsin." (History of the county, p. 102.)

OSHKOSH township, settled in the spring of 1877 and organized July 19, 1879, was named for the city of Oshkosh in Wisconsin, the county seat of Winnebago county, which commemorates the head chief of the Menominee Indians.

OTIS, formerly a small fractional township at the west side of Granite Falls, organized October 16, 1873, "named in honor of its first settler, John D. Otis," has been annexed to Stony Run.

PORTER, a village of the Northwestern railway in the south edge of Wergeland, platted in October, 1881, and incorporated February 10, 1898, was named for the L. C. Porter Milling Company, by whom its first grain warehouse was erected.

POSEN township, settled in 1868, organized May 17, 1879, received its name "from the province of Posen, formerly belonging to Poland, but now a part of the German Empire, from whence most of the settlers came." (History of the Minnesota Valley, p. 908.)

ST. LEO, a village on the line between Omro and Burton, "was named after the church, and the church was so christened in honor of Pope Leo." (History of the county, p. 247.) The church, built in 1896, is commemorative of Saint Leo, the first Pope of this name, A. D. 440-461, who is surnamed "the Great."

SANDNES township, settled in 1866, mostly from Norway, and organized March 12, 1872, bears the name (with slight change in spelling) of Sandnaes, a seaport town of southwestern Norway, adjoining the Stavanger fjord.

SIOUX AGENCY township, first permanently settled in 1865, "was set apart for organization September 4, 1866," being named Yellow Medicine, and its first township meeting was held April 2, 1867. "In March, 1877, the present boundaries were fixed and the name changed to Sioux Agency." (History of the Minnesota Valley, p. 892.) The Upper Sioux Agency was on the north side of the Yellow Medicine river and about a mile west of its mouth, in the northern part of this township. It was occupied from 1854 to 1862, and, as noted by Rose, "became a place of considerable importance and was virtually the capital of the Indian country."

SORLIEN MILLS, a hamlet of much business in the pioneer days, had a gristmill and post office on the Yellow Medicine river in the southeast part of Minnesota Falls township. E. H. Sorlien and brothers erected the mill in 1872. The post office was established in July, 1878, and E. H. Sorlien was postmaster till it was discontinued in July, 1896. (History of the county, p. 249.)

STAVANGER post office named from the fjord, city, and district of this name in southern Norway, was established about 1870 in section 27, Ree

YELLOW MEDICINE COUNTY 597

(afterward Normania), and was discontinued by a rural free delivery route in November, 1903.

STONY RUN township, settled in 1869, organized September 26, 1871, "is named for the creek that courses through it," in many places flowing over drift boulders.

SWEDE PRAIRIE township, settled in 1870, was organized January 19, 1878. "The name first given to the town was Green Prairie, but was changed March 12, 1878, to Swede Prairie," in compliment to its many immigrants from Sweden.

TYRO township, settled in August, 1872, was organized October 25, 1879. This name, meaning a beginner, is borne also by villages or hamlets in Virginia, Mississippi, Arkansas, and Kansas.

WERGELAND township, organized April 5, 1879, was then named Union, which was changed on May 1 of that year, by request of the many Norwegian settlers, "in honor of one of their native country's poets, Henrik Wergeland." He was born at Christiansand, June 17, 1808, and died at Christiania, July 12, 1845.

WOOD LAKE township, settled in 1868, organized November 1, 1873, was named for its largest lake, fringed with timber, whence the battle fought under General Sibley against the Sioux, about four miles east of this lake, September 23, 1862, has been called the battle of Wood Lake. That battle ground is marked by a monument, on the northwest quarter of section 9, Sioux Agency. The battle was followed by the flight of the hostile Sioux to Dakota and the release of the white captives, September 26, at Camp Release in Lac qui Parle county, opposite to Montevideo, likewise marked by a monument. The railway village of Wood Lake, established in the summer of 1884, before the first passenger train came on August 18, was incorporated November 28, 1891.

YELLOW MEDICINE CITY, founded in 1866 and platted June 10, 1869, was on the south side of the river of this name, about a mile west of the site of the former Yellow Medicine or Upper Sioux Agency. This village was designated as the county seat early in 1872, but in accordance with the vote of the people in 1874 the county offices were removed in December of that year to Granite Falls, which has since been the county seat. During 1875-80 the area of the Yellow Medicine village site reverted to farming land.

The mission station bearing this name, also called Pajutazee, occupied from 1853 to 1862, was in section 24 of the present Minnesota Falls township, being nearly two miles southeast of the Hazelwood mission school and its Sioux community.

STREAMS AND LAKES.

Yellow Medicine river bears this name on the map of Long's expedition in 1823 and on Nicollet's map, 1843. The latter has also the Dakota name, noted at the beginning of this chapter.

Florida creek, Hazel Run, and Stony Run, giving their names to townships, and Wood lake, whence another township is named, are noticed in the preceding pages.

Canby creek, named from the city, and the East branch of Lac qui Parle river, crossing the west part of this county, flow northward into Lac qui Parle county.

Mud creek, flowing eastward across Wergeland and Burton, and Spring creek, crossing Swede Prairie and the north edge of Normania, are tributary to the Yellow Medicine river.

The lakes of this county, occurring only in its southeastern part, include, with Wood lake, before noted, Sand and House lakes in the same township, the last being named for a pioneer; three small lakes in sections 8 and 17, Sioux Agency, lying a half mile to one and a half miles south of the Wood Lake battle ground and monument, the two northern being named High Bank and Battle lakes; a former Lake of the Woods and another long lake or marsh in Echo township, both now drained; Tyson lake or marsh, and an adjoining Twin lake, in Posen, the first being named for Joseph Tyson, an early homesteader on its south side; and a group of three lakes in Normania, of which the middle one is called Gullickson lake, for a pioneer Norwegian farmer beside it.

MINNEAPOLIS

Information of the origin and meanings of names of streets and avenues in Minneapolis, and of its boulevards, parks, and other public grounds, has been gathered from "History of the City of Minneapolis," by Isaac Atwater, 1893, two volumes, 1010 pages; "Personal Recollections of Minnesota and its People, and Early History of Minneapolis," by John H. Stevens, 1890, 433 pages; "A Half Century of Minneapolis," edited by Horace B. Hudson, 1908, 569 pages; from interviews, mostly in the autumn of 1916, with Prof. William W. Folwell, Dr. Lysander P. Foster and Edwin Clark, respectively president and secretary of the Hennepin County Territorial Association, Harlow S. Gale and John R. Gray, of the City Engineer Department, Andrew Rinker, former city engineer, Portius C. Deming and James A. Ridgway, respectively president and secretary of the Board of Park Commissioners, and David G. Gorham, deputy register of deeds of Hennepin county, president of the Native Sons of Minnesota; from the map of St. Anthony and Minneapolis in 1856, published by Chapman and Curtis, civil engineers; Books A to I, 1849 to 1885, city and county plats of surveys, in the office of the county register of deeds; and "The City Charter, Ordinances, Standing Rules and Orders of the City Council of the City of Minneapolis," revised and compiled by A. N. Merrick, city attorney, 1873, 174 pages, in which is an ordinance (pages 115-125), passed August 12, 1873, "changing the names and designations of streets," subsequent to the union of St. Anthony and Minneapolis as one city, enacted mainly for avoidance of duplication and confusion in the names of streets and avenues in the previously two municipalities, respectively east and west of the river.

In the chapter of Hennepin county, the names of St. Anthony and Minneapolis (with the earlier names suggested and somewhat used for the latter), of the Mississippi river and its islands, of St. Anthony falls, Minnehaha falls and creek, and of the several lakes and other creeks within the city area, have been duly noticed.

Streets and Avenues.

The extensive changes made in the systems of street names soon after the union of the former two cities, as above cited, are very concisely and definitely catalogued by Dr. William E. Leonard, as follows, in a paper entitled "Early Days in Minneapolis," published in the Minnesota Historical Society Collections, volume XV, 1915, pages 497-514.

"This paper may well be concluded by noting the names formerly borne by the streets (now called avenues) which run transverse to the course of the Mississippi. These were renamed numerically as avenues within the first year after the union in 1872 of St. Anthony and Minneapolis, to distinguish them conveniently from the streets which are parallel with the river, being therefore intersected by the avenues. Washington and University avenues are exceptional, being parallel with the Mississippi, so that more properly they should be called streets.

"Under dates of 1873 and 1874, maps of the enlarged city show in their order southeastward from Nicollet avenue and parallel therewith, running thus transverse to the river the following streets: Minnetonka, Helen, Oregon, California, Marshall, Cataract, Russell, Ames, Rice, Smith, Pearl, Huy, Hanson, Lake, Vine, Clay, Avon, and Lane streets, these being respectively the First to the Eighteenth avenues south, lying between Nicollet and Cedar avenues. Both the old names as streets and the new names as avenues are given on these maps, which belong to the time of transition from the old to the new.

"East of Cedar avenue on these maps are Aspen, Oak, Walnut, Elm, Maple, Pine, Spruce, Willow, Birch, and Orange streets, being respectively the present Nineteenth to the Twenty-eighth avenues south.

"In the order from Hennepin avenue to the northwest and north were Utah, Kansas, Itasca, Dakota, Nebraska, Harrison, Lewis, Seward, Marcy, Benton, the next unnamed, then Moore, Fremont, Clayton, Bingham, Breckenridge, Cass, Douglas, Buchanan, Christmas, Howard, Clay, Mary Ann, and King streets, these being renamed respectively as the First to the Twenty-fourth avenues north.

"On the St. Anthony side, Central avenue had been earlier called Bay street; and thence southeastward were Mill, Pine, Cedar, Spruce, Spring, Maple, Walnut, Aspen, Birch, Willow, Elm, and A, B, etc., to G and H streets, now respectively the First to Nineteenth avenues southeast.

"Passing northwest and north from Central avenue, in the northeast part of the city, were in succession Linden, Oak, Dakota, Todd, Dana, Wood, St. Paul, St. Anthony, St. Peter's, St. Martin, St. Genevieve, Prairie, Grove, and Lake streets, which now are, in the same order, the First to the Fourteenth avenues northeast.

"Evidently the confusion arising after the two municipalities were united as the new and greater Minneapolis, through the several duplications of street names west and east of the river, was one of the chief reasons for their renaming as avenues and under numbers for the four main divisions of the city. What was lost in the historic origins of the former names, dating from the first surveys and plats, seems to have been more than offset by the increased convenience, local significance, and systematic definiteness of the present nomenclature."

Among the personal names in the foregoing lists of former street names are Helen, in honor of Frances Helen Miller, wife of Col. John H. Stevens,† the first pioneer resident of Minneapolis on the west side of the Mississippi; Marshall, in honor of William R. Marshall,† sur-

---

†For biographic notes, see M. H. S. Collections, vol. XIV, published in 1912.

veyor of the first plat of St. Anthony Falls, October 9, 1849, and plats of Minneapolis in 1855-6, between Helen and Cedar streets, who became a colonel and general in the civil war, and later was governor of Minnesota, for whom a county is named; Russell for Roswell P. Russell,† a prominent pioneer of Minneapolis, who in the years 1854-60 resided on this street, now Seventh avenue S.; Ames, for Dr. Alfred E. Ames,† who came here in 1851, settling on a tract of 80 acres; Rice, for Henry M.† and Edmund Rice,† of St. Paul, owners of real estate platted for St. Anthony and Minneapolis; Huy, for George E. Huy,† who settled in Minneapolis in 1852, succeeded Stevens as precinct clerk of Minneapolis in 1855, and was also the county register of deeds; Hanson, for Dominicus M.† and Gilbert S. Hanson, each receiving a patent for 80 acres, April 23, 1855, crossed by the former Hanson street, now Thirteenth avenue S.; Lane, probably for Silas and Isaac E. Lane, pioneers of St. Anthony in 1849; Harrison, Lewis, Seward, Marcy, Benton, Fremont, Clayton, Bingham, Breckenridge, Cass, Douglas, Buchanan, Howard, Clay, and King, for prominent citizens and statesmen in other parts of the United States; Moore, for a pioneer family, who in the name of Rachel Moore received a patent September 7, 1855, for a tract crossed by Moore street, now Twelfth avenue N.; Christmas, in honor of Charles W. Christmas,† a land surveyor, who settled in St. Anthony in 1850 and a few years afterward took a claim extending a mile from south to north along the west side of the Mississippi, from the present Plymouth avenue to Twenty-sixth avenue N.; Todd, for Captain John B. S. Todd,† commandant of Fort Ripley in 1849-56, brigadier general of volunteers in the civil war, and governor of Dakota Territory, 1869-71, for whom Todd county is named; Dana, in honor of Napoleon J. T. Dana,† for a few months colonel of the First Minnesota regiment, and after 1862 a major general of volunteers; and Wood, for Thomas John Wood, who was graduated at West Point, 1845, served during the Mexican and civil wars, and was promoted to major general in 1865.

Hennepin and Nicollet avenues, the first following nearly the course of an earlier Territorial Road, commemorate Father Hennepin, like this county, and Joseph N. Nicollet, for whom Nicollet county is named. In 1916 the most southern part of Central avenue, Division street, and a new street, laid out to unite these, were renamed East Hennepin avenue, being a continuation of Hennepin avenue from the west side of the river northeast and east to the boundary of the city.

Lyndale avenue was named from the Lyndale farm of 1400 acres owned by Hon. William S. King, adjoining Lakes Harriet and Calhoun, which also was the source of the names of Lyndale Park and Lyndale Farmstead. The original adoption of this name for the farm was in honor of Mr. King's father, Rev. Lyndon King, an itinerant Methodist minister of northern New York, who was named for Josiah Lyndon, colonial governor of Rhode Island in 1768-9. "His administration was marked by signs of growing hostility to the British government, and especially by a correspondence between the governor and the Earl of Hillsborough, in which the former protested against the arbitrary acts of the home government." (Appleton's Cyclopaedia of American Biography.)

East from Lyndale avenue and parallel with it, running from north to south, is the following series of avenues: Garfield, named for the martyr president of the United States; Harriet, named for the adjacent lake; Grand avenue, the French word for great, hence noble, excellent; Pleasant avenue; Pillsbury avenue, named in honor of Governor Pillsbury† and others of this prominent Minneapolis family; Blaisdell, in honor of Robert Blaisdell, Sr., and his three sons, pioneers here, and lumbermen on the upper Mississippi; Nicollet avenue, before noticed; Marquette avenue, originally called Minnetonka street, later First avenue S., but renamed in 1916 for the renowned Jacques Marquette, a zealous Christian missionary to the Indians of the Great Lakes, a voyager with Joliet down the Mississippi from the Wisconsin to the Arkansas river in 1673; Stevens, in honor of Col. John H. Stevens,† before mentioned, whose statue is at the intersection of Portland avenue and Eleventh street; Second and Third avenues S.; Clinton avenue, in honor of Clinton Morrison,† a prominent business man of this city, and during nearly thirty years a bank president; Fourth and Fifth avenues; Portland, Oakland, Park, Columbus, and Chicago avenues, the last being also known as Eighth avenue S.; Elliot avenue, running south from the west side of Elliot park, which was partly donated to the city July 14, 1883, by Dr. Jacob S. Elliot† and wife; Tenth to Fifteenth avenues; Bloomington avenue, named for Bloomington township, toward which it extends; Sixteenth, Seventeenth, and Eighteenth avenues; Cedar avenue, named for red cedars formerly on the Mississippi bluffs at its north end; Longfellow avenue for the beloved American poet, who wrote of Minnehaha and the Pipestone Quarry, in this state, also for a respected family founded in this county and city by Jacob Longfellow, who came in 1852 to Getchell prairie in Brooklyn; and Nineteenth to Forty-ninth avenues, occupying a width of more than two miles in the southeast part of the city west of the river.

With the foregoing, eastward from Cedar avenue, are to be also noted four avenues, crossing these diagonally from northwest to southeast, named Hiawatha, Railroad, Snelling, and Minnehaha avenues, the last being the most northeastern. They run in parallelism with the Chicago, Milwaukee and St. Paul railroad, and lead toward Minnehaha falls and Fort Snelling, whence, and also from Longfellow's "Song of Hiawatha," celebrating the beauties of these falls, the four names are derived.

Riverside avenue, Riverside park and terrace, and their continuation southeastward by the West River Bank Parkway, are successively near and beside the great river, whence came these names.

Next may be noted Washington and Franklin avenues and Lake street. In accordance with the generalization before mentioned, that avenues are transverse to the course of the river, while streets are parallel with it, each of these should consistently be called a street. Washington avenue, commemorates George Washington. Franklin avenue, which in the numerical system would be Twentieth street, similarly honors Benjamin Franklin, but it also recalls the memory of Samuel Franklin, whose land patent for eighty acres, April 23, 1855, bordered the south side of this avenue. Furthermore, it likewise may recall Franklin Steele,† a very early and prominent citizen, and Franklin Cook†, who was an early county surveyor. Lake street, or Thirtieth street in the system of numerical nomenclature, in its western continuation skirts the north shore of Lake Calhoun, passing between that lake and the Lake of the Isles.

West from Lyndale avenue, in north to south parallelism with it, is a very interesting alphabetic series of avenues, named alike in the southwestern and the northern parts of the city west of the river, although their midway course is interrupted by railway tracks and yards. These avenues are Aldrich, named for Thomas Bailey Aldrich, poet and editor, also in honor of Cyrus Aldrich†, of this city, member of Congress in 1859-63, and postmaster of Minneapolis, 1867-71; Bryant, for the earlier poet and editor; Colfax, for the vice-president of the United States; Dupont, for the naval commander in the Mexican and civil wars; Emerson, for Ralph Waldo Emerson, essayist and poet; Fremont, for "the Pathfinder;" Girard, for the merchant and philanthropist in Philadelphia, founder of Girard College; Humboldt, for the German scientist and author, who traveled through South America and Mexico in 1799-1804; Irving, for the well known author, Washington Irving; James, for George P. R. James, an English novelist and historical writer; Knox, for Henry Knox, an artillery general in the Revolutionary War, later United States secretary of war, 1785-95; Logan, for John A. Logan, general and statesman; Morgan, in honor of George N. Morgan,† colonel of the First Minnesota regiment, September, 1862, to May, 1863, brevetted brigadier general in 1865; Newton, for Sir Isaac Newton; Oliver, for Deacon A. M. Oliver, a pioneer who came here from Missouri, platted his claim as Oliver's Park addition, and whose widow was a generous donor to the Oliver Presbyterian church and to Macalester College; Penn, for the founder of Pennsylvania; Queen avenue; Russell, for Roswell P. Russell,† before noticed as an honored pioneer, who came to Fort Snelling in 1839, and opened the first store in St. Anthony in 1847; Sheridan and Thomas avenues, for generals in the civil war; Upton, for Emory Upton, also a general in that war, afterward commandant of cadets at West Point, 1870-75; Vincent, for Thomas M. Vincent, who was graduated at West Point in 1853, and was assistant adjutant general of the United States through the civil war; Washburn avenue, in honor of Governor C. C. Washburn,† of Wisconsin, builder of a very large flouring mill in Minneapolis in 1876, and of his brother, William D. Washburn,† of this city, United States senator; and Xerxes, York, and Zenith avenues, these names being chosen simply to fill their alphabetic places.

Next westward a second alphabetic series of avenue names is begun, reaching to the city boundary. This short list comprises Abbott avenue, in honor of E. T. Abbott, Minneapolis surveyor and civil engineer, and of Seth Abbott,† who in 1883 platted an addition of this city, and whose daughter Emma† was a famous singer; Beard avenue for Henry Beach Beard, who donated to the city the greater part of the Lake Harriet boulevard; Chowen avenue, for George W. Chowen,† of this city, county register of deeds, and later clerk of the district court; and Drew, Ewing, and France avenues, the last being on the west line of the city.

Crossing the central and north part of the area of the alphabetic avenues, are several east to west avenues bearing distinctive names other than the numerical avenues north, which latter begin with the first north of Chestnut avenue. The list of these mostly short avenues, in the order from south to north, includes Lagoon avenue, close northeast of Lake Calhoun; Franklin avenue, continuing east through the city; Lincoln, Summit, Douglas, Superior, Erie, Ontario, Laurel, Hawthorne, Linden, Chestnut, Western, Plymouth, and Mississippi avenues.

The tract containing the last named avenues is also crossed by Cedar Lake road, running from southwest to northeast, and by Farwell avenue, quite short, and the longer Crystal Lake road, each running northwest.

On the north the series of numerical avenues reaches to Fifty-third avenue N., on the city boundary west of the Mississippi, and to Thirty-seventh avenue N. E., on the east side of the river. But beyond the city limit the latter series has been platted to Forty-fifth avenue N. E., or beyond this, in Fridley township, Anoka county, forming there the suburb named Columbia Heights.

Between Hennepin and Nicollet avenues, in an addition platted by Allen Harmon, July 23, 1856, was Harmon street, later renamed as Harmon place. Next southeastward are Yale place and Mary place, the latter when first platted in 1858 being named Mary street. These streets, each called a "place," run northeastward. Near them, but running due east, as the most northern in the large series of east to west streets, is Grant street, named for President Grant.

Nearly all the blocks are rectangular, and the streets and avenues straight. Notable exceptions to this general rule are several additions that occupy somewhat hilly ground, diversified by low ridges and hillocks or knolls of morainic drift. Such is a tract called Washburn Park, in the south edge of the city, surrounding the Washburn Home, an orphanage, bounded on the south by the Minnehaha creek and parkway; and other tracts of short, curving streets and avenues are the Oak Lake, Oak Park, Ridgewood, Lake View, Kenwood, Bryn Mawr, and Groveland additions.

In the vicinity of the Washburn Home are Rustic Lodge avenue, Prospect, Lynn, Belmont, and Luverne avenues, and Elmwood place.

MINNEAPOLIS

In the district of Loring Park, Lowry hill, and Kenwood Park, are Spruce place, Willow street, Oak Grove avenue, Clifton place and avenue, Groveland avenue, Dell place, Forest and Ridgewood avenues, Vineland place, Summit place, and Mount Curve avenue, names suggested by their forest trees and the irregular topography.

Adjoining Cedar Lake road and westward are Elm and Ash streets, Madeira, Antoinette, Wilton, Myrtle, Eden, and Lakeview avenues.

In Oak Lake addition are Lakeside avenue, Border, Highland, and Royalston avenues, and Holden street. This addition was platted in 1873 by Samuel C. Gale† and Chauncey W. Griggs,† of whom the former was born in Royalston, Mass. Holden, Mass., was his wife's native town.

Elwood avenue and Thomas place are in Oak Park addition, the first being named in honor of Elwood S. Corser,† who was in real estate business here during forty years.

In the hilly tract north of the North Commons are Ilion, Hillside, Willow, and Crystal Lake avenues, with McNair avenue extending thence southwest and west. The first bears the Greek name of ancient Troy, and the last honors William W. McNair,† a distinguished lawyer of this city.

Nicollet Island is nearly encircled by Island avenue, and is crossed by Merriam street, East Hennepin and Eastman avenues, Grove street, and Maple place, the last two being joined by Nicollet street. Eastman avenue honors William W. Eastman,† who settled in St. Anthony in 1854 and purchased this island; and Merriam street is named for John L. Merriam†, of St. Paul.

Continuing the catalogue to the east side of the Mississippi, which was the village and later the city of St. Anthony, until 1872, we may first note that University avenue, passing the north side of the campus and building area of the University of Minnesota, and East Hennepin avenue, of which the greater part, as before noted was originally called Division street and Central avenue, are in the groups of streets, being transverse to the groups of avenues.

University avenue also extends east in St. Paul, past the north side of the capitol, having a total length of twelve miles, and being the longest street under a single name in the Twin Cities.

Aside from the numerical systems of streets and avenues, this east side, often called East Minneapolis, has a very noteworthy group of streets named for the presidents of the United States. These streets running south and north, in chronologic sequence, are Washington, Adams, Jefferson, Madison, Monroe, Quincy (for John Quincy Adams), Jackson, Van Buren, Harrison, Tyler, Polk, Taylor, Fillmore, Pierce, Buchanan, Lincoln, Johnson, Ulysses (for Ulysses Simpson Grant, in whose honor Grant street on the west side was earlier named), Hayes, Garfield, Arthur, Cleveland, Benjamin (for Benjamin Harrison), McKinley, Roosevelt, and Taft.

A less extended alphabetic series of short west to east streets, southeast of the University campus, has Arlington and Beacon streets, names received from Boston, Mass.; the next for C is omitted, its place being taken by Washington avenue; and thence southward are Delaware, Essex, and Fulton streets. Next southward, in parallelism with the foregoing, are Dartmouth, Yale, and Hamline avenues, named for Dartmouth College and Yale and Hamline Universities.

Crossing the campus from north to south are Pleasant and Church streets; and next eastward are Union, Harvard, Walnut, Oak, Ontario. Erie, Huron, and Superior streets, the last four being named from the Great Lakes between the United States and Canada.

Southward from East Hennepin avenue and in parallelism with it, are Talmage, Como, Brook, Fairmount, and Rollins avenues, and Elm street. The first, with change in spelling, is named in honor of Tallmadge Elwell, a pioneer resident, whose sons are prominent citizens; the second, for Lake Como in St. Paul, passed in its eastern continuation; the third, for a small brook crossed by it; and the fifth, in honor of John Rollins,† who came to St. Anthony in 1848, being one of its earliest settlers, engaged in lumbering, and built a steamboat, "Governor Ramsey," to ply on the Mississippi above the falls.

North of East Hennepin avenue, parallel therewith and crossing the presidential series of streets, are Winter, Spring, and Summer streets, and Broadway, the last, like a street of St. Paul, being named from the widely known street of this name in New York City.

Adjoining the east side of the river and parallel with it, extending northwest and north, are Water street, Sibley, Ramsey, and Marshall streets, named for three early Minnesota governors, Grand, California, and Main streets, the last being the longest and at the beginning of the systems of streets for the northeast and southeast divisions of the city.

Bank street, near the river, next southeast of East Hennepin avenue, is named for its ascent of the river bank.

Only one area in East Minneapolis has broken topography of morainic drift hills and ridges. This residential tract, commonly known as Prospect Park, is at the south side of University avenue in the east edge of the city. Its curving and short streets or avenues, in their order from northwest to southeast, are St. Mary avenue, Williams and Arthur avenues, Sidney place, and Malcolm, Barton, Seymour, Orlin, Clarence, and Melbourne avenues. Adjacent southward are the short and straight Thornton street, Chandler street, Sharon avenue, and Warwick, Cecil, Bedford, and Emerald streets.

Thirty-second avenue N., in the northwest division of the city, and its direct continuation east, by a bridge over the Mississippi and by Twenty-fifth avenue N. E., were renamed in 1915 as Lowry avenue, extending thus in a west to east course across the city, honoring the late Thomas Lowry,† founder of the street railway system of the Twin Cities. His statue, at the junction of Hennepin and Lyndale avenues, near his former home, was unveiled August 18, 1915.

MINNEAPOLIS 607

BOULEVARDS AND PARKWAYS.

Nearly the entire area of this city is encircled by pleasure driveways.

Beginning with the River Road East, and crossing thence by the Franklin Avenue or Lake Street bridges to the River Road West, each of these roads being named for their following the shores of the Mississippi, the "Grand Rounds" continue by Minnehaha park, named from its falls, and the Minnehaha parkway, with Lake Nokomis park, named respectively for the Minnehaha creek and the lake, to the outlet of Lake Harriet. In Longfellow's grand poem, Nokomis was the grandmother of Hiawatha.

Thence the circuit includes the Lake Harriet boulevard, surrounding this lake, with Lyndale park and farmstead and King's highway, named for its donor, Hon. William S. King, from whose large Lyndale farm came the names of the park and farmstead, as also of Lyndale avenue.

Next are Linden Hills boulevard, named from the residential district adjoining it on the west, William Berry park, formerly called Interlachen from its position between Lakes Harriet and Calhoun, renamed in 1916 in honor of William Morse Berry,† formerly superintendent of the park system, 1885-1906, and the Lake Calhoun parkway, passing around this largest lake in the western lake chain or series of this city.

Minikahda, a club ground west of Lake Calhoun means "Beside water."

Northward this circuit of driveways comprises Dean boulevard, named in honor of A. J. Dean, one of its donors in 1892, the Lake of the Isles park, Cedar Lake boulevard, and the large Glenwood park, 586 acres, named from its glens and woods. In this park are Hillside Harbor, formerly called Brownie lake, connected with Cedar lake, Birch and Lily ponds, Glenwood lake, and the South and North Lagoons, through which Bassett creek runs, receiving also the outflow of this lake.

Memorial Drive, the part of the Grand Rounds west of Glenwood park and east to Camden park, three miles long, to be shaded with rows of elms given by Charles M. Loring, planned in October, 1919, commemorates Minneapolis soldiers of the World War.

Camden park and the adjacent residence area, to the Mississippi, are named from the city of Camden, N. J., opposite to Philadelphia.

After crossing the river, the northeastern part of the circuit is named Saint Anthony boulevard, passing through Columbia park, 185 acres, and thence southeast and south to the Stinson boulevard and Van Cleve park, and onward to the northern end of the River Road East, with which this description began. James Stinson donated the boulevard to the city in 1885, and the last named park honors Gen. Horatio P. Van Cleve† and his wife, Charlotte Ouisconsin Van Cleve.†

THE WINCHELL TRAIL.

In recognition of the public service of the late Professor Winchell,† state geologist nearly thirty years, from 1872 to 1901, and a resident of this city forty-two years, until his death May 2, 1914, a footpath along the west shore of the Mississippi river was named later in that year as the Winchell Trail, lying between the River Road West and the river, and reaching from Franklin avenue south to Minnehaha Park.

At its north entrance, a large boulder which was brought from the Mesabi Iron Range by his eldest son, Horace V. Winchell,† bears a bronze tablet, noting that the trail "was named in honor of the eminent geologist, Newton Horace Winchell, whose scientific studies along this river provided a measure for the time since the Glacial period."

Parks and other Public Grounds.

An interesting history of the inception and development of the park system of Minneapolis, by Charles M. Loring, with a postscript by William W. Folwell, is published in the Minnesota Historical Society Collections, volume XV, 1915, pages 599-608.

In addition to the numerous parks already noted on the "Grand Rounds" series of driveways, a group of parks and public grounds is connected with that circuit at the Lake of the Isles by Kenwood parkway, including Kenwood park, Bryn Mawr Meadows, which received the name of an adjoining residential area (Welsh words meaning "great hill," adopted from a town in Wales and a village near Philadelphia), the Parade grounds, 68 acres, and Loring park, 36 acres, named in honor of Charles M. Loring,† "Father of the Park System."

The many other parks and small open spaces owned by this city may be conveniently listed for reference in the following alphabetic order.

Audubon park, named for the renowned American ornithologist; Barnes place, for William A. Barnes,† who, with Elwood S. Corser† and others, platted the Oak Park addition, having this place; Barton and Bedford triangles; Bottineau field, named for Pierre Bottineau† and others of his family; Bridge square, the junction of Hennepin and Nicollet avenues, between Gateway park and the bridge of the Mississippi; Bryant square, adjoining Bryant avenue; Caleb Dorr† circle, for a prominent pioneer lumberman; Cedar Avenue triangle, and Chowen, Clarence, and Clifton triangles; Cottage park, Crystal Lake triangle, Dell park and Dell place, and Douglas triangle.

Dorilus Morrison† park, comprising eight acres, was named by its donor, Clinton Morrison,† in honor of his father, pioneer lumberman, state senator in 1864-5, and the first mayor of this city in 1867. The Minneapolis Art Institute is on the northwest part of this park.

Elliot park, seven acres, was partly deeded to the city as a donation in 1883 by Dr. Jacob S. Elliot† and his wife.

Elmwood and Euclid triangles adjoin short streets, called places, which bear these names.

Farview park, nearly 21 acres, purchased in 1883, on a hilltop in the northwest part of the city, was named by Dr. Folwell for its extensive panoramic outlook.

Farwell park adjoins Farwell avenue.

MINNEAPOLIS 609

Franklin Steele† square was donated to the city in 1883 by three daughters of the prominent pioneer of this name, who came to Minnesota in 1837 and built a suspension bridge in 1854, connecting Minneapolis and St. Anthony, the first bridge spanning the Mississippi in all its course.

The Gateway, a public ground of about one acre, between Hennepin, Nicollet, and Washington avenues, welcomes visitors and immigrants.

Glen Gale commemorates Samuel C. Gale,† in whose honor, and for his wife, as before noted, Royalston avenue and Holden street were named.

Groveland and Hiawatha triangles, Highland oval, Hillside, Humboldt, and Iagoo triangles, are mostly named from adjoining avenues, excepting the last, which is from the Shakespearean tragedy of "Othello."

Irving triangle, Jackson square, Kenwood triangle, Lakeside oval, and Laurel triangle, are named from avenues or streets.

Logan park, ten acres in East Minneapolis, purchased in 1883, commemorates Gen. John A. Logan, for whom also an avenue in the west part of the city is named.

Longfellow Gardens, a privately owned zoological garden, at the west side of Hiawatha avenue, opposite to the Minnehaha park, is open to the public by paying for admission.

Lovell square was donated to the city in 1889, by Corser, Barnes, and Lovell, who platted the Oak Park addition.

Maple Hill park, eight acres, is in the northeast division of the city, purchased in 1908.

Marshall terrace, nearly eight acres beside the Mississippi, adjoins Marshall street N. E., named for William R. Marshall,† governor of Minnesota in 1866-70.

Monroe place and Mount Curve triangle adjoin the street and avenue of these names.

Murphy square, three acres, was donated by Captain Edward Murphy† in 1857, being the earliest park of this city. He was master of the steamboat "Falls City," which made regular trips to St. Anthony and Minneapolis.

Newton triangle adjoins Newton avenue N.

Normania triangle was named through suggestion of Dr. Folwell, in compliment for the many Norwegian people living near it.

North Commons, a park of nearly 26 acres, was purchased in 1907.

Oak Lake parks, comprising two acres, were donated in the plat of that addition in 1873.

Oliver and Orlin triangles adjoin the avenues so named.

Osseo triangle, beside Hiawatha avenue, was named, like Osseo village in this county, meaning "Son of the Evening Star," in Longfellow's "Song of Hiawatha."

Powderhorn Lake park, alludes to the original outline of its lake, shown remarkably like a powderhorn and so named by the survey and plat of the Military Reservation for Fort Snelling, made under an order of Major Plympton for the War Department in 1839.

Prospect Field, five acres, is in the residential district called Prospect Park.

Rauen triangle commemorates Peter Rauen, an early German settler.

Richard Chute† square, one acre, is named in honor of a prominent pioneer who settled in St. Anthony in 1854. Its house, the museum of the Hennepin County Territorial Pioneers Association, was built by Ard Godfrey† in 1848, being the first frame house of this city.

Riverside park, 42 acres beside the Mississippi, purchased in 1883 and 1910, is at the northern end of the parkway named River Road West.

Royalston, Russell, and Rustic Lodge triangles are beside avenues so named, each being a donation to the city.

"Seven Corners" is the well known name of the wide intersection space of Washington and Cedar Avenues, with other streets, where seven street corners are seen in one view. A similar locality in St. Paul bears the same name.

Sheridan field, like the adjacent Logan park, honors a general of the civil war, for whom also Sheridan avenue is named.

Snyder triangle was named for a distinguished Minneapolis family; Stevens square, in honor of Col. John H. Stevens,† for whom the adjoining avenue is named: Stewart field, nearly four acres, for Levi M. Stewart† after his death, by whose brother it was partly donated: and Sumner field, nearly four acres, with the adjacent Sumner place, honors the well known statesman, Charles Sumner.

Svea triangle is in honor of Sweden and its immigrants.

Tower Hill, a park area of nearly five acres, comprising the highest hilltop in the Prospect Park residential district, is named for its water tower or reservoir for high pressure service.

Vineland triangle and place bear the ancient name given by the Northmen, almost five centuries before Columbus, to the northeastern coast of our continent.

Virginia triangle in the southern angle of intersection of Hennepin and Lyndale avenues, has the statue of Thomas Lowry,† for whom also Lowry avenue is named, as before noted.

Washburn Fair Oaks, a park of seven acres and a half, was a part of the home estate, named Fair Oaks, of the late Senator William D. Washburn.† It adjoins the north side of the Dorilus Morrison park, with Twenty-fourth street passing between these parks.

Washburn Park is a residence district, previously noticed.

Wilson park, about an acre, commemorates Eugene M. Wilson,† who settled here as a lawyer in 1857 and was a member of Congress, 1869-71.

Windom park, nearly nine acres, on the south side of Lowry avenue, in the northeast division of the city, is named in honor of the statesman, William Windom,† of Winona, who was United States senator and secretary of the treasury.

SAINT PAUL

Several residential districts in the city of St. Paul have been previously noticed by the chapter for Ramsey county, these being Merriam Park, Riverview or West St. Paul, St. Anthony Park, Hazel Park and Highwood, Dayton's bluff, Arlington Hills, Phalen Park, Como, Lexington, Macalester, and Groveland Parks, Hamline, St. Anthony Hill, also called the Hill district, and Seven Corners. Other residence areas having similar distinctive names are noted in the following pages.

The Mississippi river, its islands, the lakes of the city area, and Carver's cave and Fountain cave, have likewise received consideration in the Ramsey county chapter.

Information of the significance of names of streets, avenues, boulevards, and parks, as here recorded, has been derived from "History of the City of Saint Paul and of the County of Ramsey" (M. H. S. Collections, vol. IV), by John Fletcher Williams, 1876, 475 pages; "History of St. Paul," edited by Gen. C. C. Andrews, 1890, 603 and 244 pages; "Pen Pictures of St. Paul," by Major T. M. Newson, 1886, 746 pages; 'Past and Present of St. Paul," by W. B. Hennessy, 1906, 814 pages; "History of St. Paul and Vicinity," by Captain Henry A. Castle, 1912, three volumes; from George H. Hazzard, secretary of the Minnesota Territorial Pioneers Association, Edmund W. Bazille, since 1898 judge of the probate court, the late Henry S. Fairchild and Auguste L. Larpenteur, Lloyd Peabody, Cornelius M. Crowley, Edward C. Hall, William T. McMurran, Benjamin F. Meek, Duval F. Polk, William H. Wood, and many other citizens of St. Paul; and from early plats, maps, and views of St. Paul, in the Library of the Minnesota Historical Society, and in offices of the city engineer, the Board of Park Commissioners, and the Ramsey county register of deeds.

STREETS AND AVENUES.
MAPS OF 1851 AND 1857.

The oldest part of this city, called "St. Paul Proper" on the earliest map, compiled by George C. Nichols and published in 1851, as noted by Williams (page 316), was surveyed in the fall of 1847 by Ira B. and Benjamin W. Brunson,† and was placed on record April 28, 1849. This area is mapped with St. Peter's street, Wabashaw, Cedar, Minnesota, Robert, Jackson, and Sibley streets, which cross it north-northwesterly; while Water and Bench streets run eastward, adjoining the river and in parallelism with it, and Third, Fourth, Fifth, Sixth and Seventh streets run

---
†See notes of biographies in the M. H. S. Collections, vol. XIV, 1912.

east-northeastward, at right angles with the streets first named. All these streets, excepting Water street, since occupied by railways, remain today with the same names, comprising the central and most important business portion of the city.

St. Peter street, as now spelled, was named for the St. Peter or Minnesota river; Wabasha,† as now spelled, was for the hereditary Sioux or Dakota chiefs of this name, borne also by a county; Cedar street had red cedar trees on the Mississippi bluff at its southern end; Minnesota street bears the Sioux name of the river, and of the territory and state; Louis Robert† was a trader here and a steamboat captain on the Mississippi, and was the first signer and proprietor of this plat; Henry Jackson† came to St. Paul in 1842, was its first merchant, having his store on the river bank near the street that was named in his honor, and was the first postmaster; Henry Hastings Sibley,† coming to the area of Minnesota in 1834, was delegate in Congress, 1849-53, and was the first governor of this state, in 1858-60; and Bench street was named for its ascent from near the river levee, at Jackson's store, to the crest edge of the bluff near Minnesota street.

The map of 1851 includes also additions on the east, platted by Whitney and Smith in 1849, and by Norman W. Kittson† in 1851; on the northeast, platted by Benjamin F. Hoyt† in 1850, by Vandenburgh in 1851, and also by Paterson in 1851; on the north, by Robert and Randall, 1851, and Bazille and Guerin, 1850; on the northwest and west, by Rice and Irvine, in 1849 and 1851, by Leech in 1849, and Winslow and Willes in 1851.

By these additions, up to 1851, the platted area was extended to a length of two miles and a half, from Trout and Phalen creeks (the latter then called McCloud creek) at the northeast, to the corner of St. Clair and Webster streets (the latter being then named Huron street) toward the west. Its greatest width, through the eastern half, was two-thirds to three-fourths of a mile. The scale of this map is 350 feet to an inch, a mile being thus nearly sixteen inches on the map.

New street names, brought in at the east by the added plats, were Waukuta and Rosabel streets, Broadway, and Pike, Mill, John, Simpson, Charles, Brunson, and William street, running north-northwestward. Broadway was the widest, named from the most important street at that time in New York City. Wacouta street, as now spelled, commemorates a Sioux chief, for whom also a township of Goodhue county is named. The seven streets eastward from Broadway have been renamed, with one exception, being now, in the same order, Pine, Olive, John, Locust, Willius, Neill, and Kittson streets. A steam sawmill stood in 1851 at the foot of Mill street, now Olive, and the pine logs sawn there suggested the name of Pine street; Ferdinand† and Gustav Willius,† early bankers of St. Paul, are commemorated by the former Charles street, which name is now borne by another and longer street; and Edward D. Neill,† the first historian of Minnesota, and Norman W. Kittson,† sutler, fur trader, and founder of steamboat transportation on the Red river, are honored by the two most eastern streets in this list.

Northeastward this map has Grove and Somerset streets and Mississippi street, also Canada and Temperance streets, names that yet remain, which need no explanation for their origins. From near the northern end of Canada street, the New Canada road, since renamed Cortland street, ran to the principal settlement in New Canada township.

The series of numerical streets, parallel with the river, is continued by the map to Twelfth street, and by more recent names to Fourteenth street.

Westward, nearly parallel with St. Peter street, the 1851 map has the southern part of Rice street, named for Henry M. Rice,† who later was U. S. senator, for whom a county is named; Market and Washington streets, between which was "Market Square," renamed as Rice Park; and Eagle, Chestnut, and Walnut streets. Next southwestward in this series, the Pine street of 1851 has been renamed Sherman street, in honor of William Tecumseh Sherman, who conducted the march through Georgia, "from Atlanta to the sea," in 1864. Beyond are Elm and Wilkin streets, the last, running due south, being named in honor of Alexander Wilkin,† who settled here in 1849, was secretary of the territory, 1851-53, and was colonel of the Ninth Minnesota regiment, for whom Wilkin county was named.

Crossing that series and in parallelism with the Mississippi, this map has Spring street, the southwestern part of Washington street, Franklin street, named for Benjamin Franklin, Exchange street, and Fort street, named for Fort Snelling. The last, westward from the "Seven Corners," has become a part of the extension of Seventh street, now continuous to Fort Snelling; and the northeastern part of the original Fort street, leading northward from Seven Corners, has been renamed Main avenue. Oak street, next westward in 1851, has become Smith avenue, in honor of Robert A. Smith,† during many terms mayor of this city, and its continuation crosses the High Bridge of the Mississippi and thence passes south to the Dodd road. Yet farther westward, this series of streets has Pleasant street (now called an avenue) and the College avenue, which derived this name from its course passing the Episcopal mission and school of Park Place, founded by Rev. James Lloyd Breck† and others in 1850.

Streets farther west in 1851, running from north to south, parallel with Wilkin street, were Leech street, named in honor of Gen. Samuel Leech, receiver of the United States land office established at St. Croix Falls, Wis.; Forbes street, since renamed as a part of Seventh avenue, before noted; Douglas street, named for Stephen A. Douglas, who in the U. S. senate in 1848-9 had advocated the formation of this Territory; Dousman and Ann streets, the former in honor of Hercules L. Dousman (b. 1800, d. 1868), of Prairie du Chien, Wis., agent of the American Fur Company for Wisconsin, who first urged the adoption of the name Minnesota for the new Territory; Green street, which has been renamed in honor of President Garfield; Blair street, now a part of Western avenue; Erie street, near the present street of this name; and Ontario and Huron streets, names that have since disappeared from the list of this city.

Across these streets and extending from east to west, the year 1851 had Ramsey street, in honor of Governor Ramsey†; Smith and Prairie streets, now called respectively Forbes and Harrison avenues, in honor of William H. Forbes,† pioneer fur trader, general merchant, and Indian agent, and of President William Henry Harrison; McBoal street, named for James McClellan Boal,† adjutant general of Minnesota in 1851-53; Goodrich street, now an avenue, in honor of Aaron Goodrich,† chief justice of the territorial supreme court, 1849-51; Banfil street, for John Banfil, a former resident of New Orleans, who came to St. Paul in 1846, but after a few years removed to Manomin, on the Rice creek above St. Anthony, where he built a sawmill and a steamboat, "H. M. Rice," which ran on the Mississippi above the falls, but who removed in 1866 to Bayfield, Wis.; Grove street, renamed Goodhue street, in honor of James M. Goodhue,† the first editor here, commemorated also by a county; Superior, Michigan, and St. Clair streets, the last named like Lake St. Clair, between Lakes Huron and Erie, for Gen. Arthur St. Clair (b. 1734, d. 1818), who was governor of the Northwest Territory in 1789-1802; Yankee street, for a steamboat of this name, which plied between Galena and St. Paul in the autumn of 1849 and during the season of 1850, and made a very notable trip with excursionists up the Minnesota river, July 22-26, 1850; and Rice street, since renamed Von Minden street in honor of Henning Von Minden, captain in Brackett's battalion of cavalry, 1861-4, and major of Hatch's battalion, 1864-6.

In the early part of 1857 a "Map of the City of Saint Paul," which had been so incorporated by the legislature March 4, 1854, was published by Goodrich & Somers, on the scale of 800 feet to an inch. Like the map of 1851, it has Harriet, Barnes, Raspberry, and Boal islands of the Mississippi, in this descending order; and McCloud creek of that earliest map is Phalen's creek on the map of 1857, thus taking its present name.

Northeastward this map has Woodward, Patridge, Hopkins, North, and Collins streets, which yet remain, each short, running from east to west and lying in this order beyond Grove street. Yet farther north were Vine and Mt. Ida streets, the former having been since renamed Beaumont street. Herkimer avenue of 1857 is the present Lafayette avenue. The north to south streets are Bradley and Burr, yet bearing these names; Brook street, then named for Trout brook, now De Soto street; Otsego and Prospect avenues, the latter now Rivoli street; and Arkwright and Westminster streets, which, with De Soto street, are now extended north to the city boundary.

Woodward street, named after a principal avenue in Detroit, Mich., during many years had the homes of several prominent citizens, one being General Sibley, whose boyhood home was in Detroit.

An isolated plat added on the north part of the map has names of several streets and avenues, of which only Viola street and Park avenue now remain. Northwestward are Irvine and Summit avenues, Selby, Dayton, and Nelson avenues, the last three running due west; and crossing these are Farrington, Virginia, and Western avenues. Citizens commemorated were John R. Irvine,† who came here in 1843, platted several additions of the city, and for whom Irvine park was named; Jeremiah W. Selby,† owner of a farm on that St. Anthony hill; Lyman Dayton,† for whom Dayton's bluff was named; Rensselaer R. Nelson,† territorial judge, and later during nearly forty years U. S. district judge for this state; and John Farrington,† merchant and banker.

Summit avenue, the finest residence street of this city, received its name from its location, leading westward to the crest of the valley bluff, on which it lies for a half mile from the Cathedral to the University Club, thence running due west to the city boundary at the river.

Virginia avenue, the earliest named for another state, was in compliment to citizens from the "Old Dominion." Among these Virginia settlers, Henry Jackson,† for whom Jackson street was named, came in 1842; his cousin, William G. Carter, came in 1845, and died here in 1852; and James W. Simpson† came to St. Paul in 1843, and in 1849 was elected the first county treasurer.

Michigan and Mississippi streets had reference to the lake and river, without special thought of the states so named. Later other streets and avenues in St. Paul were named for states or territories, comprising Alabama, Alaska, California, Colorado, Dakota, Delaware, Florida, Idaho, Indiana, Iowa, Kansas, Kentucky, Maryland, Missouri, Montana, Nebraska, Nevada, Ohio, Oregon, Pennsylvania, Tennessee, Texas, Utah, Wisconsin, and Wyoming. Thus, with Virginia avenue, came twenty-eight street names.

On the southwest, adjoining the river between an eighth and a half of a mile above Harriet island, this map of 1857 adds a small plat having Commercial, Merchants, and Railroad streets, running from north to south, of which only one, now Merchants avenue, retains its original name, the others now being Tile street and Archer avenue; and these were crossed from east to west by streets that have since been renamed as Banning, Parsons, and Alison streets. William L. Banning† came here in 1855, and engaged in banking and railroad construction. Rev. J. P. Parsons† came in 1849, and was pastor of the First Baptist church.

The most western plat between 1851 and 1857 was a quarter of a section next beyond Western avenue and south of St. Clair street, having Richmond, Duke, Oneida, and Toronto streets, which run from north to south; also, in the intervals between these and parallel with them, were an unnamed street and First and Second streets, which now are Colborne, Erie, and Webster streets. Crossing these are Jefferson avenue and other streets that later were named Grace, Palace, Cascade, and James streets. Thomas Langdon Grace,† commemorated by Grace street, came here in

1859, as the second Roman Catholic bishop of St. Paul, which position he held during sixteen years. Jefferson avenue, in honor of President Jefferson, and Palace and James streets, names of undetermined origin, have been since extended to the west boundary of the city at the Mississippi.

West St. Paul, which was platted in 1855, being then a part of Dakota county, but nineteen years later, in 1874, annexed to this city, and to Ramsey county, was not shown on the foregoing map in 1857. It is delineated on a later map of the same year probably preceding the great financial panic and business depression which came in the autumn, stopping all real estate development in townsite platting and building.

The later map of 1857, showing small additional plats north and east of the river and the large area on the opposite side, which in 1874 was made a part of this city, is entitled "Map of St. Paul, West St. Paul and Brooklynd, compiled from the recorded plots by Von Minden & Wippermann, architects & civil engineers. St. Paul, M. T. 1857." The scale is 350 feet to an inch, as of the map in 1851. Brooklynd was a plat at the south side of the river, extending from a point opposite to the mouth of Phalen creek westward about 2,000 feet to the "Lower Ferry." Both 1857 maps show the Wabasha street bridge, on which work was begun in 1856-7 but was not completed, as related by Chaney (M. H. S. Collections, XII, 132-4), till June, 1859.

Between the dates of the earlier and later maps in 1857, the outskirts of St. Paul at the north received Williams street, Aurora and Sherburne avenues, Valley, Mt. Airy, Glencoe, and Arch streets, and Pennsylvania avenue, running in general from east to west, with L'Orient avenue (now called a street), Columbia, Linden and Warren streets, running across the foregoing from south to north. Fairview street, on the later map, is now a part of the northward extension of Jackson street; and Westerlo street, next westward, now is partly Capitol Heights street. On both of the 1857 maps, what now is Capitol boulevard was Brewster avenue.

Charles H. Williams,† who came to St. Paul in 1853, was chief engineer of the fire department in 1856-9 and 1863-4; Moses Sherburne† was judge of the United States district court for this territory, 1853-57, residing in St. Paul, and removed in 1867 to Sherburne county, which was named for him; and John Esaias Warren† came here in 1852, was U. S. district attorney for the territory, and was mayor of this city in 1863.

At the northwest, the later map adds Marshall, Iglehart, and Carroll streets, now called avenues; Rondo street; Jay and Martin streets, since respectively renamed as St. Anthony and Central avenues, the former being continued to the present west line of the city, adjoining the former municipality of St. Anthony; Fuller street, now an avenue; Arnold street and Territorial avenue, (also then and long afterward called Melrose avenue), since renamed respectively as Aurora and University avenues, the latter being extended to the city boundary, and onward northwest and north through Minneapolis; Ellen street, now the western extension of Sherburne avenue; and Charles, Edmund, and Thomas streets, the last being unnamed, though platted. Crossing the foregoing, which run from east to west, are Marion and Louis streets; Oak street, since renamed Gaultier street; Cadett street, now Jay street; and Elfelt street. The present northward continuation of Western avenue was then Annapolis street, a name now used in West St. Paul. Next westward are Arundel, Mackubin, and Kent streets, which since 1857 have been continued to the north line of the city, though with interruptions by railway tracks and shops and by other spaces that have not yet been platted. The west line of this map it at the present Dale street, which in 1857 was only partly platted and not yet named.

Citizens honored in these names were Governor Marshall,† for whom also a city and a county are named; Harwood Iglehart,† from Maryland, who was a lawyer and dealer in real estate here from 1854 to 1861, but later resided chiefly in Maryland; Charles Carroll, of Maryland, a noted patriot and signer of the Declaration of Independence; Joseph Rondo,† who came from the Selkirk settlement in 1835, was a farmer on the Fort Snelling reservation, and later purchased a claim crossed by the present street named for him in this city; Alpheus G. Fuller,† who came from Connecticut, and in 1856 built a hotel here, called the Fuller House, afterward known as the International; Edmund Rice,† for whom Edmund street was named, afterward mayor of the city and a member of Congress, who settled here in 1849, being a brother of the U. S. senator, Henry M. Rice; their sister Ellen,† Mrs William Hollinshead, of this city, who also came in 1849; their brother, Charles Rodney Rice (b. 1821, d. 1873), commemorated by Charles street, who during the territorial period was a merchant here, but afterward lived in the city of Washington; Thomas Stinson, on whose plat of an addition in July, 1856, his first name was given to an eastern part of Thomas street; Lucian Galtier,† builder of the Catholic chapel in 1841, which he dedicated to St. Paul, thereby also naming the infant village and future city; the Elfelt brothers, Abram S.† and Charles D.,† and Edwin, pioneer merchants at the beginning of the territorial period; and Charles N. Mackubin,† who came from Maryland in 1854 and engaged in banking and real estate, bringing also the names of Arundel and Kent streets, from counties in Maryland.

WEST ST. PAUL.

The area of West St. Paul on this map in 1857, comprising fifteen tracts separately platted, has many street names that are yet retained; but its several groups of streets that originally were numerically named, running from east to west or southwest, approximately in parallelism with the river, have been since renamed. Because all numerical street names are now superseded by names of personal or other distinctive derivations, the task of cataloguing them and noting their origin is greatly increased. Much of the renaming followed closely on the annexation of this area to St. Paul as its sixth ward, in 1874; but many changes and small additions have been made in the later years.

Water street, beside the river, remains; but Mill street and Fourth to Ninth streets have received later names. This series is now, in the order outward from the river, Fillmore, Fairfield, Indiana, Chicago, and Plato avenues, the Eighth and Ninth streets having been vacated to give space for railway use. Eastward from State street, which was A street in 1857, the streets running east-northeast, parallel with the river, which were then First to Ninth streets, are now, in the same order, Alabama, Tennessee, Kentucky, Texas, St. Lawrence, Constans, Florida, Utah, and Perry streets. A little farther east, beyond a narrow tract not yet platted, the streets in the course of continuation of the four last named are now Bayfield, Plymouth, Brooklyn, and Perry streets.

Crossing these series and running away from the river, to the southeast and south, are now, in the order from west to east, Hyde, Walter, and Edward streets, each renamed since 1857; South Wabasha street, then platted as Bridge street; Starkey and Custer streets, renamed from Cedar and Clay of 1857; Livingston avenue, then named as now in its southern and longer part, but near the river then called Dugas street; South Robert street, which in 1857 was called Main street in its northern part, but Washington avenue for its part running due south; Eaton avenue and Eva street, the latter being Goodhue street in 1857; Robertson street, retaining its original name; and State, Fenton, Minnetonka, Chester, Wyandotte, and Rutland streets, which in 1857 were simply lettered from A to F. The east border of the 1857 map was at Wisconsin street, which yet has this name as an avenue; but the three streets next parallel westward are renamed, being now Lowell, Court, and Missouri streets.

Personal names in the foregoing groups recall William Constans,† a merchant, who settled in St. Paul in 1850; Abraham† and Charles Perry,† father and son, who came from the Selkirk colony to Fort Snelling in 1827, and were farmers near Fountain cave after 1838; James Starkey,† who settled here in 1850, engaged in milling and railroad construction, and had charge of the first sewerage works in St. Paul; Gen. George A. Custer, who was killed by the Sioux, with all his troops, in a battle in Montana, June 25, 1876; Crawford Livingston,† banker and railroad builder, who settled here in 1870; William Dugas,† a pioneer hotel owner and ferryman, who came to St. Paul in 1844, but removed two years afterward to St. Anthony; Samuel S. Eaton, who came in 1855 and engaged in insurance; Daniel A. Robertson,† lawyer, editor, and founder of the State Horticultural Society, who settled in this city in 1850; and William Fenton,† who came in 1855, was the surveyor of West St. Paul, in association with Charles A. F. Morris,† lived here as a recluse, was a street preacher after 1880, and died in 1903.

In the plat earliest made for West St. Paul, on high land farther back from the river, the sixteen streets running east and west, in their sequence from north to south, were Wood and John streets, Delos, Isabel, Grove, Harriet, and Oak streets, George, Caroline, Greene, Elisabeth, Elm, Rose, Charles, Vine, and Mary streets. Of these names only five now remain,

Wood, Delos, Isabel, George, and Elisabeth; while the others, in their order, have been changed to Colorado, Congress, Winifred, Robie, Dearborn, Louisa, Augusta, Morton, Page, Tyler, and Curtice streets. An addition on the same map in 1857, continuing southward, extended this series of east to west streets by Clear, Spring, Grove, Cottage, Hill, Haskell, Dacotah, and Jackson streets, of which only two, Haskell and Dakota, yet remain, the others being now respectively Belvidere, Lucy, Wyoming, Annapolis, Brompton, and Bernard streets. The most noteworthy personal names of the series are Wood, for Edward H. Wood,† who in 1856, as related by Newson, was an assistant in surveys near Lake Como, then first so named, who "in 1867 settled in West St. Paul, where he taught school several terms and inaugurated the scheme to annex the West Side to the city of St. Paul;" Delos, in honor of Delos A. Monfort,† banker, who settled in St. Paul in 1857; Isabel, whose husband, Eugenio A. Johnson, a surveyor and civil engineer of this city, died in 1888, aged 69 years; Winifred, the name of the daughter of Hon. William P. Murray,† a pioneer of 1849, for whom Murray county was named; and Curtice, for David L. Curtice,† who came here in 1856 and was city engineer, 1858-59 and 1869-74. By recommendation of Curtice, the Baptist hill was removed, mostly in 1876-80, being cut down to the adjoining level, and in 1887 he published an excellent atlas of St. Paul.

Extending across the foregoing were avenues, running due south, named in sequence from east to west as Mississippi, Greenwood, Clinton, Washington, Livingston, Gorman, Gale, Hall, Stryker, Winslow, Myrtle, Bidwell, Allen, and Brown avenues. Mississippi avenue is now a part of State street; the next two names are yet retained; Washington avenue, as before noted, has become a part of South Robert street; the next two remain; Gale avenue is renamed Humboldt; Hall, Stryker, and Winslow avenues remain; Myrtle and Bidwell avenues have been changed respectively to Bidwell and Bellows streets; and Allen avenue remains, but Brown of 1857 is now Schley avenue.

Among the persons honored in these names, we may note Willis A. Gorman,† territorial governor in 1853-57; William Sprigg Hall,† who came here in 1854, was territorial superintendent of public instruction, a state senator in 1857-60, and after 1867 judge of the court of common pleas; John L. Stryker, a real estate owner; James M. Winslow,† who settled here in 1852, erected large hotels in St. Paul, St. Anthony, and St. Peter, and introduced telegraph service into this city; Ira Bidwell, a pioneer banker, who came to St. Paul in 1854, whose son Henry "at one time owned the Prescott place in West St. Paul, where he cultivated grapes and raised bees" (Newson, p. 708); Alvaren Allen,† who came in 1851, engaged in livery business, owned a stage line, and was proprietor of the Merchants' Hotel from 1875 to 1902; and Winfield Scott Schley, admiral in the U. S. navy, hero in the Spanish-American war, 1898.

Additional names on the west part of this map of West St. Paul in 1857, remaining to the present time, are Seminole, Manomin, Mohawk,

Ottawa, Cherokee, Delaware, Chippewa, and Winnebago avenues, running due south as a series in this order from east to west. Each notes a tribe or larger division of the American Indians. Each retains its original name as an avenue, excepting the last, now called Winnebago street.

Between Bidwell street, before noted, and Seminole avenue, the map in 1857 had Bellevue avenue, nearly coinciding with the present Waseca street, which is named like the county; a long unnamed avenue, now Charlton street; and Randall avenue, now represented by Ohio street and Whitall avenue. Northward, between Seminole and Manomin avenues, was Olivier avenue, now Orleans street.

Across the avenues and streets thus listed, which run north and south, the series of streets running east and west, which in 1857 were named numerically, have been renamed, including several before noted that extend much farther east, beyond Bidwell street, and also Stevens, King, Baker, Sydney, Belmont, and Winona streets, Minea avenue, and Hedge street.

Cottage street of 1857, continuing with this name, became the south line of the area annexed to St. Paul in 1874; but it has since been renamed Annapolis street, as before noted, for the capital of Maryland, the native city of Harwood Iglehart,† and probably of other early settlers of this city.

Dodd road, beginning as a street in West St. Paul and extending southwest and south to Mankato, was laid out by Captain William B. Dodd,† who was born in Montclair, N. J., in 1811, came to this state about 1851, was one of the founders of St. Peter, and was killed in the defence of New Ulm, August 23, 1862.

Other streets south and west of the river, of later dates, deserve mention, as follows.

Lamprey and Jeanne avenues, adjoining the west shore south of Dayton bluff, were named in honor of Uri Locke Lamprey and his wife. He was born in Deerfield, N. H., April 7, 1842, and died in St. Paul, March 22, 1906; was a lawyer, and was president of the Minnesota game and fish commission, 1901-06. Mrs. Jeannette Robert Lamprey is a daughter of Captain Louis Robert,† who named one of his steamboats in her honor, which plied on the Minnesota and Mississippi rivers from 1857 till 1870.

Brott street commemorates George F. Brott,† who came here in 1850, was sheriff of Ramsey county the next year, and later founded Sauk Rapids, St. Cloud, and Breckenridge.

Stickney street is named in honor of Alpheus B. Stickney,† lawyer, builder and president of railways, and organizer in 1882 of the St. Paul Union Stock Yards.

Concord street leads to South St. Paul, the site of the stock yards and packing houses.

Prescott street honors George W. Prescott,† who settled in St. Paul in 1850, was clerk of the territorial supreme court, 1854-57, and later was clerk of the U. S. district court in this state.

SAINT PAUL 621

SOUTHEASTERN PLATS.

Suburbs within the southeast part of the city area of St. Paul, lying east of the Mississippi, opposite to West St. Paul and the separately organized city of South St. Paul, which is in Dakota county, are Highwood and Oakland, beside the Chicago, Burlington and Quincy railway, platted respectively in 1887 and 1888, and Riverside Park, likewise a residence tract, adjoining the Mississippi, which was platted in the spring of 1889.

Highwood, on the ascending slope and crest of the valley bluff, has Burlington avenue, named for the railway; Upland, Howard, Brookline, Linwood, Springfield, Lenox, Highwood, and Chester avenues; and Mystic, Elmwood, Bellevue, Shawmut, Weymouth, Winthrop, Hadley, Allston, Temple, Beacon, and Woodbine streets. Ten of these names come from Massachusetts, mostly from Boston and its vicinity.

Burlington and Newport avenues, the latter forming the west border of Highwood and leading south to Newport in Washington county, extend also north through Oakland. Other streets in Oakland are the Glen road, Mystic, Piedmont, and Pond streets; Woodlawn avenue and place; Forest Hill avenue, Edgewood place, and Aftondale and Burke streets.

Riverside Park has Water street, along the river, Linda, Merrimac, Salem, and Paris streets, crossed by Basswood, Redwood, Whitewood, Blackwood, and Boxwood avenues.

DAYTON BLUFF AND EASTWARD.

For the streets and avenues in the principal additions to this city, surrounding its nucleal area already noticed as shown by the maps of 1857, we may well take a geographic order, from its eastern portions to the northeast, north, northwest, west, and southwest. Thus we shall pass in sequence from the districts of Dayton Bluff and Arlington Hills around by Hazel Park, Lakes Phalen and Como, Hamline, St. Anthony Park, Merriam and Roblyn Parks, Summit and Lexington Parks, and the Macalester and Groveland districts, to the additions along West Seventh street and opposite Fort Snelling.

Dayton Bluff and the area reaching nearly a mile eastward were platted under the names of Suburban Hills and Lyman Dayton's† addition, respectively in September, 1856, and September, 1857, the latter being the more northern and larger tract. On or adjoining the river bluff, a series of streets running from northwest to southeast, at right angles with East Seventh street, comprises Commercial street, Hoffman avenue (at first named Dayton avenue), Maria and Bates avenues, in honor of Mrs. Dayton, whose maiden name was Maria Bates, and Maple and Hope streets (originally Grove and Hill streets). Mounds boulevard, now occupying a part of the former Hoffman avenue, and Mound street, lead to the group of Indian mounds in the public park bearing this name.

North to south streets, in their order from west to east, are Arcade street (here at first called Olive and Willow streets), Mendota (originally called Oak) street, Forest street, Cypress and Earl streets (then respectively called Barton and East streets), the later being the east line of Dayton's addition, Hiawatha, Hester, Martin, Griffith, Johnson, and English streets (the last, at the east end of Suburban Hills, having originally been called East street).

James K. Hoffman† came to St. Paul at the age of twenty years, in 1851; ran the sawmill of William L. Ames† at the foot of Dayton bluff in 1856; was later a grocer, and in 1873-80 was state inspector of oil.

Gates A. Johnson,† for whom a street here was named in 1856, came the preceding year, was surveyor of numerous additions to the city, and was chief engineer of the Lake Superior and Mississippi railroad, running from St. Paul to Duluth. The place of the southern part of that street is now occupied by Johnson parkway, named in honor of John Albert Johnson,† governor of Minnesota in 1905-09; and the line of its northward continuation has now Atlantic street.

Running to the northeast, across the first of the foregoing series, in the order northward from Mounds Park, are Clermont and River streets, Urban place, McLean avenue, Short street, Cherry and Plum streets, Hudson avenue, Euclid street, Van Buren place, Conway street, and Third to Sixth streets, which last are continuous from the streets so named in the earliest and central plat of St. Paul. At the distance of a few blocks back from the crest of the bluff, several of these streets turn to a due east course, and others are parallel, forming a series transverse to the second group before noted. Thorn street borders the north side of the park, being succeeded northward by Burns avenue, Suburban street, McLean avenue, Pacific street, Hastings avenue, Wakefield and Hudson avenues, Euclid and Conway streets, Third street, Fremont street, Fourth, Fifth, and Sixth streets, and Margaret, Beech, and Minnehaha streets.

Burns avenue was named in honor of John Burns, one of the proprietors of the Suburban Hills, living, like Lyman Dayton,† on this bluff.

McLean avenue commemorates Nathaniel McLean,† who was agent at Fort Snelling for the Indians in 1849-53. McLean township, likewise named for him, adjoined this area and formed the southeast part of Ramsey county, until it was annexed to this city. Hester street, before noted in the series running north and south, has the Christian name of his wife.

Hastings and Hudson avenues were respectively in part the courses of roads to Hastings in Dakota county and Hudson in Wisconsin.

William Wakefield, coming from Rhode Island in 1856, purchased in 1860 a tract of four acres on this bluff, where he "adorned his place with beautiful trees, . . . one of the finest home surroundings in the city" (Newson, page 612).

Conway street was named for Charles R. Conway, of whom Newson gave a biographic sketch (page 143).

Fremont street honors John C. Fremont, the Republican candidate for the presidency in 1856. It is also to be noted that Van Buren place (originally called Ravine street) and its public school are named for President

Van Buren, who likewise is commemorated by the long Van Buren street, lying next south of Minnehaha street in the west part of the city.

Margaret street was at first called Pearl street, in 1857, which is the meaning of this personal name; and Minnehaha was then Lake street.

Lines of sections in the U. S. government surveys are followed by Burns avenue and Minnehaha street, lying thus exactly a mile apart; and the latter reaches from the east boundary of the city west to Prior avenue, more than eight miles, but interrupted at the middle by railway grounds.

It should be observed that in St. Paul no definite usage distinguishes these terms, avenue and street, either in respect to their width and length or the directions of their courses. The two terms are here employed promiscuously, without system or any general reasons for choice in their applications throughout all the city area.

Adjoining Dayton's addition on its east side is Sigel's addition, platted in 1880 and 1883, named in honor of Franz Sigel (b. 1824, d. 1902), a distinguished Union general of the civil war, who is also honored by the name of a township in Brown county. Several years previous to these plats he had visited in that county and in St. Paul, and his name is borne by a street extending from this tract nearly to the east line of the city. Other street names here added are Tell, Frank, Atlantic, and English streets, each running from north to south, and Hancock, Terry, and Gotzian streets, running southeast. The last three are in honor of Gen. Winfield Scott Hancock and Gen. Alfred Howe Terry, associates with Sigel in the civil war, and Conrad† and Adam Gotzian,† shoe manufacturers and wholesalers in this city, with whom Sigel visited here.

Next eastward is an addition platted in 1887, which continues the foregoing names of streets running east. Its transverse streets, in their order from west to east, are English and Clarence streets, Etna (then called Fulton) street, Birmingham and Barclay streets and Hazelwood avenue (of which the last two were then respectively Moore and Bock streets).

Thence a tract named Suburban Homes was earlier platted, in 1878, bounded on the west by the present Hazelwood avenue, with which Germain, Kennard, and Flandrau streets, and White Bear avenue, are successively parallel in this order from west to east. Kennard street was named for an attorney, Kennard Buxton, who attended to the official records of the plat; the next street was later named in honor of Charles E. Flandrau,† the eminent lawyer and justice of the state supreme court, author of a "History of Minnesota;" and White Bear avenue leads toward the lake and village so named in the northeast corner of this county.

Farther east are Hazel, Ruth, Winthrop, and East avenues, running north, the last being on the east boundary of the city area.

ARLINGTON HILLS AND EASTWARD.

North of Minnehaha street and crossed by Phalen creek, a large tract called Arlington Hills was platted in 1873, receiving its name from villages near the cities of Boston and Washington. Its west line is Edgerton street (then named Gray avenue), with which Payne, Greenbrier, Walsh and Weide avenues, and Arcade street (then Belle avenue), are parallel in this order eastward. Running due east, across the foregoing, in succession northward, are Minnehaha, Reaney, Fauquier, Dorr, Wells, York (then Searls), Sims, Case, Jenks, Lawson, Cook, and Magnolia streets (the last, on the north line of this addition, being then Hall street).

Edgerton street commemorates Erastus S. Edgerton,† a prominent banker of this city; Payne and Greenbrier avenues had been named in 1857, for their southern part, in a plat of which Rice W. Payne was one of the owners; Walsh and Weide avenues honor Vincent D. Walsh, an original owner of the Arlington Hills plat, and Charles A. B. Weide,† who as a real estate dealer sold many of its lots; Reaney street was named for Hon. John H. Reaney,† who engaged in steamboating, was a representative in the legislature in 1878, and a state senator, 1879; Fauquier street, like Payne avenue, was named in 1857, for a county of Virginia, commemorating Francis Fauquier, the colonial governor in 1758-68; Case street commemorates James A. Case,† born in the state of New York in 1823, who came to St. Paul at the age of twenty years and was a surveyor and civil engineer; Jenks street is in honor of J. Ridgway Jenks, who was a brother of the wife of Governor Ramsey and during several years was a partner as a druggist with Dr. David Day;† and Cook street was named in honor of John B. Cook,† president of the St. Paul Omnibus Company.

Between Trout brook and Arlington Hills, a plat by Edmund Rice† in 1855 named five streets crossing it from south to north, of which Clark and Jessie streets retain their original names, but the others have been renamed as parts of De Soto, Burr, and Bradley streets, in this order from west to east. Clark street was named for Martin D. Clark, who came to St. Paul in 1851, was a carpenter, and built more than two hundred houses here within the next three years (Newson, page 331); Jessie street is in honor of a daughter of Edmund Rice;† and Whitall street, on the south line of this plat in 1855, bears the family name of the wife of Henry M. Rice,† who then was the delegate of Minnesota in Congress. The first street north of Whitall was then called Douglas avenue, to honor Stephen A. Douglas, United States senator, but now forms a part of York street.

Next on the west, an addition crossed by Trout brook, including Cayuga, Genesee, and Acker streets, was platted by Edmund Rice† in 1881. The last is in honor of his wife's brother, Captain William H. Acker,† a native of New York state, who came to St. Paul in 1854, at the age of twenty-one years, was adjutant general of Minnesota in 1860-61, enlisted in the First Minnesota regiment, and was killed in battle in 1862.

Northeast of the area of Arlington Hills, a tract of 160 acres had been platted in the summer of 1856 by Harwood Iglehart,† William Sprigg Hall,† and Charles N. Mackubin.† Eight of its nine streets running east and west were named in deference or compliment to the second of these partner proprietors, for whom Hall avenue in West St. Paul had been named in 1855. The fifth or middle street in the series is Maryland, for the native state of the three partners; but all others may be considered as sprigs of trees, shrubs, or smaller flowering plants. In the entire order from south to north, they are Magnolia, Jessamine, Geranium, Rose, Maryland, Hawthorn, Orange, Hyacinth, and Ivy.

All these early street names, which may be called a bouquet of flowers, are yet retained; and several of them are applied, though interruptedly, excepting for Maryland, to the continuations of streets on the same due east lines to the city boundary. Likewise westward Geranium and Rose streets continue to Western avenue, attaining thus an extent of five miles and a half, while Maryland street runs nearly a mile farther, to Lake Como. On the east, however, it is to be noted that the place of Magnolia street is named Sanborn avenue, in honor of Gen. John B. Sanborn,† who owned land at its north side; and in the place of Ivy street beyond Lake Phalen is Autumn street, with a very short Lilac avenue next north.

Nearly a mile south of Lake Phalen and at the southeast side of its outflowing creek, John H. Tracy in 1874 platted Phalen and Tracy avenues (the former now called a street), Harvester avenue, and Brand and Kerwin streets. Here was a large manufactory, the St. Paul Harvester Works, of which Henry Brand† had charge until 1882. John Kerwin† came to Minnesota in 1857, engaged in farming and in the sale of agricultural implements, and during several years, until his death in 1908, was chairman of the Ramsey County Board of Control.

Other streets adjoining the Harvester Works, on the north side of the railway, are Stillwater and Prosperity avenues, with the short Corning avenue and Mechanic street. Within a half mile farther east are Powder street, Railroad and Hammer avenues, and Herbert and Kiefer streets, the last being named for Andrew R. Kiefer,† a captain in the civil war, who in 1893-97 was a member of Congress.

Hazel Park, which is a residence district with a tiny public park, was platted in 1886 by William L. Ames, Jr.† New street names on this plat are Ames and La Crosse avenues. Its south side is Harvester avenue, and next on the south is Keogh avenue.

Several additions of Hazel Park were platted during the next eight years, lying within the distance of about a half mile east and northeast, including Van Dyke, Hazel, Luella, and Ruth avenues.

Yet farther east, on the high land adjoining East avenue, the boundary of the city, a plat in 1892 of forty acres has in its southeast corner the northern part of Beaver lake and is bounded on the north by Maryland avenue. Another plat in 1893, of equal area, a quarter to a half mile farther north, named Harvester Heights, is traversed from west to east by Autumn street, Prospect avenue, having a far outlook southwestward over the city, Helen street, named for the wife of William L. Ames, Jr.,† and Sherwood avenue, for George W. Sherwood,† a building contractor, who owned a large stock farm, raising thoroughbred horses, on the road to Afton. Crossing these additions from south to north is Howard avenue, honoring Thomas Howard,† municipal judge in 1869-72.

Latest among noteworthy additions to this city is a tract of about 125 acres, named Beaver Lake Heights, platted in the summer of 1917, lying between a quarter of a mile and one mile southwest of Beaver lake. It is bordered on the northwest by the electric car line on Hazel avenue, running to Wildwood and Stillwater, the carriage road to Stillwater forms a part of its north line, and it is crossed centrally from south to north by Ruth avenue. The other avenues, mostly platted in curved courses, are Algonquin, Jordan, Iroquois, Manitou, Mohawk, Nokomis, Nortonia, Huron, Pedersen, and Escanaba avenues. Several of these names are received from Indian tribes; Nortonia is in compliment to John W. and William W. Norton, real estate dealers of St. Paul; and Escanaba is the aboriginal name of a river and city in Michigan.

Three short streets in this addition are named Wabasso, Bena, and Neche, Ojibway words, respectively meaning rabbit, partridge, and friend or neighbor, "one like myself." The last, which is also the name of a railway village in Pembina county, North Dakota, is pronounced in two syllables, and is a common word of greeting. In Baraga's Dictionary it is spelled *nidji,* being apparently allied with *nij* (two).

VICINITY OF LAKE PHALEN.

East of Lake Phalen, the avenues and streets running east, beyond those previously noticed, in the order northward, are Lake Como and Phalen avenue, Heron and Center streets, Mary and Vassar avenues, Keller street, and Larpenteur avenue.

Charles E. Keller,† born in St. Paul in 1858, has engaged in lumber and real estate business, and was deputy county auditor in 1901-06; and his brother, Herbert P. Keller,† was mayor of this city in 1910-14. Their father, John M. Keller, coming to St. Paul in 1856 from Germany, was a lumber dealer and had a sawmill where Third street crosses Trout brook.

The street running on the north line of the city bore originally several different names, for various parts of its extent; but in 1888 these were superseded by Minneapolis avenue, for its entire length, and in 1904, this was changed to Larpenteur avenue, in honor of Auguste Louis Larpenteur.† He came here in 1843, at the age of twenty years, engaged until 1887 in mercantile business, and for more than thirty years later was the most esteemed and beloved survivor of the early pioneers, dying February 24, 1919.

Streets running north, transverse with the foregoing, in the order east from Lake Phalen, are Overbrook, Harvard, Yale, Oxford, and Phalen avenues, McAfee, Fisher, and Schwabe streets, Hager avenue, Manton, Duncan, and Dieter streets, with others at the east before noted. Beside the trolley line leading to White Bear are Curve and Furness avenues.

VICINITY OF LAKE COMO.

On the area from Lake Phalen to Lake Como and its vicinity, for a distance of five miles originally in New Canada and Rose townships, the second and third tracts placed on sale for house lots and suburban homes were Lake Como Villas, close south of this lake, and a larger plat named simply Como, adjoining the northeast side of the lake. Each was platted by Henry McKenty,† respectively in August, 1856, and August, 1857. The former tract is bounded on the east by the present Grotto street, west by Lexington avenue, north by Union street, and south by Front street. It is now crossed by twice as many streets running north as were on the original plat, namely, in order from east to west, Jameson and Crowell avenues, Como Place, Barrett avenue, Victoria street, and Louth, Colne, Ryde, Kilburn, Chatsworth, Argyle, and Oxford streets, and Churchill avenue. None of these names appeared on the plat in 1856. Its streets running west, including those on the north and south boundaries, were named by McKenty in that order as Chestnut, Walnut, Locust, Prairie, and Front streets, of which only the last is now retained. The others have been changed respectively to Union, McKenty, Orchard, and Hatch streets, the last being in honor of Edwin A. C. Hatch,† pioneer fur trader and Indian agent.

Henry McKenty† had a genius for platting and selling "broad acres," as is well related by Newson (pages 322-6), and he deserves to be gratefully remembered for his renaming the former Sandy lake as Como; but all his street names given in 1856 for the tract of his Villas have been set aside, with one exception. The south line of the plat he called Front street, which later, with Hatch street, has been extended to the east.

In the plat of 1857, named Como, McKenty laid out eight streets running north, of which Ash and Shrub streets retain their original names, the full series and present names, in order from east to west, being Grotto, Ash, Logan, Quincy, Adams, Shrub, and Niagara streets and Lexington avenue. The transverse avenues and streets, running west, in order from the north boundary southward, are now Larpenteur avenue, Idaho, Hoyt, and Nebraska avenues, Lake Como and Phalen avenue, and Cottage and South streets. Only the last has the original name of 1857. Thus, as with Front street, we are able to account for this name, on the south line of the Como plat, though its present position, in the north part of the city, makes it seem anomalous.

Similarly North street, now in an eastern central position, was so named when it was the north border of Benjamin W. Brunson's† addition, in 1852; L'Orient street (French for "the east") was at the east side of an addition platted in 1857; and Western avenue, one of the longest in the city and far east from its west border, received the name of its part first platted, in 1853, at the west side of an addition by Lyman Dayton,† which included the early east part of Dayton avenue.

Warrendale, a relatively small neighborhood on the southwest side of Lake Como, was platted in 1885 by Cary I. Warren, who came from Louisville, Kentucky, and returned to reside there in 1896. This plat has Cross, Horton, and Van Slyke avenues, the first passing across it from east to west. The second was named for Hiler H. Horton,† a lawyer who settled here in 1878, commemorated also by one of the city parks, and the third for William A. Van Slyke,† a grain merchant, who was greatly interested in the city park system, and especially for the development of Como Park, as told glowingly by Newson (pages 487-490).

Preceding pages have presented the names of many of the streets and avenues running north on the area between Lakes Phalen and Como, but many also remain to be further noted. In their order from east to west, the following additional names in that series deserve special mention.

McMenemy street was the former name, until 1909, of a part of the present Westminster street for a mile and a half, between Case street and Larpenteur avenue. It commemorated Robert McMenemy, an immigrant from Ireland, who during many years had a fine farm beside it, raising garden produce for the St. Paul markets.

Edgemont and Sloan streets are short, lying respectively next east and west of Westminster, the second honoring a pioneer St. Paul family.

After Mississippi street, the series has Adolphus, Olivier, Agate, and Cortland streets, of which the second honors Louis M. Olivier,† register of deeds in this county, 1853-7, and John B. Olivier,† county auditor in 1872-3, and judge of probate, 1891-5, each dealing extensively in St. Paul lands and lots. Until 1874 the present Cortland street, named from a county and city in New York, had been called New Canada road, for the adjoining township and village of French Canadian people.

Next are Highland, Abell, and Sylvan streets, Park avenue, and Hawley and Rice streets, of which the fourth and the last have been previously noticed for their southern parts. The fifth honors Captain Alfred C. Hawley,† who was adjutant general of Minnesota in 1882-4.

Farther westward are Albemarle, Woodbridge, Marion, and Gaultier streets, and Matilda, Farrington, Hand, and Western avenues, of which previous mention has been made for the third, fourth, sixth, and the last. Matilda avenue bears the Christian name of Mrs. Henry M. Rice,† and her maiden surname is borne by Whitall street, as before noted. Dr. Daniel W. Hand,† who came to St. Paul in 1857, was surgeon of the First Minnesota regiment in the civil war, and in 1882-7 was professor of surgery in the state university.

The remaining list of these north to south streets includes Cumberland street, Hazzard avenue, named in honor of George H. Hazzard,† during recent years secretary of the Minnesota Territorial Pioneers, Arundel street, already noticed, Norton, Bernardine and Cohansey streets, Mackubin and Kent streets, extending with Arundel south to Summit avenue, Loeb street and Danforth avenue, and Dale, Coleman, St. Albans, and Langtry streets, the next being Grotto street, on the east side of McKenty's plats of the Villas and Como. The last, Grotto street, received its name in 1871 on the more southern plat of a large addition named Summit Park, because the extension of its course south to the Mississippi (there named Bay street) reaches the riverside very near to Fountain cave.

SAINT PAUL 629

Cottage Homes, the earliest tract platted in this vicinity, by Henry McKenty† in the summer of 1855, lying a half mile to one mile and a quarter east of Lake Como, was divided into lots of five acres, and was crossed only by Carbon and Cottage streets, names which yet remain, running east and west.

Other streets parallel with these, in the order from Maryland street northward, in addition to Hawthorn, Orange, Hyacinth, and Ivy streets, before noted, include Villard avenue, named in honor of Henry Villard,† who completed the building of the transcontinental Northern Pacific railway; Child street, South street, extended east from the Como plat, Clear street, and Denny street, named for Henry R. Denny,† U. S. marshal of this state in 1882-6, and secretary of the Minnesota Agricultural Society in 1888-9; Lake Como and Phalen avenue, crossing the distance between these lakes and resuming the same name beyond Lake Phalen to the east boundary of the city; and a series of six avenues named for states, without alphabetic or geographic system, the order for the first three being Nevada, Nebraska, and Montana, then Hoyt avenue, which commemorates Benjamin F. Hoyt,† a pioneer preacher and dealer in real estate, who platted several additions of this city, succeeded northward by Iowa, Idaho, and California avenues, the last lying next to Larpenteur avenue, which is the city boundary. With these are to be added the short Woodland avenue and Nye street.

South of Maryland street and west of Trout brook, streets running west and not previously listed, in their order from south to north, are Lafond, Blair, and Van Buren streets, Sycamore street, Lyton place, Larch and Atwater streets, Winnipeg and Manitoba avenues, Litchfield street, Milford and Wayzata streets, Topping, Burgess, and Stinson streets, and Oliver, Rock, and Acorn streets. Benjamin Lafond platted an addition in 1857, in which his name was given to the eastern end of that street; Herbert W. Topping was during many years a member of the board of park commissioners; and Thomas Stinson has been before noticed for his platting the addition that named Thomas street, in 1856.

HAMLINE AND VICINITY.

On the plats for Hamline University and its vicinity, added to the city in 1880-83, the streets and avenues running north, in their order westward from Lexington avenue or parkway, are Dunlap and Griggs streets, Syndicate, Hamline, Sheldon, Albert, Holton, Pascal, Simpson, Asbury, and Snelling avenues, Fry street and Walker, Charlotte, Aldine, Wheeler, and Fairview avenues.

Crossing this series, the names of the streets passing east and west have been already noted, for their eastern parts, from University avenue northward to Minnehaha street. Farther north are Capitol avenue, Seminary and Hubbard streets, and Wesley, Hewitt, and Taylor avenues.

Several personal names in these lists are identified with the progress of religious thought, and especially with the foundation and growth of the Methodist Episcopal church, and of this university, which represents its higher educational work for this state. Blaise Pascal (b. 1623, d. 1662), of France, was a very gifted religious author; John Wesley (1703-1791), of England, was the founder of Methodism, and his brother Charles (1708-1788) wrote many grand hymns; Francis Asbury (1745-1816), also of England, came as a missionary to the American colonies; Leonidas L. Hamline (1797-1865), of Ohio, for whom the university and this long avenue were named, was a Methodist bishop; and Matthew Simpson (1810-84), was president of a Methodist university in Indiana, 1839-48, and after 1852 was a bishop.

William Dunlap was a builder and real estate dealer here during the last fifteen years of his life, dying at the age of 78 years in 1901; Chauncey W. Griggs,† colonel in the Third Minnesota regiment, was a prominent merchant and banker in this city, and removed to Tacoma, Wash., in 1888; Lucius F. Hubbard,† of Red Wing and later of St. Paul, was governor of Minnesota in 1882-87, for whom also a county is named; Girart Hewitt† was a dealer in real estate and by pamphlets and steamboat excursions greatly promoted immigration to this state; and James W. Taylor,† who came to St. Paul in 1856, was U. S. consul in Winnipeg from 1870 until his death in 1893.

Snelling avenue runs on a section line from near Fort Snelling north six miles to the limit of the city, this name and that of the fort being in honor of Colonel Josiah Snelling,† its builder.

Northwest of the Hamline district, a tract called Midway Heights was platted in 1885, having Chelton, Tallula, and Hilles avenues, and Pennock street, running from east to west, crossed by Clayland, Tatum, and Pusey avenues, with about a third of a mile of the long Prior avenue forming its west side. The proprietors, Samuel C. Tatum and his wife, of Cincinnati, with Hannah Tatum of Philadelphia, gave their surname to an avenue; and another avenue and a street honor their friend, Pennock Pusey,† who came to St. Paul in 1854, was assistant secretary of state, 1862-72, and private secretary of Governor Pillsbury, 1876-82. Chelton avenue, with a slight change in spelling, is derived from the Chelten hills, a few miles north of Philadelphia; and Tallula is the name of a creek and waterfall in Georgia.

Beyond the lines of the Great Northern and Northern Pacific railways, the northward continuations of the south to north avenues on the Hamline plats, after a wide interruption, are again predominant names west of Como Park, there crossing an addition of 120 acres, platted in 1913 by Hon. Thomas Frankson,† who three years later was elected lieutenant governor of the state. An added avenue, extending through his plat from the earlier plats on the south and north, is named Arona, for a town in northern Italy, about 30 miles west of Como. New names applied by Frankson are McKinley, Frankson, and Bison avenues, the first for William McKinley, martyr president of the United States, and the last for a domesticated herd of several bisons, the American buffalo, brought by Frankson from his former home in Spring Valley and placed in an inclosure of Como Park. Other avenues in his addition and at the north, running from east to west, receive their names from the corresponding avenues east of Lake Como; but at the south a new series of streets includes Wynne, Breda, Albany, Almond, and Atlantis streets, with Como avenue, on which the street car line runs west from the park.

ST. ANTHONY PARK.

Southwest and west of the State Fair Ground and Agricultural College, St. Anthony Park, in the northwest edge of St. Paul and adjoining the former township and city of St. Anthony (now East Minneapolis), was platted in two parts, in the spring and late autumn of 1885. The earlier southern part was owned by Charles H. Pratt, of Minneapolis, Nathaniel P. Langford,† of St. Paul, and John H. Knapp, Andrew Tainter, and Henry Van Reed, of Menomonie, Wisconsin. The later part, called St. Anthony Park North, was platted for J. Royall McMurran, agent of a syndicate of capitalists living in Virginia, namely, Hill Carter and Major James H. Dooley, of Richmond, Brooke Doswell, of Fredericksburg, and others. Each of the owners thus named, excepting McMurran, was commemorated by an avenue or street; but Pratt street was renamed Alden in 1903, the greater part of Langford avenue (earlier extending east to Como Park) was renamed as a part of Como avenue in 1910, and Dooley avenue was changed in 1902, on request of Prof. Samuel B. Green† and others, to Commonwealth avenue, taking the name of a beautiful parkway in Boston, Mass. A part of Eustis street north of the present Great Northern railway was originally named Folwell street, in honor of William W. Folwell,† first president of the State University; but a year afterward, in 1886, it was changed, so that a street now two miles long (except interruptions by railways crossing it) was named continuously Eustis, in honor of J. Mage Eustis,† of Minneapolis, an adjacent land owner.

Because two great railways break the courses of other streets, the principal thoroughfare joining the southern and northern parts of St. Anthony Park is Raymond avenue, named in honor of Bradford Paul Raymond,† a student of Hamline at Red Wing in 1866-9, many years before its removal to this city. He was president of Lawrence University, Appleton, Wis., in 1883-89, and during the next nineteen years was president of Wesleyan University, Middletown, Conn.

Next east of the north part of Raymond avenue and beside the State Agricultural College Campus is Cleveland avenue, at first named for Heman Gibbs,† the earliest settler of the adjacent part of Rose township, but renamed in honor of Grover Cleveland, president of the United States, leaving only a short southern part, veering westward, which yet is Gibbs avenue. On the southern course of the same section line, Cleveland avenue begins again and runs through Merriam Park and onward more than three miles to the Mississippi above Fort Snelling.

Prior avenue, near the southeast limit of St. Anthony Park, was there at first called Westwood avenue, as also later in the same year 1885 it was named at the west side of Midway Heights; but that name was changed to Prior avenue in 1886, taking thus the designation given in 1882-3 to its more southward course in Merriam Park. It is in honor of Charles H. Prior, of Minneapolis, who is commemorated by the railway village of Prior Lake, in Scott county. With some interruptions, Prior avenue reaches south to the verge of the Mississippi bluff nearly opposite the fort.

In the vicinity of this north end of Prior avenue are Sherwood, Packard, Eldred, and Eastman streets; Stella, Carter, Fifield, and Raleigh streets; and Bushnell, Alfred, and Pepperell streets, with Beard court. All these streets are very short.

Between Gibbs and Raymond avenues are Bartlett, Marsh, and Everett courts, and Standish, Priscilla, and Alden streets, the last three being for pilgrims who came to Plymouth, Mass., in 1620 on the Mayflower.

South of the railways are Hersey avenue, Turner, Bradford, Endicott, and Wycliff streets, the third and fourth being names from early New England history, and the last from the dawn before the Reformation in old England; Hampden and Cromwell avenues, named for John Hampden (1594-1643) and Oliver Cromwell (1599-1658), great figures in English history; Ellis, Hunt, and Cudworth streets, the last two named for D. H. Hunt and Darius A. Cudworth, local residents; Pearl street, originally named Pym street, for John Pym (1584-1643), an English patriot; Bayless avenue, named for Vincent W. Bayless, secretary of a fuel company in Minneapolis; and Manvel and Robbins streets, for Allen Manvel,† of St. Paul, an official of the Manitoba (now Great Northern) railway, and Daniel M. Robbins,† also of St. Paul, president of a grain elevator company.

Wheeler, Lindley, and Van Reed streets, running east and west, are between the two railways, the first being named in honor of Everett P. Wheeler, a prominent attorney of New York city, who had business interests here. The second and third are very short streets, the latter being for one of the proprietors of the southern plat.

North of the railways, in addition to avenues and streets already noticed, are Scudder street, honoring Rev. John L. Scudder, in 1882-86 pastor of the First Congregational Church in Minneapolis, member of a family distinguished for its clergymen and missionaries; Blake and Gordon avenues, the former in honor of Anson Blake, of St. Paul, uncle of Mr. Pratt, who was a principal owner and agent of the south part of St. Anthony Park; Bourne avenue, for Walter B. Bourne, a clerk for the sale of lots; Keston street, Chilcombe and Pierce avenues, and Manson and Patton streets; Brompton street, Hendon avenue, and Fulham, Chelmsford, Grantham, and Hythe streets, the first three named for suburbs or parts of London, the second three for towns elsewhere in England, these names having been proposed by Manley B. Curry, of

Richmond, Va., a partner of the syndicate owning the northern plat; Buford avenue, in honor of Col. A. S. Buford, of Virginia, who served in the Confederate army; and Dudley avenue, bearing a family name long ago prominent in England, and later in American history.

This district, more than any other large part of St. Paul, is noteworthy for its streets deviating from straight and rectangular courses, on account of the diversities of the contour, which is formed by numerous irregular hillocks, ridges, and hollows, being a part of a morainic belt of the glacial drift. Thus even the chief streets, as the middle course of Raymond avenue, Scudder and Knapp streets, and Langford, Commonwealth (at first named Dooley), Carter, and Doswell avenues, in this order from southeast to northwest, the last five being named on the plats in honor of original proprietors, are curved to conform with the slopes and inequalities of the land surface.

MERRIAM PARK AND VICINITY.

Turning next south to Merriam Park and other plats in its vicinity, and thence westward to the city boundary and the Mississippi, we come to the tract platted by John L. Merriam† in 1882-83, for which his son, William R. Merriam,† later governor of the state in 1889-93, was agent. It has Wilder and Terrace Park avenues, Moore, Prior, and Howell avenues, the same on the early plat as now; but its Willius street and Laura avenue are now respectively Ferdinand street and Dewey avenue. These names commemorate Amherst H. Wilder,† who by his will, with the later wills of his widow and daughter, founded a noble charity for this city; George W. Moore,† who came to St. Paul in 1850, and after 1861 was deputy collector of customs; Charles H. Prior, previously noticed; Ferdinand Willius,† banker, who settled here in 1855; Laura E. Hancock, wife of William R. Merriam,† niece of Gen. Winfield S. Hancock; and Admiral George Dewey, hero of the capture of Manila in 1898. For the last, the change from the original name, Laura avenue, was made because of its similarity in sound with Laurel avenue, which had been earlier named, in its eastern part, in 1870. It should be added that the second wife of John L. Merriam, step-mother of Governor Merriam, was Helen M. Wilder, for whose brother, as also for herself, Wilder avenue was named.

The group of avenues running west, transverse to these here listed, had been previously named on plats farther east. Between St. Anthony avenue and the Chicago, Milwaukee and St. Paul railway are Montague place and Milwaukee and Astoria avenues, each very short.

Bordering the northeast side of Merriam Park, a smaller residential area called Union Park was platted in 1884, lying between the railway and University avenue. Its east part is crossed by Dewey avenue; the east boundary is a part of Fairview avenue (then called Pomona avenue); the southern boundary is Waltham avenue; and it also has Feronia, Lynnhurst, and Oakley avenues.

Next eastward, other small plats of 1885 and 1886 are separated by Shields avenue, named in honor of Gen. James Shields,† one of the first United States senators of Minnesota. North to south streets crossing Shields avenue, in their order from east to west, are Roy, Fry, and Pierce streets, and Aldine, Herschel, Wheeler, and Beacon avenues.

Toward the northwest, a plat in 1881 by the widow of Girart Hewitt and other owners, between the Milwaukee railway and University avenue, has Montgomery and Vandalia streets, Pillsbury and Hampden avenues, and La Salle and Carleton streets. Running from southeast to northwest, across the foregoing, are Myrtle and Wabash avenues.

In the Fourth and Fifth additions to Merriam Park, platted in 1887, and in the Capitol addition of 1890, adjoining the northwest corner of Merriam Park, are Gilbert and Cleora avenues, Corinne street, Temple court, and Ann Arbor street. The second honors a daughter of Rush B. Wheeler, dealer in real estate here since 1883; the third is named for his niece in Utica, N. Y.; and the last bears the name of a city in Michigan, where the university of that state was founded in 1837.

Next on the south, at the west side of Merriam Park, a residential tract of forty acres was platted in 1907 and named Roblyn Park for Orlando A. Robertson and Frederick B. Lynch,† its original owners. It is crossed from north to south by Finn avenue, named earlier, in its parts farther south, for William Finn, the first permanent settler of Reserve township (now the southwest part of St. Paul); and its north line is Roblyn avenue, as the western extension of Rondo street, between Pascal and Cretin avenues, was renamed in 1913.

An addition in 1889 by Daniel A. J. Baker,† lying south of University avenue and between Raymond and the west boundary of the city, has Glendale avenue, Pelham street, Cromwell avenue, Eustis and Clifford streets, and Curfew, Berry, and Emerald avenues, the last being on the Minneapolis line. These are crossed by Bayard street, with Myrtle and Wabash avenues, which have been previously noted.

Desnoyer Park, a large residential district lying south of the Milwaukee railway and bounded southwestward by the Mississippi, platted in 1887, was named for Stephen Desnoyer,† who settled here in 1843, kept a hotel, and traded with the Indians. Its streets running west and northwest, in their order from northeast to southwest, are St. Anthony avenue, Doane street, Beverly, Columbus, Glenham, Maplewood, and Otis avenues, and the Mississippi River boulevard. Transverse are the Como and River boulevard, Wentworth street, Medford, Somerville, and Glendale avenues, and Join street. Medford and Somerville are cities adjoining Boston, Mass.; and Beverly avenue is similarly named for the township and city next north of Salem, Mass.

The extensive grounds of the Town and Country Club, acquired in the summer of 1911, were formerly a part of the Desnoyer Park district, which southward, beyond Marshall avenue, has Marlboro and Montrose avenues.

SAINT PAUL 635

SUMMIT PARK AND VICINITY.

Passing eastward to the west border of the city as it was in 1857, we have the large addition named Summit Park, platted in 1871 by William S. Wright, John Wann, and several other proprietors. Its streets running north and south are Dale, St. Albans (then called Prairie street), Grotto, Avon (then Cayuga), Victoria, Milton, Chatsworth, and Oxford (then Linden) streets, and Lexington avenue, in this order from east to west. The avenues running west, across the foregoing, are Laurel, Ashland, and Portland, then named respectively Madison, Washington, and Leslie avenues; Summit, Grand, Lincoln, and Goodrich avenues, which retain their original names; Fairmount avenue, which then was Owasco; and Osceola avenue, named then as now.

Milton and Oxford are recognized as derived from England; and Chatsworth is the home of the Duke of Devonshire, in the county of Derby. Osceola was a famous Seminole warrior, who died a prisoner in Fort Moultrie, South Carolina, in 1838.

John Wann, who lived on the northwest corner of Summit avenue and Victoria street, named the latter from his admiration of the Queen of England, and in contrast his wife, to testify loyalty to the United States, named Lexington avenue for the battle on April 19, 1775, when the first shots of the American Revolution were "heard round the world." The present Portland avenue was named Leslie for their son, Thomas Leslie Wann, and after twenty-one years it was renamed as now in 1892.

Terrace Park, a smaller residence area, adjoining the southeast side of Summit Park, was platted in 1871, having Oakland street (now called an avenue), and Floral and Lawton streets. Its Heather place was platted later, by James W. Heather in 1889, so that this name, apparently of Scotch derivation, came as a personal surname. Oakland is a most characteristic term referring to the abundant oak trees of this part of Minnesota, applied also to a large cemetery in another part of the city, and to a southeastern suburb, before noticed.

Crocus Hill, platted in 1881-83 and 1889, has a circuitous street, called Crocus place, and a small public park. The name is given in the local flora, to our earliest spring flower, called also pasque flower, which means Easter flower. It is abundant through all the prairie portion of the state.

Kenwood Terrace, platted for residences in 1888-89, has Kenwood parkway and the east end of Linwood place. This small tract, at the verge of the river bluff, and the similar Crocus Hill area, thence receiving its name, adjoin the southeast corner of Summit Park. The westward extension of Linwood place, formerly called Evergreen avenue, was thus renamed in 1895.

Ridgewood Park, a residence area next westward, traversed by the Milwaukee railway, was platted in 1887, comprising Lombard avenue, Crescent court, Ridgewood avenue, parts of Grace street and Jefferson avenue, Robie street, and Baldwin court, the last two being very short, with other streets previously noticed farther north.

LEXINGTON AND MACALESTER PARKS.

From a mile and a half to more than two miles south of the Lexington Athletic Park, much used for playing baseball, on the southwest corner of University and Lexington avenues, are the residence areas named Lexington Park, including no less than eleven small plats of 1886-88. The streets and avenues running north and south, parallel with Lexington avenue and in the order westward from it, are Montcalm place, the west part of Nettleton avenue, Edgcumbe road, Griggs street, and Syndicate and Hamline avenues, of which the last three were named on earlier plats northward. Montcalm, a French general, was killed in the battle of Quebec, 1759; William Nettleton† was one of the founders of Superior, Wis., and of Duluth, and later engaged extensively in real estate business in St. Paul; and Edgcumbe road, recently improved as a parkway, formerly called South Summit avenue, was thus renamed in 1912, for a road along the high shore of Plymouth harbor, England.

Streets running west in this district, southward of Osceola avenue, before noted as the south line of Summit Park, are Sargent avenue, St. Clair street, and Lydia street; Berkeley and Stanford avenues, named for universities of California; Wellesley avenue, for the college so named near Boston; Lansing street; Jefferson avenue, for President Thomas Jefferson, reaching far east and west; Juliet, Palace, James, Randolph, and Juno streets; Niles, Armstrong, Watson, Hartford, and Bayard avenues; Scheffer and Eleanor streets; and Otto avenue, lying on a section line about two miles north of Fort Snelling. Several of these streets and avenues continue west to the River boulevard, as probably others will be so extended when the region shall be fully occupied by homes.

St. Clair street, on a section line, is named, like Lake St. Clair, between Huron and Erie, for Gen. Arthur St. Clair, who was governor of the Northwest Territory in 1789-1802; Randolph street, on a quarter section line, commemorates the Virginia family distinguished for service in the Continental Congress and in the early U. S. Congress; Bayard avenue honors a similarly eminent family of Delaware; Albert Scheffer,† of St. Paul, was a banker and a state senator; and Otto avenue is in honor of a German family bearing this surname, who held official positions in Reserve township. In 1888 the Otto family platted 40 acres at the south side of this avenue, bounded west by Cleveland avenue.

An area called Kittsondale, formerly part of a farm owned by Norman W. Kittson, for whom a county is named, was platted in 1902, nearly adjoining the Lexington Athletic Park. Next southward are Concordia College and the Central High School.

The Macalester College grounds and the residence district of Macalester Park, named like this college in honor of Charles Macalester,† a merchant of Philadelphia, platted in 1883, and an addition southeast of the college, called Sylvan Park, platted in 1886 by William E. Brimhall,† a resident market gardener and nurseryman, are traversed from

SAINT PAUL 637

north to south by Warwick, Saratoga, Brimhall, Snelling, Macalester, Vernon, and Cambridge avenues, and Amherst and Baldwin streets, with Fairview avenue at the west side of Macalester Park. The order of the list is from Pascal avenue westward. Baldwin street was named for Matthias W. Baldwin, of Philadelphia, inventor and builder of locomotives used throughout the world, principal donor for erection of the building occupied by the Baldwin School, dedicated Dec. 29, 1853, which led to the organization of this college, opened to students in 1885. Walpole street and Princeton avenue, running west, are in the south part of the college park area, the former very short, but the latter continuing west to the River boulevard. Princeton, N. J., has the largest Presbyterian university of the United States, with which this college is in close denominational affiliation.

GROVELAND AND VICINITY.

Shadow Falls Park, a small area of residences, where the Mississippi receives a cascading brook, between the two Catholic institutions of St. Thomas College and St. Paul Seminary, was platted by Archbishop Ireland† in 1911. The River boulevard here makes a detour above the falls, and the several other streets, excepting Service lane, are named from their more southern and eastern portions.

Groveland, the name of a plat by Archbishop Ireland in 1890, then comprising only about 30 acres, has been extended to a considerably larger residential area bounded on the west by Cretin avenue, beside the Seminary, named in honor of Joseph Cretin,† the first Bishop of St. Paul. About a mile distant to the south is St. Catherine's College, a Catholic college for women.

Between Macalester avenue and the river, numerous streets are found south of Summit avenue that have not been previously listed, these being Underwood and Fredericka avenues, Sue street, Dustin avenue, very short, Kenneth avenue, Sumner, Norwich, and Woodville avenues, Mt. Curve boulevard, and Woodlawn avenue. They run north and south, in westward order, and the transverse streets have been noticed eastward.

Otto's addition, before mentioned, is crossed from north to south by Berta street, and from east to west by Schneider, Moritz, and Dora avenues, with Boland avenue on its south line. The last was named in honor of Adam† and Peter Bohland,† immigrants from Germany, who were farmers in this part of the present city area, the latter being a member of the legislature in 1879-81.

Hiawatha Park, a residence addition near the Mississippi, opposite to the mouth of Minnehaha creek, platted in 1890, has Bowdoin avenue, running south, with Villard street, Magoffin and Coburn avenues, and Yale street, each short, running west. Longfellow, author of "The Song of Hiawatha," was graduated at Bowdoin College, Maine. Henry Villard† completed the building of the Northern Pacific railroad, which was grandly celebrated in St. Paul and Minneapolis on September 3,

1883. Beriah Magoffin,† a farmer in this vicinity, was a representative in the legislature in 1877, and was one of the first members of the city board of park commissioners, 1887-89.

SOUTHWESTERN ADDITIONS.

Numerous plats along the course of West Seventh street, between the central part of the city and Fort Snelling, and on the area between that street and the river, remain to be noticed.

On the valley bottomland, beneath the northern part of the High Bridge, by which Smith avenue crosses the Mississippi, are a western part of Washington street, Spring and Mill streets, the east end of St. Clair street, and Banning, Parsons, and Alison streets.

Near the north end of the bridge of the Chicago, St. Paul, Minneapolis and Omaha railway are Omaha and Barton streets.

An addition in 1873, at the west side of the Omaha railway shops, has Audubon street and Armstrong and Lee avenues, running west. Other plats next southwestward, of 1874 to 1883, have Logan and Forster streets, and the east ends of Scheffer street and Otto avenue, with Stewart and Butternut avenues, which run southwest. Stewart avenue, continuing to the vicinity of Fort Snelling bridge, was named in honor of Dr. Jacob H. Stewart,† who settled in St. Paul in 1855, was mayor in 1864, postmaster during the next five years, and a member of Congress in 1877-9.

Streets running from north to south in this part of the city, beyond Western avenue, remaining to be listed, are the short Nugent street, Daly, Drake, Warsaw, Arbor, Bay, Vance, View, Fulton, and Clifton streets, with Orrin, Canton, and Mercer streets, the last three very short.

Avenues and streets lying farther southwest, which run mostly southeastward, in courses nearly at right angles to West Seventh street, are Rogers and Hathaway avenues, May street, Vista, Alaska, and Albion avenues, Elway, Dealton, and Bee streets, very short, Glen Terrace, Parmer street, Purnell and Woolsey avenues, and Rankin, Springfield, Madison, and Alton streets, the last four having been platted in 1872.

Parallel with West Seventh street and Stewart avenue are Palmer street, Middleton avenue, Race and Adrian streets, and Benson, Agnes, Rockwood, Youngman, and Chapman avenues.

On an addition in 1886 by C. W. Youngman, Stephen Lamm, William L. Rosenberger, and John Rentz, a series of very short streets, each called a place, is platted at the southeast side of Youngman avenue, and running southeast to the verge of the valley bluff, named in southwestward order as Lamm, Jackson, Truman, Irving, Rosenberger, Lincoln, and Washington places.

Plats of 1887 and 1891, opposite to Fort Snelling, have Leonard avenue, St. Paul street, a part of Stewart avenue, and Graham, Munster, Wordsworth, and Sheridan streets, running east and west, in this order northward from the Mississippi; and a more recent plat, continuing

SAINT PAUL

north, has Field, Caulfield, Worcester, and Morgan avenues. Crossing these are Davern, Bellevue, and Fairview avenues, and southern parts of Sue street and Prior avenue, of which the last three have been earlier noted northward. Davern avenue commemorates William Davern, who was born in Ireland, June 24, 1831, and died in this city June 30, 1913. He came to America in 1848, and to St. Paul the next year; was a farmer and dairyman in Reserve township (now the southwest part of the city), living on this avenue; was a member of the legislature in 1857-8.

Parks, Boulevards, and Parkways.

The History of St. Paul, edited by Gen. C. C. Andrews, published in 1890, has a chapter on "The Parks of the City," in pages 522-542, including a part of an address by Horace W. S. Cleveland, then landscape architect of the park systems of the Twin Cities. A later paper, "History of the Parks and Public Grounds of St. Paul," by Lloyd Peabody, forms pages 609-630 in Volume XV, 1915, Minnesota Historical Society Collections. The following notes of origins of names have been gathered from these sources and from the annual reports of the Board of Park Commissioners, beginning in 1888, supplemented by interviews in the summer of 1918 with Frederick Nussbaumer, who since 1892 has been the city superintendent of parks.

Rice and Irvine parks were donated to public use by Henry M. Rice† and John R. Irvine† in their addition to St. Paul, platted July 2, 1849, being the oldest parks of the city, each designated as a "public square."

Smith park is next in age, having been included by the plat of an addition dated July 24, 1849, by Cornelius S. Whitney and Robert Smith, "who were both Illinois speculators, and never residents of St. Paul. . . . It was named for the junior member of the firm, Hon. Robert Smith, of Alton, Ill." He was born in Peterborough, N. H., June 12, 1802; removed to Illinois in 1832, and was a member of Congress, 1843-49 and 1857-59; died in Alton, Ill., December 21, 1867.

The area of Smith park was the central part of a plateau of stratified valley drift, outlined on the maps of St. Paul in 1851 and 1857, which was cut down 50 to 75 feet in the years 1876 to 1890. The plateau, extending a sixth of a mile both in length and width, was known as Baptist hill, because a Baptist church was built on its summit.

Como park, having 320 acres of land and 107 acres of water, which consists of Lake Como and the little Cozy lake, connected by a boat channel, was the earliest acquired by purchase, in 1873, with later additions, being the largest and most fully developed park in this city. Its name, received from Italy, was conferred on the lake and a plat for suburban homes by Henry McKenty† in 1856, as before noted.

Phalen park, having 216 acres of land and 222 of water, mainly acquired in 1890-94, is named from its lake and the outflowing creek. Edward Phelan† (or Phalen) owned a claim at the falls of this creek in 1840-44. His numerous successive land claims here, and his probable crime of murder, are recorded in Williams' History of St. Paul (M. H. S. Collections, vol. IV).

Indian Mounds park, purchased in 1893-1902, comprising 70 acres, has a fine group of aboriginal burial mounds on the verge of the high eastern bluff of the Mississippi valley, whence a very extensive and grand prospect is afforded, looking far up and down the bending course of the great river, and over the central and greater part of the city. A description of these mounds, with notes of excavations in them, is presented in "Minnesota in Three Centuries" (vol. I, pages 85-90).

The other parks and boulevards may be noticed advantageously in similar geographic order as the foregoing lists of street names, first considering West St. Paul, next the eastern, northern, northwestern, central western, and southwestern districts.

Cherokee Heights in West St. Paul (or Riverside, as this part of the city has been renamed) is a park acquired in 1903 to 1906, adjoining Cherokee avenue for a half mile on the crest of the river bluff.

Alice park, with Alice street encircling it, honors a daughter of William Dawson,† who platted that addition in 1879.

Prospect Terrace, close east of the preceding, is a narrow park ground adjoining the street so named; and Terrace park lies a short distance farther east.

Lamprey park, nearly five acres, is in an addition by Uri L. Lamprey in 1885, on the wide bottomland bordering the river at the east side of this Riverview district.

Harriet island of the Mississippi, having an area of 28 acres, near the center of the city, early named in honor of Harriet E. Bishop,† the first teacher here of a public school and of a Sunday school, was donated in May, 1900, by Dr. Justus Ohage,† commissioner of health, for use as a city park and playground, with public baths.

Central park, two and a third acres, was acquired in 1884, partly by donation of William Dawson and others.

Lafayette park, a space of one acre, at the south end of Lafayette avenue, purchased in 1884-5, commemorates the noble French marquis, who came to aid in achieving American independence as a special friend and associate of Washington in the Revolutionary War.

Mounds boulevard is planned to extend from East Seventh street, close east of Phalen creek, southeastward to the Indian Mounds park; and similarly a parkway named in honor of Governor John A. Johnson† will connect that park with Lake Phalen and its large park. Thence the Wheelock parkway, commemorating Joseph A. Wheelock,† who was very active for establishing the present system of city parks and boulevards, runs four miles westward to the south end of Lake Como, which forms the east part of Como park. A biographic sketch of Wheelock, with his portrait, is in the M. H. S. Collections (vol. XII, pages 787-790).

Midway parkway, a half mile long, runs from the west side of Como park to the State Fair Ground.

Lexington parkway is the enlargement of Lexington avenue for more than two miles, from Como park to Summit avenue; and thence the latter avenue is widened and beautified, being designated as Summit parkway, for two miles and a half between Lexington avenue and the River boulevard, which passes along the verge of the bluffs at the east side of the Mississippi gorge from the University in Minneapolis for about seven miles to the Fort Snelling bridge.

In the eastern part of the city, between the Johnson parkway and Trout brook, are Skidmore park, a third of an acre, platted in 1883, named for a realty dealer here, Edwin T. Skidmore; Hamm park, a fifth of an acre, beside East Seventh street, in honor of **Theodore Hamm**,† founder of a brewery; Lockwood park, three fourths of an acre, in an addition platted for H. H. Lockwood in 1883; and Stewart park, 1.36 acres, platted in 1884 and named for Dr. Jacob H. Stewart,† former mayor, postmaster, and member of Congress, who died August 25, 1884.

Between Trout brook and Lake Como are Lyton Place park, a third of an acre, named in 1883 for Michael Lyton, the former owner; Lewis park, nearly an acre, named likewise in 1883 for Robert P. Lewis,† who came to St. Paul in 1859 and has ever since engaged in law practice and as a dealer in real estate; Foundry park, one acre, platted in 1883, near the works of the St. Paul Foundry company; Stinson park, 1.2 acres, in an addition platted for Thomas Stinson in 1884; and Rogers park, 3 acres, named in 1883 for Josias N. Rogers,† a realty dealer.

In the plat of Warrendale, beside Lake Como, Cary I. Warren set aside three small park spaces at the intersections of streets, which he named as Sunshine, LeRoy, and Van Slyke triangles, the last, like the adjacent avenue, being named in honor of William A. Van Slyke,† who a few years later was the first president of the city park commission, in 1887-90.

Horton park, 3.48 acres, and Newel park, 10.43 acres, near Hamline University, are in honor of Hiler H. Horton,† and Stanford Newel,† who were early members of the board of park commissioners. Horton was afterward a state senator in 1899-1905, and Newel was U. S. minister to the Netherlands, 1897-1905.

In the addition named Midway Heights, at the west side of Newel park, are Tatum, Clayland, May, and Cato parks, each having less than an acre. The first, like an avenue crossing this addition, bears the surname of its original proprietors.

The large residential district called St. Anthony Park, forming the northwest corner of this city, has College park, three acres, nearly adjoining the State Agricultural College and Experimental Farm; Commonwealth park, four fifths of an acre, along the highest part of the avenue so named; Langford park, 9.65 acres, commemorating Nathaniel P. Langford, whose biography and portrait are in the M. H. S. Collections (vol. XV, 1915, pages 631-668); Hampden park, 3.09 acres. named for the statesman, John Hampden, of England; and several very small park spaces bounded by intersections of streets, namely, Cromwell park, and Alden, Doris, Gordon, Kendrick, Manvel, Raymond, and Sidney squares.

Merriam Terrace park, platted in 1882, containing 7.62 acres, was named in honor of John L. Merriam† and his family.

Lake Iris park, nearly two acres, named for its inclosed lakelet, and the little Feronia and Oakley squares, named from adjacent avenues, are in the residence tract of Union Park, at the south side of University avenue.

Summit park, four fifths of an acre, near the Cathedral, has the monument for soldiers of the Civil War.

About half a mile distant to the southwest, near where Summit avenue turns to a due west course, are the Portland Place, Summit Outlook, and the Point of View, each a very small park. The first has a statue of Nathan Hale, hero and martyr of the Revolutionary War; and the second and third look far away eastward and southward over the city and the valley of the Mississippi. Other little parks, within the next half mile along the verge or slope of the valley bluff, are Oakland park, between Oakland and Pleasant avenues, Crocus Hill and Webster parks, beside streets bearing these names, and Kenwood park, inclosed by the Kenwood parkway.

Holcombe park, a half mile north from the last, honors William Holcombe,† the first lieutenant governor of the state.

Linwood park, sixteen acres, acquired in 1909, and Haldeman park, an acre and a half, the latter being included in the residential area of Ridgewood Park, platted in 1887, lie on the descending slope of the bluff beyond Crocus hill. The first and a street near it, called Linwood place, receive their name from the basswood tree, the American linden; and the second commemorates Benjamin F. Haldeman, during many years a bookkeeper in this city, who died in 1909 at the age of 58 years.

Shadow Falls park, between the Mississippi and the River boulevard, is at the west end of Summit avenue.

Fountain park, beside Lexington avenue near its south end, has an area of two-fifths of an acre.

Dawson and Walsh parks, respectively containing two acres and three fourths of an acre, in an addition named West End, platted in 1884 on the north side of West Seventh street (then called Fort street), about two miles northeast of Fort Snelling, were named in honor of William Dawson† and Vincent D. Walsh, who, with Hon. Robert A. Smith and others, were original proprietors of this addition.

A few other small park spaces remain to be noticed, including Ramsey triangle, beside the street of this name, which honors Governor Ramsey,† Bay triangle, beside Bay street; and the public ground in Park Place addition, .45 of an acre, near the center of the city, where an Episcopal mission was founded by Rev. James Lloyd Breck in 1850.

DULUTH

Several villages that became parts of the present city of Duluth have been duly noted, with the dates of platting and derivation of their names, in the chapter of St. Louis county, these being Fond du Lac, Oneota, Rice's Point, Portland, Endion, Lakeside, and Lakewood, in this order from west to east.

In addition to the histories of Duluth and St. Louis county, by the late Judge Carey and by Dwight E. Woodbridge and John S. Pardee, published respectively in 1901 and 1910, which were cited for the county, information of the origins of names of streets, avenues, and parks, here presented, was gathered from plats in the office of Charles Calligan, county register of deeds, and from Henry Cleveland, city superintendent of parks, and Charles H. Drew, of the Department of Public Works, interviewed during a visit at Duluth in October, 1918.

STREETS AND AVENUES.

The earliest of the plats comprising the central part of this city was named Portland, being filed for record September 8, 1856; but its streets and avenues, running respectively from east to west and from north to south, in parallelism with the section lines, were wholly changed to diagonal courses by a new plat, surveyed by George R. Stuntz† in 1869, filed April 23, 1870. The former mostly personal names of each series were then superseded by numerical names, East Superior street and First to Ninth streets, nearly parallel with the shore of Lake Superior, being the same as now, with Third to Fourteenth avenues east as now, running across the streets.

Oneota had an earlier plat, surveyed by Henry W. Wheeler,† filed April 16, 1856, which set the example of streets running northeast to southwest, like the shore of the lake, and of St. Louis bay, crossed by avenues nearly at right angles; but the names of each series have since been changed, excepting St. Anthony street, beside the bay shore, which thus has the oldest street name in the city. Parallel with this northwestward were First to Ninth streets, which now are, in the same order, Oneota, Michigan (formerly Magellan), Superior (formerly Halifax), Rene, and Traverse streets, Grand avenue, and Fourth, Fifth and Sixth streets. The transverse avenues, coinciding mainly with the present 38th to 49th avenues west, were respectively named Cliff, Collingwood, Michigan, Huron, Fond du Lac, St. Paul, Brock, Mountain, St. Croix, Minnesota, Mississippi, Carver, Le Sueur, and Hennepin avenues.

---

†See biographic notes in the M. H. S. Collections, volume XIV, "Minnesota Biographies," published in 1912.

Next after Oneota and only a few weeks later, the original Duluth plat, surveyed by Richard Relf and filed May 29, 1856, covered a length of almost three miles on the narrow Minnesota point, which separates the Duluth harbor from the lake. Running along the southeastward extent of this sandbar point were Lake, Minnesota, and St. Louis avenues, names that yet remain. The short transverse streets, in their southward order, are Morse, Portage (at the site of the ship canal), Fulton, Oak (now Marvin), Olive, Vine, Astor, Dundee, Argyle, Dunleith, Cherry, Walnut, Elm (now Sorenson), Spruce, Pine, Pearl, St. John, Duke, St. James (now Montana), Chambers, Church, State, Jefferson (now New York), Randolph, Park (now Erie), Adams, Monroe, Murray, Clark, Warren, Williams, St. Paul (now St. George), St. Cloud, and St. Charles streets, the last being at the site of the wharf of Oatka Beach.

Superior street, named for the lake, is the most noteworthy in these lists, as the chief arterial business street of the city, having also large parts of its extent of more than ten miles occupied by residences. Grand avenue, originally meaning simply great, is six miles long in its course through the western part of the city; thence for seven miles eastward its place is mostly represented by Third street; again there was formerly an eastern Grand avenue, having a length of more than two miles, passing by the district of Lester Park, but this is now a part of East Superior street; and farther northeast for three miles, to the end of the city area, its continuation is called the North Shore road.

Buchanan street, named (before his election) for the president of the United States, was added to the transverse streets of the northern basal part of Minnesota point in a plat by William G. Cowell, filed August 16, 1856. Latest, the Industrial division of Duluth, platted in 1874, has Sutphin street, the most northern in this series, named in honor of John B. Sutphin,† who settled here in 1870.

Having in prospect the construction of the ship canal where the Ojibways and fur traders portaged their canoes and lading, Fulton street, the first south of the portage, was very appropriately named for Robert Fulton, whose genius began in 1807 the use of steamboats for travel and traffic.

Among the other miscellaneously selected names of streets crossing the long Minnesota point, Marvin is in honor of Luke Marvin,† a pioneer merchant of St. Paul, who settled at Duluth in 1861 as register of the U. S. land office; Jefferson street honored Robert E. Jefferson,† builder in 1855 of the first house on this point, the first of the Duluth village site, pictured in Carey's historical paper; and Clark street commemorates Thomas Clark, surveyor of the original plat of Superior, Wis., 1854-6, and later of Beaver Bay, Minn., whence he was a state senator in 1859-60. Clark was born in LeRay, Jefferson county, N. Y., January 6, 1814; was an assistant in geological surveys of Minnesota, 1861 and 1864, and died in Superior, Wis., December 20, 1878.

DULUTH 645

Fond du Lac, at the head of navigation, after being for more than sixty years an important post for trade with the Indians, was platted by Richard Relf in the autumn of 1856, "for the occupants of this town." Its present avenues, 126 to 135 west, were all designated as avenues on this plat, but with mostly personal names, being, in the same order, McBean, Cowell, Perry, Newton, Thompson, Paul, Morrison, Roussain, Carlton, and Superior avenues. The present Tecumseh street, on the water front, was called Water street on the plat; and the streets running from east to west, in their order northward, were Winnipeg and Ontario (renamed as Oconomowoc and Seneca), Pembina, the same as now, Erie, Huron, and Cass streets (renamed Bishop, Mohawk, and Krumseig), Itasca street, as now, and First to Ninth streets (now respectively Miles, Cherokee, Gasper, Glass, Custer, Hallenbeck, Choctaw, Callowhill, and Algonquin streets).

Annexation of Fond du Lac as a part of Duluth required much renaming of the streets, for avoidance of duplication and confusion with streets elsewhere in the city. Some of the present names are seen to be derived, like earlier names displaced, from Indian tribes, and from dealings with them in trade, treaties, and wars.

The original plat of Endion, filed for record January 14, 1857, followed the earliest survey of Portland in having its streets and avenues parallel with section lines. November 23, 1870, this plat was superseded by another conforming with the present system of streets parallel with the lake shore and crossed at right angles by avenues, like the resurvey of Portland, before noted. In the 1870 survey the present East Superior street was called Bench street. Next southeast, in the north edge of this Endion plat, is Branch street, named in honor of William Branch,† one of the proprietors of the plat, who was a director and builder of the first railroad between St. Paul and Duluth. The next south, named Center street in 1870 and later Dingwall street, for James D. Dingwall, an alderman of the city, has been renamed Greysolon road, for Daniel Greysolon Du Luth,† who is more highly commemorated by the city name. Between this and the lake are Jefferson street, as named in 1870 to honor Robert Emmet Jefferson,† whose home built in 1855 was the first in Duluth; London road, at first here called Superior street, but renamed for its passing northeastward through the suburb called London; and South and Water streets, which were named in 1870 as now. The avenues, in their series from southwest to northeast, called originally New York, Pennsylvania, Maryland, Ohio, Indiana, Missouri, Oregon, Montana, Colorado, Virginia, and Dakota avenues, have been renamed in the great system of the whole city as the 15th to 25th avenues east.

Rice's Point was platted in the autumn of 1858 for the owner, Orrin W. Rice, a younger brother of Henry M.† and Edmund Rice.† Its avenues running across the point from northeast to southwest were named for familiar Minnesota trees, in alphabetic sequence southward, being Ash, Birch, Cedar (since renamed Nelson), Elm, Lynn, (alluding to the linn or basswood, our species of the linden tree), Maple, Oak (since changed to Oie, a rare Scandinavian surname), Pine, and Spruce avenues. Farther southward, the original plat had Walnut, Vine, and Front avenues, the first being at the present southern dock line, while the former land extension surveyed for the second and third has been excavated and dredged away, its place being now a part of the passage from Duluth harbor to St. Louis bay. Transverse to these and running southeastward, the plat has First to Fifteenth streets, which now in the same order, up to the Ninth, are Rice, Garfield, Cox, and Arthur avenues, and Culpeper, Tintagel, Marquette, Raven, and Pendennis streets, but the place of the original Tenth to Fifteenth streets is a part of the harbor. On the southwest side Kittson street, adjoining Rice avenue, has been added on made land outside the former shore line.

Among these names two presidents of the United States are honored, also the Rice family, distinguished in Minnesota history, Congressman Samuel S. Cox (b. 1824, d. 1889), Thomas Culpeper, who was the colonial governor of Virginia in 1680-83, for whom a Virginia county is named, Jacques Marquette (1637-75), the devoted missionary and explorer of the Mississippi, and Norman W. Kittson,† a pioneer of Minnesota commerce, whose name is borne by the most northwestern county of this state. Two other names in the list are received from localities of Cornwall, Tintagel and Pendennis Castle.

During the ten years next after the survey of Rice's Point and including the period of the Civil War, no plats within the area of Duluth were placed on sale. In the early summer of 1869, the First division of Duluth Proper was platted for J. B. Culver,† William Nettleton,† Luke Marvin,† and George B. Sargent,† who, with their wives, and with Luther Mendenhall,† agent for the Western Land Association, signed the plat as proprietors, which was filed for record July 17. It had just the same numbered systems of streets and avenues as now, and also Superior street and Lake avenue. The latter, was extended northward from the original plat of Duluth in 1856 on Minnesota point, and became on this plat in 1869 the dividing line whence the avenues are numbered east and west. The series of avenues eastward in this First division reaches to Sixth avenue; by the resurvey of the Portland division, next eastward, filed for record in April, 1870, as before noted, this series is continued to 14th avenue east; and in the resurvey of Endion, which was filed, as also previously mentioned, in November, 1870, the series of avenues, afterward there numerically named, is extended to the 25th. By later eastern additions of the city, it now reaches to the 67th avenue east at the limit of Lester Park, distant nearly six miles and a half from Lake avenue.

The Second division was filed June 14, 1870, and the Third division August 18, 1870, which, with the First, Portland and Endion divisions, comprise the central part of the city from 25th avenue east to 28th avenue west, having together an extent of nearly five miles along the shore of the lake, the harbor, and St. Louis bay. The numerical names of the avenues and streets, the former running at right angles to the lake and harbor shore, and the latter in parallelism with the shore, leave little to be further noted for this central area.

Superior street is the starting place for the naming of the streets parallel with it and the lake, from First up to Fifteenth street as a series, lying above Superior street on the ascent from the lake and harbor. On the relatively narrow tract between Superior street and the lake, the parallel streets bear other names, not numerical, as was before noted for Endion, where this tract has its maximum width.

With geographic propriety, Michigan and Huron streets lie below and southeast of Superior in the division of "Duluth proper;" and at the southwest side of the Second division Huron street is paralleled by Helm, Courtland, and Martin streets, each short, lying in this order southeastward and including a point that projects into St. Louis bay. Helm street commemorates H. C. and Joseph Helm, who, with others, platted a small addition there in 1886; and Martin street similarly honors William P. and James M. Martin, proprietors of another small plat in 1888, on this point.

Through the Third division Mesaba avenue, named for the iron range, runs north, diagonally ascending the highland, and thence having a continuation northwestward on the Rice Lake road.

For the many plats added to the city after 1870, this consideration of names of streets and avenues may be more satisfactorily continued in the geographic order, as follows, passing from northeast to southwest.

Lester Park, principally a residence district, has the 55th to 67th avenues east, which are crossed near the lakeside by Superor street, Stearns avenue, and London road. Ozora P. Stearns,† judge of this Eleventh judicial district in 1875-94, was president of the Lakeside Land Company, by which this district was platted in four divisions in 1889 and 1890.

Several other streets here are continuations from the adjacent earlier plats on the west, London Park addition, which was filed June 6, 1888, and Crosley Park, bearing date of June 17, 1889, only three days earlier than the First division of Lester Park. These have 49th to 54th avenues east, crossed by streets which are named, in the sequence from south to north, Tioga, Otsego, Oneida, Glenwood, Juniata, Wyoming, Avondale, Oakley, Glendale, Norwood, Ivanhoe, Idlewild, Kingston, and Woodlawn streets. The first three are aboriginal names from the state of New York; Juniata is another Indian name, from a river and county of Pennsylvania; and Wyoming is from a Pennsylvania mountain range, and a valley beside it, along which flows the Susquehanna river.

London addition, surveyed in the spring of 1871 and filed September 6 of that year, has the 40th to 54th avenues east, which at first were otherwise named, in the same order, as West, Murray, Moorhead, Forbes, Sampson, Sanford, Portman, Sargent, Vail, Spencer, Lincoln, Fahnestock, Howard, Finlay, and East avenues, the first and last having reference to their location. The transverse streets, listed from south to north, are Quebec avenue, London road, Lombard street, and Luverne (formerly Puleston), Gilliat, Superior (at first called Oxford and later Cambridge), Regent, Robinson (at first mapped as Robertson), McCulloch, Gladstone, Cooke, Pitt, Jay, Dodge, Peabody and Colorado (originally Summit) streets. One of these streets commemorates Hugh McCulloch, the proprietor of this addition. Not only the name of this large plat, extending a mile and a half on the lake shore, but several of its avenue and street names, came from England.

East Duluth, platted in the summer of 1870 and filed for record September 5, less than three weeks after the Third division of "Duluth proper," and Harrison division, filed September 9, 1887, between East Duluth and Endion, lie mainly south of Superior street, having there Branch street, Greysolon road, Jefferson street, London road, and South street, the last adjoining the lake shore, all previously noticed for Endion, which has the more western mile of their extent.

In these areas are the 23rd to 39th avenues east, which on the original plats were named respectively Colorado, Virginia, Dakota, Kentucky, Massachusetts, Connecticut, Delaware, and Idaho avenues, for the Harrison division; and Vermilion, St. Louis, Superior, St. Marie, Michigan, Mackinac, Huron, St. Clair, Erie, Niagara, Ontario, and St. Lawrence avenues, for East Duluth, its first three being continuous, under different names, with the last three in the other series. It will be observed that the twelve avenues thus named in 1870 represent the entire water route from the north boundary of Minnesota, by way of Vermilion river and lake and the St. Louis river to and through the Great Lakes and down the river and gulf of St. Lawrence to the ocean. Somewhat of commendable geographic and poetic sentiment was lost when this series was displaced by merely numbered avenues.

Along and near Tischer's creek, above East Duluth, and from this creek south to Endion, are a goodly array of relatively small additions, residential plats added to the city, named, in order from north to south, Woodland Park, Hunter's Park, Princeton Place addition, Glen Avon, Oakland Park, Motor Line and Clover Hill divisions, Willard's addition, East Lawn division, Long View, Highland Park, and New Endion. Woodland avenue is a fine driveway leading through the series of these plats about four miles from Endion north past Woodland Park to the Vermilion Lake road. The name of the avenue and district refers to the originally timbered condition of all this region.

Streets of Woodland Park are named Austin, Red Wing, Faribault, Owatonna, Winona, Mankato, Wabasha, and Anoka, in southward order, with Shakopee and Crescent avenues, all named for towns in southern Minnesota, the last being for La Crescent.

Hunter's Park, named in honor of a prominent Duluth family, and Princeton Place, named for the town and university in New Jersey, have

Roslyn, Bute, Carlisle, Princeton, Wilkyns, Silcox, and Livingston avenues, running northward, with Sparkman and Spear avenues, Oxford street, and Mygatt avenue, running from east to west.

Glen Avon has Wallace, Waverly, Columbus, Abbotsford, Melrose, Harvard, and Dunedin avenues, running north and south, with St. Andrew's, Lewis, Hardy, Victoria, and Bruce streets, east and west, mostly derived from Scotland and her great author, Sir Walter Scott.

Farther south, the Motor Line division has St. Marie, Norton, Marion, and Elizabeth streets, and Niagara avenue, running west; and the Clover Hill area has Manitoba, Jackson, and Clover streets, with Allen avenue, likewise running west.

East Lawn has Kent and Garden streets, running west, with Fay, Cottage, and Snelling avenues, from north to south.

Highland Park and the adjacent plats of Long View and New Endion are parts of the general system with numbered avenues and streets.

Adjoining the Portland division and the three central plats or divisions called Duluth Proper, are numerous additions, and others lie farther west or northwest, which all may be next listed as a group.

On and near Chester creek, in descending order, are Kensington Place, Arlington Place, and Clifton Heights; additions by Charles M. Gray and others, by Jeremiah H. Triggs, Frank E. Kennedy and others, and by Clague and Prindle, each platted in 1887; an addition by Myers and Whipple in 1889; Kenwood Park and Superior View; and Chester Park, Lake View, and an addition by George W. Norton and others, these three lying at the north and west sides of the Portland division.

Between the foregoing and Miller's creek are several additions named as divisions of Duluth Heights, the earliest being platted in 1890, and relatively small residence tracts called Maple Grove, Summit Park, and Park View.

Along the course of Miller's creek are Murray Hill addition, platted in 1888, Willard and Piper's division, Brookdale, platted in 1889, Merchant's Park, a residence area, and additions by Spaulding, Fairbanks, and Walbank, the four last named being close west and southwest of the beautiful public ground named Lincoln Park.

The east to west streets of Clifton Heights and the Kensington and Arlington plats form a consecutive series, being, in southward order, Porter avenue, Persons and St. Marie streets, and Pringle, Niagara, Morgan, and Allen avenues. Transverse to these, in westward order, are Blackman, Cramer, Matthews, Hemphill, Sawyer, Florence, Backus, Bird, Arlington, Bryant, Decker, Wilson, Stanford, Lowndes, Blodgett, Gadsden, and Pickens avenues.

In Gray's addition and the next two of the foregoing list, reaching a mile and a quarter from north to south, the streets running east and west, in southward order, are St. Marie, Cleveland, Buffalo, and Toledo streets, the last three being named for the largest cities on Lake Erie; Niagara, Ohio, and Allen avenues; and Cortez, Robson, Partridge, Kelly, Hawkins,

Howitz, Davis, and Bayless streets. Running south, in sequence westward, are Triggs, Kennebec, Kentucky, Virginia, Broadway, Grant, Madison, Connecticut, and Blackman avenues.

Superior View, Kenwood Park, and Myers and Whipple's addition, have the first four east to west streets and Niagara avenue, as in Gray's addition, with Lyons street; and their avenues, running south, in westward series, are Junction, Brainerd, Mississippi, Missouri, Dodge, Kenwood, Humes, Center, Weber, Myers, and Triggs avenues. Humes and Center are names adopted in compliment for E. C. Humes, of Bellefonte, Center county, Pennsylvania, the original landowner of the third of these plats.

In the three additions noted as adjoining the Portland plat, the streets and avenues are numerically numbered, being a part of the general system for the city,

Streets running west through the northwestern part of Duluth Heights, in sequence from north to south, are Willow, Gilead, Mulberry, Locust, Linden, Myrtle, Palmetto, Palm, Orange, Lemon, and Quince streets, with Alder and Balsam streets, running southwest, and Banian street, running southeast, all being names of trees. Crossing these and running south, in westward sequence, are Arlington avenue and Niagara and Oregon streets, Highland avenue, Hugo street, and Ebony and Teak avenues, the last two being names of foreign trees. Trevanion W. Hugo,† mayor of the city in 1900-04, and his younger brother, Nicholas Frederic,† who was a representative in the legislature, 1903-08, are commemorated by the street bearing their surname.

The southeast part of this suburban area, known as the First division of Duluth Heights, has Trenton, La Salle, Winter, Bank, Buena Vista, Denver, and Portland streets, running west; and its avenues, running south, are named Winona, Beacon, Summer, Green, Highland, Bayfield, Como, Winthrop, Lewiston, and Lyon, in this order from east to west.

Brookdale and its vicinity have Prospect, Willard, Piper, Union, and Viaduct streets, Warner, Sylvan, Sycamore, and Euclid avenues, Bay View Terrace, and Forest, Marks, Cascade, Richardson, Piedmont, and West Diamond avenues, running westward; with McKinnon and Boynton avenues, Zenith, Arch, Voss, East Diamond, and Laurel avenues, and Marshall, Henry, Beltrami, Dale, and Getty streets, running southward. Piedmont avenue thence passes northwest to the city boundary, beyond which its continuation to the west is called the Hermantown road.

Walbank addition and another small residence area at its south side, named West Park, have Wellington, Wicklow, Exeter, Devonshire, Restormel, Vernon, Chestnut, Gilbert, and Carlton streets, running west, with Grand Forks, Winnipeg, Michigan, and Pacific avenues, running south.

Adjoining Oneota, and continuing two to three miles west and southwest, are numerous additions varying in size from 20 to 160 acres, which together form the large residential, manufacturing, and commercial district of West Duluth. Under this district name are seven numbered divisions and a Central division, the series having been platted in 1887 to 1889. Other tracts are named Hazelwood, Zenith Park, Whitman Park, Hall's, Dickerman's, and Stewart's additions, Belmont and Bellevue Parks, Sharp's addition, Lloyd's division, Kimberly and Stryker's additions, Oneota Park, Mineral addition, the two Bay View additions, named for their outlook across St. Louis bay, Dodge's, Macfarlane's and Stowell's additions, West End, Grassy Point, Carlton Place, Wilmington addition, Stryker and Manley's addition, in two divisions, and Cremer's addition.

Notable street names in Zenith and Whitman Parks are Ericsson, Osman, Somerville, Cass, Tillinghast, and Lovell streets, Collingwood Place, and Patterson, Chestnut, Gilbert, and Carlton streets, running westward, with Duluth and Lincoln avenues, Hughitt avenue, and Galusha, Tainter, and Hall streets, running southward.

In Dickerman's addition and others at its west side, the east to west streets, in southward order, are Martin, Gould, Stewart, Verndale, Schuylkill, Hale, and Bellevue streets, Franklin and Columbia avenues, and Albion and Medina streets. Here and in Bellevue Park, next westward, the avenues, which run to the south and southeast, are numbered from the 42nd to the 61st west. Additionally, Stewart's addition has Ella and Edna streets, respectively in the places of the 54th and 56th avenues; and Bellevue Park adds Cottage Grove avenue and West Park avenue, running southwest.

Oneota Park has La Salle, Wayne, and Nimrod streets, Fowey, High, Chippewa, Mineral, Balboa, and Mecca streets, running east and southeast, which are crossed by Granite, Tancred, Kanabec, and Park avenues, and Beulah street, running south and southwest.

Mineral addition, next southwestward, has Mineral street at its north side, with Rupley, Cardigan, Desota, and King streets, also running west, which are crossed by Hendrick and Bodmin avenues.

South of Oneota Park and Cemetery a series of streets, running east and west, includes Spencer, Highland, Huntington, Olney, Tacony, Nashua, Lexington, Elinor, Petre, Worden, Pizarro, Green, Bristol, Gosnold, Nicollet, Main, Polk, Raleigh, Redruth, Sherburne, Waseca, Fremont, Natchez, La Vaque, Pulaski, Thompson, and Milford streets, occupying a tract of two miles between the cemetery and the shore of the St. Louis river west of Grassy point. A small cyclopaedia of biography and history might well be written concerning these streets, which are crossed, wholly or in part, by the 50th to 81st avenues west.

Lying a little farther east and nearly in the course of some of the foregoing streets, are Cody, Wadena, and Ramsey streets.

Bay View, of which the first division was platted in 1888 and the second in 1890, introduced other series of streets running west. The first plat had King, Queen, Prince, Duke, and Earl streets, each a title of royalty, of which the fourth, duplicating a street in the early plat of Duluth on Minnesota point, has been changed to Clay street. These are crossed by the 69th, 71st, 73rd, 75th, and 77th avenues west. The second division continues only King street, on its north boundary, which is succeeded in southward order by Zurah, Oak, Vinland, Mitchell, Goldsmith, Ash, Godolphin, and Reed streets. Transverse with these are Fletcher, Simonds, Irwin, and Purcell avenues.

Cremer's addition, platted in 1889 by William J. Cremer and others, has Viking, Boston, Philadelphia, Baltimore, and Chicago streets, running west, crossed by Cremer and Hall avenues.

The districts farther southwest, to Fond du Lac, which was earlier noticed, have been named Ironton, Morgan Park, Gary, and New Duluth. Ironton, platted in the years 1889 to 1893, comprises four divisions and Ironton Park, with Lenroot's addition and Minnewakan and Spirit Lake additions, the last two being named from the adjacent Spirit lake and island of the St. Louis river. New Duluth was platted in 1890. The intermediate residence areas of Morgan Park and Gary, with the contiguous immense furnaces, foundries, and other workshops of the Minnesota Steel Company, are very recent additions to the city. In February, 1916, iron and steel manufacture and production of Portland cement were begun here. These new plats are named for distinguished financial leaders and industrial directors, the late John Pierpont Morgan, and his son of the same name, and Judge Elbert Henry Gary, chief executive officer for the United States Steel Corporation, of which this Minnesota company is a branch.

Streets in Ironton running west, are named Thompson, Roe, French, Warwick, Bessemer, Towne, Mesaba, Truelson, and Gogebic streets, Lenroot avenue, Beaudry street, and Swenson, Keene, Clyde, Boyd, Hulett, Kimberly, and Seaver avenues. These are crossed by the 82nd to the 98th avenues west. Other avenues, running southwest, are Barrett, Terrace, Hematite, Biwabik, York, Commonwealth, Grand, Industrial, and Furnace avenues. Kinney street runs south, and in Ironton Park the next four avenues beyond the 93rd were formerly named Leon, Lehigh, Carnegie, and Perry avenues. Transverse to the Northern Pacific railroad and the St. Louis river, Ironton, Selwood, Spring, and Matthews streets, and Traders Court, run southeast.

New Duluth has Cartaret, Fillmore, Grand, Bowser, Goodhue, Peary, Heard, McCuen, and Prescott streets, running west, crossed by the 94th to 106th avenues west.

Parks and Boulevards.

In the original plat of Duluth, on the Minnesota Point, in the spring of 1856, two small areas were reserved as public squares or parks, named Franklin and Lafayette squares, in honor of Benjamin Franklin and the Marquis Lafayette. July 4, 1868, Dr. Thomas Foster,† in a speech at a patriotic celebration in one of these parks, called the prospective Greater Duluth "the Zenith City of the Unsalted Seas."

Fond du Lac, platted in the late part of the same year, has Mission park, named like its creek tributary to the St. Louis river, for the early mission school of Ojibway children taught there by Edmund F. Ely† in 1834-39.

In London addition, by Hugh McCulloch in 1871, he designated five blocks or squares of the survey, each measuring two and seven tenths acres, to be public parks, naming them as Grosvenor, Manchester, Portman, Russell, and Washington squares. The first four names, like London, are derived from England.

Lester park, 32 acres, is singularly grand and beautiful for its pine woods and the rock gorge and falls of the two branches of Lester river.

North Shore park is a narrow strip of beach and grassy bank, extending northeast on the lake two-thirds of a mile from this river.

Congdon park, acquired in 1908, comprising, with its approaches, about 40 acres on both sides of Tischer's creek, was named in honor of Chester Adgate Congdon,† the principal donor. He was born in Rochester, N. Y., June 12, 1853; was graduated at Syracuse University, 1875; was admitted to practice law, 1877; settled in St. Paul, 1879; was assistant U. S. district attorney, 1881-86; removed to Duluth in 1892; was a representative in the legislature, 1909-11; acquired great wealth in iron ore lands; died in St. Paul, November 21, 1916.

Chester park, enlarged to 43 acres in 1905, on Chester creek above the Portland and Endion divisions of the city, has a picturesque stream gorge between perpendicular rock walls, with a noble forest of pine, spruce, and balsam fir, whose dark green is diversified by white birches.

Lake Front park, extending about a third of a mile southwest from the mouth of Chester creek, has 14 acres, acquired by the city in 1907.

Portland square, a block of two acres and a half, "dedicated in the original townsite of Portland, . . . has been made into a garden, with cement walks appropriate to a city square, a fountain with benches of concrete, shrubs and flower beds."

Cascade square, at First avenue west and Mesaba avenue, inclosed by Cascade street around its four sides, "has been made a place of rare beauty, with more elaborate masonry than in any other park." Its name refers to the cascades of a little brook which flows southeast into a corner of the harbor.

Munger park, at Fourth street and Fourth avenue west, "has the finest group of elms in the city." Its name commemorates Roger S. Munger,† for whom a village of this county is named.

Hilltop park is a single block of the city survey, at the head of the inclined railway on Seventh avenue west, "affording a magnificent outlook," acquired for the park system in 1907.

Central park, formerly called Zenith park, a tract of 20 acres, "includes a mountainous peak in the center of the boulevard system, encircled by the branching roadway high above the lake, and giving a beautiful view of the city and harbor."

Lincoln park, earlier named Garfield, has 32 acres along the ravine of Miller's creek. It honors our first martyr president.

Fairmont park, 40 acres on Kingsbury creek, acquired in 1901, bears (with slightly changed spelling) the name of a very large park on the Schuylkill river in Philadelphia.

Numerous additional small parks, smaller triangular spaces at intersections of streets, and large playgrounds adjoining public schools, are included in the list of the city's public grounds.

Duluth is widely and deservedly renowned for its far-viewing boulevard, which extends twelve miles on an ancient beach or shoreline having long reaches of gravel and sand roadbed, 470 to 475 feet above Lake Superior. By this ancient lake-graded driveway, the city park system is linked with the period, estimated about 6,000 or perhaps 10,000 years ago, when the continental ice-sheet was being finally melted away.

The report of the Board of Park Commissioners for 1911 names this drive the Rogers boulevard, in honor of William K. Rogers, from Columbus, Ohio, who became president of a bank here, was greatly interested in city improvements, and secured the construction of the earliest part of this boulevard, opened for public use in 1890, "praised as excelling any like road in the world." A short part of its course, across the Bay View addition, has been called the Bay View boulevard.

In Lester park roads leading north, toward the eastern part of the high boulevard, have been called the Oriental and Occidental boulevards, receiving these names from their course respectively along the east and west sides of Lester river; and their continuation is mapped as Snively road, in honor of Samuel F. Snively, a lawyer of Duluth and dealer in lands and city lots, who owns a large farm north of this park.

If the reader finds surprise in the length of time ago for action of storms and waves on the Glacial Lake Duluth in providing the excellent roadbed of the long and high boulevard here, such interest will be increased by the very great extent of the same beach, which has nearly the same development along all the northwest side of Lake Superior through Minnesota. On Mount Josephine, close east of Grand Portage, 140 miles from Duluth, its height is 510 feet above the lake, being the most conspicuous of the several shorelines there. Like the ancient beaches of Lake Agassiz in the Red river valley, it has a gradual ascent northeastward. While these ice-dammed lakes were being reduced to lower levels, the land was gradually uplifted by an elevation that increases from south to north and northeast.

In view of its geologic cause, with its antiquity and great length, the name High Beach boulevard seems more desirable than a personal title.

Lastly, attention may be directed to the derivation of this French word, boulevard, signifying a bulwark, from the demolition of the ancient lines of defensive fortifications that surrounded the medieval city of Paris, broad roadways being constructed in their place. Thence this name is now frequently applied to exceptionally wide avenues or streets, used as pleasure driveways, especially when they are partly decorated with flowers or belts of lawn.

INDEX

INDEX

ABBREVIATIONS: ad., addition; b., biographic; blvd., boulevard; br., brook; c., city; co., county; cr., creek; d., district; div., division; for, named for, or in honor of; gl. l., glacial lake; h., hill; id., island; l., lake; mor., moraine; mt., mount, or mountain; n., named by; p. o., post office; pk., park; pky., parkway; pt., point; q., quotation; r., river; ry., railroad, railway; sl., slough; sq., square; sta., station; t., township; tr., triangle; v. village. Obsolete names are enclosed by parentheses.

Place names appearing in the introduction and supplements in this reprint are in alphabetical order and have not been incorporated into the index. Names for Lake of the Woods County will be found under Beltrami.

Aaron, l., 182
Aastad t., for Gilbert Aastad, 391
Abbey, l., 32
Abbie, l., 591
Abbott, E. T., and Seth, for, 604
Abbott, Wilma, for, 414
Abercrombie, Gen. John J., for, b., 580
(Abert r., for John J. Abert, 511)
(Abigail, l., 168)
Abita l., 145
Accault l., 131; bay. 346
Achman l., 530
Acker, Capt. William H., for, 624
Acoma t., 316
Acorn l., 33
Acton t., 338
Ada br. and l., 99
Ada v., 381
Adams, Cuyler, for, n., l., 517; 158, 163
Adams, John, for, 605
Adams, John Quincy, for, 605
Adams, Mabel, for, 194
Adams, Rev. Moses N., 22, 164, 288, 574
Adams t. and v., 359
Addie, l., 319
(Adela l., 48)
(Adkinsville t., for Thomas Adkins, 178)
Adley, R. F., n., 396
Adley, Warren, n., 525; for, b., 529
Adley, l., 401; cr., 529
Adney l., 162
Adolph v., 477
Adrian v., 376; t., 574
Aetna t., 417
Africa, names from, 176, 456, 490, 574

Afton t., 568
Agamok l., 296
Agassiz, gl. l., 7, 8, 56, 116, 120, 218, 280, 289, 324, 331, 384, 405, 409, 429, 447, 472, 475, 505, 550, 553, 580, 654.
Agassiz t., 289
Agate bay, 294, 295; l., 162
Agder t., 327
Agnes, l., 143, 181
Agram t., 350
Ahkeek l., 78
Ahrens h., for Charles Ahrens, 163
(Aile de Corbeau, r., 154)
Aiott l., for F. Aiott, 356
Airlie v., (378), 417
Aitkin, William A., for, b., 14; 19, 21
Aitkin co., 14-21; gl. l., 21; l., 17, 19; t. and v., 14, 21; pt. and bay, Leech l., 95
Aiton, Mrs. Mary B., 372, 375
Aiton heights, for G. B. Aiton, 133
Akeley l., 141
Akeley t. and v., for H. C. Akeley, b., 242
Ako or Accault l., 131
Akron t., 53, 577
Alango t., 477
Alaska t., 35
Alba p. o., 191; t., 261
Albany t., 522
Albert l., 65, 591
(Albert sta., 477)
Albert Lea., c., t., and l., 198, 203
Alberta t., 49; v., 535
Alberts l., for Ole Alberts, 182
Albertville v., 586
Albin t., 68
Albion t., 586; l., 591

INDEX

Alborn t. and sta., 477
Alden t. and v., 199; l., 477, 499
(Alder r., 18)
Aldrich, Cyrus, for, b., 560; 603
Aldrich, Thomas Bailey, for, 603
Aldrich, l., for J. D. Aldrich, 181, 182
Aldrich t. and v., 560
Alexander, l., (48;) for T. L. Alexander, 356
Alexandria c. and t., 2, 175
Alexis l., for John P. Alexis, 110
Alfred, l., 404
Alfsborg t., 518
Alger sta., for R. A. Alger, b., 293
Algoma t., 470
Alice, l., 65, (131,) 244, 296, 389, 402, 435, 500, 580
Alice sta., 477
Alida v., 122
Alkali l., 401, 521
(All Saints c., 223)
Allen, Alvaren, for, 619
Allen, Lieut. James, for, b., 42; 97, 98; for, 133; 153; for, 246; n., 367; 502, 503, 514
Allen, Lyman, n., 340
Allen, Mrs. Saumel, for, 233
Allen, William P., for, b., 477
Allen t., 155, 477; sta., 477
Allen's bay, 42, 96; l., 246, 320
Alliance t., 114
Allibone l. and cr., for John Allibone, 573
Allie (or Alley) l., 460
Allison, Rebecca, for, 169
Alma t., 327
Alma City v., 564
Almelund v. and p. o., 108
Almond t., 53
Almora v., 391
Alpha v., 261; l., 297
Alpine l., 141
Alta Vista t., 307
Altamont moraine, 309, 420
Altermatt l., for J. B. Altermatt, 72
Alton t., 66, 564; l., 143, 337
Altona, (v. 399;) t., 417
Altura v., 581
Alvarado v., 327
Alvin, l., 181
Alvwood t., 253
Alworth l., 296
Amador t., 108
Amber l., 336
Amberger l., 295
Amboy v., 58, 63; t., 149

Amelia, l., 26, (231,) 435
America t., 470
American pt., 45
American Fur Co., 14, 95, 155, 455
American Revolution, names from, 359, 360
Ames, Dr. Alfred E., for, 601
Ames, Mrs. William L., for, 625
Amherst t., 190
Amiret t. and v., 311
Amity cr., 493
Amo t., 149
Amor t., 391
Amos l., 181
Anchor l., 500
Anderson, Mrs. Ann, for, 150
Anderson, Mathias, n., 201
Anderson l., 32, 143, 231, 434, 435; cr., 428; pt., 347; sta., 531
(Anderson v., for G. Anderson, 467)
Andover t., (359,) 421
Andrea t., 577
Andrews, Gen. C. C., 101, 148
Andrews, William H., 155; n., 159
Andrews, l., 180
(Andrus cr., 134)
Andrusia, l., 42
(Andy Johnson co., 577)
Anka, l., 182
Angle t., 35; r., 44
Angora t. and v., 477
Angus t., for R. B. Angus, b., 421; l., 591
Ann l., 85, 265, 435, 516, 590
Ann r., 265, 267
Ann t., 150
Ann Lake t., 265
Anna l., 157, 402, 530
Annalaide l., 400
Annandale v., 586
Annie, l., 404
Annie Battle l., 402
Anoka c. and t., 22, 23; co., 22-26
Ansel t. and p. o., 87
Ant id., 494
Antelope hills and moraine, 292, 310; valley, 292
Anthony t., 381
Antlers Park sta., 169
Antoinette, l., 498
Antrim t., 574
Apostle ids., Wis., 146
Appleton t. and v., 539
Aquipaguetin id., 347
Arago t. and l., for D. F. Arago, b., 243

INDEX

Arbo t., for John Arbo, 253
Arbutus sta., 477
Arc l., 141
Arch id., 145
Archibald, E. T., and J. M., n., 462
Arco v., 307
(Arcola v., 568)
Arctander t., for J. W. Arctander, b., 269
Ardenhurst t., 253
Arena t., 289
Arendahl t., 190
Argyle v., 327
Arken l., 401
Arkkola, Thomas, n., 490
Arlington t. and v., 518
Arlington Hills d., 440, 443, 623
Arlone t., 410
Armstrong, Mrs. Helen, for, 317
Armstrong, Laura, for, 104
Armstrong cr., 286; r. and bay, 494, 495
Armstrong l., for J. Armstrong, 65; 501
Armstrong sta., for Thomas H. Armstrong, b., 199
Arna t., 410
Arnesen v., for B. A. Arnesen, 36
Arnold's l., 152
Arrow l. and r., Canada, 139
Artesian wells, 116, 188
Arthur, Chester A., for, b. 265, 429, 605, 646
Arthur t., 265, 550; l., 429; sta., 477
Artichoke t. and l., 53, 56; r. and l., 499; cr. 542
Artlip l., 295
Arveson t., for Arve Arveson, 277
Arvilla, l., 342
Asbury, Bishop Francis, for, 103, 630
Asbury sta., 103
Ash l., 141, 218, 307, 337, 477, 502; cr. 466; r., 502
Ash Creek v., 466
Ash Lake t., 307; sta., 477
Ashbough, Bartlett, n., 551
Ashby v., for Gunder Ash, 213
Ashland t. and v., 172
Ashley, Ossian D., for, b., 522
Ashley cr., 434, 522; t., 522
Asia, names from, 283, 333, 458, 477, 485
Askov v., 410
Asp l., 111
Aspen l., 140; (br., 447)
Aspinwall l., for Henry Aspinwall, 324

Assiniboine bluff, 211; Indians, 281, 409
Assumption v., 81
Astor, John Jacob, 14
Athens t., 250; sta., 477
Atherton t., 578
Atkinson t., for J. Atkinson, 73; l., 341
Atlanta t., 27
Atwater v., for E. D. Atwater, 269
Auburn, l., 85
Audubon, John J., for, b., 27, 608; t. and v., 27
Augelle, Anthony, for, 130
Augsburg t., 327
Augusta sta., 81; t., 289; l., 133, 152, 168, 401, 529, 591
Aulnau, Father, 45
Ault t., 477
Aurdal t., 391
Aurora t., 531; v., 477
Austin, Gov. Horace, for, b., 363
Austin c. and t., 359; state park, 363
Austria, names from, 303, 350, 456, 469, 524
Automba t. and sta., 73
Averill v., for John T. Averill, b., 115
Avery, Carlos, 275
Avis id., 495
Avoca v., 364
Avon t. and v., 523
Axe l., 145
Ayotte, Peter, n., 164

Babbett pt., 548
Babbitt, Frances E., 353
Babcock l., 337
Baby l., 99
Bachelor l., 72
Backus v., for Edward W. Backus, 87
Bacon, D. H., n., 490
Bad Axe l., 248
Bad Water l., 104, 106, 273
Badger cr., 189, 241, 389, 422, 447, 470, 475; l., 337, 369, 422
Badger state, 4; 189, 337; t., 422; v., 470
Badoura t., 243
Bagley v., for Sumner C. Bagley, 122
Bailey, Thomas, n., 54
Bailey sta., for Orlando Bailey, b., 513
Bailly, Alexis, and Isabel, for, 168
Bain t., for William Bain, 14

Baker, B. F., fur trader, 155
Baker, Charles H., 252
Baker, Daniel A. J., n., 634
Baker, Gen. James H., quoted or cited, 3, 127, 129, 136, 179, 242, 326, 518, 539, 541
Baker, Rev. Peter, for, 263
Baker l., 143
Baker's l., for A. C. Baker, b., 319; id., 517
Baker t., for Lester H. Baker, 155; 535
Balaton v., 312
Balch, Foster L., for, 54
Bald mt., 503
Bald Bluff l., 19
Bald Eagle l., 296, 437; v., 437
Baldus t., 282
Baldwin, Matthias W., for, 637
Baldwin l., 25, 573
Baldwin t., for F. E. Baldwin, b. 514
Balkan t., 478
Balke l., 32
Ball Bluff t., 14
Ball's bluff, for Ezra Ball, 367
Ball Club l. and v., 253, 259
Ballantyne l., for J. Ballantyne, 65
Bally cr., for Samuel Bally, 144
Balm of Gilead, 3; r., 143
Balmoral v., 391
Balsam t., 14, 253
Banadad l., 141
Bancroft t., for George Bancroft, 199; cr., 204
Bandon t., 455
Banfil, John, 23; for, 614
Bangor t., 430
Banks' Pine l., 139
Banner l., 141
Banning, William L., for, b., 410, 615
Banning v., 410
Bannock t., 282
Baptism r., 295
Baptist hill, 619, 639
Baraga, Bishop F., cited, 1, 22, 42, 43, 87, 89, 92, 107, 118, 142; for, b., 143; 257, 296, 321, 324, 345, 356, 411, 474, 479, 497, 504, 626
Baraga's r., 142
Barber l., 161, 320
Barber t., for Chauncey Barber, b., 183
Barclay t., 87
Barden sta., for J. W. Barden, 507
Bardon, James, q., 73; 476; for, 503
Bardon's peak, 503

Bardwell l., 336
Barker l., 143
Barkhurst, Enoch G., n., 60
Barn bluff, 208, 211
Barnard, W. G., n., 378
Barnes, William A., for, 608
Barnes l., for W. Barnes, 85; id., 614
Barnesville t. and v., for George S. Barnes, 115
Barnett t., for M. E. Barnett, 470
Barnum t., for George G. Barnum, 74
Barr's l., 499
Barrett, J. O., cited, 550, 551, 554
Barrett v. and l., for Gen. T. H. Barrett, b., 214
Barrows sta. and mine, for W. A. Barrows, Jr., 155; l., 218
Barry t., for Edward Barry, 410; v. 54
Barsness l., for A. and O. Barsness, 181; t., for three brothers, 431
Bartlett l., 286; sta., 478; t., 543
Barto t., 470
Bartsch, John, n., 150
Bartsch l., for Jacob Bartsch, 152
Bashaw t., for Joseph Baschor, 68
Bashitanequeb l., 141
Bass br., 253
Bass ls., 20, 33 (2), 43, 100, 161, 162, (7), 189, 232, 247, 253, 267, 402, 414, 442, 500, 547 (2), 573, 591
Bass Brook t., 253
Bass Lake p. o., 189; t., 253
Bassett cr., for Joel B. Bassett, b., 232, 607; l., 500
Basswood, 24; l., 32, 297; id., 494
Bat l., 141
Bath t., 200
Battle t. and r., 36, 46; r. and l., 286; cr., 342, 442; br., 349, 516; ls., East, and West, 391; l., 598
Battle hollow, Stillwater, 572
Battle point, Lake Traverse, 553
Battle rapids, Mississippi r., 517
Battle Lake v., 391
Battle Plain t., 466
Baudette t., v., and r., 36, 42
Baumbach l., for F. von Baumbach, b., 181
Bavaria l., 85
Baxter t., for Luther L. Baxter, b., 155; for H. A. Baxter, 289; l., 251
Bay Lake t. and l., 155
Bayless, Vincent W., for, 632
Baytown t., 568; (v., 571)

INDEX

Bean l., for Joseph F. Bean, 152
Bear, Benjamin, for, 389
Bear ls., 78(2), 141, 202, 203, 253, 274, 295, 319, 320, 369, 404; r., 99, 253, 282, 501; cr., 122, 196, 319, 362, 389, 415, 547; id., 94, 101, 142, 493, 494, 517; bay, 494; narrows, 495; pt., 132
Bear Creek t. and cr., 122
Bear's Head l., 501
Bear Island l., 501
Bear Park t., 382
Bear River t. and r., 282
Bear Skin ls., E. and W., 140, 142
Bear Trap cr., 494
Bear Valley, a hamlet, 556
Beard, Henry B., for, 604
(Beardsley t., for S. A. Beardsley, 202)
Beardsley v., for W. W. Beardsley, b., 54
Bearville t., 253
Beasley, Fanning L., for, 103
Beatty, Hamilton, n., 519
Beatty l., for Robert Beatty, b. 521
Beatty t., 478
Beauford t., 58, 66
Beauharnois, Charles de, 45
Beaulieu, Emma, 156
Beaulieu t. and v., for Henry and John Beaulieu, 322; l., for A. H. Beaulieu, 324
Beauty l., 248, 257, 267, 369, 548
Beauty Shore l., 402
Beaver, former abundance, 466
Beaver l., 143, 443, 529, 534; r., 293, 295, 499; cr., 191, 197, 241, 368, 455, 459, 466, 501, 563, 581
(Beaver l. and r., 32, 119; cr., 292; ids., 517)
Beaver t., 14, 191, 282, 470; hamlet, 581
Beaver Bay v. and t., 146, 293, 295
Beaver Creek t., 466; v., 467
Beaver Dam l., 590
Beaver Falls t. and v., 455
Becker, Gen. George L., for, b., 27, 514; n., 272
Becker co., 27-33; t. and v., 514; l., 530
Becker t., for J. A. Becker, 87
Beebe l., 591
Beef bay and l., 494, 495
Beers l., 403
Bejou t. and v., 323
Belanger id., 169
Belden sta., 411
Belfast t., 364

Belgium, name from, 312; t., 422
Belgrade t., 372; v., 523
Bell l. and cr., 341
Bella l., 258
Belle l., 320, 341, 529; r., 176, 400
Belle Chester sta., 206; v., 556
Belle Creek t. and cr., 206
Belle Plaine t. and v., 507
Belle Prairie t., 351, 353
Belle River t., 176
Belle Rose id., 146
Bellevue t., 351
Bellin, map by, 53
Bellingham v., for Robert Bellingham, 289
Bellissima l., 296
(Bellville v., for E. and H. Bell, 191)
(Bellwood v., for Joseph Bell, 166)
Belmont t., for Anders Belmont, 261; l., 401
Beltrami, J. C., 4, 12, 18; for, b., 34, 35, 48, 422; q., 40; 41, 48, 97, 126, 129, 445; q., 449; 514, 517
Beltrami co., 34-48; v., 422
Peltrami id. of gl. l. Agassiz, 48
Belvidere t., 206
Belview v., 449
Bemidji c. and t., 36; l., 36, 38, 41
Ben l., 435; Ben's l., 573
Ben Wade t., 431
Bena v., 87
Benbow, W. H., n., 149
Benedict sta. and l., 243
Bennett, Mrs. Adelaide G., 420
Bennington t., 359
Benson, Jared, for, b., 540
Benson c. and t., for B. H. Benson, b., 539
Benson, l., 434, 499
Benton, Thomas H., for, b., 49, 81, 308, 601
Benton co., 49-52; l. and t., 49, 81; v., 81; l., 308, 310, 341
Benville t., 36
Bergen t., 316
Berglin's l., 180
Bergman's br., 267
Berlin t., (526,) 531
Berliner l., 85
Bern p. o., 172
Bernadotte t., 372
(Berne t., 173)
Beroun v., 411
Berry, William M., for, 607
Berry l., 152
Bertha l., 162, 274; t. and v., 543
Bertram l., 591

Besemann t., for Ernst Besemann, 74
(Bessel, l., for F. W. Bessel, 90)
Beta l., 297
Beth l., 143
Bethany v., 582
Bethel t., 23
Betty, l., 342
Beulah t., 87
Bevins or Bevens cr., 85, 520
Bidwell, Ira, for, 619
Big bay, Vermilion l., 495
(Big falls, 51)
Big fork of Rainy r., 253, 286
Big id., 44, 235, 346, 357, 415, 495, 498; l., 43, 75, 78, 143, 218, 500, 514, 530, 548, 573; pt., 46, 94, 346
Big Bass l., 324, 443
Big Bend t., 103
Big Bird l., 162
Big Cobb r., 64
Big Cormorant l., 28
Big Falls t., 282
Big Foot cr., 168
Big Fork t. and v., 253
Big Grass t., 36
Big Lake t. and v., 514
Big Pine l., 19, 251; id., 498
Big Rat l., 32
Big Rice l., 99, 163, 501
Big Rock cr., 48
Big Rush l., 32
(Big Sand Bar cr., 47)
Big Sioux r., S. D. and Iowa, 263
Big Spring cr., 72, 453
Big Stone co., 53-56; l., 7, 8, 53, 54, 56; t., 54
Big Swan l., 339
Big Trout l., 162
Big Woods, 2; t., 327
Bigelow t. and v., for C. H. Bigelow, b., 376
Biggerstaff cr., for Samuel Biggerstaff, 516
Bigsby l., 143
Bingham, Kinsley S., for, b., 150
Bingham Lake v., and l., 150
Birch bay, 494, 495; id., 146, 296, 494; r., 295, 495; cr., 411, 459; br., 99; pt., 494; pond, 607
Birch l., 19, 99, 140, 141, 162, 246; ls., Upper, and Lower, 251; 296, 297, 341, 443, 501, 516, 530, 543; Big, and Little, 547; 591
Birch t., 36; sta., for C. J. Birch, 478
Birch Bark l., 530, 547 (2)

Birch Cooley, Sioux mission, 60; t. (and v.), 456; cr., 459; battle, 460
Birch Creek t., 411
Birch Island t., 36
Birch Lake t., and l., 87
(Birch Lake City, v., 546)
Birchdale l., 162; t., 543
Bird l., 181; id., 308
Bird Island t., v., and grove, 456
Biscay v., 317
Bischoffsheim, L., and wife, for, 544
Bishop, Harriet E., for, b., 441, 640
Bishop, Gen. Judson W., n., 60, 151, 509
Bismarck t., 518
Bisson l., 32
Biwabik t. and v., 478; mines, 503
Bixby, Jacob S., for, b., 532
Bixby v., for John Bixby, b., 532
Black bay, 121, 285, 286, 495; l., 43, 162, 401, 443, 501, 591; r., 286, 406, 447; br., 349; cr., 501; pt., 145
Black Bear l., 162
Black Dog l. and v., 168
Black Duck l., r., and t., 36, 46; pt. and bay, 494; l., 502
Black Hammer t., 238
Black Hawk l., 168
Black Hoof cr. and t., 74; l., 162
Black Oak l., 106, 530
Black River t., and r., 406
Black Rush l.. 315
Blackberry t., l., and br., 253
Blackbird l., 32
Blackman l., 309
Blackwell l., for George Blackwell, 181
Bladder l., 247
Blaine t., for James G. Blaine, b., 23
Blaisdell, Robert, Sr., for, 602
Blake, Anson, for, 632
Blakeley, Capt. Russell, for, b., 507; 509
Blakeley t. and v., 507
Blanche, l., 402
Bland l., 267
Blind l., 19, 99
Block l., 401, 529
Bloody l., 369
(Bloody r., 35; l., 48)
Bloom t., for Peter Bloom, 377
Bloom's l., for Gustaf Bloom, 111
Bloomer t., 327
Bloomfield t., 191
Blooming Grove t., (398,) 564
Blooming Prairie t. and v., 532

INDEX

Blooming Valley t., 470
Bloomington t., 220
Blowers t., for A. S. Blowers, 391
Blue l., 248, 251, 258, 512; hills, 275
Blue Earth co., 57-66
Blue Earth r., 2, 57, 58, 60, 61; t. and c., 184
Blue Hill t., 514
Blue Mounds, hills, 153, 431, 435, 514; t., 431
Blueberry t., r., and l., 561
Bluff creeks, N., and S., 391, 396
Bluffton t., 391
Boal, James McClellan, for, 614 (Boal id., 614)
Bock v., 344
Boedigheimer l., 403
Bogus Brook t., and br., 344
Bohall l., for Henry Bohall, 132
Bohemia, names from, 302, 427, 464, 509
Bohland, Adam, and Peter, for, 637
Bois des Sioux r., 7, 56, 554
Bois Fort reservation, 286, 506
Boisberg, village site, 551
Bolles cr., for Lemuel Bolles, 572
Bondin t., 364
Boneset l., 465
Bonga, Jean, and George, 88
Bonny l., 573
Boom id., 228, 517
Boon Lake t., and l., 456
(Boone, l., for Capt. Nathan Boone, 203)
Boot l., 25, 32, 43, 91(2), 296, 460, 573; id., 296; cr., 566
Booth, Rev. Charles, n., 250
Borden l., for David S. Borden, 161
Borer l., for Felix A. Borer, 304
Borgholm t., 344
Borup v., for C. W. W. Borup, b., 382
Bossuot l., 304
Bottineau, Pierre, 218, 226, 608; prairie, 226
Bottle l., 248; portage, 496
Boulder l., 296, 499; cr., 499; pt., 346
Boulevard, original meaning, 654
Boundary between Ojibways and Sioux, 52; see also International Boundary
Bourne, Walter B., for, 632
Boutwell, Rev. W. T., 4, 95; for, 98; q., 101; 126; for, 132, 246; 252
Boutwell cr., 132; l., 246

Bowen, Amasa, n., 334
Bowling, name from, 40
Bowlus v., 351
Bowman, George D., n., 223
Bowstring t., l., and r., 253, 254, 286
Boxville t., for William N. Box, 327
Boy l. and r., 87, 88; bay, 94; Boy's l., 72
Boy Lake t., 87
Boy River t., 87
Boyd v., 289
Boyer l., 32
Boyington id., 592
Boynton's id., 517
Brackett, George A., n., 225
Bradbury br., 349
Bradford l., 85; t., 250, 578
Bradley l., 534; sta. and ford, 58
Bradshaw l., 511
Braham v., 250
Brainerd, Lawrence, b., 156
Brainerd c., 156
Branch, William, for, 645
Branch t., 108
Brand, Henry, for, 625
Brandon l., for John Brandon, 181
Brandon t. and v., for Ole Brandon, 176
Brandrup t., for Andrew Brandrup, 578
Brandsvold t., 422
Brandt l., for Leroy Brandt, 85; t., 422
Brandy l., 33
Branham, Jesse V., Jr., n., 339
Brant l., 141
Bratsberg, a hamlet, 191
Bray t., for D. S. Bray, b., 406
Bread and Butter state, 4
Breck, Rev. James Lloyd, for, b., 130; 613, 642
(Breck l., 130)
Breckenridge, John C., for, b., 578, 601
Breckenridge t. and v., 578
Breda sta., 478
Bredeson l., 401
Breezy pt., 233, 235
Breitung t., for Edward Breitung, b., 478
Bremen t., 411
Brenna, Ole O., n., 314
Brenner l., for A. H. Brenner, 275
(Brentwood v., 508)
Brevator sta., 478
Brewery cr., 511

Brewster, William, for, b., 377
Brewster l., 319; v., 377
Brian l., 319
Bricelyn v., for John Brice, 184
Brickton v., 344
Bridgewater t., 461
Bridgie t., 282
Briggs l., 516
(Briggs t., for Joshua Briggs, 515)
Bright l., 337
Brighton t., 372
Brimhall, William E., for, 636, 637
Brimson v., for W. H. Brimson, 478
Brisbois, Louis G., 458
Brislet t., 422
Bristol t., 191
Britt sta., 478
Britton sta. and junction, 293
Broberg, Peter, 275
Brockway, Volney J., for, 304
Brockway t., 523; (v., 527;) prairie, 530
Brodhead, John R., 344
Brofee's cr., 106
Bronseth l., 401
Bronson v., for Giles Bronson, 277
Brook, creek, of same meaning, 89
Brook Lake t., 36
Brook Park t. and v., 411
Brookfield t., 456
Brooklyn t., 220; sta., 478
Brooklyn Center v., 220
Brooks v., 446; l., 590
Brookston v., 478
Brookville t., 449
Broome l., 72
Brooten v., 523
Brother of the Hole in the Mountain, 310
Brott, George F., for, 620
Brower, Hon. Jacob V., 122; n., 127-134; b., 128; 249; q., 252; 344, 346-8, 350, 353, 390, 543, 560, 573
Brower, Josephine, for, 131
Brower id., 130
Browerville v., for A. D. Brower and his sons, b., 543
Brown, Joseph R., for, 54, 67, 551, 573; b., 67-68; q., 205; 224; n., 519; 552, 571
Brown, Oren Delavan, for, b., 184, 185
Brown, Samuel J., 55, 551
Brown co., 67-72; l., 499
Brown's bay, 235; id., 517; l., 530; cr., 573

(Brown's falls, 230, 236; cr., 236)
Brown's Creek t., and cr., 446
Brown's Valley, 7, 8, 54, 56, 550
Brown's Valley t., 54, 68; v., 68, 551
Brownie l., 232, 607
Browning cr., for J. W. Browning, 111
(Browning, l., 233)
Brownsdale v., for A. D. and H. A. Brown, b., 360
Brownsville t., for J. and C. Brown, 238
Brownton, for Capt. A. L. Brown, b., 317
Bruce sta., 467; t., for Robert Bruce, 544
Brulé bay, 145; l. and r., 143, 144; mt., 145, 147; narrows, 498
Bruno t. and v., 411
Brunson, Benjamin W., 109, 611, n., 627
Brunswick t., 265; (v., 266)
Brush id., 44; cr., 184, 469; bay and r., 494
Brush Creek t., 184
Brushvale v., for Joseph Brush, 578
Bryant, William Cullen, for, 233, 603, 608
(Bryant, l., 233;) Bryant's l., 231
Buache, map by, 53, 445, 476
Buchanan, James, for, 172, 173, 402, 478, 601, 605, 644; l., 402
(Buchanan v., 172; t., 173; townsite, 478)
Buck hill, 170; pt., 548
Buck l., 258; for Adam Buck, b., 521; 547
Buck Head l., 547
(Buckeye t., 201)
Buckman, Clarence B., for, b., 351
Buckman, l., 258; t., 351
Budd l., 133; for W. H. Budd, 336
Buffalo cr., 161, 459; r., 32, 119, 120; l., 32, 106, 119, 336, 337, 369, 456, 520, (552,) 567, 587; pt., 44; sl., 211; ridge, 370
Buffalo t. and v., 587
Buffalo delta of Lake Agassiz, 120
Buffalo fish, species, 268
(Buffalo plains, 163)
Buffalo Lake, v., 456
Buffington sta., 422
Buford, Col. A. S., for, 633
Bug l., 143; cr., 499
Buh t., for Joseph F. Buh, b., 351
Buhl v., for Frank H. Buhl, 478
Buhler, John, n., 83
Bull l., 247; run, 566

Bull Dog l., 161
Bull Moose t., 88
Bullard cr., for G. W. Bullard, 211
Bullard t., for C. E. Bullard, b., 561
Bullhead l., 320, 401, 576
Bullis l., 141
Bungo t. and br., 88
Bunker l., for Kendall Bunker, 26
Bunnell, Willard B., n., 582
Bur Oak l., 274
Buran's l., for Adolph Burandt, 85
Burbank t., for H. C. Burbank, b., 269
Burch l., 591
Burchard sta., for H. M. Burchard, 312
Burgan's l., for William P. Burgan, 180
Burke t., for Rev. T. N. Burke, 417
Burleene t., 544
Burlington t., 28; bay, 294, 295; pt., 295
Burnett sta., 478
Burnham cr., 428
Burnhamville t. and v., for David Burnham, 544
Burns, John, for, 622
Burns, Robert, for, 23, 568
Burns t., 23; (v., 71;) creeks, W., and E., 585
Burnside t., for Gen. A. E. Burnside, b., 206
Burnstown t., for J. F. Burns, 68
Burnsville t., for William Burns, 164
Burnt l., 143; Burnt Out l., 337; Burnt Land br., 349
Burntside l. and r., 501; state forest, 506
Burr l., 218; v., 593
Burrows l., 181
Burton t., 594
Burtrum v., 544
Buse t., for Ernest Buse, b., 391
Bush l., 231
Bushnell, David I., 346
Busticogan t., 254
Bustie's l., 258
Butler, Nathan, quoted, 43
Butler t., for Stephen Butler, 392
Butter l., 342
Butterfield l., 163; t. and v., for William Butterfield, 574
Butternut l., 341, 590
Butternut Valley t., 58
Buxton, Kennard, for 623
Buyck t., for Charles Buyck, 478
Buzzle t. and l., 37, 43

Bygland sta., 422
Byhre, Iver P., aid, 87
Byron, l., 320, 341
Byron t., 88, 565; v., 385

Cable l., 429
(Cabotian mts., 502, 503)
Cacaquabic l., 296
Cadotte l., 500
Cairo t., 456
Calamus cr., 179
Caldwell t. and br., 282
Caledonia t. and v., 238
Calhoun, l., for John C. Calhoun, b., 229; 236, 274
California, names from, 84, 108, 174
Calkins, F. W., n., 200
Calkins l., 337
Callaway t., for W. R. Callaway, 28
Calumet v., 254
Cambria t., 58
Cambridge t. and v., 250
Camden t., v., and p. o., 81
Camel l., 162
Cameron, Jesse, for, 519
Cameron l., 258; for Daniel Cameron, 429; t., 365
Camp l., 161, 435, 540, 591; cr. 196; t., 456
Camp Cold Water, 228, 236
Camp Comfort, 189
Camp Lake t., 540
Camp Pope, 460
Camp Release, 72, 597; t., 289
Campbell, Cyrus A., n., 176
Campbell, Patrick, for, 85
Campbell l., 32, 43, 85, 512; (t., for James Campbell, 187;) v. and t., 578
Campbell beach of Lake Agassiz, 580
Canada, names from, 30, 158, 303, 338, 373, 425, 447, 462, 550
Canby, Gen. E. R. S., for, 593; b. 594
Canby c., 594; (co., 593;) cr., 292, 598
Candor t., 392
Canestorp, Ole O., for, b., 214
Canfield, l., for Job A. Canfield, b., 567
Canfield v., and cr., for S. G. Canfield, 191, 196
Canisteo t., 172
Cannon r., 11, 134, 165, 206, 461; l., 465

Cannon t., for Thomas Cannon, 277
Cannon Ball bay, 145
Cannon City t. and v., 461
Cannon Falls t. and v., 206
(Cano r., 134)
Canoes, birch, 51
Canosia t. and l., 479
Canright l., 336
Canton t. and v., 191; (t., 313)
Canyon, a hamlet, 479
Cape Bad Luck hill, 275
Carey, Harvey, for, 152
Carey, John R., 476; q., 478, 479, 480; 644
Carey l., for Carey brothers, 152; 500
Caribou l., 140, 141, 142, 143, 258, 498; pt., 145; t., 277
Carimona t. and v., 191, 196
Carl's l., 511
Carlisle t. and v., 392
Carlos l. and t., 176, 180
Carlston t., for T. L. Carlston, 200
Carlton, Reuben B., for, b., 73, 147
Carlton co., 73-79; v., 73, 74
Carlton peak, 1, 73, 146
Carman's bay, for John Carman, 235
Carnelian l., 529, 573 (2); cr., 573
Caroline, l., 529, 591
Carp l., 162, 297; (r., 95)
Carpenter t., for Seth Carpenter, 254
Carriboo l., 258
Carrie, l., 271
Carrigan l., 590
Carroll, Charles, for, b., 192, 617
Carroll, l., 264
Carrollton t., 192
Carson, Christopher (Kit), for, 150
Carson t., and Carson City, Nev., 150
Carson's bay, 234; l., 500
Carsonville t., for G. M. Carson, 28
Carter, Hill, for, 631
Carter, William G., for, 615
Carver, Jonathan, 4, 5. 25, 53; for, b., 80; land grant, 80-81; 85; for, 229; 343, 348; q., 416; for, 443; 445, 454; q., 475; 476, 514
Carver co., 2, 80-85; cr., 81; t. and v., 81
Carver's cave, 80, 443; id., 229; l., 444, 573
Cascade r. and ls., 144; cr. and t., 386
Casco pt., 235

Case, James A., for, 624
Case, John H., quoted, 165
Casey l., 342
Cashel t., 540
Casperson p. o., 471
Cass, Gen. Lewis, 9; for, b., 86; 88, 97; for, 96; 118, 126, 443, 444, 601
Cass co., 86-101, 155
Cass co., and Casselton c., N. D., for Gen. George W. Cass, b., 117, 118
Cass l., 9, 35, 86, 91; ids., 96; 100, 101, 126
Cass Lake v., 88; Indian reservation, 101, 259
(Cassina l., 86, 96)
Castle, Capt. Henry A., 223; for, 437; 464, 570
(Castle hill, 170; v., 437, 570)
Castle Rock t., 11, 164; the Rock, 165, 170; sta., 167
Caswell, Ziba, n., 340
Cat r., 563
Cataract id., 229
Catfish bar, Lake St. Croix, 571
Cathedral bay, 295
Catholic Colonization Bureau, 551
Catlin, George, 416; for, 583
Catlin l., 516
(Catlin's Rocks, a landing, 583)
Cazenovia v., 417
Cedar bay and id., 346; id., 494, 517
Cedar bend, St. Croix r., 572
Cedar cr., 25, 162, 585; r., 13, 174, 362
Cedar l., 17, 19, 26, 143, 162, 229, 320, 333, 337, 338, 341, 357, 414, 465(2), 508, 511, 530(2), 548, 590, 591(2), 607
Cedar pt., 234(2), 235, 346; rapids, 517
Cedar sta., 25; t., 327, 333
Cedar Bend t., 471
Cedar Island l., 233, 274, 500, 530
Cedar Lake t., 508
Cedar Mills t. and v., 338
Cedar Valley t., 479
Celia, l., 435
Center cr., 189, 335; l., 370, 529, 547
(Center t., 367)
Center City v., 108
Center Creek t., and cr., 333
Centerville t. and v., 23; l., 25; (v., 558;) hamlet, 582
Central l., 370
Central Chain of lakes, 333, 335, 336

INDEX 667

Central Lakes v., 479
Central Point t., 206
Ceresco t., 58
Cerro Gordo t., 289
Ceylon v., 333
Ceynowa l., 403
Chain l., 111
Chains of lakes, 335-337
Chamberlin, Prof. T. C., n., 309
Chambers, Julius, n., 129; bay and cr., 131
Champepadan cr., 368, 380, 469
Champion t., for Henry Champion, 578
Champlain, Samuel de, 8
Champlin, Ezra T., b., 220
Champlin t. and v., 220
Chanarambie t. and cr., 365, 370
(Chanche, l., 161)
Chandler v., for J. A. Chandler, b., 365
Chaney, Josiah B., for, 132; 543, 616
Chaney bay and pt., 132
Chanhassen t., 82
Chankaska cr., 304
(Chapeau l., 203)
Chapman, Silas, map, 76
Charles, l., 401, 442
Charlestown t., 449
Charley l., 141, 180
Charlotte, l., 168, 273, 336, 435, 548, 590
Chase, Albert S., for, 477
Chase, Jonathan, for, b., 258, 349; Nehemiah, for, 349
Chase, Kelsey D., for, b., 485
Chase l., 258; br., 349(2)
Chaska t., c., l., and cr., 82
Chatfield, A. G., for, b., 192, 386; n., 507
Chatfield v., 192, 386
Chatham t., 587
Chaudiere falls, and portage, 496
(Cheevertown v., for W. A. Cheever, 226)
(Chemaun r., 134)
Cheney h., 530; p. o., for B. P. Cheney, 172
Chengwatana v., 10, 413; t. and v., 411
Cherokee l., 143; heights, 443
Cherry l., 296; cr., 304
Cherry portages, Big. and Little, 138
Cherry Grove t., 206
Chesley br., 267
Chester cr., 493, 649, 653

Chester peak, for A. H. Chester, b., 503
Chester v., 386; t., 422, 556
Chetamba cr., 459
Cheyenne, Indian tribe, 119; r., S. D., 119
Chicago bay, 145
Chief t., 323; l., 324
Chief's pt., 46
Childs, Mrs. S. B., n., 177
Childs l., for Edwin R. Childs, 180
Childs v., for Job W. Childs, 578
Chilgren t., for Albert Chilgren, 37
Chilton l., 32
Chimney rock, 169, 170(2), 197
Chippewa co., 102-106; see Ojibways
Chippewa l., 33, 102; r., 102, 105, 431, 434, 537; Indian reservation, 101, 259
Chippewa r., Wis., 11, 102
(Chippewa t., 176)
(Chippewa City v., 105)
Chippewa Falls t. and v., 431
Chisago co., 107-113; l., 107
Chisago City v., 108
Chisago Lake t., 108
Chisholm v., for A. M. Chisholm, b., 479
Choke Cherry l., 64
Chokio v., 535
Chowen, George W., for, 604, 608
Christensen l., 295
Christiania t., 261
Christina, l., 182
Christine, l., 143
Christmas, Charles W., for, 231, 601
Christmas l., 231
Chrysler l., 161
Chub l., 78, 141, 168; r., 141, 168; cr., 168
Church l., 218, 274; for C. Church, 324
Churnes p. o., for Alex. Churnes, 122
Chute, Richard, for, 610
Cingmars t., for E. F. Cingmars, 282
Circle l., 465
Civil War, see Rebellion
Clam l., 143, 337
Clara, l., 143
Clara City v., 103
Claremont t. and v., 172
Clarence, l., 32
Clarino l., 401
Clarissa v., 544
Clark, Byron F., for, 565

Clark, Martin D., for, 624
Clark, Mrs. Mary A. (Moon), for, 54; Mrs. Nathan, for, 168
Clark, Thomas, n., 142, 144, 146; q., 143; for, b., 146, 644; 293, 497
Clark, Truman, for, 335
Clark bay, 146; l., 162, 295, 511, 538
Clark t., 14, 184
Clark's Grove v., for J. M. Clark, 200
Clarke, Hopewell, 127; cr., 131
Clarkfield v., 594
(Clarksville t., for D. K. J. Clark, 54)
Classen l., 232
Clausen's l., 247
Clay, Henry, for, b., 114, 601
Clay co., 114-120; t., 243
Clay Bank sta., and Clay Pits sta., 206
Clayton, John M., for, 601
Clayton l., 337
Clayton t., for W. Z. Clayton, b., 360
Clear cr., 77; br., 122
Clear l., 19, 72, 150, 153, 162, 211, 264, 304, 320, 336, 337, 342, 369(2), 374, 380, 401, 502, 514, 520, 530, 538, 567, 573(3)
(Clear Grit, a hamlet, 192)
Clear Lake t. and v., 514
Clear River t., 471
Clearbrook v., 122, 123
Clearwater co., 121-134
Clearwater l., 43, 81, 82, 83, 84, 121(2), 140, 142, 144, 161, 162, 296, 529, 587, 591
Clearwater r., 9, 43, 121(3), 523, 587, 591
Clearwater v., 523; t. and v., 587; prairie, 592
Cleary l., 511
Clements v., for P. O. Clements, b., 449
Clementson v., for H. Clementson, 37
Cleveland, Esther, for, 424
Cleveland, Grover, for, 605, 631
Cleveland t. and v., 301
Cliff l., 141
Clifford l., 180
Clifton t., 312, 551; (townsite, 479)
Climax v., 422
Clinch, Christine, for, 143
Clinton, DeWitt, r., 134
Clinton v., 54; t., 467, 479
Clinton Falls t. and v., 532
(Clinton Lake t., 516)

Clitherall, George B., for, b., 392; n., 402
Clitherall t., v., and l., 392
Clontarf t. and v., 540
Cloquet id., 74; r. and c., 74, 498
Clothespin l., 141
Cloud l., 141
Cloudy Weather, an Ojibway, 35
Clough, Gov. D. M., for, b., 351
Clough t., 351; l., 357; id., 493
Cloustier l., 320
Clove l., 139
Clover t., 122, 243, 411
Clover Leaf t., 406
Cloverton sta., 411
Clow t., 277
Clubfoot l., 145
Coal l., 548
Cobb rs., Big, and Little, 64, 184; cr., 292
(Cobb t., 184)
Cobden v., for Richard Cobden, b., 68
(Coburg p. o., for William Coburn, 311)
Cochran, M. V., n., 588
Cochrane l., 591
Cody l., for Patrick Cody, 465
Coffee l., 78
Coggswell, Amos, n., b., 531
Cohasset v., 254
Cokato t., v., and l., 587
Colby, John, n., 571; for, 573
Colby l., 111, 141, 573; sta., 479
(Colcaspi id., 96)
Cold Spring v., 523
Cole, Charles Cameron, for, 365
Cole l., for James Cole, 78
Coleman id., 497
Coleraine v., for T. F. Cole, 254
Colfax, Schuyler, for, 269, 603
Colfax t., (27,) 269
College hill, 212, 389
Collegeville t. and v., 523
Collett l., 32
Colling, William K., n., 533
Collins, Loren W., quoted, 51; 167
Collins t., 317; cr., 559
Collinwood t. and v., 338; l., 339, 590
Collis v., 551
Cologne v., 82
Coloney, Myron, n., 177
Colorado, name from, 467
Colton, Rev. Calvin, 114
Columbia l., 25; t., 422; (townsite, 270; co., 422)
Columbia Fur Company, post, 552

INDEX 669

Columbia Heights v., 23
Columbus t., 23
Colvill, Col. William, for, b., 135; q. 208; 211
Colville t., 135, 136
Colvin t., for Frank S. Colvin, 479
Comar, James, n., 466
Comber bay and pt., for W. G. Comber, 132; id., 133
Comfort l., for Dr. J. W. Comfort, 111; t., 266
Comfrey v., 69
Como, l., 440, 639, 641; t., 327
Como Park d., 440, 626-9, 639
Compton t., for James Compton, b., 392
Comstock, S. G., for, b., 115, 327
Comstock v., 115; t., 327; l., 500
Concord t. and v., 172
Concordia College, 636
Coney Island v., and id., 82
Congdon, Chester A., for, b., 653
Conger v., 200
Conie, l., 181
Connecticut, names from, 159, 165, 172, 201, 318, 387, 533, 582, 650
Connection l., 429
Connelly t., for E. Connelly, 578; l., 592
Constance l., 591
Constans, William, for, 618
Conway, Charles R., for, 622
Cook, Alfred M., n., 449
Cook, C. P., n., 62
Cook, Charles, b., 180; for, 181; Mrs. Cook, n., 181
Cook, Charlie, and Louise, for, 180
Cook, Franklin, for, 603
Cook, Henry, for, 181
Cook, John, 135; John B., for, 624
Cook, Major Michael, for, b., 135
Cook co., 135-148
Cook l., for Charles Cook, 181
Cook v., for Wirth H. Cook, 479
Cook's bay, 234; l., 404, 499; valley, 559
Cooke, Jay, state park, for, b., 78; 117
Coombs l., for Vincent Coombs, 341
Coon cr., 25, 189; l., 25, 258, 320; pt., 548
Coon Creek t., and cr., 312
Cooper, Joseph, n., 583
Copas v., 568
Copeland's l., 296
Copley t., for Lafayette Copley, 122
Copper l., 141

Cora, l., 401
Cora Belle, l., 369
Corbeau, r. de, 154
Corbin, James P., for, 369
Corcoran t., for P. B. Corcoran, b., 221
Cordova t. and v., 301
Corinna t., 587
Corliss, Charles Mitchell, for, 579
Corliss, Eben E., for, b., 392; 394
Corliss t., 392
Cormant t., 37
Cormorant ls., 28, 31, 218; r., 46; rock, 44
Cormorant t., 28, (37)
Cornell, A. B., n., 188
(Cornell v., 412)
Cornfield id., 44
Cornish t., for C. E. and M. F. Cornish, 14; 519
Corona sta. and t., 74
Correll v., 54
Corser, Elwood S., for, 605, 608
Cosmos t., 339
Costin townsite, for John Costin, Jr., 479
Coteau des Prairies, 2, 310, 313, 416, 420
Cottage Grove t. and v., 568
Cottagewood, l. Minnetonka, 234
Cotter, Lucy, n., 468
Cotton l., 32; t., for J. B. Cotton, b., 480
Cottonwood co., 149-153
Cottonwood l., 65, 150, 218, 309, 312, 315, 521, 538, 576; cr., 106, 542; r., 149, 453
Cottonwood t., 69; v., 312
Coues, Dr. E., 6, 17, 149, 343, 354, 516
(Council l., 203)
Courage bays, N. and S., and pt., 346
Courtland t. and v., 372
Coutchiching rock formation, 287
Cow cr., 475
Cow Tongue pt., 145
Cowan's br., 19, 267; l., 375
Cowdry, l., for Samuel B. Cowdry, 180
Cowhorn l., 257
Cowley l., 233
Cox, Joseph, n., 271
Cox, Samuel S., for, 646
Cox, Ulysses O., 95; q., 490, 561
Cozy l., 441, 639
Crab l., 141, 296, 501
Craig prairie, for H. E. Craig, 517

Cramer t., for J. N. Cramer, 293
Cranberry l., 45, 548; bay, 498
Cranberry Marsh r., 140, 148
Crane id., 235, 261, 591; cr., 319, 320, 534, 566; l., 401, 502
Crate t., 103
Crawford l., 590
Cray sta., for Judge Lorin Cray, 58
Credit r., 508; l., 512
Credit River t., 508
Cree language, names from, 8, 93, 281, 294
Creek l., 337
Creek, brook, of same meaning, 89
Creighton, Thomas, n., 588
Crellin, l., 502
Cremer, William J., for, 652
Crescent springs, 133
Cretin, Bishop Joseph, for, 637
Crocker l., 162
Crocodile l., 140
Croke t., for Thomas W. Croke, b., 551
Cromwell, Oliver, for, 115, 632, 642
Cromwell v., 74; t., 115
Crook l., 274(2)
Crooked cr., 238, 415; slough, 585
Crooked l., 26, 88, 141, 157, 161, 162, 180(2), 181(2), 244, 258, 295, 298, 369, 402, 419, 496, 499, 501, 529, 547
Crooked Creek t., 238
Crooked Lake t., 88
Crooks, Ramsay, for, b., 423
Crooks, William, for, b., 423; n., 562
Crooks t., for H. S. Crooks, 456
Crookston c. and t., 423
Crosby v., for George H. Crosby, 156; t., for Ira Crosby, 411
Cross, Judson N., for, b., 216
Cross l., (72,) 140, 160, 414, 429; r., 142, 282
Cross River t., and r., 282
Crow r., 9, 154, 523, 590; cr., for Little Crow, 453; l., 523
Crow Lake t., 523
Crow River t., 523
Crow Wing co., 9, 154-163; t., 157; trading post and v., 154, 155
Crow Wing r., 9, 154, 562; l., 161; id., 154, 155, 163; series of lakes, 246, 247
Crow Wing Lake t., 243
Crowell, A. M., n., 544
Crystal bay, 235, 293, 493

Crystal, l., 60, 162, 168, 221, 258, 403, 429, 465, 512, 538; cr., 241
Crystal v., l., and prairie, 221, 232
Crystal Bay t., and bay, 293, 295
Cuba t., 28; sta., 89
Cucumber id., 141
Cudworth, D. A., for, 632
Culdrum t., 351
Culkin, William E., 498
Cullen l., 162
Culpeper, Thomas, for, 646
Culver t. and v., for J. B. Culver, b., 480
Cummings l., for A. Cummings, 521
(Cummingsville v., 386)
Curfman l., 32
Curo, James, n., 89
Currant l., 296, 368
Currie, Archibald, for, b., 365
Currie, Neil, for, b., 365
Currie v., 365
Curry, Manley B., for, 632
Curtain portage, 496
Curtice, David L., for, 619
Cushing t. and v., for Caleb Cushing, 351
Cusson v., 480
Custer, Gen. George A., for, b., 312, 618
Custer t., (290,) 312
Cut Face r., 144
Cut Foot Sioux l., 258
Cutler p. o., 15
Cuyuna iron range, 1, 157, 158, 163; v., 157
Cynthia l., 511
Cyphers sta., 89
Cypress l., 297
Cyrus v., 431; l., 435, 538

Dackins l., for Edward Dackins, 65
Dady's cr., 559
Daggett l., 162
Daggett Brook t., and br. (two), for Benjamin F. Daggett, b., 157
(Dahkotah townsite, 571)
Dahl, Ole C., for, 393
Dahler l., 163
Dahlgren, Alma, for, 327
Dahlgren t., for John A. B. Dahlgren, b., 82
Dahlquist, Louis P., n., 473
Dailey t., for Asa R. Dailey, 344
Daisy bay, 495
Dakota co., 164-170; v., 582; cr. 585; see Sioux

INDEX 671

Dakotas, names from, 3, 12, 13, 22, 53, 57, 58, 64, 66, 69, 75, 81-84, 102, 105, 106, 124, 164, 168, 169, 174, 187-9, 203, 207-210, 216, 222, 224, 225, 227, 230-2, 238, 249, 250, 262-4, 268, 273, 288, 301, 303, 308, 310, 313, 315, 317, 334, 344, 346, 365, 367, 368, 370, 374, 380, 386, 389, 419, 455, 456, 466, 520, 533, 535, 550, 552-4, 557-9, 564, 565, 569, 570, 572, 583-5, 587
Dalbo t., 250
Dale t., 150
Dalka l., 499
Dalles of St. Louis r., 78, 493, 502; St. Croix r., 112, 113, Kettle r., 415
Dalrymple, Oliver, 118
Dalton v., 393
Dam l. and br., 19
Dan Patch electric ry., 168, 510
Dan's l., 591
Dana, Charles, n., 208
Dana, Gen. N. J. T., for, 600, 601
Dane l., 72, 401
Dane Prairie t., 393
Danforth t., for N. H. Danforth, 411
(Danger l., 131)
Daniels l., 140
Danielson t., for Daniel and Nels Danielson, 339
Danube v., 456
Danvers v., 540
Danville t., 59
Darfur v., 574
Darling, l., for Andrew Darling, 180
Darling t., for W. L. Darling, b., 351
Darnen t., 535
Darwin t. and v., 339; l., 342
Dassel t. and v., for B. Dassel, 339
(Davenport l., 157, 160)
Davenport t., for Col. William Davenport, b., 157; 160
Davern, William, for, b., 639
David, l., 525
Davidson l., for D. J. Davidson, 182
Davidson t., for A. D. Davidson, 15
Daviess, Joseph Hamilton, for, b., 186
Davis, Gov. C. K., 125, 220
Davis, Jefferson, n., 373
Davis l., 141; id., 517
Davis t., for Edward N. Davis, 277

Dawson, Alice, for, 640
Dawson, William, for, b., 289, 642
Dawson c., 289
Day l., 501, 529
Dayton, Lyman, for, b., 221; 393, 439, 517, 615, 621
Dayton, Mrs. Maria Bates, for, 621
Dayton id. and rapids, 517
Dayton t. and v., 221, 587; (v., 393)
Dayton's bluff, 170, 439, 443; d., 439, 621-3
Dead l., 33, 248, 393, 403, 404; r., 393
Dead Coon l., 309, 312
Dead Fish l., 78
Dead Horse l., 258
Dead Lake t., 393
Dead Moose r., 77
Dean, A. J., for, 607
Dean, I. N., n., 507
Dean p. o. and v., for J. W. Dean, 462
Dean's l., for Matthew Dean, 512; 590
Dean Lake t., br., and ls., for Joseph Dean, 157
Death Rock, 110
Debs, Eugene V., for, 37
DeCarrie, Sabrevoir, 59
Decker l., 304
Decorah, Iowa, 59
Decoria t., for Waukon Decorah, b., 59
Deep l., 442
Deephaven v., 221
Deer, 40, 89, 169, 170
Deer cr., 77, 196, 204, 362, 393, 414
Deer l., 26, 43, 247, 257. 274, 400, 402, 548, 590; r., 257; t., 471
Deer Creek t. and v., 393
Deer Lake t., 254
Deer Park t., 406
Deer River t. and v., 254
Deerfield t., 89, 532
Deerhorn cr., 120, 580; t., 578
Deerwood v., 157; t., 277
(De Forest v., 378)
De Graff v., for Andrew De Graff, b., 540
Delafield t., 261
Delano v., for F. R. Delano, b., 587
Delavan t. and v., 184
Delaware t., 214; Indian tribe, 172
Delft v., 150
Delhi t. and v., 449
De L'Isle, G., map, 10, 12, 53, 343
Dell Grove t., 411
Dellwood v., 568

Delorme sta., for A. Delorme, 446
Delta l., 297
Deltas of gl. 1. Agassiz, 120, 324, 429
Delton t., 150
Demaray cr., for Mrs. Demaray, 132
Deming, Portius C., for, 131
Deming l., 131
De Montreville, l., 573
Denham v., 411
Denmark, names from, 542, 568
Denmark t., 568
Dennison v., for M. P. Dennison, 206, 462
Denny, Henry R., for, 629
De Noyon, Jacques, 281
Densmore, Frances, 47
Dent l., 143; v., 393
(Dent v., for Richard Dent, 178)
Dentaybow t., 282
Denver t., 467
Derham, Hugh, n., 166
Deronda bay, 145
Derrynane t., 301
Des Moines r., 12, 150, 199, 261, 337; t., 261
Des Moines River t., 365
Desnoyer, Stephen, for, 634
De Soto, Hernando, l. for, 130, 134; 614
(De Soto t., 62)
Detroit l., t., and c., 28; mt., 33
Devil cr., 465
Devil Fish l., 140, 500
Devil Track l. and r., 144
Devil's l., 181, 267, 402, 403, 414
Dewald t., for A. and H. Dewald, 377
Dewey, Admiral George, for, b., 254, 471, 633
Dewey t., 254, 471; l., 501
Dewey Lake sta., and l., 480
Dexter t. and v., 360
Diamond l., 20, 231, 233, 248, 273, 275, 304, 307
Diamond Lake t., 307
Diarrhoea r., 144
Dick t., for Mildred Dick, 15; l., 258
Dick's cr., 547
Dickinson, Leon, for, 122
Dickinson sta., for A. C. Dickinson, 588
Dickson, Robert, trading post, 551
Dieter t., for Martin V. Dieter, 471
Dillman, C., n., 312
Dilworth v., 115

Dimick's id., 517
Dingoshick l., 141
Dingwall, James D., for, 645
Dinham Lake sta., and l., 480, 500
Dinner Creek t., and cr., 282
Disappointment l., 296; h., 298
Dismal cr., 547
Division cr., 133
Dobbins cr., 362
(Dobson t., for James Dobson, 185)
Doctor's l., 111
Dodd, Capt. William B., 373; for, b., 620
Dodd, William J., n., 418
Dodd road, 620
Dodge, Augustus C., of Iowa, for, b., 171
Dodge, Gov. Henry, of Wis., for, 18, b., 171
Dodge co., 171-174; (l., 18)
Dodge Center v., 172
(Doe l., 129)
Doerfler l., 590
Dog l., 272, 304
Dog Una, for, 1, 157
Dolan, Christopher, n., 519
Doll, Anthony, for, 551
(Dolly Varden, l., 129)
Dollymount t., 551
Dolney's l., 162
Don l., 141
Donald's l., 402
Donaldson v., for H. W. Donaldson, 277
Donders l., 85
Donnelly, Ignatius, for, b., 328, 536
Donnelly t., 328; t. and v., 536
Donovan l., for John Donovan, 52
Dooley, James H., for, 631
Dopelius v., 392
Dora, l., 258, 304; t., 393
Doran v., for Michael Doran, b., 578
Dorothy sta., 446
Dorr, Caleb D., for, 608
Dorset v., 243
Dosey t., for Julius Dosey, 411
Doswell, Brooke, for, 631
Dotson sta., for Enoch Dotson, 69
Doty, Gov. James D., treaty, 375
Double bay, 145; ls., 152
Doughnut l., 296
Douglas, Stephen A., 4; b., 175; for, 165, 175, 185, 570, 601, 608, 613, 624
Douglas co., 175-182

INDEX

Douglas l., for E. Douglas, 20; sta. for James Douglas, b., 115; (t., 185, 193, 536)
Douglass t., 165,(509;) v., for Harrison Douglass, 386
Dousman, Hercules L., for, 613
(Dove r., 139)
Dover t. and v., 386; (t., 467, 532)
Dovray t. and v., 365
Dovre t. and hills, 269; moraine, 275
(Dovre Fjeld t., 396)
Dow's l., for William Dow, 248
Dower l., for Sampson Dower, 549
Downer v., 115
Downes cr., 259
Drake, Benjamin, Sr., 223
Drake, Elias F., for, 468; n., 507, 576
(Drake v., 468)
Drammen t., 307
Draper, Lyman C., 81
Dresbach t. and v., for George B. Dresbach, b., 582
Driftless area, 196, 240, 585
(Driftwood r., 11)
Dromedary hills, 549
Drum id., 287
Drummond sta., 294
Dry cr., 111, 152, 454
Dry Weather cr., 106
Dry Wood l. and cr., 542
Dryden t., 519
Dryweed id., 284, 286, 498
Dublin t., 540
Duck l., 65, 100, 143, 162, 231, 247, 337, 356, 370, 419; bay and id., 95
Dudley id., for John Dudley, 169; l., 465
Dudley t., for F. E. Dudley, b., 122; sta., 312
Duelm, a hamlet, 49
Duff l., for Bernard Duff, 521
Du Forte l., 32
Dugas, William, for, 618
Dugdale v., 423
Du Luth, Daniel Greysolon, 219, 344; for, b., 480, 481, 645
Duluth c., 480, 643-654; t., 481
Duluth, gl. l., 79, 148, 505, 654
Duluth and Iron Range ry., 503
DULUTH DISTRICTS, DIVISIONS, AND ADDITIONS: Arlington Place ad., 649; Bay View ads., 651, 654; Bellevue Park ad., 651; Belmont Park ad., 651; Brookdale ad., 649, 650; Carlton Place ad., 651; Chester Park ad., 649; Clague and Prindle ad., 649; Clifton Heights ad., 649; Clover Hill div., 648; Cremer's ad., 651, 652; Crosley Park ad., 647; Dickerman's ad., 651; Dodge's ad., 651; Duluth Heights d., 649, 650; Duluth Proper, d., 646, 647, 649; East Duluth d., 648; East Lawn div., 648, 649; Endion d., 480, 482, 643, 645-8; Fairbanks ad., 649; Fond du Lac d., 480, 483, 493, 643, 645, 652; Gary d., 652; Glen Avon ad., 648, 649; Grassy Point ad., 651; Gray and others, ad., 649, 650; Hall's ad., 651; Harrison div., 648; Hazelwood ad., 651; Highland Park ad., 648, 649; Hunter's Park ad., 648; Industrial div., 644; Ironton d., 652; Ironton Park ad., 652; Kensington Place ad., 649; Kenwood Park ad., 649, 650; Kimberly and Stryker, ad., 651; Lake View ad., 649; Lakeside d., 480, 485, 643; Lakewood d., 480; Lenroot's ad., 652; Lester Park d., 485, 493, 644, 646, 647, 653, 654; Lloyd's div., 651; London ad., 647, 653; London Park ad., 647; Long View ad., 648, 649; Macfarlane's ad., 651; Maple Grove ad., 649; Merchant's Park ad., 649; Mineral ad., 651; Minnesota Point d., 493, 644, 652; Minnewakan ad., 652; Morgan Park d., 652; Motor Line div., 648, 649; Murray Hill ad., 649; Myers and Whipple, ad., 649, 650; New Duluth d., 652; New Endion ad., 648, 649; Norton and others, ad., 649; Oakland Park ad., 648; Oneota d., 480, 487, 643, 650; Oneota Park ad., 651; Park View ad., 649; Portland div., 480, 488, 643, 646, 649, 653; Princeton Place ad., 648; Rice's Point d., 480, 489, 643, 645, 646; Sharp's ad., 651; Spaulding ad., 649; Spirit Lake ad., 652; Stewart's ad., 651; Stowell's ad., 651; Stryker and Manley, ad., 651; Summit Park ad., 649; Superior View ad., 649, 650; Triggs, Kennedy, and others, ad., 649; Walbank ad., 649, 650; West Duluth d., 650; West End ad., 651; West Park ad., 650; Whitman Park ad., 651; Willard and Piper, div., 649; Willard's ad., 648; Wilming-

ton ad., 651; Woodland Park ad., 648; Zenith Park ad., 651

DULUTH STREETS: Adams, 644; Albion, 651; Alder, 650; Algonquin, 645; Anoka, 648; Argyle, 644; Ash, 652; Astor, 644; Austin, 648; Avondale, 647; Balboa, 651; Balsam, 650; Baltimore, 652; Banian, 650; Bank, 650; Bayless, 650; Beaudry, 652; Bellevue, 651; Beltrami, 650; (Bench, 645;) Bessemer, 652; Beulah, 651; Bishop, 645; Boston, 652; Bowser, 652; Branch, 645, 648; Bristol, 651; Bruce, 649; Buchanan, 644; Buena Vista, 650; Buffalo, 649, 650; Callowhill, 645; (Cambridge, 648;) Cardigan, 651; Carlton, 650, 651; Cartaret, 652; Cascade, 653; Cass, (645,) 651; (Center, 645;) Chambers, 644; Cherokee, 645; Cherry, 644; Chestnut, 650, 651; Chicago, 652; Chippewa, 651; Choctaw, 645; Church, 644; Clark, 644; Clay, 651; Cleveland, 649, 650; Clover, 644; Cody, 651; Collingwood place, 651; Colorado, 648; Cooke, 648; Cortez, 649; Courtland, 647; Culpeper, 646; Custer, 645; Dale, 650; Davis, 650; Denver, 650; Desota, 651; Devonshire, 650; (Dingwall, 645;) Dodge, 648; Duke, 644, (651;) Dundee, 644; Dunleith, 644; Earl, 651; Edna, 651; Eighth, 643, 647; Eleventh, 647; Elinor, 651; Elizabeth, 649; Ella, 651; (Elm, 644;) Ericsson, 651; Erie, 644, (645;) Exeter, 650; Faribault, 648; Fifteenth, 647; Fifth, 643, 647; Fillmore, 652; First, 643, 647; Fourteenth, 647; Fourth, 643, 647, 653; Fowey, 651; Fremont, 651; French, 652; Fulton, 644; Galusha, 651; Garden, 649; Gasper, 645; Getty, 650; Gilbert, 650, 651; Gilead, 650; Gilliat, 648; Gladstone, 648; Glass, 645; Glendale, 647; Glenwood, 647; Godolphin, 652; Gogebic, 652; Goldsmith, 652; Goodhue, 652; Gosnold, 651; Gould, 651; Grand, 652; Green, 651; Greysolon road, 645, 648; Hale, 651; (Halifax, 643;) Hall, 651; Hallenbeck, 645; Hardy, 649; Hawkins, 649; Heard, 652; Helm, 647; Henry, 650; Hermantown road, 650; High, 651; Highland, 651; Howitz, 650; Hugo, 650; Huntington, 651; Huron, (645,) 647; Idlewild, 647; Ironton, 652; Itasca, 645; Ivanhoe, 647; Jackson, 649; Jay, 648; Jefferson, (644,) 645, 648; Juniata, 647; Kelly, 649; Kent, 649; King, 651, 652; Kingston, 647; Kinney, 652; Kittson, 646; Krumseig, 645; La Salle, 650, 651; La Vaque, 651; Lemon, 650; Lewis, 649; Lexington, 651; Linden, 650; Locust, 650; Lombard, 648; London road, 645, 647, 648; Lovell, 651; Luverne, 648; Lyons, 650; McCuen, 652; McCulloch, 648; (Magellan, 643;) Main, 651; Manitoba, 649; Mankato, 648; Marion, 649; Marquette, 646; Marshall, 650; Martin, 647, 651; Marvin, 644; Matthews, 652; Mecca, 651; Medina, 651; Mesaba, 652; Michigan, 643, 647; Miles, 645; Milford, 651; Mineral, 651; Mitchell, 652; Mohawk, 645; Monroe, 644; Montana, 644; Morse, 644; Mulberry, 650; Murray, 644; Myrtle, 650; Nashua, 651; Natchez, 651; New York, 644; Niagara, 650; Nicollet, 651; Nimrod, 651; Ninth, 643, 647; North Shore road, 644; Norton, 649; Norwood, 647; Oak, (644,) 652; Oakley, 647; Oconomowoc, 645; Olive, 644; Olney, 651; Oneida, 647; Oneota, 643; (Ontario, 645;) Orange, 650; Oregon, 650; Osman, 651; Otsego, 647; Owatonna, 648; Oxford, (648,) 649; Palm, 650; Palmetto, 650; (Park, 644;) Partridge, 649; Patterson, 651; Peabody, 648; Pearl, 644; Peary, 652; Pembina, 645; Pendennis, 646; Persons, 649; Petre, 651; Philadelphia, 652; Pine, 644; Piper, 650; Pitt, 648; Pizarro, 651; Polk, 651; Portage, 644; Portland, 650; Prescott, 652; Prince, 651; Prospect, 650; Pulaski, 651; (Puleston, 648;) Queen, 651; Quince, 650; Raleigh, 651; Ramsey, 651; Randolph, 644; Raven, 646; Red Wing, 648; Redruth, 651; Reed, 652; Regent, 648; Rene, 643; Restormel, 650; Rice

INDEX 675

Lake road, 647; (Robertson, 648;) Robinson, 648; Robson, 649; Roe, 652; Rupley, 651; St. Andrews, 649; St. Anthony, 643; St. Charles, 644; St. Cloud, 644; St. George, 644; (St. James, 644;) St. John, 644; St. Marie, 649, 650; (St. Paul, 644;) Schuylkill, 651; Second, 643, 647; Seneca, 645; Seventh, 643, 647; Sherburne, 651; Sixth, 643, 647; Snively road, 654; Somerville, 651; Sorenson, 644; South, 645, 648; Spencer, 651; Spring, 652; Spruce, 644; State, 644; Stewart, 651; (Summit, 648;) Superior, 643, 644, 645, (645,) 646-8; Sutphin, 644; Tacony, 651; Tainter, 651; Tecumseh, 645; Tenth, 647; Third, 643, 644, 647; Thirteenth, 647; Thompson, 651, 652; Tillinghast, 651; Tintagel, 646; Tioga, 647; Toledo, 649, 650; Towne, 652; Traders court, 652; Traverse, 643; Trenton, 650; Truelson, 652; Twelfth, 647; Union, 650; Vermilion Lake road, 648; Verndale, 651; Vernon, 650; Viaduct, 650; Victoria, 649; Viking, 652; Vine, 644; Vinland, 652; Wabasha, 648; Wadena, 651; Walnut, 644; Warren, 644; Warwick, 652; Waseca. 651; Water, (645,) 645; Wayne, 651; Wellington, 650; Wicklow, 650; Willard, 650; Williams, 644; Willow, 650; (Winnipeg, 645;) Winona, 648; Winter, 650; Woodlawn, 647; Worden, 651; Wyoming, 647; Zurah, 652

DULUTH AVENUES, mostly transverse to streets and to the shore of the lake, the harbor, and St. Louis bay and river, 643, 645, 646, 647: Abbotsford, 649; Allen, 649; Arch, 650; Arlington, 649, 650; Arthur, 646; Ash, 646; Backus, 649; Barrett, 652; Bay View Terrace, 650; Bayfield, 650; Beacon, 650; Birch, 646; Bird, 649; Biwabik, 652; Blackman, 649, 650; Blodgett, 649; Bodmin, 651; Boyd, 652; Boynton, 650; Brainerd, 650; Broadway, 650; (Brock, 643;) Bryant, 649; Bute, 649; Carlisle, 649; (Carlton, 645;) (Carnegie, 652;) (Carver, 643;) Cascade, 650; (Cedar, 646;) Center, 650; (Cliff, 643;) Clyde, 652; (Collingwood, 643;) (Colorado, 645, 648;) Columbia, 651; Columbus, 649; Commonwealth, 652; Como, 650; Connecticut, (648,) 650; Cottage, 649; Cottage Grove, 651; (Cowell, 645;) Cox, 646; Cramer, 649; Cremer, 652; Crescent, 648; (Dakota, 645, 648;) Decker, 649; (Delaware, 648;) Diamond, East, and West, 650; Dodge, 650; Duluth, 651; Dunedin, 649; (East, 648;) East Diamond, 650; Ebony, 650; Elm, 646; (Erie, 648;) Euclid, 650; (Fahnestock, 647;) Fay, 649; (Finlay, 648;) First to 25th E., 643, 645, 646; to 67th E., 646, 647, 648; First to 28th W., 646-7; to 81st W., 651; to 106th W., 652; to 135th W., 645; Fletcher, 652; Florence, 649; (Fond du Lac, 643;) (Forbes, 647;) Forest, 650; Franklin, 651; (Front, 646;) Furnace, 652; Gadsden, 649; Garfield, 646; Grand, 643, 644, (644,) 652; Grand Forks, 650; Granite, 651; Grant, 650; Green, 650; Hall, 652; Harvard, 649; Hematite, 652; Hemphill, 649; Hendrick, 651; (Hennepin, 643;) Highland, 650; (Howard, 648;) Hughitt, 651; Hulett, 652; Humes, 650; (Huron, 643, 648;) (Idaho, 648;) (Indiana, 645;) Industrial, 652; Irwin, 652; Junction, 650; Kanabec, 651; Keene, 652; Kennebec, 650; Kentucky, (648,) 650; Kenwood, 650; Kimberly, 652; Lake, 644, 646; Laurel, 650; (Lehigh, 652;) Lenroot, 652; (Leon, 652;) (Le Sueur, 643;) Lewiston, 650; Lincoln, (647,) 651; Livingston, 649; Lowndes, 649; Lynn, 646; Lyon, 650; (McBean, 645;) McKinnon, 650; (Mackinac, 648;) Madison, 650; Maple, 646; Marks, 650; (Maryland, 645;) Matthews, 649; (Massachusetts, 648;) Melrose, 649; Mesaba, 647, 653; Michigan, (643, 648,) 650; Minnesota, (643,) 644; Mississippi, (643,) 650; Missouri, (645,) 650; (Montana, 645;) (Moorhead, 647;) Morgan, 649; (Morrison, 645;) (Mountain, 643;) (Murray, 647;) Myers, 650; Mygatt, 649; Nelson,

646; (New York, 645;) (Newton, 645;) Niagara, (648,) 649, 650; (Oak, 646;) Ohio, (645,) 649; Oie, 646; (Ontario, 648;) (Oregon, 645;) Pacific, 650; Park, 651; (Paul, 645;) (Pennsylvania, 645;) (Perry, 645, 652;) Pickens, 649; Piedmont, 650; Pine, 646; Porter, 649; (Portman, 647;) Princeton, 649; Pringle, 649; Purcell, 652; Quebec, 648; Rice, 646; Richardson, 650; Roslyn, 649; (Roussain, 645;) (St. Clair, 648;) (St. Croix, 643;) (St. Lawrence, 648;) St. Louis, 644; (648;) (St. Marie, 648;) (St. Paul, 643;) (Sampson, 647;) (Sanford, 647;) (Sargent, 647;) Sawyer, 649; Seaver, 652; Shakopee, 648; Silcox, 649; Simonds, 652; Snelling, 649; Sparkman, 649; Spear, 649; (Spencer, 647;) Spruce, 646; Stanford, 649; Stearns, 647; Summer, 650; (Superior, 645, 648;) Swenson, 652; Sycamore, 650; Sylvan, 650; Tancred, 651; Teak, 650; Terrace, 652; (Thompson, 645;) Triggs, 650; (Vail, 647;) (Vermilion, 648;) (Vine, 646;) Virginia, (645, 648,) 650; Voss, 650; Wallace, 649; (Walnut, 646;) Warner, 650; Waverly, 649; Weber, 650; (West, 647;) West Diamond, 650; West Park, 651; Wilkyns, 649; Wilson, 649; Winnipeg, 650; Winona, 650; Winthrop, 650; Woodland, 648; York, 652; Zenith, 650

DULUTH PARKS AND BOULEVARDS: Bay View blvd., 654; Cascade sq. 653; Central pk., 653; Chester pk., 653; Congdon pk., 653; Fairmont pk., 654; Franklin sq., 652; (Garfield pk., 653;) Grosvenor sq., 653; High Beach blvd., 654; Hilltop pk., 653; Lafayette sq., 652; Lake Front pk., 653; Lester pk., 653; Lincoln pk., 649, 653; Manchester sq., 653; Mission pk., 652; Munger pk., 653; North Shore pk., 653; Occidental blvd., 654; Oriental blvd., 654; Portland sq., 653; Portman sq., 653; Rogers blvd., 654; Russell sq., 653; Washington sq., 653; (Zenith pk., 653)

Dumfries sta., 556
Dumont v., 551
Dunbar t., for W. F. Dunbar, b., 185
Duncan's l., 140
Dundas v., 462
Dundee v., 377
Dunka sta., and r., 482
Dunlap, William, for, 629, 630
Dunn l., 141, 342
Dunn t., for George W. Dunn, 393
Dunnell, Mark H., for, b., 333; n., 532
Dunnell v., 333
(Duponceau, l., 92)
Duquette v., 411
Durand t., for Charles Durand, 37
Durfee cr., for G. H. Durfee, 144
Durrie, Daniel S., 81
Du Siens, l., 124
Dutch l., 231, 590
Dutch Charley's cr., 152, 454
Dutchman l., 140
Duxbury cr., 197
Duxby p. o., 471
Dyer, Rev. John L., n., 194
Dyer, Lucius, for, 59

Eagan t., for Patrick Eagan, 165
Eagle cr., (131,) 508, 544, 547; id., 235, 591
Eagle l., 33, 59, 74, 85, 144, 147, 152, 157, 162, 163, 233, 248, 258, 274, 275, 309, 320, 337, 380, 393, 499, 516, 591
Eagle t., 74; mt., 147; rocks, 197
Eagle Bend v., 544
Eagle Creek t., 508
Eagle Lake v., 59; t., 393
Eagle Nest ls., 501
Eagle Point t., 328; l., 573
Eagle Valley t., 544
Eames, Henry H., 504
Earley, l., for William Earley, 168
(Earth Fort r., 267)
East l., 258, 295
East and West l., 141
(East Battle Lake t., 395)
East Chain t., 333; of lakes, 335, 336
East fork, Des Moines r., 337
East Grand Forks c., 423
East Greenwood l., 142
East Gull Lake t., 89
East Henderson v., 301
East Lake Lillian t., 269
East Minneapolis, 605, 606, 631

INDEX

East Palisades, l. Superior, 146
East Park t., 328
(East Richwood t., 29)
East St. Cloud, 49
East St. Peter v., 301
East Side t., 344
East Valley t., 328
Eastern t., 393
Eastman, Mrs. Mary H., quoted, 230; 252
Eastman, William W., for, 605
Easton, Elijah, n., 532
Easton v., for Jason C. Easton, b., 185
Eaton, Eber D., n., 239
Eaton, Samuel S., for, 618
Eau Claire r., Wis., 9
Ebro sta., 122
Echo l., 20, 78, 145, 181, 295, 320, 502, 537, 538, 573; t. and v., 594
Echols v., 574
Eckles t., 37
Eckloff, H. J., for, 375
Eckvoll t. and p. o., 328
Eddy, E. P., n., 190
Eddy t., for Frank M. Eddy, b., 122; p. o., 471
Eden t., 69, 417, 423; v., 172; l., 523
Eden Lake t., 523
Eden Prairie t., 221
Eden Valley v., 339, 523
Edgar cr., 233
Edgerton, Erastus S., for, 624
Edgerton v., for A. J. Edgerton, b., 417
Edgewood sta., 64
Edina v., 221
Edison t., for Thomas A. Edison, b., 540
Edna t., 393; l., 404
Edward l., 591
Edwards, Henry, n., 369
Edwards, J. N., aid, 539
Edwards t., for S. S. Edwards, 269; l., 435
Effie sta., 254
Effington t., 394
Egg ls. and r., 32; l., 573
Eggert l., 305
Eggleston, Edward, 461
Eggleston sta., 206
Egley cr., 547
Eglon t., 115
Eide l., 218
Eidsvold t., 312
Eight, l., 274
Eight Mile cr., 374
Eitzen v., 238

Eland t., 37
Elba t. and v., 582
Elbow l., 31, 143, 144, 214, 217, 247, 295, 402, 404, 414, 500, 502; r., 502
Elbow Lake t. and v., 214
Eldorado t., 536
Eldred v., for N. B. Eldred, b., 423
Eleanor, l., 319
(Eleonora l., 48)
Elephant l., 145, 502
Eleven, l., 267
Eleven towns, 406
Elfelt, A. S., C. D., and E., for, 617
Elftman, Arthur H., n., 148; for, gl. l., 299
Elgin t. and v., 556
Eli, l., for Isaac N. Eli, 548
Eliot, George, 145
Elizabeth, l., 181, 251, 271; t. and v., 394
(Elk l., now Little Rock l., 52)
Elk l., 126-131, 138, 180, 181, 204, 214, 514(2); cr., 131, 377 (2), 469; r., 514
(Elk portage and l., 138)
Elk springs, 133; Elk t., 377
Elk Horn l., 273
Elk Lake t., and l., 214
Elk River t. and v., 514
Elko v., 508
Elkton t., 116; v., 360
Elkwood t., 471
Ella l., 143, 271
Ellen l., 111, 435
Ellendale v., 532
(Ellenora, l., 182, 216)
Ellering l., 530
Ellet, Mrs. Elizabeth F., n., 221, 233
Ellingson, Knut, for, 365
Ellingson l., 218
Ellington t., 172
Elliot, Dr. Jacob S., for, 602, 608
(Elliota v., for Capt. J. W. Elliott, b., 192)
Elliott l., 500
Ellsborough t., 365
Ellsburg t., 482
Ellsmere sta., 482
Ellsworth, Eugene, for, 377
Ellsworth t., for Col. Ellsworth, 399; v., 377
Elm cr., 189, 233, 263, 333, 335; l., 331
Elm pt., 46; id., 19, 96
Elm Creek t., 333
Elm Dale t., 352
Elm Island l., 19

Elmer t., 417
Elmira t., (206,) 386
Elmo t., 394; l., 569, 572
Elmore t., for Andrew E. Elmore, b., 185
Elmwood t., 116; id., 259
Elrosa v., 524
Elsdon sta., 482
Elsie, l., 369
(Elvira, l., 244)
Elwell, Tallmadge, 352; for, 606
Ely, Rev. Edmund F., b., 482, 653
Ely c., for Arthur Ely, 482; id., 494; l., 500
(Elyria t., 191)
Elysian t., v., and l., 301; mor., 305; l., 567
Emardville, for Pierre Emard, b., 446
Embarrass r., 11, (199,) 482, (483,) 500; t. and sta., 482; l., 500
Ember l., 591
Emerald t., 185
Emerson, Ralph Waldo, for, 603
Emerson, l., 72, 576
Emily t. and l., 157; cr., 292; l., 157, 304(2), 320, 434, 435
Emma, l., 141, 342, 402, 404, (573,) 590
Emmet t., for Robert Emmet, 456
Emmons v., for Henry G. Emmons, b., 200
Empire t., 165; (v., 565; t., 594)
Encampment r. and id., 295
Enchanted id., 235
(Endion v., 482, 645, 646)
Eng l., for Erick P. Eng, 181
Engebretson, Sander, for, 408
Engelwood t., 282
England, names from, 39, 103, 115, 201, 250(2), 414, 417, 632, 635, 646, 648, 650, 653
English Grove l., for W. T. English, 180
(Enke, l., 161)
Ensign, Josiah D., for, 296
Ensign l., 296
Enstrom t., for Louis Enstrom, 471
Enterprise t., 261; hamlet, 582
Epple l., 106
Epsilon l., 297
Equality t., 446
Erdahl, Rev. Gullik M., b., 214
Erdahl t. and v., 214
Erhard v., 394
Erhard's Grove t., for A. E. Erhard, 394
Erick, l., 43

Erickson, Mandus, for, 473
Ericsburg v., 282
Ericson, Leif, 428
Ericson t., for Eric Ericson, 456
Erie t., 28; l., 324, 341; p. o., 406
Erin t., 462; l., 519, 521
Erskine l., 161; v., for J. Q. Erskine, b., 423
Erwin l., for George Erwin, 182
Eshkebugecoshe, Ojibway chief, 95
Eshquaguma l., 500
Espelee t., 328
Esquagamah t. and l., 15
Essig v., for John Essig, b., 69
Estes br., for Jonathan Estes, 349
Esther t., 424
Ethel, l., 402
Etna, a hamlet, 192
Eton sta., 417
Etter sta., for Alex. Etter, 167
Euclid t. and v., 424
Eugene t., 37
Eull's l., 591
Eunice, l., 29, 33
Eureka t., 165
Eustis J. Mage, for, 631
Evan v., 69
Evans, David C., n., 63
Evans, Matthew, n., 394
Evansville t. and v., 176
Eveleth c., 482
Even's l., 274
Evenson l., 341
Everson l., 567
(Everard l., 48)
Everglade t., 536
Evergreen t., 29, 283
Everton, Fred, n., 187
Everts t., for R. and E. A. Everts, b., 394
Ewington t., for T. C. Ewing, 261
Excel t., 328
Excelsior t. and v., 221
Eyota t. and v., 386

Fadden l., for James Fadden, 521
Fahlun t., 269
Faille l., 548
Fair Haven t. and v., 524
Fairbank, D. C., n., 172
Fairbanks, Charles W., for, b., 482
Fairbanks l., 32; v., 482
Fairfax t., 424; v., 457
Fairfield cr., for Edwin, George, and L. D. Fairfield, 179
Fairfield t., 157, 541; (v., 167)
Fairmont c. and t., 333

INDEX

Fairpoint v., 206
Fairview t., 89, 254, 312, (378)
Fairy l., 404, 545, 547
Fall r., 137, 144
Fall Lake t., and l., 294, 296
Fallon l., 341
Falls cr., 465
False Poplar r., 144
Falun t., 471
Fancher, A. N., 332
Fanny, l., 140, 251, 273; t., 424
Farden t., for Ole J. Farden, 243
Fargo c., N. D., for W. G. Fargo, b., 117
Faribault, Alexander, for, 183, b., 462
Faribault, Jean Baptiste, for, b., 183
Faribault co., 183-189; c. and t., 462
Farley sta., 37; t., for J. P. Farley, b., 424
Farm l., 296; id., 15, 495
Farm Island t. and l., 15, 20
Farmers' Alliance, 114, 115
Farming t., 524
(Farmington t., 84)
Farmington v., 167; t., 386
Farnham br. and l., for Sumner W. Farnham, b., 563
Farquhar peak, 147; l., for John Farquhar, 168
Farrington, John, for, 615
Farris v., 243
Farwell v., 431
Fauquier, Francis, for, 624
Fawn l., 162(2), 248, 544
Fawn Lake t., 544
Faxon t. (and v.), 519
Fay l., 141
Fayal t., and iron mine, 482
Featherstone t., for William Featherstone, 206
Featherstonhaugh, G. W., 4, 443, 448
Feathery l., 267
Federal Dam v., 89
Fedje l., 576
Feeley t., for Thomas J. Feeley, 254
Feldman t., 283
Felix l., 547
Felton t., for S. M. Felton, 116
Fenley shore, for W. E. Fenley, 347
Fensted l., 502
Fenton, William, for, 618
Fenton t., for P. H. Fenton, 365
Fergus, James, for, b., 394, 395
Fergus Falls, 2; c., 77, 394; t., 394
Fergus Falls moraine, 404

Fermoy sta., 483
Fern l., 43, 141
Fern t., for Richard Fern, 243; 483
Ferndale, l. Minnetonka, 235
Ferrel l., 320
Fertile v., 424
(Fever r., 510)
Field, Ira, for, 308
Field, Ira Stratton, for, b., 463
Field l., 218; t., 483
Fieldon t., 575
Fig l., 500
Fillmore, Millard, for, b., 190, 605
Fillmore co., 190-197; t., 192, 196
Fine Lakes t., 483
Finkle sta., for Henry G. Finkle, 116
Finland, names from, 16, 74, 294, 490, 491, 492
Finland v., 294
Finlayson t. and v., for David Finlayson, 411
Finn, William, for, 441, 634
Finn's glen, 441; Finn l., 141, 563
First l., 112
Fischer l., 512
Fish, Judge Daniel, 306
Fish cr., 56, 108, 592; id., 494
Fish l., 26, 108, 151, 180, 233, 264, 267(2), 304, 324, 337(2), 357(2), 401, 402, 415, 512, 530, 537, 538, 567, 573, 592
Fish Hook r. and l., 30, 32, 244, 247; pt., 145
Fish Lake t., 108
Fish Trap l., 162, 356; br., 356, 547
Fisher, Ada N., for, 381
Fisher, William H., 381; for, b., 424
Fisher t., 424
(Fisher's Landing v., 424)
Fiske l., 401
Fitzhugh l., 442
Fitzpatrick sta., 514
Fitzsimmons, Thomas, n., 202; Patrick, n., 202
Five l., 404
Five Mile cr., 56
Flacon portage, 496
Flag id., 44
Flaherty, l., 264
Flaming v., 382
Flandrau, Charles E., 4, 94; for, b., 419, 623
Flandreau cr., 419
Flat l., 32
Flat Mouth, v., Ojibway chief, 95
Flea pt., 95
Fleming l., 20; t., 15, 411

680 INDEX

Flensburg v., 352
Fletcher Boundary cr., 357
Floating Bog cr. and bay, 132
Floating Moss l., 130
Flom t., for Erik Flom, 382
Flood, James H., n., 550
Flood bay, 295
Floodwood r., 11, 483; t. and v., 483; l., 499
Flora of Minnesota, 106; Flora t., 457
Florence l., 251, 389
Florence t., (84,) 206; v., 312
Florer l., 465
Florida, names from, 274, 292, 536, 594
Florida, l., 274; cr., 292, 594; t., 594
Florida Slough l., 274
Flour l., 140, 142
(Flower l., 142)
Flowing t., 116
Floyd Is., 32
Flute Reed r., 145
Fogg l., for F. A. Fogg, 349
Foldahl t., 328
Folden t., 395
Foley v., for John Foley, b., 50
(Folle Avoine r., 18; country, 321)
Folsom, Simeon P., n., 59
Folsom, William H. C., n., 107, 265; q., 109, 110, 411, 441, 570
Folsom t., for George P. Folsom, 551
Folwell, Dr. W. W., 3, 236; n., 608, 609; for, 631
Fond du Lac reservation, 79, 506
Fond du Lac trading post and v., 73, 76; 483, 645, 652
Fool's l., 162
Foot l., for Solomon R. Foot, b., 273
Forada v., 176
Forbes, William H., for, 613, 614
Forbes v., 483; l., 500
Ford, L. M., quoted, 22
Ford br., 25; t., for Henry Ford, 266
Forest l., 232; t., 462
Forest and Prairie cr., 302
Forest area of Minnesota, 2, 118
Forests, state and national, 100, 148, 299, 506
Forest City t., 339
Forest Grove t., 283
Forest Lake t. and v., 569
Forest Prairie t., 339
Foreston v., 344

Forestville t. and v., 193
Forget-me-not, l., 33
Fork t., 328
Forsyth, Major Thomas, 11; q., 572, 583
Fort cr., 374, 459
Fort Abercrombie, N. D., 580
Fort Charlotte, 136
Fort Frances v., Ont., 283
(Fort Gaines, 355)
Fort L'Huillier, 57
Fort Ridgely, 373
Fort Ripley, 157, b., 355; v., 157
Fort St. Anthony, 34, 67; map, 168; 170, 507
Fort St. Antoine, Wis., 3
Fort St. Charles, 45
Fort Snelling, 227, 228, 236, 602; military reservation, 236
Fortier t., for Joseph Fortier, b., 594
Fosket, Mark, n., 589
Foss l., 538
Fossen l., 401
Fosston v., for Louis Foss, 424
Fossum t., 382
Foster, Dr. Thomas, n., 481, 652
Foster, William, n., 84
Foster l., 591
Foster t., for Dr. R. R. Foster, b., 185
Foster v., 54
Fountain cave, 444, 628
Fountain t. and v., 193; l., 203, 204, 590
Fountain Prairie t., 417
Fouqué, Friedrich, 65
Four Mile bay, 44; l., 98, 143, 218; cr., 469
Four Towns l., 258
Four-legged l. and cr., 125
Fourteen Mile l., 87, 98; cr., 99
Fowl portage and ls., 138, 140
Fowler, George S., 332, 333
Fox l., 33, 43, 65; ls., East, and West, 163; (203,) 232, 258, 272, 333, 337, 369, 375, 460, 465
Fox v., 471
Fox Lake t., 333
Foxhome t. and v., for R. A. Fox, 578
Framnas t., 536
France, names from, 279, 425, 433
Frances, l., 90, 98
Francis, l., 251, 304, 342, 591
Franconia t. and v., 108, 113
Frank l., 542
Frankford t. and v., 360

INDEX

Frankfort t. and v., 588
Franklin, Benjamin, for, b., 254; 603, 613, 652
Franklin, Samuel, for, 603
Franklin l., 404; t., 254, 588; v., 457
Frankson, Thomas, for, n., 630
Franquelin, J. B., map by, 10, 12, 79, 476
Franson, Eric, for, 282
Fraser l., for John Fraser, 296
Fraser t., for A. N. Fraser, 333
Frazee v., for R. L. Frazee, b., 28
Frazer bay, 494, 495
Frazier l., 132
Frear l., 143, 295
Fredenberg t., for Jacob Fredenberg, 483
(Frederica l., 48)
Frederick cr., 590
Frederick's l., for F. Ohland, 85
Freeborn, William, for, b., 198, 572
Freeborn co., 198-204; t., 200; id., 572
Freeborn l., for John Freeborn, 181; 203
Freeburg v. 238
Freedom t., 66, 565
Freeland t., for J. P. Free, 289
Freeman t., for John Freeman, 200; cr., 547
Freeport v., 524
Fremont, John C., for, 59, b., 334, 369, 515, 582, 601, 603, 622; n., 60, 308
Fremont, l., 369; 515; t., 582; (v., 59)
French, Burton, for, 594
French, Leonard, for, 123
French cr., for G. H. French, 132; 588
French l., 20, 141, 232, 233, 465, 588; rapids, 163; r., 483, 492
French sta., 395; t., for W. A. French, 483
French Lake t., 588
French River v., 483
Frenchman's bluff, 384
Frevel's l., 530
Friberg t., 395
Friday l., 296
Fridley t., for A. M. Fridley, b., 23
Friendship t., 594
Friesland sta., 411
Froberg, Alfred, n., 593
Frog and Little Frog ls., 538
Frog Rock l., 141
Frohn t., 37
Frontenac v., 207, 212

Frost l., 141; v., for C. S. Frost, 186
Frovold, l., for K. P. Frovold, 542
Fulda v., 366
Fuller, Alpheus G., for, 617
Fulton, Robert, for, 644
Funkley t., for Henry Funkley, 37; l., 43
Fur trade, 14, 135, 136, 423

Gabbro l., 296
Gabimichigama l., 141, 296
(Gager's sta., for Henry Gager, 535, 538)
Gaines, Gen. E. P., for, b., 355
Gaiter l., 567
Gale, Samuel C., for, 605, 609
Gale id., for Harlow A. Gale, 235
Galena t., 333
Gales t., for A. L. and S. S. Gale, 449
Galloway, Dr. Hector, n., 387
Galpin's l., for Rev. Charles Galpin, 231
Galtier, Father Lucian, n., quoted, 438; b., 439; for, 617
Games l., 274
Gamma l., 297
Gannett, Henry, quoted or cited, 6, 10, 202, 251, 254, 256, 258, 263, 270, 373, 565, 570, 584, 585, 589
Ganon id., for Peter Ganon, 146
Gansey l., 501
Garden id., 44, 96; l., 162, 294, 296; t., 424
Garden City, t. and v., 59
Gardner l., for Charles Gardner, 324
Garfield, James A., for, b., 176, 247, 290, 424, 602, 605, 614, 646, 653
Garfield v., 176; l., 247; t., 290, 424
Garnes t., for E. K. Garnes, 446
Garrard bluff, for Louis H. and Israel Garrard, b., 212
Garrison, Oscar E., for, 132, 158; n., 345, 348
Garrison pt., 132; t., 158
Garvin v., for H. C. Garvin, 312
Gary, Elbert H., for, 652
Gary moraine, 309; v., 382; d., 652
Gaskan l., 140
"Gate City," 584
Gates, Albert, n., 58
Gault, Z. S., aid, 372
(Gauss, l., 89)
Gaylord v., for E. W. Gaylord, 519
Geis l., 512

682 INDEX

Gem l., 501
Gemmell v., for W. H. Gemmell, 283
General features, geography of Minnesota, 1-13
Geneva, l., 177, 180; t. and v., 200
Geneva Beach v., 177
Gennessee t., 270
Genoa v., 386
Genola v., 352, 354
Gentilly t., 425
George, Capt. Sylvester A., for, 72
George, l., 26, 65, 72, 99, 141, 204, 274, 336, 401, 524, 530
George Watch l., 25
Georgetown trading post and t., 116
Georgeville v., 524
Georgia, name from, 630
German l., 251, 304, 401
Germania t., 544
Germantown t., 150
Germany, names from, 50, 70, 82 (2), 83(2), 105, 108, 117, 136, 167, 238(2), 263, 301, 327, 366, 387, 395, 411, 484, 518, 520. 525, 526, 531, 540, 588, 596
Gervais l., for Benjamin Gervais, b., 442
Gervais t., for Isaiah Gervais, b., 446
Getchell, C. S., n., 568
Getchell cr., for Nathaniel Getchell, b., 529; l., 530
Getty t., for John J. Getty, b., 524
Gheen v., for Edward H. Gheen, b., 483
Ghent v., 312
(Giant mt., 1, 147)
Giants' Kettles, Interstate pk., 113
Gibbon v., for Gen. John Gibbon, 519
Gibbs, Heman, for, 631
Gibson l., 499
Gideon's bay, for P. M. Gideon, b., 234
Gifford l., 512
Gilbert l., 162, 163, 181
Gilbert v., for E. A. Gilbert, 483
Gilbert Valley cr., 559
Gilbertson, l., 435
Gilchrist t., and l., 431; l., 591
Gilfillan, Charles D., for, 443, b., 449; 460
Gilfillan, John B., 220, 224
Gilfillan, Rev. Joseph A., for, b., 132; quoted or cited, 1, 6, 9, 17, 18, 28, 29, 31-3, 36, 48, 52, 87-90,
93, 96, 97, 99, 102, 119, 121, 124, 125, 129, 130, 132, 136-8, 140, 142-4, 146, 147, 154, 156, 159, 160, 161, 247, 256-8, 280, 281, 286, 293, 295-8, 322, 331, 343, 348, 356, 367, 390, 393, 400, 408, 412, 425, 428, 429, 445, 470, 488, 489, 493, 496-500, 504, 546, 547, 550, 560, 561, 571
Gilfillan l., 132, 443; sta.. 449
Gilfillin l., for Joseph Gilfillin, b., 65
Gill l., 126; Gill's l., 141
Gillespie br., 77
Gillford t. and v., for Mr. and Mrs. Gill, 556
Gilman, Charles A., 49, 522; for, b., 50
Gilmanton t., 50
Gilmore l., 248; cr., 585
Gilsted l., 43
Girard, Stephen, for, 395, 603
Girard t., 395; sta., 425
Girl l., 99
Glacial lakes, 7, 21, 56, 66, 79, 134, 148, 189, 218, 299, 444, 504-5, 654
Glacier Garden, 113
Gladstone l., 162; v., for W. E. Gladstone, 437
Glasgow t., 556
Glazier, Alice, for, 244; Elvira, for, 244; George, for, 244
Glazier, Willard, 126; b., 127; 134; n., 244, 246
(Glazier, l., 127, 128)
Gleason l., 232
Glen t., 15; l., 152, 231
Glencoe c. and t., 317
Glendale sta., 483; t., 508
Glendorado t., 50
(Glengarry t., 24)
Glenville v., 201
Glenwood c. and t., 2, 431
Glenwood l. and park, 232, 607
Glesne l., for Even O. Glesne, 274
Gluek's pt., 234
Glyndon v., 116
Gnat l., 43
Gneiss l., 139
Gnesen t., 483
Godfrey, Ard, n., 515
Godfrey, John, and Josephine, for, 147
Godfrey t., for W. N. Godfrey, 425
Gold washing, 174
(Gold Fish cr., 45)
Golden l., for John Golden, 25
Golden Valley, suburb of Minneapolis, 221; t., 471
Goldschmidt l., 85

INDEX 683

Goldsmith l., 304
Gonvick v., for M. O. Gonvick, 122
Good Harbor bay, 145; hill, 147
Good Hope t., 254, 382
Good Ridge t., 406
Good Road, Sioux v., 220
Good Thunder v., and ford, for Winnebago chief, 59; Sioux scout, 60
Goodhue, James M., 67; for, b., 205; 207; q., 224; for, 614
Goodhue co., 205-212; t. and v., 207
Gooding, Mrs. George, for, 168, 231
Goodland t., 254
Goodner's l., 529
Goodrich, Aaron, for, 614
Goodrich l., 162
Goose cr., 111, 203; id., 95
Goose l., 26, 85, 99, 111, 189, 204, 211, 233, 303, 304, 315, 337, 341, 357, 375, 434, 454, 511, 547, 567, 573, 591(2)
Goose Prairie t., 116
Gooseberry r., (138,) 295
Gopher state, 4
Gordon, Hanford L., 235, 581
Gordon t., for J. M. Gordon, 544
Gordonsville v., for T. J. Gordon, 201
Gorman, Gov. Willis A., for, b., 304, 619
Gorman l., 304
Gorman t., for John O. Gorman, 395
Gorman's l., for Patrick Gorman, 189
Gorton t., 215
Goslee, W. N., and J. H., n., 201
Götaholm neighborhood, 85
Gotha v., 82
Gotzian, Conrad, and Adam, for, 623
Gould, Helen, for, 96
Gould t., for M. I. Gould, 89
Gould's l., for John L. Gould, 538
Gourd l., 402
Governor's id., 146
Gowdy t., 283
Grace, Bishop Thomas L., for, b., 54, 615
Grace l., 43, 143, 248
Grace t., 103
Graceville t. and v., 54
Grafton t., 519
Graham, Judge C. C., b., 206, 207
Graham, Florence, for, 206
Graham, James D., for, 153, b., 377
Graham l., 218, 305, 377, 404

Graham t., 50
Graham Lakes t., 377
Grainwood sta. and v., 508
Gran t., 254
Granada v., 333
Granby t., 372
Grand id., 96, 517; l., 483, 498, 530
(Grand Bois, 2)
Grand Falls t., 283
Grand Forks t., 425
Grand Lake t. and sta., 483; r., 498
Grand Marais, 1; t. and v., 136
Grand Marais, marsh, 170, 442; r., 428
Grand Meadow t. and v., 360
Grand Park t., 29
Grand Plain t., 328
Grand Portage v. and trading post, 136, 148; bay and id., 146
Grand Prairie t., 377
(Grand Rapids, 51)
Grand Rapids t. and v., 254
Grandmother hill, 503
Grandrud l., 403
Grandview t., 313
Grandy v., 250
Grange, the, Barn bluff, 211; t., 417
Granger v., 193
Granite bay, 139; l., 140, 591; pt., 295, 493; t., 352
"Granite City," (v., 352;) 527
Granite Falls t. and c., 103; c., 594
Granite Ledge t., 50
Granite Rock t., 450
Grant, U. S., geologist, 282, 298, 498
Grant, Gen. Ulysses S., for, b., 213; 498, 569, 604, 605
Grant co., 213-218; t. 569
Grant l. and cr., 37; (t., 187, 209, 378)
Grant's lake, for Noah Grant, 181
Grant Valley t., 37
Granville t., 277
Grass l., 26, 43, 111, 162, 204, 231, 233, 266, 273(2), 320, 402, 415, 443, 529, 530, 592
Grass Lake t., 266
Grasston v., 266
Grassy l., 181; id., 286; narrows, 286; pt., 493
(Gratiot, l., for Gen. Charles Gratiot, 160)
Grattan t., for Henry Grattan, 255
Grave l., 99, 162, 258
Gravel l., 530, 538; (r., 34, 48)
(Gravelville v., for C. and N. Gravel, 352)
Gray, Royal C., for, 413

Gray l., 404, 548; t., for A. O. Gray, 418
Gray's l. or bay, 233
Gray Cloud id., 552, 572, 573; sl., 572
Greaney v., for Patrick Greaney, 484
Great Bend t., 150
Great Lakes, 8
Great Northern ry., 25, 540; l., 530
Great Oasis l., 369
Great Portage, 41; (r., 46)
Great Scott t., 484
Greece, names from, 105, 250, 477
Green, Prof. Samuel B., n., 631
Green l., 48, 111, 112, 133, 251, 270; (r., 57)
Green Isle t. and v., 519
Green Lake t., 270
Green Leaf t., 304
Green Meadow t., 382
Green Mountain l., 591
Green Prairie t., for C. H. Green, 352; (597)
Green Stump l., 331
Green Valley t., 29; v., 313
Green Water l., 32
Greenbush t., 344; v., 471
Greenfield t., 556, (569)
Greenfield, William H., for, b., 339; 341
Greenleafton, a hamlet, for Mary Greenleaf, 193
Greenvale t., 165
Greenwald v., 524
Greenway t., for J. C. Greenway, 255
Greenwood, George C., for, 296
Greenwood t., 122, 222; l., 140, 145, 296; r., 145; mt., 298
Greenwood Island l., 141, 142
Greer l., 162
Gregory park, Brainerd, 156; v., 156, 352
Gregory t., for Joseph Gregory, 323, 324; (for H. G. Gregory, 468)
Grey, Col. Alfred, 466
Grey Eagle t. and v., 544
Griffin, l., 542
Griffith, May, for, 90
Griggs, Chauncey W., n., 605; for, 630
Grimstad t., for John Grimstad, 472
Grindstone id., 286; r. and l., 414
Grogan v., for M. J. Grogan, 575
Groningen sta., 412

Grotto l., 401
Groseilliers l., 130, 134
Ground House r., 267
Grove l., 120, 217, 272, 404, 431, 434
Grove t., 524
Grove City v., 340
Grove Lake t., 431
Grove Park t., 425
Groveland Park d., 440, 637
Grow t., for Galusha A. Grow, b., 24
Grubb l., 181
Gruenhagen's l., 85
Grummons, Martin, for, 457
Grunard l., 403
Gudrid t., 37
Guernsey, l., 547
Gull l. and r., 43, 89, 100, 142, 296
Gull species, 142; id., 142
Gull River sta., 89
Gullickson l., 598
Gully t., 425
Gun l., 20; Gunn l., 258
Gunder p. o., 122
Gunflint l., 139
Gust l., for Gust Hagberg, 143
Gutches pt., 548
Guthrie t., for Archibald Guthrie, 243
(Guthrie t., for Sterrit Guthrie, 184)
Gwinn's bluff, 585

Haam l., 512
Haberstead l., 143
Hackberry l., 454
Hackensack v., 89
Hadler v., for Jacob Hadler, 382
Hadley v., 366
Hafften l., 233
Hagali t., 37
Hagen t., 116
Hahn l., for William Hahn, b., 521
Haldeman, Benjamin F., for, 642
Halden t., for Odin Halden, b., 484
Hale l., for James T. Hale, 258
Hale t., for John P. Hale, b., 317
Haley sta., 484
Half Moon l., 232, 342; id., 347
Halfway br., 52; pt., 46, 346
Hall, William S., for, 619; n., 624, 625
Hall l., for Edwin S. Hall, 131; for E. B. Hall, 336; (454)
Hallock t. and v., for Charles Hallock, b., 277
Halma v., 278

INDEX

Halstad t. and v., for Ole Halstad, b., 382
Halsted's bay, for F. W. and G. B. Halsted, b., 234
Halvorson l., 530
Ham l., 141, 247, 356
Ham Lake t. and l., 24
Hamburg v., 83
Hamden t., 29
Hamel v., for J. O. and W. Hamel, 222
Hamilton v., 193, 360, (510)
Hamlet l., 162
Hamlin, Lois Arlone, for, 410
Hamlin, W. H., n., 410
Hamlin t., for John R. Hamlin, 290
Hamline, Bishop L. L., for, 630
Hamline d., 440, 629-631; gl. l., 444; l., 573
Hamline University, 440, 629, 631
Hamm, Theodore, for, 641
Hammer t., 595
Hammond l., 174; t., 425; v. for Joseph Hammond, 556
Hampden, John, for, 278, 632, 641
Hampden t., 278
Hampton t., 165; v., 167
Hamre t., 37
Hanchett, Dr. Augustus H., n., 146
Hancock, Rev. J. W., quoted, 207, 208, 209; for, b., 536
Hancock, Gen. W. S., for, b., 83, 623
Hancock t., 83, (527;) v., 536
Hand, Dr. Daniel W., for, 628
Hand l., 404
Hanford l., 181
Hangaard t., for G. G. Hangaard, 122
Hanging Horn l., 78
Hanging Kettle l., 20
Hanks l., 162
Hanley Falls v., 595
Hanover v., 588
Hanrahan l., for E. Hanrahan, 512
Hanse l., 538
Hansel l., 401
Hansen, Rev. Hans P., n., 330
Hanska v., 69
Hansman l., 547
Hanson, D. M., and G. S., for, 601
Hanson, Mrs. Hilda, for, 407
Hanson, Timothy, 160
Hanson br., for G. S. Hanson, 349
Hanson l., 402, 434, 538
(Hanson sta., for Nels Hanson, 69)

Hansonville t., for John Hanson, 307
Hantho t., for H. H. Hantho, 290
Harbaugh, Springer, n., 424
Hard Scrabble pt., 234
Harder's l., 152
Harding l., for Rev. W. C. Harding, 340
Hardwick v., for J. L. Hardwick, 467
Hare l., and Nowthen p. o., for James U. Hare, 26
Harkcom cr., 174
Harlis sta., 412
Harmon, Allen, for, 604
Harmony t., 193
Harold, l., 342
Harper, C. H., n., 255
Harriet, l., 229, 236, 295; id., 441, 614
Harrigan t., 283
Harrington, l., for Lewis Harrington, b., 319, 320
Harris t. and v., for P. S. Harris, 108; t., for Duncan Harris, 255; cr., 547
Harris Lake sta. and l., 484
Harrison, Benjamin, for, 605
Harrison, William Henry, for, 601, 605, 614
Harrison, l., 404; t., for J. D. Harris, 270
Harrison's bay, 235
Harry, l., 233
Harstad l., for Lars E. Harstad, 538
Hart, D. A., n., 469
Hart l., for John and George Hart, 189; 243, 257; for Isaac Hart, 542; t., 582
Hart Lake t., 243
Hartford t., 544
Hartland t. and v., 201
Hartley l., 162
Hartshorn, Madelia, for, 575
Harvey cr., 152
Harvey t., for James Harvey, 340
Haslerud, Peter Peterson, for, b., 194
Hassan t., 222
Hassan Valley t. (and r.), 317, 319
Hassel, l., 542
(Hassler, l., for F. R. Hassler, 88)
Hastings c., 165
Hasty v., for Warren Hasty, 588
Hat pt., 146
Hatch, Edwin A. C., for, 627

Hatch, Dr. P. L., notes of birds, 154
Hatch l., for Zenas Y. Hatch, 465
Hatfield v., 418
Hattie, l., 99, 538
Haug p. o., for T. E. Haug, 472
Haugen t., for C. G. Haugen, 15
Haughey l., 232
Hausmann l., 232
Havana t. and v., 532
Havelock t., for Sir. H. Havelock, b., 103
Haven t., for John O. Haven, b., 515
Haverhill t., 386
Hawes, Eva Luverne, for, b., 467
Hawes, Philo, for, b., 468; n., 468
Hawk cr., 106, 273, 457, 459; l., 369
Hawk Bill pt., 346
Hawk Creek t., 457
Hawkinson cr., 502
Hawley, Alfred C., for, 628
Hawley v., for Gen. J. R. Hawley, b., 116
Hay cr., 46, 77, 111, 120(2), 207, 357(2), 414, 415, 475, 529, 563 (2); l., 78, 247, 573; ls., Upper, and Lower, 162
Hay Brook t., and br., 266, 267
Hay Creek t., and cr., 207
Hayden, James, n., 564
Hayden l. and br., 549; cr., 563
Hayden's l., 233
Haydenville sta., for H. L. Hayden, 290
Hayes, Rutherford B., for, b., 541; 605
Hayes, Rev. S. M., quoted, 513
Hayes t., 541; l., 567
Hayfield t. and v., 173
Hayland t., 344
Hays l., 132
Hayward t. and v., for D. Hayward, 201
Hazel v., 406
(Hazel Dell v., 397)
Hazel Park sta., 437
Hazel Run t. and v., 595
Hazeltine, Susan, for, 85
Hazelton l., 20
Hazelton t., for C. J. Hazelton, 15; 278
Hazelwood, mission station, 595
Hazzard, George H., 112, 611; for, 628
Head, George, n., 388
Head l., 403
Heart l., 126

Heath, Charles, n., 417
Heath cr., 465
Heather, James W., for, 635
(Hebbard t., for W. F. Hebbard, 378)
Hebron t., 15
Heckman sta., 313
Hector t. and v., 457
Hefta, l. of, for Mrs. Marie Hefta, 274
Hegbert t., 541
Hegg l., for Erick Hegg, 181
Hegne t., for Andrew E. Hegne, 382
Heiberg v., for J. F. Heiberg, 382
Heidelberg v., 301
Heider, Mrs. Andrea, for, 577
Heier t., for Frank Heier, 323
Height of Land t. and l., 29, 30
(Height of Land l., 124, 139)
Heim's l., for Conrad Heim, 111
Helen, l., 96, 257; t., 317
Helena t. and sta., 508; l., 567
Helga t., 243; l., 342
Helge, l., 434
Helgeland t., 425
Helm, H. C., and Joseph, for, 647
(Helvetia v., 83)
Hen l., 162
Henderson, Andrew, for, 519
Henderson, c. and t., 68, 519; l., 273
Hendricks l., t., and v., for T. A. Hendricks, b., 307; 310
Hendrickson t., for John C. Hendrickson, 243
Hendrum t. and v., 382
Henn l., 530
Hennepin, Father Louis, 5, 10, 25, 130; quoted, 209; for, b., 219; 343, 348, 553, 601
Hennepin co., 219-236; id., 229, 347;(v., 222;) l. and r., 246
Henning t., for John O. Henning, 395
Henrietta t., 243; l., 251
Henriette v., 412
Henry, Alexander, the elder, 91, 138; the younger, 149
Henry, Forest, for, 193
Henry, l., 181, 304, 524, 525, 542; for Lewis Henry, 548; 591
Henry t., 283
Henrytown, a hamlet, 193
Henryville t., for Peter Henry, 457
Henshaw l., 591
Henson l., 140
Hereford v., 215

INDEX 687

Hereim t., for Ole Hereim, 472
Herman t., 484, 650; l., 85, 502
Herman v., 215
Herman beach, Lake Agassiz, 120, 218, 505
Hernando de Soto, l., 130, 134
Heron Lake t., and l., 261
Herrick, Prof. C. L., quoted, 292; 297
Hersey t. (and v.), for S. F. Hersey, b., 377
Hewitt, Girart, for, 630; 634
Hewitt v., for Henry Hewitt, 544
Heyer's l., for Louis Heyer, 85
Hiawatha, Song of, cited, 6, 39, 43, 75, 87, 90, 118, 134, 159, 226, 230, 231, 235, 255, 258, 293, 321, 324, 367, 397, 416, 453, 561, 602, 607, 609; Myth of, 565
Hibbing c., for Frank Hibbing, b., 484
Hickey's l., 511
Hickory l., 20; t., 407
Hicks, Henry G., 224
Hidatsa Indians, Minnesota, 267
Higbie, Albert E., n., 31
Higdem t., for A. O. Higdem, 425
Higgins sta., 294; l., 320
High id., 146; l., 336
High Bank l., 598
High Beach blvd., 654
High Forest t. and v., 386
High Island cr. and l., 319, 520
High Landing t., 407
Highland, a hamlet, 193; sta., 294; l., 295; t., 556
Highland Grove t., 116
Highwater cr. and t., 150, 152
Highwood sta., 437
Hilda p. o., 407
Hill, Alfred J., 35, 57, 128; n., 130; for, 132
Hill, James J., for, b., 278
Hill l., 15, 138; pt., 132; r., 425, 428, t., 278
Hill City, v., 15
Hill Lake t., 15, 16
Hill River t., 425
Hillman t., for W. F. Hillman, 266; t., v., and br., 352
Hills, Alma, for, 564
Hills, Sylvester, n., 361
Hills, l. of the, 315
Hills v., for F. C. Hills, 467
Hillsdale id., 495; t., 582
Hillside Harbor l., 607
(Hilo t., 372)

(Hilton v., for Aaron Hilton, 62)
Hinckley, Isaac, for, b., 412
Hinckley t. and v., 410, 412
Hind, Henry Y., cited, 97
Hinds l., for Edward R. Hinds, 247
Hines sta., for William Hines, 37
Hingeley, Rev. J. B., 400
Hinman, Kelsey, n., 222
Hinsdale sta., 484
Hiram t., for Hiram Wilson, 89
Hitchcock, George, n., 172
Hitterdal v., 117
Hoag, Addie, for, 319; Marion, for, 319
Hoag, Charles, n., 223, 319
Hobart id., 357; t. and v., 395
Hobson l., 501
Hockridge l., 304
Hodge, F. W., 30, 59, 71
Hodges t., for L. B. Hodges, b., 536
Hodgson l., 460
Hoeffken's l., 85
Hoff l., 341; t., 431, (for Abel Hoff, 550)
Hoffman, James K., for, 621, 622
Hoffman l., 251
Hoffman v., for R. C. Hoffman, 215
Hokah t. and v., 12, 238
Holcombe, R. I., 22, 81, 94, 260; q., 421; 460
Holcombe, William, for, 642
Holden t., 207
Holding, Randolph, for, b., 524
Holding t., 524
Holding's Ford v., 524
Hole-in-the-Day's bluff, 357
Hole in the Mountain, 310
Holes, Andrew, n., 270
Holland, names from, 150, 270, 412, 418
Holland t., 270; v., 418
Holleque l., 181
Holley, Henry W., and wife, n., 184, 185
Hollinshead, Mrs. Ellen, for, 617
Hollow Rock cr., 145
Holloway v., 541
Holly t., for John Z. Holly, 366
Hollywood t., 83
Holman's l., 529
Holmes, Thomas A., for, b., 177; 222, 508; n., 510
Holmes, William, n., 508
Holmes l., 337

Holmes City, t., 177; l., 181
Holmesville t., for E. G. Holmes, b., 29
Holst t., for H. J. Holst, 122
Holt, Cyrus, n., 388
Holt l., 161; t., for Gilbert Holt, 193; t. and v., 328
Holy Cross t., 117
Holyoke sta. and t., 74
Home t., 70; br., 89, 100; l., 382
Home Brook t. and p. o., 89
Home Lake t., 382
Homelvig, John, for, 382
Homer l., 145; t. and v., 582
Homestead laws, 24; t., 395
Homolka p. o., for A. Homolka, 472
Homstad l., 32
Honner t., for J. S. G. Honner, b., 450
Hoodoo pt., 494
Hook l., for Isaac Hook, 320; 404
Hoop l., 342
Hoosier l., 341
Hoot l., 402
Hope t., 307; (l., 342;) sta., 533
Hopkins v., for H. H. Hopkins, b., 222; l., 576
Horace Austin state park, 363
Horn l., 78; the Horn, Pigeon r., 138
Hornby sta., for H. C. Hornby, b., 484
Hornet t., 37
Horse l., 296; Horse Leg l., 251
Horsehead l., 401
Horse-race rapids, 415
Horseshoe bay, 145; cr., 111; l., 20, 111, 140, 162, 179, 182, 218, 251, 258, 303, 342, 375, 401, 402, 454, 530, 548, 572, 573(2)
Horton, Hiler H., for, 627, 641
Horton sta., for E. H. Horton, 244; for Charles Horton, b., 387; t., for W. T. Horton, b., 536
Hosmer, J. W., n., 565
Hotchkiss, F. V., for, and n., 452
Houg l., 32
Houghton, Dr. Douglass, 91; for, 98; q., 321
(Houlton t., 457)
Houlton sta., for W. H. Houlton, b., 515
House l., 598
Houston, Samuel, for, b., 237, 238
Houston co., 237-241; t.. 238
Hovland t., 136; v., 145

Howard, Mrs. Jane Schoolcraft, for, 132
Howard, John, for, b., 588
Howard, Thomas, for, 625
Howard cr., 132; l., 25, 141, 512, 588
Howard's pt., 234
Howard Lake v., 588
Howe l., 32
Hoyt, Benjamin F., 612; for, 629
Hoyt, Daniel, n., 339
Hub l., 141
Hubbard, Gov. L. F., for, b., 242, 244, 425, 630
Hubbard co., 131, 242-248
Hubbard t. and prairie, 244; t., 425
Hubert l., for St. Hubert, 161, 162
Hubred l., for Oliver Hubred, 182
Hudson t., 177
Hudson Bay Co., 76, 116
Huey, George E., for, 601
Huff, Henry D., n., 584
Hughes, Robert H., n., 58
Hughes, Thomas, 57, 58; q., 61, 63; 64, 375
Hugo, Trevanion W., for, b., 569, 650
Hugo v., 569
Hugunin, Mrs. James H., n., 570
Hulbert, D. B., n., 166
Hull's Narrows, for Rev. S. Hull, 234
Hultgren, Nels, n., 278
Humbertson, Capt. Samuel, 63
Humboldt, Alexander, for, b., 117; 603, 609
Humboldt t., 117; v., 278, (514)
Humes, E. C., for, 650
Humiston, Ransom F., for, b., 379
Hummel, l., 72
Hungary, names from, 312, 350
Hungry l., 33
Hungry Jack l., 140
Hunt, D. H., for, 632
Hunt, W. G., n., 408
Hunt l., for Joseph Hunt, 181, 182; 304, 465
Hunter t., for James W. Hunter, b., 261
Hunter's Island, 298, 497, 505; pt., 346
Huntersville t., 561
Huntington, Henry M., for, b., 186
Huntington pt., 235
Huntley v., 186; t., 328
Huntsville t., for Bena Hunt, 425
Huot v., and Louisville t., for Louis Huot, 446

INDEX

Hurley l., 341
Hurricane l., 152
Huset l., 218
Huss t., for John Huss, 472
Hutchins, Lyle, 145
Hutchins l., 591
Hutchinson c. and t., for Asa, Judson, and John Hutchinson, b., 317, 318
Hutter sta., for H. A. Hutter, 484
Hyde, John E., for, b., 557
Hyde l., for Ernst Heyd, 85
Hyde Park t., 556
Hyland l., 231
Hystad l., for A. O. Hystad, 274

Iberia hamlet and p. o., 70
Iberville, governor of Louisiana, 57
Ice l., 112
Ice Cracking l., 32
(Iceland t., 62)
Ida, l., 33, 65, 141, 177, 180, 383, 591; t., 177
Ida Belle, l., for Mrs. H. V. Winchell, 143
Ideal t., 158
Idington sta., 484
Idun t., 15
Iglehart. Harwood, for, 617, 620; n., 624
Ihlen v., for Carl Ihlen, 418
Illinois, names from, 58, 201, 202, 208, 216, 220, 333, 378(2), 388, 419, 524, 532, 570
Illinois l., 264
Illusion l., 296
Ilstrup l., 590
Ima l., 296
Imogen v., 333; Imogene, l., 336
Ina, l., 182
Independence t., 222; l., 264; v., 484
Indian cr., 559; grove, 174; hill, 405
Indian l., 64, 378, 401, 404, 415, 521, 591
Indian legends, 235, 420, 433, 440, 441, 581
Indian reservations, 31, 66, 79, 101, 148, 259, 286, 325, 349, 506, 545
Indian Camp r., 144
Indian Jack l., 162
Indian Lake t., 378
Indian Sioux r., 502
(Indian Spring cr., 241)
Indiana, names from, 63, 546
Indus t., 283
Industrial t., 484
Inger t., 255

Inguadona t. and l., 89, 99
Inlet l., 337
Inman t., for Thomas Inman, 395
Interlachen Park v., 177
International Boundary, Cook co., 137-140; Lake co., 297, 298; St. Louis co., 496-8; Koochiching co., 286; Beltrami co., 42-45; Roseau co., 475; Kittson co., 280
International Falls c., 283
Interstate park, 112
Inver Grove t., 166; v., 167
Iona t. and v., 366; t., 544
Iosco t., 565; cr., 566
Iowa, Indian tribe, in Minnesota, 13, 119
Iowa, names from, 29, 383, 384, 424
Iowa l., 264, 336; state, 13, 199, 203
Ireland, Archbishop, 219, 220, 313; n., 364; 376, 464, 540, 551, 637
Ireland, names from, 16, 166(2), 185, 202, 301(2), 303, 351, 364(2), 378, 450, 455, 462, 519, 540(3), 541, 542, 551(2), 552(2)
Irene, l., 180
Iris, l., 642
Irish l., 141, 576
Iron l., 141, 142, 368, 501
Iron Corner l., 133
Iron Junction v., 484
Iron Mountain v., 160
Iron ore ranges, 1; Iron Range t., 255
Ironton v., 158
Irvine, John R., for, 615, 639
Irving, Mrs. A. J., for, 165
Irving, Washington, for, 41, 270, 603
Irving, l., 41; t., 270; id., 497
Isabel, l., for Isabel Bailly, 168
Isabella r., 295; l., 296, 369
Isabelle, l., 530
Isanti co., 249-251; t. and v., 250
Iselin, Adrian, for, 376
Isinours sta., for George Isenhour, 193
Island cr., 132; l. of the, 98; sta., 484
Island l., 20, 25, 33, 37, 64, 78, 100, 144, 162(2), 218(2), 248, 258(2), 259, 296, 415, 443, 499, 501, 529, 530
Island Lake t., (253), 313, 323
Island Lake v., 37; (sta., 78)
Isle v., 344; Isle Harbor t., 344
Isles, Lake of the, 229
Italy, names from, 104, 188, 222, 352, 361, 386, 440, 568, 582, 630, 639

Itasca co., 101, 252-259; 1., 4, 126, 252
Itasca moraine, 129
Itasca state park, 122, 126-134, 253
Itasca t., 122; v. and 1., 201
(Itasca townsite and sta., 24; 1., 25)
Iva Delle, l., 369
Ivanhoe v., 307
Iverson 1., 401
Iverson sta., for Ole Iverson, 74
Ives, Mrs. Ellen Dale, for, 532
Ives, Frank, n., 408
Izatys v., 344, 348

Jack 1., 143; cr., 264, 380
Jack pines, 52, 140
Jack Pine 1s., 100, 500
Jackfish id. and bay, 286; 1., 296
Jackson, Andrew, for, 42, 260, 605, 609
Jackson, Henry, 61; for, b., 260; 612, 615
Jackson, Mrs. Henry, n., 61
Jackson, Isaac, n., 190
Jackson co., 260-264; v., 260, 262
Jackson 1., for Norman L. Jackson, 64
Jackson t., (59,) 508, (509)
Jacob, 1., 404, 499
Jadis t., for Edward W. Jadis, b., 472
Jale 1., 163
James, George P. R., for, 603
James 1., 369
Jameson t., for C. S. Jameson, 283; id., 517
Jamestown t., 60
Jane, 1., 573
Janesville t. and v., 565
Jap 1., 141
Jarrett sta. (and ford), 557
Jasper 1., 141, 296; v., 418, 467; peak, 503
(Jasper t., 397)
Java 1., 143
Jay l., 141; t., for John Jay, b., 334
Jay Cooke state park, 78
Jeannette, 1., 502
Jeffers v., for George Jeffers, 150
Jefferson, Robert E., for, 644, 645
Jefferson, Thomas, for, 64, 589, 605, 616, 636
Jefferson, 1., 64, 303; t. and v., 239; (t., 583)
Jefferys, map by, 445
Jenkins l., 20; t. and v., for George W. Jenkins, 158

Jenks, Prof. Albert E., 321
Jenks, J. Ridgway, for, 624
Jennie l., 182, 341
Jessenland t., for Jesse Cameron, 519
Jessie, l., 180, 255, 273, 401
Jesuit Relations, quoted, 5
Jevne t., 15
Jewett t., for D. M. Jewett, 15; cr., 342; l., 402
Jim l., 404; Jim Cook l., 563
Jo Daviess t., 186
Joe r., 279, 280
Johanna, l., 431, 443
Johannes, l., 401
John l., 140, 402, 435, 591
Johnson, Aetna, for, 417
Johnson, Amos, for, 181
Johnson, Andrew, for, 577, 605
Johnson, Ervin H., n., 584
Johnson, Gates A., for, 622
Johnson, Mrs. Isabel, for, 619
Johnson, Gov. John Albert, for, 622, 640
Johnson, John L., n., 361
Johnson, Joseph, 406; n., 408
Johnson, Parsons K., 61
Johnson, Mrs. P. K., n., 61
Johnson l., 140, 218, 258, 273, 401 (3), 434, 502, 542
(Johnson t., for J. and A. Johnson, 186)
Johnson t., for J. O. Johnson, 425
Johnson's cr., for L. P. Johnson, 529
Johnsonville t., 450
Johnsrud, Reinhart, for, 407
Johnston, D. S. B., 217
Johnston, George, for, 98, 246
Johnston's l., 246
Jolly Ann, l., 401
Jones cr., 189; bay, 494; l., 26, 218
Jones t., 38; sta., for John T. Jones, 484
Jordan bluff and cr., 212
Jordan c., 508; t., 193, (510)
Jordan crs., N. and S., 193, 196; l., 296
Jorgenson, l., 435
Josephine l., 131, 443, 516
Josephine, mt., 147, 148. 503, 654
Jubert's l., 233
Judd, Mrs. B. S., and Mrs. W. S., for, 85
Judge sta., for Edward Judge, 387
Judson l., 318, 320
Judson t., for Adoniram Judson, b., 60

INDEX

Juggler l., 32
Julia, l., 34, 35, 41, 516
Julian sources of Red Lake r. and the Mississippi, 41, 126
Juneberry p. o., 472
Juni, Benedict, 68, 71; for, b., 72
Juni, l., 72
Junkins l., 590
Juno l., 145
Jupiter t., 278
Justus, Daniel, n., 85

Kabekona l. and r., 247
Kabetogama l., 496, 498
Kaercher, John, for, 192; n., 194
Kaginogumag l., 246
Kahra, see Kara
Kakabikans rapids, 133
Kakigo l., 141
Kalberg, Frederick S., 121; n., 123
Kalevala t., for poem of Finland, 74
Kalmar t., 387
Kanabec co., 10, 265-7; t.. 266
Kanaranzi cr., 380, 467; t. and v., 467
Kandiyohi co., 268-275; ls., 268; t. and v., 270; (townsite, 270)
Kandota t., 545
Kane l., 295, 512
Kansas l., for John Kensie, 576
Kaposia, Sioux v., 170, 442
Kara or Kahra band of Sioux, 55
Karl l., 141
Karlstad v., 278
Kasota l., 273; t. and v., 301
Kasson v., for Jabez H. Kasson, b., 173
Kathio t., 344, 348
Katrina, l., 218, 232
Kaufit l., 499
Kawasachong l., 294, 296
Kawimbash r., 143
Kawishiwi r., 296
Kearny, Stephen W., 11, 198, 363
Keating, W. H., cited, 4, 7, 12, 39, 53, 55, 58, 97, 102, 149; q., 170; 206, 209, 224, 276, 291, 292, 374, 443, 448, 455, 550, 552, 554, 581
Kedron, br., 196
Keegan, Andrew, n., 166; for, 168
Keegan, l., 168; sta., 557
Keenan sta., for C. J. Keenan, 485
Keene t., 117; cr., 493
Keewatin, iron mining v., 255
Keewaydin, Hotel, 234

Kego t., 89; l., 163
Keil t., 38
Kekequabic l., 296
Keller, C. E., and Herbert P., for, 626
Kelley, Oliver H., 418
Kelliher t., for A. O. Kelliher, 38
Kellogg v., 557
Kelly, Matthew, n., 83
Kelly l., 143, 342, 485, 500
Kelly's l., for Patrick Kelly, 182
Kelly Lake v., 485
Kelsey, James, n., 23
Kelsey t. and v., 485
Kelso l., 143; t., 519
(Kemp's id., 572)
Kennedy, Dr. V. P., n., 316
Kennedy v., for J. S. Kennedy, b., 278
Kenneth v., 467
Kennison l., 319
Keno l., 145
Kenora, Ont., 285
Kensie's l., for John Kensie, 576
Kensington v., 177; rune stone, 177
Kent, Myron R., n., 266; for, 267
Kent l., 267; v., (312,) 578
Kentucky, name from, 508
Kenyon, Dr. Thomas, n., 534
Kenyon t. and v., 207
Keoxa, Wabasha's village, 584
Kepper l., 530
Kerkhoven t. and v., 541
Kerrick t, and v., for C. M. Kerrick, b., 412
Kerry l., 521
Kertsonville t., 425
Kerwin, John, for, 625
Kettle l., 78; r., 75, 412; Upper and Lower falls, 415; falls, Rainy l., 498; cr., 562
Kettle River v., 75; t., 412; rapids, 415
Key id., 494
Keyes, Dr. Charles R., cited, 13
Keyes l., 404
Keystone t., and farm, 425
Kichi l., 43
Kid id., 494
Kiefer, Andrew R., for, 625
Kiester, Jacob A., for, b., 186
Kiester t., 186; hills and moraine, 189
Kilby l., for Benj. E. Kilby, 65
Kildare t., 541
Kilkenny t. and v., 301
Kilpatrick, l., 100

Kimball cr. and l., for Charles G. Kimball, 144; l., 162
Kimball t., for W. S. Kimball, b., 262
Kimball Prairie v., for Frye Kimball, 524
Kimberly t., for M. C. Kimberly, b., 15
Kinbrae v., 378
King, Glendy, n., 176
King, Rev. Lyndon, for, 601
King, William S., for, 341, 601, 607
King l., 258, 274, 319, 341, 530; cr., 341, 559
King t., for Ephraim King, 426
King's Cooley sta., 557
Kinghurst t., for C. M. King, 255
Kingman t., for W. H. Kingman, 457
Kingsbury cr., for W. W. Kingsbury, b., 493, 654
Kingsdale v., 412
Kingston id., 286; t. and v., 340
Kinkaid, Alexander and William, for, b., 175, 176; 181; Mary A., for, 178
Kinmount sta., 485
Kinney v., for O. D. Kinney, 485
Kinnikinnick, 448
Kintire t., 450
Kirby l., for J. P. Kirby, b., 521
Kirk l., for Thomas H. Kirk, 132
Kiskadinna l., 141, 142
Kitihi l., 43
Kittson, Norman W., for, b., 276; 381, 426, 612, 636, 646
Kittson co., 276-280; sta., 426
Kittson's pt., Stillwater, 572
Kitzville v., 485
Kjorstad l., 502
Kline t., 283
Klondike t., 158
Klossner v., for J. Klossner, b., 372
Knapp, John H., for, 631, 633
Knaus l., 530
Knife falls, 75; l., 249, 266, 297, 505; r., 266, 295, 492; pt., 295; id., 295, 493
Knife Falls t., and portage, 75
Knife Lake t., 266
Knife River v., 294
Knight, Byron, n., 451
Knobel, l., 403
Knott, James Proctor, 481; for, b., 488
Knowles l., 465
Knowlton's cr., 493

Knox, Mrs. Daniel J., n., 17
Knox, Gen. Henry, for, 603
Knute t., for Knute Nelson, 426
Knutsen l., for G. Knutsen, b., 567
Koch, Mrs. Theodor F., for, 103
Kohlman l., 442
Konig t., 38
Koniska v., 318
Koochiching co., 281-287
Koochiching r., 8, 281, 294; t., 283; (v., 283)
Koronis, l., 342, 530
Kost v., for Ferdinand A. Kost, 108
Kraemer, George, for, 524
Kraemer l., 530
Kraetz l., 232
Kragero t., for Hans H. Kragero, b., 104
Kragnes t., for A. O. Kragnes, 117
Krain t., 524
Kratka t. and v., for F. H. Kratka, b., 407
Kray's l., 530
Kreighl l., 530
Kroschel t., for H. Kroschel, 266
Kruger l., for Louis Kruger, 72
Kugler t., for Fred Kugler, 485
Kurtz, Col. John D., 117
Kurtz t., for Thomas C. Kurtz, 117
Kuzel l., 304

Labelle, l., 32
(La Biche, l., 129)
Lac qui Parle co., 288-292
Lac qui Parle, l., 11, 104, 288, 455; mission, 104; r., 292, 598; t., 290
La Crescent t. and v., 239
(La Croix cr., 456)
La Croix l., and portage, 496, 497
La Crosse c., Wis., and prairie, 239, 253
La Crosse t., 262
Lacy, l., 401
La Due's bluff, for A. D. La Due, 174
Lady l., 547
Lady Shoe and Lady Slipper ls., 315
Lafayette bay, 235; t. and v., 372
(La Fayette townsite, 119; t., 532)
La Fond, Benjamin, for, 629
La France, Joseph, 8, 9; q., 124, 281, 321
Lagarde t., for Moses Lagarde, 323
La Grand t., 177

INDEX 693

La Harpe, Bernard de., q., 10, 343
Lahontan, Baron de, 11
Laird sta., for W. H. Laird, b., 387
Lake co., 8, 293-299
(Lake r., now Little Rock cr., 52)
Lake t., (61, 186,) 557
Lake Alice t., 244
Lake Andrew t., and l., 270
Lake Belt t., 334, 336
Lake Benton t. and v., 308
Lake City, c., 557
Lake Crystal v., and l., 60
Lake Edward t., and l., 158
Lake Elizabeth t., and l., 271
Lake Elmo v., 569
Lake Emma t., 244
Lake Eunice t., and l., 29
Lake Fremont t., 334; v., 515
Lake George t., 244, 524
Lake Grove t, 323
Lake Hanska t., and l., 69, 70
Lake Hattie t., 244
Lake Henry t., 525
Lake Ida t., 383
Lake Jessie t., 255
Lake Johanna t., 431
Lake Lillian t., 269, 271
Lake Marshall t., 313
Lake Mary t., 178
Lake Park t., 29
Lake Pleasant t., 446
Lake Prairie t., 373
Lake Sarah t., 366
Lake Shore t., 290
Lake Stay t., 308
(Lake Traverse v., 551)
Lake Valley t., 552
Lake View t., 29, 75
Lake Wilson t., 366
Lakefield v., 262
Lakeland t., 569
Lakeport t., 244
Lakeside t., 16, 150; d., 485
Lakeside Park v., 426
Laketown t., 83
Lakeview v., 569
Lakeville t., 166; v., 167
Lakewood t., 38, 485
Lakin t., for F. H. Lakin, 352
Lambert l., for Louis Lambert, 442
Lambert t., for F. Lambert, b., 446
Lamberton t. and v., for H. W. Lamberton, b., 450
Lambs sta., for John and Patrick H. Lamb, 117

Lammers t., for G. A. and A. J. Lammers, 38
Lamoille v., 582
Lamphere, George N., 114; q., 119
Lamprey, Mrs. Jeannette R., for, 620
Lamprey, Uri L., for, 620, 640
Lancaster v., 279
Land t., 215
Land's End, near Ft. Snelling, 236
Lane, Silas and Isaac E., for, 601
Lane's id., 517
Lanesboro v., 193
Lanesburg t., for C. L. Lane, 302
Langdon, l., for R. V. Langdon, 232
Langdon v., for R. B. Langdon, b., 569
Langford, Nathaniel P., for, 631, 633, 641
Langhei t., 431; hill, 435
Langola t., 50
Langor t., for H. A. Langord, 38
Lanman, Charles, quoted, 230
Lansing t. and v., 360
Laona t., 472
(Laplace, r., 246)
La Pointe, Wis., treaty, 506
Laporte v., 244
La Prairie v., 255
Larch l., 141
Larkin t., for John Larkin, 378
Larpenteur, Auguste L., 611; for, b., 626
Larsmont sta., 294
Larson, Louis, n., 271; Larson l., 401
La Salle, Robert Cavelier de, 5, 6; for, 126, 134, 246, 248, 575
La Salle ls. and r., 126, 134, 246, 248; v., 575
Lashier, l., 547
Last cr., 48
Latimer, l., for A. E. Latimer, 547
Latimore, Alex F., n., 406
Latoka, l., 181
Latona p. o., 244
Latrobe, Charles J., quoted, 230; 443
Lau l., 576
Laura, l., and br., 99
Lauzer's l., 590
Lavell t., 485
(Lavinius l., 48)
Lawndale v., 578
Lawrence, l., 99, 404; for Hugh Lawrence, 258; t., 215
Lawson, Prof. Andrew C., 148

Lawson, Victor E., q., 268; 269, 275
Lax Lake sta., and l., 294, 295
Lazarus cr., 292
Lea, Albert M., cited, 11, 13; for, b., 198; 199, 203, 204, 210, 363
Lea, Luke and Pryor, 199, 375
Leaf hills, or mts., 1, 396, 405, 561; ls. and r., 396, 561, 562
Leaf Hills moraine, 404, 405
Leaf Lake t., 396
Leaf Mountain t., 396
Leaf River t. and v., 561
Leaf Valley t., 178
Leaks sta., for John Leaks, 158
Leander sta., 485
Leaping rock, 420
Leavenworth, Col. Henry, 70, 227; b., 229; 572; Mrs. Harriet, for, b., 229, 602
Leavenworth t., 70
Leavitt, l., 99
Lebanon t., 166
Le Duc, Gen. William G., 168, 169, 231
Lee, O. K., for, 446
Lee, William E., 543; for, b., 545
Lee l., 120
Lee t., for Olaf Lee., 16; another, 38; for Ole Lee, 383
Lee's Siding sta., 545
Leech, Gen. Samuel, for, 613
Leech l., 1, 35, 90; bays, points, and islands, 94-96; 100, 101
Leech l., Chisago co., 11
Leech Lake r., 35; t., 90, 100, 101
Leech Lake Agency, 95, 101; Indian reservation, 101
Leeds t., 366
Leek l., 404
Leenthrop t., 104
Left Hand r., 75
Le Hommedieu, l., 176, 177, 180
Leiding t., 485
Leigh t., for Joseph P. Leigh, 352
Le May t., for Frank Le May, 16; l., 168
Lemond t., 533
Lena l., 356, 415
Lengby v., 426
Lenhart's l., for J. F. Lenhart, 152
Lennon l., 511
Lenora v., 194
Lent t., for Harvey Lent, 108
Leo l., 140; p. o., 472
Leon l., 402
Leon t., 122, 307
Leonard, Dr. William E., 599, 600

Leonard v., 123
Leonardsville t., for Patrick Leonard, b., 552
Leora l., 499
Leota t., 378
Le Ray t., 61
Le Roy t. and v., 360; (t., 594)
Le Sauk t., 51, 525
Leslie t. and v., for J. B. Leslie, 545
Lessor t., 426
Lester r., 492, 653, 654
Lester Park d., 485, 493, 647, 654
Lester Prairie v., for J. N. Lester, 318
Le Sueur, Pierre Charles, for, 3; 13, 57, 164; for, b., 300; 343
Le Sueur co., 2, 300-305; c. and t., 302
Le Sueur l., 204; cr. or r., 302
Le Sueur Center v., 302
Lettsom, Dr. John C., 80
Levasseur, Emile, 128
Leven t., 432; l., 435
Leverett, Frank, 21, 505
Lewis, Edwin Ray, for, 285
Lewis, Eli F., n., 319
Lewis, Robert P., for, 641
Lewis, Theodore H., 128, 370
Lewis l., 267
Lewiston v., for S. J. Lewis, 582
Lewisville, for R., J., and N. Lewis, 575
Lexington t. and v., 302
Lexington Park d., 440, 636
L'Huillier, assayer, and Fort, 57
Liards, Rivère aux, two, 149
Libby t., for Mark Libby, 16
Libby's pt., Mille Lacs, 347
Liberty t., 38, 426
(Liberty t., 29, 82, 83, 201, 396)
Lida, l., and t., 396
Lieberg l., for Ole P. Lieberg, 65
Lien t., for Ole E. Lien, b., 215
Lienau l., 499
Lightfoot l., 591
Lightning l., 217, 401; ls., 434
Lillian, l., 271
Lilly l., for Terrence Lilly, b., 567
Lily cr., 337; pond, 607
Lily l., 65; ls., Lower, and Upper, 138; 258, 567, 573
Lima t., 90
Lime cr., 203, 204, 366; l., 366
Lime t., 61
(Lime t., 207)
Lime Creek v., 366
Lime Lake t., 366

INDEX

Limestone t., 308; l., 591
Lincoln, Abraham, for, 61; 175; b., 306; 328, 352, 569, 605, 635, 653
Lincoln co., 306-310
Lincoln t., 61, 328, 569; v., 352; l., 435
Lind, Gov. John, n., 122; for, 133, b., 472
Lind saddle trail, 133; t., 472
Linden t. and l., 70
Linden Grove t., 485
Linderman l., 251
Lindford t., for L. A. Lindwall, 284
Lindgren l., 274
Lindquist, Peter, n., 271
Lindsey, Mrs. Alberta, for, 535
Lindstrom v., for D. Lindstrom, b., 108
Linka, l., 434
Linn l., 111
Linneman l., 530
Linnwood l., 500
Linsell t., 329
Linwood t. and l., 24, 25
Lisbon t., (313,) 595
Lismore t. and v., 378
Litchfield, E. Darwin, for, 339, 340
Litchfield t. and v., 340
Little l., 45, 112, 375, 402
Little Bass l., 43
Little Beaver cr., 469
(Little Bemidji l., 31, 42)
Little Bowstring l., 258
Little Boy l., 88
Little Brick id., 146
Little Brulé r., 145
Little Cannon r., 211, 304
Little Cedar r., 363
Little Chippewa r., 434
Little Cobb r., 64, 566
Little Coon l., 25
Little Cormorant l., 31
Little Cottonwood r., 152
Little Crow, Sioux chief, v., 170
Little Duck l., 111
Little Elbow l., 324
Little Elk l., 130; r. and rapids, 353, 357, 545; t., 545
Little Falls c. and t., 352, 353, 394
Little Fish Trap l. and cr., 549
Little Floyd l., 32
Little fork of Rainy r., 286, 505
Little Fork v., 284
Little Horseshoe l., 111
Little Hubert l., 162
Little Jessie l., 255

Little Le Sueur r., 566
Little Long l., 98, 258
Little Man Trap l., 132, 248
Little Marais v., 294
Little Mesabi l., 501
Little Mississippi r., 125
Little Moose l., 38
Little Norway l., 99
Little Osakis l., 548
Little Oyster ls., 203
Little Partridge cr., 547
Little Pine t., l., and r., 158; r., 415
Little Rabbit l., 160, 162
Little rapids, 84, 511
Little Rock cr. and l., 52, 374
Little Rock r., 34, 374, 378; cr. and pt., 48; cr., 459
Little Rock t., 378; trading post, 459
(Little Sack r., 51)
Little Saganaga l., 141
Little Sand l., 99, 162
Little Sauk t., 51; t., v., and l., 545
Little Sioux r., 263
Little Snake r., 19, 267
Little Spirit l., 264
Little Stony l., 247
Little Swan cr., 547
Little Thunder l., 99
Little Turtle l., 258
Little Vermilion l., 246, 496; r., 496
Little Whitefish l., 99
Little Willow r., 17, 18
Livingston, Crawford, for, 618
Livonia t., 515
Lizard l., 162, 460
Lizzie, l., 400, 530
Lobster l., 180
Lobstick pt., 498
Lock's pt., 234
Locke l., 591
Lockhart t. and v., 383
Lockwood, H. H., for, 641
Lockwood, Samuel D., n., 261
Lodi t., 361
Logan, Gen. John A., for, b., 215; 603, 609
Logan t., for lakes (logans), 16; 215
Logue l., 465
Lomond, l., 125
London t. and v., 201
Lone l., 20, 324; rock, 170; mound, 389, 557
Lone Pine l., 26
Lone Tree l., and p. o., 69; 72, 104, 106, 315, 336; t., 104
Lonergan l., 534

Long, Major S. H., 3, 4, 7, 11, 12, 39, 53, 55, 58, 74, 97, 121, 125, 206, 209, 210; quoted, 211; 224, 276, 291, 295, 331, 348, 373, 374, 408, 428, 442, 444, 455, 470, 495, 496, 498, 508, 514, 550, 552, 554, 562, 581, 597
Long bay, 495; cr., 559
Long l., 20, 33, 43, 65, 83, 84, 100, 126; of Pigeon r., 137; 140, 143, 152(2), 158, 162(4), 180, 181(3), 182, 217, 222, 231(2), 232, 247, 248, 251(4), 255, 264, 267, 274(2), 295, 304, 315, 337, 341(3), 342, 357, 369(2), 384, 400, 401(2), 402(3), 404, 442, 443, 460, 500(2), 501(3), 502, 512, 516, 529, 530(3), 538, 547(2), 548(2), 573(4), 575, 576, 591
Long pt., 44, 548; prairie, 545, 549
Long siding, for E. C. Long, 345
Long Island l., 141, 142
Long Lake t., 158, 255, 575; v., 222
Long Prairie, 59, 66, 545; r., 176, 180, 545, 546; t. and v., 545
Long Rice l., 246
Long Sault rapids, Rainy r., 285
Long Water l., 98, 246
Longfellow, H. W., 6, 75, 87, 90, 118, 134, 159, 221, 226, 231, 293, 321, 324, 367, 397, 416, 451, 453, 561, 607; for, 602, 609, 637; also see Hiawatha
Longfellow, Jacob, for, 602
Longworth sta., for N. Longworth, b., 472
Longyear l., 501
Lönnrot, Elias, 74
Lonsdale v., 462
Lookout pt., 235
Loon l., 33, 43, 65, 90, 141, 247, 264, 267, 402, 403, 496, 497, 502, 567; r., 496, 502
Loon Lake t., 90
Looney l., 547
Lorain t., 378
Loretto v., 222
Loring, Charles M., for, 232; 607, 608
Loring Park l., 232
Lorne sta., for Marquis of Lorne, b., 595
Lorsung l., for Joseph Lorsung, 182
Lory l., for H. A. Lory, 251
Lost r., 123, 125, 428, 447; l., 295, 495, 501; ls., East, and West, 400; cr., 196, 502

Lottie l., 180
Loughnan's l., 320
Louisa, l., 370, 529, 591
Louisburg v., 290
Louise, l., 141, 180
Louisville t., 446, 508; (v., 509)
Louriston t., 104
Love l., 162, 384
Lovejoy l., for C. O. Lovejoy, 563
Lover's l., 180; pt. and bay, 145
Low's l., 162
Lowe's l., for Lewis Lowe, 548
Lowell t., 426
(Lower Red Cedar l., 17)
Lower Sioux Agency, 450, 453, 460
Lower Trout l., 145, 147
Lower's l., 264
Lowry, Thomas, n., 23; for, b., 432, 606, 610; statue, 606, 610
Lowry v., 432
Lowville t., for J. H. and B. M. Low, b., 366
Lucan v., 450, (473)
Lucas t., 313
Luce v., 396
Lucille id., 146
Lucknow sta., 485
Lucy, l., 85, (168)
Lum l., 141
Lumbering, 2, 22, 121, 123, 125, 137, 242, 251, 293, 410
Lund t., 178; l., 342
Lundeberg, l., 401
Lura, l., 64, 233, 529; t., 187
Lutsen t., 136
Luverne c., 467; t., 468
Luxemburg t. and v., 525
Lydiard l., 232
Lye l., 401
Lyendecker l., 133
Lyle t. and v., for Robert Lyle, 361
Lynch, Frederick B., for, 634
Lynd t. and v., for James W. Lynd, b., 313
Lynden t., 525
Lyndon, Gov. Josiah, for, b., 525, 601
Lynn t., 318
Lynwood sta., 485
Lyon, Gen. Nathaniel, for, b., 311
Lyon co., 311-315
(Lyons cr., 66)
Lyons t., 313; for Harrison Lyons, 561
Lyra t., 61, 66
Lysne v., 531
Lyton, Michael, for, 641

INDEX

Mabel v., 194; l., 304
Macalester, Charles, for, 636
Macalester College, 440, 636
Macalester Park d., 440, 636
McArthur's id., 163
McCain, Gen. Henry P., quoted, 228
McCarrahan l., for W. McCarrahan, 548
McCarron l., for J. E. McCarron, b., 442
McCauleyville t. and v., for David McCauley, b., 578; beach of Lake Agassiz, 580
(McClellan t., for Gen. G. B. McClellan, 61)
McClelland, Mrs. Eunice, for, 29, 33
(McCloud cr., 612, 614)
McCloud's l., 217, 434
McCormick t., 255; l., 530
McCracken sta., for W. McCracken, 557
McCrea t., for Andrew McCrea, b., 329
McCrery, James L., n., 186
McCrory, W. G., n., 586
McCulloch, Hugh, for, 648; n., 653
McDavitt t., for J. A. McDavitt, 485
McDonald l., 356; ls., Big, and Little, 403
McDonaldsville t., for Finnen McDonald, 383
McDougal cr., for R. McDougal, b., 566
McDougald t., for J. McDougald, 38
McFarland l., 140
McGowan l., for Daniel McGowan, 337
McGregor t., 16
McGroarty, John, n., 166
McIntosh v., 426
McIntyre, George, for, 51
McKay l., for Rev. S. A. McKay, 133
McKenty, Henry, n., b., 440; 443, 627, 629, 639
McKenty, Mrs. Johanna, for, 443
McKenty, Josephine, for, 443
Mackenzie, Alexander, 138, 139, 140, 297, 496
Mackenzie's cr., 465
McKenzie, Roderick, 45
McKinley, William, for, b., 90, 279; 605, 630
McKinley t., 90, 279
McKinley v., for brothers, 485

McKinstry l., 32
Mackubin, Charles N., for, 617; n., 624-5
McKusick, John, n., 571; for, b., 573
McKusick's l., 573
McLaughlin, Andrew C., 87
McLean, Mrs. Hester, for, 622
McLean, Nathaniel, for, b., 437, 622
McLean, Robert B., 145
(McLean t., 437, 622)
McLeod, Martin, n., 220, 317; for, b., 316
McLeod, W. W., 30
McLeod co., 316-320; t., 255
McMahon l., 511
McMenemy, Robert, for, 628
McMullen l., for W. McMullen, 133
McNabb, Francis, and others, for, 215
McNair, William W., for, 605
McPhail, Samuel, n., 238, 289, 307; 451
McPherson t., for Gen. J. B. McPherson, b., 61, 66
McQuade l., 500
Macsville t., 215
McVeigh sta., 255
Macville t., 16
Madaline, l., 357
Madelia t. and v., 575
Madison, James, for, 61, 605
Madison l., 61; t. and v., 290; (t., 311)
Madison Lake t., 61
Magdalena l., 48
Magnet id., 146; Magnetic l., 139
Magnolia t. and v., 468
Magoffin, Beriah, for, 637, 638
(Mahkahta co., 58)
Mahla l., for M. H. Mahla, 182
Mahnomen co., 321-325; t., 323
Mah-nu-sa-tia, Ojibway name for northern Minnesota, 3
Mahtomedi v., 441, 569
Mahtowa t., 75
Maiden l., 152
Maiden's Rock, Lake Pepin, 581
Maine, John, n., 193
Maine, names from, 23, 89, 225, 250 (2), 265, 327, 329, 344, 345, 372, 396, 430, 451, 515, 525, 571, 650
Maine t., 396
Maine Prairie t. and v., 525
Mainites, 344
Mallard l., 20, 123; v., 123
Mallmann's peak, for John Mallmann, 298

Mallory v., for C. P. Mallory, b., 426
Malmedard, l., 435
Malmo t., 16
Malone id., for Charles Malone, 346
Malta t., 54
Malung t. and v., 473
Mamre t. and l., 271
Man l., 573
Manannah t. and v., 340
Manchester l., 174; t., 201
Mandall l., for Lars Mandall, 111
Mandt t., for E. T. Mandt, 104
Mandus sta., 473
Maney sta., for E. J. Maney, 485
Manfred t., 290
Manganese v., 158, 160
Manganika l., 501
Manido r., 160
Manitou id., 441; r., 295
Manitou t., and rapids, Rainy r., 284
Mankato c. and t., 58, 61
Manley sta., for W. P. Manley, 468; cr., 547
(Manomin co., 23; r., 18; l., 20; cr., 47)
Manomin l., 43, 162, 296
Mansfield t., 201
Manson, l., for Andrew Manson, 542
Manston t. (and v.), 579
Mantor, Peter, Riley, and Frank, for, b., 173
Mantorville t. and v., 173
Man Trap l., 132, 244; Mantrap t., 244
Manuella l., 341
Manvel, Allen, for, 632
Many Point l., 32
Manyaska t., 334; l., 337
Maple l., 180, 181, 188, 341; ls., N. and S., 400; 426, 429, 548, 588
Maple r., 62, 64, 188; cr., 534; pt., 347; t., 90
Maple Bay v., 426
Maple Grove t., 158, 222
Maple Hill t., 137
Maple Lake t. and v., 588
Maple Plain v., 222
Maple Ridge t., 38, 250; hill, 259
Maple sugar, made by Ojibways, 40, 90, 497
Mapleton t. and v., 62; (t., 63)
Maplewood t., 396
Maraboeuf l., 139
Marble l., 296; t., 308
Marcell t., for Andrew Marcell, 255

Marcy, William L., for, 601
Marget l., 251
Marguerite l., 315
Maria l., 85, 366, 529(2), 530, 591
Marie l., 591
Marietta v., 290
Marinda, l., 140
Marine t., 570; Big Marine l., 573
Marine Mills v., 570
Marion, l., 166, 168, 319; 397, 403, 502
Marion t., for Gen. Francis Marion, 387
(Marion Lake t., 397)
Mark l., 143; Markee l., 162
Markell, Clinton, for, 479
Markham p. o., 486; l., 500
Markley l., 512
Marks, F. O., n., 62
Markville v., 412
(Marples t., for Charles Marples, 187)
Marquette, Father J., 5, 6, 8; for, 42, 602, 646
Marquette, l., 42, 126
Marschner t., 457
Marsden l., 443
Marsh l., 56, 85, 143, 162, 290; cr. 323, 384; r., 384, 428
Marsh Creek t., 323
Marsh Grove t. 329
Marshall, Gov. W. R., 270; for, 313, b., 326, 361, 600, 606, 609, 617
Marshall c., 313; co., 326-331; t., 361
Marshall, l., 32, 313, 315
Marshan l., 25; t., for Michael Marsh and wife Ann, 166
Marshfield t., for Charles Marsh and Ira Field, 308
Marten portage, 139
Martha l., 111
Martin, Henry, for, b., 332
Martin, Hon. Morgan L., n., 3, 4; for, b., 332
Martin, Nathaniel, n., 165
Martin, W. H., and wife, for, 243
Martin, William P., and J. M., for, 647
Martin co., 332-337; l., 25, 332, 336
Martin t., (27;) for John Martin, 468
Martinsburg t., 457
Marvin, Luke, for, 644
Mary cr. and l., 131

INDEX
699

Mary l., 157, 178, 180, 273, 274, 304, 320, 342, 400, 435, 530, 576, 590 (2), 591(2)
Mary t., 383
Maryland, names from, 443, 625
Maryland l., 443
Marysburg v., 302
Marysland t., 541
Marysville t., 588
Mashkenode l., 501
Mason l., 402(2); t., for M. D. Mason, 367
Massachusetts, names from, 105, 254, 302, 312, 314, 318, 362, 377, 386, 426, 437, 440, 621
Massacre id., 45
Maston's branch, Zumbro r., 174
Matawan v., 565
Matthews, James W., for, 369
Matthews, Martin I., 53, 54
Mattocks, Rev. John, 80
Mattson l., for John Mattson, 181
Maud l., 33
(Maudada v., 552)
Maughan l., for G. W. Maughan, 538
Mavie v., 407
Maxim l., 591
Maxwell bay, 235; t., for J. H. Maxwell, b., 291
May t. and l., 90, 98; t., for Morgan May, 570
Mayer v., 83
Mayfield t., for A. C. Mayfield, 407
Mayhew cr., l., and Mayhew Lake t., for George V. Mayhew, b., 50, 51
Mayhew l., for Henry Mayhew, 141, 143
Maynard v., 104; ls., 342
Mayville t., 239
Maywood t., 50
Mazaska l., 465
Mazeppa t. and v., 557
Mead, Mike, n., 469
Meadow cr., 315; t., 561
Meadow Brook t., and br., 90, 284
Meadow Land t., 38
Meadowlands t., 486
Meadows p. o., 123; t., 579
Meagher, John L., n., 302
Medford t. and v., 533
Medicine l., 43, 232
Medicine Wood (a beech tree), 572
Medina t., 223; l., 232
Meding t., for Paul Meding, 284
Medo t., for wild potato, 62, 66

Meeds l., for Alonzo D. Meeds, 141, 145
Meeker, Bradley B., for, 229, 235, b., 338
Meeker co., 338-342
Meeker id., 229, 235, 236, 338
Mehurin t., for Amasa and Lucretia S. Mehurin, b. 291
Meire Grove v., 525
Melby v., 178
Melissa, l., 33
Melon l., 297
Melrose t. and c., 525; l., 591
Melville t., 457
Memorial Drive, Minneapolis, 607
Menahga v., 561
Menan id., 494
Mendota v. and t., 166, 167, 183, 236, 518
Menominee Indians, 321, 596
Mentor v., 426
Meriden t. and v., 533
Merriam, John L., for, b., 437, 509, 605, 633, 642
Merriam, Mrs. Laura, for, 633
Merriam, Gov. W. R., for, b., 437, 633
Merriam Junction sta., 509
Merriam Park d., 437, 633-4
Merrick, A. N., 599
Merrick, George B., 374
Merrick, Rev. John A., quoted, 231
Merrifield v., 158
Merritt, Leonidas, 476; for, b., 186
Merritt townsite, for Alfred and L. Merritt, 486
Merton t., 533
Mesaba t. and v., 486, 504
Mesabi iron range, 1, 147, 298, 492, 500, 503, 504
Mesabi l., 141, 143, 147; moraine, 504
Metoswa rapids, 42
"Metropolisville," 461
(Metz p. o., 561)
Mexico, names from, 289, 327, 334
Meyer l., 401, 548
Michigan state, 4; territory, 86
Michigan, names from, 220, 626
Mickinock t., 473, 474
Micmac l., 295
Middle l., 274, 375; r., 329, 331; cr., 459, 559
Middle River t., v., and r., 329
Middletown t., 262
Middleville t., 588
Midge l., 248
Midland Junction sta., 557

Midvale v., 570
Midway cr., 77, 486; t., 151, 486
Miesville v., for John Mies, 167
Mike Drew br., 349
Mikenna l., 130
Milaca v. and t., 345
Milan v. 104
Mildred v., 90
Milford t., 70
Mill cr., 45, 529; l., 180, 548; id., 357
Mill Stone l., 591
Mille Lacs co., 343-349
Mille Lacs, l., 1, 6, 10, 17, 249, 343; bays, points, and islands, 346-8; reservation, 349
Miller, Dr. and Mrs. A. P., for, 379, 380
Miller, John, n., 372
Miller, Gov. Stephen, for, 146, 246
Miller cr., for Robert P. Miller, 493, 649, 653
Miller, l., 161, 246
Miller's l., for Herman Mueller, 85
Millersburg v., for G. W. Miller, 462
Millerville t. and v., for John Miller, 178
Milliken cr., 174
Mills l., for Titus Mills, 65
Millville v., 557
Millward t., 16
Millwood t., 525
Milo t., 345
Miloma sta., 262
Milroy v., for Gen. R. H. Milroy, b., 450
Milton t., 173 (206;) l., 273
Miltona, l., and t., 178, 179
Mina l., 180, 182
Minard l., 26
Minden t., 50
Mine cr., 72
Mineral l., 401; bluff, 585
Minerva t. and l., 123
Minikahda Club ground, 607
Minister l., 181
Mink l., 78, 403, 590, 591
Minneapolis c., 223, 227, 599-610
MINNEAPOLIS DISTRICTS, DIVISIONS, AND ADDITIONS: North and South divisions, west of the Mississippi, 600, 602, 604; Northeast and Southeast divisions, 600, 604; Bryn Mawr ad., 604, 608; Camden Park d., 607; (Cheevertown, 226;) East Minneapolis, 605, 606, 631; Groveland ad., 604; Kenwood ad., 604, 605, 608; Lake View ad., 604; Linden Hills d., 607; Nicollet Island, 605; Oak Lake ad., 604, 605; Oak Park ad., 604, 605, 608; Prospect Park d., 606, 610; Ridgewood ad., 604; (St. Anthony, 226, 326, 600, 605;) Washburn park d., 604, 610

MINNEAPOLIS STREETS: (A to H, 600;) Adams, 605; (Ames, 600, 601;) Arlington, 605; Arthur, 605; Ash, 605; (Aspen, two, 600;) (Avon, 600;) Bank, 606; (Bay, 600;) Beacon, 605; Bedford, 606; Benjamin, 605; (Benton, 600, 601;) (Bingham, 600, 601;) (Birch, two, 600;) (Breckenridge, 600, 601;) Broadway, 606; Buchanan, (600, 601), 605; California, (600,) 606; (Cass, 600, 601;) (Cataract, 600;) Cecil, 606; (Cedar, 600;) Cedar Lake road, 604; Chandler, 606; (Christmas, 600, 601;) Church, 606; (Clay, two, 600, 601;) (Clayton, 600, 601;) Cleveland, 605; Clifton place, 605; Crystal Lake road, 604; (Dakota, two, 600;) (Dana, 600, 601;) Delaware, 606; Dell place, 605; (Division, 601, 605;) Douglas, 600, 601;) Elm (two, 600,) 605, 606; Elmwood place, 604; Emerald, 606; Erie, 606; Essex, 606; Fillmore, 605; (Fremont, 600, 601;) Fulton, 606; Garfield, 605; Grand, 606; Grant, 604; Grove, (600,) 605; (Hanson, 600, 601;) (Harmon, 604;) Harmon place, 604; Harrison, (600, 601,) 605; Harvard, 606; Hayes, 605; (Helen, 600;) Holden, 605; (Howard, 600, 601;) (Huey, 600, 601;) Huron, 606; (Itasca, 600;) Jackson, 605; Jefferson, 605; Johnson, 605; (Kansas, 600;) (King, 600, 601;) Lake, (two, 600,) 603; (Lane, 600, 601;) (Lewis, 600, 601;) Lincoln, 605; (Linden, 600;) McKinley, 605; Madison, 605; Main, 606; (Maple, two, 600;) Maple place, 605; (Marcy, 600, 601;) Marshall, (600,) 606; (Mary, 604;) Mary place, 604; (Mary Ann, 600;) Merriam, 605; (Mill, 600;) (Minnetonka, 600, 602;) Monroe, 605; (Moore, 600,

601;) (Nebraska, 600;) Nicollet, 605; Oak, (two, 600,) 606; Ontario, 606; (Orange, 600;) (Oregon, 600;) (Pearl, 600;) Pierce, 605; (Pine, two, 600;) Pleasant, 606; Polk, 605; (Prairie, 600;) Quincy, 605; Ramsey, 606; (Rice, 600, 601;) Roosevelt, 605; (Russell, 600, 601;) (St. Anthony, 600;) (St. Genevieve, 600;) (St. Martin, 600;) (St. Paul, 600;) (St. Peter's, 600;) (Seward, 600, 601;) Sibley, 606; Sidney place, 606; (Smith, 600;) Spring, (600,) 606; (Spruce, two, 600;) Spruce place, 605; Summer, 606; Summit place, 605; Superior, 606; Taft, 605; Taylor, 605; Thomas place, 605; Thornton, 606; (Todd, 600, 601;) Tyler, 605; Ulysses, 605; Union, 606; (Utah, 600;) Van Buren, 605; (Vine, 600;) Vineland place, 605; Walnut, (two, 600,) 606; Warwick, 606; Washington, 605; Water, 606; (Willow, two, 600;) Winter, 606; (Wood, 600, 601;) Yale place, 604

MINNEAPOLIS AVENUES, transverse, with a few exceptions, to streets and the river, 600-603; Abbott, 604; Aldrich, 603; Antoinette, 605; Arthur, 606; Barton, 606; Beard, 604; Belmont, 604; Blaisdell, 602; Bloomington, 602; Border, 605; Brook, 606; Bryant, 603; Cedar, 600, 602; Central, 601, 605; Chestnut, 604; Chicago, 602; Chowen, 604; Clarence, 606; Clifton, 605; Clinton, 602; Colfax, 603; Columbus, 602; Como, 606; Crystal Lake, 605; Douglas, 604; Drew, 604; Dupont, 603; East Hennepin, 601, 605; Eastman, 605; Eden, 605; Elliot, 602; Elwood, 605; Emerson, 603; Erie, 604; Ewing, 604; Fairmount, 606; Farwell, 604; First to Twenty-fourth, N., 600; to Fifty-third, N., 604; First to Twenty-eighth, S., 600, 602; to Forty-ninth, S., 602; First to Fourteenth, N. E., 600; to Thirty-seventh, N. E., 604; First to Nineteenth, S. E., 600; Forest, 605; France, 604; Franklin, 603, 604; Fremont, 603; Garfield, 602; Girard, 603; Grand, 602; Groveland, 605; Harriet, 602; Hawthorne, 604; Hennepin, 600, 601; Hiawatha, 602; Highland, 605; Hillside, 605; Humboldt, 603; Ilion, 605; Irving, 603; Island, 605; James, 603; Knox, 603; Lagoon, 604; Lakeside, 605; Lakeview, 605; Laurel, 604; Lincoln, 604; Linden, 604; Logan, 603; Longfellow, 602; Lowry, 606; Luverne, 604; Lyndale, 601, 602, 603; Lynn, 604; McNair, 605; Madeira, 605; Malcolm, 606; Marquette, 602; Melbourne, 606; Minnehaha, 602; Mississippi, 604; Morgan, 603; Mount Curve, 605; Myrtle, 605; Newton, 603; Nicollet, 600, 601, 602; Oak Grove, 605; Oakland, 602; Oliver, 603; Ontario, 604; Orlin, 606; Park, 602; Penn, 603; Pillsbury, 602; Pleasant, 602; Plymouth, 604; Portland, 602; Prospect, 604; Queen, 603; Railroad, 602; Ridgewood, 605; Riverside, 602; Rollins, 606; Royalston, 605; Russell, 603; Rustic Lodge, 604; St. Mary, 606; Seymour, 606; Sharon, 606; Sheridan, 603; Snelling, 602; Stevens, 602; Summit, 604; Superior, 604; Talmage, 606; Thomas, 603; University, 600, 605; Upton, 603; Vincent, 603; Washburn, 603; Washington, 600, 603; Western, 604; Williams, 606; Willow, 605; Wilton, 605; Xerxes, 604; York, 604; Zenith, 604

MINNEAPOLIS BOULEVARDS AND PARKWAYS: Cedar Lake blvd., 607; Dean blvd., 607; Grand Rounds, 607, 608; Kenwood pky., 608; King's highway, 607; Lake Calhoun pky., 607; Lake Harriet blvd., 607; Linden Hills blvd., 607; Memorial Drive, 607; Minnehaha pky., 607; River Road East, 607; River Road West, 607; St. Anthony blvd., 607; Stinson blvd., 607; West River Bank pky., 602

MINNEAPOLIS PARKS AND OTHER PUBLIC GROUNDS: Audubon pk., Barnes place, Barton and Bedford trs., Bottineau field, Bridge sq., Bryant, sq., Bryn Mawr Meadows pk., and Caleb Dorr circle, 608; Camden pk., 607;

Cedar Avenue tr., and Chowen, Clarence, and Clifton trs., 608; Columbia pk., 607; Cottage pk., Crystal Lake tr., Dell pk., and Dell place, Douglas tr., 608; Dorilus Morrison pk., 608, 610; Elliot pk., Elmwood and Euclid trs., Farview and Farwell pks., 608; Franklin Steele sq., 609; Gateway pk., 608, 609; Glen Gale, 609; Glenwood pk., 607; Groveland and Hiawatha trs., Highland oval, Hillside, Humboldt, and Iagoo trs., 609; (Interlachen pk., 607;) Irving tr. and Jackson sq., 609; Kenwood pk., 608, and tr., 609; Lakeside oval, and Laurel tr., 609; Lake of the Isles pk., and Lake Nokomis pk., 607; Logan pk., and Longfellow Gardens, 609; Loring pk., 608; Lovell sq., 609; Lyndale pk. and farmstead, 607; Maple Hill pk., and Marshall terrace, 609; Minikahda Club ground, 607; Minnehaha pk., 607; Monroe place, Mount Curve tr., Murphy sq., Newton and Normania trs., North Commons pk., Oak Lake pks., Oliver, Orlin, and Osseo trs., 609; Parade grounds, 608; Powderhorn Lake pk., 609; Prospect field, Rauen tr., Richard Chute sq., 610; Riverside pk., 602, 610; Riverside terrace, 602; Royalston, Russell, and Rustic Lodge trs., "Seven Corners," Sheridan field, and Snyder tr., 610; statues, of Thomas Lowry, 610, and John H. Stevens, 602; Stevens sq., Stewart field, Sumner field and place, Svea tr., and Tower Hill pk., 610; Van Cleve pk., 607; Vineland tr. and place, Virginia tr., Washburn Fair Oaks pk., 610; William Berry pk., 607; Wilson pk., 610; Winchell trail, 607; Windom pk., 610
Minnehaha, 39, 231; cr., 67, 607; falls, 230, 231, 602, 607
Minneiska t. and v., 557
Minneola t., 207
Minneopa cr., falls, park, and sta., 64, 65, 66
Minneota t., 262; v., 313
Minneowah bluff, 585
Minneseka l., 264

Minnesota state, 2-4; r., 2-4, 7, 8, 53, 56, 80, 374, 520; pt., 44, 493, 644, 652
Minnesota, gl. l., 66, 189
Minnesota City v., 582
Minnesota Falls t. and sta., 104; t. (and v.), 595
Minnesota Lake, t., v., and l., 187
Minnesota Valley Historical Society, 450, 460
Minnetaga l., 273
Minnetonka, l., 67, 224; bays, points, and islands, 233-5
Minnetonka t., 224
Minnetonka Beach v., 225
Minnetrista t., 225
Minnewashta v. and l., 83; (v., 303)
Minnewaska l., 431, 435; t., 432
Minnie t., 38; l., 530
Minnie Belle, l., 341
Minnow l., 125
Mirage l., 248
Mirbat sta., 486
Misquah l., 140; hills, 147 (Missabay Heights, 1, 147)
Missabe Mountain t., 486, 504
Mission cr., 412, 493, 652; bay, 494; l., 32, 158(2), 162; t., 158
Mission Creek t., sta., and cr., 412
Mississippi r., 1, 4-6, 35; sources, 126-134; rapids and islands, Sherburne co., 516, 517
Missouri territory and state, 86
Mitchell, Rev. Edward C., 326
Mitchell, John, map, 137
Mitchell, W. H., quoted, 207, 212
Mitchell l., 157, 163, 231
Mitchell sta., for Pentecost Mitchell, 486; t., 579
Mitten l., 99
Mizpah v., 284
Moccasin br., 267; flower, 315
Moe, C. P., n., 290
Moe l., for Nels R. Moe, 120
Moe t., 178, (313)
Moenkedick l., 403
Moland t., 117
Molberg l., for Erick Molberg, 111
Mollerberg, l., 542
Mollie l., 162; Mollie Stark l., 402
Moltke t., 520
Momb's l., 32
Money cr., 196(2), 239, 585
Money Creek t. and v., 239
Monfort, Delos A., for, 619
Monker l., for Claus C. Monker, 144

INDEX 703

(Monongalia co., 268)
Monroe, James, for, 314, 605, 609
Monroe t., 314
Mons l., 547
Monson l., 32; t., for Peter Monson, 552
Monterey v., 334
Montevideo c., 104;(t., 63)
(Montezuma v., 584)
Montgomery, Gen. R., for, 302
Montgomery c. and t., 302
Monticello t. and v., 588; prairie, 592
Montrose v., 589
Monuments of the Sioux war, 1862, 460
Mooers, Hazen, trading posts, 552, 573; l., 573
(Mooers Prairie t., for J. P. Mooers, b., 587)
Moon l., 32, 141, 179, 181
Moonlight p. o., 124
Moonshine l. and t., 54, 56
Moore, George W., for, 633
Moore, Thomas, from his poem, 364
Moore l., 143, 538, 542; t., 537, 573, 590
Moorhead c. and t., for William G. Moorhead, b., 117
Moose l., 18, 38, 43, 75, 138, 258, 295, 296, 502(2), 547; mt., 138, 147; portage, 138
Moose r., 18, 77, 329, 415, 502; t., 473
Moose Creek t. and cr., 123
Moose Head l., 75; (Moosehead r., 18)
Moose Horn r., 77
Moose Island sta. and l., 537, 538
Moose Lake t., 38, 75, 90
Moose Park t., 255
Moose River t., and r., 329
Mora v., 266; l., 267
Moraines, 1, 33, 129, 153, 170, 189, 275, 292, 305, 309, 404, 420, 504
Moran l., for H. P. Moran, 78; 231, 247, 501
Moran t. and br., 545, 547
Moranville t., for P. W. Moran, 473
Morcom t., for Elisha Morcom, 486
Morgan, Gen. George N., for, 603
Morgan, John Pierpont, for, 652
Morgan cr., for Richard Morgan, 65; l., 140
Morgan t. and v., for L. H. Morgan, b., 451

(Moritzious townsite, 588, 589)
Morken t., for T. O. Morken, 118
Mormon l., 465
Morrill t., for A. C. Morrill, b., 353
Morris, Charles A. F., for, b., 537; 618
Morris, Mrs. James T., 358
Morris v. and t., 537
Morrison, Allan, for, b., 350
Morrison, Clinton, for, 602; n., 608
Morrison, Dorilus, for, 608
Morrison, William, 130, 132; for, 133, b., 350
Morrison co., 350-358
Morrison l., 32, 99; hill, 133; bay, 146
Morrison t., for Edward Morrison, 16
Morristown v., for Jonathan Morris; b., 462; l., 465
Morrow, Levi, n., 93
Morrow heights, for A. T. Morrow, 133
Morse t., for J. C. Morse, 486; l., 538
Morton v., 451, 457, 460
Moscow t., 201
Moses, l., 182, 218
Mosquito br., 100; cr., 125; rapids, 517
Moss l., 98, 140
Mother l., 231
Motley t. and v., 353
Motordale v., 83
Mott l., 567
Moulton l., 162; t., for J. P. Moulton, b., 367
Mound, hill in Rock co., 466, 468; l., 547
Mound t., 12, 468; cr., 72, 152; v., 225, 235
Mound Prairie t., 239
Mounds (hills), 170, 443
Mounds View t., 437; hills, 443
Mount Morris t., 353
Mount Pleasant t., 557
Mount Vernon t., 582
Mountain l., 138,(139,) 147, 151
Mountain, l. of the, 98
Mountain Iron v. and mine, 486, 503
Mountain Lake t., and l., 151; v., 151
Movil l., 43
Mow, Mrs. Mary Badoura, for, 243
Mower, John E., for, b., 359
Mower, Martin, b., 359
Mower co., 359-363

Moyer, Lycurgus R., 103, 104, 106, 288
Moyer t., for William Moyer, 541
Moylan t., for Patrick Moylan, 329
Mo-zo-ma-na pt., 347
Mud cr., 77, 267, 330, 374, 434, 456, 459, 465, 469, 475, 537, 542, 598
Mud l., 17, 20, 21(4), 25, 26(2), 33 (3), 39, 41, 43, 65(2), 85, 90, 99, 112, 125, 139, 161(2), 162(4), 181 (2), 189, 231, 232, 233, 248 (2), 251(2), 257, 267, 274, 304(5), 305, 320(2), 329, 336, 337(2), 341(2), 342(3), 349, 356, 369, 400, 401(2), 402(2), 403, 404, 435(2), 456, 460, 465, 475, 493, 501, 511, 516(2), 521(3), 530,(3), 534, 538, 548(2), 549, 553, 563, 573(3), 590, 591
Mud r., 17, 20, 39, 41, 46, 99, 330, 501
Mud Hen l. and cr., 500
Mud Lake t., 90, 329, (456)
(Muddy ls. and r., 17)
Mudgett t., for I. S. Mudgett, 345
Mule l., 99, 204
Mulligan t., 70
Mullin, J. C., and A. J., n., 103
Mulvey id., 347; pt., 572
Munch t., for Adolph, Emil, and Paul Munch, b., 412, 413
Munger, Roger S., for, b., 486, 653
Munger l., for Perry Munger, 337
Munson t., 525
Murdock v., for S. S. Murdock, 541
Murphy, Capt. Edward, for, 609
Murphy t., 284; l., for John Murphy, 336; 500, 511
Murray, William P., 260; for, b., 364, 367, 619
Murray co., 364-370; t., (37,) 367; sta., 487
Muscovado l., 141
Mushroom l., 93; cr., 580
Muskeg bay, 44
Muskoda sta., 118, 120
Muskrat l., 267
Muskrats, 20, 64, 133, 152, 285
Musquash l., 133
Mustinka r., 217, 400, 554
Myer's l., 180
Myhre t., for L. O. Myhre, 38
Myrtle l., 43, 502; v., 202
Mythology, names from, 40, 61, 75, 227, 287, 301, 391, 440, 452, 565, 575

Nagonab sta., for Ojibway chief, b., 487
Namekan (or Namaycan), l., 496, 498; r., 497, 502
Narrows, of Red l., 46, 47; Leech l., 94; l. Minnetonka, 234; Vermilion l., 494
Nary sta., for Thomas J. Nary, 244
Nashua v., 579
Nashville t., for A. M. Nash, 334
Nashwauk t., 255
Nassau v., 291
National forests of Minnesota, 100, 148, 299, 506
Neander l., for Nels P. Neander, 111
Nebish t. and l., 38
Nebo, mt., 549
Nebogigig l., 141
Neche v., N. D., 626
(Neenah t., 526)
Neill, Rev. E. D., 3, 88; quoted, 249, 276; 300, 345, 455; for, 612
Neill l., 231
Neimackl l., 218
Nekuk id., 493
Nelson, Carl A. A., n., 136
Nelson, Cornelius J., n., 104
Nelson, Hon. Knute, for, b., 178
Nelson, Nels K., n., 328
Nelson, Rensselaer R., for, 615
Nelson, Socrates, n., 568, 569
Nelson l., for M. Nelson, 20; for H. M. Nelson, 162; another, 162; for O. W. Nelson, 181; for John Nelson, 181, 182; 218, 401, 402, 435, 549
Nelson t., 178, 575
Nelson Park t., for James Nelson, 329
Nemadji, gl. l., 79, 505; sta. and r., 75, 505
Nemeukan l., 496
Nequawkaun l., 497
Neresen t., for Knut Neresen, 473
Nerstrand v., 463
Nesbit t., for James and Robert Nesbit, 426
(Ness t., for Ole H. Ness, 340)
Nessawae l., 348
Nessel t., for Robert Nessel, b., 108
Nest l., 274, 275
Net l., 284, 286, 415, 502(2); rs. or crs., 77, 284, 415
Net Lake t., 284; reservation, 284, 286, 506
Net River t., and r., 284
Nets for fishing, 77, 100, 126

INDEX

Netta, l., 25
Nettiewynnt l., 454
Nettleton, George E., n., 481
Nettleton, William, for, 636
Nevada l., 274; t., 361
Neving p. o., for Robert Neving, 123
Nevis t. and v., 244
New Auburn t. and v., 520
New Avon t., 451
New Brighton v., 437
New Brunswick, name from, 255
New Canada t., 437, 613
New Duluth d., 487, 652
New Folden t., 329
New Germany v., 83
New Hampshire, names from, 108, 166, 172(2), 386, 519
New Hartford t. and v., 582
New Haven t., 387
New Hope, cantonment, 227
New Independence t., 487
New Jersey, names from, 89, 637, 648
New London t. and v., 271
New Maine t., 329
New Market t., 509
New Mexico, name from, 316
New Munich v., 526
(New Paynesville v., 526)
(New Posen t., 540)
New Prague c., 302, 509
New Prairie t., 432
New Richland t. and v., 565
New Scandia t., 570
New Solum t., 329
New Sweden t., 373
New Trier v., 167
New Ulm c., 70, 80
(New Virginia t., 338)
New York, names from, 28(2), 58, 82, 165, 172, 187, 200(2), 202, 215, 239(2), 270, 314, 335, 361, 372, 386(2), 388, 417, 419, 457, 464, 467, 469, 520, 582, 583, 584(3), 589(2), 590, 647
New York Mills v. (and t.), 396
Newberg t. and v., 194
Newel, Stanford, for, 641
Newfound l., 296
Newfoundland id., 494
Newport t. and v., 570; (t., 588)
Newry t., 202; l., 204
Newson, Thomas M., quoted or cited, 198, 229, 235, 619, 622, 624, 628
Newton, Isaac, for, 603
Newton, James, for, 374

Newton l., 296; id., 357; t., 396
Nicado l., 295
Nichols, Austin R., for, 15; n., 202; for, b., 359
Nichols, Rev. H. M., n., 81
Nichols, James A., for, 487; 503
Nichols p. o., 15; t., 487; l., 499
Nickerson t. and v., for J. Q. A. Nickerson, b., 413; id., 517
Nicolet, Jean, 5, 371
Nicollet, Joseph N., for, 130, 133, 229, b., 371, 373, 601; quoted or cited, 1, 2, 4, 10-13, 17, 41, 43, 49, 55, 60, 61, 64, 65, 74, 81, 88, 90, 92, 95-97, 102, 106, 119, 121, 125-130, 134, 147, 149, 153, 154, 157, 159, 160-4, 169, 170, 174, 198, 203, 204, 206, 208, 210, 212, 224, 229, 243, 268, 292, 298, 303, 308, 334, 336-8, 342, 343, 348, 357, 362, 365-371, 374, 380, 389, 406, 408, 416, 420, 432, 448, 455-7, 466, 467, 483, 495, 503, 508, 510, 514, 520, 529, 552, 554, 559, 562, 574, 597
Nicollet co., 371-375; t. and v., 373
Nicollet cr., ls., and valley, 130; springs, 133; cr., 374
Nicollet id., 229, 605
Nicols sta., for John Nicols, 167
Nidaros t., 396
Nielsville v., 426
Ni-e-ma-da l., 131
Niggler, Mrs. Elizabeth, for, 394
Niles bay, 495
Nilsen t., 579
Nilson, l., 434
Nimrod, p. o. and hamlet, 561
Nine Mile cr., 231; l., 295
Nininger v. and t., for John Nininger, 166, 167
Nipissiquit l., 295
Nixon l., 592
Nobles, William H., for, b., 376
Nobles co., 376-380
Nobles l., for three brothers, 320
Nokay, Ojibway chief, for, 158, 159
Nokay Lake t., l., and r., 158, 159, 161
Nokomis, l., 231
Nomenclature of Itasca State Park, 129-134
No Name l., 141
Noon Day pt., 96
No-point, pt., 212
Nora t., for Knut Nora, 123; for Norway, 432
Norberg l., 106
Norcross v., 216

Norcross beach, Lake Agassiz, 218
Nord l., 20
Norden t. and p. o., 284, 407
Nordick t., for B. and G. Nordick, 579
Nordland t., 16, 314
Nore t., for K. S. and S. K. Nohre, 255
Norfolk t., 457
Norland t., 473
Norman co., 381-384; t., (383,) 413, 595
Norman p. o., for Peter Norman, 487
Normania t., 595
Normanna t., 487
Norris l., for Grafton Norris, 26
Norseth, Martin, n., 69; Mrs. Eva, for, 69
(Norsk t., 151)
Norstedt l., 274
North, John W., for, b., 463
North, Robert, n., 595
North l., 139, 211, 337, 530, 591; ridge, 503; prairie, 530; id., 553; t., 407
North branch, Sunrise r., 108, 250
North Branch t., 250; v., (68,) 109
North Fork t., 526
North Germany t., 561
North Hero t., 451
North Mankato v., 373
North Narrows, 94, 95
North Ottawa t., 216
North Prairie v., 353
North Redwood v., 451
North St. Paul v., 437
North Star state, 4, 70, 280, 408; t., 70
Northcote v., for S. H. Northcote, 279
Northern t., 38
Northern Light l., 145
(Northern Pacific Junction, 74)
Northern Pacific ry., 15, 16, 77, 78, 79, 116, 117, 156, 397, 433, 535, 569
Northfield c. and t., for J. W. North, b., 463
Northland t., 426, 487
Northome v., 284
Northrop, Pres. Cyrus, for, 299, b., 334
Northrop, mt., 299; v., 334
Northup, Anson, 119
Northwest Angle and inlet, 35, 44, 45
Northwest Fur Co., 18, 76, 95, 136

Northwestern l., 296
Northwood t., 38
Norton, Albert T., n., 166
Norton, Daniel S., n., 172; for, b., 583
Norton, Henry A., for b., 216
Norton, James L., and Matthew G., for, b., 583
Norton, John W., and Wm. W., for, 626
Norton t., 583
Norway, names from, 16, 37, 40, 104, 105, 117, 136, 137, 173, 178, 179(2), 190, 191, 194, 214, 238, 261, 269, 274, 279, 307, 312, 314, 316, 327, 328, 329(3), 365, 382 (2), 384, 391, 395, 396, 399, 407, 422, 425, 426, 427, 428, 431, 432, 459, 463, 474, 595, 596(2)
Norway br. and l., 100; l., 271, 274, 402
Norway t., 194, 279
Norway Lake t., 271
Norwegian Grove, 373; bay, 495; l., 567
Norwegian Grove t., 396
Norwood, Joseph G., 138, 139, 143, 144, 295, 357, 503
Norwood v., 83
Nourse, George A., n., 340
Nouvelle portage, 496
Nova, l., 309
Nowthen p. o., 26
Noyes sta., for J. A. Noyes, 279
Noyon, Jacques de, 8
Numedal t., 407
Nunda t., 202
Nushka sta., 90
Nymore v., for Martin Nye, 38

Oak cr., 47, 396; id., 44, 495; l., 27, 28, 33, 85, 415, 429; pt., 44; t., 526
Oak species, bur and black, 106
Oak Center, a hamlet, 558
(Oak City v., 345)
Oak Glen ls., three, 534
(Oak Glen v. and t., 532, 533)
Oak Grove t., 24, (524, 526)
Oak Hill, a hamlet, 545
(Oak Lake t., 27, 28)
Oak Lawn t., 159
Oak Leaf t., 375
Oak Park v., 50, (570;) t., 329
Oak Point l., 296
Oak Ridge, a hamlet, 583
Oak Valley t., 396

INDEX 707

Oakdale t., 570
Oakland t., 202
Oakport t., 118
Oaks l., and l. of the, 153, 367
Oaks t., for Charles Oaks, 473
Oakwood t., (353,) 558
Oasis, Great, l., 369; (grove, 366, 369)
Oatka beach, Duluth, 644
O'Brien, Dillon, 551
O'Brien l., 162
O'Brien t., for William O'Brien, 39
Observe, pt., 498
Ocano springs, 133; r., 134
Ochagach, map by, 8, 137, 282
Ocheeda, l., 368, 380
Ocheyedan cr., or r., 368, 380
Ockerson heights, for J. A. Ockerson, 133
O'Connell, Richard, n., 417
O'Connor's l., 511
Odd l., 143
Odenborg, Ole, 550, 553
Odessa t. and v., 55; (t., 544)
Odin t. and v., 575
O'Dowd l., 512
Ogechie l., 348
Ogema v., 31; t., 413
Ogilvie v., 266
Ogishke Muncie l., 296
Ogren's l., for Andrew Ogren, 111
Ohage, Dr. Justus, donor, 640
Ohio, names from, 53, 63, 90, 105, 166, 167, 190, 191, 201, 291, 301, 424, 426, 449, 649
Ojibway pt., 346; see Chippewa
Ojibways, names from, 1, 2, 3, 4, 6, 8, 9, 13, 15-20, 22, 28-33, 36-40, 42-48, 51, 52, 75, 77, 78, 86-90, 93-97, 99, 107, 110, 118-121, 124, 125, 129, 137-140, 142-7, 154, 156-160, 245, 247, 248, 256-8, 265, 266, 281, 286, 293-5, 321, 323, 331, 342, 343, 348, 367, 384, 390, 393, 397, 398, 405, 408-413, 425, 428, 429, 433, 441, 445, 447, 453, 470, 473, 474, 478, 482, 487-9, 492, 496-501, 504, 514, 529, 560-562, 571, 626
Okabena sta., 262; cr., 264, 380; ls., 379, 380
(Okaman v., 303, 565)
(Okcheeda t., 367)
Oklee v., for O. K. Lee, 446
Okshida cr., 368, 380
Olaf l., 181, 404
Olberg l., 181, 404
Olberg v., for Anton Olberg, 123
Oldenburg, Henry, 73

Olds, Mrs. Beulah, for, 87
Ole, l., 274
Olive l., 502
Oliver, A. M., for, 603
Oliver, l., 542
(Oliver's Grove, for W. G. Oliver, 165)
Olivia v., 458
Olivier, L. M., and J. B., for, 628
Olmstead, S. Baldwin, b., 385
Olmsted, David, for, b., 385
Olmsted co., 385-389
Olney t., 378
Olson, Erik, n., 215
Olson l., 218, 273, 331, 499, 538
Olstrud l., 218
Omimi, gl. l., 148
Omro t., 595
Omsrud l., 72
Omushkos, l., 129
Onamia t. and l., 345, 348
One Mile l., 401
One Pine l., 501
Onega l., 141
O'Neil pt., for John H. O'Neil, 132
O'Neill br., 349
Oneka t., 570; l., 570, 573
(Oneota v., 482, 487, 643)
Onstad, l., 402; t., for O. P. Onstad, 426
Onstine, Henry, for, 193
Ontonagon r., Mich., 256
O'Phelan, P. D., n., 551, 552(2)
Opperman l., 402
Opstead p. o., 345
Orange t., 179
Orchard l., 168, 499; cr., 363
Org sta., 378
Orion t., 387, (533)
Orleans v., 279
Ormsby v., 334, 575
Orono t. and pt., 225, 235; (v., 515)
Oronoco t., 387
Orr v., for William Orr., 488
Orrock t., for Robert Orrock, b., 515
Orth v., 256
Orton t., 561
Ortonville t. and v., for C. K. Orton, b., 55
Orwell t., 396
Osage t. and Osage Indians, 29
Osakis l. and v., 51, 179; t., 179; l., 545, 547, 548
Osauka ad., 51
Osborne t., for J. C. Osborne, 418

Oscar l., for King Oscar I, 181, 182; 368; t., for Oscar II, 397; l., 402, 403
Osceola t., 458
Oshawa t., 373
Oshkosh t., 596
Oslo hamlet and p. o., 173; v., 329
Osmund Osmundson, n., 463
Osseo v., 226
Ossowa l., 246
Ostlund's h., for Lars Ostlund, 275
Ostrander v., for W. and C. Ostrander, 194
Oteneagen t., 256
(Otis t., for John D. Otis, 596)
Otisco t. and v., 565
Otrey t., for T. and W. Otrey, 55
Otsego, (t. 62;) t. and v., 589
Ottawa Indians, 44
Ottawa t. and v., 303
Otter cr., 77, 319, 320, 363, 591; (br., 77)
Otter l., 21, 26, 140, 273, 274, 319, 404, 442, 499, 529
Otter Tail co., 390-405; t. and v., 397
Otter Tail l., 31, 390
Otter Tail r., 29, 31, 390; pt., 94, 95
(Otter Tail City, trading post, 390, 397)
Otter Track l., 297, 298, 505
Otto t., 397
(Ouchichiq r., 8)
Outing v., 159
Outlet bay, 347, 495; cr., 434
Owanka v., 367
Owasso, l., 443
Owatonna c. and t., 533; (r., 533)
Owen, David D., geological survey, 62, 143, 144, 147, 267, 495, 496, 499, 502, 504
Owens, John Algernon, 127
Owens t., for three brothers, b., 488
Owings l., 180
Ox l., 162; Ox Hide l., 258; Ox Yoke l., 225
Oxford t., 250, (398)
(Oye and Oylen post offices, 561)
Ozahtanka l., 189
Ozawindib, Ojibway guide, 96; pt., 132

Paddock t., for L. A. Paddock, 397
Page l., for William H. Page, 537
Page t., for C. H. and E. S. Page, 345
Paine, l., for Barrett C. Paine, 247
Painted rock, St. Croix r., 572
Pajutazee, Sioux mission, 597
Pale Face r., 500
Palestine, names from, 15, 115, 182, 193, 196, 271, 284, 303, 508, 528, 549, 582
Palisades, Great, 295
Palmer cr., for Frank Palmer, 106
Palmer l., 232, 247
Palmer t., for B. R. Palmer, b., 516; v., 565
Palmer's, p. o. and hamlet, 488
Palmville t., for Louis Palm, 473
Palmyra t., 458
Palo, a hamlet, 488
Panasa l., 258
Papoose l., 163
Paradise prairie, 204
(Parallel r., 514)
Parent l., 296
Parent v., for Auguste Parent, 50
Park l., 78, 530; Park Region, 2
Park Rapids v., 244
Parkdale v., 397
Parke t., 118
Parker t., for George L. Parker, 329; for George F. Parker, b., 353
Parker's l., 232
Parker's Prairie t., 397
Parks, John S., n., 62
Parkton sta., 397
Parley l., 85
Parnell t., for C. S. Parnell, b., 426, 552
Parrant, Pierre, for, 442
Parritt, Dexter, for, 360
Parry, Dr. C. C., quoted, 62; 448
Parslow's l., for S. Parslow, 233
Parsons, Rev. J. P., for, 615
Partridge, Thomas C., n., 524
Partridge, 87; bay and r., 495; cr., 197, 389; t., 413; r., 500, 547, 562
Partridge falls, 138; l., 140, 500
Pascal, Blase, for, 630
Pat's l., 465
Patchen l., 218
Patrons of Husbandry, for, 417
Patten l., 337
Patterson, Charles, trader, 458
Patterson, Robert, n., 60
Patterson l., for W. Patterson, 85
Patterson's rapids, 458, 459
Paul l., 403
Paulson, Ida, for, 383
Paulson l., 141
Paupori v., 488

INDEX 709

(Pauselim v., 558)
Paxton t., for James W. Paxton, b., 451
Pay l., 273
Payne, Edwin E., for, 526
Payne, Rice W., for, 624
Payne sta., 488
Paynesville t. and v., 526
Peabody, Lloyd, 611, 639
Peace rock, 52; t., 266
Peake, Mrs. E. Steele, quoted, 154
Pearce l., 32
Pearl l., 33, 231, 264, 526
Pearl Lake v., 526
Peary sta., for Robert E. Peary, b., 488
Pease v., 345
Peat bogs, 121, 125, 406, 447; l., 548
Pebble l., 401
Pederson, A. W., n., 69
Pelan t., for Charles H. Pelan, 279
Pelée, Isle, 169
Pelican l., 159, 182, 216, 400, 404, 435, 460, 502, 530, 534, 542, 591; cr., 400; hill, 554
Pelican pt., 46, 235; id., 94, 97, 347; r., 31, 397, 404, 502
Pelican t., 159, 397
Pelican Lake t., 216
Pelican Rapids v., 397
Pelican Rock bay, 494
Pelkey l., 357
(Pell t., for John H. Pell, 558)
Pelland v., for Joseph Pelland, 284
Pelt cr., 454
Peltier l., for C., P., and O. Peltier, 25
(Pembina co., 276)
Pembina co. and r., N. D., 276, 323
Pembina t., 323
Pencer p. o., 473
Pendergast l., 548
Penicaut, Relation by, 10, 57
Peninsula, the, and l., 94; (l., 224)
Penn, William, for, 318, 603
Penn t., 318
Pennington, Edmund, for, b., 406
Pennington co., 406-409
Pennington l., for James Pennington, 267
Pennock v., for George Pennock, 271
Pennsylvania, names from, 110, 173, 318, 406, 417, 425, 489, 647, 650
Penny l., 204

Pepin, l., 5, 10; in Le Sueur co., 305; t., 558
Peppermint cr., 43
Pepperton t., for C. A. Pepper, b., 537
Pequaywan l., 499
Pequot v., 159
Perch cr., 65, 335, 336, 576
Perch l., 33, 65, 75, 120, 162(3), 309, 336, 429, 576
Perch portage, 139
Perch Lake t., 75
Percy t., for Howard Percy, 279
Perham t. and v., for Josiah Perham, b., 397
Perley v., for George E. Perley, b., 383
Perrault sta., for C. Perrault, 447
Perrot, N., 3, 5, 10, 300
Perry, Abraham and Charles, for, 618
Perry t., for O. H. Perry, 291
Perry Lake t., and l., 159
Perth sta., 62
Pete l., 404; Peter l., 141, 232
Peter Lund cr., 204
Petersburg t., 263
Peterson l., 43; for Nels M. Peterson, 125; 143, 204, 218, 342, 402, 465
Peterson v., 194
Peyla, hamlet, for Peter Peyla, 488
Peysenski l., 247
Pfaender, William, 70
Phalen l. and cr., 440, 442, 612, 614
Phalen Park d., 440, 626, 639
Phare l., 460
Phelan, Edward, for, 440, 639
Phelps bay and id., for E. J. Phelps, b., 234
Phelps l., 162, 465
(Phelps t., for Addison Phelps, 539)
Philbrook v., 545
Phoebe l., 143
Pickard ls., 130
Pickerel l., 21, 26, 33, 144, 162, 169, 202, 203, 248, 296, 402(2), 403, 516
Pickerel Lake t., 202
Pickering bay, 92, 96; for John Pickering, b., 96
Pickle l., 296
Pickwick v., 583
Picture id., 287
Pie l., 143
Pierce, Franklin, for, 605
Pierce l., 337
Pierson l., for John Pierson, 85

INDEX

Pierz t., for F. X. Pierz, b., 354
Pig l., 162; Pig's Eye l., 442
Pigeon l., 341, 342
Pigeon r., 137, 139, 148, 259; falls, 138; bay and pt., 146
Pigeon River Indian reservation, 140, 148
Pike, Robert, n., 582
Pike, Zebulon M., 11, 12, 17, 18, 51, 52; for, b., 91; 95, 96, 154; for, 169; 206, 208, 209, 210, 343, 348, 353; for, b., 354; wintering place, 358; for, 441; 442, 514, 516, 517
Pike bay, 91, 495; cr., 45, 354; r., 488, 495
Pike id., 169, 441; t., 488
Pike ls., East and West, 140; l., 143, 161, 267, 435, 479, 508, 512
Pike Bay t., 91; Pike Creek t., 354
Pillager cr., l., and v., 91
Pillager Ojibways, 35, 51, 91, 101
Pillsbury, Gov. John S., 100; for, b., 541; 602
Pillsbury state forest, 100; t., 541
Pilot knob (or hill), 170
Pilot Grove t. and l., 187
Pilot Mound t., 194
Pimushe l., 43
Pine co., 10, 410-415
Pine cr., 196, 210, 241; cooley, 442, 573; 475, 585(2)
Pine id., 347, 494(2), 498
Pine l., 10, 19, 20, 32, 91, 111(2), 123, 139, 140, 142, 143, 145, 162 (2), 296, 357, 398; Big, and Little, 400; Big, Upper, and Lower, 413, 415; 500, 501, 530
Pine r., 10, 19, 91, 99, 100, 123, 161, 163, 413
Pine species in Minnesota, 2, 410, 529
Pine Bend sta., 167
Pine City t. and v., 413
Pine Island t. and v., 11, 207; l., 548, 549
Pine Lake t., 91, 123, 398, 413; br., 100
Pine Mountain l., 99, 100
Pine Point l., 32; pt., 95
Pine River t., 91
Pine Top t., 284
Pine Tree l., 573
(Piniddiwin r., 125)
Pioneer t., 39; cr., 232
Pipe l., 143, 341
Pipestone co., 416-420; c., 418
Pipestone quarry, 12, 416; cr. and l., 419; reservation, 101, 416

(Piquadinaw t., 16)
Pirz l., 530
Pither's pt., 286
Pitts l., 530
Pittsburg l., 141
Plainview t. and v., 558
Plantagenet, l., 246
Plantagenian fork of the Mississippi, 42, 246
Plato v., 318
Platte t. and r., 354, 357
Platte Lake t., l., and r., 159
Plaza, l., 304
(Ple, l., 246)
Pleasant l., 402, 442, 446, 447, 511, 530, 591; prairie, 334, 549
Pleasant Grove, (t., 172), t. and v., 387
Pleasant Hill t., 583
Pleasant Mound t. and p. o., 62
Pleasant Prairie t., 334
Pleasant Valley t., 361; cr., 585
Pleasant View v., 83; t., 383
Pliny t., 16
Plum l., 296, 342; cr., 284, 368, 454, 529; id., 264, 553
Plum Creek t., 284
Plum Island l., 264
Plummer v., for C. A. Plummer, 447
Plymouth t., 226
(Plympton l., for Capt. Joseph Plympton, 160, 161)
Poe l., 143
Pohlitz t., 473
Point l., 274
Point Douglas v., 570
Pointon l., 162
Pokegama, l., 129, 413; t., 256, 413; falls, 256; cr., 413
Poland, names from, 209, 464, 473, 483, 540
Polk, James K., for, b., 421; 605
Polk co., 421-429
Polk Center t., 407
Polly, l., 296
Polonia t., 473
Pomerleau l., 232
Pomme de Terre, the plant, 62, 216; t., l., and r., 216; r., 400, 537; ls., 538
Pomroy t. and l., for John Pomroy, 266
Pond, Rev. Gideon H., 3, 220, 230, 252
Pond, Rev. Samuel W., 508, 510
Pond, Samuel W., Jr., quoted, 230, 510

Ponemah v., 39
Ponto Lake t., and l., 91
Pontoria p. o., 91
Pony l., 43
Poole's l., 465
Pope, Mrs. Douglas, for, 168
Pope, Gen. John, 214, 217; for, b., 430; 434, 460
Pope co., 430-435; l., 141
Poplar cr., 47; r., 140, 143, 428, 447
Poplar l., 140, 145, 443; t. and p. o., 91
Poplar Grove t., 473
Poplar River t., 447
Poplars, silvery leaved, 30
Popple t., 123, (255)
Popple Grove t., 323
Poppleton t., 279
Populist party, 115
Poquodenaw mt., 15
Porcupine id., 146; bay and id., 494
Pork bay, 295
Port Hope t., 39
Portage bay, 347; l., 20, 100(2), 141, 162(3), 248, 258, 402; r., 77; br., 140
Portage Lake sta., l., and bay, 91, 96
Porter, Charles, for, 449
Porter cr., for George Porter, 511
Porter, (t., 200;) v., for L. C. Porter, 596
Portland d., Duluth, 488, 643, 653
Portugal, name from, 595
Posen t., 596
Possum crs., Big and Little, 511
Post bluff, for A. W. and George Post, 212
Potamo t., 39
Potato l., 248, 258, 297
Potholes, Interstate pk., 113
Potsdam v., 387; (t., 535, 536)
Poupore p. o. and v., 488
Powderhorn l., 133, 232, 609
Powell, Byron, for, 88
Powell, Rev. John W., n., 63
Powers l., 233, 342, 573
Powers t., for Gorham Powers, b., 92
Prairie area of Minnesota, 2, 118
Prairie cr., 211, 286, 465; br., 349, 547, 549; r., 17, 19, 255, 488
Prairie l., 166, 168, 204, 255, 274, 337, 403, 488; id., 169, 211; pt., Leech l., 95
Prairie Lake t., 488
Prairie View t., 579

Prairieville t., 70; (v. of Sioux, 510)
Pratt, Charles H., for, 631
Pratt sta., for W. A. Pratt, 533
Preble t., for Edward Preble, 194
Predmore sta., for J. W. Predmore, 387
Prescott, George W., for, 620
Prescott t., 187
Preston, James, n., 383
Preston t., for Luther Preston, 194
Preston Lake t., and l., 458
Priest's bay, 234
Prince l., 174
Princeton v. and t., for John S. Prince, b., 345
Prinsburg v., for Martin Prins, 271
Prior, Charles H., for, 55, b., 509, 632
Prior t., 55; l., 509, 512
Prior Lake v., 509
Prisoner's id., 347
Proctor Knott v., 488
Progress t., 75
Prospect mt., 147
Prosper t., 39; v., 194
Providence t., 291, (360)
Pseudo-Messer l., 297
Pulaski t., for C. Pulaski, b., 354; l., 591
Pullman l., for Charles Pullman, 218
Puposky, l., 34, 41, 46; l. and v., 39
Pusey, Pennock, for, 630
Putnam l., 501
Pyle, Joseph G., 278
Pym, John, for, 632

Quadna t., 16
Quam l., for P. J. Quam, 181
Quamba v., 266
(Quarry sta., 63)
Queen t., 427; bluff, 585
"Queen City," 387
Quincy t., 387
Quiring t., 39

Rabbit l., 20; pt., 46; r., 217, 580; id., 498
Rabbit Lake t., l., and r., 159
Raccoons, 25
Rachel, l., 181, 502
Racine t., (and r.), 12; t., and v., 361
Radisson, Pierre Esprit, for, 130; 164, 169

Radisson l., 130, 134; bay, 346
Radium v., 330
Rail Prairie t., for Case Rail, 354
Rainbow id., 347
Rainy l., 1, 8, 281, 287, 401, 497; islands, bays, and points, 286, 498
Rainy r., 1, 8, 44, 281, 285
(Rainy Lake c., 284)
Ramsey, Gov. Alexander, for, 24; 166, 192, 220; n., 24, 224; 361, 375; for, b., 436, 453, 454, 591, 606, 614, 642
Ramsey, Justus C., 61
Ramsey co., 436-444; t., 24; v., 361; cr. and l., 453, 454; l., 591
Ramsey state park, 454
Randall, Major B. H., quoted, 374
Randall v., for John H. Randall, b., 355; (t., 351, 355)
Randeau l., 25
Randolph t. and v., for John Randolph, 166
Ranges, iron ore, 1, 157, 163, 502-504
Ranier v., 284
Ranklev, l., 404
Ransom t., 378
Rapid r., 39, 40, 42, 284, (498)
Rapid River t., 39, 284
Rapidan t. and v., 62, 66
Rapids l., 84
Rasmusson, l., 434
Raspberry id., 441, 614
Rat l., 20, 152; Rat House l., 20
Rat Portage, Ontario, 285
Rat Root r. and bay, 121; t. and l., 284, 285
Rattle l, 141
Raven stream, 511
(Raven's Wing, r., 154)
Ravenna t., 166
Ray l., 141; t., 285
Ray's bay and pt., for Fred G. Ray, 132
Ray's l., for George E. Ray, 304
Raymond, Bradford P., for, 631
Raymond v., 271; t., for L. B. Raymond, 526
Read's Landing v., for C. R. Read, b., 558
Reading v., for Henry H. Read, 379
Ready's l., 511
Reagan, Albert B., 287
Reaney, John H., for, 624
Rebecca, l., 165, 169, 233
Rebellion, War of, 1861-5, 62, 114, 135, 136, 156

Red l., 1, 6, 34, 36, 48, 445; tributaries and points, 45-48
Red pt., Lake Superior, 145
Red r., 1, 6, 29, 56, 119, 390, 394, 445
(Red Cedar l., 9, 17, 35, 86)
Red Cedar r., 13; id., 96
Red Clover t., 75
Red Eye t. and r., 561, 562
Red Lake co., 445-447
Red Lake r., 34, 35, 41, 46, 48, 407, 408, 445
Red Lake Agency, v., 45
Red Lake Falls, c. and t., 447
Red Lake Indian reservation, 45
Red River t., 279
Red River Valley, 2, 6, 116, 118
Red Rock bay, Lake Superior, 145
Red Rock l., 141, 179, 181, 231
Red Rock t., (179,) 361, (571;) v., 570
Red Sand r., 140, 145, 148; l., 162
Red Sucker id., 286
Red Water cr., 48
Red Wing c., for Sioux chiefs, 207, 208
Redby v., 39
Redfield, Ross, for, 566
Redpath t., 552
Redstone v., 373
Redwood co., 448-454; r., 448, 451
Redwood Falls c. and t., 451
(Ree t., 595)
Reed l., 72, 402
Reed's l., for John Reed, 567
(Reed-grass r., 470)
Reedy t., for David Reedy, 285
Reep l., 32
Reeves l., 32
Reilly cr., 286
Reindeer, 142
Reiner t., 407
Reis t., for George Reis, 427
Reitz l., for Frederick Reitz, 85
Relf, Richard, 481, 644, 645
Remer t. and v., for E. N. and W. P. Remer, 92
Remund t., for Samuel Remund, b., 567
Rendsville t., 537
Reno, Gen. Jesse L., for, 162, b., 239, 432
Reno l., 162; v., 239; t., 432; sta., 489
Renova v., 361
Renville, Joseph, 104; for, b., 455, 458
Renville co., 455-460; v., 458

INDEX

Renwick, James, 153
Reque, Mrs. Linka, for, 434
Reservation r., 140, 145, 148; (l., 180)
(Reserve t., 236, 437)
Reshanau l., 25
Resser l., 401
Rest Island, 211
Retzhoff l., 218
Reunion, mt., 147
Revere v., for Paul Revere, b., 451
Reynolds t., 545
Rezac l., for Frank Rezac, 465
Rheiderland t., 105
Rhemnicha, Sioux name of Red Wing, 208
Rhinehart t., for A. C. Rhinehart, 427
Rhode Island, name from, 291
Rhodes hill, for D. C. Rhodes, 133
Rialson, Louis, and Ole, n., 314
Rice, Charles R., for, 617
Rice, Edmund, for, 601, 617, 624
Rice, Frank C., n., 244, 245
Rice, Henry M., n., 23, 25; for, 239, 441, b., 461, 601, 613, 624, 639
Rice, Mrs. Henry M., for, 624, 628
Rice, Orrin W., 22; for, b., 489, 645
Rice co., 461-465; t., 123
Rice cr., 25, 267, 441, 453, 516; bay, 94
Rice l., 16, 18, 20, 25, 26, 33(4), 43(2), 65, 72, 85(2), 124, 143, 162 (4), 169, 188(2), 202, 231(2), 233, 248; Upper, and Lower, 251; 257, 304(3), 305, 319, 337, 342, 348, 349, 357, 400(2), 403(2), 404, 435, 465, 489, 494, 502(2), 511(2), 512 (2), 516(2), 529, 530(3), 534, 548 (3), 549, 563, 566, 567, 573, 590 (3), 592
Rice r., 16, 18, 501; v. and prairie, for George T. Rice, 50
Rice's l., for Andrew Rice, 521
Rice Lake t., (61,) 489; v., 173
Rice River t., 16
Rice's Point, d., Duluth, 489, 493, 645
Riceford v., 239; cr., 240, 241
Riceland t., 202
Riceville t., 30
Rich, W. W., for, b., 398
Rich prairie, 357
Rich Valley v., 167; t., 318
Richardson, Harris, n., 284
Richardson, Nathan, 350; for, b., 355
Richardson, Robert, n., 58

Richardson l., 342; t., 355
Richardville t., for George Richards, 279
Richdale v., 398
Richfield t., (61,) 226
Richland t., (226,) 463
Richmond, (t., for John Richmond, 166;) v., 526; t. and v., 583
Richville v., 398
Richwood t., 30
Rickert l., 534
Ridgely, H., R., and T. P., for, 373
Ridgely t., and fort, 373
Rieff l., 273
Riggs, Rev. Stephen R., cited, 13, 55, 71, 82, 97, 104, 217, 227, 238, 368, 386, 564, 595
Riley, l., 231
Rima, Mrs. S., n., 68
Ringo l., 274
Ripley, Gen. Eleazar W., for, 157, b., 355
Ripley, l., for Dr. F. N. Ripley, 342
Ripley t., 173, 355; fort, 355
Ristan, Mrs. Bertha, for, 543
River t., 447
River Falls t., 407
Riverdale t., (176,) 575
Riverside t., 291, (466, 579)
Rivers sta., 489
Riverton t., 118; v., 160
Riverview d. (West St. Paul), 438, 439, 440, 611, 617-620
Roach l., 320
Roadruck, Mrs. Florence Miltona, for, 178; Irene, for, 180
Robbins, Daniel M., for, 632
Robbins bay and id., for D. H. Robbins, 347
Robbinsdale v., for A. B. Robbins, 226
Roberds l., for Wm. Roberds, 465
Robert, Capt. Louis, for, 511, 612, 620
Robert cr., 511
Roberts, Dr. T. S., notes of birds, 36, 261
Roberts t., for Michel Roberts, 579
Robertson, Col. D. A., n., 61; for, 618
Robertson, Orlando A., for, 634
Robideau l., 43
Robinson, Doane, quoted, 71, 208
Robinson, sta. and l., 489
Robinson's bay, 234
Roche, O. H., n., 379
Rochester c. and t., 387
Rock co., 466-9; t., 418

Rock cr., 111, 413; r., 12, 378, 418, 466
Rock l., 33, 161, 314, 414, 415, 501, 591
Rock Creek t. and v., 413
Rock Dell t., 388
Rock Lake t., 314
Rockford t. and v., 589
Rocksbury t. (and Rockstad p. o.), Rockville t. and v., 526
Rockwell l. (and t.), for C. H. for Martin Rockstad, 407 Rockwell, 244
Rockwell t., 383
Rockwood t., 244, 562
Rocky l., 78; pt., 36, 44
Rodman, John, n., 271
Roe, Anders, n., 261
Rogers, Albert B., n., 458
Rogers, Henry C., n., 362
Rogers, Josias N., for, 641
Rogers, William K., for, 654
Rogers l., 162, 375; for J. E., R. H., and J. Rogers, 65; for E. G. Rogers, 169
Rogers shore, for O. S. Rogers, 347
Rogers t., for Wm. A. Rogers, 92; v., 226
Roland l., for John Roland, 181
Rolette v., for Joe Rolette, 383
Rolling Forks t., 433
Rolling Green t., 334
Rolling Stone t. and v., 583; r., 583, 585
Rollins, John, for, 606
Rollins sta., 489
Rollis t., for Otto Rollis, 330
Rome t., 187
Rondo, Joseph, for, 617
Ronneby v., 51
Roome t., 427
Roosevelt, Theodore, for, 39, 49, 88, 148, 160; b., 473; 605
Roosevelt, l., 88, 161
Roosevelt t., 39, 160, (330, 472;) v., 39, 473
Root r., 11, 12, 196, 362, 389
Rosabel l., 292
Rosby sta., for Ole Rosby, 245
Roscoe t., 208; v., 526
Rose, Arthur P., 311; quoted, 466
Rose l., for Fred Rose, 72; 139, 336, 401, 404
Rose t., for Isaac Rose, b., 438; (594)
Rose Creek v., and cr., 361
Rose Dell t., 469
Rose Hill t., 151

Roseau co., 48, 470-475; v., 473
Roseau l. and r., 36, 470
Rosebud t., 427
Rosebush t. and r., 136, 144
Rosedale t., 323
Roseland t., 271
Rosemount t. and v., 166, 168
Rosendale t., 575
Roseville t., 216, 271
Rosewood t., 105; sta., 330
Rosing t., for L. A. Rosing, b., 355
Ross l., 141, 160; t., 473; sta., 566
Ross Lake t. and l., 160
Ross's Landing, for John and Samuel Ross, 239
Rost t., for Frederick Rost, 263
Rosvold l., 401
Rothsay v., 579
Round ls., 21(4), 26, 32, 33, 141, 161(2), 168, 218(2), 231, 256(3), 264, 296, 304, 337, 342, 356, 357, 369, 379, 402(2), 403, 435, 443, 548
Round Grove t. and l., 318, 521
Round Lake r., 32; t. and sta., 256, 263; v., 379
Round Mound, a hill, 554
Round Prairie t., and v., 546
Rove l., 139
Rowena v., 452
Roy, Simon, for, 324
Roy l., 162
Royal l., 140; t., 308
Royalton v., 355; t., 413
Ruble, George S., n., 201
Ruby l., 258
Ruckle's l., 590
Ruffee cr., for Charles A. Ruffee, 125
Rulien t., for William Rulien, 39
Rum r., 343, 348, 349
Rune stone, Kensington, 177
Runeberg t., for J. L. Runeberg, b., 30
(Rush bay, Leech l., 96)
Rush cr., 195, 233, 465, 534, 585; r., 109, 520
Rush l., 65, 109, 141, 160, 161, 162, 264(2), 309, 342, 369(2), 398, 402, 454, 489, 516
Rush species in Minnesota, 109
Rush City v., 109
Rush Lake t., 398; sta., 489
Rushford c. and t., 194, 195
Rushmore v., for S. M. Rushmore, 379
Rushseba t., 109

INDEX 715

Russell, Roswell P., n., 84; for, 601, 603, 610
Russell, William, n., 63
Russell l., for T. P. Russell, 161
Russell v., 314
Russia, names from, 55, 202, 427
Russia t., 427
Rustad v., for Samuel Rustad, 118
Ruth l., 157
Ruthrup sta., 118
Ruthton v., 418
Rutland t., 334
Rutledge v., 414
Rutz l., for Peter Rutz, 85
Ryder, Eben, n., 457

Sabe l., 125; Saber l., 304
Sabin v., for D. M. Sabin, b., 118; l., 500
Sable id., 44
Sac Indians, 9, 140
(Sack r., 51)
Saco sta., 534
(Sacramento v., 174)
Sacred Heart t., 458; v., and cr., 459
Saganaga falls and l., 139, 140
Sager l., 336
Saginaw v., 489; bay, 498
Saginaw, Mich., 140
Sago t., 256
Sah-ging pt., 347
(Sahlmark t., 537)
(St. Agnes t., 396)
St. Alban's bay and v., 234
St. Albans, Vt., 156
St. Anna, l., 530
(St. Anthony c., 226, 326, 600, 605, 606)
St. Anthony, (fort, 34, 67, 228, 229;) falls, 219, 230
(St. Anthony Falls v., 226, 326)
St. Anthony Hill d., 440, 443
St. Anthony Park d., 438, 631-3, 641
St. Augusta t. and v., 526; cr., 529
St. Bonifacius v., 227
St. Catherine's l., 511
St. Catherine's College, 440, 637
St. Charles t. and v., 583
St. Clair, Gen. Arthur, for, 614, 636
St. Clair ls., two, 33; v., 62
St. Cloud c., 52, 516, 526; b., 527; t., 527
St. Columba mission, 162
St. Croix l., 10, 11, 571
St. Croix r., 1, 3, 10, 572; Interstate pk., 112, 113

St. Croix River sta., 109
St. Francis t. and r., 25, 514; l., 251, (516)
St. George t., 51; hamlet, 318
St. Hilaire v., 408
St. Hubert, patron of hunters, 161
St. Hubert's Lodge, 212
St. James t. and c., 575; l., 576
St. John's t., 271; l., 272
St. John's University, 523
St. Joseph t., 279; t. and v., 527
St. Lawrence t. (and v.), 509
St. Leo v., 596
St. Louis co., 476-506; b., 476; t., 489; bay, 493, 643; l., 530
St. Louis, gl. l., 79, 505
St. Louis r., 1, 9, 75, 78, 79, 476, 493, 502, 648, 652
St. Louis Park v., 227
St. Martin t. and v., 527
St. Mary l., 500, 530; t., (509,) 566
St. Mathias t., 160
St. Michael v., 586, 589
(St. Nicholas v., 202)
St. Olaf t., 398; St. Olaf's l., 567
St. Paul c., 438, 611-642; maps of 1851 and 1857, 611-617
St. Paul Park v., 571
St. Paul Seminary, 440, 637
St. Paul and Duluth railroad, 108, 110, 569
St. Paul and Pacific railroad, 27, 423
St. Paul and Sioux City ry., 575, 576
St. PAUL DISTRICTS AND ADDITIONS:
Arlington Hills, 440, 623, 624; Baker, ad. in 1889, 634; Bazille and Guerin, ad. in 1850, 612; Beaver Lake Heights, 626; Brooklynd, 616; Brunson, ad. in 1852, 627; Cherokee Heights, 443; Como, 627; Como Park, 440, 626-9, 631; Concordia College, 636; Cottage Homes, 629; Crocus Hill, 635; Dayton, ad. in 1853, 627; Dayton Bluff, 439, 621, 623; Desnoyer Park, 634; Frankson, ad. in 1913, 630; Groveland, 440, 637; Hamline, 440, 629; Harvester Heights, 625; Hazel Park, 437, 625; Hiawatha Park, 637; Highwood, 437, 621; Hill district, 440; Hoyt, ad. in 1850, 612; Iglehart, Hall, and Mackubin, ad. in 1856, 624; Kenwood Terrace, 635; Kittson, ad. in 1851, 612; Kittsondale, 636; Lake Como Villas, 627; Leech,

ad. in 1849, 612; Lexington Park, 440, 636; Macalester Park, 440, 636; (McLean t., 437, 622;) Merriam Park, 437, 633-4; Midway Heights, 630, 641; Oakland, 621; Otto, ad., in 1888, 636, 637; Park Place ad., 613, 642; Patterson, ad. in 1851, 612; Phalen Park, 440, 626; (Reserve t., 236, 437;) Rice and Irvine, ads., 1849 and 1851, 612; Rice, Edmund, ads., 1855 and 1881, 624; Ridgewood Park, 635; Riverside Park, 621; Riverview, 438, 640; Robert and Randall, ad. in 1851, 612; Roblyn Park, 634; St. Anthony Hill, 440; St. Anthony Park, 438, 631-3, 641; St. Paul Proper, 611; Seven Corners, 440, 613; Shadow Falls Park, 637; Sigel, ad. in 1880 and 1883, 623; Stinson, ad. in 1856, 617, 629; Suburban Hills, 621; Suburban Homes, 623; Summit Park, 635; Sylvan Park, 636; Terrace Park, 635; Town and Country Club grounds, 634; Tracy, ad. in 1874, 625; Union Park, 633, 642; Vandenburgh, ad. in 1851, 612; Warrendale, 627, 641; West St. Paul, 438, 440, 616, 617-620; Whitney and Smith, ad. in 1849, 612; Winslow and Willes, ad. in 1851, 612; Youngman and others, ad. in 1886, 638.

St. Paul streets: (A, 618;) Abell, 628; Acker, 624; Acorn, 629; Adams, 627; Adolphus, 628; Adrian, 638; Aftondale, 621; Agate, 628; Alabama, 615, 618; Albany, 631; Albemarle, 628; Alden, 631, 632; Alfred, 632; Alice, 640; Alison, 615, 638; Allston, 621; Almond, 631; Alton, 638; Amherst, 637; Ann, 613; Ann Arbor, 634; Annapolis, (617,) 619, 620; Arbor, 638; Arcade, 621, 624; Arch, 616; Argyle, 627; Arkwright, 614; (Arnold, 616;) Arundel, 617, 628; Ash, 627; Atlantic, 622, 623; Atlantis, 631; Atwater, 629; Audubon, 638; Augusta, 619; Autumn, 625; Avon, 635; (B, 618;) Baker, 620; Baldwin, 637; Baldwin court, 635; Banfil, 614; Banning, 615, 638; Barclay, 623; Bartlett court, 632; Barton, (622,) 638; Bay, (628,) 638; Bayard, 634; Bayfield, 618; Beacon, 621; Beard court, 632; Bee, 638; Beech, 622; Bellevue, 621; Bellows, 619; Belmont, 620; Belvidere, 619; Bena, 626; Bench, 611, 612; Bernard, 619; Bernardine, 628; Berta, 637; Bidwell, 619, 620; Birmingham, 623; Blair, (614,) 629; (Bock, 623;) Bradford, 632; Bradley, 614, 624; Brand, 625; Breda, 631; (Bridge, 618;) Broadway, 612; Brompton, 619, 632; (Brook, 614;) Brooklyn, 618; Brott, 620; (Brunson, 612;) Burgess, 629; Burke, 621; Burr, 614, 624; Bushnell, 632; (C, 618;) (Cadett, 617;) Canada, 613; Canton, 638; Capitol Heights, 616; Carbon, 629; Carleton, 634; (Caroline, 618;) Carter, 632; Cascade, 615; Case, 624, 628; Cayuga, 624, (635;) Cedar, 611, 612, (618;) Center, 626; Charles, (612,) 616, (618;) Charlton, 620; Chatsworth, 627, 635; Chelmsford, 632; Cherry, 622; Chester, 618; Chestnut, 613, (627;) Child, 629; Clarence, 623; Clark, 624; (Clay, 618;) Clear, (619,) 629; Clermont, 622; Clifford, 634; Clifton, 638; Cohansey, 628; Colborne, 615; Coleman, 628; Collins, 614; Colne, 627; Colorado, 615, 619; Columbia, 616; Commercial, (615,) 621; Como place, 627; Concord, 620; Congress, 619; Constans, 618; Conway, 622; Cook, 624; Corinne, 634; Cortland, 613, 628; Cottage, (619, 620,) 627, 629; Court, 618; Crescent court, 635; Crocus place, 635; Cudworth, 632; Cumberland, 628; Curtice, 619; Custer, 618; Cypress, 622; (D, 618;) Dakota, 615, 619; Dale, 617, 628, 635; Daly, 638; Dealton, 638; Dearborn, 619; Delos, 618; Denny, 629; De Soto, 614, 624; Dieter, 626; Doane, 634; Dodd road, 613, 620; Dorr, 624; Douglas, 613; Dousman, 613; Drake, 638; (Dugas, 618;) Duke, 615; Duncan, 626; Dunlap, 629; (E, 618;) Eagle, 613; Earl, 622; (East, 622;) Eastman, 632; Edgcumbe road, 636; Edgemont, 628; Edgerton, 624; Edgewood place, 621; Edmund, 616; Edward, 618; Eighth, 613, (618;)

Eldred, 632; Eleanor, 636; Eleventh, 613; Elfelt, 617; Elisabeth, 618; (Ellen, 616;) Ellis, 632; Elm, 613, (618;) Elmwood, 621; Elway, 638; Endicott, 632; English, 622, 623; Erie, 614, 615; Etna, 623; Euclid, 622; Eustis, 631, 634; Eva, 618; Everett court, 632; Exchange, 613; (F, 618;) (Fairview, 616;) Fauquier, 624; Fenton, 618; Ferdinand, 633; Fifield, 632; Fifth, 611, (618,) 622; (First, 615, 618;) Fisher, 626; Flandrau, 623; Floral, 635; Florida, 615, 618; (Folwell, 631;) (Forbes, 613;) Forest, 622; Forster, 638; (Fort, 613, 642;) Fourteenth, 613; Fourth, 611, (618,) 622; Frank, 623; Franklin, 613; Fremont, 622; Front, 627; Fry, 629, 634; Fulham, 632; Fulton, (623,) 638; Garfield, 614; Gaultier, 617, 628; Genesee, 624; George, 618; Geranium, 625; Germain, 623; Glen road, 621; Glen terrace, 638; Glencoe, 616; Goodhue, 614, (618;) Gotzian, 623; Grace, 615, 635; Graham, 638; Grantham, 632; (Green, 614;) (Greene, 618;) Griffith, 622; Griggs, 629, 636; Grotto, 627, 628, 635; Grove, 613, 614, (614, 618, 619, 621;) Hadley, 621; (Hall, 624;) Hancock, 623; (Harriet, 618;) Haskell, 619; Hatch, 627; Hawley, 628; Hawthorn, 625, 629; Heather place, 635; Hedge, 620; Helen, 625; Herbert, 625; Heron, 626; Hester, 622; Hiawatha, 622; Highland, 628; (Hill, 619, 621;) Hope, 621; Hopkins, 614; Hubbard, 629; Hunt, 632; (Huron, 612;) Hyacinth, 625, 629; Hyde, 618; Hythe, 632; Irving place, 638; Isabel, 618; Ivy, 625, 629; Jackson, 611, 612, 616, (619;) Jackson place, 638; James, 615, 636; Jay, (616,) 617; Jenks, 624; Jessamine, 625; Jessie, 624; John, 612, (618;) Johnson, 622; Join, 634; Juliet, 636; Juno, 636; Keller, 626; Kennard, 623; Kent, 617, 628; Kentucky, 615, 618; Kerwin, 625; Keston, 632; Kiefer, 625; Kilburn, 627; King, 620; Kittson, 612; Knapp, 631, 633; Lafond, 629; (Lake, 623;) Lamm place, 638; Langtry, 628; Lansing, 636; Larch, 629; La Salle, 634; Lawson, 624; Lawton, 635; Leech, 613; Lincoln place, 638; Linda, 621; Linden, 616, (635;) Lindley, 632; Linwood place, 635; Litchfield, 629; Locust, 612, (627;) Loeb, 628; Logan, 627, 638; L'Orient, 616, 627; Louis, 617; Louisa, 619; Louth, 627; Lowell, 618; Lucy, 619; Lydia, 636; Lyton place, 629; McAfee, 626; McBoal, 614; Macubin, 617, 628; McKenty, 627; McMenemy, 628; Madison, 638; Magnolia, 624, 625; (Main, 618;) Manson, 632; Manton, 626; Manvel, 632; Maple, 621; Margaret, 622, 623; Marion, 617, 628; Market, 613; Marsh court, 632; Martin, (616,) 622; (Mary, 618;) Maryland, 615, 624, 625, 629; May, 638; Mechanic, 625; Mendota, 621; Mercer, 638; Merrimac, 621; Michigan, 614, 615; Milford, 629; Mill, (612, 618,) 638; Milton, 635; Minnehaha, 622, 623, 624, 629; Minnesota, 611, 612; Minnetonka, 618; Mississippi, 613, 615; Missouri, 615, 618; Montague place, 633; Montcalm place, 635; Montgomery, 634; (Moore, 623;) Morton, 619; Mound, 621; Mt. Airy, 616; Mt. Ida, 614; Munster, 638; Mystic, 621; Neche, 626; Neill, 612; (New Canada road, 613, 628;) Niagara, 627; Ninth, 613, (618;) North, 614, 627; Norton, 628; Nugent, 638; Nye, 629; (Oak, 613, 617, 618, 622;) Ohio, 615, 620; Olive, 612, (621;) Oliver, 629; Olivier, 628; Omaha, 638; Oneida, 615; (Ontario, 614;) Orange, 625, 629; Orchard, 627; Oregon, 615; Orleans, 620; Orrin, 638; Oxford, 627, 635; Pacific, 622; Packard, 632; Page, 619; Palace, 615, 636; Palmer, 638; Paris, 621; Parmer, 638; Parsons, 615, 638; Patridge, 614; Patton, 632; Pearl, (623,) 632; Pelham, 634; Pennock, 630; Pepperell, 632; Perry, 618; Phalen, 625; Piedmont, 621; Pierce, 634; (Pike, 612;) Pine, 612, (613;) Plum, 622; Plymouth, 618; Pond, 621; Powder, 625; (Prairie, 614, 627, 635;) (Pratt, 631;) Prescott,

620; Priscilla, 632; (Pym, 632;) Quincy, 627; Race, 638; (Railroad, 615;) Raleigh, 632; Ramsey, 614; Randolph, 636; Rankin, 638; (Ravine, 622;) Reaney, 624; Rice, 613, (614,) 628; Richmond, 615; River, 622; Rivoli, 614; Robbins, 632; Robert, 611, 612; Robertson, 618; Robie, 619, 635; Rock, 629; Rondo, 616, 634; Rosabel, 612; Rose, (618,) 625; Rosenberger place, 638; Roy, 634; Rutland, 618; Ryde, 627; St. Albans, 628, 635; St. Clair, 612, 614, 615, 636, 638; St. Lawrence, 618; St. Paul, 638; St. Peter, 611, 612; Salem, 621; Scheffer, 636, 638; Schwabe, 626; Scudder, 632, 633; (Searls, 624;) (Second, 615, 618;) Seminary, 629; Service lane, 637; Seventh, 611, 613 (618,) 621, 638, 642; Shawmut, 621; Sheridan, 638; Sherman, 613; Sherwood, 632; Short, 622; Shrub, 627; Sibley, 611, 612; Sigel, 623; (Simpson, 612;) Sims, 624; Sixth, 611, (618,) 622; Sloan, 628; (Smith, 614;) Somerset, 613; South, 627, 629; South Robert, 618; South Wabasha, 618; Spring, 613, (618, 619,) 638; Springfield, 638; Standish, 632; Starkey, 618; State, 618; Stella, 632; Stevens, 620; Stickney, 620; Stinson, 629; Suburban, 622; Sue, 637, 639; Superior, 614; Sycamore, 629; Sydney, 620; Sylvan, 628; Tell, 623; Temperance, 613; Temple, 621; Temple court, 634; Tennessee, 615, 618; Tenth, 613; Terry, 623; Texas, 615, 618; Third, 611, (618,) 622; Thirteenth, 613; Thomas, 616; Thorn, 622; Tile, 615; Topping, 629; Toronto, 615; Truman place, 638; Turner, 632; Twelfth, 613; Tyler, 619; Union, 627; Urban place, 622; Utah, 615, 618; Valley, 616; Van Buren, 623, 629; Van Buren place, 622; Van Reed, 632; Vance, 638; Vandalia, 634; Victoria, 627, 635; View, 638; Villard, 637; (Vine, 614, 618;) Viola, 615; Von Minden, 614; Wabasha, 611, 612, 616; Wabasso, 626; Wacouta, 612; Walnut, 613, (627;) Walpole, 637; Walter, 618; Warren, 616; Warsaw, 638; Waseca, 620; Washington, 613, 638; Washington place, 638; Water, 611, 612, 618, 621; Wayzata, 629; Webster, 612, 615; Wells, 624; Wentworth, 634; (Westerlo, 616;) Westminster, 614, 628; Weymouth, 621; Wheeler, 632; Whitall, 624; Wilkin, 613; (William, 612;) Williams, 616; Willius, 612, (633;) (Willow, 621;) Winifred, 619; Winnebago, 620; Winona, 620; Winthrop, 621; Wisconsin, 615; Wood, 618; Woodbine, 621; Woodbridge, 628; Woodlawn place, 621; Woodward, 614; Wordsworth, 638; Wyandotte, 618; Wycliff, 632; Wynne, 631; Wyoming, 615, 619; Yale, 637; Yankee, 614; York, 624

ST. PAUL AVENUES, so named indiscriminately with streets, 623; Agnes, 638; Alaska, 615, 638; Albert, 629; Albion, 638; Aldine, 629, 634; Algonquin, 626; Allen, 619; Ames, 625; Archer, 615; Armstrong, 636, 638; Arona, 630; Asbury, 629; Ashland, 635; Astoria, 633; Aurora, 616; Barrett, 627; Basswood, 621; Bates, 621; Bayard, 636; Bayless, 632; Beacon, 634; (Belle, 624;) Bellevue, (620,) 639; Benson, 638; Berkeley, 636; Berry, 634; Beverly, 634; (Bidwell, 619;) Bison, 630; Blackwood, 621; Blake, 632; Boland, 637; Bourne, 632; Bowdoin, 637; Boxwood, 621; (Brewster, 616;) Brimhall, 637; Brookline, 621; (Brown, 619;) Buford, 633; Burlington, 621; Burns, 622; Butternut, 638; California, 615, 629; Cambridge, 637; Capitol, 629; Carroll, 616; Carter, 631, 633; Caulfield, 639; Central, 616; Chapman, 638; Charlotte, 629; Chelton, 630; Cherokee, 620; Chester, 621; Chicago, 618; Chippewa, 620; Churchill, 627; Cleora, 634;; Cleveland, 631; Clinton, 619; Coburn, 637; College, 613; Columbus, 634; Commonwealth, 631, 633; Como, 631; Corning, 625; Cretin, 634, 637; Cromwell, 632, 634; Cross, 627; Crowell, 627; Curfew, 634; Curve, 626; Danforth, 628; Davern, 639; Dayton, 615, (621,) 627;

INDEX

Delaware, 615, 620; Dewey, 633; (Dooley, 631, 633;) Dora, 637; Doswell, 631, 633; (Douglas, 624;) Dudley, 633; Dustin, 637; East, 623, 625; Eaton, 618; Emerald, 634; Escanaba, 626; (Evergreen, 635;) Fairfield, 618; Fairmount, 635; Fairview, 629, 633, 637, 639; Farrington, 615, 628; Feronia, 633; Field, 639; Fillmore, 618; Finn, 634; Forbes, 614; Forest Hill, 621; Frankson, 630; Fredericka, 637; Fuller, 616; Furness, 626; (Gale, 619;) Gibbs, 631, 632; Gilbert, 634; Glendale, 634; Glenham, 634; Goodrich, 614; Gordon, 632; Gorman, 619; Grand, 635; (Gray, 624;) Greenbrier, 624; Greenwood, 619; Hager, 626; Hall, 619, 624; Hamline, 629, 636; Hammer, 625; Hampden, 632, 634; Hand, 628; Harrison, 614; Hartford, 636; Harvard, 626; Harvester, 625; Hastings, 622; Hathaway, 638; Hazel, 623, 625, 626; Hazelwood, 623; Hazzard, 628; Hendon, 632; (Herkimer, 614;) Herschel, 634; Hersey, 632; Hewitt, 629; Highwood, 621; Hoffman, 621; Holton, 629; Horton, 627; Howard, 621, 625; Howell, 633; Hoyt, 627, 629; Hudson, 622; Huron, 626; Idaho, 615, 627, 629; Iglehart, 616; Indiana, 615, 618; Iowa, 615, 629; Iroquois, 626; Irvine, 615; Jameson, 627; Jeanne, 620; Jefferson, 615, 616, 635, 636; Jordan, 626; Kansas, 615; Kenneth, 637; Keogh, 625; LaCrosse, 625; Lafayette, 614; Lake Como and Phalen, 626, 627, 629; Lamprey, 620; Langford, (631,) 633; Larpenteur, 626, 627, 628, 629; (Laura, 633:) Laurel, 635; Lee, 638; Lenox, 621; Leonard, 638; (Leslie, 635;) Lexington, 627, 629, 635, 636; Lilac, 625; Lincoln, 635; Linwood, 621; Livingston, 618, 619; Lombard, 635; Luella, 625; Lynnhurst, 633; McKinley, 630; McLean, 622; Macalester, 637; (Madison, 635;) Magoffin, 637; Main, 613; Manitoba, 629; Manitou, 626; Manomin, 619, 620; Maplewood, 634; Maria, 621; Marlboro, 634; Marshall, 616, 634; Mary, 626; Matilda, 628;

Medford, 634; (Melrose, 616;) Merchants, 615; Middleton, 638; Milwaukee, 633; Minea, 620; (Minneapolis, 626;) (Mississippi, 619;) Mohawk, 619, 626; Montana, 615, 629; Montrose, 634; Moore, 633; Morgan, 639; Moritz, 637; Myrtle, (619,) 634; Nebraska, 615, 627, 629; Nelson, 615; Nettleton, 636; Nevada, 615, 629; Newport, 621; Niles, 636; Nokomis, 626; Nortonia, 626; Norwich, 637; Oakland, 635; Oakley, 633; (Oliver, 620;) Osceola, 635, 636; Otis, 634; Otsego, 614; Ottawa, 620; Otto, 636, 638; Overbrook, 626; (Owasco, 635;) Oxford, 626; Park, 615, 628; Pascal, 629, 634, 637; Payne, 624; Pedersen, 626; Pennsylvania, 615, 616; Phalen, 626; Pillsbury, 634; Plato, 618; Pleasant, 613; (Pomona, 633;) Portland, 635; Princeton, 637; Prior, 632, 633, 639; Prospect, (614,) 625; Prosperity, 625; Purnell, 638; Railroad, 625; (Randall, 620;) Raymond, 631, 632, 633, 634; Redwood, 621; Ridgewood, 635; Roblyn, 634; Rockwood, 638; Rogers, 638; Ruth, 623, 625, 626; St. Anthony, 616, 633, 634; Sanborn, 625; Saratoga, 637; Sargent, 636; Schley, 619; Schneider, 637; Selby, 615; Seminole, 619, 620; Sheldon, 629; Sherburne, 616; Sherwood, 625; Shields, 634; Simpson, 629; Smith, 638; Snelling, 629, 630, 637; Somerville, 634; (South Summit, 636;) Springfield, 621; Stanford, 636; Stewart, 638; Stillwater, 625; Stryker, 619; Summit, 615, 628, 635; Sumner, 637; Syndicate, 629, 636; Tallula, 630; Taylor, 629; Terrace Park, 633; (Territorial, 616;) Tracy, 625; Underwood, 637; University, 616, 629, 634, 636; Upland, 621; Van Dyke, 625; Van Slyke, 627; Vassar, 626; Vernon, 637; Villard, 629; Virginia, 615; Vista, 638; Wabash, 634; Wakefield, 622; Walker, 629; Walsh, 624; Waltham, 633; Warwick, 637; (Washington, 618, 619, 635;) Watson, 636; Weide, 624; Wellesley, 636; Wesley, 629; Western, 614, 615, 617,

625, 628, 638; (Westwood, 632;) Wheeler, 629, 634; Whitall, 620; White Bear, 623; Whitewood, 621; Wilder, 633; Winnipeg, 629; Winslow, 619; Winthrop, 623; Wisconsin, 615, 618; Woodland, 629; Woodlawn, 621, 637; Woodville, 637; Woolsey, 638; Worcester, 639; Yale, 626; Youngman, 638

ST. PAUL BOULEVARDS AND PARKWAYS: Capitol blvd., 616; Como and River blvd., 634; Edgcumbe pky., 636; Johnson pky., 622, 640, 641; Kenwood pky., 635, 642; Lexington pky., 629, 641; Midway pky., 640; Mississippi River blvd., 634, 636, 637, 641, 642; Mounds blvd., 621, 640; Mt. Curve blvd., 637; Summit pky., 641; Wheelock pky., 640

ST. PAUL PARKS AND OTHER PUBLIC GROUNDS: Alden sq., 642; Alice pk., 640; Bay tr., 642; Cato pk., 641; Central pk., 640; Cherokee Heights pk., 640; Clayland pk., 641; College pk., 641; Commonwealth pk., 641; Como pk., 440, 628, 639, 640, 641; Crocus Hill pk., 642; Cromwell pk., 642; Dawson pk., 642; Doris sq., 642; Feronia sq., 642; Foundry pk., 641; Fountain pk., 642; Gordon sq., 642; Haldeman pk., 642; Hamm pk., 641; Hampden pk., 641; Harriet Island, 640; Hazel pk., 625; Holcombe pk., 642; Horton pk., 641; Indian Mounds pk., 621, 640; Irvine pk., 615, 639; Kendrick sq., 642; Kenwood pk., 642; Lafayette pk., 640; Lake Iris pk., 642; Lamprey pk., 640; Langford pk., 641; Le Roy tr., 641; Lewis pk., 641; Linwood pk., 642; Lockwood pk., 641; Lyton Place pk., 641; Manvel sq., 642; (Market sq., 613;) May pk., 641; Merriam Terrace pk., 642; monument for soldiers of the Civil War, 642; Newel pk., 641; Oakland pk., 642; Oakley sq., 642; Park place, 642; Phalen pk., 639; Point of View pk., 642; Portland Place pk., 640; Prospect Terrace pk., 640; Ramsey tr., 642; Raymond sq., 642; Rice pk., 613, 639; Rogers pk., 641; Shadow Falls pk., 637, 642; Sidney sq., 642; Skidmore pk., 641; Smith pk., 639; statue of Nathan Hale, 642; Stewart pk., 641; Stinson pk., 641; Summit pk., 642; Summit Outlook pk., 642; Sunshine tr., 641; Tatum pk., 641; Terrace pk., 640; Van Slyke tr., 641; Walsh pk., 642; Webster pk., 642

St. Peter c., 373; (r., 373)
St. Peter's cantonment, 227
(St. Peter's r., 3; trading post, 166)
(St. Pierre r., 3, 80)
St. Stephen v., 527
St. Thomas College, 440, 637
St. Vincent t., for St. Vincent de Paul, 279
St. Wendel t., 527
Sakata, l., 303
Salem t., 92, 388
Sallie, l., 33
Salo t., 16; Salol v., 473
Salt l., 292
Salter, John, n., 83; Salter, S. T., n., 457
Samson l., 401
San Francisco t. (and v.), 84
Sanborn, Gen. John B., for, 625
Sanborn l., 92; for Edwin Sanborn, 305
Sanborn prairie, 592
Sanborn v., for Sherburn Sanborn, 452
Sand bay, Rainy l., 286
Sand cr., 41, 162, 465, 499, 510; r., 415
Sand id., L. of the Woods, 44
Sand l., 78, 99, 120; Big and Little, 248; 256, 274(2), 296, 369, 404, 489, 501, 521, 530(3); 563, 573, 598
Sand pt., 212; narrows, 498; prairie, 512
Sand Bar crs., 47; l., 162
Sand Cliff pt., 46
Sand Creek t., 509
(Sand Hill l., 9, 44)
Sand Hill r., 324, 428
Sand Lake t., 256
Sand Point l., 496; (r., 212)
Sandberg l., 403
Sanders t., 408
Sandnes t., 596
Sands l., 32
Sandstone t. and v., 414
Sandsville t., for C. and M. Sand, 427
Sandwick l., for J. A. Sandwick, 258

INDEX

Sandy l., 14, 17, 18, 232, 324, 489, 516, (627)
Sandy r., 19, 48; t., 489
Sanford t., for H. F. Sanford, b., 216
Sangsue, l., 94
Santiago sta., 92; t. and v., 516
Sanwick p. o., for Aven Sanwick, 474
Sarah, l., 238, 366, 429
Saratoga, (townsite, 311;) t. and v., 583
Sardeson, F. W., 21, 505
Sargeant, Mrs. S. W., n., 575
Sargeant t. and v., for Harry N. Sargeant, b., 361
(Sargent t., 464)
Sargent's cr., 493
Sartell v., for Joseph B. Sartell, b., 51, 527
Sasse l., for W. and F. Sasse, 304
Saturday l., 296
Sauer's l., 32, 404
Sauk Indians, 9, 51, 179, 525, 545
Sauk ls., 51, 530, 547; r., 9, 51, 525, 547
Sauk Center c. and t., 51, 528
Sauk Rapids v., 9, 10; v. and t., 51
Sault t., 285
Saulteurs, Ojibways, 102
Savage, Marion W., for, 168, b., 510
Savage l., 443; v., 510
Savidge l., 304
Savanna lakes, 19; rivers, East and West, 17-19, 499; t., 30
Saw Bill lakes, 143
Sawteeth mts., 1, 146, 503
Sawyer sta., 75
Saxe sta., for Solomon Saxe, 489
(Saxton v., for Commodore Saxton, 145)
Sayers, William, 45
Scalp l., 404
Scambler t., for Robert Scambler, 398
Scandia d., 83; t., 427; l:, 538; v., 571
Scandia Valley t., 355
Scandinavian l., 434
Scanlon v., for M. J. Scanlon, b., 75
Scarlett t., 285
Schaefer, Rev. Francis J., 45
Schaff's l., 295
Schaffer l., 162
Schauer l., 233
Scheie, Rev. Andreas A., and Anthony, for, b., 381

Scheffer, Albert, for, 636
Schelin's l., 499
Schendel l., 233
Schilling l., for John Schilling, 521
Schley, Admiral W. S., for, 89, b., 92, 619
Schley sta., 89, 92
Schmidt l., 591
Schnappauf l., 233
Schneider Lake t., and l., for Frank Schneider, 323
School l., 44, 72, 112, 232, 305, 529, 576(2), 591(2)
School Grove l., 315
School Section l., 573
Schoolcraft, H. R., n., 4; q., 6; 9, 18; n., 41, 42, 52, 86; 91, 95; n., 96, 97, 98; 101, 125; n., 126; for, 130; 132, 134, 154; q., 163; 230; for, b., 245; 246, 247; q., 252, 256; 443, 444. 470; q., 487; 502, 514, 546, 565
Schoolcraft r., 42, 126, 248; id., 130; l., 248; t., 245
Schram l., 404
Schroeder t. and v., for John Schroeder, 137; l., 530
Schultz l., 273, 342, 499
Schurz, Carl, quoted, 114
Schutz l., for Matthias Schuetz, 85
Sciota t., 167
Scofield, Mrs. Mildred, for, 90
Scotch l., 304
Scotland, names from, 24, 39, 62, 63, 125, 221, 238, 244, 282, 317, 366, 377, 378, 391, 432, 450, 452, 489, 520, 544, 556(3), 568, 579, 586, 589, 649
Scott, Andrew Jackson, for, 141, 145
Scott, Thomas, for, 562
Scott, W. A., n., 378
Scott, Sir Walter, for, 307, 647, 649
Scott, Gen. Winfield, n., quoted, 228; for, 459, b., 507
Scott co., 2, 507-512; t., 537
Scott's pt., 145; l., 218
Scribner, Aaron, n., 525
Scudder, Rev. John L., for, 632
Scull l., 280
Sea Gull l., 141, 142, 501
Seaforth v., 452
Seaman, Fletcher D., n., 565
Searles v., 70
Seavey t., 16
Sebeka v., 562
Sebie l., 161
Second l., 112

Sedan v., 433
Seed l., 297
Seeley br., 25
Seely t., for P. C. Seely, b., 187
Seelye cr., for Moses Seelye, 251
Seig l., 232
Selby, J. W., for, 615
Sellards l., for Thomas Sellards, 341
Selma t., 151
Semmen, John, n., 194
Serbia, names from, 372, 523
Seven Beaver l., 500
Seven Corners, St. Paul, 440
Seven Mile l., 370
Severance, Mrs. C. A., 420
Severance, Martin J., for, b., 520, 521
Severance t., 520; l., 521
Seward, William H., for, b., 379, 601
Seward t., 379
Sewell, l., 401
Seymour l., for W. S. Seymour, 337
Sha-bosh-kung bay and pt., 347, 349
Shadow l., 181
Shadow Falls cr., 441
Shady id., 235; l., 389
Shady Oak l., 231
Shafer t., for Jacob Shafer, 109
Shakopee c., for Sioux chief, b., 510; (t., 508;) prairie, 512
Shakopee cr. and l., 106, 272, 542; l., 590
Shallow l., 32, 247; Shallow Lake r., 32
Sham l., 315
Shamano l., 356
Shambaugh, Prof. B. F., cited, 13
Shamrock t., 16
Shaokatan l. and t., 308, 310
Sharon t., 303
Shasha pt., 286
(Shaska t., 82)
Shauer l., 218
Shaw, Neal D., 22
Shaw, Col. Samuel D., n., 58
Shaw sta., 489; l., for Thomas Shaw, 580
Sha-wun-uk-u-mig cr., 132
Shea, John Gilmary, 219
Shea's l., for Timothy Shea, 305
Shelburne t., 314
Shelby t., for Isaac Shelby, b., 63 (Shelbyville v., 63)
Sheldon, Mrs. O., n., 201
Sheldon t., for J. C. Sheldon, 240; l., 592

Shell cr., 48; r., 29, 562; l., 29, 48, 502, 562
Shell City, a hamlet, 562
Shell Lake t., and l., 30
Shell River t., 562
Shell Rock t. (and v.), 202; r., 202, 203
Shelly t. and v., for John Shelly, 383
Shenango sta., 489
Shepard l., 530
Sherburn v., 334
Sherburne, Moses, for, b., 513, 516
Sherburne co., 513-517
Sheridan, Gen. Philip H., for, 247, 452, 603, 610
Sheridan, l., 247; t., 452
Sherman, Florence, for, 312
Sherman, Mrs. W. H., for, 418
Sherman, Gen. W. T., for, 452, 613
Sherman t., (for I. Sherman, 62;) 452, (558)
Sherwood, George W., for, 625
Shetek t. and l., 367
Shevlin t. and v., for T. H. Shevlin, b., 123
Sheyenne Indians, Minnesota, 119
Sheyenne r., N. D., 119
Shiba l., 98
Shible t., for Albert Shible, 541; l., 542
Shields, Gen. James, for, b., 463, 465, 634
Shields l., 465
Shieldsville t., 463; v., 464
Shine l., 162, 258
Shingle cr., 232; br., 357
Shingob l., 248
Shingobee t. and cr., 92, 248
Shirley sta., 427
Shirt l., 162
Shoal l., 258
Shoemaker l., 274
Shoepack l., 295
Shooks t., for Edward Shooks, 39
Short portage, 494
Shortiss id., 497
Shotley t. and br., 39, 47
Shotwell, Walter Scott, n., 177
Shovel Lake t., and l., 16
Sibilant l., 131
Sibley, Gov. Henry H., n., 3, 4; 27, 60; for, 160, 165, 275, b., 518, 520; quoted, 183; camp, 1863, 460; 576, 606, 612, 614
Sibley co., 518-521; t., 160, 520
Sibley l., 160, 246; state park, 275
Sibyl, l., 403
Sickle bay, 145

Side l., 501
Sieber's cr., for Rudolph Sieber, 120
Siegfried cr., for A. H. Siegfried, 130
Sigel, Gen. Franz, for, b., 71; 315, 623
Sigel t., 71; l., 315
Signalness cr., for Olaus Signalness, b., 434
Silent lakes, two, 403
Silver cr., 76, 78, 241, 295, 319, 389, 529, 566, 589, 591; id., 494
Silver l., 120, 162, 204, 210, 218, 304 (2), 319; ls., South and North, 334; 336, 349, 402(2), 404, 443, (2), 501, 521, 591
Silver t. and cr., 76, 77, 78
Silver Creek t., 294, 589
Silver Lake v., 318; t., 334
Silver Leaf t., 30
Silverton t., 408
Simon l., 324, 434, 563
Simpson, Sir George, and wife, for, 283
Simpson, James W., for, 615
Simpson, Bishop Matthew, for, 630
Simpson v., for Thomas Simpson, b., 388
Sina, l., 182
Sinclair t., 123
Sinnott t., for J. P. and P. J. Sinnott, 330
Sioux l., 341
Sioux, Prairie, 45, 53; see Dakotas
Sioux treaty, 1851, 375
Sioux war, 1862, 60, 72, 176, 525; monuments, 460
Sioux Agency t., 596
Sioux Valley t. and rivers, 263 (Sioux Wood r., 554)
Sisabagama l., and cr. or r., 18; l., 156
Siseebakwet, l., 257
Sisseton, l., 336
Sisseton Sioux, 57, 149, 336
Siverson l., 401
Six l., 404; Six Mile l., 98
Six Mile Grove t., 106, 541
Skagen t., for A. O. Skagen, 474
Skandia t., 367
Skane t., 279
Skataas l., 274
Skelton t., for J. and H. E. Skelton, 76
Skibo sta., 489
Skidmore, Edwin T., for, 641
Skifstrom l., 590

Skillman br., for two brothers, b., 559
Skogman's l., 251
Skow l., 369
Skree t., for Mikkel Skree, 118
Skull l., 274
Skunk cr., 77, 414, 529; l., 248, 264, 357, 529; r., 357, 529
Slate l., 296
Slater t., for David H. Slater, 92
Slawson l., for William Slawson, 548
Slayton t. and v., for C. W. Slayton, b., 368
Sleepy Eye c., for Sleepy Eyes, Sioux chief, b., 71
Sleepy Eye l. and cr., 72, 304, 454
Sletten t., for Paul C. Sletten, 427
Sloan l., for John Sloan. 248
Slocum, banker, n., 83
Slocum, Isaac, n., 58
(Slough cr., 197)
Smalley, Eugene V., quoted, 79; 397, 433
Smiler's rapids, 517
Smiley t., 160; for W. C. Smiley, 408
Smith, Mrs. Ann Eliza (Brainerd), for, 156
Smith, Ansel, 107; n., 108
Smith, Col. Benjamin F., n., 63
Smith, Charles W., 28
Smith, Donald A., 278
Smith, Rev. F. W., 45, 52
Smith, Henry W., for, 369
Smith, John Gregory, for, b., 156, 352
Smith, Mrs. John G., for, b., 156
Smith, Myron, n., 87
Smith, Robert, for, 639
Smith, Robert A., for, 613
Smith, Vernie, and L. W., for, b., 562
Smith, William J., n., 553
Smith l., 181, 232, 258, 337, 369, 589
Smith's bay, 235
Smith Lake v., for Eugene Smith, 589
Smith's Mill v., for Peter Smith, 566
Smithfield, (t., 556;) a hamlet, 558
Smoke l., 143
Smoky hill, 33
Smoky Hollow t., 93
Smootz, Rev. M. F., n., 283
Snail l., 443
Snake id., Lake Traverse, 553

Snake r., 10, 19, 265, 267, 331; cr., 559
Snelling, Col. Josiah, 34; for, b., 228, 630; Mrs. Snelling, for, 168
Snelling, William J., 67, 224
Snelling, Fort, 227, 228; military reservation, 236
Snipe l., 141
Snively, Samuel F., for, 654
Snow Shoe br., 267
Snowball l., 258
Snowbank l., 296
Snustad, Helga, for, 243
Snyder l., 454
Sobriquets of Minnesota, 4; St. Paul and Minneapolis, 439; Duluth, 481, 652; St. Cloud, 527; Rochester, 387; Winona, 584
Sodus t., 314
Solberg l., for Olens Solberg, 65; for A. H. Solberg, 182
Solberg's pt., 234
Solem t., 179
Soler t., 474
Solomon l., for Solomon R. Foot, 274
Solum l., for H. H. Solum, 120
Solway v., for Solway firth, 39; t., 489
Somerset t., 534
Sonmer l., 401
Sorin's bluff, for Rev. M. Sorin, b., 212
(Sorlien Mills, hamlet, for E. H. Sorlien, 596)
Soudan v. and mine, 490
South cr., 189, 335; l., 139, 320; ridge, 503
South America, names from, 105, 387
South Bend t., 63
South Branch t., 576
South Fork t., 266
South Harbor t., 345
South Haven v., 589
South Oscar l., 181
South St. Paul c., 167
South Stillwater v., 571
Southbrook t., 151
Southside t., 589
Spain, names from, 70, 122, 207, 301, 333, 581
Spalding t., for J. L. Spalding, 17
Spang t., for Matthew A. Spang, 256
Spanish-American war, 89, 92, 254
Sparta t., 105; v., 490
Spaulding townsite, 490

Spear-fish bay, 146
Spearhead lakes, 248
Spectacle l., 251
Spencer, H. H., n., 508
Spencer, John C., for, 473
Spencer l., 341; t., for W. Spencer, 17
Spencer Brook t., and br., 250
Sperry l., 273
Spicer, John M., 104, 271, 272, 314
Spicer, Russell, for, 314
Spicer l., 204; v., 272
Spider l., 100, 112, 162, 244, 258, 499; id., 347
Spirit hill, 512
Spirit id., 229, 347, 440, 493, 652
Spirit l., 20, (343,) 403, 493, 563, 652; r., 160
Spirit l., Iowa, 10, 262, 264
(Spirit Mountain cr., 291)
Spitser's l., 401
Split Hand t., l., and cr., 256
Split Rock t. and r., 76; canyon, 138; r. and pt., 295; cr., 420
Spoon l., 296, 442
Spooner t., for M. A. Spooner, 40
Sprague l., 465
Spray id., 235
Spring cr., 30, 106, 111, 120, 211, 304, 383, 384, 598; br., 280
Spring l., 112, 169, 182, 204(2), 218, 258, 267, 341, 402, 494, 502, 511, 512, 590
Spring Branch cr., 72
Spring Brook t., 280
Spring Creek t., 30, 383
Spring Grove t., 240
Spring Hill t., 528
Spring Lake t., 511
Spring Park bay, 235
Spring Prairie t., 118
Spring Ridge cr., 132
Spring Valley t. and v., 195, 631; cr., 196
Springdale t., 452
Springfield v., 71, (262;) t., 151, (382, 386)
Springvale t., 250
Springwater t., and cr., 469
Spruce r., 144, 415; cr., 179; l., 295; t., 474
Spruce Grove t., 30, 40
Spruce Hill t., 179
Spruce Valley t., 330
Spunk br., 529, ls., three, 530
Square l., 573
(Squaw l., 133)
Stacy, Edwin C., n., 200

Stacy v., for Dr. Stacy B. Collins, 109
Stafford t., for W. Stafford, 474
Stag cr., 342
Stahl's l., for Charles Stahl, 320
Stakke l., 32
Stalker l., 401
Stallcopp l., for L. E. Stallcopp, 548
Stanchfield, Daniel, for, b., 250; n., 348
Stanchfield t., brs., and ls., 250; l., 356
(Standing rock, 164)
Stanford t., 251
Stang l., 401
Stanley t., 314; v., 593
Stannard, George, n., 61
(Stanton t., for Elias Stanton, 200)
Stanton t., for William Stanton, 208
Staples t. and c., for Samuel and Isaac Staples, 546
Star id., 96; l., 145, 162, 341, 370, 398, 403, 548; t., 408
Star Lake t., 398
Starbuck v., 433
Staring l., 231
Stark, Edward W., 107; b., 109
Stark, Mrs. H. L., 375
Stark l., 162; t., for August Starck, 71; v., for Lars J. Stark, b., 109
Starkey, James, for, 618
Starlight p. o., 124
Starting pt., 47
(Starvation pt., 225, 235)
State fair ground, 631
State forests, 100, 506
State parks, 65, 78, 112, 126-134; 275, 363, 454
State Agricultural College, 631
State Line l., 264, 380
State University, 226, 605
Stately t., 71
Statues, National Statuary Hall, 49, 86, 237, 436, 461, 464
Stauffer l., 274
(Stavanger p. o., 596)
Stay l., for Frank Stay, b., 308, 309
Steamboat, Anson Northup, 119; North Star, 353
Steamboat r., 95, 98, 247; l., 98, 247
Stearns, Charles T., for, b., 522
Stearns, Ozora P., for, 647
Stearns co., 522-530
Steele, Franklin, for, b., 531, 603, 609
Steele co., 531-534; l., 304

Steen v., for J. P. and O. P. Steen, 469
Steenerson, Leif, for, 427
Steenerson t., for H. Steenerson, 40
Steffes t., 285
Stein, John, n., 335
Steinbach, Paul, n., 544
Stella, l., 280, 341
Stemmer l., 401
Stene l., for Mons L. Stene, 384
Stenerson, l., 435
Stennett, W. H., quoted or cited, 58, 59, 60, 63, 69, 71, 149, 186, 366, 386, 437, 450, 453, 507, 508, 534, 565, 566, 569, 574, 582
Stephen v., for George Stephen, b., 330
Stephens, F. J., n., 533
Sterling t., 63
Stevens, Gen. Isaac I., for, b., 535
Stevens, Col. John H., 220, 223; for 602, 610; statue, 602
Stevens, Mrs. John H., for, 600
Stevens co., 535-8; t., 537
Stevens l., 273, 342
Stevenson v., 490
Steward's cr., for H. J. Steward, b., 204
Stewart, A. T., 59
Stewart, Jacob H., for, 638, 641
Stewart, Levi M., 587; for, 610
Stewart, William, n., 564
Stewart l., for Charles Stewart, 161; r. and l., for John Stewart, 295; v., for Dr. D. A. Stewart, 318; cr., 493
Stewartville v., for Charles Stewart, 388
Stickney, Alpheus B., n., 569; for, 620
Stieger l., for Carl Stieger, 85
Stiles sta., for A. M. Stiles, b., 528
Stillwater c. and t., 571
Stillwater convention, 1848, 4, 67
Stinson, James, for, 607
Stinson, Thomas, for, 617, 629, 641
Stockhaven l., 182
Stockholm t., 589
Stockhousen l., for Hans G. von Stackhausen, 182
Stocking l., 248, 563; cr., 563
Stockton v., for J. B. Stockton, 584
Stokes t., for George Stokes, 474
Stone, Hammet, for, 105
Stone l., 180, 342, 499, 500(2), 516; sta., 63
Stoneham t., 105

Stony br., 77, 100, 217, 349, 547; cr., 100, 120, 529, 597; l., 217, 218, 247; r., 295
Stony run, 56, 597; ridge, 292; pt., 493
Stony Brook t., 217, 218
Stony Run t., 597
Stop id., 286
Storden t. and v., for Nels Storden, 151
Storer cr., 241
Stormy cr., 179
Stowe's l., for Martin Stowe, 181, 182
Stowe Prairie t., for brothers, 546
Straight l. and r., 32, 245; r., 465, 533, 534; slough, 585
Straight River t., 245
Strand t., 383
Strandquist v., for J. E. Strandquist, 330
Strathcona, Lord, 278; for, b., 474
Strathcona v., 474
Stratton l., 251
Strawberry l., 32
Stray l., 141
String ls., 153
Stringtown v., 195
Strom l., for Andrew Strom, 65
Strong cr., 516
Stroud sta., 490
Strunk's l., for H. H. Strunk, 512
Stryker, John L., for, 619
Stuart l., 401
Stubbs bay, 235
Stump r., 140; l., 530
Stuntz, George R., for, b., 490, 494, 501, 643
Stuntz t., 490; id. and bay, 494; l., 501
Sturgeon l., 211, 414, 501, (47;) r., 285, 490, 501; t., 490; portage, 495
Sturgeon, shovel-nosed, 211; rock, 490
Sturgeon Lake t. and v., 414
Sturgeon River t., 285
Sturgis br., 357
Sturtevant, Mrs. C. G. n., 29
Sucker, Charley, for, 141
Sucker cr., 46, 133, 591; bay and br., 95, 493, 494; l., 126, 143, 296, 297, 443, 475; r., 492; pt., 494
Sugar cr., 196; l., 20, 204, 401, 591
Sugar maple, 40, 82; pt., battle, 94
Sugar Bush ls., 32, 324; t., 40
Sugar Loaf pt., 145; hill, 275; mound, 389; bluff, 585
Sugar Tree ridge, 259

Sulem l., 576
Sullivan l., 357, 499; t., for Timothy Sullivan, 427
Sumac id., 347
Summerville t., 285
Summit t., 40, (452,) 534; l., 152, 246, 273, 336, 369, 379
Summit Lake t. 379
Sumner, Charles, for, 195, 583, 610
Sumner t., 195, (583)
Sumter, for Fort Sumter, 318
Sunbeam p. o., 408
Sundahl t., 384
Sundown t., 452
Sunfish l., 169, 304, 500
Sunnyside t., 579
Sunrise t., prairie, l., and r., 109, 251; branches of r., 111
Sunset pt., 234; l., 498, 573; peak, 503
Superior c., Wis., 73
Superior, l., 1, 8, 73, 293, 643, 644, 654; pts., bays, and ids., Cook co., 145, 146; Lake co., 295; St. Louis co., 492-3
Superior National Forest, 148, 299, 506
Susan, l., 85, 337, 502
Susie id., 146
Sutphin, John B., for, 644
Sutton l., 512
Svea t., 280
Sveadahl, a hamlet, 576
Sverdrup t., for George Sverdrup, b., 398
Swamp l., 100, 112, 140, 144, 500, 530; r., 140, 145; cr., 144, (331;) crs., Big, and Little, 563
Swan cr., 100; r., 256, 355, 547; r., East, and West, 500
Swan l., 26, 85, 145, 152, 189(2), 256, 273, 274(3), 309, 315, 319, 320, 337, 339, 356, 374, 401, 434, 435, 454, 521, 534, 537; Big, and Little, 547; 590
Swan Lake t., (339,) 537
Swan River v., 256; t., 355
Swanville t. and v., 356
Swartwatts l., 591
Swede l., 85, 163
Swede Grove t., 340
Swede Prairie t., 597
Swede's Forest t., 452
Sweden, names from, 15, 16, 51, 178, 250, 266, 269, 278, 279, 280, 329, 344, 356, 367, 387, 471, 473, 482, 518, 589
Sweeney l., 232

Sweet t., for Daniel E. Sweet, b., 418
Swenoda l., 435; t., 541
Swenson l., 43, 273, 274
Swetland, Melissa, for, 33
Swietzer l., 247
Swift, Gov. Henry A., for, 246, b., 539
Swift co., 539-542
Swift l., 99, 246, 342; r., 99
Swift Falls, a hamlet, 542
Swift Water t., 40
Swims l., 180
Switzerland, names from, (two) 177
Syenite id., 146; l., 296
Sykes, Mrs. Amiretta, for, 311
Sylvan l., 93, 218, 233; t., 93
Sylvia l., for Mrs. A. Townsend, 530; 591
Synnes t., 537
Syre v., 384

T lake, 404
Taarud, Nels S., n., 365
Taber sta., 490
Tabor t., 427
Taft, William H., for, b., 490, 605
Taft sta., 490
Tainter, Andrew, for, 631
Tait l., 143, 273
(Ta Kara ls., 55)
Talcott l., for Andrew Talcott, b., 153, 370
Taliaferro, Major Lawrence, 34, 35, 155, 159, 171
(Taliaferro, l., 159)
Talmadge r., for Josiah Talmadge, 492
Tamarac t. and r., 330, 331
Tamarack id., for John Tamarack, 144
Tamarack l., 25, 32, 75, 126, 251, 324, 356, 401, 402, 404, 529, 590; pt., 132
Tamarack r., 19, 47, 77, 286, 330, 415; t., 17
Tanberg t., for Christian Tanberg, 579
Tanner, George, for, 336
Tanner, John, captive of Ojibways, 44
Tanner's hill, 357
Tansem t., for John O. Tansem, b., 118
Taopi v., 362

Tara t., 542, 552
Target l., 240
Tatum, S. C., and Hannah, for, 630, 641
Taunton v., 314
Taylor, Frank B., geologist, 79, 148
Taylor, James W., for, 630
Taylor, Jesse, for, b., 110
Taylor, Joshua L., for, b., 110
Taylor, Robert, n., 63
Taylor, Zachary, for, 605
Taylor t., for James Taylor, 40; 552
Taylor's Falls v., 107, 110, 112, 113; (t., 109)
Teal l., 140
(Tears, l. of, 10)
(Tecumseh t., 61)
Tegner t., for Elias Tegner, b., 280
Teien t., for Andrew C. Teien, 280
Temperance r. and l., 143; l., 337
Ten Mile l., 45, 98, 291, 401
Ten Mile Lake t., 291
Tenhassen t., 334
Tenney v., 579
Tennis, L. L., n., 458
Tennyson l., 251
Tenstrike v., 40
(Tepeeota v., 367, 558)
Terrace pt., 145; v., 433
Terrapin l., 573
Terrebonne t., 447
Terrell l., 231
Terry, Gen. Alfred H., for, 623
Terry, Rev. C. M., 180
(Terry v., 312)
Tetonka, l., 303
Theilman v., for H. Theilman, 558
Thevot l., 501
Thief l., 9, 330, 409; r., 9, 330, 408, 409
Thief Lake t., 330
Thief River Falls c., 408
Third l., 112; r., 256, 259
Third River t., 256
Thoeny l., for Mathias Thoeny, b., 319
Thole's l., 512
Thomas, Gen. George H., for, 603
Thomas, Mrs. Mary, for, 383
Thomas l., 248, 273, 295; for Maurice Thomas, 296; 530
Thomastown t., for Thomas Scott, 562
Thompson, Clark W., for, b., 184; Mrs. Thompson, for, 188

Thompson, David, 18, 40, 42, 74; b., 76; 96, 119, 121, 125, 139, 140, 276, 297, 445, 447, 470, 496, 497, 498
Thompson l., 218, 274, 341, 499, 516, 567; cr., 241
Thompson t., (184;) for brothers, 280
Thomson t., for David Thompson, b., 76
Thoreau, Henry D., 93, 433
Thorpe, Garrett L., for, 382
Thorpe t., for Joseph Thorpe, 245
Thorson, Alice O., 433
Thorson l., 181
Thorstad l., 181
Thousand Islands, 517
Three Island l., 43
Three Lakes t., 452
Three Maidens, Pipestone, 420
Three Mile l., 98, 501; cr., 291, 315, 459
Thunder l., 93, 99, 161, 548
Thunder Lake t., 93
Thurston, Rev. J. M., n., 61
Tibbetts br., 349; for four brothers, 516; l., 369
Tidd br., 357
Tiger l., 85, 454
Tilde, l., 32
Tilden t., for S. J. Tilden, b., 427
Timber l., 264, 274, 337, 375
Timothy grass, for Timothy Hanson, 160
Timothy t., 160
Tintah t., 552; v., and beaches, 553
Tintons, l. of the, 53
(Tintonwan, v. of Sioux, 510)
Tischer's cr., 493, 648, 653
Titlow l., 521
(Tivoli t., 61)
Toad l., 30; mt., 30, 33; Toad Lake t., 30
Todd, Gen. John B. S., for, b., 543; 600, 601
Todd co., 543-9; t., for Smith Todd, 245
Todd l., for Daniel S. Todd, 320; 341
Tofte t. and v., 137
Toivola t., 490
Tokua ls., and Tokua Brothers ls., 55, 56
Tom l., 140, 401; mt., 241, 275
Toner's l., for Richard Toner, 567
Tonka Bay v., 227; bay, 234
Toombs, Thomas H., n., 216
(Toombs co., for Robert Toombs, b., 577)

Topographic names, 1, 2
Topping, Herbert W., for, 629
Toqua ls. and t., 55
Tordenskjold t., for Peder Tordenskjold, b., 398
Torfin p. o., for Iver Torfin, 474
Torgerson p. o., for M. Torgerson, 409
Torning t., 542
Torstenson l., 218
Tower, Charlemagne, Sr., and Jr., for, b., 490, 491
Tower c., 490; l., 342
Towle, J. S., and J. P., for, 451
Town and Country Club grounds, 634
Townsend, Mrs. Sylvia, for, 530
Township Corner l., 100
Trace l., for Ferdinand Trace, 547
Tracy, John H., for, 625
Tracy v., for John F. Tracy, 314
Trail (l., 203;) v., 427
"Trail City," 195
Trails of fur traders, 217
Transit t., 520
Trap l., 141
Traverse co., 550-554; l., 7, 8, 550; t., 373
Traverse l., for F. W. Traverse, 25
Traverse des Sioux, 373, 375, treaty in 1851, 199, 375
Treat, George L., letter, 178
Treaties with Ojibways, 171, 506; with Sioux, 171, 199, 375
Tree id., 494
Trelipe t., for tullibee fish, 93
Trenton l., 204, 567; (t., 55)
Triangle l., 296
Triggs, J. H., for, 649, 650
Triplet ls., 130
Tripp l., for Charles Tripp, 247
Triumph v., 335
Trondhjem t., 399
Troolin l., 251
Trosky v., 418
Trotochaud l., 32
Trott, Herman, for, b., 215
Trott cr., 25; for Joseph Trott, 516
Trout cr., 196, 559, 585 (3), 612; br., 442, (559,) 573, 614; r., 494
Trout l., 143; ls., Lower, and Little, 145; 162, 257, 494
Trout Lake t., 257
Troy t., 419, 459, (556, 559;) v., 584
Truedell slough, 169
Truman v., 335
Tucker l. and r., 141
Tuey l., 590

INDEX 729

Tulaby l., for tullibee fish, 32, 93
Tumuli t., 399
Tunsberg t., 105
Turnbull, Peter, n., and Mrs. Mary Turnbull, for, 131
Turnbull pt., 132
Turner t., for L. E. Turner, 17
Turtle cr., 204, 363, 534, 546, 547
Turtle l., 33, 40, 43, 93, 99, 120, 180, 181, 218, 232, 258; ls., South, and North, 402; 429, 443, 546, 548
Turtle r., 35, 40, 126; mt., N. D., 102
Turtle Creek t., 546
Turtle Lake t., 40, 93
Turtle River t. and l., 40
Tuscarora l., 141
Tustin, l., 304
Tuttle l., for Calvin Tuttle, 336, 337
Twelve Mile cr., 537, 554, 590
Twenty l., 20, 274
Twenty-four Mile cr., 99, 100
Twig v., 491
Twin bays, 346; bluffs, 212; peaks, 299
Twin ls., 26, 33, 43, 76. 131, 143, 145, 152, 162(3), 202, 203, 221, 232 (2), 251, 273, 280, 295, 309, 315, 323, 336, 337, 402, 403, 516, 547, 562, 573, 591(3), 598
Twin Cities, 220, 439
Twin Lakes t., 76, 323; v., 203
Twin Ports, 481, 493
Twin Valley v., 384
Twitchell, Moses, n., 23
Two pts., Leech l., 96
Two rivers, of Red l., 36, 47; Kittson co., 280; Morrison co., 356; St. Louis co., 489, 500, 501; Stearns co., 529
Two Harbor bay, 295
Two Harbors c. and t., 294
Two Inlets t. and l., 30
Two Island r., 142
Two River l., 530
Two Rivers t. and v., 356
Twohey l., 143
Tyler, John, for, 605
Tyler l., for William L. Tyler, 304
Tyler v., for C. B. Tyler, b., 309
Tynsid t., 427
Typo l., 25, 251
Tyro t., 597
Tyrone t., 303; prairie, 342
Tyrrell, J. B., geologist, 8, 76, 96, 119
Tyson l., for Joseph Tyson, 598

Udolpho t., 362
Uhlenkott's l., 530
Ulen t. and v., for Ole Ulen, b., 119
Una, dog, for, 1, 157
Underwood v., for A. J. Underwood, 399; t., 452
Undine region, 2, 62, 65; gl. l., 66
Uninhabited pt., 46
Union l., 180 (2), 429, 465; cr., 562; t., (206,) 240, (399)
Union Grove t., 340
(Union Prairie t., 533)
Upham, Warren, quoted, 113, 170, 224; for, 505
Upham, gl. l., 505
Upper Cullen l., 162
Upper Dean l., 162
Upper Hay l., 160
Upper Iowa r., 13, 197, 362
Upper Lightning l., 217, 401
Upper Rice l., 124
Upper Sioux Agency, 596
Upper Twin l., 247
Upsala v., 356
Upton, Gen. Emory, for, 603
Urn l., 296
Urness t., 179
Ushkabwahka r., 499
Utica, (t., 240;) t. and v., 584

Vadnais l., for John Vadnais, 442
Vail, James N., n., 122
Vail t., 452
Valder, Hans, n., 194
Valentine l., 443
Valhalla, of Norse mythology, 40
Vallers t., 314
Valley, Lake of the, 32
Valley t., 330
Van Buren, Mrs. John, n., 172
Van Buren, Martin, for, b., 491, 605, 622
Van Buren t., 491
Van Cleve, Mrs. Charlotte O., 510, 547; for, b., 548, 607
Van Cleve, Gen. Horatio P., for, 548, 607
Van Dusen, G. W., n., 385
Van Dyke, Mrs. James H., 175, 181
Van Loon's l., for Miner Van Loon, 181
Van Reed, Henry, for, 631
Van Slyke, William A., for, 628, 641
Vance l., 145
Vanoss l., for Francis Vanoss, 324
Varco sta., for Thomas Varco, 362

730 INDEX

Vasa t., for Gustavus Vasa, king of Sweden, b., 209; (t. and v., 571)
Vaughan, A. B., for, b., 360
Vaugondy, map by, 79, 476
Vawter v., 356
Vega t., 330
Veldt t., 330
Venoah l., 78
Venus l., 181
Verdale t., or d., 528
Verdi t,. 309
Verdon t., 17
Verendrye, Sieur de la, 8, 45; proposed for, 135; 282, 445, 470; b., 476
Vergas v., 399
Vermilion iron range, 1, 298, 503
Vermilion l., 6, 169, 491, 648; bays, pts., and ids., 494-5; 505, 511; r., 99, 169, 211, 648
Vermilion ls., Big, Little, and Upper, 99; slough, 169, 211
Vermilion moraine, 504
Vermillion t. and v., 167, 168
Vermilion Grove v., 491
Vermilion Lake t., 491; reservation, 506
Vermont, names from, 28, 59, 182, 201, 334, 355, 359, 396, 419, 451, 453, 582, 591
Vermont l., 182
Vern l., 143
Verndale v., 562
Vernon, Edward, admiral, for, b., 64; 174, 582
Vernon l., 145; t., 174
Vernon Center t. (earlier Vernon), 63
Verona t., and p. o., 188
Verrill, Charles, and H. J., n., 166
Verwyst, Father Chrysostom, 9, 18, 140; q. 142, 293; 342, 367, 504
Veseli v., 464
Vespucci, Amerigo, 134
Vesta t. and v., 452
Vick l., 273
Vickerman, W. T., n., 469
(Vicksburg v., 459)
Victor t., 589
Victoria, Queen, for, 84, 177
Victoria v., 84; l., 177, 180
Viding t., 119
Vienna t., 469
Vieux Desert, l., 246
Viking t., 330
Villard, Henry, for, b., 433, 546, 629, 637

Villard v., 433; l., 435; t., 546
Vincent, Thomas M., for, 603
Vineland v., 345; bay, 347; t., 427
Vinge l., 401
Vining v., 399
Vinland v., 84
Viola t. and v., 388
Vira, l., 296
Virginia, names from, 60, 62, 174, 457, 491, 582, 588, 589, 624, 650
Virginia c., 491; l., (48,) 85, 232, 501
Vivian, George H., 476, 491
Vivian t., 566
Vladimirof l., 20
Vlasaty sta., 174
Volen l., 401
Volney, l., 304
Von Baumbach, for, b., 181
Von Minden, Henning, for, 614; 616
Vondel br., 349
Vos l., 530

Waasa t., 491
Wabacing v., of Ojibways, 47
Wabanica t., 40
Wabano ls., 258
Wabasha, name of hereditary Sioux chiefs, 555, 612; v. and prairie, 555
Wabasha co., 555-9; c., 555, 559
Wabasha cr., 453
Wabasso v., 452
Wabedo t. and l., 93
Waboose l., 248
(Waconda l., 273)
Waconia bluff, 212; moraine, 275
Waconia l., 81, 84; t. and v., 84
Wacouta t. and v., for a Sioux chief, 209
Wade, Benjamin F., for, 431
Wadena co., 560-563; t. and v., 562
Wadena pt., 346; trading post, 560
Wagner l., 590, 591
Wagner t., for Bessie Wagner, 17
Wagoner p. o., 491
Wagonga l., 273
Wahkon v., and bay, 346, 347
Wahlsten sta., for August Wahlsten, 491
(Wahnahta co., Minn. Territory, 550)
Wahnena t., 93
Wahpeton c., N. D., 579
Waite Park v., for H. C. Waite, b., 528
Wakan id., 343, 347

INDEX

Wakefield, J. B., n., 519
Wakefield, William, for, 622
Wakefield t., for S. Wakefield, 528; (575)
Wakemup, an Ojibway, v. and bay, 495
Wakon, pt., 233
Walcott t., for Samuel Walcott, 464
Walden t., 93, 433
Waldo t. and sta., 294
Waldorf v., 566
Wales, name from, 58
Walhalla t., 40
Walker, A. P., n., 519
Walker, J. W., n., 340
Walker, Thomas B., for, b., 93; 122, 125
Walker v., and br., 93, 125; l., 320, 402
Walker Brook l., 125
Wall Lake sta., and l., 399
Wallace sta., 491
Walls t., for three brothers, 553
Walnut Grove v., 453
Walnut Lake t., and l., 188
Walsh, Vincent D., for, 624, 642
Walter t., for Henry Walter, 291
Walters v., 188
Waltham t., and v., 362
Walworth t., 31
Wanamingo t., 209
Wanan l., 501
Wanda v., 453
Wang t., 459
Wanger t., 331
Wann, John, n., 635; Mrs. Wann, n., 635
Wann, Thomas Leslie, for, 635
Wannaska, a hamlet, 474
War, names from, American Revolution, 359, 360; of 1812, 291; Mexican, 289, 334; of the Rebellion, 1861-65, 62, 114, 135, 136, 156; Spanish-American, 1898, 89, 92, 254; World, 1914-18, 83, 376, 607
War Club l., 100
War road, 102, 176, 475; see Warroad
(Waraju r., 149)
Warba v., 257
Ward's l., 319, 521; Ward t., 546
Ward Springs v., for J. W. and Martha J. Ward, 546
(Wardeville v., 524)
Warman v., for S. M. Warman, 266
Warner l., 529

(Warpool, a lake, 98)
Warren, Cary I., for, n., 627, 641
Warren, Gen. G. K., 7, 8, 56
Warren, John E., for, 616
Warren, Joseph, 285
Warren, William W., quoted, 88, 90; 91, 93, 97; q., 100; 102, 159, 258, 330, 391; q., 408-9, 517
Warren c., for Charles H. Warren, 331
Warren, gl. r., 7, 8, 56, 550, 580
Warren l., for Budd Warren, 324
Warren t., 285, 584
Warrenton t., 331
Warroad t., v., and r., 474
Warsaw t., 209, 464
(Waseata p. o., 393)
Waseca co., 564-7; c., 566
Washburn, Gov. C. C., for, 603, 604
Washburn, Hon. Israel, Jr., 9; 226
Washburn, Hon. William D., 177; for, 603, 610
Washburn, l., and br., 99, 161
Washington, George, for, b., 568; 603, 605, 613, 618, 638, 653
Washington co., 568-573
Washington, l., 64, 303, 324, 342, 520, 591; cr., 342; t., 303, (388)
Washington Lake t., 520
Washkish t., 40
Wasioja t. and v., 174
Wasuk l., 500
Watab r., 51, 52, 138, 527, 529; l., 139, 530(2); ls., Big, and Little, 530
Watab t., and trading post, 51, 52
Watap portage, 138
Water Hen r., 500
Waterbury t., 453
Waterford t. and v., 167, 168
Watermann's l., for L. Wassermann, 85
Watertown t., (24,) 160; v., 84
Waterville t. and v., 303
Watkins, F. A., 73, 78
Watkins l., 337; for Henry Watkins, 567; (t., 173;) v., 340
Watonwan co., 574-6; (t., 59)
Watonwan r., 12, 574; South branch, 576
Watopa t., 559
Watrous t., for C. B. Watrous, 285
Watson v., 105; cr., for Thomas and James Watson, 196
Waubun v., 324
Waukenabo l. and t., 17
Waukon t., 384

INDEX

Waukon Decorah, Winnebago chief, b., 59
(Waukopee, a hamlet, 195)
Waus-wau-goning bay, 146
Waverly t., 335; v., 589, 590; ls., Big, and Little, 590
Wawatasso id., 235
Wawina t., 257
Waxlax, John, for, 294
Wayburne sta., 453
Wayzata bay and v., 227
Wealthwood t. and v., 17
Weaver l., 233; v., for Wm. Weaver, 559
Webster t., for Ferris Webster, b., 464
Wedell l., 402
Wegdahl v., for H. A. Wegdahl, 105
Weide, Charles A. B., for, 624
Weimer t., 263
Weisel cr., for David Weisel, 197
Weissberger, Moritzious, for, 588
Welch, William H., b., 210
Welch t., for Abraham E. Welch, b., 209
Welcome v., for Alfred M. Welcome, 335
Weller's Spur v., 257
Wellington t., 459
Wells, James, for, 211, b., 464, 465
Wells, Verdon, for, 17
Wells cr., 211; l., and t., 464, 465
Wells v., 188
Weme v., for Hans Weme, 123
Wenaus, Effie. for, 254
Wendell v., 217
Wendt l., 403
Wergeland t., for H. Wergeland, b., 597
Wescott sta., for James Wescott, b., 168
Wesley, John and Charles, for, 630
West bay, Leech l., 95, 98; l., 274
West Albany t., v., and cr., 559
West Bank t., 542
West Chain of lakes, 335-7
West Concord v., 174
West Duluth, 650
West Greenwood l., 296
West Heron Lake t., 263
West Indian cr., 559
West Newton t., and steamboat, 374
West Saint Paul t. and c., 167
West Saint Paul d., renamed Riverview, 439, 440, 611, 616, 617-620
West Sea Gull l., 141
West Side t., 379

West Union t. and v., 546, 549
West Valley t., 331
West Virginia, names from, 268, 464
Westbrook t. and v., 151
Westerheim t., 314
Western t., 399
Western Superior gl. l., 148
Westfield t., 174
Westford t., 335
Westline t., 453
Westport t. and v., 433; l., 434
Wetmore, Irwin N., n., 388
Wetzel, Captain William, n., 39
Whalan v., for John Whaalahan, 195
Whale Tail l., 225
Wheatland t., (383,) 464
Wheaton v., for D. T. Wheaton, b., 553
Wheatville v., 384
Wheeler, C. C., n., 69, 314
Wheeler, Everett P., for, 632
Wheeler, Rush B., for, 634
Wheeler l., 273; for J. A. Wheeler, b., 567
Wheeler t., for Alonzo Wheeler, 41
Wheeling t., 464
Wheelock, Joseph A., 68; for, 640
Whetstone r., 292
Whigam, Daniel B., n., 419
Whipple, Bishop Henry B., 60, 103, 130, 162; for, 432
Whipple l., 130, 162, 432
Whiskey cr., 120(2), 580; br., 349
Whiskey l., 181; id., 494
Whitcomb, G. F., n., 327
White, A. B., n., 318
White, Almon A., n., 40
White l., for Capt. A. W. White, 203; 499, 591; t. 491.
White Bear, Ojibway chief, 432, 433
White Bear l., (432,) 440, 569; t. and v., 440,- 623
White Bear Lake t., 433
White Birch t., 285
White Earth t. and l., 31; r., 321
White Earth reservation, 31, 325
White Elk br., or cr., 18
White Elk l. and t., 17
White Face r., 499
White Fish l., 43(2), 78, 99, 143, 161(2), 258, 348, 429; (t. 158)
White Iron l., 296, 501
White Lily l., 267
White Oak t., 245; pt., l., and reservation, 258, 259
White Pine cr., 498

INDEX 733

White Rock v., S. D., 551
White Sand l., 162
White Stone l., 112
White Water cr., 303; r., 389, 557, 559, 584
Whited t., and Ogilvie v., for Oric O. Whited, b., 266
Whitefield, Edwin, and wife, for, 271, 272; n., 522, 545, 547
Whitefield t., 272
Whiteford t., 331
Whitehead l., 419
Whitely cr., and l., 162; id., 163
(Whiteville settlement, 546)
Whitewater r., 389, 584; t., (386,) 584
Whitewater Falls v., 584
Whitford, Joseph, 394, 395
Whitney, l., 320; br., 349
Whittemore, Grace, for, 103
Whittlesey, Charles, n. and q., 142; n., 147, 504
Wicker t., for Harry Wicker, 285
Wickham, mt., 292
Widness, Hans C.. for, 124
Wieb, Henry, n., 150
Wiegand l., 592
Wigwam bay, 347
Wilcox, Alvin H., 27; n., 28
Wild Cat cr. and bluff, 241
Wild Goose id, 235
(Wild Oats r., 18)
Wild rice, harvest, 124, 125, 321, 322
Wild Rice ls., 46, 47, 492, 499
Wild Rice r., 9, 47, 120; another in N. D., 120; 123, 124, 125, 321, 384
Wild Rice t., 384
Wilder, Amherst H., for, b., 263, 633
Wilder l., 296; v., 263
Wilderness l., 99
Wildwood t., 285; v., 571
(Wilhelmine v., 150)
Wilken l., for J. and W. Wilken, 182
Wilker l., 534
Wilkin, Col. Alexander, for, b., 577, 613
Wilkin co., 577-580
Wilkins l., 20
Wilkinson, Randolph A., n., 125
Wilkinson l., for R. Wilkinson, 442
Wilkinson t., for Major Melville C. Wilkinson, b., 94
Willborg p. o., for M. E. Willborg, 123
Willert l., 534
William, l., 181, 547, 591

Williams, Charles E., n., 265
Williams, Charles H., for, 616
Williams, John Fletcher, q., 67-68; 80, 192, 219, 260, 518, 539
Williams l., 247, 304, 499, 591
Williams t., for G. T. Williams, 17; for James Williams, 285
Williamson, Prof. A. W., quoted or cited, 22, 53, 249, 261, 268, 288, 301, 303, 313, 379, 439, 443, 448, 550, 564, 574, 581, 584, 593
Williamson, John P., 217, 238
Williamson, Rev. Thomas S., 104, 119, 455, 593, 595
(Williamstown t., 519)
Willie l., for U. S. Willie (or Wiley), 341
Willis l., for Abner Willis, 567
Willius, F., and G., for, 612, 633
Willmar c. and t., for Leon and Paul Willmar, 272; l., 273
Willmont t., 379
Willow cr., 62, 120, 196, 286, 389, 400, 475; r., 17, 18, 99, 414, 501; l., 103, 106, 151, 453, 529
Willow species in Minnesota, 106
(Willow Creek t., 62)
Willow Lake t., (103,) 453
Willow River v., 414
Willow Valley t., 491
Wilma t., 414
Wilmert l., 336
Wilmes l., 573
Wilmington t., 240
Wilmont v., 379
Wilpen v., 492
Wilson, Eugene M., for, 610
Wilson, Hiram, for, 89
Wilson, John L., n., 526
Wilson, Jonathan E., for, 366
Wilson, Rev. Joseph G., n., 480, 481
Wilson, Thomas, n., 172
Wilson, Warren, for, 584
Wilson, Woodrow, for, 41, b., 94
Wilson id., for Guy G. Wilson, 347; 517
Wilson l., 295, 366, 369
Wilson's l., for Samuel Wilson, 152
Wilson t., 584
Wilton v., 41; t. and v., 564, 566
Wimer l., 404
Winchell, Prof. Alexander, 138, 143, 296, 297, 501
Winchell, Alexander N., 498
Winchell, Horace V., 143, 282, 371, 498, 503, 608
Winchell, Mrs. H. V., for, 143

Winchell, Prof. N. H., 7, 57, 66; q., 75; 79, 128, 130; for, b., 134; 139, 140; for, 141, 296; n., 145, 146; q., 147; 165, 225, 267, 294; q., 297; 298, 299; q., 322, 323; 419; q., 432; 433, 494, 495, 505, 517, 529, 544, 560, 572, 607
Winchell, gl. l., 134; l., 134, 140, 145, 147
Winchell trail, Minneapolis, 607
Winchester t., 384
Wind l., 143, 296
Windemere t., 414
Windom, William, for, b., 151, 362, 610; n., 172
Windom v., 151; t., (27,) 362
Windsor t., 553
Windy l., 295
Wine l., 500
Winfield t., 459
Wing r., 400, 547, 562
Wing River l., 401; t., 562
Winger t., 428
Winkler's l., for Ignatz Winkler, 85
Winnebago t. and v. (former City), 188; t. and cr., 240; (t., 523;) prairie, 530
(Winnebago Agency, 62)
Winnebago Indians, 59, 60, 66, 191, 192; names from, 59, 191; reservation, 58, 66, 545
Winnebagoshish, l., 1, 96-98, 100, 101, 257, 259; Indian reservation, 101, 259; t., 257
Winneshiek, chief, 240; for, b., 592
Winneshiek co., Iowa, 59; (t., 58, 61;) prairie, 592
Winnewissa falls, 419
Winona co., 581-5; c. and t., 584
Winona, l., 178, 181, 585
Winslow, James M., for, 619
Winsor, Justin, 300
Winsor t., for Hans C. Widness, 124
Winsted t., v., and l., 318
Winter Road r., 42, 43, 47; l., 43
Wintermute l., for C. Wintermute, b., 538
Winthrop c., 520
Winton v., for W. C. Winton, 492
Winzer, Charles, n., 263
Wirt t., for William Wirt, 257
Wisacodé r., 144
Wisconsin, names from, 31, 58. 81, 105, 177, 215, 262, 271, 289(2), 290, 291, 314, 327, 366, 372, 387, 388, 417, 431, 458(2), 468, 490, 531, 533, 539, 551, 565, 575, 596(2)

Wisconsin pt., 44; t., 263
Wisconsin state, 3, 4, 112, 263; Historical Society Collections, 81
Wiscoy t., 584
Wita l., 64
Witchel l., 499
(Withington v., 157)
Witoka, a hamlet, 585
Wolf cr., 362, 465; sta., 492
Wolf l., 31, 42, 151, 162, 247(2), 248, 258, 341, 403, 500, 501, 530
Wolf Lake t., 31
Wolford t., for Robert Wolford, 160
Wolsfeld l., 232
Wolverine state, 4
Wolverton t., for Dr. W. D. Wolverton, 579
Wood, Edward H., for, 619
Wood, Gen. Thomas J., for, 600, 601
Wood l., 72, 182, 231, 236, 296, 315, 576, 597
Wood Lake t. and v., 597; battle ground, 597
Woodbury l., 78; cr., 204, 363
Woodbury t., for Levi Woodbury, b., 571
Woodcock l., for E. T. Woodcock, 274
Woodland t., 590
(Woodpecker l., 434)
Woodrow t., 41, 94
Woods, Major Samuel, 214, 217, 430, 432, 434
Woods, Lake of the, 1, 8, 9, 35, 41; points and islands, 44-45; 137, 516, 598
Woods t., for William W. Woods, 106
Woodside t., 399, 428
Woodstock v., 419
Woodville t., for E. G. and L. C. Wood, 566
Woolley, John G., founder of Rest Island, 211
Workman, John, n., 351
Workman t., 17
World War, 1914-18, 83, 376, 607
Worm l., 217
Worthington c., 379; t., 380
Wrenshall sta., v., and t., for C. C. Wrenshall, 77
Wright, Charles B., for, b., 77
Wright, Charles D., for, b., 396
Wright, Mrs. E. L., n., 28
Wright, George B., for, b., 77
Wright, Silas, for, b., 586

Wright co., 2, 586-592; t., 331
Wright v., for C. B. and G. B. Wright, b., 77
Wrightstown v., 399
Wuori t., 492, 504
Wyandotte t., 409
Wyanett t., 251
Wykeham t., 546
Wykoff v., for Cyrus G. Wykoff, 195
Wylie t. and v., 447
Wyman, ry. junction, for George Wyman, 492
Wyoming t. and v., 110; state, 110

Yaeger l., 563
Yankton, l., 315
Yellow Bank t. and r., 291, 292; hills, 292
(Yellow Earth r., 291)
Yellow Head r., for Ojibway guide, 42, 126, 246; v., 96; pt., 132
Yellow Medicine co., 593-8; r., 593, 597; (t., 596;) mission, 597
(Yellow Medicine City, v., 597)

York t., 195, (206, 361)
Young, Dr. Thomas M., 593
Young l., 500
Young America t., v., and l., 84
Yucatan t., 240

Zemple v., 257
(Zenith t., 408)
"Zenith City," Duluth, 481, 652
Zeta l., 297
Zierke, Charles, for, 152
Zim v., 492
Zimmerman l., 402; v., for Moses Zimmerman, 515, 516
Zion t. (and v.), 528
Zippel t., for William M. Zippel, 41
Zippel's cr., 41
Zoo l., 144
Zumbra l., 85; Heights, 234
Zumbro r., 11, 174, 199, 207, 210, 388, 559
Zumbro t., (386,) 559
Zumbro Falls v., 559
Zumbrota t. and v., 210

SUPPLEMENTS

No. 1. Minnesota Communities Incorporated since 1920

No. 2. Official Decision of the Minnesota and United States Geographic Boards, 1890–1969

1. MINNESOTA COMMUNITIES INCORPORATED SINCE 1920

THE FOLLOWING LIST of communities incorporated since 1920 was compiled from records in the Minnesota secretary of state's office, from files of the League of Minnesota Municipalities, and — for the years 1920 to 1927 — from *Village Laws and Government in Minnesota* by Harvey Walker (*Publication No. 6,* Bureau for Research in Government, University of Minnesota — 1927). An asterisk denotes place names not found in Upham's text.

Name	*County*	*Date Incorporated*
Aldrich	Wadena	March 4, 1938
*Apple Valley	Dakota	January 1, 1969
Arden Hills	Ramsey	February 13, 1951
*Babbitt	St. Louis	September 12, 1956
Baxter	Crow Wing	May 25, 1939
Beaver Bay	Lake	August 13, 1953
Bejou	Mahnomen	January 13, 1921
Belden	Pine	September 14, 1921
*Bellechester	Goodhue, Wabasha	October 5, 1955
*Birchwood	Ramsey	September 10, 1921
Biscay	McLeod	June 9, 1947
Blaine	Anoka	January 29, 1954
*Blomkest	Kandiyohi	April 7, 1952
Bloomington	Hennepin	April 8, 1953
Bock	Mille Lacs	January 30, 1923
Borup	Norman	February 15, 1951
Boy River	Cass	April 7, 1922
Branch	Chisago	March 1, 1961
Brooklyn Park	Hennepin	April 14, 1954
Brooks	Red Lake	April 7, 1955
Burnsville	Dakota	June 18, 1964
Champlin	Hennepin	October 14, 1946
*Chickamaw Beach	Cass	November 20, 1950
*Circle Pines	Anoka	April 13, 1950
*Coates	Dakota	April 7, 1953
Comstock	Clay	November 7, 1921
Conger	Freeborn	April 27, 1934
Cook	St. Louis	May 13, 1926

Name	County	Date Incorporated
*Cooley	Itasca	August 30, 1921
*Coon Rapids	Anoka	October 20, 1952
Corcoran	Hennepin	December 4, 1958
Cosmos	Meeker	September 21, 1926
Cottage Grove	Washington	July 21, 1965
*Cross Lake	Crow Wing	August 12, 1959
Dakota	Winona	May 23, 1951
Denham	Pine	March 30, 1939
Dovray	Murray	January 2, 1924
East Bethel	Anoka	June 7, 1957
East Gull Lake	Cass	May 8, 1947
Eden Prairie	Hennepin	October 22, 1962
Effie	Itasca	June 10, 1940
Eitzen	Houston	May 17, 1947
Elko	Scott	October 25, 1949
Elmdale	Morrison	April 23, 1947
Elrosa	Stearns	March 1, 1938
Emily	Crow Wing	March 7, 1957
Erhard	Otter Tail	October 13, 1949
*Falcon Heights	Ramsey	April 1, 1949
*Fifty Lakes	Crow Wing	May 10, 1949
Fort Ripley	Crow Wing	March 19, 1927
Freeborn	Freeborn	October 27, 1949
Fridley	Anoka	June 18, 1949
Garrison	Crow Wing	May 3, 1937
Garvin	Lyon	October 8, 1945
*Gem Lake	Ramsey	July 1, 1959
Gilman	Benton	February 11, 1959
*Goodview	Winona	August 8, 1946
*Greenfield	Hennepin	March 14, 1958
Greenwood	Hennepin	January 10, 1956
Gully	Polk	July 16, 1924
Halma	Kittson	September 28, 1923
*Harding	Morrison	March 15, 1938
Hayward	Freeborn	June 4, 1924
Hillman	Morrison	November 7, 1938
*Hilltop	Anoka	May 4, 1956
*Hollandale	Freeborn	February 20, 1934
*Hoyt Lakes	St. Louis	November 17, 1955
Independence	Hennepin	November 9, 1956
*Inver Grove Heights	Dakota	March 11, 1965
*Island Park	Hennepin	November 8, 1924

SUPPLEMENT NO. 1: INCORPORATED COMMUNITIES

Name	County	Date Incorporated
*Island View	Koochiching	October 30, 1939
Kenneth	Rock	July 20, 1921
Kerrick	Pine	October 22, 1946
Kettle River	Carlton	April 11, 1921
*Kingston	Meeker	September 13, 1961
Lake Elmo	Washington	December 21, 1925
*Lakeland	Washington	September 27, 1951
*Lakeland Shores	Washington	November 16, 1949
Lake Lillian	Kandiyohi	February 15, 1926
Lake St. Croix Beach	Washington	December 31, 1951
*Lake Shore	Cass	March 19, 1947
*Landfall	Washington	April 6, 1959
La Salle	Watonwan	January 25, 1921
*Lauderdale	Ramsey	January 21, 1949
Leonard	Clearwater	June 12, 1922
*Lexington	Anoka	May 12, 1950
*Lilydale	Dakota	September 13, 1951
*Lino Lakes	Anoka	May 11, 1955
Little Canada	Ramsey	October 15, 1953
*Long Beach	Pope	May 18, 1938
*Longville	Cass	March 1, 1941
Loretto	Hennepin	March 20, 1940
*Lynd	Lyon	January 4, 1954
*McGrath	Aitkin	March 26, 1923
Mahtomedi	Washington	August 14, 1931
Manchester	Freeborn	October 6, 1947
*Manhattan Beach	Crow Wing	June 24, 1941
Maple Grove	Hennepin	April 30, 1954
*Mapleview	Mower	June 6, 1946
*Maplewood	Ramsey	February 28, 1957
Meadowlands	St. Louis	October 15, 1924
Medford	Steele	May 22, 1936
*Medicine Lake	Hennepin	April 5, 1944
Medina	Hennepin	May 31, 1955
Mendota Heights	Dakota	February 21, 1956
*Miesville	Dakota	August 1, 1951
Miltona	Douglas	March 31, 1930
Minnetonka	Hennepin	August 28, 1956
Minnetrista	Hennepin	August 16, 1960
Mounds View	Ramsey	April 24, 1958
Myrtle	Freeborn	May 8, 1937
*New Hope	Hennepin	July 8, 1953

Name	County	Date Incorporated
Nimrod	Wadena	August 20, 1946
*Nisswa	Crow Wing	December 4, 1946
*North Cross Lake	Crow Wing	December 9, 1964
*North Oaks	Ramsey	July 18, 1956
Northrop	Martin	July 6, 1933
Oakdale	Washington	March 12, 1968
Oak Park Heights	Washington	April 6, 1959
Okabena	Jackson	July 30, 1938
Orono	Hennepin	November 23, 1954
*Oronoco	Olmsted	February 13, 1968
Orr	St. Louis	June 7, 1935
*Palisade	Aitkin	July 7, 1922
Pease	Mille Lacs	August 6, 1923
Pelican Lakes	Crow Wing	June 30, 1939
*Pemberton	Blue Earth	April 26, 1946
*Pine Springs	Washington	June 24, 1959
*Pleasant Lake	Stearns	July 11, 1938
Plymouth	Hennepin	May 18, 1955
Prinsburg	Kandiyohi	June 25, 1952
Quamba	Kanabec	July 11, 1952
Racine	Mower	June 30, 1959
*Regal	Kandiyohi	April 25, 1940
Roseville	Ramsey	April 19, 1948
Sabin	Clay	August 15, 1929
St. Anthony	Hennepin	November 23, 1945
St. Francis	Anoka	May 16, 1962
St. Leo	Yellow Medicine	June 6, 1940
*St. Mary's Point	Washington	October 30, 1951
*St. Rosa	Stearns	August 9, 1939
Shafer	Chisago	March 14, 1922
*Shoreview	Ramsey	April 24, 1957
*Shorewood	Hennepin	May 14, 1956
Silver Bay	Lake	October 19, 1956
*Skyline	Blue Earth	January 8, 1957
South International Falls	Koochiching	August 9, 1921
*Spring Lake Park	Anoka, Ramsey	December 31, 1953
*Spring Park	Hennepin	August 20, 1951
*Squaw Lake	Itasca	December 17, 1940
Stacy	Chisago	April 13, 1923
Steen	Rock	February 5, 1942
Stockton	Winona	August 1, 1947

Name	County	Date Incorporated
Storden	Cottonwood	June 7, 1921
Strandquist	Marshall	July 31, 1923
*Sunburg	Kandiyohi	September 8, 1951
Sunfish Lake	Dakota	June 12, 1958
Tamarack	Aitkin	July 26, 1921
Trail	Polk	April 17, 1950
*Trimont	Martin	December 16, 1958
Twin Lakes	Freeborn	April 8, 1957
*Urbank	Otter Tail	August 16, 1947
*Vadnais Heights	Ramsey	July 24, 1957
Viking	Marshall	April 12, 1921
Westport	Pope	March 13, 1926
*Willernie	Washington	February 2, 1948
*Williams	Lake of the Woods	April 1, 1922
Winger	Polk	January 5, 1921
Wolf Lake	Becker	May 12, 1949
Woodbury	Washington	March 7, 1967
*Woodland	Hennepin	December 6, 1948
Wrenshall	Carlton	March 17, 1926

2. MINNESOTA AND UNITED STATES GEOGRAPHIC BOARD DECISIONS, 1890 TO JULY 1, 1969

THE PLACE NAMES given below are the official decisions made by the United States and Minnesota geographic boards from their establishment to July 1, 1969. In addition to the correct spelling, the dates of the decisions, and a list of incorrect designations, each place has been located by township, range, and section number wherever possible.

ABITA LAKE: Cook County; T36N, R1W, Sec. 21. *Not*: Arita Lake. Minn. 1940.

ACOMA: township, McLeod County; T117N, R30W. *Not*: Aconia. U.S. *Sixth Report*, 79.

ACORN LAKE: Becker County; T138N, R40W, Sec. 20, 21, 28, 29. *Not*: Harold Lake. U.S. 1961.

AGASSA LAKE: St. Louis County; T64N, R13W, Sec. 1, 2. *Not*: Gassa Lake, Kangas Lake. U.S. *Sixth Report*, 81.

AH-GWAH-CHING: settlement, Cass County; T142N, R31W, Sec. 34, 35. *Not*: Ah Gwah Ching, Ah-Gwah-Ching. U.S. 1967.

AHSEBUN LAKE: Cass County; T140N, R25W, Sec. 13, 24. *Not*: Coon Lake. U.S. 1941–43; Minn. 1940.

ALF, LAKE: St. Louis County; T64N, R16W, Sec. 21. *Not*: Alf Lake. U.S. *Sixth Report*, 88.

ALGER LAKE: Lake County; T60N, R6W, Sec. 29, 32, 33. *Not*: Beaver Lake. U.S. 1959; Minn. 1957.

ALMA, LAKE: Pine County; T41N, R17W, Sec. 28, 33. *Not*: Larson Lake. U.S. 1963.

ALPHA LAKE: Cook County; T64N, R2W, Sec. 18. U.S. 1962.

ALSIKE LAKE: Lake County; T60N, R10W, Sec. 15. *Not*: Clover Lake. U.S. 1959; Minn. 1957.

AMERICAN POINT: in Lake of the Woods, Lake of the Woods County; T168N, R33W, Sec. 18, 19. *Not*: Lecair, Currys Fishery. U.S. *Sixth Report*, 92.

AMOEBER LAKE: Lake County; T65N, R6, 7W, Sec. 7, 8, 17, 18; 12. *Not*: Amoeba Lake, Amoebac Lake. Minn. 1940.

AMUNDSEN LAKE: St. Louis County; T68N, R19W, Sec. 23, 24, 26. *Not*: Knox Lake, Amundson Lake. U.S. 1941–43; Minn. 1940.

ANDERSON LAKE: Beltrami County; T148N, R30W, Sec. 20, 21. *Not*: Ellis Lake. Minn. 1940.

ANDREW, LAKE: Douglas County; T127N, R38W, Sec. 10–12, 14, 15. *Not*: Lake Andrews. U.S. 1967.

ANDRUSIA, LAKE: Beltrami County; T146N, R31W, Sec. 7, 8, 17–20, 29, 30. *Not*: Long Lake, Lake Andrusa, Lake Elliot Coues. U.S. 1933.

ANGUS: railroad station, Polk County; T153N, R47W, Sec. 9. *Not*: Angers. U.S. *Sixth Report*, 95.

ARROW LAKE: Lake County; T62N, R7W, Sec. 6, 7, 18. *Not*: Long Lake. U.S. *Sixth Report*, 103.

ARROWHEAD LAKE: Itasca County; T149N, R25W, Sec. 22, 23, 26. *Not*: Sand Lake. U.S. 1941–43; Minn. 1940.

ASHDICK LAKE: Lake County; T66N, R6W, Sec. 23–26. *Not*: Caribau Lake, Caribou Lake. U.S. 1959; Minn. 1957.

ASHIGAN LAKE: Lake County; T64N, R8W, Sec. 14, 15. *Not*: Bass Lake. U.S. 1959; Minn. 1957.

ASPEN LAKE: Cook County; T64N, R1W, Sec. 10–12. *Not*: Seed Lake, Aspik Lake, Spen Lake. U.S. 1941–43; Minn. 1940.

ASPEN LAKE: Itasca County; T60N, R26W, Sec. 4, 5. *Not*: Rice Lake. Minn. 1940.

ASSINIKA CREEK: Cook County; rises in T64N, R1E, Sec. 36, flows southeastward through Assinika Lake to Brule River in T63N, R2E, Sec. 21. *Not*: Stoney Creek, Stony Creek, Stoney River, Stony River. U.S. 1959; Minn. 1957.

ASSINIKA LAKE: Cook County; T63N, R1, 2E, Sec. 1, 12; 7. *Not*: Stoney Lake, Stony Lake. U.S. 1959; Minn. 1957.

ASTRID LAKE: St. Louis County; T65N, R16W, Sec. 13. *Not*: Square Lake, Astlo Lake. U.S. 1936–37.

SUPPLEMENT NO. 2: DECISIONS LIST 745

AURDAL: township, Otter Tail County; T133N, R42W. *Not*: Amdal. U.S. *Sixth Report*, 108.

AXE LAKE: Cook County; T36N, R3W, Sec. 27. *Not*: Axel Lake. Minn. 1940.

BAIRD LAKE: Lake County; T61N, R10W, Sec. 28, 29. *Not*: Spring Lake. U.S. 1959; Minn. 1957.

BAKEKANA LAKE: Lake County; T64N, R6, 7W, Sec. 6, 7; 1, 12. *Not*: Baker Lake, Hog Lake, Range Lake. U.S. 1959; Minn. 1957.

BAKER: village, Clay County; T137N, R47W, Sec. 1. *Not*: Navan. U.S. 1963.

BAKERS LAKE: McLeod County; T114N, R29W, Sec. 7, 8, 17, 18, 20. *Not*: Baker's Lake, Arms Lake, Baker Lake. U.S. 1963.

BALDWIN LAKE: Washington County; T26, 27N, R22W, Sec. 26, 35, 36. *Not*: Balden Lake, Grey Cloud Lake, Lake Balden, Lake Baldwin, Moore Lake. U.S. 1968; Minn. 1968.

BALLY CREEK: Cook County; rises in T61N, R1W, Sec. 10, flows into Cascade River in T61N, R2W, Sec. 12. *Not*: Baldy Creek, Blackwell Creek. U.S. 1962; Minn. 1940.

BALSAM LAKE: Lake County; T58N, R7W, Sec. 2, 3. *Not*: Bell Lake. U.S. 1941–43; Minn. 1940.

BANADAD LAKE: Cook County; T64N, R2, 3W, Sec. 7; 10–12. *Not*: Banner Lake, Benadad Lake. Minn. 1940.

BARDEN: village, Scott County; T115N, R22W, Sec. 12. *Not*: Bardon, Sibley, Long Lake. U.S. *Sixth Report*, 122.

BARTLET LAKE: Itasca County; T60N, R24W, Sec. 34. *Not*: Brattle Lake, Bratle Lake, Bartlett Lake. Minn. 1940.

BARWISE LAKE: Itasca County; T59N, R24W, Sec. 29, 32. *Not*: Cedar Lake. U.S. 1941–43; Minn. 1940.

BASSETT CREEK: Hennepin County; rises in Medicine Lake, T118N, R22W, Sec. 25. *Not*: Bassett's Creek. U.S. *Sixth Report*, 126.

BASSWOOD LAKE: Lake County and Ontario; T64, 65N, R9, 10W, various sections. *Not*: Bassimenau, Bois Blanc, Whitewood. U.S. 1950–54.

BATTLE CREEK LAKE: Washington County; T28N, R21W, Sec. 6. *Not*: Mud Lake. U.S. 1968; Minn. 1968.

BAYLEY BAY: in Basswood Lake, Lake County and Ontario; T64, 65N, R9W, Sec. 3, 4; 33–35. U.S. 1950–54.

BAYLIS ISLAND: in Crane Lake, St. Louis County; T67N, R17W, Sec. 13, 14, 23, 24. *Not*: Baileys Island, Bare Island, Big Bear Island. U.S. 1965.

BAYLIS LAKE: St. Louis County; T66N, R16W, Sec. 4, 5. *Not*: Rachael Lake, Ratchel Lake, Rachel Lake. U.S. *Sixth Report*, 129.

BEAR CREEK: Lake of the Woods County; rises in Manitoba, flows to Northwest Angle Inlet in T168N, R35W, Sec. 14. U.S. *Sixth Report*, 130.

BEAR LAKE: Carlton County; T46N, R18, 19W, Sec. 6; 1. *Not*: Lake Twentynine, Twenty Nine Lake. U.S. 1963.

BEAR RIVER: village, St. Louis County; T61N, R21W, Sec. 7. *Not*: Bear Lake. Minn. 1940.
BEAST LAKE: St. Louis County; T70N, R19W, Sec. 28, 33, 34. *Not*: Wilson Lake. U.S. 1941-43; Minn. 1940.
BEAVER ISLAND: in Lake Superior, Lake County; T55N, R7W, Sec. 6, 7. *Not*: Beaver Islands, Pancake Island. U.S. 1965.
BEAVER RIVER: Lake County; rises in T57N, R9W, Sec. 28, flows generally southeastward to T55N, R8W, Sec. 12. *Not*: Amiko-Zibi, Beaver, Beaver Bay River, Beaver Creek West Branch, Beaver River West Branch, West Branch Beaver Creek, West Branch Beaver River, West Fork Beaver River, West Beaver River. U.S. 1949. *See also* East Branch Beaver River, West Branch Beaver River.
BEAVER HUT LAKE: Lake County; T61N, R10, 11W, Sec. 30, 31; 25, 36. *Not*: Baird Lake, Beaver Lake. U.S. 1959; Minn. 1957.
BEETLE LAKE: Lake County; T60N, R9W, Sec. 7. *Not*: John Lake. U.S. 1941-43; Minn. 1940.
BELLEVUE: township, Morrison County; T39N, R32W. *Not*: Belle Vue. U.S. *Sixth Report,* 134.
BELTRAMI LAKE: Beltrami County; T148N, R32, 33W, Sec. 30, 31; 25, 26, 35, 36. *Not*: Gnat Lake, Gnatt Lake. U.S. 1940-41; Minn. 1940.
BERGVILLE LAKE: Itasca County; T150N, R28W, Sec. 29, 30. *Not*: Mud Lake. U.S. 1941-43; Minn. 1940.
BETA LAKE: Cook County; T64N, R2W, Sec. 18. U.S. 1962.
BETTS CHUTE: channel in Mississippi River, Winona County; T107, 108N, R7W, Sec. 6; 31. *Not*: Bett's Chute. U.S. *Sixth Report,* 139.
BEZHIK LAKE: St. Louis County; T64N, R14W, Sec. 9, 16. *Not*: Bezhick Lake. U.S. *Sixth Report,* 139.
BIAUSWAH LAKE: Itasca County; T147N, R27W, Sec. 8, 9, 16, 17. *Not*: Six Mile Lake, Lake Biauswo. U.S. 1933-34.
BIBON LAKE: St. Louis County; T66N, R13W, Sec. 26, 27. *Not*: Bibin Lake, Bibôn Lake. U.S. 1935-36.
BIG ISLAND: in Lake Minnetonka, Hennepin County; T117N, R23W, Sec. 14, 22, 23. *Not*: Meeker's Island, Morris' Island, Morse's Island. U.S. 1964.
BIG DIAMOND LAKE: Itasca County; T56N, R24W, Sec. 14, 23. *Not*: Diamond Lake. Minn. 1940.
BIG DICK LAKE: Itasca County; T59N, R26W, Sec. 2, 11. *Not*: Dick Lake. Minn. 1940.
BIG FORK RIVER: Itasca, Koochiching counties; rises in T150N, R27W, Sec. 35, Itasca County, flows into Rainy River in T70N, R26W, Sec. 32. *Not*: Bigfork River. U.S. *Sixth Report,* 142.
BIG KANDIYOHI LAKE: Kandiyohi County; T118N, R34W, Sec. 22, 23, 26-29, 31-35. *Not*: Kandiyohi Lake. U.S. 1963.
BIG KNIFE PORTAGE: between Knife and Seed lakes, Lake County and Ontario; T65N, R8W, Sec. 36. U.S. *Sixth Report,* 142.

BIG RICE LAKE: St. Louis County; T64N, R13W, Sec. 7, 8, 17, 18. Minn. 1940.
BIG SAND LAKE: Cass County; T141, 142N, R26W, Sec. 3–5, 8; 33, 34. *Not*: Sand Lake, Turtle Lake. Minn. 1940.
BIG STONE: county. *Not*: Bigstone. U.S. *Sixth Report*, 143.
BIG STONE LAKE: Big Stone County and South Dakota; T121–124N, R46–49W, various sections. *Not*: Bigstone Lake. U.S. *Sixth Report*, 143.
BIG TOO MUCH LAKE: Itasca County; T148N, R25W, Sec. 12, 13. *Not*: Tomuch Lake, Big To Much Lake, Toomuch Lake. Minn. 1940.
BIGSBY LAKE: Cook County; T61N, R2, 3W, Sec. 30, 31; 36. *Not*: Sylvia Lake, Little Caribou Lake. U.S. 1959; Minn. 1957.
BINAGAMI LAKE: Cook County; T62N, R1E, Sec. 19, 20. *Not*: Clearwater Lake, Little Clearwater Lake. U.S. 1959; Minn. 1957.
BINE LAKE: Lake County; T60N, R8W, Sec. 34 (E½). *Not*: Indian Lake, John Lake, Partridge Lake. U.S. 1959; Minn. 1957.
BIRCH LAKE: Lake County and Ontario, T64, 65N, R8, 9W, various sections. U.S. 1950–54.
BIRCH LAKE: St. Louis, Lake counties; T61N, R11–13W, various sections. U.S. *Sixth Report*, 145.
BIRCH COOLEY: township, Renville County; T112, 113N, R34W. *Not*: Birch Coolie, Birch Cooly. U.S. *Sixth Report*, 145.
BIRCHDALE: township, Todd County; T127N, R33W. *Not*: Birch Dale. U.S. *Sixth Report*, 146.
BISMARCK: township, Sibley County; T113N, R30W. *Not*: Bismark. U.S. *Sixth Report*, 146.
BLACK ISLAND LAKE: Itasca County; T58N, R25W, Sec. 4, 5, 8, 9. *Not*: Arm Lake, Moon Lake. Minn. 1940.
BLACKHAWK LAKE: Dakota County; T27N, R23W, Sec. 16, 17, 21. *Not*: Black Hawk Lake, Downing Lake. U.S. *Sixth Report*, 149.
BLACKSMITH LAKE: Cass County; T144N, R28W, Sec. 13. *Not*: Big Boy Lake. U.S. 1935–36.
BLACKWATER LAKE: Itasca County; T55N, R26W, Sec. 4, 7–10, 15–17. *Not*: Dirtywater Lake. Minn. 1940.
BLAKELEY: village, Scott County; T113N, R25W, Sec. 8. *Not*: Blakely. U.S. 1959.
BLANDIN LAKE: Itasca County; T59N, R25W, Sec. 23, 24, 25. *Not*: Craig Lake. Minn. 1940.
BLUEBILL LAKE: Itasca County; T59N, R24W, Sec. 8, 9. *Not*: Rice Lake. U.S. 1941–43; Minn. 1940.
BLUEHILL: township, Sherburne County; T35N, R27W. *Not*: Blue Hill. U.S. *Sixth Report*, 152.
BLUEWATER LAKE: Itasca County; T57N, R25W, Sec. 8, 17–20. *Not*: Blue Lake. U.S. 1941–43; Minn. 1940.
BOGBERRY LAKE: Lake County; T61, 62N, R10W, Sec. 6; 31. *Not*: Cranberry Lake. U.S. 1959; Minn. 1957.

BOIS DE SIOUX RIVER: Traverse County; flows north from Lake Traverse to T128N, R47W, joining Otter Tail River to form Red River of the North. *Not*: Boise de Sioux, Bois des Sioux, Sioux Wood, Siouxwood. U.S. *Sixth Report*, 154.

BONDIN: township, Murray County; T105N, R40W. *Not*: Bowdin. U.S. *Sixth Report*, 156.

BONE LAKE: Lake County; T61N, R6W, Sec. 13, 14. *Not*: Long Lake. U.S. 1941–43; Minn. 1940.

BONGA LAKE: Lake County; T59N, R11W, Sec. 14. *Not*: Round Lake. U.S. *Sixth Report*, 156.

BONNIE LAKE: Lake County; T65N, R7W, Sec. 27. *Not*: Portage Lake. U.S. 1941–43; Minn. 1940.

BOOT LAKE: Lake County; T64N, R8W, Sec. 16, 20, 21. *Not*: Crooked Lake. U.S. 1936–37.

BORDEN LAKE: Beltrami County; T150N, R30W, Sec. 30. *Not*: Anderson Lake. Minn. 1940.

BOSTICK CREEK: Lake of the Woods County; rises in T162N, R32W, Sec. 31, flows to Lake of the Woods in T162N, R32W, Sec. 21. *Not*: Bostedt, Bostic, Bostik, Buster, Bustig, Bostig. U.S. 1968.

BOTTLE PORTAGE: between Iron Lake and Lac la Croix, St. Louis County and Ontario; T67N, R13W. *Not*: Flacon Portage, Portage des Flacons. U.S. *Sixth Report*, 158.

BOUDER LAKE: Cook County; T62N, R3W, Sec. 19, 20. *Not*: Rush Lake, Reck Lake, Boulder Lake. U.S. 1959; Minn. 1957.

BOW LAKE: Lake County; T63N, R7W, Sec. 1, 2, 11, 12. *Not*: Hugo Lake. U.S. *Sixth Report*, 160.

BOWER TROUT LAKE: Cook County; T63N, R1W, Sec. 15, 16. *Not*: Lower Trout Lake, Brulé River Lake. Minn. 1940.

BOWMAN LAKE: Hubbard County; T145N, R32W, Sec. 13, 14. *Not*: Long Lake, Mud Lake. U.S. 1941–43; Minn. 1940.

BOXELL LAKE: Cass County; T141N, R28W, Sec. 22, 27, 28. *Not*: Craig Lake. Minn. 1940.

BOYS LAKE: Cook County; T62N, R2E, Sec. 5, 8. *Not*: Third Kimball Lake. U.S. 1959; Minn. 1957.

BRIGHT LAKE: Lake County; T64N, R11W, Sec. 31. *Not*: Clear Lake. U.S. 1959; Minn. 1957.

BROWNS BAY: in Rainy Lake, St. Louis County; T70N, R19W, Sec. 20. *Not*: Brown Bay. U.S. 1968.

BROWNS VALLEY: village, Traverse County; T125N, R49W, Sec. 32, 33. *Not*: Brown's Valley, Lake Traverse, Brown Valley, Traverse. U.S. *Sixth Report*, 167.

BRUIN LAKE: Lake County; T62N, R10W, Sec. 7, 18. *Not*: Bear Lake. U.S. 1959; Minn. 1957.

BRULE RIVER: Cook County; rises in Meeds Lake, T64N, R2W, Sec. 13, flows southeasterly into Lake Superior in T62N, R3E, Sec. 27. *Not*: Arrowhead River, Bois Brule River, Bois Brulé River, North Brule River, Brulé River, Wisacodé, Wissakode Zibi. U.S. 1961; Minn. 1960. *See also* South Brule River.

BRYANT LAKE: Hennepin County; T116N, R22W, Sec. 2, 11. *Not*: Long, Bryant's. U.S. *Sixth Report,* 168.

BUCK LAKE: St. Louis County; T63, 64N, R15W, Sec. 6; 1, 2, 11; 31. *Not*: Long Lake, Lone Lake. U.S. 1941–43; Minn. 1940.

BUCKMAN LAKE: Itasca County; T59N, R24W, Sec. 20, 21, 28, 29. *Not*: Buchman Lake, Lake Buckman. Minn. 1940.

BULLFROG LAKE: Lake County; T65N, R6W, Sec. 2, 11. *Not*: Frog Lake. U.S. 1959; Minn. 1957.

BUNGGEE LAKE: St. Louis County; T66N, R12W, Sec. 33, 34. U.S. *Sixth Report,* 174.

BUNNY LAKE: Lake County; T61N, R7W, Sec. 30, 31. *Not*: Rabbit Lake. U.S. 1959; Minn. 1957.

BURNHAMSVILLE: township, Todd County; T128N, R32W. *Not*: Burnhamville. U.S. *Sixth Report,* 176.

BURNSVILLE: township, Dakota County; T27N, R24W. *Not*: Burnesville. U.S. *Sixth Report,* 176.

BUTTERFLY LAKE: Lake County; T61N, R9W, Sec. 16 (SW¼ of SE¼). *Not*: Lake Rock, Rock Lake. U.S. 1959; Minn. 1957.

CACHE BAY: in Saganaga Lake, Cook County; T66N, R5W. U.S. *Sixth Report,* 181.

CALAMUS CREEK: Douglas County; rises in T128N, R36W, Sec. 4, flows north to T129N, R36W, Sec. 15. *Not*: Calamas Creek, Fairfield Creek. U.S. 1967.

CAMP TWENTY LAKE: Lake County; T63N, R10W, Sec. 13. *Not*: Triangle Lake. U.S. 1961.

CANAL LAKE: Lake County; T60N, R6W, Sec. 31. *Not*: Twin Lakes, Lower Twin Lake, Twin Lake. U.S. 1962; Minn. 1960.

CANOE LAKE: Lake County; T65N, R6W, Sec. 9, 10. *Not*: Clam Lake. U.S. 1959; Minn. 1957.

CARIBOU LAKE: Cook County; T65N, R1E, Sec. 32–36. *Not*: Cariboo Lake, Reindeer Lake. U.S. 1961.

CARP LAKE: Lake County and Ontario; T64N, R8, 9W, Sec. 6, 7; 1, 2, 12. *Not*: Pseudo Messer Lake, Sucker Lake, Carol Lake. U.S. 1950–54.

CARP PORTAGE: between Carp and Birch lakes, Lake County; T65N, R8W, Sec. 34. *Not*: La Carpe Portage, The Carpe Portage. U.S. *Sixth Report,* 197.

CARROT LAKE: Cook County; T64N, R2E, Sec. 17, 18. *Not*: Pants Lake. U.S. 1941–43; Minn. 1940.

CAT LAKE: Lake County; T60N, R9W, Sec. 10. *Not*: Cut Lake, Hill Lake. U.S. 1941–43; Minn. 1940.

CEDAR LAKE: Itasca County; T60N, R26W, Sec. 1. *Not*: Mud Lake. Minn. 1940.

CEDAR RIVER: Dodge County; rises in T105N, R17W, Sec. 1, flows south into Iowa. *Not*: Red Cedar River. U.S. *Sixth Report*, 205.

CERRO GORDO: township, Lac qui Parle County; T118N, R43W. *Not*: Cerrogordo. U.S. *Sixth Report*, 206.

CHAD LAKE: St. Louis County; T63, 64N, R15W, Sec. 2, 3; 34, 35. *Not*: Crab Lake, Crabbe Lake. U.S. 1936–37.

CHARLESTOWN: township, Redwood County; T109N, R36W. *Not*: Charleston. U.S. *Sixth Report*, 209.

CHAUTAUQUA LAKE: Otter Tail County; T132N, R42, 43W, Sec. 18, 19; 13, 24. *Not*: Lye Lake. U.S. *Sixth Report*, 211.

CHENGWATANA: township, Pine County; T39N, R19, 20W. *Not*: Chengwatona. U.S. *Sixth Report*, 212.

CHIPMUNK LAKE: Lake County; T60N, R10W, Sec. 12. *Not*: Shoe Lake. U.S. 1959; Minn. 1957.

CHOW LAKE: Lake County; T60N, R11W, Sec. 10 (N½ of NW¼). *Not*: Chuck Lake, Dinner Lake. U.S. 1961; Minn. 1960.

CHRISTINE LAKE: Cook County; T61N, R3W, Sec. 28, 29, 32. *Not*: Christina Lake, Lake Christine, Sucker Lake. Minn. 1940.

CHRYSLER LAKE: Crow Wing County; T44N, R29W, Sec. 1, 12. *Not*: Cryster Lake, Lake Chrysler, Pleasant Lake. U.S. 1968.

CHUCK LAKE: Cook County; T64N, R5W, Sec. 35 (NW¼ of SE¼). U.S. 1961.

CIRCLE LAKE: Lake County; T65N, R11W, Sec. 2, 3. *Not*: Round Lake, Wheel Lake. U.S. 1961; Minn. 1960.

CLARK LAKE: Lake County; T55, 56N, R10W, Sec. 5, 6; 31. *Not*: Clarke Lake. U.S. 1964.

CLEAR LAKE: Itasca County; T149, 150N, R26W, Sec. 3, 4; 33. *Not*: Killdeer Lake, Kildeer Lake. Minn. 1940.

CLEARWATER: township and village, Wright County; T122, 123N, R26, 27W. *Not*: Clear Water. U.S. *Sixth Report*, 223.

CLITHERALL: township and village, Otter Tail County; T132N, R39, 40W. *Not*: Clitheral. U.S. *Sixth Report*, 225.

CLOQUET: village, Carlton County; T49N, R17W, Sec. 14, 15, 22–24. *Not*: Colquet. U.S. *Sixth Report*, 225.

CLOUGH LAKE: Crow Wing County; T138N, R29W, Sec. 2, 3, 10, 11. *Not*: Sweet Lake, Swede Lake. U.S. 1964; Minn. 1964.

CLOVE LAKE: Cook County and Ontario; T65N, R4W, Sec. 1, 2, 11. *Not*: Cove Lake, Island Portage Lake, Pine Lake. U.S. 1950; Minn. 1940.

CLOVER CREEK: Pine County; rises in T41N, R18W, Sec. 10, flows south to Sand Creek, T40N, R18W, Sec. 19. *Not*: Hay Creek. U.S. 1964.

CLUB LAKE: Lake County; T63N, R7W, Sec. 3, 10. *Not*: Chub Lake. U.S. 1967.

COFFEE LAKE: Lake County; T61N, R6W, Sec. 10, 15, 16. *Not*: Martin Lake, Tom Lake. U.S. 1941–43; Minn. 1940.

SUPPLEMENT NO. 2: DECISIONS LIST 751

COLBY LAKE: St. Louis County; T58N, R14W, Sec. 4–9. *Not*: North Partridge Lake, Upper Partridge Lake, Partridge Lake, Partridge Lakes (one of). U.S. 1963; Minn. 1940.

COTEAU DES PRAIRIES: plateau, Jackson, Lincoln, Nobles, Pipestone counties; also parts of Marshall, Roberts, Grant, and Deuel counties, South Dakota. U.S. *Sixth Report*, 238.

COTTONWOOD RIVER: Brown, Lyon, Redwood counties; rises in T109N, R42W, Sec. 8, Lyon County, flows eastward into Minnesota River in T110N, R30W, Sec. 34. *Not*: Big Cottonwood River, Waraju River. U.S. 1963.

COUGAR LAKE: Lake County; T59N, R11W, Sec. 34, 35. *Not*: Perch Lake. U.S. 1959; Minn. 1957.

COXEY POND: St. Louis County; T64N, R13W, Sec. 29, 30. *Not*: Carey Lake. U.S. 1965.

CRAG LAKE: Cook County, T64, 65N, R4, 5W, Sec. 1; 31; 36. *Not*: Rock Lake. U.S. 1959; Minn. 1957.

CRESCENT LAKE: Cook County; T62N, R3, 4W, Sec. 19, 20, 29–31; 24, 25, 36. *Not*: Poplar River Lake, Pine Lake, West Line Lake. U.S. 1959; Minn. 1957.

CREST LAKE: Lake County; T57N, R11W, Sec. 3, 10. *Not*: Big Mud Lake, Summit Lake. U.S. 1962; Minn. 1960.

CROOKED CREEK: Pine County; formed by the junction of its East Fork and West Fork in T41N, R18W, Sec. 12, flows into St. Croix River in T41N, R17W, Sec. 32. *Not*: Crooked River. U.S. 1963. *See also* East Fork Crooked Creek, West Fork Crooked Creek.

CROOKED LAKE: Cass County; T143, 144N, R31W, Sec. 2; 34–36. *Not*: Three Lake. Minn. 1940.

CROOKED LAKE: St. Louis, Lake counties and Ontario; T66N, R11, 12W, various sections. U.S. 1950–54.

CROSS RIVER LAKE: Cook, Lake counties; T60N, R5, 6W, Sec. 7, 18; 12, 13. *Not*: Cross Lake, Nigger Lake. U.S. 1941–43; Minn. 1940.

CRUISER LAKE: St. Louis County; T69, 70N, R19W, Sec. 5, 6; 31, 32. *Not*: Trout Lake. U.S. 1941–43; Minn. 1940.

CRYSTAL LAKE: Cass, Hubbard counties; T140N, R31, 32W, Sec. 18; 13. *Not*: Williams Lake. Minn. 1940.

CRYSTAL LAKE: Cook County; T64N, R1, 2E, Sec. 1; 5–8. *Not*: Lake Fanny, Spalding Lake, Spaulding Lake. U.S. 1949–50; Minn. 1940.

CULKIN, LAKE: Lake County; T59N, R11W, Sec. 17, 20. *Not*: Snowshoe Lake, St. Louis Lake, Culkin Lake. U.S. 1966; Minn. 1937.

CUMMINGS LAKE: St. Louis County; T63, 64N, R13, 14W, Sec. 2; 31; 24–28, 32–36. *Not*: Clear Lake. U.S. 1941–43; Minn. 1940.

CURRENT LAKE: village, Murray County; T108N, R43W, Sec. 24. *Not*: Currant Lake. U.S. *Sixth Report*, 249.

CURTAIN FALLS: a waterfall between Crooked and Iron lakes, St. Louis County and Ontario; T66N, R12W, Sec. 5, 6. *Not*: Curtain Fall. U.S. 1950–54.

CYPRESS LAKE: Lake County and Ontario; T66N, R6W, Sec. 23, 26–28, 31–33. *Not*: Otter Track Lake. U.S. 1950–54.

DALEY BROOK: St. Louis County; rises in T68N, R21W, Sec. 14, flows into Kabetogama Lake in T68N, R20W, Sec. 8. *Not*: Daly Brook, Daly's Brook. U.S. *Sixth Report,* 252.

DALTON LAKE: Itasca County; T57N, R26W, Sec. 6, 7. *Not*: Dutton Lake, Outton Lake. U.S. 1941–43; Minn. 1940.

DAM FIVE LAKE: Lake County; T60N, R6W, Sec. 28, 33. *Not*: Pickerel Lake, Lake Pickeral. U.S. 1959; Minn. 1957.

DECKER LAKE: Itasca County; T148N, R29W, Sec. 7, 18. *Not*: Becker Lake. Minn. 1940.

DEER LAKE: Cook County; T64, 65N, R1E, Sec. 4, 5; 32, 33. *Not*: Moon Lake. U.S. 1949–50; Minn. 1940.

DEER YARD CREEK: Cook County; rises in Deer Yard Lake, T61N, R2W, Sec. 32, flows south and east into Lake Superior in T60N, R2W, Sec. 15. *Not*: Spruce Creek, Trout Creek. U.S. 1959; Minn. 1957.

DEER YARD LAKE: Cook County; T61N, R2W, Sec. 28, 29, 31, 32. *Not*: Trout Lake. U.S. 1959; Minn. 1957.

DEERWOOD: township, Kittson County; T159N, R46W. *Not*: Deer Wood, Dearwood. U.S. *Sixth Report,* 259.

DELAVAN: township and village, Faribault County; T104N, R27W. *Not*: Guthrie, Delevan. U.S. *Sixth Report,* 260.

DELAY LAKE: Lake County; T59N, R8W, Sec. 2. *Not*: Bear Lake. U.S. 1941–43; Minn. 1940.

DES MOINES LAKE: Beltrami County; T148N, R33W, Sec. 29. *Not*: Horseshoe Lake, Lake Horseshoe. U.S. 1961; Minn. 1960.

DEVIL TRACK LAKE: Cook County; T62N, R1W, 1E, Sec. 30, 31; 25–29, 34, 35. *Not*: Devils Track Lake, Devil's Track Lake. U.S. 1962.

DEVIL TRACK RIVER: Cook County; rises in T62N, R1E, Sec. 31, flows to T61N, R1E, Sec. 13. *Not*: Devils Track River, Devils Tract River. U.S. 1962.

DIAMOND LAKE: Aitkin County; T46N, R27W, Sec. 13. U.S. 1963.

DIN LAKE: Cook County; T64N, R4W, Sec. 21. *Not*: Dim Lake. U.S. 1967.

DIVIDE LAKE: Lake County; T59N, R7W, Sec. 7, 8. *Not*: Towney Lake, Towhey Lake, Green Lake, Toohey Lake, Twohey Lake, Twohy Lake. U.S. 1966; Minn. 1968.

DIX LAKE: Lake County; T65N, R7W, Sec. 33, 34. *Not*: Plum Lake. U.S. 1941–43; Minn. 1940.

DIXON LAKE: Itasca County; T148N, R28, 29W, Sec. 30, 31; 24, 25, 36. U.S. 1941–43; Minn. 1940.

DOCK LAKE: Itasca County; T58, 59N, R26W, Sec. 1, 2; 36. *Not*: Birch Lake. U.S. 1941–43; Minn. 1940.

DODGE CENTER CREEK: Dodge County; rises in T106N, R18W, Sec. 17, flows northeastward to T107N, R17W, Sec. 14. *Not*: South Branch Middle Fork Zumbro River, South Middle Branch Zumbro River, Zumbro River. U.S. 1961.

DOGWOOD LAKE: Cook County; T59N, R5W, Sec. 16, 17, 20, 21. *Not*: Buck Lake. U.S. 1959; Minn. 1957.

DOLNEY LAKE: Crow Wing County; T137N, R26W, Sec. 17–20. *Not*: Dolneys Lake, Dolney's Lake, Round Lake. U.S. 1962; Minn. 1962.

DOVRE: township, Kandiyohi County; T120N, R35W. *Not*: Dowe. U.S. *Sixth Report*, 271.

DOVRE LAKE: St. Louis County; T67N, R16W, Sec. 17, 20. *Not*: Echo Lake. U.S. 1941–43; Minn. 1940.

DOYLE LAKE: Lake County; T58N, R7W, Sec. 31. *Not*: Round Lake. U.S. 1941–43; Minn. 1940.

DRAGON LAKE: Lake County; T60N, R9W, Sec. 7, 8. *Not*: Duck Lake. U.S. 1941–43; Minn. 1940.

DRILLER LAKE: Lake County; T57N, R10W, Sec. 4. *Not*: Duck Lake. U.S. 1959; Minn. 1957.

DRY LAKE: St. Louis County; T63N, R12W, Sec. 4, 9. *Not*: Bass Lake (part of). U.S. 1941–43; Minn. 1940.

DUGOUT LAKE: St. Louis County; T64N, R15W, Sec. 33, 34. *Not*: Little Crab Lake, Little Pine Lake. U.S. 1936–37.

DULUTH: city, St. Louis County; T49, 50N, R13, 14W. U.S. *Sixth Report*, 274.

DUMBBELL LAKE: Lake County; T59, 60N, R7, 8W, Sec. 6, 7; 31; 1. *Not*: Dumbell Lake. U.S. 1963.

DUMBBELL RIVER: Lake County; rises in T60N, R7W, Sec. 31, flows northeasterly to Island River in T61N, R7W, Sec. 16. *Not*: Dumbell River. U.S. 1963.

DUTTON LAKE: Lake County; T65N, R6W, Sec. 5, 6. *Not*: Indian Lake, Lake Indian. U.S. 1941–43; Minn. 1940.

EAGAN: township, Dakota County; T27N, R23W. *Not*: Egan. U.S. *Sixth Report*, 278.

EAST LAKE: Itasca County; T59N, R25W, Sec. 5–8. *Not*: Fox Lake. Minn. 1940.

EAST BRANCH BEAVER RIVER: Lake County; rises in T57N, R9W, Sec. 3, flows to West Branch Beaver River in T55N, R8W, Sec. 2. *Not*: Beaver, Beaver Brook, Beaver Creek, Beaver River, Beaver River East Branch, East Beaver River, East Branch Beaver Creek, East Fork Beaver River. U.S. 1949; Minn. 1940.

EAST FORK CROOKED CREEK: Pine County; flows south into West Fork Crooked Creek in T41N, R18W, Sec. 12. *Not*: Crooked Creek, East Branch Crooked Creek, East Fork Crooked River. U.S. 1963.

EAST OTTER LAKE: Cook County; T65N, R1, 2W, Sec. 31; 36. *Not*: Mammal Lake. U.S. 1961; Minn. 1960.

EAST PIPE LAKE: Cook County; T62, 63N, R3W, Sec. 3; 34. U.S. 1962; Minn. 1962.

EAST POKEGAMA CREEK: Pine County; rises in T141N, R21W, Sec. 19, flows into Pokegama Creek in T140N, R21W, Sec. 30. *Not*: Pokegama Creek. U.S. 1963.

EAST SMITH LAKE: Itasca County; T58N, R26W, Sec. 2. *Not*: Smith Lake (part of). Minn. 1940.

ECHO LAKE: Carlton County; T46N, R19W, Sec. 27, 28, 33, 34. *Not*: Pickerel Lake. U.S. 1963.

EDDY LAKE: Lake County; T65N, R6W, Sec. 20, 21; 28, 29. *Not*: Eddie Lake. Minn. 1940.

ED SHAVE LAKE: St. Louis County; T65N, R13W, Sec. 25, 36. *Not*: Second Lake, Lake Two, Lake 2. Minn. 1957.

EGG LAKE: Itasca County; T146N, R26W, Sec. 3, 10. *Not*: Rice Lake, First Lake. Minn. 1940.

EIGHTEEN LAKE: Lake County; T60N, R8W, Sec. 28, 33, 34. *Not*: Foote Lake. U.S. 1941–43; Minn. 1940.

ELIXIR LAKE: Lake County; T60N, R6, 7W, Sec. 30, 31; 36. *Not*: Spring Lake. U.S. 1959; Minn. 1957.

ELK LAKE: Clearwater County; T143N, R36W, Sec. 15, 22, 23. *Not*: Lake Glazier, Dolly Varden Lake, Breck Lake. U.S. *Sixth Report,* 287.

ELLA HALL LAKE: Lake County; T64N, R10W, Sec. 20, 29, 30. *Not*: Annie Hall Lake, Urn Lake. U.S. 1959; Minn. 1957.

ENGLUND: village, Marshall County; T158N, R46W, Sec. 30. *Not*: England. U.S. *Sixth Report,* 290.

ERDAHL: township, Grant County; T129N, R41W. *Not*: Erdal. U.S. *Sixth Report,* 291.

ESKWAGAMA LAKE: Lake County; T62, 63N, R10W, Sec. 6; 31. *Not*: Little Clear Lake, Esquagama. U.S. 1935–36.

ESQUAGAMA LAKE: St. Louis County; T57, 58N, R16W, Sec. 4; 27, 33–35. *Not*: Esquagamah Lake, Eshquagama Lake, Eshquaguma Lake, Eskquagama Lake, Lake Eshquaguma. U.S. 1966; Minn. 1940.

ESPELIE: township, Marshall County; T154, 155N, R39W. *Not*: Espelee, Esplee. U.S. 1933–34.

EVERGREEN LAKE: Hubbard County; T144N, R34W, Sec. 8, 17. *Not*: Rat Lake. U.S. 1959; Minn. 1956.

EXPLORER LAKE: Lake County; T64N, R7, 8W, Sec. 6, 7; 1, 12. *Not*: Three Lake, Three Lakes (one of). U.S. 1959; Minn. 1957.

FAGEN LAKE: Beltrami County; T148N, R31W, Sec. 16, 21. *Not*: Foger Lake. Minn. 1940.

SUPPLEMENT NO. 2: DECISIONS LIST 755

FAITH LAKE: Lake County; T65N, R6W, Sec. 1 (NE¼). *Not*: Hope Lake, Wilderness Lake. U.S. 1961; Minn. 1960.

FALL LAKE: Lake, St. Louis counties; T63, 64N, R11, 12W, Sec. 2–4, 9–11, 16–20; 13, 24; 34–36. U.S. *Sixth Report,* 296.

FANNIE, LAKE: Isanti County; T35, 36N, R23W, Sec. 2, 3; 34, 35. *Not*: Fanny Lake, Lake Fanny. U.S. 1963.

FECTOS POINT: in Vermilion Lake, St. Louis County; T62N, R16W, Sec. 5. *Not*: Pecto's Point, Fecto Point, Pecto Point, Pectos Point. U.S. 1966; Minn. 1940.

FERGUSON POINT: in Lake Minnetonka, Hennepin County; T117N, R23W, Sec. 23. *Not*: Ferguson's Point. U.S. 1960.

FERNE LAKE: Lake County; T62N, R7W, Sec. 21, 22, 27, 28. *Not*: Maud Lake, Ferna Lake. U.S. *Sixth Report,* 300.

FINSTAD LAKE: St. Louis County; T65N, R16W, Sec. 30. *Not*: Fensted Lake, Fenstad Lake, Finsted Lake. U.S. 1964.

FISH LAKE: Dakota County; T27N, R23W, Sec. 15, 16. *Not*: Thompson Lake. U.S. *Sixth Report,* 302.

FISHER: township and village, Polk County; T150N, R48W. *Not*: Fisher Landing, Fisher's Landing. U.S. *Sixth Report,* 302.

FISHER LAKE: Lake County; T63N, R7W, Sec. 1, 2. *Not*: Oliver Lake. U.S. *Sixth Report,* 302.

FLAT HORN LAKE: Lake County; T60N, R9W, Sec. 22, 27. *Not*: Little Moose Lake. U.S. 1959; Minn. 1957.

FLOUR LAKE: Cook County; T64N, R1W, 1E, Sec. 1, 2, 11, 12; 5, 6. *Not*: Flower Lake. Minn. 1940.

FOLDAHL: township and village, Marshall County; T156N, R46W. *Not*: Foldal. U.S. *Sixth Report,* 306.

FOOL HEN LAKE: Lake County; T61N, R6W, Sec. 7, 18. *Not*: Swamp Lake. U.S. 1959; Minn. 1957.

FOOLS LAKE: Lake County; T59N, R11W, Sec. 11, 12. *Not*: Campis Lake. U.S. *Sixth Report,* 306.

FORESTVILLE: township and village, Fillmore County; T102N, R12W. *Not*: Forrestville, Fillmore. U.S. *Sixth Report,* 307.

FOURMILE BAY: in Lake of the Woods, Lake of the Woods County; T162N, R32W, Sec. 15, 16. *Not*: Four Mile Bay. U.S. 1968.

FOURTEEN, LAKE: St. Louis County; T60N, R19W, Sec. 11, 13, 14. *Not*: Crescent Lake, Lake 14. U.S. 1941–43.

FOURTOWN LAKE: Lake, St. Louis counties; T64, 65N, R11, 12W, Sec. 6; 1; 19, 30–32; 24, 25, 36. *Not*: Deer Lake. U.S. *Sixth Report,* 309.

FOWL PORTAGE: between South Fowl Lake and Pigeon River, Cook County and Ontario; T64N, R3E. U.S. *Sixth Report,* 309.

FOX LAKE: Itasca County; T59N, R25W, Sec. 8, 17. *Not*: East Lake. Minn. 1940.

FRAN LAKE: Lake County; T60N, R11W, Sec. 11 (S½ of NW¼). U.S. 1961.

FRANCIS ISLAND: in Lake Superior, Cook County; T64N, R6E, Sec. 36. *Not*: Birch Island. U.S. 1967.

FRANKLIN LAKE: St. Louis County; T67N, R18W, Sec. 11, 14. *Not*: Little Namakan Lake, Little Namekan Lake. U.S. 1941–43; Minn. 1940.

FRENCH LAKE: Cook County; T64, 65N, R5W, Sec. 3; 34, 35. *Not*: French Kakigo Lake, Kakigo Lake, Black Trout Lake. U.S. 1941–43; Minn. 1940.

FROND LAKE: Lake County; T63N, R6W, Sec. 9, 10, 15, 16. *Not*: Fern Lake, Kawishiwi River Lake. U.S. 1959; Minn. 1957.

FULL OF FISH, LAKE: Kanabec County; T41N, R23W, Sec. 10, 15. *Not*: Full of Fish Lake. U.S. 1969.

GABBRO LAKE: Lake County; T62N, R10W, Sec. 3, 9–11, 14–16, 21–23. *Not*: Gubbra Lake, Gabro Lake, Gabbre Lake. U.S. *Sixth Report*, 315.

GABIMICHIGAMI LAKE: Cook, Lake counties; T64, 65N, R5, 6W, Sec. 6; 29, 31, 32; 1, 12; 36. *Not*: Gobbemichigamme Lake, Gobbemichigomog Lake, Michigamme Lake. U.S. 1939–40.

GADBOLT LAKE: Cass County; T141N, R31W, Sec. 22, 27. *Not*: Horseshoe Lake, Bass Lake. Minn. 1940.

GANDER LAKE: Lake County; T60N, R9W, Sec. 7, 8, 17, 18. *Not*: Goose Lake, Spring Lake. U.S. 1959; Minn. 1957.

GARDEN ISLAND: in Lake of the Woods, Lake of the Woods County; T166N, R33W, Sec. 22, 23, 25–27. *Not*: Cornfield. U.S. *Sixth Report*, 317.

GARRISON: village, Crow Wing County; T44N, R28W, Sec. 13, 14. *Not*: Midland. U.S. 1963.

GEORGETOWN: township and village, Clay County; T142N, R48W. *Not*: George Town. U.S. *Sixth Report*, 321.

GERUND LAKE: Lake County; T64N, R7W, Sec. 14, 15, 22, 23. *Not*: Bass Lake. U.S. 1941–43; Minn. 1940.

GIFT LAKE: Lake County; T65N, R6W, Sec. 2 (SE¼). *Not*: Charity Lake, Turtle Lake. U.S. 1959; Minn. 1957.

GIJIK LAKE: Cass County; T141N, R28W, Sec. 25, 36. *Not*: Cedar Lake. U.S. 1948–49; Minn. 1944.

GIJIKIKI LAKE: Lake County; T65, 66N, R6W, Sec. 4, 5; 32, 33. *Not*: Cedar Lake, Gijik Lake. U.S. 1961; Minn. 1960.

GILLFORD: township, Wabasha County; T110N, R13W. *Not*: Guilford. U.S. *Sixth Report*, 324.

GILLIS LAKE: Cook County; T64, 65N, R5W, Sec. 1–3, 10, 11; 35. *Not*: Bashitanakueb Lake, Bashitanaqueb Lake, Bat Lake, Bullis Lake, Gills Lake, Gill's Lake. U.S. 1949–50; Minn. 1940.

GILSTAD LAKE: Beltrami County; T148, 149N, R30W, Sec. 5, 6; 31, 32. *Not*: Gilsted Lake, Gilstead Lake. Minn. 1940.

GLACIER LAKE: Aitkin County; T50N, R23W, Sec. 23, 26. *Not*: Turtle Lake, Glacial Lake, Turner Lake. U.S. 1968; Minn. 1966.

GLENDALE: township, Scott County; T115N, R21W. *Not*: Glendule. U.S. *Sixth Report*, 327.

GNEISS LAKE: Cook County; T66N, R4W, Sec. 26. *Not*: Round Lake. U.S. 1950; Minn. 1940.

GNESEN: township, St. Louis County; T52, 53N, R14W. *Not*: Guesen. U.S. *Sixth Report*, 327.

GOLDENEYE LAKE: Lake County; T59N, R6W, Sec. 15 (E½). *Not*: Golden Eye Lake, Duck Lake. U.S. 1959; Minn. 1957.

GOODIN ISLAND: in Mississippi River, Hennepin County; T120, 121N, R22W, Sec. 31; 5, 6. *Not*: Goodwin Island, Goodwin's Island. U.S. 1959.

GORDER LAKE: Stevens County; T124N, R43W, Sec. 25–27, 35, 36. *Not*: Frog Lake. U.S. *Sixth Report*, 330.

GRAND PORTAGE: between Pigeon River and Lake Superior, Cook County; T63, 64N, R5, 6E. U.S. *Sixth Report*, 332.

GRAND PORTAGE BAY: in Lake Superior, Cook County; T63N, R6E, Sec. 2–4, 9, 11. U.S. *Sixth Report*, 333.

GRANITE LAKE: Cook County and Ontario; T65N, R4W, Sec. 1. U.S. *Sixth Report*, 334.

GRASS LAKE: Itasca County; T60N, R26, 27W, Sec. 30, 31; 25, 36. *Not*: Shoal Lake, School Lake. Minn. 1940.

GRASSY POINT: in Vermilion Lake, St. Louis County; T63N, R16W, Sec. 31. *Not*: Grasey Point. U.S. 1966.

GREEN LAKE: Itasca County; T57N, R26W, Sec. 16. *Not*: Spring Lake. Minn. 1940.

GREENSTONE LAKE: Lake County; T63N, R10W, Sec. 15, 16, 20–22. *Not*: Stone Lake. U.S. 1959; Minn. 1957.

GREENVALE: township, Dakota County; T112N, R20W. *Not*: Green Vale. U.S. *Sixth Report*, 339.

GREY CLOUD CHANNEL: in Mississippi River, Washington County; T27N, R21, 22W, Sec. 30; 24, 25. *Not*: Grey Cloud Slough. U.S. 1968; Minn. 1968.

GROUSE LAKE: Lake County; T60N, R9W, Sec. 10, 11, 14, 15. *Not*: Section Eleven Lake. U.S. 1941–43; Minn. 1940.

GROVE: township, Stearns County; T125N, R33W. *Not*: Grave. U.S. *Sixth Report*, 342.

GULF LAKE: Cook County; T66N, R4, 5W, Sec. 30; 24, 25. *Not*: Gull Lake. Minn. 1940.

GUN CLUB LAKE: Dakota County; T27, 28N, R23W, Sec. 4, 5; 32, 33. *Not*: Marsh Lake, Slater Lake, Slater's Lake. U.S. 1963.

GUNDERSON LAKE: Itasca County; T60, 149N, R27, 25W, Sec. 3, 4; 24. *Not*: Round Lake, Lake Gunderson, Big Round Lake. Minn. 1940.

GUNFLINT LAKE: Cook County and Ontario; T65N, R2, 3, 4W, Sec. 17–19; 19, 23, 24, 26–30; 24, 25. *Not*: Gun Flint Lake. U.S. 1950–54.

GUSTAFSON LAKE: St. Louis County; T65N, R16W, Sec. 36. *Not*: Gustavson Lake. Minn. 1940.
GYPO LAKE: Lake County; T65N, R11W, Sec. 6. U.S. *Sixth Report*, 345.

HAM LAKE: Hubbard County; T150N, R32W, Sec. 18, 19. *Not*: Hay Lake. U.S. 1966; Minn. 1940.
HAMMAL LAKE: Aitkin County; T46N, R27W, Sec. 3, 9, 10. *Not*: Bass Lake, Lake Hammal, Lake Hammel. U.S. 1968.
HANGING HORN LAKE: Carlton County; T46N, R19W, Sec. 11–14. *Not*: Big Lake, Big Hanging Horn Lake, White Fish Lake, Moose Horn Lake, Hanging Horns Lake, Hanging Lake. U.S. 1963.
HANSON LAKES: Itasca County; T57N, R24, 25W, Sec. 18, 19; 12, 13. *Not*: Hansen Lakes, Hanson Lake, Middle Hansen Lake, Middle Hanson Lake, Upper Hansen Lake, Upper Hanson Lake. Minn. 1940.
HARE LAKE: Lake County; T59N, R6W, Sec. 11, 14. *Not*: Morris Lake. U.S. 1941–43; Minn. 1940.
HARRISON CREEK: Lake of the Woods County; rises in Manitoba, flows eastward to head of Northwest Angle Inlet in T168N, R35W, Sec. 15. *Not*: Harrison's Creek, Harrisson Creek. U.S. 1950–54.
HAY CREEK: Pine County; rises in T44N, R15W, Sec. 8, flows southwest to Lower Tamarack River in T42N, R16W, Sec. 31. U.S. *Sixth Report*, 357.
HAY CREEK: Pine County; rises in T42N, R18W, Sec. 7, flows southward to Little Sand Creek in T42N, R18W, Sec. 31. *Not*: Little Sand Creek. U.S. 1964.
HAY LAKE: Hubbard County; T140N, R32W, Sec. 17, 18. *Not*: Ham Lake. U.S. 1966.
HAY LAKE: St. Louis County; T59N, R16W, Sec. 28, 29. *Not*: Pike Lake, Net Lake, Nett Lake. U.S. 1941–43; Minn. 1940.
HAYWARD: township and village, Freeborn County; T102N, R20W. *Not*: Haward. U.S. *Sixth Report*, 358.
HAZEL LAKE: Lake County; T62N, R6W, Sec. 1, 2. *Not*: Northeast Lake, North East Lake, Hagel Lake. U.S. 1941–43; Minn. 1940.
HEARDING ISLAND: in Lake Superior, St. Louis County; T49N, R14W, Sec. 2. *Not*: Bird Island, Harbor Island. U.S. 1963.
HELEN LAKE: Lake County; T61N, R8W, Sec. 34. *Not*: Morse Lake. U.S. 1941–43; Minn. 1940.
HENDRICHS LAKE: Itasca County; T58N, R25W, Sec. 24, 25. *Not*: Hendricks Lake. Minn. 1940.
HENRY LAKE: Hennepin County; T120N, R23W, Sec. 28, 29, 32, 33. *Not*: Lake Harry, Harry Lake, Harvey Lake. U.S. 1959.
HENSON LAKE: Cook County; T64N, R2W, Sec. 19–22. *Not*: Hanson Lake, Benson Lake. Minn. 1940.
HERITAGE LAKE: St. Louis County; T66, 67N, R15W, Sec. 1, 2, 11, 12; 35. *Not*: Hermitage Lake. Minn. 1940.

HERRIMAN LAKE: St. Louis County; T66, 67N, R16W, Sec. 5; 31, 32. *Not*: Bug Lake. U.S. 1941–43; Minn. 1940.
HIAWATHA, LAKE: Hennepin County; T28N, R24W, Sec. 12, 13. *Not*: Hiawatha Lake, Mud Lake. U.S. 1959.
HILDA CREEK: St. Louis County; rises in T65N, R16W, Sec. 36, flows west to Vermilion River in T64N, R17W, Sec. 14. *Not*: East Creek. U.S. 1965.
HINSDALE: settlement, St. Louis County; T59N, R14W, Sec. 17 (N½). *Not*: Hinesdale. U.S. 1963.
HOGBACK LAKE: Lake County; T60N, R6W, Sec. 31. *Not*: Twin Lakes, Upper Twin Lake, Twin Lake. U.S. 1962; Minn. 1960.
HOLE-IN-THE-DAY LAKE: Crow Wing County; T135N, R29W, Sec. 23–26. *Not*: Mud Lake. U.S. 1961; Minn. 1960.
HOLE-IN-WALL LAKE: Itasca County; T59N, R26W, Sec. 27, 28. *Not*: Cranberry Lake. Minn. 1940.
HOLLAND: township, Kandiyohi County; T117N, R36W. *Not*: Hilland. U.S. *Sixth Report*, 365.
HOLLY LAKE: Cook County; T61N, R3W, Sec. 10, 15. *Not*: Twin Lake, Twin Lakes, Upper Twin Lake, Beaver Lake, Laurel Lake. U.S. 1961; Minn. 1960.
HOLMAN LAKE: Itasca County; T56N, R24W, Sec. 23, 25, 26. *Not*: Lawrence Lake. U.S. 1941–43; Minn. 1940.
HOLMES LAKE: Itasca County; T58N, R24W, Sec. 15, 22. *Not*: Lower Balsam Lake, Paul Lake. Minn. 1940.
HOLY NAME LAKE: Hennepin County; T118N, R23W, Sec. 24. *Not*: Hausman Lake, Hausmans Lake, Hausman's Lake, Hausmann Lake, Hausmanns Lake, Hansmanns Lake. U.S. 1959; Minn. 1957.
HONEYMOON ISLAND: in Burntside Lake, St. Louis County; T63N, R13W, Sec. 15, 16. U.S. 1966.
HOVDE LAKE: Cass County; T141N, R30W, Sec. 22, 23, 26, 27. *Not*: Stocking Lake. U.S. 1941–43; Minn. 1940.
HOWARD LAKE: village, Wright County; T118N, R27W, Sec. 3, 4. *Not*: Howard. U.S. *Sixth Report*, 375.
HUGHEY LAKE: Hennepin County; T118N, R24W, Sec. 7, 8. *Not*: Hughuy Lake, Huchuy Lake, Haughey Lake, Heughey Lake. U.S. 1959.

IMA LAKE: Lake County; T64N, R7, 8W, Sec. 17–20; 13, 24, 25. *Not*: Slate Lake, State Lake. U.S. *Sixth Report*, 386.
INDIANA LAKE: Lake County; T64N, R10W, Sec. 15. *Not*: Bass Lake. U.S. 1959; Minn. 1957.
INGA CREEK: Lake County; rises in Inga Lake, T60N, R9W, Sec. 2, flows northward to Mitawan Creek in T61N, R9W, Sec. 12. *Not*: Sand River. U.S. 1959; Minn. 1957.
INGA LAKE: Lake County; T60N, R9W, Sec. 2, 11. *Not*: Lone Lake, Long Lake. U.S. 1941–43; Minn. 1940.

INGUADONA LAKE: Cass County; T140, 141N, R27W, Sec. 5-8, 17, 18; 29, 32. *Not*: Lake Inguadona, Inquadona Lake, Lake Gauss, Lake Ingadonah, Upper Boy Lake. Minn. 1940.

INVER GROVE: township, Dakota County; T27N, R22W. *Not*: Invergrove. U.S. 1933.

INVER GROVE HEIGHTS: village, Dakota County; T27, 28N, R22W, Sec. 2, 3, 11; 34, 35. *Not*: Invergrove, Inver Grove. U.S. 1968.

IRON LAKE: Cook County; T64, 65N, R2W, Sec. 6; 31-34. U.S. 1961.

IRON LAKE: St. Louis County and Ontario; T66, 67N, R12, 13W, Sec. 6; 1-3, 10-13; 35. U.S. 1950-54.

ISABELLA RIVER: Lake County; rises in T61, R9W, Sec. 6, flows to T62N, R8W, Sec. 35. *Not*: Isabelle. U.S. *Sixth Report,* 392.

ITASCA LAKE: Clearwater County; T143N, R36W, Sec. 2, 10-13, 15, 24. U.S. 1940-41.

IVERSON LAKE: Cass County; T142N, R28W, Sec. 27. *Not*: Mud Lake. Minn. 1940.

JACK PINE CREEK: Lake County; rises in T60N, R8W, Sec. 20, flows northward to Mitawan Creek in T61N, R8W, Sec. 19. *Not*: Jackpine Creek. U.S. 1959; Minn. 1957.

JAIL LAKE: Cass, Crow Wing counties; T138, 139N, R29W, Sec. 1, 2; 35, 36. *Not*: Gail Lake, Big Lake, Rice Lake, Big Rice Lake. U.S. 1964; Minn. 1964.

JENNY LAKE: Lake County; T65N, R6W, Sec. 27, 28. *Not*: Jean Lake, Lake Jean. U.S. 1959; Minn. 1957.

JERRY LAKE: Cook County; T64N, R5W, Sec. 11-14. U.S. *Sixth Report,* 398.

JO DAVIESS: township, Faribault County; T102N, R28W. *Not*: Jo Davis, Jo Davies, Joe Daviess. U.S. *Sixth Report,* 399.

JOHNSON CREEK: St. Louis County; rises in Sand Lake in T60N, R18W, Sec. 28, flows to T61N, R18W, Sec. 32. *Not*: Little Fork River, South Branch of the Little Fork of Rainy River, South Branch Little Fork River. U.S. 1966.

JONVICK CREEK: Cook County; rises in T60N, R3W, Sec. 12, flows southeasterly to Lake Superior in T60N, R2W, Sec. 19. *Not*: Caribou Creek. U.S. 1959; Minn. 1957.

JORDAN LAKE: Lake County; T64N, R8W, Sec. 23, 24, 26. *Not*: Tordan Lake. Minn. 1940.

JORGENS LAKE: St. Louis County; T69N, R20W, Sec. 1, 11, 12. *Not*: Beaver Lake, Jorgen Lake. U.S. 1941-43; Minn. 1940.

JUNCO CREEK: Cook County; rises in Musquash Lake, T63N, R1E, Sec. 29, flows southwest from Junco Lake to Devil Track Lake in T62N, R1W, Sec. 28. *Not*: Swamp River, Swamp Creek. U.S. 1959; Minn. 1957.

JUNCO LAKE: Cook County; T62N, R1W, Sec. 11-13. *Not*: Swamp Lake. U.S. 1959; Minn. 1957.

SUPPLEMENT NO. 2: DECISIONS LIST 761

KABEKONA LAKE: Hubbard County; T142, 143N, R32, 33W, Sec. 4, 5; 29–34; 24, 25. *Not*: Kabecona Lake, Garfield Lake. Minn. 1940.

KABETOGAMA LAKE: Koochiching, St. Louis counties; T68–70N, R19–22W, various sections. *Not*: Kabatogama Lake, Kabet-Togo-ma Lake, Kabetogame Lake. U.S. *Sixth Report*, 404.

KABUSTASA LAKE: St. Louis County; T66N, R17W, Sec. 21, 22, 27, 28. *Not*: Rice Lake. U.S. *Sixth Report*, 405.

KADUNCE CREEK: Cook County; rises in T62N, R2E, Sec. 9, flows south and empties into Lake Superior in T61N, R2E, Sec. 2. *Not*: Diarrhea River, Diarrhoea River, Cadunce Creek, Greenwood River. U.S. 1941–43; Minn. 1940.

KALEVALA: township, Carlton County; T47N, R20W. *Not*: Kalavala. U.S. *Sixth Report*, 409.

KALLIO LAKE: Lake County; T64N, R6W, Sec. 23–26. *Not*: Cliff Lake, Spring Lake. U.S. 1959; Minn. 1957.

KANGAS BAY: in Birch Lake, St. Louis County; T61N, R12W, Sec. 22. *Not*: Kingas Bay, Kings Bay. U.S. 1966.

KARL LAKE: Cook County; T64N, R3, 4W, Sec. 18, 19; 13, 24. *Not*: Carl Lake. Minn. 1940.

KATHERINE LAKE: Lake County; T57N, R9W, Sec. 3, 9, 10. *Not*: Grass Lake. U.S. 1941–43; Minn. 1940.

KATYDID LAKE: Lake County; T60N, R7W, Sec. 35 (NW¼). *Not*: Square Lake, Spring Lake. U.S. 1959; Minn. 1957.

KAWISHIWI LAKE: Lake County; T62N, R6W, Sec. 16, 17, 20, 21. U.S. *Sixth Report*, 418. *See also* South Kawishiwi Lake.

KAWISHIWI RIVER: Lake County; rises in T62N, R6W, flows north and west to Fall Lake in T63N, R11W. U.S. *Sixth Report*, 418.

KAYOSKH LAKE: Lake County; T62N, R9W, Sec. 9, 16. *Not*: Little Gull Lake. U.S. 1959; Minn. 1957.

KEENE CREEK: Pine County; rises in Nemadji State Forest, T43N, R16W, Sec. 19, flows southwest into Lower Tamarack River in T42N, R17W, Sec. 16. U.S. *Sixth Report*, 420.

KEENE LAKE: Pine County; T41N, R17W, Sec. 11, 14. *Not*: Keen Lake. U.S. 1963.

KEGAN LAKE: Dakota County; T115N, R19W, Sec. 20, 21. *Not*: Keegans Lake, Keegan Lake. U.S. *Sixth Report*, 421.

KEKEKABIC LAKE: Lake County; T64, 65N, R6, 7W, Sec. 2–4, 11; 29–32; 34–36. *Not*: Hawk Lake, Cacaquabic Lake, Kekequabic Lake, Caraquabic Lake, Kekekobic Lake. U.S. *Sixth Report*, 421.

KEMO LAKE: Cook County; T63N, R1W, Sec. 27, 34, 35. *Not*: Keno Lake, Clubfoot Lake, Club Foot Lake. Minn. 1940.

KENNEY BROOK: Pine County; flows into Crooked Creek in T41N, R17W, Sec. 19. *Not*: Kenny's Creek, Kennys Creek. U.S. 1963.

KENNEY LAKE: Pine County; T41N, R17W, Sec. 17. *Not*: Kenivey Lake. U.S. 1963.

KENOGAMA LAKE: Itasca County; T146, 147N, R29W, Sec. 4, 5, 8, 9; 32, 33. *Not*: Long Lake, Maple Lake. U.S. 1941–43; Minn. 1940.

KETTLE FALLS: a waterfall between Namakan and Rainy lakes, St. Louis County and Ontario; T70N, R18W, Sec. 27, 33, 34. *Not*: Chaudiere Falls, Kettle Fall. U.S. 1950–54.

KETTLE FALLS PORTAGE: between Namakan and Rainy lakes, St. Louis County and Ontario; T70N, R18W, Sec. 27, 33, 34. *Not*: Chaudiere Portage, Bare Portage. U.S. *Sixth Report,* 424.

KILKENNY: township and village, Le Sueur County; T110N, R23W. *Not*: Kilkeny, Killkeny. U.S. *Sixth Report,* 427.

KIMBALL CREEK: Cook County; rises in Kimball Lake, T62N, R2E, Sec. 17, flows south to Lake Superior in T61N, R2E, Sec. 10. *Not*: Kimball River, Kimballs Creek. Minn. 1940.

KINDLE LAKE: Cook County; T64N, R2E, Sec. 31 (NW¼). *Not*: Fire Lake. U.S. 1959; Minn. 1957.

KINOGAMI LAKE: Cook County; T62N, R3W, Sec. 8–10, 16, 17. *Not*: Long Lake, Willow Lake. U.S. 1962; Minn. 1962.

KINTIRE: township, Redwood County; T113N, R37W. *Not*: Knitire, Kentrie. U.S. *Sixth Report,* 429.

KITCHI CREEK: Itasca County; rises in T147N, R29W, Sec. 19, flows south to Burns Lake in T146N, R29W, Sec. 6. *Not*: Beaver Creek. Minn. 1940.

KITIGAN LAKE: Lake County; T60N, R9W, Sec. 11–14. *Not*: Pickerel Lake, Lower Sand Lake, Sand Lake. U.S. 1959; Minn. 1957.

KIVANDEBA LAKE: Lake County; T64N, R6W, Sec. 34, 35. *Not*: Pan Lake. U.S. *Sixth Report,* 431.

KJOSTAD LAKE: St. Louis County; T65N, R18W, Sec. 13, 14, 23, 24. *Not*: Kjorstad Lake. Minn. 1940.

KNIFE LAKE: Lake County and Ontario; T65N, R7, 8W, various sections. *Not*: Big Knife Lake. U.S. 1950–54.

KOOCHICHING: county. U.S. *Sixth Report,* 435.

KOOCHICHING FALLS: in Rainy River, Koochiching County and Ontario; T171N, R24W. *Not*: Chaudiere Falls, Chaudron Falls, Koochiching Fall. U.S. 1950–54.

KRAGNES: settlement, Clay County; T141N, R48W, Sec. 34. *Not*: Kragness. U.S. 1963.

KRAGNES: township, Clay County; T141N, R48W. *Not*: Kragness, Woodland. U.S. *Sixth Report,* 437.

LABRADOR POND: Lake County; T61N, R10W, Sec. 29 (NE¼). *Not*: Bog Pond. U.S. 1959; Minn. 1957.

LAC-A-ROY LAKE: Itasca County; T149N, R25W, Sec. 14, 15. *Not*: Davis Lake, Lac-a-roy Lake, Lac-A-Roy Lake. U.S. 1966; Minn. 1940.

SUPPLEMENT NO. 2: DECISIONS LIST 763

LAC LA CROIX: St. Louis County and Ontario; T66–68N, R13–16W, various sections. *Not*: Cross Lake, Kekwakwan Lake, Lake LaCroix, Nameukan Lake, Namoukan Lake, Ne-qua-kaun Lake, Nequaquon Lake, Nequawkaun Lake, Lake Lac La Croix, Lac LaCroix, Lake La-Croix, Lac La Croix. U.S. 1950–54.

LAC QUI PARLE: township and village, Lac qui Parle County; T118, 119N, R42W. *Not*: Lac-qui-parle. U.S. *Sixth Report*, 442.

LAKE OF THE WOODS: Lake of the Woods, Roseau counties, Manitoba and Ontario; T162–168N, R32–37W, various sections. U.S. 1950–54.

LAKE ST. CROIX BEACH: village, Washington County; T28N, R20W, Sec. 11, 14. *Not*: Lake Saint Croix Beach, St. Croix Beach. U.S. 1968.

LAKETOWN: township, Carver County; T116N, R24W. *Not*: Lake Town. U.S. *Sixth Report*, 445.

LAKEVILLE: township and village, Dakota County; T114N, R20, 21W. *Not*: Lake Ville, Fairfield. U.S. *Sixth Report*, 445.

LANGDON LAKE: Hennepin County; T117N, R24W, Sec. 14, 23. *Not*: Lake Landon, Lake Langdon. U.S. 1960.

LA SALLE: village, Watonwan County; T107N, R31W, Sec. 16, 17. *Not*: Lasalle, LaSalle. U.S. 1968.

LEATHERLEAF LAKE: Lake County; T61N, R10W, Sec. 29 (E½). *Not*: Leather Leaf Lake, Bog Lake. U.S. 1959, Minn. 1957.

LEDGE LAKE: Lake County; T64N, R6W, Sec. 16, 17. *Not*: Prune Lake. U.S. 1941–43; Minn. 1940.

LEG LAKE: Lake County; T64N, R6W, Sec. 12. *Not*: Leo Lake. U.S. 1959; Minn. 1957.

LEGION LAKE: Hennepin County; T116, 117N, R24W, Sec. 5; 32. *Not*: Mud Lake. U.S. 1957–58; Minn. 1957.

LEMAY LAKE: Dakota County; T28N, R23W, Sec. 27, 34. *Not*: Lake Lemay, Le May Lake. U.S. *Sixth Report*, 454.

LENA LAKE: Lake County; T60N, R8W, Sec. 5, 6. *Not*: Lone Lake, Leona Lake. U.S. 1941–43; Minn. 1940.

LEORA LAKE: St. Louis County; T53N, R16W, Sec. 5, 6. *Not*: Elora Lake. U.S. 1963.

LE SUEUR: county. *Not*: Lesueur. U.S. *Sixth Report*, 456.

LE SUEUR CREEK: Le Sueur County; joins Minnesota River from the east in T112N, R25W, Sec. 31. *Not*: Lesueur. U.S. *Sixth Report*, 456.

LE SUEUR RIVER: Blue Earth, Waseca, Freeborn counties; joins Blue Earth River from east in T108N, R27W, Sec. 26. *Not*: Lesueur River. U.S. *Sixth Report*, 456.

LEVEAUX MOUNTAIN: Cook County; elevation 1,625 feet, T59N, R4W, Sec. 11. U.S. *Sixth Report*, 456.

LICHEN LAKE: Cook County; T62N, R3W, Sec. 16, 20, 21. *Not*: Beaver Lake. U.S. 1959; Minn. 1957.

LILLIAN LAKE: Itasca County; T56N, R27W, Sec. 11, 12. *Not*: Mud Lake. Minn. 1940.

LILY LAKES: Cook County and Ontario; T65N, R2E, Sec. 13. Individually known as Fan and Vaseux lakes. *Not*: Lily Ponds. U.S. 1950–54.

LIME CREEK: Freeborn County; rises in Bear Lake, T101N, R22W, Sec. 20, flows south, leaving Minnesota in T101N, R23W, Sec. 35. *Not*: Winnebago River. U.S. 1961.

LITTLE CARIBOU LAKE: Cook County; T65N, R1E, Sec. 36. *Not*: Grebe Lake. U.S. 1961; Minn. 1960.

LITTLE DEVIL TRACK RIVER: Cook County; rises in T61N, R1W, Sec. 11, flows generally eastward to T61N, R1E, Sec. 10. *Not*: Little Devils Track River, South Branch Devils Track River. U.S. 1962.

LITTLE DIXON LAKE: Itasca County; T148N, R29W, Sec. 13, 24. *Not*: Otter Lake. U.S. 1941–43; Minn. 1940.

LITTLE DRUM LAKE: Itasca County; T55N, R27W, Sec. 12, 13. *Not*: Two Routes Lake, Drombeater Lake, Drumbeater Lake. U.S. 1941–43; Minn. 1940.

LITTLE EAST LAKE: Itasca County; T59N, R25W, Sec. 4, 5, 8, 9. *Not*: Long Lake, Little Long Lake. Minn. 1940.

LITTLE ESQUAGAMA LAKE: St. Louis County; T57, 58N, R16W, Sec. 3; 34. *Not*: Little Eshquagama Lake, Little Eskquagama Lake, Little Esquaganmah Lake, Little Lake Eshquagama. U.S. 1966; Minn. 1940.

LITTLE FORK RIVER: Koochiching, St. Louis counties; rises in T62N, R17W, Sec. 22, flows northwest to Rainy River in T70N, R25W, Sec. 29. *Not*: Little Fork of Rainy River, Littlefork River, Ningtawonani, North Branch Little Fork River. U.S. 1963.

LITTLE INDIAN SIOUX RIVER: St. Louis County; rises in Otter Lake, T64N, R14W, Sec. 29, flows northerly to Upper Pauness Lake, T66N, R15W, Sec. 22. *Not*: Loon River, Indian Sioux River, Little Indian River, Indian Soo River, Sioux River. U.S. 1964.

LITTLE IRON LAKE: Cook County; T64, 65N, R2, 3W, Sec. 6; 31; 1, 2; 35, 36. *Not*: Iron Lake, Oxide Lake. U.S. 1961; Minn. 1960.

LITTLE KNIFE PORTAGE: between Cypress and Knife lakes, Lake County and Ontario; T66N, R6W, Sec. 31, 32. U.S. *Sixth Report,* 465.

LITTLE LONG LAKE: Itasca County; T57, 58N, R26W, Sec. 1; 25, 26, 35, 36. *Not*: Long Lake. Minn. 1940.

LITTLE MESABA LAKE: St. Louis County; T59N, R15W, Sec. 27, 28. *Not*: Little Mesabi Lake, Old Mesaba Lake, Mesaba Lake, Mesabe Lake. U.S. 1963; Minn. 1941.

LITTLE MUD HEN LAKE: St. Louis County; T56N, R16W, Sec. 11, 12. *Not*: Little Mud Lake, Little Mudhen Lake. Minn. 1940.

LITTLE PONY RIVER: St. Louis County; rises in Bootleg Lake in T64N, R15W, Sec. 1, flows north to Little Indian Sioux River in T65N, R15W, Sec. 13. Minn. 1940.

SUPPLEMENT NO. 2: DECISIONS LIST 765

LITTLE RANIER LAKE: Itasca County; T59N, R26W, Sec. 7, 18. *Not*: Little Rainy Lake. U.S. 1941–43; Minn. 1940.

LITTLE SAGANAGA LAKE: Cook County; T64N, R5, 6W, Sec. 5–9, 15–19; 12, 13, 24. *Not*: Little Sagana Lake, Little Segana Lake. Minn. 1940.

LITTLE SAND CREEK: Pine County; rises in T42N, R18W, Sec. 17, flows generally southward to Sand Creek, T40N, R19W, Sec. 12. U.S. 1964.

LITTLE SANDY LAKE: St. Louis County; T59N, R18W, Sec. 2, 3, 10, 11. *Not*: West Sandy Lake, Sandy Lake, Twin Lake. Minn. 1940.

LITTLE SISEEBAKWET LAKE: Itasca County; T54N, R27W, Sec. 11, 13, 14. *Not*: Quam-Butch-e-Mag-Es-Mug Lake, Little Sugar Lake, Little Sissebakwet Lake, Quam-butch-e-mages-mug Lake, Quan-butch-e-mages-mug Lake. U.S. 1941–43; Minn. 1940.

LITTLE STEWART RIVER: Lake County; rises in T53N, R11W, Sec. 9, flows generally southeastward to T53N, R10W, Sec. 29. *Not*: Wabegan Creek. U.S. 1964.

LITTLE SWIFT LAKE: Cass County; T141, 142N, R27W, Sec. 1; 36. *Not*: Kidney Lake. Minn. 1940.

LITTLE TOO MUCH LAKE: Itasca County; T59, 148N, R25, 27W, Sec. 3, 4; 24. *Not*: Prestidge Lake, Gunderson Lake. Minn. 1940.

LITTLE TWIN LAKE: Cass County; T144N, R31W, Sec. 11, 12. *Not*: South Twin Lake. Minn. 1940.

LITTLE VERMILION LAKE: St. Louis County and Ontario; T67N, R16W, Sec. 6–8, 16, 17, 20, 21, 28. *Not*: Little Vermillion Lake, Vermilion Lake, Vermillion Lake. U.S. 1950–54.

LITTLE WABANA LAKE: Itasca County; T57N, R25W, Sec. 22, 23, 26, 27. *Not*: Clearwater Lake, Little Wabano Lake. U.S. 1941–43; Minn. 1940.

LITTLE WAMPUS LAKE: Lake County; T60N, R10W, Sec. 28 (S½). *Not*: Little Pine Lake. U.S. 1964.

LIZZIE LAKE: Cass, Crow Wing counties; T138, 139N, R29W, Sec. 2, 3; 34, 35. *Not*: Jale Lake, Jake Lake, Jute Lake, Jail Lake, Jule Lake, Gail Lake. U.S. 1964; Minn. 1964.

LOBO LAKE: Lake County; T59N, R11W, Sec. 22, 23. *Not*: Swamp Lake. U.S. *Sixth Report,* 468.

LOCATOR LAKE: St. Louis County; T70N, R21W, Sec. 22, 23. *Not*: Cranberry Lake. U.S. 1941–43; Minn. 1940.

LOCKE LAKE: Wright County; T122N, R26W, Sec. 21, 22, 28. *Not*: Lock Lake. U.S. 1963.

LOGGER LAKE: Cook County; T63N, R1E, Sec. 14, 15. *Not*: Rock Lake. U.S. 1959; Minn. 1957.

LON, LAKE: St. Louis County; T64N, R16W, Sec. 16, 17. *Not*: Lon Lake. U.S. *Sixth Report,* 471.

LONG LAKE: Itasca County; T60N, R24W, Sec. 21. *Not*: Bass Lake. Minn. 1940.

LONG PORTAGE: between Rose and Rove lakes, Cook County and Ontario; T65N, R1E, Sec. 19 to T65N, R1W, Sec. 24. *Not*: Grand Neuf, Great New, New

Grande Portage, Grand Portage Neuf, Grand New Portage. U.S. *Sixth Report,* 472.

LONG SAULT RAPIDS: in Rainy River, Koochiching County and Ontario; T160N, R27W, Sec. 23. *Not*: Long Sault. U.S. 1950–54.

LOOKOUT LAKE: Lake County; T58N, R7W, Sec. 32. *Not*: Chub Lake, Corner Lake, Spruce Lake. U.S. 1959; Minn. 1957.

LOON LAKE: St. Louis County and Ontario; T66, 67N, R15W, Sec. 3–6; 26–28, 31–35. U.S. 1950–54.

LOST LAKE: Beltrami County; T146N, R31W, Sec. 14, 15, 22, 23. *Not*: Cox Lake, Big Lost Lake. Minn. 1940.

LOTUS LAKE: Carver County; T116N, R23W, Sec. 1, 12. *Not*: Long Lake. U.S. 1960.

LOURISTON: township and village, Chippewa County; T119N, R38W. *Not*: Lorriston. U.S. *Sixth Report,* 476.

LOWER BADGER CREEK: Red Lake County; rises at junction of ditches in Polk County, T149N, R43W, Sec. 3, flows northwest to Clearwater River, T151N, R44W, Sec. 36. *Not*: Badger Creek. U.S. 1967.

LOWER PAUNESS LAKE: St. Louis County; T66N, R15W, Sec. 15, 16, 21, 22. *Not*: Dauness Lake, Upper Pauness Lake, Upper Pouness Lake, Pauness Lake. U.S. 1964.

LOWER SUCKER LAKE: Cass County; T144, 145N, R29, 30W, Sec. 31; 2; 25, 35, 36. *Not*: Big Sucker Lake, Mud Lake. U.S. 1933.

LOWER TAMARACK RIVER: Pine County; rises in T44N, R17W, Sec. 1, flows south then southeast to join St. Croix River in T41N, R16W, Sec. 18. *Not*: Tamarack Creek, Tamarack River. U.S. *Sixth Report,* 478.

LOWVILLE: township, Murray County; T107N, R42W. *Not*: Lordville, Low Ville, Stowville. U.S. *Sixth Report,* 478.

LUNAR LAKE: Lake County; T65N, R6W, Sec. 4. *Not*: Moon Lake. U.S. 1959; Minn. 1957.

LUPUS LAKE: Lake County; T59, 60N, R6W, Sec. 6; 31. *Not*: Wolf Lake. U.S. 1959; Minn. 1957.

LUSTER LAKE: Lake County; T60N, R10W, Sec. 25 (NW¼). *Not*: Silver Lake. U.S. 1959; Minn. 1957.

LUVERNE: township and city, Rock County; T102N, R45W. *Not*: Lu Verne. U.S. *Sixth Report,* 481.

McAVITY LAKE: Itasca County; T56, 57N, R26W, Sec. 2; 35. *Not*: Crooked Lake. U.S. 1941–43; Minn. 1940.

McCACKRON BROOK: Cass County; rises in T141N, R25W, Sec. 14, flows to Willow River in T141N, R25W, Sec. 35. *Not*: McCacken Brook. Minn. 1940.

McCARTHEY LAKE: Cass County; T140N, R28W, Sec. 13, 24. *Not*: McCarthy Lake, Lake McCarthey. U.S. 1966; Minn. 1940.

McDERMOTT CREEK: Pine County; rises in T44N, R16W, flows southwest to

SUPPLEMENT NO. 2: DECISIONS LIST

Lower Tamarack River in T42N, R17W, Sec. 27. *Not*: West Fork. U.S. *Sixth Report*, 484.

McKEOWN LAKE: Cass County; T140N, R29W, Sec. 3, 10, 11. *Not*: Barrow Lake. Minn. 1940.

McKEWEN LAKE: Itasca County; T59N, R26W, Sec. 34, 35. *Not*: Johnson Lake. Minn. 1940.

McMAHON LAKE: Scott County; T113, 114N, R22W, Sec. 1; 35, 36. *Not*: Carl's Lake, Carls Lake, Karls Lake. U.S. 1963.

McMANUS ISLAND: in Namakan Lake, St. Louis County; T69N, R18W, Sec. 30. *Not*: Sheen Point. U.S. 1969.

MACSVILLE: township, Grant County; T127N, R43W. *Not*: Maesville. U.S. *Sixth Report*, 487.

MADDEN LAKE: Lake County; T63N, R10W, Sec. 9, 10, 15, 16. *Not*: Aladden Lake. Minn. 1940.

MAGNET ISLAND: in Lake Superior, Cook County; T63N, R7E, Sec. 3, 4. *Not*: Belle Rose Island. U.S. 1967.

MAGNETIC LAKE: Cook County and Ontario; T65N, R3, 4W, Sec. 19; 13, 24. *Not*: Magnetic Bay. U.S. 1950–54.

MAGNUSONS ISLAND: in Lake of the Woods, Lake of the Woods County; T168N, R34W, Sec. 23, 24. *Not*: American Point. U.S. *Sixth Report*, 489.

MAHPIYATA ISLAND: in Lake Minnetonka, Hennepin County; T117N, R23W, Sec. 22. *Not*: Big Island. U.S. 1964; Minn. 1964.

MAINGAN LAKE: Lake County; T65N, R11W, Sec. 4, 5, 8. U.S. *Sixth Report*, 490.

MAKI CREEK: St. Louis County; rises in T61N, R18W, Sec. 24, flows to Puutio Creek in T61N, R18W, Sec. 36. U.S. 1961.

MAKWA LAKE: Lake County; T64N, R6W, Sec. 23, 26, 27. *Not*: Bear Lake, Bean Lake, Black Bear Lake. U.S. 1961; Minn. 1960.

MANITOU RAPIDS: in Rainy River, Koochiching County; T160N, R26W, Sec. 36. *Not*: Manitou Rapid. U.S. 1950–54.

MANITOU RIVER: Lake County; rises in Round Island Lake, T59N, R8W, Sec. 12, flows southeast into Lake Superior in T57N, R6W, Sec. 11. Minn. 1940. *See also* South Branch Manitou River.

MANIWAKI LAKE: Lake County; T62N, R7W, Sec. 3, 4, 9, 10. *Not*: Miniwaki Lake. Minn. 1940.

MARGARET, LAKE: Cass County; T135N, R29W, Sec. 17, 20, 29, 30. *Not*: Lake Kilpatrick, Kilpatrick Lake, Kilpatric Lake, Margaret Lake. U.S. 1962; Minn. 1962.

MARINE ON ST. CROIX: township and village, Washington County; T31, 32N, R19, 20W. *Not*: Marine Mills, Marine, Marine-on-Saint Croix, Marine On Saint Croix, Marine on Saint Croix. U.S. 1968.

MARKHAM LAKE: St. Louis County; T56N, R15W, Sec. 14, 15, 22, 23. *Not*: Markeham Lake. Minn. 1940.

MAUDE LAKE: St. Louis County; T65N, R16W, Sec. 14, 23. *Not*: Maud Lake, Mosquito Lake. U.S. 1936–37.

MAYFLY LAKE: Lake County; T61N, R9W, Sec. 21 (NW¼). *Not*: Little Rock Lake. U.S. 1959; Minn. 1957.

MEADOW CREEK: Lyon, Redwood counties; rises in Lake Marshall, T111N, R41W, Sec. 36, flows generally east-southeastward to Cottonwood River in T110N, R39W, Sec. 16. *Not*: Cottonwood River. U.S. 1963.

MEDIAN LAKE: Lake County; T64N, R6W, Sec. 13, 14. *Not*: Mediak Lake, Mediar Lake. U.S. 1967.

MELON LAKE: Lake County and Ontario; T65N, R8W, Sec. 35. U.S. 1950–54.

MERRIAM BAY: in Basswood Lake, Lake County; T64, 65N, R9W. U.S. *Sixth Report*, 513.

MERRITT, LAKE: St. Louis County; T63, 64N, R16W, Sec. 3; 34. *Not*: Lake Merrit, Burik Lake, Burke Lake, Sea Gull Lake. U.S. *Sixth Report*, 514.

MESABI: range of hills, St. Louis, Itasca counties. *Not*: Masab, Mesaba Heights, Mesabi Heights, Missabay Heights, Missaube Heights. U.S. *Sixth Report*, 515.

MICMAC LAKE: Lake County; T56N, R7W, Sec. 8, 17. *Not*: Mic Mac Lake, Lake Micmac. U.S. 1964.

MIDDLE BRANCH RUSH RIVER: Sibley County; rises in T113N, R31W, flows to Rush River in T112N, R27W, Sec. 16. *Not*: Middle Fork Rush River, North Branch Rush River. U.S. 1963.

MIDDLE FORK ZUMBRO RIVER: Olmsted, Dodge, and Goodhue counties; rises in T108N, R18W, Sec. 30, flows eastward joining South Fork to form the Zumbro River in T108N, R14W, Sec. 14. *Not*: Middle Branch Zumbro River, North Middle Branch Zumbro River, North Zumbro River. U.S. 1961.

MIDDLE SUCKER LAKE: Cass County; T145N, R29, 30W, Sec. 30; 24, 25. *Not*: Little Sucker Lake, Mud Lake. U.S. 1933.

MILLE LACS: county. *Not*: Millelacs. U.S. *Sixth Report*, 520.

MILLE LACS LAKE: Aitkin, Crow Wing, Mille Lacs counties; T42–45N, R25–28W, various sections. *Not*: Millelacs Lake. U.S. *Sixth Report*, 520.

MINISOGAMA LAKE: Itasca County; T147N, R29W, Sec. 27, 34. *Not*: Island Lake. U.S. 1941–43; Minn. 1940.

MINNEAPOLIS: city, Hennepin County; T28, 29N, R20, 21W. U.S. 1934–35.

MINNEOTA: village, Lyon County; T113N, R43W, Sec. 25, 26, 35, 36. *Not*: Minnesota, Nordland. U.S. *Sixth Report*, 522.

MINNETOGA LAKE: Hennepin County; T117N, R22W, Sec. 26, 27. *Not*: Mud Lake, Wynn Lake. U.S. 1964; Minn. 1964.

MINNEWAWA, LAKE: Aitkin County; T49N, R23W, Sec. 16, 20–23, 26–29, 32, 33. *Not*: Rice Lake. U.S. *Sixth Report*, 522.

MISSIONARY LAKE: Lake County; T64N, R7, 8W, Sec. 6; 1. *Not*: Three Lake, Three Lakes (one of). U.S. 1959; Minn. 1957.

MISTLETOE LAKE: Cook County; T61N, R3W, Sec. 15, 16. *Not*: Twin Lake, Twin Lakes, Lower Twin Lake. U.S. 1961; Minn. 1960.

MITAWAN CREEK: Lake County; rises in Mitawan Lake, T60N, R9W, Sec. 14, flows northward to Isabella River in T62N, R9W, Sec. 35. *Not*: Sand Creek, Sand River. U.S. 1959; Minn. 1957.

MITAWAN LAKE: Lake County; T60N, R9W, Sec. 13, 14, 23, 24. *Not*: Pickerel Lake, Sand Lake, Upper Sand Lake. U.S. 1959; Minn. 1957.

MONKER LAKE: Cook County; T61, 62N, R1E, Sec. 6; 31. *Not*: Monkey Lake, South Devil Track Lake. Minn. 1940.

MOOERS LAKE: Washington County; T27N, R21, 22W, Sec. 30; 25, 26. *Not*: Balden Lake, Baldwin Lake, Balsam Lake, Medicine Wood Lake, Moore Lake. U.S. 1968; Minn. 1968.

MOONEY LAKE: Hennepin County; T118N, R22, 23W, Sec. 30; 25. *Not*: Keegan Lake, Kegan Lake, Mooneys Lake, Mooney's Lake. U.S. 1964.

MOORE LAKE: Cook County; T62N, R4W, Sec. 23, 24. *Not*: Moores Lake, Moore's Lake, Moors Lake, Moorse Lake, Roothouse Lake, Root House Lake. U.S. 1941–43; Minn. 1940.

MOOSE LAKE: Cook County and Ontario; T65N, R2, 3E, Sec. 24; 19–21, 27, 28. *Not*: Elk Lake. U.S. 1950–54.

MOOSE PORTAGE: between Moose and North Fowl lakes, Cook County and Ontario; T65N, R3E, Sec. 26, 27. *Not*: Elk Portage. U.S. *Sixth Report*, 530.

MOOSE RIVER: Carlton, Pine counties; rises in Moosehead Lake, T46N, R19W, Sec. 29, joins Kettle River in T45N, R20W, Sec. 23. *Not*: Moose Horn River, Moosehorn River. U.S. *Sixth Report*, 530.

MOOSECAMP LAKE: Lake, St. Louis counties; T65N, R11, 12W, Sec. 7, 18; 12, 13. *Not*: Moose Lake. U.S. 1941–43; Minn. 1940.

MOOSEHEAD LAKE: Carlton County; T46N, R19W, Sec. 20, 21, 28, 29. *Not*: Moose Head Lake, Moose Lake. U.S. 1963.

MORCOM LAKE: St. Louis County; T55N, R16W, Sec. 9, 10, 15, 16. *Not*: Pale Face Lake, Paleface Lake. U.S. 1941–43; Minn. 1940.

MOSOMO LAKE: Itasca County; T147N, R27W, Sec. 8, 17. *Not*: Lake Mosamo. Minn. 1940.

MOTHER LAKE: Hennepin County; T28N, R24W, Sec. 24, 25. *Not*: Muther Lake. U.S. *Sixth Report*, 533.

MOUNTAIN LAKE: Cook County and Ontario; T65N, R1, 2E, Sec. 23, 24; 14, 15, 19–23. *Not*: Hill Lake. U.S. 1950–54.

MUDRO LAKE: St. Louis County; T64N, R12W, Sec. 11–14. Minn. 1940.

MUELLER LAKE: Lake County; T65N, R6W, Sec. 25, 26. *Not*: Fox Lake, Agamok Lake, Cherry Lake. U.S. 1941–43; Minn. 1940.

MUKOODA LAKE: St. Louis County; T68N, R17W, Sec. 26, 27, 35, 36. *Not*: Trout Lake, American Trout Lake, Muksota Lake, Lake Mukcoda, Lake Mukooda. U.S. 1941–43; Minn. 1940.

MUSHGEE LAKE: Itasca County; T148N, R26W, Sec. 27, 34. *Not*: Buck Lake. U.S. 1949; Minn. 1942.

NABEK LAKE: Lake County; T65N, R6W, Sec. 14, 15. *Not*: Bear Lake. U.S. 1959; Minn. 1957.

NAGEL LAKE: Itasca County; T55, 56N, R25W, Sec. 6; 31. *Not*: Lost Lake. U.S. 1941–43; Minn. 1940.

NAMAKAN LAKE: St. Louis County and Ontario; T68–70N, R17–19W, various sections. *Not*: Namecan Lake, Nameukan Lake, Lake Namaycan, Namekan Lake, Sturgeon Lake. U.S. 1950–54.

NAWAKWA LAKE: Lake County; T65, 66N, R6W, Sec. 1; 35, 36. *Not*: Crooked Lake. U.S. 1959; Minn. 1957.

NEESH LAKE: St. Louis County; T64N, R14W, Sec. 16. *Not*: Meesh Lake. U.S. *Sixth Report*, 547.

NEEWIN LAKE: St. Louis County; T64N, R14W, Sec. 22, 27. U.S. *Sixth Report*, 547.

NELSON LAKE: Pope County; T124N, R38W, Sec. 21, 22, 27, 28. *Not*: Lake Nelson, Barsness Lake. Minn. 1969.

NETT LAKE: village, Koochiching, St. Louis counties; T65N, R21, 22W, Sec. 18, 19; 13, 24. *Not*: Net Lake. U.S. *Sixth Report*, 549.

NEW MARKET: village, Scott County; T113N, R21W, Sec. 20, 21, 28. *Not*: Newmarket. U.S. 1950.

NEW PRAGUE: city, Le Sueur, Scott counties; T112, 113N, R23W, Sec. 3; 34. *Not*: Prague. U.S. *Sixth Report*, 552.

NIBIN LAKE: St. Louis County; T66N, R13W, Sec. 27. *Not*: Neeben Lake. U.S. *Sixth Report*, 552.

NICADO, LAKE: Lake County; T56N, R7W, Sec. 6. *Not*: Lake Nigado, Nigadoo Lake, Nicado Lake. Minn. 1940.

NICHOLS LAKE: St. Louis County; T53N, R17W, Sec. 5–8. *Not*: Nichol Lake, Lake Nichols, Nicholas Lake. U.S. 1963.

NICOLS: settlement, Dakota County; T27N, R23W, Sec. 18. *Not*: Nicol, Nichols, Nicol's. U.S. 1968.

NIGH LAKE: St. Louis County; T65N, R15, 16W, Sec. 7, 18; 13. *Not*: Lake Marie. U.S. *Sixth Report*, 553.

NIKI LAKE: St. Louis, Lake counties; T65N, R11, 12W, Sec. 6; 1. *Not*: Nicki Lake, Sturgeon Lake. U.S. *Sixth Report*, 553.

NINEMILE CREEK: Lake County; rises in T59N, R6W, Sec. 27, flows southwest to Manitou River in T58N, R6W, Sec. 17. *Not*: Nine Mile Creek, Nine Mile River. U.S. 1966; Minn. 1940.

NINEMILE LAKE: Lake County; T59N, R6W, Sec. 21, 22, 27. *Not*: Nine Mile Lake. U.S. 1966.

NIPISIQUIT LAKE: Lake County; T56N, R7W, Sec. 8. *Not*: Lake Nipissiquit, Nippissiquit Lake, Nipissiquit Lake. U.S. 1964.

NISWI LAKE: St. Louis County; T64N, R14W, Sec. 16, 21. *Not*: Neswebet Lake, Nisswi Lake. U.S. 1935–36.

NOKASIPPI RIVER: Crow Wing County; rises in Long Lake, T44N, R30W, Sec.

27, flows southwest to Mississippi River in T43N, R32W, Sec. 27. *Not*: Nokay River, Nokaysippi River, Nokay Sebie River, Noka Sippi River, Noka Sipi River, Scrub Oak River, Wokeosiby River, Profit River, Nokay Sibe River, Long River, Nankesele River, Wokco-sibi River, Nunkesebe River, Anokeseba River. U.S. *Sixth Report,* 556.

NOKOMIS, LAKE: Hennepin County; T28N, R24W, Sec. 13, 14, 23, 24. *Not*: Amelia Lake, Lake Amelia, Emelia Lake, Nokomis Lake. U.S. 1959.

NORTH LAKE: Cook County and Ontario; T65N, R2W, Sec. 16, 20–22. *Not*: Mountain Lake, Hauteur de Terre Lake. U.S. 1950–54.

NORTH BRANCH MIDDLE FORK ZUMBRO RIVER: Dodge, Goodhue counties; rises in T109N, R18W, Sec. 21, flows generally eastward to T109N, R15W, Sec. 31. *Not*: North Middle Branch. U.S. 1961.

NORTH BRANCH SUNRISE RIVER: Chisago, Isanti counties; rises in T134N, R23W, Sec. 1, flows to T35N, R20W, Sec. 17. *Not*: Hay Creek, North Branch of Sunrise River, North Branch of the Sunrise River. U.S. 1963.

NORTH CORMORANT RIVER: Beltrami, Itasca counties; rises in T150N, R29W, Sec. 35, flows west to Black Duck River in T151N, R32W, Sec. 3. *Not*: Cormorant River, North Branch Cormorant River, Cormant River. Minn. 1940.

NORTH FORK WATONWAN RIVER: Cottonwood, Watonwan counties; rises in T107N, R35W, Sec. 28, flows generally eastward to Watonwan River in T107N, R32W, Sec. 14. *Not*: North Branch North Fork Watonwan River, North Branch Watonwan River, North Fork River. U.S. 1962.

NORTH FORK ZUMBRO RIVER: Goodhue, Rice, Wabasha counties; rises in T109N, R20W, Sec. 27, flows generally eastward to Zumbro River in T109N, R14W, Sec. 10. *Not*: North Branch Zumbro River, Zumbro River. U.S. 1961.

NORTH FOWL LAKE: Cook County and Ontario; T64, 65N, R3E, Sec. 1, 2; 26, 27, 35. *Not*: Hen Lake. U.S. 1950–54.

NORTH TEMPERANCE LAKE: Cook County; T63N, R3, 4W, Sec. 7, 18; 12, 13. *Not*: Temperance Lake, Surveyors' Lake. U.S. 1961.

NORTH TURTLE RIVER: Beltrami County; rises in T147N, R31W, Sec. 1, flows into Turtle River in T147N, R31W, Sec. 23. *Not*: North Branch Turtle River. Minn. 1940.

NORTH TWIN LAKE: Beltrami County; T148N, R31W, Sec. 27, 28, 33, 34. *Not*: Twin Lake, Twin Lakes (one of). Minn. 1940.

NORTH WILDER LAKE: Lake County; T62N, R8W, Sec. 5–7. *Not*: Wilder Lakes (one of). U.S. 1959; Minn. 1957.

NORTHWEST ANGLE: Lake of the Woods County; T166–168N, R33–35W. U.S. *Sixth Report,* 562.

NORTHWEST ANGLE INLET: Lake of the Woods County; T168N, R34, 35W. *Not*: Angle River. U.S. 1950–54.

NUSHKA LAKE: Cass County; T145N, R27W, Sec. 33, 34. *Not*: Rice Lake. U.S. 1935–36.

ODEIMA LAKE: Lake County; T60N, R8W, Sec. 34, 35. *Not*: Heart Lake. U.S. 1959; Minn. 1957.

ODODIKOSSI LAKE: Cass County; T141N, R26W, Sec. 8. *Not*: Kidney Lake. Minn. 1944.

O'DONNELL LAKE: Itasca County; T60N, R24W, Sec. 28 (SE¼). *Not*: Laura Lake, Spring Lake. U.S. 1941–43; Minn. 1940.

OGISHKEMUNCIE LAKE: Lake County; T65N, R6W, Sec. 13, 22–24, 26, 27. *Not*: Kingfisher, Ogishki Muncie. U.S. *Sixth Report,* 568.

OJIBWAY LAKE: Lake County; T63N, R9, 10W, Sec. 7, 18; 11–14. *Not*: Twin Lakes, Twin Lake, Northwestern Lake, North Twin Lake, Triangle Lake, Upper Twin Lake. U.S. 1961; Minn. 1960.

OLE LAKE: St. Louis County; T63, 64N, R13W, Sec. 5, 6; 32. Minn. 1940.

O'LEARY LAKE: St. Louis County; T68, 69N, R17W, Sec. 4; 32, 33. *Not*: Hammer Lake. U.S. 1941–43; Minn. 1940.

OMEGA LAKE: Cook County; T64N, R2, 3W, Sec. 19, 30; 23–25. *Not*: Onega Lake, Nebogigig Lake. U.S. 1962; Minn. 1940.

O'NEILS POINT: on Star Island in Cass Lake, Beltrami County; T146N, R31W; Sec. 25. *Not*: O'Neills Point. Minn. 1940.

ONE LAKE: Cass County; T140N, R30W, Sec. 20, 29. *Not*: Padgett Lake, Paquet Lake, Pequet Lake, Little Whitefish Lake, Poquet Lake. Minn. 1940.

ONE LOAF LAKE: Itasca County; T148N, R27W, Sec. 31. *Not*: One Leaf Lake. Minn. 1940.

ONE PINE LAKE: St. Louis County; T62N, R12W, Sec. 28, 32–34. *Not*: Pine Lake. U.S. 1941–43; Minn. 1940.

ORGAN LAKE: Lake County; T61N, R6W, Sec. 24, 25. *Not*: Heart Lake, Little Frear Lake. U.S. 1962; Minn. 1960.

OSBORNE: township, Pipestone County; T105N, R44W. *Not*: Osborn. U.S. *Sixth Report,* 576.

OSIER LAKE: Lake County; T59N, R8W, Sec. 30, 31. *Not*: Trout Lake. U.S. 1959; Minn. 1957.

OSLO LAKE: St. Louis County; T70N, R19W, Sec. 29, 30. *Not*: Brown Lake. U.S. 1941–43; Minn. 1940.

OSSAWINNAMAKEE LAKE: Crow Wing County; T136, 137N, R28W, Sec. 2–5; 27, 33–36. *Not*: Long Lake. Minn. 1944.

OTTER TAIL RIVER: Becker, Otter Tail, Wilkin counties; rises in T139N, R39W, Sec. 6, joins Red River of the North in T132N, R47W, Sec. 8. *Not*: Ottertail River, North Red River, Red River, Red River of the North, Otter-tail River. U.S. *Sixth Report,* 577.

OTTERTAIL: village, Otter Tail County; T134N, R39W, Sec. 10–15. *Not*: Otter Tail. U.S. 1950.

OTTO LAKE: St. Louis County; T56N, R13W, Sec. 21, 22. *Not*: Greenwood Lake. U.S. 1941–43; Minn. 1940.

OVA LAKE: Lake County; T60N, R9W, Sec. 9, 10. *Not*: Finn Lake. U.S. 1941–43; Minn. 1940.

PAGAMI LAKE: Lake County; T63N, R9, 10W, Sec. 31; 36. *Not*: Pogami Lake, School Section Lake. U.S. *Sixth Report*, 580.

PAKWENE LAKE: Lake County; T65N, R11W, Sec. 5. *Not*: Pakwéne. U.S. 1935–36.

PALEFACE RIVER: St. Louis County; rises in T56N, R15W, Sec. 27, flows to Whiteface River in T54N, R17W, Sec. 9. *Not*: Pale Face River. U.S. *Sixth Report*, 582.

PANCORE LAKE: Cook County; T61N, R4W, Sec. 22, 27. *Not*: Lost Lake. U.S. 1941–43; Minn. 1940.

PANGI LAKE: Lake County; T62N, R9W, Sec. 20, 29. *Not*: Bass Lake. U.S. *Sixth Report*, 585.

PAPOOSE LAKE: Lake, St. Louis counties; T66N, R11, 12W, Sec. 31; 36. *Not*: Pappoose Lake. U.S. 1964.

PAQUET LAKE: Cass County; T140N, R30W, Sec. 29. *Not*: One Lake, Padgett Lake, Poquet Lake. U.S. 1966.

PARENT LAKE: Lake County; T63N, R8, 9W, Sec. 6, 7; 1, 12. *Not*: Lac La Mar, Round Lake. U.S. *Sixth Report*, 589.

PARTRIDGE CREEK: Pine County; rises in T43N, R19W, Sec. 23, flows southward into Sand Creek in T42N, R19W, Sec. 27. *Not*: Little Sand Creek. U.S. 1964.

PARTRIDGE: falls and portage, in Pigeon River, Cook County and Ontario; T64N, R4E, Sec. 30, 31. U.S. 1950–54.

PAULINE LAKE: St. Louis County; T65N, R16W, Sec. 12. *Not*: Nigh Lake, Lower Nigh Lake. U.S. 1936–37.

PAUNESS LAKE. *See* Lower Pauness Lake, Upper Pauness Lake.

PEAVEY LAKE: Lake County; T59N, R7W, Sec. 3, 4. *Not*: Long Lake. U.S. 1959; Minn. 1957.

PELLET ISLAND: in Lake Superior, Lake County; T55N, R7W, Sec. 7. U.S. 1957.

PELT LAKE: Lake County; T62N, R8W, Sec. 27, 28. *Not*: Wolf Lake. U.S. 1959; Minn. 1957.

PEPIN: township, Wabasha County; T111N, R11W. *Not*: Reads, Reed's, Read's Landing. U.S. 1950.

PEQUOT LAKES: village, Crow Wing County; T136N, R29W, Sec. 10, 15. *Not*: Pequot, Sibley. U.S. 1950.

PERCH LAKE: St. Louis County; T61N, R12W, Sec. 18, 19. *Not*: Spruce Lake. U.S. 1963.

PERENT LAKE: Lake County; T61, 62N, R6, 7W, Sec. 4–9; 1; 31, 32; 36. *Not*: Parent Lake. U.S. 1959; Minn. 1957.

PERENT RIVER: Lake County; rises in Perent Lake, T61N, R7W, Sec. 1, flows westward to Isabella Lake in T62N, R7W, Sec. 31. *Not*: Parent River. U.S. 1959; Minn. 1957.

PFEIFFER LAKE: St. Louis County; T61N, R17W, Sec. 23. *Not*: Clearwater Lake. U.S. 1941–43; Minn. 1940.

PHALEN, LAKE: in St. Paul, Ramsey County; T29N, R22W, Sec. 16, 21. *Not*: Phaline Lake, Phelans Lake, Phalen Lake, Lake Roberts, Lake Goodhue, Phalins Lake. U.S. *Sixth Report,* 600.

PHANTOM LAKE: Lake County; T57, 58N, R10W, Sec. 3; 34. *Not*: Muck Lake, Swamp Lake. U.S. 1964.

PICKERAL CREEK: Lake of the Woods County; flows entirely in T167N, R33W, Sec. 19. U.S. *Sixth Report,* 601.

PICKET LAKE: St. Louis County; T65N, R16W, Sec. 21, 22, 27–29. *Not*: Pickett Lake, Morgan Lake. U.S. *Sixth Report,* 601.

PICKETTS LAKE: St. Louis County; T63N, R12W, Sec. 12. *Not*: Rochghe Lake. U.S. 1966.

PIERZ LAKE: Cook County; T64N, R1, 2E, Sec. 12; 7. *Not*: Beaver Lake. U.S. 1959; Minn. 1957.

PIETRO LAKE: Lake County; T62N, R9W, Sec. 7, 8, 17, 18. *Not*: Pietra Lake. Minn. 1940.

PIGEON BAY: in Lake Superior, Cook County and Ontario; T64N, R7E, Sec. 25–28. U.S. 1950–54.

PIGEON FALLS: a waterfall in Pigeon River, Cook County and Ontario; T64N, R7E, Sec. 30. *Not*: High Falls. U.S. 1950–54.

PIGEON POINT: in Lake Superior, Cook County; T64N, R7E, Sec. 25. *Not*: Pointe au Tourtre. U.S. *Sixth Report,* 602.

PIGEON RIVER: Cook County and Ontario; rises in South Fowl Lake, T64N, R3E, Sec. 12, flows to Lake Superior in T64N, R7E, Sec. 29. U.S. 1950–54.

PIGS EYE ISLAND NUMBER ONE: in Mississippi River, Ramsey County; T28N, R22W, Sec. 9, 16. *Not*: Pig Eye Island Number One. U.S. 1962.

PIGS EYE ISLAND NUMBER TWO: in Mississippi River, Ramsey County; T28N, R22W, Sec. 22. *Not*: Pig Eye Island Number Two. U.S. 1962.

PIGS EYE LAKE: Mississippi River bottom, Ramsey County; T28N, R22W, Sec. 10, 11, 14, 15, 22, 23. *Not*: Pig Eye Lake, Pig's Eye Lake, Grand Marais. U.S. *Sixth Report,* 602.

PIKE LAKE: Lake County; T60N, R10W, Sec. 13, 14, 24. *Not*: Moose Larson Lake. U.S. 1936.

PILLSBERY LAKE: Cook County; T64N, R2W, Sec. 21, 22. *Not*: Pillsbury Lake, Pittsburg Lake. Minn. 1940.

PINE CREEK: Lake, St. Louis counties; rises in T55N, R11W, Sec. 6, flows generally westward to Cloquet River in T55N, R12W, Sec. 17. *Not*: Stewart Branch Cloquet River, Stewart Branch, Stewart Brook, Little Stewart River, Stewart River. U.S. 1964.

PIONEER LAKE: St. Louis County; T54N, R16W, Sec. 22. *Not*: Lake 22, Antila Lake. U.S. 1957–58; Minn. 1957.

PIPE LAKE: Cook County; T62N, R3W, Sec. 4, 5. *Not*: Midpipe Lake, Mid Pipe Lake, Middle Pipe Lake. U.S. 1962; Minn. 1940.

PITCHA LAKE: Lake County; T60N, R10W, Sec. 19, 20, 29, 30. *Not*: Camp Seven Lake, Long Lake, Mud Lake. U.S. 1959; Minn. 1957.

PITFALL LAKE: Lake County; T65N, R6W, Sec. 11. *Not*: Trap Lake. U.S. 1959; Minn. 1957.

PLACID, LAKE: reservoir in Crow Wing River, Cass, Morrison counties; T133N, R30, 31W, various sections. *Not*: Casmer Lake, Pillager Dam Reservoir. U.S. 1968; Minn. 1966.

PLAISTED LAKE: Washington County; T31N, R21W, Sec. 25. *Not*: Reier's Lake, Reiers Lake, North School Section Lake. Minn. 1969.

PLANTATION LAKE: Itasca County; T58N, R25W, Sec. 23, 26. *Not*: Crane Lake, Otter Lake. U.S. 1941–43; Minn. 1940.

PLEASANT MOUND: township, Blue Earth County; T105N, R29W. *Not*: Pleasant Mounds. U.S. *Sixth Report,* 609.

POKEGAMA CREEK: Kanabec, Pine counties; rises in T41N, R22W, Kanabec County, flows generally southeastward to Pokegama Lake in T39N, R22W, Sec. 13. U.S. 1963.

POPLAR CREEK: Lake of the Woods County; rises in T168N, R35W, Sec. 34, flows into Lake of the Woods in T168N, R35W, Sec. 24. U.S. 1950–54.

PORTAGE LAKE: Lake County and Ontario; T65N, R8W, Sec. 35, 36. *Not*: Potato Lake. U.S. 1950–54.

PORTAGE RIVER: Carlton County; rises in Lost Lake, T46N, R18W, Sec. 5, flows to Moosehead Lake in T46N, R19W, Sec. 21 (SW¼). *Not*: Partridge River, Mud Creek. U.S. 1963.

PRAIRIE VIEW: township, Wilkin County; T136N, R45W. *Not*: Prairieview. U.S. *Sixth Report,* 618.

PUUTIO CREEK: St. Louis County; rises in T61N, R17W, Sec. 28, flows southwestward to Rice River in T60N, R18W, Sec. 2. *Not*: Walberg Creek. U.S. 1961.

RABIDEAU LAKE: Beltrami County; T148N, R30, 31W, Sec. 8, 9, 16–20; 13. *Not*: Lake Gladys, Robideau Lake, Rabidew Lake, Minn. 1940.

RAHKOS LAKE: Itasca County; T58N, R24W, Sec. 13. *Not*: Lower Balsam Lake. Minn. 1940.

RAINY LAKE: Koochiching, St. Louis counties and Ontario; T70, 71N, R17–24W, various sections. *Not*: Lac la Pluie. U.S. 1950–54.

RAINY RIVER: Koochiching, Lake of the Woods counties and Ontario; flows from Lake of the Woods in T162N, R32W, Sec. 24 to Rainy Lake in T7N, R24W, Sec. 25. *Not*: Lac la Pluie. U.S. 1950–54.

RANGE LINE LAKE: St. Louis County; T67N, R14, 15W, Sec. 30, 31; 25, 36. Minn. 1940.

RANIER LAKE: Itasca County; T59N, R26W, Sec. 17, 18, 20. *Not*: Rainy Lake, Big Rainy Lake, Big Ranier Lake. U.S. 1941–43; Minn. 1940.

RAT LAKE: Cook County and Ontario; T65N, R1W, Sec. 19. U.S. 1950–54.

RAVEN LAKE: Lake County; T64N, R6W, Sec. 7, 18. *Not*: Link Lake, Linx Lake, Lynx Lake. U.S. 1941–43; Minn. 1940.

RAVENNA: township, Dakota County; T114, 115N, R16W. *Not*: Ravanna. U.S. *Sixth Report,* 634.

READS LANDING: village, Wabasha County; T111N, R11W, Sec. 24. *Not*: Reeds Landing, Reads, Read's Landing, Reeds, Pepin, Read's. U.S. 1950.

RED RIVER OF THE NORTH: Wilkin, Clay, Norman, Polk, Marshall, Kittson counties; forms border with North Dakota, leaving Minnesota in Kittson County, 164N, R51W, Sec. 26. *Not*: Red River. U.S. 1950–54.

REDCOAT LAKE: Cook County; T63N, R2E, Sec. 15 (SW¼). *Not*: Fox Lake. U.S. 1959; Minn. 1957.

REDEYE RIVER: Becker, Otter Tail, Wadena counties; rises in Wolf Lake, T139N, R38W, Sec. 25, flows southeast to join Leaf River in T135N, R33W, Sec. 19. *Not*: Red Eye River. U.S. 1967.

REDSKIN LAKE: Lake County; T60N, R8W, Sec. 35 (SW¼). *Not*: Byron Lake, Indian Lake. U.S. 1959; Minn. 1957.

REGAN: railroad station, Dakota County; T27N, R24W, Sec. 34. *Not*: Reagan. U.S. *Sixth Report,* 639.

REMUND LAKE: Waseca County; T108N, R22W, Sec. 8, 9. *Not*: Hemund Lake, Redmund Lake. U.S. 1963.

RICE BAY: in Vermilion Lake, St. Louis County; T63N, R15W, Sec. 34, 35. *Not*: Rice Lake. U.S. 1941–43; Minn. 1940.

RICE LAKE: Dodge, Steele counties; T107N, R18, 19W, Sec. 6, 7; 1, 11–14. *Not*: Hobson. U.S. 1963.

RICE RIVER: St. Louis County; rises in T60N, R17W, Sec. 1. flows northwest, joining South Branch Little Fork River in T62N, R19W, Sec. 21. *Not*: South Branch Little Fork River. U.S. 1966.

RICES POINT: in Lake Superior, St. Louis County; T49, 50N, R14W, Sec. 3, 4; 33. *Not*: Rice's Point, Rice Point. U.S. 1940.

RICHEY LAKE: Cook County; T60N, R5W, Sec. 20. Minn. 1940.

RICHFIELD LAKE: Hennepin County; T28N, R24W, Sec. 21, 27, 28. *Not*: Grass Lake. U.S. 1964; Minn. 1964.

RIDGELY: township, Nicollet County; T111N, R32W. *Not*: Ridgley. U.S. *Sixth Report,* 642.

RIPPLE LAKE: Aitkin County; T46N, R26, 27W, Sec. 17–20; 13, 24. *Not*: Diamond Lake, Mud Lake. U.S. 1963; Minn. 1962.

RIPPLE RIVER: Aitkin County; rises in T46N, R27W, Sec. 24, flows to Mississippi

River in T47N, R27W, Sec. 24. *Not*: Mud River, Muddy River, Mud Creek, Ripple Creek. U.S. 1962; Minn. 1962.

RIVERTON: township, Clay County; T139N, R46W. *Not*: Reverton. U.S. *Sixth Report*, 644.

ROADSIDE LAKE: Beltrami County; T147N, R31, 32W, Sec. 6; 1. *Not*: Loon Lake, Long Lake, Turtle River Lake. U.S. 1941–43; Minn. 1940.

ROBERTSON LAKE: Hubbard County; T143N, R33W, Sec. 32. Minn. 1956.

ROCK ISLAND LAKE: Lake County; T63N, R9W, Sec. 33. *Not*: One Island Lake. U.S. 1959; Minn. 1957.

ROGERS LAKE: Dakota County; T28N, R23W, Sec. 26, 35. *Not*: Roger's Lake, Roger Lake. U.S. *Sixth Report*, 647.

ROLLINGSTONE: township and village, Winona County; T107, 108N, R8W. *Not*: Rolling Stone. U.S. *Sixth Report*, 648.

ROOME: township, Polk County; T149N, R48W. *Not*: Rome. U.S. *Sixth Report*, 649.

ROSE LAKE: Cook County and Ontario; T65N, R1W, Sec. 19–24, 27. *Not*: Mud Lake, Rosa Lake. U.S. 1950–54.

ROSEAU RIVER: Lake of the Woods, Beltrami, Roseau, Kittson counties; rises in T158N, R35W, Sec. 5, flows northwesterly into Manitoba at T164N, R45W, Sec. 29. *Not*: North Fork. U.S. 1950–54.

ROSEMOUNT: township and village, Dakota County; T115N, R18, 19W. *Not*: Rosemont. U.S. *Sixth Report*, 650.

ROTA LAKE: Lake County; T58N, R9W, Sec. 2, 3. *Not*: Round Lake. U.S. 1959; Minn. 1957.

ROVE LAKE: Cook County and Ontario; T65N, R1E, Sec. 19, 20, 29. *Not*: Rose Lake, Watab Lake, Watap Lake. U.S. 1950; Minn. 1940.

RUM RIVER: Anoka, Isanti, Sherburne, Mille Lacs counties; rises in T142N, R27W, Sec. 8, Mille Lacs County, flows into Mississippi River in T31N, R25W, Sec. 12. *Not*: Run River. U.S. *Sixth Report*, 652.

RUSH RIVER: Sibley County; flows from T112N, R27W, Sec. 16 into Minnesota River, T112N, R26W, Sec. 13. *Not*: North Branch Rush River, North Fork Rush River. U.S. 1963. *See also* Middle Branch Rush River.

RUSTAD: settlement, Clay County; T138N, R48W, Sec. 28. *Not*: Kurtz, Elmer Station. U.S. 1963.

SABIN LAKE: St. Louis County; T58N, R15W, Sec. 5, 6. Minn. 1940.

SABLE LAKE: Lake County; T63N, R8W, Sec. 1. U.S. *Sixth Report*, 655.

SAGANAGA LAKE: Cook, Lake counties and Ontario; T66, 67N, R4, 5W, various sections. *Not*: Kaseiganah Lake, Saisaginaga Lake, Seiganaga Lake, Seiganagaw Lake, Seiganagooh Lake, Lake Saganaga, Big Saganaga Lake, Seiganagah Lake, Seiganagan Lake. U.S. 1950–54.

SAGUS LAKE: Lake County; T64N, R6, 7W, Sec. 19; 13, 24. *Not*: Peterson Lake, Little Sagus Lake. U.S. 1941–43; Minn. 1940.

St. Hilaire: village, Pennington County; T152N, R43, 44W, Sec. 6; 1. *Not*: St. Hiliare. U.S. *Sixth Report,* 658.

St. Paul: city, Ramsey County; T28, 29N, R22, 23W. *Not*: Pig's Eye, St. Paul's Landing, St. Paul's. U.S. *Sixth Report,* 659.

Salem Creek: Olmsted, Dodge counties; rises in T106N, R17W, Sec. 26, flows eastward to South Fork Zumbro River, T106N, R15W, Sec. 24. *Not*: South Fork Zumbro River, West Branch South Fork Zumbro River. U.S. 1961.

Sand Bay: in Rainy Lake, Koochiching County and Ontario; T71N, R24W. U.S. 1950–54.

Sand Creek: Pine County; rises in T44N, R17W, Sec. 19, flows southward to St. Croix River in T40N, R18W, Sec. 19. *Not*: Big Sand Creek, Sand River. U.S. 1964.

Sand Lake: Crow Wing County; T138N, R27W, Sec. 25, 36. *Not*: Bass Lake. U.S. 1962; Minn. 1962.

Sand Hill River: Mahnomen, Norman, Polk counties; rises in Sand Hill Lake, T147N, R40W, Sec. 28, flows west-northwestward joining Red River of the North in T148N, R49W, Sec. 36. *Not*: Sandhill River. U.S. 1965.

Sand Point Lake: St. Louis County and Ontario; T67–69N, R16, 17W, various sections. *Not*: Sand Points Lake. U.S. 1950–54.

Sandnes: township, Yellow Medicine County; T114N, R40W. *Not*: Sannes, Sennes. U.S. *Sixth Report,* 665.

Sandwick Lake: Itasca County; T60N, R25W, Sec. 5–8. *Not*: Sandwich Lake, Sandwick Lakes, Coon Lake. Minn. 1940.

Sandy Lake: Sherburne County; T35N, R26W, Sec. 25, 36. *Not*: Lake Sandy; Lake Sand. U.S. 1963.

Sauk Centre: city and township, Stearns County; T126N, R34W. *Not*: Sauk Center. U.S. 1934–35.

Sawbill Creek: Cook County; rises in Sawbill Lake, T62N, R4W, Sec. 7, flows southeastward to Temperance River in T62N, R4W, Sec. 28. *Not*: North Branch Temperance River, West Branch Temperance River. U.S. 1941–43; Minn. 1940.

Sawtooth Bluff: Cook County; elevation 1,500 feet, T61N, R1E, Sec. 16. *Not*: Saw Teeth Bluff, Sawteeth Bluff. U.S. 1968.

Sawtooth Mountains: Cook, Lake counties; range of hills extending from the area of Grand Marais in T61N, R1E, southwest to T55N, R8W near Beaver Bay. *Not*: Fond du lac Mountains, Misquah Hills, North Shore Mountains, Sawteeth Mountains, Sawtooth Range. U.S. 1968.

Scarp Lake: Lake County; T60N, R6W, Sec. 31, 32. *Not*: Cliff Lake. U.S. 1959; Minn. 1957.

Schlamn Lake: St. Louis County; T63N, R14W, Sec. 8, 9. *Not*: Sclamm Lake, Schlamm Lake, Schlamp Lake. U.S. 1966; Minn. 1940.

Schoolcraft River: Hubbard, Beltrami counties; rises in Schoolcraft Lake T143N, R34W, Sec. 32, flows north to Lake Irving in T146N, R33W, Sec.

SUPPLEMENT NO. 2: DECISIONS LIST 779

17. *Not*: Laplace, Ozawindib, Plantagenian Fork, Yellow Head, Yellowhead. U.S. *Sixth Report*, 677.

SCHRAM LAKE: Beltrami County; T146N, R30W, Sec. 28, 33. *Not*: Schramm Lake. Minn. 1940.

SCHUTZ LAKE: Carver County; T116N, R23, 24W, Sec. 7; 1, 12. *Not*: Schultz Lake, Shutz Lake, Goldschmidt Lake, Schulz Lake, Goldsmith's Lake. U.S. 1960.

SEA GULL LAKE: Cook County; T65, 66N, R4, 5W, various sections. *Not*: Gull Lake. Minn. 1940.

SECTION TWELVE LAKE: Lake County; T63N, R10W, Sec. 12. *Not*: Camp Twenty Lake, Section 02 Lake, Section 12 Lake. U.S. 1961.

SEED LAKE: Lake County and Ontario; T65N, R8W, Sec. 35. U.S. 1950–54.

SHADY OAK LAKE: Hennepin County; T117S, R22W, Sec. 26, 35. *Not*: Shady Lake. U.S. *Sixth Report*, 684.

SHALLOW POND LAKE: Itasca County; T149N, R28W, Sec. 5, 6, 8. *Not*: Shallow Lake. Minn. 1940.

SHAMROCK LAKE: Lake County; T60, 61N, R10W, Sec. 4; 33. *Not*: Kelly Lake. U.S. 1959; Minn. 1957.

SHAOKATAN: township, Lincoln County; T111N, R46W. *Not*: Shaokaton. U.S. *Sixth Report*, 685.

SHEEN ISLAND: in Namakan Lake, St. Louis County; T69N, R18W, Sec. 30. *Not*: Sheen Point. U.S. 1969.

SHEEN POINT: peninsula in Namakan Lake, St. Louis County; T69N, R18W, Sec. 29–32. U.S. 1969.

SHERMANS CORNER: settlement, St. Louis County; T61N, R18W, Sec. 8. *Not*: Sherman Corner. U.S. 1966.

SHOEPACK LAKE: St. Louis County; T69, 70N, R20W, Sec. 3; 33–35. *Not*: Bootjack Lake, Boot Jack Lake, Shoe Pack Lake, Shoepac Lake. U.S. 1968.

SHOKO LAKE: Cook County; T64N, R1W, Sec. 14, 15. *Not*: Arrow Lake, Mile Post Lake. U.S. 1941–43; Minn. 1940.

SHUMWAY LAKE: Aitkin County; T50N, R22W, Sec. 8, 9. *Not*: Green Lake. U.S. 1968; Minn. 1966.

SILVER CREEK: Carlton County; rises in T46N, R21W, Sec. 6, flows east-southeast to Kettle River in T46N, R20W, Sec. 16. *Not*: Otter Brook. U.S. 1964.

SILVER LAKE: Beltrami County; T146N, R31W, Sec. 9, 16. *Not*: Cowling Lake. Minn. 1940.

SILVER ISLAND LAKE: Lake County; T60, 61N, R6, 7W, Sec. 5; 19, 20, 29–32; 25, 36. *Not*: Island Lake, Bellissima Lake. Minn. 1940.

SINNEEG LAKE: St. Louis County; T65, 66N, R12W, Sec. 2; 35. *Not*: Thunder Lake. U.S. 1941–43; Minn. 1940.

SISEEBAKWET LAKE: Itasca County; T54N, R26W, Sec. 16–21. *Not*: Lake Siseebakwet, Sissebakwet Lake, Sugar Lake, Sisi Bakwet Lake. U.S. 1941–43; Minn. 1940.

SKANDIA: township, Murray County; T108N, R42W. *Not*: Scandia. U.S. *Sixth Report*, 698.

SKIMERHORN LAKE: Itasca County; T149N, R29W, Sec. 31. *Not*: Shallow Lake, Grass Lake. Minn. 1940.

SLEEPY EYE: city and lake, Brown County; T110N, R32W, Sec. 29–32. *Not*: Sleepyeye, Sleepy Eye Lake, Lorena, Loreno, Leonora. U.S. *Sixth Report*, 699.

SMITH BAR: post light in Mississippi River, Dakota County; 5 miles below mouth of St. Croix River. *Not*: Smith's Bar. U.S. *Sixth Report*, 701.

SNAIL LAKE: Ramsey County; T30N, R23W, Sec. 23, 24. *Not*: Maryland Lake, Snake Lake, Lake Avoca, Lake Maryland. U.S. 1941–43.

SNELLING LAKE: Hennepin County; T28N, R23W, Sec. 28, 29. *Not*: Gun Club Lake, Gunclub Lake, Soldier's Lake, Soldiers Lake, Government Lake, G. I. Lake. U.S. 1962; Minn. 1962.

SOLEM: township, Douglas County; T127N, R40W. *Not*: Solum. U.S. *Sixth Report*, 705.

SOURCE LAKE: Lake County; T58N, R10W, Sec. 25, 26. *Not*: Indian Lake. U.S. 1959; Minn. 1957.

SOUTH LAKE: Cook County and Ontario; T65N, R1, 2W, Sec. 19; 21–24, 27, 28. U.S. 1950–54.

SOUTH BRANCH BUFFALO RIVER: Clay, Otter Tail, Wilkin counties; rises in T135N, R44W, Sec. 4, flows to T140N, R47W, Sec. 33. *Not*: South Buffalo River, Willow River (upper), Stony Creek (upper), Buffalo Creek, Deerhorn Creek. U.S. 1965.

SOUTH BRANCH MANITOU RIVER: Lake County; rises in T58N, R8W, Sec. 1, flows east to Manitou River in T58N, R7W, Sec. 9. Minn. 1940.

SOUTH BRANCH MIDDLE FORK ZUMBRO RIVER: Olmsted, Dodge counties; rises in T107N, R18W, Sec. 8, flows generally east and northeast joining Middle Fork Zumbro River in T108N, R14W, Sec. 17. *Not*: Rice Lake Branch Zumbro River, South Middle Branch Zumbro River, South Middle Fork Zumbro River. U.S. 1961.

SOUTH BRANCH SUNRISE RIVER: Chisago, Anoka counties; rises in Anoka County, flows into Sunrise Pool No. 1 in T33N, R21W, Sec. 9. U.S. 1963.

SOUTH BRULE RIVER: Cook County; rises in Brule Lake, T63N, R2W, Sec. 17, flows easterly into Brule River in T63N, R1E, Sec. 22. *Not*: Arrowhead, Bois Brule, Bois Brulé, Brulé, Brule, South Arrowhead, South Branch Brule River, Wisacodé, Wissakode Zibi. U.S. 1961; Minn. 1960.

SOUTH FORK WATONWAN RIVER: Watonwan, Cottonwood, Martin counties; rises in Fish Lake, T105N, R35W, Sec. 34, joins Watonwan River in T107N, R30W, Sec. 29. *Not*: South Branch Watonwan River. U.S. 1962.

SOUTH FORK ZUMBRO RIVER: Olmsted, Dodge counties; rises in T105N, R17W, Sec. 2, flows northeast and north joining Middle Fork to form the Zumbro River in T108N, R14W, Sec. 14. *Not*: South Branch Zumbro River. U.S. 1961.

SUPPLEMENT NO. 2: DECISIONS LIST   781

SOUTH FOWL LAKE: Cook County and Ontario; T64, 65N, R3E, Sec. 1, 2, 12; 35. *Not*: Cock Lake, Fowl Lake. U.S. 1950–54.

SOUTH KAWISHIWI RIVER: Lake County; rises from Kawishiwi River in T63N, R10W, Sec. 26, flows southwest and north to White Iron Lake, and thence east to rejoin Kawishiwi River in T63N, R11W, Sec. 32. U.S. *Sixth Report,* 710.

SOUTH TEMPERANCE LAKE: Cook County; T63N, R3, 4W, Sec. 18; 13, 14, 24. *Not*: Temperance Lake, Georgia Lake. U.S. 1961.

SOUTH TWIN LAKE: Beltrami County; T147, 148N, R31W, Sec. 2, 3; 34, 35. *Not*: Twin Lake. Minn. 1940.

SOUTH WILDER LAKE: Lake County; T62N, R8W, Sec. 7, 8, 17. *Not*: Wilder Lakes (one of). U.S. 1959; Minn. 1957.

SPAULDING LAKE: Cook County; T64N, R2E, Sec. 5, 6. *Not*: Lake Marinda, Lake Miranda, Sarah Lake, Spalding Lake. U.S. 1949–50; Minn. 1940.

SPECKLED TROUT LAKE: Cook County; T63N, R5E, Sec. 7, 8. *Not*: Speckle Trout Lake, South Trout Lake. U.S. 1950; Minn. 1940.

SPHAGNUM LAKE: Lake County; T61N, R9W, Sec. 28. *Not*: Lost Lake, Spaghum Lake. U.S. 1941–43; Minn. 1940.

SPLASH LAKE: Lake County; T64N, R8, 9W, Sec. 7; 12. *Not*: Little Iron Lake. U.S. 1959; Minn. 1957.

SPRAGUE CREEK: Roseau County; rises in Canada, crosses border in T164N, R39W, Sec. 27, joins Roseau River in T163N, R40W, Sec. 14. *Not*: Mud Creek, Muddy, Northeast Roseau River, North Fork, North Fork Roseau, Roseau River, Sprague River. U.S. 1950–54.

SPRINGSTEEL ISLAND: in Lake of the Woods, Roseau County; T163N, R36W, Sec. 9. *Not*: Springsteel Point. U.S. 1968.

STARING LAKE: Hennepin County; T116N, R22W, Sec. 21, 22. *Not*: Staring's Lake, Starings Lake, Starring Lake, Starring's Lake, Starrings Lake. U.S. 1968; Minn. 1968.

STARLIGHT LAKE: Lake County; T63N, R8W, Sec. 9, 10, 15, 16. *Not*: Star Lake, Starr Lake. U.S. 1959; Minn. 1957.

STATE ISLAND: in Burntside Lake, St. Louis County; T63N, R13W, Sec. 16. *Not*: Honeymoon Island. U.S. 1966.

STATE LAKE: Cook County; T63, 64N, R2W, Sec. 1; 35, 36. Minn. 1940.

STEM LAKE: Cook County; T62, 63N, R3, 4W, Sec. 6; 31; 36. *Not*: Pipe Lake. U.S. 1962; Minn. 1962.

STEPHENS CREEK: St. Louis County; rises in T59N, R15W, Sec. 23, flows south to T59N, R15W, Sec. 35 (NE¼). *Not*: Stevens Creek. U.S. 1963.

STEWART RIVER: Lake County; rises in Stewart Lake, T54N, R11W, Sec. 4, flows south and southeast into Lake Superior in T53N, R10W, Sec. 29. *Not*: Steward River, Stewards River, Stewarts River. U.S. 1964.

STUB LAKE: Lake County; T63N, R11W, Sec. 11, 14, 15. *Not*: Stump Lake. U.S. 1959; Minn. 1957.

STUMBLE CREEK: Cook County; rises in T59N, R5W, Sec. 7, 8, flows southeasterly, joining Cross River in T59N, R5W, Sec. 26. *Not*: Four Mile Creek, Fourmile Creek. U.S. 1959; Minn. 1957.

SUCKER LAKES: Cass County; T145N, R29, 30W, various sections. U.S. 1933. *See also* Lower Sucker Lake, Middle Sucker Lake, Upper Sucker Lake.

SUGAR LAKE: Cass County; T142, 143N, R25W, Sec. 4; 27, 28, 33, 34. *Not*: Little Sugar Lake. Minn. 1940.

SUGAR LAKE: Itasca County; T146N, R29W, Sec. 13, 14, 23–26. *Not*: Little Lake, Lake Raven, Raven Lake, Overflow Lake. Minn. 1940.

SUMPET LAKE: Lake County; T61N, R7W, Sec. 10, 15. *Not*: Marsh Lake. U.S. 1959; Minn. 1957.

SUNDLING CREEK: Cook County; rises in T61N, R1W, Sec. 11, flows to T61N, R2W, Sec. 13 (SE¼). *Not*: Bally Creek. U.S. 1962; Minn. 1962.

SUNRISE RIVER: Chisago, Washington counties; rises in Forest Lake, T23N, R21W, flows north to St. Croix River in T36N, R20W, Sec. 32. *Not*: South Branch Sunrise River. U.S. 1963. *See also* North Branch Sunrise River, South Branch Sunrise River.

SUOMI LAKE: Itasca County; T58N, R27W, Sec. 25. *Not*: Round Lake, Soumi Lake. U.S. 1941–43; Minn. 1940.

SUPERIOR, LAKE: St. Louis, Lake, Cook counties; T49–64N, R1–8E, 1–14W, various sections. *Not*: Lac Superieur, Superior Lake. U.S. *Sixth Report,* 729.

SURBER LAKE: Cook County; T65N, R2W, Sec. 34. *Not*: Lake X. U.S. 1962; Minn. 1962.

SVERDRUP: township, Otter Tail County; T133N, R41W. *Not*: Swerdrup, Norman. U.S. *Sixth Report,* 731.

SWALLOW LAKE: Lake County; T60N, R10W, Sec. 10, 11. *Not*: Deep Lake. U.S. 1959; Minn. 1957.

SWAMP LAKE: Lake County and Ontario; T66N, R5, 6W, Sec. 19; 24, 25. U.S. 1950–54.

SWAMP PORTAGE: between Swamp and Cypress lakes, Lake County; T66N, R6W, Sec. 24. U.S. 1950–54.

SWANSONS BAY: in Sand Point Lake, St. Louis County; T68N, R17W, Sec. 2. *Not*: Steege Bay, Staege Bay. U.S. 1965.

SWIFT LAKE: Cass County; T142N, R27W, Sec. 15, 16, 21, 22, 26, 27. *Not*: Big Swift Lake. Minn. 1940.

SWIFT POINT: in Lake Minnetonka, Hennepin County; T117N, R23W, Sec. 24. *Not*: Ferguson Point, Swifts Point. U.S. 1960.

SYLVANIA LAKE: Lake County; T61N, R7, 8W, Sec. 31; 36. *Not*: Long Lake. U.S. 1959; Minn. 1957.

SYNNES: township, Stevens County; T123N, R43W. *Not*: Symes. U.S. *Sixth Report,* 735.

T LAKE: Lake County; T61N, R6W, Sec. 21, 28, 29. *Not*: Tee Lake. U.S. 1966; Minn. 1940.

SUPPLEMENT NO. 2: DECISIONS LIST   783

TADPOLE LAKE: Itasca County; T57N, R25W, Sec. 25, 26. *Not*: Clear Lake. Minn. 1940.

TALMOON: community, Itasca County; T59N, R27W, Sec. 9, 10, 15. *Not*: Allens Corner, Hayslips Corner, Mack's, Tallmoon. U.S. 1966; Minn. 1940.

TAMARACK RIVER. *See* Lower Tamarack, Upper Tamarack.

TANAGER LAKE: Hennepin County; T117N, R23W, Sec. 10, 11. *Not*: Mud Lake. U.S. 1960; Minn. 1959.

TARA: township, Swift County; T122N, R41W. *Not*: Tava, Ridgeville. U.S. *Sixth Report*, 744.

TEMPERANCE RIVER LAKE: Cook County; T62N, R4W, Sec. 26, 27. *Not*: Temperance Lake, Descent Lake, Prohibition Lake. U.S. 1961; Minn. 1960.

TEN LAKE: Beltrami County; T146N, R31W, Sec. 10. *Not*: Burton Lake. Minn. 1940.

TETAGOUCHE LAKE: Lake County; T56N, R7W, Sec. 7, 18. *Not*: Jitcagouche Lake, Teteagouche Lake. U.S. 1941–43; Minn. 1940.

THIMBLE LAKE: Itasca County; T62N, R24, 25W, Sec. 7; 12. *Not*: Timber Lake, Big Timber Lake. U.S. 1966; Minn. 1940.

THUNDER LAKE: St. Louis County; T65N, R12W, Sec. 3, 10. *Not*: Sinneeg Lake. Minn. 1940.

THUNDERBIRD LAKE: Lake County; T59N, R6W, Sec. 16. *Not*: Thunder Bird Lake, Long Lake. U.S. 1959; Minn. 1957.

TIN CAN MIKE LAKE: Lake County; T64N, R11W, Sec. 5, 8. *Not*: Mike Lake, Murphy Lake. U.S. 1961; Minn. 1960.

TITLOW LAKE: Sibley County; T113N, R28W, Sec. 20–22, 27–29. *Not*: Titloe Lake, Tillow Lake, Lake Titlow. U.S. 1963.

TOFTE LAKE: Lake County; T63, 64N, R10W, Sec. 2, 3, 10, 11; 35. *Not*: Clear Lake. U.S. 1936–37.

TOMAHAWK LAKE: Lake County; T62N, R7W, Sec. 26. *Not*: Sand Lake. U.S. 1941–43; Minn. 1940.

TOOHEY CREEK: Cook County; rises in Toohey Lake, T60N, R5W, Sec. 3, flows south to Fourmile Lake, T60N, R5W, Sec. 10. *Not*: Towhey Creek, Twohey Creek, Twohy Creek. U.S. 1966.

TOOHEY LAKE: Cook County; T60, 61N, R5W, Sec. 3, 4; 33, 34. *Not*: Twohey Lake, Twohy Lake, Towhey Lake, Towney Lake, Green Lake. U.S. 1966; Minn. 1966.

TOPAZ LAKE: Lake County; T65N, R6W, Sec. 8, 9. *Not*: Star Lake, Stark Lake. U.S. 1959; Minn. 1957.

TOPPER LAKE: Cook County; T65N, R2W, Sec. 27. *Not*: South Round Lake. U.S. 1962; Minn. 1960.

TOQUA: township, Big Stone County; T124N, R47W. *Not*: Tokua, Tokna. U.S. *Sixth Report*, 763.

TOWNLINE LAKE: Lake County; T62, 63N, R6W, Sec. 4; 33. *Not*: Towline Lake. U.S. 1961.

TRADER LAKE: Lake County; T64N, R7, 8W, Sec. 6, 7; 1, 12. *Not*: Three Lake, Three Lakes (one of). U.S. 1959; Minn. 1957.

TRESTLE LAKE: Itasca County; T149N, R25W, Sec. 15, 16, 21. *Not*: Fox Lake. U.S. 1941–43; Minn. 1940.

TRIANGLE LAKE: Lake County; T63N, R10W, Sec. 13, 14, 23, 24. *Not*: Lower Twin Lake, Twin Lakes. U.S. 1961.

TRIDENT LAKE: Lake County; T64N, R8W, Sec. 3, 4. *Not*: Triangle Lake. U.S. 1959; Minn. 1957.

TRIEGLAFF LAKE: Becker County; T138N, R40W, Sec. 23, 24. *Not*: Trisglaff Lake. U.S. 1962; Minn. 1962.

TROTT BROOK: Anoka, Sherburne counties; rises in Eagle Lake, T33N, R26W, Sec. 13, flows south, then east-southeast to Rum River in T32N, R25W, Sec. 1. *Not*: Trout Brook. U.S. 1963.

TROY: township, Pipestone County; T107N, R46, 47W. *Not*: Tracy. U.S. *Sixth Report*, 769.

TURPELA LAKE: St. Louis County; T57, 58N, R15W, Sec. 3; 34. U.S. 1960; Minn. 1959.

TURTLE CREEK: Todd County; rises in T129N, R33W, Sec. 22, joins Long Prairie River in T131N, R33W, Sec. 2. *Not*: Eagle River. U.S. *Sixth Report*, 775.

TUSTIN, LAKE: Le Sueur County; T109N, R24W, Sec. 35, 36. *Not*: Tustin Lake, Lake Custan, Perch Lake. U.S. 1963.

TUTTLE LAKE: Itasca County; T146N, R26W, Sec. 29. *Not*: Little Little Ball Club Lake. U.S. 1935–36.

TWENTYNINE, LAKE: Carlton County; T47N, R18W, Sec. 28, 29. *Not*: Twenty Nine Lake, Twenty-Nine Lake. U.S. 1963.

TWIN LAKE: Cass County; T144, 145N, R31W, Sec. 1, 2, 11; 36. Minn. 1940.

TWIN LAKES: Anoka, Sherburne counties; T33N, R25, 26W, Sec. 19; 24. *Not*: Twin Lake. U.S. 1963.

TWO DEER LAKE: Lake County; T60N, R10W, Sec. 14. *Not*: Pickerel Lake. U.S. 1959; Minn. 1957.

ULEN: township and village, Clay County; T142N, R44W. *Not*: Uhlen. U.S. *Sixth Report*, 780.

UPLAND LAKE: Lake County; T57N, R11W, Sec. 1, 12. *Not*: Little Mud Lake. U.S. 1959; Minn. 1957.

UPPER BADGER CREEK: Polk County; rises in Badger Lake, T149N, R42W, Sec. 34, flows north to T149N, R43W, Sec. 1. *Not*: Badger Creek. U.S. 1967.

UPPER IOWA RIVER: Fillmore County; enters Minnesota in T101N, R11W, Sec. 34, leaving in T101N, R10W, Sec. 31. *Not*: Oneota. U.S. *Sixth Report*, 783.

UPPER PAUNESS LAKE: St. Louis County; T66N, R15W, Sec. 15, 16, 21, 22. *Not*: Dauness Lake, Lower Pauness Lake, Lower Pouness Lake, Pauness Lake. U.S. 1964.

SUPPLEMENT NO. 2: DECISIONS LIST 785

UPPER SUCKER LAKE: Cass County; T145N, R29, 30W, Sec. 19; 24. *Not*: Mud Lake. U.S. 1933.

UPPER TAMARACK RIVER: Pine County; enters Minnesota from east in T42N, R15W, Sec. 6, flows southwest into St. Croix River in T41N, R16W, Sec. 36. *Not*: Tamarack Creek, Tamarack River. U.S. *Sixth Report*, 784.

VARIETY LAKE: Cass County; T140N, R31W, Sec. 32, 33. *Not*: Pickerel Lake. U.S. 1941; Minn. 1940.

VELVET LAKE: Crow Wing County; T137N, R27W, Sec. 24, 25. *Not*: Phelps Lake, Phelps Velvet Lake. U.S. 1962; Minn. 1962.

VERA LAKE: Lake County; T64N, R8W, Sec. 1–3. *Not*: Lake Vira. U.S. 1936–37.

VERMILION LAKE: St. Louis County; T61–63N, R14–16W, various sections. *Not*: Vermillion Lake, Lake Vermilion. U.S. 1963; Minn. 1940.

WABANA LAKE: Itasca County; T57N, R25W, Sec. 4, 8, 9, 15–17, 20–23, 29. *Not*: Wabano Lake. U.S. 1941–43; Minn. 1940.

WABANG LAKE: St. Louis County; T67N, R13W, Sec. 30, 31. *Not*: Wabun. U.S. 1935–36.

WABEGON LAKE: Cass County; T142N, R30W, Sec. 21, 28. *Not*: Mud Lake. U.S. 1941–43; Minn. 1940.

WABOSONS LAKE: Lake County; T65, 66N, R11W, Sec. 3; 34. *Not*: Rabbit Lake. U.S. 1959; Minn. 1957.

WADOP LAKE: Lake County; T60N, R10W, Sec. 24, 25. *Not*: Alder Lake, Silver Lake. U.S. 1959; Minn. 1957.

WAGOSH LAKE: St. Louis County; T65N, R21W, Sec. 1. U.S. *Sixth Report*, 793.

WAHNESHIN LAKE: Cass County; T142N, R26W, Sec. 15, 22. *Not*: Lost Lake. U.S. 1941–43; Minn. 1940.

WAKEMUP NARROWS: in Vermilion Lake, St. Louis County; T63N, R17, 18W, Sec. 29–32. *Not*: Williams Narrows. U.S. 1966.

WALBERG CREEK: St. Louis County; rises in T61N, R17W, Sec. 31, flows northwestward to T61N, R17W, Sec. 30. U.S. 1961.

WALCOTT: township and village, Rice County; T160N, R20W. *Not*: Wolcott. U.S. *Sixth Report*, 799.

WALTERS LAKE: Itasca County; T60N, R24W, Sec. 22, 23. *Not*: Kelly Lake, Waters Lake, Wallace Lake. U.S. 1941–43; Minn. 1940.

WAMPUS LAKE: Lake County; T60N, R10W, Sec. 28, 29, 32, 33. *Not*: Pine Lake. U.S. *Sixth Report*, 800.

WANIHIGAN LAKE: Cook County; T64N, R2, 3W, Sec. 31; 36. *Not*: Sham Lake, Trap Lake. U.S. 1959; Minn. 1957.

WANLESS LAKE: Lake County; T60N, R6W, Sec. 18, 19. *Not*: Wanlas Lake. Minn. 1940.

WARROAD RIVER: Roseau County; formed by east and west branches in T162N, R36W, Sec. 5, flows north, then east into Lake of the Woods in T163N, R36W,

Sec. 28. *Not*: River Warroad, War Road River, West Branch Warroad River. U.S. 1968. *See also* West Branch Warroad River.

WASSERMANN LAKE: Carver County; T116N, R24W, Sec. 23. *Not*: Wasserman Lake, Waterman Lake, Watermann Lake, Watermans Lake, Waterman's Lake, Watermann's Lake. U.S. 1963.

WATAP LAKE: Cook County and Ontario; T64N, R1E, Sec. 21, 22. *Not*: Rove Lake, Watab Lake. U.S. 1950.

WATERS ISLAND: in Burntside Lake, St. Louis County; T63N, R13W, Sec. 21, 22. *Not*: Hall Island. U.S. 1966.

WATONWAN LAKE: Lake County; T62N, R6W, Sec. 15, 16, 21, 22. *Not*: Wantonwan Lake, Long Lake. U.S. *Sixth Report,* 804.

WATONWAN RIVER: Watonwan, Blue Earth, Cottonwood counties; rises in T106N, R36W, Sec. 5, flows generally eastward to T107N, R27W, Sec. 18. *Not*: North Fork Watonwan River, South Fork Watonwan River. U.S. 1962. *See also* North Fork Watonwan River, South Fork Watonwan River.

WAWA LAKE: Cass County; T141N, R29W, Sec. 9, 10, 15, 16. *Not*: Goose Lake, Mud Lake, Haka-Wash-Te Lake, Hoko-Wash Lake, Hoko-Wash-Te Lake. U.S. 1949; Minn. 1944.

WAWATOSA ISLAND: in Lake Minnetonka, Hennepin County; T117N, R24W, Sec. 30. *Not*: Dunlap's Island. U.S. *Sixth Report,* 805.

WAX LAKE: Cass County; T141N, R27W, Sec. 13, 24. *Not*: Beauty Lake. U.S. 1941–43; Minn. 1940.

WEAPON LAKE: Lake County; T60N, R8W, Sec. 27. *Not*: Tomahawk Lake. U.S. 1959; Minn. 1957.

WEGWOS LAKE: Cass County; T140N, R31W, Sec. 30, 31. *Not*: Birch Lake. U.S. 1949; Minn. 1944.

WEST BRANCH BEAVER RIVER: Lake County; rises in T55N, R9W, Sec. 4, joins East Branch Beaver River in T55N, R8W, Sec. 2. *Not*: Beaver Creek, Beaver River, Lennox Creek. U.S. 1966; Minn. 1940.

WEST BRANCH SUNRISE RIVER: Chisago, Anoka, Isanti counties; rises in T34N, R22W, Sec. 5, flows into Sunrise Pool No. 1 in T34N, R21W, Sec. 33. U.S. 1963.

WEST BRANCH WARROAD RIVER: Lake of the Woods, Roseau counties; rises in T160N, R36W, Sec. 9, flows north, joining East Branch to form the Warroad River in T162N, R36W, Sec. 5. *Not*: Clear River, River Warroad, Warroad River. U.S. 1968.

WEST FORK CROOKED CREEK: Pine County; rises in T43N, R18W, Sec. 11, flows south-southeast to join East Fork in T41N, R18W, Sec. 12. *Not*: Crooked Creek, West Fork Crooked River, West Branch Crooked Creek. U.S. 1963.

WEST MINNEAPOLIS: village, Hennepin County; T117N, R21, 22W, Sec. 19, 24, 25. *Not*: Bushnell. U.S. *Sixth Report,* 810.

WEST PIPE LAKE: Cook County; T62, 63N, R3W, Sec. 5; 32. U.S. 1962; Minn. 1962.

SUPPLEMENT NO. 2: DECISIONS LIST 787

WESTBANK: township, Swift County; T120N, R41W. *Not*: West Bank, Springdale. U.S. *Sixth Report*, 808.

WHALETAIL LAKE: Hennepin County; T117N, R24W, Sec. 16, 17, 20, 21. *Not*: Hiawatha Lake, Whale Tail Lake. U.S. 1959.

WHISPER LAKE: St. Louis County; T61N, R12W, Sec. 19. *Not*: Perch Lake. U.S. 1963.

WHITE BEAR LAKE: city, Ramsey County; T30N, R22W. *Not*: White Bear, White Bear City. U.S. *Sixth Report*, 813.

WHITE IRON LAKE: St. Louis, Lake counties; T62, 63N, R11, 12W, various sections. U.S. *Sixth Report*, 814.

WHITE PINE LAKE: Cook County; T61N, R3W, Sec. 19, 20, 29, 30. *Not*: Big Lake. U.S. 1949; Minn. 1940.

WHITEFACE RESERVOIR: in Whiteface River, St. Louis County; T55N, R15W, Sec. 2. *Not*: Minnesota Power and Light Company Reservoir, White Face River Reservoir, Whiteface River Reservoir. U.S. 1963.

WHITEFACE RIVER: St. Louis County; rises in T55N, R15W, Sec. 2, flows southwesterly, joining St. Louis River in T52N, R20W, Sec. 24. *Not*: White Face River, Big White Face River. U.S. *Sixth Report*, 814.

WHITEWATER LAKE: St. Louis County; T58N, R14, 15W, Sec. 7, 17-19; 13, 24. *Not*: South Partridge Lake, Lower Partridge Lake, Partridge Lake, Partridge Lakes (one of), Sunfish Lake, White Water Lake. U.S. 1941-43; Minn. 1940.

WILBUR BROOK: Pine County; rises in T41N, R18W, Sec. 23, flows generally southward, then eastward, to Crooked Creek, T41N, R17W, Sec. 29. *Not*: Wilbur Creek. U.S. 1963.

WILDERNESS LAKE: Itasca County; T147N, R28W, Sec. 4. *Not*: Tank Lake. U.S. 1941-43; Minn. 1940.

WILDS ISLAND: post light in Mississippi River, Winona County. *Not*: Wild's Island. U.S. *Sixth Report*, 818.

WILLIAMS LAKE: Cook County; T61N, R3W, Sec. 3, 4. *Not*: Mad Lake, Mud Lake. U.S. 1941-43; Minn. 1940.

WILMONT: township, Nobles County; T104N, R42W. *Not*: Willmont. U.S. *Sixth Report*, 820.

WINCHESTER LAKE: St. Louis County; T64N, R17, 18W, Sec. 7, 8, 17, 18; 12, 13. *Not*: Eight Lake. U.S. 1941-43; Minn. 1940.

WINDIGO, LAKE: Beltrami County; T146N, R31W, Sec. 35, 36. *Not*: Lake Helen. U.S. 1934.

WINKLE LAKE: St. Louis County; T53N, R16W, Sec. 5, 8. *Not*: Little Leora Lake, South Elora Lake, South Leora Lake. U.S. 1963.

WINNIBIGOSHISH, LAKE: Cass, Itasca counties; T145-147N, R26-29W, various sections. *Not*: Lake Winnebagoshish, Lake Winepegoos, Winnipeg Lake, Lake Winnipec, Lake Winnepec, Little Winnepeek Lake, Lake Winnepeg, Lake Winnipeg, Lake Winebigoshish, Lake Winnebagooshish. U.S. *Sixth Report*, 822.

WINTERS LANDING: Winona County [La Crosse County, Wisconsin?]. *Not*: Winter's. U.S. *Sixth Report,* 822.

WIRT: post office, Itasca County; T149N, R26W, Sec. 10, 15. *Not*: Stanley, Wirth. Minn. 1940.

WIRT LAKE: Itasca County; T150N, R26W, Sec. 35. *Not*: Beaver Lake. U.S. 1941-43; Minn. 1940.

WISINI LAKE: Lake County; T64N, R7W, Sec. 11-14. *Not*: Crocus Lake. U.S. 1941-43; Minn. 1940.

WIYAPKA LAKE: St. Louis County; T68N, R18W, Sec. 7. *Not*: Wiyapko Lake, Wiyarka Lake. U.S. 1968.

WOLF CREEK: Pine County; rises in T43N, R18W, Sec. 29, flows south-southeastward to West Fork Crooked Creek, T42N, R18W, Sec. 16. *Not*: West Fork Crooked Creek, West Fork Crooked River. U.S. 1963.

WOLF PACK ISLANDS: in Namakan Lake, St. Louis County; T69N, R18W, Sec. 29, 30. *Not*: McManus Island, Wolf Island. U.S. 1969.

WOOD LAKE: Lake County; T64N, R10W, Sec. 25-28, 34. *Not*: Pine Lake. U.S. 1941-43; Minn. 1940.

WOODCOCK LAKE: Lake County; T55N, R11W, Sec. 6. *Not*: Pine Lake. U.S. 1961; Minn. 1960.

WRIGHT LAKE: Otter Tail County; T133N, R43W, Sec. 25, 35, 36. *Not*: Stump Lake. U.S. 1968; Minn. 1966.

WYANETT: township and village, Isanti County; T36N, R25W. *Not*: Wyanette. U.S. *Sixth Report,* 826.

WYE LAKE: Lake County; T60N, R6W, Sec. 7, 8. *Not*: Spring Lake. U. S. 1959; Minn. 1957.

ZEBULON PIKE LAKE: reservoir in Mississippi River, Morrison County; T128, 129N, R29, 30W, various sections. U.S. 1968; Minn. 1968.

ZEPHYR LAKE: Lake, Cook counties; T66N, R5, 6W, Sec. 19, 30; 24, 25. *Not*: Wind Lake. U.S. 1959; Minn. 1957.

ZUMBRO RIVER: Wabasha, Olmsted counties; formed by junction of its South Fork and Middle Fork at Oronoco in T108N, R14, 15W, flows into Mississippi River in T110N, R9W, Sec. 32. *Not*: Embarras, Zambre, Zumbroto. U.S. 1961. *See also* various forks.